BUTLER'S
LIVES OF THE SAINTS

BUTLER'S
LIVES OF THE SAINTS

COMPLETE EDITION

EDITED, REVISED AND SUPPLEMENTED BY

HERBERT THURSTON, S.J.

AND

DONALD ATTWATER

VOLUME II
APRIL · MAY · JUNE

General Index in Volume IV

CHRISTIAN CLASSICS, INC.
Westminster, Maryland

REPRINTED 1980
NIHIL OBSTAT: PATRICIVS MORRIS, S.T.D., L.S.S.
CENSOR DEPVTATVS
IMPRIMATVR: E. MORROGH BERNARD
VICARIVS GENERALIS
WESTMONASTERII: DIE XXIII FEBRVARII MCMLIII

Christian Classics, Inc.
P.O. BOX 30
WESTMINSTER, MD. 21157

LIBRARY OF CONGRESS CATALOG CARD NUMBER: 56-5383

© 1956, BURNS AND OATES, LONDON

ISBN: 0 87061 047 3 (U.S.A.)

PRINTED IN THE UNITED STATES OF AMERICA
NOBLE OFFSET PRINTERS INC.

CONTENTS OF VOLUME II

APRIL

JUNE

BIBLIOGRAPHICAL ABBREVIATIONS

Acta Sanctorum. — This without qualification refers to the *Acta Sanctorum* of the Bollandists.

BHG. — The *Bibliotheca hagiographica graeca* of the Bollandists.

BHL. — The *Bibliotheca hagiographica latina* of the Bollandists.

BHO. — The *Bibliotheca hagiographica orientalis* of the Bollandists.

Burton and Pollen, LEM. — *Lives of the English Martyrs,* second series, ed. E. H. Burton and J. H. Pollen.

Camm, LEM. — *Lives of the English Martyrs,* first series, ed. Bede Camm.

CMH. — H. Delehaye's Commentary on the Hieronymian Martyrology, in the *Acta Sanctorum,* November, volume ii, part 2.

DAC. — *Dictionnaire d'Archéologie chrétienne et de Liturgie,* ed. F. Cabrol and H. Leclercq.

DCB. — *A Dictionary of Christian Biography,* ed. William Smith and Henry Wace.

DHG. — *Dictionnaire d'Histoire et de Géographie ecclésiastiques,* ed. A. Baudrillart *et al.*

DNB. — The *Dictionary of National Biography,* ed. Leslie Stephen *et al.*

DTC. — *Dictionnaire de Théologie catholique,* ed. A. Vacant *et al.*

KSS. — *Kalendars of Scottish Saints,* ed. A. P. Forbes.

LBS. — *Lives of the British Saints,* by S. Baring-Gould and John Fisher.

LIS. — *Lives of the Irish Saints,* by John O'Hanlon.

Mabillon. — *Acta Sanctorum Ordinis Sancti Benedicti,* ed. J. Mabillon.

MGH. — *Monumenta Germaniae Historica,* ed. G. H. Pertz *et al.*

MMP. — *Memoirs of Missionary Priests,* by Richard Challoner, referred to in the edition of 1924, ed. J. H. Pollen.

PG. — *Patrologia graeca,* ed. J. P. Migne.

PL. — *Patrologia latina,* ed. J. P. Migne.

REPSJ. — *Records of the English Province of the Society of Jesus,* ed. Henry Foley.

Ruinart. — *Acta primorum martyrum sincera et selecta,* ed. T. Ruinart.

Stanton's *Menology.* — *A Menology of England and Wales,* by Richard Stanton.

VSH. — *Vitae Sanctorum Hiberniae,* ed. Charles Plummer.

Father H. Delehaye's *Les origines du culte des martyrs* is referred to in the " deuxième édition revue " of 1933.

There is an English translation by Mrs V. M. Crawford of Father Delehaye's *Les légendes hagiographiques* (" The Legends of the Saints "), made from the first edition. The third French edition (1927) is revised and is therefore sometimes referred to.

The English title of the work herein referred to as " Léon, *L'Auréole séraphique* (Eng. trans.) " is *Lives of the Saints and Blessed of the Three Orders of St Francis,* by Father Léon (Vieu) de Clary.   A corrected and enlarged edition of this work in Italian, by Father G. C. Guzzo, began publication in 1951 : *Aureola serafica*. By 1954 four volumes had appeared, covering January–August.

It has not been deemed necessary to give every reference to such standard works as the *Dictionary of Christian Biography*, the *Dictionnaires* published by Letouzey, and A. Fliche and V. Martin's *Histoire de l'Église*, though these are often referred to in the bibliographical notes.   The first two volumes of Fliche and Martin, by J. Lebreton and J. Zeiller, have been translated into English by Dr E. C. Messenger (*The History of the Primitive Church*, 4 vols.), and the first two English volumes of the continuation, *The Church in the Christian Roman Empire*, are also published.

The reader may here be reminded once for all that for all modern saints and *beati* the surest source of information on the more strictly spiritual side is the *summarium de virtutibus* with the criticisms of the *Promotor fidei* which are printed in the process of beatification.   Copies of these are occasionally to be met with in national or private libraries, though they are not published or offered for sale to the general public.

For all saints named in the Roman Martyrology the standard short reference is in the *Acta Sanctorum, Decembris Propylaeum: Martyrologium Romanum ad formam editionis typicae scholiis historicis instructum* (1940).   This great work provides a running commentary on the entries in the Roman Martyrology, correcting where necessary conclusions expressed in the sixty-odd volumes of the *Acta Sanctorum*, and anticipating much that will be said at greater length in those volumes that have yet to appear ; and there are summary bibliographies throughout.   It is indispensable for all serious study and reference.

BUTLER'S
LIVES OF THE SAINTS

APRIL

1 : ST MELITO, Bishop of Sardis   (c. A.D. 180 ?)

EUSEBIUS and other ecclesiastical writers greatly commend the writings of St Melito, Bishop of Sardis in Lydia, who during the second century wrote an Apology for Christianity addressed to the Emperor Marcus Aurelius and many other works, theological and ethical. Eusebius and St Jerome give the titles or the subjects of a number of these writings, but of the books themselves little has survived but a few fragments. According to Tertullian, who was rather disdainful of his oratorical diction and style, St Melito was regarded as a prophet by many people. His name occurs in some of the old *martyrologia*, but beyond the fact that he was unmarried and was said to have ruled his conduct by the teaching of the Holy Spirit, nothing whatever is known of his life or death.

Owing to the similarity between the names of Sardis and Sardinia, St Melito has often been confused with a fictitious namesake reputed to have been a pupil of St Boniface, the first bishop of Cagliari, and to have suffered martyrdom in Sardinia under Domitian.

There is a very full article on Melito, concerned of course principally with the writings attributed to him, in DTC., vol. x, cc. 540–547, to which the writer, E. Amann, appends a full bibliography. See also G. Salmon in DCB., vol. iii, pp. 894–900, and Bardenhewer, *Altkirchliche Literatur*, vol. i, pp. 546–557.

ST WALARICUS, or VALÉRY, Abbot   (c. A.D. 620)

ST WALARICUS or Valéry, whose body William the Conqueror caused to be publicly exposed that the saint might obtain a favourable wind for his English expedition, was born in a humble home in the Auvergne. Somehow he learned to read, and he is said to have procured a psalter, the contents of which he committed to memory while tending sheep. His uncle one day took him to visit the monastery of Autumo, but when the time came for returning, the boy insisted upon staying behind ; so there he was allowed to remain and to continue his education, though it is doubtful whether he ever took the habit there. Some years later he left to enter the abbey of St Germanus near Auxerre, but his sojourn does not seem to have been a pro-tracted one. It was not unusual in those days for monks voluntarily to go from one monastery to another ; some indeed were vagrants by nature who could never settle anywhere, but many of them were men striving after perfection, who were only eager to find a director capable of assisting them to attain their goal. Of this number was Walaricus. The renown of St Columban and of the life led by his followers at Luxeuil determined him to seek out the great Irishman and to place himself under his rule. With him went his friend Bobo, a nobleman who had been converted by him and who had abandoned his possessions to join him. At Luxeuil,

I

where they found the leader and the spiritual life they sought, they settled down happily.   To Walaricus fell the duty of cultivating part of the garden.   The flourishing condition of his allotment, when the rest of the estate was being devoured by insects, was regarded as miraculous, and is said to have induced St Columban, who already had a high opinion of him, to profess him after an unusually short novitiate.

When King Theodoric expelled the abbot from his monastery, allowing only the Irish and the Bretons to accompany him, Walaricus, not wishing to remain on at Luxeuil without St Columban, obtained leave to join a monk called Waldolanus, who was about to start on a mission of evangelization.   Receiving permission to settle in Neustria, they preached freely to the people, and Walaricus's eloquence and miracles gained many converts.   It was not long, however, before he began to feel again the call to retire from the world, but this time he thought it his vocation to be a hermit.   By the advice of Bishop Berchundus he chose a solitary spot near the sea, at the mouth of the river Somme, where he proposed to live in solitude ; but he could not remain hidden.   Disciples discovered him and cells sprang up around, which developed into the celebrated abbey of Leuconaus.   St Walaricus would occasionally issue forth to preach missions in the countryside, and so successful were his efforts that he is said to have evangelized not only what is now known as the Pas-de-Calais, but the whole eastern shore of the English Channel.

Tall and ascetic-looking, the holy man was noted for his singular gentleness which tempered the stern Rule of St Columban with excellent results.   Animals were attracted to him : birds perched on his shoulders and ate from his hand, and often the good abbot would gently warn off an intruding visitor with the words, " Do let these innocent creatures eat their meal in peace ".

After ruling his monastery for six years or more, St Walaricus passed to his rest about the year 620.   Numerous miracles reported after his death quickly spread his *cultus*, at least two French towns, St-Valéry-sur-Somme and St-Valéry-en-Caux, being named after him.   King Richard Cœur-de-Lion transferred his relics to the latter town, which is in Normandy, but they were afterwards restored to St-Valéry-sur-Somme, on the site of the abbey of Leuconaus.

We are told that a life of St Walaricus was written by Raginbertus, who became abbot of Leuconaus not long after the death of the saint.   It was formerly believed that this document was preserved in substance by a later writer, who re-edited it in a new setting and in a more correct style.   Bruno Krusch, however, seems to have proved that this later life dates only from the eleventh century and is a fabrication which borrows freely from other hagiographical materials which have nothing to do with St Walaricus.   See MGH., *Scriptores Merov.*, vol. iv, pp. 157–175 ; where a more critical text than that of the Bollandists and Mabillon may also be found.   For some criticisms of B. Krusch's edition see Wattenbach-Levison, *Deutschlands Geschichtsquellen im Mittelalter Vorzeit und Karolinger*, vol. i (1952), p. 137.

ST MACARIUS THE WONDER-WORKER   (*c.* A.D. 830)

MACARIUS the Wonder-worker was a native of Constantinople.   He received an excellent education, showing special aptitude for the study of the Holy Scriptures, " the whole of which ", we read, " he ran through in a short time ".   Afterwards, leaving the city, he betook himself to the monastery of Pelekete where he dropped his baptismal name of Christopher to assume that of Macarius.   A model monk, he was chosen abbot and soon became celebrated for his miracles of healing. Crowds flocked to Pelekete to be cured of diseases both of body and of mind.   The patriarch of Constantinople, St Tarasius, who had received many reports of his sanctity and miracles, greatly desiring to see him, dispatched to be his escort the patrician Paul, who had once been cured by the abbot and whose wife had recently been restored to health by him after she had been given over by the physicians. When the two saints met, Tarasius gave Macarius his blessing and, before allowing him to return, ordained him priest.   He was not destined to remain long at peace in his cloister.   The Emperor Leo the Armenian attacked in turn all the prominent supporters of the *cultus* of holy images, and Macarius was tortured in various ways and kept in prison until the emperor's death.   His successor, Michael the Stammerer, released the saint and tried by promises and threats to win him over. Finding, however, that he remained inflexible, the emperor banished him to the island of Aphusia off the shore of Bithynia, where on August 18 he died in exile ; the precise year is unknown.

A Greek life of St Macarius by the monk Sabas was edited in the *Analecta Bollandiana*, vol. xvi (1897), pp. 140–163.   Its historical character is confirmed by certain letters of Theodore Studites.   See the *Analecta Bollandiana*, vol. xxxii (1913), pp. 270–273 ; and cf. *Échos d'Orient*, i (1898), pp. 274–280.   April 1 seems to have been the day of his translation.

ST HUGH, BISHOP OF GRENOBLE   (A.D. 1132)

ST HUGH was born at Châteauneuf, near Valence in the Dauphiné, in the year 1052. His father, Odilo, after being twice married, became a Carthusian, and died at the age of 100, receiving viaticum from his son in whose arms he passed away.   After an education begun in Valence and completed with distinction in foreign centres of learning, Hugh was presented to a canonry in the cathedral of Valence though still a layman—such benefices at that period being often conferred on young students without orders.   Very young, good-looking, and extremely bashful, he soon won all hearts by his courtesy and by the modesty which led him to conceal and underrate his talents and learning.   The bishop of Die, another Hugh, was so charmed by his namesake when he came to Valence that he insisted upon attaching him to his household.   The prelate soon proved the young canon's worth by entrusting him with some difficult negotiations in the campaign then directed against simony ; and in 1080 he took him to a synod at Avignon, called to consider, amongst other matters, the disorders which had crept into the vacant see of Grenoble.   The council and the delegates from Grenoble severally and collectively appear to have looked on Canon Hugh as the one man who was capable of dealing with the disorders complained of ; but though unanimously elected it was with the greatest reluctance that he consented to accept the office.   The legate himself conferred on him holy orders up to the priesthood, and took him to Rome that he might receive consecration from the pope.   The kindness of the reception he met emboldened the young bishop elect to consult St Gregory VII about temptations to blasphemy which sometimes beset him, causing him great distress and, as he considered, rendering him unfit for the high office to which he was called.   The pontiff reassured him, explaining that God permitted these trials to purify him and render him a more fitting instrument for the divine purposes.   These particular temptations continued to assault him until his last illness, but he never yielded to them in any way.

The Countess Matilda gave the twenty-eight-year-old bishop his crozier and some books, including the *De officiis ministrorum* of St Ambrose and a psalter to

3

which were appended the commentaries of St Augustine. Immediately after his consecration, St Hugh hurried off to his diocese, but he was appalled by the state of his flock. The gravest sins were committed without shame ; simony and usury were rampant ; the clergy openly flouted the obligation to celibacy ; the people were uninstructed ; laymen had seized church property and the see was almost penniless. It was indeed a herculean task that lay before the saint. For two years he laboured unremittingly to redress abuses by preaching, by denunciations, by rigorous fasts and by constant prayer. The excellent results he was obtaining were patent to all but to himself : he only saw his failures and blamed his own incompetence. Discouraged, he quietly withdrew to the Cluniac abbey of Chaise-Dieu, where he received the Benedictine habit. He did not remain there long, for Pope Gregory commanded him to resume his pastoral charge and return to Grenoble. Coming out of his solitude, like another Moses from the mountain, he seemed—so men declared—to preach with greater fervour and success than before. It was to St Hugh of Grenoble that St Bruno and his companions addressed themselves when they decided to forsake the world, and it was he who granted to them the desert called the Chartreuse which gave its name to their order. The bishop became greatly attached to the monks : it was his delight to visit them in their solitude, joining in their exercises and performing the most menial offices. Sometimes he would linger so long in these congenial surroundings that St Bruno was constrained to remind him of his flock and of his episcopal duties. These periods of retreat were the bright oases in a hard and anxious life.

With the clergy and the common people St Hugh was most successful, but the nobles continued to withstand him to the end. Moreover, for the last forty years of his life he suffered almost unremittingly from headaches complicated by gastric trouble, and was tormented by severe temptations. Nevertheless occasionally he was granted sensible spiritual consolations which filled his heart with joy. During his sermons it was not unusual to see the whole congregation in tears, whilst individuals would be moved to make public confession on the spot. Of sin he had the utmost horror, and his loathing of detraction was so great that he disliked the duty of listening to official reports and closed his ears to the news of the day. Temporal things always seemed to him dull and irksome as compared with the heavenly things on which his heart was set. He besought pope after pope to release him from office. One and all refused point-blank. Honorius II, to whom he pleaded his age and infirmities, replied that he preferred to retain him as bishop of Grenoble—old and ill— rather than have any younger or stronger man in his place.

A generous almsgiver, St Hugh in a time of famine sold a gold chalice as well as rings and precious stones from his church treasury ; and rich men were stirred by his example to give liberally to feed the hungry and supply the needs of the diocese. Although at the end of life his soul was further purified by a lingering illness of a very painful character, Hugh never uttered a word of complaint, nor would he speak of what he endured. His only concern was for others. His humility was all the more striking because everyone approached him with the utmost reverence and affection. In reply to someone who asked, " Why do you weep so bitterly—you who never offended God by any wilful sin ? " he replied, " Vanity and inordinate affections alone are enough to damn a soul. Only through God's mercy can we hope to be saved, and should we ever cease to implore it ? " A short time before his death he lost his memory for everything but prayer, and would recite the psalter or the Lord's Prayer without intermission. St Hugh died on April 1, 1132, **two** months before attaining the age of eighty, having been a bishop for fifty-two years. Pope Innocent II canonized him two years later.

The main authority for the life of St Hugh is the Latin biography by Guigo, prior of the Grande Chartreuse, who died only five years after the saint himself. This life is printed in the *Acta Sanctorum*, April, vol. i, and elsewhere. See also Albert du Boys, *Vie de St Hugues* (1837) ; Bellet in the *Bulletin Soc. Archéol. Drôme* (1894), xxviii, 5–31, and Marion, *Chartulaire de l'Eglise de Grenoble* (1869). Hugh is reckoned amongst ecclesiastical writers chiefly on the strength of this cartulary, or collection of charters, copies of which, accompanied by curious historical notes, are preserved in Grenoble Library. The bishop is often associated with St Bruno as co-founder of the Grande Chartreuse.

ST HUGH OF BONNEVAUX, ABBOT   (A.D. 1194)

IN one of his letters St Bernard of Clairvaux mentions with great praise a novice called Hugh, who had renounced considerable riches and entered the abbey of Mézières at a very early age against the wishes of his relations. He was nephew to St Hugh of Grenoble. Once, when greatly troubled by temptations and longings to return to the world, he entered a church to pray for light and help. As he raised his eyes to the altar, he beheld above it a figure which he recognized to be that of our Lady, and then, beside her, appeared the form of her divine Son. The Mother of Mercy, with a look of great kindness, addressed him, saying, " Bear yourself like a man and let your heart be comforted in the Lord ; rest assured that you will be troubled no more by these temptations." Hugh afterwards gave himself up to such severe penances that his health broke down and he seemed to be losing his memory. He owed his recovery to the wise common-sense of St Bernard, who ordered him off to the infirmary with instructions that he should be properly tended and allowed to speak to anyone he liked.

Not long afterwards he was made abbot of Bonnevaux, and in Hugh's care the abbey became very flourishing. It was noted that the abbot could read men's thoughts and was quick to detect any evil spirit which had access to the minds of his brethren. The stories that have come down to us testify to his powers of divination and exorcism. Like so many of the great monastic luminaries, both men and women, Hugh did not confine his interests to his own house or even to his order. Moved by what he felt to be divine inspiration he went to Venice in 1177, there to act as mediator between Pope Alexander III and the Emperor Frederick Barbarossa. To him is due the credit of negotiating between them a peace which has become historic. St Hugh died in 1194, and his ancient *cultus* was approved in 1907.

In the *Acta Sanctorum*, April, vol. i, certain meagre details have been collected from the chroniclers Helinandus, Vincent of Beauvais, etc. On the other hand in vol. xi of the *Cistercienser-Chronik* (1899) G. Müller has compiled an adequate account, distributed through several numbers, drawing upon the cartularies of Bonnevaux and Léoncel, which have been published by Canon Ulysse Chevalier. And see the unpublished *vita* in *Collectanea O.C.R.*, vol. vi (1939), pp. 214–218, edited by A. Dimier, and that writer's *St Hugues de Bonnevaux* (1941).

ST GILBERT, BISHOP OF CAITHNESS   (A.D. 1245)

FOR his alleged defence of the liberty of the Scottish church, when threatened with subordination to England, St Gilbert was formerly held in honour by his fellow-countrymen as a great patriot. Born in Moray, he received holy orders and became archdeacon of Moray. Legend declared that while still a young man he was summoned with the heads of the Scottish church to a council at Northampton in

1176. As spokesman for the Scottish bishops he opposed with fervour and eloquence a proposal that the northern prelates should be suffragans to the archbishop of York. From the time that Scotland had received the Christian faith it had been free, he maintained, and was subject to no outside authority except that of the pope. It would be iniquitous to place it under an English metropolitan—especially since the English and the Scots were constantly at war. He seems to have carried his point. There was, no doubt, an ecclesiastic named Gilbert who made such a speech, but it is barely conceivable that he can be the man who was made bishop of Caithness in 1223.

According to the *Aberdeen Breviary*, St Gilbert was high steward to several monarchs, and a legend relates that enemies maliciously burnt the books in which he kept his accounts, hoping thereby to discredit him, but that the books were restored intact in answer to his prayers. After the death of Bishop Adam, who was murdered, King Alexander nominated Gilbert bishop of Caithness, and he ruled that northern diocese wisely and well for twenty years. He built several hospices for the poor as well as the cathedral of Dornoch, and both by preaching and example did much to civilize his flock.

As he lay dying, he said to those who stood by him : " Three maxims which I have always tried to observe I now commend to you : first, never to hurt anyone and, if injured, never to seek revenge ; secondly, to bear patiently whatever suffering God may inflict, remembering that He chastises every son whom He receives ; and finally to obey those in authority so as not to be a stumbling-block to others."

See Forbes, KSS., pp. 355–356, the *Aberdeen Breviary* (·854), and the DNB. (vol. xxi, p. 317), with the references there indicated.

ST CATHERINE OF PALMA, Virgin   (A.D. 1574)

THE whole life of Catherine Tomàs—from the moment of her birth in the little village of Valdemuzza until her death at Palma—was spent in the Balearic island of Majorca. Her parents died when Catherine, their seventh child, was seven years old, leaving her unprovided for. Sad tales are told of the indignities to which she was subjected in the house of her paternal uncle, to whose custody she was transferred. Young as she was, she became a regular little drudge whom the very servants were encouraged to overwork and to slight. Nevertheless she bore her sufferings with unfailing sweetness and patience. When she was about fifteen years old, visions of St Antony and of her patroness St Catherine awoke aspirations after the religious life which she confided to a holy hermit priest, Father Antony Castagneda. Thinking that time was required as a test of her vocation, he replied that she would receive a reply in due course if she would continue to commend her case to God, as he himself would do. She meekly agreed, but she had to wait for a long time—a delay which was the more trying because the unkindness of her relations was increased by their fear of losing her services. Father Antony, however, had not forgotten her, although he found it difficult to find a convent which could afford to take a dowerless girl. As a preliminary step, he arranged for Catherine to enter the service of a family in Palma where no hindrances would be placed in the way of her spiritual life. The daughter of the house taught her to read and write, but soon became her disciple in religious matters, for Catherine had already advanced very far on the road to perfection.

Eventually several convents offered to open their doors to Catherine almost at the same moment, and she elected to join the canonesses of St Augustine in their convent of St Mary Magdalen at Palma.   She was then in her twentieth year. From the moment of her admission she won the veneration of all by her sanctity and their love by her humility and eagerness to serve others.   At first there was nothing about the convent life of Catherine Tomàs to distinguish her from any other holy nun, but she soon began to be subject to a number of strange phenomena which are carefully described in the records of her life.   Annually, for thirteen or fifteen days before the feast of St Catherine of Alexandria, she was observed to lie in a profound trance and always, after making her communion, she would remain in an ecstasy which usually lasted for the greater part of the day and occasionally extended to several days or even to a fortnight.   Sometimes she seemed to be in a cataleptic state, giving no signs of life, but at other times she would move about with her feet together and her eyes shut—sometimes holding converse as with celestial spirits and oblivious of all around, at other times answering quite intelligently questions that were put to her.   She also possessed the gift of prophecy.

Alternating with these occurrences were severe trials and assaults from the powers of darkness.   Not only did she suffer from evil suggestions and alarming hallucinations or phantoms, but she was subjected to physical violence of the most distressing nature.   On such occasions fearful shrieks and sounds were heard by the other nuns who, however, could never see the attackers although they witnessed the results and tried to alleviate St Catherine's sufferings.   But she tried never to allow her experiences to interfere with the punctual discharge of her duties.   The death of St Catherine Tomàs, which she had foretold, took place when she was forty-one.   She was beatified in 1792 and canonized in 1930.

The bull of canonization, which is printed in the *Acta Apostolicae Sedis*, vol. xxii (1930), pp. 371–380, gives a summary of her life and details of the miracles approved in the last stages of the process.   Early biographies were written by Canon Salvador Abrines, who had been her confessor, and by Father Pedro Caldes.   Both are freely quoted in the documents of the official process, the earliest portions of which appear to have been printed in 1669. There was a *Ristretto della Vita della Beata Caterina Tomas* published in Rome at the time of the beatification.

BD LUDOVIC PAVONI, Founder of the Sons of Mary Immaculate of Brescia   (A.D. 1849)

THIS forerunner of St John Bosco in the education and care of boys, especially the orphaned and neglected, was born at Brescia in Lombardy in 1784.   His parents were Alexander Pavoni and Lelia Pontecarali, and the family was of noble descent, with a sufficiency of property to maintain its position.   Ludovic while still young showed a serious disposition ;   his sister Paolina said of him that " Ludovic was always a good religious youngster, while I was always a scamp " ;   and as a youth he already outlined his vocation when, during summer holidays at Alfianello, he played with the peasants' children and taught them the catechism.   On another occasion he threw his shirt out of the window to a beggar shivering in the street below.   He had a taste and some capacity for the fine arts and might have become a painter or an architect, but probably nobody was surprised when he decided to study for the priesthood.   This he did under the Dominicans (all the Lombard seminaries were closed in consequence of the revolution), and he was ordained priest in 1807.

Don Pavoni received no benefice, but ministered as required in the various parishes of Brescia ; and especially he helped in the several " oratories " (a combination of boys' club, Sunday-school and church) which had been started by the Oratorian father Manelli and others, work for which he showed a marked ability. In 1818, when he was only thirty-four years old, he was nominated to a canonry in Brescia cathedral and was made rector of the parish of St Barnabas.   Adjoining the church was a former Augustinian monastery, of which a corner served as rectory and the remainder was used as a military store ; and the new rector conceived the project of turning this building into a " permanent oratory " or institute, that is, a full-time home wherein boys who were destitute, abandoned or otherwise in need of care could be looked after, taught a trade and prepared for the world in a decent family atmosphere.   Such a scheme bristled with difficulties, and Canon Pavoni laid it at the foot of the Crucifix—and the Figure seemed to say to him, " Go on ! "

Mgr Nava, the bishop, promised his support,* and Pavoni began his institute in a small part of the monastery that he called " the rat-hole ", choosing printing as the trade that his boys should learn.   The next twenty years is a tale, on the one hand, of encouraging progress, and, on the other, of maddening negotiations with the civil authorities with the object, firstly, of getting the printing-press licensed, and secondly, of obtaining the use of the whole of the monastery buildings for the growing orphanage.   In those days Lombardy was still under Austrian rule, the French Revolution and Napoleon were more than living memories, and Joseph II of Austria (" Our brother the sacristan "), though dead, still spoke.   Among a people agitating for independence the authorities viewed an Italian printing-press with grave suspicion, if not alarm ; as for the buildings, the Austrian governor, though an admirer of Canon Pavoni, was a good Josephinist and would not easily release to the Church a property of which the state had deprived her.   And then there were the ordinary bureaucratic conditions—in quintuplicate.†   The press was licensed in 1823 (it had already been working, whether or no), but it was not till 1841 that the city council of Brescia granted the rest of the building required. This gave room for a school of the " three R's ", a school of design, and a school of music, which, with previous building and other work, Canon Pavoni was able to set up through the generosity of benefactors, of whom his own sister, Paolina Trivellini, and Bishop Nava were among the foremost, though the institute was not always free from money troubles.

In 1832 the work of the printing-press attracted favourable notice at the Brescia Exhibition, and in the following year Pope Gregory XVI commended the institute as *Cosa buona*, " A good thing " ; but in 1836 a great strain was put on its resources when there was a cholera epidemic in Brescia and hundreds of children lost their homes.   Among those who distinguished themselves as nurses at this time was Paola di Rosa, foundress of the Handmaids of Charity (December 15), and it was she who inspired Mgr Pinzoni to organize a school for deaf-and-dumb boys.   Canon Pavoni was asked to take over the responsibility for this undertaking, which he did. He also took over the Mercy Orphanage at the request of the civil governor, and it

---

* At a meeting of the Brescia Academy held at the Jesuit college there in 1858, Mr Ronchi acclaimed the holy partnership of Bishop Nava and Canon Pavoni in a hundred hexameters.

† The institute had to put up with all sorts of vexations.   At the carnival of 1828, a circus was allowed to camp itself in the courtyard of the monastery.   Fancy trying to keep boys in order with that going on under their windows.

was this generous action that at last shamed the city council into conveying the St Barnabas building to him, freehold and as a gift.

Ludovic Pavoni was a man of middle-height, well and strongly built, with rather silky hair ; his features strongly marked and expressive, with a mouth that had a smile playing about it.   By nature he was hot and impulsive, and his words came easily and decisively ; but he had schooled himself to patience and calmness, and so gave an impression of restrained energy.   He was what would be called today a man of good general culture, versatile but well-balanced, neither superficial nor deeply learned.   His ideal of education was a broad one, to dispose a person *in his wholeness* to be *really* good ; and it is significant that, fifty years before " *Rerum novarum* ", he grasped the religious significance of social justice and set an example by his own dealings with his employees.   Some of his boys were literally the scourings of the streets, and these had to be made good men, good workmen, good citizens, good Christians.   Like St John Bosco after him, Canon Pavoni's methods were encouraging and preventive rather than repressive ; he preferred gentleness to severity.   " Rigorism ", he said, " keeps Heaven empty."   For all that, his means of discipline and vigilance might seem excessive to some ; but who will dare say they were unnecessary with such tough material as some of it was ?   He aimed at a family and not an institution (those were the days of Oliver Twist in England), and one has only to read of some of his actual dealings with his pupils to detect a holy man at work and to see him " loving the children with all his heart, and being loved by them ".   He was relentless in expelling really vicious characters, lest their fellows be corrupted—but they were not left to sink or swim : he continued to watch over them outside the institute.

If one feels that Rodriguez's *Treatise on Perfection* is a rather unhappy choice of spiritual reading for youths, comfort may be found elsewhere in the fact that the cook and kitchen staff were considered of such importance that they were under the immediate control of the director, and that good food, punctuality and good manners to the boys were their first duties ; nor was a " discreet measure of wine " regarded as superfluous.   Not only that, but Canon Pavoni encouraged play-acting among his charges' recreations.   This was looking for trouble from the *bien-pensants* of mid-nineteenth-century Italy, and it required the presence of the bishop, the seminarists and the pupils of the Jesuit college at the first performance to confound—but not to silence—the critics.

It had been for a long time in Ludovic Pavoni's mind that he ought to establish a religious society of some kind to carry on the work which he had begun, and he gradually elaborated a rule and constitutions for a congregation of priests and of laybrothers who should work at their own trades.   After long prayer and deep consideration he opened his mind to Mgr Nava and to Cardinal Angelo Mai ; both of them encouraged the project, and he decided to go ahead in the face of the adverse criticism of other, less wise, people, some of whom thought that, while it was all right for religious to teach boys the sciences and letters, it was not all right for religious to teach boys the fine and useful arts.   Was it not St Teresa who asked to be protected from pious fools ?

Premises for a novitiate were acquired at Saiano, a few miles from Brescia. Canon Pavoni restored the old buildings, established a farm colony, and transferred his deaf-mutes to Saiano, and in 1844 the Holy See gave permission for novices to be received.   But such things could not be done in Austrian dominions without a further permission—that of the civil power ; and so it was not till another three years had passed that the Congregation of Sons of Mary Immaculate was formally founded.* On December 8, 1847, Ludovic Pavoni, already named superior general, made his religious profession.   On the previous day he had resigned his canonry, and conveyed the title to his house in Brescia and all his other private property, together with the buildings at St Barnabas's and Saiano, to the new congregation as a body ; and with his canonical cross he no doubt put off also the decoration of a knight of the Iron Crown, which his Imperial Majesty Ferdinand I had conferred on him in 1844.   On which occasion Don Pavoni had remarked privately, " Why didn't the emperor send me a sack of flour to make *polenta* for my boys instead of this ? "

These happy events were not long over when Lombardy was convulsed by a revolt against Austrian domination.   For a year the situation became daily more threatening ; in January 1849 the government imposed a heavy fine on the city of Brescia ; feeling ran so high on both sides that Bd Ludovic thought it prudent to close his beloved printing works : and on March 26 the storm broke.   The people rose, and the " Ten Days of Brescia " began.   On the following day Bd Ludovic gathered all his charges together, and in a storm of wind and rain they set out for Saiano.   At Torricelle, where Paolina Trivellini lived, she wanted to get a carriage for her ageing brother : he refused it, " No, I can go on on foot like my youngsters".   At length, wet through and worn out, the sad procession reached its destination, and Father Pavoni went up the hill to look out over burning Brescia, in the midst of which was the institute that had been his life's work for thirty years.   At that moment he felt the first spasm of that weakening of his heart that in a few days was to end his course.

The rector of St Mary's, Father Amus, sent him to bed, and Bd Ludovic obediently went (it was the first time he had enjoyed the refinement of linen sheets since he was a young man).   Daily he weakened, and a week later, surrounded by his weeping brethren and boys, Bd Ludovic Pavoni died, in his sixty-sixth year. It was April 1, 1849, Palm Sunday ; on the previous day and night the dying man had heard the roar of guns bombarding Brescia echoing in the hills around.

The body was buried at Saiano, but afterwards translated to Brescia, where it now rests in the Immacolata church, and his cause was introduced at Rome in 1919. Twenty-eight years later, in 1947, Ludovic Pavoni was solemnly beatified.

There seems to be nothing about Bd Ludovic Pavoni except in Italian.   A full " life ", *Un Apostolo della Gioventù Derelitta,* by Canon Luigi Traverso, was published at Monza in 1928 ; this is summarized in a booklet by Giovanni della Cioppa, *Lodovico Pavoni* (1946), and a few misstatements of fact are corrected.   A selection of the *beato's* letters (*Lettere del Servo di Dio P. Lodovico Pavoni* (1945) should be read by all attracted by this sympathetic character, of whom little is known outside his own country.

2 : ST FRANCIS OF PAOLA, Founder of the Minim Friars
(A.D. 1507)

S T FRANCIS was born about the year 1416 at Paola, a small town in Calabria. His parents were humble, industrious people who made it their chief aim to love and to serve God. As they were still childless after several years of married life, they prayed earnestly for a son, and when at last a boy was born to them, they

* This congregation must not be confused with that of the Sons of the Immaculate Virgin Mary, founded at Luçon by the Venerable Louis Baudouin in 1828.

named him after St Francis of Assisi, whose intercession they had specially sought. In his thirteenth year he was placed in the Franciscan friary at San Marco, where he learnt to read and where he laid the foundation of the austere life which he ever afterwards led ; although he had not professed the rule of the order, he seemed even at that tender age to outstrip the religious themselves in a scrupulous observance of its requirements.   After spending a year there he accompanied his parents on a pilgrimage which included Assisi and Rome.   Upon his return to Paola, with their consent, he retired first to a place about half a mile from the town, and after-wards to a more remote seclusion by the sea, where he occupied a cave.   He was scarcely fifteen years old.   Before he was twenty, he was joined by two other men.   The neighbours built them three cells and a chapel in which they sang the divine praises and in which Mass was offered for them by a priest from the nearest church.

This date, 1452, is reckoned as that of the foundation of his order.   Nearly seventeen years later, when the number of disciples had been augmented, a church and a monastery were built for them in the same place, with the sanction of the archbishop of Cosenza.   So greatly were they beloved by the people that the whole countryside joined in the work of construction.   Several miracles are said to have been worked by St Francis during the erection of the building, one or two of which were vouched for in the process of canonization.   When the house was finished, the saint set himself to establish regular discipline in the community, whilst never mitigating anything of the austerity he practised.   Though his bed was no longer a rock, it was a plank or the bare ground, with a log or a stone by way of a pillow. Only in extreme old age would he allow himself a mat.   Penance, charity and humility formed the basis of his rule : charity was the motto he chose ; but humility was the virtue which he inculcated continually on his followers.   In addition to the three usual monastic obligations he imposed upon them a fourth, which bound them to observe a perpetual Lent, with abstinence not only from flesh but also from eggs and anything made with milk.   Fasting he regarded as the royal road to self-conquest and, deploring as he always did the relaxation in the strict rule of Lent which the Church had been obliged to concede, he hoped that the abstinence of his followers might set a good example as well as make some sort of reparation for the lukewarmness of so many Christians.

Besides the gift of miracles St Francis was endowed with that of prophecy, and long afterwards, writing to Pope Leo X for the canonization of St Francis, the Bishop of Grenoble (uncle to Bayard, the " Chevalier sans peur et sans reproche ") wrote, " Most holy Father, he revealed to me many things which were known only to God and to myself ".   Pope Paul II sent one of his chamberlains into Calabria to inquire about the truth of the wonderful things that were reported of the saint. Upon seeing a visitor approach, St Francis, who was busy with the masons over the construction of his church, left his work to greet him.   The envoy attempted to kiss his hand, but this Francis would not allow ; he protested that it was for him to kiss the hands which for some thirty years had been sanctified by offering the holy Sacrifice.   The chamberlain, surprised that Francis should know how long he, a stranger, had been a priest, did not disclose his mission, but asked to speak with him and was led within the enclosure.   Here he expatiated eloquently on the dangers of singularity, and censured Francis's way of life as too austere for human nature. The saint attempted humbly to vindicate his rule and then, to prove what the grace of God would enable single-minded men to bear, he lifted out of the fire some burning coals and held them for some time in his hands unscathed. It may be noted that there is record of several similar examples of his immunity from the effects of fire. The chamberlain returned full of veneration for the holy man, and the new order received the sanction of the Holy See in 1474. At that time the community was composed of uneducated men, with only one priest. They were then called Hermits of St Francis of Assisi, and it was not until 1492 that their name was changed to that of " Minims ", at the desire of the founder, who wished his followers to be reckoned as the least (*minimi*) in the household of God.

St Francis made several other foundations in southern Italy and Sicily but he was threatened with a serious check to his activities ; for Ferdinand, King of Naples, annoyed at some wholesome admonitions he and two of his sons had received from Francis, gave orders for him to be arrested and brought a prisoner to Naples. The official arrived to execute his order, but was so impressed with the saint's personality and humility that, returning awestruck without his prisoner, he dissuaded Ferdinand from interfering in any way with so holy a man. Indeed all Italy was then ringing with the praises of St Francis as a saint, a prophet, and a wonder-worker.

It happened in 1481 that Louis XI, King of France, was slowly dying, after an apoplectic fit. Never had anyone a stronger passion for life or a greater dread of death, and so irritable and impatient was he that everyone feared to approach him. Realizing that he was steadily growing worse, he sent into Calabria to beg St Francis to come and heal him, making many promises to assist him and his order. Then, as his request was not acceded to, he appealed to Pope Sixtus IV, who told Francis to go. He at once set out ; and King Louis gave ten thousand crowns to the herald who announced the saint's arrival in his dominions, and sent the dauphin to escort him to Plessis-les-Tours. Louis, falling on his knees, besought Francis to heal him. The saint replied that the lives of kings are in the hands of God and have their appointed limits ; prayer should be addressed to Him. Many interviews followed between the sovereign and his guest. Although Francis was an unlearned man, Philip de Commines, who often heard him, wrote that his words were so full of wisdom that all present were convinced that the Holy Ghost spoke through his lips. By his prayers and example he wrought a change of heart in the king, who died in resignation in his arms. Charles VIII honoured Francis as his father had done, and would do nothing in the affairs of his conscience or even in state matters without his advice. He built for his friars a monastery in the park of Plessis and another at Amboise, at the spot where they had first met. Moreover, in Rome, he built for the Minims the monastery of Santa Trinità del Monte on the Pincian Hill, to which none but Frenchmen might be admitted.

St Francis passed twenty-five years in France, and died there. On Palm Sunday 1507 he fell ill, and on Maundy Thursday assembled his brethren and exhorted them to the love of God, to charity and to a strict observance of all the duties of their rule. Then he received viaticum barefoot with a rope round his neck, according to the custom of his order. He died on the following day, Good Friday, being then ninety-one years of age. His canonization took place in 1519.

Besides the rule which St Francis drew up for his friars, with a *correctorium* or method of enjoining penances and a ceremonial, he also composed a rule for nuns, and regulations for a third order of persons living in the world. Today the number of members of the Order of Minims is considerably reduced : they are mostly found in Italy.

In the *Acta Sanctorum*, April, vol. i, the Bollandists have printed a great part of the depositions made by witnesses in the process of canonization. Although the saint was canonized only twelve years after his death, still the advanced age to which he lived rendered it difficult to procure contemporary evidence as to his early life ; those who had known him when he founded the Order of Minims were nearly all dead. Still the facts of his later career are well known, not only from the depositions but from the chronicles, letters and other documents of the period. Modern biographies are numerous, and among them may be mentioned those of Dabert (1875), Ferrante (1881), Rolland (1874), Pradier (1903), Porpora (1901) and G. M. Roberti (1915). Much information concerning the foundations of the Minims may be gathered from the volumes of G. M. Roberti, *Disegno storico dell' Ordine dei Minimi*, 1902, 1909, etc.

SS. APPHIAN AND THEODOSIA, MARTYRS   (A.D. 306)

AMONGST the martyrs of Palestine whom Eusebius knew personally and whose sufferings he has described, there are two who seem to have made a special impression upon him by reason of their tender age. One was Apphian, or Apian, a youth in his twentieth year, and the other was a girl of eighteen called Theodosia.

Apphian, born in Lycia, had passed through the then famous schools of Berytus in Phoenicia, where he had become a Christian, and he went to live at Caesarea when he was eighteen. Not long afterwards there came instructions to the governor of the city that everyone should attend the public sacrifices. Thereupon Apphian, communicating his design to no one—" not even to us ", says Eusebius, with whom he lived—went to the place where Urban the governor was offering the sacrifice, and, slipping unnoticed through the guards, laid hold of the magistrate's arm and stopped him, exclaiming that it was impious to neglect the worship of the true God to sacrifice to idols. The guards fell upon him, beat him and kicked him, and he was thrown into a dark dungeon, where he remained twenty-four hours with his feet in the stocks. The following day, when his face had become so swollen with blows as to be unrecognizable, his sides were torn until his bones and entrails were exposed. To all interrogations he made but one reply : " I am a servant of Christ ". Lighted pieces of flax dipped in oil were next applied to his feet, but though the fire burnt to his bones his constancy could not be shaken. When urged to sacrifice he only said, " I confess Christ, the one God, and the same God with the Father ". Finding no weakening of resolution, the judge condemned him to be cast into the sea. Immediately after the sentence had been carried out there ensued a prodigy of which Eusebius says there were as many witnesses as there were inhabitants of Caesarea. The sea and city were shaken by an earthquake, and though the saint's feet were weighted down by heavy stones, his body was cast up on the shore.

Of Theodosia, who appears to have suffered also under Maximinus, Eusebius writes in the following words : " After the persecution had lasted over five years, on the . . . fourth day before the nones of April—actually on the day of the Lord's resurrection—there came into Caesarea a holy and very devoted girl called Theodosia, a native of Tyre. She approached some prisoners, who were sitting before the pretorium awaiting sentence of death, with the intention of greeting them and also probably of asking them to remember her when they came into the presence of God. She was set upon by the soldiers as though she had done something impious or criminal, and was brought before the president. He was in a savage mood and, moved by some cruel impulse, he condemned her to horrible tortures, her sides and her breasts being torn to the bone by means of iron teeth. Then, as she was still breathing and her face bore a happy smile, he caused her to be thrown into the sea."

All this is taken from Eusebius in *The Martyrs of Palestine*. Two texts are preserved to us which may conveniently be consulted in E. Grapin's edition in the series *Textes et Documents pour l'Étude historique du Christianisme*, vol. iii, pp. 183–227. See also the *Analecta Bollandiana*, vol. xvi (1897), pp. 122–127.

ST MARY OF EGYPT   (FIFTH CENTURY ?)

THE story of St Mary of Egypt seems to be based upon a short and not incredible account contained in the Life of St Cyriacus, written by his disciple Cyril of Scythopolis. The holy man had retired with his followers into the wild and apparently uninhabited desert beyond Jordan. One day two of his disciples suddenly saw a human figure which escaped into some bushes, but which they afterwards tracked into a cave. The figure told them not to approach because she was a woman and naked, but upon being interrogated she informed them that her name was Mary, that she was a great sinner who had been a public singer and actress, and that she had come there to expiate her former life. The two returned to tell St Cyriacus what they had seen and heard. Upon the occasion of a second visit which they paid to the cave they found her lying dead and they buried her on the spot.

Round about this narrative there grew up an elaborate legend which attained enormous popularity in the middle ages and which is illustrated on the old glass windows of the cathedrals of Bourges, Auxerre and elsewhere. It may be summarized as follows :

In the reign of Theodosius the Younger, there lived in Palestine a holy monk and priest named Zosimus who, having served God with great fervour in the same house for fifty-three years, was divinely directed to leave his monastery for one near the Jordan, where he might learn how to advance still further on the path of holiness. He found that the members of this community on the first Sunday in Lent after Mass used to disperse in the desert to pass in solitude and penance the time until Palm Sunday. It was at that season, about the year 430, that Zosimus found himself a twenty days' distance from his monastery, and sat down one day at noon to say his psalms and to rest. Perceiving suddenly what appeared to be a human form he made the sign of the cross and finished his psalms. Then, looking up, he saw a white-haired, sun-tanned figure which he took to be a hermit, but which ran away as he went towards it. He had nearly overtaken it and was near enough to crave its blessing, when it exclaimed, " Father Zosimus, I am a woman : throw your mantle to cover me that you may come near me ". Surprised that she should know his name, he complied, and they entered into conversation. In reply to his inquiries the woman told him her strange story with many expressions of shame and penitence : " My country ", she said, " is Egypt. At the age of twelve, while my father and mother were still living, I went without their consent to Alexandria. I cannot think without trembling of the first steps by which I fell into sin or of the excesses which followed." She then described how she had lived as a public prostitute for seventeen years, not for money, but to gratify her lust. At the age of about twenty-eight, curiosity led her to join a band of people who were going to celebrate at Jerusalem the feast of the Holy Cross—and even on the journey she continued her evil courses, corrupting some of the pilgrims. Upon their arrival in

14

Jerusalem she tried to enter the church with the rest of the congregation, but an invisible force held her back.   After two or three ineffectual attempts, she withdrew into a corner of the outer court, and for the first time a full realization of her sinfulness swept over her.   Raising her eyes to an *eikon* of the Blessed Virgin Mary she besought with tears the help of the Mother of God, vowing herself to a life of penance.   With a lightened heart she was now able without any difficulty to enter the church to venerate the cross, and as she returned to the *eikon* to give thanks to our Lady she heard a voice which said, " Go over Jordan and thou shalt find rest ".

At a baker's where she bought loaves she inquired the way to the Jordan, and started off forthwith, arriving that same night at the church of St John the Baptist on the bank of the river.   Here she made her communion and crossed the Jordan into the wilderness, where she had remained ever since—about forty-seven years, as far as she could judge.   She had seen no human being and had lived on edible plants and on dates.   The winter cold and the summer heat had sorely afflicted her unprotected body, and she had often been tortured by thirst.   At such times she had been tempted to regret the luxuries and the wines of Egypt in which she had formerly indulged.   These and other assaults beset her night and day almost unremittingly for seventeen years, but she had implored the intercession of the Blessed Virgin and the divine assistance had never failed her.   She could not read, and had never had any human instruction in holy things, but God Himself had taught her the mysteries of faith.   At her request, Zosimus undertook not to divulge what she had said until after her death, and promised to meet her again beside the Jordan on the Maundy Thursday of the following year to give her holy communion.

The next Lent, Zosimus made his way to the selected meeting-place, bearing the Blessed Sacrament, and that same Maundy Thursday evening beheld Mary standing on the opposite bank of Jordan.   After she had made the sign of the cross, she proceeded to walk upon the water until she reached dry ground beside the astonished priest.   She received communion with deep devotion, following it by the recitation of the opening words of the *Nunc dimittis*.   From a basket of dates, figs and lentils which Zosimus offered, she would accept only three lentils ; and she thanked him for all he had done and commended herself to his prayers.   Then, with a final entreaty that he would return a year later to the spot where they had first met, she departed over the river as she had come.   But when Zosimus went back into the desert to keep this second appointment, he found Mary's dead body stretched out upon the ground, whilst beside her on the sand were traced these words : " Father Zosimus, bury the body of lowly Mary.   Render earth to earth and pray for me.   I died the night of the Lord's Passion, after receiving the divine and mystic Banquet."   The monk had no spade, but a lion from the desert came to his assistance and with its claws helped him to dig her grave.   Zosimus resumed his mantle, which he treasured henceforth as a holy relic, and returned to tell his brethren all his experiences.   He continued for many years to serve God in his monastery until a happy death released him in the hundredth year of his age.

This legend has had a remarkable diffusion and popularity in the East.   In its developed form it seems to have been the composition of St Sophronius, Patriarch of Jerusalem, who died in A.D. 638.   Besides the digression referred to above, which Cyril of Scythopolis introduced into his Life of St Cyriacus, Sophronius had before him a somewhat similar story told by John Moschus in the *Pratum Spirituale*.   This nucleus was elaborated into a narrative of respectable dimensions with the aid of sundry borrowings from the Life of St Paul of Thebes.   St John Damascene, who died in the middle of the eighth century, makes long quotations from the developed Life of St Mary of Egypt and apparently regarded it as an authentic record. A good account of the whole matter is furnished by H. Leclercq in DAC., vol. x (1932), cc. 2128–2136, where a full bibliography will be found. See also the *Acta Sanctorum*, April, vol. i; and A. B. Bujila, *Rutebeuf : La Vie de sainte Marie l'Égyptienne* (1949).

ST NICETIUS, or NIZIER, Bishop of Lyons   (A.D. 573)

St Nicetius, or Nizier, a great-uncle to St Gregory of Tours, was descended from a Burgundian family and had been destined for the Church from an early age. Even after he was ordained priest, he continued to live in his own home with his widowed mother, whom he obeyed as implicitly as the lowliest of her servants. Although he valued letters so highly that he insisted that every boy born on the estate should learn to read and to know the psalms, yet he made a practice of personally assisting the servants and dependents in their manual labours, that he might carry out the apostolic precept, and have something to give to those that suffered need. When St Sacerdos, bishop of Lyons, lay on his death-bed in Paris, he was visited by King Childebert who urged him to nominate a successor. The aged prelate accordingly named his nephew Nicetius, who in due time was approved and consecrated. A man of blameless life, he was a determined opponent of loose and uncharitable speech, which he denounced on every possible occasion. He became famous for his power of exorcising unclean spirits ; and in the course of an episcopate which lasted nearly twenty years St Nicetius revived and improved ecclesiastical chant in his diocese. St Gregory of Tours relates a number of miracles that occurred at his tomb.

See the *Acta Sanctorum*, April, vol. i, where a short anonymous life is printed, as well as an account by Gregory of Tours. The former has been more critically edited by B. Krusch in MGH., *Scriptores Merov.*, vol. iii, pp. 521–524. See also Duchesne, *Fastes Épiscopaux*, vol. ii, pp. 166–167 ; Hefele-Leclercq, *Conciles*, vol. iii, pp. 182–184 ; and especially A. Coville, *Recherches sur l'Histoire de Lyon* (1928), pp. 323–346.

BD JOHN PAYNE, Martyr   (A.D. 1582)

Peterborough appears to have been the birthplace of Bd John Payne, but nothing is known of his family, except that he had a brother who was an ardent Protestant —a fact which has given rise to the conjecture that he himself was a convert.

We first hear of him as a seminarist at Douai, where he arrived in 1574 for his theological training. Less than three weeks after his ordination to the priesthood he was sent on the English mission, his destination being Essex, whilst that of Bd Cuthbert Mayne, his fellow-traveller, was Devonshire. At Ingatestone, in the house of Lady Petre, whose steward he was supposed to be, Bd John had his headquarters, but he also found a lodging in London. He seems to have been very active, and his efforts, unlike those of many of the other martyrs, were crowned with immediate and visible success. As he writes in one of his letters : " On all sides, in daily increasing numbers, a great many are reconciled to the Catholic faith, to the amazement of many of the heretics ", and he adds that this augmentation makes it essential that Douai should send more priests to minister to them. Less than a year after his arrival, he was arrested at Lady Petre's and imprisoned, but was released within four weeks and left England some nine months later—why and for how long a period history does not tell. We know that he was back in Essex by Christmas 1579, for the man who afterwards betrayed him stated that he first came across the martyr at Lady Petre's at that date, and there seems no reason to doubt the statement.   Ingatestone Hall was then a regular refuge for priests, and its priests' hiding-place, 14 feet by 2 feet and 10 feet in height, was accidentally rediscovered in 1855.

Mr Payne's second and final arrest was in Warwickshire on a charge of conspiracy, but Walsingham, who examined him, reported to Burleigh that he thought the accusation baseless.   Nevertheless, as it was clear that he was a priest from Douai, it was deemed undesirable to let him go, although the law declaring it treason to be ordained abroad had not yet been passed.   Accordingly a fresh charge of plotting to murder the queen, the lord treasurer and Walsingham was trumped up by his denouncer, who pretended that Payne had tried to enlist him in the conspiracy. This informer was John Eliot—Judas Eliot as he came to be called—who had occupied positions of trust at Lady Petre's and in other Catholic families, but was a profligate, an embezzler and a murderer.   To escape punishment and to obtain money, he denounced no less than thirty priests and caused the capture of Bd Edmund Campion.   On this man's accusation alone, Mr Payne suffered eight months' imprisonment in the Tower without being tried.   Several times he was tortured, notably on August 31, when, according to the Diary of the Tower, " John Payne priest was most violently tormented on the rack ".

On the night of March 20, 1582, he was roused from sleep and hurried off to Chelmsford gaol, without being allowed to dress or to take his purse, which was appropriated by Lady Hopton.   At the assizes, Eliot repeated his charge : there was no other witness, neither was there any attempt made to obtain one.   The martyr declared his innocence and protested that it was against divine and human law that he should be condemned on the evidence of one man, and he a notoriously infamous character.   But his fate had already been sealed : sentence of death was passed, the date of the execution fixed for April 2, and it was duly carried out.   The crowd, who were well affected towards him, interfered to prevent the hangman from quartering and disembowelling him before he was dead.   The feast of Bd John Payne is kept in the dioceses of Northampton and Brentwood (on the morrow).

See Challoner, MMP., pp. 39–44, and B. Camm, LEM. (1905), ii, pp. 424–442.

BD LEOPOLD OF GAICHE   (A.D. 1815)

BD LEOPOLD was born at Gaiche in the diocese of Perugia, the son of humble parents, and was christened John.   A neighbouring priest helped him with his education and in 1751, when he was eighteen, he received the Franciscan habit in the friary at Cibotola, taking the name Leopold.   After he became a priest in 1757 he was sent to preach Lenten courses of sermons which soon made him famous. As the result of his eloquence and fervour, numerous conversions took place, enemies were reconciled, and penitents besieged his confessional.   For ten years, from 1768 when he was made papal missioner in the States of the Church, he held missions in several dioceses, and even after he had become minister provincial he continued his apostolic labours.   Fired by the example of Bd Thomas of Cori and of St Leonard of Port Maurice he was anxious to found a house to which missioners and preachers could retire for their annual retreat and where other brethren and friends of the order could come for spiritual refreshment.   He had, however, many difficulties to overcome and disappointments to meet before he could realize his desire, on the lonely hill of Monte Luco, near Spoleto.

When in 1808 Napoleon invaded Rome and imprisoned Pope Pius VII, religious houses were suppressed and their occupants turned out. Bd Leopold, a venerable old man of seventy-seven, was obliged to abandon his beloved convent, and with three of his brethren to live in a miserable hut in Spoleto. While there he acted as assistant to a parish priest, but afterwards he had charge of an entire parish whose pastor had been driven out by the French. Then he was himself imprisoned for refusing to take an oath which he considered unlawful. His imprisonment, however, was of short duration, for we soon find him giving missions once more. His fame was enhanced by his prophetical powers and by strange phenomena which attended him : for example, when he was preaching his head often appeared to his congregation as though it were crowned with thorns.

With the fall of Napoleon, Bd Leopold hurried back to Monte Luco, where he set about trying to establish things as they had been before ; but he only survived for a few months, dying on April 15, 1815, in his eighty-third year. The numerous miracles reported to have taken place at his grave caused the speedy introduction of the process of his beatification, which reached a favourable conclusion in 1893.

Abundant information is provided by the documents printed for the process of beatification ; and there is a life by Fr M. Antonio da Vicenza. See also Kempf, *Holiness of the Church in the Nineteenth Century*, pp. 95–96, and Seeböck, *Die Herrlichkeit der Katholischen Kirche*, pp. 212–213.

3 : ST PANCRAS, Bishop of Taormina, Martyr　　　(*c.* A.D. 90 ?)

WE have no trustworthy records of the life and death of this St Pancras (Pancratius) who, though less well known than his Roman namesake, is greatly honoured in Sicily. According to his legendary history he was a native of Antioch and was converted and baptized together with his parents by St Peter, who sent him to evangelize Sicily, consecrating him the first bishop of Taormina. There he preached, destroyed the idols, and, by his eloquence and miracles, converted Boniface, the city prefect, who helped him to build a church. After he had baptized a great number, he was stoned to death by brigands who came down from the mountains and captured him by guile.

A panegyric purporting to give biographical details is printed in the *Acta Sanctorum*, April, vol. i ; but while this information is quite unreliable, there seems to have been an early *cultus*. This St Pancratius is twice mentioned in the " Hieronymianum ", and even as far off as Georgia we find mention of him as a disciple of St Peter. His proper day seems to have been July 8 ; see the stone calendar of Nap ɩ ɛand the *Acta Sanctorum*, November, vol. ii, part 2, p. 359. The Greek text of the panegyric by Theophanes is in Migne, PG., vol. 132, cc. 989 *seq.*

ST SIXTUS, or XYSTUS, I, Pope and Martyr　　　(*c.* A.D. 127)

St Xystus I succeeded Pope St Alexander I about the end of the reign of Trajan, and governed the Church for some ten years at a period when the papal dignity was the common prelude to martyrdom. In all the old martyrologies he is honoured as a martyr, but we have no particulars about his life or death. He was by birth a Roman, his father's house in the ancient Via Lata having occupied, it is supposed, the site now covered by the church of St Mary-in-Broad-Street. The *Liber Pontificalis* credits him with having laid down as ordinances that none but the clergy should touch the sacred vessels, and that the people should join in when the priest had intoned the *Sanctus* at Mass. The Sixtus mentioned in the canon of the Mass was probably not this pope but St Sixtus II, whose martyrdom was more widely famous.

See the *Liber Pontificalis* (ed. Duchesne), vol. i, pp. 56 and 128, and the *Acta Sanctorum*, November, vol. ii, pars posterior, pp. 173 and 177.

SS. AGAPE, CHIONIA and IRENE, VIRGINS AND MARTYRS (A.D. 304)

IN the year 303, the Emperor Diocletian issued a decree rendering it an offence punishable by death to possess or retain any portion of the sacred Christian writings. Now there were living at that time at Thessalonica in Macedonia three Christian sisters, Agape, Chionia and Irene, the daughters of pagan parents, who owned several volumes of the Holy Scriptures. These books were kept so carefully concealed that they were not discovered until the following year when the house was searched after the sisters had been arrested upon another charge.

One day, when Dulcitius the governor had taken his seat on the tribune, his secretary Artemesius read the charge-sheet, which had been handed in by the public informer. It ran as follows : " The pensioner Cassander to Dulcitius, President of Macedonia, greeting. I send to your Highness six Christian women and one man who have refused to eat meat sacrificed to the gods. Their names are Agape, Chionia, Irene, Cassia, Philippa and Eutychia, and the man is called Agatho."

The president said to the women, who had been arrested, " Fools, how can you be so mad as to disobey the commands of the emperors ? " Then, turning to the man, he asked, " Why will you not eat of the meat offered to the gods, like other subjects ? " " Because I am a Christian," replied Agatho. "Do you adhere to your determination ? " "Certainly I do." Dulcitius next questioned Agape as to her convictions. " I believe in the living God," was her answer, " and I will not lose all the merit of my past life by one evil action." " And you, Chionia, what have you to say for yourself ? " " That I believe in the living God and therefore I cannot obey the emperor's orders." Irene replied when asked why she did not comply, " Because I was afraid of offending God." " What do you say, Cassia ? " inquired the judge. " That I desire to save my soul." " Then will you not partake of the sacred offerings ? " " No, indeed, I will not." Philippa declared that she would rather die than obey, and so did Eutychia, a young woman recently widowed who was about to become a mother. Because of her condition, she was separated from her companions and taken back to prison, while Dulcitius proceeded to press the others further. " Agape ", he inquired, " what have you decided ? Will you act as we do, who are obedient and dutiful to the emperor ? " " It is not right to obey Satan ", she answered, " I am not to be influenced by anything that you can say." " And you, Chionia ", persisted the president, " what is your ultimate decision ? " " My decision remains unchanged." " Have you not some books or writings relating to the religion of the impious Christians ? " he asked. " We have none : the emperor now on the throne has taken them all from us ", was the reply. To inquiries as to who had converted them to Christianity Chionia would only say, " Our Lord Jesus Christ."

Then Dulcitius gave sentence : " I condemn Agape and Chionia to be burnt alive for having out of malice and obstinacy acted in contravention of the divine edicts of our lords the Emperors and Caesars, and for continuing to profess the rash and false religion of the Christians, which all pious persons abhor. As for the other four ", he added, " let them be kept in close captivity during my pleasure."

After the martyrdom of her elder sisters, Irene was again brought before the president, who said to her, " Your folly is patent enough now, for you retained in your possession all those books, parchments, and writings relating to the doctrine of the impious Christians which you were forced to acknowledge when they were produced before you, although you had previously denied that you had any . . . Yet even now, notwithstanding your crimes, you may find pardon if you will worship the gods. . . . Are you prepared to do so ? " " No ", replied Irene, " for those who do so are in danger of hell fire." " Who persuaded you to hide those books and papers for so long ? " " Almighty God, who has commanded us to love Him unto death. For that reason we prefer to be burnt alive rather than give up the Holy Scriptures and betray Him." " Who knew that you had those writings hidden away ? " " Nobody ", replied Irene, " except Almighty God ; for we concealed them even from our servants lest they should inform against us." " Where did you hide yourselves last year when the emperors' edict was first published ? " " Where it pleased God : in the mountains." " With whom did you live ? " persisted the judge. " We were in the open air—sometimes on one mountain, sometimes on another." " Who supplied you with food ? " " God, who gives food to all flesh." " Was your father privy to it ? " " No, he had not the least idea of it." " Which of your neighbours was in the secret ? " " Inquire in the neighbourhood and make your search." " After you returned from the mountains did you read those books to anyone ? " " They were hidden in the house, but we dared not produce them : we were in great trouble because we could no longer read them day and night as we had been accustomed to do."

Irene's sentence was a more cruel one than that of her sisters. Dulcitius declared that she like them had incurred the death penalty for having concealed the books, but that her sufferings should be more lingering. He therefore ordered that she should be stripped and exposed in a house of ill fame which was kept closely guarded. As, however, she appeared to be miraculously protected from molestation, the governor afterwards caused her to be put to death. The acts say that she suffered at the stake, being compelled to throw herself into the flames. But this is improbable, and some later versions speak of her being shot in the throat with an arrow.

As we read of these noble women who preferred to die rather than yield up their copies of the Sacred Scriptures, and as we consider the loving care lavished by the monks of a later generation upon copying and illuminating the gospels, we may with advantage question ourselves as to the value which we attach to God's written word. Irene and her sisters were distressed when they could not read the sacred books at all hours. Many of us in these latter ages do not even read them every day although we have every inducement and encouragement to do so. The very facilities which we have for obtaining cheap and well-printed Bibles seem to render us less appreciative and less studious of the word of God—in spite of the exhortations of our pastors. There is a salutary lesson for all in the story of Agape, Chionia and Irene.

The Greek text of the *acta* of these martyrs was discovered and edited in 1902 by Pio Franchi de' Cavalieri in part ix of *Studi e Testi*. It is admitted on all hands that the document was compiled from genuine and official records, but the Latin translation reproduced by

Ruinart in his *Acta Martyrum Sincera* is not altogether satisfactory.   An English version
of the Greek may be found in A. J. Mason, *Historic Martyrs of the Primitive Church* (1905),
pp. 341–346.   The names of Chionia and Agape occur in the old Syriac martyrologium, or
" Breviarium ", of the beginning of the fifth century, entered under April 2.   Irene's name
was perhaps omitted because she suffered later and separately.   Nothing is recorded of the
fate of the other four.   See the *Acta Sanctorum*, November, vol. ii, pars posterior (1932),
pp. 169–170 ; and also Delehaye, *Les Passions des Martyrs . . .*, pp. 141–143.

ST BURGUNDOFARA, or FARE, Virgin   (A.D. 657)

Amongst the courtiers of King Theodebert II one of the foremost was Count
Agneric, three of whose children were destined to be honoured by the Church.
They were St Cagnoald of Laon, St Faro of Meaux, and a daughter called Burgundofara (" Fare " in France) who as a child had received a blessing from St Columban
when he was a guest at Agneric's house.   The girl was resolved to lead the religious
life, but she had to face opposition and even persecution from her father, who wished
to bestow her in marriage.   The struggle caused her health to give way and she
suffered from a prolonged malady which was cured by St Eustace.   Even then the
count did not at once surrender ; but eventually Burgundofara had her way, and
her father became so reconciled to her vocation that he built for her a convent which
he richly endowed.   Of this house, young as she was, she became abbess—in
accordance with the custom of the time—and throughout the thirty-seven years of
her rule she proved herself a capable and saintly superior.   The convent, which in
its early days kept the Rule of St Columban, was known by the name of Evoriacum,
but after the death of St Burgundofara it was renamed in her honour and developed
into the celebrated Benedictine abbey of Faremoutiers.

There are early materials for the life of this saint, particularly an account of the wonderful
works wrought at Faremoutiers, written by Abbot Jonas of Bobbio.   It is printed by Mabillon
in the *Acta Sanctorum O.S.B.*, and has been more recently edited by B. Krusch in MGH.,
Scriptores Merov., vol. iv.   St Fare is also mentioned by Bede, *Hist. Eccles.*, iii, ch. 8.   Probably this reference by the great English writer, coupled with some confusion between
Eboracum (York) and Evoriacum, led to the extraordinary blunder in earlier editions of the
Roman Martyrology which stated that St Burgundofara died in England.   An admirable
modern account is that of H. M. Delsart, *Sainte Fare, sa vie et son culte* (1911).

ST NICETAS, Abbot   (A.D. 824)

The parents of St Nicetas were residents of Caesarea in Bithynia, but his
mother died when he was a week old, and his father, a very few years later,
retired into a monastery.   The boy, brought up from infancy in monastic austerity,
responded eagerly to the teaching he received, and entered the monastery of
Medikion on Mount Olympus in Asia Minor.   It had been founded not long
before by an eminent abbot named Nicephorus, who was subsequently honoured as
a saint.   In 790 Nicetas was ordained priest by St Tarasius and rose to be coadjutor
to Nicephorus and then his successor.   From the peaceful life of prayer which he
led with his monks Nicetas was summoned to Constantinople, together with other
important heads of monasteries, by the iconoclastic Emperor Leo the Armenian,
who demanded their adherence to the usurper whom he had thrust into the seat of
the banished patriarch St Nicephorus.   Upon their refusal Nicetas was sent to a
fortress in Anatolia, where he was confined in an uncovered enclosure, and had to
lie on the earth exposed to the snow and rain.   Brought back to Constantinople, he
allowed himself to be over-persuaded by his brother abbots and to be imposed upon

by imperial guile : they all received communion from the so-called patriarch and were allowed to return to their monasteries.

Nicetas, however, promptly recognized his mistake. He embarked, it is true, on a vessel bound for the island of Proconnesus, but his conscience drove him back to Constantinople, and there publicly to retract his adherence to the usurper and to protest that he would never abandon the tradition of the fathers in the *cultus* of sacred images. He was in 813 banished to an island, where he languished for six years in a dark dungeon. His only food was a little mouldy bread tossed through the grating, and his drink stagnant water. In this martyrdom he lingered until Michael the Stammerer, upon his accession to the throne, released Nicetas with many other prisoners, and the holy man returned to the neighbourhood of Constantinople. There he shut himself up in a hermitage where he lived until he went to his reward.

See the *Acta Sanctorum*, April, vol. i, where a Greek biography of St Nicetas is printed and translated. It was apparently written shortly after his death by a disciple of his named Theosterictus. The substance of three letters from Theodore Studites addressed to St Nicetas was published by Mai in his *Nova Patrum Bibliotheca*, vol. viii, letters 176, 195, 196. See also C. Van de Vorst in the *Analecta Bollandiana*, vol. xxxi, pp. 149–155, and vol. xxxii, pp. 44–45.

ST RICHARD OF WYCHE, Bishop of Chichester　(A.D. 1253)

RICHARD DE WYCHE, or Richard of Burford, as he is sometimes called, was born *c.* 1197 at Wyche, the present Droitwich, then as now famous for its brine-springs. His father was a landed proprietor or small squire, but both he and his wife died when their children were very young, leaving the estate in the charge of a negligent guardian who allowed it to go to rack and ruin. Richard, the younger son, although addicted to study from childhood, was of a much more virile temperament than his brother, and, as soon as he realized the state of affairs he literally put his hand to the plough and worked like a common labourer until by sheer industry and good management he had retrieved the family fortunes. In a fit of gratitude, the elder, Robert, made over to him the title deeds, but when Richard discovered that a wealthy bride was being found for him and also that Robert was repenting of his generosity, he resigned to him both the land and the lady, departing almost penniless to take up a new life in the University of Oxford. Poverty was no drawback, social or educational, in a medieval seat of learning, and Richard was wont in after days to characterize those years at Oxford as the happiest of his life. Little did he reck that he was sometimes hungry, that being unable to afford a fire he had to run about in winter to keep warm, or that he and the companions who shared his room had but one college gown which they took it in turns to wear at lectures. They were athirst for learning, and they had great masters at Oxford in those days. Grosseteste was lecturing in the Franciscan house of studies, and the Dominicans, who arrived in the city in 1221, at once gathered round them a host of brilliant men. We are not told how it happened that, in the short interval between Richard's arrival and Edmund Rich's departure for Salisbury, the unknown freshman came into contact with the great university chancellor, but there seems no reason to doubt that the acquaintance was then begun which ripened to a life-long friendship.

From Oxford Richard went to Paris, but returned to his *alma mater* to take his M.A. degree, and then, some years later, proceeded to Bologna to study canon law in what was regarded as the chief law school of Europe.   He made a stay in that city for seven years, receiving the degree of doctor and winning general esteem, but when one of his tutors offered to make him his heir and to give him his daughter in marriage, Richard, who felt himself called to a celibate life, made a courteous excuse and returned to Oxford.   There his career had been watched with interest. Almost immediately he was appointed chancellor of the university, and soon afterwards both St Edmund Rich, now archbishop of Canterbury, and Grosseteste, who had become bishop of Lincoln, invited him to become their chancellor.   He accepted Edmund's offer and henceforth became his close companion and righthand man, relieving him as much as he could of his heavy burdens.   In the words of the Dominican Ralph Bocking, afterwards St Richard's confessor and biographer, " Each leaned upon the other—the saint upon the saint : the master upon the disciple, the disciple upon the master : the father on the son, and the son on the father."

St Edmund needed all his chancellor's help and sympathy in face of his well-nigh overwhelming difficulties, the greatest of which arose from Henry III's reprehensible and obstinate practice of either keeping benefices vacant that he might enjoy their revenues or else filling them with unworthy favourites of his own.   When, after many ineffectual struggles, the archbishop, sick and despairing, retired to the Cistercian monastery of Pontigny, St Richard accompanied him and nursed him until his death.   Unwilling to remain on without his master, the ex-chancellor then left Pontigny for the Dominican house of studies in Orleans, where he continued reading and lecturing for two years, and it was in the friars' church that he was ordained priest in 1243.   Although he certainly contemplated eventually joining the Order of Preachers, he returned to England, for some reason unknown, to work as a parish priest at Deal, the prebendal stall of which had probably been conferred upon him by St Edmund, as it was in the gift of the archbishop.   A man of his outstanding merits and qualifications could not long remain in obscurity, and he was shortly afterwards recalled to his former chancellorship by the new archbishop of Canterbury, Boniface of Savoy.

In 1244 Ralph Neville, bishop of Chichester, died, and Henry III, by putting pressure on the canons, obtained the election of Robert Passelewe, a worthless man who, according to Matthew Paris, " had obtained the king's favour in a wonderful degree by an unjust inquisition by which he added some thousands of marks to the royal treasury."   The archbishop refused to confirm the election and called a chapter of his suffragans who declared the previous election invalid, and chose Richard, the primate's nominee, to fill the vacant see.   Upon hearing the news, King Henry was violently enraged : he kept in his own hands all the temporalities and forbade the admission of St Richard to any barony or secular possession attached to his see.   In vain did the bishop elect himself approach the monarch on two separate occasions : he could obtain neither the confirmation of his election nor the restoration of the revenues to which he was entitled.   At last both he and the king carried the case to Pope Innocent IV, who was presiding over the Council of Lyons, and he decided in favour of St Richard, whom he consecrated himself on March 5, 1245.   Landing once more in England the new bishop was met by the news that the king, far from giving up the temporalities, had forbidden anyone to lend St Richard money or even to give him houseroom.   At Chichester he found the palace gates closed against him : those who would gladly have helped him feared the sovereign's anger, and it seemed as though he would have to wander about his diocese a homeless outcast. However, a good priest, Simon of Tarring, opened his house to him, and Richard, as Bocking informs us, " took shelter under this hospitable roof, sharing the meals of a stranger, warming his feet at another man's hearth ".

From this modest centre St Richard worked for two years like a missionary bishop, visiting fisherfolk and downsmen, travelling about mainly on foot, and succeeding under great difficulties in holding synods—as we learn from the Constitutions of St Richard, a body of statutes drawn up at this period and dealing with the various abuses which had come to his notice. Only when the pope threatened to excommunicate him would Henry acknowledge the bishop and yield up the temporalities, but even then much of the money which should have been restored to him remained unpaid until after his death. Still, St Richard's position was now totally changed : he was enthroned and could henceforth dispense some of that general hospitality combined with liberal almsgiving which was expected of a medieval prelate. His own austerity remained unaltered, and, while his guests feasted, he kept to his simple fare from which flesh meat was rigorously excluded. When he saw poultry or young animals being conveyed to his kitchen he would say, half sadly and half humorously, " Poor little innocent creatures, if you were reasoning beings and could speak, how you would curse us ! For we are the cause of your death, and what have you done to deserve it ? " His dress was as plain as he could make it : lamb's wool took the place of the usual fur, and next to his skin he wore a hair shirt and a sort of iron cuirass.

In the course of his eight years' episcopate he won the affection of his people to a remarkable extent, but though fatherly and tender he could be very stern when he discovered avarice, heresy or immorality amongst his clergy. Not even the intercession of the archbishop and of the king could induce him to mitigate the punishment of a priest who had sinned against chastity. His objection to nepotism was so strong that he never would give preferment to any of his relations, always instancing the example given by the Pastor of pastors, who gave the keys, not to His cousin St John, but to St Peter, who was no relation. His charity was boundless. When his steward complained that his alms exceeded his income he bade him sell his gold and silver dishes, adding, " There is my horse too ; he is in good condition and should fetch a good price. Sell him also, and bring me the money for the poor." Of himself and of his own powers he had the lowest opinion, and it has been noticed that of the numerous miracles with which he has been credited the majority were performed at the request or at the suggestion of other people.

To the strenuous duties of his office, the pope added that of preaching a new crusade against the Saracens, and it was upon reaching Dover after conducting a strenuous campaign along the coast that St Richard was seized with a fever which he knew would prove fatal. He died at the house for poor priests and pilgrims called the Maison-Dieu, surrounded on his death-bed by Ralph Bocking, Simon of Tarring, and other devoted friends. He was then in his fifty-fifth year, and he was canonized only nine years later. No vestige of his relics or of his tomb at Chichester has survived. St Richard's feast is kept in the dioceses of Westminster, Birmingham and Southwark.

Two lives of St Richard are printed in the *Acta Sanctorum*, April, vol. i, that by Ralph Bocking, and another which is found in Capgrave's *Nova Legenda Angliae*. This last seems to be a copy of an early biography written before the canonization. There is an excellent account of St Richard in J. H. Newman's " Lives of the English Saints ", the authorship of which has been assigned sometimes to Father Dalgairns, sometimes to R. Ornsby. The fullest modern biography is that of M. R. Capes, *Richard of Wyche* (1913). Further useful bibliographical references are given in DNB. and in the *Dictionary of English Church History.*

BD GANDULF OF BINASCO (A.D. 1260)

THE Sicilians have a great veneration for this Gandulf, a Franciscan who, though born at Binasco near Milan, lived and died upon their island. He was one of those who entered the order while the Seraphic Father was still alive, and the life he led was one of great self-abnegation. Alarm at hearing himself commended induced him to embrace the solitary life, lest he should be tempted to vainglory. With one companion, Brother Pascal, he left the friary at Palermo and set out for the wild district in which he had determined to settle. Afterwards from time to time he would emerge from his retreat to evangelize the people of the neighbouring districts, upon whom his discourses and miracles made a profound impression. Once while he was preaching at Polizzi, the sparrows chattered so loudly that the congregation could not hear the sermon. Bd Gandulf appealed to the birds to be quiet, and we are told that they kept silence until the conclusion of the service. On that occasion the holy man told the people that he was addressing them for the last time ; and in fact, immediately upon his return to the hospital of St Nicholas where he was staying he was seized with fever, and died on Holy Saturday as he had foretold, in 1260.

Afterwards, when his body was enshrined, the watchers declared that during the night there had flown into the church a number of swallows who had parted into groups and had sung, in alternating choirs, a *Te Deum* of their own.

Some account of this *beato* will be found in the *Acta Sanctorum*, September, vol. v. See also Léon, *Auréole séraphique* (Eng. trans.), vol. iii, pp. 201–205, and Mazara, *Leggendario Francescano* (1679), vol. ii, pp. 472–476.

BD JOHN OF PENNA (A.D. 1271)

PENNA in the March of Ancona was the birthplace of this holy Minorite. Impressed by the teaching of one of the early followers of St Francis of Assisi, he sought admission into his order and received the habit in the convent of Recanati. From Italy he was afterwards sent to Provence. In France, where he laboured for twenty-five years, he founded several houses of the order, and won all hearts by his exemplary life as well as by his kindly and courteous manners. Recalled to Italy he gave himself up, as far as he could, to prayer and retirement. The good friar's later years were tried by aridity and by a lingering illness which was of a very painful kind, but which he bore with perfect resignation. Ultimately he was rewarded by spiritual consolations and by the assurance that he had accomplished his purgatory on earth. As the hour of death drew near, his cell was illuminated with a celestial light, and he passed to glory with uplifted hands and with words of thanksgiving upon his lips. His *cultus* was approved by Pope Pius VII.

The story of Bd John of Penna fills a long chapter (45) in the *Fioretti*. See also Léon, *Auréole Séraphique* (Eng. trans.), vol. iii, pp. 276–278, and Mazara, *Leggendario Francescano* (1679), vol. i, pp. 474–476.

4 : ST ISIDORE, Bishop of Seville, Doctor of the Church   (A.D. 636)

IT was said of St Isidore by his disciple and friend St Braulio that he appeared to have been specially raised up by God to stem the current of barbarism and ferocity which everywhere followed the arms of the Goths who had settled in Spain.   His father, Severian, who came from Cartagena, was probably of Roman origin, but he was closely connected with the Visigothic kings.   Two of St Isidore's brothers, Leander, who was greatly his senior, and Fulgentius, became, like himself, saints as well as bishops, and of his sisters one was St Florentina, abbess of many convents.   Isidore's education was entrusted to his brother Leander, who seems to have been a somewhat severe master.   Once, the story runs, the little lad ran away to escape from his brother's castigations and from lessons which he found difficulty in remembering ;   and though he returned, with a new determination, after looking at the holes worn in rock by the continual dripping of water, even then, we are told, Leander found it desirable to shut him up in a cell to prevent him from straying :   but that may only mean that he sent him to complete his education in a monastery.

The system, whatever it may have been, at any rate had good results, for Isidore became the most learned man of his age and, what is even more remarkable in the circumstances, an ardent educationist.   Although it is almost certain that he never was a monk, he had a great love for the religious orders, and at their request drew up a code of rules for them which bore his name and was generally followed throughout Spain.   In it he insists that no distinction must be made in monasteries between freemen and bondmen—all of them are equal in the sight of God.   It seems probable that he assisted St Leander in ruling the diocese of Seville, and then succeeded to it after his brother's death.   During the thirty-seven years of his episcopate, which extended through the reigns of six kings, he completed the work begun by St Leander of converting the Visigoths from Arianism to Catholicism. He also continued his brother's practice of settling the discipline of the Spanish church in councils, the arrangement and organization of which were largely due to Leander and Isidore.   As models of representative government these synods have attracted the favourable notice of those interested in the origins of the modern parliamentary system.

St Isidore presided over the second Council of Seville in 619 and again over the fourth Council of Toledo in 633, where he was given precedence over the archbishop of Toledo on the ground of his exceptional merit as the greatest teacher in Spain. Many of the enactments of the council emanated from St Isidore himself, notably the decree that a seminary or cathedral school should be established in every diocese.   The aged prelate's educational scheme was extraordinarily wide and progressive :   far from desiring a mere counterpart of the conventional classical curriculum, his system embraced every known branch of knowledge.   The liberal arts, medicine, and law were to be taught as well as Hebrew and Greek ;   and Aristotle was studied in the Spanish schools long before he was reintroduced by the Arabs.

St Isidore seems to have foreseen that unity of religion and a comprehensive educational system would weld together the heterogeneous elements which threatened to disintegrate his country, and it was mainly thanks to him that Spain was a centre of culture when the rest of Europe seemed to be lapsing into barbarism.

His crowning contribution to education was the compilation of a sort of encyclopedia, called the Etymologies or Origins, which gathered into compact form all the knowledge of his age. He has sometimes been called " The Schoolmaster of the Middle Ages ", and until almost the middle of the sixteenth century this work remained a favourite text-book. St Isidore was a voluminous writer, his earlier works including a dictionary of synonyms, a treatise on astronomy and physical geography, a summary of the principal events of the world from the creation, a biography of illustrious men, a book of Old and New Testament worthies, his rules for monks, extensive theological and ecclesiastical works, and the history of the Goths, Vandals and Suevi. Of all these writings the most valuable to us at the present day is undoubtedly his history of the Goths, which is our only source of information for one period of Visigothic history. Another great service which St Isidore rendered to the church in Spain was the completion of the Mozarabic missal and breviary which St Leander had begun to adapt for the use of the Goths from the earlier Spanish liturgy.

Although he lived to be almost eighty years of age, the holy bishop would remit none of his austere practices, even after his health had begun to break down. During the last six months of his life, he increased his charities to such an extent that from morning to night his house was crowded by all the poor of the countryside. When he felt that his end was drawing near, he invited two bishops to come to see him. In their company he went to the church where one of them covered him with sackcloth, while the other put ashes upon his head. Thus clad in the habit of penance, he raised his hands towards Heaven, praying earnestly and aloud for the forgiveness of his sins. Afterwards he received viaticum, commended himself to the prayers of those present, forgave his debtors, exhorted the people to charity, and distributed to the poor the rest of his possessions. He then returned to his house where he shortly afterwards peacefully departed this life.

St Isidore was declared a doctor of the Church in 1722, and he is named in the canon of the Mozarabic Mass still in use at Toledo. Some notes on St Isidore was one of the works on which the Venerable Bede was engaged just before his death.

No very satisfactory early materials exist for a biography of St Isidore. We have an account of his death by Redemptus and a panegyric by his disciple Braulio, but the life attributed to Luke, Bishop of Tuy, is a poor affair, and, being compiled many hundred years after the saint's death, is quite unreliable. It is printed in the *Acta Sanctorum*, April, vol. i. For a full bibliography and for further details of his life and work, see DTC., vol. viii, cc. 98–111 ; and P. Séjourné, *St Isidore de Séville* (1929). A *Miscellanea Isidoriana*, in several languages, was published in Rome in 1936.

SS. AGATHOPUS and THEODULUS, Martyrs   (A.D. 303)

THE cult of these martyrs is attested before the year 411 by the Syriac " Breviarium ". We find them also mentioned in the " Hieronymianum ", though only the name of Theodulus appears in the marble calendar of Naples. In the Roman Martyrology we have the entry : " At Thessalonica, of the holy martyrs Agathopus, deacon, and Theodulus, lector, who under the Emperor Maximian and the governor Faustinus were for their confession of the Christian faith drowned in the sea with stones tied to their necks." There is preserved among the Greek manuscripts of the Vatican Library what purports to be the *passio* of these martyrs. The slight historical details therein contained which recount the reiterated solicitations of the governor Faustus, the demand that they should surrender the

Christian scriptures, the tortures endured and derided by the victims, and finally the miraculous recovery of their bodies from the sea after the sentence of drowning had been carried out, seem to be entirely conventional and so far unreliable.

The Greek *passio* with a Latin translation is printed in the *Acta Sanctorum*, April, vol. i. An abridgment is to be found in the synaxaries. See also the *pars posterior* (1932) of the *Acta Sanctorum* for November, vol. ii, pp. 173-174.

ST TIGERNACH, BISHOP   (A.D. 549)

IN the neighbourhood of Clones in County Monaghan the memory of St Tigernach or Tierney is held in great honour, but the account of his life was written from tradition centuries after his death and cannot be considered historically accurate. He is said to have been of royal race, and St Conleth of Kildare baptized him, St Brigid being his godmother. Taken prisoner by pirates when he was still a boy, he was carried as a slave to a British king who gave him his liberty. He then became the disciple of Monennus in the monastery of Rosnat in Scotland. From a pilgrimage to Rome he returned to Ireland, and was consecrated bishop at Clogher in succession to St Macartan, but he lived at the monastery of Clones which he had founded. Like St Macartan he seems to have been surnamed " Fer dá chrích "—man of two districts. In his old age he lost his sight and spent his time in continual prayer and contemplation. There still remain at Clones some ruins of a monastery and also of a round tower known until comparatively recently as Cloichteach or St Tierney's Clacker.

The Latin life originally printed in the *Acta Sanctorum*, April, vol. i, has been more critically edited by Plummer, VSH., vol. ii, pp. 262-269 ; see also the introduction, pp. lxxxviii *seq.* There are also some useful references in Father John Ryan's *Irish Monasticism* and in Whitley Stokes's *The Martyrology of Oengus*, p. 111.

ST PLATO, ABBOT   (A.D. 814)

THE parents of St Plato died in Constantinople when he was thirteen years old, and an uncle, who was the imperial treasurer, took charge of him and trained him to be his assistant ; but at the age of twenty-four the young man abandoned all his worldly prospects to enter upon the religious life. He sold his estates, and, after he had divided the proceeds between his two sisters and the poor, he set out for Bithynia to the monastery of Symboleon on Mount Olympus. When he had proved himself a perfect monk by performing the meanest offices and by receiving in silence punishment for faults he had not committed, he was set to the congenial task of copying books and making extracts from the works of the fathers.

Upon the death of the abbot Theoctistus in 770 he was chosen to succeed him, although he was only thirty-six. It was a time of tribulation and danger for orthodox monks, but the secluded position of the monastery appears to have protected him from the persecution of the iconoclast emperor, Constantine Copronymus. In 775 St Plato visited Constantinople, where he was received with great honour, being offered another monastery as well as the bishopric of Nicomedia, both of which he refused : he would not even be ordained priest. Afterwards, however, he was induced to leave Symboleon to become abbot of the Sakkudion which had been founded near Constantinople by the children of his sister Theoctista. This post, which he held for twelve years, he resigned to his nephew St Theodore Studites.

This was about the time that the Emperor Constantine Porphyrogenitus divorced his wife Mary to marry Theodota. Uncle and nephew became leaders of the monastic party which practically excommunicated the sovereign and the imperial vengeance fell upon St Plato, who was imprisoned and exiled. By the time he was released his brethren had been obliged, by the attacks of the Saracens, to leave Sakkudion for the greater security of the monastery of Studius. Thither St Plato returned to place himself once more under his nephew. He elected to live apart from the other monks in a cell where he spent his time in prayer and manual work; but he continued to oppose imperial misdoings, and suffered therefor. Eventually by the Emperor Nicephorus he was banished to the isles of the Bosphorus, although he was old and ill. For four years he bore his hardships with exemplary patience, being constantly and ignominiously moved from one place to another. In 811 Michael I gave orders that St Plato should be released. In Constantinople he was received with all possible marks of respect, but for the rest of his life he was bedridden and lived in great retirement. Among his visitors was the patriarch St Nicephorus, whose election he had formerly opposed, but who now came to commend himself to his prayers. St Plato died on April 4, 814, and St Theodore preached his funeral oration.

The only biographical account preserved to us is the panegyric by St Theodore Studites which may be found with a Latin translation in the *Acta Sanctorum*, April, vol. i. But there are many references to St Plato in other documents of the period, and there has been, indirectly at least, considerable discussion of the part he played in the religious disturbances of that age; see *e.g.* C. Van de Vorst in *Analecta Bollandiana*, vol. xxxii (1913), pp. 27–62 and 439–447; and J. Pargoire in the *Byzantinische Zeitschrift*, vol. viii (1899), pp. 98–101. See also articles by Fr Pargoire in *Échos d'Orient*, vol. ii (1899), pp. 253 *seq.*, and vol. iv (1901), pp. 164 *seq.*

BD PETER, BISHOP OF POITIERS   (A.D. 1115)

ALTHOUGH his *cultus* seems never to have been officially sanctioned by the Church, Peter II of Poitiers has a feast in that diocese on account of the holiness of his life and the stand that he made for justice and good morals. King Philip I of France having repudiated his wife Bertha and entered into a union with Bertrada de Montfort, Bd Peter was a leader, with St Ivo of Chartres, St Bernard of Tiron and Bd Robert of Arbrissel, in convening a council to consider the matter. In vain did William the Troubadour, Count of Poitou, break in on its deliberations and try with his men-at-arms to intimidate the fathers. The assembly denounced the king's adulterous union and pronounced excommunication against him.

It was in Bd Peter's diocese that Robert of Arbrissel had settled, and it was with the encouragement and help of the holy bishop that he founded the abbey of Fontevrault. Indeed Peter went himself to Rome in 1106 to obtain sanction for the new establishment, of which he came to be reckoned one of the founders.

Peter never ceased to oppose the vices of those in high places. Especially did he protest against the enormities of William of Poitou, who threatened his life, sword in hand. "Strike: I am ready", said the bishop. The count did not dare to carry out his threat, but he succeeded in exiling Bd Peter to the castle of Chauvigny, where he died two years later.

There is no early biography of Bishop Peter, but some information may be obtained concerning him from the chroniclers, and from the Life of Robert of Arbrissel. William of Malmesbury in his *Gesta Regum* (§ 439) calls Peter "a man of eminent holiness" and reproduces some highly laudatory verses written in his honour. See also Auber, *Vies des Saints de l'Église de Poitiers* (1858).

ST BENEDICT THE BLACK　　(A.D. 1589)

BENEDICT was born in a village near Messina in Sicily. His parents were good Christians, but African slaves of a rich landowner whose name (Manasseri) they bore, according to the prevalent custom. Christopher's master had made him foreman over his other servants and had promised that his eldest son, Benedict, should be free. The baby grew up such a sweet-tempered, devout child that when he was only ten years old he was called " The Holy Black " (*Il moro santo*), a nickname which clung to him all his life. One day, when he was about twenty-one, he was grossly insulted by some neighbours, who taunted him with his colour and the status of his parents. There happened to be passing at the time a young man called Lanzi, who had retired from the world with a few companions to live the life of a hermit in imitation of St Francis of Assisi. He was greatly impressed by the gentleness of Benedict's replies and, addressing the mockers, he said, " You make fun of this poor black man now ; but I can tell you that ere long you will hear great things of him ". Soon afterwards, at Lanzi's invitation, Benedict sold his few possessions and went to join the solitaries.

Several times in the ensuing years the hermits were obliged to shift their quarters, and at last they settled on Montepellegrino near Palermo, already hallowed by having sheltered St Rosalia. Here Lanzi died, and the community chose Benedict as their superior, very much against his will. But when he was about thirty-eight, Pope Pius IV decreed that the hermits must either disperse or join some order. Benedict chose to join the Friars Minor of the Observance, and found a welcome as a lay-brother in the convent of St Mary near Palermo. At first he was employed as cook, a post which suited his retiring nature and which gave him opportunities for little deeds of kindness, but his extraordinary goodness could not long escape notice. His face when he was in chapel often shone with an unearthly light, and food seemed to multiply miraculously under his hands.

In 1578, when the Friars Minor of the Observance held their chapter at Palermo, it was decided to convert the house of St Mary into a convent of the reform. This necessitated the appointment of a very wise guardian, and the choice of the chapter fell upon Benedict, a lay-brother who could neither read nor write. He himself was greatly perturbed at the appointment, but was obliged under obedience to accept. The choice was abundantly justified. Benedict proved to be an ideal superior, for his judgement was sound and his admonitions were so tactfully and wisely given that while never resented they were always taken to heart. His reputation for sanctity and miracles quickly spread over Sicily, and when he went to attend the provincial chapter at Girgenti clergy and people turned out to meet him, men and women struggling to kiss his hand or to obtain a fragment of his habit as a relic.

Relieved of the office of guardian, St Benedict was made vicar of the convent and novice-master. To this post also he proved himself fully equal. An infused sacred science enabled him to expound the Holy Scriptures to the edification of priests and novices alike, and his intuitive grasp of deep theological truths often astonished learned inquirers. It was known that he could read men's thoughts, and this power, coupled with great sympathy, made him a successful director of novices. Nevertheless he was glad when he was released and allowed to return to the kitchen, although his position was scarcely that of the obscure cook of earlier years. Now, all day long, he was beset by visitors of all conditions—the poor demanding alms, the sick seeking to be healed, and distinguished persons requesting his advice or his prayers. Though he never refused to see those who asked for him, he shrank from marks of respect, and when travelling would cover his face with his hood and if possible choose the night that he might not be recognized. Throughout his life he continued the austerities of his hermit days. In the matter of food, however, he was wont to say that the best form of mortification was not to deprive oneself of it, but to desist after eating a little, adding that it was right to partake of food given in alms, as a token of gratitude and to give pleasure to the donors.

Benedict " The Holy Black " died in 1589 at the age of sixty-three after a short illness. He was chosen as patron by the Negroes of North America and as protector by the town of Palermo, having been canonized in 1807.

See the life (*Vita di San Benedetto di San Fradello*) by F Giovanni da Capistrano, published in 1808 ; that by Father B. Nicolosi (1907) ; and Léon, *Auréole Séraphique* (Eng. trans.), ii, pp. 14–31.

5 : ST VINCENT FERRER (A.D. 1419)

THE descendant of an Englishman or a Scotsman settled in Spain, St Vincent Ferrer was born at Valencia, probably in the year 1350. Inspired by prophecies of his future greatness, his parents instilled into him an intense devotion to our Lord and His blessed Mother and a great love for the poor. Moreover they made him the dispenser of their bountiful alms, and from them also he learnt the rigorous Wednesday and Saturday fast which he continued to practise all his life. On the intellectual side he was almost equally precocious. He entered the Dominican priory of Valencia, where he received the habit in 1367, and before he was twenty-one he was appointed reader in philosophy at Lerida, the most famous university in Catalonia. Whilst still occupying that chair he published two treatises, both of which were considered of great merit. At Barcelona, whither he was afterwards transferred, he was set to preach, although he was still only a deacon. The city was suffering from famine : corn which had been despatched by sea had not arrived and the people were nearly desperate. St Vincent, in the course of a sermon in the open air, foretold that the ships would come in that day before nightfall. His prior censured him severely for making predictions, but the ships duly appeared—to the joy of the people who rushed to the priory to acclaim the prophet. His superiors, however, deemed it wise to transfer him to Toulouse, where he remained for a year. He was then recalled to his own country, and his lectures and sermons met with extraordinary success. Nevertheless it was to him a time of trial. Not only was he assailed by temptations from the hidden powers of darkness, but he was also exposed to the blandishments of certain women who became attached to him—his good looks were exceptional—and strove first to beguile him and then to blacken his name. From these trials the saint emerged braced for the strenuous life which lay before him, as well as for the priestly office which was conferred upon him. He soon became famous as a preacher, whose eloquence roused to penitence and fervour multitudes of careless Catholics, besides converting to the Christian faith a number of Jews, notably the Rabbi Paul of Burgos, who died bishop of Cartagena in 1435.

This was the time of the " great schism ", when rival popes were reigning at Rome and Avignon and when even great saints were divided in their allegiance.

That terrible scandal had begun in 1378 when, upon the death of Gregory XI, sixteen of the twenty-three cardinals had hastily elected Urban VI in deference to the popular cry for an Italian pope.   Under the plea that they had been terrorized, they then, with the other cardinals, held a conclave at which they elected Cardinal Robert of Geneva, a Frenchman.   He took the name of Clement VII and ruled at Avignon, whilst Urban reigned in Rome.   St Vincent Ferrer, who had been amongst those who recognized Clement, naturally upon his death accepted as pope his successor, Peter de Luna or Benedict XIII as he was called, who summoned the Dominican to his side.*

St Vincent duly arrived in Avignon where he had great favour shown him, including the offer of a bishopric, which he refused ; but he found his position very difficult.   He soon realized that Benedict by his obstinacy was hindering all efforts that were being made towards unity.   In vain did Vincent urge him to come to some sort of understanding with his rival in Rome.   Even when a council of theologians in Paris declared against his claim, the Avignon pontiff would not stir an inch.   The strain upon the saint as his confessor and adviser was so great that he fell ill.   Upon his recovery he with great difficulty obtained permission to leave the court and devote himself to missionary work.   His object was not primarily to escape from the intrigues and worries of the papal court, but to obey a direct call, for it is said that during his illness our Lord had appeared to him in a vision with St Dominic and St Francis and, after making him understand that he was to go and preach penance as those two had done, had then instantaneously restored him to health.   He set forth from Avignon in 1399 and preached to enormous congregations in Carpentras, Arles, Aix, Marseilles.   Besides the inhabitants of the districts he visited, his audience consisted of a number of men, women and even children who followed him from place to place.   These people, at first a heterogeneous crowd, were gradually weeded out, organized and brought under rule until, as " Penitents of Master Vincent ", they became valuable helpers, when necessary staying behind in places where the mission had been held to consolidate the good work begun.   It is worthy of note that, in a lax age, no breath of suspicion appears to have attached to any member of that mixed company.   Several priests travelled with the party, forming a choir and hearing confessions.

Between 1401 and 1403 the saint was preaching in the Dauphiné, in Savoy and in the Alpine valleys : he then went on to Lucerne, Lausanne, Tarentaise, Grenoble and Turin.   Everywhere crowds flocked to hear him ; everywhere innumerable conversions and remarkable miracles were reported.   Vincent preached mainly on sin, death, hell, eternity, and especially the speedy approach of the day of judgement ; he spoke with such energy that some of his hearers fainted with fear, whilst the sobs of his congregation often compelled him to pause, but his teaching penetrated beyond the emotions and bore fruit in many cases of genuine conversion and amendment of life.   At the Grande Chartreuse, which he visited several times, his brother Boniface being prior, the Carthusian Annals record that " God worked wonders by means of these two brothers.   Those who were converted by the preaching of the one, received the religious habit at the hands of the other."

In 1405 St Vincent was in Genoa, from whence he reached a port from which he could sail for Flanders.   Amongst other reforms he induced the Ligurian ladies to modify their fantastic head-dress—" the greatest of all his marvellous deeds ",

---

* Because of their anomalous position this Clement VII and Benedict XIII are not referred to as antipopes but as " called popes in their obedience ".

as one of his biographers avers.   In the Netherlands he wrought so many miracles that an hour was set apart every day for the healing of the sick.   It has also been supposed that he visited England, Scotland and Ireland, but of this there is no shadow of proof.   Although we know from the saint himself that beyond his native language he had learnt only some Latin and a little Hebrew, yet he would seem to have possessed the gift of tongues, for we have it on the authority of reliable writers that all his hearers, French, Germans, Italians and the rest, understood every word he spoke, and that his voice carried so well that it could be clearly heard at enormous distances.   It is impossible here to follow him in all his wanderings.   In fact he pursued no definite order, but visited and revisited places as the spirit moved him or as he was requested.   In 1407 he returned to Spain.

Grenada was then under Moorish rule, but Vincent preached there, with the result that 8000 Moors are said to have asked to be baptized.   In Seville and Cordova the missions had to be conducted in the open air, because no church could accommodate the congregations.   At Valencia, which he revisited after fifteen years, he preached, worked many miracles, and healed the dissensions which were rending the town.

According to a letter from the magistrates of Orihuela, the effects of his sermons were marvellous : gambling, blasphemy and vice were banished, whilst on all hands enemies were being reconciled.   In Salamanca he converted many Jews, and it was here that, in the course of an impassioned open-air sermon on his favourite topic, St Vincent declared himself to be the angel of the Judgement foretold by St John (Apoc. xiv 6).   As some of his hearers began to protest, he summoned the bearers who were carrying a dead woman to her burial and adjured the corpse to testify to the truth of his words.   The body was seen to revive for a moment to give the confirmation required, and then to close its eyes once more in death.   It is almost unnecessary to add that the saint laid no claim to the nature of a celestial being, but only to the angelic office of a messenger or herald—believing, as he did, that he was the instrument chosen by God to announce the impending end of the world.

St Vincent of course had never ceased being deeply concerned at the disunity within the Church, especially since after 1409 there had been no less than three claimants to the papacy, to the great scandal of Christendom.   At last the Council of Constance met in 1414 to deal with the matter and proceeded to depose one of them, John XXIII, and to demand the resignation of the other two with a view to a new election.   Gregory XII expressed his willingness, but Benedict XIII still held out.   St Vincent went to Perpignan to entreat him to abdicate, but in vain.   Thereupon, being asked by King Ferdinand of Castile and Aragon to give his own judgement in the matter, the saint declared that because Benedict was hindering the union which was vital to the Church, the faithful were justified in withdrawing their allegiance.   Ferdinand acted accordingly, and at length Benedict, Peter de Luna, found himself deposed.   " But for you ", wrote Gerson to St Vincent, " this union could never have been achieved."

The last three years of the saint's life were spent in France.   Brittany and Normandy were the scene of the last labours of this " legate from the side of Christ ".   He was so worn and weak that he could scarcely walk without help, but in the pulpit he spoke with as much vigour and eloquence as though he were in the prime of life.   When, early in 1419, he returned to Vannes after a course of sermons in Nantes, it was clear that he was dying, and on the Wednesday in Passion Week

1419 he passed away, being then in his seventieth year. His death was greeted by an outburst of popular veneration, and in 1455 St Vincent Ferrer was canonized. Amid all the honours and applause which were lavished upon him, St Vincent was remarkable for his humility. It seemed to him that his whole life had been evil. " I am a plague-spot in soul and body ; everything in me reeks of corruption through the abomination of my sins and injustice ", he laments in his treatise on the spiritual life. It is ever thus with the great saints. The nearer they are to God, the baser do they appear in their own eyes.

According to Dr H. Finke, a most competent historian of this period, no satisfactory life of St Vincent Ferrer has yet been written. His story even now is overlaid with legend ; Peter Razzano, who compiled the first biography thirty-six years after the saint's death, set a very bad example of credulity, which was followed by too many of those who came after him. A collection of the depositions taken in 1453 and 1454 for the process of canonization has been printed by Fr H. Fages (1904) and other documents (1905), as well as his works (1909), but the French life by the same friar (1901) by no means corresponds to the requirements of modern criticism. Other materials have been studied by R. Chabas in the *Revista de Archivos* . . ., 1902–1903. A short English life, based on that of Fages, was published by Fr S. Hogan (1911). More recent accounts are those of R. Johannet (1930), of M. M. Gorce (1924 and 1935, " Les Saints " series), and S. Brettle (1924)—on which see the *Analecta Bollandiana*, xliv (1926), pp. 216–218—and there is a valuable note by H. Finke in the *Gustav Schnürer Festschrift* (1930) on St Vincent's sermons in 1413. St Vincent also figures largely in Mortier's *Histoire des Maîtres Généraux O.P.*, vol. iv. A characteristic study by H. Ghéon has been translated into English.

ST DERFEL GADARN   (Sixth Century ?)

DERFEL GADARN, if he died a monk on Bardsey, was first a warrior, for he is frequently referred to by the Welsh bards for his prowess in the field (his surname means " the mighty "), and he is said to have distinguished himself at the battle of Camlan, " in which Arthur and Medrod perished ". But it is all very shadowy and legendary, and there would be no point in mentioning St Derfel and his folk-lore here were it not for the curious association with Bd John Forest (May 22).

Before the Reformation there was a wooden image of St Derfel in the church of Llandderfel in Merioneth, and in 1538 Mr Commissary Price wrote to Thomas Cromwell asking what should be done about this image of Derfel, " in whom the people have so great confidence, hope and trust that they come daily in pilgrimage unto him, some with kine, others with oxen, or horses, and the rest with money. . . . The innocent people have been sore allured and enticed to worship the said image, in so much that there is a common saying as yet amongst them, that whosoever will offer anything to the said image of Derfel Gadarn he hath power to fetch him or them that so offers out of Hell when they be damned."

If this superstition was really attached to it, one can for once sympathize with Cromwell when he ordered it to be brought up to London and burnt. And in spite of the vehement protests of the people of Llandderfel (Price says they offered him forty pounds if they might keep it) to London it was taken.

On May 22, 1538, the Franciscan friar Bd John Forest was burned at Smithfield for denying the king's ecclesiastical supremacy, and part of the fuel whose flames consumed him was the " huge and great " statue of Derfel. Now there was a saying in Wales that this image would one day set a *forest* afire, " which prophecy now took effect, for he set this friar Forest on fire, and consumed him to nothing ".

The chronicler Hall goes on to say that some verses were nailed to the gallows, of which the first stanza ran :—

> David Derfel Gatheren,
> As sayeth the Welshman,
> Fetched outlaws out of Hell.
> Now is he come with spear and shield
> In harness to burn in Smithfield,
> For in Wales he may not dwell:

The statue was an equestrian one, and the horse was not sent to London.   Part of it, very much mutilated, still remains at Llandderfel.   St Derfel's feast was on April 5, and formerly on Easter Tuesday the wooden horse was taken in procession to the neighbouring Bryn Sant (Holy Hill) and there fixed up so that the children could have rides on it.

Cotton MS. Cleopatra E., iv ;   Wright, *Suppression of the Monasteries ;*   Gairdner's *Letters and Papers . . . of the Reign of Henry VIII ;*   Hall's *Chronicles ;*   all summarized, with other references, by Baring-Gould and Fisher in LBS., vol. ii, pp. 333–336.

ST ETHELBURGA, ABBESS OF LYMINGE, MATRON   (*c.* A.D. 647)

ST ETHELBURGA was the daughter of St Augustine's convert, King Ethelbert of Kent and of his wife Bertha.   Ethelburga, also called Tata, was given in marriage to Edwin, the pagan king of Northumbria, and St Paulinus, one of St Augustine's companions, accompanied her as chaplain.   Although Edwin was well affected towards Christianity, he hesitated so long before accepting the faith that Pope Boniface V wrote expressly to Ethelburga, urging her to do her utmost to bring about his conversion.   But it was not until 627 that Edwin himself received baptism. During the rest of his reign, Christianity made progress throughout Northumbria, encouraged as it was by the royal couple, but when Edwin had been killed at Hatfield Chase, his pagan adversaries overran the land.   The queen and St Paulinus found themselves obliged to return to Kent where Ethelburga founded the abbey of Lyminge, which she ruled until her death.

We know nothing of St Ethelburga but what Bede (*Hist. Eccles.* ii, ch. 9 *seq.*) and Thomas of Elmham (pp. 176–177) have recorded.

ST GERALD OF SAUVE-MAJEURE, ABBOT   (A.D. 1095)

CORBIE in Picardy was the birthplace of St Gerald, who became first a pupil and then a monk in its great abbey.   Quite suddenly he was attacked by excruciating pains, the symptoms of which, as described by his biographer, suggest a severe attack of shingles in the head, with the acute neuralgia which so often follows it. He could get no rest or sleep by day or by night, and it seemed to him as though he were losing his reason.   Doctors bled him and dosed him, but afforded him no relief.   Worst of all, he could no longer pray.   Feeling that all he could do for God was to minister to others, he undertook, in honour of the Holy Trinity, the care of three poor men whom he looked after.   His abbot chose him as companion to go with him to Rome, where he hoped the sufferer might be cured.   Together they visited the tombs of the Apostles, and at the hands of St Leo IX Gerald was ordained priest.   But from time to time the terrible headaches recurred, until one day when —at the intercession, he was convinced, of St Adelard, whose life he had written—

the pains left him as suddenly as they had come, never to trouble him again. After this, in thanksgiving he redoubled his prayers and mortifications. In a vision he beheld our Lord come down from the crucifix towards him, he felt Him place His hand on his head, and heard Him say, " Son, be comforted in the Lord and in the power of His might ". A pilgrimage to Jerusalem was another source of inspiration and consolation.

Soon after his return St Gerald was chosen abbot by the monks of the abbey of St Vincent at Laon, but he found them lax and unwilling to submit to discipline. Unable to reform them, he resigned, and with some companions started southward in search of a suitable spot for a new foundation ; they continued their way until they reached Aquitaine. There, not far from the present city of Bordeaux, on a tract of forest land given them by William VII, Count of Poitou, they in 1079 founded the abbey of Sauve-Majeure (Silva Major), of which Gerald became the first abbot. The monks reclaimed the land and acted as missionaries to the inhabitants of the neighbouring districts, Abbot Gerald being foremost as a preacher and confessor. He instituted the practice of offering Mass and reciting the office of the dead for thirty days after the death of any member of the community, and he also ordered that bread and wine should be served for a whole year for the deceased member and given to the poor. This custom spread to other monasteries and even to parish churches, but after a time the offerings, placed on the bier or on the tomb, were no longer given to the poor but to the priest. St Gerald was canonized in 1197.

Our information comes mainly from two medieval Latin lives of the saint, one written by an anonymous contemporary, and the other somewhat later by the monk Christian. They are printed in the *Acta Sanctorum*, April, vol. i. See also Cirot de la Ville, *Histoire de St Gérard* . . . (1869), and F. Moniquet, *Un Fondateur de ville* . . . (1895).

ST ALBERT, Bishop of Montecorvino   (A.D. 1127)

IN the early days of Montecorvino in Apulia, when it was developing into a town, the father of St Albert took up his residence there with his little son. Albert grew up to be so highly esteemed that upon the death of the bishop he was unanimously chosen to be his successor. After a time he lost his sight, but although bereft of physical vision he was endowed with second sight and the gift of prophecy. Albert's fame became widespread mainly owing to two miracles with which he was credited. On a hot summer's day he had asked for a drink of water which his servant fetched from the spring. " My son ", said the bishop, when he had tasted it, " I asked for water and you have given me wine." The man declared that he had offered him water, and brought him some more. That also became converted into wine. Soon afterwards a citizen, taken captive and imprisoned, called upon the name of the bishop ; and a heavenly visitant carried him off from his prison in the Abruzzi and set him down near Montecorvino. The following morning he went to thank the bishop, who said, " Do not thank me, my son, but give thanks to God, who with His great might raises up the downtrodden and releases the fettered ".

In St Albert's old age he was given as vicar a priest called Crescentius. He was an unscrupulous man whose one hope was that the aged prelate would die soon that he might succeed him. Instead of assisting the old bishop he and his satellites persecuted him by playing cruel practical jokes. The good man bore all with patience, although he prophesied that Crescentius would not long enjoy the bishopric he coveted.

The people of Montecorvino loved their pastor to the end. When it was known that he was dying, men, women and children gathered round weeping. The old saint gave them his benediction with a parting injunction that they should live in piety and justice and then passed away as though in sleep.

The only account of St Albert which we now possess was written three or four hundred years after his death by one of his successors in the united dioceses of Montecorvino and Vulturaria. This was Alexander Gerardinus, a prolific author as Ughelli shows. However, he seems only to have put into more classical form a life of Albert which was compiled by Bishop Richard, the next but one to follow him at Montecorvino. It is printed in the *Acta Sanctorum*, April, vol. i, and by Ughelli, *Italia Sacra*, vol. viii (1662), cc. 469–474.

BD JULIANA OF MOUNT CORNILLON, Virgin (A.D. 1258)

The introduction of the feast of Corpus Christi was primarily due to one woman, whose mind first conceived it and whose efforts brought about its observance. Juliana was born near Liège in 1192, but being left an orphan at the age of five, she was placed by guardians in the care of the nuns of Mount Cornillon, a double Augustinian monastery of men and women devoted to the care of the sick, more especially of lepers. To keep Juliana and her sister Agnes from contact with the patients, the superior sent them to a dependent farm near Amercoeur, where they were in the kindly charge of a Sister Sapientia, who also taught them. Agnes died young ; Juliana grew up into a studious girl who had an intense devotion to the Blessed Sacrament and who loved to pore over volumes of St Augustine, St Bernard and other fathers on the library shelves. Strangely enough, from the time when she was about sixteen she was haunted day and night by the appearance of a bright moon streaked with a dark band. Occasionally she feared lest it might be a device of the Devil to distract her from prayer, but usually she felt convinced that it had some deep spiritual meaning if only she could grasp it. At last she had a dream or vision in which our Lord explained that the moon was the Christian year with its round of festivals and that the black band denoted the absence of the one holy day required to complete the cycle—a feast in honour of the Blessed Sacrament.

The years passed and Juliana became a nun at Mount Cornillon ; but she was unknown, without influence and in no position to do anything in the matter of the desired feast. Then in 1225 she was elected prioress and began to speak about what she felt to be her mission to some of her friends, notably to Bd Eva, a recluse who lived beside St Martin's church on the opposite bank of the river, and to a saintly woman, Isabel of Huy, whom she had received into her community. Encouraged no doubt by the support of these two, she opened her heart to a learned canon of St Martin's, John of Lausanne, asking him to consult theologians as to the propriety of such a feast. James Pantaleon (afterwards Pope Urban IV), Hugh of St Cher, the Dominican prior provincial, Bishop Guy of Cambrai, chancellor of the University of Paris, with other learned men, were approached, and decided that there was no theological or canonical objection to the institution of a festival in honour of the Blessed Sacrament. On the other hand opposition arose in other quarters. Although John of Cornillon composed an office for the day which was actually adopted by the canons of St Martin's, and although Hugh of St Cher preached and spoke on her behalf, Juliana was criticized as a visionary, and worse. Feeling ran high against her even in the monastery, the constitution of which was somewhat peculiar. Whilst the ultimate direction of brethren and sisters was in the hands of the prior, the burgomaster and citizens seem to have had a voice in the management of the hospital, the revenues of which, however, were administered by the prioress.　A new prior, Roger by name, accused Juliana of falsifying the accounts, of making away with the title-deeds, and of misappropriating the funds to further the promotion of a feast which nobody wanted.　These accusations so infuriated the people of Liège that they compelled Juliana to leave.　Bishop Robert caused an inquiry to be made into the matter.　This resulted in the recall of Juliana to Cornillon, the transference of the prior to the hospital of Huy, and in 1246 the proclamation of the new festival for the diocese of Liège.　After the death of the bishop, however, the persecution was renewed and Bd Juliana was driven from Cornillon altogether.

With three of the sisters, Isabel of Huy, Agnes and Otilia, she wandered from one place to another until they found a shelter at Namur.　Here for some time they lived upon alms, but the abbess of Salzinnes came to their rescue and, espousing Juliana's cause, obtained for her from Cornillon a grant from the dowry she had formerly brought to the convent.　Misfortune, however, continued to dog her steps—misfortune which she foresaw and foretold.　During the siege of Namur by the troops of Henry II of Luxemburg, Salzinnes was burnt down and Juliana was forced to escape with the abbess to Fosses, where she lived as a recluse for the rest of her days in poverty and sickness.　She died on April 5, 1258, in the presence of the abbess and of a faithful companion called Ermentrude.

Juliana's great mission was carried on and completed by her old friend Eva, the recluse of St Martin's.　After the elevation to the papacy of Urban IV, who as James Pantaleon had been one of Juliana's earliest supporters, Eva, through the bishop of Liège, begged him to sanction the new feast of the Blessed Sacrament. He did so ; and afterwards, in recognition of the part she had taken, he sent her his bull of authorization together with the beautiful office for Corpus Christi which St Thomas Aquinas had composed at his desire.　The bull was confirmed in 1312 by the Council of Vienne under Pope Clement V, and the celebration of the feast of Corpus Christi has from that time become of universal obligation throughout the Western church, and most Catholics of the Eastern rite have adopted it too.　The observance of a feast in honour of Bd Juliana was allowed by the Holy See in 1869.

A narrative originally compiled in French but translated into Latin by John of Lausanne is printed in the *Acta Sanctorum* (April, vol. i) and forms the principal source for the incidents here recorded.　See also Clotilde de Sainte-Julienne, *Sainte Julienne de Cornillon* (1928) ; and E. Denis, *La vraie histoire de ste Julienne* . . . (1935).　There is an account in Flemish by J. Coenen (1946).

BD CRESCENTIA OF KAUFBEUREN, Virgin　(A.D. 1744)

IT was in the humble home of wool-weavers at Kaufbeuren in Bavaria that Crescentia Höss first saw the light in 1682, but if her parents were lacking in this world's goods, they could set their children an example of simple piety which Crescentia— or Anna as she was baptized—was quick to follow.　At an early age, as she knelt in the chapel of the local convent of Franciscan nuns, a voice from the crucifix had said to her, " This shall be your dwelling-place ".　When, however, her father applied that she might be received there, he was informed that the poverty of the house rendered a dowry essential—and a dowry he could not supply.　Crescentia was content to wait, working at the family trade until she was twenty-one.　The promise was then fulfilled in an unexpected way.　Beside the convent was a tavern the noise from which was a constant annoyance to the nuns.　When they would have bought it up, a prohibitive price was set upon it by the owner. Eventually it came into their possession through the benevolence of the Protestant burgomaster who, as the only token of gratitude which he would accept, asked them to admit Crescentia, saying it would be a pity for such an innocent lamb to remain in the world. Her wish was thus accomplished and she entered the third order regular of St Francis.

Her life for the next few years was to be one of humiliations and persecution, for the superioress and the older nuns could not forget that she had come to them penniless. They taunted her with being a beggar, gave her the most disagreeable work, and then called her a hypocrite. At first she had a little cell, but that was taken away to be given to a novice who had brought money. For three years she had to beg first one sister and then another to allow her to sleep on the floor of her cell: then she was allowed a damp dark little corner of her own. Taking all humiliations as her due, Crescentia refused the sympathy of some of the younger nuns when they exclaimed at the treatment meted out to her. In time, however, another superioress was appointed, who had more charity and discrimination. In time the nuns recognized that they had a saint amongst them and eventually chose her as novice mistress and finally as superioress. She had many visions and ecstasies, besides a mystical experience of the sufferings of our Lord which lasted every Friday from nine until three, culminating often in complete unconsciousness. On the other hand she suffered greatly from the assaults of the powers of evil.

Unkindly criticism of others Crescentia always repressed, invariably defending the absent. Stern to herself, she yet said to her daughters, " The practices most pleasing to God are those which He himself imposes—to bear meekly and patiently the adversities which He sends or which our neighbours inflict on us ". Gradually her influence spread beyond the walls of her convent, and people who came to consult her went away impressed by her wisdom and spoke of her to others : leaders in church and state visited the weaver's daughter or corresponded with her, and to this day her tomb is visited by pilgrims. Pope Leo XIII beatified her in 1900.

The decree of beatification, giving a summary of the life of Crescentia Höss, is printed in the *Analecta Ecclesiastica*, viii (1900), pp. 455–457. Besides the documents published for the Congregation of Rites in the course of the process, some unprinted materials connected with the first stages of the inquiry have been edited by Alfred Schröder in the *Hagiographischer Jahresbericht* for 1903, pp. 1–111. There are also sundry popular lives of the *beata* in German, e.g., that by Jeiler, which has been translated into Italian, and others by Offner, Seeböck and P. Gatz (1930).

6 : CXX MARTYRS IN PERSIA (A.D. 345)

WE do not know the names of any of these martyrs, but it was generally believed that at Seleucia-Ctesiphon under the Persian King Sapor II more than a hundred victims were put to death on the same day. There were among them nine consecrated virgins, and the rest were priests, deacons or monks. Refusing to worship the sun, they had been left for six months in filthy dungeons. However, a wealthy and devout woman, Yazdandocta by name, came to their aid by sending them food. She seems to have managed to discover the date which was fixed for the final ordeal. Arranging that a generous meal should be provided for them on the day before, she came herself to visit them and presented to each one a suit of festival white garments. On the morrow at dawn she came again, and gave them the news that this was the day on which they were to suffer, urging them to implore with all their hearts the support of God's fortifying grace so that they might be ready to shed their blood in so glorious a cause. " As for myself ", she added, " I ask most earnestly that you by your prayers will obtain for me from God the happiness of meeting you all again before His heavenly throne."

At the place of execution the confessors were again promised their freedom if only they would worship the sun, but they proudly replied that the robes they wore were only the outward expression of the feelings with which they were prepared to surrender their lives in the cause of their Master. The martyrs perished by decapitation ; and that night Yazdandocta found means to remove their bodies and to bury them at a distance where they would be safe from profanation.

Although this story is free from the sort of miraculous element which usually awakens suspicion, it contains certain improbabilities, and, as Father Peeters has shown (*Analecta Bollandiana*, vol. xliii, 1925, pp. 261–304), the Adiabene cycle of martyr-acts to which this belongs is by no means uniformly trustworthy. The Syriac text was first published by E. Assemani in his *Acta martyrum orientalium*, i, p. 100, and it has also been edited by Bedjan without a translation. The early Greek versions of the same acts have been edited by Delehaye in the *Patrologia Orientalis*, vol. ii (1905). French translation in H. Leclercq, *Les Martyrs*, t. iii.

ST MARCELLINUS, MARTYR   (A.D. 413)

SEVERAL of the works of St Augustine, including his great book *On the City of God*, are dedicated to his friend Marcellinus, secretary of state to the Emperor Honorius. Moreover we still have the encomiums upon St Marcellinus pronounced by St Augustine and St Jerome after his martyrdom. In the year 409, the emperor had granted liberty of public worship to the Donatists, an ultra-puritan party in the Church who refused to readmit to communion penitents who, after baptism, had fallen into mortal sin, and especially those who had failed in time of persecution. The Donatists in North Africa had taken advantage of this permission to oppress and illtreat the orthodox, who appealed to the emperor. Marcellinus was sent to Carthage to preside over a conference of Catholic and Donatist bishops and to act as judge. After a three days' parley he decided against the Donatists, whose privileges were revoked and who were ordered to return to the communion of their Catholic brethren. It fell to the lot of Marcellinus and of his brother Apringius to enforce the decision, and they proceeded to do so with a severity which the Roman law justified but which, it must be admitted, drew upon them remonstrances from St Augustine. In revenge the Donatists accused them of being implicated in the rebellion of Heraclian, and the general Marinus, who was dealing with the insurrection, cast them both into prison. St Augustine, who visited them in their captivity, tried in vain to save them : they were taken from prison and executed without a trial. The emperor afterwards severely censured Marinus and vindicated Marcellinus as " a man of glorious memory " ; his name was added to the Roman Martyrology by Cardinal Baronius.

See the *Acta Sanctorum*, April, vol. i, where the more relevant passages in the correspondence and writings of St Augustine and St Jerome are collected ; and also DCB., vol. iii, pp. 806–807.

ST CELESTINE I, POPE   (A.D. 432)

IN the Roman Martyrology the commemoration of this pope, which formerly occurred on April 6, has been transferred to July 27, the day of his death. It is, however, on April 6 that his feast is still observed in Ireland. Of his private life we know little or nothing. He was born in Campania, and he had been for some time a conspicuous figure as deacon in Rome before he was elected pope in September 422. During the ten years of his pontificate he showed considerable energy and he had often to encounter opposition. The bishops of Africa, who had previously raised difficulties about the appeals of priests to Rome, remonstrated again at the pope's seemingly precipitate and ill-advised action in the case of Apiarius, but it seems certain that St Augustine in particular entertained for Celestine an affectionate veneration which is conspicuous in his letters. In counteracting the heretical movements of his times, notably in the measures taken against Pelagianism and against Nestorius, Celestine acted vigorously. A council held at Rome in 430 may be regarded as a prealiminry to the oecumenical assembly at Ephesus, and to this last vitally important gathering he despatched three legates of high standing to represent the Apostolic See. He encouraged St Germanus of Auxerre to make vigorous opposition to the spread of Pelagianism and wrote himself a tractate of dogmatic importance dealing with the heresy in its more diluted form known as semi-Pelagianism. We may trace to him the germs of the recognition of the Divine Office as an obligation incumbent upon all clergy of the higher ranks. There seems little likelihood that it was Pope Celestine who sent St Patrick to Ireland, but he must have had the spiritual needs of that country in his thoughts, for he commissioned Palladius to minister there to the people who already believed in Christ, just before St Patrick began his great work.

See the *Acta Sanctorum*, April, vol. i ; Duchesne's notes in his edition of the *Liber Pontificalis*, vol. i, pp. 230–231 ; Hefele-Leclercq, *Conciles*, vol. ii, pp. 196 *seq.* ; Cabrol in DAC., vol. ii, cc. 2794–2802 ; Portalié in DTC., vol. ii, cc. 2052–2061 ; and *Revue Bénédictine*, vol. xli, pp. 156–170. The so-called *Capitula Caelestini* condemning semi-Pelagian doctrine are probably not the work of Celestine himself, but rather have St Prosper of Aquitaine for their author.

ST EUTYCHIUS, Patriarch of Constantinople (A.D. 582)

ALTHOUGH the name of this Eutychius is not commemorated in the Roman Martyrology, and although his career belongs more to church history than to hagiography, still he has always been honoured as a saint among the Greeks (and at Venice, which claims his relics), and he set a noble example of resistance to the Emperor Justinian's pretensions to figure as arbiter in theological matters. Eutychius became a monk at Amasea in Pontus, having previously been ordained priest ; and in 552 he was sent to Constantinople as the representative of his bishop ; he there attracted the notice of Justinian who, on the death of the Patriarch Mennas, had Eutychius consecrated in his place. At the fifth oecumenical council, which met at Constantinople in 553, Eutychius presided along with the patriarchs of Alexandria and Antioch, Pope Vigilius having, for reasons readily intelligible in view of the complications of that disturbed period, refused to attend. Some years later in the intricate theological controversies still connected with the monophysite heresy, Eutychius found himself in conflict with the emperor. The patriarch would not give way, and he was banished to an island in the Propontis. There he is stated by his biographer to have worked many miracles. He was only restored to his see when Justinian was dead, after twelve years of exile. Towards the end of his days Eutychius was engaged in controversy with Gregory, then the representative of the Holy See at Constantinople, better known after his succession to the papacy as Pope St Gregory the Great. Eutychius before his death is said to have admitted his error.

There is a fairly lengthy biography of the saint by his chaplain Eustratius printed in Greek with a Latin translation in the *Acta Sanctorum*, April, vol. i. For the controversies of the times, consult Hefele-Leclercq, *Conciles*, vol. iii, pp. 1–145, and also Duchesne, *L'Église au VIème siècle* (1925), pp. 156–218.

ST PRUDENTIUS, BISHOP OF TROYES   (A.D. 861)

ST PRUDENTIUS was one of the most learned prelates of the Gallican church in the ninth century ; and if, amid the intricacies of the predestination controversy in which he was involved, he steered a somewhat wavering course, it must be remembered that the question was a difficult one and that Prudentius appears to have been willing to accept the verdict of the Church even when it ran counter to his own conclusions. He was by birth a Spaniard, christened Galindo. About the year 840 or 845 he was elected bishop of Troyes, and in a sermon he preached upon St Maura he speaks of himself as occupied in hearing confessions and administering the last sacraments in addition to performing his strictly episcopal duties. He must already have won a considerable reputation as a theologian, for he was summoned by Bishop Hincmar of Reims to consider the case of the monk Gottschalk who had been condemned for teaching that Christ had died only for the elect, whilst the greater part of mankind had been irredeemably doomed by God from all eternity to sin and Hell. · Gottschalk had been tortured and imprisoned, and Prudentius thought the punishment excessive—especially the excommunication which Hincmar had launched—and he seems to have been among those who suspected Hincmar of inclining towards the contrary error of semi-Pelagianism or the denial of the necessity for divine grace. In the disputes that followed St Prudentius played a conspicuous part, and a book he wrote to correct the errors of John Scotus Erigena is still extant.

Apart from his controversial efforts St Prudentius worked hard for the discipline of the Church and for the reformation of manners. He died on April 6, 861, and his feast is still kept at Troyes, but he is not commemorated in the Roman Martyrology, nor is he included by the Bollandists in their *Acta Sanctorum*.

The life of St Prudentius has to be pieced together from the chronicles and documents of the period, but the editors of his theological tractates and other works have generally prefaced them by some kind of memoir. See *e.g.* Migne, PL., vol. cxv, and Ebert, *Literatur des Mittelalters*, vol. ii. There is a full bibliography of the Predestination controversy in Hefele-Leclercq, *Conciles*, vol. iv, p. 138, and cf. the whole of Book xxii.

BD NOTKER BALBULUS   (A.D. 912)

IN the days when Grimoald was abbot of Saint-Gall, the parents of Bd Notker placed their young son in its school. The boy was delicate, with an impediment in his speech from which he derived his nickname of Balbulus, and he seems to have been already what the monk Ekkehard (IV) described him to have been in later life, " weakly in body but not in mind, stammering of tongue but not of intellect, pressing forward boldly in things divine—a vessel filled with the Holy Ghost without equal in his time ". With his companions and lifelong friends, Tutilo and Radpert, he studied music under Marcellus, the Irishman, and the trio afterwards did much to develop the singing-school of Saint-Gall which had hitherto mainly confined itself to trying to maintain north of the Alps the form of ecclesiastical music as used in Rome. They were all three professed, and afterwards taught in the schools ; Notker was also librarian and guest-master. Charles the Fat, who was fond of visiting Saint-Gall, had a great regard for Notker whom he often consulted in his spiritual and even in his temporal difficulties, without, however, always following his advice. One day a messenger arrived from the monarch while the holy man was busy weeding his garden and planting and watering. " Tell the emperor to do what I am now doing ", was the answer he sent back, and Charles, who was no fool, was not at a loss to understand his meaning. The court chaplain, a learned but conceited man, thought to confound the monk whose influence with his master he resented. " Tell me, you who are so learned, what God is now doing ", he asked him in the presence of a large gathering. " He is doing now what He has done in the past, He is putting down the proud and exalting the humble ", was the ready reply : the chaplain beat a hasty retreat amid general laughter.

It was thought at one time that Notker was the inventor of the sequence or " prose " which fits into the music of the Alleluia *jubilus* between the epistle and the gospel at Mass, but it is now established that he composed his sequences on a model he found in an antiphonary brought to Saint-Gall by a fugitive monk when Jumièges was burnt down. To Notker belongs the credit of introducing sequences into Germany, of developing them, and of composing some thirty-eight or more original ones of his own. His other works comprise a martyrology, some hymns, and the completion of Echambert's Chronicle. A metrical biography of St Gall is also attributed to him as well as the *Gesta Caroli Magni* by an anonymous monk of Saint-Gall, but, as there were several other monks there of the name of Notker who also were writers, it is extremely difficult to allocate the works which became connected with their name.

So greatly was Bd Notker beloved that for a long time after his death in 912 his brethren could not speak of him without tears. His *cultus* was confirmed in 1512.

The life of Notker by Ekkehard V, who lived long after his time, is printed in the *Acta Sanctorum*, April, vol. i, but the biographical notice in Mabillon's *Acta Sanctorum O.S.B.* is also valuable. On Notker's musical and literary work much has been written. P. von Winterfeld in the *Neues Archiv* (1902) does not hesitate to call him the greatest poet of the middle ages. Valuable bibliographical references will be found in Julian's *Dictionary of Hymnology ;* in W. H. Frere, *The Winchester Troper* (H. Bradshaw Society) ; in DTC., vol. xi, cc. 805–806 ; DAC., vol. xi, cc. 1615–1623, and vol. xii. cc. 1727–1732 ; and in the *Analecta Hymnica* of Dreves and Blume, vol. liii. See also Manitius, *Geschichte des lateinischen Literatur des Mittelalters*, vol. i, § 48.

ST WILLIAM OF ESKILL, ABBOT (A.D. 1203)

ON this day the Roman Martyrology mentions the death in Denmark of St William, " famous for his life and miracles ". He was born about 1125 at Saint-Germain, Crépy-en-Valois, and became a canon of the collegiate church of St Genevieve in Paris. In 1148 Suger, abbot of Saint-Denis, carrying out the wishes of the pope, Bd Eugenius III, established canons regular in this church, and William was one of those who accepted a more austere and regular life with enthusiasm. In time his reputation for canonical discipline and holiness of life reached so far as Denmark, for, about 1170, he received a visit from a young Dane, Saxo Grammaticus, who was to become famous as an historian. Saxo had been sent by the bishop of Roskilde, Absalom or Axel, to invite William to undertake the restoration of discipline in the monastic houses of his diocese. William agreed, and began his labours with the canons regular at Eskilsoe on the Ise fiord, where his delicate task was successfully carried out, but only after a hard struggle. His so-called canons regular followed no rule, kept no enclosure, and observed no discipline. Two of them he was obliged to expel, but gradually by patience he won over the rest to a stricter life. He had many other difficulties created by the severity of the climate, the persecutions of powerful men, and his own interior trials. Nevertheless in the thirty years that he discharged the office of abbot, he had the consolation of seeing many of his brethren walk with fervour in his footsteps.

Having established the monastery of St Thomas on Seeland, William undertook to reform other religious houses, and in all his very considerable difficulties he had the support of Axel, who had become archbishop of Lund. During his later years he left Denmark for a time, having embroiled himself in some semi-political affairs ; but he returned to his abbey, where he died peacefully on April 6, 1203.

St William of Eskill (who must be distinguished from St William of Roskilde, September 2) was canonized in 1224. His feast is observed in the modern diocese of Copenhagen, which in 1952 replaced the vicariate apostolic of Denmark, on the occasion of the eighth centenary of the Scandinavian ecclesiastical reorganization by Nicholas Breakspear.

William's biography, written by one of his canons some years after the saint's death, is printed in the *Acta Sanctorum*, April, vol. i ; but a better text has been edited by C. Gertz in his *Vitae Sanctorum Danorum* (1910) : the writer seems to have considerably embellished his facts. For the writings attributed to St William, see Migne, PL., vol. ccix, cc. 655–746.

BD CATHERINE OF PALLANZA, Virgin   (A.D. 1478)

MORE destructive than the many wars which devastated medieval Europe was the dread disease called plague which, with varying severity, was of constant recurrence, sometimes sweeping away entire populations. During one of these epidemics there perished near Pallanza in the diocese of Novara a whole family except one little child of the name of Catherine. She was rescued by the local lord, who entrusted her to a Milanese lady who adopted and educated her. When Catherine was in her fifteenth year she was so profoundly touched by a sermon on the sufferings of our Lord that she then and there resolved to consecrate her life to His service. Her benefactress was now dead and there was no one to hinder her, so she withdrew to the mountain district above Varese, where the great St Ambrose, it was said, had once erected an altar in honour of the Mother of God. From time to time men had lived there as hermits, but she was the first woman to settle in that wilderness, and for the next fifteen years she led a life of the utmost austerity. She fasted for ten months of the year, living even at less penitential seasons on presents of fish which were brought to her, for she seldom left her retreat. Hidden as she strove to be, other women collected round Catherine to imitate her example and to become her disciples. Eventually she gathered them into a community which adopted the Augustinian rule and was known as the convent of Santa Maria di Monte. She died at the age of forty, after being prioress for four years. During her life Blessed Catherine was endowed with the gift of prophecy, and her *cultus* was approved in 1769.

See the *Acta Sanctorum*, April, vol. i, where a life of the *beata* written in Italian by Cesare Tettamanzi has been translated into Latin. Cf. also Sevesi in *Studi Francescani*, vol. xxv (1928), pp. 389–449.

7 : ST HEGESIPPUS   (*c.* A.D. 180)

IT is as the reputed Father of Church History that St Hegesippus is chiefly remembered to-day.   By birth a Jew, and a member of the church of Jerusalem, he travelled to Rome, and there spent nearly twenty years, from the pontificate of St Anicetus to that of St Eleutherius.   In 177 he returned to the East, where he died in extreme old age, probably at Jerusalem.   In the course of his travels, he seems to have visited the principal Christian centres in the West as well as in the East, and he noted with satisfaction that, although disturbances had been caused by individual heretics, hitherto no episcopal see or particular church had fallen into error : everywhere he had found the unity of the faith as it had been delivered by our Lord to the saints.   Unfortunately only a few chapters remain of the five books which he wrote on the history of the Church from the passion of our Lord down to his own time, but the work was highly esteemed by Eusebius and others, who drew largely upon it.   He was a man filled with the spirit of the apostles and with a love of humility " which ", says St Jerome, " he expressed by the simplicity of his style ".   St Hegesippus is named in the Roman Martyrology to-day.

The scant notices concerning St Hegesippus furnished by St Jerome and others are collected in the *Acta Sanctorum*, April, vol. i.   See also Abbot J. Chapman in the *Revue Bénédictine*, xviii (1901) and xix (1902) ; and Bardenhewer, *Gesch. der altkirch. Literatur*, vol. i, pp. 385–392.   Another work in five books formerly attributed to Hegesippus, is a Latin rendering of Josephus on the Jewish War.   This was a blunder, due to the fact that the name Iosippus was miswritten Egesippus and eventually Hegesippus.

ST APHRAATES   (*c.* A.D. 345)

ACCORDING to the Bollandists, followed by Alban Butler, we owe our knowledge of the history of St Aphraates to Theodoret, who recalled how, as a boy, he had been taken by his mother to visit the saint and how Aphraates had opened his door to bless them, promising to intercede with God on their behalf.   In his later years Theodoret continued to invoke that intercession, believing that it had become even more potent since the holy man had gone to God.

Aphraates came of a Persian family, but after his conversion to Christianity he settled at Edessa in Mesopotamia, then a stronghold of the faith, hoping to discover the most perfect way of serving God.   When he had come to the conclusion that this could best be done in solitude, he shut himself up in a cell outside the city walls, where he gave himself up to penance and heavenly contemplation.   His food consisted of bread, eaten after sunset ; only in old age did he add a few vegetables ; his bed was a mat on the ground, and his clothing one coarse garment.   After some time he changed his residence to a hermitage beside a monastery near Antioch in Syria, and gradually people began to resort to him there for advice.   Anthemius, who afterwards became consul for the East, once brought back from Persia a garment which he presented to the hermit as a product of his native land.   Aphraates asked him whether he thought it would be reasonable to exchange a faithful old servant for a new one merely because he was a fellow countryman.   " Certainly not ", replied Anthemius.   " Then take back your tunic ", said the recluse, " for I have one which I have used for sixteen years, and I do not need more than one."

When the Emperor Valens had banished the bishop St Meletius and the Arian persecution was making great havoc of the church in Antioch, St Aphraates left his retreat to come to the assistance of Flavian and Diodorus who were governing the distressed Catholics during the exile of their pastor. His reputation for sanctity and miracles gave great weight to his actions and words. As the Arians had taken possession of their churches, the faithful were reduced to worshipping beside the river Orontes or in the large open space outside the city which was used for military exercises. One day, as St Aphraates was hurrying along the road which led from the city to this parade-ground, he was stopped by order of the emperor, who happened to be standing in the portico of his palace which overlooked the road. Valens inquired whither he was going : " To pray for the world and the emperor ", replied the recluse. The monarch then asked him how it happened that one dressed as a monk was gadding about far away from his cell. To this Aphraates answered with a parable : " If I were a maiden secluded in my father's house, and saw it take fire, would you recommend me to sit still and let it burn ? It is not I who am to blame, but rather you who have kindled the flames which I am striving to extinguish. We are doing nothing contrary to our profession when we gather together and nourish the adherents of the true faith."

The emperor made no reply, but one of his servants reviled the venerable man, whom he threatened to kill. Shortly afterwards the same attendant was accidentally scalded to death, which so terrified the superstitious Valens that he refused to listen to the Arians when they tried to persuade him to banish St Aphraates. He was also greatly impressed by the miracles wrought by the hermit, who not only healed men and women but also—or at least so it was reported—cured the emperor's favourite horse.

Whether the Aphraates, described as above by Theodoret in his *Philotheus* and his *Ecclesiastical History*, is identical with the early Syriac writer whose homilies or dissertations are preserved to us, remains a great problem. These homilies, as all scholars agree, belong to the years 336–345. Valens died in 378 and Theodoret seems to have been born in 386 at the earliest. It is difficult to suppose that the latter, as a little boy, could have been taken to receive the blessing of the author of the homilies. On the other hand we know very little about the history of the great writer. He seems to have been invested with some ecclesiastical authority and was very possibly a bishop. The statement, however, that he lived near Mosul cannot be depended on. There is also an Aphraates mentioned in the Syriac " Breviarium ", seemingly a martyr in the early years of the persecution under Sapor. The works of Aphraates may best be consulted in Parisot's edition, Syriac and Latin, in the *Patrologia Syriaca*, vols. i and ii. See also articles by Dom Connolly and F. C. Burkitt in the *Journal of Theological Studies*, vols. vi and vii ; and Bardenhewer, *Geschichte der altkirchlichen Literatur*, vol. iv, pp. 327–342.

ST GEORGE THE YOUNGER, Bishop of Mitylene (c. A.D. 816)

Lesbos in ancient days was the birthplace of several celebrated men and of one famous woman. Pittacus, one of the seven wise men of Greece, was born at its capital Mitylene, whilst the poet Alcaeon, the poetess Sappho, and the historian Theophanes were all natives of that same island. Moreover, three saints bearing the name of George occupied the bishopric of Mitylene within a hundred years. George the Younger was a man of position who had devoted his wealth to the relief of the sick and poor and had entered a monastery, from which he was taken to rule over the church of Lesbos as bishop of Mitylene. In that capacity he was remarkable for his generosity in almsgiving, for his singular humility, and for the rigorous and prolonged fasts which caused men to say that he must be an angel, because he lived without food or drink. From the outbreak of the iconoclastic persecution under Leo the Armenian he was a staunch upholder of Catholic tradition, encouraging his flock to venerate the sacred images. For this reason he was exiled to the Chersonese, where he died about the year 816. His body was afterwards brought back to Mitylene where, according to the Greek account, it wrought so many cures that the saint was called " the doctor of incurable diseases and the great exorcist of unclean spirits ".

Our information, derived principally from the Greek Menaion, is not very satisfactory. See the *Acta Sanctorum*, April, vol. i, and Nilles, *Kalendarium Manuale*, vol. i, p. 134.

ST CELSUS, or CEALLACH, Archbishop of Armagh   (A.D. 1129)

Celsus is the Latin name given to Ceallach mac Aedha, in whose family the see of Armagh had become hereditary for several generations. Like his eight predecessors, Celsus himself was a layman when he succeeded to the see at the age of twenty-six in 1105 ; but he was then consecrated bishop and proved a good one. " He was a worthy and God-fearing man ", wrote St Bernard of Clairvaux. He was assiduous in conducting visitations, in conserving the temporalities of his see, and in restoring ecclesiastical discipline. For this last purpose he attended a great synod at Rath Breasail, whereat there were said to be no less than fifty bishops present, and Gilbert of Limerick presided as papal legate. Neither the liturgical reforms of this council nor the diocesan organization and boundaries that it drew up were well received. The Annals of the Four Masters says that St Celsus rebuilt the cathedral of Armagh. He lived in very troubled times and was called on to mediate between the warring Irish princes, while he himself suffered from the depredations of the O'Rourkes and O'Briens.

In all his labours St Celsus was supported by St Malachy, first as his archdeacon and then as bishop of Connor. On his death-bed at Ardpatrick in Munster in 1129, Celsus broke the evil custom of hereditary succession by nominating Malachy to succeed him at Armagh. By his own wish he was buried at Lismore.

The name of St Celsus was added by Cardinal Baronius to the Roman Martyrology, where it now appears on the day of his death, April 1. His feast is kept throughout Ireland to-day.

See *Acta Sanctorum*, April 6 ; St Bernard's life of St Malachy (Migne, PL., vol. clxxxii, col. 1086 ; DNB., vol. ix, p. 418 ; O'Hanlon, LIS., vol. iv, p. 43 ; and all modern lives of St Malachy.

ST AYBERT   (A.D. 1140)

St Aybert or Aibert was born in 1060 at Espain, a village in the diocese of Tournai. From infancy his heart was wholly given to God. At night the little boy would rise from bed and slip away to pray without attracting the notice of his parents ; when he got older he played truant from caring for his father's herds to go to church. One day a wandering minstrel sang in his hearing a lay about the life of a hermit—St Theobald of Provins—who had lately died. Forthwith there sprang up in Aybert's heart a desire to imitate the recluse. He accordingly sought out a priest called John who belonged to the abbey of Crespin, but who was permitted to live as a solitary. Father John accepted the youth as a companion and together they lived a most austere and penitential life.

The abbot of Crespin had to go to Rome some time later and as his companions he chose the two hermits ; and the party set off barefoot. The hardships they endured caused John to fall ill on the road, but he was nursed back to health by the kindly monks of Vallombrosa.　Not long after their return, Aybert was moved by a dream or vision to seek admittance into the abbey itself, and for twenty-five years he was procurator and cellarer, dispensing hospitality and good cheer to others although never modifying his own austerities ; he was always happy and very cheerful.　The time came, however, when he felt the call to return to the solitary life which he had abandoned.　With the abbot's leave, he built himself a hermitage in a barren district, and there he lived for twenty-two years more.

St Aybert's holiness began to attract visitors, who found themselves greatly helped by his spiritual advice and made him known to others.　Bishops and laymen, grand ladies and canonesses, scholars and humble peasants flocked to him in such numbers that Bishop Burchard of Cambrai promoted him to the priesthood, providing him with a chapel beside his cell.　Moreover Pope Innocent II granted him leave to absolve reserved cases—a right which he only exercised in exceptional circumstances.　God crowned Aybert's long penance with a happy death in the eightieth year of his age.

One phase of Aybert's devotional practice is of great interest in its bearing on the controversy concerning the origin of the rosary.　It is recorded that the saint used to repeat the *Ave Maria* fifty times in succession, accompanying each *Ave* with a prostration.　A mention in the same context of his habit of dividing his recitation of the whole psalter into fifties makes the allusion still more significant.

The Latin biography from which all our information is derived was written by Robert, Archdeacon of Ostrevant, shortly after the saint's death.　The text may be consulted most conveniently in the *Acta Sanctorum*, April, vol. i.　See also the *Biographie nationale de Belgique*, vol. i.

BD HERMAN JOSEPH　(A.D. 1241)

AMONGST the German mystics of the twelfth and thirteenth centuries, special interest attaches to Bd Herman Joseph, not so much for his writings as for his visions, which were later a source of inspiration even to poets and painters.　Herman, to give him his baptismal name, was born in Cologne, and lived from his seventh year until his death in extreme old age apparently in continual intercourse with the denizens of Heaven.　As a little boy he would enter a church and converse familiarly with our Lady and the Holy Child, as he knelt before their statue.　Once, indeed, when he offered them an apple he had the joy of seeing the hand of the Madonna extended to accept it.　Sometimes he was uplifted to another plane and permitted to play with the Infant Saviour and the angels ; and on one bitter winter's day when he came to church barefoot, his parents being very poor, a kindly voice, which he took to be that of the Mother of Mercy, bade him look under a stone near by and he would find money wherewith to buy shoes.　He looked, and the coins were there !

At the age of twelve, Herman offered himself to the Premonstratensian monastery of Steinfeld, but as he was far too young to receive the habit he was sent on to one of the order's houses in Friesland to study.　There he profited by the general education that was imparted, though he deplored the time spent over profane literature : all study seemed to him unprofitable if it did not lead to the knowledge of God.　His schooling completed, he returned to Steinfeld, where he was professed and afterwards set to serve the brethren in the refectory.　His duties were exactly performed, but he was perturbed to find that they left him very little leisure for prayer.   He was reassured by a vision in which our Lady told him that he could do nothing more pleasing to God than to wait upon others in charity.   Afterwards he was promoted to be sacristan, an office after his own heart, because he was able to spend the greater part of the day in church.   His life was so blameless and his innocence so candid that he was jestingly called " Joseph "—a nickname he modestly disclaimed until it was confirmed by a vision in which, in the character of an earthly Joseph, he was mystically espoused by our Lady with a ring.   This is the scene which Van Dyck has painted in a celebrated picture.   It is not known at what date Herman received ordination, but the offering of the Holy Sacrifice was to him a time of extraordinary exaltation.   Often he would be rapt in ecstasy, and would remain so long in that condition that it came to be increasingly difficult to find anyone who was willing to act as his server.   Nevertheless he gained the love of his brethren for his eagerness to do kindnesses to others.   Visionary as he was, he had a practical side, and, as he was a clever mechanic, he would go from monastery to monastery adjusting or repairing the clocks for them.   He is said also to have composed a number of prayers as well as hymns and one or two mystical treatises, including one on the Canticle of Canticles which, though it has not come down to us, was greatly admired.   He also wrote a hymn in honour of St Ursula and her maidens, whose reputed relics are venerated in his native city and whose *cultus* he did much to spread.   On the other hand the two books of revelations concerning their lives and death sometimes attributed to him are probably by another hand ; some, indeed, have claimed that they were no more than a very ill-considered joke.

At no time robust, Bd Herman Joseph's health became seriously affected by his fasts and austerities.   Severe headaches attacked him, and his digestion became so impaired that he ate nothing and seemed a living skeleton.   However, God granted him a reprieve from suffering towards the end, prolonging his life for nine years, and this was the period of his chief literary output.   He had been sent in 1241 to the Cistercian nuns at Hoven for Passiontide and Easter when he was taken ill with fever from which he never recovered.   The process of Herman's canonization was introduced but never completed ; his *cultus*, however, has been authoritatively sanctioned.

We are fortunate in possessing a detailed biography of Bd Herman Joseph which was written by a contemporary, said to have been the prior of Steinfeld.   It is printed with some other materials in the *Acta Sanctorum*, April, vol. i.   Other adaptations and condensations based on this primitive life were produced at a later period, notably one by Raso Bonus Vicinus (Goetgebuer).   The legend as presented in German by F. Kaulen has a charm and simplicity which reminds one of the *Little Flowers of St Francis :*   English translation by Wilfrid Galway (1878).   There are popular modern German lives by Pösl and others, and in French by Timmermans (1900) and Petit (1929).   See also Michael, *Geschichte des deutschen Volkes . . .*, vol. iii, pp. 211 *seq.* ; R. van Waefelghem, *Répertoire de l'Ordre de Prémontré* (1930) ; and *Histoire littéraire de la France*, vol. xxi, p. 583.

BD URSULINA, Virgin   (a.d. 1410)

Of the intrepid women who made noble efforts to end the scandals of the " Babylonish Captivity " of Avignon and of the Great Schism which ensued, not the least courageous, though certainly the youngest, was Bd Ursulina of Parma.   From her tenth year she had enjoyed heavenly visions and mystical experiences, and when she was fifteen a supernatural voice several times bade her go to Avignon to urge upon Clement VII the renunciation of his claim to the papacy.   A vision which was vouchsafed to her on Easter day decided her purpose. With two companions, besides her mother who accompanied her on all her subsequent travels, the girl made the toilsome journey over the Alps and succeeded in obtaining an audience with Clement more than once. Her efforts to persuade him proving fruitless, she went back to Parma, but almost immediately proceeded to Rome where she delivered a similar message to the true pope, Boniface IX. He received her graciously and appears to have encouraged her to make another attempt to win over his rival. Thereupon she undertook a second expedition to Avignon, with no better success than before. Indeed this time she was separated from her mother, was accused of sorcery, and narrowly escaped a trial. Another journey to Rome was followed by a somewhat perilous pilgrimage to the Holy Land. If she and her mother had hoped to settle down in Parma on their return they were doomed to disappointment, for civil war broke out in the city and they were expelled. They made their way to Bologna and then to Verona, which Bd Ursulina seems to have made her home until her death at the age of thirty-five.

Our information comes almost entirely from the Latin life by Simon Zanachi, a Carthusian of Parma. It is printed in the *Acta Sanctorum*, April, vol. i. A popular adaptation was published by H. M. Garofani in 1897, *Vita e Viaggi della B. Orsolina di Parma*.

BD WILLIAM OF SCICLI   (A.D. 1411)

WILLIAM CUFITELLA was a Franciscan tertiary who became a hermit near Scicli in Sicily, and spent about seventy years in his little cell, giving himself up to prayer and to very severe mortifications. He lived on the vegetables which he cultivated in his garden and on a small part of what the faithful brought to him. He seldom left his hermitage except to visit and relieve the sick poor for whom he had great compassion, or to tend the adjacent chapel of our Lady of Pity which had been committed to his charge. Many people came to him for guidance and direction in their spiritual life. A very close friendship united him to another saintly solitary, Bd Conrad of Piacenza, who would come over from Pizzoni to pass Lent with him.

Bd William was ninety-five years of age when he died. The people of Scicli, hearing the sound of bells, hurried out and found the old man dead on his knees, hands joined in prayer, surrounded by beams of heavenly light. The town, which afterwards made him its protector in thanksgiving for preservation from plague, still keeps his feast. His *cultus* was approved in 1537.

See the *Acta Sanctorum*, April, vol. i (under April 4), where some fragments are printed from the beatification process ; *cf.* also Léon, *Auréole Séraphique* (Eng. trans.), vol. ii, pp. 34–35.

BB. ALEXANDER RAWLINS and HENRY WALPOLE, MARTYRS (A.D. 1595)

ALEXANDER RAWLINS, secular priest, and Henry Walpole, Jesuit, who suffered martyrdom together in 1595, were men of good family, born, the one on the borders of Worcestershire and Gloucestershire, and the other in Norfolk. Whereas Rawlins seems to have gone directly to the English College at Rheims to prepare to receive holy orders, Walpole, who was intended for the law, continued his education at Cambridge and then took chambers at Gray's Inn. Realizing that he was becoming an object of suspicion to the authorities and feeling himself called to the priesthood, he proceeded to Rheims and then to Rome, where he entered the Society of Jesus. After taking his final vows, he was sent on missions, first to Lorraine and then to the Netherlands, where he was captured by Calvinists and imprisoned for a year. Upon being liberated, he asked to be allowed to go to England, but he was sent to teach in English seminaries at Seville and Valladolid. After another mission to Flanders, the long-desired permission was accorded, and he set out for England, landing at Flamborough Head on December 4, 1593. Within twenty-four hours he was arrested and was taken prisoner to York.

In reply to interrogations Father Walpole owned quite frankly that he was a Jesuit priest, and that he had come to gain souls to God. Thereupon he was imprisoned, first at York and then in the Tower of London, where he was tortured fourteen times. In these straits he seems to have shown a certain weakness, but it is clear that he betrayed no one and never surrendered the faith in any essential point. The brutality of his torturer Topcliffe was such that the stern lieutenant of the Tower in pity gave him a little straw to lie on, and intimated to his relations that he was without bed or covering in the depth of winter. After a year's confinement he was taken back to York, tried at the Mid-Lent Assizes, and condemned to death on a charge of treason. It was decided that he should suffer at the same time as Mr Rawlins, who, ever since his ordination in March 1590, had been labouring in the English mission, and had been arrested about the date of Walpole's return from the Tower to York Castle. They were drawn to execution on the same hurdle, but, lest they should have the consolation of speaking to each other, they were laid with the head of the one beside the feet of the other. Bd Alexander suffered first ; Bd Henry, obliged to look on while the usual barbarities were carried out upon his fellow-martyr, displayed the same fortitude as his brother priest.

See Challoner's MMP., pp. 217–227 ; and, for Walpole especially, the publications of the Catholic Record Society, vol. v, *Documents relating to the English Martyrs*, pp. 244–269, etc. *Cf.* also A. Jessopp, *One Generation of a Norfolk House* (1878), and John Gerard's autobiography (1951).

BB. EDWARD OLDCORNE and RALPH ASHLEY, Martyrs (A.D. 1606)

A York man by birth, Edward Oldcorne pursued his ecclesiastical studies first at Rheims and then in Rome, where, after a stay of six years, he was ordained priest with a view to proceeding at once to the English mission. As he was very desirous of joining the Society of Jesus, Father Aquaviva admitted him without requiring the usual period of noviciate, because of the perilous nature of the enterprise to which he was committed. He landed in England with Father Gerard, but they separated almost immediately, and Father Oldcorne was sent to Worcester, where for seventeen years, under the name of Hall, he laboured zealously and had some hairbreadth escapes. He was successful in reconciling many lapsed Catholics and in converting a number of Protestants, amongst others Mrs Dorothy Abington, formerly one of Queen Elizabeth's ladies and a sister of the Catholic gentleman whose house at Henlip became Oldcorne's headquarters during the time he spent in Worcestershire. After the discovery of the Gunpowder Plot there was a great recrudescence of hostility to Catholics, and a proclamation was issued directed more particularly against Father Garnet, the superior of the English Jesuits, who was charged with knowledge of the plot. Garnet came to Henlip, and when the house was searched he was found in the priests' hiding-hole together with Father Oldcorne

—their place of concealment having been betrayed by a prisoner who hoped to save his own life by turning informer.   Father Oldcorne was taken to Worcester and then to the Tower of London.   Although he was racked five times, he could not be shaken in his repudiation of any cognizance of the scheme of the conspirators, and in reply to a charge of having approved of the plot, he persistently denied having either known or approved of it.   He was nevertheless found guilty and sentenced to be hanged, drawn and quartered, and with him was condemned and executed also his servant, Ralph Ashley, a Jesuit lay-brother, against whom nothing could be proved except that he was in attendance upon the father.   Littleton, the man upon whose information Father Oldcorne had been caught and upon whose evidence he had been condemned, publicly asked pardon for his treachery and false accusations, and died with the martyrs.   Bd Edward was cut down and butchered while still alive, and the different parts of his body set up upon the gates of the city of Worcester.

See Challoner's MMP., pp. 289–291 ; John Morris, *Life of Father John Gerard ;* Foley, REPSJ., vol. iv ; and Gerard's autobiography (1951).

8 : ST DIONYSIUS, Bishop of Corinth   (*c.* A.D. 180)

ST DIONYSIUS, bishop of Corinth, flourished in the reign of the Emperor Marcus Aurelius, and was one of the foremost leaders of the Church in the second century. Besides instructing and guiding his own flock he wrote letters to the churches of Athens, Lacedaemon, Nicomedia, Knossus and Rome, as well as to the Christians of Gortyna and Amastris and to a lady called Chrysophora.   It is in the *Ecclesiastical History* of Eusebius that are contained the few extracts from the writings of St Dionysius which have come down to us.   In a letter thanking the church of Rome, then under the pontificate of St Soter, for continuing to send alms as it had done in the past, the bishop of Corinth writes : " From the earliest times you have made it your practice to bestow alms everywhere and to provide for the necessities of many churches.   Following the example set by your fathers you send relief to the needy, especially to those who labour in the mines.   Your blessed Bishop Soter is so far from lagging behind his predecessors in this respect that he actually outstrips them—to say nothing of the consolation and advice which, with fatherly affection, he tenders to all who come to him.   On this morning we celebrated together the Lord's Day and read your letter, even as we read the one formerly written to us by Clement."   In other words, they read aloud these letters of instruction in church after the lessons from the Holy Scriptures and the celebration of the Divine Mysteries.   The heresies of the first three centuries arose mainly from the erroneous principles of pagan philosophy, and St Dionysius was at pains to point out the source of these errors, showing from what particular school of philosophy each heresy took its rise.   " It is not surprising that the text of Holy Scripture should have been corrupted by forgers ", he says, alluding to the Marcionites, " when they have not spared the works of a far less exalted authority."   Although Dionysius appears to have died in peace, the Greeks venerate him as a martyr because he suffered much for the faith.

See the *Acta Sanctorum,* April, vol. i, where the text of Eusebius is quoted ; Bardenhewer, *Geschichte der altkirchlichen Literatur,* vol. i, pp. 235 and 785 ; DCB., vol. i, pp. 849–850 ; DAC., vol. viii, cc. 2745–2747.

ST PERPETUUS, Bishop of Tours (c. A.D. 494)

ST PERPETUUS succeeded Eustochius in the bishopric of Tours. During the thirty years of more that he ruled over the diocese he worked hard to spread the Catholic faith, to enforce discipline, and to regulate the fasts and festivals to be observed in his see. Among other provisions, a third fast day—probably Monday—was to be observed weekly from the feast of St Martin until Christmas day. This is interesting as showing the antiquity of the observance of Advent. St Gregory of Tours, writing a hundred and twenty years later, says that these regulations were still kept in his time. St Perpetuus had a great veneration for St Martin of Tours, in whose honour he enlarged or rebuilt the basilica which bore his name. As the church which St Britius had erected over St Martin's tomb was too small to accommodate the throngs of pilgrims, the bishop caused his relics to be translated with great solemnity to the new building at its consecration about the year 491 : it had taken nearly twenty-two years to build.

The saint's death is said to have been hastened by grief at the invasions of the Goths and the spread of Arianism. Some fourteen or fifteen years earlier he is said to have made a will, still extant, which, if genuine, would be of considerable interest. In it he professes to remit all debts owing to him and liberates his serfs : then, having bequeathed to his church his library besides several farms, and established a trust for the maintenance of lamps and the purchase of sacred vessels, he declares the poor his heirs. It begins : " In the name of Jesus Christ, Amen. I, Perpetuus, a sinner, priest of the church of Tours, would not depart without a last will and testament lest the poor should be defrauded. . . ." Towards the end he apostrophizes them : " You, my most beloved brethren, my crown, my joy, Christ's poor, ye needy, beggars, sick, widows and orphans ! You do I name and make my heirs. Of all I possess except the things especially allocated above, of my fields, pastures, groves, vineyards, houses, gardens, waters, mills, of my gold, silver and garments I constitute you my heirs. . . ." To his sister Fidia Julia Perpetua he leaves a little gold cross with relics, and to a church a silver dove for containing the Blessed Sacrament—a gift suggesting the prevalence at that date and in that diocese of the practice of reserving the Blessed Sacrament in a vessel shaped like a dove and hanging over the altar.

It is distressing to have to add that this document, accepted as genuine by d'Achéry, by Henschenius in the *Acta Sanctorum*, by Alban Butler, and even by the *Dictionary of Christian Biography* in 1887, is a shameless fabrication perpetrated by Jerome Vignier in the seventeenth century. It can only serve to illustrate the need of a rigidly critical examination of our hagiographical sources at all periods of history.

For the life of Perpetuus see the *Acta Sanctorum*, April, vol. i ; and *cf.* the *Analecta Bollandiana*, vol. xxxviii (1920), pp. 121–128, with Duchesne, *Fastes Episcopaux*, vol. ii, pp. 300–301. On the supposed will consult Havet, *Bibliothèque de l'École des Chartes*, vol. xlvi (1885), pp. 207–224. The epitaph, which has also received unmerited recognition, is equally a forgery.

ST WALTER OF PONTOISE, Abbot (A.D. 1095)

IN studying the lives of the saints, we not infrequently meet with men and women whose lifelong aspiration it is to serve God in solitude, but who are recalled again and again by the voice of an authority which they dare not gainsay, and are forced to shoulder responsibilities from which they shrink, in a world from which they fain would flee.   Such a saint was Walter (Gautier) of Pontoise.   A Picard by birth, he received a liberal education at various centres of learning and became a popular professor of philosophy and rhetoric.   Then he entered the abbey of Rebais-en-Brie, and was afterwards compelled by King Philip I to become the first abbot of a new monastery near Pontoise.   Although, in accordance with the custom of the time, he received his investiture from the sovereign, the new abbot placed his hand not under but over that of the king, and said : " It is from God, not from your Majesty, that I accept the charge of this church ".   His courageous words, far from offending Philip, won his approval ; but the very honour in which he was held by persons in high office was a source of anxiety to Walter, and some time later he fled secretly from Pontoise and took refuge at Cluny, then under the rule of St Hugh, hoping there to lead a hidden life.   His refuge was, however, discovered by his monks, who fetched him back to Pontoise.   From the cares of office he would retire occasionally to a grotto in the abbey grounds, hoping for a little solitude ; but his visitors followed him there, and he took to flight once more.   This time he buried himself in a hermitage on an island in the Loire, but again he was forced to return.

Some time later, St Walter went to Rome, where he requested St Gregory VII to relieve him of his burden.   Instead of doing so, the pope told him to use the talents God had bestowed upon him, and bade him resume his charge.   From that time Walter resigned himself to his fate.   The mortifications he would have wished to practise in solitude were more than compensated for by the persecutions he had to undergo in consequence of his fearless opposition to simony and to evil-living among the secular clergy ; there was even one occasion when he was mobbed, beaten and thrown into prison, but his friends procured his release.   In spite of advancing age he never relaxed but rather increased the austerity of his habits ; he rarely sat down in church, but when his aged limbs would no longer support him, he leant upon his pastoral staff.   After the other monks had retired at the close of the night offices, he would remain behind, lost in contemplation, until he sank to the ground, where in the morning he would sometimes be found lying helpless. His last public effort was to found, in honour of our Lady, a convent for women at Bertaucourt.   He succeeded in building a church with a small house, but the community was not actually established there until after his death, which occurred on Good Friday 1095.

Two lives which seem to be of contemporary authorship have been printed by the Bollandists (in the *Acta Sanctorum*, April, vol. i) and by Mabillon.   A more correct text of the first and older of these biographies has been edited by I. Hess, in the *Studien und Mittheilungen aus dem Benedictiner und dem Cistercienser Orden*, vol. xx (1899), pp. 297–406.

BD CLEMENT OF OSIMO   (A.D. 1291)

BD CLEMENT was probably born at Sant' Elpidio in the March of Ancona, although his name is closely connected with Osimo where he would appear to have made a prolonged stay.   In 1270 and in 1284 he was elected prior general of the Augustinian Hermits, whose constitutions he drew up or revised.   He was consequently regarded as the second founder of the order.   It is also stated that he acted as confessor to Cardinal Benedict Gaetani, afterwards Pope Boniface VIII, who held him in great esteem.   Clement lived to extreme old age and died at Orvieto.

Jordan of Quedlinburg says that seventy years after his death, his remains were enshrined by order of Pope Nicholas IV on account of the miracles that were reported, and that the municipality of Orvieto caused some houses to be demolished and the road to the friars' church to be widened to make room for the huge crowds who thronged the building upon that occasion.

As in the case of many other holy men belonging to the Augustinian Order, little is known of the life of Bd Clement. The few data which may be found in Jordan of Quedlinburg's *Vitae Fratrum* have been extracted :1 the short notice which appears in the *Acta Sanctorum*, April, vol. i. See also Hélyot, *Ordres Monastiques*, vol. iii (1721), pp. 15-16.

BD JULIAN OF ST AUGUSTINE   (A.D. 1606)

BD JULIAN MARTINET, who was descended from a long line of French knights, was born in the Castilian town of Medinaceli, where his family were living in such reduced circumstances that they were glad to apprentice him in his boyhood to a tailor. However, at an early age he sought admittance into the Franciscan convent of his native town and was permitted to try his vocation. The extraordinary devotional exercises and strange austerities to which he was addicted were looked at askance by his superiors who, judging him to be mentally unbalanced, dismissed him as unsuitable. From Medinaceli he went to Santorcaz, where he plied his trade until he made the acquaintance of Father Francis de Torrez, a Franciscan who was conducting a mission in the district. The friar recognized the young tailor's capacities and invited his assistance. During the rest of the mission Julian went up and down the streets, ringing a bell and inviting the inhabitants to come and listen to the preacher. Through the influence of Father de Torrez, the young man was received into another Franciscan house, the convent of our Lady of Salceda. Here history repeated itself : Julian's practices gave rise to the notion that he was crazy, and he was accordingly sent away. Disappointed but undaunted, he built himself a hermitage and lived his austere life in solitude, occasionally emerging to go with other beggars to the convent to ask for a little food.

Eventually the sanctity and growing reputation of the hermit induced the Franciscan superiors to welcome him back into the house. After a year's noviciate he was professed, as Brother Julian-of-St-Augustine, but he never sought the priesthood. He was left free to give himself up to his self-chosen mortifications, and lacerated his body with every instrument of torture he could devise ; he took his few hours of rest either in the open air or else leaning against a wall or in one of the confessionals in the church. From time to time Father Torrez would enlist his help on his missionary tours, and the lay-brother was found to be possessed of an eloquence which went straight to the hearts and consciences of his audience. His fame spread rapidly, and Queen Margaret, the mother of Philip IV, expressed a desire to see him. Very unwillingly did Julian go to court at the command of his superiors, but when he found himself there he was too much embarrassed to utter a word. In 1606 he was taken very ill on the road two leagues from Alcala de Henares. Refusing all offers of transport he managed to drag himself as far as the friary of St Didacus, and there he died. At once he was honoured as a saint, but the process of his beatification was not formally concluded until 1825.

The documents printed in the process of beatification form the most reliable source of information, and from these Father Joseph Vidal in 1825 compiled a popular life of Bd Julian in Italian. See also Léon, *Auréole Séraphique* (Eng. trans.), vol. ii, pp. 47–59 ; and Mazzara, *Leggendario Francescano*, vol. i (1676), pp. 518–520.

BD JULIA BILLIART, Virgin, Co-Foundress of the Institute of
Notre Dame of Namur   (a.d. 1816)

The origin of the Institute of Notre Dame was once described by Cardinal Sterckx
as a breath of the apostolic spirit upon the heart of a woman who knew how to
believe and how to love ". That woman was Bd Mary Rose Julia Billiart. She
came of a family of fairly well-to-do peasant farmers, who also owned a little'shop
at Cuvilly in Picardy, where she was born in 1751. Reading and writing she learnt
from her uncle, the village schoolmaster, but her special delight was in religious
instruction and the things of God. By the time she was seven, she was in the habit
of explaining the catechism to other children less intelligent than herself. The
parish priest encouraged these good instincts, and allowed her to make her first
communion at the age of nine—a rare privilege in those days. He also permitted
her to take a vow of chastity when she was fourteen. Although Julia had to work
very hard, especially after heavy losses had impoverished her family, yet she always
found time to visit the sick, to teach the ignorant and to pray. Indeed, she had
already begun to earn the title by which she was afterwards known, " The Saint of
Cuvilly ".
      Suddenly a complete change came over her hitherto active existence. As the
result of shock caused by the firing of a gun through a window at her father, beside
whom she was sitting, there came upon her a mysterious illness, attended with great
pain, which gradually deprived her of the use of her limbs. Thus reduced to the
condition of an invalid, she lived a life of even closer union with God, continuing
on her sick-bed to catechize the children, to give wonderfully wise spiritual advice
to visitors, and to urge all to practise frequent communion. " Qu'il est bon le
bon Dieu ! " was a saying of hers long remembered and often quoted. In 1790,
when the curé of Cuvilly was superseded by a so-called constitutional priest who
had taken the oath prescribed by the revolutionary authorities, it was mainly Julia's
influence which induced the people to boycott the schismatic intruder. For that
reason and because she was known to have helped to find hiding-places for fugitive
priests, she became specially obnoxious to the Jacobins, who went so far as to
threaten to burn her alive. She was with difficulty smuggled out of the house,
hidden in a haycart, and taken to Compiègne, where she was hunted from one
lodging to another until at last one day they heard her exclaim, " Dear Lord, will
you not find me a corner in Paradise, since there is no room for me on earth ? "
The hardships she had to undergo so aggravated her malady that for several months
she almost completely lost her power of speech.
      She was, however, to enjoy a short period of peace. In the first lull which
followed the end of the Reign of Terror, an old friend rescued Julia and brought
her to Amiens to the house of Viscount Blin de Bourdon. In that hospitable
home the invalid recovered her speech, and there she met a sensitive and highly-
educated woman, Frances Blin de Bourdon, Viscountess de Gézaincourt, who was
henceforth to be her close friend and her associate in all her work. In the sickroom, where the Holy Sacrifice was daily offered, gathered a little party of women
who were inspired by the invalid and spent their time and money in good works ;
but a recrudescence of persecution scattered them, and forced Julia and her new
friend to retire to a house belonging to the Doria family at Bettencourt. There the
catechism classes were resumed and practically all the villagers were brought back
to their religious duties through the efforts of these two devoted girls.

During their stay at Bettencourt, they were several times visited by Father Joseph Varin, who was immensely struck by the personality and capabilities of Julia. He was convinced that God intended her to do great things. Under his direction, as soon as they could return to Amiens, were laid the foundations of the Institute of Notre Dame which was to devote itself primarily to the spiritual care of poor children, but also to the Christian education of girls of all classes and to the training of religious teachers. The rules were in some respects a great departure from those of existing orders, notably in the abolition of the distinction between choir and lay sisters. Soon several postulants joined them, an orphanage was opened, and evening catechism-classes started. " My daughters, " exclaimed Mother Julia, " think how few priests there are now, and how many poor children are sunk in the grossest ignorance. We must make it our task to strive to win them ! " In 1804, when the Fathers of the Faith held a great mission in Amiens, they entrusted the teaching of the women to the Sisters of Notre Dame. The close of that mission was followed by an event that made a great sensation. Father Enfantin asked Bd Julia to join him in a novena for an unknown intention. On the fifth day—the feast of the Sacred Heart—he approached the invalid of twenty-two years' standing and said to her, " Mother, if you have any faith, take one step in honour of the Sacred Heart of Jesus ". She at once got up, and realized that she was completely cured.

Her former activity now fully restored, Mother Julia was able not only to consolidate and extend the new institute, but also to give her personal assistance to the missions which were conducted by the Fathers of the Faith in other towns, until their activities in that direction were checked by the action of the government. The educational work of the sisters continued to increase rapidly ; convents were opened by them at Namur, Ghent and Tournai, and everything seemed to augur well for their future when a disastrous set-back was experienced which threatened the very existence of the new community. Father Varin had been obliged to leave Amiens, and the post of confessor to the Sisters of Notre Dame fell to a capable but most injudicious, self-opinionated young priest, who tried to upset the rules of the congregation ; when gently remonstrated with, he turned against the foundress. He even managed for a time to estrange from her many who had been her warm friends. Among these was the Bishop of Amiens, who now virtually demanded her withdrawal from his diocese. Accompanied by nearly all the sisters she accordingly retired to the branch house at Namur, where the bishop of that city received her warmly. Before long Bd Julia was fully vindicated and she was invited to return to Amiens ; but it was found impracticable to restart the work there, so Namur became permanently the mother-house. The remaining seven years of the holy woman's life were spent in training her daughters and in founding new convents, fifteen of which were established during her lifetime. " Mother Julia is one of those souls who can do more for God's Church in a few years than others can do in a century ", said the Bishop of Namur, who knew her worth. It is recorded that in the interest of her institute she made no less than one hundred and twenty journeys.

In 1816 it became evident to herself and to her community that she was failing fast. Mother Blin de Bourdon was also ill at the time, but whereas Bd Julia's earthly course had run, her faithful friend was to be restored to health to carry on the great work. On April 8, while she was gently repeating the *Magnificat*, the foundress of the Institute of Notre Dame of Namur passed to her reward. She was beatified in 1906.

Lives of Bd Julia Billiart are numerous in French, English and German. That by Fr Charles Clair, s.j., *La bse Mère Julie Billiart* (1906), must not be confused with another written in English by a member of the order and edited by Fr James Clare, s.j. (1909). The French biography by Fr C. Clair was supplemented and re-edited by Fr Griselle (1907). In German the best life is that by B. Arens (1908). More recent accounts are by T. Réjalot (1922), Sr F. de Chantal (*Julie Billiart and Her Institute*, 1939), and M. G. Carroll, *The Charred Wood* (1951).

9 : ST MARY OF CLEOPHAS, Matron (First Century)

TO Mary of Cleophas whose name stands first in the Roman Martyrology on this day no general liturgical recognition is accorded, though her feast is kept by the Passionists, and by the Latins in Palestine. She seems to have been the wife of one Cleophas, who may or may not be identical with the Cleophas who is named as one of the two disciples who went to Emmaus on the day of our Lord's resurrection. Her identity among the various Marys mentioned by the evangelists is a matter of discussion among biblical commentators. The martyrology contents itself with saying that " Blessed John the Evangelist calls [her] sister of the most holy Mary, Mother of God, and relates that she stood with her by the cross of Jesus ". But it is possible that the sister of the mother of Jesus mentioned (John xix 25) was in fact a fourth, unnamed, woman.

Round the name of Mary of Cleophas all sorts of legendary excrescences gathered in later days. She was said to have travelled to Spain with St James the Greater, to have died at Ciudad Rodrigo, and to have been venerated with great honour at Compostela. On the other hand another extravagant legend connects her with the coming of SS. Lazarus, Mary Magdalen and Martha to Provence, and her body was believed to repose at Saintes-Maries near the mouth of the Rhone.

See the *Acta Sanctorum*, April, vol. i ; Moroni, *Dizionario di Erudizione*, vol. xciv, pp. 10–60 ; Vigouroux, *Dictionnaire de la Bible*, vol. iv, cc. 818–819 ; Durand, *L'Enfance de Jésus Christ* (1908).

ST WALDETRUDIS, or WAUDRU, Widow (*c.* A.D. 688)

St Waldetrudis, called in French Waltrude or Waudru, who is venerated in Belgium, especially at Mons of which she is patron, belonged to a family of remarkable holiness. Her parents were St Walbert and St Bertilia, her sister St Aldegundis of Maubeuge, her husband St Vincent Madelgar, and their four children St Landericus, St Dentelinus, St Aldetrudis and St Madelberta, the last two named both being abbess of Maubeuge. She married a young nobleman called Madelgar, with whom she led a happy life of devotion and good works. Some time after the birth of the last of their children, Madelgar withdrew into the abbey of Haumont which he had founded, taking the name of Vincent.

Waldetrudis remained in the world two years longer than her husband and then she also withdrew, retiring into a very humble little house, built in accordance with her instructions, where she lived in poverty and simplicity. Her sister repeatedly invited her to join her at Maubeuge, but she wished for greater austerity than she could have at the abbey. Her solitude was so often broken in upon by those who sought her advice and direction that she eventually founded a convent. This place, which afterwards became known as Chateaulieu (Castri locus in Monte), was in the centre of what is now the town of Mons. Throughout her life St Waldetrudis was greatly given to works of mercy, and she became celebrated for the miracles of healing which were wrought through her both before and after her death.

There are two Latin lives of St Waldetrudis ; the first, written in the ninth century, has only been printed in *Analectes pour servir à l'histoire ecclésiastique de la Belgique*, vol. iv, pp. 218–231 ; the second, at one time wrongly attributed to Philip de Harveng, is in fact a later adaptation of the former. It has been printed in the *Acta Sanctorum*, April, vol. i, and by Mabillon. See especially L. Van der Essen, *Saints Mérovingiens de Belgique*, pp. 231–237, and Berlière, *Monasticon Belge*, vol. i, pp. 327–328.

ST HUGH, Bishop of Rouen   (A.D. 730)

HISTORY has preserved few details about St Hugh of Rouen, who owed much of the fame he enjoyed among his contemporaries to his family connections. The son of Drogo, Duke of Burgundy, he was the grandson on the paternal side of Pepin de Herstal and nephew of Charles Martel. He was made *primicerius* of the church of Metz, and subsequently, no doubt through the influence of his uncle Charles, bishop of Rouen, Paris and Bayeux, and abbot of Fontenelle and Jumièges. To be a pluralist in those days was unfortunately only too common, but Hugh, far from profiting by the revenues to which he became entitled, expended his own considerable wealth for the benefit of the churches which he governed. The Chronicle of Fontenelle, which is our chief source of information, expatiates upon the generous gifts with which he endowed that abbey alone. He died in the abbey of Jumièges in 730.

Our chief source of information is the *Gesta Abbatum* of the abbey of Fontenelle. The biography written by Bishop Baudri of Dol four hundred years after the death of the saint is of little worth. See the *Acta Sanctorum*, April, vol. i. The life by Baudri is printed in Migne, PL., vol. clxvi, cc. 1163–1172. See also Duchesne, *Fastes Épiscopaux*, vol. ii, pp. 208 and 460.

ST GAUCHERIUS, Abbot   (A.D. 1140)

ST GAUCHERIUS was only eighteen when he abandoned the world to live the solitary life. He was born at Meulan-sur-Seine, where he received a good and religious education. His director sent him to his own master, Humbert, one of the canons of Limoges, who happened to be staying in the neighbourhood. That wise man not only encouraged the youth, but offered to assist him in carrying out his heart's desire by taking him back to the Limousin district which was suitable for the life of retirement which he was contemplating. After spending a night in prayer at the tomb of St Leonard of Limoges, Gaucherius and a friend called Germond struck out into the wild forest region which stretched away for miles without any human habitation. In a particularly remote and inaccessible spot, they constructed a hermitage, and there they lived for several years unknown and forgotten. But gradually, as knowledge of the hermits' holy life spread, cells sprang up round about to accommodate disciples and visitors. Many holy men were trained in this community, which became known as Aureil. To them, and to a convent he founded for women, Gaucherius gave the rule of the canons and canonesses of St Augustine. St Lambert of Angoulême, and St Faucherus were amongst the disciples of St Gaucherius, and it was he who gave St Stephen of Grandmont his

hermitage of Muret.   The saint's death took place as the result of a fall from his
horse when, as an old man of eighty, he was returning to Aureil from a visit to
Limoges.   He was canonized in 1194.

There is an earlier and fuller Latin life than that printed in the *Acta Sanctorum*, April,
vol. i, but it only exists in manuscript and in a fragmentary condition.   See the Catalogue
of Paris Hagiographical MSS., vol. ii, p. 626.

BD UBALD OF FLORENCE   (A.D. 1315)

ONE of the most prominent leaders of the Ghibelline party in Florence in the year
1276 was the young Ubald Adimari.   Well favoured by nature and fortune and
belonging to a distinguished family, he had up to the age of thirty led a turbulent
life with dissipated companions.   One day, however, as he was listening to the
preaching of St Philip Benizi, he was struck to the heart with shame for the past,
and, with one of those sudden impulses to which generous souls are prone, he then
and there vowed that he would never again bear arms.   Attaching himself to St
Philip, who admitted him into the Servite Order, he undertook severe penances to
atone for his sins and to tame his proud and haughty spirit.   In after years those
about him noted that he had grown so gentle that when he appeared in the garden
of the monastery of Monte Senario the birds would perch upon his head and hands
and shoulders.   He had the gift of miracles, and it is recorded that once, when it
was his turn to fetch water from the spring to serve to the brethren in the refectory
and accidentally broke the pitcher, he filled his scapular with water and carried it
safely home.   There was enough, we are told, to satisfy the thirst of all.

St Philip dearly loved his devoted disciple.   Not only did he make him for
several years the companion of his journeys, but he chose him for his confessor.
As Philip lay sick at Todi, Ubald was warned by a supernatural premonition that
his master was dying and hastened to his bedside.   When the saint asked for his
" book ", eager hands offered the Bible, the Breviary and the rosary ; but Ubald
knew better, and gave him the book from which he had learnt all his wisdom—the
crucifix : and on that " book " he fixed his failing eyes until they finally closed in
death.   Ubald survived him for thirty years at Monte Senario.   His *cultus* was
confirmed in 1821.

See Gianni-Garbi, *Annales Ordinis Servorum B.V.M.*, vol. i, pp. 228–229 ; Spörr,
Lebensbilder aus dem Servitenorden, pp. 437 *seq.*   Most of the lives of St Philip Benizi (*e.g.*
that of P. Soulier) also contain some mention of Bd Ubald.

BD THOMAS OF TOLENTINO, MARTYR   (A.D. 1321)

AMONG the missionary pioneers who in the early fourteenth century strove to
spread Christianity in the Far East was the Franciscan, Thomas of Tolentino, whose
memory is still venerated by the faithful in India, the country in which he received
the crown of martyrdom.   From the time he had entered the Order of Friars
Minor in early youth, Thomas had been known as a truly apostolic man, and when
the ruler of Armenia sent to ask the Minorite minister-general for some priests to
fortify true religion in his realm, Thomas was chosen for the mission with four of
his brethren.   Their labours were blessed with success, many schismatics being
reconciled and infidels converted.   Armenia, however, was being seriously threatened by the Saracens, and Thomas came back to Europe to solicit help from Pope
Nicholas IV and the kings of England and France.

Although he duly returned to the Armenian mission with twelve other Franciscans, Thomas subsequently travelled farther afield to Persia. Again he was recalled or sent back to Italy, but this time it was to report to Pope Clement V with a view to a further advance into Tartary and China. His embassy resulted in the nomination of an ecclesiastical hierarchy consisting of John of Monte Corvino as archbishop and papal legate for the East, with seven Franciscans as suffragans. In the meantime Bd Thomas had returned to the field of his labours, full of zeal for the conversion of India and China. He appears to have been making for Ceylon and Cathay, but the ship was driven by contrary winds to Salsette Island, near Bombay. Thomas was seized by the Saracens with several of his brethren and imprisoned. After being scourged and exposed to the burning rays of the sun, the holy man was beheaded. Bd Odoric of Pordenone afterwards recovered his body and translated it to Xaitou. The *cultus* was approved in 1894.

There are various letters of Jordan de Severac, and others, which supply information concerning Bd Thomas ; see BHL., nn. 8257–8268. Some portion of these is printed in the *Acta Sanctorum*, April, vol. i (under April 1), and others in the *Analecta Franciscana*, vol. iii. Further materials are available in the volumes of Fr Jerome Golubovich, *Bibliotheca bio-bibliographica della Terra Santa e dell' Oriente Francescano*. See also Léon, *Auréole Séraphique* (Eng. trans.), vol. ii, pp. 61–64. On Bd Odoric of Pordenone, see under January 28 and the bibliography thereto appended, much of which has also a bearing upon the subject of the present notice.

BD ANTONY PAVONI, Martyr (A.D. 1374)

Antony Pavoni was born at Savigliano in Piedmont and entered, while still young, the Dominican priory there. His reputation for fervour and learning caused him to be appointed inquisitor general over Piedmont and Liguria : as such he was called upon to refute and pass judgement on the opponents of the faith, notably the Vaudois. In the zealous performance of his office he made many enemies, as he himself knew full well. At Easter 1374, in the little town of Bricherasio he prophesied his own approaching death. He bade the barber who was shaving him give him a fine tonsure because he was invited to a marriage feast. The man who, like all those of his trade, was well up in the local news, exclaimed in surprise that no wedding was about to take place in the neighbourhood. " All the same I can assure you that I am telling you the truth ", was Antony's reply. A few days later, on Low Sunday, as he left the church in which he had just offered Mass and preached, he was set upon by seven armed men, who killed him. His tomb was the scene of miracles (one of the beneficiaries being Bd Haymo Taparelli) ; and the *cultus* was authorized in 1856.

See the *Acta Sanctorum*, April, vol. i, and *Archivio storico italiano*, 3rd series, vol. xii, pp. 29 *seq.* A fuller bibliography in Taurisano, *Catalogus hagiographicus O.P.* There is a short English account in Procter, *Lives of the Dominican Saints*, pp. 85–87.

10 : ST BADEMUS, Abbot (A.D. 376)

ONE of the victims of the persecution under King Sapor II of Persia was a holy abbot whose name is latinized as Bademus. He was a citizen of Bethlapat, who had founded near the city a monastery over which he ruled with great repute for sanctity. He was apprehended with seven of his monks, condemned to be beaten daily, loaded with chains, and imprisoned in a dungeon. About the same time a Christian at the Persian court, Nersan, was also apprehended because he refused to worship the sun. At first he showed constancy, but at the sight of torture his resolution failed and he promised to conform. To test his sincerity Sapor suggested that he should kill Bademus, promising that he should be restored to favour and to his former possessions if he would comply. Nersan consented ; a sword was placed in his hand and the abbot was brought into his cell. As Nersan advanced to plunge the weapon into his victim's body, terror seized upon him and he stood for a time motionless, unable to raise his arm. Bademus remained calm, and fixing his eyes upon his would-be assailant he said, " Nersan ! To what depths of wickedness you must have sunk when you can not only deny God but can also kill His servants. Willingly do I give myself to be a martyr for Christ, but I could have wished that it might have been by some other hand than yours ! " Nersan, however, hardened his heart and made a thrust at the saint, but his arm was so unsteady that he struck several times before he inflicted a mortal wound.

S. E. Assemani in his *Acta Martyrum Orientalium* was the first to make known the Syriac text of these " acts ", but they have also been printed by Bedjan. The Greek translation has been edited by Fr Delehaye in vol. ii of the *Patrologia Orientalis*. See also the *Acta Sanctorum*, April, vol. i, and BHO., 131 ; BHG., 210.

THE MARTYRS UNDER THE DANES   (*c.* A.D. 870)

IN one of their numerous descents upon Anglo-Saxon England, the Danes made their way up the Thames as far as the abbey of Chertsey, where they massacred Beocca the abbot, a priest called Hethor, and a number of monks. There are said to have been as many as ninety victims. They are reckoned as martyrs because the Danes showed special ferocity towards those whom they regarded as the representatives of Christianity. At about the same period similar massacres occurred in different parts of England. At Medeshamstede, the site of the modern Peterborough, Abbot Hedda was slain with all his community, to the number of eighty-four. There were also raids made into the fen country, and at Bardney, Ely and probably at Croyland all the religious were exterminated. In the abbey church of Thorney in Cambridgeshire were venerated the relics of three anchorets of whom tradition declared that they had suffered martyrdom in the same year, 870, at the hands of the Danes. The very lack of details in our chronicles is probably due to the desolation almost everywhere created among those who alone could make any pretence to scholarship.

Only small and scattered fragments of information are available concerning these raids, *e.g.* in the Anglo-Saxon Chronicle, in William of Malmesbury, *Gesta Pontificum*, in Brompton and similar sources. See Stanton's *Menology*, pp. 150–151 ; and for the invasions F. M. Stenton, *Anglo-Saxon England* (1943), pp. 243 *seq.* The best-known victim was the East Anglian king, St Edmund (November 20).

ST MACARIUS, or MACAIRE, OF GHENT   (A.D. 1012)

ST MACARIUS (Macaire) is popular throughout Flanders, where he is regarded as patron against epidemic diseases of all kinds. Very little is actually known about him but, as frequently happens in the case of uncanonized saints honoured locally, fiction steps in where history is lacking. He is supposed to have been archbishop of Antioch, and it is possible that the Macarius who about the year 970 was presiding over the church of Antioch in Pisidia may have nominated and consecrated this younger namesake as his successor. He was certainly never archbishop of Antioch in Syria. To escape the honours which threatened his humility—says the legend—he distributed all his property to the poor and went on a pilgrimage to Jerusalem. There he was captured, tortured and imprisoned by the Saracens ; but making his escape he came to Europe, which he traversed, performing many wonderful miracles on the way. Thus he passed through Mainz, Cologne, Malines, Cambrai and Tournai until he reached Ghent. All we can be sure about is that in this latter city a Macarius was hospitably received as a poor pilgrim by the monks of Saint-Bavon, who allowed him to remain in their hospice, and that he fell a victim to the plague which was ravaging the country. As the pestilence ceased directly after his death, as he had prophesied would be the case, he was held to have offered his life to God in expiation for the sins of the people.

See the *Acta Sanctorum*, April, vol. i, where two Latin accounts of his life are printed. The first of these, by Erembold, a monk of Ghent, was written in 1047 ; the second, a very extravagant document, was produced in 1067 when his remains were more honourably enshrined. *Cf.* the volume of *Aufsätze* printed in remembrance of G. Waitz (1886), pp. 642 *seq.* There are some small popular lives of St Macaire in Flemish and in French, notably one by J. J. De Smet (1867).

ST FULBERT, BISHOP OF CHARTRES (A.D. 1029)

WE learn from St Fulbert of Chartres himself that he was of humble extraction, but we know little of his early years beyond the fact that he was born in Italy and spent his boyhood there. He was later on a student in Rheims and must have been one of its most distinguished scholars, for when the celebrated Gerbert, who taught him mathematics and philosophy, was raised to the papacy under the title of Silvester II, he summoned Fulbert to his side. When another pope succeeded, Fulbert returned to France, where Bishop Odo of Chartres bestowed upon him a canonry and appointed him chancellor. Moreover, the cathedral schools of Chartres were placed under his care, and he soon made them the greatest educational centre in France, attracting pupils from Germany, Italy and England. Regarded as a paragon of learning and described as a reincarnation of Socrates and Plato, he stood as a bulwark against the rationalizing tendencies of his day, although one at least of his pupils, the notorious Berengarius, afterwards lapsed into heresy. Upon the death of Bishop Roger, Fulbert was chosen to succeed him in the see of Chartres. In his humility the prelate elect wrote to Abbot St Odilo of Cluny that he trembled at the prospect of leading others in the way of holiness when he stumbled so repeatedly himself, but he was obliged to accept the office.

Fulbert's influence was now immense, for besides retaining direction of the school he became the recognized counsellor of the spiritual and temporal leaders of France. Yet he never ceased to deplore his unfitness for the position he held, and was wont to describe himself as " the very little bishop of a very great church ". External affairs were never allowed to interfere with the duty he owed to his diocese : he preached regularly from his cathedral pulpit and exerted himself to spread instruction in the territories under his jurisdiction. When, soon after his elevation, the cathedral of Chartres was burnt down, he at once set about rebuilding it with great magnificence, though this is not the cathedral which is now one of the glories of Christendom ; people of all classes came to his assistance, including Canute, King of England, who contributed a large sum. St Fulbert had a great devotion to our Lady, in whose honour he composed several hymns, and when the beautiful new cathedral was opened he caused the recently introduced feast of her birthday to be celebrated there with great solemnity, as well as to be observed throughout the diocese.

Like most of the more eminent churchmen of his century he was an outspoken opponent of simony and of bestowing ecclesiastical endowments upon laymen. After an episcopate of nearly twenty-two years, he died on April 10, 1029. The writings of St Fulbert include a number of letters, a brief penitential, nine sermons, a collection of passages from the Bible dealing with the Trinity, the Incarnation and the Eucharist, and also some hymns and proses.

There is no ancient life of St Fulbert, but a great deal of biographical material is contained in his letters and in the chronicles of the period. See especially A. Clerval, *Les Ecoles de Chartres au moyen âge* (1895), pp. 30–102, and the article of the same writer in DTC., vol. vi (1920), cc. 964–967. *Cf.* also Pfister, *De Fulberti Carnotensis ep. vita et operibus* (1885). Fulbert's hymn " Chorus novae Hierusalem " was included in the Sarum Breviary, and an English translation of it, " Ye choirs of New Jerusalem ", has been often reprinted in modern times. Fulbert's works are conveniently accessible in Migne, PL., vol. cxli. Some useful comments will be found in J. de Ghellinck, *Le Mouvement Théologique du XII* Siècle* (1914), pp. 31–38.

ST PATERNUS OF ABDINGHOF (A.D. 1058)

MANY ecclesiastical writers make mention of the recluse St Paternus, whose death seems to have left a deep impression on his contemporaries, notably on St Peter Damian and Bd Marianus Scotus. By birth he was probably an Irishman, but he found his way to Westphalia, where he was one of the first monks to enter the monastery of Abdinghof founded by St Meinwerk. Feeling called to complete retirement, he obtained leave to be enclosed as a solitary in a cell adjoining the abbey. He prophesied the destruction by fire of the city within thirty days unless the inhabitants would turn from their sins, but was laughed at as a visionary and an alarmist. On the Friday before Palm Sunday 1058, fires broke out simultaneously in seven parts of the town, which was completely destroyed ; the monastery itself was burnt down. The monks were saved, except Paternus, who refused to break his life-vow of enclosure—burnt to death by the fire or possibly suffocated by the smoke. Marianus Scotus says that he visited the ruins a fortnight after the fire, and prayed on the very mat whereon the recluse had suffered and died.

The little we know of St Paternus has been brought together in the *Acta Sanctorum*, April, vol. i, and again by Mabillon. The information is mainly derived from Marianus Scotus and Peter Damian. See also Greve, *Geschichte der Benedict. Abtei Abdinghof* (1894), pp. 33–34 ; and Gougaud, *Gaelic Pioneers of Christianity*, p. 89.

BD ANTONY NEYROT, MARTYR (A.D. 1460)

ANTONY NEYROT was born at Rivoli in Piedmont, and entered the Dominican priory of San Marco in Florence, then under the direction of St Antoninus. After being professed he was sent to one of the houses of the order in Sicily. Between Naples and Sicily his ship was boarded by pirates, who carried him to Tunis, where he was sold as a slave. He succeeded in obtaining his freedom, but only to fall into a worse captivity, for the study of the Koran led him to abjure his faith and to become a Mohammedan. For several months he had practised the religion of the false prophet when his eyes were suddenly opened, in consequence, it is said, of a vision he had of St Antoninus. Smitten with contrition, he at once sent away his wife, did penance, and resumed the daily recitation of the office. Then he went before the ruler of Tunis in his friar's habit and, in the presence of a great crowd, openly renounced his heresy and proclaimed the religion of Jesus Christ as the one true faith. Arguments, promises and threats were employed without being able to shake him. Eventually he was condemned to death, and perished by stoning and by sword cuts as he knelt in prayer with hands upraised. His body was given over to the flames, but portions of his relics which remained unconsumed were sold to Genoese merchants, who took them back to Italy. The *cultus* of Bd Antony was approved in 1767.

In the *Acta Sanctorum*, August, vol. vi, two accounts are printed of the martyrdom of Bd Antony ; but a still more valuable source has been edited in the *Analecta Bollandiana*, vol. xxiv (1905), pp. 357–374 : it is a letter addressed in 1461 to Pope Pius II by Peter Ranzano, prior provincial of the Dominicans in Sicily. See also Procter, *Dominican Saints*, pp. 87–90.

BD MARK FANTUCCI (A.D. 1479)

AMONGST the Franciscan leaders of the fifteenth century a special place must be assigned to Bd Mark Fantucci of Bologna, to whom was mainly due the preservation of the Observance as a separate body when it seemed on the point of being compulsorily merged into the Conventual branch. After having received an excellent education to fit him for the good position and large fortune to which he was left sole heir, he had given up all his worldly advantages at the age of twenty-six to receive the habit of St Francis. Three years after his profession, he was chosen guardian of Monte Colombo, the spot where St Francis had received the rule of his order. So successful was he in converting sinners that he was given permission to preach outside his province by St John Capistran, then vicar general of the Observants in Italy.

Having served twice as minister provincial, Bd Mark was elected vicar general in succession to Capistran, and showed himself zealous in enforcing strict observance of the rule : the various reforms he brought about all tended to revive the spirit of the founder. After the taking of Constantinople so many Franciscans had been enslaved by the Turks, that Mark wrote to all his provincials urging them to appeal for alms to ransom the captives ; but in answer to a request for instructions how to act in the danger zone, he sent word to Franciscan missionaries in places threatened by victorious Islam bidding them remain boldly at their posts and to face what might betide. He was able to execute a long-cherished plan to form a convent of Poor Clares in Bologna. St Catherine of Bologna came with some of her nuns from Ferrara to establish it, and found in Bd Mark one who could give her all the assistance she needed. He visited as commissary all the friaries in Candia, Rhodes and Palestine, and on his return to Italy he was elected vicar general for the second time. Never sparing himself he undertook long and tiring expeditions to Bosnia, Dalmatia, Austria and Poland, often travelling long distances on foot. Pope Paul II wished to make him a cardinal, but he fled to Sicily to avoid being forced to accept an honour from which he shrank.

The next pope, Sixtus IV, formed a project which was even less acceptable, for he had set his heart upon uniting all Franciscans into one body, without requiring any reform from the Conventuals. At a meeting convened to settle the matter,

Bd Mark used all his eloquence to defeat the proposal, but apparently in vain.   At last, in tears, throwing down the book of the rule at the pope's feet, he exclaimed, " Oh my Seraphic Father, defend your own rule, since I, miserable man that I am, cannot defend it " ; and thereupon left the hall.   The gesture accomplished what argument had failed to do ; the assembly broke up without arriving at a decision, and the scheme fell through.   In 1479, while delivering a Lenten mission in Piacenza, Bd Mark was taken ill and died at the convent of the Observance outside the city.   His *cultus* was confirmed in 1868.

Bd Mark is very fully dealt with under different years in Wadding's *Annales Ordinis Minorum ;* and a summary account may be found in Mazzara, *Leggendario Francescano,* vol. i (1676), pp. 431–440.   See also Léon, *Auréole Séraphique* (Eng. trans.), vol. ii, pp. 1–13. Sundry letters and other references have been published by Faloci Pulignani in his *Miscellanea francescana,* vol. xiv (1913), and also in the *Archivum Franciscanum Historicum,* vol. xxi (1928).   Fr Mark is said to have been one of the founders of *monti di pietà* to combat oppression ef the poor by usury.

ST MICHAEL DE SANCTIS   (A.D. 1625)

THIS Michael was born at Vich in Catalonia in 1589 or 1591, and when six years old announced that he had decided to be a monk when he grew up ; his mother having told him about St Francis of Assisi he set himself to imitate that saint in ways unsuitable to his years.   Doubtless his prudent parents restrained his ardour, but he retained his enthusiasm for St Francis.   When his father and mother died, leaving him to the guardianship of an uncle, he was put in the service of a merchant. Young Michael had no fads about being above " mere trade " and did his work well ; but whenever he was not at it he was doing works of devotion : assisting at the Divine Office when he could, and saying the Little Office of our Lady every day. His master was thoroughly edified, held up Michael as a pattern to his family, and raised no objection to the boy joining the Trinitarian friars at Barcelona ; he took his vows at the monastery of St Lambert at Saragossa in 1607.

About this time Bd John-Baptist-of-the-Conception had rallied many of the Trinitarians of Spain to his congregation of reformed Trinitarians, whose greater austerity was indicated by the wearing of sandals instead of shoes.   One of these discalced brothers coming to St Lambert's to be ordained, Michael was moved to offer himself for their harder life.   His superiors gave the necessary permission, he was received into the novitiate at Madrid, and some time later he renewed his vows with them at Alcalà.   He studied at Seville and Salamanca, was ordained priest, and his virtues and ability caused him to be twice named superior of the convent at Valladolid.   His religious not only loved him as a father but revered him as a saint, and he set them a special example of devotion to the Blessed Sacrament.   Several times he was rapt in ecstasy during Mass, and he was God's instrument in the working of a number of miracles during life and after his death, which took place on April 10, 1625, when he was only thirty-six years old.   St Michael de Sanctis was canonized in 1862, and he is described in the Roman Martyrology to-day as " remarkable for innocence of life, wonderful penitence, and love for God ".

The postulator of the cause, Fr Niccolò della Vergine, in the year of the beatification 1779), published a *Ristretto istorico della vita, virtù e miracoli del B. Michele de Santi,* in which, for example, details are given of the saint's levitations.   A devotional tractate of his on " The Peace of the Soul " has been discovered and printed by Fr Antonino de la Asuncion.   St Michael's feast is kept in the Trinitarian Order on July 5.

11: ST LEO THE GREAT, POPE AND DOCTOR OF THE CHURCH (A.D. 461)

THE sagacity of Leo I, his successful defence of the Catholic faith against heresy, as well as his political intervention with Attila the Hun and Genseric the Vandal, raised the prestige of the Holy See to unprecedented heights and earned for him the title of " the Great ", a distinction accorded by posterity to only two other popes, St Gregory I and St Nicholas I. The Church has honoured St Leo by including him amongst her doctors on the strength of his masterly expositions of Christian doctrine, many extracts from which are incorporated in the Breviary lessons. St Leo's family was probably Tuscan, but he seems to have been born in Rome, as he always speaks of it as his " patria ". Of his early years and of the date of his ordination to the priesthood there are no records. It is clear from his writings that he received a good education, although it did not include Greek. We hear of him first as deacon under St Celestine I and then under Sixtus III, occupying a position so important that St Cyril wrote directly to him, and Cassian dedicated to him his treatise against Nestorius. Moreover, in 440, when the quarrels between the two imperial generals, Aetius and Albinus, threatened to leave Gaul at the mercy of the barbarians, Leo was sent to make peace between them. At the time of the death of Sixtus III he was still in Gaul, whither a deputation was sent to announce to him his election to the chair of St Peter.

Immediately after his consecration on September 29, 440, he began to display his exceptional powers as a pastor and ruler. Preaching was at that time mainly confined to bishops, and he set about it systematically, instructing the faithful of Rome whom he purposed to make a pattern for other churches. In the ninety-six genuine sermons which have come down to us, we find him laying stress on almsgiving and other social aspects of Christian life, as well as expounding Catholic doctrines—especially that of the Incarnation. Some idea of the extraordinary vigilance of the holy pontiff over the Church and its necessities in every part of the empire can be gathered from the 143 letters written by him, and the 30 letters written to him, which have fortunately been preserved. About the period that he was dealing with the Manichaeans in Rome, he was writing to the Bishop of Aquileia advising him how to deal with Pelagianism, which had made a reappearance in his diocese.

From Spain St Turibius, Bishop of Astorga, sent him a copy of a letter he had circulated with reference to Priscillianism—a sect which had made great headway in Spain, some of the clergy being favourable to it. Its tenets seem to have combined astrology with fatalism and with a Manichaean theory of the evil of matter. In his reply the pope refuted the Priscillianist doctrines at considerable length, and, after describing the measures he had taken against the Manichaeans, advised the summoning of a council of bishops to combat the heresy. In the affairs of Gaul he was called upon several times to interfere : twice he had occasion to quash the proceedings of St Hilary, Bishop of Arles, who as metropolitan had exceeded his powers. Several letters are addressed to Anastasius, Bishop of Thessalonica, confirming his vicariate over the bishops of Illyricum ; on one occasion recommending him to be more tactful and considerate, and on another reminding him that bishops had a right to appeal to Rome, " according to ancient tradition ". In

446 he wrote to the African church of Mauretania, forbidding the appointment of laymen to the episcopate, and of any man who had been twice married or who had married a widow, and dealing with such a delicate matter as the treatment of consecrated virgins who had been outraged by the barbarians.　In a letter addressed to the bishops of Sicily, in consequence of complaints from the clergy of Palermo and Taormina, he lays down the axiom that church property may not be alienated by a bishop without the consent of all his clergy.

In these and in all Leo's pronouncements, couched in authoritative and almost stern language, there is no personal note, no uncertainty : it is not the man who seems to speak, but the successor of Peter.　Therein lies the secret of his greatness, that which gives unity to his career.　Yet one little human touch, though it be only a tradition, may not be deemed out of place, illustrating as it does the extreme importance the saint attached to the selection of suitable candidates for holy orders. In the *Spiritual Meadow* of John Moschus, Amos, Patriarch of Jerusalem, is quoted as saying : " I have found it written that the blessed Pope Leo, equal to the angels, watched and prayed forty days at the tomb of St Peter, begging through the inter-cession of that apostle to obtain of God the pardon of his sins.　After that period St Peter, in a vision, said to him : ' Your sins are forgiven by God, except those committed in conferring holy orders : of these you will still have to render a strict account '."　St Leo prohibited the ordination of slaves or of men who had been employed in unlawful or unseemly occupations, and caused the in-sertion into the canon law of a special clause restricting elevation to the priesthood to candidates of mature age who had been thoroughly tested and had laboured in the service of the Church, giving evidence of submission to rule and love of discipline.

But the holy man, as pontiff of the Universal Church, found himself called upon to deal with difficulties in the East far greater than any which had hitherto met him in the West.　In the year 448, he received a letter from a Constantinopolitan abbot, called Eutyches, complaining of a recrudescence of the Nestorian heresy.　St Leo replied in guarded terms, promising to make inquiries.　The next year came another communication from Eutyches, duplicates of which were sent to the patriarchs of Alexandria and Jerusalem.　In this he protested against a sentence of excommunica-tion which had been passed upon him by St Flavian, Patriarch of Constantinople, at the instance of Eusebius of Dorylaeum, and asked to be reinstated.　The appeal was supported by a letter from the Emperor Theodosius II.　As no official notice of the proceedings at Constantinople had reached Rome, Leo wrote to St Flavian, who sent a report of the synod at which Eutyches had been sentenced.　From this it was abundantly clear that he had fallen into the error of denying the two natures of Christ—a heresy the reverse of Nestorianism.　A council was now summoned at Ephesus by the Emperor Theodosius, ostensibly to inquire into the matter, but it was packed with the friends of Eutyches, and presided over by one of his strongest supporters, Dioscorus, Patriarch of Alexandria.　This gathering, nicknamed " The Robber Synod ", acquitted Eutyches and condemned St Flavian, who was moreover subjected to such physical violence that he died soon after.　The pope's legates, on their refusal to subscribe to the unjust sentence, were not allowed to read St Leo's letter.　As soon as the proceedings of the synod became known to the pope, he declared their decisions null and void.　This he followed up by a letter of remon-strance to the emperor in which he said : " Leave to the bishops the liberty of defending the faith : no worldly power or terrors will ever succeed in destroying it.

Protect the Church and seek to preserve its peace that Christ in His turn may protect your empire ".

Two years later, under the Emperor Marcian, a general council was held at Chalcedon.   Six hundred bishops or more were present, and St Leo was represented by his legates.   In this assembly the memory of St Flavian was vindicated and Dioscorus was declared excommunicated and deposed.   On June 13, 449, St Leo had written to St Flavian a doctrinal letter in which he had clearly set out the Catholic faith with regard to the natures of our Lord, steering clear of the errors of Nestorianism and Eutychianism.   This pronouncement, which has become famous as " The Dogmatic Letter " or " The Tome of St Leo ", had been suppressed by Dioscorus, but was read by the legates to the Council of Chalcedon.   " Peter has spoken by Leo ! " exclaimed the assembled bishops, when they had heard this lucid explanation of the two-fold nature of Christ, which has become for all subsequent ages the Church's official teaching.

In the meantime serious political events had been happening in the West, and were being met by St Leo with the same firmness and wisdom.   Attila with his Huns in 452 entered Italy, burning Aquileia and filling the country with blood and desolation.   After sacking Milan and razing Pavia, he set out with his army to assault the capital.   Panic seized the whole population : the general Aetius did nothing.   All eyes turned to Leo—the one strong man—and the emperor, Valentinian III, and senate ordered him to negotiate with the enemy.   Upheld as usual by the sense of his sacred office, and without a moment's hesitation, he started out from the capital, accompanied by Avienus the consul, Trigetius the governor of the city, and some of his priests, and came face to face with the invaders on the site of the present town of Peschiera.   The pope and his clergy interviewed the dreaded foe and induced him to retire and to accept an annual tribute instead of entering the holy city.   Rome was freed for the moment, but not for long.   Three years later, the Vandal Genseric (Gaiseric) appeared with an army before its walls, now almost defenceless.   This time St Leo's intervention was not so successful, but he obtained from the barbarian chief an undertaking to be satisfied with pillaging the city and to restrain his troops from slaughter and incendiarism.   The Vandals withdrew after fifteen days, taking back to Africa many captives as well as immense booty.

St Leo immediately set about the task of repairing the damage and of finding a remedy for the evils caused by the barbarians.   He sent priests to minister to the captives in Africa and alms to assist them.   He also replaced, as far as he could, the vessels and ornaments of the devastated churches.   It was characteristic of his trust in God that he was never discouraged, and that he maintained an unruffled equanimity even in the most difficult moments.   In the twenty-one years of his pontificate he had won the love and veneration of rich and poor, emperors and barbarians, clergy and lay folk alike.   He died on November 10, 461, and his relics are preserved in the Vatican basilica.   He is, however, commemorated on this day, which is that of one of the translations of his remains which have since taken place. His Anglican biographer, Dr Jalland, sums up Leo's personal character under four aspects—" his indomitable energy, his magnanimity, his consistency and his devotion to simple duty ".   His exposition of the true doctrine of the incarnation of the Son of God was a " moment " of the highest importance in Christian history, and among all his personal achievements, " there was none greater than the success with which he vindicated the claim of the Roman see to a primacy in the sphere of doctrine ". This great pope was declared a doctor of the Church, rather belatedly, in 1754.

Amongst the sermons of St Leo which have been preserved is one which he preached on the festival of St Peter and St Paul, not long after the retreat of Attila. He begins by contrasting the fervour of the Romans at the moment of their deliverance with their increasing forgetfulness, and reminds them of the ingratitude of the nine lepers. " Therefore, my beloved ", he goes on to say, " lest you incur the like reproach, return to the Saviour : remember the marvels He has wrought amongst you. Beware of attributing your deliverance to the stars, as some people impiously do, but refer it only to the boundless mercy of God who softened the furious hearts of the barbarians. Your past negligence must be atoned for by an expiation which exceeds the offence. Let us use the respite accorded by our kind Master to work at amending our lives, so that St Peter and all the saints who have succoured us in countless afflictions may second the tender supplications which we address on your behalf to the God of mercy through our Lord Jesus Christ."

Despite the prominent part played by St Leo in the history of his times, we have nothing in the nature of an early biography. The account given of him in the *Liber Pontificalis* amounts to very little. On a notice preserved in the Greek *Menaia* see the *Analecta Bollandiana*, vol. xxix (1910), pp. 400–408. A convenient summary of the saint's career and character is that of A. Régnier (1910) in the series " Les Saints ". For a fuller bibliography see the excellent article of Mgr Batiffol in DTC., vol. ix, cc. 218–301. Naturally Pope Leo is accorded a conspicuous place in such general works as Duchesne's *Histoire ancienne de l'Eglise* (Eng. trans.), vol. iii ; Hefele-Leclercq, *Conciles*, vol. ii ; and Bardenhewer, *Geschichte der altkirchlichen Literatur*, vol. iv. Special attention must be called to C. H. Turner's discussion of the dogmatic letters of St Leo in the *Miscellanea Ceriani* (1910) and to the most valuable *Life and Times of St Leo the Great* (1941), by the Rev. T. G. Jalland, which contains a bibliography.

ST BARSANUPHIUS (c. A.D. 550)

THE Greeks held St Barsanuphius in so great honour that his eikon was placed beside those of St Ephraem and St Antony in the church of the Holy Wisdom at Constantinople. He was an Egyptian by birth, who lived in a cell adjoining a monastery at Gaza in Palestine, in the time of the Emperor Justinian. He communicated with no one except by writing, so that the story got around that he neither ate nor drank earthly food. Evagrius relates that Eustochius, Patriarch of Jerusalem, doubting whether anyone could really be leading such a life, caused the wall of the cell to be broken through, whereupon flames burst out and consumed the unfortunate masons for their curiosity. A less absurd version of this story says that Barsanuphius invited the doubters into his cell and demonstrated the actuality of his existence by washing their feet.

Whatever his own austerities, the anchorite's written advice to others was to eat, drink, sleep and clothe themselves sufficiently. He was particularly resorted to by those who required assurance of the forgiveness of their sins, a subject on which Barsanuphius had often to write.

We have to depend on references in Evagrius (*Eccl. Hist.*, iv, 33), the Life of St Dositheus (February 23), and what can be gathered from the saint's " letters ", on which see two articles by S. Vailhé in *Échos d'Orient*, vol. vii (1904), pp. 268 *seq.*, and vol. viii (1905), pp. 14 *seq.* The so-called " acts " of Barsanuphius are characterized by the Bollandists as partly fabulous and partly doubtful (*Acta Sanctorum*, April, vol. ii), while Fr Vailhé regards them as a tissue of fictions. In MS. 5290, *fonds latin*, of the Bibliothèque Nationale, Paris, is contained a fanciful and no doubt wholly fictitious account of one Barsanorius, seemingly to be identified with the hermit referred to by Evagrius. This text has been printed in the *Catalogus Codicum Hagiog. Paris*, vol. i, pp. 525–535. The spiritual teaching of Barsanuphius and of his friend John the Prophet is of considerable interest; *cf.* the article *s.v.* " Barsanuphe " by Fr I. Hausherr in the *Dictionnaire de spiritualité*, vol. i (1938); and *Writings from the Philokalia* (1951), pp. 341–381.

ST ISAAC OF SPOLETO   (*c.* A.D. 550)

THE ilex-covered slopes of Monte Luco, considered sacred since pagan times, are honeycombed by caves which sheltered many a Christian solitary in the early middle ages. One of the most famous of these recluses was St Isaac, a man well known to St Gregory's friend St Eleutherius, who furnished the particulars about the hermit which are contained in the *Dialogues*. Isaac was a Syrian, who left his native land in consequence of the monophysite persecution to take up his residence in Italy. Upon his first arrival in Spoleto he entered a church, where he remained for three days and three nights, absorbed in prayer. Mistrusting his motives, one of the custodians of the building called him a hypocrite, struck him, and drove him from the church. Retribution immediately overtook the man, for the Devil entered into him and would not leave until St Isaac had stretched himself upon the body of his assailant. " Isaac is driving me out ! " exclaimed the evil spirit, thus disclosing to the inhabitants of Spoleto the identity of the stranger. The townsfolk, convinced that they had in their midst a very holy man, offered him presents and would have built him a monastery, but he refused all gifts and retired to a cave on Monte Luco. After several years spent in solitude, he had a vision of our Lady in which she bade him train disciples. He then became the director of a kind of *laura*, although he never founded a monastery. Several times his followers asked him to sanction their acceptance of offerings from the faithful, but he always replied, " A monk who wants earthly possessions is not a monk at all ". The holy man was endowed with the gifts of prophecy and miracles.

All that we know of St Isaac is derived from the third book of the *Dialogues* of St Gregory. See also the *Acta Sanctorum*, April, vol. ii.

ST GODEBERTA, VIRGIN   (*c.* A.D. 700)

WHEN the parents of St Godeberta considered that their daughter had reached a marriageable age, they took her to court in order that a suitable match might be arranged for her. That the maiden herself had a vocation for the religious life did not enter into their calculations, but St Eligius, Bishop of Noyon, who arrived during the deliberations and was perhaps in her confidence, slipped off his ring and, giving it to Godeberta, announced that he was thus affiancing her to our Lord Jesus Christ. She, greatly delighted, at once begged the prelate to give her the veil and to become her spiritual director. No serious opposition seems to have been made by her parents, who were no doubt well satisfied when King Clotaire III announced his intention of bestowing upon her his house of Noyon for a convent. Very soon there gathered round her twelve maidens, who led a life of prayer and mortification which must have contributed much to the Christian influences at work in a district which had hitherto remained partially pagan. When a terrible plague had broken out at Noyon, Godeberta urged the clergy to proclaim a three days' fast and general penance. Her suggestion was adopted and the scourge abated. This was followed later on by a great fire.   Godeberta was ill at the time, but she caused herself to be carried to the place where the flames were raging furiously and quenched them—tradition says—by making the sign of the cross.   During her life, the saint had a great reputation as a wonder-worker, and ever since her death she has been invoked in the diocese of Noyon against calamities of all sorts, but especially against drought and epidemics.

There is a Latin life of St Godeberta which has been printed in the *Acta Sanctorum*, April, vol. ii ; its authorship is ascribed to Radbod II, Bishop of Noyon.   See also Laffineur, *Vie de Ste Godeberthe* (1856) and Corblet, *Hagiographie d'Amiens* (1870), vol. ii, pp. 550–569.

ST GUTHLAC   (A.D. 714)

THE great Norman abbey of Croyland or Crowland, the ruins of which are still standing, replaced more than one earlier monastery on the site sanctified by the life and death of the holy hermit St Guthlac.   Whilst it was the monks who reclaimed the swamp, joining the island to the mainland and rendering it arable and fertile, it was in the name of the recluse, their patron, that they obtained from the council of the realm permission to make of Croyland a sanctuary of refuge where fugitives could be secure from their pursuers.

St Guthlac, who was of noble race, joined the army of Ethelred of Mercia as a fighting man when he was very young.   At the age of twenty-four, however, he laid down his arms to enter the double monastery of Repton, at that time under the rule of the abbess Elfrida.   The handsome young novice, though amiable and courteous to all, was at first unpopular owing to his austerity and especially to his total abstinence from any intoxicating drink, but as soon as his brethren came to know him better they appreciated his sincerity and goodness.   For two years he remained at Repton, acquiring monastic discipline and studying the Scriptures, and then he was seized with the desire to take up the life of a hermit.   He was told of a dismal island in the Fens, described as being so dank and so haunted by monsters and evil spirits that no one had hitherto been able to live in it.   He persuaded his informant to take him there in a fishing boat, and decided that it was the place he sought.   He returned with two or three companions to Croyland, where he was to end his days.   With certain modifications necessitated by the difference in place and climate his life reproduced that of the fathers of the desert, and in addition to severe interior trials he experienced violent temptations, not unlike those which St Athanasius describes of St Antony.   Moreover, he was savagely attacked by wild beings whom he regarded as monsters, but who seem to have been the descendants of Britons who had fled into the Fens to avoid their Saxon conquerors.   On the other hand God gave the recluse great spiritual consolations, besides bestowing upon him the gifts of prophecy and miracles.   St Hedda, Bishop of Dorchester, conferred holy orders upon him when he had been six years on the island.   In his solitude St Guthlac possessed a great attraction for wild nature : the fish in the marshes would swim towards him at his call, and he was constantly surrounded by birds, who flocked into his cell, ate from his hands, and built their nests in the places he selected.   When the crows robbed him of some of his few possessions, he bore with their depredations, " deeming that an example of patience ought to be set not only to men but also to birds and beasts ".   One day, as he was talking with a man called Wilfrid, two swallows alighted on his shoulders and then perched on his arms and knees, chattering all the time as though quite at home. In reply to Wilfrid's exclamations of surprise St Guthlac said, " Have you not read that he who elects to be unknown of men becomes known of wild creatures and is visited by angels ? For he who is frequented by men cannot be frequented by the holy angels."

When the saint had been living as a hermit for a period variously computed as fifteen and twenty-one years, God revealed to him the date of his death, which was very near. It also became known in some way to Edburga, abbess of Repton, for she sent him a leaden coffin and a shroud. On the Wednesday in Holy Week 714, he sent word to his sister St Pega, inviting her to come to his funeral. Although she had been living as an anchoress at Peakirk (Pegkirk), close to Croyland, her brother had always refrained from seeing her, deeming it desirable that they should not meet in this world that they might meet with greater joy in the next. On the seventh day of his illness, after taking viaticum from his altar, he passed to his eternal reward. His burial was attended by St Pega and by his disciples, Cissa, Egbert, Bettelin and Tatwin, who occupied cells not far from that of their master. St Guthlac's tomb became a great place of pilgrimage, especially after Ceolnoth, Archbishop of Canterbury, had been cured of ague through the intercession of Guthlac in the year 851.

There is a trustworthy life of St Guthlac written in the eighth century by Felix which is printed both by Mabillon, *Acta Sanctorum O.S.B.* (vol. iii, part 1, pp. 264–284) and by the Bollandists. Though little fresh information is obtainable from any other source, there are two Anglo-Saxon poems of contemporary date which have been attributed to Cynewulf (on which see the *Cambridge History of English Literature*, vol. i, p. 58, etc.), which are of great literary interest. Other lives, such as that by Peter of Blois, have no historical value. See also W. de Gray Birch, *Memorials of St Guthlac of Crowland* (1881) and his edition of Felix's *vita ;* DNB., vol. xxiii, p. 373 ; and DCB., vol. ii, pp. 823–826. From the frequent occurrence of the name of St Guthlac in English calendars it is plain that there was a very general popular *cultus.* A new edition of the Felix *vita*, by B. Colgrave, is announced.

BD WALTMAN, ABBOT (A.D. 1138)

TOWARDS the close of the first quarter of the twelfth century a layman called Tanchelm originated a new sect in Antwerp, which gained a considerable following. Its adherents held that bishops and priests were unnecessary and denied the efficacy of the sacraments, whilst permitting themselves great relaxation of morals. The archbishop of Cambrai, in whose diocese Antwerp then lay, greatly perturbed at the progress of the heresy, persuaded the canons of St Michael's in the city to enlist the help of St Norbert to combat the evil. In response to the invitation, the great Premonstratensian founder duly arrived with two of his disciples, Evermod and a learned and pious canon of the name of Waltman. Thanks to the zeal and preaching of these three, the people were soon won back to the faith, the sect lost its hold, and Tanchelm had to beat an ignominious retreat. As a token of their gratitude the secular canons presented St Michael's to St Norbert, they themselves retiring to Notre-Dame, now the cathedral. Waltman became abbot of the newly-formed Premonstratensian establishment.

No independent account of the activities of Bd Waltman seems to have come down to us from early times, but we hear of him in the Life of St Norbert (see the *Acta Sanctorum*, June, vol. i) and in the notices which chroniclers have devoted to the heresy of Tanchelm. *Cf.* I. van Spillbeeck, *Vie de saint Norbert ;* *tableaux historiques du XIIᵉ siècle* (1898), and C. J. Kirkfleet, *History of St Norbert* (1916).

BD RAINERIUS INCLUSUS   (A.D. 1237)

ADJOINING the cathedral of Osnabrück in the early part of the thirteenth century was a hermit's cell, with a squint which commanded a view of the altar inside the church.   Shut up (*inclusus*) for twenty-two years in the narrow enclosure lived a recluse called Rainerius (in English, Rayner) who, by his extraordinary austerities even more than by the few words he allowed himself to utter, recalled many a sinner and worldly man to repentance and newness of life.   Although he had lived blamelessly from childhood, Rainerius used every device he could imagine to chastise and mortify his flesh.   On his naked body he wore a shirt of chain-mail and hair, concealed by a coarse habit, and he scourged himself regularly until the blood ran.   When asked why he thus tortured his body, he would reply, " As our Lord Jesus Christ suffered in all His limbs for me, so do I wish, out of love for Him, to suffer in all my members ".   On Sundays, Tuesdays and Thursdays he fasted on bread and vegetables, on Mondays, Wednesdays and Saturdays on bread and beer, while on Fridays he took only bread and water. He daily recited the psalter and so many other prayers for the living and the dead that sometimes he had not time enough to eat.   He observed absolute silence except on feast-days, when he spoke a little but only for edification, usually keeping a stone in his mouth lest he might be tempted to vain words ; his requirements were made known by nods and signs.   Bd Rainerius is said to have died in 1237.

See the *Acta Sanctorum*, April, vol. ii, and Strunck, *Westphalia Sancta*, vol. ii, pp. 192–195.

BD GEORGE GERVASE, MARTYR   (A.D. 1608)

GEORGE GERVASE (Jervis) was born in 1569 at the port of Bosham in Sussex, in the register of whose famous parish church the entry of his christening may still be read.   He was apparently brought up a Protestant, or else left the Church for a time, though his mother belonged to the well-known Catholic family of Shelley that gave Bd Edward Shelley to the Church.   Challoner relates that at the age of twelve George was kidnapped by pirates and carried off to the West Indies for the next twelve years of his life.   What really happened was that, when he was twenty-six, he was with Sir Francis Drake's last and disastrous expedition to the Indies, which left Plymouth in 1595 and for which George may well have been " pressed ", as he seems to have gone against his will.   On his return he served for nearly two years in Flanders, with the Spanish army this time, and apparently it was not till the beginning of 1599 that he " enrolled himself in a better kind of service and became a soldier of Christ in the English College of Douay ".

Mr Gervase was ordained priest at Cambrai in 1603 and in the following year was sent on the mission.   He ministered in various parts of the country for two years, till he was arrested at Haggerston ; his examination by the dean of Durham is still extant, and valuable for Gervase's own testimony about himself.   Then he was imprisoned in London, till July 1606 when, with other priests, including several future martyrs, he was banished the realm.   George Gervase then made a pilgrimage to Rome, and it is likely that there he determined to offer himself to the English Benedictines ; for in the same year, 1607, between returning to Douay in July and again setting out for the mission in September, he was duly clothed a monk by the prior general, Dom Augustine Bradshaw.   On account of the opposition of the

English College to the Benedictines, this was done without the knowledge of the college authorities.

Father George had been back in England only two months when he was taken up and committed to the Gatehouse prison at Westminster. At his trial at the Old Bailey he refused the oath of allegiance, tendered in the form which had been condemned by the Holy See, while protesting his loyalty to the Crown ; and when pressed for his opinion on the pope's deposing power, replied, " I say that the pope can depose kings and emperors when they deserve it ". He also admitted that he was a priest, and so was condemned to death without more ado.

His confessor, Robert Chamberlain, records that as the rope was put round his neck Father George stretched out his arms and looked upward, standing like a monastic novice at his profession, singing the *Suscipe*. And so, " flinging out his hands like the wings of a bird ", he met his passion.

Bd George Gervase, the protomartyr of St Gregory's, Douay (now St. Gregory's, Downside), suffered on April 11, 1608. It was noted that at the same day and hour a fire consumed much of the town of Bury St Edmunds, where the martyr had spent much of his youth.

Camm gives a full account in *Nine Martyr Monks* (1931), drawing on Pollen's *Acts of the English Martyrs*, letters in the *Westminster Archives*, vol. ix, the *Middlesex County Records*, vol. ii, an Italian account of the trial and execution in the Record Office, a letter of the Spanish ambassador, Don Pedro de Zuniga, in the Vatican Library, and other sources. The last-named library has a manuscript account of the martyr written from the persecutors' point of view : Camm gives a translation of this.

ST GEMMA GALGANI, Virgin   (A.D. 1903)

THE short life of this saint, who was born at Camigliano in Tuscany in 1878, and died at Lucca at the age of twenty-five, was in one sense uneventful. It is a story of very fervent piety, charity and continuous suffering. These sufferings were caused partly by ill-health, partly by the poverty into which her family fell, partly by the scoffing of those who took offence at her practices of devotion, ecstasies and other phenomena, partly by what she believed to be the physical assaults of the Devil. But she had the consolation of constant communion with our Lord, who spoke to her as if He were corporeally present, and she also met with much kindness from the Giannini family, who in her last years after her father's death treated her almost as an adopted daughter.

Gemma's ill-health seems to have been congenital ; she suffered from tuberculosis of the spine with aggravated curvature. The doctors despaired of any remedy, but she was cured (instantaneously and, it was then believed, completely) after an apparition of St Gabriel-of-the-Sorrows, to whom she was very devout. She earnestly desired to be a Passionist nun, but, the miracle notwithstanding, she could never obtain that medical certificate of sound health which was very wisely required before admission into the noviceship. She had periodically recurring stigmata from June 1899 to February 1901, as well as the marks of our Lord's scourging at a later time. She was also at one period obsessed by the Devil, and in these attacks she even spat upon the crucifix and broke her confessor's rosary. On the other hand, her normal state was one of great spiritual peace and love. During her many ecstasies she used to commune with her heavenly visitants in a low sweet voice, and the bystanders often took down her words in writing. After a long and painful illness St Gemma died very peacefully on Holy Saturday, April 11, 1903.

A great popular *cultus*, stimulated by the accounts which were written of her by her spiritual directors, followed shortly after St Gemma Galgani's death. She was beatified in 1933, and canonized in 1940. Her cause met with considerable opposition on account of the very extraordinary nature of some of her experiences. It is noteworthy that the Congregation of Rites, in declaring that Gemma practised the Christian virtues in a heroic degree, expressly refrained from passing any judgement upon the preternatural character of the phenomena recorded of her. This is a matter, the congregation added, upon which no decision is ever made.

For English readers the two fullest and most accessible biographies, both translations from the Italian, are those by Father Germanus, C.P. (1914) and Father Amadeus, C.P. (1935). The later Italian editions of the first of these contain a considerable amount of matter not found in the translation. For a fuller insight into Gemma's devotional spirit see *Lettere ed Estasi della beata Gemma Galgani* (1909), edited by Fr Germanus. There are other lives in English by Bishop Leo Prosperpio (1941) and Fr P. Coghlan (1949) ; Sr M. St Michael's *Portrait of St Gemma* (1950) is made from her letters and reported speech. The decree of beatification is in *Acta Apostolicae Sedis*, vol. xxv (1933), pp. 363–367 ; and see also vol. xxiv (1932), p. 57. Cf. H. Thurston, *Physical Phenomena of Mysticism* (1952).

12 : ST JULIUS I, Pope   (A.D. 352)

THE name of Pope St Julius stands in the Roman Martyrology to-day with the notice that he laboured much for the Catholic faith against the Arians. He was the son of a Roman citizen named Rusticus, and succeeded Pope St Mark in 337. In the following year St Athanasius, who had been exiled at the instance of the Arians, returned to his see of Alexandria, but found himself opposed by an Arian or semi-Arian hierarch whose intrusion had been obtained by Bishop Eusebius of Nicomedia. In response to the request of the followers of Eusebius, Pope Julius convoked a synod to examine into the matter, but the very people who had asked for the council refrained from attending it. The case of St Athanasius was, however, very carefully examined in their absence ; and the letter which the pope subsequently sent to the Eusebian bishops in the East has been characterized by Tillemont as " one of the finest monuments of ecclesiastical antiquity ", and by Monsignor Batiffol as " a model of weightiness, wisdom and charity ". Calmly and impartially he meets their accusations one by one and refutes them. Towards the end he states the procedure they ought to have followed. " Are you not aware that it is customary that we should first be written to, that from hence what is just may be defined ? . . . Whereas you expect us to approve condemnations in which we had no part. This is not according to the precepts of Paul or the tradition of the fathers. All this is strange and new. Allow me to speak as I do : I write what I write in the common interest, and what I now signify is what we have received from the blessed apostle Peter."

The council at Sardica (Sofia) convened in 342 by the emperors of the East and West, vindicated St Athanasius, and endorsed the statement, previously made by St Julius, that any bishop deposed by a synod of his province has a right to appeal to the bishop of Rome. Nevertheless it was not until the year 346 that St Athanasius was able to return to Alexandria. On his way thither he passed through

Rome, where he was cordially received by Pope Julius, who wrote a touching letter
to the clergy and faithful of Alexandria, congratulating them on the return of their
holy bishop, picturing the reception they would give him, and praying for God's
blessing on them and on their children.

St Julius built several churches in Rome, notably the Basilica Julia, now the
church of the Twelve Apostles, and the basilica of St Valentine in the Flaminian
Way. He died on April 12, 352. His body was buried at first in the cemetery
of Calepodius, but was afterwards translated to Santa Maria in Trastevere which
he had enlarged and beautified.

The story of the life of St Julius belongs to general church history and may best be
studied in such works as Hefele-Leclercq, *Histoire des Conciles* ; Grisar, *Geschichte Roms
und der Päpste* (Eng. trans.) ; Duchesne in his edition of the *Liber Pontificalis* and in his
Histoire ancienne de l'Eglise (Eng. trans.) ; J. P. Kirsch, *Die Kirche in der antiken Griechisch-
Römischen Kulturwelt* ; and P. Batiffol, *La paix constantinienne*.

ST ZENO, BISHOP OF VERONA   (A.D. 371)

IN the *Dialogues* of St Gregory and in several martyrologies St Zeno, bishop of
Verona, is styled a martyr, but St Ambrose, who was his contemporary, in a letter
addressed to his successor Syagrius speaks of his happy death. Furthermore, in
an ancient missal of Verona, St Zeno is honoured only as a confessor. Living as
he did in the days of Constantius, Julian and Valens, he may well have merited
the title of martyr by suffering in the persecutions they waged, even if he did not
die a violent death.

From a panegyric he delivered on St Arcadius, a Mauretanian martyr, it has
been conjectured that St Zeno was born in Africa ; and from the excellent flowing
Latin of his writings and from the quotations he makes from Virgil, it is evident that
he received a good classical education. He seems to have been made bishop of
Verona in 362. We gather a number of interesting particulars about him and about
his people from a collection of his *tractatus*, short familiar discourses delivered to
his flock. We learn that he baptized every year a great number of pagans, and
that he exerted himself with zeal and success against the Arians, who had been
emboldened by the favours they had enjoyed under the Emperor Constantius.
When he had in a great measure purged the church of Verona from heresy and
heathenism, his flock increased to an extent which necessitated the building of a
large basilica. Contributions flowed in freely from the citizens, whose habitual
liberality had become so great that their houses were always open to poor strangers,
whilst none of their fellow citizens ever had occasion to apply for relief, so promptly
were their wants forestalled. Their bishop congratulated them upon thus laying up
for themselves treasure in Heaven. After the battle of Adrianople in 378, when
the Goths defeated Valens with terrible slaughter, the barbarians made numerous
captives in the neighbouring provinces of Illyricum and Thrace. It appears to
have been on this occasion that, through the bountiful charity of the inhabitants of
Verona, many of the prisoners were ransomed from slavery, some rescued from a
cruel death, and others freed from hard labour. Though this probably occurred
after the death of St Zeno, the self-sacrifice of the townsmen may be traced to his
inspiring zeal and example.

St Zeno himself always chose to live in great poverty. He often speaks of the
clergy he trained and of the priests, his fellow-labourers, to whom offerings were
allotted at Easter. He alludes to the ordinations he performed at the paschal season,

as well as to the solemn reconciliation of penitents, which also took place in Holy Week. St Ambrose makes mention of virgins, living in Verona in their own houses and wearing the veil, who had been consecrated to God by St Zeno, as well as of others who dwelt in a convent of which he was both the founder and the director. This was before St Ambrose had established anything of the kind in Milan. St Zeno inveighed against the abuses of the *agape* or love-feast, which had become a scandal, and also against the practice of interrupting funeral Masses by loud lamentations. Many of the customs of the period are recorded in these discourses. It would appear to have been still usual, at any rate in Verona, to immerse the whole body at baptism, the water being warmed for the purpose, and St Zeno is the only writer to allude to the habit of giving medals to the newly baptized.

St Gregory the Great describes a remarkable miracle which occurred two centuries after St Zeno's death, related to him by John the Patrician, who was an eye-witness of it. In the year 598 the river Adige threatened to submerge Verona. The people flocked to the church of their holy bishop and patron, Zeno. The waters seemed to respect the building for, although they rose outside as high as the windows, they never penetrated into the church but stood like a solid wall. The people remained within in prayer until, after twenty-four hours, the waters once more subsided. This miracle and others greatly increased the general devotion to the saint, and in the reign of King Pepin, Charlemagne's son, a new church was built to contain his relics, which are still preserved there in a subterranean chapel. St Zeno is usually represented with a fishing-rod, from the end of which a fish is hanging. The emblem is accounted for locally by the tradition that the saint was fond of fishing in the Adige, but the fish may possibly be symbolical of baptism.

See the *Acta Sanctorum*, April, vol. ii, and some other scattered biographical materials which are duly registered in BHL., nn. 9001–9013. The best general account is that of Bigelmair, *Zeno von Verona* (1904); but *cf.* Bardenhewer, *Geschichte der altkirchlichen Literatur*, vol. iii, pp. 478–481, and DCB., vol. iv.

ST SABAS THE GOTH, MARTYR   (A.D. 372)

THE Goths in the third century swarmed over the Danube and established themselves in the Roman provinces of Dacia and Moesia, making expeditions from time to time into Asia Minor, especially into Galatia and Cappadocia, from which they brought back Christian slaves, priests and lay people. These prisoners soon began to make converts amongst their conquerors, with the result that Christian churches were founded. In 370 the ruler of one section of the Goths raised a persecution against his Christian subjects, out of revenge, it is supposed, for a declaration of war launched against him by the Roman emperor. The Greeks commemorate fifty-one Gothic martyrs, the most famous of whom were St Sabas and St Nicetas. Sabas, who had been converted to Christianity in early youth, acted as cantor or lector to the priest Sansala. When, at the outset of the persecution, the magistrates ordered the Christians to eat meat sacrificed to idols, certain pagans, who had Christian relations whom they wished to save, persuaded the officials to give them meat which had not been offered to idols. Sabas loudly denounced this ambiguous proceeding : not only did he himself refuse to eat, but he declared that those who consented to do so had betrayed the faith. Some of the Christians applauded him, but others were so much displeased that they obliged him to withdraw from the town. He was, however, soon allowed to return. The following year, when the persecution broke out again, some of the principal inhabitants offered to swear that there were no Christians in the town. As they were about to take the oath, Sabas presented himself and said, " Let no one swear for me : I am a Christian ! " The officer asked the bystanders how much he was worth, and, upon learning that he had nothing but the clothes he wore, contemptuously released him, remarking, " Such a fellow can do us neither good nor harm ".

A couple of years later the attacks upon the Christians were renewed. Three days after Easter, there arrived in the town a band of soldiers under the command of one Atharidus. They broke into the lodging of the priest Sansala, with whom Sabas was staying after they had spent the festival together. Sansala was surprised in his sleep, bound, and thrown into a cart, whilst Sabas was pulled out of bed, dragged naked through the thorn-brakes, and belaboured with sticks. In the morning he said to his persecutors, " Did you not drag me naked over rough and thorny ground ? Look and see if my feet are wounded or if the blows you gave me have left bruises upon my body." They examined him, but could not perceive the slightest mark. Determined to make him suffer, they took the axle-trees of a cart by way of a rack, and having fastened his hands and feet to their extremities, tortured him for a considerable part of the night. When at last they got tired, the woman with whom they lodged, out of compassion, unbound Sabas but he refused to escape. The following day he was suspended to a beam of the house by his hands. Afterwards there was set before him and Sansala some meat that had been offered to idols. Both refused to touch it, Sabas exclaiming, " This meat is as impure and profane as Atharidus who sent it ". Thereupon one of the soldiers struck at his breast with his javelin with such violence that all thought he must have been killed. The holy man, however, remained unhurt, and said, " Did you think you had slain me ? I felt no more than if that javelin had been a skein of wool."

As soon as Atharidus heard what had happened he gave orders that Sabas should be put to death, and he was accordingly led away to the river to be drowned. When they reached the river bank, one of the officials said to the others, " Why should we not let this man go ? He is innocent, and Atharidus would never be any the wiser ! " Sabas, however, remonstrated with the man for not carrying out his orders. " I can see what you cannot see ", he said. " I perceive people on the opposite side of the river who are ready to receive my soul and to conduct me to glory : they are only waiting for the moment when it will leave my body." The executioners then plunged him into the river, and held him under the water with a plank which they had fastened about his neck. The scene of the martyrdom of St Sabas seems to have been at Targoviste, north-west of the city of Bucarest in what is now Rumania.

Although the account of the martyrdom of St Sabas takes the form of a letter which in certain phrases recalls the letter of the Smyrnaeans describing the death of St Polycarp, Father Delehaye regards the substance of the document as authentic and reliable. He printed a critical revision of the Greek text in the *Analecta Bollandiana*, vol. xxxi (1912), pp. 216–221, and on pp. 288–291 of the same article added some valuable comments. Amongst other things he has shown (*cf. Analecta Bollandiana*, xxiii (1904), pp. 96–98) that the suggestion of H. Boehmer-Romundt, in *Neue Jahrbücher*, etc., vol. xi, p. 275, assigning the composition of the *passio* to Ulfilas, cannot be accepted. The text may also be found in G. Krüger's edition of R. Knopf's *Ausgewählte Martyrerakten* (1929).

SS. ALFERIUS AND OTHERS, ABBOTS OF LA CAVA (ELEVENTH-THIRTEENTH CENTURIES)

OF the holy abbots of La Cava who are honoured upon April 12, November 16 and other dates a special notice can only be given here of St Alferius, the founder of the abbey, although his immediate successors, Leo I of Lucca, Peter I of Polycastro and Constabilis of Castelabbate were all saints ; whilst eight later abbots, Simeon, Falco, Marinus, Benincasa, Peter II, Balsamus, Leonard and Leo II all received the title of Blessed.

Alferius belonged to the Pappacarboni family which was descended from the ancient Lombard princes.   Sent by Gisulf, duke of Salerno, as ambassador to the French court, he fell dangerously ill, and vowed that if he should regain his health he would embrace the religious life.   Upon his recovery he entered the abbey of Cluny, then under the rule of St Odilo, but was recalled by the duke of Salerno, who wished him to reform the monasteries in the principality.   The task appeared beyond his power, and he retired about the year 1011 to a lonely spot, picturesquely situated in the mountainous region about three miles north-west of Salerno, where he was soon joined by disciples.   Of these he would only accept twelve—at any rate at first—but they formed the nucleus around which gradually grew the abbey of La Cava which afterwards attained to great celebrity.   Alferius is said to have lived to the age of 120 and to have died on Maundy Thursday, alone in his cell, after he had celebrated Mass and washed the feet of his brethren.   Only a very few years after his death there were, in south Italy and Sicily, over 30 abbeys and churches dependent upon La Cava and 3000 monks.   Amongst his disciples had been Desiderius, who subsequently became Pope Victor III and a *beatus*.

The *cultus* of the sainted abbots of La Cava was confirmed in 1893, that of the *beati* in 1928.

There is a somewhat legendary life of St Alferius, written by Abbot Hugh of Venosa, *c*. 1140. It has been printed in the *Acta Sanctorum*, April, vol. ii, and by Mabillon.   A new edition of this and the lives of other abbots by Hugh was printed at La Cava in 1912 and again, edited by D. M. Cerasoli, at Bologna in 1941 (*Rerum italicarum scriptores*, vol. vi, part 5).   But see E. Sackur, *Die Cluniacenser*, vol. ii, pp. 472 seq.   Very little is known of the individual histories of the *beati*, though they are mentioned in the *Annales Cavenses*, of which an abridgement is printed in Ughelli, *Italia Sacra*, vol. vii, cc. 520–522.   See also *Acta Sanctae Sedis*, vol. xxvi (1893), p. 369 and *Acta Apostolicae Sedis*, vol. xx (1928), p. 304.

BD ANDREW OF MONTEREALE (A.D. 1480)

ANDREW of Montereale was born at Mascioni in the diocese of Rieti and joined the Hermits of St Augustine when he was only fourteen.   For fifty years he preached the gospel in Italy and in France.   The Augustinian roll of honour describes him as " remarkable for his patience in suffering, for his extraordinary austerity of life, for his great learning and especially for his success in preaching the word of God ".   It is recorded of him that he never went to see any public show or spectacle, and that he never laughed.   We are also told that when he died the church bells began to toll of their own accord and continued sounding at intervals for twenty-four hours.   The Augustinian Joseph Pamphili, who in 1570 was consecrated bishop of Segni, states in his *Chronica O.F.E.A.* that in his day, a hundred years after Andrew's death, the body of the holy man, with the cloak that covered it, remained as immune from decay as it was at the moment when he expired.   So great was the desire of those who had known Bd Andrew to visit his remains, and so numerous were the miracles wrought beside the bier, that a whole month elapsed before the interment actually took place.   His *cultus* was confirmed in 1764.

In the *Acta Sanctorum*, April, vol. ii, a brief account of Bd Andrew, published in Italian by S. Ricetelli (1614), has been translated into Latin.   See also L. Torelli, *Ristretto delle Vite degli Huomini* . . . *O.F.E.A.* (1647), pp. 380–382.

BD ANGELO OF CHIVASSO   (A.D. 1495)

THE little town of Chivasso was the birthplace of Angelo Carletti, whose parents belonged to the Piedmontese nobility.   He was educated at the University of Bologna, where he received the degrees of doctor of civil and of canon law, and upon his return to his native Piedmont he was made a senator.   As long as his mother was alive he led an exemplary life in the world, spending his time in his magisterial duties, in prayer and in visiting the sick, but after her death he divided his possessions between his elder brother and the poor, and retired into a Franciscan friary of the Observance at Genoa.   Bd Angelo's superiors soon realized that they had in him a recruit of exceptional merit as well as of great missionary zeal, and it was not long before he was admitted to the priesthood.   At once he embarked upon a strenuous evangelistic campaign.   Full of eloquence and zeal, he made his way into remote villages in the Piedmontese mountains and valleys, regardless of weather and of the roughness of the way.   The poor he greatly loved : he sought them out, visited them in sickness, and would often beg on their behalf.   He helped them in many ways, notably by encouraging the introduction of *monti di pietà* to save them from the clutches of money-lenders.   His penitents, however, were not confined to the poor.   St Catherine of Genoa consulted him, and Charles I, Duke of Savoy, chose him to be his confessor.   His so-called *Summa Angelica*, a book of moral theology which he wrote, was much used.   Bd Angelo filled a number of offices, and as superior he was extremely zealous in preserving the purity of the rule ; his outstanding capabilities caused him to be three times re-elected vicar general.

When, after the taking of Otranto by the fleet of Mohammed II, Pope Sixtus IV appealed for recruits to fight the threatening forces of Islam, the Observants proved themselves specially zealous in rousing the people to meet the crisis, but it was Bd Angelo who always chose the places of greatest danger for his activities.   Moreover, when in 1491, at the age of eighty, he had accepted the office of commissary apostolic to evangelize the Waldensians in the Piedmontese valleys, he displayed a fervour and intrepidity which were rewarded by a surprising measure of success.   Many heretics as well as lapsed Catholics were brought back to the faith, so that Pope Innocent VIII wished to raise him to the episcopate, but he could not be induced to consent.

At last, in 1493, Bd Angelo was able to lay down office and to prepare his soul for death.   He had always been humble : even as vicar general he would only wear the cast-off habits of others and delighted in doing the lowliest work.   Now he begged to be allowed to go and beg for the poor.   His last two years were spent at the convent of Cuneo in Piedmont where he died at the age of 84.   His *cultus* was approved in 1753.

The external facts of Bd Angelo's career are duly recorded in Wadding's *Annales Ordinis Minorum*.   The best available biography is that of C. Pellegrino, *Vita del beato Angelo*

Carletti (1888).   See also Léon, *Auréole Séraphique* (Eng. trans.), vol. ii, pp. 69–76.   It is recorded that when Luther in 1520 publicly burnt the papal bull of excommunication he also threw into the flames the *Summa* of St Thomas and the *Summa Angelica* of Angelo of Chivasso : it was, Luther declared, a devilish work.   On this *Summa Angelica* see DTC., vol. i, cc. 1271–1272.

13 : ST HERMENEGILD, Martyr   (A.D. 585)

HERMENEGILD and his brother Reccared were the two sons of the Visigothic king of Spain, Leovigild, by his first wife Theodosia.   They were educated by their father in the Arian heresy, but Hermenegild married a zealous Catholic, Indegundis or Ingunda, daughter of Sigebert, king of Austrasia ; his conversion to the true faith was due as much to her example and prayers as to the teaching of St Leander, archbishop of Seville.   Leovigild was furious when he heard of his son's open profession of the faith, and called upon him to resign all his dignities and possessions.   This Hermenegild refused to do.   He raised the standard of revolt and, as the Arians were all-powerful in Visigothic Spain, he sent St Leander to Constantinople to obtain support and assistance.   Disappointed in that quarter, Hermenegild implored the help of the Roman generals who, with a small army, still ruled the strip of Spanish land along the Mediterranean coast which remained in the possession of the Empire.   They took his wife and infant son as hostages and made him fair promises which they failed to fulfil.   For over a year Hermenegild was besieged in Seville by his father's troops, and when he could hold out no longer he fled to the Roman camp—only to be warned that those he had reckoned upon as his friends had been bribed by Leovigild to betray him.   Despairing of all human aid, he entered a church and sought refuge at the altar. Leovigild did not venture to violate the sanctuary, but permitted his younger son Reccared, who was still an Arian, to go to his brother with an offer of forgiveness if he would submit and ask for pardon.   Hermenegild took his father at his word and a reconciliation took place, the genuineness of which there seems no reason to doubt. Leovigild appears to have restored his elder son to some measure of his former dignities ; but the king's second wife, Gosvinda, soon succeeded in estranging him once more from the unfortunate prince, and Hermenegild was imprisoned at Tarragona.   He was no longer accused of treason but of heresy, his liberty being offered to him at the price of recantation.   With fervent prayer he asked God to give him fortitude in his combat for the truth, adding voluntary mortifications to his enforced sufferings and clothing himself in sackcloth.

At Easter his father sent him an Arian bishop, offering to restore him to favour if he would receive communion from the prelate.   Upon learning that Hermenegild had absolutely refused, Leovigild fell into one of the paroxysms of rage to which he was subject, and despatched soldiers to the prison with orders to put the young prince to death.   They found him fully prepared and quite resigned to his fate. He was killed instantaneously by one blow from an axe.   St Gregory the Great attributes to the merits of St Hermenegild the conversion of his brother Reccared and of the whole of Visigothic Spain.   Leovigild was stung with remorse for his crime, and although he never actually renounced Arianism, yet when he was on his death-bed he commended his son Reccared to St Leander, desiring him to convert him to the orthodox faith.

It is impossible to do otherwise than condemn the conduct of Hermenegild in taking up arms against his own father, but, as St Gregory of Tours has pointed out, his guilt was expiated by his heroic sufferings and death. Another Gregory, the great pope of that name, remarked of him that he only began to be truly a king when he became a martyr.

The question of Hermenegild's title to be honoured as a martyr has been discussed with a certain amount of acrimony. Despite the account given by St Gregory the Great in his *Dialogues* (bk iii, ch. 31), other early writers even in Spain itself—notably the abbot of Vallclara, Johannes Biclarensis (in Florez, *España Sagrada*, vi, p. 384), Isidore of Seville, and Paul of Merida—seem only to suggest that Hermenegild was a rebel and put to death as such. An excellent summary of the question will be found in DCB., vol. ii, pp. 921–924. This is based mainly upon an article by F. Görres in *Zeitschrift f. hist. Theologie*, vol. i, 1873. In *Razón y Fe* Father R. Rochel (see especially vol. vii, 1903) vehemently replied to this criticism, but Father Albert Poncelet in the *Analecta Bollandiana*, xxiii (1904), pp. 360–361, found much that was unsatisfactory in this attempted vindication. A more moderate view is that of Gams in his *Kirchengeschichte Spaniens*. It should perhaps be mentioned that the best edition of the chronicle of Johannes Biclarensis is that edited by Mommsen in MGH., *Auctores antiquissimi*, vol. xi. A tradition of much later date identifies Seville as the scene of the "martyrdom" of St Hermenegild; but Johannes Biclarensis, a contemporary, expressly declares that he was put to death at Tarragona. See *Analecta Bollandiana*, xxiii, p. 360. Pope Benedict XIV's commission recommended that the feast of this saint be removed from the general calendar.

SS. CARPUS, PAPYLUS AND AGATHONICE, MARTYRS (*c.* A.D. 170 OR 250)

IN the reign either of Marcus Aurelius or of Decius, a bishop, Carpus, from Gurdos in Lydia, and Papylus, a deacon from Thyateira, were together brought before the Roman governor at Pergamos in Asia Minor. Carpus, when he was asked his name, replied, " My first and noblest name is that of Christian : but if you want to know my worldly name, it is Carpus ". The proconsul invited him to offer sacrifice. " I am a Christian ", replied the prisoner. " I worship Christ, the Son of God, who came in these latter times to save us and who has delivered us from the snares of the Devil. I do not sacrifice to idols like these." The governor ordered him to obey the emperor's commands without more ado. " The gods that have not made heaven and earth shall perish ", protested Carpus, quoting from the prophet Jeremias, and he declared that the living do not sacrifice to the dead. " Do you think the gods are dead ? " asked the magistrate. " They were never even living men that they should die ", retorted the martyr, when he was cut short and delivered to the torturers to be strung up and flayed.

The governor then cross-examined Papylus, who said he was a citizen of Thyateira. " Have you any children ? " " Yes, many." A bystander explained that this was a Christian mode of speech and that he meant that he had children according to the faith. " I have children according to God in every city and province ", insisted the deacon. " Will you sacrifice or will you not ? " asked the proconsul impatiently ; and Papylus made reply, " I have served God from my youth and have never sacrificed to idols. I am a Christian and that is the only answer you will get from me—there is nothing greater or nobler that I could say." He also was hung up and tortured. When it became evident that nothing could shake their fortitude, they were condemned to be burnt at the stake. Papylus was the first to pass to his reward. As Carpus was fastened to the stake there came over his face an expression of such great joy that a bystander asked him what he was smiling at. He replied, " I saw the glory of God and was glad ".* When the flames were leaping up, he cried aloud with his dying breath, " Blessed art thou, Lord Jesus Christ, Son of God, because thou hast deigned to give to me, a sinner, this part with thee."

Then the governor had the God-fearing Agathonice brought before him, and she too refused to sacrifice to the gods. The bystanders urged her to spare herself and remember her children ; but she answered, " My children have God, and He will look after them ". The proconsul threatened her with a death like the others, but Agathonice remained unmoved. So she too was taken to the place of execution, and when her clothing was removed the crowd marvelled at her beauty.

As the fire was kindled, Agathonice exclaimed, " Help me, Lord Jesus Christ, since I must bear this for thee ". And as she prayed thus a third time her spirit departed.

These simple martyr-acts rank as belonging to almost the highest class of those which are preserved to us. One has, however, to add " almost ", for, as the texts published by Pio Franchi de' Cavalieri in *Studi e Testi*, no. 33 (1920) clearly show, all the existing recensions have undergone some process of retrenchment or amplification. Of the antiquity of the cult, the mention by Eusebius (*Hist. Eccl.*, iv, 15) and in the Syriac " Breviarium " (where the martyrs are spoken of as forming part of the older tradition) supplies adequate proof. We do not know for certain whether they belong to the time of Marcus Aurelius or of Decius. See upon the whole question the discussion by Delehaye in *Les Passions des Martyrs et les genres littéraires*, pp. 136–142, and the comments of Pio Franchi mentioned above. *Cf.* Harnack in *Texte und Untersuchungen*, vol. iii, n. 4 ; but the newly recovered Latin text rules out his hypothesis of a Montanist origin. This text, together with the two best Greek texts, is printed in *Analecta Bollandiana*, vol. lviii (1940), pp. 142–176, introduced by Fr Delehaye.

ST MARTIUS, OR MARS, ABBOT   (*c.* A.D. 530)

THE memory of St Martius or Mars, abbot of Clermont in the Auvergne, has been preserved by St Gregory of Tours, whose father when a boy had been cured by him of a fever. From early youth, Martius had resolved to give himself to God, and upon attaining manhood he retired from the world to lead the solitary life ; he hewed himself a hermitage in the mountain side and carved the stone bed upon which he lay. His sanctity and spiritual gifts attracted disciples who gradually formed themselves into a community, whose time was divided between prayer and the cultivation of the soil, which they converted from a desert into a flourishing garden. St Gregory of Tours tells the following anecdote. One night a thief broke into the monastery enclosure and set about rifling its apples, onions, garlic and herbs. When he had collected as much as he could carry, he attempted to depart, but was unable to find his way out in the dark. He therefore lay down on the ground to await the daylight. In the meantime Abbot Martius in his cell was fully aware of all that had happened. At the break of dawn, he summoned the prior and told him to go into the garden to release a bull which had found its way in. " Do not hurt him ", he added, " and let him have all he wants, for it is written, ' Thou shalt not muzzle the ox that treadeth out thy corn ! ' " The prior went forth and came upon the thief, who started up on seeing him, threw down his booty and attempted to escape. He was, however, caught by the briars. The monk smilingly released and reassured him. Then, after picking up the scattered spoil, he led the culprit to the gate where he laid the pack upon the man's shoulders

* Another version attributes these words to Papylus.

saying, " Go in peace, and give up your evil ways ". St Martius lived to the age of ninety, and his tomb was the scene of many miracles.

All that we know concerning St Mars is found in the *Vitae Patrum* of St Gregory of Tours, ch. xiv; and see the *Acta Sanctorum*, April, vol. ii.

BD IDA OF BOULOGNE, WIDOW   (A.D. 1113)

IDA of Boulogne may well be called a daughter and a mother of kings, for both her parents were descended from Charlemagne, two of her sons, Godfrey and Baldwin, became kings of Jerusalem, and her granddaughter Matilda was destined to be queen consort of England.   Ida herself was the child of Godfrey IV, Duke of Lorraine, by his first wife Doda, and at the age of seventeen she was given in marriage to Eustace II, Count of Boulogne.   Their union seems to have been a happy one, and Countess Ida regarded it as her paramount duty to train her children in the paths of holiness and to set them the example of liberal almsgiving to the poor.   She had the good fortune to have as her spiritual adviser one of the greatest men of the age, St Anselm, abbot of Bec in Normandy, afterwards archbishop of Canterbury, some of whose letters to Ida have been preserved in his correspondence. The death of Count Eustace left his widow the control of valuable property, much of which she expended in the relief of the needy and in the construction of monasteries.   Thus she founded Saint-Wulmer at Boulogne and Vasconvilliers, restored Samer and Our Lady of the Chapel, Calais, besides bestowing generous benefactions upon Saint-Bertin, Bouillon and Afflighem.

Bd Ida gave herself ardently to prayer for the success of the First Crusade, and it is recorded that, while she was making intercession for the safety of her son Godfrey of Bouillon, it was revealed to her that he was at that very moment making his victorious entry into Jerusalem.   Although as the years passed Ida retired more and more from the world (she had once visited England), she does not appear ever to have actually taken the veil.   She died when she was over seventy, at the close of a long and painful illness, and was buried in the church of the monastery of St Vaast.

There are two short lives of Bd Ida printed in the *Acta Sanctorum*, April, vol. ii.   The first is attributed to a monk of St Vaast, a contemporary, the other was compiled by the canon regular John Gielemans, at a much later date.   The best popular account is that of F. Ducatel *Vie de Ste Ide de Lorraine* (1900).

BD JAMES OF CERTALDO, ABBOT   (A.D. 1292)

ALTHOUGH born at Certaldo near Florence, Bd James spent practically all his life at Volterra, which his parents had made their home.   He was in the habit of accompanying his father and mother to the church of St Clement and St Justus, served by Camaldolese monks, and he early developed a vocation to the religious life.   In the year 1230 he was received into the order.   His devotion and austerity greatly edified all who came into contact with him, and so strongly affected his father that he resigned his property to his two remaining sons to enter the monastery, where he spent the last years of his life as a lay-brother.   Bd James was placed in charge of the parish, where he discharged his duties with great wisdom, leading many souls into the paths of holiness.   Twice he refused the post of abbot, and although he was obliged to accept office when elected for the third time, he resigned shortly afterwards to become once more parish priest.   One of his brothers joined the Knights of St John of Jerusalem, but left them after six months to begin again more humbly as a lay-brother at St Justus. Bd James survived this brother for ten years, dying in 1292.

See the *Acta Sanctorum*, April, vol. ii. There is also an Italian life, printed early in the seventeenth century by S. Razzi.

BD IDA OF LOUVAIN, VIRGIN   (A.D. 1300 ?)

IT is curious that two saints, bearing the same not very common name and separated from each other by a considerable interval of time, should have died on the same day of the year ; but in both cases the thirteenth day of April is definitely set down by their respective biographers as that of their departure from this world.

The account preserved of Bd Ida of Louvain is, it must be confessed, open to some suspicion, partly because we have no external corroboration of any of the incidents recorded, and partly because it abounds in marvels of a very astonishing character. She was a maiden born of a well-to-do family in Louvain, and she is said to have been marked out from her earliest years by God's special graces. Though she had much to suffer from her father and sisters, who did not approve of her devotional practices, her superabundant charity and extreme asceticism, she pursued her way of life unfalteringly, guided, as she believed, by the spirit of God. Among her observances was that of genuflecting or prostrating herself repeatedly before a picture of our Lady, reciting the Hail Mary at each genuflection, a form of salutation which she sometimes reiterated over 1000 times in one day. Her devotion to the sacred Passion was ardent beyond belief and earned for her the gift of the stigmata in hands, feet and side, as well, it seems, as the marks of the crown of thorns. She strove to hide them, but finding that they could not altogether be concealed, she obtained by her prayers the withdrawal of the external signs, though the pain which accompanied them still continued. Her love for the Blessed Eucharist was not less remarkable. More than once her biographer speaks of her having received communion miraculously, and it is noteworthy that the practice of communicating under both kinds is represented as still surviving, apparently after 1250, in the neighbourhood of Louvain and Mechlin. On one occasion Ida is said, in her desire to possess our Lord, to have lowered the pyx in which the Blessed Sacrament was hanging above the altar and to have attempted, though without success, to open it.

All dates are sadly lacking in Bd Ida's biography, and we do not know at what age she entered the Cistercian convent of Roosendael near Mechlin, nor how old she was when she died, nor whether the year 1300 assigned for her death is not the error of some transcriber. In her religious life she was remarkable for her ecstasies and miracles. She was seen radiant with heavenly light, she is said to have known the secrets of hearts, and a fragrant perfume was often perceived by those who came near her. There seems to be no doubt that her tomb became a place of pilgrimage after her death, though all traces of it appear to have been swept away by the Gueux in 1580.

The biography of Bd Ida which is printed in the *Acta Sanctorum*, April, vol. ii, purports to have been compiled from memoranda carefully recorded by her confessor, Hugh by name. It is an interesting document from the point of view of the student of mystical theology and its atmosphere certainly corresponds with what we find in many similar records of the thirteenth century. See also an article by C. Kolb in the *Cistercienser Chronik*, vol. v (1893), pp. 129–140.

BD MARGARET OF CITTÀ-DI-CASTELLO, VIRGIN   (A.D. 1320)

IT must have been about the year 1293 when some women of Città-di-Castello in Umbria, who had gone one day to pray in their parish church, found within a destitute blind child of about six or seven who had been abandoned there by her parents. The kind souls were filled with pity for the little waif, and, poor though they were, they took charge of her—first one family and then another sheltering and feeding her until she became practically the adopted child of the village. One and all declared that, far from being a burden, little Margaret brought a blessing upon those who befriended her. Some years later the nuns of a local convent offered her a home. The girl herself rejoiced at the prospect of living with religious, but her joy was short-lived. The community was lax and worldly : Margaret's fervour was a tacit reproach to them, nor did she bring them the profit they had anticipated. Neglect was succeeded by petty persecution, and then by active calumny. Finally she was driven forth ignominiously to face the world once more.

However, her old friends rallied round her. One couple offered her a settled home, which became her permanent residence. At the age of fifteen Margaret received the habit of a tertiary from the Dominican fathers, who had lately established themselves in Città-di-Castello, and thenceforth she lived a life entirely devoted to God. More than ever did God's benediction rest upon her. She cured another tertiary of an affliction of the eyes which had baffled medical skill, and her mantle extinguished a fire which had broken out in her foster-parents' house. In her desire to show her gratitude to the people of Città-di-Castello she undertook to look after the children whilst their parents were at work. Her little school prospered wonderfully, for she understood children, being very simple herself. She set them little tasks which she helped them to perform ; she instructed them in their duty to God and to man, instilling into them her own great devotion to the sacred Childhood, and she taught them the psalms which, in spite of her blindness, she had learnt by heart at the convent. We are told that when at prayer she was frequently raised a foot or more from the ground, remaining thus for a long time. Thus she lived, practically unknown outside her own neighbourhood, until the age of thirty-three, when she died amidst the friends who loved her, and was buried by their wish in the parish church, where many remarkable miracles were wrought at her tomb. The *cultus* of Bd Margaret was confirmed in 1609.

The principal document we possess concerning Bd Margaret is a sketch of her life, written in the fourteenth century, which has been printed in the *Analecta Bollandiana*, vol. xix (1900), pp. 21–36. See also the *Acta Sanctorum*, April, vol. ii, and Procter, *Dominican Saints*, pp. 90–93, as well as Ganay, *Les Bienheureuses Dominicaines*. It is probable that the Franciscan Ubertino di Casale in an enthusiastic tribute which he pays in his *Arbor Vitae* to a devout mystic of Città-di-Castello was referring to Bd Margaret. An interesting popular account of the *beata* by W. R. Bonniwell, *The Story of Margaret of Metola*, was published in America in 1952 ; it is based on a biography discovered by Fr Bonniwell and differs in some particulars from the account given above. Cf. *Analecta Bollandiana*, vol. lxx (1952), p. 456.

BB. JOHN LOCKWOOD AND EDMUND CATHERICK, MARTYRS   (A.D. 1642)

BOTH these noble martyrs were Yorkshiremen. Lockwood, who sometimes used his mother's family name of Lassels, was born in 1561. He had studied at Douai and at Rome, and before his final apprehension had twice been arrested and imprisoned. After his first confinement he was banished in 1610, but returning to England he was again taken and this time condemned to death. He was, however, reprieved and kept in prison until he regained his liberty, we know not how. Resuming his apostolic labours, he was finally captured at the house of a Mrs Catesby, being then eighty-one years old. Catherick was a much younger man, and when, after his studies at Douai, he came to the English mission about the year 1635 he was only thirty years of age. After seven years of labour he also fell into the hands of the pursuivants and was brought before Justice Dodsworth, a connection of his by marriage, who committed him to York Castle and afterwards very discreditably gave evidence against him founded on his own private knowledge. Both the prisoners were condemned to death for their priesthood. When they came to the scaffold at York, the elder, thinking he saw signs of some weakening in his companion, claimed in virtue of his years the privilege of suffering first, and Bd Edmund, thus encouraged, met his end with entire firmness. Some portion of their relics, secured by Mary Ward's community, were conveyed to the convent of her institute at Augsburg, where they still remain. The body, or part of it, of Bd John Lockwood is at Downside.

See Challoner, MMP., pp. 411–416, and also Stanton's *Menology*, pp. 155–157.

14 : ST JUSTIN MARTYR   (*c.* A.D. 165)

PRE-EMINENT amongst those who suffered death for the faith in the reign of Marcus Aurelius stands the layman who has become famous as St Justin Martyr, the first great Christian apologist known to us by works of any considerable length. His own writings give us interesting particulars of his early life, including the circumstances which led to his conversion. He tells us that he was in one sense a Samaritan, being a native of Flavia Neapolis (Nablus, near the ancient Sichem), but he knew no Hebrew and his parents, who were pagans, seem to have been of Greek origin. They were able to give their son a liberal education, of which he took full advantage, devoting himself specially to rhetoric and to reading poetry and history. Afterwards a thirst for knowledge induced him to apply himself to philosophy. For some time he studied the system of the Stoics, but abandoned it when he found that it could teach him nothing about God. A peripatetic master to whom he next addressed himself disgusted him at the outset by his eager demand for fees. In the school of Pythagoras he was told that a preliminary knowledge of music, geometry and astronomy would be required, but an eminent Platonist undertook to lead him to the science of God. One day, as he was walking in a field near the sea-shore—perhaps at Ephesus—pondering one of Plato's maxims, he turned round and saw, following in his wake, a venerable-looking old man with whom he soon found himself discussing the problem uppermost in his mind. The stranger aroused his interest by telling him of a philosophy nobler and more satisfying than any he had hitherto studied. It was one which had been revealed by God to the Hebrew prophets of old and had reached its consummation in Jesus Christ. He concluded by urging the young man to pray fervently that the doors of light might be opened to allow him to obtain the knowledge which God alone can give. The old man's words inspired Justin with a desire to study the

Scriptures and to know more about the Christians. His attention had already been attracted to them. " Even at the time when I was content with the doctrines of Plato ", he writes, " when I heard Christians accused and saw them fearlessly meet death and all that is considered terrible, I felt that such men could not possibly have been leading the life of vicious pleasure with which they were credited." He seems to have been about thirty when he actually embraced the Christian faith, but we know neither the date nor the scene of his baptism. Probably it was at Ephesus or at Alexandria, which he is known to have visited.

Up to this period, although there had been a few Christian apologists, very little was known to the outside world about the beliefs and practices of the followers of our Lord. The early Christians, many of whom were simple and unlearned, were satisfied to bear misrepresentation in order to protect their sacred mysteries from profanation. Justin, on the other hand, was convinced from his own experience that there were many who would gladly accept Christianity if it were properly expounded to them. Moreover, to quote his own words, " It is our duty to make known our doctrine, lest we incur the guilt and the punishment of those who have sinned through ignorance ". Consequently, in his oral teaching as well as in his writings, he openly set forth the faith of the Christians and even described what took place at their secret meetings. Still wearing the cloak of a philosopher, he appears to have travelled in various lands where he held disputations with pagans, heretics and Jews, but eventually he came to Rome. Here he argued in public with a Cynic called Crescens whom he convicted of ignorance as well as of wilful misrepresentation. It is thought that it was mainly through the efforts of Crescens, of whose enmity he was well aware, that Justin was apprehended during a second visit to Rome. After a bold confession followed by refusal to sacrifice to the gods, he was condemned to be beheaded. With him perished six other Christians, five men and one woman. The exact date of their execution is not recorded, but St Justin is commemorated in the Roman martyrology on April 14, the day following the feast of St Carpus, whose name immediately precedes his in the Chronicle of Eusebius.

Of the writings of Justin Martyr, the only treatises which have survived intact are two Apologies and the Dialogue with Trypho. His great Apology, to which the second seems to have been an appendix, is addressed to the Emperor Antoninus, to his two sons, and to the Roman senate and people. In it he protests against the condemnation of Christians simply on the score of their religion or of unsubstantiated charges. After vindicating them from accusations of atheism and immorality he goes on to insist that, far from being a danger to the state, they are peaceable subjects whose loyalty to the emperor is based on the teaching of our Lord. Towards the end he describes the rite of baptism and of the Sunday services, including the Eucharistic Sacrifice and the distribution of alms. His third book is a vindication of Christianity as opposed to Judaism, in the form of a dialogue with a Jew called Trypho. A treatise which he wrote against heresy seems to have been utilized by Irenaeus.

The acts of St Justin's trial and martyrdom are among the most valuable and authentic which have come down to us. When he and his companions were brought before the Roman prefect, Rusticus, he was urged to submit to the gods and obey the emperors, to which he replied that nobody can incur blame by following the law of Christ.

RUSTICUS : What branch of learning do you study ?

JUSTIN : I have studied all in turn.   But I finished by deciding on the Christian teaching, however disagreeable it may be to those who are deceived by error.

RUSTICUS : And that is the learning that you love, you foolish man ?

JUSTIN : Yes.   I follow the Christians because they have the truth.

RUSTICUS : What is this teaching ?

Justin then explained that Christians believe in the one creator God, and confess His Son, Jesus Christ, of whom the prophets spoke, the bringer of salvation and judge of mankind.   Rusticus asked where the Christian assemblies took place.

JUSTIN : Wherever they can.   Do you suppose we all meet in the same place ? Not a bit of it.   The God of the Christians is not found in any particular place : He is invisible, He is everywhere in Heaven and earth, and His faithful ones praise and worship Him everywhere and anywhere.

RUSTICUS : All right then : tell me where you foregather with your followers.

JUSTIN : I have always stayed at the house of a man called Martin, just by Timothy's baths.   This is the second time I have been in Rome, and I have never stayed anywhere else.   Anybody who wants to can find me and hear the true doctrine there.

RUSTICUS : You, then, are a Christian ?

JUSTIN : Yes, I am a Christian.

After ascertaining from the others that they also were Christians, Rusticus turned again to Justin and said : " Listen, you who are said to be eloquent and who believes that he has the truth—if I have you beaten and beheaded, do you believe that you will then go up to Heaven ? "

JUSTIN : If I suffer as you say, I hope to receive the reward of those who keep Christ's commandments.   I know that all who do that will remain in God's grace even to the consummation of all things.

RUSTICUS : So you think that you will go up to Heaven, there to receive a reward ?

JUSTIN : I don't think it, I know it.   I have no doubt about it whatever.

RUSTICUS : Very well.   Come here and sacrifice to the gods.

JUSTIN : Nobody in his senses gives up truth for falsehood.

RUSTICUS : If you don't do as I tell you, you will be tortured without mercy.

JUSTIN : We ask nothing better than to suffer for the sake of our Lord Jesus Christ and so to be saved.   If we do this we can stand confidently and quietly before the fearful judgement-seat of that same God and Saviour, when in accordance with divine ordering all this world will pass away.

The others agreed with what Justin had said.   And so they were sentenced to be scourged and then beheaded, which was carried out at the common place of execution, fulfilling their final witness to Christ.   Some of the faithful took up their bodies secretly and buried them in a fitting place, upheld by the grace of our Lord Jesus Christ, to whom belongs glory for ever and ever.   Amen.

As might be expected, a very considerable literature has gathered round a martyred apologist whose life and writings present so many problems as do those of St Justin.   The bibliography which is appended to the article " Justin " by G. Bardy in DTC., vol. viii (1924), cc. 2228–2277, may be recommended as very thorough.   Apart from the martyrdom we know hardly anything about St Justin beyond what he tells us himself in the Dialogue with Trypho.   St Irenaeus, Eusebius, St Jerome and others mention him, but supply little in the way of fresh information.   The text of the acts of his martyrdom is printed in the *Acta Sanctorum* (June, vol. i), but other copies have since been collated by P. Franchi de' Cavalieri (in *Studi e Testi*, vol. viii) and by Prof. Burkitt (in the *Journal of Theological*

Studies, 1910, vol. xi, pp. 61–66). There are excellent studies of Justin's life and writings by Fr Lagrange (in the series " Les Saints ") ; J. Rivière, *St Justin et les Apologistes du II*ᵉᵐᵉ *siècle* (1907) ; A. Béry, *St Justin, sa vie et sa doctrine* (1911) ; and others. The Acts of St Justin are edited or translated in most of the modern collections of acts of the martyrs, *e.g.* those of Krüger-Knopf, Owen, Monceaux. See also especially Delehaye, *Les Passions des Martyrs et les Genres Littéraires*, pp. 119–121. It is curious that no cult of St Justin Martyr seems to have left any traces in Rome itself : he is not mentioned in the Philocalian calendar nor in the " Hieronymianum ". There is an excellent little book by Fr C. C. Martindale, *St Justin the Martyr* (1923), and translations of the Apology and of the Dialogue with Trypho have been published in America in recent years.

SS. TIBURTIUS, VALERIUS and MAXIMUS, MARTYRS
(DATE UNKNOWN)

THE holy martyrs Tiburtius, Valerius and Maximus have been honoured by the Church from an early date, and the Catacomb of St Callixtus in which their bodies were found at Rome was known at one time as the Cemetery of Tiburtius. In several of the old martyrologies, Valerius (or Valerianus) is described as the brother of Tiburtius and the bridegroom of St Cecilia, but nothing certain is known about them, their very dates being doubtful. Their story, as it is generally told, forms part of the legend of St Cecilia, which first became current in the fourth century, to which period her *acta* belong : this document can by no means be regarded as trustworthy or even founded on authentic materials. It is instructive to contrast the sober and convincing account of the trial and death of St Justin, most of which is printed above, with the very different sort of tale, with its improbable details, that enshrines the names of Tiburtius, Valerius and Maximus.

See the account of St Cecilia with its bibliography on November 22 herein (vol. iv).

ST ARDALION, MARTYR (*c.* A.D. 300)

AMONGST the early martyrs we meet with several instances of actors who were converted to Christianity while they were turning into ridicule upon the stage the sufferings of the confessors and the truths of the Catholic faith. One of these was a man named Ardalion, who lived in the days of the Emperor Maximinian. One day he had been personating with great spirit a Christian who had refused to renounce his faith and was about to be executed. The excellence of his acting aroused the enthusiasm of his audience but, as he stood to receive the applause, he was suddenly convinced of the truth of Christianity. Addressing the people he cried out in a loud voice that he was himself a Christian. Brought before the judge, he adhered to his confession, and was burnt alive in some eastern city, the name of which has not been handed down to us. The whole story is probably a fiction.

See the *Acta Sanctorum*, April, vol. ii. The eulogium accorded to St Ardalion in the Roman Martyrology was borrowed by Baronius from Greek sources.

ST LAMBERT, ARCHBISHOP OF LYONS (A.D. 688)

ST LAMBERT was sent by his parents at an early age to the French court, where he won the favour of King Clotaire III. After a few years, however, he abandoned the world to enter the abbey of Fontenelle, then under the rule of St Wandregisilis whom he succeeded as abbot. Amongst many holy men who were his disciples may be mentioned St Erembert and the English St Condedus, the former of whom resigned the bishopric of Toulouse to come and serve under him.　Upon the death of St Genesius, about the year 679, Lambert was nominated archbishop of Lyons.　The records of his episcopacy have perished, so that we have no certain details about his later years, but he appears to have been in the habit of retiring from time to time for spiritual refreshment to the abbey of Donzère, which he had founded as a branch of Fontenelle.

There is a fragment of a life of St Lambert, or Landebertus, which has been printed by Mabillon and in the *Acta Sanctorum*, April, vol. ii.　See also Duchesne, *Fastes Épiscopaux*, ii, pp. 170–171.

ST BERNARD OF TIRON, Abbot　　(A.D. 1117)

BERNARD of Tiron, also known as Bernard of Abbeville, had a troubled and chequered career.　In early life he had been a monk of St Cyprian's, near Poitiers, and then prior of St Sabinus, the lax discipline of which he strove to correct.　The desire for the eremitic life caused him to leave the monastery and to enter a kind of Thebaïd in the forest of Craon.　He was, however, persuaded to return to St Cyprian's, of which he was made abbot.　Claims of Cluny to which he could not agree induced him to resign and he returned to Craon, from whence he went on preaching missions with Bd Robert of Arbrissel and others.　On land given him in the forest of Tiron he in 1109 built a monastery in which the Rule of St Benedict was strictly kept.　The new community flourished and spread outside of France, including a cell on Caldey Island, whose church returned to Catholic hands in 1913 and the feast of this St Bernard was revived there.

We have an unsatisfactory Latin life of this St Bernard compiled from earlier materials by G. Grossus, which has been printed in the *Acta Sanctorum*, April, vol. ii.　See also Corblet, *Hagiographie d'Amiens*, vol. i, pp. 271–307, and vol. iv, pp. 699–700 ; as well as J. von Walter, *Die Ersten Wanderprediger Frankreichs* (1906).　*Cf.* D. Knowles, *The Monastic Order in England* (1949), pp. 200–202, 227.

BD LANVINUS　　(A.D. 1120)

IN 1893 Pope Leo XIII confirmed the *cultus* of a Carthusian monk, Bd Lanvinus, who though little known to the world at large has always been held high in honour in his own order.　He was a Norman by birth who seems to have made his way south to the Grande Chartreuse about the year 1090, and thence accompanied St Bruno to Calabria.　When the holy founder died there in 1101, Lanvinus was elected to succeed him in the government of the two charterhouses which the order at that time possessed in the south of Italy.　Some little difference of opinion had preceded this election, and we possess more than one letter addressed to the new superior by Pope Paschal II, congratulating the brethren on this peaceful solution and admonishing them not to presume too much upon the austerity of their rule, but ever to seek perfect concord and union with God.　In 1102 Lanvinus was summoned to Rome to attend a synod.　Other letters of the same pontiff were despatched to him in 1104 commending his zeal in carrying out the pope's injunctions, and entrusting to his care a difficult negotiation which concerned one of the bishops of that province.　In 1105 he was further appointed visitor of all monastic houses in Calabria and charged with the duty of restoring strict discipline ; while eight years later he again came to Rome and obtained from Pope Paschal a bull to protect the houses of the Carthusians from molestation. He died greatly revered on April 11, 1120, but his feast is kept in the order on this day.

A good deal of space is devoted to Bd Lanvinus in the *Annales Ordinis Cartusiensis* by Dom Le Couteulx (vol. i) as well as in other chronicles of the order.

ST CARADOC (A.D. 1124)

As a young man St Caradoc lived at the court of Rhys ap Tewdwr, prince of South Wales, where he occupied the honourable post of harper. One day he fell into disgrace with his master who blamed him for the loss of two favourite greyhounds and threatened to kill him. Thus brought to realize the folly of trusting in the favour of earthly princes, Caradoc resolved from henceforth to give his services only to the King of kings. He accordingly abandoned the court and repaired to Llandaff, where he received the tonsure from the bishop who sent him to serve in the church of St Teilo. Afterwards he spent some years as a hermit near the abandoned church of St Cenydd in Gower and then retired with some companions to the still more remote solitude of an island off the coast of Pembroke. Here they suffered from Norse raiders, and St Caradoc eventually settled in St Ismael's cell at Haroldston, of which he was given charge. Like so many other solitaries Caradoc had unusual power over the lower animals, illustrated on one occasion by his mastering a pack of hounds " by a gentle movement of his hand ", when they were quite out of the owner's control.

St Caradoc was buried with great honour in the cathedral church of St David, where the remains of his shrine may be seen. A still extant letter of Pope Innocent III directs certain abbots to make inquiry into the life and miracles of this Welsh hermit.

A brief account of St Caradoc by Capgrave (*Nova Legenda Angliae*) has been reprinted in the *Acta Sanctorum*, April, vol. ii. He is mentioned in a twelfth-century calendar of Welsh saints and by Giraldus Cambrensis (*Itinerary through Wales*, bk i, cap. 11), who seems also to have written a life of him, not now extant. See LBS., vol. ii, pp. 75–78.

ST BÉNEZET (A.D. 1184)

THE boyhood of Bénezet, or Little Benedict the Bridge Builder, was spent in minding his mother's sheep either in Savoy or in the Ardenne. He was a pious lad, thoughtful beyond his years, and seems to have reflected much on the perils encountered by people who sought to cross the Rhône. One day, during an eclipse of the sun, he heard a voice which addressed him three times out of the darkness, bidding him go to Avignon and build a bridge over the river which was extremely rapid there. The construction and the repair of bridges was regarded in the middle ages as a work of mercy, for which rich men were often urged to make provision in their wills ; but Bénezet was only an ignorant, undersized youth, without experience, influence or money. Nevertheless he did not hesitate to obey the call. As may be imagined, the Bishop of Avignon, to whom he addressed himself upon his arrival in the city, was not disposed at first to take him seriously, but the lad was able by miracles to prove his mission to the good bishop's satisfaction ; and with his approval the work of building a stone bridge over the Rhône was begun in A.D. 1177. For seven years little Benedict directed the operations, and when he died in 1184 the main difficulties of the enterprise had been overcome.

His body was buried upon the bridge itself, which was not completed until four years after his death. The wonders which attended the construction from the moment of the laying of the foundations and the miracles wrought at Bénezet's tomb induced the city fathers to build upon the bridge a chapel, in which his body lay for nearly 500 years. In 1669, when part of the bridge was washed away, the coffin was rescued and when it was opened the following year the body was found to be incorrupt. It was afterwards translated to the church of the Celestine monks. The Order of Bridge Brothers, the constitutions of which were approved in 1189, regarded St Bénezet as their founder, and he is reckoned one of the patrons of Avignon.

The brief document which supplies these and other details is of early, almost contemporary date, and is preserved in the municipal archives of Avignon. It is printed in the *Acta Sanctorum*, April, vol. ii, and also by some other more modern editors. We have further a summary of the evidence of witnesses given in an episcopal inquiry of the year 1230 in view of Bénezet's beatification, as well as the testimony of chronicles such as that of Robert of Auxerre under the years 1177 and 1184. See A. B. de Saint-Venant, *St Bénezet, Patron des Ingénieurs* (1889) ; Lanthéric, *Le Rhône, histoire d'un fleuve* (1892), pp. 556–562 ; and an article on " St Bénezet and his Biographer " in the *Catholic World* for December 1907. For the further curious adventures of the relics, see Baudot and Chaussin, *Vies des Saints* . . . vol. iv (1946), p. 341.

BD PETER GONZALEZ   (A.D. 1246)

SPANISH and Portuguese sailors have a great veneration for Bd Peter Gonzalez, whom they invoke as St Elmo or St Telmo—a pseudonym which he shares with another patron of mariners, St Erasmus. Peter came of a noble Castilian family and was educated by his maternal uncle, the Bishop of Astorga, who was more concerned with his material than with his spiritual advancement. Appointed canon of the cathedral whilst still under age, the young man came proudly riding into Astorga on Christmas day in splendid array to assume his new dignity. Great, however, was his mortification when his horse stumbled and threw him into the mire amid the jeers of the populace. " If the world mocks at me, I will mock at the world ", he is reported to have exclaimed in words which were prophetic ; for the incident opened his eyes to his own vanity and led to a complete change of heart. Resigning his office, he entered the order of St Dominic, and in due time he was professed and sent forth to preach. From the outset his ministrations were abundantly blessed.

King St Ferdinand III was so impressed by him that he appointed him his chaplain. The friar immediately set about the difficult task of reforming the morals of the courtiers and of the soldiers—in the face of great opposition from the younger nobles. He also preached the crusade against the Moors and contributed much to the success of Ferdinand's campaigns by his prudent advice, by his prayers, and by the good spirit he instilled. He was with the army during the siege of Cordova, and at the surrender of the city exerted all his influence to restrain the victorious soldiers from excesses, whilst the clemency of the terms granted to the vanquished must be attributed in large measure to him. As soon as he could obtain leave, Bd Peter quitted the court to devote the rest of his life to evangelizing the country districts, especially Galicia and the coast. Often the churches could not contain the people who flocked to hear him, and he had to preach in the open air. Very specially did he love sailors, whom he visited on board their vessels. His last weeks on earth were spent at Tuy, where he died on Easter Sunday, 1246.   His *cultus* was confirmed in 1741.

Florez, *España Sagrada*, vol. xxiii, pp. 245–285, has printed an early Latin biography of Bd Peter together with a collection of miracles wrought at the shrine which seems to have been compiled in 1258.   See also Mortier, *Maîtres Généraux O.P.*, vol. i, pp. 401–403 ; Taurisano, *Catalogus Hagiographicus O.P.*, and Procter, *Lives of Dominican Saints*, pp. 94–96. It seems certain from what Father Papebroch has written in the *Acta Sanctorum*, April, vol. ii, that it was only in the sixteenth century that Bd Peter Gonzalez began to be spoken of as St Elmo : *cf.* St Erasmus, on June 2.

SS. JOHN, ANTONY and EUSTACE, Martyrs   (A.D. 1342)

The young men, John, Antony and Eustace, were officials in the household of Duke Olgierd, who eventually ruled Lithuania and was the father of the famous Jagiello. Like most of their fellow-countrymen they had been heathen, but they were converted to Christianity and baptized.   Because of their fidelity to their new faith, and especially because they refused to partake of forbidden food on days of fasting, they were cast into prison.   After enduring many trials they were condemned to death.   John was hanged on April 14, his brother Antony on June 14, whilst Eustace, who was still young, was cruelly tortured before his execution on December 13.   The martyrs suffered at Vilna, about the year 1342, and were buried in the famous church of the Holy Trinity in that city.   They are honoured not only by the Lithuanians but also by the Russians.

See the *Acta Sanctorum*, April, vol. ii ; and *cf.* Maltsev, *Menologium der Orthodox-Katholischen Kirche des Morgenlandes*, as well as Martynov, *Annus Ecclesiasticus Graeco-Slavicus*.

BD LYDWINA OF SCHIEDAM, Virgin   (A.D. 1433)

The *cultus* of Bd Lydwina has spread far beyond the limits of her native land, for she has come to be regarded as the special patroness of that company of chosen souls who live a more or less hidden life of intense suffering in expiation of the sins of others.   She herself is described in the special office for her feast as " a prodigy of human misery and of heroic patience ".

The only girl in a family of nine children, she was born at Schiedam in Holland on Palm Sunday 1380.   Her father was a labourer who eked out his scanty means by acting as night-watchman, but he was an exemplary Christian, and so high-minded that in after years he always refused to touch the offerings brought to his daughter, maintaining that she ought to be free to distribute them in alms to those who were in still greater poverty.   Up to the age of fifteen there seems to have been nothing to distinguish Lydwina from any other good, lively and pretty girl beyond the fact that she had already taken a vow of virginity.   During the exceptionally severe winter of 1395–1396 she suffered from a serious illness from which, however, she had entirely recovered, when some of her friends came to invite her to join them in a skating party on the frozen canal.   They had started off gaily and were resting on their skates when a late comer, hurrying to overtake them, collided with Lydwina, causing her to fall and to break one of the ribs of her right side.   She was carried home and tenderly nursed, but in spite of all the care she received complications set in and she grew steadily worse.   An internal abscess formed and then burst, inducing violent vomiting which left the patient completely exhausted.

This was succeeded by agonizing headaches, toothache and pains in every part of the body accompanied by fever and unendurable thirst. There was no position in which she could obtain the slightest relief. Poor as her parents were, they called in doctors who tried to diagnose and alleviate her diseases, but they were obliged to confess that they were baffled. One of them indeed, Andrew of Delft, declared that in his opinion all human treatment was useless and only served to increase the financial burdens of a poor family.

Lydwina herself at first was far from realizing her great vocation, and felt all the desire for health and the repugnance to suffering natural to a girl of her age, besides shrinking from the trouble and expense she was entailing upon her parents. Light came to her gradually, through the ministrations of a good priest, Father John Pot, who seems to have been the curate of the parish. From the outset of her illness he visited her regularly, and in simple language urged her to fix her mind on the sufferings of our Lord and to unite her sufferings with His. Obediently she set about acquiring the habit of constant meditation upon the Passion, and after about three years it was borne in upon her that God was calling her to be a victim for the sins of others. As soon as she grasped this tremendous truth, she accepted her vocation with enthusiasm; her sufferings from henceforth became her greatest joy and, as she admitted, if a single Hail Mary could have gained her recovery, she would not have uttered it. To her involuntary mortifications she added others of her own choice, such as lying on bare planks instead of on the feather bed provided for her.

After she had become completely bedridden, Father John would bring holy communion to her at first twice a year and then every two months, as well as on the great festivals. In the words of her biographer Brugman, " meditation on the Passion and reception of the Eucharist became, as it were, the two arms with which Lydwina embraced her Beloved ". She was to need all the spiritual support she received, for when she was nineteen her maladies assumed even more strange and alarming proportions. Spasms of pain which convulsed and contorted her body, besides constant vomiting at times, brought on a syncope of the heart which left her utterly prostrate. Nothing remained of her former beauty, for she was disfigured by a fissure which extended from the top of the forehead to the middle of her nose, and the lower lip became partly severed from the chin. One eye was completely blind, whilst the other was so sensitive that she could not bear even the reflection from the fire. She could no longer raise herself in bed or move any limb except the left arm, and on the right shoulder another abscess formed which mortified and caused almost unbearable neuritis. Symptoms of gravel and of tertian fever also supervened.

It was as though the dissolution of the grave had begun and this condition was to continue for the rest of her life. Even then, as in later ages, her case aroused the interest of the medical world, and specialists examined her and prescribed for her ; for it was not long before the fame of her extraordinary sufferings and invincible patience spread far beyond her native town, attracting the attention of William VI, Count of Holland, and his wife Margaret of Burgundy, who sent their own doctor, Godfrey de la Haye—a clever and kind physician nicknamed Godfrey Zonderdank or " Don't Mention It ", from the reply he used to make to the thanks of poor people from whom he would take no fees.* He and a friend succeeded, by

---

* We are reminded of the legend of the early martyrs, SS. Cosmas and Damian, " the moneyless physicians ", who took no fees.

poultices, in healing gangrenous sores which had appeared on the patient's body, but this only caused the body to swell and brought on dropsy. One trial was spared to her : she was never misunderstood or neglected by her family. Their simple piety could not fail to recognize her sanctity and received its reward even in this world. It seems nothing less than a miracle that Lydwina's revolting symptoms, the full description of which we spare the reader, evoked no disgust in those who ministered to her. On the contrary, they maintained that her poor putrefying body emitted a fragrant perfume and that, although natural light had to be rigidly excluded, Lydwina's sickroom was often irradiated by a celestial brilliancy so vivid that, on more than one occasion, neighbours raised the cry of fire. Other abnormal and supernatural elements began to enter into the invalid's life. In the early stages of her illness she could eat a little solid food, but soon she was reduced to liquids— wine at first and then only Meuse water. Finally and for the last nineteen years of her life—according to the sworn deposition of witnesses—she practically depended for nourishment upon holy communion. She now developed powers of healing, of television and of prophecy. About the year 1407 she began to have ecstasies and mystical visions. While her body lay in prolonged cataleptic trances, her spirit communed with our Lord, with the saints, and with her guardian angel, or it would visit the holy places of Rome and Palestine or else churches near at hand. Now she would help our Lord to carry His cross on Calvary, now she would witness the pains of purgatory and would be given a foretaste of the joys of Heaven. Two points are emphasized by her biographers : never, in all her raptures, did she lose sight of her vocation, and always those spiritual privileges were followed by increase of suffering. Acclaimed as she was even then as a saint, she was not destined to escape detraction, which came in a very painful form. A new parish priest was appointed to Schiedam, one Master Andrew, a Premonstratensian from Marien- werd. He was a worldly, sensual man, totally unable to understand Lydwina, against whom he at once conceived a violent prejudice. He chose to regard her as a hypocrite, deprived her for a time of holy communion, and went so far as to ask his congregation to pray for her as the victim of diabolical hallucinations. The people of Schiedam, however, who loved and honoured her, would have driven him from the city if the magistrates had not interfered to protect him. As the result of an inquiry held by the ecclesiastical authorities, Lydwina's good faith was fully vindicated, and she was permitted from that time onwards to receive her com- munion fortnightly. Another great trial to her affectionate heart was the death of all her near relations one after another. Her mother, though a good woman, had died in anxiety about her future state, and Lydwina on her behalf added to her other mortifications a tight horsehair girdle which she continued to wear for the rest of her life. She seems to have sorrowed most of all for her young niece Petronilla, whose death resulted from injuries which she had sustained in protecting her aunt against the attacks and insults of two soldiers, who had forced their way into the sickroom. At length the time drew near for Lydwina's release : for seven years she had been virtually sleepless, so acute were her sufferings. During the course of Easter Tuesday 1433 she became rapidly worse, and shortly before three in the afternoon, Petronilla's little brother ran to fetch a priest. He came almost immediately, but realized at once that all was over : she had died, as she had hoped to die—alone.

The *cultus* of Bd Lydwina, which may be said to have begun during her life, was promoted after her death by the biographies written by her cousin John Gerlac, by Thomas à Kempis, and by Brugman, as well as by the untiring efforts of a physician, the son of that Godfrey Zonderdank whose patient she had formerly been. It was he who, in fulfilment of a wish very dear to her heart, built a hospital on the site of her humble home.

The biography of Bd Lydwina compiled by John Brugman has been printed, both in its first and latest form, by the Bollandists in the *Acta Sanctorum*, April, vol. ii ; and they have also given extracts from the memoir by Thomas à Kempis. John Gerlac's narrative is in Dutch and was first printed at Delft in 1487. Full bibliographical details are provided in the excellent little volume *Sainte Lydwine* contributed by Hubert Meuffels to the series " Les Saints " (1925). This is by far the best popular life, and it corrects in many details the extravagances and inaccuracies of Huysmans' *Sainte Lydwine de Schiedam* which has gone through so many editions. There are several other lives of less value. That by Thomas à Kempis has been translated into English by Dom Vincent Scully (1912), with a useful introduction. In this introduction may be found a translation of the striking official document drawn up in 1421 by the municipality of Schiedam attesting among other things that " within the seven years last passed she (Lydwina) has used no food or drink at all nor does use any at present ". Although she is quite commonly called *Saint* Lydwina, she has never been officially canonized, but her *cultus* was formally confirmed by Pope Leo XIII in 1890.

15 : SS. BASILISSA AND ANASTASIA, MARTYRS   (*c.* A.D. 65 ?)

ACCORDING to their traditional history, Basilissa and Anastasia were noble Roman matrons who were converted to Christianity by the teaching of St Peter and St Paul. After the martyrdom of the apostles, the two women removed their bodies by night and caused them to be honourably buried. For this action, which became known to the authorities, they were cast into prison. When they were brought before the tribunal of Nero, they fearlessly acknowledged that they were Christians and were condemned by him to be cruelly mutilated and then beheaded.

Although these saints stand first in the Roman Martyrology on this day, it must be confessed that their very existence is extremely doubtful. We know nothing of them except through Greek sources which offer no guarantee of reliability. The various entries in the Greek *Menaia* are collected in the *Acta Sanctorum*, April, vol. ii ; and see also the *Synaxarium Constantinopolitanae*, edited by Fr Delehaye in the *Acta Sanctorum* for November, vol. ii, c. 106, where this commemoration is assigned to April 17.

ST PADARN, OR PATERN, BISHOP IN CEREDIGION   (FIFTH-SIXTH CENTURY)

THE existing life of Padarn, a saint formerly much honoured in Wales, was written at Llanbadarn Fawr, probably about the year 1120 ; it is a fusion of earlier legends of two separate people, St Paternus, an abbot-bishop in Wales, and another St Paternus, a fifth-century bishop at Vannes in Brittany. This document is a collection of untrustworthy tales and traditions. According to it Padarn was born in Letavia (Brittany ; or possibly south-east Wales), the son of Petran and Gwen ; his father afterwards went off to Ireland to live as a hermit, leaving his wife to bring up their little boy in his native land. As soon as he had attained manhood, Padarn announced his intention of following his father's example. With some companions he sailed away to Wales, where they decided to settle, and he founded a monastery at a place in Cardiganshire which became known as Llanbadarn Fawr, *i.e.* the great church of Paternus. Not only was he abbot but he is said to have been the first bishop of the region, ruling over it for twenty-one years. It is related of him that he went about the country like a true missionary, preaching the gospel to all sorts and conditions of men, " without pay or reward ", and that he was famous for his charity and mortifications. The monastery of Llanbadarn, near Aberystwyth, certainly became very influential, and Rhygyfarch's Life of St David and the *Book of Llandaff* both witness to its importance. It did not finally disappear until between 1188 and 1247.

The story that St Padarn accompanied St David and St Teilo on a pilgrimage to Jerusalem, where he received from the patriarch a staff and a " tunic " (which was subsequently coveted by " a certain *tyrannus* named Arthur "), is unquestionably a fable, but it appears in the Lives of St David and of St Teilo. According to this confused story St Padarn, after founding other monasteries and churches in Wales, returned in his old age to Brittany where, before he died, he became bishop of Vannes, but through jealousy was forced to take refuge among the Franks. Another tradition says he was buried on Ynys Enlli, that is, Bardsey.

The *Vita Paterni* has been printed by Rees in his *Lives of the Cambro-British Saints*, critically supplemented by Kuno Meyer in *Y Cymmrodor*, vol. xiii (1900), pp. 88 *seq.* ; the text, with a translation, is also in A. W. Wade-Evans, *Vitae Sanctorum Britanniae . . .* (1944). Canon Doble's excellent examination of the problem, *St Patern* (1940), modifies some of the views of F. Duine in his *Memento des sources hagiographiques de . . . Bretagne* (1918), and *cf. Analecta Bollandiana*, vol. lxvii (1949), pp. 388 *seq.* See also LBS., vol. iv, pp. 39–51 ; and F. R. Lewis, *Short History of the Church of Llanbadarn Fawr* (1937). There is an account of Llanbadarn in 1188 in the Welsh *Itinerary* of Giraldus, bk ii, cap. 4.

ST RUADAN OF LOTHRA, Abbot   (*c.* A.D. 584)

St Ruadan, who was born in the western part of Leinster, was one of the chief disciples of St Finian of Clonard. In the district now known as County Tipperary he founded the monastery of Lothra, into which he gathered one hundred and fifty monks who divided their time between prayer and manual work. In virtue of his office as abbot he enjoyed episcopal honour and is reckoned as one of the twelve apostles of Ireland.

His Latin life, written centuries after his death, is wholly unreliable from the point of view of the historian. Unless the researches of scholars discover some new evidence, we must rest content with the eulogy contained in the *Félire* of St Oengus : " An excellent flame that waneth not ; that vanquisheth urgent desires : fair was the precious stone, Ruadan, lamp of Lothra ". In reference to one incident in the extravagant stories handed down to us, Father John Ryan in his *Irish Monasticism* observes that " this saint has secured an unenviable notoriety in Irish hagiographical literature because of the leading part ascribed to him in a fantastic encounter with the civil authorities at Tara ". It is, however, satisfactory to note that this preposterous contest in vituperation has been shown to be historically impossible.

There is a Latin life preserved in the Codex Salmanticensis and other MSS. and also a life in Irish. Both have been edited by C. Plummer—the former in VSH., vol. ii, pp. 240–252 ; the latter in his *Bethada Náem n-Érenn*, vol. i, pp. 316–329, with a translation in vol. ii. See also the *Acta Sanctorum*, April, vol. ii, and MacNeill, *Phases*, p. 234.

ST HUNNA, Matron   (*c.* A.D. 679)

St Hunna, or Huva, came of the reigning ducal family of Alsace and was married to a nobleman, Huno of Hunnaweyer, a village in the diocese of Strasbourg. Because she undertook to do the washing for her needy neighbours, she was nick-named by her contemporaries " The Holy Washerwoman ". Her family seems to have been influenced by St Deodatus (Dié), Bishop of Nevers, for St Hunna's son, who was his namesake, was baptized by him and subsequently entered the monastery which he founded at Ebersheim. St Hunna died in 679 and was canonized in 1520 by Leo X at the instance of Duke Ulric of Würtemberg.

It is difficult to find satisfactory authority for what is recounted above. There is mention of Hunus and of " his holy wife " in the eleventh-century Life of St Deodatus of Nevers, and Henschenius in his note on the passage quotes a French work of John Ruyms upon the saints of the Vosges. See the *Acta Sanctorum*, June, vol. iv (3rd ed.), p. 731 ; and *Analecta Bollandiana*, vol. lxvi, pp. 343-345. There seems, however, to be a local *cultus* of St Hunna, and the Abbé Hunckler in his *Saints d'Alsace* writes on the subject at some length.

16 : SS. OPTATUS AND HIS COMPANIONS, AND ST ENCRATIS, VIRGIN, MARTYRS   (A.D. 304)

IT was the proud boast of the poet Prudentius that no town in all Spain could rival his own city of Saragossa for the number of its citizens who had won the martyr's crown. During the persecution of Diocletian St Optatus and seven-teen others thus witnessed to Christ on the same day in the year 304, under the governor Dacian. Prudentius celebrated their memory in verse and records their names—four of them were called Saturninus. We are not told how they died, but two others, Caius and Crementius, succumbed to injuries received under torture.

In the same long poem Prudentius mentions a certain Encratis, about whom he supplies more information. She was clearly a woman of extraordinary spirit who, in some way, bore energetic witness to her faith ; but Prudentius does not tell us what she said and did to merit his admiring epithet of *virgo violenta*, " a vehement maiden ", and to provoke the savage fury of her persecutors. She was subjected to the most appalling tortures. After the usual gashing and scraping, her sides were torn with the iron claws, her left breast cut off, her entrails exposed, and part of her liver dragged out. (The poet informs us that he had himself seen the relic, which was preserved in one of the churches of Saragossa.) She was taken back to her prison, but the governor would not allow her to be put out of her suffering. So great was her vitality that she lived on after her wounds had begun to mortify. Indeed it would seem as though she had survived the persecution, for Prudentius speaks of her house as having been the shrine of a living martyr. It is doubtful whether Encratis suffered in the persecution of Diocletian. The vivid description given by Prudentius supports the theory that she lived at a period much nearer to his own.

See the *Acta Sanctorum*, April, vol. ii, where the poem of Prudentius is quoted at length ; and *cf.* also Delehaye, *Les Origines du Culte des Martyrs*, pp. 363-364, together with Férotin, *Le liber mozarabicus Sacramentorum*, especially col. 276. The name of St Encratis takes a variety of forms and she was clearly held in great honour throughout Spain and the Basses Pyrénées. The acts of the Saragossan group of martyrs to which she belongs are printed in the *Acta Sanctorum*, April, vol. ii (text and appendix), and another recension in November, vol. i, pp. 642–649. See also Florez, *España Sagrada*, vol. xxx, pp. 260–267, and V. Dubarat, *Études hist. relig. Bayonne*, vol. i, pp. 188 *seq.*

ST TURIBIUS, Bishop of Astorga (*c.* A.D. 450)

St Turibius became bishop of Astorga when the errors of the Priscillianists were gaining many adherents in various parts of Spain. Based on forged apostolic writings, this heresy was a subtle form of Manichaeism which seems to have attracted both laymen and clergy : even Dictinus, the previous bishop of Astorga, is said at one time to have defended its teachings. St Turibius, on the other hand, came forward as an uncompromising champion of the Catholic faith. Not only did he boldly expose and denounce the new doctrines, but he took strong action against the leaders of the movement. He then appealed for support to Pope St Leo the Great, to whom he sent a report of the measures he was adopting. Leo in reply wrote a long epistle in which he categorically condemned the tenets of the Priscillianists. Mainly as a result of the efforts of St Turibius, thus backed by the authority of Rome, the spread of this heresy was checked, and the bishop was able to devote his energies to the enforcement of discipline amongst his clergy and the reform of morals amongst his people. His death occurred about the year 450.

An account of St Turibius is given in the *Acta Sanctorum*, April, vol. ii ; but see more especially the short essay of Fr V. De Buck in the *Acta Sanctorum*, October, vol. xiii, pp. 226–230. There are three Spanish saints called Turibius, and much confusion between them : cf. *Analecta Bollandiana*, vol. lix (1941), pp. 34–37.

ST PATERNUS, or PAIR, Bishop of Avranches (A.D. 564)

The leading facts in the life of St Paternus, bishop of Avranches, are much more surely established than anything we read in the account of St Padarn (April 15) though the two have been confused and are mentioned in many martyrologies on the same day. This Paternus came from Poitiers, where his father occupied some official position. The boy entered the monastery of Ansion in Poitou. After some time, however, he and another monk, St Scubilio, withdrew to lead an eremitical life in the wild country round Coutances in Normandy. There they settled in Scissy, near Granville, attracting other recruits until an abbey was constituted, which later became known as Saint-Pair. Paternus was elected abbot and busied himself in founding other religious houses which had an excellent influence upon the paganism around him. At the age of seventy Paternus was appointed bishop of Avranches and lived for thirteen years afterwards. We know that he attended a council in Paris, and he was probably brought into personal relation with King Childebert. He is said to have died at Eastertide on the same day as his friend St Scubilio, and they were both buried together in the church at Scissy.

A life of St Paternus was written by Venantius Fortunatus. The uninterpolated text has been edited by Bruno Krusch in MGH., *Auctores Antiquissimi*, vol. iv, part 2, pp. 33–37. See also Duchesne, *Fastes Épiscopaux*, vol. ii, p. 223. His anniversary is assigned to April 15 in certain manuscripts of the " Hieronymianum " which derive from Fontenelle, but the Roman Martyrology commemorates this St Paternus on April 16. See *Analecta Bollandiana*, vol. lxvii, pp. 384–400.

ST FRUCTUOSUS, Archbishop of Braga   (A.D. 665)

THE son of a Spanish general of the Visigothic kings, Fructuosus from boyhood
desired to consecrate himself to God, and the early death of his parents left him
free to follow his vocation.   He accordingly prepared himself in the school which
Conantius, bishop of Palencia, had established.   The young man had a large
inheritance, part of which was distributed to the poor and to his liberated slaves,
whilst the remainder was devoted to the foundation of monasteries.   Of these the
first was on his own estate in the mountains near Vierzo.   He himself undertook
the direction of this house, which was called Complutum, until he saw it thoroughly
well settled.   He then resigned and retired into the wilderness, where he led a most
austere life after the manner of the hermits of old.   In spite of his efforts to live lost
to the world, he could never remain long hidden.   Once he was discovered by a
hunter, who was about to discharge an arrow at what he took to be a wild animal
until he noticed the hands uplifted in prayer.   On another occasion, we are told,
the saint had penetrated far into the forest when his hiding-place was betrayed by
the joyful cries of some jays, who had recognized in fresh surroundings one who
had made friends with them in the monastery garden.

These stories may or may not be true, but they serve to emphasize the fact that
wherever he went disciples came to him.   For these he built a number of monasteries, as well as a convent for women, called Nona, because it was nine miles from
the sea.   Amongst those who applied to St Fructuosus were entire families—
parents with their children—all expressing themselves desirous to embrace the
religious life.   They must have been rather a source of embarrassment, for not
all had vocations in the ordinary sense of the word, some indeed being mainly
concerned with escaping military service or tyrannical exactions.   Actually these
family monasteries proved so attractive that the provincial governor persuaded the
king to issue an enactment making permission to enter the religious life dependent
upon the royal consent.   St Fructuosus drew up two sets of regulations, a very
strict code for Complutum, much influenced by the Benedictine rule, but exacting
practically blind obedience, and another for his other foundations.   In it he lays
down certain conditions for the family monasteries.   The men with their little
sons must inhabit a part of the buildings entirely separate from that occupied by
the women and their infant daughters, whilst all children who have reached the age
of reason must be instructed in the rule, and then transferred to another house of
the order as oblates—*oblati a parentibus.*

Realizing that solitude was out of the question for him as long as he remained
in his own country, St Fructuosus determined to settle as a hermit in Egypt, and
was on the point of starting when he received a royal order prohibiting his departure.
The monarch, who held him in high esteem, summoned him to the court, directing
that he should be closely watched lest he should slip away unnoticed ; and very
soon afterwards he was chosen bishop of Dumium.   In 656 he became archbishop
of Braga, and in that same year he took part in the Council of Toledo.   At first in
his diocesan work he found himself faced by much opposition, which almost
amounted to persecution ; but his patience and meekness eventually won over his
opponents.   As his last hours drew near, he caused himself to be carried into a
church, where he died lying on a cross of ashes.

There is a short life of St Fructuosus, attributed to Abbot Valerius of Alcala, who was
a contemporary of the saint.   It is printed in the *Acta Sanctorum*, April, vol. ii, and also

by Mabillon and others, and, with a translation by Sister F. C. Nock, it was published at Washington, D.C., in 1946. See further Gams, *Kirchengeschichte Spaniens*, vol. ii, part 2, pp. 152–158, and A. C. Amaral, *Vida e regras religiosas de S. Fructuoso* (1805).

ST MAGNUS OF ORKNEY, MARTYR   (A.D. 1116)

IN the second half of the eleventh century the Orkney Islands were governed by two brothers, Paul and Erling, who, like their subjects, were Christians, at any rate nominally.   Erling had two sons, Magnus, our saint, and Erlend, whilst Paul had one son, Haakon, a young man of such an ambitious and quarrelsome disposition that his father sent him to the Norwegian court to put an end to his intrigues against his kinsmen.   Time and distance only increased Haakon's animosity, and he found King Magnus Barefoot eager to adopt his suggestion of equipping a force to subdue, or at least harry, the isles and coasts of Scotland.   King Magnus, with his young guest on board, set sail for the Orkneys, which he subdued ; and he made Magnus Erlingsson and his brother Erlend accompany the fleet on a piratical cruise to the Hebrides and then along the western coast of Scotland and the north of England.

Opposite Anglesey the earls of Chester and Shrewsbury with a large body of Welshmen came out to give battle.   In the fight which ensued St Magnus refused to take part, saying that he would not injure those who had never injured him. Thereupon the king, scornfully dubbing him a coward, dismissed him to the hold, where he sat reading his psalter during the engagement.   Soon afterwards he managed to escape from his captors by jumping into the sea and swimming to land. He found his way to the court of King Malcolm III of Scotland, by whom he was kindly received.   Either there or in the house of a bishop where he lived for some time, Magnus was led to repent of the excesses of his youth, and to enter upon a course of penitence and prayer which he pursued until his death.

After King Magnus Barefoot had been killed in battle against the Irish, his son Sigurd allowed Haakon to return to the Orkneys, of which he wished to be the sole ruler.   But Magnus, whose brother Erlend had also been slain, gathered a body of men and proceeded to his native country, where he vindicated his right to share in the government of the islands.   Although the two cousins could unite against a common foe, disputes often arose between them.   At last Haakon, whose overbearing spirit could no longer brook a rival, invited Magnus to meet him with a few followers on the island of Egilsay, under pretext of cementing a lasting peace. Magnus unsuspectingly complied, but was overpowered by a large band of men brought by Haakon and was treacherously slain, refusing to resist.   The cathedral of Kirkwall, where he was buried (and where what seem to have been his bones were found in 1919), and many other churches have been dedicated in honour of St Magnus, who was regarded as a martyr, in spite of the fact that he was murdered on political rather than on religious grounds.   He is said to have appeared to Robert Bruce with a promise of victory, on the eve of Bannockburn, and his feast is still observed in the diocese of Aberdeen.

The sources for the story of St Magnus are much more satisfactory than would be expected. The Latin *legenda* from the Aberdeen Breviary, together with the hymns, etc., have been reprinted in the *Acta Sanctorum*, April, vol. ii ; and the *legenda* has also been edited from another manuscript by Sir G. W. Dasent in vol. ii of the *Orkneyinga Saga* (Rolls Series). But the narrative itself is based upon an old Icelandic text, of which Prof. Vigfusson says : " Its more learned and less classic style must not blind us to its early date.   It must have been composed when the holy earl's death was still within the memory of living men and while interest about him was still very great." A certain Rodbert expanded this narrative and added to it. He was himself an Orkney man and seems to have written in 1136, twenty years after St Magnus's death. Portions of the Rodbert life are translated and incorporated in the longer Magnus Saga. Both these sagas are printed and translated in the volumes of the Rolls Series mentioned above. See also G. Walker, *St Magnus, Kirkwall* (1926). A full and excellent study by J. Mooney, *St Magnus, Earl of Orkney*, was published in 1935 ; and see the same writer's *The Cathedral and Royal Burgh of Kirkwall* (2nd edn. 1947).

ST DROGO, OR DRUON   (A.D. 1189)

THE patron of shepherds, St Drogo was a Fleming of noble parentage, but his father died before he was born, whilst his mother did not survive his birth. When he was ten years old, he learned that his mother's life had been sacrificed to save his, and the poor child immediately imagined himself to have been her murderer. Indeed so great was his distress that, in the words of his biographer, " he used to weep most bitterly, accusing himself of every crime ". Happily as he grew older these morbid fancies did not prevent him from casting himself in simple trust on the mercy of God, even while he sought to expiate his transgressions and subdue his body by fasting, by prayer and by distributing to the poor whatever money he received. He was about eighteen when he embarked on the penitential life of a pilgrim. In this manner he visited the chief holy places in several lands. The change of scene, the open-air exercise and the interest aroused in him by the people he met, as well as by the lives of the saints whose shrines he visited, must have been beneficial to a growing lad overmuch given to introspection, quite apart from the direct spiritual blessings which he derived from his devotion. After a time, however, Drogo settled down at Sebourg, near Valenciennes, where he hired himself out as a shepherd to a benevolent lady called Elizabeth de la Haire. In spite of his humble position he soon came to be regarded with great esteem by his mistress and the inhabitants of the district. The people regarded him as a saint, and declared that whilst he was tending his flocks in the fields he had yet been seen assisting at the holy Sacrifice in distant churches. This afterwards gave rise to a local saying, " Not being St Drogo, I cannot be in two places at the same time ".

At the end of six years, the holy man resumed his pilgrimages, returning from time to time to revisit his patroness. He had made the journey to Rome nine times before his travels were ended by a terrible affliction, a peculiarly repulsive hernia which could not be hidden. He was then at Sebourg, and he immediately retired from the sight of his fellow-creatures into a cell built against the church, provided with a " squint " by means of which he could assist at Mass without entering the building or becoming an object of embarrassment to the other worshippers. From his seclusion Drogo never emerged, even when the church caught fire, but on barley bread and water he lived for forty years, suffering greatly but perfectly resigned. From the moment of his death he was popularly honoured as a saint, and his tomb has been a favourite place of pilgrimage ever since.

All our information is, practically speaking, derived from a brief Latin life compiled in 1320, which has been printed in the *Acta Sanctorum*, April, vol. ii. There are short popular accounts of this saint published both in French and in Flemish.

ST CONTARDO   (A.D. 1249)

AMONGST the many holy men who in the first half of the thirteenth century gave up the riches of this world to embrace holy poverty must be reckoned St Contardo the Pilgrim, a member of the Este family of Ferrara.   With two companions he set out to make a pilgrimage to Compostela, but as he climbed the hill which afterwards bore his name and looked down upon the town of Broni, then in the diocese of Piacenza, he prayed in prophetic words that he might die in that beautiful place if God willed that he should end his days away from his own land.   Almost immediately afterwards he was seized with pains which became so acute that the party were obliged to stay in the hostelry of Broni.   When it became evident that St Contardo's illness was likely to be a prolonged one, his two friends sorrowfully bade him farewell and continued on their way.   The landlord, not knowing who he was and fearing lest his groans should frighten away strangers, caused him to be removed to a wretched hut in the neighbourhood, where he lay on a little straw, destitute and abandoned but resigned, until God was pleased to release him from his sufferings.   His identity was disclosed after his death and his tomb was honoured by miracles.

A short Latin account purporting to have been written by a certain Peter de Crosnis in the fourteenth century is printed in the *Acta Sanctorum*, April, vol. ii.   From this source other popular lives have been derived.

BD JOACHIM OF SIENA   (A.D. 1305)

BD JOACHIM was a native of Siena and a member of the great Piccolomini family. Even as a child he showed a singular devotion to the Blessed Virgin, before whose image and altar he loved to pray, and in his charity to the poor he showed himself no less precocious.   So constantly did he ask the aid of his parents for those in distress that at last his father, half in jest, bade him restrain his demands or he would reduce his family to poverty.   The good man was touched but somewhat taken aback when his little son replied, " But, father, you have told me yourself that what we give to the poor we give to Jesus Christ.   Can we refuse Him anything ? "

At the age of fourteen Joachim received the Servite habit at the hands of St Philip Benizi, and from the first day of his entrance into the monastery he was a pattern of all the virtues, but especially of prayerfulness and humility.   So unworthy did he consider himself of the priesthood that no efforts could overcome his refusal to seek ordination, although it was his delight to serve at Mass.   Sometimes he would fall into an ecstasy while the holy sacrifice was being offered.   The most disagreeable offices were his delight, for his constant endeavour was to remain hidden from the world.   Unable to avoid the respect the people of Siena insisted upon showing him, he entreated his superior to send him to some distant house of the order, where he hoped to pass unnoticed.   He was accordingly sent to Arezzo, but his stay there was a brief one.   No sooner had the people of Siena realized Joachim's disappearance than they raised such an outcry that it became necessary to recall him.   From that time until his death he remained in his native city, to edify and support it by his prayers as well as by his example.   He died in 1305 in his forty-seventh year.

The earliest life is one that is believed to have been written by Christopher de Parma, a contemporary.   It has been edited by Fr Soulier in the *Analecta Bollandiana*, vol. xiii (1894), pp. 383–397.   In the *Acta Sanctorum*, April, vol. ii, will be found an account dating from the fifteenth century compiled by Paul Attavanti, and there is yet another fifteenth-century narrative by Nicholas Borghesi.

BD WILLIAM OF POLIZZI   (*c.* A.D. 1317)

WILLIAM GNOFFI was born at Polizzi, near Palermo, and, after being a hermit for a short time near Castelbuono, became a mendicant religious. A temptation to sin presented to him by a woman on one of his begging journeys produced such imaginative disorder that he left his friary, intending to return to secular life. But in consequence of an alarming dream he instead withdrew to a solitary life at various lonely places in the Sicilian mountains. Having thus lived most austerely for eleven years, Bd William died in 1317 (or 1318). He is venerated as the patron of Castelbuono.

No early biography has survived, but the Bollandists, in *Acta Sanctorum*, April, vol. ii, print two lives abbreviated from compilations of the seventeenth century. See also Cajetanus, *Vitae Sanctorum Siculae*, vol. ii, pp. 230–233, and notes 79–80.

BD ARCHANGELO OF BOLOGNA   (A.D. 1513)

THE martyrology for the canons regular of St Augustine records under the date of April 16 the name of Bd Archangelo, whose relics lie in the church of St Ambrose in Gubbio and who was conspicuous for his holy life, his prophetical gifts and his spirit of Christian brotherly love. He is generally identified with a certain Archangelo Canetuli of Bologna, of whom we read that he entered the religious state after his life had been providentially preserved when, in the course of a civil riot, his father and brothers were killed. In the Venetian house of the order he held the post of guestmaster, and was once called upon to entertain his father's murderer, whom he recognized at first sight. Banishing all feelings of resentment he treated this visitor with the utmost kindness and with the courtesy which he would have accorded to an honoured friend. Bd Archangelo is said to have been nominated for the archbishopric of Florence, but he never held that dignity. He lived for some years in the monastery of St Ambrose at Gubbio, and died at Castiglione, near Arezzo, in 1513.

A tolerably full account of this *beato* has been compiled by the Bollandists in the *Acta Sanctorum*, October, vol. xiii, pp. 186–193.

ST BENEDICT JOSEPH LABRE   (A.D. 1783)

AMETTES, in the eighteenth century a village in the diocese of Boulogne-sur-Mer, was the birthplace in 1748 of Benedict Joseph Labre, the eldest of the fifteen children of a local shopkeeper of good standing. His parents sent him at the age of twelve to pursue his studies with his uncle, the parish priest of Érin. Here he became so completely absorbed in the Holy Scriptures and the lives of the saints that his uncle had to insist upon the importance of Latin and of secular subjects generally in the education of a candidate for holy orders. The boy, however, had already begun to realize a call to serve God in complete abandonment of the world. The good curé died of cholera, after he and his nephew had spent themselves in assisting other victims of the epidemic in the parish, and Benedict Joseph returned home. His one ambition was now to retire into the most austere religious order he could find. At the age of eighteen, having wrung a reluctant consent from his parents, he started off in mid-winter to walk sixty miles to La Trappe. Here disappointment awaited him : he was too young, he was told, to be admitted. Subsequent attempts to join the Carthusians and the Cistercians were not much more successful. Thrice indeed he was permitted to make trial of his vocation, but he was obviously unsuited to community life : devout indeed he was, but somewhat eccentric ; the confinement of the cell told on his health as well as on his spirits ; he became reduced to a shadow, and his superiors had no option but to dismiss him. " God's will be done ", he said, as he took a final farewell of the Cistercians of Septfons in 1770.

Benedict now determined to go on pilgrimage to Rome, walking all the way and living on alms. He set out accordingly, staying among other places at Ars, where he met Mr Vianney, father of the future curé. Having crossed the Alps into Italy, he wrote from Piedmont a touching letter to his parents—the last they ever received from him. In it he apologized for the uneasiness he may have caused them and announced his intention of trying to enter an Italian monastery. This he does not appear to have done, for his true vocation began to dawn upon him. Not by shutting himself up in any cloister was he to abandon the world, but by obeying the counsels of perfection without turning his back on the world. Literally and in spirit he must follow the example of our Lord and so many of His saints. With this object in view he embarked upon a life of pilgrimages which led him to the principal shrines in western Europe. Oblivious of wind and weather, he travelled everywhere on foot, carrying neither purse nor scrip nor yet provisions for the way. Often he slept in the open air upon the bare ground ; at best he took his rest in a shed or a garret, for he could rarely be induced to accept a bed. He wished to be homeless like his Master. He saluted no man by the way : unless specially moved to do so, he seldom opened his lips except to acknowledge or distribute to others the alms which he had received. As he made his way along the roads absorbed in meditation, or spent whole days of prayer in churches, he was so entirely lost to his surroundings that once, in his later years when he was kneeling before a crucifix, an artist was able to paint the portrait which has preserved his likeness for later generations. His clothing consisted of a ragged old cloak and of broken shoes, whilst his two or three books were carried with his few other possessions in an old sack slung over his back. Was it not written, " Be not solicitous for your body—what you shall put on ? " As for that body, Benedict Joseph carried his neglect of it to a degree which provided him with a form of mortification of the flesh more galling than any hairshirt, besides earning the contempt and avoidance which he actually desired. No one could possibly have a lower opinion of him than he held of himself. He seldom begged ; if charitable people failed to offer him food, he would pick up orange peel, cabbage stalks, or mouldy fruit from refuse heaps, or would do without. If they gave him money he usually passed it on. A donor of a trifling coin afterwards confessed to having belaboured him with a stick for having, as he thought, shown his contempt at the smallness of the gift by handing it over to another. Benedict bore the beating without a word.

For three years and more the young man wandered about western Europe, not aimlessly, but going from shrine to shrine in Italy, Switzerland, Germany, France, Spain, to Loreto, Assisi, Bari, Einsiedeln, Aix, Compostela. Nor was an undeserved beating an isolated example of ill-treatment. At Moulins he was suspected of theft, and turned out of the church ; in Gascony he was arrested for assaulting an injured man whom he had in fact been helping. But he attracted the attention he wished to avoid by an apparently miraculous multiplication of bread for some poor people and by the healing of a confirmed invalid.

In the year 1774, after a fifth visit to Einsiedeln, his pilgrimages ceased and he remained in Rome, except for an annual journey to Loreto. His nights were now spent in the ruins of the Colosseum, his days in the various churches of the city. So constantly was he to be seen wherever the Quarant' Ore was in progress that the Romans nicknamed him " the saint of the Forty Hours ". Many people who knew nothing about him testified after his death to the inspiration they had received from seeing him absorbed in contemplation before the Blessed Sacrament or a crucifix. Increasing infirmities obliged Benedict Joseph to accept the night shelter of a hospice for poor men, and his obedience as well as his true piety greatly impressed those in charge. It was noticed that he always came last to receive his portion of soup, and that often he would give it away to someone he thought more hungry than himself.

At the beginning of Lent 1783, Benedict contracted a chill with a violent cough but he would abandon none of his religious observances. On the Wednesday in Holy Week he managed to attend Mass in his favourite church, Santa Maria dei Monti, but was overcome with faintness. Sympathizers gathered round him as he sat on the steps outside the church, and a butcher who lived near by removed him to his own house. It was quite clear that Benedict was dying. He received the last sacraments and passed away peacefully about eight o'clock in the evening. He was thirty-five years old. Scarcely had he breathed his last when children in the street were heard to raise the cry, " The saint is dead ", and the chorus was taken up all over the city. Within an incredibly short period the name of St Benedict Joseph Labre became known throughout Christendom, and his fame was enhanced by the account of " the beggar of Rome ", which was written by one who had been his confessor during the closing years of his life. He was canonized in 1883, exactly a century later.

In the case of St Benedict Joseph several volumes of beatification documents are accessible at the British Museum. They were printed between 1820 and 1840 and anyone who examines them will find that the circumstances of the saint's unusual career were subjected to very rigorous scrutiny and criticism. There are many biographies. One of the best is that in German by N. Heim. There are others in French by Desnoyers (2 vols.), E. Rosière, and F. Audiger (1906), Canon Gaquère (1936), and P. Doyère (1948); that in the series " Les Saints " cannot be recommended without reserves. An account of Labre was translated into English so soon as 1785, by the Rev. Mr James Barnard, vicar general of the London district; the latest biography in English is by A. de la Gorce (tr. R. Sheed, 1952).

ST BERNADETTE, Virgin   (A.D. 1879)

THE story of the appearings of our Blessed Lady at Lourdes has already been told here in connection with the feast now kept throughout the Western church on February 11. But on the anniversary of the death of the humble intermediary through whom the message of Heaven was communicated to the world, a few words must be said regarding this chosen soul, whose merits were known to God, but hidden for the most part from the eyes of her fellow men. She was born on January 7, 1844, the oldest of a family of six, and though christened Marie Bernarde, was known to the family and neighbours by the pet name of Bernadette. The father was by trade a miller, and in 1844 he rented a mill of his own, but thrift and efficiency were not the distinguishing virtues of either Francis Soubirous or his wife, Louise Casterot, then still in her teens and eighteen years younger than her husband.   Bernadette was always a most delicate girl, afflicted with asthma and other ailments, and the fact that she was one of the sufferers in the cholera epidemic of 1854 cannot have helped to make her more robust.   Meanwhile the family was gradually sinking into dire poverty, which probably had for one result that Bernadette's education, even in a measure her religious education, was sadly neglected. At the date of the first apparition (February 11, 1858) the family were living in the dark airless basement of a dilapidated building in the rue des Petits Fossés. The child herself, though fourteen years of age, had not yet made her first communion and was regarded as a very dull pupil, but she was notably good, obedient and kind to her younger brothers and sisters, in spite of the fact that she was continually ailing.

The apparitions and the popular excitement which accompanied them did eventually have some effect in relieving the destitution of the Soubirous family, for people interested themselves to find work for the father ; but for Bernadette, apart from the spiritual consolation of these visions, which had come to an end in less than a couple of months, they left a heavy load of embarrassment from the ceaseless and indiscreet questionings which allowed her no peace.   People wanted to cross-examine her about the three secrets our Lady had imparted, they wanted to press money upon her, they wanted to interview her at all sorts of hours, they wanted her to bless them or their sick folk, they even tried to cut pieces from her dress. It was a strange form of ordeal, but for a sensitive child, and Bernadette even at eighteen was no more than a child, it was in truth a martyrdom.   As a measure of protection, she was after a while taken to reside with the nuns at the hospice (1861–1866), but even there there were often visitors who could not be denied.   Sister Victorine, to whose charge she was specially confided, has recorded how " she nearly always shrank from the task of replying to the questions of those who came to see her, if only on account of the fatigue which these conversations entailed. Every effort of this sort told upon her chest and was liable to bring on a bad attack of asthma.   When I took her down to the parlour, I used to see her come to a standstill near the door, and the tears, big heavy drops, welled up into her eyes— ' Come ', I would say to her, ' be brave '.   Then she wiped away the tears, came into the room, bade a pleasant welcome to her visitors and answered everything she was asked, without a hint of impatience at their importunate questions or showing irritation when her word was doubted."

Earlier than this, in 1859, the year after the apparitions, we have a singularly interesting account left by an English non-Catholic visitor of the impression Bernadette made upon people who had come prepared to find nothing but hysteria or imposture.   The account is taken from a contemporary entry in a diary.   The writer says :

I ought before this to have spoken more particularly of the little girl herself.   She was a pretty-looking child, 14 years of age [she was in reality 15½], with large, dreamy eyes, and a quiet, sedate demeanour, which added some years to her appearance and seemed altogether unnatural in so small a figure.   She welcomed us with the air of one long accustomed to receive strangers, and bid us follow her into an upper room of the humble cottage attached to her father's mill.   Two bright, happy little urchins—her brothers —were playing about and seemed no way abashed at our entrance. . . . The child offered us seats, while she herself stood by the window and answered briefly the questions I put to her, but volunteered very few remarks of her own. . . . We offered her a small donation, which she politely refused, nor would she allow us to give anything to her little brothers—and we were assured that neither the parents, nor their child, although very poor, will ever receive anything from strangers. . . . We certainly left her in the conviction that we had been talking with a most amiable little girl, and one superior to her age and station, both in manner and education ; and whatever may be the true account of the apparition, as far as the girl herself is concerned, we feel quite convinced of the sincerity of her faith in it.

Protestant visitors seem to have shown delicacy and consideration by comparison with some of the Catholic ecclesiastics who came to converse with Bernadette. Here is an example left on record by a certain curé who spent a day at Lourdes in January 1860, and who seemed to think that by his interest in the apparitions he was rendering a service to the poor girl herself and to the Church at large. He summoned the child, though he had been told she was poorly and suffering from a nasty cough, to come to him at his hotel through howling wind and pelting rain, and after cross-questioning her for the best part of two hours about the apparitions, the fountain, and the Blessed Virgin's three secrets, the interview according to his own volunteered statement ended as follows :

" My child, I must have quite worn you out with my questions. Please accept these three louis d'or to remunerate you for your trouble."—" No, monsieur, I cannot take anything."

Here Bernadette expressed herself with an energy which showed that I had deeply wounded her self-respect. I tried to press the money upon her, but her silence, eloquent both of the pain she felt and of suppressed indignation, made it clear to me that I could insist no further. So I replaced the coins in my purse, and I went on :

" My child, will you show me the medals you wear in our Lady's honour ? " —" They are at home. They took them from me to lay upon some sick people, and they cut the string from which they all hung."

" Well, will you let me see your rosary ? "

Bernadette took out her simple rosary with a medal at the end of it.

" Now will you not let me have this rosary ? I will give you the price of it directly."—" No, monsieur, I have no wish either to give you my rosary, or to sell it to you."

" Oh, but I should so much like to have some souvenir of you. I have come such a long way to see you. You really ought to let me have your rosary."

In the end she surrendered it. I clutched this heavenly booty upon which the child's tears had fallen more than once and which had been the instrument of so many grateful and heartfelt prayers in the presence of Mary herself, for Bernadette had fingered this rosary again and again when the apparition had kept count upon a rosary of her own in the grotto of Massabielle. It seemed to me then, it seems to me now, and it always will seem to me, that in this I possess a treasure of great price.

" Will you permit me, my child, to refund you the cost of the rosary ? Please accept this small coin."—" No, monsieur, I will buy myself another with my own money."

But even this was not the climax. The curé's account of the interview continues thus :

"My child, will you let me show you my scapular ? I wonder if yours is made the same way."—" No, monsieur, mine is a double one."
"Show it me." Bernadette modestly fishes up one end of her scapular, which is, as she said, made with double strings.
"God be praised, my daughter. Now I know a very pious soul who would esteem it such a happiness to possess half your scapular. As you see, it can easily be divided."—" Oh, but please. . . ."—" As a great favour will you not give me half of it ? There will be plenty left, for you will still have a whole scapular." "Monsieur, would you be willing to cut in two the rosary I have just given you ? "—" No." "Well, I cannot divide my scapular either."
I understood that I had to give way and must press the matter no further. I told the child that I would give her my blessing, and she received it, kneeling on both knees, with all the reverence of an angel.

If Bernadette, then sixteen years old, was not tingling with indignation all over, she must already have reached a very high stage of virtue, or of resignation to the peculiar form of trial by which her soul was to be purified. Everything we know of her points to the fact that she was an exceptionally sensitive child. In 1864 she offered herself, under advice, to the sisters of Notre-Dame de Nevers. Attacks of illness postponed her departure from Lourdes, but in 1866 she was allowed to join the novitiate in the mother-house of the order. Separation from her family and from the grotto cost her much, but with her fellow-novices at Nevers she was gay, while remaining still the humble and patient child she had always been. Her ill-health continued, so that within four months of her arrival she received the last sacraments and by dispensation was permitted to take her first vows. She recovered, however, and had strength enough to act as infirmarian and afterwards as sacristan, but the asthma from which she suffered never lost its hold, and before the end came she suffered grievously from further complications.

Characteristic of Bernadette were her simplicity of a truly child-like kind, her peasant "sanity", and her self-effacement. She likened herself to a broom : "Our Lady used me. They have put me back in my corner. I am happpy there, and stop there. . . ." But even at Nevers she had sometimes to resort to little stratagems to avoid "publicity". Though her heart was always centred in Lourdes, she had no part in the celebrations connected with the consecration of the basilica in 1876. The abstention seems to have been in large measure her own voluntary choice ; she preferred to efface herself. But who shall say how much the deprivation cost her ? There are few words more pathetic than the cry of Bernadette from her cell at Nevers : "Oh ! si je pouvais voir sans être vue." "Oh! if only I could see without being seen." The conjecture suggests itself strongly that one of Bernadette's "secrets" must have been this, that she was never of her own free will to do anything which would attract to herself the notice of other people.

Bernadette Soubirous died on April 16, 1879 ; she was thirty-five years old. In 1933 she was canonized, and she now appears in the Church's official records as St Mary Bernarda : but in the hearts and on the lips of the faithful she is always St Bernadette.

Apart from the sworn testimonies of witnesses printed in the process of beatification, the most reliable evidence we possess concerning St Bernadette is probably that collected by Fr L. J. M. Cros in his *Histoire de Notre-Dame de Lourdes* (3 vols., 1925-1927). Numerous biographies exist in many languages. One of the earliest was that of Henri Lasserre (very unreliable), one of the latest that of Fr H. Petitot, *The True Story of St Bernadette* (1949). Other widely-read accounts are Mgr Ricard's *La vraie Bernadette* (1896), a reply to Émile Zola ; *Bernadette Soubirous*, by Jean Barbet, who wrote largely from local knowledge ; *La confidente de l'Immaculée* (1921), by a nun of Nevers (Eng. trans.) ; and Abbé J. Blazy's life (Eng. trans., 1926). A very popular novel by Franz Werfel, *Song of Bernadette* (1942), was criticized by Dom Bede Lebbe in *The Soul of Bernadette* (1947). Other popular biographies are those by F. Parkinson Keyes, *Sublime Shepherdess* (1940), and Mrs M. G. Blanton, *Bernadette of Lourdes* (1939). But for a sensitive and reliable summary Fr C. C. Martindale's C.T.S. booklet cannot be bettered. For further particulars of the interviews with St Bernadette quoted above, see *The Month*, June 1924, pp. 526–535, and July 1924, pp. 26–36.

17 : ST ANICETUS, Pope and Martyr   (*c.* A.D. 165)

ST ANICETUS was raised to the chair of St Peter in the latter part of the reign of the Emperor Antoninus Pius. He is styled a martyr in the Roman and other martyrologies and, if he did not actually shed his blood for the faith, he at least purchased the title of martyr by the sufferings and trials he endured. His efforts appear to have been specially directed to combating the errors of Valentine and Marcion and to protecting his flock from heresy. It was whilst he was pope that St Polycarp, the great bishop of Smyrna, came to Rome in connection with the controversy about the date of Easter. The conference which took place led to no settlement, but, to quote the words of Eusebius, " the bonds of charity were not broken ". St Anicetus is said to have been a Syrian.

See the *Acta Sanctorum*, April, vol. ii, and the *Liber Pontificalis* with Mgr Duchesne's introduction and notes.

SS. MAPPALICUS and his Companions, Martyrs   (*c.* A.D. 250)

THE persecution under Decius was the most systematic and general attack which Christianity had yet experienced. The emperor had determined to exterminate completely a fast-increasing body which he regarded as a menace because it obeyed an authority other than his own. On one specified day every denizen of the empire was ordered to sacrifice to the gods and to the genius of the emperor, suspected persons being specially summoned by name, and severe penalties being decreed for those who refused. As soon as news of the edict arrived in Carthage, St Cyprian, the bishop, knowing that he would be the first to be arrested, withdrew into a hiding-place outside the city from whence he could direct and support his flock. The full rigour of the edict was not experienced until the arrival of the proconsul in April 250. He was not content to remain in the city, but made a tour throughout the province, using such severity that many who had hitherto remained faithful fell away. The protomartyr of this persecution in Carthage was a confessor of the name of Mappalicus, whom St Cyprian in his Epistle to Martyrs and Confessors singles out for special praise. After having undergone the torture of the iron claw he was brought before the tribunal, to whom he announced triumphantly that on the morrow they would witness a contest indeed. The following day he was again tortured and perished under the infliction. He was soon followed by other martyrs who gained their crown in various ways, one under torture, one in the mines, and fifteen who died of starvation and of the filthy conditions they endured when herded in two terrible cells.

We know little of these martyrs beyond what we learn from the correspondence of St Cyprian (ed. Hartel), pp. 492, 534, 541. Their names occur in the Calendarium Cathaginense and in the " Hieronymianum ".

ST INNOCENT, Bishop of Tortona   (c. A.D. 350)

The parents of St Innocent at Tortona in the north of Italy, although they were Christians living in times of persecution, were by imperial licence exempted from molestation. The exemption granted to the parents did not extend to the children, and after the death of his father and mother Innocent was summoned to appear before the magistrates. As the young man steadfastly refused to sacrifice to the gods, he was tortured and sentenced to perish at the stake. During the night before his execution he had a dream of his father, who bade him go at once to Rome, where he would find safety. He awoke to find his guards fast asleep, and easily succeeded in making his escape. Upon his arrival in Rome he was kindly received by Pope St Miltiades. Pope St Silvester raised him to the diaconate, and after the accession of the Emperor Constantine he was sent back to Tortona as bishop. During the twenty-eight years of his episcopate he showed great zeal in spreading the faith, in building churches, and in converting pagan temples into Christian sanctuaries.

We owe these details to a late and quite untrustworthy life of St Innocent which is printed in the *Acta Sanctorum*, April, vol. ii. But Father F. Savio has shown in the *Analecta Bollandiana*, vol. xv (1896), pp. 377–384, that the saint really existed and that there are germs of truth in the legend, though the story is a fiction. See on the other hand the brochure of Canon V. Legé (1913) to which Fr Savio subsequently replied.

SS. DONNAN and his Companions, Martyrs   (A.D. 618)

St Donnan was one of the many Irishmen who followed St Columba to Iona. Afterwards, with fifty-two companions, he founded a monastery on the island of Eigg in the Inner Hebrides. They were all slaughtered by some robbers, who descended on them while the abbot was celebrating the Holy Mysteries on the night of Easter. St Donnan was allowed to finish the sacrifice, and then gathered his brethren into the refectory, which seems to have been set on fire, the robbers slaying with the sword those who tried to escape. A story says that the raid was instigated by a woman who had formerly pastured sheep on the island and resented the loss of it to the monks.

The *Félire* of Oengus gives April 17 as the date of the massacre, and other old calendars record this date as their feast-day. Several Scottish churches were dedicated in honour of St Donnan and there is a Kildonan and a St Donnan's well on Eigg ; his feast is still observed in the diocese of Argyll and the Isles.

See Forbes, KSS., p. 325 ; O'Hanlon, LIS., vol. iv, p. 550 ; and Whitley Stokes, *Martyrology of Oengus*, pp. 114–117. On the date, see *Analecta Bollandiana*, vol. lxiii, pp. 121–122 ; and for the text, *ibid.*, li, 126.

ST ROBERT OF CHAISE-DIEU, Abbot   (A.D. 1067)

The founder and first abbot of the monastery of Chaise-Dieu in Auvergne was Robert de Turlande, who after a blameless youth was raised to the priesthood, becoming a canon of the church of St Julian at Brioude. His fervent charity showed itself in his zeal for the public worship of God as well as in his devotion to the sick poor. At one time he contemplated assuming the religious habit at Cluny, but he never seems actually to have taken the step. In order to obtain guidance as to his vocation he made a pilgrimage to the tombs of the Apostles in Rome. Upon his return he was consulted by a knight called Stephen, who was anxious to know what he ought to do to expiate his past sins. When St Robert advised him to leave the world to serve God in the solitary life, Stephen promptly declared himself quite ready to do so, provided Robert would accompany him. This appeared to the saint to be the direct answer to his prayer for light, and he acknowledged that he had for some time been considering the matter.

Stephen set to work enthusiastically, and not only won a second recruit in the person of another knight, but also discovered a suitable place for their settlement in a deserted spot beside a ruined church some five leagues from Brioude. Here they built themselves cells, and embarked on a life of prayer and of manual work, which soon provided for their simple wants and enabled them to assist the poor. Within three years, the fame of the hermits had attracted so many disciples that it became necessary to organize a monastery. People came forward with donations, and buildings arose which developed into the great abbey of Chaise-Dieu, with 300 monks to whom St Robert gave the Benedictine rule. Chaise-Dieu became the mother-house of other monasteries, but in 1640 the congregation was absorbed in that of Saint-Maur.

The Life of St Robert was written within thirty years of his death by Marbod, bishop of Rennes. It is printed in the *Acta Sanctorum*, April, vol. iii (under April 24), and by Mabillon (*Acta Sanctorum O.S.B.*, vol. vi, part 2, pp. 188–197). There is also, *ibidem*, another sketch of his history by Bernard, a monk of Chaise-Dieu, with a collection of his miracles. *Cf. Bulletin historique et scientifique d'Auvergne*, 1906, pp. 47, 72, 82, 116.

ST STEPHEN HARDING, Abbot of Cîteaux, Co-Founder of the Cistercian Order   (A.D. 1134)

St Stephen Harding, the Englishman who helped to found the monastery of Cîteaux, and who actually framed the Cistercian constitution, was educated at the abbey of Sherborne in Dorsetshire. Nothing is known of his parentage or family. He seems to have left the abbey without any very definite idea of becoming a monk, and went first to Scotland and then to Paris, probably to study and to see something of the world. With a friend, he made a journey to Rome which was, in the true sense, a pilgrimage, for we are told that the two young men used every day to recite the whole psalter together. On the way back, as they passed through a forest in Burgundy, they came upon a collection of rough huts, inhabited by monks who were living a life of poverty, their time being divided between prayer and the hard manual work which provided them with vegetables. Their self-abnegation and austerity made an immediate appeal to Stephen, and, leaving his friend to continue his journey alone, he remained at Molesmes and threw in his lot with the monks. In St Robert the abbot and St Alberic the prior he found kindred spirits, and all rejoiced in their holy fellowship of prayer and mortification as well as in a poverty which sometimes amounted to absolute want. After some years, however, it seemed to Stephen and to some of the others that the spirit of the place had departed; and in 1098 Abbot Robert accompanied by Alberic, Stephen and four others, went to Lyons and, in an interview with Archbishop Hugh, who was also the papal legate in France, they applied for permission to leave Molesmes. He at once appreciated their aims and gave them the authorization in a document the terms of which have been preserved. St Robert released the brethren from their vows of obedience to him, and he and twenty of the monks left Molesmes. It is not certain whether they allowed themselves to be led by chance, or whether they had already selected as their future home the loneliest and most uncultivated spot they knew. In any case they found their way to Cîteaux, then a gloomy place in the heart of the forest, far removed from any human habitation. Rainald, the lord of Beaune, willingly gave them the site, and Odo, Duke of Burgundy, who had heard of them from Archbishop Hugh, sent some workmen to assist them in building their monastery.

On March 21, 1098, the new abbey was inaugurated, with Robert as abbot, Alberic as prior, and Stephen as sub-prior, but the following year the monks of Molesmes, finding that they fared very badly without their former abbot, petitioned Rome that Robert should be sent back to them. He had never really been a leader in the migration to Cîteaux and he seems to have been glad to return to Molesmes, to judge from an allusion in a contemporary letter to Robert's " wonted fickleness ".

Alberic now became abbot of Cîteaux with Stephen as prior, but the troubles of the new foundation were only beginning. It took time to convert the virgin forest into arable land, and the brethren were often reduced to great straits. Nevertheless they kept a good heart and continued to serve God according to the strict rule of St Benedict, reinforced by usages of their own.

In 1109 Bd Alberic died and Stephen was elected abbot in his place. His first act was to decree that magnates should no longer be permitted to hold their courts at Cîteaux—thus apparently cutting off the abbey's greatest earthly support and alienating for a time Odo's successor, Duke Hugh. His second measure was even more severe. He forbade the use of anything costly in the service of God : there must be nothing which tended to pomp. Chalices where to be silver gilt, chasubles of good common stuff, and so forth. But the immediate result of these regulations was to discourage visitors and to dry up still further the supply of novices—already a source of anxiety. The day came when starvation stared them in the face, but the monks remained loyal. Then the abbot made a great venture of faith. He bade one of the brethren go to the market of Vézelay and there buy three horses and three waggons, which he was to bring back laden with the necessaries of life. When the monk asked for the money required, the abbot replied he had only threepence. The brother obediently started forth, and upon his arrival in Vézelay told his errand to a friend who lived there. The good man immediately rushed to the bedside of a rich neighbour who was dying, and induced him to give a sum which covered all the purchases required.

But their numbers still diminished. A mysterious disease appeared amongst them which carried off one monk after another, until even Stephen's stout heart quailed before the prospect of the future, and he began to wonder if he were really doing the will of God. Addressing a dying monk the abbot asked him to bring back word from beyond the grave to let him know the divine will—if God would allow it. Soon after his death the monk appeared to Stephen as he was out in the fields, and assured him not only that his way of life was pleasing to God but that recruits would soon come who, " like bees swarming in haste and overflowing the hive, would fly away and spread themselves through many parts of the world ". Thus assured, Stephen was satisfied to wait for the fulfilment of the prophecy. Certainly no one could have foreseen how dramatically that answer would come.

At the monastery gates appeared one day a troop of thirty men, who announced to the astonished porter that they had come to crave admittance and to offer themselves to the religious life. They were all of noble lineage, mostly also in their early prime, and they had as their leader and spokesman a young man of singular beauty whose name was Bernard. He had been moved to give up the world, but being a youth of keen affections he had no mind to enter the way of perfection himself and leave his friends outside. One after another, he had gained over his brothers, his uncle, and a number of his acquaintances. This was the turning-point : from henceforth there was no lack of novices and no fear of starvation, for the new foundation was drawing upon itself the attention and admiration of France. It was also the culminating event in St Stephen's history : his personality almost disappears in the two great tasks now before him—the training of St Bernard and the constitution of the Cistercian Order.

Increasing numbers soon necessitated a daughter house, and a foundation was made at Pontigny. Two other houses, Morimond and then Clairvaux, followed, and to the general surprise Stephen appointed Bernard abbot of Clairvaux, although he was only twenty-four years of age. To bind these monasteries to Cîteaux, Stephen instituted an annual general chapter which the heads of the affiliated abbeys were bound to attend. In 1119, when nine abbeys had sprung from Cîteaux and Clairvaux, St Stephen drew up a body of statutes, the Charter of Charity, which both organized the Cistercians as an order and regulated their mode of life.

It was only when he was old and very nearly blind that St Stephen laid down his pastoral staff to prepare for the end. As he lay on his death-bed, he heard some of the monks round him extolling him and saying that he would be able to enter fearlessly into the presence of God. Raising himself, he rebuked them, saying, " Indeed, I assure you that I am going to God as trembling and as anxious as if I had never done any good. For if there has been in me any good at all, and if any fruit has been produced from my littleness, it was through the help of the grace of God : and I fear greatly lest perhaps I have husbanded that grace less jealously and less humbly than I ought to have done." These were his last words before he went to his reward. As well as by the Cistercians, the feast of St Stephen Harding is kept in the dioceses of Westminster and (on March 28) Plymouth. He was canonized in 1623.

Materials for the study of the early history of the Cistercian Order are tolerably ample. We have the *Exordium Parvum*, the *Exordium Magnum*, and the works of such chroniclers as William of Malmesbury and Ordericus Vitalis, as well as a life of St Robert of Molesmes. For English readers Father Dalgairns contributed to the " Lives of English Saints " series an excellent biography of St Stephen Harding ; this was reprinted separately with additional notes by Fr Herbert Thurston in 1898, and was reissued in U.S.A. in 1946. Several important articles upon the early days of Cîteaux have been contributed to the periodical *Die Cistercienser-Chronik* by P. Gregor Müller, notably that entitled " Citeaux unter dem Abte Alberich ", vol. xxi (1909), nn. 239–243. For the Charter of Charity, see D. Knowles, *The Monastic Order in England* (1949), pp. 208–216.

BD EBERHARD OF MARCHTHAL, Abbot   (A.D. 1178)

As early as the year 1100 the counts of Swabia had built or restored a minster at Marchthal on the southern bank of the Danube and installed in it secular canons. In time the foundation languished : canons died and were not replaced, others voluntarily abandoned the house—" preferring fat oxen to lean ", as the old chronicler expresses it.   At last it became derelict and entirely deserted.   The sight of the ruined buildings in which the praises of God were no longer chanted was a source of grief to Elizabeth, the wife of Hugo, Count of Tübingen ; and at her request Hugo rebuilt the monastery, which he handed over to the Premonstratensians of Roth as a thank-offering for his success in battle.   The gift was a valuable one, including four churches, large tracts of land, and fishing rights in the Danube.   Over the twelve canons who came from Roth was set Eberhard of Wolfegg, a very holy man who had given up great riches and the dignity of archdeacon to enter the Premonstratensian Order.   He ruled Marchthal with great success for twelve years and died in the year 1178.

There seems to be no formal biography of Eberhard, nor has there ever been any authoritative recognition of his claim to be liturgically honoured, but an account of him is given in the *Acta Sanctorum*, April, vol. ii.   See also F. Walter, *Geschichte des Klosters Obermarchtal*, pp. 5–7, and J. Vochezer, *Geschichte des Hauses Waldburg*, vol. i, pp. 5–6.

BD JAMES OF CERQUETO   (A.D. 1367)

HISTORY has little to tell concerning Bd James of Cerqueto, who entered the order of the Hermits of St Augustine at Perugia when still very young and lived until extreme old age a life almost entirely devoted to prayer.   It was to his prayers that his brethren attributed the permission they received sometimes to wear white habits in honour of the Blessed Virgin.   Like many other saints who have led the eremitic life he had great power over animals.   During his open-air preaching it was noticed that the very frogs ceased their croaking at his bidding, to allow his words to be heard by those for whom they were intended.   He died in the church of St Augustine at Perugia on April 17, 1367.   Owing to the number of miracles reported as having taken place at his tomb, Horatius, bishop of Perugia, caused his body to be enshrined in 1754 and carried in solemn procession through the city.

The *cultus* of Bd James was confirmed in 1895.   The decree, giving a brief sketch of his life, may be found in the *Analecta Ecclesiastica* for 1895, pp. 253–254.   A short account of the *beato* was printed in the same year by A. Rotelli, *Il beato Giacomo da Cerqueto*.

BD CLARE OF PISA, WIDOW   (A.D. 1419)

THIS Bd Clare was the child of Peter Gambacorta, who became virtually head of the Pisan republic, and she was born in 1362 ; Bd Peter of Pisa (Gambacorta junior ; June 17) was her brother, seven years older than herself.   To provide for the future of his little daughter, familiarly known as Thora (short for Theodora), her father betrothed her to Simon de Massa, a wealthy youth of good family, although the child was only seven years old.   Yet, young as she was, she was wont to slip off her betrothal ring during Mass and murmur, " Lord, thou knowest that I desire no love but thine ".   At the age of twelve when she was sent to her husband's home, she had already begun to practise severe mortifications.   Her mother-in-law was kind, but upon discovering that Thora was over-lavish in her gifts to the poor she ceased to allow her access to the household stores.   Her charitable instincts thus thwarted in one direction, the young bride joined a band of ladies who ministered to the sick, and she took as her special charge a poor woman afflicted with a distressing form of cancer.   Thora's wedded life was of short duration : she and her husband fell ill of an epidemic disease which cost him his life. As she was only fifteen her relations set about arranging another marriage, but she was old enough to assert herself, and her decision to remain a widow was strengthened by a letter from St Catherine of Siena, whose acquaintance she had made when that holy woman had visited Pisa.

As a first step, Thora cut off her hair and distributed her fine clothes to the poor —much to the indignation of her mother- and sisters-in-law. Then, secretly, through the intermediary of a servant, she arranged for admission into the Poor Clares. Stealing out of the house she made her way to the convent, where she was immediately clothed with the habit, assuming at the same time the name of Clare, by which she was from thenceforth to be known. The following day her brothers appeared at the gates to demand her return, and the terrified nuns let her down over the wall into the hands of her kinsmen, who took her home in disgrace. Although she was kept a prisoner in her father's house for five months, neither threats nor starvation could shake her determination. At last Peter Gambacorta relented, and not only allowed his daughter to enter the Dominican priory of Holy Cross, but promised to build another house of the order. She now became associated with Mary Mancini, also a widow, and destined like herself to be raised to the altars of the Church. The teaching of St Catherine of Siena strongly influenced the two women who, when they were transferred to Gambacorta's new foundation in 1382, succeeded in inaugurating observance of their rule in its primitive austerity. This house, in which Bd Clare was at first sub-prioress and then prioress, became the training centre for many saintly women who afterwards carried the reform movement to other Italian cities. To this day, enclosed Dominican nuns are often spoken of in Italy as " Sisters of Pisa ". They led a contemplative life of prayer, manual work and study : " Never forget ", said Bd Clare's director, " that in our order very few have become saints who were not likewise scholars."

During the rest of her life, the holy prioress was beset by financial difficulties in connection with her convent, which required alterations and extensions. Nevertheless, when a large sum of money came into her hands with the option of using it for the priory, she preferred to give it for the establishment of a foundling hospital. Perhaps, however, her most conspicuous virtues were her sense of duty and her forgiving spirit—both of which she displayed to a heroic degree in exceptional circumstances. Gambacorta, in the midst of his efforts to maintain peace in the city, was treacherously slain by Giacomo Appiano, whose fortune he had made and whom he had refused to mistrust ; two of his sons were done to death by the miscreant's supporters, whilst a third escaped, closely followed by the enemy, to the door of Bd Clare's convent at which he knocked for admission. Recognizing that her first duty was to protect her daughters from the mob, the prioress refused to break the enclosure. Her brother was hewn down at the threshold, and the shock brought on her a severe illness. But Clare could forgive so completely that she invited Appiano to send her a dish from his table that she might seal her forgiveness by partaking of his bread. In later years, when his widow and daughters were reduced to great straits, she opened the convent doors to receive them.

Bd Clare was a great sufferer towards the close of her life, and as she lay on her death-bed with outstretched arms, she was heard to murmur, " My Jesus, here I am upon the cross ". Just before she died, however, her face was illuminated

with a radiant smile and she blessed her daughters absent as well as present.   She
had reached the age of fifty-seven years.   Her *cultus* was confirmed in 1830.

There is an Italian life by a contemporary, herself a nun, which has been translated
into Latin and printed in the *Acta Sanctorum*, April, vol. ii, and there are also a few of
Clare's letters, which have been published.   See further M. C. de Ganay, *Les Bienheureuses
Dominicaines* (1913), pp. 193–238 ; and Procter, *Lives of the Dominican Saints*, pp. 96–100.
A full bibliography will be found in Taurisano, *Catalogus hagiographicus O.P.*, p. 34.

18 : ST APOLLONIUS THE APOLOGIST, MARTYR   (c. A.D. 185)

THE Emperor Marcus Aurelius had persecuted the Christians on principle,
but his son Commodus, who succeeded him about the year 180, although
a vicious man, showed himself not unfavourably disposed towards them.
During the cessation of active persecution under his reign, the number of the
faithful greatly increased, many men of rank enlisting themselves under the banner
of the cross.   Amongst these was a Roman senator called Apollonius, who was well
versed in philosophy as well as in the Holy Scriptures.   In the midst of the peace
which the Church was enjoying, he was denounced as a Christian by one of his own
slaves to Perennis, the praetorian prefect.   The laws against the Christians had
not been repealed and, although the slave was promptly put to death as an informer,
Perennis called upon Apollonius to renounce his religion.   As the saint refused,
the prefect referred him to the judgement of the Roman senate.   In their presence
the martyr who, possibly on account of his learning and social position, seems to
have been treated with a certain exceptional consideration, debated with Perennis
and boldly gave an account of his faith.   As Apollonius persisted in his refusal to
offer sacrifice, he was condemned and decapitated ; another, less probable, account
tells us that he was put to death by having his legs crushed.

In the opinion of hagiographical scholars the dialogue between the martyr and
his judge bears every mark of having been extracted from an authentic record taken
down by a stenographer.   Alban Butler in the eighteenth century could not have
known of this recently discovered document, and a quotation from the fearless
words, spoken on the threshold of death by the Christian apologist so many hundred
years ago, may well supply the place of any later homily.   We borrow the slightly
contracted, but substantially exact, translation of the late Canon A. J. Mason.

Death, said the martyr, was appointed for all ; and Christians practised themselves for it in dying daily.   So far were the heathen calumnies against Christianity
from being true, that Christians would not allow themselves a single impure glance,
nor listen to a bad word.   He said that it was no worse to die for the true God than
to die of fever, or dysentery, or any other disease.   " Are you then bent upon
death ? " asked Perennis.   " No ", said Apollonius, " I enjoy life ; but love of life
does not make me afraid to die.   There is nothing better than life—the life eternal,
which gives immortality to the soul which has lived well here."   The prefect
confessed that he did not understand.   " I am heartily sorry for you ", said the
prisoner ; " so insensible are you to the beauties of grace.   Only the seeing heart
can appreciate the Word of God as the seeing eye the light."

Here a brother philosopher of the Cynic school interrupted Apollonius, and said
that such language was an insult to the understanding, though Apollonius himself
thought that he was uttering profound truths.   " I have learned to pray, and not

to insult," Apollonius answered, "only to the senseless does the truth appear to be an insult." The judge besought him to explain himself clearly. Then Apollonius answered with what Eusebius justly calls a most eloquent defence of the faith.

"The Word of God", he said, "who brought into existence men's souls and bodies, became man in Judea—our Saviour Jesus Christ. Perfectly righteous and filled with divine wisdom, He lovingly taught us what the God of all is like, and what is the end of virtue, befitting the souls of men with a view to social order and dignity. By His own suffering He put a stop to sins in their very beginning. He taught us to stop anger, to moderate desire, to chastise the love of pleasure. He taught us to relieve sorrow, to be generous, to promote charity, to put away vainglory, to abstain from taking revenge, to despise death—not when inflicted for wrongdoing, but in patient endurance of the wrongdoing of others. He taught us to obey the law laid down by Himself, to honour the king, to worship the immortal God, and Him only, to believe our souls to be immortal, to look forward to judgement after death, to expect the reward of the toils of virtue to be given by God after the resurrection of those who have lived good lives. All this He taught us plainly, and gave us convincing reasons for it ; and won great glory for this excellence. But He incurred the envy of the unnurtured like the righteous men and philosophers before Him. For the righteous are unserviceable to the unrighteous ; as the fools unjustly say in a certain proverb "—here Apollonius refers to a passage in the Book of Wisdom—" ' Let us lie in wait for the righteous, because he is not for our turn.' And not only so, but it was said by one of the Greeks "—a speaker in the *Republic* of Plato—" ' the righteous man shall be scourged, tortured, bound, have his eyes put out, and at last be crucified.' As the Athenian sycophants persuaded the multitude and unjustly sentenced Socrates, so our Master and Saviour was sentenced to death by some of the wicked who reproached Him as they had reproached the prophets before Him. . . . We," he concluded, "have hastened to honour Him because we have learned from Him lofty commandments, of which we were ignorant before, and are under no delusion. Yet if it were a delusion, as you say, which tells us that the soul is immortal, and that there is a judgement after death, and a reward of virtue at the resurrection, and that God is the Judge, we would gladly be carried away by such a lie as that, which has taught us to live good lives awaiting the hope of the future even while suffering adversities."

Although from Eusebius, Rufinus, and St Jerome something was known of this discussion with Apollonius in the presence of the senate, no accurate report was believed to survive until F. C. Conybeare translated an Armenian text which had in 1874 been printed by the Mekhitarist monks (see Conybeare, *The Apology and Acts of Apollonius*, etc., 1894, pp. 29–48). Shortly afterwards the Bollandists found a copy of the Greek text in a Paris MS. and edited it in the *Analecta Bollandiana*, vol. xiv (1895), pp. 284–294. The two texts attracted great attention among scholars and have been many times re-edited and translated. See the admirable account of these acts which is furnished by Father Delehaye in his *Les Passions des Martyrs et les genres littéraires* (1921), pp. 125–136. While he strongly upholds the substantial authenticity of the dialogue, he points out how both in the Greek and the Armenian the process of adaptation and falsification has already begun. He also supplies a sufficient bibliography of the contribution made to the discussion by Harnack, Mommsen, Klette, Geffcken, and others. See also A. J. Mason, *Historic Martyrs of the Primitive Church* (1905), pp. 70–75.

SS. ELEUTHERIUS AND HIS COMPANIONS, MARTYRS   (NO DATE)

THE story of St Eleutherius and his companions is one of those pious romances of Greek origin which were accepted as veracious in a subsequent uncritical age and attained to great popularity.   It follows conventional lines and may be summarized as a specimen of such fables.   Eleutherius was a Christian, the son of a Roman widow called Anthia, and was educated by a certain Bishop Dynamius.   A deacon at sixteen, a priest at eighteen, the young man was consecrated bishop of Illyrium at the age of twenty.   After having converted and baptized an imperial official sent to arrest him, Eleutherius was brought before the Emperor Hadrian, who caused him to be bound with outstretched limbs upon a red-hot iron bedstead.   The martyr's bonds, however, broke spontaneously, and he stood up and harangued the people.   Hadrian then sent for a large grid, and after promises and threats he offered Eleutherius the alternative of either recanting or being roasted to death. The young bishop never faltered, but the fire died out of itself and could not be rekindled.   Thereupon he was shut up in a hot oven from which he emerged two hours later entirely unscathed.   The enraged emperor ordered him to be tied by the feet behind a waggon drawn by wild horses, which took him up into a mountain where an angel released him and where the beasts of the forest gathered round him like lambs.   There he remained until he was discovered by hunters and delivered to the imperial soldiers.   During the public games he was exposed in the amphitheatre, but a lion and a lioness, let loose upon him, only licked his hands and feet.   Eventually he was clubbed to death with eleven companions, his mother Anthia perishing by the sword soon afterwards.

These fictitious acts may be read in the *Acta Sanctorum*, April, vol. ii, and *cf.* Delehaye, *Les Légendes Hagiographiques* (3rd ed., 1927), p. 77.

ST LASERIAN, LAISREN OR MOLAISSE, Bishop of Leighlin (A.D. 639)

The early history of St Laisren is very uncertain in view of the discrepancy between the various accounts which have come down to us.   He is said to have spent several years at Iona, and then to have proceeded to Rome where he received ordination from Pope St Gregory the Great.   We next find him at Leighlin, on the banks of the Barrow, in a monastery presided over by its founder, St Goban.   At a synod held at White Fields in the immediate vicinity, St Laisren was foremost in upholding the Roman date for keeping Easter as against the Columban usage still widely prevalent in Ireland.   The conference, which was conducted with great courtesy on both sides, could come to no conclusion, and it was decided to send St Laisren with a deputation to refer the matter to the pope.   On this second visit to Rome, the saint was consecrated bishop by Honorius and appointed papal legate for Ireland. In this capacity he would seem to have succeeded in practically settling the paschal controversy as far as the south of Ireland was concerned.   About two years after the synod, St Goban resigned the government of the monastery to St Laisren, who ruled it until his death.   His feast is kept throughout Ireland.

Lamlash Bay and the sea-bathing resort of Lamlash on the island of Arran off the south-west coast of Scotland have been said to derive their name from St Lamliss, a hermit who, at some period in the seventh century, occupied a cell in the district where the present village stands.   Although this is stated by Butler, who refers in support of his assertion to " memoirs in the Scottish College at Paris ", it seems much more probable that the name commemorates the Irish bishop St Laisren of Leighlin.

The Latin life of St Laisren, printed in the *Acta Sanctorum*, April, vol. ii, curiously says nothing of the saint's connection with the paschal controversy, though this is much insisted on in other sources. See Plummer, *Irish Litanies* (1925), p. 120. The text in the Codex Salmanticensis is only fragmentary. *Cf.* also O'Hanlon, LIS., vol. iv, pp. 203 *seq.*, and Forbes, KSS., pp. 407–409 ; but mainly W. J. Watson, *History of the Celtic Place-Names of Scotland* (1926), pp. 305–307.

ST IDESBALD, ABBOT   (A.D. 1167)

THE celebrated abbey of our Lady of the Dunes arose from a small settlement formed in 1107 by a hermit called Ligerius on the sand-hills between Dunkirk and Nieuport. The monks followed the Savigny reform until 1137, when the monastery, which had been transferred to a neighbouring spot, became affiliated to the Cistercians. Thither there came one day from Furnes a canon of the church of St Walburga, Idesbald by name, asking to be given the monastic habit. He was a man no longer young, and with aristocratic connections, but it was not long before he won the affectionate esteem of the whole abbey by his meekness, his wisdom and his integrity. The post of cantor, which he held, was dear to him, for the Divine Office was his passion : he would become so much absorbed in it as to be oblivious to all things else. He eventually became abbot, and the monastery prospered greatly under his rule, his prestige being so great that outsiders eagerly assisted him in carrying out his schemes ; and privileges were granted to the abbey by Pope Alexander III. When St Idesbald died, his brethren, in deference to his great sanctity, departed from the custom of the order and laid him in a coffin which they buried in their church. His body, which was found to be incorrupt 450 years after his death, now lies at Bruges.

There seems to be no early life of St Idesbald, but an account of him is given in the *Acta Sanctorum*, April, vol. ii. There is a good book in Flemish by J. De Cuyper, *Idesbald van der Gracht* (1946).

ST GALDINUS, ARCHBISHOP OF MILAN AND CARDINAL   (A.D. 1176)

MILAN honours as one of its principal patrons the holy Galdinus, whose name appears associated with those of St Ambrose and St Charles Borromeo at the close of every litany of the Milanese rite. A member of the famous Della Scala family, he occupied the posts of chancellor and archdeacon under two archbishops of Milan, winning the confidence of clergy and people by the manner in which he shouldered his responsibilities at a very difficult epoch. When Pope Alexander III was elected in 1159, a few dissentient cardinals promptly elected a rival pope more favourable to the pretensions of the Emperor Frederick Barbarossa. Milan had already offended the emperor by claiming the right to select its own magistrates, but when the citizens acknowledged Alexander III he became further incensed against them. Archbishop Hubert and his archdeacon Galdinus were obliged to withdraw into exile, and the following year Frederick, with a great army, invested the city, which surrendered after a siege. It was by his orders that the reputed bodies of the Three Magi were then removed from the church of St Eustorgius to Cologne, where the greater part of these " relics " still remain.

In 1165 Galdinus was created cardinal, and the following year, upon the death of Archbishop Hubert, he was appointed his successor. In vain he pleaded the state of his health, enfeebled by the hardships he had undergone : Alexander consecrated him with his own hands. The new prelate made it his first care to comfort and encourage his distressed flock ; the Lombard states had entered into a league to rebuild Milan, and St Galdinus threw himself heart and soul into the new undertaking.   Nor did the distracted state of the commonwealth hinder St Galdinus from attending assiduously to his pastoral duties.   He preached constantly, and assisted the poor whom he sought out in their miserable homes. Amongst his clergy he enforced discipline, which had inevitably become relaxed during the troublous times through which they had been passing.   His wisdom and eloquence, which had at first been mainly directed towards healing the schism, were afterwards exerted to confute the doctrines of the Cathari, then widely prevalent in Lombardy.   On the last day of his life, although too weak to celebrate Mass, he succeeded in delivering an impassioned sermon against false doctrine.   The effort was too much for him : he lost consciousness before he could leave the pulpit, and died as the Mass was ending.

In the very year of St Galdinus's death the imperial army was routed by the Lombard league at the battle of Legnano.   And at the celebrated meeting which took place in Venice in 1177, Barbarossa abjured the schism, and made his peace with the Church.   That the pope placed his foot upon the emperor's neck in any but in a metaphorical sense is now discredited by all sober historians. The incident, which would have been utterly inconsistent with Alexander III's magnanimous character, is not mentioned by any contemporary writer.

A short biography of early date is printed in the *Acta Sanctorum* (April, vol. ii) with copious annotations.   See also Ughelli, *Italia Sacra*, vol. iv, cc. 219–226, and L. Marazza, *La Lega Lombarda e S. Galdino* (1897).

BD JAMES OF LODI   (A.D. 1404)

As a young man, James Oldi took a prominent part in the social gaieties of his native town, Lodi, concerning himself very little with religion ; he painted, he sang, he played the lute, and there was no better dancer in all the land.   Moreover he had married a lady, Catherine by name, who was equally addicted to amusement.   A severe epidemic of plague destroyed the amenities of the town, and James went to stay with his father-in-law in the country.   Happening to enter a local church which contained a reproduction of the Holy Sepulchre, James said to a companion, " Let us see which is the taller—Christ or I ".   With these flippant words he lay down at full length on the tomb—but when he stood up again he was a changed man.   From that moment he shunned all his former pleasures.   He scourged himself, spent hours in church, painted sacred pictures, and undertook the care of a sick priest, who taught him Latin.

The example of her husband, as well as the death of their two girls of plague, led to the conversion of Catherine.   They took a vow of continence, became Franciscan tertiaries, and converted their house into a church, Catherine's dresses being cut up for vestments, whilst her jewels were given to adorn the sacred vessels. James himself was raised to the priesthood, after he had lived for some time an austere life of piety and good works with a band of friends who gathered round him. Misunderstandings with neighbouring Franciscan regulars, who suspected them of attempting to found a new branch of the order, obliged them to leave the town for the suburb of Old Lodi, where Bd James served a church.   The upheaval caused by the civil war, however, eventually led to their return to Lodi, where this good priest spent his last years devoting himself to the sick and to the prisoners-of-war.

He died of an illness contracted from a patient he was attending, and was buried in St Julian's, the church which he had founded.

An Italian life written by the confessor of Bd James is preserved in a Latin translation in the *Acta Sanctorum*, April, vol. ii. See the valuable little book *B. Giacomo Oldi da Lodi* (1933), by P. M. Sevesi.

BD ANDREW HIBERNON (A.D. 1602)

ANDREW HIBERNON came of noble Spanish stock, but his parents, who lived at Alcantarilla, near Murcia, were so poor that at a very early age the boy hired himself out to an uncle, in order to contribute to the support of his family. He had gradually amassed a sum sufficient to provide a dowry for his sister, and was taking it home in triumph, when he was set upon by thieves who robbed him of all. Bitterly disappointed, he now began to realize the uncertainty of earthly riches compared with the heavenly treasure which is eternal. He entered a house of Conventual Franciscans which he soon left to pass to a convent of the Alcantarine reform, where he was professed as a lay-brother. He sought to live a hidden life of self-effacement, humility and prayer, but God was pleased to glorify him by giving him the gifts of prophecy and of miracles. Many owed their conversion to him. The holy man foretold the date of his own death, which occurred at Gandia when he was in his sixty-eighth year.

St Pascal Baylon and Bd John de Ribera made Andrew's name widely known ; but he had been locally honoured as a saint even in his life-time, and he was beatified in 1791.

There is a life by Fr Vincent Mondina, the postulator of the cause, *Vita del B. Andrea Ibernon* (1791), and see also Léon, *Auréole Séraphique* (Eng. trans.), vol. ii, pp. 77–83.

BD MARY OF THE INCARNATION, WIDOW (A.D. 1618)

To Barbara Acarie—*la belle Acarie*—afterwards known as Bd Mary-of-the-Incarnation, is due the credit of having introduced into France the Carmelites of the reform initiated in Spain by St Teresa. She also had some part in establishing in Paris the Ursulines and the Oratorians. The daughter of Nicholas Avrillot, a high government official, Barbara showed unusual piety and astonished the nuns of her aunt's convent at Longchamps, where she was educated, by her austerities when, as a girl of twelve, she was preparing for her first communion. She would fain have embraced the religious life, preferably as a Franciscan at Longchamps, or failing that as a nursing sister of the poor at the Hôtel-Dieu in Paris, but her parents had other plans for the only one of their children they had been able to rear. She complied with their wishes, saying resignedly, " If I am unworthy through my sins to be the bride of Christ, I can at least be His servant ". At the age of seventeen she was given in marriage to Peter Acarie, an aristocratic young advocate who held an important post in the treasury. He was a man of piety and charity who did much to help the exiled English Catholics reduced to poverty by the penal laws of Queen Elizabeth ; but though so well-meaning he was also rather foolish, and he caused his wife no little suffering. However, the marriage was on the whole a happy one, and Madame Acarie proved herself a devoted wife and mother. She took so much trouble over the spiritual training of her six children that she was asked if she intended them all for the religious life. " I am preparing them to carry out God's

will . . ." was her reply. " A religious vocation can only come from God."
Eventually all her three daughters entered the Carmelite Order, whilst of her three
sons one became a priest and the other two maintained throughout their careers in
the world the principles they had imbibed in childhood.   Her glowing piety seems
to have communicated itself to her whole household, whose welfare she constantly
sought and whom she nursed with the utmost tenderness when they were ill.   Her
personal maid, Andrée Levoix, in particular became her associate in her devotions
and charities.

Great temporal trials were in store for this happy family circle.   Peter Acarie
had been a prominent supporter of the Catholic League, on whose behalf he had
incurred heavy financial liabilities.   After the accession of Henry IV he was
banished from Paris, and his property was immediately seized by his creditors.
Madame Acarie and her children were at one time reduced to such extremities that
they had not enough to eat.   The intrepid wife rose to the occasion.   Herself
conducting the defence of her husband in the courts, she proved his innocence of
the charge of conspiracy against the king, and was able to help him to compound
with his creditors.   She even obtained leave for him to return to Paris, with a
diminished fortune indeed but with an untarnished name.   Madame Acarie's
far-reaching but discriminating charity became so widely known that she was
entrusted by many people with the distribution of their alms.   Mary of Medici
and Henry IV themselves honoured her with their esteem, and she was able to obtain from them the sanction and help required to bring the Carmelite nuns to Paris.
Her sympathies were so wide that they included every kind of person : she fed the
hungry, she befriended the fallen, she assisted " decayed " gentlefolk, she watched
beside the dying, she instructed heretics, she encouraged religious of every order.

Madame Acarie was moved to work for the introduction of the Teresian
Carmelites into France by two visions of St Teresa ; it was nearly three years from
the second of these to the opening of the convent of Spanish nuns in Paris in
November 1604. Four more foundations elsewhere followed during the next five
years.   Madame Acarie was not only the prime mover in bringing all this about :
she also trained young women for the Carmelite life—she was, in fact, a sort of un-
official married novice-mistress.   Among her advisers and helpers at this time were
St Francis de Sales and Peter de Bérulle, the founder of the French Oratorians.

It was not then surprising that soon after her husband died in 1613 she asked
to be received among the Carmelites, as a lay-sister.   But she was a nun for only
four years ; Barbara Acarie was essentially a woman who attained holiness in the
married state—she was a saint before ever she put on the habit of Carmel.   Taking
the name of Mary-of-the-Incarnation, she entered the convent at Amiens, where
her eldest daughter was shortly after appointed sub-prioress.   Sister Mary was
the first to promise her obedience, and she was happy to scour the pots and pans
in the house she had helped to found—yet she could walk only with difficulty and
great pain, through having three times broken a leg over twenty years before.
Afterwards, owing to regrettable disagreements with Father de Bérulle, she was
transferred to Pontoise.

Underlying the outward activities of Bd Mary was a mystical life of a high order.
Great spiritual truths were revealed to her whilst she was in a state of contemplation
bordering upon ecstasy.   These effects of the life of grace already showed themselves in the early years of her married life, and occasioned misunderstandings in
her family and grave trials for her.   Among the well-known spiritual directors who

helped her was that Capuchin from Canfield in Essex, Father Benet Fitch. In February 1618 she developed symptoms of apoplexy and paralysis which showed that her end was near. When the prioress asked her to bless the nuns gathered about her bedside she first raised her eyes and hands to Heaven with the prayer, " Lord, forgive me the bad example I have set ". After giving her blessing she added, " If it should please Almighty God to admit me to eternal bliss I will ask that the will of His divine Son should be accomplished in each one of you ". At three o'clock on Easter morning she received her last communion, and died whilst being anointed. She was fifty-two years old. Barbara Acarie was beatified in 1791.

There are many biographies of Madame Acarie, beginning with that of André du Val (1621 ; 1893). It will be sufficient to mention those of Boucher, Cadoudal, Griselle, and the summary by E. de Broglie in the series " Les Saints ". But Fr Bruno's *La belle Acarie* (1942) is by far the best life, and it contains a very full bibliography. Mother Mary's influence upon her generation was sufficiently great to claim notice in such works as Pastor's *Geschichte der Päpste*, vols. xi and xii, and in H. Bremond, *Histoire littéraire du sentiment religieux en France*, vol. ii (Eng. trans.), pp. 193–262. There is an excellent life in English, *Barbe Acarie* (1953), by L. C. Sheppard.

19 : ST LEO IX, POPE   (A.D. 1054)

ALSACE, at that period a part of the Holy Roman Empire, was the birth-place of St Leo IX in the year 1002. His father Hugh, who was closely related to the emperor, and his mother Heilewide were a pious and cultured pair of whom it is recorded, as though it were somewhat unusual, that they spoke fluent French as well as their own German tongue. At the age of five, Bruno, as he was called, was sent to a school presided over by Berthold, Bishop of Toul. He displayed exceptional abilities and was placed under the special charge of a much older cousin, Adalbert, afterwards bishop of Metz. One experience of his boyhood made a profound impression upon the future pope. He was on a visit to his home when he contracted severe blood-poisoning caused by the bite of some reptile. While he lay between life and death he had a vision of St Benedict, who touched him with a cross, and when he came to himself the boy found that he was completely cured. His studies ended, he was appointed to a canonry of St Stephen's, Toul. When in 1026 the Emperor Conrad II went to Italy to quell a rebellion in Lombardy, Bruno, although now a deacon, was given command of the corps furnished by the aged bishop of Toul. His success in handling the men gave him a reputation for military skill which, in the light of future events, was perhaps unfortunate. While the army was still in Italy, Bishop Heriman died and the clergy and people of Toul immediately elected Bruno to be his successor. On Ascension day, 1027, amid the rejoicings of the people, he entered Toul to be enthroned in the cathedral over which he was to rule for twenty years. His first pastoral work was to enforce a stricter mode of life amongst his clergy, regular as well as secular. Inspired, no doubt, by his grateful devotion to St Benedict, he held the religious life in the utmost veneration, and did much to revive discipline and fervour in the great monasteries of his diocese, into which he introduced the reform of Cluny.

In the summer of 1048 Pope Damasus II died after a pontificate of twenty-three days, and the Emperor Henry III chose his kinsman Bruno of Toul as his successor.

He set out for Rome, stopping at Cluny on the way, where he was joined by the monk Hildebrand, afterwards Pope St Gregory VII. His nomination having been endorsed in due form, Bruno was enthroned, taking the name of Leo IX, early in 1049. For many years the growing evil of simony in the Church had been exercising the minds of good men, lay as well as ecclesiastical. The mischief had reached such alarming proportions that it needed a strong hand to grapple with it. But Leo had no hesitation. Shortly after his accession, he called a synod in Rome which anathematized and deprived beneficed clergy guilty of simony, besides dealing sternly with the relaxation of the rule of celibacy. The collegiate life, which as a young man he had helped Bishop Heriman to uphold at Toul, he now recommended to the secular clergy throughout the Church. Moreover, as he was quite aware that to bring about the reforms he required would necessitate something more than the mere issue of orders from Rome, he embarked upon a kind of visitation of Western Christendom in order that he might personally enforce his regulations and arouse the conscience of those in authority. Besides the reformation of morals, which was his principal theme, he urged the extension of preaching and the better rendering of the sacred chant, an object dear to his heart. In another sphere of activity St Leo was confronted with the necessity of condemning the doctrines of Berengarius of Tours, who denied Christ's real presence in the Eucharist. Twice more did the energetic pope cross the Alps, once to revisit his former see of Toul and on the other occasion to attempt a reconciliation between Henry III and King Andrew of Hungary—well was he called *Peregrinus apostolicus*, " the Apostolic Pilgrim ".

Leo obtained for the patrimony of St Peter possession of Benevento and other territories in southern Italy, thus ultimately increasing the temporal power of the papacy. To himself they proved only a great embarrassment, for they were ravaged by the Normans. He led an army against the invaders, but was defeated and captured at Civitella and was detained for a while by his captors at Benevento. This was a blow to Leo's prestige, and St Peter Damian and others criticized him severely—if battles were necessary, they said, they should be fought by the emperor, not by the vicar of Christ.

This was the time chosen by Michael Cerularius, patriarch of Constantinople, to accuse the Western church of heresy on the ground of certain points of discipline and ritual practice in which it differed from the Eastern church. Pope Leo answered in a long and indignant but not immoderate letter, and it was characteristic of him that he then began to study Greek the better to understand the arguments of his accusers. But though this was the beginning of the final separation of Christian East and West, St Leo did not live to see the further developments that followed the arrival in Constantinople of the legates whom he sent thither. His health was by this time shattered. He ordered that his bed and a coffin should be placed side by side in St Peter's, and here he passed away peacefully before the high altar on April 19, 1054.

" Heaven has opened for the pontiff that this world was not worthy to keep : the glory of the saints is his ", declared Didier, abbot of Monte Cassino, and in so saying he was echoing the voice of the multitude. All mourned him, seventy miraculous cures were claimed within forty days of Leo's death, and in 1087 Bd Victor III confirmed the popular canonization by ordering the mortal remains of St Leo IX to be solemnly enshrined.

It was Leo who first promulgated the proposal to vest the election of future popes exclusively in the Roman cardinals—a suggestion which became law five years after his death. Amongst the monarchs with whom St Leo maintained friendly relations was St Edward the Confessor, whom he authorized to refound Westminster Abbey in lieu of a pilgrimage he had undertaken to make to Rome. During his pontificate King MacBeth is said to have visited the Holy See—perhaps in expiation of his crimes.

The sources for the life of St Leo IX are much too varied to be enumerated in detail. It must be sufficient to give a general reference to BHL., nn. 4818–4829, and to the notice prefixed to the excellent summary of this pontificate in Mgr H. K. Mann's *Lives of the Popes in the Middle Ages*, vol. vi, pp. 19–182. For the ascetical aspects of the pope's life the earlier portion of Wibert's biography is particularly valuable, and so also are the documents published by Fr A. Poncelet in the *Analecta Bollandiana*, vol. xxv (1906), pp. 258–297. Though ignorant of these last-named materials, O. Delarc's book, *Un pape alsacien* (1876), may still be recommended for its thorough grasp of the conditions of the time ; E. Martin's volume, *St Léon IX*, in the series " Les Saints ", is a convenient handbook. For anyone who wishes to make a study of the subject the works of Martens, Drehmann, Hauck and Brucker, written from quite different standpoints, would also have to be consulted. L. Sittler and P. Stintzi, *St. Léon IX* (1950), is a useful series of studies and excerpts, some with special reference to Alsace.

ST EXPEDITUS (No Date)

It is perhaps necessary to mention St Expeditus, because at one time there was much talk of such a saint, and some good people were led to believe that, when there was need of haste, an undertaking committed to his patronage was likely to meet with prompt settlement. Without going into detail, two definite statements may be made in this matter. The first is that we have no adequate reason to think that any such saint was ever invoked in the early Christian centuries ; in fact it is more than doubtful whether the saint ever existed. We may own that in the " Hieronymianum " the name Expeditus occurs among a group of martyrs both on the 18th and the 19th of April, being assigned in the one case to Rome, and in the other to Melitene in Armenia ; but there is no vestige of any tradition which would corroborate either mention, whereas there is much to suggest that in both lists the introduction of the name is merely a copyist's blunder. Hundreds of similar blunders have been quite definitely proved to exist in the same document.

The second statement has reference to a story which pretends to explain the origin of this " devotion " by an incident of modern date. A packing-case, we are told, containing a *corpo santo* from the catacombs, was sent to a community of nuns in Paris. The date of its dispatch was indicated by the use of the word " spedito ", but the recipients mistook this for the name of the martyr and set to work with great energy to propagate his cult. From these simple beginnings, it is asserted, a devotion to St Expeditus spread rapidly through many Catholic countries. In answer to this it should be pointed out that though the recognition of St Expeditus as the patron of dispatch depends beyond doubt upon a *calembour* or play upon words—there are many similar examples in popular hagiology—still the particular story about the Paris nuns falls to pieces, because as far back as 1781 this supposed martyr, St Expeditus, was chosen patron of the town of Acireale in Sicily, and because pictures of him were in existence in Germany in the eighteenth century which plainly depicted him as a saint to be invoked against procrastination.

Regarding the supposed martyr himself, see the *Analecta Bollandiana*, vol. xxv (1906), pp. 90–98, and the *Acta Sanctorum*, November, vol. ii, part 2, p. 198. The story of the French nuns was told in the *Fortnightly Review*, Oct. 1906, p. 705 ; on which *cf. The Month*,

Nov. 1906, pp. 544–546. Delehaye, in his *Legends of the Saints*, pp. 47–49, gives examples of the developments in popular devotion which have resulted from a play upon words or from a name that has been misunderstood.

ST URSMAR, ABBOT AND BISHOP   (A.D. 713)

THE abbey of Lobbes, one of the most famous in Belgium, was founded by St Landelin in 654. We do not know the name of his immediate successor, but in 689, or shortly afterwards, the government of the abbey was entrusted to St Ursmar, who may, or may not, have been already a bishop. Though various biographies of him were written a century or two later, we learn singularly little about his early history, but conventional phrases about his sanctity, austerity and apostolic zeal occur in abundance. We are told that he consecrated the abbey church of Lobbes in honour of SS. Peter and Paul on August 26, 697, and that he afterwards built a separate church for the people upon the hill-side. Ursmar is also credited with the foundation of other monasteries, and much is said about his missionary work in evangelizing Flanders.

The various lives of St Ursmar have been printed by Mabillon in the *Acta Sanctorum O.S.B.*, vol. iii, part 1, pp. 248–355, and part 2, pp. 608–611. There are also several collections of miracles. But see especially U. Berlière, *Monasticon Belge*, vol. i, pp. 200–201 ; Van der Essen, *Études critiques . . . méroving.*, pp. 71–73 and 76–82 ; and G. Morin in the *Analecta Bollandiana*, vol. xxiii (1904), pp. 315–319. There is also a modern life by C. L. Declèves (1886).

ST GEROLDUS   (A.D. 978)

THE little village of Sankt-Gerold near Mitternach in the Wallgau continues to draw numbers of pilgrims to venerate the tomb of the tenth-century hermit who, with his two sons, lies buried in the church. Various legends have grown up about him but a few details of his life seem to be well established. Geroldus came of the Rhetian family of the counts of Sax, and he was a middle-aged man when he decided to retire from the world to live as a recluse. For years he occupied a hermitage which he had erected in the forest, on a plot of ground given him by his friend and neighbour Count Otto. His own land he had bestowed upon the Benedictine abbey of Einsiedeln, in which his sons Cuno and Ulric were monks, the gift having been sealed by the placing of a basketful of the soil upon our Lady's altar. After the death of Geroldus, his sons obtained permission to occupy their father's cell and to watch over his tomb. In later years, when the forest was cleared, the abbots of Einsiedeln, several of whom were members of the hermit's family, established a church upon the spot. The building was desecrated and reduced to ruin at the Reformation, but in 1663 Abbot Placid of Einsiedeln enshrined the saint's body in a new church beside the relics of Cuno and Ulric.

There is no ancient biography, but an account has been pieced together from various sources in the *Acta Sanctorum*, April, vol. ii ; and see Ringholz, *Geschichte von Einsiedeln*, vol. i.

ST ALPHEGE, ARCHBISHOP OF CANTERBURY, MARTYR   (A.D. 1012)

ST ALPHEGE (Aelfheah ; Elphege) when a young man entered the monastery of Deerhurst in Gloucestershire. Afterwards he withdrew to a deserted place near Bath as a solitary, and eventually became abbot of the monastery at Bath which had been refounded by St Dunstan.   As an abbot Alphege would never tolerate the slightest relaxation of the rule, for he realized how easily a small concession may begin to undermine the regular observance of a religious house ;   he used to say that it was far better for a man to remain in the world than for him to become an imperfect monk.

Upon the death of St Ethelwold in 984, St Dunstan obliged Alphege to accept the bishopric of Winchester, although he was only thirty years of age and shrank from the responsibility.   In this position his high qualities and exceptional abilities found a wider scope.   His liberality to the poor was so great that during the period of his episcopate there were no beggars in the diocese of Winchester.   Adhering to the austerity of his monastic days, he became so thin through prolonged fasts that men declared they could see through his hands when he uplifted them at Mass. The holy prelate had ruled his see wisely for twenty-two years when he was translated to Canterbury in succession to Archbishop Aelfric.   In order to be invested with the pallium, he paid a visit to Rome, where he was received by Pope John XVIII.

At this period England was suffering severely from the ravages of the Danes. Joining forces in 1011 with the rebel earl Edric, they marched into Kent and laid siege to Canterbury ;   the leading citizens urged St Alphege to seek safety in flight. This he absolutely refused to do.   The city was betrayed, when a terrible massacre ensued, men and women, old and young, being put to the sword.   St Alphege hastened to the place where the worst deeds of cruelty were being perpetrated. Pressing through the crowd, he appealed to the Danes to cease their carnage : " Spare those poor innocent victims ", he exclaimed.   " Turn your fury rather against me."   He was immediately seized, roughly handled, and then confined in a dungeon.   Several months later he was released from prison because a mysterious epidemic had broken out amongst the Danes, but although he cured many of the sick by prayer and by giving them blessed bread, the barbarians demanded three thousand gold crowns for his ransom.   The archbishop declared that the country was too poor to pay such a sum.   He was therefore taken to Greenwich and upon a second refusal to pay the money demanded he was barbarously put to death, though a Dane, Thorkell the Tall, tried to save him.   The Anglo-Saxon Chronicle breaks into verse in recording his tragic end :

> Then was he captive . who had been the head
> Of the English race . and of Christendom.
> There was misery to be seen . where bliss had been before
> In that unhappy city . whence came to us first
> Christendom and happiness . in the sight of God and man.

His body was recovered and buried at St Paul's in London, but was translated to Canterbury with great honour by the Danish King Canute in 1023.   That St Alphege did not actually die for the faith was pointed out by one of his successors, Lanfranc, to St Anselm, but the latter replied that in his opinion to die for justice was tantamount to martyrdom.   The English always regarded the holy man as a martyr, and as such his name appears in the Roman Martyrology, while his feast is nowadays observed in the dioceses of Westminster, Clifton, Portsmouth and Southwark.

The Latin Life of St Alphege written by Osbern, a monk of Christchurch, Canterbury, about the year 1087 is most correctly printed in Wharton's *Anglia Sacra* (vol. ii, pp. 122–142). As Freeman has pointed out (*Norman Conquest*, vol. i, pp. 658–660) Osbern cannot be regarded as a trustworthy source ; the information we obtain from the Anglo-Saxon Chronicle, Thietmar and Adam of Bremen is more reliable.   See also Stanton's *Menology*, pp. 164–166, where the references given to English calendars show that the cult of the martyr was general throughout the country.

BD BERNARD THE PENITENT   (A.D. 1182)

NOTHING is known of the early years of this Bernard except that he was born in the diocese of Maguelone in Provence, and even his contemporary biographer could never ascertain of what crimes he had been guilty beyond his participation in a rising which had resulted in the death of an unpopular governor.   We have, however, the exact wording of the certificate which he obtained from his bishop before entering upon his penitential life.

John, by the grace of God Bishop of Maguelone, to all the pastors and faithful of the Catholic Church, eternal salvation in the Lord.   Be it known to you all that in expiation of the horrible crimes committed by him, we have imposed upon Bernard, the bearer of this present letter, the following penance.   He is to go barefoot for seven years : he is not to wear a shirt for the rest of his life : he is to observe the forty days before the Birthday of our Saviour like a Lenten fast : he is to abstain from meat and fat on Wednesdays and from everything but bread and a little wine on Fridays.   On the Fridays of Lent and Embertide he shall drink nothing but water, and on all Saturdays which are not great festivals he shall take no meat or fat unless illness requires it.   Therefore we ask you of your charity in Jesus Christ, for the redemption of your souls and in a spirit of compassion, to give to this very poor penitent the necessary food and clothing and to shorten his penance so far as reason may allow.   Given at Maguelone in the year of the Incarnation of our Lord 1170 in the month of October.   In force for seven years only.

In the garb of a penitent and loaded with heavy iron fetters, Bernard undertook a number of pilgrimages, during which he endured and even courted hardships of all sorts.   Three times, it is said, he visited Jerusalem, and once went as far as India to implore the intercession of St Thomas.   At last one day when he arrived at Saint-Omer, it was revealed to him that his travels were now to cease.   A generous citizen gave him a little house abutting on the monastery of Saint-Bertin, and the monks allowed him access at all hours to their church.   He was always the first at the night offices and he would stand barelegged and barefooted on the stone flags even in the depth of winter when his flesh was cracked and frozen with the cold. He loved to make himself useful by nursing the poor or by cleaning the churches. Bernard came to be a familiar and popular figure as he passed through the streets on his errands of mercy, replying to all greetings with the words, " God grant us all a good end ".   The time came when he ventured to ask the monks to give him the habit, and they welcomed him, for they regarded him as a saint.   Towards the end of his life he was endowed with the gift of prophecy and many miracles were attributed to him ; and after his death the church was thronged by such crowds that the monks had the utmost difficulty in proceeding with the funeral : everyone was begging for some fragment of his garments or for something he had used.   Bd Bernard's biographer testifies that he had been an eye-witness of many of the wonderful cures which he relates.

This life printed in the *Acta Sanctorum*, April, vol. ii, purports to have been written by one John, a monk of the abbey of Saint-Bertin.

BD CONRAD OF ASCOLI   (A.D. 1289)

THE power of foreseeing the future is a gift which is seldom bestowed upon the young, but Conrad Miliani of Ascoli was a mere boy when, as we are told, he knelt before a peasant lad called Jerome Masci and greeted him, whether in jest or earnest, as destined to become pope. The prophecy was fulfilled in time, for Jerome in due course occupied the chair of St Peter as Nicholas IV. Although Conrad was of noble birth, there sprang up between the two youths a close friendship which was to prove lifelong. Together they entered the Franciscan Order, together they were professed, together they studied, and they received their doctor's degree at Perugia on the same day.

Conrad began his public career as a preacher in Rome but, called to the mission-field, he obtained leave of Jerome, by this time minister general of the order, to attempt to evangelize Libya. His success in northern Africa was great : many thousands are said to have been converted by his teaching and miracles. His external activities were the outcome of a life of extreme austerity and of so great a devotion to the Sacred Passion that he was sometimes allowed to behold our Lord crowned with thorns and to take part in His sufferings. Recalled to Italy, probably for reasons of health, he was selected to accompany Jerome, who was proceeding to France as papal legate ; then the envoys returned to Rome, where Conrad spent a couple of years till he was sent to Paris to deliver lectures in theology. Besides attending to his professorial duties he found time to preach in the churches and to visit the sick poor in the hospitals. In 1289 Jerome, now pope, sent for his friend, whom he wished to have in the college of cardinals, but Conrad fell ill before he could reach Rome and died in his native town of Ascoli. His *cultus* was approved by Pope Pius VI.

There is an account of Conrad in the *Acta Sanctorum*, April, vol. ii, but for fuller details we have to turn to Wadding (*Annales Minorum*, vol. v, pp. 212–215) and the other chroniclers of the order. See also Léon, *Auréole Séraphique* (Eng. trans.), vol. ii, pp. 83–88.

BD JAMES DUCKETT, MARTYR   (A.D. 1602)

BD JAMES DUCKETT has a special interest because most of his sentences of imprisonment, as well as his death, were the result of his persistent efforts to keep alive and to spread the faith by the dissemination of Catholic books. A north-countryman, born at Gilfortriggs in Westmorland, he was apprenticed to a printer in London. The perusal of a book called *The Firm Foundation of the Catholic Religion* so shattered his belief in the reformed religion in which he had been bred that he ceased to go to the Protestant services at which he had formerly been a regular attendant. The clergyman in charge of St Edmund's, Lombard Street, to whom he was denounced, sent for the young man, but Duckett frankly told him that he should continue to stay away from church until he had heard more convincing arguments in favour of Protestantism than any hitherto advanced. He was sentenced to two terms of imprisonment, the first at Bridewell and the second in the Compter, his liberation being due in both cases to the intervention of his master who, however, afterwards thought it wiser to break his articles and to sever connection with him. Duckett then sought instruction from an aged priest, Mr Weekes, a prisoner in the Gatehouse, by whom he was reconciled to the Church within two months.

His life is described as having been in all respects most exemplary. He married a Catholic widow to whom he was greatly attached and it is from their son, afterwards prior of the Carthusians at Nieuport, that we have the particulars of his trial and death. His main occupation was dealing in books with which, we are told, " he furnished Catholics as well for their own comfort and instruction as for the assistance of their neighbours' souls ". This work was fraught with such great danger that out of the twelve years of his wedded life he spent nine in prisons in various parts of the country. His final apprehension and conviction were due to the accusations of Peter Bullock, who had bound some books for him and who, being under sentence of death for some offence, seems to have hoped to purchase a reprieve by turning informer. The immediate charge that he had published Father Southwell's " Supplications " to the queen was untrue, but Duckett readily acknowledged that he had had other Catholic books in his possession.

The jury at first refused to convict on the evidence of only one witness, but Chief Justice Popham bade them reconsider their verdict. Thereupon they declared Bd James guilty of felony and he was sentenced to death. To his weeping wife who came to him in prison he said, " If I were made the queen's secretary or treasurer you would not weep. Do but keep yourself God's servant and in the unity of God's Church, and I shall be able to do you more good, being now to go to the King of kings. . . . I take it for a great favour from Almighty God that I am placed among the thieves, as He himself, my Lord and Master, was." He desired her to bear no resentment towards his betrayer who, in spite of his treachery, was to be executed with him. Upon their arrival at Tyburn, to which they were drawn in the same cart—his wife at Holborn Bars bringing him out a pint of wine—he assured Bullock of his forgiveness, and, after exhorting him to die a Catholic, kissed him when they both had the ropes round their necks.

See Challoner, MMP., pp. 261–264 ; Pollen, *Acts of English Martyrs* (1891), pp. 238–248 ; *Publications* of the Catholic Record Society, vol. v, pp. 390–391 ; and M. M. Merrick, *James Duckett* (1947).

20 : ST MARCELLINUS, BISHOP OF EMBRUN (*c.* A.D. 374)

S T MARCELLINUS, venerated as the first bishop of Embrun, was an African priest who, with two companions, St Vincent and St Domninus, evangelized a considerable part of the district known in later times as the Dauphiné. Marcellinus made Embrun his headquarters, building first an oratory on a cliff above the town and afterwards a large church for the accommodation of the citizens, all of whom were converted from paganism by him and by St Domninus. The church had a baptistery in which many miracles of healing took place. St Gregory of Tours and St Ado of Vienne both state that even in their days the font used to fill spontaneously to overflowing on Holy Saturday and at Christmas with water which had wonderful medicinal properties. In consequence of his sanctity and zeal, St Marcellinus was raised to the episcopate by the exiled St Eusebius of Vercelli. St Marcellinus too, during his later years, suffered persecution from the Arians ; ultimately the aged bishop was obliged to escape, and lived for the rest of his life in hiding in the Auvergne Mountains, from whence he made occasional nocturnal visits to Embrun to advise and encourage his faithful clergy and people.

The short life of St Marcellinus, which is printed in the *Acta Sanctorum* (April, vol. ii), is an early document and trustworthy. See Duchesne, *Fastes Épiscopaux*, vol. i, pp. 290–291.

ST MARCIAN, OR MARIAN   (*c.* A.D. 488)

WHEN St Mamertinus was abbot of the monastery which St Germanus had founded at Auxerre, there came to him a young man called Marcian, a fugitive from Bourges then occupied by the Visigoths.   St Mamertinus gave him the habit, and the novice edified all by his piety and obedience.   The abbot, wishing to test him, gave him the lowest possible post—that of cowman and shepherd in the abbey farm at Mérille. Marcian accepted the work cheerfully, and it was noticed that the beasts under his charge throve and multiplied astonishingly.   He seemed to have a strange power over all animals.   The birds flocked to eat out of his hands : bears and wolves departed at his command ; and when a hunted wild boar fled to him for protection, he defended it from its assailants and set it free.   After his death the abbey took the name of this humble monk.

A short biography is printed in the *Acta Sanctorum*, April, vol. ii.

ST CAEDWALLA   (A.D. 689)

ENGLISH-SPEAKING visitors to the crypt of St Peter's at Rome often have their attention called to the epitaph which eulogizes an English king buried in that hallowed spot.   Caedwalla in 685 began a campaign to obtain and to enlarge the West Saxon kingdom.   After several years of savage fighting he made a pilgrimage to Rome, where he received baptism at the hands of Pope St Sergius I on Easter eve in the year 689.   The king was taken ill almost immediately afterwards, and died— as Bede tells us he had wished to die—while still wearing his white baptismal garment.   He was buried in the archbasilica, and his long metrical epitaph (without the prose addition given by Bede) has been preserved from the original stone in old St Peter's.   Caedwalla was the first of several Anglo-Saxon kings who are recorded to have left their kingdoms to go *ad limina Apostolorum*, but there is no evidence that there was any ancient *cultus* of him.

Bede in his *Ecclesiastical History* supplies all our information ; see Plummer's edition and notes.   The king's name is found spelt in over twenty different ways.   For the epitaph, *cf.* F. J. E. Raby, *History of Secular Latin Poetry in the Middle Ages*, vol. i, p. 159.

BD HUGH OF ANZY   (*c.* A.D. 930)

THIS Hugh was educated at the abbey of Saint-Savin in Poitou : there he grew up, received the habit and was ordained priest.   An able organizer and administrator, he was sent to assist Abbot Arnulf in reforming the monastery of St Martin at Autun, and afterwards in a similar capacity to accompany Bd Berno to Baume-les-Messieurs in the diocese of Besançon.   When Duke William of Aquitaine presented Cluny to Berno, Hugh helped him to organize the new foundation.   His last appointment was to be prior of Anzy-le-Duc.   The building of a hospital and other houses is ascribed to Bd Hugh, who obtained a great reputation for his wisdom and miracles. He made war relentlessly upon the idolatrous superstitions which still lingered on amongst the people, especially upon the orgies of the first day of January and on St John's eve.   This holy prior, who lived to a great age, spent his last three years in retirement, preparing for death.   The exact date of his passing is uncertain.

This Hugh is sometimes called Hugh of Poitiers from his birthplace, but there is another Hugh of Poitiers.   The Bollandists print his life in the *Acta Sanctorum*, April, vol. ii.   See also Mabillon in *Acta Sanctorum O.S.B.*, vol. v, pp. 92–104, and F. Cucherat, *Le B. Hugues de Poitiers* (1862).

ST HILDEGUND, Virgin   (A.D. 1188)

THE *cultus* of St Hildegund has never been approved, but on account of its romantic nature her story was popular in the later middle ages. She was the daughter of a knight of Neuss on the Rhine, who after his wife's death decided to make a pilgrimage to the Holy Land, accompanied by his little girl, then twelve years old. For her protection he dressed her as a boy and called her Joseph. The knight died on the way home, and the man to whom he commended the child robbed her and deserted her at Tyre.   However, by some means or other—the accounts are conflicting—she managed to find her way back to Europe, still posing as a boy. After this, " Joseph " became servant to an old canon of Cologne, starting with him on a visit to the pope, then at Verona, and undergoing extraordinary adventures on the way.   She was condemned to death as a supposed robber, was saved by undergoing the ordeal of red-hot iron, was then actually hanged by the robber's confederates, but being cut down finally reached Verona.   Returning to Germany, she was persuaded to try her vocation at Schönau by a female recluse, or as others say, by an old man who had become a lay-brother in the abbey.   She received the Cistercian habit and remained at Schönau until her death, although she made two or three attempts to run away, apparently fearing that her sex would be discovered.   She never took vows, but died a novice.   Only after her death was it discovered that she was a woman.   Her life was written by the monk who had been charged to instruct her because of her ignorance.   To him as well as to the prior she had confided her adventures, but not her sex.

Strange as this story is, it cannot be altogether apocryphal. Besides the long narrative printed in the *Acta Sanctorum*, April, vol. ii, we have a metrical life (in the *Neues Archiv*, vol. vi, pp. 533–536), another recension in prose (in Catalogue of Brussels MSS., vol. ii, pp. 92–95) and, most important of all, an account by Engelhard, abbot of Ebrach, who wrote in 1188, the very year in which the novice died.   This was discovered and edited for the first time by J. Schwartzer in the *Neues Archiv*, vol. vi, pp. 516–521.   See also an article by Father Thurston in *The Month* for February 1916, pp. 145–155.   Caesarius of Heisterbach refers to the story in his *Dialogus miraculorum* (Eng. trans., 1929).

ST AGNES OF MONTEPULCIANO, Virgin   (A.D. 1317)

IN the little Tuscan village of Gracchiano-Vecchio, some three miles from Montepulciano, there was born about the year 1268 to a well-to-do couple a little girl who was destined to become one of the great women saints of the Order of Preachers. When she was nine years old she induced her parents to place her in a convent at Montepulciano, occupied by a community of austere nuns who were popularly nicknamed *Sacchine*, from the coarse material of their habits.   Her religious formation was entrusted to an experienced old sister called Margaret, and she soon edified the whole house by her exceptional progress.   Moreover she was wise beyond her years and was made housekeeper when she was only fourteen.   One day there arrived at the convent a request from Procena that a nun might be sent to take charge of a new convent in their town.   Sister Margaret, who was selected for the purpose, stipulated that she should have Agnes as her assistant, and as soon as it became known that Agnes was at Procena, a number of girls offered themselves to the new foundation, and before long she was elected abbess. A special dispensation had to be obtained from Pope Nicholas IV to authorize the appointment of a girl of fifteen to such a post. From that moment Agnes redoubled her austerities. For fifteen years she lived on bread and water, sleeping on the ground with a stone for a pillow. It was only when she was overtaken by a very severe illness which she bore with exemplary patience that she consented to mitigate her penances. Numerous were the extraordinary graces conferred upon Mother Agnes. Once, in a vision, she was allowed to hold the Infant Saviour in her arms, on several occasions it was reported she received holy communion from an angel, and her nuns declared that they had many times seen her in ecstasy uplifted from the ground. They also bore testimony to the miracles she had wrought, notably the supernatural provision of bread and oil for the convent when food ran short. One of the most curious manifestations recorded of her was that on certain occasions after her raptures her cloak and the place where she was kneeling were covered with white " manna ". She looked, we are told, as if she had been out of doors in a heavy snow-storm.

In the meantime the inhabitants of Montepulciano were becoming anxious to bring back to their town a fellow citizen whose fame had by now become widespread. It was ascertained that Agnes was favourably disposed towards a proposal to build a convent for her ; and as she had by this time realized the lack of permanence inherent in communities like her own, attached to no great order though practising the Rule of St Augustine, it was decided at her suggestion that the new convent should be placed under Dominican patronage. The building was erected on the site previously occupied by several houses of ill fame which had been a disgrace to the town, and as soon as it was completed Agnes bade farewell to Procena.

Upon her arrival at Montepulciano Agnes was installed as prioress, a post she continued to fill until her death. Several remarkable prophecies and cures attributed to the saint belong to this period of her life, and the priory at Montepulciano flourished greatly under her rule. A painful illness afflicted her later days, but she never allowed it to interfere with her usual occupations. It had been preceded by a vision in which an angel had led her under an olive tree and had offered her a cup, saying, " Drink this chalice, spouse of Christ : the Lord Jesus drank it for you ". In compliance with the entreaties of her anxious daughters she resorted to some medicinal springs in the neighbourhood—the convent was not enclosed—but she derived no benefit from them and returned to Montepulciano to die. To the weeping nuns who surrounded her death-bed she said with a sweet smile, " If you loved me, you would be glad because I am about to enter the glory of my Spouse. Do not grieve over much at my departure : I shall not lose sight of you. You will find that I have not abandoned you and you will possess me for ever." She had reached the age of forty-nine.

Amongst the countless pilgrims who visited the tomb of St Agnes may be mentioned the Emperor Charles IV and St Catherine of Siena, who held her in great veneration. When St Catherine visited the shrine it is recorded that as she stooped to kiss the foot of the incorrupt body, the foot lifted itself to meet her lips : the incident has been made famous by several painters. St Agnes was canonized in 1726.

Owing to the comparatively late date at which St Agnes was canonized, the main documents of the process are accessible in printed form. The principal item is a biography by Bd Raymund of Capua, who some fifty years after her death was confessor to the convent. This is also printed in the *Acta Sanctorum*, April, vol. ii.   There are some lives, mostly Italian, of later date, *e.g.* that by G. Bartoli, *Istoria di S. Agnese di Montepulciano* (1779), and one in German by A. Walz (1922).   See also Künstle, *Ikonographie*, vol. ii, pp. 42–43 and Procter, *Lives of Dominican Saints*, pp. 100–103.

BD SIMON OF TODI   (A.D. 1322)

SIMON RINALDUCCI of Todi joined the Hermits of St Augustine in the year 1280. He was a distinguished preacher and became prior of several houses of his order besides being at one time provincial of Umbria.   In a general chapter grave accusations were made against him in his absence by some of his brethren.   Although he could have cleared himself, he chose rather to suffer in silence than to court an inquiry which would certainly have caused scandal and might have led to dissensions in the order.   Bd Simon died at Bologna and many cures took place at his tomb.

See the notice in the *Acta Sanctorum*, April, vol. ii, where an account is printed of the miracles alleged to have been worked at his intercession.   The *confirmatio cultus* was accorded in 1833.

BB. JAMES BELL AND JOHN FINCH, MARTYRS   (A.D. 1584)

A NATIVE of Warrington, educated at Oxford, James Bell was ordained to the priesthood in the days of Queen Mary.   Upon the accession of Elizabeth, he conformed to the state religion, under which he held appointments in several places, but on being reconciled to the Church he was allowed to resume his priestly duties. He had been working zealously for about two years when he was apprehended by a pursuivant who brought him before a magistrate, and he was accordingly sent to Lancaster gaol to await the Lent assizes.   At the trial he acknowledged his priesthood and refused to acknowledge Elizabeth's ecclesiastical supremacy.   When the judge sentenced him to death for high treason, Father Bell said, " I beg your Lordship would add to the sentence that my lips and the tops of my fingers be cut off for having sworn and subscribed to the articles of heretics, contrary both to my conscience and to God's truth ".

Bd John Finch was also a native of Lancashire, but a married layman, a yeoman farmer.   He was reconciled to the Church and was zealous in winning converts as well as in helping priests, to whom he acted as clerk and catechist.   He was arrested, tried at Lancaster with Bd James Bell, condemned for treason, and executed with him on April 20, 1584.

See Challoner, MMP., pp. 100–102 ; Burton and Pollen, LEM., vol. i, pp. 107–126 ; and *Publications* of the Catholic Record Society, vol. v, pp. 74–81, etc.

BB. ROBERT WATKINSON AND FRANCIS PAGE, MARTYRS (A.D. 1602)

ROBERT WATKINSON and Francis Page suffered martyrdom together at Tyburn on April 20, 1602, for the offence of being Catholic priests who were exercising their ministry in England.

Robert Watkinson (who used the alias of John Wilson) was born at Hemingborough in Yorkshire.   He was ordained at Arras, and sent upon the English mission in 1602. Always a delicate man, he was under the care of a physician in London when he was arrested. The previous day he had been accosted in the street by a stranger of venerable appearance, who said, " Jesus bless you, sir : you seem to be sick and troubled with many infirmities ; but be of good cheer, for within four days you shall be cured of all "—a prophecy which was fulfilled on the following Tuesday, when he received the martyr's crown.

Francis Page appears to have been born at Antwerp, although his family belonged to Harrow-on-the-Hill. He was intended for the law and was brought up a Protestant, but after he had formed an attachment to a Catholic gentlewoman he was induced to study her religion. He became a Catholic, gave up all his worldly prospects, and went to Douai, where he was ordained and allowed to return to England. He was betrayed by a woman, tried at the sessions, and condemned to death. In prison he was visited first by extraordinary spiritual consolations and then by great desolation. When told to prepare for execution his peace returned, and he died cheerfully after making a profession of faith and a declaration that he had vowed himself to the Society of Jesus.

See Challoner, MMP., pp. 262–268 ; *Publications* of the Catholic Record Society, vol. v, pp. 375–381 and 390–391.

21 : ST ANSELM, ARCHBISHOP OF CANTERBURY AND DOCTOR OF THE CHURCH (A.D. 1109)

IF the Norman invaders deprived the English nation of its liberty and of many temporal advantages, it must be owned that they brought into it some of its greatest leaders in church and state. Amongst these must be numbered the two archbishops of Canterbury, Lanfranc and his immediate successor. St Anselm was born at Aosta in Piedmont about the year 1033. He wished to enter a monastery when he was fifteen years old, but the abbot to whom he applied refused to accept him, apprehending his father's displeasure. The desire which had been thus thwarted left him for a time, he grew careless about religion, and lived a worldly, if not dissipated, life, of which in after years he never ceased to repent. There was no sympathy between him and his father, who by his harshness practically drove him from home, after his mother's death, to prosecute his studies in Burgundy. Three years later he went to Bec in Normandy attracted by the fame of its great abbot Lanfranc, whose pupil, disciple and friend he became, and also a monk at Bec at the age of twenty-seven in 1060. He had only been a religious for three years when Lanfranc was appointed abbot of St Stephen's at Caen, and he himself was elected prior of Bec. At this promotion several of the monks murmured on account of his youth ; but his patience and gentleness won the allegiance of all, including his bitterest opponent, an undisciplined young man called Osbern whom he gradually led on to strictness of life and whom he nursed with the utmost tenderness in his last illness. An original and independent thinker, endowed with profound learning, St Anselm was the greatest theologian of his age and the " father of Scholasticism " ; as a metaphysician he surpassed all Christian doctors since the days of St Augustine. Whilst still prior of Bec, he wrote his *Monologium*, in which he gave metaphysical proofs of the existence and nature of God, his *Proslogium*, or contemplation of God's attributes, as well as treatises on truth, on freewill, on the origin of evil, and a work on the art of reasoning. With regard to the training of the young, he held quite modern views. To a neighbouring abbot, who was lamenting the poor success which attended his educational efforts, he said : " If you planted a tree in your garden, and bound it on all sides, so that it could not spread out its branches, what kind of a tree would it prove when in after years you gave it room to spread ? Would it not be useless, with its boughs all twisted and tangled ? . . . But that is how you treat your boys . . . cramping them with fears and blows, debarring them also from the enjoyment of any freedom."

In 1078, after he had been prior for fifteen years, Anselm was chosen abbot of Bec. This entailed occasional visits to England, where the abbey possessed property and where his friend Lanfranc was now archbishop of Canterbury. Eadmer, an English monk, from that time forward his devoted disciple and after- wards his biographer, says that he had a method of his own of giving very simple instructions, pointed with homely illustrations, which even the simplest could understand. Anselm was in England in 1092, three years after Lanfranc's death, when the see of Canterbury was being kept vacant for the sake of its revenues by King William Rufus, who in reply to all requests to appoint Anselm swore " By the Holy Face of Lucca "—his favourite oath—that neither Anselm nor anyone else should be archbishop of Canterbury as long as he himself lived. He was, however, induced to change his mind by a sudden illness that brought him to death's door. Stricken with fear, he promised that in future he would govern according to law and nominated Anselm to the archbishopric. The good abbot pleaded his age, ill- health and unfitness for the management of public affairs ; but the bishops and others present forced the pastoral staff into his hand and bore him away to the church where they sang a *Te Deum.*

But the heart of Rufus, though temporarily softened by the fear of death, had not really changed. The new archbishop had not long been installed when the king, with a view to wresting the duchy of Normandy out of his brother Robert's hands, began to make large demands for supplies. Not content with Anselm's offer of five hundred marks (a large sum in those days) the monarch required him to pay a thousand, as the price of his nomination to the see. St Anselm absolutely refused to comply. Moreover, he did not hesitate to urge the king to fill the vacant abbeys and to sanction the convening of those synods whose office it was to repress abuses among clergy and laity. The king angrily replied that his abbeys were no more to be extorted from him than his crown, and from that moment he sought to deprive Anselm of his see. He succeeded in detaching from their obedience a number of time-serving bishops, but when he bade the barons disavow the action of the primate he was met with a blank refusal. An attempt to persuade Pope Urban II to depose the saint was equally futile. The very legate who was charged to tell William that his desire could not be granted brought the pallium which rendered Anselm's position unassailable.

Finding that King William was determined on every possible occasion to oppress the Church unless the clergy would yield to his will, St Anselm sought per- mission to leave the country that he might consult the Holy See. Twice he was met with refusal, but eventually he was told by the monarch that he might depart if he liked, but that if he did so his revenues would be confiscated and he would never be allowed to return. Nevertheless he set out from Canterbury in October 1097, accompanied by Eadmer and another monk called Baldwin. On his way, he stayed first with St Hugh, abbot of Cluny, and then with another Hugh, archbishop of

Lyons. Upon his arrival in Rome, he laid his case before the pope, who not only assured him of his protection, but wrote to the English king to demand Anselm's re-establishment in his rights and possessions. It was while the archbishop was staying in a Campanian monastery, whither he had betaken himself from Rome for the benefit of his health, that he completed his famous book, *Cur Deus Homo*, the most famous treatise on the Incarnation ever written. Despairing of doing any good at Canterbury, and convinced that he could serve God better in a private capacity, he asked the pope to relieve him of his office, but his request was refused, although, as it was obviously impossible for him to return to England at the moment, he was allowed to remain in his Campanian retreat. While there Anselm attended the Council of Bari in 1098, and distinguished himself by his dealing with the difficulties of the Italo-Greek bishops on the matter of the *Filioque*. The council proceeded to denounce the king of England for his simony, his oppression of the Church, his persecution of Anselm and his personal depravity. A solemn anathema was only prevented by the entreaties of the archbishop, who persuaded Pope Urban to confine himself to a threat of excommunication.

The death of William Rufus put an end to St Anselm's exile, and he came back to England amid the rejoicings of king and people. The harmony did not last long. Difficulties arose as soon as Henry I wanted Anselm to be reinvested by him and to make the customary homage for his see. This was contrary to the enactments of a Roman synod in 1099 which had forbidden lay investiture in respect of cathedrals and abbeys, and the archbishop refused. But at this time great apprehension was being felt at the threatened invasion of England by Robert of Normandy, whom many of the barons were not indisposed to support. Eager to have the Church on his side, Henry made lavish promises of future obedience to the Holy See, whilst Anselm did his utmost to prevent a rebellion. Although, as Eadmer points out, Henry owed the retention of his crown in no small measure to St Anselm, yet, as soon as all danger of invasion was passed, he renewed his claim to the right of investiture. The archbishop, on the other hand, absolutely declined to consecrate bishops nominated by the king unless they were canonically elected ; and the divergence grew daily more acute. At last Anselm was persuaded to go in person to lay the questions before the pope, Henry at the same time sending a deputy to state his own case. After due consideration Paschal II confirmed his predecessor's decisions, and Henry thereupon sent word to St Anselm forbidding his return if he continued recalcitrant, and pronouncing the confiscation of his revenues. Eventually the rumour that St Anselm was about to excommunicate him seems thoroughly to have alarmed the English monarch, and at a meeting in Normandy some sort of reconciliation took place. Afterwards in England at a royal council the king renounced the right of investiture to bishoprics or abbeys, whilst Anselm, with the pope's consent, agreed that English bishops should be free to do homage for their temporal possessions. The pact thus made was loyally kept by King Henry, who came to regard the saint with such confidence that he made him regent during an absence in Normandy in 1108. Anselm's health, however, had long been failing— he was by this time an old man—and he died the following year, 1109, amongst the monks of Canterbury.

His was a character of singular charm. It was conspicuous for a sympathy and sincerity which won him the affection of men of all classes and nationalities. His care extended to the very poorest of his people. He was one of the first to stand forward as an opponent of the slave trade. When in 1102 he held a national council at Westminster, primarily for settling ecclesiastical affairs, the archbishop obtained the passing of a resolution to prohibit the practice of selling men like cattle. St Anselm was in 1720 declared a doctor of the Church, though never formally canonized. In Dante's *Paradiso* we find him among the spirits of light and power in the sphere of the sun, next to St John Chrysostom. Eadmer tells a story of him coming upon a boy who had tied a thread to a bird's leg and was jerking it back when it tried to fly. Anselm indignantly snapped the thread and, " ecce filum rumpitur, avis avolat, puer plorat, pater exsultat "—" the bird flies away, the boy howls, and the father rejoices ". The body of the great archbishop is believed still to be in the cathedral church at Canterbury, in the chapel known as St Anselm's, on the south-east side of the high altar.

For our knowledge of the religious and personal character of St Anselm we are almost entirely indebted to the *Historia Novorum* and the *Vita Anselmi* of Eadmer (the best text is that edited in the Rolls Series by Martin Rule), and to the saint's own most attractive letters (edited originally by Dom Gerberon and reprinted in Migne, PL., vols. clviii and clix). A full life of St Anselm in two volumes was published by Martin Rule in 1883, and there are other slighter sketches both in English and in French, such as J. Clayton's (1933) and Cochin in " Les Saints " series. From a non-Catholic standpoint the sympathetic volume by Dean Church (1873), may be commended. For a bibliography of the many studies devoted to St Anselm from a literary, philosophical and theological point of view, see DTC., vol. i, and the *Lexikon für Theologie und Kirche*, vol. i, cc. 467–468. A definitive edition of the saint's *opera omnia* has been completed by Fr Francis Schmitt, o.f.m., in 6 volumes, and Dom A. Stolz has made an excellent study of Anselm's thought (Munich, 1937). Fr Ragey's *Histoire de S. Anselme* (2 vols., 1892) must be used with caution.

SS. SIMEON BARSABAE, Bishop of Seleucia-Ctesiphon, and his Companions, Martyrs   (A.D. 341)

PERHAPS the longest individual notice which occurs in the Roman Martyrology is that devoted to a group of Persian martyrs on this day. It runs as follows : " In Persia the birthday of St Simeon, Bishop of Seleucia and Ctesiphon, who was taken by command of Sapor, King of the Persians, loaded with chains, and brought before iniquitous tribunals. As he refused to worship the sun, and bore testimony to Jesus Christ with clear and constant voice, he was first of all kept for a long time in prison with a hundred others, whereof some were bishops, others priests, others clerics of divers ranks ; then when Usthazanes, the king's tutor, who some time before had lapsed from the faith, but whom the bishop had recalled to repentance, had suffered martyrdom with constancy, on the next day, which was the anniversary of the Lord's passion, the others were all beheaded before the eyes of Simeon, who meanwhile zealously exhorted each of them ; and lastly he himself was beheaded. With him there suffered moreover the men of renown Abdechalas and Ananias, his priests ; Pusicius also, the overseer of the king's workmen, fell by a cruel death, because he had strengthened Ananias when he was wavering, wherefore his neck was severed and his tongue removed ; and after him his daughter also was slain who was a holy virgin."

A hardly less lengthy eulogy is accorded on the next day to another group of Persian martyrs. St Simeon, called Barsabae, *i.e.* son of the fuller, is mentioned in the first place among the martyrs in the little supplement annexed to the Syriac " Breviarium " of A.D. 412 under the heading " The Names of our Masters the Confessors, Bishops of Persia ". There can be no question as to the reality and the cruelty of the persecution which was renewed by Sapor II in 340 or 341, for we hear much about it in Sozomen and other authorities.

The best text of the Passion of St Simeon Barsabae is probably that edited by M. Kmosko in vol. ii of *Patrologia Syriaca*, pp. 661–690. The document had been published long ago by E. Assemani in his *Acta martyrum orientalium*, and there is also an Armenian translation. As has been pointed out by Fr Peeters in the *Analecta Bollandiana* (vol. xxix, pp. 151–156, and vol. xliii, pp. 264–268) as well as in the *Acta Sanctorum*, November, vol. iv, pp. 419–421, several interesting problems arise out of these acts. In particular the name which appears in the Roman Martyrology as Usthazanes and in the Syriac as Guhistazad is probably identical with the name Azadas which figures in the list of Persian martyrs on the next day. A French translation of the acts is printed in Dom Leclercq's *Les Martyrs*, vol. iii, pp. 145–162.

ST ANASTASIUS I, Patriarch of Antioch   (A.D. 599)

St Anastasius I was a man of much learning and piety. According to Evagrius he was little given to speech, and when people discussed temporal affairs in his presence he seemed to have neither ears to hear nor tongue to make answer ; yet he had a great gift for comforting the afflicted. Anastasius was banished from his see for twenty-three years for opposing erroneous teaching that had the support of the Emperors Justinian I and Justin II, but was restored by the Emperor Maurice at the instance of his friend and correspondent Pope St Gregory I. Several of the bishop's letters and sermons have survived.

This Anastasius is often confused (*e.g.*, apparently, in the Roman Martyrology) with St Anastasius the Sinaite, who was a hermit on Mount Sinai a century later. He was afterwards called the " New Moses ", and some of his writings against Monophysism and other works are extant. He died *c.* 700.

Most of what is known concerning the Patriarch Anastasius is recorded by Evagrius and Theophanes. For both saints see the *Acta Sanctorum*, April, vol. ii, DCB., vol. i, DTC., vol. i, and DHG., vol. ii.

ST BEUNO, Abbot   (*c.* A.D. 640)

As in the case of so many of the Celtic saints, the Life of Beuno is a fantastic narrative which merits no confidence. At the very beginning an angel comes to announce to his parents, who had long given up any hope of offspring, that a son is to be born to them. The boy grows up, quits them to be educated in a monastery, and then founds a community himself. But one would judge from the confused record presented to us that he was never long resident in any one place. He moves about and obtains grants of land, upon which he builds churches or founds monasteries. He is thus brought into relation with such prominent figures in Welsh history as Iddon ab Ynyr Gwent and Cadwallon. The most famous incident in the legend is the restoration of St Winifred after her head had been cut off by Caradoc. But this marvel does not stand alone. There are two other occasions on which it is narrated that the dead were brought back to life again by the prayers of the saint.

There can, however, be no doubt that the example and the energetic preaching of St Beuno made a deep impression upon his countrymen in North Wales. He was especially honoured at Clynnog Fawr, where he is believed to have founded some sort of monastery, and which seems most probably to have been the place of his burial. For centuries afterwards, practices, sometimes of a more or less superstitious nature, survived in districts where St Beuno's memory was still revered. Lambs and calves bearing a particular mark were given to the saint's

representatives and then redeemed for a price ; so that an informer writing in the
days of Queen Elizabeth complains that people were very eager to buy these beasts
because, as they held, " Beyno his cattell prosper marvellous well ".   Even two
centuries later this still went on, and the money so realized was put by the church-
wardens into a great chest, called " Cyff Beuno ", for charitable uses.   At the same
period (*c.* 1770) Pennant records how people venerated what was believed to be St
Beuno's tomb at Clynnog Fawr.   " It was customary ", he says, " to cover it with
rushes and leave on it till morning sick children, after making them first undergo
ablution in the neighbouring holy well ; and I myself once saw on it a feather bed,
on which a poor paralytic from Merionethshire had lain the whole night, after
undergoing the same ceremony."   In excavations carried out at Clynnog shortly
before 1914, an ancient square-headed oblong chamber was discovered with walls
three feet thick, and we are told that this probably was " a specimen of the earliest
type of tiny basilica such as might well have been erected in the seventh century ".
St Beuno's feast is kept in the diocese of Menevia.

We have a Welsh life of St Beuno, the earliest copy of which dates only from 1346.
The translation of this by A. W. Wade-Evans, printed in the *Archaeologia Cambrensis*,
vol. lxxxv (1930), pp. 315–341, with the notes appended, is the most valuable contribution
which has been made to St Beuno's history.   The Welsh text is printed in Mr Wade-Evans's
Vitae Sanctorum Brittaniae (1944), and see his *Welsh Christian Origins* (1934), pp. 170–176.
See also J. H. Pollen in *The Month*, vol. lxxx (1894), pp. 235–247 ; LBS., vol. i, pp.
208–221 ; and *Analecta Bollandiana*, vol. lxix, pp. 428–431.

ST MALRUBIUS, or MAELRUBHA, Abbot   (A.D. 722)

LIKE so many other saints who laboured in Scotland, St Maelrubha was by birth
an Irishman, and it was at St Comgall's monastery of Bangor in County Down that
he became a monk.   When twenty-nine years of age he went to Scotland, spending
some time, it is said, at Iona before proceeding to the mainland.   At Applecross in
Ross he established a mission station with a church and monastery, and this became
his headquarters for the rest of his life.   He preached the gospel zealously to the
Picts, extending his labours even to Skye, where his memory was long honoured.
The whole coast between Applecross and Loch Broom came to regard Maelrubha
as its patron saint, and the great impression made by his austerity and teaching is
clear from the number of places which are called after him, such as Maree, Mulruby,
Mary, Mury, Murray, Summuruff, Summereve.   The beautiful island of Eilean
Maree in Loch Maree upon which he built a church contains a spring, known as St
Maelrubha's well, which was famous until quite recent times for its healing pro-
perties, especially in cases of insanity.   For fifty-one years the holy man ruled as
abbot of Applecross, dying at the age of eighty a death which was probably a natural
one, though some accounts call him a martyr.   A hillock called Claodh Maree at
Applecross is pointed out as his grave.   His feast is observed in the diocese of
Aberdeen.

See Forbes, KSS., pp. 382–383 ; Reeves in *Proceedings of Soc. Antiquaries, Scotland,*
vol. iii (1861), pp. 258 *seq. ;* and O'Hanlon, LIS., vol. iv, pp. 255 *seq.* ; and also W. J.
Watson, *History of the Celtic Place-Names of Scotland* (1926), passim.

ST CONRAD OF PARZHAM   (A.D. 1894)

IN its external aspects nothing could offer less of sensation or romantic interest
than the life of this humble Capuchin lay-brother.   Born in the Bavarian village of

Parzham of pious parents, simple folk, but not indigent, Conrad was the ninth and youngest of the family. In his early years he set an example of conscientious industry and of great devotion to the Mother of God. After his parents' death, he entered the noviceship of the Capuchins, being then thirty-one years of age, took his solemn vows in 1852, and shortly afterwards was sent to Altötting, famous for a much venerated shrine of our Lady. There for forty years he discharged the duties of porter, an office which, owing to the multitude of pilgrims who were continually coming and going, offered endless opportunities for the exercise of charity, patience, tact and apostolic zeal. In all these respects he left an ineffaceable impression of self-abnegation and union with God. He seemed to have the gift of reading hearts, and there were occasions on which he manifested a strange knowledge of the future. Worn out with his labours he fell grievously ill in 1894 and died on April 21 of that year. Perhaps the most conclusive testimony to St Conrad's exceptional virtue is the fact that, though the process of beatification was held up by the war of 1914–1918, he was canonized in 1934, only forty years after his death.

The decree of beatification containing a brief biographical sketch is printed in the *Acta Apostolicae Sedis*, vol. xxii (1930), pp. 319–323. See Fr Felice da Porretta, *Il B. Corrado da Parzham* (1930), and Fr Dunstan, *St Conrad of Parzham* (1934).

22 : SS. SOTER AND CAIUS, POPES AND MARTYRS　　(A.D. 174 AND 296)

ST SOTER was raised to the papacy upon the death of St Anicetus. Eusebius has preserved parts of a letter of thanks addressed to the Romans by St Dionysius, bishop of Corinth, in which allusion is made to the pope's fatherly kindness and liberality, especially to those who suffered for the faith. St Dionysius promises that a letter which St Soter had written to him should be read in the assemblies of the Corinthians together with that of Pope St Clement. It has been contended by some that what is known to us as the second epistle of St Clement is no other than this letter. The church honours Soter as a martyr, but no account of his death has been preserved.

Of the life of St Caius, the successor of St Eutychian in the apostolic see, nothing is known. According to a late tradition he was a Dalmatian and a relation of the Emperor Diocletian. Owing to the fury of the persecution in his days, he is said to have lived for eight years concealed in the catacombs and to have been honoured as a martyr because of his sufferings. His epitaph, found in a fragmentary state in the catacomb of St Callixtus, clearly names, in accord with the " Depositio Episcoporum " of the Philocalian calendar, April 22 as the date of his interment.

The little we know about these two popes will be found in the *Acta Sanctorum*, April, vol. iii ; and in the text and notes of Duchesne's edition of the *Liber Pontificalis*. See also on St Caius—De Rossi, *Roma Sotterranea*, vol. iii, pp. 115, 120, and 263 *seq.* ; G. Schneider in *Nuovo Bullettino di archeolog. crist.*, vol. xiii (1902), pp. 147–168 ; and Leclercq in DAC., vol. ii, cc. 1736–1740 ; and vol. vi, cc. 33–37.

SS. EPIPODIUS AND ALEXANDER, MARTYRS　　(A.D. 178)

THE persecution of Christians during the reign of Marcus Aurelius raged with special severity in the city of Lyons. Amongst the victims were two young men, Epipodius and Alexander. They had been friends from childhood, and after the martyrdom of St Pothinus and his companions they left Lyons for a neighbouring town, where they lay hid in the house of a widow. They were eventually arrested, Epipodius in trying to escape losing a shoe, which was treasured as a relic. When brought before the governor they readily acknowledged themselves to be Christians. The people raised an outcry, but the governor marvelled that in spite of the tortures and executions which had already taken place men were still willing to profess Christianity. Having separated the two, he addressed Epipodius, who as the younger appeared the weaker, and by cajolery sought to overcome his resolution. The martyr remaining unmoved, the exasperated magistrate ordered him to be struck on the mouth, but with bleeding lips Epipodius continued to profess his faith until he was stretched on the rack and his sides torn by iron claws. Then, to satisfy the people who clamoured for his death, the governor ordered him to be beheaded. Two days later came the turn of his friend. Reminded of the fate of Epipodius, he thanked God for his example and expressed a fervent desire to join him. Although three executioners took turns in scourging Alexander as he lay on the rack with his legs extended, yet with undaunted courage he repeated his declaration of faith and his abhorrence of idols. He was sentenced to be crucified, but died the moment his mutilated limbs were fastened to the cross.

The acts of these martyrs have been printed both in the *Acta Sanctorum*, April, vol. iii, and by Ruinart. Delehaye describes them as " pas très importants " (*Origines du Culte des Martyrs*, p. 352).

ST LEONIDES, Martyr   (A.D. 202)

THE most illustrious of the Alexandrian martyrs who suffered during the reign of the Emperor Severus was a learned Christian philosopher called Leonides. He was a married man, and the eldest of his seven sons was the great scholar Origen, whom he loved dearly and educated himself with the utmost care. When the persecution was at its height at Alexandria under Laetus, governor of Egypt, Leonides was cast into prison. Origen, at that time only seventeen years old, was consumed by a desire for martyrdom, and so eager to go forth to seek it that his mother locked up all his clothes to keep him at home. He then wrote a touching letter to his father exhorting him to accept with courage and joy the crown that was offered him, adding, " Take heed, sir, that you do not, for our sakes, change your mind ". Leonides was beheaded in the year 202, his property being confiscated and his family reduced to great poverty.

Nearly all that we know of St Leonides is derived from bk vi of Eusebius's *Ecclesiastical History*.

ST AGAPITUS I, Pope   (A.D. 536)

ST AGAPITUS, son of a Roman priest called Gordian, was a deacon of the church of SS. John and Paul when he was elected to the chair of St Peter on the death of John II in 535. He was already an old man, and he survived for less than eleven months, most of which time was taken up by a visit to Constantinople on behalf of the Ostrogothic King Theodahad. Agapitus had to pawn some church vessels to pay the expenses of his journey, and his political mission was not successful. But he did manage, by standing up to the great Justinian, to get the monophysite patriarch Anthimus removed from the see of Constantinople, and Agapitus himself consecrated the monk St Mennas in his place.   He died in Constantinople, and his body was brought back to Rome.   The most important thing known about St Agapitus personally is that in the opinion of Pope St Gregory I he was " a trumpet of the gospel and a herald of righteousness ".

St Agapitus was formerly named in the Roman Martyrology on September 20, and the notice of him in the *Acta Sanctorum* will be found under that day (vol. vi).   See also the *Liber Pontificalis* with Duchesne's notes ; Grisar, *Geschichte Roms und der Päpste* (Eng. trans.), § 326, etc. ; and DHG., vol. i, cc. 887–890.

ST THEODORE OF SYKEON, BISHOP OF ANASTASIOPOLIS   (A.D. 613)

ST THEODORE was born in the Galatian town of Sykeon in Asia Minor, the son of a harlot who kept an inn.   From infancy he was so given to prayer that as a schoolboy he often deprived himself of his meal to spend the dinner hour in church.   At an early age he shut himself up, first in a cellar of his mother's house and then in a cave under a disused chapel.   The desire to escape still more completely from the world led him subsequently to take up his abode for a time on a desert mountain.   He assumed the monastic habit when on a pilgrimage to Jerusalem, and received ordination to the priesthood from his own bishop.   His life was extremely austere. Vegetables were his only food, but of these he partook most sparingly, and he wore an iron girdle about his body.   Endowed with the gifts of prophecy and of miracles, he obtained by his prayers, when on a second visit to the Holy Land, an abundant fall of rain after a severe drought.

Several monasteries were founded by St Theodore, notably one near an ancient chapel dedicated in honour of St George, to whom he had a great devotion, and another at his native town of Sykeon.   Over the latter he ruled as abbot, although he continued to reside mainly in a remote and secluded cell.   Maurice, the general of the armies of the Emperor Tiberius, upon his return from his victorious campaign in Persia, visited the saint, who foretold to him his accession to the imperial throne.   When the prophecy was fulfilled in 582, Maurice did not fail to commend himself and his empire to the holy man's prayers.   By main force Theodore was consecrated bishop of Anastasiopolis—a post for which he felt himself totally unfitted—but after ten years he succeeded in obtaining leave to resign.   From Sykeon whither he joyfully retired he was recalled to Constantinople to bless the emperor and senate, and he then cured one of the emperor's sons of a skin disease, supposed to be leprosy.   St Theodore died at Sykeon on April 22, 613.   He had done much to propagate and popularize the *cultus* of St George.

There is a long account of this St Theodore, written by a contemporary. Perhaps for modern taste it is too much a succession of wonders, anecdotes and encounters with demoniacs, and it is not free from what Dr Baynes calls that " portentous rhetoric which often makes the reading of Byzantine hagiography a weariness of the flesh ".   But it is a fascinating work for all that and, again to quote Dr. Baynes, " the best picture known to us of life in Asia Minor in the Byzantine period before the Arab invasions of the empire ".

In the *Acta Sanctorum* for April, vol. iii, is the Latin translation of the Greek biography, which purports to have been written by a disciple of the saint, Eleusius, called George. The Greek text has been published by Theophilus Joannis, and there is an excellent English version, a little abridged, in E. Dawes and N. H. Baynes, *Three Byzantine Saints* (1948). There is also the Greek text of a lengthy " Encomium " by Nicephorus Scevophylax which adds other details.   This has been edited in the *Analecta Bollandiana*, vol. xx (1901), pp. 249–272.

ST OPPORTUNA, Virgin and Abbess   (*c.* A.D. 770)

St Opportuna was born near Hyesmes in Normandy. At an early age she entered a Benedictine convent near Almenèches, receiving the veil from her brother Chrodegang, bishop of Séez. As a simple nun and afterwards as abbess she edified the whole community by her piety and austerity. Her brother the bishop came to a violent end : he was murdered ; and the tragic fate of this brother to whom she was warmly attached was so great a shock to St Opportuna that she died shortly afterwards, leaving behind the memory of a life of humility, obedience, mortification and prayer. The legends which grew up about her after her death, as well as many reputed miracles, made the saint very popular in France.

There is a life by Adalelmus, Bishop of Séez (best text in Mabillon, vol. iii, part 2, pp. 222–231), but the prominence given to the miraculous element does not inspire confidence. See also L. de la Sicotière, *La vie de ste Opportune* (1867), and Duchesne, *Fastes Épiscopaux*, vol. ii, pp. 231–234.

BD WOLFHELM, Abbot   (A.D. 1091)

Bd Wolfhelm was educated at the cathedral school of Cologne, and after his confirmation, which made a great impression upon him, he determined to consecrate himself to God. He secretly left Cologne where he was well known, and received the habit from Abbot Bernard in the monastery of St Maximinus at Trier. Powerful representations led to his recall to Cologne, where he became a monk in the abbey of St Pantaleon, then under the rule of his uncle Henry. He had been there but a short time when he was made abbot of Gladbach, from whence he was chosen to rule the abbey of Siegburg ; but he found himself overburdened with secular affairs and preferred to retire to the secluded monastery of Brauweiler, where he remained until his death. He was remarkable for his devotion to the rule and for his love of the Bible, the study of which he urged upon all those under his charge. An admirable superior, he instilled into others what he practised himself—a life well balanced between action and contemplation. He was unflinching in maintaining the rights of the Church, whilst never resenting personal slights. Moreover, although he was intensely strict with himself, he was considerate with others and as lenient as was compatible with discipline. In a letter which he addressed to the abbot of Gladbach upon the errors of Berengarius he said : " In order to see the bread and the wine, he [Berengarius] uses the eyes of the body, but at the same time he closes the eyes of the soul and so he does not see the Body and Blood of the Lord ".

Bd Wolfhelm died at the age of seventy-one. His literary activity was considerable and has left many traces in the controversies of the time.

A full but rather characterless life of Wolfhelm, written for edification after the manner of that period by Conrad, a monk of Brauweiler, is printed by Mabillon, by the Bollandists, and in Pertz, MGH., *Scriptores*, vol. xii, pp. 180-195. Wolfhelm played a sufficiently conspicuous part in the history of the times to be noticed in such a work as Hauck's *Kirchengeschichte Deutschlands*, vol. iii, pp. 964-965.

BD FRANCIS OF FABRIANO   (*c.* A.D. 1322)

In the year 1251 there was born at Fabriano to a physician Compagno Venimbeni and his wife Margaret a baby who received the name of Francis. The child, who is said to have come into the world laughing instead of crying, grew up a devout and studious boy.   He entered the Order of Friars Minor when only sixteen, and became equally distinguished for his sanctity and for his learning.   At the close of his novitiate he went to Assisi to gain the Portiuncula indulgence.   There he met Brother Leo, the secretary and confessor of the holy founder, and as the result of their conversations he afterwards wrote a treatise in defence of the indulgence.   Bd Francis, who dearly loved books, is said to have been the first Franciscan to form a library.   An eloquent and persuasive preacher, he succeeded in inducing three of his nephews to relinquish worldly prospects and to become Minorites like himself.   He had a great devotion to the holy souls for whom he celebrated requiem Mass with the utmost fervour.   His own death took place after a lingering fever when he was seventy-one years of age, and his ancient *cultus* was approved in 1775.

A life of Blessed Francis was written by Dominic of Fessis, one of the nephews mentioned above.   This was printed in the *Acta Sanctorum*, April, vol. iii, from a very unsatisfactory copy.   See also Léon, *Auréole Séraphique* (Eng. trans.), vol. ii, pp. 171–175 ; Tassi, *Vita del B. Francesco Venimbeni* (1893) ; and especially the few pages devoted to Bd Francis by Sabatier in his edition of Francis Bartholi, *Tractatus de Indulgentia S. Mariae de Portiuncula*, preface, pp. lxvi–lxix.

BD BARTHOLOMEW OF CERVERE, MARTYR   (A.D. 1466)

THE Dominican priory of Savigliano in Piedmont has had three martyrs, all inquisitors.   Bartholomew of Cervere was actually born at Savigliano, his father being lord of Ruffia, Cervere and Rosano.   At an early age he entered the priory, and was sent to study at Turin, where he attained the unusual distinction of receiving on one and the same day his licentiate, his doctor's degree, and his admission to the magisterial college, as may be seen in the university register.   His exceptional qualifications led to his appointment to the position of inquisitor, which was one fraught with considerable danger, owing to the number of determined heretics in Piedmont.   Bartholomew himself was aware of the fate that awaited him.   On the morning after he had received a summons to go to Cervere, he made what was intended to be a last confession to one of his brethren, adding," They call me Bartholomew of Cervere, although I have never been in the place.   But I am going there to-day as inquisitor, and there I shall die."   His enemies were in fact lying in wait for him, and Bartholomew was murdered as he approached the town.   His ancient *cultus* was approved by Pope Pius IX.

There is a short account of the *beato* in the *Acta Sanctorum*, April, vol. ii, and in Procter, *Lives of Dominican Saints*, pp. 103–105.   See also Taurisano, *Catalogus Hagiographicus O.P.*, p. 42, and C. F. Savio, *Storia Compendiosa di Savigliano* (1925).

23 : ST GEORGE, MARTYR, PROTECTOR OF THE KINGDOM OF ENGLAND (A.D. 303 ?)

THROUGHOUT Europe in the later middle ages the story of St George was best known in the form in which it was presented in the *Legenda Aurea* of Bd James de Voragine.   William Caxton translated the work and printed it.   Therein we are told that St George was a Christian knight and that he was born in Cappadocia.   It chanced, however, that he was riding one day in the province of Lybia, and there he came upon a city called Sylene, near which was a marshy swamp. In this lived a dragon " which envenomed all the country ". The people had mustered together to attack and kill it, but its breath was so terrible that all had fled. To prevent its coming nearer they supplied it every day with two sheep, but when the sheep grew scarce, a human victim had to be substituted. This victim was selected by lot, and the lot just then had fallen on the king's own daughter. No one was willing to take her place, and the maiden had gone forth dressed as a bride to meet her doom. Then St George, coming upon the scene, attacked the dragon and transfixed it with his lance. Further, he borrowed the maiden's girdle, fastened it round the dragon's neck, and with this aid she led the monster captive into the city. " It followed her as if it had been a meek beast and debonair." The people in mortal terror were about to take to flight, but St George told them to have no fear. If only they would believe in Jesus Christ and be baptized, he would slay the dragon. The king and all his subjects gladly assented. The dragon was killed and four ox-carts were needed to carry the carcass to a safe distance. " Then were there well XV thousand men baptized without women and children." The king offered St George great treasures, but he bade them be given to the poor instead. Before taking his leave the good knight left behind four behests : that the king should maintain churches, that he should honour priests, that he should himself diligently attend religious services, and that he should show compassion to the poor.

At this period under the Emperors Diocletian and Maximian a great persecution began against the Christians. George, seeing that some were terrified into apostasy, in order to set a good example went boldly into a public place and cried out, " All the gods of the paynims and gentiles are devils. My God made the heavens and is very God." Datianus the " provost " arrested him and failing to move him by cajolery had him strung up and beaten with clubs and then tortured with red-hot irons. Our Saviour, however, came in the night to restore him to health. Next a magician was brought to prepare a potion for George with deadly poison, but the draught took no effect and the magician, being converted, himself died a martyr. Then followed an attempt to crush the saint between two spiked wheels, and after that to boil him to death in a caldron of molten lead : but without any result. So Datianus once more had recourse to promises and soft words, and George, pretending to be shaken, let them think that he was willing to offer sacrifice. All the people of the city assembled in the temple to witness the surrender of this obstinate blasphemer of the gods ; but George prayed, and fire coming down from Heaven destroyed the building, the idols and the heathen priests, while the earth opened at the same time to swallow them up. Datianus's wife witnessing these things was converted ; but her husband ordered the saint to be decapitated, which took place without difficulty, though Datianus himself returning from the scene was consumed by fire from Heaven.

This is a comparatively mild version of the Acts of St George, which existed from an early date in a great variety of forms. It should be noted, however, that the story of the dragon, though given so much prominence, was a later accretion, of which we have no sure traces before the twelfth century. This puts out of court the attempts made by many folklorists to present St George as no more than a christianized survival of pagan mythology, of Theseus, for example, or Hercules, the former of whom vanquished the Minotaur, the latter the hydra of Lerna. There is every reason to believe that St George was a real martyr who suffered at Diospolis (*i.e.* Lydda) in Palestine, probably before the time of Constantine. Beyond this there seems to be nothing which can be affirmed with any confidence. The cult is certainly early, though the martyr is not mentioned in the Syriac " Breviarium ". But his name (on April 25) is entered in the " Hieronymianum " and assigned to Diospolis, and such pilgrims as Theodosius, the so-called Antoninus and Arculf, from the sixth to the eighth century, all speak of Lydda or Diospolis as the seat of the veneration of St George and as the resting place of his relics. The idea that St George was a Cappadocian and that his *acta* were compiled in Cappadocia " is entirely the responsibility of the compiler of the *acta* who confused the martyr with his namesake, the celebrated George of Cappadocia, the Arian intruder into the see of Alexandria and enemy of St Athanasius " (Father H. Delehaye).

It is not quite clear how St George came to be specially chosen as the patron saint of England. His fame had certainly travelled to the British Isles long before the Norman Conquest. The *Félire* of Oengus, under April 23, speaks of " George, a sun of victories with thirty great thousands ", while Abbot Aelfric tells the whole extravagant story in a metrical homily. William of Malmesbury states that Saints George and Demetrius, " the martyr knights ", were seen assisting the Franks at the battle of Antioch in 1098, and it seems likely that the crusaders, notably King Richard I, came back from the east with a great idea of the power of St George's intercession. At the national synod of Oxford in 1222 St George's day was included among the lesser holidays, and in 1415 the constitution of Archbishop Chichele made it one of the chief feasts of the year. In the interval King Edward III had founded the Order of the Garter, of which St George has always been the patron. During the seventeenth and eighteenth centuries (till 1778) his feast was a holiday of obligation for English Catholics, and Pope Benedict XIV recognized him as the Protector of the Kingdom.

In 1960 this feast was removed from the Calendar of Saints by the Sacred Congregation of Rites.

A very great number of recensions of the supposed Acts of St George exist not only in Greek and Latin, but in Syriac, Coptic, Armenian, Ethiopic, etc., differing often very widely in their contents. See on these texts K. Krumbacher, " Der heilige Georg " in the *Abhandlungen der K. bayerischen Akademie*, vol. xxv, n. 3. Probably the most important contribution to the very considerable literature of the subject is that of H. Delehaye, *Les Légendes grecques des saints militaires* (1909), pp. 45–76, in which a number of bibliographical references are given in the footnotes. Sir E. A. Wallis Budge published a volume, *St George of Lydda* (1930), which is concerned mainly with the Ethiopic texts bearing on St George. See also as representing the more popular aspects of the subject G. F. Hill, *St George the Martyr* (1915) and G. J. Marcus, *Saint George of England* (1929). There is an excellent article by Father Thurston in the *Catholic Encyclopaedia*, vol. vi.

SS. FELIX, FORTUNATUS AND ACHILLEUS, MARTYRS (A.D. 212)

FELIX, a priest, and two deacons, Fortunatus and Achilleus, were sent by St Irenaeus, bishop of Lyons, at the beginning of the third century, to Valence in the district afterwards known as the Dauphiné to evangelize its inhabitants. They all three suffered martyrdom in the reign of Caracalla about the year 212. That is all that is actually known about these saints, but legend has supplied additional details. According to their reputed " acts ", after they had by their preaching and miracles converted a great proportion of the heathen people, they were arrested. From prison they were liberated by angels, at whose bidding they cast down the idols in the temples, destroying with hammers the images of Mercury and Saturn and a valuable amber statue of Jupiter. For this they were promptly seized: their legs were broken, they were tortured on wheels and subjected by day and by night to acrid and suffocating fumes. As they survived all these torments they were eventually beheaded.

An even more fantastic legend than that related connects St Felix, St Fortunatus and St Achilleus with Valencia in Spain. The remains there venerated are certainly those of other saints.

The acts are printed in the *Acta Sanctorum*, April, vol. iii ; though the narrative is of no value, these three martyrs are commemorated and connected with Valence in the " Hieronymianum ". See the *Acta Sanctorum*, November, vol. ii, part 2, p. 205.

ST IBAR, BISHOP OF BEGGERY   (FIFTH CENTURY)

IT is difficult to reconstruct more than the barest outlines of the life of St Ibar from the legendary and often conflicting material at our disposal. The saint was one of the pre-Patrician missionaries in Ireland according to some, but it seems more probable that he was a disciple of St Patrick. Ibar is best known for his association with the island of Beg-Eire (Beggery), where he had a famous monastic school. After a life divided between active labours and monastic contemplation, the holy man died at an advanced age, but the date of his death is uncertain. Beg-Eire means " little Ireland ", and a story is told that when Ibar had a dispute with St Patrick, the great apostle said to him, " Thou shalt not be in Erin " ; to which Ibar replied, " Erin shall be the name of the place in which I am wont to be ".

There is a short account of St Ibar in the *Acta Sanctorum*, April, vol. iii. See also the *Félire* of Oengus (ed. Stokes), pp. 108 and 119 ; O'Hanlon, LIS., vol. iv, pp. 456 *seq.* ; and scattered references in J. Ryan, *Irish Monasticism* (1931). The best summary of the evidence is in Kenney, *Sources for the Early History of Ireland*, vol. i, pp. 310–311.

ST GERARD, BISHOP OF TOUL   (A.D. 994)

COLOGNE was the birthplace of St Gerard in 935. He was educated in the cathedral school with a view to the priesthood, but was led definitely to vow himself to a life of penance and devotion after his mother had been struck dead by lightning—a catastrophe which he regarded (perhaps rather curiously) as a punishment for his own sins. Having joined the community of canons who served the church of St Peter, which was the cathedral, he was in 963 promoted to the bishopric of Toul by Bruno, archbishop of Cologne. St Gerard relaxed none of his former observances, devoting much time to the Divine Office and other regular prayer ; the Bible and the lives of the saints he read daily. Yet his duties were exceedingly onerous, entailing not only the spiritual charge of his diocese, but also its temporal government and the administration of justice.

St Gerard had a great gift for preaching, which he exercised not only in Toul itself but in neighbouring country churches. He rebuilt his cathedral church of St Stephen, enriched the ancient monastery of Saint-Evre, and completed his predecessor's foundation of Saint-Mansuy. His great charity was specially displayed during a famine in 982, and during the pestilence by which it was followed. The Hôtel-Dieu, the oldest hospital in Toul, was one of his foundations. St Gerard pursued the policy of his predecessor St Gauzlin in endeavouring to make of Toul a centre of learning. For that purpose he induced a number of Greek and Irish monks to settle in his diocese. Partly through the instructions given by these strangers in the science of those days and in the Greek language Toul became famous both for scholarship and piety. St Gerard ruled his diocese for thirty-one years and died in the year 994 after a life of great holiness and of unrelenting self-mortification.

St Gerard is an early case of a formal canonization by the Holy See. Pope St Leo IX, who was one of the successors of Gerard in the see of Toul, gave an account in 1050 to the Roman synod there assembled of the vision of the monk Albizo to whom St Gerard had appeared in glory. The assembled fathers thereupon declared unanimously that " the same Lord Gerard was a holy man numbered by God amongst the saints and that he ought to be numbered and venerated among the saints by men also ".

The best text of the Life of St Gerard (which was written by a contemporary, Widric, abbot of Saint-Evre) is that printed in Pertz, MGH., *Scriptores*, vol. iv, pp. 490–505 ; but see also the introductory matter and notes in the *Acta Sanctorum*, April, vol. iii. For the canonization, see H. Delehaye, *Sanctus* (1927), p. 187 ; and E. W. Kemp. *Canonization and Authority* . . . (1948), pp. 62–64.

ST ADALBERT, BISHOP OF PRAGUE, MARTYR   (A.D. 997)

ST ADALBERT was born of a noble family in Bohemia in 956 and received in baptism the name of Voytiekh. He was sent to be educated under St Adalbert at Magdeburg, who gave him his own name at confirmation. On the death of the archbishop the young man returned to Bohemia with a library of books he had collected, and two years later he was ordained subdeacon by Bishop Thietmar of Prague, who died in 982. Adalbert, though so young, was elected to the vacant bishopric. He had been much impressed by the death-bed scruples of Thietmar as to whether he had neglected his episcopal duties, and " It is easy to wear a mitre and carry a crozier ", Adalbert was heard to say, " but it is a terrible thing to have to give account of a bishopric to the Judge of the living and the dead ". Barefoot he entered Prague, where he was received with enthusiasm by Boleslaus II of Bohemia and the people. His first care was to divide the revenues of his see into four parts, of which one was devoted to the upkeep of the fabric and ornaments of the church, a second to the maintenance of his canons, a third to the relief of the poor, whilst the fourth portion was reserved for his own use and for that of his household and guests.

After his consecration at Mainz Adalbert had met St Majolus, abbot of Cluny, at Pavia, and had been fired with Cluniac ideals ; but though he preached assiduously and visited the poor in their homes and the prisoners in their dungeons, he seemed unable to make any impression upon his flock, some of whom were still heathen, while many of the rest were Christian only in name. Thoroughly discouraged, he left his diocese in 990 and went to Rome. A good bishop, of course, does not abandon his charge in the face of pastoral difficulties, and there is evidence that there were serious political complications behind Adalbert's action.

In Italy he came under the influence of the Greek abbot St Nilus at Vallelucio and, together with his step-brother Gaudentius, the bishop became a monk of the abbey of SS. Boniface and Alexis in Rome. But soon Duke Boleslaus asked for his return, and at the bidding of Pope John XV Adalbert returned to Prague, on the understanding, it is said, that he should receive proper support from the civil power. He was well received, and at once proceeded to establish the famous Benedictine abbey of Brevnov, whose church he consecrated in 993. But difficulties again arose, culminating when a noblewoman, convicted of adultery, took refuge with the bishop to escape the sentence of death that was the penalty in those barbarous times. Adalbert sheltered her in the church of some nuns, and defied her accusers in the name of penitence and sanctuary. But the unhappy woman was dragged from the altar and slain on the spot. Adalbert thereupon excommunicated the principals in the affair; and this so aggravated the malice of his political opponents that he had to leave Prague a second time.

St Adalbert went back to his monastery in Rome, and there he remained as prior until a synod under Pope Gregory V, on the insistence of his metropolitan, St Willigis of Mainz, ordered him back again. He was prepared to obey; but it was agreed that he should be free to go and preach the gospel to the heathen if he found it impossible to return to Bohemia, for a powerful section of the citizens of Prague had massacred a number of his kinsmen and burnt their castles. To go amongst them against their will was only to provoke further bloodshed, and therefore the saint turned aside to visit his friend Duke Boleslaus of Poland, by whose advice he sent to Prague to inquire if the people would admit him and obey him as their bishop. They replied with threats, callously adding that they were too bad to mend their ways. Under the patronage of Duke Boleslaus, St Adalbert then directed his efforts to the conversion of pagan Prussians in Pomerania. With his two companions, Benedict and Gaudentius, he made some converts in Danzig, but also met with opposition, for they were regarded with suspicion as Polish spies and told to leave the country. But they refused to abandon their Christian mission, and very soon, on April 23, 997, St Adalbert and his brethren were done to death. Traditionally this happened not far from Königsberg, at a spot between Fischausen and Pillau, but it is more likely to have been somewhere between the Elbing canal and the Nogat river. Adalbert's body was thrown into the water and, being washed up on the Polish coast, it was eventually enshrined at Gniezno; in 1039 the relics were translated (by force) to Prague.

The importance of St Adalbert in the history of central Europe has perhaps been insufficiently appreciated. He was intimate with the Emperor Otto III, and appears to have entered into that monarch's scheme for a *renovatio imperii Romanorum* and the christianization and unification of the remoter parts of Europe. Adalbert sent missionaries to the Magyars and visited them himself, and was the " remote " inspiration of King St Stephen. St Bruno of Querfurt (who wrote his life) was his friend and devoted follower, as was St Astrik, the first archbishop of Hungary; and his memory was influential in Poland, where the foundation of a monastery, either at Miedrzyrzecze in Poznania or at Trzemeszno, is attributed to him. There was some *cultus* of him even in Kiev. The name of St Adalbert has also been associated with Czech and Polish hymnody; one thing seems certain, that he was not opposed to the use of the Slavonic liturgy in the tradition of SS. Cyril and Methodius: hostility to that was rather a product of the Gregorian reformist movement, half a century later. But above all he was a holy man and a martyr, who gave his life rather than cease to witness to Christ; and the wide extent of his *cultus* is the measure of his appreciation.

The sources available for the life of St Adalbert are unusually abundant and early; it must suffice here to give a reference to BHL., nn. 37–56, where the different items are carefully enumerated. There are two contemporary lives, by St Bruno of Querfurt and the Roman monk John Canaparius. The best modern biography is that of H. G. Voigt, *Adalbert von Prag* (1898), which includes a detailed list of sources. See also B. Bretholz, *Geschichte Böhmens und Mährens* . . . (1912); R. Hennig, " Die Missionsfahrt des hl. Adalbert ins Preussenland " in *Forschungen zur Preussischen und Brandenburgischen Geschichte*, vol. xlvii (1935), pp. 139–148; and the *Cambridge History of Poland*, vol. i (1950), pp. 66–68 and *passim*. But the most up-to-date account is F. Dvornik, *The Making of Central and Eastern Europe* (1949), pp. 97–135 and *passim*.

BD GILES OF ASSISI   (A.D. 1262)

OF all the early companions of Francis of Assisi there was no other so dear to his heart as the simple brother whom he called " our Knight of the Round Table ". A young man of singular piety and purity of life, Giles had admired his fellow citizen Francis from afar, but had not ventured to approach him until he learnt that his own friends Bernard and Peter had become his associates, pledged to live with him a life of poverty.   Giles promptly resolved to do likewise.   Going forth out of the city he met the master, and they were deep in conversation when they were accosted by a beggar woman.   " Give her your coat ", said St Francis, when it became clear that neither of them had any money ; and the would-be disciple immediately obeyed.   The test was sufficient : the following day Giles received the habit.   At first he remained with St Francis, accompanying him on his evangelistic tours in the March of Ancona and other places not far from Assisi, but a sermon in which the founder bade his disciples go forth into the world decided Giles to make a pilgrimage to Compostela.   He may be said to have worked his way thither and back, for whenever it was possible he requited alms by personal service ; and he shared everything he received or possessed, including his cloak—regardless of the mockery aroused by his grotesque appearance.   Upon his return to Italy Giles was sent to Rome, where he earned his living by such work as carrying water and hewing wood.   A visit to the Holy Land was followed by a mission to Tunis to convert the Saracens.   The expedition proved a failure ; the Christian residents feared lest they themselves should suffer from the resentment of the Moslems, and, so far from assisting or even welcoming the missionaries, they forced them to return to their ships before they had even begun their mission.   The rest of Brother Giles's life was spent in Italy, mainly at Fabriano, at Rieti and at Perugia, where he died.

Simple though he was and devoid of book-learning, Bd Giles was endowed with an infused wisdom which caused him to be consulted by persons of all conditions. Experience soon taught those who sought his advice to avoid certain topics or words, the very mention of which sent the friar into an ecstasy, during which he appeared lost to the world.   Even the street urchins knew this, and would shout " Paradise ! Paradise ! " when they saw him.   He held learned men in veneration, and once asked St Bonaventure whether the love of ignorant folk for God could equal that of a scholar.   " Yes, indeed ", was the reply.   " A poor illiterate old woman can love Him better than a learned doctor of the Church."   Delighted at this response, Brother Giles rushed to the garden gate which overlooked the entrance to the city and shouted, " Listen, all you good old women !   You can love God better than Brother Bonaventure ! "   He then was rapt in an ecstasy which lasted for three hours.   As far as possible he lived a retired life, in the company of one disciple who afterwards declared that, in all the twenty years they spent together, his master had never uttered a vain word.   His love of silence was indeed remarkable.   A beautiful story relates that St Louis of France on his way to the Holy Land secretly disembarked in Italy to visit its shrines.   At Perugia he sought out Brother Giles, of whom he had heard much.   Having clasped each other in loving embrace, they knelt side by side in prayer and then parted, without having outwardly exchanged a single word.

All through his life Bd Giles was subject to fierce temptations of the Devil, but as a soldier of Christ he took it as a matter of course that he should have to fight his Master's enemy.   Idleness he hated.   When he was living at Rieti, the Cardinal Bishop of Tusculum constantly desired his company at his table, but Giles would only come if he could earn his dinner.   On a very rainy day his host assured him that, since work in the fields was impossible, he would have for once to accept a free meal.   His guest was not so easily put off.   Slipping into the cardinal's kitchen, which he found extremely dirty, Giles helped to give it a good cleaning before returning to his host's table.

The poignant sorrow which he felt at the death of St Francis was followed that same year by the greatest joy of his life, for our Lord appeared to him at Cetona, looking as He had looked upon earth.   Afterwards Giles used to tell the brethren that he had been born four times—on his actual birthday, at his baptism, at the taking of the habit, and on the day he had beheld our Lord.   The golden sayings of Brother Giles, many of which have been preserved, have been often published ; they display deep spirituality combined with shrewd insight.   His *cultus* was confirmed by Pope Pius VI.

The sources for the Life of Blessed Giles are so numerous that no account can be given here.   The main element is a biography, written, it seems, in its primitive form by Brother Leo, but preserved in two distinct recensions known as the Long Life and the Short Life. A full discussion of these and of the other materials will be found in W. W. Seton, *Blessed Giles of Assisi* (1918), who attributes the priority to the Short Life and prints a Latin text and translation.   The Long Life is incorporated in the *Chronica XXIV Generalium*, edited at Quaracchi in 1897.   See also *The Little Flowers of St Francis* (numerous editions) and Léon, *Auréole Séraphique* (Eng. trans.), vol. ii, pp. 89–101.

BD HELEN OF UDINE, Widow   (A.D. 1458)

THE life of Bd Helen up to the age of forty offers a strong contrast to the rude austerity which she afterwards embraced.   A member of the Valentini family of Udine, in north-eastern Italy, she was given in marriage at the age of fifteen to a knight called Antony dei Cavalcanti, and during the twenty-five years of a happy wedded life she appears to have led a normal existence as the mother of a large family of children.   The death of her husband came as a great blow ; she then cut off her beautiful hair, which she laid on the bier together with her jewelled head-dress, saying, " For love of you alone have I worn these : take them down into the earth with you ! "   She decided to become a tertiary of the Hermits of St Augustine, and from that moment devoted herself to works of charity, prayer and mortification.

With the consent of her director Helen took a vow of perpetual silence, which she observed all the year round except on Christmas night.   It is quite clear, however, that this did not extend to her actual household, which included her servants and her sister Perfecta, from whose account many of the details of her religious life are derived.   Great trials beset her at this period.   She was terrified by loud noises and beset by temptations to commit suicide ; at times she was discovered lying bruised upon the ground, twice with a broken leg.   Once as she was crossing a bridge on her way to church she was precipitated into the river, but she scrambled out and attended Mass as usual, regardless of her dripping clothes. But if she was much tried by temptations she was still more consoled by spiritual joys and ecstasies.   She appears also to have been endowed with the gift of healing, many sick persons having been cured at her intercession.   During the last three years of her life she was unable to rise from her bed of stones and straw.   She died at the age of sixty-two on April 23, 1458.

In the *Acta Sanctorum*, April, vol. iii, two lives are printed, the longer and earlier being a translation from an Italian original.   Though they profess to be derived from contemporary sources, they do not leave the impression of being very reliable documents.

24 : ST FIDELIS OF SIGMARINGEN, MARTYR (A.D. 1622)

THE Congregation *de Propaganda Fide* honours as its protomartyr the Capuchin priest St Fidelis, otherwise known as Mark Rey. A native of Sigmaringen in Hohenzollern and a youth of great promise, he was sent to the university of Freiburg in Breisgau, where he taught philosophy whilst he was working for a legal degree. Already he had begun to lead a penitential life, wearing a hair shirt and abstaining from wine. In 1604 he was appointed tutor to a small party of aristocratic Swabian youths who wished to complete their education by supplementary studies in the chief cities of western Europe. During this tour, which seems to have lasted for six years, he won the affection and esteem of his companions, to whom he set the example of religious devotion and of liberality towards the poor, to whom he sometimes gave the clothes off his back. Upon his return to Germany, he took his degree as doctor of laws, and began to practise as an advocate at Ensisheim in Upper Alsace. He soon became known for his integrity and for his studied avoidance of the invective and personalities then too often employed to damage an opponent's case. His espousal of the cause of the oppressed earned him the nickname of The Poor Man's Lawyer ; but the unscrupulous and crooked expedients adopted by his colleagues gave him a disgust for the law, and he decided to enter the Capuchin branch of the Franciscan Order, of which his brother George was already a member. After having received holy orders Mark took the habit, together with the name of Fidelis, chosen in allusion to the promise of a crown of life to those who persevere (Apoc. ii, 10).

Father Fidelis's constant prayer was that he might be preserved from sloth or lukewarmness : " Woe betide me if I should prove myself but a half-hearted soldier in the service of my thorn-crowned Captain ! " he was heard to exclaim. His patrimony was divided into two portions, one of which was distributed to the poor, whilst the other was given to the bishop in aid of needy seminarists. As soon as his theological course was completed, the young Capuchin was employed in preaching and in hearing confessions. He was appointed guardian successively at Rheinfelden, Freiburg and Feldkirch, and whilst he held this last office he not only brought about a reform in the town and in several outlying districts, but also converted numerous Protestants. His great devotion to the sick, many of whom he cured during a severe epidemic, still further enhanced his reputation, and at the request of the bishop of Chur his superiors sent him to preach among the Zwinglians of the Grisons, with eight other Capuchins. This first attempt since the Reformation to reclaim that land from heresy was received by the leading Protestants with threats of violence which Fidelis affected to disregard, although fully aware of the fate that probably awaited him.

From the outset the mission was abundantly blessed, and the newly established Congregation for the Spreading of the Faith formally appointed Father Fidelis leader of the Grisons enterprise. Day after day he gathered fresh recruits into the Church, his success being attributable even more to the prayers in which he spent his nights than to his daily sermons and instructions. The wonderful effects of his zeal inflamed the rage of his adversaries. They roused the peasants against him by representing him as the opponent of their national aspirations for independence and the agent of the Austrian emperor, to whose rule he was said to have counselled submission. St Fidelis, who had been warned, spent several nights in prayer before the Blessed Sacrament or before his crucifix. On April 24, 1622, he preached at Grüsch.   At the close of his sermon, which he had delivered with more than his customary fire, he stood silent for some time in an ecstasy with his eyes looking upwards.   He had spoken in a sermon at Feldkirch of his approaching death and had signed his last letter, " Brother Fidelis who will soon be food for worms ".   He then proceeded to Sewis, and was in the midst of a sermon on " One Lord, one faith, one baptism ", when a gun was fired at him ; but the bullet missed, lodging in the wall.

There was a great tumult, the Austrian soldiers who were about the place were set upon, and a Protestant offered to shelter Fidelis, who thanked him but declined, saying his life was in God's hands.   He tried to retake the road back to Grüsch, but was attacked by a score of armed men, clamouring that he should repudiate his faith. " I came here to enlighten you, not to accept your errors ", was the reply, and he was struck down, calling on God to forgive his murderers as they mangled his body with their weapons.   He was forty-five years old.

The conversion of a Zwinglian minister who was present was one of the first fruits of the martyrdom of St Fidelis of Sigmaringen, who was canonized by Pope Benedict XIV.

The most reliable account of St Fidelis of Sigmaringen seems to be that of F. della Scala, *Der hl. Fidelis von Sigmaringen* (1896).   Much use has been made of this work in the more popular account written by Fr F. de la Motte-Servolex, *St Fidèle de Sigmaringen* (1901).   See also *Nel terzo centenario di san Fedele da Sigmaringa* (1922).   There are several other lives, especially in German, *e.g.* that by B. Gossens (1933), and *cf.* Léon, *Auréole séraphique* (Eng. trans.), vol. ii, pp. 101–104, as also J. G. Mayer, *Geschichte des Bistums Chur* (1914), pp. 399–405.

ST MELLITUS, Archbishop of Canterbury   (a.d. 624)

St Mellitus was a Roman abbot—presumably from the monastery of St Andrew— whom Pope St Gregory the Great despatched to England in 601 at the head of a second band of missionaries to assist St Augustine.   When he had laboured for three years in Kent, he was appointed first bishop of London or of the East Saxons, and baptized King Sabert as well as many of his subjects.   At the death of Sabert his three sons, who had never been baptized, openly reverted to idolatry.   Nevertheless they demanded that Mellitus should give them the Blessed Sacrament— " the fine white bread " they called it—as he had been accustomed to give It to their father.   Upon his refusal they banished him from the kingdom.   Mellitus retired to France, but was soon recalled to Kent, the scene of his earlier labours, and succeeded St Laurence as archbishop of Canterbury in 619.   While prostrate with gout, he stopped by his prayers a great conflagration which was threatening to destroy the city.   The feast of this saint is kept in the dioceses of Westminster, Brentwood and Southwark.

See the *Ecclesiastical History* of Bede with Plummer's notes.

ST IVO, Bishop   (No date)

The town of Saint Ives in Huntingdonshire recalls the memory of a saint who was —supposing indeed that he ever existed—quite a different person from the St Ia who accounts for the Saint Ives in west Cornwall.   All that we can be reasonably sure of is that in accord with some supposed dream or vision (though the vision may well have been invented afterwards) certain bones and episcopal insignia were dug up at Slepe, close to the abbey of Ramsey, about the year 1001 and were enshrined in the abbey church.

In the vision St Ivo had disclosed his name and history. He was a Persian and a bishop, who had, with three companions, run away from the comfort and honour he enjoyed in his own country and eventually found his way to England. There he had settled in the wild fen country, and after being mocked at first for his barbarous speech, had been left alone to live or die unnoticed. After the bones had been removed from the spot where they had lain hidden, a spring appeared at which many miracles were reported. William of Malmesbury tells us that he had been an eye-witness of the remarkable cure of a man suffering from dropsy.

This story became well known after the Norman conquest, but no satisfactory evidence is producible and the whole thing is very suspicious. Since before 1281 this Ivo has been regarded as the patron of Saint Ive, near Liskeard in east Cornwall, probably taking the place of some local patron. Saint Ives in Hampshire is not a saint's name, says Ekwall, but probably a derivative of Old English *ifig*, ivy.

An abbot of Ramsey, Withman, having gone as a pilgrim to Jerusalem in 1021 heard so much of the fame of St Ivo in the East that on his return he wrote a life of him. This was reproduced in more polished style by Goscelin when at Canterbury, and from an imperfect copy his account has been printed in the *Acta Sanctorum*, June, vol. ii. See DCB., vol. iii, p. 324; G. H. Doble, *St Yvo* (1935); and remarks in *Analecta Bollandiana*, vol. liv (1936), p. 202.

ST EGBERT, Bishop (A.D. 729)

ONE of the many Englishmen who in Anglo-Saxon days crossed the sea to acquire sanctity and learning in Ireland was a young monk from Lindisfarne called Egbert. Whilst living at the monastery of Rathmelsigi, during a terrible epidemic of plague, he vowed that if God would grant him time for repentance he would never return to his native land. After his ordination to the priesthood he conceived an ardent desire to evangelize Friesland and the north of Germany. But it was revealed to him that Providence had another design for him, and he abandoned the enterprise to St Wigbert, St Willibrord and others. His own task was to be less glorious, but no less difficult. The great paschal controversy had ended in the general acceptance of the Roman use throughout the British Isles. The celebrated monastery of Iona alone held out, even the efforts of their own abbot Adamnan having been unable to shake the adherence of the monks to the Columban tradition. Thither went St Egbert, who spent the last thirteen years of his life upon the island. By his patient reasoning, enhanced by his reputation for holiness and learning, he succeeded where all others had failed. The very day on which he died, an old man of ninety, the brethren of Iona were keeping Easter day for the first time with the rest of the Western church. It was April 24, 729. His feast is observed in the dioceses of Hexham and Argyll, as a confessor though Bede says he was a bishop.

We know little more than can be learnt from Bede, *Hist. Eccl.*, bks. iii–v, with Plummer's notes. See also Forbes, KSS., p. 331.

ST WILLIAM FIRMATUS (*c.* A.D. 1090)

CANONRIES in the eleventh century were not always reserved for the clergy, and William Firmatus, a gifted young citizen of Tours, was appointed a canon of St Venantius at a very early age, before he had decided upon his future career. He took up soldiering and then medicine, till a dream or vision in which he beheld the

Devil, in the form of an ape, sitting upon his money chest, revealed to him an unconscious tendency to avarice. Immediately he threw up his profession and withdrew into retirement with his widowed mother. At her death he embraced a still more austere mode of life, residing as a hermit in a wood at Laval in Mayenne, where he suffered much from his neighbours, especially from the wiles and accusations of a wicked woman. After a first pilgrimage to Jerusalem, he occupied solitary cells in various parts of Brittany and France—notably at Vitré, Savigny and Mantilly—earning a great reputation for sanctity. A second visit to the Holy Land was followed by a return to Mantilly. St William's power over animals led the peasants to appeal to him for the protection of their gardens and fields from the depredations of wild creatures. We read that with a gentle tap he would admonish the hares and goats that frisked about him and the birds as they nestled for warmth in the folds of his habit. In the case of a particularly destructive wild boar he adopted sterner measures. Leading it by the ear he shut it up in a cell, bidding it fast all night, and, when he set it free in the morning, the beast was cured for ever of its marauding proclivities ! St William died at a date which appears to have been 1090 or a little earlier.

A life is printed in the *Acta Sanctorum*, April, vol. iii, which is attributed to Stephen de Fougères. See also E. A. Pigeon, *Vies des Saints du diocèse de Coutances*, vol. ii, p. 398.

ST MARY EUPHRASIA PELLETIER, Virgin, Foundress of the Institute of Our Lady of Charity of the Good Shepherd (A.D. 1868)

Rose Virginia Pelletier was born in 1796 in the island of Noirmoutier off the coast of Brittany ; her parents had been forced to seek shelter there in the war of La Vendée. Having been sent to school at Tours, Rose came to learn something of the Convent of the Refuge. This belonged to a religious congregation founded in 1641 by St John Eudes for the rescue of " fallen " women and the protection of those in danger. It was known as the Institute of Our Lady of Charity of the Refuge, and it had a house in Tours. Rose joined the noviceship there in 1814, and some eleven years later, when she was still only twenty-nine, was elected superior. In this office she was prevailed upon to make a new foundation at Angers and she herself went temporarily to take over a house of refuge which had existed there years before under the invocation of the Good Shepherd. Her success was marvellous, but there was a sad reaction when she was compelled to leave Angers and return to her own proper community at Tours. In the end, after much negotiation and rather painful controversy, Mother Pelletier was made prioress of the new foundation. Coming before long to realize the difficulties which would hamper their work if each house, as was the case with the Institute of Our Lady of Charity, stood alone, remaining under control of the bishop of the diocese and training its own novices, Mother St Euphrasia (as she was now called) became convinced that a centralized organization was necessary, having one common noviceship, and a superior general who could transfer subjects from one house to another as need required. In spite of strong opposition and the anguish of mind entailed by taking so independent a line, Mother Euphrasia stood firm in what she clearly saw to be a wiser policy to promote the great cause they had at heart.

While deeply humble and respectful of authority, the young prioress, who, as one of her admirers said, " était de taille à gouverner un royaume ", succeeded, God's providence helping, in creating at Angers what was virtually a new institute,

" of the Good Shepherd ".   Papal approbation was obtained in 1835, and the developments were rapid, immense good being visibly effected wherever new foundations were made.   When Mother Euphrasia died in 1868, the Good Shepherd nuns numbered 2760 and were known all over the world.   In all her manifold trials and difficulties, including charges of rash innovation, personal ambition and impatience of authority, St Mary Euphrasia displayed heroic fortitude, cheerfulness and trust in God ;   " Having brought to birth all our young sisters in the Cross ", she said once, " I love them more than life itself.   And the root of that love is in God and in the knowledge of my own unworthiness, for I realize that at the age at which they are professed I could not have supported such deprivations and hard work."   She was canonized in 1940.

There are full biographies in French, both in two volumes, by Mgr Pasquier (1894) and by Canon Portais (1895), and a more recent one (1946) by G. Bernoville in which use has been made of unpublished beatification documents ; shorter ones by E. Georges (1942) and H. Joly (1933) in the " Les Saints " series.   A religious of the congregation published a life in English in 1933, and *Redemption* (1940), by G. F. Powers, is a good popular account of the saint ; the biography by A. M. Clarke is founded on the books of Pasquier and Portais.

25 : ST MARK, Evangelist   (*c.* A.D. 74)

FOR our knowledge of the personal history of St Mark, the author of the second gospel, we are dependent more or less upon conjecture.   It is generally believed that he must be identical with the " John surnamed Mark " of Acts xii 12 and 25, and that the Mary whose house in Jerusalem was a kind of rendezvous for the apostles was consequently his mother.   From Col. iv 10 we learn that Mark was a kinsman of St Barnabas who, as stated in Acts iv 36, was a Levite and a Cypriot, and from this it is not unlikely that St Mark was of a levitical family himself.   When Paul and Barnabas returned to Antioch, after leaving in Jerusalem the alms they had brought, they took John surnamed Mark with them, and in their apostolic mission at Salamis in Cyprus, Mark helped them in their ministry (Acts xiii 5), but when they were at Perga in Pamphylia he left and returned to Jerusalem (Acts xiii 13).   St Paul seems consequently to have suspected Mark of a certain instability, and later, when preparing for a visitation of the churches in Cilicia and the rest of Asia Minor, he refused to include John Mark, though Barnabas desired his company.   The difference of opinion ended in Barnabas separating from St Paul and going with Mark again to Cyprus.   None the less when Paul was undergoing his first captivity in Rome, Mark was with him and a help to him (Col. iv 10).   Also in his second Roman captivity, shortly before his martyrdom, St Paul writes to Timothy, then at Ephesus, enjoining him to " take Mark and bring him with thee, for he is profitable to me for the ministry ".

On the other hand tradition testifies strongly in the sense that the author of the second gospel was intimately associated with St Peter.   Clement of Alexandria (as reported by Eusebius), Irenaeus and Papias speak of St Mark as the interpreter or mouthpiece of St Peter, though Papias declares that Mark had not heard the Lord and had not been His disciple.   In spite of this last utterance, many commentators incline to the view that the young man (Mark xiv 51) who followed our Lord after His arrest was no other than Mark himself.   What is certain is that St Peter, writing from Rome (1 Peter v 13), speaks of " my son Mark " who apparently

was there with him.   We can hardly doubt that this was the evangelist, and there
is at any rate nothing which conclusively shows that this young man is a different
person from the " John surnamed Mark " of the Acts.

Turning to more uncertain documents, we have in the first place to note a
curiously sober narrative—sober in the sense that the miraculous element is very
restrained and the local knowledge exceptional—which purports to have been
written by the same John Mark to give an account of that second visit of Barnabas
and himself to Cyprus, which ended in the martyrdom of the former, here assigned
to A.D. 53.   It is noteworthy that the compiler of this apocryphal " passion " had
apparently no idea that Mark was himself the author of the second gospel, for great
prominence is given to the possession by Barnabas of a record of our Lord's sayings
and doings which he had obtained from St Matthew.   This seems an unlikely detail
to be invented and put in the mouth of one who was himself known to be one of the
four evangelists.   On the other hand the concluding passage represents Mark as
sailing for Alexandria and there devoting himself to the work of teaching others
" what he had learned from the apostles of Christ ".

That St Mark lived for some years in Alexandria and became bishop of that see
is an ancient tradition, though his connection with their native city is not mentioned
either by Clement of Alexandria or by Origen.   Eusebius, however, records it, and
so also does the ancient Latin preface to the vulgate of St Mark's Gospel.   This
last notice, referring to some personal deformity of the evangelist, mentioned also
at an earlier date by Hippolytus, suggests that it was a mutilation self-inflicted to
prevent his ordination to the priesthood of which he deemed himself unworthy.
But while it is quite probable that St Mark did end his days as bishop of Alexandria,
we can put no confidence in the " acts " of his supposed martyrdom.   These are
briefly summarized in the notice which still stands in the Roman Martyrology :
" At Alexandria, the birthday of St Mark the Evangelist, who was the disciple and
interpreter of Peter the Apostle.   He was sent for to Rome by the brethren and
there wrote a gospel, and having finished it, went into Egypt.   He was the first
to preach Christ at Alexandria and formed a church there.   Later he was arrested
for his faith in Christ, bound with cords and grievously tortured by being dragged
over stones.   Then, while shut up in prison, he was comforted by the visit of an
angel, and finally, after our Lord Himself had appeared to him, he was called to the
heavenly kingdom in the eighth year of Nero."

The city of Venice claims to possess the body of St Mark which is supposed to
have been brought there from Alexandria early in the ninth century.   The authenticity of the remains preserved for so many hundred years has not passed unquestioned, and in any case it may be doubted whether the percolation of water, which
for long periods rendered the subterranean *confessio* where they repose quite
inaccessible, has not wrought irreparable damage to the frail contents of the shrine.
It is certain, however, that St Mark has been honoured from time immemorial as
principal patron of the city.   St Mark's emblem, the lion, like the emblems of the
other evangelists, is of very ancient date.   Already in the time of St Augustine and
St Jerome, " the four living creatures " of Apoc. iv 7-8 were held to be typical of
the evangelists, and these holy doctors were reduced to tracing a connection between
St Mark and his lion by the consideration that St Mark's Gospel begins with a
mention of the desert and that the lion is lord of the desert.

On St Mark's day are celebrated the *litaniae majores*, but it should be pointed
out that this solemn procession, formerly associated with a fast, has no connection

of origin with the festival of the holy evangelist. It is not improbable that the *litaniae majores* date back in Rome to the time of St Gregory the Great or even earlier, whereas the liturgical recognition of St Mark on this day was only introduced at a much later period. There can be no reasonable doubt, as Mgr Duchesne long ago pointed out, that the ceremony and prayers of the litany (*i.e.* supplications) are no more than the christianized adaptation of the Robigalia occurring on the same day, which are commemorated in Ovid's *Fasti*. Of this pagan procession and lustration something has been said under Candlemas day, February 2.

In the martyrologies and liturgical tradition of both East and West, Mark the Evangelist and John Mark are regarded as being separate persons. John Mark is in the Greek *Menaion* on September 27, and on the same date the Roman Martyrology has : " At Byblos in Phoenicia, St Mark the bishop, who by blessed Luke is also called John and who was the son of that blessed Mary whose memory is noted on June 29 ". That he became a bishop at Byblos or elsewhere is a tradition of the Greeks, from whom the West acquired it.

The so-called " acts " and other apocryphal documents connected with St Mark are printed in the *Acta Sanctorum*, April, vol. iii ; see also September, vol. vii. The text of the *passio* of St Barnabas attributed to John Mark will be found in the same collection in the second volume for June, under Barnabas, and it has also been edited by Tischendorf in his *Acta Apostolorum Apocrypha*, vol. iii, pp. 292 *seq.* See further the *Dictionnaire de la Bible* and DTC., under " Marc " ; and amongst non-Catholic contributions to the subject the introduction to St Mark's Gospel by C. H. Turner in Bishop Gore's *New Commentary on Holy Scripture* (1928) may be specially recommended, as well as the article by F. Chase in Hastings's *Dictionary of the Bible*. For the relics of St Mark at Venice *cf.* G. Pavanello, in the *Rivista della Città di Venezia*, August, 1928 ; and Moroni, *Dizionario di Erudizione*, vol. xc, pp. 265–268.

ST ANIANUS, BISHOP OF ALEXANDRIA   (FIRST CENTURY)

ACCORDING to the so-called " Acts of St Mark ", St Anianus, the second bishop of Alexandria, had been a shoemaker, whose hand, wounded by an awl, had been healed by the evangelist at his first entrance into the city. Other writers, on the other hand, assert that St Anianus was an Alexandrian of noble family. He is said to have been consecrated bishop in order that he might govern during the absence of St Mark, whom he afterwards succeeded. Eusebius speaks of him as " a man well pleasing to God and admirable in all things ", and Epiphanius mentions a church in Alexandria built in his honour.

See the *Acta Sanctorum*, April, vol. iii.

ST HERIBALD, BISHOP OF AUXERRE   (*c.* A.D. 857)

AN ancient Gallican martyrology asserts of St Heribald that the light of his virtues, hidden for a time in a monastic cell, afterwards spread its rays over the whole of Gaul and drew upon him not only the love but the wonder of his contemporaries. From the abbey of St Germanus, which he ruled, he was promoted to the bishopric of Auxerre ; and he enshrined in a more worthy place the body of St Germanus. The exact date of his death is uncertain.

See Mabillon, *Acta Sanctorum O.S.B.*, vol. iv, part 2, pp. 573–578, and Duchesne, *Fastes Épiscopaux*, vol. ii, pp. 445–446.

BB. ROBERT ANDERTON AND WILLIAM MARSDEN, MAR-
TYRS (A.D. 1586)

ROBERT ANDERTON and William Marsden were two young Lancashire men who were ordained priests at Rheims and sent upon the English mission. The ship which was conveying them to England was driven out of her course to the shore of the Isle of Wight, where the passengers were obliged to disembark. Suspicion at once fell upon the two young men : they were taken before a magistrate to be questioned, and, as they did not deny that they were priests, they were sent to prison. At their trial they protested not only that they had made a forced landing, but also that at the time of their arrest they had not been in England for the statutory period which would bring them within the scope of the penal law. Although this was actually the case, they were found guilty of treason and sentenced to death. A reprieve, however, was granted until the will of the Privy Council could be ascertained, and the prisoners were sent up to London for further examination. In the end they were executed in the Isle of Wight on April 25, 1586, their cheerful fortitude on the scaffold producing a profound impression upon all who witnessed it.

See Challoner, MMP., pp. 114–115 ; Burton and Pollen, LEM., vol. i, pp. 202–210. Fr Pollen in his *Acts of English Martyrs*, pp. 75–80, prints in full the proclamation which was posted up at the time of their execution.

26 : SS. CLETUS AND MARCELLINUS, POPES AND MARTYRS (*c.* A.D. 91 AND A.D. 304)

THE exact order in the succession of the earliest popes has never been satisfactorily established, and it is still a moot point whether St Cletus was the third or the fourth occupant of the chair of St Peter. The fact that he is sometimes referred to by the name of Cletus and sometimes by the Greek equivalent of Anencletus has further confused the issue. It is now, however, agreed that the names belong to the same pope, and that he died about the year 91—probably as a martyr during the reign of Domitian. Nothing else is known about him. He is named, as the third pope, in the present canon of the Mass, and the name Anacletus has now been expunged from the list of popes in the *Annuario Pontificio*.

St Marcellinus followed St Caius in the bishopric of Rome in 296, and reigned eight years. Theodoret states that he acquired great glory in the stormy times of Diocletian's persecution ; on the other hand it was generally believed throughout the middle ages that under fierce trial he yielded up the holy books and offered incense to the gods. The legend, fostered by the Donatists, that he afterwards acknowledged his guilt at a certain Council of Sinuessa, pronouncing at the same time his own deposition, is now universally discredited, no such council having ever taken place ; but ancient breviaries and catalogues of popes certainly allude to the fall of Marcellinus and to his subsequent repentance crowned by martyrdom. If, as seems more than probable, he was guilty of a temporary lapse, he expiated it by a holy death and is honoured as a saint and a martyr, though his actual martyrdom is far from certain. He was buried in the cemetery of St Priscilla which he built or enlarged.

The *Liber Pontificalis* with Mgr Duchesne's introduction and notes supplies the most reliable information concerning the early popes. See also Grisar, *Geschichte Roms und der*

Päpste (Eng. trans.), §§ 185 and 467 ; and E. Casper, *Die älteste röm. Bischofsliste* (1926). It is curious that the name of Marcellinus does not occur in the list of A.D. 354 headed " Depositio Episcoporum " ; his name is omitted from the new Benedictine calendar approved in 1915.

ST PETER, Bishop of Braga   (*c*. A.D. 350 ?)

The principal patron of Braga in Portugal is one of its former bishops, Peter by name, who probably lived in the fourth century and whose relics were translated in 1552 by Balthasar Limpo, archbishop of Braga, from Rates to Braga, where the body was placed in a marble tomb and the head in a silver casket.   Nothing is known of his real history, but local tradition represents him to have been a disciple of St James the Greater, consecrated as the first bishop of Braga, and to have suffered martyrdom after he had baptized and had cured of leprosy the daughter of the king of the district.

It is plain that if St Peter had been a disciple of St James the Greater, he could not have died in 350 ; but see the *Acta Sanctorum*, April, vol. iii, and Florez, *España Sagrada*, vol. iii, pp. 404–405.

ST RICHARIUS, or RIQUIER, Abbot   (*c*. A.D. 645)

The town of Abbeville claims to derive its name from the abbey of St Richarius or Riquier, which once owned the land upon which the city now stands.   The saint was born at Celles, near Amiens, at a period when the population of the district was still largely pagan.   Two Irish priests who landed on the coast and sought to pass through the country met with a hostile reception, and would have been seriously ill-treated had not Richarius protected them.   In return they gave him instruction, as a result of which he was inspired with a desire to become a priest.   After a very penitential preparation he received holy orders and then made a stay of some length in England, apparently to perfect himself in the science of the saints.   Upon his return to France, he began to preach with extraordinary zeal and with great success. He strongly influenced St Adalbald and St Rictrudis, and to King Dagobert he spoke on the dangers and vanities of this world, warning him of his responsibilities. " He who has to obey will only have to render account to God of himself ", he declared, " but he who commands will also have to answer for all his subjects ". With increasing age came the desire to yield up the charge of the abbey he had founded at Celles, and so Richarius withdrew to a hermitage, in which he spent the rest of his life in the company of a disciple called Sigobard.   Over this cell afterwards rose the monastery of Forest-Montiers, between Rue and Crécy.

We have two noteworthy accounts of St Riquier, the one by Alcuin, the other by Angilramnus ; they are printed both in the *Acta Sanctorum*, April, vol. iii, and by Mabillon. See also Corblet, *Hagiographie d'Amiens*, vol. iii, pp. 417–462 ; and MGH., *Scriptores Merov.*, vol. vii, pp. 438–453, for the rhymed *vita* by Hariulf.

ST PASCHASIUS RADBERTUS, Abbot   (*c*. A.D. 860)

St Radbertus was adopted, when left as a motherless babe on their doorstep, by the nuns of Notre-Dame at Soissons, who sent him to be educated by the monks of St Peter in that same city.   He seems to have become engrossed in the Latin classics, and he lived for several years in the world before deciding to enter the religious life.   He received the habit at Corbie and turned his attention to sacred studies, in which he became very proficient.   The abbot St Adalhard and his brother Wala who succeeded him made Radbertus their confidant and their travelling companion on their journeys, whilst he repaid their trust by devoted affection. It was he who after their death wrote the biographies of the two holy abbots.   In 822 he was taken by his superiors to aid in the foundation of New Corbie in Westphalia, and during the years that he was instructor of novices he made the Corbie schools very famous.   He assumed as a prefix the name of Paschasius in deference to the custom then prevalent amongst French men of letters of adopting a classical or scriptural name.   Although Radbertus would never suffer himself to be promoted to the priesthood, yet he was elected to be abbot of Corbie—a post which he found difficult and uncongenial.   Gladly at the close of seven years did he lay down his crozier to retire to the abbey of Saint-Riquier where he could write in peace. His last years, however, were spent at Corbie.   St Paschasius Radbertus was a prolific writer.   Amongst his works are lengthy commentaries on St Matthew and on the forty-fourth psalm, a treatise on the book of Lamentations, the two biographies already mentioned, and a famous book, *De Corpore et Sanguine Christi*.

A short life of Paschasius Radbertus has been edited by Mabillon and in Pertz, MGH., *Scriptores*, vol. xv, pp. 452–454.   See also the *Acta Sanctorum*, April, vol. iii.   Paschasius's eucharistic teaching has been much discussed : on this see Ernst, *Die Lehre d. h. Paschasius Radbertus* (1896).

BD JOHN I, BISHOP OF VALENCE   (A.D. 1146)

LYONS was the birthplace of this John, who when a young canon in the cathedral of his native city made a vow to join the community of Cîteaux, but mistrust of his power of perseverance led him to seek to compound with his conscience by a pilgrimage to Compostela instead.   Vocation, however, was too strong : he had a dream or vision of so terrifying a character that he set off for Cîteaux in the middle of the night.   He proved himself an exemplary monk, and was sent to found the abbey of Bonnevaux.

The diocese of Valence had been suffering under an unworthy bishop called Eustace, whose extravagance and harshness had drawn upon him the reproaches of St Bernard and the excommunication of the Holy See.   He nevertheless clung to office, until the exasperated people in 1141 drove him from his cathedral city.   Three days later the abbot of Bonnevaux was taken off to the cathedral, where he was consecrated in spite of his strong remonstrances. The choice proved an excellent one.   He was a devoted spiritual pastor and a merciful temporal ruler.   When his officials sometimes complained of his leniency, he would remind them that severity had been overdone in the past and that those who are called upon to judge the evildoer might not always be able to resist if faced with his temptations.   The *cultus* of Bd John was approved in 1901.

A life of this holy bishop, written by one Giraudus, has been printed by Martène and Durand in their *Thesaurus novus anecdotorum*, vol. iii, pp. 1693–1702.   See also Nadal, *Histoire hagiologique de Valence*, pp. 273 *seq.*, and such Cistercian historians as Manrique and Le Nain.

ST FRANCA OF PIACENZA, Virgin and Abbess (A.D. 1218)

FRANCA VISALTA was only seven years old when she was placed in the Benedictine convent of St Syrus at Piacenza and fourteen when she was professed. Young though she was, she had already outstripped all her sisters in obedience, devotion and self-denial. After the death of the abbess she was chosen superior, and for a short time all went well. But the zealous young abbess soon began to tighten the reins of discipline, prohibiting amongst other luxurious innovations the practice of cooking vegetables in wine. So bitter was the opposition that Franca was actually deposed in favour of the bishop's sister, who did not share her reforming spirit. For years Franca had to suffer calumny and misrepresentation, as well as severe interior trials. Her one earthly solace was a young girl called Carentia who used to visit her. By her advice Carentia underwent a year's novitiate in the Cistercian convent at Rapallo, and then persuaded her parents to build for the order a house at Montelana which she entered, while it was arranged that St Franca should be transferred from St Syrus to rule the new foundation. Later the community settled at Pittoli. They kept the Cistercian rule in all its poverty and austerity, but even that was not enough for the abbess. Night after night she would go to the chapel to spend in prayer hours which others devoted to sleep. Her daughters, marking with dismay her failing health, bade the sacristan withhold the key, but it would have required more than a key to keep her from her vigil. She died in 1218, and Pope Gregory X, Carentia's kinsman, sanctioned her *cultus* for Piacenza.

In the *Acta Sanctorum*, April, vol. iii, are printed a letter of a contemporary Cistercian prior recounting a vision of one of his monks to whom was revealed the glory of St Franca Visalta, and also a lengthy biography by Father Bertram Recoldi, written in 1336.

BB. DOMINIC and GREGORY (A.D. 1300)

DOMINIC and Gregory were two Dominican friars, living in the first century of the order, who were impelled by zeal for souls to leave their Castilian priory to preach the gospel in Aragon. Their labours lay specially in out-of-the-way districts among the hill folk inhabiting the steep southern spurs of the Pyrenees. Penniless and barefoot they went from hamlet to hamlet, giving spiritual instruction and receiving frugal hospitality. They had taken refuge under a cliff during a severe thunder-storm when a fall of rock buried them beneath it. The ringing of bells startled the inhabitants of the nearest villages, and a strange light is said to have revealed the scene of the catastrophe. The bodies of the two missionaries were recovered and buried at Besiano, where they have ever since been venerated, and their *cultus* was confirmed in 1854.

There is a short account of these *beati* in Seeböck, *Die Herrlichkeit der Katholischen Kirche*, p. 139, and in Procter, *Lives of Dominican Saints*, pp. 106–107. For a fuller bibliography see Taurisano, *Catalogus Hagiographicus O.P.*, p. 23.

BD ALDA, or ALDOBRANDESCA, Widow (A.D. 1309)

THE tomb of Bd Alda was formerly a great centre of devotion in the church of St Thomas at Siena. She was a matron of good position who, upon finding herself a childless widow, retired into a little house outside the walls of Siena. There she devoted herself to almsgiving, and by mortifications tried to fill up the chalice of the sufferings of Christ. She had many visions in which she beheld scenes in the earthly life of our Lord. Gradually she gave away all her possessions and finally she determined to sacrifice her solitude, and went to live in the hospital that she might devote herself to nursing the sick poor. She still continued to be subject to ecstasies. When first she was seen in a state of trance resembling catalepsy, some members of the staff were sceptical and scoffed—even going so far as to pinch her, pierce her with needles, and apply lighted candles to her hands. When she recovered consciousness she felt intense pain from the wounds thus made, but all she said to her tormentors was, " God forgive you ". The experiments were not repeated. Before her death Bd Alda won the veneration of all, and many were the cures attributed to her ministrations.

A short life was published in 1584 by G. Lombardelli : this has been translated into Latin and printed in the *Acta Sanctorum*, April, vol. iii.

ST STEPHEN, Bishop of Perm   (A.D. 1396)

It is related in the life of St Sergius of Radonezh that a bishop was one day travelling to Moscow and, coming level with Sergius's monastery, but some seven miles away, he stopped on his road, bowed low in the direction of Sergius, and said, " Peace be with you, brother in God ". At the same moment St Sergius stood up in the refectory and, bowing towards the far-off road, said, " Be of good cheer, shepherd of Christ's flock. The peace of God be always with you." Later he explained to his brethren that the Bishop Stephen on his way to Moscow had saluted their monastery and called down blessings on them.

From their early Christian days the Russians had sent out missions to the heathen, such as the Mongols and Finns, and in the revival of this zeal during the fourteenth century the outstanding figure was this bishop St Stephen. He was a monk of Rostov, who sometime after 1370 went to preach the gospel to the Zyriane or Permiaks, a people who lived far to the east of the Volga river but south-west of the Ural mountains, among whom he had been born though himself a Russian.

St Stephen was a very worthy successor of St Cyril and St Methodius and his missionary methods are reminiscent of theirs. He believed, as his biographer tells us, that every people should worship God in its own tongue, since languages also are from God, and so one of his first undertakings was to translate the necessary parts of the liturgical services into the language of the Zyriane, and portions of the Holy Scriptures likewise. So convinced was Stephen that every people has its own peculiar contribution to make to God's service that he would not give his converts even the Russian characters : instead he invented an alphabet of letters based on details in the patterns of their embroideries and carvings. And he established schools wherein the use of this alphabet could be learned. Like other Russian missionaries St Stephen used the celebration of public worship as an initial means of attracting the heathen by its beauty and impressive solemnity. He distinguished himself not only as a missionary, but also as a champion of the downtrodden and oppressed so far away as Novgorod and Moscow.

In 1383 his work was recognized by the conferring of episcopal orders, and he became the first bishop of Perm, where he had to oppose by writing and preaching the people called Strigolniks, the first Russian dissenters, who had much in common with the Lollards and Hussites. St Stephen died at Moscow in 1396.

For bibliographical notes on Russian saints, see under St Sergius of Radonezh on September 25.

27 : ST PETER CANISIUS, Doctor of the Church　(A.D. 1597)

ST PETER CANISIUS has been called the Second Apostle of Germany—
our English St Boniface being the first—but he is also honoured as one of
the creators of a Catholic press : he was, moreover, the first " literary "
Jesuit—the forerunner of a great band of writers.　Born in the year 1521 at Nijmegen in Holland, then a German Reichstadt in the archdiocese of Cologne, he was
the eldest son of Jacob Kanis, who had been ennobled after acting as tutor to the
sons of the Duke of Lorraine and who was nine times burgomaster of Nijmegen.
Although Peter had the misfortune to lose his mother at an early age, his father's
second wife proved an excellent stepmother, and he grew up having before his eyes
the fear of God.　He accuses himself of having wasted time as a boy in unprofitable
amusement, but in view of the fact that he took his master of arts degree at Cologne
University when he was only nineteen, it is difficult to believe that he was ever really
idle.　To please his father, who wished him to be a lawyer, he proceeded to Louvain,
where for a few months he studied canon law.　Realizing, however, that he was not
called to this career he refused marriage, took a vow of celibacy, and returned to
Cologne to read theology.　Great interest had been aroused in the Rhineland towns
by the preaching of Bd Peter Faber (Favre), the first disciple of St Ignatius;
Canisius attended an Ignatian retreat which Faber gave at Mainz, and during the
second week made a vow to join the new order.　Admitted as a novice, he lived
for some years a community life in Cologne, spending his time in prayer, in study,
in visiting the sick and instructing the ignorant.　The money which he inherited
upon his father's death was devoted to the relief of the poor and the necessities of
the house.　He had already begun to write, his first publications having been
editions of the works of St Cyril of Alexandria and St Leo the Great.*　After his
ordination to the priesthood, he came into prominence for his preaching ; and as a
delegate to the Council of Trent he had attended two of its sessions, the one at Trent
and the other at Bologna, when he was summoned to Rome by St Ignatius, who
retained him by his side for five months and proved him to be a model religious,
prepared to go anywhere and to do anything.　He was sent to Messina to teach in
the first Jesuit school known to history, but very shortly was recalled to Rome for
his solemn profession and to be given a more important charge.

　　The order was to return to Germany, he having been selected to go to Ingolstadt
with two brother Jesuits, in response to an urgent appeal from Duke William IV of
Bavaria for Catholic professors capable of counteracting the heretical teaching which
was permeating the schools.　Not only was Peter Canisius successful in reforming
the university, of which he was made rector and afterwards vice-chancellor, but he
also effected a real religious revival amongst the people by his sermons, his catechizing, and his campaign against the sale of immoral or heretical books.　Great
was the general regret when in 1552 the saint was withdrawn to undertake, at the
request of King Ferdinand, a somewhat similar mission in Vienna.　He found that
great city in a worse condition than Ingolstadt.　Many parishes were without
clergy, and the Jesuits had to supply the lack as well as to teach in their newly-
founded college.　Not a single priest had been ordained for twenty years ; monasteries lay desolate ; members of the religious orders were jeered at in the streets ;

---

* That he was the editor of the Cologne, 1543, edition of John Tauler's sermons has
not been proved.

nine-tenths of the inhabitants had abandoned the faith, whilst the few who still regarded themselves as Catholics had, for the most part, ceased to practise their religion. At first Peter Canisius preached to almost empty churches, partly because of the general disaffection and partly because his Rhineland German grated on the ears of the Viennese; but he found his way to the heart of the people by his indefatigable ministrations to the sick and dying during an outbreak of the plague. The energy and enterprise of the man was astounding; he was concerned about everything and everybody, from lecturing in the university to visiting the neglected criminals in the jails. The king, the nuncio, the pope himself would fain have seen him appointed to the vacant see of Vienna, but St Ignatius could be induced only to allow him to administer the diocese for one year, and that without episcopal orders, title or emoluments. It was about this period that St Peter began work on his famous catechism, or Summary of Christian Doctrine, published in 1555; this was followed by a Shorter and a Shortest Catechism—both of which attained enormous popularity. These catechisms were to be to the Catholic Reformation what Luther's catechisms were to the Protestant Reformation; they were reprinted over two hundred times and translated into fifteen languages (including English, Braid Scots, Hindustani and Japanese) even during the author's lifetime. And he never by violently or rudely attacking his opponents, either in these catechisms or in any of his instructions, roused hostility towards the truths he wished to commend to his hearers.

In Prague, whither he had gone to assist in founding a college, he learnt with dismay that he had been appointed provincial of a new province which was to include South Germany, Austria and Bohemia. He wrote to St Ignatius: " I am entirely lacking in the tact, prudence and decision essential for ruling others. My temper is hasty and fiery, and my inexperience renders me quite unsuitable for the post." St Ignatius, however, knew better. In the course of his two years' residence in Prague, Peter Canisius in great measure won back the city to the faith, and he established the college on such excellent lines that even Protestants were glad to send their sons to it. In 1557 he went by special invitation to Worms to take part in a discussion between Catholic and Protestant divines, although he was firmly convinced from past experience that all such conferences on doctrine were worse than useless, the heated discussions which always took place only widening the chasm between the disputants. It is quite impossible in limited space to follow the saint on his numerous journeys as provincial, or to provide any adequate survey of his extraordinary activities. Father James Brodrick calculates that he covered 6000 miles during 1555–1558, and 20,000 in thirty years—on foot and on horseback. Canisius was wont to say—no doubt in answer to those who thought he was over-worked—" If you have too much to do, with God's help you will find time to do it all ".

Apart from the colleges he actually founded or inaugurated, he prepared the way for many others. In 1559, at the wish of King Ferdinand, he took up his residence in Augsburg, and this town continued to be his headquarters for six years. Here again the lamp of faith was rekindled by his efforts as he encouraged the faithful, reclaimed the lapsed, and converted many heretics. Moreover he succeeded in persuading the *Reichstag* to decree the restoration of the public schools, which had been destroyed by the Protestants. Whilst he strove most strenuously to prevent the dissemination of immoral and unorthodox literature he encouraged good books to the utmost of his ability, for he clearly foresaw the future importance of the press.

Amongst the works he himself produced at the time may be mentioned a selection of St Jerome's letters, a " Manual for Catholics ", a martyrology and a revision of the Augsburg Breviary. The General Prayer which he composed is still recited in Germany on Sundays. At the close of his term of office as provincial, St Peter took up his abode at Dillingen in Bavaria, where the Jesuits not only had a college of their own but also directed the university. The town had for him the additional attraction of being the favourite place of residence of Cardinal Otto Truchsess who had long been his close friend. He occupied himself mainly in teaching, in hearing confessions, and in the composition of the first of a series of books he had undertaken by order of his superiors. They were intended as a reply to a strongly anti-Catholic history of Christianity which was being published by certain Protestant writers commonly known as the Centuriators of Magdeburg—" the first and worst of all Protestant church histories ". This work he continued afterwards whilst acting as court chaplain for some years at Innsbruck, and until 1577, when he was dispensed from proceeding with it on the score of his health. There seems to have been no curtailment of his activities in other directions, for we find him still preaching, giving missions, accompanying the provincial on his visitations, and even filling the post of vice-provincial.

Canisius was at Dillingen when, in the year 1580, he was instructed to go to Fribourg in Switzerland. That city, which was the capital of a Catholic canton wedged in between two powerful Protestant neighbours, had long desired a college for its sons, but had been handicapped by lack of funds and other difficulties. These obstacles were surmounted within a few years by St Peter, who obtained the money, selected the site, and superintended the erection of the splendid college which developed into the present University of Fribourg. He was, however, neither its rector nor one of its professors, although always keenly interested in its progress. For over eight years his principal work was preaching : on Sundays and festivals he delivered sermons in the cathedral, on weekdays he visited other parts of the canton. It may confidently be asserted that to St Peter Canisius is due the credit of having retained Fribourg in the Catholic fold at a critical period of its history. Increasing bodily infirmities obliged him to give up preaching, and in 1591 a paralytic seizure brought him to the brink of the grave, but he recovered sufficiently to continue writing, with the help of a secretary, until shortly before his death, which took place on December 21, 1597.

St Peter Canisius was canonized and declared a doctor of the Church in 1925. Among the general considerations which arise from his life and personality one of the most important is still his insistence on the spirit and manner in which Christian apologetics and controversy should be conducted. St Ignatius himself had stressed the necessity for " an example of charity and Christian moderation to be given in Germany " ; and among the practical points laid down by Canisius was that it is a mistake " to bring up in conversation subjects to which the Protestants have an antipathy . . . such as confession, satisfaction, purgatory, indulgences, monastic vows and pilgrimages ; the reason being that, like fever patients, they have infected palates and so are incapable of judging aright about such foods. Their need, as that of children, is for milk, and they should be led gently and gradually to those dogmas about which there is dispute ". Canisius was stern towards the leaders and propagators of heresy, and like most other people in those days he was prepared to use force to repress their activities. But the rank and file who had been born in Lutheranism, or had drifted into it, were another matter. He spent a lifetime opposing heresy and restoring Catholic faith and life : and he declared of the Germans that " Certainly an infinite number of them adhere to the new sectaries and err in religious belief, but they do so in such a way as proves that their errors proceed from ignorance rather than malice. They err, I repeat, but without contention, without wilfulness, without obstinacy." And even those who were more consciously and defiantly unorthodox should not be met, he wrote, " in a temper of asperity or . . . with discourtesy, for this is nothing else than the reverse of Christ's example inasmuch as it is to break the bruised reed and quench the smoking flax ".

The activities of St Peter Canisius were so intimately bound up with the whole religious history of Central Europe in his day that no bibliography can be anything but superficial. It is, however, necessary to call attention to the collection of his letters edited in eight stout volumes by Fr O. Braunsberger, with abundant footnotes and marvellously detailed indexes. There is also useful material in the book of J. Metzler, *Die Bekenntnisse des heiligen P. Canisius und sein Testament*, and in many of the volumes of the *Monumenta Historica S.J.* Among biographies, which in the German tongue especially are very numerous, may be mentioned those of O. Braunsberger, J. Metzler and A. O. Pfülf. In French there are lives by L. Michel, J. Genoud and E. Morand. The neglect of Canisius by English writers has now been amply compensated for by Fr James Brodrick's magnificent, definitive and most readable work, *St Peter Canisius* (1935). There is a smaller popular book by W. Reany, *A Champion of the Church* (1931).

ST ANTHIMUS, Bishop of Nicomedia   (A.D. 303)

The persecution under Diocletian and Maximian was waged with particular ferocity at Nicomedia in Bithynia, where the emperors had a favourite residence. When the edict was first posted up, it was torn down by a Christian, moved by a zeal which Lactantius condemns but Eusebius commends. From that time the faithful could neither buy nor sell, draw water or grind corn without being called upon to offer incense to the gods. Eusebius, after relating that Anthimus the bishop was beheaded for confessing the Christian faith, states that an immense number of other martyrs perished also. He adds : " In those days, I do not know how, a fire broke out in the palace, and a false report was spread that we originated it. By the emperor's orders all who were servants of God perished in masses, some by the sword, others by fire. A certain number of men and women, spurred on by an inexplicable divine inspiration, are said to have rushed into the blazing pyre. Innumerable others, bound and placed on rafts or planks, were drowned in the sea." Nearly the whole of the Christian population proved faithful and won the crown of martyrdom. With St Anthimus are also sometimes associated eleven of his fellow-martyrs.

See the *Acta Sanctorum*, April, vol. iii, where besides the allusions of Eusebius and the martyrologies, there is printed a late Greek text of the supposed Acts of St Anthimus. The unreliable legend of SS. Indes and Domna speaks of letters addressed to these martyrs by St Anthimus, but there is no reason to believe him to have been an author. Consequently a curious fragment which Cardinal G. Mercati edited in *Studi e Testi*, n. 5 (1901), and which purports to be part of a dissertation " on the Holy Church " by St Anthimus, is not likely to be authentic. See Bardenhewer, *Geschichte der altkirchlichen Literatur*, vol. ii, pp. 333–334.

ST ASICUS, or TASSACH, Bishop of Elphin   (c. A.D. 470)

St Asicus (Tassach) is the principal patron of Elphin in County Roscommon, and is traditionally regarded as having been the first bishop of that diocese. From some of the early lives of St Patrick it appears that he was one of the great apostle's earliest disciples in Ireland, that he was married, and that he was a clever brass-worker or copper-smith.   He was placed over the church of Elphin, but it is uncertain whether he became a bishop before or after the death of St Patrick. According to one account he resigned his see because he had told an untruth, according to another he presided over an episcopal seminary or monastery; in any case he seems to have failed as a ruler, and he fled to the island of Rathlin O'Birne in Donegal Bay, where he lived in solitude for seven years.   When his monks found him and took him back, he died on the way at Raith Cungi, or Racoon.   The *Félire* of Oengus commemorates St Asicus (on April 14) in these terms : " The royal bishop, Tassach, gave when he came unto him the body of Christ, the truly strong King, at the communion unto Patrick ".   His feast is observed in all Ireland.

There seems to be no proper biography of Asicus, but he is mentioned more than once in Tirechan's collections in the *Book of Armagh* and in the Tripartite Life of St Patrick. See also references in J. Ryan's *Irish Monasticism* (1931), and O'Hanlon, LIS., vol. iv, pp. 406 *seq.*

ST MAUGHOLD, OR MACCUL, BISHOP OF MAN   (c. A.D. 498)

IT is from some of the early lives of St Patrick that we derive the little we know of St Maccul, or Maughold.   A bloodthirsty and wicked freebooter, he was converted by the apostle of Ireland.   As a penance, and to cut him off from his evil associates, St Patrick bade him leave his native land, and he embarked alone, without rudder or oars, in a leather-covered coracle which bore him to the shores of the Isle of Man. Two missionaries had already been sent there by St Patrick, and they gave a kindly reception to the new-comer, who, until their death, led an austere penitential life in that part of the island which afterwards adopted his name.   He is said to have been chosen bishop by the general consent of the Manx people and to have done much by his example and labours to extend the Church of Christ in this land.   To him is attributed the division of the diocese into seventeen parishes.   His feast is kept in the archdiocese of Liverpool, which includes Man.

The name of this saint is very variously written.   He is mentioned (under April 25) in the *Félire* of Oengus as " a rod of gold, a vast ingot, the great Bishop MacCaille ".   Forbes in KSS., p. 380, gives a notice of him under " Machalus ".   See also O'Hanlon, LIS., vol. iv, p. 478.

ST FLORIBERT, BISHOP OF LIÈGE   (A.D. 746)

THE parents of St Floribert were St Hubert and his wife Floribane who died at the birth of her son.   Nothing is known of his earlier years, a tradition that he was abbot of Stavelot and of St Peter's, Ghent, being almost certainly based on confusion between him and some of his namesakes.   He succeeded Hubert as bishop of Liège, which he ruled for eighteen years.   He enshrined the bodies of his father, of his great-aunt St Oda and of St Landoaldus and his companions.   The saint is described as a man of great humility, a lover of the poor, and " vehement in correcting ".

A short account of St Floribert, compiled from various sources, is printed in the *Acta Sanctorum*, April, vol. iii, under April 25.   There seems to be no formal biography of early date.   *Cf.* Duchesne, *Fastes Épiscopaux*, vol. iii, p. 192.

ST STEPHEN PECHERSKY, Bishop of Vladimir   (A.D. 1094)

This Stephen was a disciple of St Theodosius at the monastery of the Caves at Kiev. He absorbed so much of the spirit of his master and walked so closely in his footsteps that when Theodosius died in the year 1074, Stephen was unanimously chosen to take his place at the head of the community. Hitherto he had been engaged in such offices as those of sacristan and precentor, for he was skilled in singing and knowledge of the rites of worship, and one of his first undertakings was to finish building the church which St Theodosius had begun. But after only four years St Stephen was displaced, for what reason is not known. Thereupon he established a new community at Klov, conducting it on the principles he had learned from St Theodosius. This monastery was known as the Blakhernae, from the dedication of its church in honour of our Lady of Blakhernae (a famous shrine church in Constantinople).

St Stephen became bishop of Vladimir in Volhynia in 1091, and died only three years later, leaving a great reputation for the holiness of his life.

From Martynov's *Annus ecclesiasticus Graeco-Slavicus* in *Acta Sanctorum*, October, xi.

ST ZITA, Virgin   (A.D. 1278)

It was in a humble household, as pious as it was poor, that St Zita, the patroness of domestic workers, first saw the light. Her parents were devout Christians, her elder sister afterwards became a Cistercian nun, and her uncle Graziano was a hermit who was locally regarded as a saint. As for Zita herself, it was enough for her mother to say to the child, " This is pleasing to God " or " That would displease God ", to ensure her immediate obedience. At the age of twelve, she went to be a servant at Lucca, eight miles from her native village of Monte Sagrati, in the house of Pagano di Fatinelli, who carried on a wool and silk-weaving business. From the outset she formed the habit of rising during the night for prayer and of attending daily the first Mass at the church of San Frediano. The good food with which she was provided she would distribute to the poor, and more often than not she slept on the bare ground, her bed having been given up to a beggar. For some years she had much to bear from her fellow servants, who despised her way of living, regarded her industry as a silent reproach to themselves, and resented her open abhorrence of evil suggestions and foul language. They even succeeded for a time in prejudicing her employers against her. But she bore all her trials uncomplainingly. After a man-servant had made dishonourable advances from which she had defended herself by scratching his face, she made no attempt to explain or justify her action when her master inquired the cause of the man's disfigurement. Gradually her patience overcame the hostility of the household, and her master and mistress came to realize what a treasure they possessed in Zita.

Her work indeed was part of her religion. In after life she was wont to say, " A servant is not good if she is not industrious : work-shy piety in people of our position is sham piety." The children of the family were committed to her care, and she was made housekeeper. One day the master suddenly expressed his intention of inspecting the stock of beans, for which he thought he could obtain a good sale. Every Christian family in that land and at that period gave food to the hungry, but Zita, as she acknowledged to her mistress, had been led by pity to make considerable inroads on the beans, and Pagano had a violent temper. She could but tremble in her shoes and send up an earnest prayer to Heaven. But no diminution could be detected in the store : that it had been miraculously replenished seemed the only possible explanation. On another occasion when she had unduly protracted her devotions, forgetting that it was baking day, she hurried home to find that she had been forestalled : a row of loaves had been prepared and lay ready to be placed in the oven.

One bitterly cold Christmas eve when Zita insisted upon going to church, her master threw his fur coat over her, bidding her not to lose it. In the entrance to San Frediano she came upon a scantily clad man, whose teeth were chattering with the cold. As he laid an appealing hand upon the coat, Zita immediately placed it upon his shoulders, telling him that he might retain it until she came out of church. When the service was over, neither the man nor the coat were anywhere to be seen. Crestfallen, Zita returned home to encounter the reproaches of Pagano, who was naturally extremely annoyed at so serious a loss. He was about to sit down to his Christmas dinner a few hours later, when a stranger appeared at the door of the room, bearing on his arm the fur coat which he handed to Zita. Master and maid eagerly addressed him, but he disappeared from their sight as suddenly as he had come, leaving in the hearts of all who had seen him a wonderful celestial joy. Since that day the people of Lucca have given the name of " The Angel Door " to the portal of San Frediano in which St Zita met the stranger.

In time Zita became the friend and adviser of the whole house, and the only person who could cope with the master in his rages ; but the general veneration with which she was regarded embarrassed her far more than the slights she had had to bear in her earlier years. On the other hand, she found herself relieved of much of her domestic work and free to visit to her heart's content the sick, the poor and the prisoners. She had a special devotion to criminals under sentence of death, on whose behalf she would spend hours of prayer. In such works of mercy and in divine contemplation she spent the evening of her life. She died very peacefully, on April 27, 1278. She was sixty years of age and had served the same family for forty-eight years. The body of St Zita lies in the church of San Frediano at Lucca, which she had attended so regularly for the greater part of her life.

The principal source is the biography by Fatinellus de Fatinellis printed in the *Acta Sanctorum*, April, vol. iii ; but there are many lives of more recent date, notably that of Bartolommeo Fiorito in 1752, and in quite modern times those of Toussaint (1902) and Ledóchowski (1911). See also the *Analecta Bollandiana*, vol. xlviii (1930), pp. 229–230.

BD PETER ARMENGOL　(A.D. 1304)

IT is very difficult to credit the story of Bd Peter Armengol as it is recounted in Mercedarian sources. He is alleged to have been born about the year 1238 of the family of the counts of Urgel at Guardia in Catalonia, and while yet in his teens to have joined a band of brigands. When King James of Aragon in 1258 sought to pass through that district, an armed guard was sent on ahead under the command of Peter's father. They encountered the brigands, and father and son were on the point of engaging in combat when Peter recognized his opponent. Stricken with remorse, he implored pardon, was converted and spent the rest of his life in doing penance, joining, for that purpose, the Order of Mercedarians (for the redemption of captives). Twice he was sent to Africa to ransom prisoners in captivity among the Moors. On the second occasion, the money he had taken with him was insufficient to secure the release of eighteen young boys ;

whereupon he volunteered to remain as a hostage himself until his companion returned with the ransom demanded.   But the religious who brought it only arrived in time to learn that Peter had been hanged as a defaulter some days before. He went to secure the remains of the martyr, but discovered on cutting the body down that Peter was still living.   He was allowed to return to his fellow religious at Guardia, and there living on for ten years, with twisted neck and contorted limbs, he gave a wonderful example of virtue.   His *cultus* was formally approved in 1686, and his name has since been inserted in the Roman Martyrology.

A sufficient account of Peter Armengol is given in the *Acta Sanctorum*, September, vol. i ; but doubts may very well be felt regarding the authenticity of most of the scanty documents there reprinted from the process of beatification.   Cf. under St Peter Nolasco, on January 28, concerning the early records of the Mercedarian Order.   A short account of Bd Peter in French, by J. Cartier, appeared in 1898.

BD ANTONY OF SIENA   (A.D. 1311)

A MEMBER of one of the principal Sienese families, Bd Antony de' Patrizi entered the Order of the Hermits of St Augustine and afterwards became superior of their house at Monteciano.   The only notable fact which seems to be recorded of him is that he was possessed by a very great desire of conversing with another holy hermit, Peter of Camerata.   He set out to find him, fell grievously ill upon the way, but after fervent prayer was miraculously restored and was able to accomplish the object of his journey.   The meeting of the two men is compared by his biographer to the meeting of St Paul the Hermit and St Antony at the very beginning of Christian ascetic history.   This Antony lived a very holy life and died in the year 1311.

There is a short biography printed in the *Acta Sanctorum*, April, vol. iii (under April 30) but it is mainly taken up with the miracles wrought after the hermit's death.   See also G. Ballati, *Vita, miracoli e grazie del B. Antonio Patrizi* (1728).

BD JAMES OF BITETTO   (*c.* A.D. 1485)

ALTHOUGH a native of Dalmatia, whence he is sometimes called " the Slav " or " the Illyrian ", Bd James spent the greater part of his life on the opposite coast of the Adriatic, where he became a lay-brother of the Friars Minor of the Observance at Bitetto, a small town nine miles from Bari.   Through humility, self-denial and contemplation he attained to great holiness.   He was favoured by God with a prophetic spirit and, according to the deposition of a fellow friar in the process for his beatification, he was seen on occasions upraised from the ground when engaged in prayer.   In another house of the order, at Conversano, he was employed for some years as cook.   The sight of the kitchen fire led him at times to contemplate the flames of Hell and on other occasions to soar in spirit to the highest Heaven to dwell on the consuming fire of eternal love.   Thus he often fell into ecstasies over his work, standing motionless and entirely absorbed in God.   Afterwards Bd James was transferred back to Bitetto, where he closed a holy life by a happy death.   Many miracles were ascribed to his intercession, and in the garden at Bitetto there used to be a juniper tree which he had planted, the berries of which were said to possess healing properties.   He was beatified by Pope Innocent XII.

The notice of James de Bitetto in the *Acta Sanctorum*, April, vol. iii, is interesting because this is one of the cases in which the Bollandists have had access to the documents submitted for the beatification process, and have been able to print the evidence of the various witnesses. See also Léon, *Auréole Séraphique* (Eng. trans.), vol. ii, pp. 104–105.

BD OSANNA OF CATTARO, VIRGIN   (A.D. 1565)

CATHERINE COSIE was a Montenegrin girl born in 1493, the daughter of dissident Orthodox parents. Her early years seem to have been spent mostly with the flocks and herds, but later she was allowed by her parents to enter the service of a Catholic lady at Cattaro, where she made herself beloved. After seven years she undertook the seclusion of an anchoress, first in a cell adjoining the church of St Bartholomew, and afterwards in one attached to the church of St Paul. On becoming a Dominican tertiary she had taken the name of Osanna in veneration for Bd Osanna Andreasi, who had died not long before, in 1505. Young women and matrons crowded to her anchorage and were guided by her counsels. Her prayers, it was believed, protected the city from the inroads of Turks and other raiders. She had much to suffer, both from the assaults of Satan within and from calumny without, but she was graced with many supernatural gifts, such as that of prophecy. Finally after a grievous illness of two months borne with exemplary patience, she went to her reward on April 27, 1565. The *cultus* was confirmed in 1928.

The decree in the *Acta Apostolicae Sedis*, vol. xx (1928), pp. 39–42, sets out the above facts and appeals to the testimony of earlier authors, in particular to Father Bazzi in 1589 and to Father Cerva in 1738, who have borne witness to the holiness of her life and to the veneration uninterruptedly shown since her death.

ST TURIBIUS, ARCHBISHOP OF LIMA   (A.D. 1606)

ST TURIBIUS is, equally with St Rose of Lima, the first known saint of the New World. It is true that he was not born on the American continent, and not canonized until fifty-five years after her; but they lived in the same place at the same time, Turibius died first, and it was he who conferred the sacrament of confirmation on Rose. His memory is held in great veneration throughout Peru, for although he did not plant Christianity in that land he greatly promoted it, and cleansed the Church there from grave abuses which were sapping its vitality and bringing discredit upon its name; his feast is, moreover, observed throughout South America.

Turibius, Toribio Alfonso de Mogrobejo, was born in 1538 at Mayorga in Spain. His childhood and youth were notably religious, but he had no intention of becoming a priest and was, in fact, educated for the law. He was so brilliant a scholar that he became professor of law in the University of Salamanca, and while there he attracted the notice of King Philip II (widower of Mary I of England), who eventually made him chief judge of the ecclesiastical court of the Inquisition at Granada. This was a surprising position for a layman to hold, and it was not a pleasant or easy post for anyone, lay or cleric. But it led to an even more surprising development. After some years the archbishopric of Lima in the Spanish colony of Peru became vacant. Turibius had carried out his judge's duties so well, and displayed such a fine missionary spirit, that it was decided to send him to Peru as archbishop : he seemed to be the one person who had force of character sufficient to remedy the serious scandals which stood in the way of the conversion of the Peruvians.

Turibius himself was shocked by the decision, and he wrote forthwith to the royal council, pleading his incapacity and appealing to the canons which forbade the promotion of laymen to ecclesiastical dignities. His objections were overruled ; he received all the orders and episcopal consecration, and immediately afterwards sailed for Peru. Arriving in Lima in 1581, it did not take him long to realize the arduous nature of the charge which had been laid upon him. His diocese stretched for some 400 miles along the coast, and inland amongst the spurs of the Andes, a most difficult country to traverse. Far more serious, however, than the physical difficulties were those created by the attitude of the Spanish conquerors towards the native population. With few exceptions the officials and colonists had come there to make their fortunes, and they made the Indians serve that purpose by every sort of extortion and tyranny. Communications with the central authority at home were incredibly slow. The most flagrant abuses might continue for years without the possibility of redress and, the Spaniards quarrelling continually among themselves and sending home contradictory reports, it was often impossible for the supreme Council of the Indies to know whom to believe. Worse than all the sense of religion seemed to be completely lost, and the example given to the natives was one of almost universal rapacity and self-indulgence.

The clergy themselves were often among the most notorious offenders, and it was the first care of Turibius to restore ecclesiastical discipline. He at once undertook a visitation of his diocese, and was inflexible in regard to scandals amongst the clergy. Without respect of persons, he reproved injustice and vice, using his authority always to protect the poor from oppression. He naturally suffered persecution from those in power, who often thwarted him in the discharge of his duties, but by resolution and patience he overcame their opposition in the end. To those who tried to twist God's law to make it accord with their evil practice he would oppose the words of Tertullian : " Christ said, ' I am the truth '. He did not say, ' I am the custom '." The archbishop succeeded in eradicating some of the worst abuses, and he founded numerous churches, religious houses and hospitals ; in 1591 he established at Lima the first ecclesiastical seminary in the New World.

Right on into old age St Turibius continued to study the Indian dialects so that he could address the people in their own speech and not through an interpreter. Thus he succeeded in making many conversions. In order to teach his flock he would sometimes stay two or three days in a place where he had neither bed nor sufficient food. Every part of his vast diocese was visited, and when danger threatened from marauders or physical obstacles he would say that Christ came from Heaven to save man and that we ought not to fear danger for His glory. The archbishop offered Mass daily, even when on a journey, and always with intense fervour, and every morning he made his confession to his chaplain. Among those St Turibius confirmed, as well as St Rose, are said to have been Bd Martin Porres and Bd John Massias. From 1590 he had the help of another great missionary, the Franciscan St Francis Solano, whose denunciations of the wickedness of Lima so alarmed the people that the viceroy had to call on the archbishop to calm them. The charities of St Turibius were large, and he had feeling for the sensitive pride of the Spaniards in his flock. He knew that many were shy of making their poverty or other needs known, that they did not like to accept public charity or help from those they knew : so he did all he could to assist them privately, without their knowing from whom their benefactions came.

St Turibius was in his sixty-eighth year when he fell ill at Pacasmayo, far to the north of Lima. Working to the last, he struggled as far as Santa, where he realized the end was at hand. He made his will, giving his personal belongings to his servants and all the rest of his property for the benefit of the poor. He asked to be carried into the church to receive viaticum, and was then brought back to bed and anointed. While those about him sang the psalm, " I was glad when they said unto me, We will go into the house of the Lord ", St Turibius died on March 23, 1606. In 1726 he was canonized.

The four volumes compiled by Mgr C. G. Irigoyen, *Santo Toribio ; Obra escrita con motivo del tercer centenario de la muerte del Santo Arzobispo de Lima* (1906) are of the first importance, most of the documents being previously unpublished. But see also the less exhaustive biographies by Fr Cyprian de Herrera and A. Nicoselli, and in French that by T. Bérengier (1872).

28 : ST PAUL OF THE CROSS, Founder of the Barefooted Clerks of the Holy Cross and Passion (A.D. 1775)

THE founder of the Passionists, St Paul-of-the-Cross, was born at Ovada in the republic of Genoa in 1694—the year which saw also the birth of Voltaire. Paul Francis, as he was called, was the eldest son of Luke Danei, a business man of good family, and his wife, both exemplary Christians. Whenever little Paul shed tears of pain or annoyance his mother used to show him the crucifix with a few simple words about the sufferings of our Lord, and thus she instilled into his infant mind the germs of that devotion to the Sacred Passion which was to rule his life. The father would read aloud the lives of the saints to his large family of children, whom he often cautioned against gambling and fighting. Although Paul seems to have been one of those chosen souls who have given themselves to God almost from babyhood, yet at the age of fifteen he was led by a sermon to conclude that he was not corresponding to grace. Accordingly, after making a general confession, he embarked on a life of austerity, sleeping on the bare ground, rising at midnight, spending hours in prayer, and scourging himself. In all these practices he was imitated by his brother John Baptist, his junior by two years. He also formed a society for mutual sanctification among the youths of the neighbour-hood, several of whom afterwards joined religious communities. In 1714 Paul went to Venice in response to the appeal of Pope Clement XI for volunteers to fight in the Venetian army against the Turks, but a year later he obtained his discharge, having discovered that the army was not his vocation. Convinced that he was not meant to lead the ordinary life in the world he refused a good inheritance and a promising marriage ; but before he or his directors could perceive his true vocation he was to spend (at Castellazzo in Lombardy, then his home) several years in almost unbroken prayer which sometimes attained to the highest degree of contemplation.

During the summer of 1720, in three extraordinarily vivid visions, Paul beheld a black habit with the name of Jesus in white characters, surmounted by a white cross, emblazoned upon the breast. On the third occasion our Lady, attired in the tunic, told him that he was to found a congregation, the members of which would wear that habit and would mourn continually for the passion and death of her Son. A written description of these visions was submitted to the bishop of Alessandria, who consulted several spiritual guides, including Paul's former director, the Capuchin Father Columban of Genoa. In view of the heroic life of virtue and prayer led by the young man since his childhood, all agreed that the call must have

178

come from God.   The bishop therefore authorized him to follow his vocation and invested him with the black habit, stipulating, however, that the badge was not to be worn until papal approval had been obtained.   Paul's next step was to compose a rule for the future congregation.   He retired for a forty days' retreat into a dark, damp, triangular cell adjoining the sacristy of St Charles's church at Castellazzo, where he lived on bread and water and slept on straw.   The rules which he drew up at that time, without book or earthly guide, are substantially the regulations followed by the Passionists to-day.   It was during this retreat that the saint first felt impelled to pray for the conversion of England : " That country is always before my eyes ", he said in later years.   " If England again becomes Catholic, immeasurable will be the benefits to Holy Church."

For a short time after the retreat he remained with John Baptist and another disciple in the neighbourhood of Castellazzo, rendering assistance to the local clergy by catechizing the children and giving missions, which were very successful. Nevertheless he soon realized that if he wished to carry out his vocation he must seek the highest sanction.   Bareheaded, barefoot and penniless, he set out for Rome, refusing the escort of John Baptist beyond Genoa.   Upon his arrival he presented himself at the Vatican, but as he had not thought of providing himself with an introduction or credentials he was turned away.   He accepted the rebuff as a sign that his hour was not yet come, and started on his homeward journey, visiting on the way the solitary slopes of Monte Argentaro, which the sea almost severs from the mainland.   So great was the attraction he felt to this spot that he soon returned to it, accompanied by John Baptist, to lead in one of its derelict hermitages a life almost as austere as that of the fathers in the desert.   They left for a time to stay in Rome, where they were ordained to the sacred ministry, but in 1727 they made their way back to Monte Argentaro, prepared to start their first house of retreat on the strength of the papal permission Paul had received to accept novices.

Numerous were the difficulties with which they had to contend.   Their first recruits found the life too hard and all withdrew ; war was threatening ; benefactors who had offered assistance declared themselves unable to fulfil their undertakings ; a serious epidemic broke out in the nearest villages.   Paul and John Baptist, who had received faculties for missionary work soon after they had left Rome, went about fearlessly ministering to the dying, nursing the sick, and reconciling sinners to God.   The missions they thus inaugurated proved so fruitful that more distant towns applied for the services of the missioners.   Fresh novices came —not all of whom remained—and in 1737 the first Passionist Retreat (as their monasteries are called) was completed.   The little band could now move from its inadequate quarters in the old hermitage.   From this time onwards there was a steady progress, although many trials and disappointments had still to be faced. In 1741 Pope Benedict XIV granted a general approbation to the rules after their severity had been somewhat mitigated, and immediately a number of promising candidates offered themselves.   Six years later, when the congregation had three houses, the first general chapter was held.   By this time the fame of the Passionists, of their missions and of their austerity, was spreading throughout Italy.   St Paul himself evangelized in person nearly every town in the Papal States as well as a great part of Tuscany, taking always as his theme the Sacred Passion.   When, cross in hand, with arms outstretched, he preached about the sufferings of Christ, his words seemed to pierce the stoniest hearts : and when he scourged himself pitilessly in public for the offences of the people, hardened soldiers and even bandits wept, confessing their sins. " Father, I have been in great battles without ever flinching at the cannon's roar ", exclaimed an officer who was attending one of the missions. " But when I listen to you I tremble from head to foot." Afterwards in the confessional the apostle would deal tenderly with his penitents, confirming them in their good resolutions, leading them on to amendment of life and suggesting practical aids to perseverance.

St Paul-of-the-Cross was endowed with extraordinary gifts. He prophesied future events, healed the sick, and even during his lifetime appeared on various occasions in vision to persons far away. In the cities which he visited crowds followed him, desiring to touch him or to carry off some fragment of his habit as a relic, but he deprecated all tokens of esteem. In 1765 he had the grief of losing John Baptist, from whom he had scarcely ever been separated and to whom he was united by a bond of love as rare as it was beautiful. Unlike in disposition, the one brother seemed the complement of the other as they strove side by side to attain to perfection. Since their ordination they had been each other's confessors, inflicting penances and reproofs in turn. Once only had a shadow of disagreement ever arisen between them, and that was upon the only occasion John Baptist ever ventured to praise his brother to his face. St Paul's humility was so deeply wounded that he put them both to penance, forbidding his brother to approach him. Not until the third day, when John Baptist crept on his knees to implore pardon, did the cloud lift—never to descend again. It was in memory of the close association between the two men that Pope Clement XIV long afterwards bestowed upon St Paul-of-the-Cross the Roman basilica dedicated in the names of Saints John and Paul.

The new institute in 1769 received from Clement XIV the final authorization which placed it on the same footing as other approved religious institutes. Now St Paul would fain have retired into solitude, for his health was failing and he thought that his work was done. His sons, however, would have no other superior, whilst the pope, who was greatly attached to him, insisted upon his spending part of the year in Rome. During the latter part of his life, he was much preoccupied by arrangements for the establishment of Passionist nuns. After many disappointments the first house was opened at Corneto in 1771, but the founder was not well enough to be present, nor did he ever see his spiritual daughters in their habit. So ill was he indeed during this year, that he sent to ask for the papal blessing, only to be told by Pope Clement that he must live a little longer because he could not yet be spared. The saint actually rallied and survived for three years, dying in Rome on October 18, 1775, at the age of eighty. His canonization took place in 1867.

Apart from the depositions of witnesses in the process of beatification, the most important contribution which has been made to the history of the founder of the Passionists is the publication in 1924 of his letters, in four volumes : *Lettere di S. Paolo della Croce, disposte ed annotate dal P. Amadeo della Madre del Buon Pastore*. In particular the spiritual journal of the forty days' retreat made at Castellazzo in 1720 is worthy of attention as enabling the reader better than any other document to enter into the workings of St Paul's soul. Other biographies are numerous in most European languages. The earliest was that written by St Vincent Strambi of which an English version in three volumes was published in 1853 in the Oratorian series. A revised edition of the English life by Father Pius a Spiritu Sancto was issued in 1924, and there is a study by Father Edmund, C.P., *Hunter of Souls* (1946). Several others might be cited, but the religious names of their authors, such as " Father Pius of the Name of Mary ", " Father Louis of Jesus Agonizing ", not to speak of " Father Amadeus of the Mother of the Good Shepherd ", mentioned above, do not encourage the bibliographer to make a long catalogue.

SS. VITALIS AND VALERIA, MARTYRS   (SECOND CENTURY ?)

SINCE this St Vitalis is named in the canon of the Mass according to the Milanese rite, is commemorated in the Roman rite to-day, and is the titular saint of the famous basilica of San Vitale at Ravenna, he should be mentioned here, though nothing certain is known about him beyond the fact that he and St Valeria were early martyrs, probably at or near Milan.

The spurious letter of St Ambrose which purports to narrate the history of the twin martyrs SS. Gervase and Protase states incorrectly that Vitalis and Valeria were their parents.   According to the legend, Vitalis was a soldier who, when the physician St Ursicinus of Ravenna wavered when faced with death for Christ, encouraged him to stand firm.   The governor accordingly ordered Vitalis to be racked and then buried alive, which was done.   His wife, St Valeria, was set upon by pagans near Milan, and died from their brutal treatment.   These things are said to have happened during the persecution under Nero, but the second century, under Marcus Aurelius, is a more likely date for their martyrdom.

The story of St Vitalis is discussed in the *Acta Sanctorum*, April, vol. iii, and by Tillemont in his *Mémoires*, vol. ii.   See also the *Analecta Bollandiana*, vol. xlvi (1928), pp. 55–59.

ST POLLIO, MARTYR   (A.D. 304)

THE scene of the martyrdom of St Pollio was the ancient town of Cybalae or Cibalis in Lower Pannonia (now Mikanovici in Yugoslavia), the birth-place of the Emperors Gratian, Valentinian and Valens.   He was a lector in the church, and, after the martyrdom of his bishop Eusebius, he became the leader of those Christians in the diocese who disregarded the edicts of Diocletian.   He was accordingly brought before Probus the president, before whom he made a bold confession.   Because he refused to offer sacrifice to the gods and to render divine honours to the emperors he was condemned to death, and was burnt at the stake a few years after the martyrdom of Eusebius.

There can be no doubt about the historical existence of St Pollio, although his reputed acts may not deserve to be included, as Ruinart ranks them, among the *acta sincera*.   The text is printed in the *Acta Sanctorum*, April, vol. iii, and also by Ruinart.   Pollio unquestionably figures in the "Hieronymianum".   As to Eusebius, there may be some confusion with a presbyter who is commemorated on this day in the Syriac "Breviarium", who suffered at Nicomedia.

SS. THEODORA AND DIDYMUS, MARTYRS   (A.D. 304 ?)

ACCORDING to the legend Theodora was a beautiful maiden of Alexandria who, because during the persecution of Diocletian she refused to sacrifice to the gods, was sentenced to exposure in a house of ill-fame.   She was rescued from the brothel by one Didymus, who changed clothes with her ; but on reaching a place of safety Theodora fell dead from shock.   Didymus was soon detected, and was put to death by beheading.

Alban Butler retells this story at some length, following Ruinart, who included the "acts" in his *Acta martyrum sincera ;* but later scholars, *e.g.* Father Delehaye, regard them as purely fictitious.

The so-called acts are in Ruinart and the *Acta Sanctorum*, April, vol. iii.   Father Delehaye suggests a comparison with the Acts of SS. Alexander and Antonina in the *Acta Sanctorum*, May, vol. i.

ST CRONAN OF ROSCREA, Abbot   (c. A.D. 626)

St Cronan of Roscrea was one of the greatest Irishmen of his age, but for the history of his life we have nothing more reliable than accounts compiled centuries after his death, apparently from oral traditions rather than from written records. His father's name was Odran, and the saint was born in the district of Ely O'Carroll, in Offaly. Cronan made his first monastic settlement at Puayd, where he lived for some time, but afterwards he showed his charity in a fashion as practical as it was unusual, for we read that he built as many as fifty houses, which he relinquished one after another to anchorites who required homes. Moreover, he would take nothing away with him when he left these houses, and actually made one of his disciples do penance for the rest of his life because he had removed a sackful of things which he thought might prove useful. St Cronan seems to have established communities at Lusmag in Offaly and at Monahincha near Roscrea, where a flourishing abbey, to which a school was attached, may perhaps be traced to his foundation. Not far off, beside the present bog of Monela, he built himself a cell at Seanross, and here he was visited by St Molua to whom he gave viaticum. Cronan became blind a few years before his death, which took place when he was an extremely old man. One of the strangest incidents recorded of St Cronan is thus summarized by Father John Ryan in his *Irish Monasticism* (1931) : " He worked a miracle to provide his guests with beer, and the result was so successful that they all became inebriated ".

There is a Latin life printed in the *Acta Sanctorum*, April, vol. iii, and re-edited by Plummer in VSH., vol. ii, pp. 22–31. See also O'Hanlon, LIS., vol. iv, pp. 516 *seq.*, and D. F. Gleeson, *Roscrea* (1947).

ST PAMPHILUS, Bishop of Sulmona   (c. A.D. 700)

During the last quarter of the seventh century there was living in the Abruzzi a bishop called Pamphilus, who ruled over the united dioceses of Sulmona and Corfinium. He was a very holy man, a zealous teacher, austere in his life and generous to the poor, but he aroused hostility by introducing certain innovations. On Sunday mornings he would rise shortly after midnight and, after the solemn singing of the night offices, he would proceed at once to celebrate Mass. Then he would distribute alms, and at daybreak would provide for the poor a meal which he shared with his guests. Some of his clergy and people strongly objected to this hour for offering the holy Sacrifice. They pointed out that no other bishop in Italy had Mass celebrated before the second or third hour. They actually went so far as to denounce him as an Arian to the pope, before whom he was summoned. So completely did Pamphilus succeed in vindicating his orthodoxy that the pontiff sent him home with a liberal donation for his poor. St Pamphilus was greatly venerated in his own neighbourhood, and his *cultus* afterwards spread to Germany.

See the *Acta Sanctorum*, April, vol. iii, where a short Latin life is printed, but of no great authority.

ST CYRIL, Bishop of Turov   (A.D. 1182)

Cyril of Turov is one of the three outstanding figures in Russian Christian culture before the Mongol invasions (the other two are Clement Smoliatich and Hilarion, both metropolitans of Kiev). But in spite of this practically nothing is known about his life : if anybody wrote his biography it has not survived, and the chronicles tell us nothing. He lived during the middle of the twelfth century, and was first a monk, then a recluse, and left his cell to be bishop of Turov, a town not far from Kiev. Professor Fedotov says of him that " From his writings one receives the impression of a man who stands very remote from life, even from the moral needs of life, and who is entirely elevated to the sphere of religious worship and thought, with its dogmatic or would-be dogmatic mysteries : he is a unique example of theological devotion in ancient Russia ".

It is remarkable about St Cyril of Turov that " he is nothing but an exponent of the Greek tradition on the Russian soil ", lacking any specifically Russian feature. Whether in fact he knew Greek and read the Greek fathers of the Church in the original tongue is debated : but on the whole it seems that he probably did not, and the extent of his patristic learning is undetermined. But he was the best biblical scholar among the early Russian writers, though Fedotov points out some remarkable inaccuracies. His interpretation was allegorical, and he carried it to extravagant lengths. His ascetical ideals, at any rate for monks, emphasized spiritual mortification, especially by way of obedience as the outward fruit of humility : " You are a piece of cloth, and you may be conscious of yourself only until someone picks you up : do not worry if you are then torn up for footwear ".

But it was as a preacher that St Cyril of Turov was most famous, and he faith-fully followed his Greek models in their rhetoric and flowing oratory ; but he never " unbends " as, for example, St John Chrysostom so often does, and he so ignores the practical application of his theology to human life that some have dismissed his sermons as pure oratory—overlooking that St Cyril was really carried away by the contemplation of divine mysteries. The balance, both in manner and matter, is somewhat restored by certain prayers which he wrote ; their language is more straightforward and they are predominantly concerned with the writer's sinfulness and need of forgiveness. It was to bring forgiveness and salvation that God became man and died on the cross, and it was this divine salvation that provides the theme for some of the finest passages in Cyril's sermons.

What part St Cyril of Turov took in the ecclesiastical affairs of his time is not known ; it is recorded that he wrote certain letters about them, but they have been lost. He died in the year 1182.

There is a good deal about St Cyril and his sermons and writings in Professor Fedotov's *The Russian Religious Mind* (1946), especially at pages 69–84 and 136–141. *Cf.* also general bibliographical notes under St Sergius of Radonezh on September 25.

BD LUCHESIO (A.D. 1260)

THE Val d'Elsa, then Florentine territory, was the birth-place of Luchesio, or Lucius, the first Franciscan tertiary. As a young man he was wholly engrossed in worldly interests, especially politics and money-making. So unpopular did he make himself by his violent partisanship of the Guelf cause that he found it advis-able to leave Gaggiano, his native place, and to settle in Poggibonsi, where he carried on business as a provision merchant and money-lender. Then, when he was between thirty and forty a change came over him, partly perhaps as the result of the death of his children. His heart was touched by divine grace and he began to take interest in works of mercy, such as nursing the sick and visiting the prisons. He even gave away to the poor all his possessions, except a piece of land which he determined to cultivate himself.

Soon afterwards St Francis of Assisi came to Poggibonsi. He had for some time contemplated the necessity of forming an association for persons desiring to live the religious life in the world, but Luchesio and his wife Bonadonna were actually, it is said, the first man and woman to receive from the Seraphic Father the habit and cord of the third order. From that moment they gave themselves up to a penitential and charitable life. Sometimes Luchesio would give away every scrap of food that was in the house, and at first Bonadonna would demur, for she did not at once rise to such perfect trust in divine Providence : but experience taught her that God supplies His faithful children with their daily bread. Her husband attained to great sanctity, and was rewarded by ecstasies and the gift of healing. When it became evident that he had not long to live, his wife begged him to wait a little for her, so that she who had shared his sufferings here might participate in his happiness above. Her wish was granted, and she died shortly before her husband passed to his reward. Bd Luchesio's *cultus* was confirmed in 1694.

Though a life of Bd Luchesio seems to have been written by a contemporary it has unfortunately not been preserved, and we are dependent upon that compiled a century later by Father Bartholomew Tolomei which is printed in the *Acta Sanctorum*, April, vol. iii. It is to be noted that this text by no means clearly asserts that Luchesio and his wife were the first to receive the habit as tertiaries ; it rather implies the contrary. See also F. Van den Borne, *Die Anfänge des Franziskanischen Dritten Ordens* (1925), and Léon, *Auréole Séraphique* (Eng. trans.), vol. ii, pp. 131–137.

ST LOUIS MARY OF MONTFORT, FOUNDER OF THE COMPANY OF MARY AND OF THE DAUGHTERS OF WISDOM　　(A.D. 1716)

ST LOUIS MARY was the eldest of the eight children of John Baptist Grignion, and was born in modest circumstances at Montfort, then in the diocese of Saint-Malo, in 1673. After being educated at the Jesuit college in Rennes, he went at the age of twenty to Paris to prepare for the priesthood ; but being unable through poverty to gain admittance to the seminary of Saint-Sulpice, he entered a small institution conducted by the Abbé de la Barmondière. At the abbé's death he moved to a still more Spartan establishment : real penury reigned, and the wretched food was cooked by the students, who all in turn " had the pleasure of poisoning themselves ", as one of them afterwards ironically observed. Louis himself fell so dangerously ill that he had to be removed to the hospital. When at last he recovered, it was made possible for him to enter Saint-Sulpice to complete his religious course. We find him selected as one of the two exemplary students who were annually sent on pilgrimage to one of our Lady's shrines, on this occasion Chartres.

His success while still a seminarist in giving catechetical instruction to the roughest and most undiscplined children in Paris, confirmed Louis Grignion in the desire to undertake apostolic work. Therefore, after his ordination in 1700, he spent a short time at Nantes with a priest, who trained men for home missions, before proceeding to Poitiers, where he was appointed chaplain to the hospital. In this institution for nursing the sick poor he soon produced a much-needed reformation, and organized from amongst the female staff and residents the nucleus of the congregation of Daughters of the Divine Wisdom, for whom he compiled a rule. Nevertheless the very improvements he introduced aroused resentment, and he was obliged to resign his post. At once he began to give missions to the poor, who flocked to hear him, but the bishop of Poitiers, at the instigation of the critics of Father Grignion, forbade him to preach in his diocese. Undismayed, he set off on foot for Rome to seek authority from Pope Clement XI, who received him encouragingly and sent him back to France with the title of missionary apostolic. As Poitiers remained closed to him, he returned to his native Brittany, where he embarked on a course of missions which he continued almost uninterruptedly until his death.

Although the majority of parishes received St Louis Mary with open arms, adverse criticism continued to dog his steps, and he found himself excluded from certain churches and even dioceses by ecclesiastics of Jansenist proclivities. Moreover, his methods sometimes startled the conventional. He would invite his audience to bring their irreligious books to be burnt on a great pyre surmounted by an effigy of the Devil represented as a society-woman; or he would himself realistically act the part of a dying sinner whose soul was being contended for by the Devil and his guardian angel, personated by two other priests standing beside his prostrate form. But, if he seemed to appeal to the emotions, the response he elicited was frequently practical and lasting. It often expressed itself in the restoration of some dilapidated church, in the setting up of huge memorial crosses, in liberal alms to the poor and in a real spiritual revival. Nearly sixty years after the holy man's death, the curé of Saint-Lô declared that many of his parishioners still practised the devotions Louis had inculcated in one of his missions. The first and foremost of these was the rosary, for the recitation of which he established numerous confraternities. Then there were hymns or metrical prayers of his own composition, many of which are sung to this day in parts of France. It seems to have been his great love for the rosary which led him to become a tertiary of the order of St Dominic.

But St Louis did not confine his evangelistic efforts to his missions—he believed in preaching the word of God in season and out of season. On one occasion, when travelling on a market-boat between Rouen and Dinant, he asked his fellow passengers, who were singing obscene songs, to join him in the rosary. Twice they answered his invitation with jeers, but eventually they not only recited it reverently on their knees, but also listened attentively to the homily with which he followed it. Another day it was a rough alfresco dance which he brought to an end in the same way. Perhaps his greatest triumphs were won in the Calvinistic stronghold of La Rochelle, where he held several crowded missions in rapid succession, and reconciled a number of Protestants to the Church. St Louis had long desired to form an association of missionary priests, but it was only a few years before his death that he succeeded in attaching to himself a few ordained men who became the first Missionaries of the Company of Mary. He was in the midst of a mission at Saint-Laurent-sur-Sèvre when he was attacked by a sudden illness which proved fatal. He was only forty-three years of age when he died in 1716.

Apart from his verses and hymns, St Louis Mary Grignion's chief literary work was the well-known treatise on " True Devotion to the Blessed Virgin ", in which a renewal of interest was caused by his canonization in 1947.

Leaving out of account earlier biographies, such as those of the contemporary J. Grandet and of P. de Clorivière (1775), special mention must be made of A. Laveille's *Le b. L.-M. Grignion de Montfort d'après des documents inédits* (1907) ; but there are many other lives in French, among the more recent being those by G. Bernoville (1946) and Fr Morineau (1947). L. Jac's volume in the series " Les Saints " can also be recommended. There is a long life in Italian by Cardinal E. Tisserant (1943). The fullest work in English is Dr Cruikshank's *Bd Louis Marie Grignon de Montfort and His Devotion* (2 vols., 1892); see also a shorter life by Fr E. C. Bolger (1952). For the testament dictated by the saint just before he died, see *Analecta Bollandiana*, vol. lxviii (1950), pp. 464–474.

ST PETER MARY CHANEL, Martyr   (A.D. 1841)

THE first martyr of Oceania and of the Society of Mary, Peter Louis Mary Chanel, was born in 1803 in the diocese of Belley.   Set to mind his father's sheep from the age of seven, he was one day noticed by the Abbé Trompier, parish priest of Cras, who was struck by his intelligence and piety, and obtained leave from the boy's parents to educate him in the little Latin school which he had started.   " He was the flower of my flock ", the curé was wont afterwards to declare, and indeed both as a student at Cras and in the seminary Peter won the affectionate esteem of masters and pupils alike.   A bishop who was very well acquainted with him said, " He had a heart of gold with the simple faith of a child, and he led the life of an angel ".   A year after his ordination he was appointed to the parish of Crozet—a district which bore a bad reputation.   In the three years he remained there he brought about a great revival of religion, his devotion to the sick opening to him many doors which would otherwise have remained closed.   But his heart had long been set on missionary work, and in 1831 he joined the Marists, who had recently formed themselves into a society for evangelistic work at home and abroad.   His aspirations were not at once realized, for he was given professorial work for five years in the seminary of Belley.

However, in 1836, Pope Gregory XVI gave canonical approval to the new congregation, and St Peter was one of a small band of missionaries commissioned to carry the faith to the islands of the Pacific.   Peter with one companion went to the island of Futuna in the New Hebrides.   They were well received by the people, whose confidence they gained by healing the sick.   But after the missionaries had acquired the language and had begun to teach, the chieftain's jealousy was aroused.   Suspicion turned to hatred when his own son expressed a desire for baptism, and on April 28, 1841, he sent a band of warriors, one of whom felled St Peter with his club and the rest cut up the martyr's body with their hatchets.   The missionary's death swiftly completed the work he had begun, and within a few months the whole island was Christian.   Peter was canonized in 1954, and his feast is kept in Australia and New Zealand as well as by the Marists.

There is a French biography by C. Nicolet (1920).   See also J. Hervier, *Les missions maristes en Océanie* (1902) ; and F. Gilmore, *The Martyr of Futuna* (1917).

29 : ST PETER OF VERONA, Martyr   (A.D. 1252)

ST PETER Martyr was born at Verona in 1205 of parents who belonged to the sect of the Cathari, a heresy which closely resembled that of the Albigenses and included amongst its tenets a denial that the material world had been created by God.   The child was sent to a Catholic school, in spite of the remonstrances of an uncle who discovered by questioning the little boy that he had not only learnt the Apostles' Creed, but was prepared stoutly to maintain in the orthodox sense the article " Creator of Heaven and earth ".   At Bologna University Peter found himself exposed to temptations of another sort amid licentious companions, and soon decided to seek admission into the Order of Preachers.   Having received the habit from St Dominic himself, the young novice entered with zeal into the practices of the religious life.   He was always studying, reading, praying, serving the sick, or performing such offices as sweeping the house.

Later on we find him active as a preacher all over Lombardy. A heavy trial befell him when he was forbidden to teach, and was banished to a remote priory on a false accusation of having received strangers and even women into his cell. Once, as he knelt before the crucifix, he exclaimed, " Lord, thou knowest that I am not guilty. Why dost thou permit me to be falsely accused ? " The reply came, " And I, Peter, what did I do to deserve my passion and death ? " Rebuked yet consoled, the friar regained courage, and soon afterwards his innocence was vindicated. His preaching from that time was more successful than ever, as he went from town to town rousing the careless, converting sinners, and bringing back the lapsed into the fold. To the fame of his eloquence was soon added his reputation as a wonder-worker. When he appeared in public he was almost crushed to death by the crowds who flocked to him, some to ask his blessing, others to offer the sick for him to cure, others to receive his instruction.

About the year 1234 Pope Gregory IX appointed Peter inquisitor general for the Milanese territories. So zealously and well did he accomplish his duties that his jurisdiction was extended to cover the greater part of northern Italy. We find him at Bologna, Cremona, Ravenna, Genoa, Venice and even in the Marches of Ancona, preaching the faith, arguing with heretics, denouncing and reconciling them. Great as was the success which everywhere crowned his efforts, Peter was well aware that he had aroused bitter enmity, and he often prayed for the grace to die as a martyr. When preaching on Palm Sunday, 1252, he announced publicly that a conspiracy was on foot against him, a price having been set on his head. " Let them do their worst ", he added, " I shall be more powerful dead than alive ".

As he was going from Como to Milan a fortnight later Peter was waylaid in a wood near Barlassina by two assassins, one of whom, Carino, struck him on the head with a bill-hook and then attacked his companion, a friar named Dominic. Grievously wounded, but still conscious, Peter Martyr commended himself and his murderer to God in the words of St Stephen. Afterwards, if we may believe a very old tradition, with a finger dipped in his own blood he was tracing on the ground the words *Credo in Deum* when his assailant despatched him with another blow. It was April 6, 1252, and the martyr had just completed his forty-sixth year. His companion, Brother Dominic, survived him only a few days.

Pope Innocent IV canonized St Peter of Verona in the year after his death. His murderer, Carino, fled to Forlì, where repentance overtook him ; he abjured his heresy, became a Dominican lay-brother, and died so holy a death that his memory was venerated. So recently as 1934 his head was translated from Forlì to Balsamo, his birthplace near Milan, where there is some *cultus* of him.

In the *Acta Sanctorum*, April, vol. iii, are printed a number of documents, including the bull of canonization and a biography by Fr Thomas Agni of Lentino, a contemporary. See also Mortier, *Maîtres Généraux O.P.*, vol. iii, pp. 140–166 ; *Monumenta Historica O.P.*, vol. i, pp. 236 *seq.* A fuller bibliography will be found in Taurisano, *Catalogus Hagiographicus O.P.*, p. 13. St Peter is depicted by Fra Angelico in a famous painting with wounded head and his finger on his lips, but there are many other types of representation, for which see Künstle, *Ikonographie*, vol. ii. See S. Orlandi, *S. Pietro martire da Verona : Leggenda di fr. Tommaso Agni . . .* (1952), and other recent work.

ST WILFRID THE YOUNGER, BISHOP OF YORK   (*c.* A.D. 744)

AMONGST the bishops mentioned by the Venerable Bede as having been educated at Whitby Abbey under the rule of St Hilda was Wilfrid the Younger, the favourite disciple of St John of Beverley.   He was appointed bishop's chaplain and ruled the establishment of cathedral clergy.   As the years went by, he was employed more or less in the capacity of a coadjutor by St John, who before finally retiring to Beverley nominated him to be his successor.   St Wilfrid showed great zeal in instructing his people ; and like his predecessor he eventually laid down his office to end his days in a monastery—presumably Ripon—where he died.   There seems to be only one old calendar known in which this bishop's name appears.

See Mabillon, *Acta Sanctorum O.S.B.*, vol. iii, part 2, p. 506.   There are also brief references to St Wilfrid II in Simeon of Durham and William of Malmesbury, *Gesta Pontificum.*   See Stanton's *Menology*, pp. 185–186.

ST HUGH THE GREAT, Abbot of Cluny   (A.D. 1109)

HONOURED as adviser by nine popes, consulted and venerated by all the sovereigns of western Europe, entrusted with the ultimate control of two hundred monasteries, St Hugh during the sixty years that he was abbot of Cluny raised its prestige to extraordinary heights.   He was born in 1024, the eldest son of the Count of Semur, and the boy showed so evident a vocation to the religious life that he was allowed to enter the monastery of Cluny, then under St Odilo, when he was fourteen.   At the age of twenty he was ordained priest, and before attaining his majority he had risen to be prior.   Five years later, upon the death of St Odilo, he was unanimously chosen abbot by his brethren.

Soon after his promotion Hugh took part in the Council of Rheims, presided over by Pope St Leo IX.   Placed second in rank amongst the abbots, the youthful superior of Cluny championed the reforms called for by the supreme pontiff, and denounced the prevalence of simony together with the relaxation of clerical celibacy in such eloquent terms that he was loudly applauded by the assembled dignitaries —many of whom had purchased their own offices.   Hugh accompanied the pope back to Italy, and in Rome he took part in the synod which pronounced the first condemnation of the errors of Berengarius of Tours.   In 1057 we find him at Cologne as godfather to the emperor's infant son, afterwards Henry IV ; a little later he is in Hungary, negotiating as papal legate a peace between King Andrew and the emperor ; and in February 1058 he is summoned to the death-bed of Pope Stephen X in Florence.   With the accession of St Gregory VII, who had been a monk at Cluny, the tie between St Hugh and the papacy became still closer.   The two men worked together heart and soul to remedy abuses and to rescue the Church from subservience to the state.   During the bitter feud between Gregory and the Emperor Henry IV, the holy abbot never relaxed his efforts to reconcile the two adversaries, both of whom loved and trusted him.   In a letter addressed to St Hugh by the disappointed monarch shortly before his death he wrote : " Oh, that it were granted to us to behold once more with our bodily eyes your angelic face ; to kneel before you ; to lay this head, which you once held over the font, upon your breast, bewailing our sins and telling our sorrows ! "

Notwithstanding his numerous enforced absences from Cluny, St Hugh raised his monks to a high level of religious perfection which was maintained throughout his life.   On one occasion St Peter Damian, when in France, characteristically suggested that Hugh should make the rule more severe.   " Come and stay with us for a week before you form your judgement ", was the abbot's answer.   The invitation was accepted and the point was not pressed.   In 1068 St Hugh fixed the usages for the whole Cluniac congregation. New houses sprang up in France, Switzerland, Germany, Spain and Italy, and older foundations affiliated themselves to Cluny that they might profit by its discipline and privileges. It is to this period that is to be ascribed the building of the first English Cluniac priory at Lewes. St Hugh personally established a convent for women at Marcigny with strict enclosure. So faithfully was the rule kept by the nuns, of whom St Hugh's sister was the first prioress, that they refused to leave the building when it was partially destroyed by fire. Another institution established by the saint was a leper hospital, in which he loved to wait upon the sick with his own hands.

Few men have been so universally esteemed. He was publicly commended and thanked for his services at the Roman synod of 1081 and at the Council of Clermont in 1095, and he was the first to whom St Anselm of Canterbury turned in his troubles two years later. Posterity has confirmed the verdict of his contemporaries. In a beautiful character sketch, his disciple Heribert thus describes him: " Insatiable in reading, indefatigable in prayer, he employed every moment for his own progress or for the good of his neighbour. It is hard to say which was the greater, his prudence or his simplicity. Never did he speak an idle word : never did he perform a questionable act. Anger—except against sin—he never knew. His advice even when addressed to individuals was serviceable to all. There was in him more of the father than of the judge, more of clemency than of severity. He was tall of stature and striking in appearance, but his spiritual endowments far surpassed his bodily graces. When he was silent, he was conversing with God : when he talked he spoke of God and in God. He could always deal with whatever he undertook, for he gave it his entire attention. He loved in their due order— God above and beyond all, his neighbour equally with himself, and the world beneath his feet."

A true Benedictine, St Hugh omitted nothing to ensure the worthy fulfilment of the Church's worship, and it was he who first introduced the singing of the *Veni Creator* during Terce at Pentecost—a practice now general throughout the Western church. To the age of eighty-five St Hugh continued to rule over his order, his mental faculties undimmed but with gradually increasing bodily weakness. When at length he knew that his last hour was approaching he received viaticum, took leave of his sons, and asked to be carried into the church, where he lay upon sackcloth and ashes until death released his soul to pass to eternal glory on April 29, 1109. He was canonized in 1120.

Even apart from the chroniclers there are abundant materials for the life of St Hugh. There is a sketch by Gilo (printed in Pertz, MGH., *Scriptores*, vol. xv, pp. 937–940) ; a longer account by Rainaldus, abbot of Vézelay, and a biography by Hildebert of Le Mans (both in the *Acta Sanctorum*, April, vol. iii) ; together with many minor documents. See BHL., nn. 4007–4015 ; and also L'Huillier, *Vie de St Hugues* (1888) ; Sackur, *Die Cluniacenser*, vol. i.

ST ROBERT OF MOLESMES, ABBOT   (A.D. 1110)

ROBERT of Molesmes, who is honoured as one of the founders of the Cistercian Order, was born *c.* 1024 of noble parents at or near Troyes in Champagne. At the age of fifteen he took the Benedictine habit at Moutier-la-Celle, and made such rapid progress that he was named prior after the completion of his novitiate, although he was one of the youngest members of the community. Later he was appointed abbot of the daughter house of St Michael of Tonnerre, the discipline of which had become relaxed. He had been striving with little success to effect a reformation when he received a request from some hermits living in the wood of Collan that he would instruct them in the Rule of St Benedict. Only too gladly would he have acceded to their petition, but his monks opposed his departure and he was soon afterwards recalled to Moutier-la-Celle. In the meantime the hermits appealed to Rome with such success that Alexander II issued a decree appointing Robert their superior. One of his first tasks was to remove the little community from Collan, which was very unhealthy, to the forest of Molesmes, where they built themselves wooden cells and a small oratory. This was in 1075.

In those early days their austerity was extreme and their poverty so great that often they had not enough to eat. It was not long, however, before the fame of their life spread through the neighbouring districts. Headed by the bishop of Troyes, the local magnates vied with one another in supplying their needs, whilst numerous applications were made for admission. This sudden prosperity, however, proved unfortunate. Unsuitable candidates were accepted, little luxuries were introduced, and discipline suffered accordingly. Discouraged at finding his remonstrances unheeded, Robert retired for a time to a hermitage, but returned to Molesmes at the request of his monks, who had not prospered in his absence and promised to obey him in future. But as their desire for his return was based only upon temporal advantage, it produced no permanent amelioration in their conduct. Eventually a zealous minority, headed by St Alberic and St Stephen Harding, approached St Robert asking permission to go away to some place where they could live up to their profession. He expressed his eagerness to join them, and went with a deputation to Lyons to consult Archbishop Hugh, the papal legate. The prelate not only gave his sanction, but encouraged them to leave Molesmes and persevere in their determination to practise strictly the Rule of St Benedict. Thus authorized Robert, after formally resigning his pastoral staff, set out with twenty monks for Cîteaux (Cistercium), a wild forest district, watered by a little river, at a distance of five leagues from Dijon. There they began on March 21, 1098, to build some wooden huts, engaging themselves to live according to the strictest interpretation of the Benedictine rule. Walter, bishop of Chalon, declared the new foundation an abbey, investing Robert with the dignity of abbot ; and thus originated the great Cistercian Order.

A year later the monks of Molesmes sent representatives to Rome to ask for the return of their former abbot Robert. They asserted that religious observance had suffered greatly in his absence, and that the good of their souls as well as the prosperity of the house depended upon his presence. Pope Urban II referred the matter to Archbishop Hugh, requesting him, if he thought fit, to arrange for Robert to be transferred, and the holy man accordingly went back to Molesmes, accompanied by two monks who " did not like the wilderness ". There is some evidence that St Robert too was not unwilling to leave, but that he afterwards regretted Cîteaux is clear from a letter he wrote to his Cistercian brethren in which he says : " I should sadden you too much if I could use my tongue as a pen, my tears as ink and my heart as paper. . . . I am here in body because obedience demands it, but my soul is with you." Nevertheless his return to Molesmes bore good fruit, for the monks had learnt their lesson and lived in pious submission to his rule until his death at the age of ninety-two on March 21, 1110. He was canonized in 1222.

A life of St Robert (written by a monk of Molesmes, whose name has not been preserved, in the twelfth century) is printed in the *Acta Sanctorum*, April, vol. iii. See also Dalgairns,

Life of St Stephen Harding (1898) ; Duplus, *Saints de Dijon ;* and an article by W. Williams in the *Journal of Theological Studies,* vol. xxxvii (1936), pp. 404–412).

ST JOSEPH COTTOLENGO, FOUNDER OF THE SOCIETIES OF THE LITTLE HOUSE OF DIVINE PROVIDENCE   (A.D. 1842)

ON a September day of the year 1827 a priest was called to give the last sacraments to a young Frenchwoman, who had been taken ill at Turin when travelling from Milan to Lyons with her husband and three little children, and who died in a squalid slum from lack of adequate care.   The priest was Canon Joseph Benedict Cottolengo, a native of Bra in Piedmont.   He was a great lover of the poor, and was shocked to discover that no institution in Turin was available for such cases. Though without private means he promptly hired five rooms in a house called Volta Rossa with the aid of a lady who supplied several beds.   A doctor and a chemist having offered their services, a little hospital was opened with five patients. Soon it became necessary to take more rooms and to organize the charitable voluntary helpers into a permanent male and female nursing staff.   The men Canon Cottolengo called Brothers of St Vincent, whilst the women, who before long received a rule, a habit and a superior, were designated Daughters of St Vincent de Paul, or Vincentian Sisters.

In 1831 cholera broke out in Turin, and fear of infection from the crowded inmates of Volta Rossa induced the civic authorities to close the hospital.   The canon was unperturbed : " In my country they say that cabbages increase and multiply by transplantation ", he remarked.   " We must change our quarters." During the epidemic the Vincentians nursed the cholera-stricken in their homes, but afterwards the Cottolengo Hospital was transferred to Valdocco, then outside Turin.   The canon called the house he bought the Piccola Casa, or Little House of Divine Providence, and placed over the entrance the words : " Caritas Christi urget nos ".   To accommodate the ever-increasing number of patients other buildings gradually arose alongside, bearing such distinctive names as the House of Faith, the House of Hope, Madonna's House, Bethlehem.   But it was not only the sick whom Don Cottolengo was to shelter in what he sometimes called his Noah's Ark, but epileptics, the deaf and dumb, orphans, waifs and distressed persons of all sorts.   For the various classes he started special homes, besides providing hospices for the aged, many of them blind and crippled.   Two houses were devoted to idiots—whom the canon always tactfully called his " good boys and girls "—and a rescue home was started, from among the inmates of which a religious congregation was formed under the patronage of St Thais.   The great block of buildings constituted what a French writer described as a University of Christian Charity, but the founder continued to call it the Piccola Casa.   He never attributed its success to his own powers of organization, being entirely convinced that he was merely a tool in the hands of God.   That conviction he once set forth in graphic words to the Vincentian Sisters.   " We are like the marionettes of a puppet-show.   As long as they are held by a hand from above they walk, jump, dance and give signs of agility and life : they represent . . . now a king, now a clown . . . but as soon as the performance is over they are dropped and huddled together ingloriously in a dusty corner.   So it is with us : amid the multiplicity of our various functions we are held and moved by the hand of Providence.   Our duty is to enter into its designs, to play the part assigned to us . . . and respond promptly and trustfully to the impulses received from on high."

Although he directed everything, yet Don Cottolengo kept no books or accounts, the money he received being promptly spent and never invested. He went so far as to refuse royal patronage for his work, because it was already under the patronage of the King of kings. Repeatedly but in vain did his well-wishers counsel prudence with a view to safeguarding the future of his works : over and over again his creditors pressed him sorely, the cash-box was empty, and provisions threatened to run short. The holy man trusted to God and was never disappointed. Moreover he *had* safeguarded the future of the Piccola Casa by ensuring a treasury not of money but of prayers. In response to what he conceived to be a call from above he had founded, in connection with his organization, several religious communities, the main purpose of which was to pray for all necessities. These new societies included the Daughters of Compassion, who intercede for the dying, the " suffragists " of the Holy Souls to gain relief for the departed in Purgatory, the Daughters of the Good Shepherd who by prayers and active work assist those in moral danger, and a very strict community of Carmelites, whose penance and prayer are offered on behalf of the Church. For men he established the Hermits of the Holy Rosary and the Congregation of Priests of the Holy Trinity.

Joseph Cottolengo was in his fifty-sixth year when he realized that he was dying, typhoid fever having exhausted a body already weakened by hard work and austerity. Without a shadow of anxiety about his great work, he calmly handed over his authority to his successor, bade farewell to his spiritual children, and set out for Chieri, where he died nine days later in the house of his brother, Canon Louis Cottolengo. Nearly all his numerous foundations are flourishing to this day, and thousands of poor persons are still sheltered in the precincts of the Piccola Casa. St Joseph Cottolengo was canonized in 1934.

The most complete life is that written in Italian by P. Gastaldi in three volumes (1910 ; French trans., 1934). A shorter French account was compiled for the beatification in 1917 by J. Guillermin. For English readers there is an abridgement of Gastaldi and a sketch by Lady Herbert. See also S. Ballario, *L'apostolo della carità* (1934).

30 : ST CATHERINE OF SIENA, Virgin   (A.D. 1380)

ST ĆATHERINE was born in Siena on the feast of the Annunciation 1347, she and a twin sister who did not long survive her birth being the youngest of twenty-five children. Their father, Giacomo Benincasa, a well-to-do dyer, lived with his wife Lapa, daughter of a now forgotten poet, in the spacious house which the piety of the Sienese has preserved almost intact to the present day. Catherine as a little girl is described as having been very merry, and sometimes on her way up or downstairs she used to kneel on every step to repeat a Hail Mary. She was only six years old when she had the remarkable mystical experience which may be said to have sealed her vocation. In the company of her brother Stephen she was returning from a visit to her married sister Bonaventura when she suddenly came to a dead stop, standing as though spellbound in the road, with her eyes gazing up into the sky, utterly oblivious to the repeated calls of the boy who, having walked on ahead, had turned round to find that she was not following. Only after he had gone back and had seized her by the hand did she wake up as from a dream. " Oh ! " she cried, " if you had seen what I saw you would not have done that ! " Then she burst into tears because the vision had faded—a vision in which she had beheld our Lord seated in glory with St Peter, St Paul and St John.   The Saviour had smiled upon the child : He had extended His hand to bless her . . . and from that moment Catherine was entirely His.   In vain did her shrewish mother seek to inspire her with the interests common to girls of her age : she cared but for prayer and solitude, only mingling with other children in order to lead them to share her own devotion.

When she had reached the age of twelve, her parents urged her to devote more care to her personal appearance.   In order to please her mother and Bonaventura she submitted for a time to have her hair dressed and to be decked out in the fashion, but she soon repented of her concession.   Uncompromisingly she now declared that she would never marry, and as her parents still persisted in trying to find her a husband she cut off her golden-brown hair—her chief beauty.   The family, roused to indignation, tried to overcome her resolution by petty persecution. She was harried and scolded from morning to night, set to do all the menial work of the house, and because she was known to love privacy she was never allowed to be alone, even her little bedroom being taken from her.   All these trials she bore with patience which nothing could ever ruffle.   Long afterwards, in her treatise on divine Providence, more commonly known as " The Dialogue ", she said that God had taught her to build in her soul a refuge in which she could dwell so peacefully that no storm or tribulation could ever really disturb her.   At last her father realized that further opposition was useless, and Catherine was allowed to lead the life to which she felt called.   In the small room now ceded for her use, a cell-like apartment which she kept shuttered and dimly lighted, she gave herself up to prayer and fasting, took the discipline and slept upon boards.   With some difficulty she obtained what she had ardently desired—permission to receive the habit of a Dominican tertiary, and after her admission she still further increased her mortifications, in accordance with the spirit of that then rigorously penitential rule.

Sometimes now Catherine was favoured by celestial visions and consolations, but often she was subjected to fierce trials.   Loathsome forms and enticing figures presented themselves to her imagination, whilst the most degrading temptations assailed her.   She passed through long intervals of desolation, during which God would appear to have abandoned her altogether.   " Oh Lord, where wert thou when my heart was so sorely vexed with foul and hateful temptations ? " she asked our Lord, as He manifested himself once more to her after a series of such trials. " Daughter ", He replied, " I was in thy heart, fortifying thee by my grace " ; and He assured her that He would from thenceforth be with her more openly, because the time of her probation was drawing to a close.   On Shrove Tuesday, 1366, while Siena was keeping carnival, she was praying in her room when the Saviour appeared to her again, accompanied by His blessed Mother and a crowd of the heavenly host. Taking the girl's hand, our Lady held it up to her Son who placed a ring upon it and espoused Catherine to Himself, bidding her to be of good courage, for she was now armed with faith to overcome the assaults of the enemy.   The ring remained visible to her though invisible to others.   This spiritual betrothal marked the end of the years of solitude and preparation.   Very shortly afterwards, it was revealed to Catherine that she must now go forth into the world to promote the salvation of her neighbour, and she began gradually to mix again with her fellow creatures. Like the other tertiaries she undertook to nurse in the hospitals, and she always chose for preference the cases from which they were apt to shrink.   Amongst these was a woman afflicted with a repulsive form of cancer and a leper called Tecca—

both of whom rewarded her loving care by ingratitude, abusing her to her face and spreading scandal about her behind her back.   In the end, however, they were won by her devotion.

" I desire to become more closely united to thee through charity towards thy neighbour ", our Lord had said, and Catherine's public life in no way interfered with her union with Him.   Bd Raymund of Capua tells us that the only difference it made was that " God began from that time to manifest Himself to her, not merely when she was alone, as formerly, but when she was in public ".   Often in the family circle, oftener still in church after she had made her communion, she was rapt in prolonged ecstasy, and whilst at prayer she was seen by many persons upraised from the ground.   Gradually there gathered round her a band of friends and disciples—her Fellowship or Family, all of whom called her " Mamma ". Prominent amongst them were her Dominican confessors, Thomas della Fonte and Bartholomew Dominici, the Augustinian Father Tantucci, Matthew Cenni, rector of the Misericordia hospital, Andrew Vanni, the artist to whom posterity is indebted for the loveliest of all the pictures of the saint, the aristocratic young poet Neri di Landoccio dei Pagliaresi, her own sister-in-law Lisa Colombini, the noble widow Alessia Saracini, the English William Flete, an Austin hermit, and the aged recluse Father Santi, popularly known as " the Saint ", who frequently left his solitude to be near Catherine because, to quote his own words, he found greater peace of mind and perseverance in virtue by following her than he had ever found in his cell.   The tenderest affection bound the holy woman to those whom she regarded as her spiritual family—children given to her by God that she might lead them to perfection.   She not only read their thoughts, but she frequently knew their temptations when they were absent, and it was to keep in touch with them that she seems to have dictated her earliest letters.

As may be readily supposed, public opinion in Siena was sharply divided about Catherine, especially at this period.   Although many acclaimed her as a saint, some dubbed her a fanatic, whilst others loudly denounced her as a hypocrite, even some of her own order.   It may have been in consequence of accusations made against her that she was summoned to Florence, to appear before the chapter general of the Dominicans.   If any charges were made, they were certainly disproved, and shortly afterwards the new lector to Siena, Bd Raymund of Capua, was appointed her confessor.   Their association was a happy one for both.   The learned Dominican became not only her director but in a great measure her disciple, whilst she obtained through him the support of the order.   In later life he was to be the master general of the Dominicans and the biographer of his spiritual daughter.

Catherine's return to Siena almost coincided with the outbreak of a terrible epidemic of plague, during the course of which she devoted herself to relieving the sufferers, as did also the rest of her circle.   " Never did she appear more admirable than at this time ", wrote Thomas Caffarini, who had known her from her early girlhood.   " She was always with the plague-stricken : she prepared them for death ; she buried them with her own hands.   I myself witnessed the joy with which she nursed them and the wonderful efficacy of her words, which wrought many conversions."   Amongst those who owed their recovery to her were Bd Raymund himself, Matthew Cenni, Father Santi and Father Bartholomew, all of whom had contracted the disease through tending others.   But Catherine's care for the dying was not confined to the sick.   She made it a regular practice to visit in prison those condemned to execution, in order that she might lead them to make their peace with God.   A young Perugian knight, Nicholas di Toldo, sentenced to death for speaking lightly of the Sienese government, was the best-known example, vividly related in the best-known of the saint's letters.   At her persuasion he made his confession, assisted at Mass and received the Lord's Body.   The night before execution Catherine comforted and encouraged him as he leaned his head upon her breast.   And on the morrow she was at the scaffold ; and Nicholas, seeing her pray for him, laughed with joy, and as he murmured " Jesus and Catherine " she received his severed head into her hands.   " Then I saw God-and-man, as one sees the brightness of the sun, receiving that soul in the fire of His divine love."

Such things as these, coupled with her reputation for holiness and wonders, had by this time won for her a unique place in the estimation of her fellow citizens, many of whom proudly called her " La Beata Popolana " and resorted to her in their various difficulties.   So numerous were the cases of conscience with which she dealt that three Dominicans were specially charged to hear the confessions of those who were induced by her to amend their lives.   Moreover, because of her success in healing feuds, she was constantly being called upon to arbitrate at a time when every man's hand seemed to be against his neighbour.   It was partly no doubt with a view to turning the belligerent energies of Christendom from fratricidal struggles that Catherine was moved to throw herself energetically into Pope Gregory XI's appeal for another crusade to wrest the Holy Sepulchre from the Turks.   Her efforts in this direction brought her into direct correspondence with the pontiff himself.

In February 1375 she accepted an invitation to visit Pisa, where she was welcomed with enthusiasm and where her very presence brought about a religious revival.   She had only been in the city a few days when she had another of those great spiritual experiences which appear to have preluded new developments in her career.   After making her communion in the little church of St Christina, she had been looking at the crucifix, rapt in meditation, when suddenly there seemed to come from it five blood-red rays which pierced her hands, feet and heart, causing such acute pain that she swooned.   The wounds remained as stigmata, apparent to herself alone during her life, but clearly visible after her death.

She was still at Pisa when she received word that the people of Florence and Perugia had entered into a league against the Holy See and its French legates ; and Bologna, Viterbo, Ancona, together with other cities, not without provocation from the mismanagement of papal officials, promptly rallied to the insurgents.   That Lucca as well as Pisa and Siena held back for a time was largely due to the untiring efforts of Catherine, who paid a special visit to Lucca besides writing numerous letters of exhortation to all three towns.   From Avignon, after an unsuccessful appeal to the Florentines, Pope Gregory despatched his legate Cardinal Robert of Geneva with an army, and laid Florence under an interdict.*   This ban soon entailed such serious effects upon the city that its rulers in alarm sent to Siena, to accept Catherine's offer to become their mediatrix with the Holy See.   Always ready to act as peacemaker, she promptly set out for Florence.   The magistrates promised she should be followed to Avignon by their ambassadors, but these gentlemen set out only after a protracted delay.   Catherine arrived at Avignon on June 18, 1376, and soon had a conference with Pope Gregory, to whom she had already written six times, " in an intolerably dictatorial tone, a little sweetened with

---

* In this unhappy business the pope hired the services and force of the English free-booter, John Hawkwood.

expressions of her perfect Christian deference." But the Florentines proved fickle and insincere ; their ambassadors disclaimed Catherine, and the pope's peace terms were so severe that nothing could be done.

Although the immediate purpose of her visit to Avignon had thus failed, Catherine's efforts in another direction were crowned with success. Many of the religious, social and political troubles under which Europe was groaning were to a great degree attributable to the fact that for seventy-four years the popes had been absent from Rome, living in Avignon, where the curia had become almost entirely French. It was a state of things deplored by all earnest Christians outside France, and the greatest men of the age had remonstrated against it in vain. Gregory XI had indeed himself proposed to transfer his residence to the Holy City, but had been deterred by the opposition of his French cardinals. Since Catherine in her previous letters had urged his return to Rome, it was only natural that the pope should talk with her on the subject when they came face to face. "Fulfil what you have promised", was her reply—recalling to him, it is said, a vow which he had never disclosed to any human being. Gregory decided to act without loss of time. On September 13, 1376, he started from Avignon to travel by water to Rome, Catherine and her friends leaving the city on the same day to return overland to Siena. The two parties met again, almost accidentally, in Genoa, where Catherine was detained by the illness of two of her secretaries, Neri di Landoccio and Stephen Maconi, a young Sienese nobleman whom she had converted and who had become the most ardent of her followers, and perhaps the most beloved— except Alessia. It was a month before she was back in Siena, from whence she continued to write to Pope Gregory, exhorting him to contribute by all means possible to the peace of Italy. By his special desire she went again to Florence, still rent by factions and obstinate in its disobedience. There she remained for some time, amidst daily murders and confiscations, in danger of her life but ever undaunted, even when swords were drawn against her. Finally she did indeed establish peace with the Holy See, although not during Gregory's reign, but in that of his successor.

After this memorable reconciliation the saint returned to Siena where, as Raymund of Capua tells us, " she occupied herself actively in the composition of a book which she dictated under the inspiration of the Holy Ghost ". This was the very celebrated mystical work, written in four treatises, known as the " Dialogue of St Catherine ". That she was favoured with some infused knowledge had indeed already been made clear on several occasions—in Siena, at Avignon and in Genoa—when learned theologians had plied her with hard questions, and had retired disconcerted with the wisdom of her replies. Her health had long since become so seriously impaired that she was never free from pain : yet her emaciated face habitually bore a happy and even smiling expression, and her personal charm was as winning as ever.

But within two years of the ending of the papal " captivity " at Avignon began the scandal of the great schism which followed the death of Gregory XI in 1378, when Urban VI was chosen in Rome and a rival pope was set up in Avignon by certain cardinals who declared Urban's election illegal. Christendom was divided into two camps, and Catherine wore herself out in her efforts to obtain for Urban the recognition which was his due. Letter after letter she addressed to the princes and leaders of the various European countries. To Urban himself she continued to write, sometimes to urge him to bear up under his trials, sometimes admonishing him to abate a harshness which was alienating even his supporters. Far from resenting her reproof, the pope told her to come to Rome that he might profit by her advice and assistance. In obedience to the call she took up her residence in the City, labouring indefatigably by her prayers, exhortations and letters to gain fresh adherents to the true pontiff. Her life, however, was almost ended. Early in 1380 she had a strange seizure, when a visible presentment of the ship of the Church seemed to crush her to the earth and she offered herself a victim for it. After this she never really recovered. On April 21 there supervened a paralytic stroke which disabled her from the waist downwards, and eight days later, at the age of thirty-three, St Catherine of Siena passed away in the arms of Alessia Saracini.*

Besides the Dialogue mentioned above, about 400 of St Catherine's letters are still extant, many of them of great interest and historical value, and all of them remarkable for the beauty of their diction ; they are addressed to popes and princes, priests and soldiers, religious and men and women in the world, and are indeed " the most complete expression of Catherine's many-sided personality ". Those, especially, addressed to Gregory XI show a remarkable combination of deep respect, outspokenness and familiarity—" my sweet babbo " she calls the pontiff. Catherine has been called " the greatest woman in Christendom ", and her spiritual significance can hardly be overrated ; but it is perhaps open to question whether she had as much political and social influence as is sometimes attributed to her. As Father B. de Gaiffier has written : " It is Catherine's devotion to the cause of Christ's Church that makes her such a noble figure ". That Church canonized her in 1461.

Nearly all the more painstaking English biographers of St Catherine—for example, Mother Frances Raphael Drane (1887), Professor E. G. Gardner (1907), and Alice Curtayne —discuss the question of sources in some detail. The most important materials for her life are supplied by the *Legenda Major* of Bd Raymund of Capua, her confessor ; the *Supplementum* by Thomas Caffarini ; the *Legenda Minor*, which is also Caffarini's ; the *Processus Contestationum super sanctitatem et doctrinam Catharinae de Senis ;* and the *Miracoli.* There is also, of course, the great collection of Catherine's letters, with regard to which both the dating and the determination of the primitive text is often a matter of great difficulty, as well as many other documents of considerable, if minor, importance. Some little commotion was caused by the extremely drastic criticism to which these sources were subjected by Dr Robert Fawtier. Many of his strictures appeared in the form of articles or contributions to the proceedings of learned societies, and he himself re-edited some of the less familiar texts, e.g. the *Legenda Minor,* but the most notable points of attack are set out in two larger volumes under the common title, *Sainte Catherine de Sienne : Essai de critique des sources.* The earlier volume deals with the *Sources hagiographiques* (1921), the later with *Les œuvres de Ste Catherine* (1930). Criticisms of Dr Fawtier's many useful comments will be found in the appendix to Alice Curtayne's *Saint Catherine of Siena* (1929), an excellent book, where an essay of Fr Taurisano is reprinted in the original Italian. Cf. also the *Analecta Bollandiana,* vol. xlix (1930), pp. 448–451. Other useful contributions are those of J. Joergensen, *Sainte Catherine de Sienne* (Eng. trans., 1938) ; E. de Santis Rosmini, *Santa Caterina da Siena* (1930) ; and F. Valli, *L'infanzia e la puerizia di S. Caterina* (1931). Among more recent books must be mentioned N. M. Denis-Boulet, *La carrière politique de ste Catherine de Sienne* (1939) ; M. de la Bedoyère, *Catherine, Saint of Siena* (1946) ; and a full popular life in Italian by Fr Taurisano (1948). *La double expérience de Catherine Benincasa* (1948), by R. Fawtier and L. Canet, is a full statement from a different approach. Canon J. Leclercq's *Ste Catherine de Sienne* (1922) still retains its worth. There is an English edition of the *Dialogue* by Algar Thorold. There is an excellent concise account

* The date of Catherine's birth, and therefore her age, was questioned by Robert Fawtier. On this point, see *Analecta Bollandiana,* vol. xl (1922), pp. 365–411.

of certain problems connected with St Catherine's life, by Fr M. H. Laurent, in DHG., vol. xi, cc. 1517–1521. For the sources of the *Dialogue*, consult A. Grion, *Santa Caterina da Siena : Dottrina e fonti* (1953). For other recent works, see *Analecta Bollandiana*, vol. lxix (1951), pp. 182–191.

ST MAXIMUS, Martyr   (A.D. 250)

THE Roman Martyrology states that the passion of this martyr took place at Ephesus on this day, though his *acta* say distinctly that it was on May 14. Moreover, there is a possibility that it happened at Lampsacus rather than Ephesus, a point not cleared up by the contemporary account of the trial, which is extant in a rather touched-up but substantially authentic form.

When the Emperor Decius issued his decree against Christians a certain Maximus, a small man of business and a true servant of God, voluntarily gave himself up in Asia (Minor). He was brought before the proconsul Optimus, and when asked his name and condition answered, " Maximus. Born a freeman, but a slave of Christ."

OPTIMUS : What is your occupation ?

MAXIMUS : I am a man of the people, and I live by trading.

OPTIMUS : Are you a Christian ?

MAXIMUS : Yes, but an unworthy one.

OPTIMUS : Don't you know the recent decrees of the invincible emperors ?

MAXIMUS : Which ones ?

OPTIMUS : Those which order all Christians to give up their empty super-stition, to acknowledge the true and supreme prince, and to worship the gods.

MAXIMUS : I know the impious edict issued by the king of this world, and that is why I have surrendered myself.

OPTIMUS : Sacrifice to the gods.

MAXIMUS : I sacrifice to only one God, to whom I am happy to have sacrificed since my childhood.

OPTIMUS : If you sacrifice you will be set free. If not, you will be tortured to death.

MAXIMUS : That is what I have always wanted. I have given myself up so that I may exchange this short and miserable life for life everlasting.

Then the proconsul had him flogged, and when that effected nothing Maximus was hung up on the instrument of torture called the horse. But he remained firm, and so Optimus pronounced sentence : " Maximus has refused to obey the law and to sacrifice to the great Diana : the Divine Clemency [*i.e.*, the Emperor] there-fore ordains that he be stoned to death as a warning to other Christians ". So he was taken outside the city and thus slain, while he glorified and gave thanks to God.

The text of the *acta* is in the *Acta Sanctorum* and Ruinart's *Acta sincera*. Other refer-ences and notes can be found in Leclercq, *Les Martyrs*, vol. ii.

SS. MARIAN AND JAMES, Martyrs   (A.D. 259)

THESE two martyrs suffered during the persecution of Valerian at Lambesa in Numidia. Marian (Marianus) was a reader, James a deacon, and they were arrested at Cirta (modern Constantine in Algeria) and put to torture. Marian was treated with special savagery, apparently because he was suspected of being a deacon too. He told the writer of his *acta* that, falling asleep after his torments, he had a dream in which he was invited up to the scaffold by St Cyprian, who had suffered at Carthage in the previous year. James also had a vision of his approaching triumph.

After being interviewed by the governor they were sent to Lambesa, some eighty miles away, where they were sentenced to death. The scene of their martyrdom was a hollow in a river valley, where " the high ground on either side served for seats as in a theatre ". So many others were put to death at the same time that they were drawn up in rows for execution, so that " the blade of the impious murderer might behead the faithful, one after another, in a rush of fury ". Before his turn came, Marian spoke with the voice of prophecy of the avenging misfortunes that would come upon the slaughterers of the righteous ; and his dead body was embraced and kissed by his mother, " rightly named Mary, blessed both in son and name ".

The Passion of SS. Marian and James and their fellows is an authentic document of great interest, written by one who shared their imprisonment. The ancient Calendar of Carthage commemorates them on May 6, but the Roman Martyrology, following the " Hieronymianum ", names them on April 30 ; other martyrs mentioned in the *passio*, e.g. SS. Agapius and Secundinus, are named on the previous day. The cathedral of Gubbio in Umbria is dedicated in honour of SS. Marian and James, and claims to have their relics.

The *passio* is printed by Ruinart in his *Acta sincera* and by Gebhardt in *Acta martyrum selecta;* see also P. Franchi de Cavalieri in *Studi e Testi* (1900). There is an English translation in E. C. E. Owen, *Some Authentic Acts of the Early Martyrs* (1927).

ST EUTROPIUS, Bishop of Saintes, Martyr   (Third Century)

THE town of Saintes in south-west France honours as its first bishop St Eutropius, who was sent from Rome in the third century to evangelize the inhabitants and who suffered martyrdom either at their hands or by order of the Roman authorities. The story locally told is that St Eutropius accompanied St Denis to France to share his apostolic labours. The people of Saintes, to whom he preached, expelled him from their city, and he went to live in a cell on a neighbouring rock where he gave himself to prayer and to instructing those who would listen. Amongst others he converted and baptized the Roman governor's daughter, Eustella. When the girl's father discovered that she was a Christian he drove her from his house, and charged the butchers of Saintes to slay Eutropius. Eustella found him dead with his skull split by an axe, and she buried his remains in his cell.

In the *Acta Sanctorum*, April, vol. iii, will be found what purports to be an early Latin life of St Eutropius, but no reliance can be placed upon it. St Gregory of Tours, however, in his *Gloria Martyrum*, ch. 55, bears witness to the translation of the saint's relics in the sixth century, as does Venantius Fortunatus. *Cf.* Duchesne, *Fastes Épiscopaux*, vol. ii, p. 138 ; and *Analecta Bollandiana*, vol. lxix (1951), pp. 57–66. Both Gregory and Venantius seem to have written the name " Eutropis ".

BD HILDEGARD, Matron   (A.D. 783)

HISTORY has but little to tell us about Bd Hildegard, the girl of seventeen whom Charlemagne married after his repudiation of the Lombard princess Hermengard. Even her parentage is uncertain, although she was probably connected with the dukes of Swabia. She is said to have been extremely beautiful, and as good as she was fair. Of her nine children, one became Louis the Debonair and three predeceased her. Hildegard was very friendly with St Boniface's kinswoman, the abbess St Lioba. She died in 783 at Thionville (Diedenhofen) on the Moselle, and her relics were subsequently translated to the abbey of Kempten in Swabia, of which she had been a benefactress. Hildegard was greatly revered during her lifetime, and her shrine was a place of pilgrimage.

The legendary or fictitious element is very conspicuous in the life of Hildegard printed in the *Acta Sanctorum*, April, vol. iii, and the story cannot be trusted wherever it goes beyond the data furnished in the chronicles and other sources. Hildegard, of course, figures to some extent in all the modern lives of Charlemagne.

ST FORANNAN, Abbot   (A.D. 982)

The abbey of Waulsort on the Meuse must have been closely connected with Ireland in its early days, for several of its abbots came to it from that country, including St Maccallan, St Cadroe and St Forannan, who occupied for a time the Irish bishopric of Domhnach-Mòr, a diocese or monastery which has not hitherto been identified. He is said to have been led to abandon his native land by a dream, in which an angel showed him a beautiful valley that was to be his home. With twelve companions he left Ireland and made his way to the mouth of the river Meuse, up which he sailed as far as Waulsort. In this beautiful spot, which charms the tourist who takes the river trip between Namur and Givet, the saint recognized the Vallis Decora of his vision. He was hospitably received by the monks there.

He appears to have been appointed abbot of Waulsort in 962. Business connected with his monastery afterwards took him to Rome, and on his way back he stayed for a time at the abbey of Gorze in Lorraine. His object appears to have been to obtain training for himself and his companions in the Rule of St Benedict, with a view to reforming the discipline of Waulsort, which had become relaxed. St Forannan raised his abbey to great sanctity and glory, and obtained from the Christian princes the privilege of the Truce of God, which gave security of life and limb to all bona-fide pilgrims to Waulsort on the annual festival and during its octave.

There is quite a lengthy life printed both by Mabillon and in the *Acta Sanctorum*, April, vol. iii. See also O'Hanlon, LIS., vol. iv, pp. 552 *seq.*, and Gougaud, *Gaelic Pioneers of Christianity*, pp. 37, 83–84, and *Les saints irlandais hors d 'Irlande*, p. 103.

ST GUALFARDUS OR WOLFHARD   (A.D. 1127)

About the year 1096 there arrived at Verona, in the train of a party of German merchants, a saddler from Augsburg called Gualfardus (Wolfhard), who took up his abode in the city. All that he earned by his trade, apart from what was necessary for bare subsistence, he gave to the poor, and he led so holy a life that he was regarded with veneration. Shocked to find himself treated as a saint, he secretly left Verona to seek a spot where he could serve God unobserved by men. In a forest on the river Adige he lived as a hermit for years, until he was recognized by some boatmen whose vessel ran aground near his hut. The Veronese induced him to return into their midst and he eventually became a hermit-monk of the Camaldolese priory of the Holy Redeemer. There he spent the last ten years of his life.

Famous for miracles during his life, St Guaifardus became even more famous for them after his death.

No other source of information seems available beside the short Latin life printed in the *Acta Sanctorum*, April, vol. iii.

BB. FRANCIS DICKENSON AND MILES GERARD, MARTYRS
(A.D. 1590)

NATIVES respectively of Yorkshire and of Lancashire, Francis Dickenson and Miles Gerard crossed over to France to be educated for the priesthood in the Douai college at Rheims.   In 1589, six years after Gerard's ordination, they were despatched on the English mission, but the ship on which they embarked was wrecked, passengers as well as crew being cast up on the Kentish coast.   Either on suspicion or on information, Dickenson and Gerard were promptly arrested and cast into prison.   Brought up for trial, they were condemned to death as traitors for the offence of coming to England as priests.   They suffered martyrdom together at Rochester, on April 13 or 30, 1590.

See Challoner, MMP., p. 162.   There is further interesting information in the state papers which preserve a record of the examinations of these two martyrs.   See Catholic Record Society *Publications*, vol. v, pp. 171–173 ; and *cf.* Pollen, *Acts of English Martyrs*, pp. 314–315.

BD BENEDICT OF URBINO   (A.D. 1625)

THE father of Benedict of Urbino was a member of the princely family of the Passionei, and his mother was Magdalen Cibò.   The little boy, Martin by name, lost both his parents before he was seven, but he was left in charge of guardians who brought him up carefully.   In the University of Perugia, where he studied philosophy, as well as at Padua, where he graduated in jurisprudence, he was known as a young man of exemplary conduct.   After taking his doctor's degree he went to Rome, but finding no satisfaction in the legal career which he had chosen he decided to seek admission to the Capuchin friary at Fossombrone.   This was not readily conceded on account of the opposition of his relations, but the habit was bestowed upon him at Fano in 1584.   It was then that he took the name of Benedict. Even then his difficulties were by no means ended.   During his novitiate he became so ill that it seemed as though he would have to leave, and although he made a good recovery it was thought that he was too delicate to be professed.   That he was eventually allowed to take the vows was due entirely to the novice-master, who emphasized the extraordinary piety of the young neophyte.

Friar Benedict was for three years specially attached to the vicar general, St Laurence of Brindisi, to accompany him on his visitations in Austria and Bohemia. The missionary sermons which Benedict preached at that time brought about many conversions amongst heretics and lax Catholics.   He had a great zeal for the care of God's house, and would sometimes, even when he was a superior, take a broom and sweep out the church.   He frequently preached on the passion of our Lord, upon which he meditated daily for an hour, lying on the ground with his face to the earth, and his most ardent desire was that every heart should be consumed with the fire of love which Christ came on earth to kindle.   In the year 1625 he set forth in very severe weather to preach the Lenten sermons at Sassocorbaro, although he was in very poor health.   He began his course on Ash Wednesday, but was too ill to proceed.   He was therefore taken back to Fossombrone, where he died on April 30.   One of Bd Benedict's favourite sayings was : " He that hopes and trusts in God can never be lost ".   He was beatified in 1867.

More than one account of his life was published in 1867, *e.g.* those by Eusebio a Montesanto and Pellegrino da Forli ; a later book is that of Eugenio de Potenza (1920). *Cf.* also Ernest-Marie de Beaulieu, *Liber Memorialis O.M.Cap.* (1928), pp. 258–260 ; and Léon, *Auréole Séraphique* (Eng. trans.), vol. ii, pp. 147–150.

MAY

1 : ST. JOSEPH THE WORKMAN *(see 19 March)*

SS. PHILIP AND JAMES, APOSTLES *(transferred to 11 May)*

ST PHILIP the apostle came from Bethsaida in Galilee, and seems to have belonged to a little group of earnest men who had already fallen under the influence of St John the Baptist.   In the synoptic gospels there is no mention of Philip except in the list of apostles which occurs in each.   But St John's gospel introduces his name several times, recording in particular that the call of Philip came the day after that given to St Peter and St Andrew.   Jesus, we are told, " found Philip " and said to him, " Follow me ".   More than a century and a half later Clement of Alexandria avers that St Philip was the young man who, when our Lord said to him, " Follow me ", begged leave to go home first and bury his father, which occasioned the reply, " Let the dead bury their dead ; but go thou and preach the kingdom of God " (Luke ix 60).   It seems probable that this identification was based on no firmer ground than the use of the phrase " Follow me " in both cases. The position of the incident of the rebuke ("Let the dead ", etc.) in the narrative of St Luke, and also in that of St Matthew, clearly suggests that it occurred some time after the beginning of the public life, when our Lord was already attended by His little company of apostles.   On the other hand, St Philip was certainly called before the marriage feast at Cana, though, as our Saviour Himself declared, His hour had not yet come, *i.e.* He had not yet embarked on the public activities of His great mission.

From the account given by the evangelist, we should naturally infer that Philip responded without hesitation to the call he had received.   Though his knowledge was imperfect, so much so that he describes Jesus as " the son of Joseph of Nazareth ", he goes at once to find his friend Nathanael (in all probability to be identified with the apostle Bartholomew) and tells him, " We have found him of whom Moses, in the law and the prophets did write ", being plainly satisfied that this was in truth the Messias.   At the same time Philip gives proof of a sober discretion in his missionary zeal.   He does not attempt to force his discovery upon unwilling ears. When Nathanael objects, " Can anything good come from Nazareth ? " his answer is not indignant declamation, but an appeal for personal inquiry—" Come and see ". In the description of the feeding of the five thousand Philip figures again.   " When Jesus ", we are told, " had lifted up His eyes and seen that a very great multitude cometh to Him, He said to Philip, ' Whence shall we buy bread that these may eat ? ' And this He said to try him ; for He Himself knew what He would do."   Once more we get an impression of the sober literalness of St Philip's mental outlook when he replies : " Two hundred pennyworth of bread is not sufficient for them that every one may take a little ".   It is in accord with the same amiable type of character which hesitates before responsibilities that, when certain Gentiles among the crowds who thronged to Jerusalem for the pasch came to Philip saying, " Sir, we would see Jesus ", we find him reluctant to deal with the request without taking counsel. " Philip cometh and telleth Andrew. Again Andrew and Philip told Jesus." Finally another glimpse is afforded us of the apostle's earnestness and devotion conjoined with defective spiritual insight, when on the evening before the Passion our Lord announced, " No man cometh to the Father but by me. If you had known me, you would without doubt have known my Father also : and from henceforth you shall know Him, and you have seen Him." Philip saith to Him : " Lord, show us the Father, and it is enough for us ". Jesus saith to him : " Have I been so long a time with you ; and have you not known me ? Philip, he that seeth me seeth the Father also. How sayest thou : Show us the Father ? " (John xiv 6–9).

Apart from the fact that St Philip is named with the other apostles who spent ten days in the upper room awaiting the coming of the Holy Ghost at Pentecost, this is all we know about him with any degree of certainty.

On the other hand, Eusebius, the church historian, and some other early writers, have preserved a few details which tradition connected with the later life of Philip. The most reliable of these is the belief that he preached the gospel in Phrygia, and died at Hierapolis, where he was also buried. Sir W. M. Ramsay found among the tombs of that city a fragmentary inscription which refers to a church there dedicated in honour of St Philip. We know also that Polycrates, bishop of Ephesus, writing to Pope Victor towards the close of the second century, refers to two daughters of St Philip the Apostle, who had lived in virginity until old age at Hierapolis, and mentions also another daughter who was buried in his own city of Ephesus. Papias, who was himself bishop of Hierapolis, seems to have known personally the daughters of St Philip and to have learnt from them of a miracle attributed to him, no less than the raising of a dead man to life. Heracleon, the gnostic, about the year 180, maintained that the apostles Philip, Matthew and Thomas died a natural death, but Clement of Alexandria contradicted this, and the opinion commonly accepted at a later date was that Philip was crucified head downwards under Domitian. One fact which introduces much uncertainty into these obscure fragments of evidence is the confusion which undoubtedly arose between Philip the Apostle and Philip the Deacon, sometimes also called " the Evangelist ", who figures so prominently in chapter viii of the Acts of the Apostles. Both, in particular, are alleged to have had daughters who enjoyed exceptional consideration in the early Church. It is stated that the remains of St Philip the Apostle were eventually brought to Rome, and that they have been preserved there in the basilica of the Apostles since the time of Pope Pelagius (A.D. 561). A late apocryphal document in Greek, dating from the close of the fourth century at earliest, purports to recount the missionary activities of St Philip in Greece, as well as in the land of the Parthians and elsewhere, but it echoes the received tradition so far as regards his death and burial at Hierapolis.

The apostle St James—the Less, or the younger—here associated with St Philip, is most commonly held to be the same individual who is variously designated " James, the son of Alpheus " (*e.g.* Matt. x 3, and Acts i 13), and " James, the brother of the Lord " (Matt. xiii 55 ; Gal. i 19). He may also possibly be identical with James, son of Mary and brother of Joseph (Mark xv 40). This, however, is not the place to discuss the rather intricate problem of the " brethren of our Lord " and the questions connected with it. It may be assumed then, as Alban Butler infers, that the apostle James who became bishop of Jerusalem (Acts xv and xxi 18) was the son of Alpheus and " brother " (*i.e.* first cousin) of Jesus Christ. Although no prominence is given to this James in the gospel narrative, we learn from St Paul that he was favoured with a special appearing of our Lord before the Ascension. Further, when St Paul, three years after his conversion, went up to Jerusalem and was still regarded with some suspicion by the apostles who remained there, James, with St Peter, seems to have bid him a cordial welcome. Later we learn that Peter, after his escape from prison, sent a special intimation to James, apparently as to one whose pre-eminence was recognized among the Christians of the holy city. At what is called the Council of Jerusalem, where it was decided that the Gentiles who accepted Christian teaching need not be circumcised, it was St James who, after listening to St Peter's advice, voiced the conclusion of the assembly in the words, " it hath seemed good to the Holy Ghost and to us " (Acts xv). He was, in fact, the bishop of Jerusalem, as Clement of Alexandria and Eusebius expressly state. Even Josephus, the Jewish historian, bears testimony to the repute in which James was held, and declares, so Eusebius asserts, that the terrible calamities which fell upon the people of that city were a retribution for their treatment of one " who was the most righteous of men ". The story of his martyrdom, as told by Hegesippus in the latter part of the second century, has been preserved by Eusebius, and runs as follows :

Together with the apostles, James, our Lord's brother, succeeded to the government of the Church. He received the name of " the Just " from all men from the time of our Lord even to our own ; for there were many called James. Now he was holy from his mother's womb, drank no wine nor strong drink nor ate anything in which was life. No razor came upon his head ; he anointed himself not with oil, and used no bath. To him alone it was permitted to enter the holy place ; for he wore nothing woollen, but linen garments [*i.e.* the priestly robes]. And alone he entered into the sanctuary and was found on his knees asking forgiveness on behalf of the people, so that his knees became hard like a camel's, for he was continually bending the knee in worship to God and asking forgiveness for the people. In fact, on account of his exceeding great justice he was called " the Just " and " Oblias ", that is to say, bulwark of the people.

We learn further from Hegesippus that :

As many as came to believe did so through James. When, therefore, many also of the rulers were believers, there was an uproar among the Jews and scribes and pharisees, for they said : " There is danger that the whole people should expect Jesus as the Christ ". Coming together, therefore, they said to James : " We beseech thee, restrain the people, for they are gone astray unto Jesus, imagining that he is the Christ. We beseech thee to persuade all who come for the day of the Passover concerning Jesus, for in thee do we all put our trust. For we bear thee witness, as do all the people, that thou art just and that thou acceptest not the person of any. Persuade, therefore, the multitude that they go not astray concerning Jesus. For, of a truth, the people, and we all, put our trust in thee. Stand, therefore, upon the pinnacle of the temple, that from thy lofty station thou mayest be evident, and thy words may easily be heard by all the people. For on account of the Passover all the tribes, with the Gentiles also, have come together." Therefore the aforesaid scribes and pharisees set James upon the pinnacle of the temple, and cried aloud to him saying : " O Just One, in whom we ought all to put our trust, inasmuch as the people is gone astray after Jesus who was crucified, tell us what is the door of Jesus " (*cf.* John x 1–9). And he replied with a loud voice : " Why ask ye me concerning the Son of Man, since He sitteth in Heaven on the right hand of the Mighty Power, and shall come on the clouds of Heaven ? " And when many were fully persuaded and gave glory at the testimony of James and said : " Hosanna to the son of David ", then once more the same scribes and pharisees said among themselves : " We do ill in affording such a testimony to Jesus. Let us rather go up and cast him down, that being affrighted they may not believe him." And they cried aloud saying : " Ho, ho, even the Just One has gone astray ! " And they fulfilled the scripture that is written in Isaias : " Let us take away the just one, for he is troublesome to us. Therefore they shall eat the fruit of their doings." Going up therefore they cast the Just One down. And they said to each other : " Let us stone James the Just ". And they began to stone him, for the fall did not kill him. But turning he kneeled down and said : " I beseech thee, O Lord God, Father, forgive them, for they know not what they do ". And while they thus were stoning him, one of the priests of the sons of Rechab, the son of Rachabim, who had witness borne to them by Jeremias the prophet, cried aloud, saying : " Cease ye ; what do ye ? The Just One is praying on your behalf." And one of them, a fuller, took the stick with which he beat out the clothes, and brought it down on the Just One's head. Thus he was martyred. And they buried him at the spot beside the temple, and his monument still remains beside the temple.

The story is told somewhat differently by Josephus, who says nothing about James's having been thrown down from the pinnacle of the temple. He informs us, however, that he was stoned to death, and assigns this to the year 62. In relation to the festivals kept by the Church liturgically under the designation of " St Peter's Chair ", it is interesting to note that Eusebius speaks of the " throne ", or chair, of St James as still preserved and venerated by the Christians of Jerusalem. This St James is commonly held to be the author of the epistle in the New Testament which bears his name and which, by its insistence on good works, was highly obnoxious to those who preached the doctrine of justification by faith alone.

Outside the New Testament, and such not wholly reliable traditions as we find recorded in the pages of Eusebius, there is very little we can appeal to as sources for the history of either St Philip or St James. In the *Acta Sanctorum*, May, vol. i, the Bollandists have gathered up most of the allusions to be met with in the early ecclesiastical writers. The apocryphal Acts of St Philip, which probably date from the third or fourth century, have been edited by R. A. Lipsius in his *Apokryphen Apostelgeschichten und Apostellegenden*, vol. ii, part 2, pp. 1–90. See also E. Hennecke, *Neutestamentliche Apokryphen* (2nd edn., 1924) ; and the *Handbuch* brought out by the same editor. The life of the two apostles is discussed in nearly all scriptural encyclopaedias, such, for example, as the *Dictionnaire de la Bible* with its supplements. The authorship of the canonical Epistle of St James has been the subject of much heated discussion. The matter does not concern us here, and the text of the epistle itself throws little light upon the history or character of the writer who penned it. As the martyrdom of St James the Less is commonly assigned to the year A.D. 62 or 63, the epistle, on the assumption that he is the author, must be of early date. Mgr Duchesne has suggested that the association of St James with St Philip on May 1, which is common both to the Gelasian and the Gregorian Sacramentaries, may be traced to the dedication of the church " of the Apostles " at Rome by Pope John III, *c.* A.D. 563. This church, though later spoken of vaguely as the church " of the Apostles ", was originally dedicated in honour of SS. Philip and James in particular ; the inscription long preserved there said :

Quisquis lector adest Jacobi pariterque Philippi
Cernat apostolicum lumen inesse locis.

But there are indications in certain manuscripts of the Hieronymianum and in other documents that Philip's name on May 1 once stood alone, and that James is a later addition.

ST AMATOR, or AMATRE, BISHOP OF AUXERRE   (A.D. 418)

FOR details of the life of St Amator we have to rely upon a biography written 160
years after his death by an African priest called Stephen. The contents of the
narrative prove it to have been for the most part an audacious fiction. Amator,
we read, was the only son of distinguished citizens of Auxerre, who affianced him
to a young heiress named Martha, although he had expressed a strong disinclination
for the married state. On the wedding day the guests assembled, and the aged
Bishop Valerian came to perform the ceremony. Accidentally or providentially
Valerian, instead of reading the nuptial blessing, recited the form which was used
in the ordination of deacons—a mistake which was noticed only by the bride and
bridegroom. When the service was over the young couple agreed to live a life of
virginity, and Martha within a short time retired into a convent. Amator, after
having laboured for some years as a priest, was elected bishop of Auxerre. In the
course of a long episcopate he converted the remaining pagans of the district,
performed many miracles, and built churches. He is said, on reliable evidence,
to have ordained St Patrick up to the priesthood.

The governor of Auxerre during St Amator's later years was Germanus, a
high-spirited young patriciar wholly devoted to hunting. That all men might
admire his prowess he continued, although he was a Christian, to observe the pagan
custom of hanging the heads of the animals he killed on a pear-tree in the middle
of the city—an offering to Woden. This caused great scandal, and St Amator,
after having repeatedly remonstrated with Germanus, had the tree cut down during
the governor's absence. Greatly incensed, the young man on his return threatened
to kill the bishop, who thought it advisable to retire for a time from the city. He
was now well advanced in years, and had been for some time desirous of handing
on his office to another. While he was staying at Autun with the provincial prefect,
Julius, it was suddenly borne in upon him—by revelation or by intuition—that the
worthy successor he was seeking was none other than Germanus himself. Having
obtained the sanction of his host, under whom the governor of Auxerre served,
Amator returned to Auxerre where, at his summons, the people—Germanus
included—came to him in the cathedral. All arms having been laid down outside
at the bishop's request, the doors were shut, and the prelate, with the help of some
of his clergy, seized Germanus, stripped him of his secular garb, gave him the
tonsure, and pronounced him bishop designate of Auxerre.

St Amator's work was now done. He had laboured for many years, and had
secured as his successor one who was destined to become the greatest of all the
bishops of Auxerre. A few days later the aged saint asked to be conveyed once
more into his cathedral, where he peacefully breathed his last. The body of St
Amator was laid with his predecessors in the ancient cemetery on the Entrains road.

The Latin life written by Stephen is printed in the *Acta Sanctorum*, May, vol. i. Its
extravagant details are, of course, quite fabulous, but there is no reason to doubt St Amator's
historical existence. Mgr Duchesne in his *Fastes Épiscopaux* (vol. ii, pp. 427–446) speaks
well of the episcopal lists of Auxerre. See also DHG., vol. ii, *c.* 981, and Father Delehaye's
commentary on the *Hieronymianum* (p. 224) in which martyrology St Amator is commemorated. But especially consult R. Louis on " L'Église d'Auxerre . . . avant S.

Germain " in *S. Germain d'Auxerre et son temps* (1951), and his *Les églises d'Auxerre . . . au xie siècle* (1952).

ST BRIEUC, OR BRIOCUS, ABBOT   (SIXTH CENTURY)

ALTHOUGH some writers have striven to prove that St Brieuc was of Irish descent, it is now commonly admitted that he probably was born in Cardiganshire. A life of him, which purports to be written by a contemporary but which is certainly of much later date, perhaps the eleventh century, describes his career in some detail. The saint, who in this Latin narrative is generally called Brioccius, but also Brio-maglus,* is said to have been the son of noble parents, pagans, but good and charitable people. Before his birth an angel appeared, first to his mother and then to his father, in their sleep, demanding of them that the child should be sent to France to be brought up by a St Germanus. When in due course he had been ordained priest, a vision in his sleep recalled him to his own country, and there he converted his parents to Christianity, seemingly as a consequence of the miracles of healing which he wrought. After a while he was bidden by an angel to return to " Latium ", † and accordingly he set sail with no less than 168 disciples whom he had gathered about him. On the journey the ship's progress was suddenly arrested in the middle of the night. Great consternation prevailed, but they eventually discovered that they had struck an obstacle, which was really the Devil, who, in the form of a huge monster, was lying right across their course. Yielding to the prayers of the saint this primitive sea-serpent, though with a very bad grace, vanished into thin air. " *Evanescit ut fumus* ", is the biographer's phrase.

Pursuing their journey, they landed at some unidentified place where the local chieftain, named Conan, was converted from paganism by Brieuc's miracles. This, however, was not their final destination, and they sailed on to a little estuary on the coast of Brittany near Tréguier, where they settled and built a monastery, of which St Brieuc became abbot. A flourishing and fervent community was formed, but before long news came of a grievous pestilence which was devastating his native land. His family implored him to visit them once again, and he, though very reluctantly, yielded to their entreaties, leaving his nephew, St Tugdual, to rule the abbey in his absence. His parents were consoled, and the pestilence was arrested by his prayers, but he would not consent to abide with them long. He was gladly welcomed back in Brittany, where he determined to found another monastery in a different part of the country. It is said that eighty-four volunteers accompanied him, who all travelled by sea, and, finding a suitable spot with a good water supply, proceeded to encamp and make themselves at home. The ruler of the district, Rigual, was at first infuriated by this invasion, but falling ill himself he was cured by St Brieuc. Having further discovered that he was a blood relation he became his warm friend and patron. We are told, however, that Brieuc, after the founda-tion of the new abbey on the lands which the chieftain bestowed, assisted Rigual on his death-bed, and himself, to the great sorrow of his brethren, passed away shortly after. He is said to have been then one hundred years old. All this is supposed to have happened on the site of the present cathedral and town of Saint-Brieuc, but in the middle of the ninth century the saint's remains, for fear of the Norman marauders, were translated to Angers. In 1210 a portion of the relics was given

* Briomaglus seems to be the full form of the name, Briocus the hypocoristic abbreviation so common among Celtic peoples.
† Which may mean Brittany.

back by the monks of Angers, and they are preserved in the cathedral to this day. It is possible that St Brieuc was a missionary bishop, but the see which bears his name was not formed until many centuries later.

The complete text of the *Vita S. Brioci* was printed for the first time in the *Analecta Bollandiana*, vol. ii (1883), pp. 161–190. In the same collection, vol. xxiii (1904), pp. 246–251, is an interesting fragment in verse of a life in which he is called " Briomaglus ". From this we learn that when his remains were exhumed (*c.* 853[?]) he was found wearing a dalmatic, a fact which pointed to episcopal consecration. See also Duchesne, *Fastes Épiscopaux*, vol. ii, pp. 269 and 390 ; LBS., vol. i, p. 288 ; du Bois de la Villerabel, *Vie de Saint Brieuc ;* Gougaud, *Christianity in Celtic Lands* (1932), p. 115. Most valuable of all, however, is the essay of G. H. Doble, *St Brioc* (1929). At least one Cornish church is dedicated in honour of St Brieuc, *viz.* St Breoke (but not Breage) ; one in Cardiganshire, Llandyfriog ; and one in Gloucestershire, St Briavels.

ST SIGISMUND OF BURGUNDY   (A.D. 524)

THE kingdom of Burgundy at the beginning of the sixth century comprized a great portion of south-eastern France and of south-western Switzerland. It was ruled by a prince of Vandal extraction named Gundebald, who was an Arian, but a year before his death his son and successor, Sigismund, was converted to the Catholic faith by St Avitus, Bishop of Vienne. But Sigismund seems to have remained something of a barbarian—subject at times to uncontrollable fits of rage. On one occasion, when worked upon by the false accusations of his second wife, he ordered his son Sigeric to be strangled. No sooner had the deed been perpetrated than Sigismund came to his senses and was overpowered with horror and remorse. Perhaps the greatest service Sigismund rendered to the Church was the virtual refounding of the monastery of St Maurice at Agaunum in the present canton of Valais ; he endowed it liberally and, in order that the *laus perennis*, the unbroken chant, should be celebrated within its walls, he brought to it monks from Lérins, Gigny, Ile-Barbe and Condat.* When the church was dedicated St Avitus preached a sermon of which fragments are still preserved.

Sigismund in his repentance had prayed that God would punish him in this life, and his prayer was granted. The three kings of France, sons of Clovis, declared war against him with the avowed intention of avenging their maternal grandfather, Chilperic, whom Sigismund's father had put to death, and of conquering Burgundy. Sigismund, after he had been defeated in battle, escaped in the direction of Agaunum. For a time he lived as a hermit in the vicinity of St Maurice, but eventually he was captured and taken to Orleans. There he was put to death by King Clodomir, in spite of the remonstrances of St Avitus. His body was thrown into a well, from which it was recovered, and his relics are now preserved at Prague in Bohemia. St Sigismund is not only named in the Roman Martyrology but is even called a martyr.

There is a *Passio Sancti Sigismundi* which is a valuable historical document compiled by a monk of Agaunum. It is printed in the *Acta Sanctorum*, May, vol. i, but more critically

* The *laus perennis* was an arrangement in certain religious houses by which the praises of God never ceased. Relays of monks or nuns were so timed to succeed each other that the chanting of the divine office went on night and day without intermission ; this was only practicable where communities contained an unusually large number of members. The practice seems to have been of eastern origin, but it found much favour in houses in which the Celtic traditions were strong, and it was also particularly associated with Agaunum. In the course of centuries this observance died out everywhere. *Cf.* St Alexander Akimetes (January 15).

edited by Bruno Krusch in MGH., *Scriptores Merov.*, vol. ii, pp. 333–340. We also learn something from Gregory of Tours, both in his *Historia Francorum*, bk. iii, and in his *De Gloria Martyrum*, ch. 74. A full bibliography is available in H. Leclercq's article on Agaunum in the DAC., vol. i, cc. 850–871, and in Hefele-Leclercq, *Histoire des Conciles*, vol. ii, pp. 1017–1022 and pp. 1031–1042.

ST MARCULF, OR MARCOUL, ABBOT   (*c.* A.D. 558)

THE name of St Marcoul was formerly celebrated throughout the length and breadth of France because for centuries it was usual for the king, after his coronation at Rheims, to proceed to Corbeny to venerate the relics of St Marcoul, in whose honour a novena was observed by the sovereign in person or, vicariously, by his grand-almoner. It was through St Marcoul that the king was popularly believed to derive the gift of healing known as " touching for the King's Evil ", or scrofula. As recently as 1825, after the coronation of Charles X at Rheims, the relics were brought to the hospital of St Marcoul at Rheims, and the novena was kept. Afterwards the monarch laid his hands on a number of patients, making the sign of the cross and saying : " Le roi te touche : Dieu te guérisse ".

Marcoul was born at Bayeux of noble parents. At the age of thirty he was ordained by Possessor, bishop of Coutances, who sent him forth to preach as a kind of diocesan missioner. Although successful in winning souls, Marcoul always longed for solitude and closer union with God, and would retire to a lonely island, where he would spend his days as a hermit. After some time he obtained from King Childebert a grant of land at Nanteuil, on which he built some huts for a few disciples who also wished to live a retired life. From this small nucleus there soon grew a great monastery. Many of the monks continued to live, like their founder, the eremitic life, and several of them, including St Helier, went to settle in the island of Jersey. We read that St Marcoul at one period stayed there with them, and by his intercession saved the inhabitants from a raid of marauding Saxons. So violent a storm arose when he prayed that the invaders were dashed to pieces on the rocks. Marcoul died about the year 558, on May 1, and tradition says that his two most faithful disciples, St Domardus and St Cariulfus (St Criou), passed away on the same day. St Marcoul was regarded as a patron who cured skin diseases, and as late as 1680 sufferers made pilgrimages to his shrine at Nanteuil and bathed in the springs connected with the church. The shrine was completely destroyed by the revolutionaries in 1793.

Mabillon and the Bollandists in the *Acta Sanctorum* (May, vol. i) have printed an ancient life of St Marculf, which, however, as B. Baedorf has shown, can hardly be older than the early ninth century. A somewhat expanded recension is also included in the same collection. Consult further F. Duine, *Mémento des sources hagiographiques de Bretagne*, p. 44. Popular accounts have been published by C. Gautier (1899) and H. Scholl (1932).

ST THEODARD, ARCHBISHOP OF NARBONNE   (A.D. 893)

THE birthplace of St Theodard (" Audard ") was Montauriol, a little town which formerly occupied a site covered by the present city of Montauban. He appears to have studied law at Toulouse, for we first hear of him as the advocate retained by the cathedral authorities in a curious suit brought against them by the Jews of Toulouse, who, not unnaturally, objected to a sort of religious pageant in the course of which a Jew was publicly struck on the face before the cathedral doors. This ceremony took place three times a year—at Christmas, on Good Friday, and on the feast of the Assumption. Archbishop Sigebold, who came to Toulouse for the hearing of the case, was so greatly taken with the young lawyer that he took him back with him to Narbonne. Soon afterwards Theodard received holy orders and became Sigebold's archdeacon. The Montauban breviary describes him as " an eye to the blind, feet to the lame, a father of the poor, and the consoler of the afflicted ". Greatly beloved by all, he was unanimously chosen archbishop of Narbonne at the death of Sigebold, who had nominated him as his successor. The perils which then beset travellers did not deter the newly-elected prelate from undertaking a visit to Rome, where he received the pallium.

As an archbishop he worked unremittingly to repair the ravages wrought by the Saracens and to revive the drooping faith of the people. He practically rebuilt his cathedral, and in 886 restored the bishopric of Ausona (now Vich) which had long fallen into abeyance. To buy back those who were taken captive by the Saracens in their raids, and to feed the hungry during a three years' famine, he not only spent his whole income, but also sold some of the vessels and other treasures of his church. The strenuous life he led and his anxieties for his flock seriously impaired his health ; he could not sleep and suffered from continual fever. It was thought that he might recover in his native air, and he accordingly returned to Montauriol. The monks of St Martin received him joyfully, but they soon realized that he had only come back to die. After making a general confession in the presence of all the brethren St Theodard passed peacefully away as if in sleep. Afterwards the abbey was renamed St Audard in his honour.

The life of St Theodard printed in the *Acta Sanctorum*, May, vol. i, dates only from the close of the eleventh century. See also *Gallia Christiana*, vol. vi, pp. 19–22, and Duchesne, *Fastes Épiscopaux*, vol. i, p. 306. A popular account of the saint has been written in French by J. A. Guyard (1887).

ST PEREGRINE LAZIOSI   (A.D. 1345)

THE only son of well-to-do parents, St Peregrine Laziosi was born in 1260 at Forlì, in the Romagna. As a young man he took an active part in the politics of his native city, which belonged to the anti-papal party. On the occasion of a popular rising, St Philip Benizi, who had been sent by the pope to act as a mediator, was severely mishandled by the popular leaders, and Peregrine himself struck him on the face with his fist. The holy Servite's only reply was to offer the other cheek—an action which brought his assailant to immediate repentance, and from that time Peregrine was a reformed character. Turning away from his worldly companions, he spent hours upon his knees in the chapel of our Lady in the cathedral. One day the Blessed Virgin herself appeared to him in that place, and addressed him, saying, " Go to Siena : there you will find the devout men who call themselves my servants : attach yourself to them ". Peregrine instantly obeyed. Having received the Servite habit, he set about following with zeal the path of perfection. It became his guiding principle that one must never rest in the way of virtue, but must press on to the appointed goal. It is said that for thirty years he never sat down, and as far as he could he observed silence and solitude.

After he had spent some years in Siena, his superiors sent him to Forlì to found a new house for the order. By this time he had been ordained and had proved himself to be an ideal priest—fervent in the celebration of the holy mysteries, eloquent in preaching, untiring in reconciling sinners. A great affliction now befell him in the form of cancer of the foot, which, besides being excruciatingly painful, made him an object of repulsion to his neighbours. He bore this trial without a murmur.   At last the surgeons decided that the only thing to do was to cut off the foot.   St Peregrine spent the night before the operation in trustful prayer ; he then sank into a light slumber, from which he awoke completely cured—to the amazement of the doctors, who testified that they could no longer detect any trace of the disease.   This miracle greatly enhanced the reputation which the holy man had already acquired by his exemplary life.   He lived to the age of 80, and was canonized in 1726.

The Bollandists in the *Acta Sanctorum*, April, vol. iii, were able to print some portion of the documents presented in the cause of the canonization of St Peregrine.   Many Italian accounts of the saint have been published, mostly devotional rather than historically critical ; for example, B. Albicini, *Vita e Morte del B. Pellegrino Laziosi* (1648) ; F. A. Monsignani, *Notizie della Vita, Morte e Miracoli, etc.* (1727).   See also Giani, *Annales FF. Servorum B.V.M.*, vol. i, pp. 285 *seq.*

2 : ST ATHANASIUS, ARCHBISHOP OF ALEXANDRIA, DOCTOR OF THE CHURCH (A.D. 373)

ST ATHANASIUS, " the Champion of Orthodoxy ", was probably born about the year 297 at Alexandria.   Of his family nothing is known except that his parents were Christians, and that he had a brother called Peter.   All that has come down to us concerning his childhood is a tradition, preserved by Rufinus, to the effect that he first attracted the notice of Bishop Alexander when he was " playing at church " on the beach with other little boys.   The truth of this is more than questionable ; at the time of Alexander's accession Athanasius must have been at least fifteen or sixteen years old.   Whether or not he owed his training to the bishop, it is certain that he received an excellent education, which embraced Greek literature and philosophy, rhetoric, jurisprudence and Christian doctrine. His familiarity with the text of the Bible was quite exceptional.   We have it on his own authority that he learnt theology from teachers who had been confessors during the persecution under Maximian, which had raged in Alexandria when he was almost an infant.   It is interesting to note that from his early youth Athanasius appears to have had close relations with the hermits of the desert—more especially with the great St Antony.   " I was his disciple ", he wrote, " and like Eliseus I poured water on the hands of that other Elias."   The friendship he then formed. with the holy men was to prove of inestimable assistance to him in later life.   But it is not until the year 318, when he was about 21, that Athanasius makes his first actual appearance upon the stage of history.   He then received the diaconate, and he was appointed secretary to Bishop Alexander.   It was probably at this period that he produced his first literary work, the famous treatise on the Incarnation, in which he expounded the redemptive work of Christ.

It was probably about the year 323 that scandal began to be aroused in Alexandria by the priest of the church of Baukalis, Arius by name, who was publicly teaching that the Word of God is not eternal, that He was created in time by the Eternal Father, and that therefore He could only figuratively be described as the Son of God.   The bishop demanded a statement of these doctrines, which he laid first before the Alexandrian clergy and afterwards before a council of Egyptian bishops.   With only two dissentients the assembly condemned the heresy, deposing Arius together with eleven priests and deacons who adhered to his tenets.   The heresiarch retired to Caesarea, where he continued to propagate his teaching, having enlisted the support of Eusebius of Nicomedia and other Syrian prelates. In Egypt he had won over the Meletians, a disaffected body, and many of the " intellectuals ", whilst his doctrines, embodied in hymns or songs set to popular tunes, were popularized in the market-place and carried by sailors and traders in an incredibly short time all along the Mediterranean shores. That Athanasius, as the bishop's archdeacon and secretary, already took a prominent part in the struggle, and that he even composed the encyclical letter announcing the condemnation of Arius, has been assumed with a great show of probability. All that is actually certain, however, is that he was present, as attendant upon his bishop, at the great Council of Nicaea in which the true doctrine of the Church was set forth, the sentence of excommunication against Arius confirmed, and the confession of faith known as the Nicene Creed promulgated and subscribed. It is unlikely that Athanasius actually participated in the discussions of this assembly of bishops in which he had not even a seat, but even if he did not exercise any influence upon the council it assuredly influenced him, and, as a modern writer has well said, the rest of his life was at one and the same time a testimony to the divinity of the Saviour and a heroic testimony to the profession of the Nicene fathers.

Shortly after the close of the council Alexander died, and Athanasius, whom he had nominated as his successor, was chosen bishop of Alexandria, although he was not yet thirty years old. Almost immediately he undertook a visitation of his enormous diocese, including the Thebaïd and other great monastic settlements, where he was warmly welcomed as being himself an ascetic. He also appointed a bishop for Ethiopia, a country in which the Christian faith had recently found a footing. Nevertheless almost from the first he was faced by dissensions and opposition. In spite of his strenuous efforts to bring about union, the Meletians continued their schism and made common cause with the heretics, whilst Arianism, though temporarily crushed by the Council of Nicaea, soon reappeared with renewed vigour in Egypt as well as in Asia Minor, where it had powerful support. In 330 the Arian bishop of Nicomedia, Eusebius, returned from exile and succeeded in persuading the Emperor Constantine, whose favourite residence was in his diocese, to write to Athanasius, bidding him re-admit Arius into communion. The bishop replied that the Catholic Church could hold no communion with heretics who attacked the divinity of Christ. Eusebius then addressed an ingratiating letter to Athanasius, in which he sought to justify Arius ; but neither his flattering words nor the threats he induced the emperor to utter could shake the determination of the lion-hearted though weakly-looking young bishop whom Julian the Apostate, at a later date, was angrily to stigmatize as " that mannikin ".

The bishop of Nicomedia's next move was to write to the Egyptian Meletians urging them to carry out a design they had formed of impeaching Athanasius. They responded by bringing against him charges of having exacted a tribute of linen for use in his church, of having sent gold to a certain Philomenus, suspected of treason against the emperor, and of having authorized one of his deputies to destroy a chalice which was being used at the altar by a Meletian priest called Iskhyras. In a trial before the emperor, Athanasius cleared himself of all these accusations and returned in triumph to Alexandria, bearing with him a commendatory letter from Constantinople. His enemies, however, were not discouraged. He was now charged with having murdered a Meletian bishop, Arsenius, and was cited to attend a council at Caesarea. Aware that his supposed victim was alive and in hiding,

Athanasius ignored the summons. Nevertheless he found himself compelled by a command from the emperor to appear before another council summoned at Tyre in 335—an assembly which, as it turned out, was packed by his opponents and presided over by an Arian who had usurped the see of Antioch. Various offences were preferred against him, of which the first was that of the broken chalice. Several of the charges he disposed of at once : in regard to others he demanded time in which to obtain evidence. Realizing, however, that his condemnation had been decided beforehand, he abruptly left the assembly and embarked for Constantinople. Upon his arrival he accosted the emperor in the street in the attitude of a suppliant, and obtained an interview. So completely did he seem to have vindicated himself that Constantine, in reply to a letter from the Council of Tyre announcing that Athanasius had been condemned and deposed, wrote to the signatories a severe reply summoning them to Constantinople for a retrial of the case. Then, for some reason which has never been satisfactorily cleared up, the monarch suddenly changed his mind. Ecclesiastical writers naturally shrank from attaching blame to the first Christian emperor, but it would appear that he took umbrage at the outspoken language of Athanasius in a further interview. Before the first letter could reach its destination, a second one was despatched which confirmed the sentences of the Council of Tyre and banished Athanasius to Trier in Belgian Gaul.

History records nothing about this first exile, which lasted two years, except that the saint was hospitably received by the local bishop and that he kept in touch with his flock by letters.

In 337 the Emperor Constantine died, and his empire was divided between his three sons, Constantine II, Constantius and Constans. The various exiled prelates were immediately recalled, and one of the first acts of Constantine II was to restore Athanasius to his see. The bishop re-entered his diocesan city in seeming triumph, but his enemies were as relentless as ever, and Eusebius of Nicomedia completely won over the Emperor Constantius, within whose jurisdiction Alexandria was situated. Athanasius was accused before the monarch of raising sedition, of promoting bloodshed and of detaining for his own use corn which was destined for widows and the poor. His old adversary Eusebius furthermore obtained from a council which met at Antioch a second sentence of deposition, and the ratification of the election of an Arian bishop of Alexandria. By this assembly a letter was written to Pope St Julius inviting his intervention and the condemnation of Athanasius. This was followed by an encyclical, drawn up by the orthodox Egyptian hierarchy and sent to the pope and the other Catholic bishops, in which the case for Athanasius was duly set forth. The Roman pontiff replied accepting the suggestion of the Eusebians that a synod should be held to settle the question.

In the meantime a Cappadocian named Gregory had been installed in the see of Alexandria ; and in the face of the scenes of violence and sacrilege that ensued, Athanasius betook himself to Rome to await the hearing of his case. The synod was duly summoned, but as the Eusebians who had demanded it failed to appear, it was held without them. The result was the complete vindication of the saint—a declaration which was afterwards endorsed by the Council of Sardica. Nevertheless he was unable to return to Alexandria till after the death of the Cappadocian Gregory, and then only because the Emperor Constantius, on the eve of a war with Persia, thought it politic to propitiate his brother Constans by restoring Athanasius to his see.   After an absence of eight years the bishop returned to Alexandria amidst scenes of unparalleled rejoicing, and for three or four years the wars and disturbances in which the rulers of the empire were involved left him in comparatively peaceful possession of his chair.   But the murder of Constans removed the most powerful support òf orthodoxy, and Constantius, once he felt himself securely master of the west and of the east, set himself deliberately to crush the man whom he had come to regard as a personal enemy.   At Arles in 353 he obtained the condemnation of the saint from a council of time-serving prelates, and again in 355 at Milan where he declared himself to be the accuser of Athanasius; of a third council St Jerome wrote, " The whole world groaned and marvelled to find itself Arian ".   The few friendly bishops were exiled, including Pope Liberius, who was kept in isolation in Thrace until, broken in body and spirit, he was temporarily beguiled into acquiescence with the censure.

In Egypt Athanasius held on with the support of his clergy and people, but not for long.   One night, when he was celebrating a vigil in church, soldiers forced open the doors, killing some of the congregation and wounding others.   Athanasius escaped—he never knew how—and disappeared into the desert, where the watchful care of the monks kept him safely hidden for six years.   If during that time the world had few tidings of him, he was kept well informed of all that was going on, and his untiring activity, repressed in one direction, expressed itself in literary form : to this period are ascribed many of his chief writings.

The death of Constantius in 361 was followed soon afterwards by the murder, at the hands of the populace, of the Arian who had usurped the Alexandrian see. The new emperor, Julian, had revoked the sentences of banishment enacted by his predecessor, and Athanasius returned to his city.   But it was only for a few months. The Apostate's plans for the paganizing of the Christian world could make little way as long as the champion of the Catholic faith ruled in Egypt.   Julian therefore banished him as " a disturber of the peace and an enemy of the gods ", and Athanasius once more sought refuge in the desert.   He only narrowly escaped capture. He was in a boat on the Nile when his companions in great alarm called his attention to an imperial galley which was fast overhauling them.   Athanasius, unperturbed, bade them turn the boat and row towards it.   The pursuers shouted out, asking for information about the fugitive.   " He is not far off ", was the reply.   " Row fast if you want to overtake him."   The stratagem succeeded.   During this fourth exile Athanasius seems to have explored the Thebaïd from end to end.   He was at Antinopolis when he was informed by two solitaries of the death of Julian, who had at that moment expired, slain by an arrow in Persia.

At once he returned to Alexandria, and some months later he proceeded to Antioch at the invitation of the Emperor Jovian, who had revoked his sentence of banishment.   Jovian's reign, however, was a short one ; and the Emperor Valens in May 365 issued an order banishing all the orthodox bishops who had been exiled by Constantius and restored by his successors.   Again Athanasius was forced to withdraw.   The ecclesiastical writer Socrates says that he concealed himself in the vault in which his father lay buried, but a more probable account states that he remained in a villa in one of the suburbs of Alexandria.   Four months later Valens revoked his edict—possibly fearing a rising among the Egyptians, who had become devotedly attached to their much-persecuted bishop.   With great demonstrations of joy the people escorted him back.   Five times Athanasius had been banished ; seventeen years he had spent in exile : but for the last seven years of his life he was left in the unchallenged occupation of his see.   It was probably at this time that he wrote the Life of St Antony.

St Athanasius died in Alexandria on May 2, 373, and his body was subsequently translated first to Constantinople and then to Venice.

The greatest man of his age and one of the greatest religious leaders of any age, Athanasius of Alexandria rendered services to the Church the value of which can scarcely be exaggerated, for he defended the faith against almost overwhelming odds and emerged triumphant. Most aptly has he been described by Cardinal Newman as " a principal instrument after the Apostles by which the sacred truths of Christianity have been conveyed and secured to the world ".   Although the writings of St Athanasius deal mainly with controversy, there is beneath this war of words a deep spiritual feeling which comes to the surface at every turn and reveals the high purpose of him who writes.   Take, for example, his reply to the objections which the Arians raised from the texts : " Let this chalice pass from me ", or " Why hast thou forsaken me ? "

Is it not extravagant to admire the courage of the servants of the Word, yet to say that that Word Himself was in terror, through whom they despised death ?   For that most enduring purpose and courage of the holy martyrs demonstrates that the Godhead was not in terror but that the Saviour took away our terror.   For as He abolished death by death, and by human means all human evils, so by this so-called terror did He remove our terror, and brought about for us that never more should men fear death.   His word and deed go together. . . . For human were the sounds : " Let this chalice pass from me ", and " Why hast thou forsaken me ? " and divine the action whereby He, the same being, did cause the sun to fail and the dead to rise.   And so He said humanly : " Now is my soul troubled " ; and He said divinely : " I have power to lay down my life and power to take it again ".   For to be troubled was proper to the flesh, but to have power to lay down His life and take it again when He would, was no property of man, but of the Word's power.   For man dies not at his own arbitrament, but by necessity of nature and against his will ; but the Lord being Himself immortal, not having a mortal flesh, had it at His own free will, as God, to become separate from the body and to take it again, when He would. . . . And He let His own body suffer, for therefore did He come, that in the flesh He might suffer, and henceforth the flesh might be made impassible and immortal ; and that contumely and the other troubles might fall upon Him, but come short of others after Him, being by Him annulled utterly ; and that henceforth men might for ever abide incorruptible, as a temple of the Word.

The principal source of information for the life of St Athanasius is the collection of his own writings, but his activities were so interwoven with not only the religious, but the secular history of his times that the range of authorities to be consulted is very wide. For English readers Cardinal Newman in his Anglican days, both in his special work on St Athanasius and in his tract on the " Causes of the Rise and Successes of Arianism ", rendered the whole complicated situation intelligible.   There is also a brilliantly written chapter on St Athanasius in Dr A. Fortescue's volume, *The Greek Fathers* (1908).   Two excellent little monographs have appeared in France, by F. Cavallera (1908) and by G. Bardy (1914) in the series " Les Saints ".   Reference should also be made to four valuable papers by E. Schwartz in the *Nachrichten* of the Göttingen Akademie from 1904 to 1911.   For a fuller bibliography, see Bardenhewer in the latest edition of his *Patrologie*, or in his larger work, *Geschichte der altkirchlichen Literatur*, and for a survey of more recent work, F. L. Cross, *The Study of St Athanasius* (1945).

SS. EXSUPERIUS AND ZOË, MARTYRS (*c*. A.D. 135)

EXSUPERIUS, or rather Hesperus, and his wife Zoë were slaves of a rich man named Catalus, who lived in the reign of the Emperor Hadrian at Attalia, a town of Pamphylia in Asia Minor. They had been born Christians, and though negligent themselves, they brought up their two sons, Cyriacus and Theodulus in the faith. Having been shamed out of their religious indifference by the example of their children, they refused to accept food offered to the gods, which their master sent them on the occasion of the birth of his son. Thereupon they were arrested and brought up for trial. All made a bold confession. After the two boys had been tortured in the presence of their parents, all four were roasted to death in a furnace. Justinian built a church in Constantinople dedicated in honour of St Zoë—presumably to contain her remains—but some of the relics of all these martyrs appear to have been translated to Clermont, where they are still venerated.

Although these saints seem to be commemorated on May 2 in all the synaxaries (see in particular the *Synaxarium Constantinopolitanum*, ed. Delehaye, cc. 649–650), and a Greek *passio* is printed in the *Acta Sanctorum*, May, vol. i, the account seems to be historically worthless. It is difficult to understand how the father's name, Hesperus, which appears in all the manuscripts, has been transformed into Exsuperius in the Roman Martyrology.

ST WALDEBERT, ABBOT (*c*. A.D. 665)

AMONGST the successors of St Columban in the monastery of Luxeuil the most famous during his life and the most revered after his death was St Waldebert (Walbert, Gaubert), the third abbot. This is partly due to the fact that his long rule coincided with the most glorious period of the abbey's history and partly to the numerous miracles attributed to the saint. Objects he had touched—notably his wooden drinking bowl—were long venerated for their healing properties, and in the tenth century Anso, a Luxeuil monk, wrote a book about the wonders the saint had wrought.

Waldebert was a young Frankish nobleman, who in military attire appeared at Luxeuil to ask admittance of the abbot, St Eustace, and when he laid aside his weapons to receive the habit they were suspended from the roof of the church, where they remained for centuries. He proved so exemplary a monk that he obtained permission to lead the eremitic life about three miles from the abbey. After the death of St Eustace and the refusal of St Gall to become his successor, the brethren chose St Waldebert as their superior. For forty years he ruled them wisely and well. Under his government the Rule of St Columban was superseded by that of St Benedict, and he obtained for Luxeuil from Pope John IV the privilege, already conceded to Lérins and Agaunum, of being free from episcopal control. He had bestowed his own estates upon the abbey, which was also enriched during his lifetime by many benefactions. Such assistance was indeed needed, because Luxeuil itself could not contain or support all who sought to enter it ; parties of monks were continually being sent out from it to found fresh houses in other parts of France. Even over nunneries St Waldebert was called to exercise control, and it was with his help that St Salaberga founded her great convent at Laon. The holy abbot died about the year 665.

An account of the life and miracles of St Waldebert was written 300 years after his death by Abbot Adso ; this has been printed by Mabillon, and in the *Acta Sanctorum*, May, vol. i. See also J. B. Clerc, *Ermitage et vie de S. Valbert* (1861) ; H. Baumont, *Étude historique sur Luxeuil* (1896) ; J. Poinsotte, *Les Abbés de Luxeuil* (1900).

ST ULTAN, Abbot   (A.D. 686)

St Ultan (or Ultain) and his more celebrated brothers, St Fursey and St Foillan, were Irish monks who crossed over to East Anglia, where they founded the abbey of Burgh Castle, near Yarmouth, on territory bestowed upon them by King Sigberct or Sigebert I.   In consequence of raids by the Mercians, St Fursey went to France, where he died.   When St Foillan and St Ultan visited their brother's tomb at Péronne on their way back from a pilgrimage to Rome, they were warmly welcomed by Bd Itta and St Gertrude at Nivelles, who offered them land at Fosses on which to build a monastery and a hospice for strangers.   Ultan became the abbot of Fosses.   We are told that by supernatural revelation he knew of the death of St Foillan, who was murdered by robbers in the forest of Seneffe, and he foretold to St Gertrude, at her request, the day of her own death.   He said that St Patrick was preparing to welcome her, and in point of fact she died on March 17.   St Ultan later became abbot of, and died at, Péronne, but his relics were subsequently translated to Fosses.

What we know of St Ultan is mainly gleaned from the life of St Fursey and from that of St Gertrude of Nivelles.   These texts have been edited by Bruno Krusch in the second and the fourth volume of MGH., *Scriptores Merov.*   See also Gougaud, *Christianity in Celtic Lands*, pp. 147–148, *Les saints irlandais hors d'Irlande*, and *Gaelic Pioneers*, pp. 128–131 ; and *cf.* J. F. Kenney, *The Sources for the Early History of Ireland*, vol. i, pp. 502–505.

ST WIBORADA, Virgin and Martyr   (A.D. 926)

Klingnau, in the Swiss canton of Aargau, was the birthplace of St Wiborada, who is called in French Guiborat and in German Weibrath.   Her parents belonged to the Swabian nobility, and she led a retired life in the house of her father and mother. After one of her brothers, Hatto by name, had decided to be a priest she made his clothes and also worked for the monastery of St Gall, where he prosecuted his studies.   Many of the books in the abbey library were covered by her.   Upon the death of her parents, Wiborada joined this brother, who had been made provost of the church of St Magnus, and he taught her Latin so that she could join him in saying the offices.   Their house became a kind of hospital to which Hatto would bring patients for Wiborada to tend.   After the brother and sister had made a pilgrimage to Rome, Hatto resolved to take the habit at St Gall, largely through Wiborada's influence.   She, on the other hand, remained for some years longer in the world, though not of it.   It may have been at this period—but more probably, as certain writers have argued, after she became a recluse—that she came into touch with St Ulric, who had been sent, as a delicate little lad of seven, to the monastic school of St Gall.   We read that she prophesied his future elevation to the episcopate, and in after years he regarded her as his spiritual mother.

According to some of the saint's biographers—but not the earliest—she suffered so severely from calumnies against her character that she underwent trial by ordeal at Constance to clear herself of the charges.   Whether the story be true or false, she decided to withdraw into solitude that she might serve God without distraction. At first she took up her abode in an anchorhold on a mountain not far from St Gall, but in 915 she occupied a cell beside the church of St Magnus ; there she remained for the rest of her life, practising extraordinary mortifications.   Many visitors came to see her, attracted by the fame of her miracles and prophecies.   Other recluses settled near her, but only one of them was admitted to any sort of companionship.

This was a woman called Rachildis, a niece of St Notker Balbulus. She was brought to St Wiborada suffering from a disease which the doctors had pronounced incurable. Having apparently been cured by the ministrations of the recluse, she could never be induced to leave her benefactress. But after the death of the latter the malady returned with so many complications that she seemed a second Job, owing to the multiplicity of her diseases and the patience with which she bore them.

St Wiborada foretold her own death at the hands of the invading Hungarians, adding that Rachildis would be left unmolested. Her warnings enabled the clergy of St Magnus and the monks of St Gall to escape in time, but she herself refused to leave her cell. The barbarians burnt the church and, having made an opening in the roof of the hermitage, entered it as she knelt in prayer. They struck her on the head with a hatchet and left her dying ; Rachildis, however, remained unharmed and survived her friend for twenty-one years. St Wiborada was canonized in 1047.

There is good evidence for most of the details given above. Hartmann, a monk of St Gall, who first wrote a sketch of her life—it is printed by Mabillon and in the *Acta Sanctorum*, May, vol. i—was almost a contemporary. A later life by Hepidannus is less reliable. But we have also other references to St Wiborada, for example, in Gerhard's *Life of St Ulric of Augsburg* and in Ekkehard (iv), *Casus S. Galli*. This last is printed by G. Meyer v. Knonau, *St Gallische Geschichtsquellen*, iii. See also A. Schröder's valuable article in the *Historisches Jahrbuch*, vol. xxii (1901), pp. 276–284, and A. Fäh, *Die hl. Wiborada* (1926).

BD CONRAD OF SELDENBÜREN (A.D. 1126)

THE celebrated Benedictine abbey of Engelberg, in Unterwalden, owed its foundation to Bd Conrad, a scion of the princely family of Seldenbüren. Conrad resolved to devote part of his patrimony to building a monastery, and tradition says that the site was revealed to him by our Lady in a vision. For some unrecorded reason, delay must have occurred in the construction, for although the work was begun in 1082 it was not completed until 1120. After devoting the rest of his fortune to establishing a convent for women, the founder went to Rome where he obtained recognition and privileges for his houses. He then retired from the world, receiving from St Adelhelmus the habit of a lay brother. From his peaceful retreat Conrad emerged at the bidding of his superior to meet a claim which had been made on some of the property he had bestowed upon the abbey. At Zürich he went unsuspectingly to a meeting arranged by his opponents, who fell upon him and killed him. The body of Bd Conrad was brought back to Engelberg, where it remained incorrupt until the abbey was burnt down in 1729.

There is no early life of Bd Conrad, but a short account is furnished in the *Acta Sanctorum*, May, vol. i. See also two papers by A. Brackmann in the *Abhandlungen* of the Prussian Academy for 1928, and the sketch by B. Egger, *Konrad von Seldenbüren* (1926). The abbey at Mount Angel in Oregon was founded from Engelberg, as was Conception in Missouri.

ST MAFALDA (A.D. 1252)

IN the year 1215, at the age of eleven, Princess Mafalda (*i.e.* Matilda), daughter of King Sancho I of Portugal, was married to her kinsman King Henry I of Castile, who was like herself a minor. The marriage was annulled the following year on the ground of the consanguinity of the parties, and Mafalda returned to her own country, where she took the veil in the Benedictine convent of Arouca. As religious observance had become greatly relaxed, she induced the community to adopt the Cistercian rule. Her own life was one of extreme austerity. The whole of the large income bestowed upon her by her father was devoted to pious and charitable uses. She restored the cathedral of Oporto, founded a hostel for pilgrims, erected a bridge over the Talmeda and built an institution for the support of twelve widows at Arouca. When she felt that her last hour was approaching she directed, according to a common medieval practice, that she should be laid on ashes. Her last words were, " Lord, I hope in thee ". Her body after death shone with a wonderful radiance, and when it was exposed in 1617 it is said to have been as flexible and fresh as though the holy woman had only just died. Mafalda's *cultus* was confirmed in 1793.

A notice of Mafalda, compiled mainly from late Cistercian sources, will be found in the appendix to the first volume for May in the *Acta Sanctorum*. An account of her, with her sisters SS. Teresa and Sanchia, is also contained in *Portugal glorioso e illustrado, etc.*, by J. P. Bayao (1727).

3 : THE FINDING OF THE HOLY CROSS (*c.* A.D. 326)

THE feast of the *Inventio*, that is to say the discovery, of the Holy Cross, which is kept on May 3 with the rite of a double of the second class, would seem to take precedence of the September feast, the " Exaltation ", which is only observed as a greater double. There is, however, a good deal of evidence which suggests that the September feast is the more primitive celebration, and that a certain confusion has arisen between the two incidents in the history of the Holy Cross which these festivals purport to commemorate. Strictly speaking, neither of them seems at first to have been directly connected with the discovery of the cross. The September feast took its rise from the solemn dedication in A.D. 335 of the churches which Constantine, encouraged by his mother, St Helen, had caused to be built on the site of the Holy Sepulchre. We cannot be sure that the dedication was carried out precisely on September 14. The month, however, was September, and seeing that in the time of the pilgrim Etheria, fifty years later, the annual commemoration of this inaugurating ceremony lasted for a week, there is clearly no reason to be particular to a day or two. In any case, Etheria herself tells us : " The dedication of these holy churches is therefore celebrated with the highest honour, and also because the cross of our Lord was found on this same day. And it was so ordained that, when the holy churches above mentioned were consecrated, that should also be the day when the cross of our Lord had been found, in order that the whole celebration should be made together, with all rejoicing, on the self-same day." From this it would follow that the discovery of the cross was honoured at Jerusalem in September, and the pilgrim Theodosius, about A.D. 530, speaking expressly of the *inventio crucis*, bears witness to the same fact.

But at present we commemorate in September an entirely different event, to wit, the recovery in 629 by the Emperor Heraclius of the relics of the cross which some years before had been carried off from Jerusalem by Chosroes II, King of Persia. The Roman Martyrology and the lessons of the Breviary are explicit on the point. There is, however, reason to think that under the style " Exaltation of the Cross " we have reference to the physical act of the lifting (ὕψωσις) of the sacred relic when it was exhibited for the veneration of the people, and it is also probable that this designation was used in connection with the feast before the time of Heraclius.

As for the actual finding, with which we are here concerned, there is a distressing absence of early information. The Pilgrim of Bordeaux, in 333, says nothing of the cross.   Eusebius, the historian, from whom, as a contemporary, we should have expected to learn much, makes no reference to the discovery, though he seems to know about the three separate places of worship within the Holy Sepulchre pre-cincts.   Thus, in stating that Constantine " adorned a shrine sacred to the salutary emblem ", he may well be supposed to refer to that chapel, " Golgotha ", in which as Etheria tells us, the relics of the cross were preserved.   St Cyril, Bishop of Jerusalem, in his catechetical lectures which were delivered, about the year 346, on the very site where our Saviour was crucified, refers more than once to the wood of the cross.   " It has been distributed ", he declares, " fragment by fragment, from this spot and has already nearly filled the world."   Furthermore, in his letter to Constantius, he expressly states that " the saving wood of the cross was found at Jerusalem in the time of Constantine ".   In all this there is no mention of St Helen, who died in 330.   The first, perhaps, to ascribe the discovery to her active inter-vention is St Ambrose, in his sermon *De Obitu Theodosii*, preached in 395 ; but about that date or a little later we find many others, John Chrysostom, Rufinus, Paulinus of Nola, and Cassiodorus, together with the church historians Socrates, Sozomen and Theodoret—but notably not St Jerome, who lived on the spot—all repeating similar stories of the recovery of the cross in which St Helen plays a principal part.   Unfortunately, the details of these accounts are by no means always in agreement.   St Ambrose and St John Chrysostom inform us that in the excava-tions which were undertaken at the instance of St Helen, three crosses were dis-covered.   They add that to the one in the middle the " title " was still attached, and that in this way our Saviour's cross was clearly identified.   On the other hand, Rufinus, who is followed in this by Socrates, reports that in accordance with a special inspiration St Helen directed that excavations should be made in a certain place, that three crosses were found and an inscription, but there was no way of deciding to which of the three the inscription belonged.   The bishop of Jerusalem, Macarius, thereupon had a dying woman brought to the spot.   She was made to touch the three crosses, and at the contact of the third she was healed, so that it was made plain to all that this was the cross of our Saviour.   There are other diverg-ences, at about the same date, regarding the miracle of healing by which the true cross was identified, the finding and disposal of the nails, etc.   On the whole, it seems probable that the statements made more than sixty years after the event by writers bent mainly on edification were a good deal influenced by certain apocryphal documents which must already have been in circulation.

The most notable of these is the tractate *De inventione crucis dominicae* which is mentioned (*c.* 550) in the pseudo-Gelasian decree *De recipiendis et non recipiendis libris* as a writing to be regarded with mistrust.   There can be no doubt that this little tractate was widely read.   The compiler of the first redaction of the *Liber Pontificalis* (*c.* A.D. 532) must have had it in his hands, and he quotes from it in the account he gives of Pope Eusebius.   It must also have been known to those who blunderingly revised the *Hieronymianum* at Auxerre early in the seventh century.[*]   Neglecting the anachronisms in which the narrative abounds, the story in brief runs thus.   The Emperor Constantine, in conflict with hordes of barbarians on the Danube, was in grave danger of defeat.   There appeared to him, however, a vision of a brilliant cross in the sky, with the legend " In this sign thou shalt conquer ".

[*] It is curious to find Mgr Duchesne stating in his *Origines* (*Christian Worship*, p. 275, n. 2 ; and *cf.* the *Liber Pontificalis*, vol. i, p. 378, n. 29) that " in the Epternach MS. there is no mention of this festival of the cross ".   It occurs there on May 7, and also on the same day in St Willibrord's Calendar.

He was thereupon victorious, was instructed and baptized by Pope Eusebius in Rome, and out of gratitude despatched his mother, St Helen, to Jerusalem, to search for the relics of the holy cross.   All the inhabitants professed ignorance of its whereabouts, but at last, by dint of threats she prevailed upon a learned Jew named Judas to reveal what he knew.   They dug twenty fathoms deep and discovered three crosses.   The identity of the true cross is determined by its raising a dead man to life.   Judas is thereupon converted, and, as the bishop of Jerusalem happened just then to die, St Helen selects this new convert, who is henceforth called Cyriacus, or Quiriacus, to govern that see in his place.   Pope Eusebius is summoned from Rome to Jerusalem to consecrate him bishop, and shortly after-wards, through the miraculous appearance of a brilliant light, the hiding-place of the holy nails is also revealed.   St Helen, having made generous donations to the holy places and the poor of Jerusalem, happened to die not long afterwards, charging all faithful Christians as her last behest to hold festival every year on May 3 (*quinto nonas Maii*), the day on which the cross was found.   Before the year 450, Sozomen (bk. ii, ch. i) seems to have been acquainted with this story of the Jew who revealed the hiding-place of the cross.   He does not denounce it as a fabrication, but quietly passes it by as less probable.

Another apocryphal story which bears, though less directly, on the finding of the cross, is introduced, somewhat as a digression, into the document known as *The Doctrine of Addai*, of Syrian origin.   What we are told here is that Protonike, the wife of the Emperor Claudius Caesar, less than ten years after our Lord's ascension, went to the Holy Land, compelled the Jews to reveal where the crosses were hidden, and distinguished that of our Saviour by a miracle wrought upon her own daughter. It is contended that this legend has suggested the story of St Helen and the dis-covery of the cross in the time of Constantine.   Mgr Duchesne believed that the *Doctrine of Addai* was earlier in date than the *De inventione crucis dominicae*, but there are strong arguments for the contrary opinion.

In view of all this very unsatisfactory evidence, the most probable suggestion seems to be that the holy cross with the title was found during the excavations rendered necessary by the construction of Constantine's basilica on Mount Calvary. Such a discovery, which may well have involved some period of doubt and inquiry while the authenticity of the find was being discussed, is likely to have given rise to multifarious conjectures and rumours which before long took written shape in the *De inventione* tractate.   It is probable that St Helen's share in the transaction actually amounted to no more than what we should gather from Etheria's statement when she speaks of " the building which Constantine, under his mother's auspices (*sub praesentia matris suae*) embellished with gold and mosaics and precious marbles". The credit of a victory is often given to a sovereign, though it is his generals and troops who have done all the fighting.   What is certain in the whole matter is that from the middle of the fourth century reputed relics of the true cross spread through the world.   This we know not only from St Cyril's reiterated statement, but also from dated inscriptions in Africa and elsewhere.   Still more convincing is the evidence that before the end of the same century the stem of the cross and the title were both venerated in Jerusalem with intense devotion.   Etheria's account of the ceremony is the description of an eye-witness about the year 385 ; but only a dozen years or so later we have in the Life of St Porphyrius of Gaza another testimony to the veneration with which the relic was regarded by its custodians.   And again, after nearly two centuries, the pilgrim, commonly, if incorrectly, known as

Antoninus of Piacenza, tells us how " we adored (adoravimus) and kissed " the wood of the cross and handled its title.

In a Motu Proprio of John XXIII dated July 25, 1960, this feast was dropped from the Roman Calendar.

There is a considerable literature bearing upon the matters here discussed. For much of this the reader may conveniently be referred to the bibliographical references in Dom Leclercq's article in DAC., vol. iii, cc. 3131–3139. See also the *Acta Sanctorum*, May, vol. i ; Duchesne, *Liber Pontificalis*, vol. i, pp. cvii–cix and pp. 75, 167, 378 ; Kellner, *Heortology* (1908), pp. 333–341 ; J. Straubinger, *Die Kreuzauffindungslegende* (1912) ; A. Halusa, *Das Kreuzesholz in Geschichte und Legende* (1926) ; H. Thurston in *The Month*, May 1930, pp. 420–429. It is generally held that this feast of the Finding of the Cross on May 3 is not of Roman origin, since it is lacking in the Gregorian Sacramentary, but, so far as its prevalence in the West is concerned, must have arisen in Gaul. It occurs in the *Félire* of Oengus and in most MSS. of the *Hieronymianum*. In the Epternach MS., however, it is assigned, as noted above, to May 7. This seems to have reference to a feast celebrated in Jerusalem and among the Armenians, in memory of the luminous cross in the heavens which appeared on May 7, 351, as St Cyril describes in his letter to the Emperor Constantius. As for the date, May 3, it is impossible not to believe that it is closely connected with the mention of that precise day in the apocryphal tract, *De inventione crucis dominicae*. The earliest notice of a cross festival in the West seems to be the mention of a " dies sanctae crucis " in a lectionary of Silos, c. 650.

SS. ALEXANDER, EVENTIUS AND THEODULUS, MARTYRS
(c. A.D. 113 ?)

IN the Roman Martyrology the second announcement for this day, May 3, runs : " At Rome, on the Via Nomentana, the passion of the holy martyrs Alexander the Pope, Eventius and Theodulus, priests ; whereof Alexander, after suffering fetters, imprisonment, the rack and torture by hooks and the flame, was, under the Emperor Hadrian and the judge Aurelian, pierced with many sharp points in all his limbs, and slain, but Eventius and Theodulus, after long imprisonment, were tried by fire and at last beheaded ". Although the whole of this notice has practically speaking been repeated in successive martyrologies for more than 1200 years, it unfortunately reposes upon a so-called *passio* of the martyrs which is a mere work of fiction and historically worthless. The Alexander mentioned is assumed to have been the pope, but this is almost certainly an error. In the *Hieronymianum* the name Eventius stands first, and in a fragmentary inscription found in 1855 on the spot indicated as that of the burial in the Via Nomentana, another name must have come before Alexander's ; in neither is he styled *episcopus*. There were, no doubt, three martyrs interred on this spot, but we know nothing beyond their names. Of Pope Alexander I the *Liber Pontificalis* tells us very little. It attributes to him the insertion of the clause " Qui pridie quam pateretur " in the canon of the Mass, and the custom of using holy water in private houses, but if it indicates the seventh milestone along the Via Nomentana as the place of his interment, it has borrowed this from some recension of the quite unreliable *passio*.

The *passio* itself is printed in the *Acta Sanctorum*, May, vol. i. But consult also Duchesne, *Liber Pontificalis*, vol. i, p. xci ; Quentin, *Les Martyrologes historiques*, p. 58 and *passim ;* Delehaye, CMH., pp. 227–228 ; and Marucchi, *Il Cimitero e la Basilica di S. Alessandro alla Via Nomentana* (1922).

SS. TIMOTHY AND MAURA, MARTYRS   (c. A.D. 286)

THE cruel edicts of Diocletian against the Christians were enforced with great severity in Upper Egypt by Arrian, the prefect of the Thebaïd. Amongst his victims were a young couple named Timothy and Maura, who were ardent students of the Holy Scriptures, Timothy being a lector of the church at Penapeis, near Antinoë. They had only been married twenty days when Timothy was taken before the governor and bidden to deliver up the sacred books that they might be publicly burned. Upon his refusal, red-hot iron instruments were thrust into his ears, his eyelids were cut off and other tortures applied to him. As he remained steadfast, Maura was sent for that she might break down his resolution by her entreaties. Far from obeying the governor's orders, she declared herself willing to die with her husband. After her hair had been torn out, she and Timothy were nailed to a wall where they died, after lingering for nine days.

There was a considerable *cultus* of these martyrs in the East, though its introduction at Constantinople seems to have been relatively late. The Greek " acts " have been printed in the *Acta Sanctorum*, May, vol. i (appendix), but see also the *Synaxarium Constantinopolitanum* (ed. Delehaye), cc. 649–652.

ST JUVENAL, BISHOP OF NARNI   (*c.* A.D. 376)

THE chief patron of Narni and the titular of its cathedral is its first bishop, St Juvenal, whose oratory and original tomb are still venerated in the city. His history has been confused with that of other saintly prelates of the same name, and a connected biography compiled by the Bollandists, from fragmentary notices in print and manuscript, is quite obviously legendary in parts. According to this account, Juvenal, who was both a priest and a physician, came from the East to Narni, where he was hospitably entertained by a woman called Philadelphia. At the request of the Christian inhabitants, Pope Damasus made Narni into a spearate diocese and consecrated St Juvenal to be its bishop. One day, as he was passing a brazen bull in front of a temple dedicated to Bacchus, a pagan priest struck him in the mouth with the hilt of his sword because the saint refused to sacrifice to the gods. The bishop held the weapon with his teeth, and the priest, in a violent effort to withdraw his blade, cut his own throat. This incident led to the immediate conversion of the heathen bystanders. In the fifth year of his pontificate, troops of Ligurians and Sarmatians who had captured Terni proceeded to invest Narni. St Juvenal climbed upon the city wall, where he chanted Psalm xxxiv and prayed aloud for the town. Scarcely had the people responded Amen, when a great thunderstorm broke out, with torrents of rain, in which 3000 of the assailants perished. Thus was Narni saved. The saint ruled his diocese for seven years, dying about 376. St Gregory the Great speaks of him more than once and styles him martyr, but he seems to have made the mistake of identifying him with a namesake who suffered death for the faith at Benevento.

The Bollandists have collected much archaeological material bearing on the cult of St Juvenal. See the *Acta Sanctorum*, May, vol. i ; and also Lanzoni, *Le Diocesi d'Italia*, vol. i, pp. 402 *seq.* ; the *Römische Quartalschrift*, 1905, pp. 42–49, and 1911, pp. 51–71. *Cf.* the *Neues Archiv*, 1919, pp. 526–555.

ST PHILIP OF ZELL   (EIGHTH CENTURY)

DURING the reign of Charlemagne's father, King Pepin, there was living in the Rhenish palatinate, not far from the present city of Worms, a hermit named Philip who had an extraordinary reputation for sanctity and miracles. An Englishman by birth, he had settled in the Nahegau after he had made a pilgrimage to Rome, where he was ordained priest.   Amongst those who sought out the recluse was King Pepin himself who, according to the legend, often visited him and conversed familiarly with him about holy things.   The historian of St Philip, who wrote a century after his death, states that through his intercourse with the hermit, Pepin " began to fear as well as to love God and to place all his hope in Him ".   As is so often the case with solitaires, Philip exercised a great attraction over the wild creatures of the forest : birds perched on his shoulder and ate from his hands, whilst hares frisked about him and licked his feet.   He was joined in his solitude by another priest, Horskolf by name, who served God with him in prayer and helped to cultivate the land.   One evening, thieves stole the two oxen which the hermits kept to aid them in their labours.   All night long the miscreants wandered about the woods, unable to find their way out, and in the morning they discovered that they were back again in front of the hermitage.   In dismay they threw themselves at St Philip's feet, begging forgiveness.   The holy man reassured them, entertained them as guests and sped them on their way.   Gradually disciples gathered round the two hermits and a church was built.

A story is told that Horskolf, on his return from a journey, found Philip dead and lying in his coffin.   With tears the disciple besought his master to give him the usual blessing which, for some reason, had been omitted when they had last parted. In reply the corpse sat up and said, " Go forth in peace, and may God prosper you abundantly in all things.   Take care of this place as long as you live.   Safe and sound you shall go forth ; safe and sound shall you return."   Then, having given the desired blessing, he sank back into death.   Horskolf continued to reside in the hermitage until, at the age of 100, he passed away to rejoin his master.   On the site of the cells was built a monastery, and then a collegiate church, in the midst of what became the parish of Zell, *i.e.* cell, named after St Philip's hermitage.

The author of the life of St Philip which is printed in the *Acta Sanctorum*, May, vol. i, is not known, but he was certainly not a contemporary, as has sometimes been stated.   This text, with other materials, has been more critically edited by A. Hofmeister in the supplementary volume (*Scriptores*, vol. xxx, part 2, pp. 796–805) of Pertz, MGH.   Some useful information concerning St Philip and his *cultus* was printed in various numbers of *Der Katholik* of Mainz, in 1887, 1896, 1898 and 1899.

4 : THE MARTYRS OF ENGLAND AND WALES   (A.D. 1535-1681)

IN addition to local feasts of individuals and groups there is to-day observed throughout England and Wales a collective festival, with proper Mass, of all the beatified among our martyrs from the Carthusians and others of 1535 to (at present) Bd William Howard in 1680 and Bd Oliver Plunket in 1681.

Already, while the persecution was at its height, Pope Gregory XIII informally approved certain recognitions of martyrdom, such as the public display of pictures of the victims in the church of the English College at Rome ;* and in 1642 Pope

* These pictures are mentioned several times in these pages.   They were a series of frescoes or wall-paintings of English saints and martyrs, made at the expense of George Gilbert, a friend of Bd Edmund Campion, and painted by Circiniani ; Pope Gregory XIII gave permission for the inclusion of the English martyrs of between 1535 and 1583.   The pictures were destroyed at the end of the eighteenth century, but a book of engravings of them (made in 1584) was preserved, and the equivalent beatification of certain martyrs was made on the strength of this evidence of ancient approved *cultus*.

Urban VIII began a formal inquiry, which came to nothing because of the Civil War. Not till over three hundred years later, in 1874, was an ordinary process begun, when Cardinal Manning, Archbishop of Westminster, sent a list of 360 names to Rome, with the evidence. In December 1886 the Holy See announced that 44 of these names had been referred back (*dilati*); but of the remainder, 54 (9 more were added later) were recognized as having been equivalently beatified by the actions of Pope Gregory XIII in 1583 mentioned above, which *cultus* Pope Leo XIII now confirmed. Of the remaining 253 one, Archbishop Plunket, was separately beatified in 1920. The evidence concerning the rest was exhaustively examined in Rome, and on December 15, 1929, the centenary year of Catholic Emancipation, 136 more were solemnly beatified. There are therefore now, apart from the *dilati*, 116 undecided cases from the list submitted in 1874. But in 1889 a second and separate list of presumptive martyrs was drawn up, whose process continues ; these number 242, and are known as the *praetermissi*. It includes the last confessor to die in prison, Father Matthew Atkinson, Franciscan, who died in Hurst Castle in 1729 after thirty years' imprisonment.

The 200 martyrs beatified to date (of whom, of course, two have since been canonized, Fisher and More) are made up as follows : 2 bishops, 84 secular priests, 7 more secular priests who became regulars (6 Jesuits, one Benedictine), 16 Benedictine monks, 18 Carthusians (including 6 lay-brothers), one Bridgettine, 3 Franciscans, one Austin friar, one Minim friar, 19 Jesuits (2 lay-brothers), 44 laymen and 4 laywomen. Of these persons some twenty were Welsh and the remainder mostly English. They are all referred to individually herein, either separately or as members of groups, *e.g.* the London Martyrs of 1588.

The best general books are Bishop Challoner's *Memoirs of Missionary Priests* (1741), edition by Fr J. H. Pollen, s.j., 1924 ; *Lives of the English Martyrs*, first series from 1535 to 1583, in 2 volumes, edited by Dom Bede Camm (1904–5) ; second series 1583–1603 unfinished : vol. i, edited by Canon E. H. Burton and Fr Pollen (1914) ; T. P. Ellis, *The Catholic Martyrs of Wales* (1933). Fr Pollen's *Acts of English Martyrs* (1891) is a valuable collection of contemporary documents.

ST MONICA, WIDOW (A.D. 387)

THE Church is doubly indebted to St Monica, the ideal of wifely forbearance and holy widowhood, whom we commemorate upon this day, for she not only gave bodily life to the great teacher Augustine, but she was also God's principal instrument in bringing about his spiritual birth by grace. She was born in North Africa —probably at Tagaste, sixty miles from Carthage—of Christian parents, in the year 332. Her early training was entrusted to a faithful retainer who treated her young charges wisely, if somewhat strictly. Amongst the regulations she inculcated was that of never drinking between meals. " It is water you want now ", she would say, " but when you become mistresses of the cellar you will want wine—not water —and the habit will remain with you." But when Monica grew old enough to be charged with the duty of drawing wine for the household, she disregarded the excellent maxim, and from taking occasional secret sips in the cellar, she soon came to drinking whole cupfuls with relish. One day, however, a slave who had watched her and with whom she was having an altercation, called her a wine-bibber. The shaft struck home : Monica was overwhelmed with shame and never again gave way to the temptation. Indeed, from the day of her baptism, which took place soon afterwards, she seems to have lived a life exemplary in every particular.

As soon as she had reached a marriageable age, her parents gave her as wife to a citizen of Tagaste, Patricius by name, a pagan not without generous qualities, but violent-tempered and dissolute. Monica had much to put up with from him, but she bore all with the patience of a strong, well-disciplined character. He, on his part, though inclined to criticize her piety and liberality to the poor, always regarded her with respect and never laid a hand upon her, even in his worst fits of rage. When other matrons came to complain of their husbands and to show the marks of blows they had received, she did not hesitate to tell them that they very often brought this treatment upon themselves by their tongues. In the long run, Monica's prayers and example resulted in winning over to Christianity not only her husband, but also her cantankerous mother-in-law, whose presence as a permanent inmate of the house had added considerably to the younger woman's difficulties. Patricius died a holy death in 371, the year after his baptism. Of their children, at least three survived, two sons and a daughter, and it was in the elder son, Augustine, that the parents' ambitions centred, for he was brilliantly clever, and they were resolved to give him the best possible education. Nevertheless, his waywardness, his love of pleasure and his fits of idleness caused his mother great anxiety. He had been admitted a catechumen in early youth and once, when he was thought to be dying, arrangements were made for his baptism, but his sudden recovery caused it to be deferred indefinitely. At the date of his father's death he was seventeen and a student in Carthage, devoting himself especially to rhetoric. Two years later Monica was cut to the heart at the news that Augustine was leading a wicked life, and had as well embraced the Manichean heresy. For a time after his return to Tagaste she went so far as to refuse to let him live in her house or eat at her table that she might not have to listen to his blasphemies. But she relented as the result of a consoling vision which was vouchsafed to her. She seemed to be standing on a wooden beam bemoaning her son's downfall when she was accosted by a radiant being who questioned her as to the cause of her grief. He then bade her dry her eyes and added, " Your son is with you ". Casting her eyes towards the spot he indicated, she beheld Augustine standing on the beam beside her. Afterwards, when she told the dream to Augustine he flippantly remarked that they might easily be together if Monica would give up her faith, but she promptly replied, " He did not say that I was with you : he said that you were with me ".

Her ready retort made a great impression upon her son, who in later days regarded it as an inspiration. This happened about the end of 377, almost nine years before Augustine's conversion. During all that time Monica never ceased her efforts on his behalf. She stormed heaven by her prayers and tears : she fasted : she watched : she importuned the clergy to argue with him, even though they assured her that it was useless in his actual state of mind. " The heart of the young man is at present too stubborn, but God's time will come ", was the reply of a wise bishop who had formerly been a Manichean himself. Then, as she persisted, he said in words which have become famous : " Go now, I beg of you : it is not possible that the son of so many tears should perish ". This reply and the assurance she had received in the vision gave her the encouragement she was sorely needing, for there was as yet in her elder son no indication of any change of heart.

Augustine was twenty-nine years old when he resolved to go to Rome to teach rhetoric. Monica, though opposed to the plan because she feared it would delay his conversion, was determined to accompany him if he persisted in going, and followed him to the port of embarkation. Augustine, on the other hand, had made up his mind to go without her.   He accordingly resorted to an unworthy stratagem. He pretended he was only going to speed a parting friend, and whilst Monica was spending the night in prayer in the church of St Cyprian, he set sail alone.   " I deceived her with a lie ", he wrote afterwards in his *Confessions*, " while she was weeping and praying for me ".   Deeply grieved as Monica was when she discovered how she had been tricked, she was still resolved to follow him, but she reached Rome only to find that the bird had flown.   Augustine had gone on to Milan.   There he came under the influence of the great bishop St Ambrose.   When Monica at last tracked her son down, it was to learn from his own lips, to her unspeakable joy, that he was no longer a Manichean.   Though he declared that he was not yet a Catholic Christian, she replied with equanimity that he would certainly be one before she died.

To St Ambrose she turned with heartfelt gratitude and found in him a true father in God.   She deferred to him in all things, abandoning at his wish practices which had become dear to her.   For instance, she had been in the habit of carrying wine, bread and vegetables to the tombs of the martyrs in Africa and had begun to do the same in Milan, when she was told that St Ambrose had forbidden the practice as tending to intemperance and as approximating too much to the heathen *parentalia*.   She desisted at once, though Augustine doubted whether she would have given in so promptly to anyone else.   At Tagaste she had always kept the Saturday fast, which was customary there as well as in Rome.   Perceiving that it was not observed in Milan, she induced Augustine to question St Ambrose as to what she herself ought to do.   The reply she received has been incorporated into canon law :   " When I am here, I do not fast on Saturday, but I fast when I am in Rome ;   do the same, and always follow the custom and discipline of the Church as it is observed in the particular locality in which you find yourself ".   St Ambrose, on his part, had the highest opinion of St Monica and was never tired of singing her praises to her son.   In Milan as in Tagaste, she was foremost among the devout women, and when the Arian queen mother, Justina, was persecuting St Ambrose, Monica was one of those who undertook long vigils on his behalf, prepared to die with him or for him.

At last, in August 386, there came the long-desired moment when Augustine announced his complete acceptance of the Catholic faith.   For some time previously Monica had been trying to arrange for him a suitable marriage, but he now declared that he would from henceforth live a celibate life.   Then, when the schools rose for the season of the vintage, he retired with his mother and some of his friends to the villa of one of the party named Verecundius at Cassiciacum.   There the time of preparation before Augustine's baptism was spent in religious and philosophical conversations, some of which are recorded in the *Confessions*.   In all these talks Monica took part, displaying remarkable penetration and judgement and showing herself to be exceptionally well versed in the Holy Scriptures.   At Easter, 387, St Ambrose baptized St Augustine, together with several of his friends, and soon afterwards the party set out to return to Africa.   They made their way to Ostia, there to await a ship, but Monica's life was drawing to an end, though no one but herself suspected it.   In a conversation with Augustine shortly before her last illness she said, " Son, nothing in this world now affords me delight.   I do not know what there is now left for me to do or why I am still here, all my hopes in this world being now fulfilled.   All I wished to live for was that I might see you a Catholic and a child of Heaven.   God has granted me more than this in making you despise earthly felicity and consecrate yourself to His service."

Monica had often expressed a desire to be buried beside Patricius, and therefore one day, as she was expatiating on the happiness of death, she was asked if she would not be afraid to die and be buried in a place so far from home. " Nothing is far from God ", she replied, " neither am I afraid that God will not find my body to raise it with the rest." Five days later she was taken ill, and she suffered acutely until the ninth day, when she passed to her eternal reward. She was fifty-five years of age. Augustine, who closed her eyes, restrained his own tears and those of his son Adeodatus, deeming a display of grief out of place at the funeral of one who had died so holy a death. But afterwards, when he was alone and began to think of all her love and care for her children, he broke down altogether for a short time. He writes : " If any one thinks it wrong that I thus wept for my mother some small part of an hour—a mother who for many years had wept for me that I might live to thee, O Lord—let him not deride me. But if his charity is great, let him weep also for my sins before thee." In the *Confessions*, Augustine asks the prayers of his readers for Monica and Patricius, but it is her prayers which have been invoked by successive generations of the faithful who venerate her as a special patroness of married women and as a pattern for all Christian mothers.

We know practically nothing of St Monica apart from what can be gleaned from St Augustine's own writings and especially from bk. ix of the *Confessions*. A letter reviewing her life and describing her last moments, which purports to have been addressed by St Augustine to his sister, Perpetua, is certainly not authentic. The text of this will be found in the *Acta Sanctorum*, May, vol. i, and elsewhere. In the article " Monique " in DAC., vol. xi, cc. 2332–2356, Dom H. Leclercq has collected a good deal of information concerning Tagaste, now known as Suk Arrhas, and the newly discovered foundations of a basilica at Carthage. It is difficult, however, to see what connection this has with St Monica, beyond the fact that the name " St Monica's " has, in modern times, been given to a chapel in the neighbourhood. It must be confessed that little or no trace can be found of a *cultus* of St Monica before the translation of her remains from Ostia to Rome, which is alleged to have taken place in 1430. Her body thus translated is believed to rest in the church of S. Agostino. Of the many lives of St Monica which have been written in modern times that by Mgr Bougaud (Eng. trans., 1896) may be specially recommended. There are others by F. A. M. Forbes (1915) and by E. Procter (1931), not to speak of those in French, German and Italian.

ST CYRIACUS, OR JUDAS QUIRIACUS, BISHOP (A.D. 133 ?)

THE principal patron of Ancona, St Judas Cyriacus, may possibly have been a local bishop who died or was killed during a pilgrimage to Jerusalem. On the other hand, he has been conjecturally identified with Judas, bishop of Jerusalem, who was slain during a riot in 133. The local tradition of Ancona, however, connects its patron with Judas Quiriacus, a legendary Jew who is supposed to have revealed to the Empress Helen the place in which the Holy Cross lay hidden, and after being baptized and made bishop of Jerusalem, to have suffered martyrdom under Julian the Apostate. A fantastic account of his dialogue with the Emperor Julian, and of the torments endured by him and his mother Anna, is furnished in the so-called " acts " of his martyrdom. Ancona is said to owe to the Empress Galla Placidia the relics of its patron, but the saint's head was brought over from Jerusalem by Henry, Count of Champagne, who built a church in the town of Provins to contain it.

The text of the *De inventione crucis dominicae*, the second part of which is concerned with the martyrdom of Judas Cyriacus, has been printed both in Latin and in Greek in the *Acta Sanctorum*, May, vol. i. See also E. Pigoulewsky in the *Revue de l'Orient chrétien*, 1929, pp. 305–356. The legend of Judas Cyriacus has already been referred to above, under the Finding of the Cross on May 3.

ST PELAGIA OF TARSUS, VIRGIN AND MARTYR   (A.D. 304 ?)

THE story of St Pelagia of Tarsus is one of those Greek romances which appear to have been originally fabricated to supply edifying fiction for the Christian public. She is described as the beautiful daughter of pagan parents who sought to betroth her to the son of the Emperor Diocletian.   She did not wish to marry and obtained permission to go away on a visit to her former nurse.   She seized the occasion to seek instruction from a bishop called Clino, who baptized her and gave her holy communion.   When on her return it transpired that she was a Christian her fiancé committed suicide and her mother denounced her to the emperor.   So lovely was the maiden that Diocletian, instead of punishing her, would fain have married her, but she rejected his addresses and refused to abandon her faith.   She was therefore roasted to death in a red-hot brazen bull.   Her remains were cast forth, but lions guarded them until they were rescued by the bishop, who buried them with honour on a mountain near the city.

There are many Pelagias, upon one of whom—Pelagia of Antioch—St John Chrysostom pronounced a panegyric.   The stories of the others are almost entirely legendary, and are confused one with another.   No data are preserved, in this case of Tarsus, upon which any reasonable presumption of a historic foundation can be based.   The attempt, however, to reduce all these hagiographic fables to a recrudescence of the worship of Aphrodite is quite unreasonable.

The theories of H. Usener in his *Legenden der heiligen Pelagia* (1897) and other folk-lorists need to be controlled by such comments as Fr Delehaye has published in his *Légendes Hagiographiques* (1927), pp. 186–195.   There is, moreover, nothing suggestive of Aphrodite in these particular " acts ", printed in the *Acta Sanctorum*, May, vol. i, as the fabulous history of Pelagia of Tarsus.

ST FLORIAN, MARTYR   (A.D. 304)

THE Saint Florian commemorated in the Roman Martyrology on this day was an officer of the Roman army, who occupied a high administrative post in Noricum, now part of Austria, and who suffered death for the faith in the days of Diocletian. His legendary " acts " state that he gave himself up at Lorch to the soldiers of Aquilinus, the governor, when they were rounding up the Christians, and that after making a bold confession he was twice scourged, half-flayed alive and finally thrown into the river Enns with a stone round his neck.   His body, recovered and buried by a pious woman, was eventually removed to the Augustinian abbey of St Florian, near Linz.   It is said to have been at a later date translated to Rome, and Pope Lucius III, in 1138, gave some of the saint's relics to King Casimir of Poland and to the Bishop of Cracow.   Since that time St Florian has been regarded as a patron of Poland as well as of Linz and of Upper Austria.   In these translations there may have been some confusion with other reputed saints of the same name, but there has been great popular devotion to St Florian in many parts of central Europe, and the tradition as to his martyrdom not far from the spot where the Enns flows into the Danube is ancient and reliable.   Many miracles of healing are attributed to his intercession and he is invoked as a powerful protector in danger from fire or water.

In contrast to so many reputed Diocletian martyrs there is solid ground for the belief that Florian suffered at Lauriacum (Lorch).   His " acts ", first printed in the *Acta Sanctorum*, May, vol. i, have been critically edited by Bruno Krusch in MGH., *Scriptores Merov.*, vol. iii, pp. 68–71.   They date from the end of the eighth century, but are admitted to have an historical foundation. There is also under May 4 a clear mention of his name and the manner of his martyrdom in the *Hieronymianum*. There has been much discussion of the case in the *Neues Archiv* and other learned German periodicals. For references, see the *Lexikon für Theologie und Kirche*, vol. iv (1932), cc. 42–43. Consult further J. Zeiller, *Les Origines chrétiennes dans les Provinces Danubiennes* (1919).

ST VENERIUS, Bishop of Milan   (A.D. 409)

The second bishop of Milan after St Ambrose was St Venerius, who was one of his deacons and who succeeded St Simplician in 400. Very little is known about him, but his *cultus* received a great impetus when St Charles Borromeo elevated his relics in 1579 and translated them to the cathedral. The saint enjoyed the friendship of St Paulinus of Nola, of St Delphinus of Bordeaux and of St Chromatius of Aquileia, and was a warm sympathizer with St John Chrysostom in his sufferings. When the bishops of Africa, assembled at Carthage in 401, appealed for the support of Pope Anastasius, they also addressed a similar appeal to Bishop Venerius. The Christian poet Ennodius celebrated his praises and describes him as a man of singular eloquence.

All these testimonies are gathered up in the account furnished in the *Acta Sanctorum*, May, vol. i.

ST GODEHARD, or GOTHARD, Bishop of Hildesheim   (A.D. 1038)

The birthplace of St Godehard was the Bavarian village of Reichersdorf, where his father was an employee in the service of the canons, who at that period occupied what had formerly been the Benedictine abbey of Nieder-Altaich. The boy was educated by the canons and showed so much promise that he attracted the notice of the bishops of Passau and Regensburg and the favour of Archbishop Frederick of Salzburg. The last named not only took him to Rome, but also made him provost of the canons at the age of nineteen. When, mainly through the efforts of the three prelates, the Benedictine rule was restored in Nieder-Altaich in 990, Godehard, by this time a priest, received the monastic habit together with several other canons. He rose to be abbot, his installation being honoured by the presence of St Henry, then duke of Bavaria—afterwards emperor—who always held him in the utmost esteem. A girdle worked for him by the Empress Cunegund was long venerated as a relic. The excellent order kept by Godehard at Nieder-Altaich prompted St Henry to send him to reform the monasteries of Tegernsee, in the diocese of Freising, Hersfeld, in Thuringia, and Kremsmünster in the diocese of Passau. This difficult task he accomplished satisfactorily whilst retaining the direction of Nieder-Altaich, which was ruled by a deputy during his long absences. In the course of twenty-five years he formed nine abbots for various houses.

Then came the call to a very different life. St Bernwald, bishop of Hildesheim, died in 1022, and the Emperor Henry immediately decided to nominate Godehard to be his successor. In vain did the abbot plead his age and lack of suitable qualifications; he was obliged to comply with the wishes of the monarch, supported by the local clergy. Although he was sixty years of age he threw himself into the work of his diocese with the zest and energy of a young man. He built and restored churches : he did much to foster education, especially in the cathedral school ; he established such strict order in his chapter that it resembled a monastery ; and, on a swampy piece of land which he reclaimed on the outskirts of Hildesheim, he built a hospice where the sick and poor were tenderly cared for. He had a great love for the really necessitous, but he looked with less favour on able-bodied professional tramps ; he called them " peripatetics ", and would not allow them to stay for more than two or three days in the hospice. The holy bishop died in 1038 and was canonized in 1131. It is generally agreed that the celebrated Pass of St Gothard takes its name from a chapel built upon its summit by the dukes of Bavaria and dedicated in honour of the great prelate of Hildesheim.

We have a full and trustworthy account of St Gothard written by his devoted disciple, Wolfher. There are, in fact, two lives by the same author, the one compiled before Gothard's death, the other revised and completed some thirty years later. Both are printed in Pertz, MGH., *Scriptores*, vol. xi, pp. 167–218. There are also some letters by and to him which have survived and which have been printed in MGH., *Epistolae Selectae*, vol. iii, pp. 59–70 and 105–110. St Gothard figures prominently in the third volume of Hauck's *Kirchengeschichte Deutschlands*. There are also modern biographies by F. K. Sulzbeck (1863) and O. J. Blecher (1931). See further the *Acta Sanctorum*, May, vol. i, and E. Tomek, *Studien z. Reform d. deutsch. Klöster*, vol. i (1910), pp. 23 *seq*.

BD CATHERINE OF PARC-AUX-DAMES, Virgin (Early Thirteenth Century)

Bd Catherine of Parc-aux-Dames was the daughter of Jewish parents, resident in the city of Louvain. Amongst the constant visitors to their house was the duke of Brabant's chaplain, Master Rayner, with whom his host used to have long discussions on religious subjects. From the time she was five years old, little Rachel— as she was then called—was an attentive listener to these talks and one day the priest, noticing her eager expression, said to her, " Rachel, would you like to become a Christian ? " " Yes—if you would tell me how ! " was the prompt reply. From that time Master Rayner began to give her instruction in the faith as occasion offered. Rachel's parents, however, became uneasy at the change which was taking place in their child, and when she was in her seventh year decided to send her away beyond the Rhine, to remove her from Christian influences. Rachel was greatly distressed at the prospect, but one night she had a vision of our Lady, who gave her a staff and bade her escape. The girl arose at once, slipped out of the house and made her way to the priest, by whom she was taken to the Cistercian nuns in the abbey of Parc-aux-Dames, a mile and a half from Louvain. There she was baptized and clothed with the habit of the order, assuming the name of Catherine. Her parents appealed to the bishop of Louvain, to the duke of Brabant and even to Pope Honorius, that their daughter might be restored to them—at any rate till she was twelve years old. The bishop and the duke favoured the claim, but it was successfully opposed by Engelbert, archbishop of Cologne, and William, abbot of Clairvaux. Catherine accordingly remained at Parc-aux-Dames until her death, and became famous for her visions and miracles.

See the account in the *Acta Sanctorum*, May, vol. i, which is mainly compiled from such Cistercian sources as Caesarius of Heisterbach and Henriquez. But the Dominican Thomas de Cantimpré also vouches for the truth of the story, from his personal knowledge of Catherine.

BD GREGORY OF VERUCCHIO (A.D. 1343)

The father of Bd Gregory dei Celli of Verucchio died before his son was four years old, and the child was brought up by a mother whose one object was to train him for God. When he was fifteen, they decided to dedicate themselves to St Augustine and St Monica : Gregory received the habit of the Hermits of St Augustine, whilst his mother spent their fortune in founding as well as endowing a house for the order at Verucchio. For ten years Gregory lived in the monastery, leading an exemplary life and converting many sinners who had been led away into heresy. But after his mother's death, the brethren, instigated by jealousy at his success, or perhaps by resentment at his strictness, ungratefully drove him out of the house which had been built from the proceeds of his patrimony. Homeless and destitute, he made his way to the Franciscans of Monte Carnerio, near Reati, by whom he was so kindly received that he settled down permanently amongst them. He lived to extreme old age, dying, it is alleged, at the age of 118. It is averred that the mule which was bearing his coffin to the burial ground at Reati suddenly broke away and as though driven by an unseen force, carried its load back to Verucchio, where its arrival was announced by the spontaneous ringing of all the church bells. By local custom Bd Gregory is invoked as a patron when rain is needed.

The account of this *beatus* printed in the *Acta Sanctorum*, May, vol. i, depends mainly upon a document, attested by a notary public of the Celli family, which was forwarded to the Bollandists by Father H. Torelli, the historiographer of the Hermits of St Augustine. It must be confessed that there are suspicious features about this notarial instrument, but there can be no doubt that the *cultus* of Bd Gregory, alleged to have been signalized by many miraculous cures, was formally confirmed by Pope Clement XIV in 1769.

BD MICHAEL GIEDROYĆ (A.D. 1485)

THE history of Bd MichaelGiedroyć is the story of his infirmities and his austerities. Born at Giedroyc Castle, near Vilna in Lithuania, the only son of noble parents, it soon became evident that he could never bear arms, being a dwarf and very delicate. Moreover, an accident at a very early age deprived him of the use of one of his feet. His father and mother therefore destined him for the Church, and his natural piety pointed in the same direction.   His studies being frequently interrupted by ill-health and the lack of good teachers, the boy occupied himself in making sacred vessels for the church when he was not engaged in prayer.   Weakly as he was, he had begun almost from childhood to practise mortification, speaking seldom, fasting strictly four days in the week and living as far as possible in retirement. He joined the canons regular of St Augustine in the monastery of our Lady of Metro at Cracow, but was permitted at his request to take up his abode in a cell adjoining the church.   There, in a space so restricted that he could scarcely lie down, he spent the rest of his life, only leaving his cell to go to church, and on very rare occasions to converse with holy men.   He never ate meat, living on vegetables, or else on bread and salt.   His austerities were extreme and were never relaxed during illness or in his old age.   Moreover, he suffered much physical and mental torment from evil spirits.   On the other hand, God gave him great consolations : once, it is said, our Lord spoke to him from the crucifix, and he was endowed with the gifts of prophecy and miracles.

An account of this *beatus*, based on materials which do not seem to be altogether reliable, is given in the *Acta Sanctorum*, May, vol. i.   The canons of our Lady of Metro were members of a penitential order of which a brief description may be found in Hélyot, *Ordres religieux*, vol. ii (1849), pp. 562–567.

5 : ST PIUS V, Pope   (A.D. 1572)

MICHAEL GHISLIERI was born in 1504 at Bosco, in the diocese of Tortona, and received the Dominican habit at the age of fourteen in the priory of Voghera.   After his ordination to the priesthood he was lector in theology and philosophy for sixteen years, and for a considerable time was employed as novice master and in governing houses of the order—everywhere endeavouring to maintain the spirit of the founder.   In 1556 he was chosen bishop of Nepi and Sutri, and the following year was appointed inquisitor general, and also cardinal—in order, as he ruefully remarked, that irons should be riveted to his feet to prevent him from creeping back into the peace of the cloister.   Pope Pius IV transferred him to the Piedmontese bishopric of Mondovi—a church reduced almost to ruin by the ravages of war.   Within a short time of his accession the newly-appointed prelate had done much to restore calm and prosperity in his diocese, but he was soon recalled to Rome in connection with other business.   Here, though his opinions were often at variance with those of Pius IV, he never shrank from openly stating his convictions.

In December 1565 Pius IV died, and Michael Ghislieri was chosen pope, largely through the efforts of St. Charles Borromeo, who saw in him the reformer of whom the Church stood in need.   He took the name of Pius V, and from the outset made it abundantly clear that he was determined to enforce the letter as well as the spirit of the recommendations of the Council of Trent.   On the occasion of his coronation, the largesses usually scattered indiscriminately amongst the crowd were bestowed upon hospitals and the really poor, whilst the money which was wont to be spent in providing a banquet for the cardinals, ambassadors and other great persons was sent to the poorer convents of the city.   One of his first injunctions was that all bishops should reside in their dioceses, and parish priests in the cures to which they had been appointed—severe penalties being imposed for disobedience. The new pope's activities extended from a drastic purge of the Roman *curia* to the clearing of the papal states of brigands, from legislation against prostitution to the forbiddance of bull-fighting.   In a time of famine, he imported from Sicily and France at his own expense large quantities of corn, a considerable proportion of which was distributed gratis to the poor or was sold under cost price.   A determined opponent of nepotism, he kept his relatives at a distance, and although he was persuaded to follow tradition by making one of his nephews a cardinal, he gave him little influence or power.   In the new Breviary which was published in 1568, certain saints' days and some extravagant legends were omitted and lessons from the Holy Scriptures regained their proper place, whilst the Missal, issued two years later, was as much a restoration of ancient usage as a revision adapted to the needs of the time.*   To Pius the Church owed the best edition of St Thomas Aquinas which had yet appeared and the solemn recognition of St Thomas as a doctor of the Church.   So severe were the penalties inflicted for every breach of order or morals that he was accused of wanting to turn Rome into a monastery.   That he succeeded as well as he did was largely owing to the popular veneration for his personal holiness : even when he was ill and old he fasted throughout Advent as well as through Lent, and he prayed with such fervour that he was popularly

* This Roman liturgy was imposed on the whole Western church, except where local and proper uses could show a prescription of two hundred years, *e.g.* in the pope's own order, the Dominicans.

supposed to obtain from God whatever he asked. In the hospitals, which he visited frequently, he loved to tend the sick with his own hands.

Reforms such as those enumerated might seem more than enough to engross the attention of any one man, but they were not even the main preoccupation of St Pius V. Throughout his pontificate two menacing shadows were ever before his eyes—the spread of Protestantism and the inroads of the Turks. To counteract these dangers he laboured untiringly; the Inquisition received fresh encouragement, and the learned Baius, whose writings were condemned, only saved himself by recantation. Nevertheless this pope's success against Protestantism was not all effected by such drastic means, for he is said to have converted an Englishman simply by the dignity and holiness of his appearance. The catechism, too, which had been ordered by the Council of Trent was completed during his pontificate, and he at once ordered translations to be made into foreign tongues. Moreover, he made the catechetical instruction of the young a duty incumbent on all parish priests. Conservative in most of his views, he was notably ahead of his contemporaries in the importance he attached to adequate instruction as a preliminary to adult baptism.

By the terms used when Pius V re-issued the bull " In cena Domini " (1568), it was made clear that as pope he claimed a certain suzerainty over secular princes. For a long time he cherished hopes of winning to the faith Queen Elizabeth of England, but in 1570 he issued a bull of excommunication (" Regnans in excelsis ") against her, absolving her subjects from their allegiance and forbidding them to recognize her as their sovereign. This was undoubtedly an error of judgement due to imperfect knowledge of English feeling and of the conditions which obtained in that country. Its only result was to increase the difficulties of loyal English Catholics and to lend some appearance of justification to the accusation of treason so frequently brought against them ; and to aggravate those controversies about oaths and tests which vexed and weakened their body from the Oath of Obedience in 1606 until Emancipation in 1829 : the suspicion which the bull raised about the civil loyalty of Catholics has not quite disappeared even to-day. Several English martyrs died protesting their loyalty to the queen, and when in 1588 the Spanish Armada set out, with the encouragement of Pope Sixtus V, to (incidentally) enforce the sentence of Pius V by establishing Spanish dominion in England, English Catholics at home were in general no more anxious for its success than were their compatriots. All Europe, indeed, had gone a long way since St Gregory VII and Henry IV, Alexander III and Barbarossa, Innocent III and John of England, since Boniface VIII and " Unam sanctam " ; it was nearer the time when a pope, Pius IX, would declare that : " Nowadays no one any longer thinks of the right of deposing princes that the Holy See formerly exercised—and the Supreme Pontiff thinks of it less than anyone."

Pius V's disappointment in England was compensated for in the following year when, aided politically and materially by the Holy See, Don John of Austria and Marcantonio Colonna broke the Turkish power in the Mediterranean. Their force, which comprised 20,000 soldiers, sailed from Corfu and came upon the Turks in the Gulf of Lepanto. There, in one of the world's greatest maritime battles, the Ottoman fleet was completely defeated. From the moment the expedition started the pope had prayed for it almost unceasingly—often with uplifted hands like Moses on the mountain. He had also prescribed public devotions and private fasts and, at the very hour that the contest was raging, the procession of the rosary in the church of the Minerva was pouring forth petitions for victory. Meanwhile the pope himself was conversing on business with some of his cardinals ; but on a sudden he turned from them abruptly, opened a window and remained standing for some time with his eyes fixed upon the sky. Then, closing the casement, he said, " This is not a moment in which to talk business : let us give thanks to God for the victory He has granted to the arms of the Christians ". To commemorate the great deliverance he afterwards inserted the words " Help of Christians " in the Litany of Our Lady and instituted the festival of the Holy Rosary. The victory was won on October 7, 1571. In the following year the pope was struck down by a painful disorder from which he had long suffered and which his austerities had aggravated : it carried him off on May 1, 1572, at the age of sixty-eight.

St Pius V was canonized in 1712, the last pope to be raised to the Church's altars till the beatification of Pius X. The monastic austerity of Pius V's earlier days was continued throughout his life,* his personal kindness and religious devotion were known to all, and his care for the poor and sick and unfortunate went beyond monetary aid to personal attention to them. There was another, a hard side to his character, and of this some historians have made more than enough. But under his rule, with the help and example of such men as St Philip Neri, Rome again became worthy of being the Apostolic City and chief see of the Church of Christ, and the effects of the Council of Trent began to be widely felt. We have an interesting tribute to the new atmosphere in Rome in a letter written in 1570 to his family in Spain by Dr Martin Azpilcueta, a near relative of St Francis Xavier. He was a much-travelled man, and he speaks in the very highest terms of the inhabitants, of their good behaviour and religious spirit. In no such tone did visitors write in the days of Leo X or Paul III. And the change was ultimately chiefly due to St Pius V.

St Pius V played so important a part in the history of his times that anything like a full bibliography is out of the question. A list of all the older books and articles may be found in Emilio Calvi's *Bibliografia di Roma*, and the more important are cited in the eighth volume of Pastor's *Geschichte der Päpste* (and its English translation), which is entirely devoted to this pontiff. It is only necessary here to refer to the *Summarium de Virtutibus* printed in the process of beatification for the Congregation of Sacred Rites, and to the lives by Catena and Gabutius, which are included in the *Acta Sanctorum*, May, vol. i, together with some other materials of a more miscellaneous character. A particularly valuable article by Fr Van Ortroy, which includes the earliest known sketch of the life of St Pius, will be found in the *Analecta Bollandiana*, vol. xxxiii (1914), pp. 187–215. There is an excellent biography by G. Grente (1914) in the series " Les Saints ", and a booklet in English by C. M. Antony (1911). It is curious to notice that in the bibliography appended to the account of St Pius V in the *Catholic Encyclopedia* the first work mentioned is the life by Joseph Mendham (1832). This is, in fact, a bitter indictment of the pontiff himself, and of the Catholic Church, in the course of which we read, for example, that the Little Office of Our Lady sanctioned by the pope " is as disgusting a concentration of blasphemy and idolatry as deforms any part of the papal services ", and in which complaint is also made of " the brutish bigotry and sanguinary intolerance of this pontiff ".

ST HILARY, BISHOP OF ARLES (A.D. 449)

THE birthplace of St Hilary of Arles is not known, but he came of a noble family and was nearly related to St Honoratus, the founder and first abbot of the monastery of Lérins. Having received an excellent education and being endowed with exceptional abilities, he had the prospect of a successful career in the world. But

* The white cassock now worn by the popes is said to derive from Pius V's white Dominican habit.

St Honoratus, who had always loved him, was convinced that he was called to the special service of God. The holy abbot actually abandoned for a short time his island retreat to seek out his young kinsman with the object of inducing him to embrace the religious life. Hilary, however, seemed proof against all his entreaties and fears. " I will obtain from God what you will not concede ! " the monk exclaimed as they bade each other farewell. His prayers were quickly answered. Two or three days later Hilary found himself a prey to a violent interior contest. " On the one side I felt that the Lord was calling me, whilst on the other hand the seductions of the world held me back ", he afterwards wrote. " My will swayed backwards and forwards, now consenting, now refusing. But at last Christ triumphed in me." Once he had definitely made up his mind, he had never looked back : he distributed to the poor the proceeds of his patrimony, which he sold to his brother, and then went to join St Honoratus at Lérins. He has left us a description of the holy, happy life led there by the monks, amongst whom, as it turned out, he was not destined to remain very long. In 426 St Honoratus was elected bishop of Arles and being an old man, greatly desired the assistance and companionship of his favourite relation. Hilary was loth to leave Lérins, but Honoratus went in person to fetch him and they remained together until the bishop's death. Grieved though he was at the loss of his spiritual father, the young monk rejoiced at the prospect of returning to his abbey. He had started on his journey when he was overtaken by messengers, sent by the citizens of Arles, who desired to have him for their archbishop. He was obliged to consent and was duly consecrated, although only twenty-nine years of age.

In his new station Hilary observed the austerities of the cloister, while carrying out with immense energy all the duties of his office. He allowed himself only the bare necessaries of life, wore the same cloak summer and winter, travelled everywhere on foot. Besides observing the canonical hours for prayer, he set aside stated times for manual work, the proceeds of which he gave to the poor. So great was his anxiety to ransom captives that he sold even the church plate to obtain money, contenting himself with a chalice and paten of glass. A great orator, he yet knew how to adapt his language, when necessary, so as to be understood by the most ignorant. Besides building monasteries, he was indefatigable in his visitation of them, being determined everywhere to keep up a high standard of discipline and morals amongst his suffragans and clergy. He presided over several church councils ; but his very zeal, and, perhaps, a somewhat autocratic temper, caused him on more than one occasion to act in a way which had serious consequences for himself. The limits of his province as metropolitan of Southern Gaul had never been satisfactorily settled, and once, when he was on a visitation in debatable territory, he deposed a certain bishop called Chelidonius on the plea that before he had received holy orders he had married a widow and, as a magistrate, had passed a death sentence. Either of these charges, if substantiated, would have disqualified him for the episcopate. Chelidonius forthwith set out for Rome, where he cleared himself of the imputations to the satisfaction of Pope St Leo the Great. As soon as St Hilary realized that the prelate he had deposed had gone to the Holy City, he followed him thither. To settle the matter a council was called, which Hilary attended—not, however, to defend his action, but to contend that the case ought to have been tried by the papal commissaries in Gaul. He did not even await the verdict. Realizing that he was being kept under supervision, and fearing lest he might be forced to communicate with Chelidonius, he left Rome secretly and returned to Arles. Judgement was given against him, and soon afterwards another complaint against him reached the Holy See. Whilst a Gaulish bishop called Projectus was still living—though apparently at the point of death—Hilary had appointed another bishop to the see. The sick man recovered, and there were two prelates claiming the same diocese. Hilary supported his own nominee, perhaps because the other claimant was too infirm to carry out his duties, but St Leo, to whom the matter was referred, rightly judged that Hilary's proceedings had been irregular and were likely to lead to schism. He therefore censured him, forbade him to appoint any more bishops and transferred the dignity of metropolitan to the bishop of Fréjus.

We know little about St Hilary's last years, except that he continued to labour in his own diocese with the same zeal as before, and that he died in his forty-ninth year. It is clear that a reconciliation must have taken place with the pope, for St Leo, writing to his successor at Arles, refers to the late bishop as " Hilary of sacred memory ". Attempts have sometimes been made, though on very insufficient grounds, to brand St Hilary as a semi-Pelagian. It is true that he took exception to the terms in which St Augustine stated the doctrine of predestination, but his views were strictly orthodox.

The life of St Hilary which is printed in the *Acta Sanctorum*, May, vol. ii, and is there attributed to one Honoratus, supposed to have been bishop of Marseilles, is probably the composition of a certain Reverentius at the beginning of the sixth century. It is a work written for edification, purporting to be the memoirs of a contemporary, but unreliable as a record of historical facts. See on all this B. Kolon, *Die Vita S. Hilarii Arelatensis* (1925) and also *cf.* Hefele-Leclercq, *Histoire des Conciles*, vol. ii, pp. 477–478, with Bardenhewer, *Altkirchlichen Literatur*, vol. iv, p. 571.

ST MAURUNTIUS, ABBOT   (A.D. 701)

ST MAURUNTIUS (Mauront) was born in Flanders in the year 634, eldest son of St Adalbald and St Rictrudis. At the court of King Clovis II and Queen Bathildis, where he spent his youth, he occupied several important posts in the royal household. Upon the death of his father he returned to Flanders to settle his affairs and to make arrangements for a projected marriage. But God designed him for the religious life, and the instrument by whose guidance the young man realized his true vocation was St Amandus, bishop of Maestricht, who was at that time living a retired life in the monastery of Elnone. Mauruntius was so deeply moved by a sermon preached by the holy prelate that he decided to retire forthwith into the monastery of Marchiennes. There he was raised to the diaconate. On his estate of Merville in the diocese of Thérouanne, he built the abbey of Breuil, of which he was the first abbot. When St Amatus was banished from Sens by King Thierry III, he was committed to the care of St Mauruntius, who held him in such high esteem that he resigned to him the post of superior and lived under his obedience until the death of that holy bishop in 690. Mauruntius then resumed the direction of Breuil. In compliance with the dying injunction of St Rictrudis, he also retained the supervision of the double monastery of Marchiennes, where his sister, St Clotsindis, ruled as abbess. He was actually staying at Marchiennes when he was seized with the illness of which he died.

The account of St Mauruntius in the *Acta Sanctorum*, May, vol. ii, is almost entirely derived from the biography of St Rictrudis, concerning whom see later in this volume, under May 12.

ST AVERTINUS (A.D. 1180 ?)

IN the *Acta Sanctorum* under May 5, as well as in a number of less important collections, we find mention of a St Avertinus, who is still commemorated on this day in the diocese of Tours. The story told of him is briefly this. St Thomas of Canterbury, in his exile and in all his troubles, was attended by a Gilbertine canon named Avertinus, whom he had raised to the diaconate. Avertinus accompanied his patron to the Synod of Tours in 1163, and after the martyrdom of the archbishop he settled in Touraine, near Vençay, where he consecrated himself to the service of the poor and strangers. He seems to have ended his days as a solitary. He is invoked against dizziness and headache, and a number of *ex votos*, which were still to be seen in the church of St Avertin, near Tours, in the seventeenth century, bore witness to the existence at one time of a very considerable popular *cultus*.

As a curious illustration of the manner in which baseless conjecture or folk tales come to pass for sober history, it seemed worth while to make brief mention of St Avertinus. There may well have been a hermit of that name who was venerated near Tours and in some other parts of France. But there is not a shadow of evidence for attributing to him any connection with St Thomas of Canterbury. In the vast mass of materials printed concerning the great archbishop in the Rolls Series (nine volumes in all) no mention can be found of an Avertinus. Neither is it likely that a devoted disciple and associate of the saint could have escaped notice in the very detailed modern lives written by Father John Morris and Dom A. L'Huillier.

ST ANGELO, MARTYR (A.D. 1220)

ST ANGELO, who was one of the early members of the Carmelite Order, suffered martyrdom for the faith at Leocata, in Sicily. The story of his life, as it has come down to us, is not very reliable. It may be summarized as follows : The parents of St Angelo were Jews of Jerusalem who were converted to Christianity by a vision of our Lady. She told them that the Messias they were awaiting had already come and had redeemed His people, and she promised them two sons, who would grow up as flourishing olive-trees on the heights of Carmel—the one as a patriarch and the other as a glorious martyr. From childhood the twins displayed great mental and spiritual gifts. When, at the age of eighteen, they entered the Carmelite Order, they already spoke Greek, Latin and Hebrew. After Angelo had been a hermit on Mount Carmel for five years, our Lord appeared to him and bade him go to Sicily, where he would have the grace to offer the sacrifice of his life. The saint immediately obeyed the call. During his journey from the East, as well as after his arrival in Sicily, he converted many sinners by his teaching, no less than by his miracles. At Palermo over 200 Jews sought baptism as the result of his eloquence. Similar success attended his efforts in Leocata, but he aroused the fury of a man called Berengarius, whose shameless wickedness he had denounced. As he was preaching to a crowd, a band of ruffians headed by Berengarius broke through the throng and stabbed him. Mortally wounded, Angelo fell on his knees, praying for the people, but especially for his murderer.

St Angelo is commemorated as a martyr in the Roman Martyrology on this day. The legend is printed from Carmelite sources in the *Acta Sanctorum*, May, vol. ii. See also the *Analecta Bollandiana*, vol. xvii (1898), p. 315, and DHG., vol. iii, cc. 6–9.

ST JUTTA, WIDOW (A.D. 1260)

AMONGST the numerous women who were inspired by the example of St Elizabeth of Hungary, one of the most remarkable was St Jutta, or Judith, patroness of Prussia.

Like her great exemplar she was a native of Thuringia, having been born at Sanger-hausen, to the south-west of Eisleben.　Married at the age of fifteen to a man of noble rank, she proved an admirable wife, besides being a great benefactress to the poor.　Once, in a vision, our Lord had said to her, " Follow me " ; and she strove not only to obey Him herself, but to lead her household to do the same.　In the early days of her married life, her husband had remonstrated with her for the simplicity of her dress, but she gradually won him over to her own point of view. He was actually on a pilgrimage to the Holy Land when he died—to the great grief of his widow, who was left to bring up her children alone.

As they grew up, one after another entered religious orders, and Jutta was left free to follow the call which she had long cherished in her heart.　She gave every-thing she possessed to the poor, and then, clad in a miserable dress, she begged bread for herself and the poor from those who had been her dependents.　Though some scoffed, others treated her with reverence, knowing what she had given up, and she resolved to go forth among strangers in order that she might be despised by all.　As she wandered on, walking barefoot in summer and winter, she relieved on the road many tramps by dressing their wounds and feeding them with food supplied to her in charity.　At last she made her way into Prussia, the land of the Teutonic Knights, whose grand-master, Hanno of Sangerhausen, was a relation of her own.　There she settled as a solitary in a ruinous building on the shore of a sheet of water called the Bielcza, half a mile or so from Kulmsee.

St Jutta received wonderful graces, for besides being favoured with many visions and revelations, she was given an infused understanding of the Holy Scriptures.　She once said that three things could bring one very near to God— painful illness, exile from home in a remote corner of a foreign land, and poverty voluntarily assumed for God's sake.　The inhabitants of the neighbouring villages who passed her dwelling declared that they had often seen her raised from the ground, as if upheld by angels.　On Sundays she attended the church at Kulmsee, and she had as her directors at first a Franciscan, John Lobedau, and afterwards a Dominican, Henry Heidenreich.　For four years she remained in her solitude, praying fervently for the conversion of the heathen and the perseverance of the newly baptized.　Then she was seized by a fever which proved fatal.　Many miracles were recorded as having taken place at her grave, and she has been associated in the veneration of the Prussian Catholics with Bd John Lobedau and with another female recluse, Bd Dorothy of Marienwerder.

The very full account of this recluse printed in the *Acta Sanctorum* is a translation of a Polish life by Father Szembek.　This claims to have been based upon a mass of materials collected for the process of canonization, but the originals unfortunately could not be traced by the Bollandists at the date at which they wrote. See also the *Mittheilungen des Vereins f. Gesch., etc., v. Sangerhausen*, vol. i (1881), pp. 82 seq. ; P. Funk, in *Festschrift für W. Goetz* (1927), pp. 81–84 ; and a sketch by H. Westpfahl, *Jutta von Sangerhausen* (1938).

6 : ST JOHN BEFORE THE LATIN GATE　(A.D. 94 ?)

IN the Roman Martyrology for May 6 the first announcement takes the following form : " At Rome, of St John before the Latin Gate, who, at the command of Domitian, was brought in fetters from Ephesus to Rome, and by the verdict of the Senate, was cast into a cauldron of boiling oil before that gate, and came forth thence more hale and more hearty (*purior atque vegetior*) than he entered it ".　The phrase is that of St Jerome (*Adversus Jovinianum*, i, 26), and it is based upon the still earlier statement of Tertullian (*De praescriptionibus*, ch. 36). Alban Butler, in common with the Bollandists and the most critical scholars of his time, such as Tillemont, raises no question as to the historic fact and lays stress upon it as an equivalent martyrdom. His devotional treatment of the subject may be here recapitulated.

When the two sons of Zebedee, James and John, strangers as yet to the mystery of the cross and the nature of Christ's kingdom, had, through their mother's lips, petitioned for places of honour in the day of His triumph, He asked them if they were prepared to drink of His cup. They answered boldly, assuring their master that they were ready to undergo anything for His sake. Our Lord thereupon promised them that their sincerity should be put to trial and that they should both be partakers of the cup of His sufferings. This was literally fulfilled in St James on his being put to death for the faith by Herod, and this day's festival records in part the manner in which it was verified in St John. It may, indeed, be said that this favourite disciple who so tenderly loved his Master, had already had experience of the bitterness of the chalice when he was present on Calvary. But our Saviour's prediction was to be fulfilled in a more particular manner, which should entitle him to the merit and crown of martyrdom, the instrument of this trial, postponed for more than half a century, being Domitian, the last of the twelve Caesars.

He was a tyrant, detestable on account of his cruelty, and he was the author of the second general persecution of the Church. St John, the only surviving apostle, who was famous for the veneration paid to him while he governed the churches of Asia, was arrested at Ephesus and sent prisoner to Rome about the year 94. Regardless of his victim's great age and gentle bearing, the emperor condemned him to a barbarous form of death. He was probably first scourged, according to the Roman custom, and then thrown into a cauldron of boiling oil. We cannot doubt that St John exulted in the thought of laying down his life for the faith and rejoining the Master whom he loved. God accepted his oblation and in some sense crowned his desire. He conferred on him the merit of martyrdom, but suspended the operation of the fire, as he had formerly preserved the three children from hurt in the Babylonian furnace. The seething oil was changed into a refreshing bath, so that Domitian, who entertained a great idea of the power of magic, and who, it is alleged, had previously found himself baffled by some prodigy when Apollonius of Tyana was brought before him, now contented himself with banishing the apostle to the island of Patmos. Under the mild rule of Domitian's successor, Nerva, St John is believed to have returned to Ephesus and there peacefully to have fallen asleep in the Lord.

The localization of the alleged miracle outside the Latin gate is certainly not historical, for the Porta Latina belongs to the walls of Aurelian, two centuries later than St John's time. This particular festival cannot be traced farther back in the Roman church than the sacramentary of Pope Adrian, towards the close of the eighth century. There is a church of St John at the Porta Latina, replacing an older one which owed its existence to that pontiff and presumably was dedicated on this day. Mgr Duchesne suggests that the choice of this date (May 6) is connected with the occurrence in the Byzantine calendar of a feast on May 8, commemorating a miracle of St John at Ephesus. In the so-called *Missale Gothicum* there is a Mass of St John the Evangelist which must have fallen in May, not long after that of the Finding of the Cross. The incident of the boiling oil seems originally to have belonged to certain apocryphal but early " Acts of John ", of which we now only possess fragments.

In a *Motu Proprio* of *John XXIII* dated July 25, 1960, this feast was dropped from the Roman Calendar.

See L. Duchesne, *Liber Pontificalis*, vol. i, pp. 508, 521, and *Christian Worship* (1920), pp. 281–282. On the general question, see K. A. Kellner, *Heortology* (1908), p. 298.

ST EVODIUS, Bishop of Antioch　　(*c*. A.D. 64 ?)

WE learn from Origen and from Eusebius that the predecessor of St Ignatius the God-bearer in the see of Antioch was Evodius, who had been ordained and consecrated by the Apostles themselves—doubtless when St Peter was about to leave Antioch for Rome. Later writers have tried to identify Evodius with the Evodias or Evodia mentioned by St Paul in his epistle to the Philippians—though this person was almost certainly a woman—and have also described him as a martyr. According to tradition, he was one of the seventy disciples sent out by our Lord to preach. He is supposed to have coined the word "Christian", which, as we know from the Acts of the Apostles, was first used in Antioch to denote members of the Church of Christ. This is stated by the chronicler Malalas, who wrote in the latter part of the sixth century, and we further learn from him that St Peter happened to be passing through Antioch at the time when St Evodius died, and that he thereupon consecrated St Ignatius to be bishop in his room. If this be true, Evodius must have died before A.D. 64.

There is a short notice in the *Acta Sanctorum*, May, vol. i ; but consult also G. Salmon in DCB., vol. ii, p. 428, and Harnack, *Chronologie d. Altchrist. Literatur*, vol. i, p. 94, as well as *Die Zeit des Ignatius* by the same author.

ST EDBERT, Bishop of Lindisfarne　　(A.D. 698)

THE Venerable Bede, writing of St Edbert, states that he was remarkable for his knowledge of the Bible, as well as for his faithful observance of the divine precepts. All his life long he was extremely generous to the poor, for whose benefit he set aside a tenth part of his possessions. Ordained successor to St Cuthbert in the see of Lindisfarne, he governed wisely for eleven years, and covered with lead St Finan's great wooden cathedral church which had previously been thatched only with reeds, Scottish fashion. He made it a practice to retire twice a year for forty days of solitary prayer to the retreat—probably the tiny island known as St Cuthbert's Isle—where his great predecessor had spent some time before finally withdrawing to Farne. When the relics of St Cuthbert were found incorrupt, St Edbert gave instructions that the body should be put into a new coffin which was to be raised above the pavement for greater veneration. He added that the space below would not long remain empty. Scarcely had his orders been carried out when he was seized with a fever which proved mortal, and his own remains were laid in the empty grave. A commemoration of St Edbert is made to-day in the diocese of Hexham.

All our information is, practically speaking, derived from Bede in his *Historia Ecclesiastica*, bk iv. C. Plummer in his notes, Canon Raine in DCB., the *Acta Sanctorum*, May, vol. i, and Symeon of Durham add very little. St Edbert's relics shared the wanderings of those of St Cuthbert, and ultimately rested with them at Durham.

ST PETRONAX, Abbot of Monte Cassino　　(*c*. A.D. 747)

THE second founder of the abbey of Monte Cassino, St Petronax, was a native of Brescia. When on a visit to Rome he seems to have been induced by Pope St

Gregory II to make a pilgrimage to the tomb of St Benedict, in the year 717. There, among the ruins of the old monastery which had been destroyed by the Lombards in 581, he found a few solitaries, who elected him their superior. Other disciples soon gathered round them. Through the generosity of prominent nobles, chief amongst whom was the Lombard duke of Beneventum, and with the strong support of three popes, he succeeded in rebuilding Monte Cassino, which, under his long and vigorous rule, regained its old eminence. The English St Willibald, afterwards bishop of Eichstätt, received the habit at his hands. St Sturmius, founder of the abbey of Fulda, spent some time at Monte Cassino learning the primitive Benedictine rule, and great men of all kinds, princes as well as ecclesiastics, stayed within its hospitable walls. St Petronax ruled over the community until his death, the date of which was probably 747. Recent investigation has shown that St Willibald himself, during the ten years he spent at Monte Cassino, contributed much to the restoration of Benedictine discipline and to the general development of this great abbey.

The more relevant texts in Paul Warnefrid's *Historia Langobardorum* have been extracted by the Bollandists, and by Mabillon, vol. iii, part 1, pp. 693–698. But see especially Abbot J. Chapman, " La Restauration du Mont Cassin par l'Abbé Petronax " in the *Revue Bénédictine*, vol. xxi (1904), pp. 74–80, and H. Leclercq in DAC., vol. xi, cc. 3451–3468.

BD PRUDENCE, VIRGIN   (A.D. 1492)

THE life of Bd Prudence seems to have been quite uneventful, and her fame rests entirely upon the miracles she is reported to have wrought after her death. A member of the noble Milanese family of the Casatori, she joined the Hermitesses of St Augustine in her native city. She was promoted to be superior of the convent of St Mark at Como, and succeeded in settling the dissensions which were dividing the two communities. Her zeal was displayed not only amongst her nuns, whom she ruled with great prudence, but also in bringing about the restoration of the church of the Visitation at Como. Full of years, labours and merits, she passed to her eternal reward after she had governed the house at Como for thirty-eight years.

Here the Bollandists, apparently with good reason, complain of the lack of materials. though the Augustinian historiographer, Father A. Torelli, had done his best to help them. Their account is printed in vol. ii for May.

BB. EDWARD JONES AND ANTONY MIDDLETON, MARTYRS (A.D. 1590)

EDWARD JONES was a Welshman from the diocese of St Asaph, and Antony Middleton was a Yorkshireman. Both were educated at the Douai College in Rheims, raised to the priesthood and chosen for the English mission. Middleton came to London in 1586, and owing to his juvenile appearance and small stature was able to labour for a considerable time without rousing suspicion. Jones, who followed two years later, at once made a name for himself as a fervent and eloquent preacher. They were tracked down by spies who professed to be Catholics, and they appear to have been hanged before the doors of the houses in Fleet Street and Clerkenwell within which they had been arrested, the words " For Treason and Foreign Invasion " being posted up in large letters as an explanation of this summary " justice " which, as attested by witnesses present at the trial, was full of irregularities. Middleton, whose request that he might address the people was refused, called God to witness that he died simply and solely for the Catholic faith and for being a priest and preacher of the true religion. He then prayed that his death might obtain the forgiveness of his sins, the advancement of the Catholic faith and the conversion of heretics. According to the testimony of eye-witnesses, he was flung off the ladder, cut down, and disembowelled while still alive. They died on May 6, 1590.

The account originally given by Challoner in MMP., pp. 162–163 is not altogether accurate. See the fuller narrative printed by the Catholic Record Society, vol. v, pp. 182–186, and *cf.* Pollen, *Acts of English Martyrs*, pp. 308–309 and 315–317. It appears that Bd Edward Jones was sentenced in virtue of his own confession that he was a priest, made under torture.

7 : ST STANISLAUS, BISHOP OF CRACOW, MARTYR   (A.D. 1079)

THE *cultus* of St Stanislaus is widespread in Poland—especially in his episcopal city of Cracow, which honours him as principal patron and preserves the greater part of his relics in the cathedral. His biography, written some four hundred years after his death, by St Casimir's tutor, the historian John Dlugosz, seems to be an uncritical compilation from various earlier writings and from oral tradition, for it contains several conflicting statements, besides a certain amount of matter which is obviously purely legendary.

Stanislaus Szczepanowski was born on July 26, 1030, at Szczepanow. He came of noble parents, who had been childless for many years until this son was vouchsafed to them in answer to prayer. They devoted him from his birth to the service of God, and encouraged in every way the piety which he evinced from early childhood. He was educated at Gnesen and afterwards, we are told, " at the University of Paris ", which at that time had not yet come into existence. Eventually he was ordained priest by Lampert Zula, bishop of Cracow, who gave him a canonry in the cathedral and subsequently appointed him his preacher and archdeacon. The eloquence of the young priest and his saintly example brought about a great reformation of morals amongst his penitents—clergy as well as laity flocking to him from all quarters for spiritual advice. Bishop Lampert wished to resign the episcopal office in his favour, but Stanislaus refused to consider the suggestion. However, upon Lampert's death, he could not resist the will of the people seconded by an order from Pope Alexander II, and he was consecrated bishop in 1072. He proved himself a zealous apostle, indefatigable in preaching, strict in maintaining discipline, and regular in his visitations. His house was always crowded with the poor, and he kept a list of widows and other distressed persons to whom he systematically distributed gifts.

Poland at that epoch was ruled by Boleslaus II, a prince whose finer qualities were completely eclipsed by his unbridled lust and savage cruelty. Stanislaus alone ventured to beard the tyrant and to remonstrate with him at the scandal his conduct was causing. At first the king endeavoured to vindicate his behaviour, but when pressed more closely he made some show of repentance. The good effects of the admonition, however, soon wore off : Boleslaus relapsed into his evil ways. There were acts of rapacity and political injustice which brought him into conflict with the bishop and at length he perpetrated an outrage which caused general indignation. A certain nobleman had a wife who was very beautiful.

Upon this lady Boleslaus cast lustful eyes, and when she repelled his advances he caused her to be carried off by force and lodged in his palace. The Polish nobles called upon the archbishop of Gnesen and the court prelates to expostulate with the monarch. Fear of offending the king closed their lips, and the people openly accused them of conniving at the crime. St Stanislaus, when appealed to, had no such hesitation ; he went again to Boleslaus and rebuked him for his sin. He closed his exhortation by reminding the prince that if he persisted in his evil courses he would bring upon himself the censure of the Church, with the sentence of excommunication.

The threat roused the king to fury. He declared that a man who could address his sovereign in such terms was more fit to be a swineherd than a shepherd of souls, and cut short the interview with threats. He first had recourse to slander—if we may believe a story related by the saint's later historians. St Stanislaus, we are told, had bought some land for the Church from a certain Peter, who died soon after the transaction. It was suggested to the deceased man's nephews that they should claim back the land on pretence that it had not been paid for. The case came up before Boleslaus : no witnesses for the defence were allowed to be heard and the verdict seemed a foregone conclusion, when, in answer to a dramatic appeal from St Stanislaus, the dead man appeared before the court in his grave-clothes and vindicated the bishop. If we can credit this story we are further asked to believe that the marvel produced no permanent change of heart in Boleslaus, whose barbarity had only increased with time.

At last, finding all remonstrance useless, Stanislaus launched against him a formal sentence of excommunication. The tyrant professed to disregard the ban, but when he entered the cathedral of Cracow he found that the services were at once suspended by order of the bishop. Furious with rage, he pursued the saint to the little chapel of St Michael outside the city, where he was celebrating Mass, and ordered some of his guards to enter and slay him. The men, however, returned, saying that they could not kill the saint as he was surrounded by a heavenly light. Upbraiding them for cowardice, the king himself entered the building and dispatched the bishop with his own hand. The guards then cut the body into pieces and scattered them abroad to be devoured by beasts of prey. Protected, it is said, by eagles, the sacred relics were rescued three days later by the cathedral canons and privately buried at the door of the chapel in which Stanislaus had been slain.

The above summarizes the story of the martyrdom of St Stanislaus as it is commonly told. Considerable discussion was caused in Poland by the publication in 1904 of an historical work by Professor Wojchiechowski in the course of which he maintained that Stanislaus had been guilty of treason, had plotted to dethrone his sovereign, and had therefore rightly been put to death. To this charge Professor Miodonski and others replied with vigour. But there seems no doubt that there were some political considerations behind the murder of St Stanislaus, though the whole business is very uncertain and obscure. It is not true that the action of Boleslaus led to an immediate rising of the people which drove him from Poland ; but it certainly hastened his fall from power. Pope St Gregory VII laid the country under an interdict, and nearly two centuries later, in 1253, St Stanislaus was canonized by Pope Innocent IV.

The long life of St Stanislaus by John Dlugosz is printed in the *Acta Sanctorum*, May, vol. ii. Two shorter but earlier biographies have since been discovered and published.

For details see Poncelet, BHL., nn. 7832–7842. The action of Pope St Gregory VII has been studied in the seventh volume of Gfrörer's *Kirchengeschichte*, pp. 557 *seq.* *Cf.* also the *Cambridge History of Poland*, vol. i (1950). Polish biographies of the saint are numerous, but little seems to have been written in other languages.

ST DOMITIAN, Bishop of Maestricht   (*c.* A.D. 560)

THE principal patron of Huy on the Meuse is St Domitian, whose relics still repose in a beautiful medieval reliquary in the church of our Lady. A native of France, the saint was elected bishop of Tongres, but his episcopal seat was afterwards removed to Maestricht. At the Synod of Orleans in 549 he distinguished himself for the skilful manner in which he refuted the doctrines of heretics. He evangelized the Meuse valley, converting numerous pagans, besides building churches and hospices in his diocese. When, towards the close of a severe famine, the well-to-do were ceasing to relieve their poorer neighbours lest they themselves should suffer from shortage, the holy bishop made an eloquent and successful appeal to their generosity, rebuking their lack of faith and prophesying a plentiful harvest. Tradition attributes to St Domitian the slaying of a terrible monster, which was causing great distress by poisoning the drinking-water of Huy ; a procession still takes place to the place beside a spring where the saint overcame this real or metaphorical dragon.

The formal biographies of St Domitian printed in the *Acta Sanctorum*, May, vol. ii, are all very late. A few notices in the *Gesta Ep. Leodiensium* (see Pertz, MGH., *Scriptores*, vol. vii, p. 178, and vol. xxv, pp. 26–27) are more reliable. See also Duchesne, *Fastes Épiscopaux*, vol. iii, p. 189.

ST LIUDHARD, Bishop   (*c.* A.D. 602)

WE know definitely from Bede that when King Ethelbert of Kent married the Frankish princess Bertha, who was the daughter of Charibert, King of Paris, a stipulation was made that she should be free to practise her own Christian religion, and that she should bring with her her chaplain, Liudhard, who is stated to have been a bishop. According to later traditions he died at Canterbury, and St Laurence, St Augustine's immediate successor in the see, removed the body of Liudhard into the church of the monastery of SS. Peter and Paul, where it was placed with that of Bertha in the *porticus* of St Martin. This is practically all we know of Liudhard, though such writers as William of Malmesbury attributed to him a considerable influence in preparing the way for the Kentish king's eventual acceptance of Christianity on the coming of St Augustine. In the martyrologies of the ninth century, however, we find on February 4 mention of " the passion of St Liphard, martyr, archbishop of Canterbury ", and this at a later date meets us in the form of a story that this Archbishop Liphard on his way back to England after a visit to Rome was waylaid and suffered a violent death in the neighbourhood of Cambrai. There certainly was no Liphard who was archbishop of Canterbury, and it is impossible to reach any definite conclusion as to the identity of this Liphard or the fact of the alleged martyrdom. The feast of " St Liphard, bishop and martyr ", has, however, for a long time past been kept in the diocese of Cambrai.

See C. Plummer's note in his edition of Bede's *Historia Ecclesiastica*, vol. ii, p. 42 ; Stanton, *Menology*, pp. 51–52 and 200–201 ; C. J. Destombes, *Vies des Saints des diocèses de Cambrai et d'Arras*, vol. i, pp. 158 *seq.* St Liphard, under the name of Liefardus, was represented in the old paintings in the English College, Rome.

SS. SERENICUS AND SERENUS   (*c.* A.D. 669 AND 680)

SERENICUS, or Cerenicus, and his brother Serenus, or Seneridus, were young patricians from Spoleto who abandoned their family and their possessions at the bidding, it is said, of an angel, and betook themselves to Rome.   The tombs of the Apostles were at that time under the care of the Benedictines, with whom the two strangers were brought into contact and from whom they received the habit.   For some time they lived the community life in Rome, edifying their brethren by their youthful piety, but before long they withdrew, still under angelic guidance, to seek a new home beyond the Alps in France.   On the site of the present town of Château Gontier, in the diocese of Angers, and subsequently in the forest of Charnie, near the village of Saulges in Maine, they led a life of extreme self-abnegation as solitaries.   But, desirous though they were of remaining lost to the world, the fame of their sanctity began to attract visitors, who disturbed their solitude.   So strongly did Serenicus feel the call to greater seclusion that he bade farewell to his brother, from whom he had never previously been parted, and struck out into the unknown region of Hyesmes, accompanied by a child whom he had baptized and who would not leave him.   On a spot surrounded by boulders, situated over the river Sarthe and approached only by a narrow path, he determined to make his abode.   He was soon to discover that solitude was not for him.   Disciples gathered round, and he became the head of a large community of monks, whom he taught to recite the full psalmody, consisting of the complete Roman use in addition to all the Benedictine offices.   He continued to rule over the monastery he had founded until his death which occurred when he was very old, about the year 669.

In the meantime his brother Serenus had remained in his hermitage at Saulges, his fasts and austerities winning for him many graces, including visions, ecstasies and miracles.   When the countryside was stricken by pestilence, famine and drought, following on the horrors of the civil war, St Berarius, bishop of Le Mans, besought the intercession of the recluse.   The cleansing rain which cleared away the infection and refreshed the earth was attributed by the grateful people to the prayers of St Serenus, whose reputation as a wonder-worker was greatly enhanced. Like St Serenicus, he lived to old age, and as he lay dying, sounds of celestial music are said to have been plainly heard by those who were near him at the time.

The not very convincing narrative, compiled seemingly in the eighth century, which is here summarized, has been printed by the Bollandists and in Mabillon, *Acta Sanctorum O.S.B.*, vol. ii, pp. 572–578.

ST JOHN OF BEVERLEY, BISHOP OF YORK   (A.D. 721)

FEW native saints enjoyed a greater reputation in Catholic England than St John of Beverley, whose shrine was one of the favourite places of pilgrimage until the Reformation.   The learned Alcuin had an extraordinary devotion to him and celebrated his miracles in verse, whilst Athelstan ascribed to him his victory over the Scots and Henry V his defeat of the French at Agincourt.   At the instance of the latter, a synod in 1416 ordered his feast to be kept throughout England.   The saint was born at Harpham, a village in Yorkshire.   As a young man, he was attracted to Kent by the famous school of St Theodore in which he became a distinguished student under the holy abbot Adrian.   Upon his return to his own county, he entered the double abbey of Whitby, then under the rule of the Abbess Hilda.

His exceptional abilities marked him out for preferment, and after the death of St Eata he was appointed bishop of Hexham. Whatever time he could spare from the duties of his office he devoted to heavenly contemplation, retiring for that purpose at stated periods to a cell beside the church of St Michael beyond the Tyne, near Hexham. Often he would be accompanied by some poor person, whom he would serve, and once he took with him a youth who seems to have suffered from a loathsome form of ringworm and who had never been able to speak. The bishop taught him to say " Géa "—the Anglo-Saxon equivalent for " Yes ". From this beginning he led him on to pronounce the letters of the alphabet and then to enunciate syllables and words. In this manner the youth gradually acquired the use of speech and was at the same time cured of the malady which disfigured him.

After the death of St Bosa, John was appointed bishop of York. The Venerable Bede, who received holy orders from St John when bishop of Hexham, refers to him at some length in his *Ecclesiastical History*, giving ample testimony to his sanctity, and recounting several miracles which had been described to him by such reliable eye-witnesses as the abbots of Beverley and of Tynemouth. After St John had been translated to York he continued his practice of a periodical retirement from the world for spiritual refreshment. He chose for his retreat an abbey which he had built at Beverley, then a forest. In 717, when he was much worn by age and fatigue, St John resigned his bishopric to his chaplain, St Wilfrid the Younger, and retired to Beverley, where he spent the four last years of his life in the faithful performance of all monastic duties. He died on May 7, 721. His feast is kept in the diocese of Hexham to-day, and in other northern dioceses on October 25, the date of the translation of his relics in 1037.

The *Ecclesiastical History* of Bede is our most reliable source of information. More than three centuries later Folcard, a monk of St Bertin then resident in England, wrote a life of John of Beverley, followed by a long series of miracles. This, together with other documents, has been edited by Canon Raine for the Rolls Series in *The Historians of the Church of York*, vol. i. See also Raine's two volumes on Hexham in the Surtees Society publications. Entries in the calendars (for which consult Stanton's *Menology*, p. 201) give evidence of a widespread *cultus* of St John of Beverley from an early date. Stanton (p. 676) speaks of the discovery of certain relics as late as the year 1664. There is a charming reference to the saint in Dame Julian's *Revelations*, ch.38.

BD ROSE VENERINI, Virgin (A.D. 1728)

Bd Rose was born at Viterbo in 1656, the daughter of Godfrey Venerini, a physician. Upon the death of a young man who had been paying court to her, she entered a convent, but after a few months had to return home to look after her widowed mother. Rose used to gather the women and girls of the neighbourhood to say the rosary together in the evenings, and when she found how ignorant many of them were of their religion she began to instruct them. She was directed by Father Ignatius Martinelli, a Jesuit, who convinced her that her vocation was as a teacher "in the world" rather than as a contemplative in a convent; whereupon in 1685, with two helpers, Rose opened a free school for girls in Viterbo : it soon became a success.

Bd Rose had the gift of ready and persuasive speech, and a real ability to teach and to teach others to teach, and was not daunted by any difficulty when the service of God was in question. Her reputation spread, and in 1692 she was invited by Cardinal Barbarigo to advise and help in the training of teachers and organizing of schools in his diocese of Montefiascone. Here she was the mentor and friend of Lucy Filippini, who became foundress of an institute of *maestre pie* and was canonized in 1930.   Rose organized a number of schools in various places, sometimes in the face of opposition that resorted to force in unbelievable fashion— the teachers were shot at with bows and their house fired.   Her patience and trust overcame all obstacles, and in 1713 she made a foundation in Rome that received the praise of Pope Clement XI himself.   It was in Rome that she died, on May 7, 1728 ; her reputation of holiness was confirmed by miracles, and in 1952 she was beatified.   It was not till some time after her death that Bd Rose's lay school-teachers were organized as a religious congregation : they are found in America as well as in Italy, for the Venerini Sisters have worked among Italian immigrants since early in the twentieth century.

There is a short account of Bd Rose in the decree of beatification, printed in the *Acta Apostolicae Sedis*, vol. xliv (1952), pp. 405–409.

8 : THE APPEARING OF ST MICHAEL THE ARCHANGEL
(A.D. 492 ?)

WHEN people had become familiar with the idea that Michael the Arch-angel was not only the captain of the heavenly host and the great protector, but also the arbiter of man's destinies on the threshold of the world to come (*cf.* his feast on September 29), some public and external manifestation of the appeals made to this beneficent influence in private could not long be delayed. Any nucleus provided by an alleged miraculous happening would awaken ready response and would suffice to crystallize into one determined form the latent devotion of the crowd.   There are indications of an early cult of St Michael, connecting him with the wonders wrought by the hot springs of Phrygia, notably at Hierapolis, and it seems certain that already in the fourth century a church was dedicated under his name near Constantinople, possibly in the lifetime of the first Christian emperor, Constantine.   This impulse came from the East, though there is evidence that a basilica in honour of St Michael was constructed near Rome at the sixth milestone along the Via Salaria at an early date.   Several Masses, appar-ently connected with this shrine, or possibly with others bearing the same dedication within the city, are provided in the earliest Roman Mass-book, the so-called *Leonianum*, and are assigned to the end of September.   Whether the dedication on Mount Garganus, in Apulia, where Greek influences were dominant, is older than this cannot be easily determined.   According to the written legend, still sum-marized in the Breviary, it occurred in the time of Pope Gelasius (492–496).   A bull which had strayed from the herd of a certain rich land-owner found its way into a cave near the summit of the eminence called Mount Garganus.   In the search which was made for it portents occurred by which the archangel manifested his desire that this spot should be consecrated in his honour.   Numberless miracles were believed to have been wrought in the cave or crypt, where a spring trickled which was accredited with healing virtue.   That the fame of this shrine soon spread all over the West is manifested by the fact that Mount Garganus is mentioned in one of the oldest manuscripts of the *Hieronymianum* in connection with the feast of St Michael on September 29.   Even in England the Anglo-Saxon collection of ser-mons called the Blickling Homilies, written before the end of the tenth century, supplied an account of Mount Garganus and its crypt chapel, from which, to quote a modern English version, we may learn that : " There was also from the same stone of the church roof, at the north side of the altar, a very pleasant and clear stream issuing, used by those who still dwell in that place. Beside this piece of water was a glass vessel hung on a silver chain, which received this joy-giving tide, and it was the custom of this people when they had been houselled (*i.e.* had received holy communion) that they by steps should ascend to the glass vessel and there take and taste the heavenly fluid." This is an interesting piece of evidence for the fact that long before communion under both kinds was abolished for the laity, it was customary to take a draught of water after receiving the Precious Blood, or more probably, under Greek influences, after receiving the dipped Host, which is still the usual manner of administering the sacrament of the Eucharist in the East.

In a Motu Proprio of John XXIII dated July 25, 1960, this feast was dropped from the Roman Calendar.

The full text of the legend is printed in Ughelli, vol. vii, cc. 1107–1111, and in the *Acta Sanctorum*, September, vol. viii ; on which *cf.* Ebert, *Geschichte der Literatur des Mittelalters*, vol. ii, p. 358. See also K. A. Kellner, *Heortology* (1908), pp. 328–332, and H. Leclercq in DAC., vol. xi, cc. 903–907. There has been confusion between this feast and that of St Michael on September 29, and Pope Benedict XIV proposed to suppress to-day's observance, which has in fact now been done in the Benedictine calendar. There can be little doubt that the story of the foundation of Saint-Michel au Péril de Mer, the famous Mont-Saint-Michel near Avranches, which is traditionally dated 709, was based on the legend of Monte Gargano. At what date St Michael's Mount at Marazion in Cornwall received its name is not certainly known ; but it may have been before Robert of Mortain presented the Mount to the monks of St Michael *in Periculo Maris* (Mont-Saint-Michel) *c.* 1086, if that charter be genuine: see T. Taylor, *The Celtic Christianity of Cornwall* (1916), pp. 141-168. See also Taylor's *St Michael's Mount* (1932) ; and J. R. Fletcher, *Short History of St Michael's Mount* (1951).

ST VICTOR MAURUS, Martyr   (A.D. 303 ?)

St Ambrose says of St Victor that he was one of the patrons of Milan, and as such he is associated with St Felix and St Nabor. According to tradition, he was a native of Mauretania, and was called Maurus to distinguish him from other confessors of the name of Victor. He is stated to have been a soldier in the Praetorian guard, a Christian from his youth, and to have been arrested for the faith when quite an old man. After enduring severe tortures, he suffered martyrdom by decapitation under Maximian in Milan about the year 303. His body was buried by order of the bishop, St Maternus, beside a little wood, and a church was afterwards built over his remains. St Gregory of Tours tells us that God honoured his tomb by many miracles. St Charles Borromeo caused the relics to be translated in 1576 to the new church in Milan which had then been recently built by the Olivetan monks and which still bears St Victor's name.

In the *passio* of this martyr we have the usual fantastic accumulation of torments. He is said, for example, to have been basted with molten lead, which instantaneously cooled on touching his flesh, and did him no sort of harm. Nevertheless, the fact of his martyrdom and early veneration at Milan is beyond doubt.

There is quite a considerable literature concerning St Victor the Moor, for which see CMH., p. 238. Consult especially F. Savio, *I santi Martiri di Milano* (1906), pp. 3–24 and 59–65. The *passio* is printed in the *Acta Sanctorum*, May, vol. ii.

ST ACACIUS, or AGATHUS, Martyr   (A.D. 303 OR 305)

With the exception of St Mucius, St Acacius, or Agathus, is the only genuine ancient martyr of Byzantium. He was a Cappadocian, a centurion in the imperial army, who perished for the faith during the persecution under Diocletian and Maximian. He suffered alone, and the seventy-seven companions who are commonly associated with him must be referred elsewhere. According to his so-called " acts ", which, however, are not trustworthy, he was denounced by the tribune Firmus at Perinthus in Thrace, where he was cruelly tortured under the judge Bibienus. He was then taken to Byzantium, publicly scourged and finally beheaded.

Constantinople contained two, if not three, churches dedicated in honour of St Acacius, one of which was built by Constantine the Great. It was nicknamed " the Walnut ", because built into its structure was the walnut tree upon which the saint was said to have been suspended for his flagellation.

The Greek text of the Acts of Acacius is printed in the *Acta Sanctorum*, May, vol. ii, and there is also an ancient Syriac version edited by P. Bedjan. See what has been written concerning this martyr by Delehaye in the *Analecta Bollandiana*, vol. xxxi (1912), p. 228, as well as in his *Origines du Culte des Martyrs*, pp. 233–236, and in his CMH., p. 239. This martyr's name is found both in the ancient Syriac *Breviarium* of *c.* 412, and in the Spanish calendar of Carmona. *Cf.* also Salaville, " Les Églises de St Acace " in *Échos d'Orient*, vol. xi, pp. 105 *seq.*

ST GIBRIAN   (*c.* A.D. 515)

TOWARDS the end of the fifth century—so we are told—there arrived in Brittany from Ireland a family consisting of seven brothers and three sisters, all of whom had abandoned their native land that they might serve God more freely in a strange country. The men were St Gibrian, St Helan, St Tressan, St German, St Veran, St Abran and St Petran, and the women's names were Francla, Pomptia and Posemna. St Gibrian, who was the eldest and a priest, was their leader. They eventually settled as solitaries in the forest land near the Marne, living alone, but not so far apart that they could not visit each other from time to time. Gibrian's hermitage was at the junction of the Coole and the Marne. He died in his retreat after a life of prayer and austerity, and a chapel was erected over his tomb. To preserve his relics from the ravages of the Normans they were afterwards removed to the abbey of St Remigius at Rheims, where they remained until the French Revolution, when they were scattered and lost.

The Bollandists deal with this alleged family of saints in the *Acta Sanctorum*, May, vol. ii, printing what purports to be their story from a medieval manuscript at Rheims. A collection of reputed miracles at the shrine after the translation to Rheims is to be found in an appendix to the seventh volume for May. Dom Gougaud, in his *Gaelic Pioneers of Christianity*, p. 4, seems to be right in treating the account as legendary, but these saints are still liturgically commemorated in some French dioceses, notably at Rheims itself. See also O'Hanlon, LIS., vol. v, p. 129.

ST DESIDERATUS, BISHOP OF BOURGES   (*c.* A.D. 550)

ST DESIDERATUS (Désiré) was one of a holy trio, his two brothers, Desiderius and Deodatus, being locally venerated as saints, although there is no mention of any one of the three in the Roman Martyrology. They were the sons, we are told, of a worthy couple of Soissons, who not only devoted their time and possessions to relieving the poor, but practically turned their house into a hospital. Desideratus attached himself to the court of King Clotaire, to whom he became a sort of secretary of state, and over whom he exercised a most salutary influence. In the midst of the splendours by which he was surrounded he lived a mortified life, and he used the great powers with which he was entrusted to stamp out heresy and to punish simony. On various occasions he expressed a desire to retire into a monastery, but the proposal was always vetoed by the king, who declared that he ought rather to consult the public weal than to indulge his own private inclinations. Upon the death of St Arcadius in 541, Desideratus was chosen bishop of Bourges, and during the nine years of his episcopate he acquired a great reputation as a peacemaker and wonder-worker. The holy bishop took part in various synods—notably the fifth Council of Orleans and the second of Auvergne, both of which dealt with the errors of Nestorius and Eutyches, besides providing for the restoration of ecclesiastical discipline. In his old age St Desideratus obtained as vicar a young priest named Flavian, whose untimely death hastened his own end. He died on May 8, probably in the year 550.

The narrative printed in the *Acta Sanctorum*, May, vol. ii, is of late date and unreliable ; but there can be no question of the historical existence and pious activity of St Desideratus. See Duchesne, *Fastes Épiscopaux*, vol. ii, p. 28.

ST BONIFACE IV, POPE   (A.D. 615)

NOT very much is known to us about the saintly pope who ruled the Church for six years under the title of Boniface IV. He was the son of a physician and a native of the " city " of Valeria in the Abruzzi. He is supposed to have been a pupil of St Gregory the Great in Rome, and the Benedictines accordingly claim him as a member of their order. His reign was signalized by the conversion of the Pantheon—the temple erected by Marcus Agrippa in honour of all the Roman deities—into a Christian church, dedicated in honour of our Lady and All Martyrs. The building was bestowed by the Emperor Phocas upon the Roman pontiff, who consecrated it on May 13, 609, as recorded in the Roman Martyrology (the church is now often called Santa Maria Rotonda, from its shape). At a synod of Italian bishops, summoned primarily for the restoration of discipline, St Boniface conferred with St Mellitus, bishop of London, then on a visit to Rome, about the affairs of the English church. Boniface IV was the recipient of a famous and much-discussed letter from St Columban, which combines remarkable expressions of devotion and loyalty to the Holy See with unwarrantable insinuations of laxity in the matter of doctrine. This holy pope was buried in the portico of St Peter's, but his remains were afterwards transferred to the interior of the basilica.

In the *Acta Sanctorum* Boniface is noticed on May 25 (May, vol. vi), but a more up-to-date account of his pontificate will be found in Mann, *The Lives of the Popes*, vol. i, pp. 268–279. See also Duchesne, *Liber Pontificalis*, vol. i, pp. 317–318 ; and Laux, *Der hl. Kolumban* (1919), or in an earlier English form, *The Life and Writings of St Columban* (1914).

ST BENEDICT II, POPE   (A.D. 685)

POPE St Benedict II was brought up from infancy in the service of the Church and became at an early age proficient in the Holy Scriptures, as also in ecclesiastical chant, for which he was an enthusiast. A Roman by birth, he took part in the government of the Church under Popes St Agatho and St Leo II. After the death of the latter in 683, he was elected to the chair of St Peter, his virtues, his liberality and his intellectual abilities marking him out as specially suited to fill that sacred office. In accordance with ancient custom, the popes were at that time still chosen by the clergy and people of Rome, the consent of the Christian emperor being also required.   The embassies between Rome and Constantinople necessary before this sanction could be obtained frequently entailed not only inconvenience, but also delay, and nearly a year elapsed between the death of Pope Leo and the consecration of Benedict II.   One of the successful efforts of the new pontiff was to induce the Emperor Constantine IV to issue a decree enacting that, for the future, the suffrages of the clergy and people of Rome should suffice for the election of the pope, the necessity for imperial confirmation being abolished or else its delegation to the exarch in Italy being allowed.   But there were further examples of imperial ratification.

So great was the emperor's regard for St Benedict that he sent him locks of the hair of his two sons, Justinian and Heraclius—thus signifying to him, according to the symbolism of the time, that they were the Holy Father's spiritual sons.   St Benedict strove to win back to the true faith Macarius, Patriarch of Antioch, who had been deposed for heresy, and in his short pontificate (eleven months) he found time to restore several of the Roman churches.   He was also interested in the English church, upholding the cause of St Wilfrid of York.   St Benedict II died on May 8, 685, and was buried in St Peter's.

The *Acta Sanctorum* treat Pope St Benedict II under May 7 (vol. ii).   The *Liber Pontificalis* (Duchesne, vol. i, pp. 363–365) is our principal authority ; but see also Muratori, *Annales*, ad. ann. 684, and Hefele-Leclercq, *Histoire des Conciles*, vol. iii, pp. 549 *seq.*   Mgr Mann in his *Lives of the Popes*, vol. i, part 2, pp. 54–63, has gathered all the available information.

SS. WIRO AND PLECHELM, BISHOPS, AND ST OTGER (EIGHTH CENTURY)

WITH respect to the birthplace of St Wiro we can only say that it was somewhere in the British Isles, for whereas Alcuin asserts that he was a Northumbrian, certain other writers declare that he was a Scotsman and others that he was a native of County Clare in Ireland.   We read that from his earliest youth he modelled himself upon St Patrick, St Cuthbert and St Columban.   After his ordination he went with another priest, St Plechelm (probably also a Northumbrian) and a deacon, St Otger, to Rome, where he and St Plechelm are said to have been consecrated to be regionary bishops.   When they had laboured for some time in their native land, the three friends—perhaps at the suggestion of St Willibrord—passed over to the Netherlands, where they spent part of their time evangelizing the lower valley of the Meuse, and the rest in retirement and prayer.   Pepin of Herstal gave them St Peter's Hill, afterwards called the Odilienberg, at a league's distance from Roermond, and there they built several cells and a church.   Pepin is said to have held Wiro in such great veneration that he appointed him his director and made it a rule to repair to him barefoot every Lent, and at other times, to receive penance from him or from St Plechelm.

A medieval biography of St Wiro is printed in the *Acta Sanctorum*, May, vol. ii, and of Plechelm in July, vol. iv, but they are late and unreliable.   See rather Van der Essen, *Étude critique et littéraire sur les vitae des saints mérovingiens*, pp. 105–109 ; I. Snieders, " L'Influence de l'hagiographie irlandaise ", in the *Revue d'Histoire Ecclésiastique*, vol. xxiv (1928), pp. 849–850 ; and W. Levison, *England and the Continent* . . . (1946), pp. 82–83.

ST PETER, ARCHBISHOP OF TARENTAISE (A.D. 1175)

ST PETER of Tarentaise, one of the glories of the Cistercian Order, was born near Vienne in the French province of the Dauphiné.   He early displayed a remarkable memory, coupled with a great inclination for religious studies, and at the age of twenty he entered the abbey of Bonnevaux.   With great zeal he embraced the austerities of the rule, edifying all who came into contact with him by his charity, his humility and his modesty.   After a time, his father and the other two sons followed Peter to Bonnevaux, whilst his mother, with the only daughter, entered a neighbouring Cistercian nunnery.   Besides these members of his own humble family, men of high rank were led by the example of Peter to become monks at Bonnevaux.   He was not quite thirty when he was chosen superior of a new house built at Tamié, in the desert mountains of Tarentaise.   It overlooked the pass which was then the chief route from Geneva to Savoy, and the monks were able to be of great use to travellers.   There, with the help of Amadeus III, Count of Savoy, who held him in high esteem, he founded a hospice for the sick and for strangers, in which he was wont to wait upon his guests with his own hands.

In 1142 came his election to the archbishopric of Tarentaise, and Peter was compelled by St Bernard and the general chapter of his order, though much against the grain, to accept the office.   He found the diocese in a deplorable state, due mainly to the mismanagement of his predecessor, an unworthy man who had eventually to be deposed.   Parish churches were in the hands of laymen, the poor were neglected, and the clergy, who ought to have stemmed the general tide of iniquity, too often promoted irregularity by their evil example.   In place of the cathedral clergy whom he found lax and careless, St Peter substituted canons regular of St Augustine, and he soon made his chapter a model of good order.   He undertook the constant visitation of his diocese ; recovered property which had been alienated ; appointed good priests to various parishes ; made excellent founda- tions for the education of the young and the relief of the poor ; and everywhere pro- vided for the due celebration of the services of the Church.   The author of his life, who was his constant companion at this period, testifies to numerous miracles which he wrought, mainly in curing the sick and multiplying provisions in time of famine.

Apprehension at finding himself honoured as a wonder-worker, and the natural longing of a monk for solitude, turned his mind back to the cloister and in 1155, after he had administered the diocese for thirteen years, Peter suddenly disappeared, leaving no trace behind.   Actually he had made his way to a remote Cistercian abbey in Switzerland, where, being yet unknown, he was accepted as a lay-brother. Great was the dismay throughout the diocese of Tarentaise when the departure of the archbishop became known, and diligent was the search made for him throughout the religious houses of the neighbouring provinces.   Not until a year later was he discovered.   His identity having been revealed to his new superiors, Peter was obliged to leave and to return to his see, where he was greeted with great joy.   He took up his duties more zealously than ever.   The poor were ever his first considera- tion : twice in bitterly cold weather he gave away his own habit at the risk of his life.   He rebuilt the hospice of the Little St Bernard and founded other similar refuges for travellers in the Alps.   He also inaugurated a practice, kept up until the French Revolution—and even a little after—of making a free distribution of bread and soup during the months preceding the harvest, when food was scarce in many parts of his hilly diocese.   The dole came to be called " May bread ".   All his life he continued to dress and to live like a Cistercian, replacing manual labour by the spiritual functions of his office.

Essentially a man of peace, St Peter had a singular gift for allaying seemingly implacable enmities and on several occasions averted bloodshed by reconciling contending parties. His chief political efforts, however, were directed to supporting the cause of the true pope, Alexander III, against the pretensions of the antipope, Victor, who had behind him the redoubtable Emperor Frederick Barbarossa. At one time, indeed, it seemed as though the archbishop of Tarentaise was the only subject of the empire who dared openly to oppose the pretender, but it soon became apparent that he carried with him the whole of the great Cistercian Order. To establish the claims of the true pontiff, St Peter preached in Alsace, Lorraine, Burgundy and many parts of Italy, the effect of his words being enhanced by miracles of healing. He also spoke out fearlessly in various councils and even in the presence of the emperor himself, who was so far impressed by his sanctity and courage as to permit in him a freedom of speech he would endure from no one else.

It was not granted to the saint to die amongst his mountain flock. His reputation as a peacemaker led Alexander III to send him in 1174 to try to effect a reconciliation between King Louis VII of France and Henry II of England. St Peter, though he was old, set out at once, preaching everywhere on his way. As he approached Chaumont in the Vexin, where the French court was being held, he was met by King Louis and by Prince Henry, the rebellious heir to the English throne. The latter, alighting from his horse to receive the archbishop's blessing, asked for the saint's old cloak, which he reverently kissed. Both at Chaumont and at Gisors where he interviewed the English king, St Peter was treated with utmost honour, but the reconciliation for which he laboured did not take place until after his death. As he was returning to his diocese he was taken ill on the road near Besançon, and died as he was being carried into the abbey of Bellevaux. This St Peter was canonized in 1191.

Our most copious and trustworthy source of information is the life written by the Cistercian, Geoffrey of Auxerre, Abbot of Hautecombe, in response to the request of Pope Lucius III. It is printed in the *Acta Sanctorum*, and we know that it was completed before 1185, that is, within ten years of the death of the saint. But there are besides this many references to St Peter in the correspondence, chronicles and hagiographical literature of the time. Even a man like Walter Map, who was prone to write of the Cistercians with the utmost bitterness, speaks with reverence of St Peter of Tarentaise. See *The Life of St Hugh of Lincoln* (Quarterly Series), pp. 625–626, and in the same work an account of the relations between St Hugh, the Carthusian, and his Cistercian brother bishop (pp. 60–64, etc.). Consult further Le Couteulx, *Annales Ordinis Cartusiensis*, vol. ii *passim* ; G. Müller, *Leben des hl. Petrus von Tarentaise* (1892) ; and the biographies in French by Dom M. A. Dimier (1935) and H. Brultey (1945).

9 : ST GREGORY NAZIANZEN, BISHOP OF CONSTANTINOPLE, DOCTOR OF THE CHURCH (A.D. 390)

IN view of his resolute defence of the truths promulgated by the Council of Nicaea, St Gregory Nazianzen has been declared a doctor of the Church and has also been surnamed " the Theologian "—a title which he shares with the Apostle St John. Born about the year 329 at Arianzus in Cappadocia, he was the son of St Nonna and of St Gregory the Elder, a landowner and magistrate who, being converted to Christianity by his wife, had been raised to the priesthood and for forty-five years was bishop of Nazianzus. The younger Gregory and his brother, St Caesarius, received the best education available. Having studied together for a time at Caesarea in Cappadocia, where they made the acquaintance of St Basil, Gregory, who was intended for the law, went to Caesarea in Palestine, which had a famous rhetorical school, and then went on to join his brother at Alexandria.　It was usual for scholars to pass from one great educational centre to another, and Gregory, after a short stay in Egypt, decided to complete his training in Athens.　As the vessel which bore him rolled tempest-tossed for days, the young man realized with terror the danger he ran of losing not only his body, but also his soul, being still unbaptized.　But he probably shared the views of many pious men of that period with regard to the difficulty of obtaining forgiveness for post-baptismal sin, for he does not appear to have been baptized until many years later.　During the greater part of the ten years Gregory spent in Athens he enjoyed the companionship of St Basil, who became his intimate friend.　Another but less congenial fellow student was the future Emperor Julian, whose affectations and extravagances even then disgusted the serious young Cappadocians.　Gregory was thirty when he left Athens, having learnt all that its masters could teach him.　It is not clear with what plans he returned to Nazianzus ; if he had intended to practise law or to teach rhetoric, he soon changed his mind.　He had always been earnestly devout, but about this time he was led to adopt a much more austere mode of life —apparently as the result of a great religious experience, possibly his baptism. Consequently when Basil, who was living the life of a solitary in Pontus, on the river Iris, invited him to join him, Gregory responded eagerly to the call.　In a wildly beautiful spot which Basil has described in graphic language, the two friends spent a couple of fruitful years in prayer and study, compiling a collection of extracts from Origen and adumbrating that life which was to form the basis of all Christian monastic life in the East, and through St Benedict was to influence the West.

From this peaceful existence Gregory was called home to assist his father—then over eighty years old—in the management of his diocese and estate.　Not content, however, with the help his son could give him as a layman, the aged bishop, with the connivance of certain members of his flock, ordained him priest more or less by force.　Taken by surprise, and terrified at finding himself invested with a dignity from which he had always shrunk in the consciousness of his own unworthiness, he acted on the impulse of the moment and fled to his friend Basil.　Ten weeks later, however, he returned to shoulder his responsibilities in obedience to what he realized was a call from on high.　The apology he wrote for his flight is a treatise on the priesthood which has been drawn upon by countless writers on the same subject from St John Chrysostom to St Gregory the Great down to our own day.　An incident was soon to show how much his assistance was needed.　The old prelate, like many others, had been led to give his assent to the decisions of the Council of Rimini in the hope of conciliating the semi-Arians.　This gave great offence to many of the most zealous Catholics—especially the monks—and it was entirely due to Gregory's tact that a schism was averted.　His oration on the occasion of the reconciliation is still extant, as are also two funeral discourses he delivered at that period of his life, the one, in 369, on his brother Caesarius, who had been the imperial physician at Constantinople, and the other on his sister, St Gorgonia.

In the year 370 St Basil was elected metropolitan of Caesarea.　At that period the Emperor Valens and the procurator Modestus were doing their utmost to introduce Arianism into Cappadocia and were finding Basil the chief obstacle in their way.　To diminish his influence, Cappadocia was divided into two, Tyana being made the capital of a new province.　Anthimus, bishop of Tyana, promptly claimed archiepiscopal jurisdiction over the newly-established province, whilst St

Basil maintained that the civil division did not affect his own authority as metropolitan.   It seems to have been solely to consolidate his position by settling a friend on disputed territory that he nominated Gregory to a new bishopric which he established at Sasima, a miserable unhealthy town on the borderland between the two provinces.   Gregory did, indeed, very reluctantly submit to consecration, but he never went to Sasima, the governor of which was an open adversary.   In reply to the reproaches of St Basil, who accused him of slackness, he declared that he was not disposed to fight for a church.   Gregory was deeply hurt at the treatment he had received, and although he became reconciled to St Basil, the friendship was never again the same.   He actually remained at Nazianzus, acting as coadjutor until his father's death the following year.   He had long desired to live a solitary life, but was induced to carry on the government of Nazianzus until a new bishop was appointed.   His health, however, broke down in 375 and he withdrew to Seleucia, the capital of Isauria, where he spent five years.

The death of the persecuting Emperor Valens brought peace once more to the Church, and it was decided to send learned and zealous men to those cities and provinces where the faith had suffered the greatest set-back.   It was realized that the church of Constantinople was of all others the most desolate, having been dominated by Arian teachers for between thirty and forty years, and being without a church in which to assemble the few orthodox who remained in it.   At the suggestion of several bishops, an invitation was sent to St Gregory to come and rebuild the faith.   To the sensitive peace-loving recluse the prospect of being plunged into that whirlpool of intrigue, corruption and violence must, indeed, have seemed appalling, and at first he declined to leave his solitude.   Eventually, however, he was induced to consent, but his trials were to begin with his entrance into Constantinople, for as he made his appearance, poorly clad, bald, and prematurely bent, he was ill received by a populace accustomed to dignity and splendour At first he lodged with relations in a house which he soon converted into a church. and to which he gave the name of Anastasia—the place where the faith would rise again.   In this small building he preached and taught his little flock, and it was here that he delivered the celebrated Sermons on the Trinity which won for him the title of Theologian—meaning in effect one who apprehends aright the divinity of our Lord Jesus Christ.   Gradually his audience increased and the fame of his eloquence spread.   On the other hand, the Arians and Apollinarists pursued him unrelentingly with slanders, insults and even personal violence.   They broke into his church ; they pelted him in the streets and dragged him before the magistrates as a brawler.   He comforted himself by reflecting that if his adversaries were the stronger party, he had the better cause : though they had the churches, God was with him ; if they had the populace on their side, the angels were on his. Moreover, he won the esteem of some of the greatest men of the age : St Evagrius of Pontus came to serve him as archdeacon, and St Jerome, arriving in Constantinople from the deserts of Syria, was glad to sit at his feet and learn of him.

Yet trials of all sorts continued to beset the Catholic champion, from his own party as well as from heretics.   A certain Maximus, an adventurer in whom he had believed and whom he had publicly praised, actually tried to supersede him by obtaining consecration from some passing bishops and causing himself to be proclaimed while St Gregory was ill.   The would-be usurper was promptly driven out, but St Gregory himself was greatly chagrined and mortified, especially as Maximus had won the ear of some whom Gregory had regarded as his friends.

Early in the year 380 the Emperor Theodosius was baptized by the orthodox bishop of Thessalonica and shortly afterwards he promulgated an edict to his Byzantine subjects, bidding them observe the Catholic faith as professed by the pope of Rome and the archbishop of Alexandria. This he followed up when he came to Constantinople by giving the Arian bishop the option of subscribing to the Nicene faith or leaving the city. The prelate chose the latter course, and Theodosius determined to instal Gregory in his place. Hitherto he had been a bishop in Constantinople, but not the bishop of Constantinople. The nomination having been confirmed synodically, St Gregory was solemnly installed in the cathedral of the Holy Wisdom amid the acclamations of the people. He did not, however, retain the seat for many months. His old enemies rose against him, and fresh hostility was aroused by his decision in the matter of the vacant see of Antioch. The validity of his election was contested, and attempts were actually made upon his life. Always a lover of peace, and fearing lest the unrest should lead to bloodshed, Gregory determined to lay down his office. " If my tenure of the see of Constantinople is leading to disturbance ", he cried out in the assembly, " I am willing, like Jonas, to be thrown into the waves to still the tempest, although I did not raise it. If all followed my example, the Church would enjoy tranquillity. This dignity I never desired ; I assumed the charge much against my will. If you think fit, I am most ready to depart." Having obtained the emperor's reluctant consent, he then prepared to leave the city, after delivering a dignified and touching farewell to the citizens. His work there was done : he had rekindled the torch of the true faith in Constantinople when it was well-nigh extinguished and had kept it burning at the Church's darkest hour. It was characteristic of his magnanimity that he always maintained cordial relations with his successor Nectarius, a man who, in every respect but birth, was his inferior.

For some time after leaving Constantinople, Gregory divided his time between his parental estate upon which he was born and the city of Nazianzus, which was still without a bishop ; but after the year 383, when through his efforts his cousin Eulalius was appointed to fill the see, he retired completely into private life, leading a secluded existence and taking much delight in his garden, with its fountain and shaded grove. Yet he practised at the same time severe mortifications, never wearing shoes or seeing a fire. Towards the end of his life he wrote a number of religious poems, partly for his own pleasure, partly for the edification of others. They have considerable biographical and literary interest, because in them he recounts his life and sufferings, and they are written in graceful verses which occasionally rise to sublimity. Upon them, upon his orations and upon his excellent letters, his reputation as a writer has rested through the centuries. He died in his retreat in the year 390, and his remains, which were first translated from Nazianzus to Constantinople, now repose at St Peter's in Rome.

St Gregory greatly loved to dwell upon the condescension of God to men. " Admire the exceeding goodness of God ", he writes in one of his letters. " He vouchsafes to accept our desires as though they were a thing of great value. He burns with an ardent longing that we should desire and love Him, and He receives the petitions we send up for His benefits as though they were a benefit to Himself and a favour we did Him. He gives with a greater joy than the joy with which we receive. Only let us not be too apathetic in our petitions, or set too narrow bounds to our requests : nor let us ask for frivolous things which it would be unworthy of God's greatness to propose that He should grant us."

St Gregory's own letters and writings (notably the long poem, *De Vita Sua*, of nearly two thousand verses) are the principal source of information regarding his life. Unfortunately the great Benedictine edition of his works suffered many setbacks at the time when it was being prepared for the press. Successive editors died, and the first volume, containing the sermons, only appeared in 1778. Hence before the second volume was ready the French Revolution had occurred, and it did not see the light until 1840. The Academy of Cracow has undertaken a new critical edition. Many of the earlier manuscripts of St Gregory Nazianzen, some of which belong to the ninth century, are embellished with miniatures. On these the article of Dom Leclercq, which reproduces many of the drawings, may conveniently be consulted ; see DAC., vol. vi, cc. 1667–1710. For English readers Cardinal Newman's essay in his *Historical Sketches*, vol. iii, pp. 50–94, and the article of H. W. Watkins in DCB., vol. ii, pp. 741–761, will always be of value. See also C. Ullmann, *Gregory of Nazianzus* (1851) ; A. Benoit, *S. Grégoire de Nazianze* (1885), and other French biographies by M. Guignet (1911) and P. Gallay (1943) ; E. Fleury, *Hellénisme et christianisme : S. Grégoire et son temps* (1930) ; and L. Duchesne, *History of the Early Church* (vol. ii, 1912). A fuller bibliography is provided by Bardenhewer both in his *Patrologie* and in his *Geschichte der altkirchlichen Literatur*, vol. iii (2nd ed.), pp. 162–188 and 671.

ST BEATUS   (A.D. 112 ?)

St BEATENBERG, above the lake of Thun, derives its name from St Beatus, a hermit who, at an early date, is said to have occupied a cave on its slope and died there— supposedly about the year 112. A whole legendary history afterwards grew up about him. It was believed that he had been baptized in England by the Apostle St Barnabas, and that he had been sent to evangelize Switzerland by St Peter, who ordained him priest in Rome. His cave, where he was reputed to have slain a dragon, became a favourite place of pilgrimage, until it was closed by the Zwinglians. His *cultus* was then transferred to Lungern in Oberwalden, and St Peter Canisius did much to revive and propagate it. Modern research, however, has revealed that the tradition of St Beatus as the apostle of Switzerland is a late one, extending back no farther than the middle of the eleventh century— if so far.

The Swiss St Beatus is often confused with a namesake, honoured on the same day, *viz.* St Beatus of Vendôme, who preached the gospel first on the shores of the Garonne, then at Vendôme and Nantes, and who is stated to have died at Chevresson, near Laon, about the close of the third century. This St Beatus seems to have a better claim to be regarded as historical, for his name undoubtedly was entered on this day in the *Hieronymianum*, and his legend has seemingly supplied much that is attributed to the Swiss Beatus.

Both these legends are dealt with in the *Acta Sanctorum*, May, vol. ii. The *cultus* of the Swiss St Beatus is apparently still active, and he is regarded as a sort of national patron. See, on the relations between these two supposed hermit missionaries, the *Analecta Bollandiana*, vol. xxvi (1907), pp. 423–453 ; O. Scheiwiller in the *Zeitschrift f. Schweizer. Kirchengeschichte*, vol. v (1911), pp. 21–52 ; and on the folklore aspects, Bächtold-Stäubli, *Handwörterbuch des deutschen Aberglaubens*, vol. i, pp. 964–966.

ST PACHOMIUS, ABBOT   (A.D. 348)

ALTHOUGH St Antony is often reckoned the founder of Christian monasticism, that title belongs more properly to St Pachomius, called " the Elder ", for he was the first—not, indeed, to gather round him communities of Christian ascetics on a large scale—but to organize them and draw up in writing a rule for their common use. He was born of heathen parents in the Upper Thebaïd about the year 292, and when he was twenty was conscripted for the emperor's army.   As he and other recruits were being conveyed down the Nile under wretched conditions, they received great kindness from the Christians of Latopolis (Esneh), who were moved with compassion for them.   This disinterested charity Pachomius never forgot ; and as soon as the army was disbanded, he made his way back home to Khenoboskion (Kasr as-Syad), where there was a Christian church, and enrolled himself among the catechumens.   After his baptism his one preoccupation was how best to correspond with the grace he had received.   Having heard that an old hermit called Palaemon was serving God with great perfection in the desert, he sought him out and begged him to receive him as a disciple.   The old man set before him the hardships of the life, but Pachomius was not to be deterred.   Having promised obedience, he received the habit.   The life they led together was one of extreme austerity : their diet was bread and salt ; they drank no wine and used no oil ; they always watched half the night and frequently passed the whole of it without sleep.   Sometimes they would repeat the entire psalter together ; at other times they would occupy themselves in manual labour accompanied by interior prayer.

One day when Pachomius was visiting, as he occasionally did, a vast uninhabited desert on the banks of the Nile called Tabennisi, he is said to have heard a voice bidding him begin a monastery there, and about the same time he had a vision of an angel who gave him certain instructions regarding the religious life.*   These revelations he imparted to Palaemon, who accompanied him to Tabennisi about the year 318, helped him to construct a cell and remained with him for some time before returning to his solitude.

The first disciple to receive the habit at Tabennisi from St Pachomius was his own eldest brother John : others followed, and within a comparatively short time the number of his monks exceeded one hundred.   He led them to an eminent degree of perfection, mainly through his own fervent spirit and example.   He passed fifteen years without ever lying down, taking his short rest sitting on a stone, and from the moment of his conversion he never ate a full meal.   Yet his rule for others was graduated according to their capacity, for he refused no applicant on the score of age or weakliness.   He established six other monasteries in the Thebaïd, and from the year 336 resided often at Pabau, near Thebes, which became a larger and even more famous community than Tabennisi.   He built for the benefit of the poor shepherds a church in which for some time he acted as lector, but he could never be induced to offer himself for the priesthood, or to present any of his monks for ordination, although he was always prepared to give the habit to men who were already priests.   He zealously opposed the Arians, and in 333 had a visit from St Athanasius.   For the benefit of his sister whom, however, he never would see, he built a nunnery on the opposite side of the Nile.   Cited to appear before a council of bishops at Latopolis to answer certain accusations, he displayed such humility in his replies to his calumniators that all present marvelled.   Humility and patience were indeed virtues which he practised in a heroic degree ; and miracles of healing took place at his intercession.

* Some rationalist critics, laying stress upon the fact that the saint is said before his baptism to have resided in a little temple of Serapis, have sought to draw the inference that the whole monastic idea was an importation from paganism ; but, as Ladeuze and others have pointed out, Pachomius lived there after his thoughts had been turned to Christianity. The building referred to was probably only an abandoned shrine.

Pachomius died on May 15, 348, of an epidemic disease which had already carried off many of his brethren. He had lived to see three thousand monks in the nine monasteries under his charge. Cassian tells us that the larger his communities were, the more perfect was the observance of discipline, all obeying the superior more readily than any single person could be found to do elsewhere. To help in maintaining this discipline St Pachomius had a system of registering each monk in one of 24 lettered categories: " ι ", for example, indicated a simple, innocent type, " χ ", a difficult and stubborn character. The monks lived together three in a cell, grouped according to trades, and assembled together for the two night offices and for Mass on Saturdays and Sundays. Much emphasis was laid on Bible-reading and learning passages by heart; in general the monks were drawn from rough and rude material.

The story of the angel who appeared to Pachomius, bidding him gather young monks about him at Tabennisi, has not everywhere found acceptance; and still more difficulty has been raised over the brass tablet which the angel is supposed to have brought him and which is said to have been inscribed with a summary of the rule he was to follow. None the less, such an account of its contents as we read in the *Lausiac History* of Palladius cannot have been a mere burlesque of the practices observed by the monks. The source of the rule may be legendary and it may be difficult to determine what its authentic provisions actually were. But there is a fair measure of resemblance among the texts handed down in Greek or in Ethiopic when compared with the amplified Sahidic original, which St Jerome translated by means of an interpreter and which we only know through this translation. There is probably some foundation for that mitigation of austerity according to the capacity of the subject which Palladius makes so prominent. The angel-borne tablet is said to have enjoined: " Thou shalt allow each man to eat and drink according to his strength; and proportionately to the strength of the eaters appoint to them their labours. And prevent no man either from fasting or eating. However, assign the tasks that need strength to those who are stronger and eat, and to the weaker and more ascetic such as the weak can manage." So, too, we have probably a glimpse of the practice actually followed, when Palladius quotes further: " Let them sleep not lying down full length, but let them make sloping chairs easily constructed and put their legs on them and thus sleep in a sitting posture ". Or again : " As they eat, let them cover their heads with their hoods, lest one brother see another chewing. A monk is not allowed to talk at meals, nor let his eye wander beyond his plate or the table." What is certain is that St Benedict's Rule, which has shaped nearly all surviving monasticism in the West, borrowed a good deal from Pachomius. Abbot Cuthbert Butler, in his edition of the *Regula S. Benedicti*, makes thirty-two references to St Jerome's *Pachomiana*, and several phrases in the rule can be traced to Pachomian sources, while the spirit of the so-called Angelic Rule is even more noticeable therein.

Of all the early saints of the East it is St Pachomius who seems of recent years to have attracted most attention. New discoveries have been made especially of Coptic (*i.e.* Sahidic) texts, though for the most part these unfortunately are only fragmentary. Other manuscripts previously neglected have now been collated in many different redactions and languages. The older generation of Bollandists (in the *Acta Sanctorum*, May, vol. iii) did a great deal, but in the seventeenth century no exhaustive research of oriental sources was possible. Their modern representatives, however, have published a thoroughly satisfactory edition of *St Pachomii Vitae Graecae* (1932), edited by Fr F. Halkin. With this great advance may be associated the not less important study of L. T. Lefort, *S. Pachomii Vitae Sahidice Scriptae* (published in two parts in the *Corpus Scriptorum Christianorum Orientalium*, 1933 and 1934), in the same series his edition of a Bohairic life of Pachomius (1925), and his *Vies coptes de*

S. Pacôme (1943) : these are discussed in *Analecta Bollandiana*, vol. lii (1934), pp. 286–320, and vol. lxiv (1946), pp. 258–277. A further piece of research is that of A. Boon, *Pachomiana latina* (1932), an essay on St Jerome's translation of the Rule with an appendix on the Greek and Coptic versions ; see also B. Albers, *S. Pachomii . . . Regulae Monasticae* (1923). Amongst a multitude of somewhat older studies the essay of F. Ladeuze, *Le Cénobitisme Pakhômien*, deserves special mention, and H. Leclercq in his long article " Monachisme " in DAC., vol. xi (1933), especially in cc. 1807–1831, has brought together a number of valuable bibliographical references. There are also biographies, with slight variations, in Syriac and Arabic. M. Amélineau, who was among the first to take account of the Coptic texts, published in 1887 an *Étude historique sur S. Pachôme*. After the sixteenth-centenary celebrations in Egypt in 1948 a volume of lectures, *Pachomiana*, by scholars of several nationalities and ecclesiastical obediences was published. For the Angelic Rule and Western monachism, see J. McCann's *St Benedict* (1938), pp. 152 *ss.* and *passim*. In spite, however, of the research bestowed upon the subject, the life and work of St Pachomius still remain very much of a problem, as such an authority as Fr Paul Peeters is the first to confess.

ST GERONTIUS, Bishop of Cervia   (A.D. 501)

ALL that is known of St Gerontius is that he was bishop of Cervia (Ficocle) in the archdiocese of Ravenna, and that he was murdered by " ungodly men "—presumably bandits—at Cagli, on the Flaminian Way, near Ancona, as he was returning from a synod in Rome, presided over by Pope St Symmachus. A Benedictine abbey, dedicated in his honour, was afterwards erected on the spot where he fell, and the Church honours him as a martyr.

What the Bollandists are able to tell us regarding St Gerontius has much more to do with his cult than with his personal history. See the *Acta Sanctorum*, May, vol. ii, and Ughelli, *Italia Sacra*, vol. ii, c. 486. The saint is locally held in great honour.

BD NICHOLAS ALBERGATI, Bishop of Bologna and Cardinal   (A.D. 1443)

EVEN before 1744, when his cult was formally approved, Bd Nicholas Albergati was held in great veneration by the Carthusians and by the Augustinian friars. A Bolognese of good family, he had begun to study for the law, but decided at the age of twenty to enter the Carthusian Order. He rose to be superior of several houses, and in 1417 the clergy and citizens of Bologna chose him for their bishop—a dignity which only the express command of his superiors could induce him to accept. He always retained his monastic austerity, lived simply in a small house and sought out the poor in their homes. Pope Martin V and his successors in the chair of St Peter charged him with important diplomatic missions which he accomplished with conspicuous success. In 1426 he was raised to the dignity of a cardinal. Thomas Parentucelli of Sarzana, whom he had educated, chose the name of Nicholas when he was elected pope, out of gratitude and veneration for his generous patron. So great was the cardinal's reputation as a mediator that he was sent as papal legate to foreign courts as well as to Italian states that were at variance, and was called " the Angel of Peace ". In the capacity of legate he took part in the Council of Bâle, and he also opened the Council of Ferrara where, and at Florence, he had much to do with the reconciliation of the Greeks. Pope Eugenius IV held him in the highest esteem ; he consulted him in almost all things, made him chief penitentiary, and came to see him frequently when he was ill.

Bd Nicholas died in Siena, when visiting a house belonging to the Augustinians, whose protector he was. Although it was an unprecedented thing for a pope to attend the obsequies of a cardinal, Eugenius IV took part in the funeral services at

Bologna, being present also at his actual burial.   Cardinal Albergati was a great patron of learning and the author of several literary works.

A full biography as well as a panegyric will be found in the *Acta Sanctorum*, May, vol. ii, and another panegyric in the *Analecta Bollandiana*, vol. vii (1888), pp. 381–386.   A long account is also given in Le Couteulx, *Annales Ordinis Cartusiensis*, vol. vii.   See further Pastor, *History of the Popes*, vol. ii.

10 : ST ANTONINUS, ARCHBISHOP OF FLORENCE   (A.D. 1459)

OF all the prelates who through many centuries have ruled the diocese of Florence, no one has gained so great and lasting a hold upon the loving veneration of the Florentines as St Antoninus.   His father, a citizen of good family, who was notary to the republic, was called Nicholas Pierozzi, and he himself received in baptism the name of Antony.   The diminutive Antonino, which clung to him all his life, was given him in childhood because of his small stature and gentle disposition.   A serious boy, much addicted to prayer, he loved to listen to the sermons of Bd John Dominici, then prior of Santa Maria Novella, and when he was fifteen he asked the friar to admit him to the Dominican Order. The saintly John, judging him too weakly for the life, tried to put him off by bidding him study for a time and learn the *Decretum Gratiani ;* but when, within a year, the lad returned, having committed the whole of the treatise to memory, he was received without further hesitation.   He was the first postulant to take the habit in the new priory at Fiesole, which Bd John Dominici had built.   For the novitiate Antonino was sent to Cortona, where he had as novice master Bd Laurence of Ripafratta and as companions Bd Peter Capucci and the future great artist Fra Angelico da Fiesole. Antoninus early gave evidence of exceptional gifts as a scholar and as a leader.   He was chosen when very young to govern the great convent of the Minerva in Rome ; and afterwards he was successively prior at Naples, Gaeta, Cortona, Siena, Fiesole and Florence.   As superior of the reformed Tuscan and Neapolitan congregations, and also as prior provincial of the whole Roman province, he zealously enforced the measures initiated by Bd John Dominici with a view to restoring the primitive rule.   At Florence in 1436 he founded the famous convent of San Marco in buildings taken over from the Silvestrines, but practically rebuilt by him after designs by Michelozzi and decorated with the frescoes of Fra Angelico.

The adjacent late thirteenth-century church was rebuilt with great magnificence by Cosimo de' Medici to serve the new Dominican house.   In addition to his official duties, St Antoninus preached often and wrote works which made him famous among his contemporaries.   He was consulted from Rome and from all quarters, especially in intricate cases of canon law.   Pope Eugenius IV summoned him to attend the general Council of Florence, and he assisted at all its sessions. He was occupied with reforming houses in the province of Naples when he learnt to his dismay that the pope had nominated him to be archbishop of Florence.   In vain did he plead incapacity, ill-health and advancing years ; Eugenius was inflexible and left him no freedom of choice.   He was consecrated in March 1446 amid the rejoicings of the citizens.

In his new capacity St Antoninus continued to practise all the observances of his rule, as far as his duties would permit.   The most rigid simplicity reigned where he resided : his household consisted of six persons only ; he had no plate or horses ; even the one mule which served the needs of the whole establishment was often sold to assist the poor, but as often bought back by some well-to-do citizen and restored to its charitable owner.   He gave audience daily to all comers, whilst declaring himself especially the protector of the poor, at whose disposal he kept his purse and granaries.   When these were exhausted he gave away his furniture and his clothes.   To assist the needy who were ashamed to beg, he had established a sort of " S.V.P.", under the patronage of St Martin, which has been the means of supporting thousands of families in reduced circumstances.

Although naturally gentle, the saint was firm and courageous when circumstances demanded it.   He put down gambling in his diocese, was the determined foe of both usury and magic, and reformed abuses of all kinds.   In addition to preaching nearly every Sunday and festival, he visited his whole diocese once a year, always on foot.   His reputation for wisdom and integrity was such that he was unceasingly consulted by those in authority, laymen as well as ecclesiastics ; and his decisions were so judicious that they won for him the title of " the Counsellor ". When Pope Eugenius IV was dying he summoned Antoninus to Rome, received from him the last sacraments and died in his arms.   Nicholas V sought his advice on matters of church and state, forbade any appeal to be made to Rome from the archbishop's judgements, and declared that Antonino in his lifetime was as worthy of canonization as the dead Bernardino (da Siena), whom he was about to raise to the altars. Pius II nominated him to a commission charged with reforming the Roman court. In no less esteem was he held by the Florentine government, who charged him with important embassies on behalf of the republic and would have sent him as their representative to the emperor if illness had not prevented him from leaving Florence.

During a severe epidemic of plague which lasted over a year, the saintly archbishop laboured untiringly to assist the sufferers, inspiring by his example the clergy to do the same.   Very many of the friars of Santa Maria Novella, Fiesole and San Marco were carried off, and as usual famine followed upon the heels of the epidemic. The saint stripped himself of almost everything and obtained substantial relief for the victims from Pope Nicholas V, who never refused him any request.   For two or three years from 1453 Florence was shaken by frequent earthquakes and a violent storm wrought havoc in one quarter of the city.   St Antoninus maintained the most distressed of the victims, rebuilt their houses and gave them a fresh start. He also cured a number of sick persons, for all knew that he possessed the gift of miracles.   Cosimo de' Medici publicly asserted that the preservation of the republic from the dangers which threatened it was largely due to the merits and prayers of the holy archbishop.   St Antoninus was canonized in 1523.

In the *Acta Sanctorum*, May, vol. i, there is printed a life of St Antoninus by Francis Castiglione, one of his household, together with a supplement by Leonard de Seruberti, and some extracts from the process of canonization.   There are a good many other sources of information in the chronicles, correspondence, diaries, etc., of the period, few of which were accessible in the seventeenth century.   By far the best attempt to utilize these materials is that made by the Abbé Raoul Morçay in his substantial work, *Saint Antonin* (1914).   This is a very satisfactory biography, embodying many details which were recorded by the archbishop's notary, Baldovino Baldovini, in a memoir which has only come to light in recent years.   A shorter account has been contributed to the series " Les Saints " by A. Masseron (1926).   See also the many references to St Antoninus in vol. i of Pastor's *Geschichte der Päpste* (vol. ii of the English translation) and also in Mortier's *Histoire des Maîtres Généraux O.P.*   On the literary work of the saint see DTC., vol. i, cc. 1451–1453, and also J. B. Walker, *The Chronicles of St Antoninus* (1933), who covers rather more ground than Schaube, the first and more scholarly explorer in this field.   For a fuller bibliography dealing with the early literature see Taurisano, *Catalogus Hagiographicus O.P.*   St Antoninus is important as a practical moralist, and in *Social Theories of the Middle Ages* (1926) Fr Bede Jarrett throws light on his moral and social teaching for the general reader ; see also the same writer's little book in Jack's People's Books series, *Medieval Socialism* (1913), and his *St Antonio and Medieval Economics* (1914).

ST CALEPODIUS, Martyr   (A.D. 222)

The reputed founder of the Roman cemetery which bears his name, St Calepodius was a Roman priest who, according to the legendary Acts of Pope St Callistus, suffered martyrdom during the reign of Alexander Severus as the result of a fanatical attack by the populace upon the Christians.   He was decapitated and his body cast into the Tiber, from whence it was rescued and brought to Pope Callistus by a fisherman who had caught it in his net.   Amongst a number of companions who are said to have perished in the same outbreak were the consul Palmatius, his family and forty-two members of his household, the senator Simplicius, with sixty-eight of his dependents, and a couple named Felix and Blandina.   The reputed relics of St Calepodius are to be found in the Roman churches of Santa Maria in Trastevere and San Pancrazio, as well as in the cathedral of Taranto.

There was undoubtedly a small catacomb which bore the name of Calepodius situated on the Via Aurelia, three miles from the city, and there is early and trustworthy evidence that Pope St Callistus I was buried there.   Beyond that we know very little.   See Duchesne, *Liber Pontificalis*, vol. i, pp. 141–142 ; CMH., pp. 555–556 ; and Dom Leclercq in DAC., vol. ii, cc. 1593–1595.

SS. GORDIAN and EPIMACHUS, Martyrs   (A.D. ? and 250)

Practically speaking, all the martyrologies, etc., of the Western church from the sixth century onwards make mention of SS. Gordian and Epimachus, who are also commemorated in the Roman Martyrology on this day.   Epimachus is said to have been thrown into a lime kiln at Alexandria in 250 with a certain Alexander, after they had endured cruel tortures for the faith.   The body of St Epimachus was subsequently taken to Rome.   St Gordian was beheaded in Rome and his body was placed with that of St Epimachus in the same tomb.   The greater part of their remains were afterwards given by St Hildegard, Charlemagne's wife, to the abbey of Kempten, in Bavaria, which she had restored.   The so-called " acts " of these two saints are spurious.

In contrast to the martyrs last mentioned, the historic existence and cult of SS. Gordian and Epimachus can raise no doubts.   The epitaph of Pope Damasus on St Gordian is still preserved to us, and describes the martyr as little more than a boy, whereas the legendary " acts " present him as having been the *vicarius*, the responsible minister, of the Emperor Julian.

See on the whole matter the text and notes of CMH., p. 244.   The acts are printed in the *Acta Sanctorum*, May, vol. ii.   There seems no sufficient reason to suppose, as Butler did, that the two martyrs were separated by a century in time.   *Cf.* J. P. Kirsch, *Der Stadtrömische christliche Festkalender*, pp. 54–55.

SS. ALPHIUS and his Companions, Martyrs   (A.D. 251)

The principal patrons of Vaste in the diocese of Otranto, and of Lentini, in Sicily, are SS. Alphius, Philadelphus and Cyrinus, who were martyred at the latter place and were probably natives of the former.   The various accounts of them which have come down to us are conflicting and quite unreliable. According to one legend, they and their sister St Benedicta, after being well instructed in the Christian faith by their father and a certain Onesimus, were apprehended with a number of companions during the Decian persecution and were taken to Rome. There they endured severe torture and were then removed to Pozzuoli, near Naples, where Onesimus and some of the party suffered martyrdom. The rest were transferred to Sicily and again tried and tortured. Their bold confession of faith caused the conversion of many spectators, including twenty soldiers. Eventually Alphius, who was twenty-two, died as the result of having his tongue torn out, Philadelphus, who was twenty-one, was roasted to death, and Cyrinus, who was nineteen, was boiled to death in a vessel full of hot pitch. In 1517 three bodies were discovered, and being identified with these saints, were elevated with great pomp at Lentini, a town seventeen miles south-west of Catania.

Although these alleged martyrs are duly entered in the Roman Martyrology, and their story occupies altogether some sixty folio pages in the *Acta Sanctorum* (May, vol. ii), there is no reliable evidence of early *cultus*. Their " acts " must be regarded as nothing better than a pious Greek romance. See DHG., vol. ii, c. 676.

ST CATALD, Bishop of Taranto, and ST CONLETH, Bishop of Kildare   (*c.* A.D. 685 ? and *c.* A.D. 520)

THESE two saints, far apart in time and space, but both sons of Ireland, are to-day celebrated together by the Church in that country. St Catald (Cathal) was a learned monk who for some time taught in the great school of Lismore. Resigning his post with a view to seeking greater retirement, he undertook a pilgrimage to Jerusalem. On his way home he was chosen bishop of Tarentum or Taranto, not in the sixth century as certain Italian writers have asserted, much less in the second, but towards the close of the seventh. He is said to have been an excellent prelate and several miracles were attributed to him. St Catald is titular saint of Taranto cathedral, being reckoned the second bishop of the diocese, and his *cultus* is very widely spread in Italy.

History has preserved few reliable details concerning St Conleth (Conlaed), who was, like many of the early Irish ecclesiastics, a clever worker in metals. He was living the life of a solitary at Old Connell on the Liffey when he came into touch with St Brigid, who at once formed a very high opinion of him. Their intercourse ripened into friendship. A gloss on the Félire of Oengus calls St Conlaed " St Brigid's chief artificer " ; but, if she knew how to utilize his artistic talents in making sacred vessels, she knew still better how to employ his spiritual gifts, for she obtained his help as bishop over her people at Kildare. A leaf appended to the Martyrology of Donegal describes St Conlaed as " brazier of Brigid, first bishop of Celldara and archbishop also "—meaning, perhaps, that he became head over the regionary bishops and abbots in that district of Ireland. Tradition ascribes to St Conlaed the fashioning of the crozier afterwards owned by St Finbar of Termon Barry and now preserved in the museum of the Royal Irish Academy. In the gloss upon the Félire of Oengus the curious statement is made that St Conlaed was devoured by wolves when he persisted in undertaking a journey to Rome against St Brigid's wishes. This seems to be an attempt to explain the name Conlaed, *i.e.* " half (*leth*) to wolves (*coin*) ", and the gloss states further that his previous name was Roncenn.

St Catald is another of those cases in which we know next to nothing of the life of the saint, but have long accounts of the veneration paid to what were believed to be his relics. See the *Acta Sanctorum*, May, vol. ii ; O'Hanlon LIS., vol. v, p. 185 ; and Ughelli, *Italia Sacra*, vol. ix, cc. 162–168 ; with A. Tommasini, *Irish Saints in Italy* (1937), pp. 401–432. He was honoured also at Seurre and Auxerre in France (where he is called " St Cartault") because some portion of his relics are said to have been brought there. On the obscure question of thê date at which he lived, consult J. F. Kenney, *The Sources for the Early History of Ireland* (1929), vol. i, p. 185. There are no materials apparently for the life of St Conlaed except casual allusions in Cogitosus's account of St Brigid and other similar sources. See, however, Healy, *Ireland's Ancient Schools and Scholars*, pp. 112–118 ; Gougaud, *Christianity in Celtic Lands ;* and Kenney, *op. cit.*

ST SOLANGIA, Virgin and Martyr   (A.D. 880)

St Solangia (Solange), who is sometimes called the St Geneviève of Berry, is also the patroness of that province of France. The child of vine-dressers, poorly endowed with this world's goods, she was born at Villemont, near Bourges. She dedicated herself to God from early childhood and took a vow of chastity at an early age. Her occupation was to mind her father's sheep as they grazed on the pasturages. It is said that she was attended by a guiding star which shone over her head with special brilliancy as the hour of prayer approached. Besides having a great power over animals, she was endowed with the gift of healing and effected many cures. Reports of her beauty and sanctity reached the ears of Bernard, one of the sons of the count of Poitiers, and he came on horseback to make advances to her as she was alone with her flock. When she resisted, he caught her up and set her in the saddle before him, but she succeeded in slipping from his horse, sustaining serious injury in her fall. The young man then despatched her with his hunting-knife. According to the legend, the girl afterwards arose and carried her head in her hands as far as the church of Saint-Martin-du-Cros, in the cemetery of which an altar was erected in her honour about the year 1281. A field near her home in which she liked to pray received the name of " Le Champ de Sainte Solange ".

That St Solangia has enjoyed much popular veneration in Bourges and surrounding districts is made clear by the number of devotional brochures published about her. See, for example, the *Vie de Sainte Solange*, written by Joseph Bernard de Montmélian, which has appeared in more than one edition. There is an account of this martyr in the *Acta Sanctorum*, May, vol. ii, but the evidence there furnished is very unsatisfactory. See Ombline P. de la Villéon, *Sainte Solange, protectrice du Berry* (1948).

BD BEATRICE OF ESTE, Virgin   (A.D. 1226)

The childhood of Bd Beatrice of Este cannot have been a happy one. Her mother died when she was an infant, her father, the Marquis Azzo of Este, when she was six ; and her elder brother, Aldobrandino, her natural protector, was poisoned when she was ten. The charge of the little girl devolved partly on her step-mother and partly on a paternal aunt. From the time of her father's death Beatrice would only wear the simplest clothes, absolutely refusing to put on the adornments which belonged to a girl of her rank. As she approached a marriageable age her relations, desirous of extending the power of the great house of Este, began to consider a suitable match for her, in spite of her protestations that she wished to live the religious life. Despairing of overcoming the opposition of her surviving brother, Beatrice secretly left home and made her way to the Benedictine abbey of

Solarola, where she received the habit at the age of fourteen. A year and a half later, she and ten other sisters were transferred to Gemmola, a quiet place less exposed to warlike attacks and worldly interruptions. There Beatrice spent the remainder of her short life, dying when she was in her twentieth year. In 1578 her relics were translated to Padua, where they are held in great veneration. Her cult was approved in 1763.

A life by a contemporary, one Albert, a religious at Verona, was printed for the first time by G. Brunacci in 1767. The narrative in the *Acta Sanctorum* is translated from the Italian of Bishop Tomasini, who wrote in the middle of the seventeenth century. See also P. Balan, *La B. Beatrice d' Este* (1878).

BD JOHN OF AVILA   (A.D. 1569)

AMONGST the great religious leaders of sixteenth-century Spain, one of the most influential and most eloquent was Bd John of Avila, the friend of St Ignatius Loyola and the spiritual adviser of St Teresa, St John of God, St Francis Borgia, St Peter of Alcantara and of Louis of Granada, who became his biographer. He was born in New Castile at Almodovar-del-Campo of wealthy parents, who sent him at the age of fourteen to Salamanca University to prepare to take up law. This career, however, had no attraction for the boy and he returned home, where for three years he gave himself up to devotional exercises and austerities. Then, at the suggestion of a Franciscan who was greatly impressed by his piety, he went to Alcalà to study philosophy and theology. There he had as his master the celebrated Dominic Soto; there also he laid the foundation of a life-long friendship with Peter Guerrero, afterwards archbishop of Granada. His parents died while he was still at Alcalà, leaving him their sole heir, but no sooner had he been ordained priest than he distributed the proceeds of his inheritance to the poor. From the moment he began to preach it was clear that he possessed extraordinary oratorical powers, and when he expressed a desire to go as a missionary to Mexico, the archbishop of Seville bade him remain in Spain and evangelize his fellow countrymen. Appointed missioner for Andalusia, he laboured indefatigably for nine years in this great province. Rich and poor, young and old, learned and unlearned, saints and sinners—all flocked to hear him. Countless souls were brought by him to penance and amendment of life, whilst many were led into the path of perfection under his direction. When he preached, he spoke like one inspired and, indeed, the only preparation he ever made for his sermons was his daily meditation of four hours. To a young priest who asked him how to become a good preacher, he replied that the only way he knew was to love God very much.

By his fearless denunciation of vice in high places, he made for himself some bitter enemies who actually succeeded in obtaining his imprisonment by the Inquisition at Seville on a charge of preaching rigorism and the exclusion of the rich from the kingdom of Heaven. The accusation could not be substantiated, and his first public appearance after his release was made the occasion for an extraordinary popular ovation. When his time in Andalusia was completed, Bd John devoted himself to giving what were practically missions, in all parts of Spain but especially in the cities. Moreover, he kept up a vast correspondence with his spiritual children and other persons who desired his advice. For the last seventeen years of his life he was in constant pain which he bore with unflinching patience. Of his writings the most celebrated are a collection of his letters and a treatise entitled *Audi Filia*, which he drew up for Doña Sancha Carillo, a rich and beautiful young woman who under his direction had given up great worldly prospects at court to lead a life of prayer and solitude under her father's roof.

Ever since his beatification in 1894 the Society of Jesus has kept John of Avila's feast almost as that of one of her own members, and indeed, as Don Vincente Garcia shows, Bd John had fully determined at the age of fifty-nine to enter the Society, but was deterred by the rigorism and rather extravagant attitude of Father Bustamente, the then provincial of Andalusia. His devotion to the order and its founder, however, did not in any way slacken. He was attended by a Jesuit in his last hours and left his body to be buried in their church at Montilla.

Our best sources of information are the *summarium de virtutibus* in the process of beatification, the writings of Bd John himself and the sketch of his life written by his friend and
contemporary, Louis de Granada. His writings may most conveniently be consulted in the
bulky work—there are 2199 pages—*Obras del B. Maestro Juan de Avila*, published at Madrid
in 1927. His spiritual letters are one of the classics of Spanish literature and were reprinted
in the series of *Classicos Castellanos* in 1912. The preface of this volume, by Don V. Garcia
de Diego, is also a valuable contribution, especially from the point of view of chronology,
to the biography of this master of the spiritual life. His life by Father degli Oddi, has been
translated into English (1898). A more recent life, by Father J. M. de Buck, appeared at
Louvain in 1927; and a small collection of his letters was translated by the Benedictine
nuns of Stanbrook and published in 1904, with a preface by Cardinal Gasquet. Bd John's
gifts as a preacher cannot fairly be judged by his extant sermons, which for the most part
are merely imperfect reports taken down by his auditors.

11: SS. PHILIP AND JAMES (see p. 203ff. Vol. II)

ST MAMERTUS, BISHOP OF VIENNE   (c. A.D. 475)

WE do not know much about the life of St Mamertus. He was the elder brother of Claudian, the poet, author of *De statu animae*, whom he ordained priest, and both brothers seem to have enjoyed a deserved reputation for learning as well as piety. In 463 trouble arose in connection with the consecration of a bishop to the see of Die, which Pope St Leo I not long before had transferred from the province of Vienne to that of Arles. It was complained to Pope St Hilarus that Mamertus, without justification, had consecrated a new bishop for Die. A council of bishops was held at Arles to inquire into the matter and a report was sent to Rome. Though Hilarus wrote rather severely and declared that Mamertus deserved to be deposed for his usurpation, no change was, in fact, made, and the new bishop of Die was allowed to retain his see after confirmation from Arles. Somewhat later than this we learn that Mamertus translated to Vienne the remains of the martyr Ferreolus, who had been put to death in that part of the country a century or two earlier. But that which more than anything else has made the name of St Mamertus well known in ecclesiastical history is his institution of the penitential processions on what we now call the Rogation Days, the three days preceding the feast of the Ascension. These are the *Litaniae minores*, which in the time of Pope St Leo III (795–816) were adopted in Rome itself, Frankish influence, under the Emperor Charlemagne, thus making itself felt throughout the whole of western Christendom.

That St Mamertus was the real author of the Rogation processions is proved by an abundance of early testimony. We have a letter addressed to him by St Sidonius Apollinaris, in which he speaks of these supplications which the bishop had instituted and which had proved so efficacious a remedy in the panic which had seized upon the populace. He enlarges at the same time on the courage this shepherd of his people had shown by standing his ground when others were taking to flight. St Avitus, who himself became bishop of Vienne only fifteen years after Mamertus's death, and who as a child had received baptism at his hands, preached a homily, still preserved to us, on one of the occasions when the Rogation processions came round. From him we learn in some detail of the tribulations with which the country had been afflicted at the time of their institution. He speaks of earthquake, of repeated conflagrations and of the wild deer taking refuge in the busy haunts of men. Very naturally, according to the ideas of the period, St Mamertus had interpreted these calamities as the judgement of God upon the sins of the people, and the remedy he proposed was entirely of a penitential character. He obliged all to fast, and to join in a long procession of young and old during which many psalms were sung. The example set at Vienne was almost immediately followed in other parts of France, and in time became universal in the West. At the first Council of Orleans, held in 511, the twenty-seventh decree prescribes that all churches are to celebrate these Rogation days before the feast of the Ascension. A strict fast is to be kept on all three days as in the time of Lent, and no work is to be done, even by those of servile condition, in order that they may be free to be present in church and take part in the processions ; in particular all clerics who absent themselves from these offices are to be punished as the bishop may direct. From the writings of contemporaries, or of such historians as St Gregory of Tours, it is clear that Mamertus was looked upon not only as a holy and self-sacrificing pastor of souls, but also as a leader who possessed both tact and courage. St Avitus in his homily is full of admiration for the sound judgement he displayed in reconciling both the secular officials and the people to an observance which imposed so heavy a tax upon their good will.

In the *Acta Sanctorum*, May, vol. ii, nearly all the early references to St Mamertus will be found collected. As to the Rogation Days, see K. A. Kellner, *Heortology*, pp. 189–194 ; but Edmund Bishop does well to point out (*Liturgica Historica*, pp. 128–130) that we must be on our guard against attaching to the word " litanies ", as used in connection with the Rogations, the meaning which it bears now. " So far as I can read ", he says, " there is no indication whatever that litanies were at the first institution sung on these three days at all." " In a word ", he adds, " so far as the original testimonies go, the substance of the devotion of the Rogations was psalm-singing, with, perhaps, the prayers or collects which in some quarters accompanied the singing of psalms." *Cf.* also Abbot Cabrol's article " Litanies ", in DAC., as well as what has previously been said herein under February 2 (Candlemas) and April 25 (St Mark).

ST COMGALL, ABBOT OF BANGOR   (A.D. 603)

ST COMGALL, one of the founders of Irish monasticism, was born in Ulster about the year 517, and spent some years under the direction of St Fintan in the monastery of Cluain Eidnech or Cloneenagh at the foot of the Slieve Bloom range. He was ordained priest by a certain Bishop Lugid, who is said to have deterred him from dedicating himself to missionary work in Britain. For a time he retired to an island in Lough Erne where he and some companions practised such austerities that seven of them died of hunger and cold. In response to the remonstrances of Bishop Lugid, Comgall relaxed his rule for his disciples, though not for himself. Emerging from his retreat, he founded the great abbey of Bennchor, or Bangor, which became the largest and most famous monastery in Ireland. No less than three thousand monks are said to have lived under the government of St Comgall at Bangor and in its daughter houses.

The holiest men of the age sought the friendship of the Abbot of Bangor and great saints owed their training to him—notably St Columban, who afterwards carried the tradition of Bangor to France and Italy. St Comgall seems to have carried out his early missionary aspirations by accompanying St Colmcille on an expedition to Inverness, where they preached the Gospel to a Pictish chieftain called Brude, and he is stated to have founded a monastery in a place called the Land of Heth (Tiree). St Comgall continued to rule Bangor until his death, although during the last years of his life he endured terrible sufferings, apparently as the result of his great austerities. He also became totally deaf. He died in 603, and his feast is kept throughout Ireland.

A curious alphabetical hymn in honour of the saint ("*Hymnus sancti Comgalli abbatis nostri*") occurs in the Bangor Antiphonary. The D stanza runs thus:

> Doctus in Dei legibus : divinis dictionibus,
> Ditatus sanctis opibus, Deo semper placentibus,
> Dedicatus in moribus : Dei Stephanus hagius
> Docebat sic et caeteros : Dicta docta operibus.

The date of this manuscript can be accurately fixed as between A.D. 680 and 691. One living word of St Comgall's seems to have been preserved in a gloss upon the *Félire* of Oengus ; in reference to the death of his confessor, he remarked : " My soul-friend has died and I am headless, and ye, too, are headless, for a man without a soul-friend is a body without a head ".

There is a Latin life of St Comgall which is printed in the *Acta Sanctorum*, May, vol. ii, and also in C. Plummer's VSH., vol. ii, pp. 3–21. The rule attributed to St Comgall, or what purports to be a metrical version of it, has been edited by J. Strachan in the periodical *Ériu*, vol. i (1904), pp. 191–208. See also J. Ryan, *Irish Monasticism* (1931), and Dom Gougaud, *Christianity in Celtic Lands* (1933), in both of which works many references to St Comgall and his monks will be found in the index. In Forbes, KSS., there is a lengthy account of St Comgall (pp. 308–310) drawn largely from the legends of the Aberdeen Breviary. See also *Analecta Bollandiana*, vol. lii (1934), pp. 343–356. For the hymn referred to, see Henry Bradshaw Society publications, vol. ii (1895), pp. 6–19 and notes.

ST ASAPH, BISHOP (SEVENTH CENTURY)

WHEN St Kentigern returned to Glasgow from Llanelwy in Denbighshire (if indeed he was ever there), he is said to have left that monastery in charge of St Asaph. Of this Asaph very little is known, though there is evidence that he was an important person in North Wales, cousin of St Deiniol and St Tysilio and grandson of Pabo Post Prydyn, " the prop of Pictland ". When the Normans developed an episcopal see at Llanelwy, St Asaph was claimed as the successor of its first bishop, St Kentigern, and the see has ever since been known by his name. The second recorded bishop of the diocese of St Asaph was Geoffrey of Monmouth, in whose *History of the Kings of Britain* there is no mention of Llanelwy or any ancient see there.

What, if anything, Asaph actually had to do with Llanelwy is not certainly known : Llanasa in Flintshire may have been the principal scene of his activity. The *Red Book of Asaph*, said to have been originally compiled early in the fourteenth century, refers to " the charm of his conversation, the symmetry, vigour and grace of his body, the holiness and virtue of his heart, and the witness of his miracles ".

Unexpectedly enough, St Asaph's name figures in the Roman Martyrology on May 1, where " Elwy " is stated to be in England.   His feast is observed to-day in the diocese of Menevia.

The Bollandists, in their brief account of this saint (*Acta Sanctorum*, May, vol. i, p. 84) draw mainly on the legends in the Aberdeen Breviary.   See A. P. Forbes, KSS., pp. 271-272 ; LBS., vol. i, pp. 177-185 ; and A. W. Wade-Evans, *Welsh Christian Origins* (1934), pp. 191-194.

ST GENGULF, OR GENGOUL   (A.D. 760)

ST GENGULF was a Burgundian knight, so greatly beloved by Pepin the Short, at that time mayor of the palace, that he used to sleep in the great man's tent during his campaigns.   Gengulf is said to have been married to a woman of rank in whom for a long time he trusted, but she proved scandalously unfaithful to him.   Finding remonstrances and appeals useless, he quietly withdrew from her to a castle of his at Avallon (the birthplace of St Hugh of Lincoln, between Auxerre and Autun), after making suitable provision for her maintenance.   There he spent his time in penitential exercises and his money in alms.   He died—so the legend avers—from a wound inflicted by his wife's lover who, at her instigation, broke in upon him one night to murder him as he lay in bed.   The fame of St Gengulf afterwards spread to Holland, Belgium and Savoy as the result of the distribution of his relics and the miracles with which he was credited.

The short biography printed in the *Acta Sanctorum*, May, vol. ii, seems to be largely fabulous ; it has been critically edited by W. Levison in MGH., *Scriptores Merov.*, vol. vii, pp. 142 *seq.*   The famous nun Hroswitha of Gandersheim, at the close of the tenth century, wrote an account of the martyrdom in elegiac verse (see Winterfeld's edition of her works, 1902, pp. 32 *seq.*).   The *cultus* of St Gengulf was widespread both in France and Germany. For the folk-lore which has gathered round his name see Bächtold-Stäubli, *Handwörterbuch des deutschen Aberglaubens*, vol. iii, pp. 289-290.

ST MAJOLUS, OR MAYEUL, ABBOT OF CLUNY   (A.D. 994)

PROVENCE in the early part of the tenth century suffered terribly from the incursions of the Saracens, and St Majolus, who at an early age was left heir to large estates near Riez, was obliged to take refuge with relatives who lived at Mâcon, in Burgundy. There he received the tonsure and a canonry from his uncle Bishop Berno, by whom he was afterwards sent to Lyons to study philosophy under a celebrated master, Antony, abbot of L'Isle Barbe.   Upon his return to Mâcon he was made archdeacon, although he was still young, and when the see of Besançon fell vacant he was selected to fill it.   To avoid being forcibly consecrated to a dignity for which he felt himself unfitted, he fled to the abbey of Cluny, to which his father had been a benefactor.   There he received the habit and was appointed by Abbot Aymard librarian and procurator.   In this double capacity he not only had direction of the studies and care of the treasury, but he also conducted all important business outside the monastery.   In the course of the various journeys he was obliged to make, he won golden opinions for his humility and wisdom.   As St Berno,* the first abbot of Cluny, had chosen St Odo to be his coadjutor, and St Odo in his turn had selected Aymard, so Aymard, when he lost his sight, raised St Majolus to the dignity of joint abbot.

* Berno was not then an uncommon name, and it may be well to point out that Berno, abbot of Cluny, was quite a different person from the Berno, bishop of Mâcon, mentioned before.

His wisdom and virtue gained him the respect of the great men of the age. The Emperor Otto the Great placed entire confidence in him and gave him supervision over all the monasteries in Germany and other parts of the empire. The Empress St Adelaide and her son Otto II had no less esteem for the holy abbot, who succeeded in reconciling them when they were at variance. By virtue of the privileges bestowed upon the congregation of which he was the head, Majolus was able to reform a great number of monasteries, many of which adopted the Cluniac life. Otto II was anxious that he should be chosen pope, but could not overcome his opposition ; to all that could be urged he replied that he knew how little fitted he was to fill so high an office and how different his manners were from those of the Romans. A man of great scholarship, he did much to foster learning. Three years before his death he appointed St Odilo his coadjutor, and from that time gave himself up to the exercises of penance and contemplation. He could not, however, disregard the express request of Hugh Capet, King of France, that he would undertake a journey to settle reforms in the abbey of St Denis, near Paris. On the way thither he fell ill and died at the abbey of Souvigny on May 11, 994. At his funeral in the church of St Peter at Souvigny, the king of France himself was present.

There is abundant material for the life of St Majolus. Three separate biographies of early date are printed in the *Acta Sanctorum*, May, vol. ii, a compendious account of which is furnished in BHL., nn. 5177–5187. Upon the complicated problem of the relations of these lives a valuable note was contributed by L. Traube to the *Neues Archiv. . . .*, vol. xvii (1892), pp. 402–407. See also J. H. Pignot, *Histoire de l'Ordre de Cluny*, vol. i, pp. 236–303 ; E. Sackur, *Die Cluniacenser*, vol. i, pp. 205–256 ; S. Hilpisch, *Geschichte des Ben. Mönchtums*, pp. 170 *seq.* A hymn written by St Odilo on St Majolus has been printed by Dom G. Morin in the *Revue Bénédictine*, vol. xxxviii (1926), pp. 56–57. See also Zimmermann, *Kalendarium Benedictinum*, vol. ii, pp. 171–173.

ST ANSFRID, Bishop of Utrecht   (A.D. 1010)

IN early life St Ansfrid was a warrior, noted for his success in suppressing brigands and pirates, and for this reason high in the favour of the Emperors Otto III and Henry II. He was count of Brabant and when the see of Utrecht fell vacant at the death of Bishop Baldwin the emperor suggested that he should be appointed to succeed him. In spite of his opposition he was consecrated bishop in 994. He founded a convent for nuns at Thorn near Roermond and the abbey of Hohorst, or Heiligenberg, to which he retired when blindness came upon him. It was there also he died. At the time of his burial a number of citizens of Utrecht came to Heiligenberg ; seizing their opportunity when the people of the neighbourhood were busily engaged in extinguishing a conflagration which had broken out at that moment (perhaps not accidentally) they took possession of the venerated remains and carried them off. When the Heiligen monks discovered their loss, a fierce pursuit was on the point of taking place, but the Abbess of Thorn by her prayerful entreaties succeeded in preventing the threatened rescue by force of arms. St Ansfrid accordingly was peacefully interred in his own episcopal cathedral at Utrecht.

What is printed in the *Acta Sanctorum*, May, vol. i, as a fragmentary life of St Ansfrid is in reality merely an extract from the *De diversitate temporum* of the Benedictine monk Albert of St Symphorian at Metz. He was a contemporary who wrote in 1022, and though he does not tell us very much, the substance of what he says is trustworthy.

ST WALTER OF L'ESTERP, ABBOT   (A.D. 1070)

ST WALTER (Gautier) was born at the castle of Conflans on the Vienne, the chief seat of his family, which was one of the foremost in Aquitaine. For his education he was sent to the Augustinian canons at Dorat where he had Bd Israel as his master and where he received the habit. The ill-will of an unreasonable superior led him to retire to Conflans, but he was soon afterwards elected abbot of L'Esterp, a position he held for thirty-eight years. He had an ardent zeal for souls, and his influence spread far beyond the walls of his monastery. So great was his reputation for converting sinners that Pope Victor II granted him special faculties for dealing with penitents—including the right to excommunicate and to restore to communion. For the last seven years of his life he was blind, but he continued his activities until his death.

His biographer tells us that while yet a young monk St Walter made a pilgrimage to Jerusalem, in the course of which journey rumour seems to have credited him with some remarkable miracles. Driven to land on a desolate shore, he and his companions had nothing to eat, but a strange bird flew over them and dropped at his feet a fish which was so large that Walter by himself could not even lift it from the ground. This gentle saint's compassion for human infirmity and error was unbounded; and when his companions, absorbed in external tasks, forgot that a day was Friday and had prepared a meal of meat, he not only allowed them to eat it, saying that they might count on the indulgence of the great St Martin whose feast it was, but he set them the example by partaking of it himself. One of the company, scandalized and rigorist, hotly denounced this concession, but immediately after lost the whole sum of money he was carrying in his purse, a calamity which the writer treats as a divine rebuke to his self-righteousness. What is certain is that Abbot Walter is repeatedly referred to by the chroniclers of that age as a man of outstanding holiness, whose undertakings were marvellously blessed by Heaven.

The biography, ascribed to the famous Bishop Marbod, who was a contemporary, is printed in the *Acta Sanctorum*, May, vol. ii.

BD ALBERT OF BERGAMO   (A.D. 1279)

BD ALBERT OF BERGAMO was a peasant farmer who lived an exemplary life amongst his neighbours in the Valle d'Ogna and became a Dominican tertiary. Though married he had no children, and he had much to bear from a shrewish wife, as well as from other relations who resented his liberality to the poor. In later life he went on pilgrimages to Rome and Jerusalem and is said to have visited Compostela eight times, always supporting himself on the way by the work of his hands. Eventually he settled in Cremona, where he became closely associated with another holy man, Bd Homobonus, and where he died in the year 1279. He was famous in Cremona for his miracles. Some of the wonders which he is said to have worked in his lifetime are certainly of a very remarkable and unusual character. For example, in the *Short Lives of Dominican Saints*, edited by Fr John Proctor, O.P., we read : " One day he was carrying a barrel of wine to the house of a poor woman, when it accidentally slipped from his shoulder and broke to pieces on the road. ' King of Glory, come to my assistance ', exclaimed the holy man, according to his wont in all difficulties. Then he gathered up the broken pieces of wood, adjusted them in their proper places, and collected the spilt wine in his hands so that not a drop was lost."

In the Prato edition of the *Opera Omnia* of Pope Benedict XIV, vol. vi (1842), pp. 35–36, will be found a summary of the evidence presented to establish the fact of the immemorial *cultus* paid to Bd Albert of Bergamo. The documents submitted at that time were printed for the Congregation of Rites, and the decree of confirmation is dated May 9, 1748. See also the *Année Dominicaine* (1891), pp. 375–381. A short notice of Bd Albert will also be found in the *Acta Sanctorum*, May, vol. ii.

BD VIVALDO   (A.D. 1300)

VIVALDO, or Ubaldo, was a disciple and fellow townsman of Bd Bartolo of San Gemignano whom he nursed for twenty years through a particularly distressing form of leprosy. Afterwards he lived as a solitary inside a hollow chestnut-tree at Montajone, in Tuscany. One day as a huntsman was seeking game in the mountains, his hounds discovered the hermit, who was kneeling in his retreat in an attitude of prayer, but was quite dead. It is stated that at the moment his soul passed to God the bells of Montajone began ringing of themselves and never ceased pealing until the huntsman came in with the news of the discovery of the body. Bd Vivaldo had been attached to the third order of St Francis, and the Observants built a convent on the site where he had lived and died.

The brief account printed in the *Acta Sanctorum*, May, vol. i, seems to contain all that has been recorded of Bd Vivaldo. The decree by which Pope Pius X confirmed his *cultus* may be read in the *Analecta Ecclesiastica* for 1908, p. 145, but it adds nothing material to the facts mentioned above. Neither is anything further to be learnt from the article of Father Ghilardi in the *Miscellanea Storica della Valdelsa*, vol. xi (1903), pp. 38–42.

BD BENINCASA   (A.D. 1426)

BD BENINCASA, a member of one of the great Florentine families, entered the Servite Order at a very early age and when twenty-five was permitted to embrace the life of a hermit on the mountain of Montagnata, near Siena. There he gave himself up to prayer, but was greatly tried by diabolical assaults. Through a little window he gave spiritual advice to the men who resorted to him—with women he would have no dealings—and healed the sick by the sign of the cross or by holy water. Realizing, however, that the Devil was tempting him to pride, he retired to another spot much more difficult of access. His death is said to have been announced to the people in the plain by the spontaneous ringing of the church bells and by a light which streamed from his cave.

An account of Bd Benincasa is given in the *Acta Sanctorum*, May, vol. vii, supplement. This is almost entirely based on Father A. Giani, *Annales Ordinis Servorum*. In the seventeenth century the local veneration of Bd Benincasa at Montechielo, where he was buried, seems almost to have died out. This was explained at the time by the fact that a rumour was in circulation that his authentic relics had been stolen. The *cultus* was, however, officially sanctioned in 1829. There is a short life by L. Raffaelli (1927).

BD ALOYSIUS RABATA   (A.D. 1490)

FEW incidents seem to have marked the life of Bd Aloysius Rabata. Admitted to the Carmelite Order as a young man at Trapani, in Sicily, he was afterwards prior of the friary at Randazzo. He lived on bread and water and was remarkable for his humility, his patience and his zeal for souls. As superior he insisted upon performing such tasks as road-mending and begging for alms. He took the sins of his penitents so much to heart that when a poor man confessed to a theft for which he was unable to make restitution, his ghostly father himself approached the injured party and with tears continued to implore forgiveness until it was granted. He died from the after-effects of a blow on the head inflicted by a scoundrel whom he refused to bring to justice; he would not even disclose the identity of the perpetrator of the outrage.

A tolerably full notice is printed in the *Acta Sanctorum*, May, vol. ii. It is mainly derived from the materials which were collected in 1533 and 1573 with a view to canonization, which never took place. The *cultus* was confirmed in the nineteenth century under Pope Gregory XVI.

BD LADISLAUS OF GIELNIOW   (A.D. 1505)

ONE of the principal patrons of Poland, Galicia and Lithuania is Bd Ladislaus of Gielniow, a Pole born in the year 1440, who, after being educated in the University of Warsaw, entered the Franciscan convent of the strict observance founded in that city by St John Capistran. He was several times elected provincial and drew up a revised constitution which received the approbation of the general chapter held in Urbino in 1498. At the request of Duke Alexander, Ladislaus sent out a picked body of friars to evangelize Lithuania. Before they started he warned them that the example of personal holiness must always precede the preaching of the gospel. The mission was greatly blessed : not only were thousands of pagans baptized, but many schismatics were reconciled. Bd Ladislaus himself was an ardent missioner and a man of great eloquence, and when he became guardian at Warsaw he was in great request as a preacher. He delivered sermons in every part of Poland, and wrote both in Latin and in Polish ; he also composed hymns which were sung by the people at evening services. His favourite topic was the Passion and his best-loved text, " Jesus of Nazareth, the King of the Jews ".

In 1498 Poland was in great danger : the Tartars had made a league with the Turks and were advancing with an army of 70,000 men. Ladislaus called upon the panic-stricken population to pray and to put their trust in God, who alone could deliver them. The invading army was encamped between the Pruth and the Dniester when suddenly the waters of both rose up in flood, inundating the country. This was followed by an intense frost and then by a blinding snowstorm. Thousands of the enemy's men and horses were drowned, thousands more perished of cold, and the miserable remnant was easily defeated and almost exterminated by the Wallachian Prince Stephen. The victory was generally ascribed to the prayers of Bd Ladislaus, whose prestige was enormously enhanced. His brethren often beheld him raised from the ground in ecstasy and on the Good Friday before his death, as he was preaching to an immense congregation, he was seen to be lifted into the air and to hang there as though crucified. Afterwards when he slowly sank to the ground he was so weak that he had to be carried to the convent infirmary, where he died a month later, mourned by the whole city. He was beatified in 1586.

A very ample life, published in Latin by the Franciscan Father Vincent Morawski, at the beginning of the seventeenth century, has been reprinted in the *Acta Sanctorum*, May, vol. i. There is also a brief account by Fr Léon in his *Auréole Séraphique* (Eng. trans.), vol. iv, pp. 335–337. The *Lexikon für Theologie und Kirche* mentions two modern writers, C. Bogdalski and K. Kantak, who in recent works dealing with the Franciscan missions in Poland have specially called attention to Bd Ladislaus. These books, however, are written in Polish.

THE ENGLISH CARTHUSIAN MARTYRS, WITH BB. RICHARD REYNOLDS AND JOHN HAILE (A.D. 1535-1540)

To the Carthusian Order belongs the honour of having furnished the first martyr of the Tudor persecution in the person of JOHN HOUGHTON, prior of the London Charterhouse. After him, on the same day and at the same place, were martyred two other Carthusian priors, as well as JOHN HAILE, vicar of Isleworth, and a Bridgettine monk named RICHARD REYNOLDS.

John Houghton, who was a native of Essex and a graduate of Cambridge University, had been a secular priest for four years when he entered the London Charterhouse. There he spent twenty years of religious life, being conspicuous even amongst his austere brethren for his mortification, his patience and his humility. Maurice Chauncy, a fellow monk, has left us an edifying record of his heroic virtues, together with an interesting description of his person and bearing. He was short of stature, we read, graceful, venerable of countenance, modest in demeanour and winning of speech. In spite of his ardent desire to remain hidden, he was marked out for preferment, and was elected prior of the Charterhouse of Beauvale, in Nottinghamshire. Upon the death of John Batmanson a few months later, he was recalled by the unanimous vote of the brethren to become prior of the London Charterhouse, and shortly afterwards he was nominated visitor of the English province of the order.

In the summer of 1533 a royal proclamation was issued ordering the adhesion by oath of every person over the age of sixteen to the Act of Succession, which recognized Anne Boleyn as the lawful queen and her children as heirs to the throne. The cloistered monks of the Charterhouse may well have thought that, as politics were outside their province, the edict did not affect them. For about eight months they actually seem to have remained unmolested. Their great reputation, however, and the influence they wielded as directors of souls then decided King Henry and his officials to demand their assent. Royal commissioners accordingly presented themselves at the Charterhouse and questioned the superiors.

In his reply, the prior, whilst disclaiming any desire or intention of interfering with the king's affairs, admitted that he could not see how the marriage with Catherine of Aragon, properly solemnized as it had been, and for so many years unquestioned, could suddenly have become invalid. On the strength of this remark he was summarily arrested and imprisoned in the Tower with his procurator, HUMPHREY MIDDLEMORE. A month later, in deference to the decision of learned and devout men who deemed that the succession to the throne was not a cause for which they should sacrifice their lives, the two prisoners agreed to take the oath with the added proviso, " as far as the law of God permits ". Thereupon they were allowed to return to the Charterhouse, where, after a little hesitation on the part of several of the monks, the whole community made the required declaration in its modified form. During the short period of peace which followed, Houghton was under no illusion as to his future ; the night before his release from the Tower it had been revealed to him in a dream that he would return within a twelvemonth and would end his days in prison.

On February 1 of the following year there came into force another act of Parliament—much more far-reaching than the Act of Succession. It was called the Act of Supremacy and declared it to be high treason to deny that the King was the sole and supreme head of the Church in England. That this was a very different thing from a question of mere temporal succession to the English throne, Prior Houghton fully realized. Summoning his spiritual sons to the chapter-house, he warned them that they would probably all be shortly faced with the alternative between death and apostasy. He then declared a solemn triduum, during which they were to prepare for the approaching trial; and on the third day, while their prior was celebrating the holy Mysteries, there came " a soft whisper of air, which some perceived with their bodily senses, while all experienced its sweet influence upon their hearts ".

John Houghton determined to make a personal appeal to Thomas Cromwell, the king's chief secretary, in the hope of obtaining exemption from the oath of supremacy, or at least a mitigation of it. He took with him two priors who had come to London to consult him about the affairs of their monasteries : they were ROBERT LAWRENCE, a London monk, Houghton's successor at Beauvale, and AUGUSTINE WEBSTER, trained at Sheen, but now prior of the charterhouse in the Isle of Axholme. Cromwell, who was aware that King Henry was greatly incensed against the Carthusians, received them roughly, and summarily cutting short Prior Houghton's opening remarks, ordered them all three to be committed to the Tower, although Lawrence and Webster had not opened their lips. An interrogatory at the Rolls three weeks later was followed by a visit to the Tower of Cromwell himself and the king's commissaries, bearing with them a copy of the oath. By this time the priors had been joined in their captivity by Richard Reynolds, a distinguished and learned Bridgettine monk from the monastery of Syon, whose singular holiness was reflected in the angelic beauty of his countenance. Cardinal Pole, who was his intimate friend, declared that he was the only religious in England well versed in the three languages " in which all liberal learning is comprised ". Called upon to take the oath, the prisoners said they would do so if they might add the saving clause " as far as the law of God allows ". " I admit of no condition ", was Cromwell's reply. " Whether the law of God permits or not, you must take the oath without reservation." This they absolutely refused to do, and they were accordingly committed for trial.

When, on April 29, they came before the court at Westminster Hall, they were accused of denying that Henry VIII was supreme head on earth of the Church of England. To this charge they made no defence, but the jury showed the utmost reluctance to condemn them, only consenting to declare them guilty of high treason when Cromwell appeared in person and terrified them into submission. Sentence of death was then passed upon the four monks and upon an aged secular priest, John Haile, vicar of Isleworth, who was accused of uttering slanderous words against the king, the queen and the council. Their execution was fixed to take place at Tyburn on May 4, every expedient being adopted to degrade them in the eyes of the populace. They were dragged to the scaffold, lying on their backs on hurdles, still wearing their habits—a thing hitherto unheard of in a Christian country. Arrived at the foot of the gallows, Bd John Houghton embraced his executioner, who craved his forgiveness, and having testified that he was suffering for conscience because he was unwilling to deny a doctrine of the Church, he met his death with the utmost fortitude. After being strung up, he was cut down and disembowelled while still alive. In fact he was conscious and still able to speak when his heart was torn out. The rest of the martyrs showed the same courage. All refused a pardon proffered at the last moment at the price of acknowledging the king's supremacy. Special efforts had been made to break down the constancy of

Bd RICHARD REYNOLDS, who, as he was the last to be executed, was obliged to witness the barbarities inflicted on his companions. Their remains were parboiled, divided, and exposed in various parts of the city, an arm of Bd John Houghton being posted over the chief entrance of his monastery.

On the very day of the execution of the priors, one of the commissaries visited the Charterhouse to interrogate and examine the three monks who had taken over the government, namely, HUMPHREY MIDDLEMORE, WILLIAM EXMEW, the late prior's confessor, and SEBASTIAN NEWDIGATE, once a favourite courtier in the palace of Henry VIII. Their replies were deemed unsatisfactory and three weeks later they were committed to the Marshalsea prison, where for over a fortnight they were chained to columns by the neck and feet, unable to sit or lie down, and never released for a moment. Newdigate had a special trial to undergo, for King Henry came to the prison in disguise and tried to win him over. All three came up for trial on June 12, were convicted of high treason, and were executed on June 19.

No further executions took place for some time, but the monks were not left to themselves. Resident commissioners were placed over them, their books were taken away, and in the words of Maurice Chauncy, " they never knew what it was to be free from vexation for a single hour ". A monk from Sheen, who had taken the oath of supremacy, was placed over them as prior, whilst several of the most resolute of the monks were sent to other houses. Amongst these were two priests, JOHN ROCHESTER and WILLIAM WALWORTH, who were transferred to Hull. In consequence of an imprudent letter which the former addressed from there to the Duke of Norfolk, he and his brother monk were arrested, tried at York, condemned and executed on May 11, 1537, two years after the death of Bd John Houghton.

In the meantime the constant pressure brought to bear upon the London community had been gradually breaking down the constancy of the majority, and on May 18, 1537, nineteen of the monks, besides the prior, consented to take the oath. There still, however, remained a heroic minority of ten who continued staunch. Three of them were priests—THOMAS JOHNSON, RICHARD BEER and THOMAS GREEN or Greenwood ; one was a deacon, JOHN DAVY, and the rest were the lay brothers ROBERT SALT, WILLIAM GREENWOOD, THOMAS REDING, THOMAS SCRYVEN, WALTER PIERSON and WILLIAM HORN. They were imprisoned in the Marshalsea, tied to posts and left to starve to death. For a time they were kept alive by the heroism of Sir Thomas More's adopted daughter, Margaret Clement, who, after bribing the gaoler, obtained access to the prison in the disguise of a milkmaid and fed the prisoners by placing food in their mouths. The warder, however, became alarmed when the king expressed surprise that the captives were still alive, and Margaret was refused admission. One after the other the monks died of neglect and starvation, until only William Horn remained. He was removed to the Tower, where he was treated with less inhumanity, but three years later he was attainted, condemned for denying the royal supremacy, and executed at Tyburn on August 4, 1540. He was the last of the eighteen who make up the roll of the English Carthusian martyrs.

A general feast of these martyrs is kept to-day in the archdiocese of Westminster and by the Carthusians. Bd John Houghton is celebrated in the diocese of Brentwood, BB. John Rochester and William Walworth in Leeds and Middlesbrough, Bd Richard Reynolds separately in Westminster (May 14), Bd John Haile in Brentwood (May 21), and BB. Sebastian Newdigate and Humphrey Middlemore in Birmingham (June 19).

Apart from the state papers in Record Office and elsewhere, all of which are calendared in the *Letters and Papers, Foreign and Domestic : the Reign of Henry VIII,* our principal authority is the narrative of Dom Maurice Chauncy, *Historia aliquot nostri saeculi Martyrum.* Fr Van Ortroy, in the *Analecta Bollandiana,* vols. vi, xiv, and xxii, has studied the slight variations in the different recensions of Chauncy's work. The story is also retold with supplementary details by L. Hendriks, *The London Charterhouse* (1889), and by V. Doreau, *Henri VIII et les Martyrs de la Chartreuse* (1890). See also Fr. John Morris, S.J., *Troubles of our Catholic Forefathers,* vol. i, pp. 3–29 ; Camm, LEM., vol. i, pp. 1–46 ; and E. M. Thompson, *The Carthusian Order in England* (1930). The same writer contributes an introduction to an unpublished manuscript of Chauncy's, *Brevis et fidelis narratio,* edited by G. W. S. Curtis (1935). For Bd Richard Reynolds see A. Hamilton, *The Angel of Syon* (1905) and M. J. R. Fletcher, *The Story of . . . Syon Abbey* (1933). D. B. Christie, *While the World Revolves* (1932), is a popular account of Bd John Houghton. There is an admirable brief summary in R. W. Chambers, *Thomas More* (1935), pp. 320–332.

ST FRANCIS DI GIROLAMO   (A.D. 1716)

A BOUNDLESS zeal for the conversion of sinners and a tender love for the poor, the sick and the oppressed were the outstanding characteristics of St Francis di Girolamo, the eloquent Jesuit missioner whom the inhabitants of the Two Sicilies venerate to this day as, in a special sense, the apostle of Naples. The eldest of a family of eleven, he was born in 1642 at Grottaglie, near Taranto. After he had made his first communion, at the age of twelve, he was received into the house of some secular priests in the neighbourhood who lived a community life. The good fathers were not slow to perceive that their young charge was no ordinary boy ; from leaving him in charge of their church they promoted him to teaching the catechism, and he received the tonsure when he was barely sixteen. With a view to learning canon and civil law, he went to Naples in the company of a brother who desired to study under an eminent painter. In 1666 Francis was ordained priest, for which a dispensation had to be obtained as he was not yet twenty-four. For the next five years he taught at Naples in the Jesuit Collegio dei Nobili. The impression he made there upon his pupils may be gauged from the fact that the boys habitually spoke of him among themselves as " the holy priest ". At the age of twenty-eight, having overcome the opposition of his parents, he entered the Society of Jesus.

During the first year of novitiate Francis was subjected to exceptionally severe tests by his superiors, who were so completely satisfied that at its close they sent him to help the celebrated preacher Father Agnello Bruno in his mission work. From 1671 till 1674, the two priests laboured untiringly and with great success, mainly amongst the peasants of the province of Otranto. At the close of that mission Francis was recalled to Naples where he completed his theological studies and was professed. He was now appointed preacher at the Neapolitan church known as the Gesù Nuovo. It was his ardent desire to be sent to Japan, when there was talk of attempting a new missionary effort in that land which had ruthlessly exterminated every Christian teacher who landed on its shores, but he was told by his superiors that he must regard the kingdom of Naples as his India and Japan. It was, indeed, to be the scene of his untiring activities for the remaining forty years of his life.

From the outset his preaching attracted huge congregations and was rewarded by such excellent results that he was set to train other missionaries. In the provinces he conducted at least 100 missions, but the people of Naples would never allow him to be long absent from their city. Wherever he went, men and women hung upon his lips and crowded to his confessional; and it was confidently asserted that at least four hundred hardened sinners were annually reclaimed through his efforts. He would visit the prisons, the hospitals and even the galleys, in one of which—a Spanish one—he brought to the faith twenty Turkish prisoners. Moreover, he did not hesitate to track down sinners to the very haunts of vice, in which it sometimes happened that he was very roughly handled. Often he would preach in the streets—occasionally on the spur of the moment. Once, in the middle of a stormy night, he felt irresistibly moved to turn out and preach in the dark in an apparently deserted part of the town. The following day there came to his confessional a young woman who had been living a sinful life, but had been conscience-stricken when through her open window she had heard his stirring appeal of the previous evening. Amid his numerous penitents of all classes, perhaps the most remarkable was a woman, French by birth, called Mary Alvira Cassier. She had murdered her father and had afterwards served in the Spanish army, disguised as a man. Under the direction of St Francis she not only was brought to penitence, but attained to a high degree of holiness.

The effects of the preaching of the holy Jesuit were enhanced by his reputation as a wonder-worker, but he consistently disclaimed any extraordinary powers, attributing the numerous cures which attended his ministrations to the intercession of St Cyrus (January 31), for whom he had a special veneration. St Francis di Girolamo died at the age of seventy-four, after much suffering, and his remains were interred in the Jesuit church of Naples where they still lie. He was canonized in 1839.

There is a valuable report drawn up by the saint himself to acquaint his superiors with the more striking manifestations of God's grace during fifteen years of his missionary labours. These " Brevi Notizie " have been printed by Father Boero in his book *S. Francesco di Girolamo e le sue Missioni* (1882). We have also two Italian lives written by fellow Jesuits who had known the saint intimately ; that by Stradiotti appeared in 1719, and that by Bagnati in 1725. Among more modern contributions, the *Vita di San Francesco di Girolamo*, by Father degli Oddi, has been perhaps the most widely circulated, but J. Bach's *Histoire de S. François de Geronimo* (1867), is the most complete. See further the convenient *Raccolta di Avvenimenti singolari e Documenti autentici*, collected by Canon Alfonso Muzzarelli (1806), as well as the life by C. de Bonis. In English there is a biography by A. M. Clarke which appeared in the " Quarterly Series " in 1891, and an admirable article by the Bollandist Father Van Ortroy in the *Catholic Encyclopedia*.

ST IGNATIUS OF LACONI   (A.D. 1781)

LACONI is beautifully situated a little south of the middle of the island of Sardinia. Two hundred and fifty years ago it was little more than a large village, with narrow winding streets between the peasant cottages, adjoining the park and mansion of the local nobleman, the Marquis of Laconi. Living in the Via Prezzu was a man named Matthew Cadello Peis, who was married to Ann Mary Sanna Casu. They were respectable people, very hard-working and very poor, and they had three sons and six daughters. One who knew them personally said they were " a household of saints " ; that, no doubt, must not be taken too literally ; but one of the children, the second born, was in fact to be raised to the Church's altars.

This boy was born on December 17, 1701. He was christened Francis Ignatius Vincent, and was known at home by his last name. Little is known of his early

281

years, except that he was a " child of the fields ", early becoming acquainted with
hard work on his father's land.   Physically, Vincent was delicate and his healthy
life failed to strengthen him ; all the witnesses speak of his being thin and pale.
It was precisely this poor health that was the occasion of his seriously determining
to " enter religion ".   Vincent's mother is said to have promised her son to St
Francis of Assisi at birth, and she certainly used to speak to him of one day wearing
the habit of *Il Poverello*.   Accordingly when, being about seventeen or eighteen
years old, he was taken seriously ill, he offered himself to St Francis should he
recover.   But on regaining his health, his father was unwilling to part with him :
" We did not promise to do anything in a hurry ", said the prudent Matthew.
" To-day or to-morrow, this year or later on, it all comes to the same thing.   There's
no need to keep your promise at once."   But on an autumn day in 1721 something
happened to strengthen Vincent's determination.   He was riding out to look at
his father's cattle when, at a rather dangerous part of the road, his horse bolted.
Vincent lost control altogether and thought he would certainly be killed ; but for
no apparent reason the horse pulled up suddenly, and then jogged on quietly as
before.   In this the young man saw the finger of God.

A few days later, in spite of his father's expostulations, Vincent made his way to
Buoncammino, near Cagliari, and there asked to be admitted to the Capuchin
branch of the Order of Friars Minor.   After some delay he was clothed in 'the
habit of St Francis, as Brother Ignatius, at St Benedict's friary.   It was one
of those beautiful homely little houses of friars such as are still to be found in
parts of Italy.

At first Brother Ignatius got on well, under the eye of a sympathetic and discerning novice-master.   But his successor in office was less understanding : he
suspected Brother Ignatius of insincerity, and was of the opinion that he was not
physically strong enough for Franciscan life.   As the end of his novitiate approached
it looked as if Brother Ignatius would be rejected for profession, but he redoubled
his efforts to carry out all he was called on to do : and so at the end of 1722 he was
allowed to make his vows.   Brother Ignatius was specially attached to St Benedict's;
but after profession he was sent for short periods to other neighbouring houses, the
bigger friary, St Antony's, at Buoncammino, Cagliari, Iglesias.   It was at the
last-named place that rumours of wonders began to be associated with the young
laybrother, and when he was sent out to collect alms people not only gave to him
but asked him to come again.   Near the village of Sant' Antioco there is a hillock
called to this day Brother Ignatius's Hill, though why is not known.   From
Iglesias he was sent back to Cagliari, where for fifteen years he worked in the
weaving-shed.   The life of a laybrother is likely in any case to be uneventful, and
during this period practically nothing is known of Brother Ignatius beyond his
steady progress in the love of God.

Then came a change which gave him opportunity more widely to extend this
love in terms of his human fellows.   He was already a " friar " ; he had now to
be a " brother " as well.   A man of solitude and silence, working quietly within
monastery walls, he had to go out into the world, travel around on foot, and commend himself and his mission to all and sundry.   In 1741 he was sent out from St
Antony's at Buoncammino to quest for alms, and that proved to be the chief external
occupation of the remaining forty years of his life.   It is easy enough to dress up
a " begging son of St Francis " in a spurious romanticism : the reality is rather
different.   You are liable to have the door slammed in your face, to be assailed with

abuse; you are at the mercy of the weather and the miles no less than of the moods and whims of men and women. Brother Ignatius made of this humbling task a real apostolate: he was consulted by those in difficulties, he visited the sick and reproved sinners and taught the ignorant, enemies were reconciled, he took back alms to support his brethren, and God was glorified. For people loved Brother Ignatius. And outstandingly children loved him and he loved them. More than one happy mother claimed that her barrenness had been taken away through the prayers of Ignatius of Laconi.

A Capuchiness, who well remembered him coming to her home when she was seven years old, recorded that St Ignatius was of medium height, with slight features, his hair and beard white. He carried a forked stick and was upright in his gait, easy in manner, and " gentle and caressing with children ". His simplicity was truly Franciscan, and the measuredness of his speech reflected the serene calm of his mind. His daily activity was sufficiently trying, but the solitude he lacked then he found at night, when contemplation of divine things often reduced sleep to a few hours, and that on a shake-down bed with a log for pillow.

There is the testimony of an onlooker, Brother Francis Mary of Iglesias, for St Ignatius being lifted from the ground in prayer, and the account bears the stamp of accuracy: " Then it was time for the night office ", it ends, " and at the sound of the bell Brother Ignatius slowly moved down to the ground and went into choir with the others." Numerous marvels are attributed to him, and attested in the process of beatification. Many of them were cures of ill-health, so much so that Father Emmanuel of Iglesias and others said that Brother Ignatius seemed to be the general medical practitioner of the whole neighbourhood, and the laybrother had often to protest that " I am not a doctor. What can I do ? " What he did was to recommend some simple remedy, to exhort to trust in God, or to pray, " If it be God's will, may you be healed ".

There was in Cagliari a rich and unscrupulous money-lender, named Franchino, at whose house St Ignatius deliberately never called in his quest for alms. Regarding this as a public slight, Franchino complained to the father guardian of St Antony's, who, not knowing the reason for the omission, told Brother Ignatius to remedy it. He obeyed without argument, and came back from Franchino's house with a sack full of food. This he brought to the guardian and poured out at his feet—when it was seen to be dripping with blood. " What is the meaning of this ? " asked the guardian in astonishment. " Father guardian ", explained Brother Ignatius " this is the blood of the poor. And that is why I ask for nothing from that house."

From the early spring of 1781, when he was in his eightieth year, the health of St Ignatius began seriously to fail, and he visited his beloved sister Mary Agnes, a Poor Clare, telling her it was the last time they would meet on earth. He took to his bed, and on May 11, at the hour of our Lord's agony on the cross, he put his hands together, murmured, " It is the Agony ! " and died. St Ignatius of Laconi was canonized in 1951.

A *Vita del Ven. Fra Ignazio da Laconi*, by F. Sequi, was published at Cagliari in 1870. Another, by Father G. de Dominicis, in 1929, was based on documents of the process and local research. Another, by R. Branca, appeared at Turin in 1932. The official biography, published in 1940, was written by Father Samuel of Chiaramonte and gathers in a convenient form all that is of general interest about St Ignatius ; but the work is somewhat verbose, spun out and repetitive for English taste. A German Protestant minister, Joseph Fues, who was in Sardinia in 1773–76, published a series of descriptive letters (Leipzig,

1780) which contain very valuable contemporary information about Ignatius ; they were translated into Italian in 1899. A life in French by Father Majella was published in Belgium in 1946.

12 : SS. NEREUS, ACHILLEUS AND DOMITILLA, MARTYRS (FIRST CENTURY ?)

THE *cultus* of SS. Nereus and Achilleus is very ancient, going back, we may say with certainty, to the fourth century. It was on the occasion of their festival, which was observed with some solemnity in Rome two hundred years later, that St Gregory the Great delivered his twenty-eighth homily. " These saints, before whom we are assembled ", he says, " despised the world and trampled it under their feet when peace, riches and health gave it charms." The church in which he spoke was built over their tomb in the cemetery of Domitilla, on the Via Ardeatina. A new church was built by Leo III about the year 800 and this lay in ruins when Baronius, who derived from it his title as cardinal, rebuilt it and restored to it the relics of SS. Nereus and Achilleus which had been removed to the church of St Adrian.

Nereus and Achilleus were pretorian soldiers—as we know from the inscription Pope St Damasus placed on their tomb—but their legendary " acts " suppose them to have been attached as eunuchs to the household of Flavia Domitilla and to have shared her banishment. Of this lady, who was the great-niece of the Emperor Domitian,* Eusebius writes : " In the fifteenth year of Domitian, for professing Christ, Flavia Domitilla, the niece of Flavius Clemens, one of the consuls of Rome at that time, was transported with many others to the island of Pontia ", *i.e.* Ponza. St Jerome describes her banishment as one long martyrdom. Nerva and Trajan were perhaps unwilling to restore the relations of Domitian when they recalled the other exiles. The " acts " report that Nereus, Achilleus and Domitilla were removed to the island of Terracina, where the first two were beheaded during the reign of Trajan, whilst Domitilla was burnt because she refused to sacrifice to idols. This story probably found its starting-point in the fact that the bodies of the two former martyrs were buried in a family vault, which burying-place later became known as the cemetery of Domitilla. The excavations of de Rossi in that catacomb in 1874 resulted in the discovery of their empty tomb in the underground church constructed by Pope St Siricius in 390.

All, therefore, that we can with any confidence affirm regarding SS. Nereus and Achilleus is what we can gather from the inscription which Pope Damasus wrote in their honour towards the close of the fourth century. The text is known from the reports of travellers who read it when the slab was still entire, but the broken fragments which de Rossi found in his excavation of the cemetery of Domitilla in the last century are sufficient to identify it beyond possible doubt. Its terms run as follows, in English : " The martyrs Nereus and Achilleus had enrolled themselves in the army and exercised the cruel office of carrying out the orders of the

---

* The opinion now more generally accepted holds that there were two Christian women who bore the name of Flavia Domitilla. The elder was the daughter of a sister of Domitian and Titus, and she, as the wife of Flavius Clemens, was banished to the island of Pandatania. We learn this from Dion Cassius. The second Domitilla was a niece by marriage of the first, and it is she who was banished to Ponza, a fate which St Jerome seems to regard as equivalent to martyrdom.

tyrant, being ever ready through the constraint of fear to obey his will.   O miracle of faith ! Suddenly they cease from their fury, they become converted, they fly from the camp of their wicked leader ; they throw away their shields, their armour and their blood-stained javelins.   Confessing the faith of Christ, they rejoice to bear testimony to its triumph.   Learn now from the words of Damasus what great things the glory of Christ can accomplish."

The legendary story of Nereus and Achilleus, and the discovery of the cemetery of Domitilla with which it is connected, have given rise to a considerable literature.   The " acts ", printed in the *Acta Sanctorum*, May, vol. iii, have been since edited or commented upon by such scholars as Wirth (1890) ; Achelis, in *Texte und Untersuchungen*, vol. xi, pt. 2 (1892) ; Schaefer, in the *Römische Quartalschrift*, vol. viii (1894), pp. 89–119 ; P. Franchi de' Cavalieri, in *Note Agiografiche*, no. 3 (1909), etc.   *Cf.* also J. P. Kirsch, *Die römischen Titelkirchen* (1918), pp. 90–94 ; Huelsen, *Le Chiese di Roma nel medio evo*, pp. 388–389, etc., and CMH., p. 249.   Abundant references to the archaeological literature devoted to the cemetery of Domitilla will be found in Leclercq's article in DAC., vol. iv (1921), cc. 1409–1443.

ST PANCRAS, Martyr   (A.D. 304 ?)

WE have no reliable information concerning St Pancras, whose martyrdom is celebrated on this day.   The story, as it is usually told, is based upon his so-called " acts " which were fabricated long after his death and contain serious anachronisms.   He is supposed to have been a Syrian or Phrygian orphan who was brought by an uncle to Rome, where both were converted to Christianity.   Pancras was, it is said, in his fourteenth year when he was beheaded for the faith under Diocletian.   He was buried in the cemetery of Calepodius, which afterwards took his name, and about the year 500 a basilica was built or rebuilt over his tomb by Pope Symmachus.   St Augustine dedicated in his honour the first church he erected in Canterbury and some fifty years later Pope St Vitalian sent to Oswy, king of Northumberland, a portion of the martyr's relics, the distribution of which seems to have propagated his *cultus* in England.   St Gregory of Tours, who called St Pancras " the avenger of perjuries ", asserted that God, by a perpetual miracle, visibly punished false oaths made in the presence of his relics.

Pancras's tomb in Rome was near the second milestone along the Via Auralia, and the church of Pope Symmachus was very handsomely restored by Pope Honorius (625–638) ; the inscription commemorating the fact is known to us. Pope St Gregory the Great had previously built a monastery for Benedictines under his invocation, and it seems likely that the dedication of the church erected by St Augustine at Canterbury may have been suggested by a remembrance of the Roman community in which he had lived.   Another well-known cemetery that bore his name was that in London, where many penal-times Catholics were buried ; its church gave its name to the district and so to the railway station.

The " acts ", which exist both in Latin and in Greek and in more than one recension, may be read in the *Acta Sanctorum*, May, vol. iii.   They are discussed with the Greek text by P. Franchi de' Cavalieri in *Studi e Testi*, vol. xix, pp. 77–120.   See also *Analecta Bollandiana*, vol. lx, pp. 258–261.

ST EPIPHANIUS, Bishop of Salamis   (A.D. 403)

ST EPIPHANIUS was born at Besanduk, a village near Eleutheropolis in Palestine, about the year 310.   In order to qualify himself for the study of the Holy Scriptures he acquired in his youth a knowledge of Hebrew, Coptic, Syriac, Greek and Latin.

Frequent interviews with solitaries, whom he used to visit, gave him a strong inclination to the religious life, which he embraced very young. Even if, as one of his biographers asserts, he made his first essay of monasticism in Palestine, it is certain that he soon went to Egypt to perfect himself in ascetical discipline by staying with one or more of the desert communities. He returned to Palestine about the year 333, was ordained priest and built at Eleutheropolis a monastery, of which he became superior. The mortifications he practised seemed to some of his disciples to overtax his strength, but in answer to their expostulations he would say, " God gives not the kingdom of Heaven except on condition that we labour : and all we can do bears no proportion to the crown we are striving for ". To his bodily austerities he added an indefatigable application to prayer and study, and most of the books then current passed through his hands. In the course of his reading he was shocked by the errors he detected in the writings of Origen. His reaction was violent, and he ever afterwards regarded Origen as the fountain-head of all the heresies that were afflicting the Church.

Epiphanius in his monastery came to be regarded as the oracle of Palestine and the neighbouring countries ; it was asserted that no one ever visited him without receiving spiritual comfort. Indeed, his reputation spread to more distant lands, and in the year 367 he was chosen bishop of Salamis, or Constantia as it was then called, in Cyprus. He continued, however, to govern his community at Eleutheropolis which he visited from time to time. His charity to the poor is described as boundless and many persons made him the dispenser of their alms. The widow St Olympias bestowed upon him a valuable gift of land and money for that purpose. The veneration which all men had for his sanctity exempted him from the persecution of the Arian Emperor Valens ; and he was almost the only orthodox bishop on the eastern shores of the Mediterranean who was not molested during that reign. In 376 he undertook a journey to Antioch in a vain endeavour to convert Vitalis, the Apollinarist bishop ; and six years later he accompanied St Paulinus of Antioch to Rome, where they attended a council summoned by Pope Damasus. They stayed in the house of St Jerome's friend, the widow St Paula, whom St Epiphanius was able to entertain in Cyprus three years afterwards, when she was on her way to Palestine to rejoin her spiritual father.

Saint though he was, the bishop was a violent partisan and his prejudices led him, as an old man, to take action in ways which were—to say the least—regrettable. Thus, after having stayed as an honoured guest with John, bishop of Jerusalem, he had the bad taste to preach a sermon in the metropolitan church, attacking his host, whom he suspected of sympathy with Origenism. Then, having withdrawn to Bethlehem, he proceeded to commit the ecclesiastical offence of ordaining, in a diocese not his own, Paulinian, the brother of St Jerome. The complaints of the bishop and the scandal caused obliged him to take the newly-ordained priest back with him to exercise his ministry in Cyprus. On another occasion, being incensed at the sight of a picture of our Lord or of a saint on the curtain over the door of a village church, he tore it to pieces, recommending that it should be used as a shroud. It is true that he subsequently replaced the curtain by another, but we are not told what the villagers thought of the exchange. Finally, he allowed himself to be used as a tool by the unscrupulous Theophilus of Alexandria, and to appear in his stead at Constantinople to impeach the four " Tall Brothers ", who had escaped from the persecution of Theophilus and had appealed to the emperor. Epiphanius, on his arrival, refused the proffered hospitality of St John Chrysostom because he had protected the fugitive monks, but when he was brought face to face with the Tall Brothers and asked to state his charges against them, he was obliged to make the humiliating admission that he had read none of their books and knew nothing whatever of their doctrines ! In a somewhat chastened spirit he set out shortly afterwards to return to Salamis, but he died on the voyage home.

The fame of St Epiphanius rests chiefly upon his writings, the principal of which are the *Anchoratus*, a treatise designed to confirm unsettled minds in the true faith ; the *Panarium*, or medicine-chest against all heresies ; the Book of Weights and Measures, which depicts many ancient Jewish customs and measures ; and an essay on the precious stones set in the breastplate of the Jewish high priest. These works, which were formerly much esteemed, show the writer to have amassed a vast amount of information, but today he seems to be regrettably lacking in judgement and the gift of clear exposition. Well might St Jerome describe him as " a last relic of ancient piety ! "

The so-called biography of St Epiphanius attributed to a supposed Bishop Polybius is historically worthless and has not been printed in the account given of the saint in the *Acta Sanctorum*, May, vol. iii. For our knowledge of his life we have to go to the church historians, such as Sozomen, and the controversialists who occupied themselves with the writings of Origen and with the history of St John Chrysostom. A critical edition of the works of Epiphanius, for which the Prussian Academy of Sciences took the responsibility, makes but slow progress. For more detailed information regarding the saint's life and writings, see DTC., vol. v (1913), cc. 363–365 ; Bardenhewer, *Geschichte der altkirchlichen Literatur*, vol. iii, pp. 293–302 ; and P. Maas in the *Byzantinische Zeitschrift*, vol. 30 (1930), pp. 279–286. There is an excellent article in DCB., vol. ii, pp. 149–156, by R. A. Lipsius.

ST MODOALDUS, Bishop of Trier (c. A.D. 640)

AQUITAINE was the birthplace of the holy bishop St Modoaldus, who is also known as Modowaldus and Romoaldus. He seems to have belonged to a family of high rank which was prolific in saints, for one of his sisters was the abbess St Severa and the other was Bd Iduberga, wife of Pepin of Landen and mother of St Gertrude of Nivelles. Modoaldus came to be frequently received at the court of King Dagobert, where he met St Arnulf of Metz and St Cunibert of Cologne, with whom he formed a close friendship. Dagobert esteemed the young ecclesiastic so highly that he nominated him to the see of Trier (Trèves), but this mark of favour did not prevent the saint from constantly remonstrating with his royal patron for his personal licentiousness and the loose morals of his court. In the course of time his strictures touched the king's heart : he became sincerely penitent and tried to make amends for the past. Not only did he take St Modoaldus as his spiritual father and adviser, but he also gave him grants of land and money with which to make religious foundations. Few incidents in the life of St Modoaldus have come down to us, and even the dates of his consecration and death are doubtful. However, he was certainly present at the Council of Rheims in 625. He ordained the martyr St Germanus of Grandval, whom he had brought up, and gave hospitality to St Desiderius of Cahors, as may be gathered from the letter of thanks afterwards written to him by his guest. St Modoaldus died after an episcopate which the Bollandists conjecture to have extended approximately from 622 to 640.

The very sketchy biography of St Modoaldus, written more than 400 years after his death by Abbot Stephen of Liège, is of no particular historical value. It is printed with the usual introduction and commentary in the *Acta Sanctorum*, May, vol. iii.

ST RICTRUDIS, WIDOW   (A.D. 688)

THE family of St Rictrudis was one of the most illustrious in Gascony, and her parents were devout as well as wealthy.   In her father's house when she was a young girl Rictrudis met one who was to be her director for a great part of her life. This was St Amandus, then an exile from the territory of King Dagobert, whose licentious conduct he had condemned ; the prelate was evangelizing the Gascons, many of whom were still pagans.   Later on there arrived another distinguished visitor in the person of St Adalbald, a young French nobleman in great favour with King Clovis.   He obtained from his hosts the hand of Rictrudis in spite of the opposition of relations who viewed with disfavour any alliance with a Frank.   The home to which Adalbald took his bride was Ostrevant in Flanders, and there four children were born to them— Mauront, Eusebia, Clotsind and Adalsind, all of whom, like their parents, were destined to be honoured in later times as saints. After his return from exile St Amandus would come now and then to stay with this remarkable family, whose holy and happy life is described in glowing terms by the tenth-century compiler of the life of St Rictrudis.   She had been married sixteen years when Adalbald, on a visit to Gascony, was murdered by some of her relations who had never forgiven him for his successful wooing.   The blow was a terrible one to St Rictrudis.   She told St Amandus that she wished to retire into a convent, but he advised her to wait until her son was old enough to take up his residence at court.   This delay entailed on her a severe trial in later years, when King Clovis II suddenly made up his mind to give her in marriage to one of his favourites, for she was still attractive and very wealthy.   The king's commands in such cases were law, and Rictrudis pleaded with him in vain.   Eventually, however, St Amandus persuaded the monarch to allow her to follow her vocation, and Rictrudis joyfully set out for Marchiennes, where she had founded a double monastery, for men and women.   There she received the veil from St Amandus.   Her two younger daughters, Adalsind and Clotsind, accompanied her, but Eusebia remained with her paternal grandmother, St Gertrude, at Hamage.   After a few years at court Mauront decided that he too wished to abandon the world and it was at Marchiennes, in his mother's presence, that he received the tonsure.   Adalsind died young, but Clotsind lived to become abbess ot Marchiennes when St Rictrudis passed to her reward at the age of seventy-six.

The life of St Rictrudis, which was written by Hucbald of Elnone in 907, seems to represent a sincere attempt to arrive at historical truth, however greatly the biographer was hampered by the lack of materials, most of which are said to have perished when Marchiennes was raided and burnt by the Normans in 881.   See the admirable discussion of the subject by L. Van der Essen in the *Revue d'Histoire ecclésiastique*, vol. xix (1923), especially pp. 543–550 ; and in the same author's *Étude critique . . . des Saints mérovingiens* (1907), pp. 260–267.   Hucbald's life, with other materials, may be read in the *Acta Sanctorum*, May, vol. iii.   W. Levison, in MGH., *Scriptores Merov.*, vol. vi, has only re-edited the prologue. St Rictrudis is sometimes confused with St Rotrudis, a saint venerated at Saint-Bertin and Saint-Omer, about whose life nothing at all is known.

ST GERMANUS, PATRIARCH OF CONSTANTINOPLE   (A.D. 732)

ST GERMANUS was the son of a senator of Constantinople, was educated for the priesthood, and was for some time attached to the metropolitan church ; but after his father's death, at a date which is not recorded, he was appointed bishop of Cyzicus.   Nicephorus and Theophanes assert that he countenanced the attempts made by the Emperor Philippicus to spread the monothelite heresy ; this, however, seems inconsistent with the bishop's subsequent unflinching defence of orthodoxy, and the encomium passed upon him by the second oecumenical Council of Nicaea in 787.   Under Anastasius II Germanus was translated from Cyzicus to the see of Constantinople.   Within a year of his accession he called a synod of 100 bishops at which the true doctrine of the Church was asserted against the monothelite heresy.

After Leo the Isaurian had ascended the imperial throne in 717, St Germanus crowned him in the church of the Holy Wisdom, and the emperor solemnly swore to preserve the Catholic faith.   Ten years later, when Leo declared himself in sympathy with the iconoclasts and set himself against the veneration of images, St Germanus reminded him of the vow he had made.   In spite of this remonstrance, the emperor issued an edict prohibiting the outward display of reverence to religious statues and pictures, all of which were to be raised to a height which precluded the public from kissing them.   A later and still more drastic decree ordered the general destruction of sacred images and the whitewashing of church walls.   The patriarch, though a very old man, spoke out fearlessly in defence of images and wrote letters upholding the Catholic tradition to bishops inclined to favour the iconoclasts.   In one of these, to Thomas of Claudiopolis, he says : " Pictures are history in figure and tend to the sole glory of the heavenly Father.   When we show reverence to representations of Jesus Christ we do not worship the colours laid upon the wood : we are venerating the invisible God who is in the bosom of the Father : Him we worship in spirit and in truth."   In reply to an epistle he addressed to Pope St Gregory II, St Germanus received an answer, still preserved to us, in which the pope expresses his deep appreciation of the patriarch's vindication of Catholic doctrine and tradition.

Over and over again did Leo attempt to win over the aged prelate, but finally, in 730, realizing that his efforts remained fruitless, he practically compelled St Germanus to relinquish his office.   The saint then retired to his paternal home, where he spent the remainder of his life in monastic seclusion, preparing for his death which took place when he was over ninety.   Of his writings, the greater part of which have perished, the best known was an apology for St Gregory of Nyssa against the Origenists ; Baronius described them as having kindled a beacon which illuminated the whole Catholic Church.

A medieval life of St Germanus in Greek was edited by A. Papadopoulos Kerameus in 1881, but it is of little value.   The statement, for example, that the patriarch, to escape from the resentment of the Emperor Leo, took refuge in a convent of nuns at Cyzicus, and wearing their habit was quite unrecognizable because he already looked like a wizened old woman, can hardly be credited, especially in view of the oriental insistence on episcopal beards.   Our surest source of information is to be found in such letters of the period as have been preserved, and in the proceedings of the councils.   There is an excellent article on St Germanus in DTC., vol. vi (1920), cc. 1300–1309 ; to this a full bibliography is appended, as also in Bardenhewer, *Geschichte der altkirchlichen Literatur*, vol. v, pp. 48–51. See also Hefele-Leclercq, *Histoire des Conciles*, vol. iii, pp. 599 *seq.*

ST DOMINIC OF THE CAUSEWAY   (*c.* A.D. 1109)

ST DOMINIC DE LA CALZADA, " of the Causeway ", was so called from the road which he made for pilgrims on their way to Compostela.   He was a native of Villoria in the Spanish Basque country, and as a young man had made several unsuccessful attempts to become a Benedictine, his uncouth appearance and his ignorance causing him to be rejected wherever he applied.   He then went to live as a solitary in a hermitage of his own construction, surrounded by a garden which he cultivated. When St Gregory of Ostia came to preach in north-eastern Spain, Dominic attached himself to him, and remained with him until St Gregory's death.   Bereft of his master, Dominic was again cast upon his own resources.   Not far from his former hermitage lay the wilderness of Bureba through which many of the pilgrims had to pass to reach the shrine of St James.   It was virgin forest and was dangerous not only because no proper road traversed it, but also because the undergrowth and trees afforded a lurking place for bandits.   Here Dominic took up his abode. Having built himself a cabin and an oratory, he set about felling trees and building a good road.   So successful were his efforts that settlers began to gather round him ; with their help he was able to construct also a hospice and a bridge.   He died about the year 1109, and his grave, which he had made himself, became famous for miracles.   The town of S. Domingo de la Calzada which grew up round his shrine was at one time important enough to be the seat of a bishopric, now transferred to Calahorra.

The account in the *Acta Sanctorum*, May, vol. iii, is derived mainly from a set of breviary lessons and from a life compiled by Louis de la Vega in 1606.   See also the *Encyclopedia Europeo-Americana*, vol. xviii, p. 1846.

BD FRANCIS PATRIZZI   (A.D. 1328)

AMONG the holy men who have shed lustre on the Servite Order not the least notable was Bd Francis Arrighetto, descended from a branch of a noble Sienese family, the Patrizzi, by which last name he is more commonly known.   He was drawn to God while still a boy on listening to a sermon preached by the Dominican Bd Ambrose Sansedoni.   Francis had a great desire to hide himself in some desert place, but he knew that duty required him to remain with his mother, who was a widow and blind.   After her death he, at the age of twenty-two, was received into the Order of Servants of Mary by St Philip Benizi, and became in a short time famous as a missioner and preacher.   His confessional was crowded, and popularity seems to have caused some jealousy and criticism amongst his brethren.   Sensitive and perplexed, for fear he was giving scandal, he besought the guidance of our Blessed Lady, and was thereupon afflicted with sudden deafness.   This infirmity was not permanent, but he took it as a sign that it was by the use of his tongue and not of his ears that God wished to be served.   He had a wonderful gift for preaching moving sermons with little or no preparation, and he was indefatigable in exercising it.   Though relentless in inflicting pain upon his body by taking the discipline and in other ways, he held that it was a mistake to starve himself : he needed all his strength to do the work committed to him.   He foresaw that he would die on the feast of the Ascension, 1328, but he went out to preach on that day as he had been asked to do ; he collapsed by the roadside as he went.   The touching story of his end is told by his biographer in great detail.   His whole life was spent in Siena, where he is still venerated.   The *cultus* was approved in 1743.

All that is likely to be known concerning Bd Francis may be read in the text and annotations of the life edited in the *Analecta Bollandiana*, vol. xiv (1895), pp. 167–197, by Father Soulier, o.s.m.   The author of this biography was Father Christopher de Palma, a contemporary.

BD GEMMA OF SOLMONA, Virgin (A.D. 1429)

Solmona in the Abruzzi, which was Ovid's native place, has also given birth to a very different type of character in the person of Bd Gemma, a holy recluse who lived and died there, whose relics are still venerated in the church of St John. Gemma's parents were peasants who encouraged their little girl's precocious piety and set her to mind the sheep—an occupation which gave her ample leisure for prayer and contemplation. According to tradition, when she was twelve years old, her beauty attracted the notice of a local count called Roger, who sent his servants to kidnap her. Brought into his presence, God lent a marvellous power to her words, and she succeeded in so greatly impressing him that he undertook to build her a hermitage. Whatever truth there may be in that story, it is clearly established that she lived a holy life for forty-two years in a cell adjoining the church. The *cultus* which continued uninterrupted after her death was formally approved in 1890.

A short notice of this *beata* will be found in the *Acta Sanctorum*, May, vol. iii. The decree, which amounts to an equivalent beatification, may be read in the *Acta Sanctae Sedis*, vol. xxiii (1890), p. 48. A little book about Gemma was published by B. Silvestri at Prato in 1896.

BD JANE OF PORTUGAL, Virgin (A.D. 1490)

Bd Jane of Portugal came into the world heiress to the throne of her father, Alphonsus V, and although a brother was born three years later the boy's delicacy, and the untimely death of the children's mother, Elizabeth of Coïmbra, made it seem not unlikely that the young princess would eventually become queen ; and no pains were spared to fit her for the high position she might be called on to fill. Nevertheless, from childhood Jane took little pleasure in earthly things, caring only for what concerned the service of God. Unknown to all but two or three members of her suite, she wore a hair-shirt, used the discipline and spent hours of the night in prayer. When, at the age of sixteen, she found that her father was making plans for her marriage she asked him to permit her to embrace the religious life, but was met by a point-blank refusal. Alphonsus did not, however, for the moment, press her to marry and allowed her to lead a secluded life in the palace.

In 1471 King Alphonsus and Prince John started on a punitive expedition against the African Moors, leaving Jane, then nineteen years of age, as regent. The campaign was successful : and in the midst of the public rejoicings which followed their return, the princess again asked permission to retire into a convent. She obtained from her father a conditional consent, and, though it was for a time suspended owing to the objections of Prince John, Bd Jane, the moment she felt secure, took prompt action. She distributed her personal effects and set out for the Bernardine convent of Odivellas, on her way to her ultimate objective, the Dominican priory of Aveiro. Jane entered the priory on August 4, 1472, but she was not allowed by her family to take vows, or to give up control of her property. For a long time she did not even dare to receive the habit. Nevertheless, as far as she could, she led the life of a simple sister, always seeking to perform the most lowly tasks. Her income she devoted to charity, especially to redeeming captives. Her peace was repeatedly disturbed by her relations, who could never resign themselves to her refusing the marriages which continued to be suggested for her : Maximilian, king of the Romans, and Richard III, king of England, are said to have been amongst the suitors.   Moreover, Jane's family seem to have been genuinely concerned about her health, and they insisted upon making her leave Aveiro—never a salubrious place—when the plague was raging there.   She died at the age of thirty-eight, of a fever supposed to have been contracted from contaminated or poisoned water given to her on her way home after a visit to court, by a woman of position whom she had banished from the town of Aveiro because of her scandalous life.   The *cultus* of Bd Jane was authorized in 1693.

The most authentic account of the life of Bd Jane is that by Margaret Pineria, who had been one of her ladies-in-waiting.   It was written in Portuguese, but in the *Acta Sanctorum*, May, vol. vii, it is accessible in a Latin translation.   See also a popular French life, by de Belloc, with a number of engravings (1897) ; M. C. de Ganay, *Les Bienheureuses Dominicaines* (1913), pp. 279–304 ; and a brief sketch in J. Procter, *Lives of Dominican Saints*, pp. 122–126.

BD JOHN STONE, Martyr   (A.D. 1539 ?)

John Stone's portrait and name are found in the old engravings representing the English martyrs as formerly depicted on the walls of the church of St Thomas in the English College at Rome ; but beyond the fact that he was an Austin friar, a doctor of theology, and that he died a martyr little is known about him.   It was in all probability to him that Bishop Ingworth, the king's sequestrator, referred in a letter to Cromwell in December 1538, when he complained of the insolence of one of the Austin friars at Canterbury, who " still held and still desired to die for it, that the King may not be head of the Church of England ".   In his *Dialogi sex . . .* (1566) Nicholas Harpsfield, archdeacon of Canterbury, states that Stone, after he had prayed and fasted for three days in prison, " heard a voice, though he saw nobody, which addressed him by name, and admonished him to be brave of heart and not to hesitate with constancy to suffer death for that belief which he had professed ".   " These things I learned from a serious and trustworthy man, who is even now living, to whom Stone himself related them."

It was formerly supposed that Bd John suffered on May 12, 1538, and on this date the Augustinian friars keep his feast ; but both Ingworth's letter and the account-book of the city chamberlain of Canterbury seem to imply that he was still alive at December 14, 1538.   The account-book notes the expenses of " ffryer Stone's " execution, fifteen items, including " for a Halter to hang hym . . . 1d ".

In the Catholic Record Society's publications, vol. 45 (1950), Fr L. E. Whatmore prints a translation of the passage from Harpsfield, a corrected transcription from the Canterbury account-book, and other things bearing on John Stone, with references and comments.

13: ST ROBERT BELLARMINE, Archbishop of Capua and Cardinal, Doctor of the Church   (A.D. 1621)

ONE of the greatest polemical theologians the Church has ever produced, and her foremost controversialist against the doctrines of the Protestant Reformation, was Robert Francis Romulus Bellarmine, whose feast is kept upon this day.   Born in 1542 at Montepulciano in Tuscany, of a noble but impoverished family, he was the son of Vincent Bellarmino and Cynthia Cervini, half-sister to Pope Marcellus II.   Even as a boy Robert showed great promise. He knew Virgil by heart, he wrote good Latin verses, he played the violin, and he could hold his own in public disputations, to the great admiration of his fellow-citizens.   Moreover, he was so deeply devout that in 1559, when Robert was seventeen, the rector of the Jesuit college at Montepulciano described him in a letter as " the best of our school, and not far from the kingdom of Heaven ".   It was his ambition to enter the Society of Jesus, but he had to encounter strong opposition from his father, who had formed other plans for his son.   Robert's mother, however, was on his side, and eventually he obtained the permission he desired.   In 1560 he went to Rome to present himself to the father general of the order, by whom his noviciate was curtailed to enable him to pass almost immediately into the Roman College to enter upon the customary studies.

Ill-health dogged his steps from the cradle to the grave, and his delicacy became so pronounced that, at the close of his three years of philosophy, his superiors sent him to Florence to recruit his strength in his native Tuscan air, whilst at the same time teaching boys and giving lectures on rhetoric and on the Latin poets.   Twelve months afterwards he was transferred to Mondovi in Piedmont.   There he discovered that he was expected to instruct his pupils in Cicero and Demosthenes.   He knew no Greek except the letters of the alphabet, but with characteristic obedience and energy he set to work to study at night the grammar lesson he was expected to give the next day.   Father Bellarmine strongly objected to the flogging of boys, and himself never did so.   In addition to teaching he preached sermons which attracted crowds.   Amongst the congregation on one occasion was his provincial superior, Father Adorno, who promptly transferred him to Padua that he might prepare himself in that famous university town to receive ordination.   Again he studied and preached, but before the completion of his course he was bidden by the father general, St Francis Borgia, to proceed at once to Louvain in Belgium to finish his studies there and to preach to the undergraduates, with a view to counteracting the dangerous doctrines which were being propagated by Dr Michael Baius, the chancellor, and others.   It is interesting to note that on his journey he had as companion for part of the way the Englishman William Allen, afterwards to become like himself a cardinal.   From the time of his arrival at Louvain until his departure seven years later, Robert's sermons were extraordinarily popular, although they were delivered in Latin, and although the preacher had no physical advantages to commend him, for he was small of stature and had to stand on a stool in the pulpit to make himself properly seen and heard.   But men declared that his face shone with a strange light as he spoke and that his words seemed like those of one inspired.

After his ordination at Ghent in 1570, he was given a professorship in the University of Louvain—the first Jesuit to hold such a post—and began a course of lectures on the *Summa* of St Thomas Aquinas, which were at the same time brilliant expositions of doctrine and a vehicle through which he could, and did, controvert the teachings of Baius on such matters as grace, free will and papal authority. In contrast to the controversial brutality of the time he never made personal attacks on his enemies or mentioned them by name.   Not content with the great labour entailed on him by his sermons and lectures, St Robert during his stay at Louvain taught himself Hebrew and embarked upon a thorough study of the Holy Scriptures and of the Fathers.   To assist the studies of others he also made time to write a Hebrew grammar, which became extremely popular.

A serious breakdown in health, however, necessitated his recall to Italy and there, in spite of the efforts of St Charles Borromeo to secure his services for Milan, he was appointed to the recently established chair of controversial theology at the

Roman College. For eleven years, from 1576, he laboured untiringly, giving lectures and preparing the four great volumes of his *Disputations on the Controversies* of the Christian faith which, even three hundred years later, the great ecclesiastical historian Hefele described as " the most complete defence of Catholic teaching yet published ". It showed such profound acquaintance with the Bible, the Fathers, and the heretical writers, that many of his opponents could never bring themselves to believe that it was the work of one man. They even suggested that his name was an anagram covering a syndicate of learned and wily Jesuits. The work was one urgently needed at that particular moment, because the leading Reformers had recently published a series of volumes purporting to show, by an appeal to history, that Protestantism truly represented the Church of the Apostles. As these were published at Magdeburg, and as each volume covered a century, the series became known as the " Centuries of Magdeburg ". The answer which Baronius set out to furnish in the field of history, St Robert Bellarmine supplied in the field of dogmatics. The success of his *Controversies* was instantaneous : laymen and clergy, Catholics and Protestants, read the volumes with avidity, and even in Elizabethan England, where the work was prohibited, a London bookseller declared, " I have made more money out of this Jesuit than out of all the other divines put together ".

In 1589 he was separated for a while from his books to be sent with Cardinal Cajetanus on a diplomatic embassy to France, then in the throes of war between Henry of Navarre and the League. No tangible results came of the mission, but the party had the experience of being in Paris for eight months during the siege, when, to quote St Robert's own words, they " did practically nothing though they suffered a very great deal ". As opposed to Cardinal Cajetanus, who had Spanish sympathies, St Robert was openly in favour of trying to make terms with the king of Navarre if he would become a Catholic, but within a very short time of the raising of the siege the members of the mission were recalled to Rome by the death of Pope Sixtus V. Soon afterwards we find St Robert taking the leading part on a papal commission appointed by Pope Clement VIII to edit and make ready for publication the new revision of the Vulgate Bible, which had been called for by the Council of Trent. An edition had indeed already been completed during the reign of Sixtus V and under that pope's immediate supervision, but it contained many errors due to defective scholarship and to a fear of making important alterations in the current text. Moreover, it was never in general circulation. The revised version, as produced by the commission and issued with the *imprimatur* of Clement VIII, is the Latin Bible as we have it to-day, with a preface composed by St Robert himseli. He was then living at the Roman College, where, as official spiritual director to the house, he had been brought into close contact with St Aloysius Gonzaga, whose death-bed he attended and to whom he was so deeply attached that in his will he asked to be buried at the feet of the youthful saint, " once my dear ghostly child ".

Recognition of Bellarmine's great qualities followed quickly. In 1592 he was made rector of the Roman College ; in 1594 he was made provincial of Naples ; and three years later he returned to Rome in the capacity of theologian to Clement VIII, at whose express desire he wrote his two celebrated catechisms, one of which is still in general use throughout Italy. These catechisms are said to have been translated more frequently than any other literary work except the Bible and the *Imitation of Christ*. In 1598, to his great dismay, he was nominated a cardinal by Clement VIII on the ground that " he had not his equal for learning ". Though obliged to occupy apartments in the Vatican and to keep up some sort of an establishment, he relaxed none of his former austerities. Moreover, he limited his household and expenses to what was barely essential : he lived on bread and garlic —the food of the poor ; and he denied himself a fire even in the depth of winter. Once he ransomed a soldier who had deserted from the army ; and he used the hangings of his rooms to clothe poor people, remarking, " The walls won't catch cold ".

In 1602 he was, somewhat unexpectedly, appointed archbishop of Capua, and within four days of his consecration he left Rome to take up his new charge. Admirable as the holy man appears in every relation of life, it is perhaps as shepherd of his immense flock that he makes the greatest appeal to our sympathy. Laying aside his books, the great scholar, who had no pastoral experience, set about evangelizing his people with all the zeal of a young missionary, whilst initiating the reforms decreed by the Council of Trent. He preached constantly, he made visitations, he exhorted the clergy, he catechized the children, he sought out the necessitous, whose wants he supplied, and he won the love of all classes. He was not destined, however, to remain long away from Rome. Paul V, who was elected pope three years later, at once insisted upon retaining Cardinal Bellarmine by his side, and the archbishop accordingly resigned his see. From that time onwards, as head of the Vatican Library and as a member of almost every congregation, he took a prominent part in all the affairs of the Holy See. When Venice ventured arbitrarily to abrogate the rights of the Church, and was placed under an interdict, St Robert became the pope's great champion in a pamphlet contest with the Republic's theologian, the famous Servite, Fra Paolo Sarpi. A still more important adversary was James I of England. Cardinal Bellarmine had remonstrated with his friend, the Archpriest Blackwell, for taking the oath of allegiance to James—an oath purposely so worded as to deny to the pope all jurisdiction over temporals. King James, who fancied himself as a controversialist, rushed into the fray with two books in defence of the oath, both of which were answered by Cardinal Bellarmine. In the earlier rejoinder, St Robert, writing in the somewhat lighter vein that so became him, made humorous references to the monarch's bad Latin ; but his second treatise was a serious and crushing retort, covering every point in the controversy. Standing out consistently and uncompromisingly as a champion of papal supremacy in all things spiritual, Bellarmine nevertheless held views on temporal authority which were displeasing to extremists of both parties. Because he maintained that the pope's jurisdiction over foreign rulers was indirect, he lost favour with Sixtus V, and because, in opposition to the Scots jurist, Barclay, he denied the divine right of kings, his book, De potestate papae, was publicly burnt by the parlement of Paris.

The saint was on friendly terms with Galileo Galilei, who dedicated to him one of his books. He was called upon, indeed, to admonish the great astronomer in the year 1616, but his admonition, which was accepted with a good grace, amounted to a caution against putting forward, otherwise than as a hypothesis, theories not yet fully proved. Well would it have been for Galileo if he had continued to act in accordance with that advice. It would be impossible in limited space even to enumerate the various activities of St Robert during these later years. He continued to write, but his works were no longer controversial. He completed a commentary on the Psalms and wrote five spiritual books, all of which, including the last, on the Art of Dying, were soon translated into English. When it became clear that his days were drawing to a close, he was allowed to retire to the Jesuit novitiate of St Andrew.   There he died, at the age of seventy-nine, on September 17, 1621—on the day which, at his special request, had been set aside as the feast of the Stigmata of St Francis of Assisi.   St Robert Bellarmine was canonized in 1930, and declared a doctor of the Church in 1931.

It hardly needs saying that the sources of information for such a career are far too copious to be specified in detail.   The mere fact that the beatification was opposed, and in this way retarded, by a certain school of theologians who did not find themselves in harmony with Bellarmine's views, has had the result of multiplying to a quite unusual extent the printed documents connected with the process.   Besides these quasi-official materials and the seventeenth century lives, notably those by Fuligatti (1624) and Daniel Bartoli (1678), it will be sufficient to call attention to the brief autobiography of the saint written in 1613 at the pressing instance of Father Mutius Vitelleschi.   This may most conveniently be consulted in the valuable work of Father Le Bachelet, *Bellarmin avant son Cardinalat* (1911); Le Bachelet supplemented this with another important collection of documents, entitled *Auctarium Bellarminianum* (1913).   For English readers the work which supersedes all others and which is as exhaustive in its range as it is attractive in treatment, is the *Life of Robert Bellarmine*, by Father James Brodrick (2 vols. 1928).   The Congregation of Sacred Rites issued an imposing volume, *De S. Roberto Bellarmino Univ. Eccl. Doctore* (1931), setting out the grounds on which Bellarmine was enrolled among the doctors of the Church; this includes (pp. xxi–xxxii) what is in effect a very full bibliography.   St Bellarmine's Tor in the parish of Cardinham, Cornwall, is a curious modern corruption of St Bartholomew, titular of a neighbouring church.

ST GLYCERIA, Virgin and Martyr   (*c.* A.D. 177)

THE Greek " acts " which are our sole authority for the life of St Glyceria, are unfortunately quite unreliable, and all that can be asserted definitely is that she was a Christian maiden who suffered martyrdom at Heraclea in the Propontis towards the close of the second century.   The legend follows conventional lines : She is said to have been the daughter of a Roman official of senatorial rank living at Trajanopolis in Thrace.   She openly avowed her faith, in the presence of Sabinus the prefect, who caused her to be led to the temple of Jupiter that she might sacrifice.   Instead of doing so, she threw down the statue of the god and broke it. She was hung up by the hair and beaten with iron rods, but sustained no harm. Deprived of food by her jailers in prison, she was fed by an angel.   When placed in a hot oven the fire was promptly extinguished.   Her hair was then dragged out and she was exposed to wild beasts, but she died before they could reach her.   A splendid church was set up to her honour at Heraclea.

In his *Origines du Culte des Martyrs* (pp. 244–245) Delehaye remarks that nothing could be more clearly demonstrated than the early *cultus* of St Glyceria at Heraclea.   The Emperor Maurice visited the shrine in 591 and Heraclius in 610, while there is mention of St Glyceria's tomb as a centre of devotion in the Passion of the Forty Martyrs of Heraclea.   On the other hand the story printed with the Greek text in the *Acta Sanctorum*, May, vol. iii, is, as stated above, no more than a pious fiction.   *Cf.* also the *Byzantinische Zeitschrift*, vol. vi (1897), pp. 96–99.

ST MUCIUS, Martyr   (A.D. 304)

ST MUCIUS, or Mocius, was a Christian priest who suffered at Constantinople during the persecution of Diocletian, and his *cultus* goes back to very early times.   This is all we know for certain about the saint, for his so-called " acts " are undoubtedly spurious.   In them we read that St Mucius was an eloquent Christian preacher at Amphipolis in Macedonia, and that, on the occasion of the feast of Bacchus, he overthrew the deity's altar, casting the votive offerings on the ground. The crowd would have rent him to pieces had not the proconsul interfered to have him arrested. The tribunal which tried him condemned him to be burnt alive, but he walked unscathed in the flames accompanied by three strangers, whilst the prefect and his attendants were consumed by the fire. The martyr was then sent to Heraclea, where he was tortured on the wheel and afterwards exposed to the wild beasts, which refused to touch him. Eventually he was conveyed to Constantinople and there beheaded.

> Delehaye, in the *Analecta Bollandiana*, vol. xxxi (1912), pp. 163–187 and 225–232, devotes considerable space to St Mucius. He first prints the best text of the " acts " together with the panegyric of a certain Michael, and then points out that the obviously fictitious acts do not detract from the historic character of the martyr himself. There undoubtedly was a church dedicated to Mucius in Constantinople at the end of the fourth century, and this may have been built by the Emperor Constantine. Further, it is pretty certain that the martyr is mentioned at about the same date in the ancient Syriac martyrology, though his name, one knows not how, has been transformed into " Maximus ". He is also mentioned in the *Hieronymianum*.

ST SERVATIUS, or SERVAIS, BISHOP OF TONGRES (A.D. 384)

IT is recorded of St Servatius, supposed to be an Armenian by birth, that he gave hospitality to St Athanasius during his banishment, and that he defended the great patriarch's cause and the Catholic faith at the Council of Sardica. After the murder of Constans, the usurper Magnentius sent him and another bishop as envoys to Alexandria to plead his cause with the Emperor Constantius. Nothing came of the embassy, but Servatius was able, while in Egypt, to renew his intercourse with St Athanasius. In the year 359 we find him at the Council of Rimini, valiantly holding out, together with St Phoebadius, Bishop of Agen, against the Arian majority, and equally deceived by the formula there signed, until enlightened by St Hilary of Poitiers.

St Gregory of Tours relates that St Servatius foretold the invasion of Gaul by the Huns, and that he strove to avert the calamity by fasting and prayer and a pilgrimage to Rome. This penitential journey he undertook with the object of commending his flock to the care of the two great apostles. Almost immediately after his return to Tongres he contracted fever and died, either in his episcopal city or, according to some authorities, in Maestricht. That same year Tongres was plundered and partially destroyed in a raid ; it was not, however, till seventy years later, when Attila with his Huns overran and ravaged the country, that the supposed prophecy was completely fulfilled.

The *cultus* of St Servatius was very considerable during the middle ages in the Low Countries, and many legends grew up about him. His relics are preserved in a beautiful ancient reliquary at Maestricht, where his staff, his drinking cup and his silver key are also treasured. According to tradition the key was given to him when in Rome by St Peter in a vision, but it is actually one of the " Claves Confessionis S. Petri ", which popes have from time to time bestowed on those they wished to honour, and which contained filings from the chains of St Peter. The drinking cup, on the other hand, was popularly supposed to have been the gift of an angel and to have the property of healing fever.

> The " acts " of St Servatius, printed in part in the *Acta Sanctorum*, May, vol. iii, are only a compilation of Herigerus, Abbot of Lobbes, in the tenth century. Several older

texts, however, have since been discovered and have been edited in the *Analecta Bollandiana*, vol. i (1882), pp. 88–112, and in G. Kurth, *Deux Biographies de St Servais* (1881). See also G. Kurth, *Nouvelles Recherches sur S. Servais* (1884) ; A. Proost, *Saint Servais* (1891) ; F. Wilhelm (1910), G. Gorris (1923) ; Duchesne, *Fastes Episcopaux*, vol. iii, p. 188 ; and *Analecta Bollandiana*, vol. lv (1937), pp. 117–120.   There has undoubtedly been a very widespread *cultus* of St Servais and the literature is considerable.   On St Peter's keys, *cf.* DAC., vol. iii, c. 1861.

ST JOHN THE SILENT   (A.D. 558)

St John derived the surname by which he is designated from his great love of silence and recollection.* He was born in the year 454, at Nicopolis in Armenia, of a family which had supplied generals and governors for that part of the empire. After the death of his parents he built a monastery in which, at the age of eighteen, he shut himself up with ten companions.   Here, under the direction of their youthful superior, the little community led a most edifying life of devotion and hard work.   The great reputation St John acquired for sanctity and leadership led the archbishop of Sebaste to consecrate him bishop of Colonia in Armenia, much against his will, when he was only twenty-eight.   For nine years he exercised his episcopal functions, zealously instructing his flock, depriving himself of even the necessaries of life that he might relieve the poor, and continuing to practise as far as possible the austerities of his former life.   Then his inability to remedy certain evils, combined with a strong desire for a secluded life, decided him to lay down his charge.   Instead of returning to Armenia he quietly went to Jerusalem—uncertain as to his future vocation.

His biographer assures us that whilst John was watching one night in prayer he saw before him a bright cross in the air and heard a voice which said, " If thou desirest to be saved, follow this light ".   The cross then moved before him, and at length directed him to the laura (monastery) of St Sabas.   Convinced that he now knew God's will, St John immediately betook himself to the laura, which contained one hundred and fifty monks.   He was then thirty-eight years old.   St Sabas at first placed him under the steward to fetch water, carry stone, and serve the workmen in building a new hospital.   John came and went like a beast of burden, remaining ever recollected in God, always cheerful and silent.   After this test, the experienced superior made him guestmaster ; the holy man served everyone as though he were serving Christ Himself.   By this time St Sabas recognized that his novice was on the road to perfection and, in order to give him opportunities for uninterrupted contemplation, he allowed him to occupy a separate hermitage.   During five consecutive days of the week, which he passed fasting, John never left his cell ; but on Saturdays and Sundays he attended public worship in church.   After three years spent in this eremitic life, he was made steward of the laura.   The business which this office entailed was no distraction to him : so great was his love for God that his mind was fixed on Him continually and without effort.

Four years later St Sabas thought him worthy of the priesthood and decided to present him to the Patriarch Elias.   Upon their arrival at the church of Mount Calvary, where the ordination was to take place, John said to the patriarch, " Holy father, I have something to impart to you in private : afterwards, if you judge me suitable, I will receive holy orders ".   The patriarch granted him a private

---

* At least by the first half of the seventh century this name, " Hesychast ", had become a technical term for those who followed a certain spiritual tradition in the East.   John is sometimes called the Sabaïte.

interview, and St John, when he had bound him to secrecy, said, " Father, I have been consecrated bishop : but on account of my many sins I have fled and have sought out this desert to await the coming of the Lord ". Elias was startled, and having summoned St Sabas, declared, " I cannot ordain this man, because of certain particulars he has communicated to me ". St Sabas returned home deeply grieved because he feared that John must have committed some terrible crime, but in answer to his earnest prayer the truth was made known to him by revelation. He was, however, directed not to divulge the secret to others.

In the year 503 the factious spirit of certain turbulent monks obliged St Sabas to leave his laura ; St John at the same time withdrew into a neighbouring desert, where he spent six years. When St Sabas was recalled to his community, St John returned to the laura and there lived in his cell for forty years. Experience had taught him that a soul accustomed to speak to God alone finds only bitterness and emptiness in worldly intercourse. Moreover his love of obscurity and his humility made him desire more than ever to live unknown. Nevertheless the fame of his sanctity made it impossible for him to realize his ambition, and he now no longer refused to see those who resorted to him for advice. Amongst these was Cyril of Scythopolis, who wrote the saint's life when he had reached the great age of 104, whilst still preserving the vigour of mind which had always characterized him. Cyril relates that he himself in early manhood had consulted the hermit as to his choice of a career. St John advised him to enter the monastery of St Euthymius. Instead, Cyril went to a small monastery on the bank of the Jordan. There he at once contracted a fever of which he nearly died. But St John appeared to him in his sleep and, after a gentle reprimand, told him that if he repaired at once to St Euthymius he would regain his health and win God's favour. The next morning, he set out for the aforesaid monastery, and found that he had entirely recovered. The same author also describes how, in his presence, St John exorcized an evil spirit from a child by making on its forehead the sign of the cross with oil. Both by example and precept St John led many souls to God, and continued in his hermitage to emulate, as far as this mortal state will allow, the glorious employment of the heavenly spirits in an uninterrupted exercise of love and praise. He passed to their blessed company in A.D. 558—having lived in solitude for seventy-six years, interrupted only by the nine years of his episcopate.

Cyril of Scythopolis, the biographer from whom we derive all our knowledge of St John, seems to have entered the monastery of St Euthymius in 544 and to have passed on to the laura at Jerusalem in 554. Though credulous, like all men of his generation, delighting in marvels, he was a conscientious reporter of what he believed to be the truth. The biography he wrote is printed in the *Acta Sanctorum*, May, vol. iii. See also Ehrhard in the *Römische Quartalschrift*, vol. vii (1893), pp. 32 *seq.* ; and the text of Cyril in E. Schwartz, *Kyrillos von Skythopolis* (1939).

ST ERCONWALD, BISHOP OF LONDON (c. A.D. 686)

ST ERCONWALD is said to have been the son of the East Anglian prince Anna. He left his own country for the kingdom of the East Saxons, where he spent his fortune in founding two monasteries, the one for men at Chertsey in Surrey, and the other for women at Barking in Essex. Over the latter he set his sister St Ethelburga, and over the former he himself ruled as abbot until 675, when St Theodore consecrated him bishop of London. During the eleven years that he presided over the see, he did much to increase the buildings and repute of St Paul's, his cathedral church.

Bede says that God honoured Erconwald with miracles, and that even in his own day healing properties were attributed to the litter in which the holy bishop had been carried when he was ill. His feast is still observed in the dioceses of Westminster, Brentwood and (on May 11) Southwark.

Our most reliable authority is Bede, *Eccl. History*, iv, 6 ; but some further information may be gleaned from charters and other sources. See DCB., vol. ii, pp. 177–179 ; DNB., vol. xvii, p. 390 ; and Stanton's *Menology*, pp. 187 and 189, and supplement.

ST EUTHYMIUS THE ENLIGHTENER, ABBOT   (A.D. 1028)

THIS Euthymius was the son of that St John the Iberian who is noticed herein on July 12. As there narrated, Euthymius accompanied his father on his retirement to Mount Athos, and helped him in the foundation there of the famous monastery Iviron for monks from their native Iberia (Georgia).* On the death of John about the year 1002, Euthymius succeeded him as abbot.

Under his care Iviron grew and prospered, attracting recruits from Palestine and Armenia as well as Iberia, and Euthymius had to weed out a considerable number of wealthy young men whose idea of the monastic life was that it was one of elegant retirement and repose. The biography of himself and his father, written by the hieromonk George the Hagiorite about 1040, devotes a good deal of space to common-form eulogy of the virtues of these holy men, but a reasonably living picture of St Euthymius nevertheless emerges. He appears as a firm but not severe superior, who directed more by example than by precept and who knew the importance of keeping an eye on details. Remarkably enough for those days and a wine-drinking country, he was what is now called a teetotaller ; but he was none the less careful that the wine ration, which each monk had with his dinner as a matter of course, should be of good quality and not unduly watered. Another practical point was that beardless youths should not be employed as workmen around the monastery : " I know that grown men must be paid higher wages, but it is better to spend more money than to expose our brethren to possible harm ".

The work of predilection of St Euthymius was the translation of sacred books from Greek into Iberian, and George the Hagiorite names over sixty for which the Iberian church was indebted to him. Among them were biblical commentaries, writings of St Basil, St Gregory of Nyssa, St Ephrem and St John Damascene, the *Institutes* of St John Cassian, and the *Dialogues* of Pope St Gregory the Great. One of his translations, from Iberian into Greek this time, has an interest for hagiology : this was the so-called *History of Saints Barlaam and Josaphat* (Joasaph), imaginary people whose names Cardinal Baronius unfortunately added to the Roman Martyrology (November 27). Naturally enough, St Euthymius found that his duties as abbot seriously interfered with his work of translation, and after he had directed Iviron for fourteen years he resigned his charge, on the plea that the church of his people was crying out for more books that only he could efficiently supply.

Unfortunately his successor in the abbacy precipitated disturbances between Iberians and Greeks among the monks, and St Euthymius was summoned to Constantinople by the Emperor Constantine VIII to explain the situation. While there he was thrown from his mule and sustained injuries from which he died,

* The homeland of Joseph Stalin, *vere* Yugashvili, who was born near Tiflis.

on May 13, 1028. His body was taken back to Mount Athos, and eventually enshrined in the church of the All-Holy Mother of God.

For bibliographical notes, see July 12, *loc. cit.* A French translation of the life by George the Hagiorite was published in *Irénikon*, vol. vi, no. 5, vol. vii, nos. 1, 2 and 4 (1929–30). " Hagiorite " (the epithet is also given to St Euthymius's father, St John) means Athonite, Mount Athos being commonly called in Greek *Hagion Oros*, the Holy Mountain. Iviron still exists as a monastery of the Orthodox Church, but Iberian monks have been long ago displaced by Greeks.

BD IMELDA, VIRGIN   (A.D. 1333)

THE patroness of fervent first communion, Bd Imelda, came of one of the oldest families in Bologna : her father was Count Egano Lambertini, and her mother was Castora Galuzzi. Even as a tiny child she showed unusual piety, taking delight in prayer and slipping off to a quiet corner of the house, which she adorned with flowers and pictures to make it into a little oratory. When she was nine she was placed, at her own wish, in the Dominican convent in Val di Pietra, to be trained there by the nuns. Her disposition soon endeared her to all, whilst the zeal with which she entered into all the religious life of the house greatly edified the sisters. Her special devotion was to the eucharistic presence of our Lord at Mass and in the tabernacle. To receive our Lord in holy communion became the consuming desire of her heart, but the custom of the place and time had fixed twelve as the earliest age for a first communion. She would sometimes exclaim : " Tell me, can anyone receive Jesus into his heart and not die ? "

When she was eleven years old she was present with the rest of the community at the Ascension-day Mass. All the others had received their communion : only Imelda was left unsatisfied. The nuns were preparing to leave the church when some of them were startled to see what appeared to be a Sacred Host hovering in the air above Imelda, as she knelt before the closed tabernacle absorbed in prayer. Quickly they attracted the attention of the priest, who hurried forward with a paten on which to receive It. In the face of such a miracle he could not do otherwise than give to Imelda her first communion, which was also her last. For the rapture with which she received her Lord was so great that it broke her heart : she sank unconscious to the ground, and when loving hands upraised her, it was found that she was dead.

The Bollandists in the *Acta Sanctorum*, May, vol. iii, inserted a notice of Bd Imelda on the ground of a long-established *cultus*, though the formal papal confirmation did not occur until 1826. Many devotional booklets—notably those by Lataste (1889), Corsini (1892), Wilms (1925), and T. Alfonsi (1927)—have been published concerning her ; but see more especially M. C. de Ganay, *Les Bienheureuses Dominicaines* (1913), pp. 145–152. There is also a short account in Procter, *Lives of Dominican Saints*, pp. 259–262, and a devotional sketch, R. Zeller, *Imelda Lambertini* (1930).

BD JULIAN OF NORWICH, VIRGIN   (c. A.D. 1423)

APART from the autobiographical details given in the *Revelations of Divine Love*, history has preserved few records of the holy woman known as Dame Julian of Norwich. She lived as a strict recluse in the anchoress-house attached to the old church of St Julian, and had even in her lifetime a reputation for great sanctity. She is said to have survived to an advanced age, having two maids to wait upon her when she was old, but the actual date of her death is unknown, as is also her parentage.   That she was certainly living at the age of seventy appears from a notice prefixed to a manuscript of her book purporting to have been transcribed by a contemporary, and now in the British Museum.   It runs : " Here es a vision schewed be the goodenes of God to a deuoute Woman and hir name es Julyan that es recluse atte Norwyche and yitt ys on lyfe.   Anno dni millmo CCCCXIIIº.   In the whilke Vision er fulle many comfortabylle wordes and gretly styrrande to alle thaye that desyres to be crystes looverse."

At the beginning of her book Julian states that before she received what she calls the " shewings ", she had desired three gifts from God—that He would grant her a greater realization of Christ's sufferings, that He would send her a severe illness which would bring her to death's door and detach her from earthly things, and that He would give her the three wounds of " very contrition ", of " kind compassion ", and of " wilful longing towards God ".   The first two aspirations in course of time passed from her mind, but the third remained ever with her.

When she was thirty and a half years old she actually did contract a malady so serious that her life was despaired of.   On the fourth day she received the last sacraments, and on the seventh she seemed to be sinking.   All she had strength to do was to keep her eyes fixed on the crucifix.   Then, quite suddenly, all her pains left her, and between four and nine o'clock in the morning of May 8, or the 13th, 1373, she had a succession of fifteen distinct visions or shewings, concluded by a sixteenth during the night after the following day.   These visions for the most part presented different aspects of our Lord's passion, which, while producing in her the compunction she had desired, brought her wonderful peace and joy, although their full significance did not unfold itself until long afterwards.   " And from that time that it was shewed ", she writes, " I desired oftentimes to learn what was our Lord's meaning.   And fifteen years after, and more, I was answered in ghostly understanding, saying thus : ' Wouldst thou learn thy Lord's meaning in this thing ? Learn it well : love was His meaning.   Who shewed it thee ?   Love. What shewed He thee ?   Love.   Wherefore shewed it He ? For love.   Hold thee therein and thou shalt learn and know more in the same.   But thou shalt never know nor learn therein other thing without end.'   Thus was I learned that Love was our Lord's meaning."   Elsewhere she speaks of being inwardly instructed for twenty years all but three months.   At the time when the visions came she was, according to her own account, " a simple creature that colde no letters ", in other words, illiterate, but in the years that elapsed before she wrote her book she must have acquired a considerable knowledge of the Christian mystics, for while her style and her message are her own she often uses their terminology and adopts their distinctions.

Professor Edmund Gardner has pointed out one passage which indicates familiarity with the letters of her great contemporary St Catherine of Siena, and there are several others which appear to have been suggested by the teaching of Eckhart.   It would have been strange indeed if she had remained uninfluenced by the spiritual revival on the continent, for Norwich, as the second largest city in England and the centre of the woollen trade, was in close and constant communication with the Low Countries.   Anchoresses, although they never left their houses, could and did hold intercourse through a window with the outside world, and one who like Julian was famous as a saint and a visionary would undoubtedly receive many visits from strangers, ecclesiastics and layfolk.   The book which she eventually produced remains perhaps the most beautiful and certainly the tenderest exposition of divine love that has ever been written in the English language. From beholding God's charity as exhibited to mankind in the passion of our Incarnate Lord, she rises to the contemplation of His eternal, all-embracing, all-directing, all-creating love. Even what had been a sore perplexity to her—lapses into sin on the part of those called to be saints—she sees to be somehow " behovable " because God has permitted them, and because such failures can be translated through contrition into increased love and humility. To a distressful world Julian sought to pass on words of consolation with which our Lord had comforted her own soul : " I can make all thing well : I will make all thing well : I shall make all thing well : and thou shalt see thyself that all manner of thing shall be well ".

There has been no known public *cultus* of Dame Julian ; the epithet Blessed sometimes given to her can only be justified as a title of affection.

Four manuscripts are known of Mother Julian's *Revelations of Divine Love*. That dated 1413 is shorter than the others, which were all copies made at a much later period ; probably it represents a primitive text which was subsequently expanded by her. The first printed edition was by Dom Serenus Cressy in 1670, reprinted in 1902 with a preface by Fr G. Tyrrell. Miss G. Warrack (1901) and Dom Roger Hudleston (1927) have edited the text afresh, and there has been a French translation (1910). The shorter text was edited by the Rev. Dundas Harford, *The Shewings of Lady Julian* (1925). See further Dom D. Knowles, *English Mystics* (1927). For a reference to Julian in *The Book of Margery Kempe*, see E.E.T.S. edition, pp. 42–43.

ST PETER REGALATUS   (A.D. 1456)

ST PETER REGALATUS came of a noble family settled at Valladolid in Spain. He lost his father in infancy, and when he was in his thirteenth year he obtained, though with difficulty, his mother's permission to enter the Franciscan convent of his native city. He soon became distinguished amongst his brethren for his fervour. When Peter Villacretios, after initiating a rigorous reform at Aguilar in the diocese of Osma, founded another convent at Tribulos on the Douro—which seemed to most people more like a prison than a monastery—our saint at his own earnest request was allowed to form one of the community. By the austerity of his penances, his assiduity in prayer, and his frequent ecstasies, in which he is said to have been often raised from the ground, he seems to have equalled the most eminent saints of his order, and he lived in constant union with God. Upon the death of Father Villacretios he succeeded him in the government of his reformed congregation, and died at Aguilar on March 30, 1456, in the sixty-sixth year of his age. He was called Regalatus on account of the zeal with which he enforced the rule.

The Bollandists (*Acta Sanctorum*, March, vol. iii) print only a Latin translation of the Spanish life by Antony Daza (1627), with some extracts from the process then instituted before the auditors of the Rota. Several Spanish biographies have since appeared, notably one by J. Infantes (1854). See also the bull of canonization issued by Benedict XIV, and many references in that pontiff's great treatise *De Beatificatione etc. Sanctorum ;* and Léon, *Auréole Séraphique* (Eng. trans.), vol. ii, pp. 150–159. St Peter's feast is now kept by the Friars Minor on March 30.

ST ANDREW HUBERT FOURNET, Co-Founder of the Daughters of the Cross   (A.D. 1834)

IN studying the lives of those who have been raised to the altars of the Church we find many instances of men and women who from childhood have felt drawn to the mode of life they afterwards adopted ; but occasionally we come across individuals who began by experiencing a positive aversion from what subsequently proved to be their vocation.   To this latter category belonged St Andrew Hubert Fournet. He was born on December 6, 1752, at Maillé, near Poitiers, of well-to-do parents. Possibly his good mother rather overdid her pious instructions and her laudation of the priestly office, for little Andrew was frankly bored by religion : he wished neither to pray nor to learn : all he wanted to do was to amuse himself.   In a book belonging to him when a lad, and preserved as a relic, may be read the following words written in his childish handwriting : " This book belongs to Andrew Hubert Fournet, a good boy, though he is not going to be a priest or a monk ! "   At school his idleness and frivolity led him into many scrapes, and one day he ran away—only to be brought back in disgrace to receive a thrashing.   Later on he went to Poitiers, ostensibly to study philosophy and law, but his main study was to get as much pleasure out of life as possible.   Once he enlisted and was bought out.   Then his mother tried to obtain some secretarial work for him : his handwriting, however, was too bad.   Almost in despair his family sent him to an uncle, a parish priest in a lonely, poverty-stricken parish.   This was the turning-point in his life.

The uncle was a holy man, who won his nephew's confidence, and succeeded so well in drawing out the good that underlay his frivolity that before long Andrew appeared a changed character.   He set himself to study theology, was ordained priest, and became his uncle's curate.   After serving a second and more strenuous cure he was nominated parish priest in his native town of Maillé in 1781.   His liberality to the poor and his winning personality soon endeared him to the whole parish.   For a time he continued to entertain friends at a well-appointed table, but the casual criticism of a beggar led him to give away all his silver and every article of furniture that was not absolutely necessary.   From that time forward he and his mother, his sister, and a curate led an almost conventual life in the presbytery.   His simplicity soon extended itself from his manner of life to his speech.   " Your Reverence used to preach so finely that no one understood you ", his sacristan remarked one day.   " Nowadays we can all follow every word you say."

This peaceful, happy existence came to an end with the French Revolution. St Andrew refused to take the oath which the new government required of the clergy, and was consequently outlawed.   Only by stealth could he minister to his flock—now in the woods, now in a barn, now in a humble cottage—and always at the risk of his life.   Towards the end of 1792, at the bidding of his bishop, he retired to Spain, but after an absence of five years he decided that he could no longer leave his flock unshepherded.   Secretly he made his way back to his parish, which he entered at dead of night.   The news of his return spread like wildfire and his ministrations were sought on all hands.   The danger, however, was greater than ever ; the pursuivants were constantly on his track : and on several occasions he only escaped by the skin of his teeth.   Once, as he was sitting by a cottage fire, the bailiffs entered in search of him.   The good woman of the house promptly boxed his ears for an idle churl, and bade him give his place to the gentlemen while he went off to mind the cattle.   The ruse succeeded ; but in telling the story St Andrew was wont to add : " She had a heavy hand : she made me see stars ! " Another day he eluded capture by feigning to be a corpse.   The officials sent in search of him drew back at the sight of a shrouded figure on a bed surrounded by candles and kneeling women.

The accession to power of Napoleon Bonaparte brought relief to the faithful, for the First Consul soon realized that it was politic to make terms with the Church. Fournet openly took control of his parish and presbytery, and set himself to rekindle the embers of religion.   He gave many missions, and was untiring in the pulpit and confessional.   In all his efforts he was ably seconded by St Elizabeth Bichier des Ages, who under his guidance formed a congregation of women pledged to teach children and to look after the sick and poor.   St Andrew directed the sisters and drew up their rule ; they became known as the Daughters of the Cross, but the foundress liked to call them Sisters of St Andrew.

When Abbé Fournet had reached the age of sixty-eight, fatigue and increasing infirmities induced him to resign his parish work at Maillé and to retire to La Puye. Here he not only devoted himself to the new community but also gave assistance in the adjoining parishes, and became spiritual adviser to many souls, clergy as well as layfolk.   In the process of beatification some remarkable evidence was given of the miraculous multiplication of food, and especially of grain, effected by the prayers of St Andrew when the nuns among whom he resided needed bread for themselves and their children.   He died on May 13, 1834, and was canonized on June 4, 1933.

A biographical summary in some detail is included in the bull of canonization : it may be found in the *Acta Apostolicae Sedis*, vol. xxv (1933), pp. 417–428.   See also L. Rigaud, *Vie de A. H. Fournet* (1885) ; an anonymous Italian life, *Il beato Andrea Uberto Fournet* (1885) ; and the bibliography of St Elizabeth Bichier, on August 26.

14 : ST PONTIUS, MARTYR   (THIRD CENTURY ?)

ST PONTIUS was long believed to be an illustrious primitive martyr who suffered in the persecution of Valerian about the year 258 at Cimella, a city afterwards destroyed by the Lombards but rebuilt in modern times as Cimiez on the French Riviera, near Nice.   According to his legendary history he was the son of a Roman senator, and was instructed in the Christian faith as a lad by Pope Pontian.   Upon the death of his father he gave away his inheritance to the poor, devoting himself to good works.   He was greatly esteemed by the Emperor Philip and by his son—both of whom he converted to Christianity.   After the murder of his royal patron he fled to Cimella, but was arrested as a Christian and condemned to be tortured and exposed to the wild beasts.   As the creatures would not attack him, the governor ordered him to be beheaded.

Here again we find in the Roman Martyrology a name which in Alban Butler's time was reputed to be that of " an illustrious primitive martyr ".   On the other hand modern hagiography, as represented by the Bollandist Father Delehaye, tells us that the " acts" (printed in the *Acta Sanctorum*, May, vol. iii) are historically worthless and cannot be of older date than the sixth century, though they pretend to have been written by a contemporary, an eye-witness of the martyrdom.   Neither in this case is there any adequate evidence of early *cultus*.   See *Analecta Bollandiana*, vol. xxv (1906), pp. 201–203.

ST BONIFACE OF TARSUS, MARTYR   (A.D. 306 ?)

ST BONIFACE of Tarsus seems to have found no public *cultus* before the ninth century although he is said to have suffered in 306, and his reputed acts, even if they contain a substratum of truth, are obviously embellished with fictitious details.   The story may be summarized as follows : There was living in Rome about the beginning of the fourth century a wealthy young woman named Aglaë, beautiful, well-born, and so fond of attracting attention that on three occasions she entertained the city with public shows at her own expense. Her chief steward was a man called Boniface, with whom she lived on terms of undue intimacy. He was dissolute and given to intemperance, but, on the other hand, he was liberal, hospitable, and extremely kind to the poor. One day Aglaë summoned him and bade him go to the East and fetch the relics of some of the martyrs. " For ", she said, " I have heard tell that they who honour those that suffer for Jesus Christ will have a share in their glory. In the East His servants daily suffer torments and lay down their lives for Him." Boniface prepared to obey, and, having collected a considerable sum of money, he bade farewell to Aglaë, adding, " I will not fail to bring back relics of martyrs if I find any, but what if my own body should be brought to you as one of them ? " From that time he was a changed man, and during his long voyage he neither ate meat nor drank wine, spending much of his time in prayer and fasting.

The Church at that period enjoyed peace in the West, but in the East the persecution inaugurated under Diocletian was being continued under Galerius Maximian and Maximinus Daia. It raged most fiercely in Cilicia under an inhuman governor of the name of Simplicius. Boniface accordingly directed his steps to Tarsus, the capital of that province. On arriving at the city he went straight to the court of the governor. Simplicius was found sitting on the judgement-seat, and twenty Christians were being tortured before him. Boniface ran towards them, exclaiming, " Great is the God of the Christians ! Great is the martyrs' God ! and you, servants of Jesus, pray for me that I may join with you in fighting the Devil ! " The angry governor caused him to be arrested and ordered that sharpened reeds should be thrust under his nails and molten lead poured down his throat. The people, revolted by so much cruelty, began to cry out, " Great is the God of the Christians ! " Simplicius, in some alarm, hastily withdrew, fearing a tumult ; but the following day he called for Boniface again and condemned him to be cast into a cauldron of boiling pitch from which, however, he emerged unscathed. Finally, a soldier cut off the martyr's head with his sword. The body was bought by his servants, embalmed and conveyed back to Italy. Half a mile from Rome, on the Latin Way, it was met by Aglaë, accompanied by a procession bearing lighted torches. In that place she erected a church to enshrine the sacred relics, and when she herself died, after leading a penitential life for fifteen years, her remains were laid beside his. In 1603 their reputed relics were found, with those of St Alexius, in the church which formerly bore the name of St Boniface, but is now known as Sant' Alessio.

The account here given, abbreviated from Alban Butler, was published by him, apparently without the least misgiving, as a narrative derived from " the authentic acts " of the martyr. Delehaye, and other modern authorities, pronounce the story to be no more than a pious fiction. The " acts " are to be found in the *Acta Sanctorum*, May, vol. iii. See further Duchesne, *Mélanges d'Archéologie*, 1890, pp. 2–10, and the *Nuovo Bullettino di archeologia crist.*, vol. vi (1900), pp. 205–234. The story was very popular in the middle ages and gave rise to much folklore ; on which consult Bächtold-Stäubli, *Handwörterbuch des deut. Aberglaubens*, vol. i, pp. 1475 *seq.*

ST CARTHAGE, CARTHACH, OR MOCHUDA, BISHOP
(A.D. 637)

St CARTHACH appears to have adopted the name of his master, St Carthach the Elder, who for his part called his disciple Mochuda, " my Cuda "—Cuda being presumably the younger man's actual name.   A native of Castlemaine in Kerry, he is said to have been employed as a swineherd for his father, when he came under the care of St Carthach the Elder, from whom he received his monastic training, and by whom he was afterwards ordained priest.   About the year 590, he went to live as a hermit at a place called Kiltulagh, but the jealousy of two neighbouring bishops caused him to withdraw, and he spent a year at Bangor under the direction of St Comgall.   He then visited other monasteries, and by the advice of St Colman Elo, with whom he made some stay, he decided to establish himself at Rahan in Offaly.   There, about the year 595, he founded a monastery in which he gradually assembled (it is said) over eight hundred monks.   For these disciples he drew up a rule which is still extant, and remains one of the great treasures of the Irish Church.   It is in the form of a metrical poem, 420 to 580 lines long, and is divided into nine sections ;   but the form in which it has survived cannot possibly go back to the seventh century.   The monks, who lived almost entirely on the vegetables they cultivated themselves, led a most austere life, not unlike that afterwards adopted by the Cistercians.   Among them were a number of Britons, two of whom, thinking it was time they had a new abbot, attempted to drown their holy founder in the river Cloddagh.

Besides having charge of this monastery, St Carthach seems to have been bishop over the Fircall district ; but after forty years of existence there the settlement at Rahan came to an end.   The abbot-bishop and his monks were expelled by the chieftain Blathmac through considerations of local politics, not uninfluenced by neighbouring monasteries jealous of the prosperity and repute of Rahan.   At Easter 635 St Carthach led his community out to seek a new home.   After some wandering, the great party arrived at the banks of the river Blackwater, where the prince of the Decies gave them a tract of land for a new monastery.   St Carthach remained with them for two years, laying the foundation for the great abbey and school of Lismore, which was to become famous throughout Christendom.   But he found the noise of the building operations so troublesome that he had to withdraw to a cave in the glen called Mochuda's Inch.   He died on May 14, 637.

St Carthach is regarded as the founder of the episcopal see of Lismore, which was united to that of Waterford in 1363.   From the lustre shed upon it by the sanctity and miracles of Carthach, Lismore came to be regarded in after-ages as a holy city—a reputation well sustained by its great school and monastery.   Thither flocked from all parts of Ireland and England crowds of eager young students, and many older men who desired to end their days within its hallowed walls.   The saint's feast is kept throughout Ireland.

Materials for the life of St Carthach are relatively speaking abundant.   There are two Latin lives, both of which are printed in the *Acta Sanctorum*, May, vol. iii, while the longer has been re-edited by C. Plummer in his VSH., vol. i, pp. 170–199.   There is also an Irish life (not a direct translation of either of these) which may be found in Plummer's *Bethada Náem nÉrenn*, vol. i, pp. 291–299, with an English translation in vol. ii.   The Rule mentioned above has been printed with an English translation in the *Irish Ecclesiastical Record*, 4th ser., vol. xxvii (1910), pp. 495–517, and elsewhere.   See also Kenney, *Sources for the Early History of Ireland*, vol. i, pp. 473–475, and especially Plummer's preface to VSH., pp. lxv–lxviii. There is a very useful book by a Cistercian, Fr Carthage, *The Story of St Carthage* (1937).

ST EREMBERT, BISHOP OF TOULOUSE   (c. A.D. 672)

AMONGST the many good men who received the Benedictine habit at Fontenelle Abbey from the hands of its founder St Wandrille one of the most distinguished was a youth called Erembert, a native of Waucourt, near Poissy, in the department of Seine-et-Oise. He was not, however, suffered to remain undisturbed in his monastic retreat, for King Clotaire III summoned him to become bishop of Toulouse. One incident in his episcopal life alone has come down to us. He was on a visit to his brother Gamard in his birthplace when a fire broke out which threatened to destroy the town. St Erembert prostrated himself in prayer in the church of St Saturninus and then emerged holding his pastoral cross erect. Immediately the wind veered, the flames died down, and the people flocked to the church praising God. Ill-health induced St Erembert to resign office in 668. He retired to Fontenelle, and there he remained until his death. His brother Gamard, with his two sons, afterwards entered Fontenelle, upon which they bestowed all the family estates.

A Latin life compiled at Fontenelle a century and a half later is not historically of much value. It has been printed by Mabillon and in the *Acta Sanctorum*, May, vol. iii, and it was re-edited in 1910 by W. Levison in MGH., *Scriptores Merov.*, vol. v, pp. 652 seq. See also Duchesne, *Fastes épiscopaux*, vol. i, p. 307.

BD GILES OF PORTUGAL   (A.D. 1265)

DURING the reign of Sancho the Great, King of Portugal, one of the monarch's most trusted counsellors was Rodrigues de Vagliaditos, the governor of Coïmbra. This nobleman had several sons, of whom the third, Giles, or Aegidius, was destined for the Church, and he was sent to study at Coïmbra, where he at once attracted attention by his brilliant abilities. The king bestowed upon him a canonry and other benefices, but the young man himself was far more concerned with experimental science than with theology. He therefore elected to go to Paris to qualify for medicine. He had started on his journey and had proceeded but a little way when he fell in with a stranger, whom he afterwards considered to be the Devil. The man induced him to go to Toledo instead of to France. In that city Giles took up his abode, and not only studied alchemy and physics but also became deeply interested in necromancy and the black arts. He appears to have plunged into every form of evil, and he so completely turned his back upon religion that he drew up a document which purported to be a pact with Satan and sealed it with his blood. After seven years in Toledo Giles reverted to his original design, and in Paris practised as a physician with considerable success. Before long, however, his conscience began to prick him. One night he had an alarming dream in which a gigantic spectre threatened him, crying out, " Amend your life ". Upon awaking he tried to disregard the warning as a mere nightmare, but the vision was repeated a night or two later. This time the spectre shouted, " I shall kill you unless you amend your life ! " " I *will* amend it ! " exclaimed Giles as he awoke, and he kept his word. Without delay he burnt his magical books, destroyed the phials which contained his potions and set out on foot to return to Portugal.

After a long journey he arrived, footsore and weary, at Valencia in Spain, where he was hospitably received by the Dominican friars. There Giles sought absolution for his sins of the past and there he received the habit. The rest of his life was edifying in the extreme. He had indeed to face fierce trials from the powers of darkness, and the memory of his iniquitous pact often tempted him to despair of salvation, but he persevered in prayer and mortification. After seven years he was granted a vision in which our Lady restored to him the sinister document, and his anxiety on that score was allayed for ever.   Soon after his profession Bd Giles was sent to Santarem in Portugal ; at a later date he spent some time in the Parisian house of his order, where he contracted a warm friendship with Bd Humbert de Romans, the future master general of the Friars Preachers.   Giles was elected prior provincial for Portugal, but he soon laid down the charge on the score of age.   In his last years, which were spent at Santarem, the holy man was favoured with frequent ecstasies, and showed himself to be endowed with the gift of prophecy. His *cultus* was approved in 1748.

The resemblance which this story bears to such popular legends as that of Cyprian and Justina (September 26), not to speak of Faust and other fictions of similar purport, renders its more sensational elements very open to question.   The lengthy narrative which the Bellandists (*Acta Sanctorum*, May, vol. iii) have borrowed from Father Resendio seems to lack any reliable corroboration.   The same type of story is to be found in Procter, *Lives of Dominican Saints*, pp. 130–133.

BD PETRONILLA OF MONCEL, Virgin   (A.D. 1355)

VERY little seems to be known about Bd Petronilla except that she belonged to the family of the counts of Troyes, and that she was the first abbess of the convent of Le Moncel in Oise, founded by King Philip le Bel, but not completed for occupation until the reign of Louis of Valois.   Down to the time of their dispersion at the French Revolution, the Poor Clares of Moncel regarded Bd Petronilla as their special protector and patroness, and the Franciscans still observe her feast.

See H. L. Fautrat, " L'Abbaye du Moncel ", in *Mémoires com. archéo. Senlis*, vol. vi (1892), pp. 1–24 ; *Gallia Christiana* (nova), vol. ix, pp. 852–856.

BD MAGDALEN DI CANOSSA, Virgin, Foundress of the Canossian Daughters of Charity   (A.D. 1835)

IN the foothills of the Appenine mountains, some eighteen miles from Parma, stand the few remains of the once mighty castle of Canossa.   It was here, while the guest of Matilda, Countess of Tuscany, in the winter of 1076–77, that Pope St Gregory VII received that ostensible submission of Henry IV of Germany whose circumstances have been so much exaggerated and significance misunderstood.   And it was the family of this Countess Matilda that seven hundred years later produced Magdalen Gabriela, Marchioness of Canossa, a " valiant woman " of a somewhat different stamp.

Her parents were the Marquis Ottavio and his wife Teresa Szlukhe, and her birth was at Verona, in 1774.   There is still in existence a portrait of Magdalen at the age of four, an attractive, rather imperious-looking child, with strongly marked features, dressed in the complicated clothes of a grown woman as was the eighteenth-century (and later) way with children.   After looking at it, one is not surprised to learn that little Magdalen, while frank and straightforward, was also stubborn, wilful and quick-tempered.   Her nurse remarked in later years, " It's a marvel to me how that naughty little thing has changed.   I didn't think she would ever be tamed."

A boy and two more girls were born to Magdalen's parents and then, when he was only thirty-nine, her father died.   This was a sad blow to Magdalen, and it was followed two years later by another : her mother married again and went to live with her new husband, the Marquis Zanetti, in Mantua, leaving her children to the care of their uncles. Magdalen, who was now eight, with her elder sister Laura, was put in charge of a governess, a woman who " took out " on Magdalen a spite she had for someone who had criticized her inadequate religious instruction of the children. It was six years before Uncle Jerome found out how badly his second niece was being treated, and dismissed the governess. Apparently Magdalen had never said a word, and would not let her sisters do so. Perhaps these years of domestic tyranny had something to do with the period of painful sickness that followed them, during which Magdalen " took stock " with herself : she was definite that she did not wish to marry, but was not sure that she wanted to be a nun, which in those days still generally meant joining an enclosed order. She did eventually go into the Carmelite convent at Conegliano, but it was soon recognized that she had no vocation for that life, and she returned home again.

During the revolutionary wars the Canossas went to Venice for a time, and after they had returned they were visited by Napoleon Bonaparte at their mansion in Verona. Napoleon showed respect and indeed admiration for the marchioness, and she felt encouraged to ask a favour of him : it was that he would assign to her the empty convent of St Joseph in Verona, as a centre for work for poor people and neglected children, whose sad state she set vividly before him. And he granted the request.

The reason for this action went back to the time when she was in Venice. There Magdalen had had a vision, or a dream as she herself called it, in which she saw our Lady surrounded by six religious in a brown dress ; it then seemed to her that our Lady took the religious two by two to a church filled with girls and women, to a hospital, and to a hall full of ragged children, telling them to work there, but especially in the third. Magdalen at once took this as a divinely appointed programme, and henceforward spent her time giving religious instruction, working in hospitals and looking after children. She was soon joined by other young women ; but she saw that if the work was to go on and be made permanent by means of a congregation it was necessary to have a proper house for the purpose. And at a time when he was turning monks and nuns out of their convents, Napoleon made this possible by his own gift.

Magdalen was now thirty-four years old, and it was not easy for her to leave the Canossa household, where among other responsibilities was an orphaned baby cousin. Her family looked on her projects as rather undignified for one of her birth. Pope Pius XI seems to have been glancing sideways at this when, in his address at the reading of the decree which declared Magdalen di Canossa's virtues to have been heroic, he quoted the great man " who was humble enough to serve the poor at table with his own hands, but not quite humble enough to sit at table with them ". A remark which, as his Holiness added, " suggests a lot of things and goes a long way ". Magdalen's brother Boniface was especially sad that she should leave them. But it was done, and on May 8, 1808 Magdalen and her few companions opened the doors of their house to the poor girls of the San Zeno quarter, Verona's " east end ". They began by teaching them the simplest prayers and the elements of the Christian faith, with a little reading, writing and sewing, and within a few months the effects of this centre of goodness and decency were seen in the quarter.

Good news spreads no less than bad, and before long Venice asked for a centre like Verona's. By this time other associates had joined Sister Magdalen and, after some hesitation, she extended the work accordingly. Over a period of twenty-five years other foundations followed, at Milan, Bergamo, Trent and elsewhere in northern Italy and, especially in the early days, the sisters were often too few for the work ; it was the foundress herself who would come to the rescue, working in the scullery or anywhere with what she called her two servants—by which must be understood her own two hands. She had a predilection for the dirtiest and most troublesome children, and would look after them from the combing of their hair to the brushing of their minds, so that to this day a specially difficult child is known in the congregation as " One of our holy foundress's ".

In amplifying his words quoted above Pope Pius XI said that " Many are charitable enough to help and even to serve the poor, but few are able deliberately to become poor with the poor ", and that that is exactly what Bd Magdalen did. Such a life can only grow from a rooted interior humility, and it was through no will of hers that others came to know how she had to struggle with her quick imagination and keen senses—to say nothing of unavoidable external distractions— to attain the degree of religious recollection that was hers. In fact she reached a high state of contemplation : on several known occasions she was rapt in ecstasy and at least once was seen to be lifted from the ground. Such an intense life of the soul was not inconsistent (only through misunderstanding could it be supposed to be) with a life of daily cares in which it was possible, for example, for her to be held up at pistol-point in the parlour. This actually happened. Mother Magdalen found a refuge for a penitent girl who had been seduced. The young man concerned threatened her with a pistol to disclose the girl's whereabouts. " If you want to kill me, here I am ", she replied. " But are you really brave enough ? " He slunk away, leaving the weapon behind, and before long he too had answered the call to repentance.

Bd Magdalen told her Daughters of Charity that their mission on earth was to make Jesus Christ known to little children, and they primarily concerned themselves with those who were poor and neglected. But she also opened high-schools and colleges, made special provision for the deaf-and-dumb, and organized closed retreats for women and girls. After her death the congregation also undertook work on the foreign missions. At Venice in 1831 Bd Magdalen even launched a small congregation of men, which carries on similar work among boys.

At the end of 1834 Bd Magdalen was taken ill at Bergamo ; she struggled back to the mother house at Verona, and by passion-week in the following year she knew she was dying. Nobody else, neither her religious nor her medical advisers, thought so ; but she asked for the last sacraments, and having received them the end came suddenly. For some years Mother Magdalen had been bent almost double and could sleep only in a sitting position. On the evening of April 10, 1835 she asked to be helped to her knees while she joined in her daughters' prayers, and thus, with an exclamation of joy, she died, leaning on the arms of Mother Annetta.*· She was beatified in 1941.

There are several biographies in Italian, but the above account relies on *A Short Life of the Venerable Servant of God Magdalen, Marchioness of Canossa*, written by a sister of her congregation and published at Bangalore in India in 1933. It includes translations of the decree of 1927 pronouncing the heroism of Mother Magdalen's virtues and of the address given by Pope Pius XI to the Canossian Daughters of Charity to mark that occasion.

* As a little girl Annetta had declared she would rather burn down the convent than be a nun. Whereupon Mother Magdalen had foretold, " One day you will be one of us. And you will be there to help me when I die."

ST MICHAEL GARICOÏTS, FOUNDER OF THE PRIESTS OF THE SACRED HEART OF BÉTHARRAM   (A.D. 1863)

TOWARDS the close of the eighteenth century, and in the early part of the nineteenth, there was living in the Lower Pyrenees, at the hamlet of Ibarra, a family of poor peasants named Garicoïts.   Their cottage was humble enough to human eyes, but God's blessing must have rested upon it because its hospitable door was always open to receive the proscribed priests who, from time to time during the French Revolution and the years immediately following, came to minister in secret to the faithful.   Here on April 15, 1797, there was born to Arnold and Gratianne Garicoïts their eldest son Michael.   Life is hard in those mountain regions, and the boy was a mere child when he was hired out to be shepherd-boy to a farmer.   His own often expressed desire was to be a priest, but his parents always replied, " No, we are too poor ".   The old grandmother thought otherwise.   One day she went to talk the matter over with the parish priest of Saint-Palais, who in times past had often found a hiding-place in the Garicoïts' cottage.   Through his efforts the boy was received first into the College of S. Palais and afterwards at Bayonne, arrangements having been made that he should be no charge upon his parents but should earn his expenses by working out of school hours for the clergy and in the bishop's kitchen.   It was a strenuous time for the young peasant, but he was clever and healthy.   Moreover, he was working to attain his heart's desire.   Philosophy he studied at Aire and theology in the *grand séminaire* at Dax, where he was nicknamed " Our Aloysius Gonzaga ".   Whilst still a seminarist he took a class in a preparatory school near by, and in December 1823 he was ordained priest in Bayonne cathedral by Bishop d'Astros.

Michael's first parochial experience was gained at Cambo, whither he was sent to act as *vicaire* to the *curé*, who was in feeble health.   In the two years he remained there he did much to revive religion, combating Jansenism by the custom of frequent communion as well as by introducing Sacred Heart devotions.   He tackled freethinkers with so much fervour that one of them was heard to exclaim, " That devil would give his life to save the soul of an enemy ! "   Father Garicoïts' next call was to a professorship in the senior seminary for priests at Bétharram, and then to be superior—a congenial post which he filled with conspicuous ability and success. The bishop, however, suddenly decided to merge the seminary with that of Bayonne, and Michael Garicoïts found himself with two other priests left alone to carry on the services.

During this period, when he was more or less stranded, there began to take shape in his mind a scheme for training priests to do mission work among the people. With two or three companions he started to live a community life, and then, in order that he might better know God's will, he went to Toulouse to attend a retreat given by Father Le Blanc, a Jesuit.   To this good priest he opened his heart, and was encouraged to persevere.   " You will be the father of a congregation that will be our sister ", said the Jesuit, and Father Garicoïts drew up in 1838 a constitution largely based on that of the sons of St Ignatius.   Like them, his missionaries were to take life vows and to spread far and wide.   Associates gathered round him at Bétharram, and all seemed promising, when a check came from an unexpected quarter.   The bishop who had been his patron and had ordained him was replaced by another, who viewed with disapproval this idea of founding a new congregation. His constitutions were subjected to a fundamental revision, he was told to confine himself to the diocese, and to work only under the direction of the bishop.   Not till 1852 was the community allowed to choose its own superior, and even then it was tied down by regulations which hampered its activity.   Father Garicoïts submitted, but with a heavy heart.   " What pangs accompany the birth of a congregation ! " he once said to one of his sons ; but generally he bore his trials in silence.   He died on Ascension-day, May 14, 1863.

Fourteen years later the Society of Priests of the Sacred Heart of Bétharram was approved by the Holy See on the lines the founder had laid down.   St Michael Garicoïts, who was at one time spiritual director of the Basque house of the Daughters of the Cross at Igon, received much encouragement in his foundation from St Elizabeth Bichier des Ages, and he was all his life a close friend of her congregation in the Basque country.   Both of them were canonized in the year 1947.

The brief of beatification, which contains a detailed biographical summary, will be found in the *Acta Apostolicae Sedis*, vol. xv (1932), pp. 263–269.   Lives of the saint have been written in French by B. Bourdenne (1921) and the Abbé Bordachar (1926) ; there is a life in English by C. Otis-Cox (1935), another by J. F. Makepeace, and a brief sketch, *The Saint of Bétharram* (1938), by Fr P. E. Collier.   See also P. Mazoyer, *Lourdes et Bétharram* (1895), especially pp. 272 *ss.*

ST MARY MAZZARELLO, Virgin, Co-Foundress of the Daughters of Our Lady Help of Christians   (A.D. 1881)

MORNESE is a mountain village in the south of Piedmont, near the border of Liguria and not far from Genoa.   There lived there in the first half of the nineteenth century a certain energetic, hard-headed and honest peasant named Joseph Mazzarello and his wife Maddalena Calcagno, and to them was born in 1837 the first of several children, who was christened with the names Mary Dominica.   Six years later the family moved to a new home on a hill, the Valponasca, some way out of Mornese, and here Mary was brought up, working long hours in the fields and vineyards so that she developed considerable physical toughness and strength.

From the Valponasca to Mornese church is a long and hard walk, even by the short cut, but Mary Mazzarello was assiduous in her attendance there and assisted at Mass daily whenever it was possible for her to do so.   When the parish priest, Don Pestarino, started a Marian sodality she was one of the five foundation members, and her example attracted others, for her gentleness, modesty and lively mind made her a popular young woman.   This sodality of Daughters of Mary Immaculate, with its rule of life, was a result of an interview that Don Pestarino had with Don Bosco at Turin, thereby making the first link in the chain that was to bind St John Bosco with St Mary Mazzarello.   This was in 1855, when she was seventeen.   Five years later the spiritual quality of the sodalists was put to the test, for a fierce epidemic of typhoid broke out in Mornese.   Mary was asked to go and nurse her uncle and his family, who had sickened.   She was rather frightened at the prospect, but she went, and when she had carried out the task " like a Sister of Charity ", herself caught the fever and was near to death.

During her long convalescence Mary began to realize that she would not be strong enough to work in the fields again, and with her friend Petronilla she decided to learn dressmaking.   This they did, and started a small business in the village which was so successful that they soon were taking the local girls as pupils and assistants.   And so, seemingly by accident, these two peasant girls in a remote village began to do for girls what Don Bosco was doing for boys, and with the same spirit and methods. " Laugh and play and dash about as much as you like ", they said to their younger pupils, " but be ever so careful not to do or say anything that would be displeasing to God." And on an autumn evening in 1865 Don Bosco himself with some of his boys came on a holiday excursion to Mornese. The Daughters of Mary Immaculate knelt for his blessing, and Mary Mazzarello said, " I feel that Don Bosco is a saint ".

On that saint's advice, the parish priest, Don Pestarino, put up a building for a boys' college in Mornese. But Don Bosco had been talking with Pope Pius IX about his project for a congregation of nuns to carry out among girls the educational work that the Salesians were doing for boys ; and it so happened that the bishop of Acqui, Mgr Sciandra, for good reasons of his own, did not want a college in Mornese. Accordingly, on May 29, 1872, the people of Mornese woke up to find that the new building was occupied by a community of nuns. Its nucleus was drawn from among the local Daughters of Mary Immaculate ; Mary Mazzarello, now thirty-five years old, was the superioress, and the convent was on the very site where, years before, she had had some sort of vision of a building filled with children being looked after by habited religious. Thus began the congregation of the Daughters of Our Lady Help of Christians, sometimes called Salesian Sisters.

They did not have an easy start. The villagers were indignant that their college had not materialized and that the building had been given to nuns, " usurpers " drawn from the ranks of the village sodality. In the words of St John Bosco, they were subjected to annoyances, mocked at, and cold-shouldered even by their own relatives. Two months later he and the bishop visited the new establishment, and Sister Mary, Sister Petronilla and nine others took triennial vows ; and Don Bosco preached. John Bosco was a saint, an educationist, and on any showing a very great man. He chose as head of his new congregation a country sempstress who, on her own testimony, could hardly write. " Wisdom is justified of her children." By 1878 six of the Mornese sisters were found suitable to accompany the second Salesian mission to the Indians of the Argentine, and in the following year the Mornese community had outgrown its accommodation. The mother house was therefore reconstituted in a former Capuchin friary at Nizza Monferrato, and Mother Mary left her home in tears.

During the lifetime of St Mary Mazzarello thirteen other convents of the congregation were opened in Italy and France (within sixty years there were over 800 throughout the world), and in each one the spirit and methods of St Francis of Sales and St John Bosco were faithfully followed. Their principal work was teaching, but as time went by any work for the good of the young came to engage their attention and activity, and a simple naturalness and gentleness distinguishes it all—encouragement and guidance, not repression ; the example of Christ, not the stick. Continual busyness, in however good work, calls for a certain firmness and simplicity of character, else it may degenerate into " activism " and the fullness of really Christian life be smothered : the plain hard-working peasant upbringing of Mother Mary Mazzarello must have been of very great value to her in guiding the destinies of her congregation in its early days. She would attribute all her success to God ; but others may remember that God allows Himself to be dependent in some measure on the grace-strengthened quality of the instruments whom He chooses.

Early in 1881 Mother Mary accompanied some of her nuns to Marseilles, to see them off to South America. She found the voyage from Genoa trying, and the miserable lodging at Marseilles worse, and she was plainly ill. She took Don Bosco's advice in going to a convent of the congregation between Marseilles and Toulon, and was in bed there for six weeks, very ill indeed. She was able at length to get back to Nizza Monferrato, but before doing so had asked Don Bosco whether she was ever likely to recover. He answered in a parable, of which the meaning was, " No ; it is the office of a superior to lead, even in death ". She grasped his hand, and said nothing.

On April 27 she received the last anointing, and observed cheerfully to the priest, " Now you've given me my passport I can go any time, can't I ? " But a few days before the end she suffered a grievous temptation to despair ; she emerged shaken and weak, but steadfast, singing faintly to herself the hymn *Chi ama Maria contento sarà*, " Those who love Mary shall be happy ". A few days later, on May 14, 1881, Mother Mary of Mornese died, at the age of only forty-four. She was canonized in 1951, and her body is now enshrined side by side with that of St John Bosco in Turin.

Maria Mazzarello : Life and Times, by the Rev. Dr H. L. Hughes (1933), consists, as to three-quarters, of " times ", *i.e.* historical background ; the remaining quarter, of " life ", is also useful. A pamphlet by Father J. B. Calvi (Salesian Press, Battersea) adds a few more facts. See also the numerous biographies of St John Bosco. The official life of St Mary of Mornese was written by Don Ferdinand Maccono, under the title *Suor Maria Mazzarello*, and there is a full-length study by Don Eugenio Ceria.

15 : ST JOHN BAPTIST DE LA SALLE, Founder of the Brothers of the Christian Schools (A.D. 1719)

THE founder of the Institute of the Brothers of the Christian Schools was born at Rheims on April 30, 1651. His parents were both of noble family. From the instructions of a devout mother, the boy, John Baptist, early gave evidence of such piety that he was designated for the priesthood. He received the tonsure when he was only eleven, and became a member of the cathedral chapter of Rheims at the age of sixteen ; in 1670 he entered the seminary of St Sulpice in Paris, being ordained priest in 1678. A young man of striking appearance, well connected, refined and scholarly, he seemed assured of a life of dignified ease or of high preferment in the Church. But God in His providence had other designs for him—of which he himself had no presentiment, apparently not even when one of his fellow canons on his deathbed committed to his care the spiritual direction of a girls' orphanage and school as well as of the sisters who conducted it.

But in 1679 he met a layman, Adrian Nyel, who had come to Rheims with the idea of opening a school for poor boys. Canon de la Salle gave him every encouragement, and, somewhat prematurely, two schools were started. Gradually the young canon became more and more drawn into the work and grew interested in the seven masters who taught in these schools. He rented a house for them, fed them from his own table, and tried to instil into them the high educational ideals which were gradually taking shape in his own mind. In 1681, though their uncouth manners repelled him, he decided to invite them to live in his own home that he might have them under his constant supervision. The result must have been a great disappointment. Not only did two of his brothers indignantly leave his house—a step he may have anticipated, for "ushers" were then ranked with pot-boys and hucksters—but five of the schoolmasters soon took their departure, unable or unwilling to submit to a discipline for which they had never bargained. The reformer waited, and his patience was rewarded. Other men of a better type presented themselves, and these formed the nucleus of what was to prove a new congregation. To house them the saint gave up his paternal home, and moved with them to more suitable premises in the Rue Neuve. As the movement became known, requests began to come in from outside for schoolmasters trained on the new method, and de la Salle found his time fully engrossed. Partly for that reason, and partly because he realized the contrast his disciples drew between his assured official income and their own uncertain position, he decided to give up his canonry. This he did.

The next question for consideration was the use he should make of his private fortune, which he no longer wished to retain for his own use. Should he employ it for the infant community, or should he give it away ? He went to Paris to consult Father Barré, a saintly man greatly interested in education, whose advice had helped him in the past. Father Barré was strongly opposed to the idea of endowment. " Si vous fondez, vous fondrez " (" If you endow, you will founder "), he said, and the saint, after fervent prayer for light, determined to sell all he had and to distribute the proceeds to the poor—who at that time were in the direst need, as a famine was raging in Champagne. His life from that time became even more austere. He had naturally a very delicate palate, but he deliberately starved himself until hunger enabled him to swallow any food, however coarse or ill-prepared.

Four schools were soon opened, but de la Salle's great problem at this stage was that of training teachers. Eventually he called a conference of twelve of his men, and it was decided to make provisional regulations, with a vow of obedience yearly renewable until vocations became certain. At the same time a name was decided upon for members of the community. They were to be called the Brothers of the Christian Schools. The first serious trial that befell them was illness amongst the brothers. De la Salle seems to have attributed this visitation to his own incapacity to rule, and he consequently persuaded his disciples to elect another superior. No sooner, however, did this become known than the archiepiscopal vicar general ordered him to resume his office. His wisdom and his guiding hand were indeed necessary, for external pressure was about to cause unforeseen developments in the new congregation—developments which would greatly widen its field of operation. Hitherto recruits had been full-grown men, but now applications began to be received from boys between the ages of fifteen and twenty. To reject promising lads at a malleable age might mean losing them altogether, and yet they were not old enough to be subjected to a rule framed for adults. De la Salle, in 1685, accordingly decided to set up a junior novitiate. He lodged the youths in an adjoining house, gave them a simple rule of life, and entrusted their training to a wise brother, whilst retaining supervision of them himself. But soon there appeared another class of candidate who also, like the boys, could not well be refused and who likewise required to be dealt with apart. These were young men who were sent by their parish priests to the saint with a request that he would train them as schoolmasters, and send them back to teach in their own villages. He accepted them, found them a domicile, undertook their training, and thus founded the first training-college for teachers, at Rheims in 1687 ; others followed, at Paris (1699) and at Saint-Denis (1709).

All this time the work of teaching poor boys had been steadily going on, although hitherto it had been restricted to Rheims. In 1688 the saint, at the request of the curé of St Sulpice in Paris, took over a school in that parish. It was the last of seven free schools founded by M. Olier, which had eventually been compelled to close for lack of satisfactory teachers. The brothers were so successful that a second school was opened in the same district. The control of these Paris foundations was entrusted to Brother L'Heureux, a gifted and capable man whom de la Salle designed to be his successor, and whom he was about to present for ordination. It had been his intention to have priests in his institution to take charge of each house, but Brother L'Heureux's unexpected death made him doubt whether his design had been according to God's will. After much prayer it was borne in upon him that if his order was to confine itself strictly to the work of teaching, for which it had been founded, and to remain free from " caste " distinctions the brothers must continue to be laymen. He therefore laid down the statute—perhaps the most self-denying ordinance which could be imposed upon a community of men— that no Brother of the Christian Schools should ever be a priest, and that no priest should ever become a member of the order. That regulation is in force to this day. Troubles which had affected the work during the founder's absence in Paris led him afterwards to take a house at Vaugirard to serve as a retreat where his sons could come to recruit body and spirit ; it also became the novitiate-house. Here, about 1695, de la Salle drew up the first draft of the matured rule, with provision for the taking of life vows. Here also he wrote his manual on the *Conduct of Schools* in which he sets forth the system of education to be carried out—a system which revolutionized elementary education and is successfully pursued at the present day. It replaced the old method of individual instruction by class teaching and the " simultaneous method ", it insisted on silence while the lessons were being given, and it taught in French and through French—not through Latin. Up to this period the schools opened by the brothers had all been intended for poor children, but in 1698 a new departure was made at the request of King James II of England, then an exile in France. He wanted a college for the sons of his Irish adherents, and at his request the saint opened a school for fifty boys of gentle birth. About the same time he started for the benefit of youths of the artisan class the first " Sunday academy ", in which more advanced instruction was combined with religious teaching and exercises, and it at once became extremely popular.

St John Baptist de la Salle had not been able to carry out all these schemes without experiencing many trials. He had heartrending disappointments and defections amongst his disciples, and bitter opposition from the secular school-masters, who resented his intrusion into what they regarded as their special preserves. At one time the very existence of the institute seems to have been jeopardized through the injudicious action of two brothers occupying posts of authority. Complaints of undue severity towards novices reached the archbishop of Paris, who sent his vicar general to make investigations. The brothers unanimously exonerated their superior from blame in the matter, but the vicar general was prejudiced and drew up an unfavourable report. The result was that St John Baptist was told to regard himself as deposed—a verdict he received without a murmur. When, however, the vicar attempted to impose on the brothers a new superior—an outsider from Lyons—they indignantly exclaimed that M. de la Salle was their superior, and that they would one and all walk out of the house rather than accept another.   Though the saint afterwards induced them to make a formal submission, the fresh appointment was allowed to lapse, and the founder remained in charge of his congregation.   Somewhat later than this the removal of the novitiate from Vaugirard to larger premises inside Paris, together with the opening of new schools in connection with it, led to a violent organized attack on the Paris schools in which the lay schoolmasters were joined by the Jansenists, and by those who, on principle, were opposed to education other than manual for the children of the poor.   St John Baptist found himself involved in a series of law-suits, and obliged to close all his Parisian schools and houses.   Eventually the storm died down, the persecution ended as suddenly as it had begun, and before long the brothers were able to resume and even extend their educational work in the capital.

Elsewhere the institute had been steadily developing.   As early as 1700 Brother Drolin had been sent to found a school in Rome, and in France schools were started at Avignon, at Calais, in Languedoc, in Provence, at Rouen, and at Dijon.   In 1705 the novitiate was transferred to St Yon in Rouen.   There a boarding-school was opened, and an establishment for troublesome boys, which afterwards developed into a reformatory-school.   From these beginnings grew the present world-wide organization, the largest teaching-order of the Church, working from primary schools to university-colleges.   In 1717 the founder decided finally to resign ; from that moment he would give no orders, and lived like the humblest of the brothers. He taught novices and boarders, for whom he wrote several books, including a method of mental prayer.   St John Baptist lived at an important period in the history of spirituality in France, and he came under the influence of Bérulle, Olier and the so-called French " school " of de Rancé and of the Jesuits, his friends Canon Nicholas Roland and the Minim friar Nicholas Barré being specially influential.   On the negative side he was distinguished by his strong opposition to Jansenism, illustrated positively by his advocacy of frequent and even daily communion.   In Lent, 1719, St John Baptist suffered a good deal from asthma and rheumatism, but would give up none of his habitual austerities.   Then he met with an accident, and gradually grew weaker.   He passed away on Good Friday, April 7, 1719, in the sixty-eighth year of his age.

The example of St John Baptist de la Salle may well lead everyone of us to ask himself : " What have I done to help and to encourage this most necessary and divine work ?   What sacrifices am I prepared to make that the Christian education of our children may be carried on in spite of all the hindrances and hostilities which beset it ? "   The Church has shown her appreciation of the character of this man, a thinker and initiator of the first importance in the history of education, by canonizing him in 1900, and giving his feast to the whole Western church ; and in 1950 Pope Pius XII declared him the heavenly patron of all school-teachers.

There is no lack of excellent lives of St John Baptist de la Salle, especially in French. The foundation of all is the biography by J. B. Blain, the intimate friend of the saint, which appeared in 1733.   Of modern works the most important is probably that of J. Guibert, *Histoire de St Jean Baptiste de la Salle* (1900).   Shorter works are those of A. Delaire (1900) in the series " Les Saints ", F. Laudet (1929), and G. Bernoville (1944).   In English, Francis Thompson's sketch was republished in 1911, and there are other good biographies ; but the best and most thorough work is Dr W. J. Battersby's *De la Salle*, vol. i (1945), as educational pioneer, vol. ii (1950), as saint and spiritual writer, vol. iii (1952), letters and documents.

SS. TORQUATUS AND HIS COMPANIONS, MARTYRS (FIRST CENTURY ?)

THE first Christian missionaries to attempt the evangelization of Spain are said to have been seven holy men who had been specially commissioned by St Peter and St Paul, and sent forth for that purpose. According to the legend the party kept together until they reached Guadix in Granada, where they encamped in a field whilst their servants went into the town to buy food. The inhabitants, however, came out to attack them, and followed them to the river. A miraculously-erected stone bridge enabled the Christians to escape, but it collapsed when their pursuers attempted to cross it. Afterwards the missionaries separated, each one selecting a different district in which he laboured and was made bishop. Torquatus chose Guadix as the field of his labours, and is honoured on this day in association with his companions, all six of whom, however, have also special feasts of their own. St Torquatus and the other bishops appear to have suffered martyrdom.

For this story we have only the authority of a set of medieval breviary lessons, printed in the *Acta Sanctorum*, May, vol. iii. There is no trace of early *cultus* to confirm it. See J. P. Kirsch, *Kirchengeschichte*, vol. i, p. 307, n. 25.

ST ISIDORE OF CHIOS, MARTYR (A.D. 251 ?)

THE Isidore named in this day's martyrology appears to have been a native of Alexandria. We are told that he was a commissariat officer in the army of the Emperor Decius, and went to Chios with the fleet, which was under the command of Numerius. Whilst he was staying in the island he was discovered to be a Christian, and was denounced to Numerius by his captain. Placed on trial, he showed great constancy, threats and promises proving equally unavailing. As he refused to sacrifice, his tongue was cut out and he was beheaded. His body was sunk in a well, but it was recovered by the Christians. It was then interred by a soldier called Ammianus, who was afterwards martyred at Cyzicus, and by a woman, St Myrope, who is said to have been flogged to death because of her charity in giving Christian burial to martyrs. The well became famous for its healing properties, and over the tomb of St Isidore a basilica was erected. In the fifth century, as the result of a vision or dream, St Marcian, who was at that time treasurer of the cathedral of Constantinople, dedicated to St Isidore a chapel in a church he was building in honour of St Irene. From Constantinople the *cultus* of St Isidore spread to Russia. In 1525 Christian merchants conveyed the relics of St Isidore to San Marco in Venice, where they are said to be still preserved.

It is to be feared that in this case again the *passio* (printed in the *Acta Sanctorum*, May, vol. iii) is no better than a pious romance. But the *cultus* is relatively early and identified with Chios. St Isidore was known even to St Gregory of Tours. See Delehaye, *Origines du Culte des Martyrs*, pp. 226, etc.; and *Recueil des historiens des Croisades, Occident*, vol. v, pp. 321–334.

SS. PETER OF LAMPSACUS AND HIS COMPANIONS, MARTYRS (A.D. 251)

DURING the persecution under Decius there was living at Lampsacus on the Hellespont a young Christian of lofty character and noble appearance called Peter. Brought before Olympius, the proconsul, and bidden to sacrifice to Venus, he refused, and made a spirited attack upon the worship of so licentious a deity, the

319

words of which are quoted in his " acts ".   He was tortured on the wheel and then beheaded.   Immediately afterwards at Troas the same proconsul had to deal with three other Christians, whose names were Nicomachus, Andrew and Paul.   They declared themselves to be Christians, but under torture Nicomachus abjured his faith.   Dionysia, a girl of sixteen, who was present, exclaimed in horror at his defection ; she was promptly arrested, and on being questioned avowed herself a Christian.   As she refused to sacrifice, she was condemned like Andrew and Paul to die on the morrow.   In the meantime she was given over for the night to the tender mercies of two young men, who were allowed to insult her as they would. But by the mercy of God she was protected from harm.   The following morning Andrew and Paul were taken from prison, delivered to the mob, and stoned outside the city walls.   Dionysia followed, desiring to die with them, but by order of the proconsul she was brought back and beheaded within the city.

Whatever be thought of this rather suspicious document (printed in the *Acta Sanctorum*, May, vol. iii), these martyrs found their way into the *Hieronymianum ;* see Delehaye's commentary, p. 256.   The fact that they, or at least one of the group, suffered at Lampsacus can hardly be doubted.

ST HILARY OF GALEATA, ABBOT   (A.D. 558)

A COPY of St Paul's epistles, which came into the hands of this St Hilary when he was twelve years old, first inspired him to abandon the world in order to serve God in solitude.   Shortly afterwards he heard that gospel read in church, in which our Lord says that if anyone would be His disciple he must hate father, mother and his own life.   Uncertain as to the exact meaning of the words he consulted a pious old man, who hesitated to expound this counsel of perfection to a lad of his years. But the boy insisted, and received the explanation he sought.   Confirmed in his previous conviction, Hilary immediately forsook his Tuscan home, crossed the Apennines, and took up his abode in a hermitage beside the river Ronco.   Afterwards he fashioned a cell for himself on a neighbouring mountain peak.   Gradually disciples gathered round, and for their sake he built a monastery on land granted by a nobleman of Ravenna whom he had freed from an evil spirit, and who had been converted, together with his household.   This abbey, which he named Galeata, was subsequently called after him, Sant' Ilaro.   He gave his monks no written rule, but they continued to observe the way of life instituted by him—a round of praise, prayer and manual work.   According to a popular legend, he was always visibly protected by his guardian angel in times of danger—notably when Theodoric the Goth threatened to destroy him and his monastery because he refused to pay tribute. The conqueror was certainly favourably impressed by the saint, for he not only besought his prayers but also gave him territory for the enlargement of his abbey. St Hilary died in 558, at the age of eighty-two, and his body was translated in 1495, seven years after the time when the monastery passed into the hands of the Camaldolese Order.

There seems no reason to doubt that the short life, which purports to be written by Paul, a disciple of St Hilary, is a substantially faithful record.   It is printed in the *Acta Sanctorum*, May, vol. iii.

SS. DYMPNA AND GEREBERNUS, MARTYRS   (*c.* A.D. 650 ?)

IN the town of Gheel, twenty-five miles from Antwerp, great honour is paid to St Dympna, whose body, and that of St Gerebernus, buried in two ancient marble sarcophagi, were there discovered, or re-discovered, in the thirteenth century. Widespread interest was taken in them because the elevation of the relics of St Dympna was followed, it is alleged, by the restoration to normal health of a number of epileptics, lunatics and persons under malign influence who visited her shrine. Ever since then she has been regarded as the patroness of the insane, and the inhabitants of Gheel have been distinguished by the kindly provision they have made for those so afflicted. As early as the close of the thirteenth century an infirmary was built for their accommodation and at the present time the town possesses a first-class state sanatorium for the care and supervision of mental defectives, the greater number of whom lead contented and useful lives as boarders in the homes of farmers or other local residents, whom they assist by their labour and whose family life they share. The body of St Dympna is preserved in a silver reliquary in the church which bears her name. Only the head of St Gerebernus now rests there, his other remains having been removed to Sonsbeck in the diocese of Münster.

The true history of these saints is probably lost, but popular belief, reaching back to the date of the finding of their relics, has attached to them a story which, with local variations, is to be found in the folk-lore of many European countries. Briefly summarized, it runs as follows. Dympna was the daughter of a pagan Irish, British or Armorican king and of a Christian princess who died when their child was very young, though not before she had been instructed in the Christian faith and baptized. As she grew up, her extraordinary resemblance to her dead mother whom he had idolized awakened an unlawful passion in her father. Consequently, by the advice of St Gerebernus, her confessor, she fled from home to avoid further danger. Accompanied by the priest and attended by the court jester and his wife, she embarked in a ship which conveyed them to Antwerp. From thence they made their way south-east, through a tract of wild forest country, until they reached a little oratory dedicated to St Martin and built on a site now covered by the town of Gheel. Here they settled, intending to live as solitaries. In the meantime, however, Dympna's father had started in pursuit and in due time arrived at Antwerp, from whence he sent out spies who discovered the refuge of the fugitives. The clue by which they were traced was the use of strange coins similar to those which the spies themselves proffered in payment. Coming upon them unawares, the king first tried by cajolery to persuade his daughter to return with him. She refused, and as she was supported by St Gerebernus, the tyrant ordered his attendants to kill them both. The men promptly despatched the priest, but hesitated to attack the princess. Thereupon the unnatural father struck off his daughter's head with his own sword. The bodies of the saints, which were left exposed on the ground, were afterwards buried by angelic or human hands in the place where they had perished.

This story is treated by Delehaye in his *Légendes Hagiographiques* (Eng. trans., pp. 9, 105, 157) as an almost typical example of the infiltrations of folklore into hagiography. The text of the legend is in the *Acta Sanctorum*, May, vol. iii. See further Van der Essen, *Étude critique sur les Vies des Saints méroving.*, pp. 313–320 ; Künstle, *Ikonographie*, vol. ii, pp. 190–192 ; and Janssens, *Gheel in Beeld en Schrift* (1903). An interesting feature in the case is the fact that lunatics who go to Gheel to be healed are made to pass through an archway immediately underneath the shrine of the saint. One finds many early examples, even at Jerusalem itself, in which the squeezing through some narrow aperture is believed to be a condition for obtaining special favour. Dympna is not to be identified with the Irish St Damhnait (Damnat of Tedavnet), but her feast is observed throughout Ireland.

SS. BERTHA AND RUPERT   (*c.* A.D. 840 ?)

THE history of St Rupert and St Bertha was written and their *cultus* popularized some three hundred years after their death by St Hildegard, who spent the latter part of her life on the Rupertsberg.   According to this account, Rupert was the son of a pagan father and of a Christian mother called Bertha, who came of the family of the dukes of Lorraine and owned much property beside the Rhine and the Nahe. Her husband having been killed in battle when their son was still an infant, Bertha devoted herself entirely to his education.   So eagerly did the boy respond to the Christian instruction he received that the rôles of teacher and pupil were practically reversed.   " Look, mother ! those are all your children ! " he would say as ragged little beggars gathered round them, and once, in reply to his mother's suggestion of building a church, he exclaimed, " But first of all we must obey God and give our bread to the hungry and clothe the naked ".   These words produced such an impression on St Bertha that she immediately established several hospices for the poor.   When Rupert was twelve, he and his mother went to Rome to visit the tombs of the apostles.   Upon their return they made several religious foundations and gave away the rest of their possessions.   Accompanied by his mother, Rupert then retired to live as a hermit in the hilly country near Bingen, which was afterwards called the Rupertsberg.   He was only twenty years of age when he died. St Bertha continued to serve God in the same place for another twenty-five years, and when she, too, passed away, she was buried beside her son in a convent which they had built beside the Nahe.

> The text of St Hildegard's narrative is in the *Acta Sanctorum*, May, vol. iii.   See also P. Bruder, *St Rupertus Büchlein* (1883).

ST HALLVARD, MARTYR   (A.D. 1043)

IN Norway St Hallvard (Halward) was formerly held in great honour, and its capital, Oslo, is still under his patronage.   His history is shrouded in obscurity, but tradition has supplied us with an account of his death.   He is said to have been the son of one Vebjörn of Husaby, and to have been engaged in trading with the various Baltic islands.   He was about to cross the Drammenfjord one day when he was accosted by a woman, who besought him to receive her into his boat and save her from her enemies.   As she appeared to be in terrible distress and was obviously with child, he acceded to her request.   Before they could start, three men came running down to the shore demanding the surrender of the woman, whom they accused of theft.   She denied the charge, and Hallvard refused to deliver her over to their vengeance, though he said he was willing to give them the value of what she was accused of stealing.   Thereupon one of the men drew his bow and shot first one and then the other dead.   After they had attached a heavy stone to Hallvard's neck, they flung his body into the sea, but it floated on the water ; this drew attention to what had happened, and the young man was revered as a martyr in defence of an innocent person.   St Hallvard's relics were afterwards taken to Oslo where a stone church was built to enshrine them early in the twelfth century.

> However slight and legendary the account may seem which is printed in the *Acta Sanctorum*, May, vol. iii, and in Storm, *Monumenta historica Norvegiae*, there can be no question that the church of St Hallvard at Oslo was held in great honour.   See the *Hacon Saga* (Rolls Series), § 288 ; and S. Undset, *Saga of Saints* (1934), pp. 149–162.

ST ISAIAS, Bishop of Rostov   (A.D. 1090)

THIS Isaias, a native of Kiev, was a monk in the monastery of the Caves during the lifetime of its founders, St Antony and St Theodosius. Because of his capability and exemplary piety he was called to be abbot of St Demetrius in the same city in 1062, and fifteen years later was chosen bishop of Rostov. Here he devoted all his energies to bringing the gospel to the heathen, carrying on the work of his predecessor, St Leontius. He not only baptized many neophytes, but concerned himself with the further instruction and confirmation in the faith of those who were already Christians. His preaching is said to have been reinforced by many miracles, and he was tireless in bodily no less than in spiritual works of mercy in every part of his eparchy. Isaias was venerated as a saint from his death in 1090, and about seventy years later his body was enshrined in the cathedral church of Rostov.

From Martynov's *Annus ecclesiasticus Graeco-Slavicus* in *Acta Sanctorum*, October, vol. xi. *Cf.* St Sergius, September 25, and bibliography.

ST ISIDORE THE HUSBANDMAN   (A.D. 1130)

In the United States of America this feast is celebrated on 25 October.

THE patron of Madrid was born in the Spanish capital of poor parents, and was christened Isidore after the celebrated archbishop of Seville. Although unable to procure educational advantages for their son, his father and mother early instilled into his mind a great horror of sin and a love of prayer. As soon as he was old enough to work, Isidore entered the service of John de Vergas, a wealthy resident of Madrid, as a farm labourer on his estate outside the city, and with that one employer he remained all his life. He married a girl as poor and as good as himself, but after the birth of one son, who died young, they agreed to serve God in perfect continence. Isidore's whole life was a model of Christian perfection lived in the world. He would rise early to go to church, and all day long, whilst his hand guided the plough, he would be communing with God, with his guardian angel or with the holy saints. Public holidays he would spend in visiting the churches of Madrid and the neighbouring districts. Kind and helpful though he always was to others, he did not escape detraction. His fellow workmen complained that his attendance at church caused him to be late in starting work. To test the truth of this accusation, de Vergas hid himself to watch. He saw that Isidore did actually arrive after his fellow labourers, and he was advancing to upbraid him for his irregularity when he was surprised, we are told, to see a second team of snow-white oxen led by unknown figures ploughing beside that driven by Isidore. As he stood watching, rooted to the ground, the strange team disappeared and he realized that supernatural help had supplied all that was lacking. Other people also reported having seen angels assisting Isidore, and John de Vergas came to revere his servant who, it is said, worked miracles for the benefit of his employer and his family.

The saint's liberality to the poor was so great that he was wont to share his meals with them, often reserving for himself only the scraps they left over. On one occasion, when he had been invited to a confraternity dinner, he remained so long in church absorbed in prayer that the feast was nearly over before he made his appearance—followed by a train of beggars. His hosts expostulated, saying that they had reserved for him his portion, but that they could not possibly feed the whole crowd. St Isidore replied that there would be ample for himself and for Christ's poor. So, indeed, it happened, for when the food was produced there was enough and to spare for them all.   Amongst the numerous stories told of the holy man is one which illustrates his love for animals.   On a snowy winter's day, as he was carrying a sack of corn to be ground, he saw a number of birds perched disconsolately on the bare branches, obviously unable to find anything to eat.   Isidore opened the sack and, in spite of the jeers of a companion, poured out half its contents upon the ground.   When, however, they reached their destination the sack proved to be still full and the corn, when ground, produced double the usual amount of flour.

St Isidore died on May 15, 1130.   His wife survived him for several years and, like him, is honoured as a saint.   In Spain she is venerated as Santa Maria de la Cabeza, because her head (Sp. *cabeza*) is often carried in procession in times of drought.   Forty years after the death of St Isidore his body was transferred to a more honourable shrine, and a great impetus was given to his *cultus* by the report of many miracles worked through his intercession.   In 1211 he is said to have appeared in a vision to King Alphonsus of Castile, then fighting the Moors in the pass of Navas de Tolosa, and to have shown him an unknown path by means of which he was able to surprise and defeat the enemy.   More than four hundred years later, King Philip III of Spain was taken so ill at Casaribios del Monte that his life was despaired of by the physicians.   Thereupon the shrine of St Isidore was carried in solemn procession from Madrid to the sick monarch's room ; at the hour the relics were removed from the church of St Andrew, the fever left the king, and when they were brought into his presence he recovered completely.   The Spanish royal family had long desired to have St Isidore formally enrolled amongst the saints, and in March 1622 he was duly canonized together with St Ignatius, St Francis Xavier, St Teresa and St Philip Neri.   In Spain this holy quintet are commonly spoken of as " The Five Saints ".

The foundation document upon which our knowledge of the saint is almost entirely based is a life by "John the Deacon", probably identical with the Franciscan writer Johannes Aegidius of Zamora.   It is printed in the *Acta Sanctorum*, May, vol. iii, but as it was compiled a century and a half after St Isidore's death it cannot be regarded as a very trustworthy record.   A critical edition of this Latin text was published by Fr F. Fita, in the *Boletin de la Real Academia de la Historia*, vol. ix (1886), pp. 102–152.   Lives in Spanish (including several poetical settings by Lope de Vega) and in Italian are numerous.   The best biography is said to be that by Father J. Bleda (1622), and there is a more modern account in French by J. P. Toussaint (1901).   But by far the most satisfactory treatment of the points of interest in the history of St Isidore is that published by Fr Garcia Villada in *Razón y Fe*, January to May, 1922.   He in particular supplies very full details regarding the preservation of the body of the saint : it is mummified, but still entire.

BD MAGDALEN ALBRIZZI, Virgin   (A.D. 1465)

The Albrici or Albrizzi family to which Bd Magdalen belonged ranked among the nobility, and her father was a distinguished citizen of her native city, Como.   After the death of her father and mother, she decided to retire from the world, and she selected the convent of St Margaret, a house at Como which was considered suitable for a woman of her rank.   She had actually reached the door, when she distinctly heard a voice say to her three times, " Magdalen, turn your steps to Brunate : that is where you must go ".   There existed, as she well knew, a very poor convent situated in an isolated spot up in the mountains at Brunate, and thither accordingly she betook herself.   It contained only a few nuns, but after Bd Magdalen's reception the numbers increased considerably.   She was soon chosen superior, and was able to affiliate the community to the Hermits of St Augustine.

Lack of the bare necessities of life sometimes obliged the nuns to make begging expeditions into Como, where they were liable to be detained for the night by bad weather ; so to obviate the undesirable necessity of their having to accept casual hospitality from strangers, and also to provide a hospice for young women stranded in Como without a home, Magdalen founded a kind of daughter house in the city, though she herself remained at Brunate.   Hers was a hidden life, but she was endowed with supernatural gifts which precluded her from remaining as unknown as she could have wished.   She healed the sick and foretold the future, while her trust in God was so perfect that many miracles were wrought in immediate response to her prayers.   She also was constantly urging her nuns to frequent communion. Bd Magdalen appears to have died on May 15, 1465, at an advanced age, after a long and painful illness.

The account printed in the *Acta Sanctorum*, May, vol. iii, is a transcript from the life written by Father Paul Olmo in 1484.   The cult of Bd Magdalen was confirmed in 1907 and the decree may be read in the *Analecta Ecclesiastica*, vol. xvi (1908), pp. 19–20.   A life by G. B. Melloni was published at Bologna in 1764.

16 : ST UBALD, Bishop of Gubbio   (A.D. 1160)

WE are fortunate in possessing an excellent and reliable biography of Ubald Baldassini, bishop of Gubbio, compiled by Theobald, his immediate successor.   The saint, descended from a noble family in Gubbio, became an orphan at an early age and was educated by his uncle, also bishop of the same see, in the cathedral school.   Having completed his studies, he was ordained priest and appointed dean of the cathedral, young though he was, that he might reform the canons amongst whom grave irregularities were rampant.   The task was no easy one, but he succeeded before long in persuading three of the canons to join him in a common life.   Then, that he might obtain experience in the management of a well-conducted household, he resided for three months with a community of regular canons which had been established by Peter de Honestis in the territory of Ravenna.   The rule which they followed he brought back to Gubbio, and within a short time it was accepted by the whole chapter.   A few years later, after their house and cloisters had been burnt down, Ubald thought it a favourable moment to retire from his post into some solitude.   With this object in view he made his way to Fonte Avellano where he communicated his intention to Peter of Rimini.   That great servant of God, however, regarded the plan as a dangerous temptation and exhorted him to return to the post in which God had placed him for the benefit of others.   The saint accordingly returned to Gubbio, and rendered his chapter more flourishing than it had ever been before.   In 1126 St Ubald was chosen bishop of Perugia ; but he hid himself so that the deputies from that city could not find him ; then he went to Rome, threw himself at the feet of Pope Honorius II and begged that he might be excused.   His request was granted ; but when, two years later, the see of Gubbio fell vacant, the pope himself directed that the clergy should elect Ubald.

In his new office the saint displayed all the virtues of a true successor to the apostles, but perhaps his most distinguishing characteristic was a mildness and patience which made him appear insensible to injuries and affronts.   On one occasion workmen repairing the city wall encroached upon his vineyard and were

injuring his vines.   He gently drew their attention to this.   Thereupon the foreman, who probably did not recognize him, became abusive and pushed him so
roughly that he fell into a pool of liquid mortar.   He rose up, splashed all over with
lime and dirt, and without a word of expostulation returned to his house.   Eye-
witnesses, however, reported the incident and the citizens clamoured loudly that
the foreman should be punished.   So great was the popular indignation that a
severe sentence seemed a foregone conclusion, when St Ubald appeared in court and
claimed that, since the offence had been committed against an ecclesiastic, it came
under his jurisdiction as bishop.   Then, turning to the culprit, he bade him give him
the kiss of peace in token of reconciliation, and, after a prayer that God would forgive
him that and all his other trespasses, he directed that the man should be set at liberty.

The saint often defended his people in public dangers.   The Emperor Frederick
Barbarossa during his wars in Italy had sacked the city of Spoleto and threatened
to subject Gubbio to a similar fate.   Ubald met the emperor on the road and
diverted the tyrant from his purpose.   During the last two years of his life, the
holy bishop suffered from a complication of painful diseases which he bore with
heroic patience.   On Easter day 1160, although very ill, he rose to celebrate Mass,
and, that he might not disappoint his people, preached and gave them his blessing.
He was carried back to bed, from which he never rose again.   At Pentecost, as he
lay dying, the whole population of Gubbio filed past his couch, anxious to take a
last farewell of one whom each individual regarded as his dear father in God.
Ubald died on May 16, 1160, and the people who flocked to his funeral from far
and wide were eye-witnesses of the many miracles God performed at his tomb.

The life by Bishop Theobald is printed in the *Acta Sanctorum*, May, vol. iii, and there
is a further collection of miracles in vol. vii.   A modern Italian biography was published
by Gianpaoli in 1885.   On the curious confusion between St Ubald and the " St Theobald "
who is honoured as the patron of Thann, in Alsace, see H. Lempfrid in *Mittheilungen d.
Gesellschaft f. Erhalt. d. gesch. Denkmäler im Elsass*, vol. xxi (1903), pp. 1–128.

ST PEREGRINE, BISHOP OF AUXERRE, MARTYR   (*c.* A.D. 261)

AN accepted legend states that the first bishop of Auxerre, St Peregrine, was
consecrated by Pope Sixtus II and was sent from Rome at the request of the
Christians resident in that part of Gaul.   Landing at Marseilles, he preached the
gospel in that city, as well as in Lyons on his way.   During his episcopate the
greater part of the inhabitants of Auxerre are said to have been converted to
Christianity.   He built a church on the banks of the Yonne and evangelized all the
surrounding country.   In the mountainous district of the Puisaye, some ten
leagues or more south-west of Auxerre, stood the town of Intaranum—the present
Entrains—at a point where several roads met.   The Roman prefect had a palace
there and the place had become a great centre for the worship of Roman deities.
On the occasion of the dedication of a new temple to Jupiter, St Peregrine went to
the town and appealed to the populace to abandon idolatry.   He was seized,
brought before the governor and condemned to death.   After being cruelly
tortured he was beheaded.

This account is based upon two texts, one of which is printed in the *Acta Sanctorum*,
May, vol. iii, while the other may most conveniently be consulted in Migne, PL., vol. 138,
cc. 219–221.   There is no reason to doubt the fact of the martyrdom, for the *Hieronymianum*
commemorates it on this day and informs us that it took place at the " vicus Baiacus "
(Bouhy), where Peregrine was buried.   See also Duchesne, *Fastes Épiscopaux*, vol. ii, p. 431.

ST POSSIDIUS, Bishop of Calama   (c. A.D. 440)

Except that he was a native of proconsular Africa and a pupil of St Augustine at Hippo, nothing is known of the early history of St Possidius.   It seems to have been about the year 397 that he was made bishop of Calama in Numidia, a diocese greatly disturbed by the factions of the Donatists as well as by pagan opposition. He was closely associated with Augustine in his struggles against heresy, and suffered personal violence in an attempt made upon his life by the extremists amongst the Donatists.   For the energy he displayed against Pelagianism at the synod of Mileve in 416 he was commended by Pope Innocent I.   He made a religious foundation at Calama on the lines of St Augustine's community at Hippo.

When in 429 the Vandals passed over from Spain into Africa, they quickly made themselves masters of Mauritania, Numidia, and the proconsular province except the strong fortresses of Carthage, Cirta and Hippo.   Calama was destroyed, and Possidius took refuge with his lifelong friend St Augustine, who died not long afterwards in his arms whilst the barbarians were besieging Hippo.   Prosper, in his chronicle, states that Possidius and two other bishops were driven from their sees by the Arian Genseric.   The saint died in exile : he was alive in 437, but the date of his death is unknown.   Tradition reports that he spent the close of his life in Italy, dying at Mirandola.   St Possidius wrote a short life of St Augustine and left a catalogue of his writings.

What we know of St Possidius is gathered from miscellaneous sources, but especially from the works of St Augustine.   See the *Acta Sanctorum*, May, vol. iv.   There is a good notice of Possidius in DCB., vol. iv, pp. 445–446.

ST GERMERIUS, Bishop of Toulouse   (A.D. 560 ?)

St Germerius (Germier) was only thirty years old when he is said to have become bishop of Toulouse, and to have occupied the see for fifty years.   Although a native of Angoulême, he had been educated at Toulouse, whither he had migrated in early boyhood.   Very shortly after his consecration, he was summoned to the court of Clovis, the first Christian king of France, and was treated with great respect by the monarch, who entertained him for three weeks and loaded him with gifts for his churches.   He also bestowed upon him the district of Dux (?) near Toulouse and as much land for a cemetery as seven yoke of oxen could till in a day.   At Dux, Germerius built a church with three altars which he placed under the patronage of St Saturninus, the first bishop of Toulouse.   We read that, on the day of its dedication, it was lighted by three hundred wax candles and that a number of sick persons were restored to health.   At a later period the holy bishop founded a monastery at Dux, besides a second church, of St Martin.   A great lover of the poor, he appointed almoners whose special work it was to assist the needy.   In all his good works St Germerius was ably seconded by his two favourite disciples, Dulcidius and Pretiosus.   He died and was buried in his monastery at Dux.   The *cultus* of St Germerius goes back to a very early date.

There is every reason to be distrustful of the life printed in the *Acta Sanctorum*, May, vol. iii.   No Germerius can be found in the episcopal lists of Toulouse.   As against C. Douais, *Mémoires Soc. Antiq. France*, 1890, pp. 1–134, see L. Saltet in *Annales du Midi*, vol. xiii (1901), pp. 145–175.

ST BRENDAN, ABBOT OF CLONFERT   (A.D. 577 OR 583)

THERE is hardly any Irish saint whose name is more widely known than that of St Brendan, though it is to be feared that this exceptional prominence is due rather to the popularity of the saga, called his *Navigatio* (sea-voyage), admittedly a fiction, than to the tradition of his saintliness.   His life is preserved to us in several varying texts, Latin and Irish, but even when we eliminate the extravagances of the *Navigatio* which have been incorporated in some of these accounts, the residue is far from producing the impression of a sober historical record.   The early Bollandists who, like other scholars of that generation, were indulgent in their attitude towards the marvellous, decided against printing the full biography in their *Acta Sanctorum*, on the ground that it was " fabulous ".   On the other hand, it is certain that St Brendan was a real personage, and that he exercised great influence amongst his contemporaries in the sixth century.   He was probably born near Tralee on the west coast of Ireland, and Findlugh is given as his father's name.   For five years as a tiny child he was committed to the care of St Ita, and after that he was watched over by Bishop Erc who had already baptized him as an infant and who was in due time to ordain him priest.   St Jarlath of Tuam is also named as one of the holy men whom he visited with the view of obtaining edification and counsel.

To determine the chronological sequence of events is quite impossible, but we should be led to infer that shortly after being raised to the priesthood, St Brendan assumed the habit of a monk and gathered followers around him in a settled community.   How he could have left these behind to start off with sixty chosen companions in skin-covered coracles to discover the Isles of the Blessed is a difficulty which does not seem to have troubled his biographers.   One or other of these speaks of two separate voyages, though the first expedition is said to have lasted for five or seven years, as a sort of floating monastery.   At the same time, while it is ridiculous to suppose, as some fervent advocates of the legend have done, that the abbot sailed to the Canaries or travelled north-west to the coast of Greenland, so competent an authority as Dr J. F. Kenney states : " It is reasonably certain that Brendan himself made a voyage to the Scottish isles and perhaps to the Strathclyde, Cumbria or Wales ".   We know at any rate that Adamnan, writing little more than a century after St Brendan's death, describes him as visiting St Columba in the little island of Himba, or Hinba, in Argyll ; this island has not been identified, and on the point of this visit Adamnan has the Old Life against him. The biographers, whose narratives are probably later in date, discourse at considerable length of a visit he paid to St Gildas in Britain and of the marvels which happened on that occasion.

The most reliable fact which we can connect with the life of St Brendan is his foundation of a monastic community at Clonfert in 559 (?).   His biographers speak of his governing a community of three thousand monks.   He is also said to have had a rule of life dictated to him by an angel.   We know nothing of its nature, but we are told that the rule was followed " down to the present day " by those who succeeded him in the office of abbot.   There seems, again, no sufficient reason for questioning the statement that he did not die at Clonfert, but that God called him to his reward when he was paying a visit to his sister, Brig, who governed a community at Enach Duin.   After offering Mass, he said, " Commend my departure in your prayers " ; and Brig replied, " What do you fear ? "   " I fear ", he said, " if I go alone, if the journey be dark, the unknown region, the presence of the

328

King, and the sentence of the Judge." Foreseeing that attempts would be made to detain his body, he directed that his death should be kept secret for a time, while his remains were taken back to Clonfert in a cart, disguised as luggage he was sending on in advance of his own return. St Brendan's feast is observed throughout Ireland.

The biographical materials, which are relatively abundant, consist principally of two Latin lives, edited by C. Plummer in his VSH., vol. i, pp. 90–151, and vol. ii, pp. 270–292 ; that edited by P. Grosjean, in the *Analecta Bollandiana*, vol. xlviii (1930), pp. 99–121 ; an Irish life edited by Whitley Stokes in the *Lismore Lives*, pp. 99–115, and a second Irish life edited by Charles Plummer in his *Bethada Náem n-Érenn*, vol. i, pp. 44–95. Plummer has also provided a valuable discussion of the problems arising from these texts: see the prefaces of the two works mentioned and also the *Zeitschrift für Celtische Philologie*, vol. v (1905), pp. 124–141. The literature occasioned by the story of St Brendan, and especially by the *Navigatio*, which in the middle ages was translated into almost all European languages and has points of contact with the sagas current in Arabic, is very extensive. Consult further J. F. Kenney, *Sources for the Early History of Ireland*, i, pp. 408–412 ; Nutt and Meyer, *The Voyage of Bran* (1897) ; Schirmer, *Zur Brendanus Legende* (1888) ; and L. Gougaud, *Les Saints irlandais hors d'Irlande* (1936), pp. 6–15. An attractive little illustrated volume is that of J. Wilkie, *S. Brendan the Voyager and his Mystic Quest* (1916), and G. A. Little's *Brendan the Navigator* (1945) is an interesting " interpretation " by a maritime scholar, but is insufficiently critical, (See review in *Analecta Bollandiana*, vol. lxiv, pp. 290–293).

ST DOMNOLUS, BISHOP OF LE MANS　　(A.D. 581)

THE various accounts we have of the career of St Domnolus are somewhat conflicting, and it seems clear that our sources of information are unreliable. He was probably abbot of a monastery in Paris when he attracted the favourable notice of King Clotaire I, who offered him the see of Avignon. This he refused, but the king afterwards bestowed upon him the bishopric of Le Mans, which he held for twenty-one years. He built several churches and a hospice on the Sarthe for poor pilgrims. Attached to it was a monastery with a church, to the dedication of which he invited his special friend, St Germanus of Paris. We find him taking part in the Council of Tours in 566. St Gregory of Tours speaks of Domnolus as having reached a high pitch of sanctity and working many miracles, and we have also two apparently authentic charters of his.

The biographical materials supplied by the *vita* (printed in the *Acta Sanctorum*, May, vol. iii), and by the *Actus Pont. Cenom. (ibid.*), are altogether untrustworthy and are almost certainly compilations fabricated by the chorepiscopus David more than two centuries later, though they profess to be written by a contemporary. See on all this, Havet, in the *Bibl. de l'École des Chartes*, vol. liv, pp. 688–692 ; Celier, in *Revue Historique et archéol. du Maine*, vol. lv (1904), pp. 375–391 ; A. Poncelet, in the *Analecta Bollandiana*, vol. xxiv (1905), pp. 515–516 ; and Duchesne, *Fastes Épiscopaux*, vol. ii, p. 337.

ST CARANTOC, OR CARANNOG, ABBOT　　(SIXTH CENTURY)

ST CARANTOC was a Welsh abbot, formerly venerated in Cardiganshire where he founded the church of Llangrannog. He lived for some time in Ireland, but returned to Britain and made a religious settlement at a place called Cernach, which may have been either Carhampton in Somerset or the Cornish village of Crantock, which still has the saint's well and celebrates Crantock Feast on May 16 ; but the Welsh story puts Cernach in Ireland, deriving its name from an Irish version of the saint's name. It also associates Carantoc with Arthur. At a later date he is said to have passed over to Brittany. This is confirmed by a statement in the Life of St Guenael to the effect that when that holy man returned to Brittany from Britain, after collecting a number of disciples and books, he proceeded at once to pay a visit to St Carantoc. Moreover there is in Brittany a widespread *cultus* of Carantoc, sometimes in association with St Tenenan. Eventually, however, he died, we are told, " in his renowned monastery, the best of all his monasteries, which is called the monastery of Cernach ".

For the least unreliable information available about St Carantoc see the brochure of Canon Doble and C. G. Henderson in the Cornish Saints series (1928). The text printed with interpolations from an early twelfth-century *vita* originating in Cardigan in the *Acta Sanctorum*, May, vol. iii, is of very doubtful historical value ; a better text is that given in an appendix to J. T. Evans's volume on the church plate of Cardiganshire ; *cf.* too A. W. Wade-Evans, *Vitae Sanctorum Britanniae* (1944). See also Armitage Robinson in the *Downside Review*, vol. xlvi (1928), pp. 234–243 ; he shows that the saint was closely connected with Carhampton in west Somerset.

ST HONORATUS, Bishop of Amiens (*c.* A.D. 600)

THE famous Faubourg and Rue Saint-Honoré in Paris derive their name from St Honoratus who was bishop of Amiens at the close of the sixth century. History has little to tell us about him except that he was born at Port-le-Grand in the diocese of Amiens where he also died, and that he elevated the relics of SS. Fuscianus, Victoricus and Gentianus, which a priest called Lupicinus had discovered after they had been forgotten for three hundred years. The *cultus* of St Honoratus received a great impetus and became widespread in France in consequence of a number of remarkable cures which followed the elevation of his own body in 1060, and which were attributed to his agency. In 1204 Reynold Cherez and his wife Sybil placed under his patronage the church they built in Paris. Nearly a hundred years later another bishop of Amiens, William of Mâcon, dedicated in honour of his saintly predecessor the charterhouse he was building at Abbeville. St Honoratus is generally regarded in France as the patron of bakers, confectioners, corn chandlers and of all trades that deal with flour, and his appropriate emblem in art is a baker's peel.

The materials for this history, printed in the *Acta Sanctorum*, May, vol. iii, are altogether late and unreliable. See, however, Duchesne, *Fastes Épiscopaux*, vol. iii, p. 125 ; and H. Josse, *La Légende de S. Honoré* (1879).

ST SIMON STOCK (A.D. 1265)

ALTHOUGH St Simon Stock was undoubtedly a very active member of the Carmelite Order at a critical period of its history, and although his alleged connection with the brown scapular revelation (or promise) has made his name familiar to Catholics, we know very little in detail of his life and character. When he died at Bordeaux on May 16, 1265, he is said to have been a hundred years old, but this statement of a Carmelite catalogue of saints compiled upwards of a century and a half after the event is hardly sufficient to establish a longevity so unusual. It is hard to believe that he could have been elected prior general of the order at the age of eighty-two travelling afterwards not only to many different parts of England, but to Sicily, Bologna and Gascony. In the same authority we read that St Simon, being a strict vegetarian, when a cooked fish was on one occasion set before him, he told them to throw it into the river again, whereupon it swam away fully restored to life. Neither can we attach much more importance to another statement in the same context that Simon was called Stock because as a boy he had adopted the life of an anchoret, making his home in the hollow trunk of a tree.   All that has to do with the saint before the year 1247 is conjectural.

It is probable enough, as Father Benedict Zimmerman supposes, that after a short period spent as a hermit in England, he made his way to the Holy Land, and having there come into contact with some of the primitive Carmelites whose original profession was eremitical, he joined their organization as a religious.   When the hostility of the Saracens made life impossible for the brethren, we know that their settlements in the East were broken up and that nearly all returned to Europe.   In these circumstances St Simon seems to have come back to his native Kent, and being evidently a man of vigour as well as of exceptional holiness, he was elected superior-general, in succession to Alan, when a chapter was held at Aylesford in 1247.

His period of rule was marked by wonderful developments of the Carmelite Order.   As Father Benedict notes : " St Simon established houses in four University towns, Cambridge, Oxford, Paris and Bologna, with the result that a very large number of young, and probably immature, men joined the order.   A considerable number of foundations were made in England, Ireland, perhaps also in Scotland, in Spain, and in various countries on the continent " We have every reason to believe that about the same time the rule, which was originally drafted for hermits primarily intent upon their own individual perfection, had to be substantially modified now that the members of the order were becoming mendicant friars, busied with preaching and the work of the ministry.   This revision was carried through and a preliminary approval was granted by Pope Innocent IV in the year 1247 itself.   In 1252 a letter of protection was obtained from the same pontiff to secure them from the molestations of certain of the clergy, for the success of the White Friars had provoked jealousy and hostility in many quarters.

It was also at this time of stress and trial that our Lady is believed to have honoured St Simon with the declaration of an extraordinary privilege.   We are told that she appeared to him holding the scapular of the order in her hand, and that she said : " This shall be a privilege unto thee and all Carmelites ; he who dies in this habit shall be saved ".   This is not the place to embark upon the discussion of a controversy which has lasted for centuries.   It must be admitted that the evidence adduced in favour of this celebrated vision is not entirely satisfactory. There is no contemporary or quasi-contemporary document which attests or refers to it.   On the other hand the wearing of the brown scapular of the Carmelites has become a widespread devotion in the Church and has been enriched with indulgences by many different popes.   St Simon's devotion to our Lady is exemplified by two antiphons, the *Flos Carmeli* and the *Ave stella matutina*, which are unhesitatingly attributed to his authorship and which are employed liturgically by the Calced Carmelites.   The saint has never been formally canonized, and his name is not in the Roman Martyrology, but his feast by permission of the Holy See is kept in the Carmelite Order and the dioceses of Birmingham, Northampton and Southwark.   We are told that after his death many miracles were wrought beside his grave at Bordeaux, from which city what remained of his relics were solemnly translated to the restored Carmelite friary at Aylesford in Kent in 1951.

Almost everything which is evidential in connection with the life of St Simon will be found cited in the *Monumenta Historica Carmelitana* (1907) of Fr Benedict Zimmerman, O.D.C. ; see also his article in *The Month* for October 1927 and his " De sacro Scapulari Carmelitano " in *Analecta O.C.D.*, vol. ii (1927-28), pp. 70-89.   The conservative Carmelite position in the scapular controversy is best presented by Fr B. M. Xiberta in *De visione sti Simonis Stock* (1950). On the other side, see Fr H. Thurston in *The Month*, June and July 1927. For documentation, *Études carmélitaines*, t. xiii (1928), pp. 1 *seq.*

ST JOHN NEPOMUCEN, MARTYR   (A.D. 1393)

ST JOHN NEPOMUCEN was born in Bohemia, probably between the years 1340 and 1350. The appellation by which he is distinguished is derived from his native town of Nepomuk, or Pomuk, but his family name was actually Wölflein or Welflin. He studied at the University of Prague which had recently been founded by the Emperor Charles IV, king of Bohemia. Later on we find him occupying various ecclesiastical posts, and eventually he was appointed vicar general to the archbishop of Prague, John of Genzenstein (Jenstein).

The Emperor Charles IV had died at Prague in 1378, and had been succeeded by his son Wenceslaus IV, a vicious young man who gave way unrestrainedly to fits of rage or caprice in which he would perpetrate acts of savage cruelty. It is said that John of Pomuk received from Wenceslaus the offer of the bishopric of Litomerice, which he refused. There seems no evidence for this, or for the statement that he was appointed almoner and confessor to the king's wife. Shamelessly unfaithful himself, Wenceslaus was intensely jealous, and harboured suspicions of his young wife, whose conduct was irreproachable. A tradition, widely credited in Bohemia to this day, attributes the martyrdom of St John Nepomucen to the resentment aroused in the king by the holy man's uncompromising refusal to reveal to him the substance of the queen's confessions. On the other hand, no mention of this appears in the contemporary documents, or indeed for forty years after John's violent death. Thereafter, history and legend became so entangled that a theory (now abandoned) was evolved whereby there were two canons of Prague, both named John, who at ten years' interval both suffered death in the same way, in consequence of differing circumstances.

The only contemporary evidence about the circumstances of St John's murder comes from a report sent to Rome by Archbishop John of Genzenstein relating to his own difficulties with his sovereign, King Wenceslaus. It is an *ex parte* statement, but even so it appears that these grave difficulties arose principally from matters of material interests about which the archbishop was willing to concede but little. It appears further that St John Nepomucen's cruel death was no more than an incident in this rather disedifying series of quarrels. He was obedient to his ecclesiastical superior, and fell a victim to the king's anger in consequence.

In 1393 Wenceslaus resolved to found a new diocese at Kladrau, in order to give a bishopric to one of his favourites. To furnish a cathedral and endowment he proposed to confiscate the church and revenues of the ancient Benedictine abbey of Kladrau as soon as the abbot, who was very old, should die. This proposal was strenuously opposed by Archbishop John of Genzenstein and by St John Nepomucen as his vicar general. Acting under instructions from them, the monks, immediately after the abbot's death, proceeded to the election of a new superior. The archbishop and his two vicars general ratified the appointment so promptly that the king was informed at the same moment of the death of the one abbot and the institution of the new. Wenceslaus sent envoys to the archbishop, who came to an agreement with them, but then, for reasons unknown, the king had one of his tempests of rage. He confronted the two vicars general and other dignitaries of the chapter and, after striking the aged dean, Boheslaus, on the head with the hilt of his sword, ordered them to be tortured: it is likely that he suspected some conspiracy against himself and wanted to get information about it. He with his own hand wreaked his fury on St John and his coadjutor Nicholas Puchnik, by applying a burning torch to their sides.

Then Wenceslaus came to himself, and he released his victims on condition they should say nothing of his mishandling of them. But John Nepomucen was already dying of the injuries he had received, and so, to get rid of the evidence, he was made away with. His body was trussed up, " like a wheel ", his heels tied to his head ; lest he should cry out a gag was forced into his mouth, and he was then borne secretly through the streets to the Karlsbrücke and cast into the river Moldau. This was on March 20, 1393. In the morning the body was washed ashore, and it was immediately recognized. It was later buried in the cathedral of St Vitus, where it still is. On the old bridge the place from which he was thrown is marked by a metal plate adorned with seven stars, in reference to the story that on the night of his murder seven stars hovered over the water. St John Nepomucen is principal patron of Bohemia, where he is invoked against floods and against slander, as well as for help to make a good confession.

The account which the *Acta Sanctorum*, May, vol. iii, furnishes of St John Nepomucen is not altogether trustworthy. The Bollandists were not permitted to have access to the archives at Prague, and they have followed Fr B. Balbinus and the materials which, from unsatisfactory sources, were first presented for the confirmation of *cultus*. Even in the bull of canonization (1729) the death of this martyr is alleged to have taken place in 1383, whereas it certainly occurred in 1393. On the other hand, there is no solid reason for supposing that there were two different Johns, canons of the cathedral, who have been confused. But the controversy, which has been conducted with much acrimony, is too intricate to be discussed here at length. A convenient statement of the whole question is available in the little volume of J. Weisskopf, *S. Johannes von Nepomuk* (1931) and also in W. A. Frind, *Der hl. Johannes von Nepomuk* (1929) ; but the most recent and weighty contribution is that of P. de Vooght, " Jean de Pomuk ", in *Revue d'histoire ecclésiastqiue*, vol. xlviii (1953), nos. 3–4, pp. 777–795. John of Jenstein's report to Rome was found in the Vatican archives in 1752 and printed as an appendix to M. Pelzel's *Lebensgeschichte des Römischen und Böhmischen Königs Wenceslaus*, vol. i (1788), pp. 145–164. A good bibliography and discussion of the earlier writers on the question will be found in the *Kirchenlexikon*, vol. vi, pp. 1725–1742. See also J. P. Kirsch in the *Catholic Encyclopaedia*, vol. viii, pp. 467–468.

17: ST PASCHAL BAYLON   (A.D. 1592)

THE notice of St Paschal Baylon in the Roman Martyrology tells us not only that he was a man of wonderful innocence and austerity of life, but also that he has been proclaimed by the Holy See patron of all eucharistic congresses and confraternities of the Blessed Sacrament. It is a striking fact that a humble friar, of peasant birth, who was never even a priest, whose name in his own day was hardly known to any but his townsfolk in a corner of Spain, should now from his place in Heaven preside over those imposing assemblies of the Catholic Church.

Thanks mainly to his fellow religious, superior and biographer, Father Ximenes, we are well informed regarding Paschal's early days. He first saw the light at Torre Hermosa, on the borders of Castile and Aragon, on a Whitsunday, and to that accident he seems to have owed his Christian name, for in Spain, as well as in Italy, the term *Pascua* is given to other great feasts of the year besides Easter.   So the little son born to Martin Baylon and his wife Elizabeth Jubera was called Pascual, just as we are told that the famous Cervantes was christened Miguel because he came into the world on St Michael's day.   The pious couple possessed little in the way of worldly goods, but they owned a flock of sheep, and from his seventh to his twenty-fourth year Paschal, first as the deputy of his own father, and then serving other employers, led the life of a shepherd.   Some of the incidents ascribed to that time are probably legendary, but one or two certain facts stand out : for example, that this shepherd lad, who never had any schooling, taught himself to read and write, being determined to recite the Little Office of our Lady, the central feature of the *Horae B. Mariae Virginis*, then the prayer-book universally in use among lay-folk.   It was noticed with surprise that he went barefoot despite the briars and stony mountain tracks, lived on the poorest fare, fasted often, and wore under his shepherd's cloak some sort of imitation of a friar's habit.   He could not always get to Mass, but when he was unable to leave his charge in the early morning he knelt for long spaces of time absorbed in prayer, his eyes fixed upon the distant sanctuary of Nuestra Señora de la Sierra where the holy sacrifice was being offered.   Fifty years afterwards an aged shepherd who had known Paschal in those days deposed that on such occasions the angels more than once brought to the lad the Blessed Sacrament suspended in the air above a chalice, that he might gaze upon and venerate It.   He is also alleged to have had a vision of saints, identified by conjecture with St Francis and St Clare, who directed him to offer himself to God in the Order of Friars Minor.   More convincing than this testimony is the evidence given of his scrupulous sense of justice.   The damage which his beasts occasionally caused to the vines or growing crops was to him a continual source of worry.   He insisted that compensation should be made to the owners and often paid for it out of his own slender wage.   In that matter his fellows, though they respected him for it, thought he went to absurd lengths.

When Paschal, seemingly about the age of eighteen or nineteen, first sought admission among the barefooted Friars Minor, St Peter of Alcantara, the author of the reform, was still living.   The austerity of the rule which he had revived was only equalled by the fervour of those who practised it.   Probably the friars of the Loreto convent, knowing nothing of the young shepherd who came from a district two hundred miles away, doubted his fortitude.   At any rate, they put him off, but when they admitted him some few years later, they soon realized that God had committed a treasure to their keeping.   The community lived at the level of the first fervour of the reform, but Brother Paschal even in this ascetical atmosphere was recognized as being eminent in every religious virtue.   One is apt to regard with some distrust the extravagant eulogiums of hagiographers, but no discerning reader can make himself acquainted with the description which Father Ximenes has left of his friend without feeling that we have here no conventional panegyric, but a straightforward statement of his own inmost conviction.   In charity towards all, Paschal was a marvel even to those mortified men who shared the same hard external conditions and were bound by the same rule.   In what he deemed to be matters of conscience he was inflexible.   There is the story of the ladies who, when Paschal was porter, came to the door to ask the father guardian to come down to hear their confessions.   " Tell them ", said the guardian, " that I am out."   " I will tell them ", amended Paschal, " that your Reverence is engaged."   " No ", the

guardian insisted, " tell them that I am not at home." " Forgive me, Father ",
objected the brother very humbly and respectfully, " I must not say that, for that
would not be the truth and would be a venial sin " ; and thereupon he returned to
the door in perfect peace of mind.   It is such little flashes of independence which
relieve the monotony of the catalogue of virtues, and enable us to see something of
the human element in a soul so exalted and purified.

It is pleasant, too, to read of the little devices by which Paschal schemed to
secure special delicacies for the sick, the poor, and those whom he regarded as
exceptionally deserving, as well as of the tears sometimes seen in the eyes of this
austere man, who normally repressed all signs of emotion, when he was brought
into contact with some pathetically hard case.   Although, it seems, he never
laughed, still he was gay, and there was nothing gloomy about his devotion or even
his spirit of penance.   Ximenes tells us how on one occasion when Paschal was
refectorian and had shut himself in to lay the tables, another friar, peeping through
the buttery-hatch, caught sight of the good brother executing an elaborate dance,
like a second *jongleur de Notre-Dame*, leaping high and moving rhythmically backwards and forwards, before the statue of our Lady which stood over the refectory
door.   The intruder withdrew noiselessly, but coming in again a few minutes later
with the customary salutation, " Praised be Jesus Christ ", he found Paschal with
so radiant a countenance that the memory of the scene was a spur to his devotion
for many days afterwards.   It is no small tribute that Father Ximenes, who
was himself a minister provincial of the Alcantarines within little more than
half a century of their inauguration, says of St Paschal : " In no single case do I
remember to have noted even the least fault in him, though I lived with him
in several of our houses and was his companion on two long journeys ; such
journeys being commonly an occasion when a man, worn out with fatigue and
the monotony, allows himself some indulgence which is not entirely free from
blame ".

It is, however, as the Saint of the Eucharist that St Paschal is best remembered
outside his own country.   Many years before the great work of annual eucharistic
congresses was instituted and our saint was nominated its patron, the title-page of
Father Salmeron's Spanish biography bore the heading *Vida del Santo del Sacra-
mento S. Pascual Bailon.*   The long hours which he spent before the tabernacle,
kneeling without support, his clasped hands held up in front of, or higher than, his
face, had left a deep impression upon his brethren.   No wonder that he was for
them the " Saint of the Blessed Sacrament ".   The recognition of this special
characteristic goes back to his earliest biographer.   Ximenes tells us how the good
brother, whenever he had a moment free from his other duties, invariably made
his way to the church to honour the presence of our Lord, how it was his delight
to serve Mass after Mass in succession beginning with the very earliest, how he
stayed behind in choir when after Matins and Lauds the rest of the community
had retired again to sleep, and how the dawn found him there still on his knees,
eager as soon as the bell rang to visit the altars at which the Holy Sacrifice was to be
offered.

Father Ximenes prints some specimens, too lengthy to quote, of the simple
heartfelt prayers recited by Paschal at the time of communion.   Whether they
were his own composition, as his biographer supposes, is not so clear.   The saint
had long kept what he himself calls a *cartapacio* (a home-made scrap-book, formed,
it seems, out of odds and ends of paper which he had rescued from the rubbish-heap)

and in this he noted down in a beautiful handwriting certain prayers and reflections which he had either come across in his reading or had composed himself. One at least of these books—there seem to have been two—is still preserved. Shortly after Paschal's death some of these prayers were brought to the notice of Bd John de Ribera, then archbishop of Valencia. He was so impressed that he begged to have a relic of this holy lay-brother who, it seemed to him, had achieved so perfect an understanding of spiritual things. When a relic was brought him by Father Ximenes, the archbishop said to him, " Ah ! Father Provincial, what are we to do ? These simple souls are wresting Heaven from our hands. There is nothing for it but to burn our books." To which Ximenes answered, " My Lord, it is not the books that are in fault, but our own pride. Let us burn that."

St Paschal, the Saint of the Eucharist, had, it appears, some experience in his own person of the ferocity with which Protestant reformers sometimes manifested their dislike of the sacraments and of faithful sons of the Church. He was on one occasion sent into France as the bearer of an important communication to Father Christopher de Cheffontaines, the very learned Breton scholar who at that time was minister general of the Observants. For a friar wearing the habit of his order the journey across France at that time, when the wars of religion had reached their most acute phase, was extremely dangerous, and the choice for such an errand of a simple lay-brother, who certainly did not know any French, remains a mystery. Perhaps his superior believed that his simplicity and trust in God would carry him through where more diplomatic methods would fail. He succeeded in his mission, but was very roughly handled ; on several occasions barely escaping with his life. At one town in particular, where he was stoned by a party of Huguenots, he seems to have sustained an injury to his shoulder which was a cause of suffering for the rest of his days. At Orleans, we are told by most of his biographers, even by Ximenes, he was questioned as to his belief in the Blessed Sacrament, and when he unhesitatingly made profession of his faith, his opponents instituted a sort of formal disputation in which they were worsted by the good brother, who was preternaturally aided from on high. Here again in their fury the Huguenots stoned him, but he escaped, because all their missiles fell wide of the mark. It seems, however, a little difficult to believe in such a disputation in argumentative form with citation of authorities.

St Paschal died, as he was born, on a Whitsunday, in the friary at Villareal. He was fifty-two years old. It was held to be significant of his life-long devotion to the Blessed Sacrament that, with the holy name of Jesus on his lips, he passed away just as the bell was tolling to announce the consecration at the high Mass. He had long been honoured as a saint, partly owing to the miracles of all kinds attributed to him in life, especially in his dealings with the sick and poor, and these miracles were multiplied beside his bier. There can be little doubt that the unusually great number of remarkable cures, reported then and later, influenced ecclesiastical authorities to take unwontedly speedy action in the matter of his beatification. He was in fact beatified in 1618, before St Peter of Alcantara, the author of the reform to which he belonged, though Peter had died thirty years earlier than he. Perhaps a bizarre factor which intervened in the case, causing considerable popular excitement, contributed to this. It was universally believed that curious knockings (*golpes*) proceeded from Paschal's tomb, which knockings were invested with portentous significance. This phenomenon is said to have continued for a couple of centuries, and his later biographers devote much space to the *golpes* and their interpretation. St Paschal's canonization took place in 1690.

Our information concerning St Paschal comes almost entirely from the life by Father Ximenes and the process of beatification. A Latin version of Ximenes' biography, somewhat abridged, is printed in the *Acta Sanctorum*, May, vol. iv. Lives in Spanish, Italian and French are numerous, *e.g.* those by Salmeron, Olmi, Briganti, Beaufays, Du Lys and L. A. de Porrentruy ; this last has been translated from the French by O. Staniforth, under the title of *The Saint of the Eucharist* (1908). See also O. Englebert's French sketch (1944), and Léon, *Auréole séraphique* (Eng. trans.), vol. ii, pp. 177–197. Probably the best modern life is that written in German by Father Grötcken (1909).

ST MADRON, or MADERN   (Sixth Century ?)

THIS saint, who has given his name to a large parish in the extreme south-west of England and to its unusually interesting church (the mother church of Penzance) has not been satisfactorily identified and nothing is known for certain about his life. Alban Butler does not venture beyond connecting him with Brittany. Some claim him to be the Welsh St Padarn ; others say he is the same as St Medran, brother of St Odran, a disciple of St Kieran of Saighir—on the assumption that the last named was identical in his turn with St Piran. Professor Loth inclined to the view, and Canon Doble agreed, that Madron was Matronus, a disciple of St Tudwal who went with his master to Brittany and was buried close to him at Tréguier.

In any case St Madron is of interest because of the persistence of a *cultus* associated with his well and chapel. This well is out among the fields three-quarters of a mile north-west of Madron churchtown. Close by is the chapel or baptistery, of which the remains are of great interest : water from the spring flows through it at the west end, where there is a sort of tiny structural baptistery in the angle of the south and west walls. The repute of this sanctuary for miraculous occurrences did not end with the Reformation : and if John Norden the topographer wrote in 1584 that Madron was " coye of his cures ", less than sixty years later a happening there caused widespread interest. The Anglican bishop of Exeter, Dr Joseph Hall, himself examined it in 1641, and wrote in a treatise *On the Invisible World :*

> The commerce which we have with the good spirits is not now discerned by the eyes, but is, like themselves, spiritual. Yet not so, but that even in bodily occasions, we have many times insensible helps from them : in such manner as that by the effects we can boldly say : " Here hath been an angel, though we see him not." Of this kind was that (no less than miraculous) cure which at St Madern's in Cornwall was wrought upon a poor cripple, John Trelille, whereof (besides the attestation of many hundreds of neighbours) I took a strict and personal examination in that last visitation which I either did or ever shall hold. This man, that for sixteen years together, was fain to walk upon his hands, by reason of the close contraction of his legs (upon three admonitions in a dream to wash in that well) was suddenly so restored to his limbs that I saw him able to walk and get his own maintenance. I found here was no art nor collusion : the thing done, the author invisible.

A more detailed description of the same cure is given by another writer, Francis Coventry, in a book entitled *Paralipomena Philosophica de Mundo Peripatetico*

(Antwerp, 1652).* It appears that the story of the miracle came to the ears of King Charles I, who caused further inquiries to be made, from which it was ascertained that :

A certain boy of twelve years old, called John Trelille . . . as they were playing at football, snatching up the ball ran away with it : whereupon a girl in anger struck him with a thick stick on the back-bone, and so bruised or broke it that for sixteen years after he was forced to go creeping on the ground. In this condition he arrived to the twenty-eighth year of his age, when he dreamed that if he did but bathe in St Madern's well, or in the stream running from it, he should recover his former strength and health. This is a place in Cornwall from the remains of ancient devotion still frequented by Protestants on the Thursdays in May, and especially on the feast of Corpus Christi ; near to which well is a chapel dedicated to St Madern, where is yet an altar, and right against it a grassy hillock (made every year anew by the country people) which they call St Madern's bed. The chapel roof is quite decayed ; but a kind of thorn of itself shooting forth of the old walls so extends its boughs that it covers the whole chapel and supplies as it were a roof. On a Thursday in May, assisted by one Berriman his neighbour, entertaining great hopes from his dream, thither he crept, and lying before the altar, and praying very fervently that he might regain his health and the strength of his limbs, he washed his whole body in the stream that flowed from the well and ran through the chapel : after which, having slept about an hour and a half on St Madern's bed, through the extremity of pain he felt in his nerves and arteries, he began to cry out ; and his companions helping and lifting him up, he perceived his hams and joints somewhat extended and himself become stronger, in so much that, partly with his feet, partly with his hands, he went much more erect than before. Before the following Thursday he got two crutches, resting on which he could make shift to walk, which before he could not do. And coming to the chapel as before, after having bathed himself he slept on the same bed, and awaking found himself much stronger and upright ; and so leaving one crutch in the chapel, he went home with the other. The third Thursday he returned to the chapel and bathed as before, slept, and when he awoke rose up quite cured : yea, grew so strong that he wrought day-labour among the hired servants ; and four years after listed himself a soldier in the king's army, where he behaved himself with great stoutness, both of mind and body ; at length in 1644 he was slain at Lyme in Dorsetshire.

For a long time the local Wesleyan Methodists have met annually for a service at St Madron's chapel on the first two Sundays of May, and since about 1920 the Anglicans do the like on St John's day in summer. A child was baptized there in June 1951. On the other hand, the custom, especially during May month, of passing children through the spring water to alleviate skin affections has also been observed within living memory, and young people still visit the well and drop pins and little crosses therein, though no doubt " more from the pleasure of each other's

* Francis Coventry was none other than Christopher Davenport, better known as Francis a Sancta Clara, the Franciscan Recollect who was chaplain to Queen Henrietta Maria and sought to interpret the Thirty-Nine Articles in a Catholic sense. Apparently on the strength of a statement by Alban Butler, the judicious Dr Oliver states in his *Collections* (1857) that Father Francis " lived in Cornwall before the civil wars ". This seems to be a mistake.

company than from any real faith " in its power of divination. But those customs go back in all probability to long before St Madron may have built his chapel and hermitage here, to a time when no child in these islands had yet been christened.

See Canon H. R. Jennings, *Historical Notes on Madron* . . . (1936) ; LBS., vol. iii, pp. 396–398 ; W. Scawen in an appendix to D. Gilbert's *Parochial History of Cornwall* (1838) ; R. Hunt, *Popular Romances of the West of England* (1903), pp. 294–295 ; A. K. H. Jenkin, *Cornwall and Its People* (1945), pp. 309–310.

BD RATHO OF ANDECHS   (A.D. 953)

THE famous pilgrimage-place of Grafrath in Bavaria derives its name from Bd Ratho, Graf von Andechs, who is buried there and whose intercession is sought at his shrine by countless invalids, especially by those suffering from hernia and stone. The *beatus*, whose name is also written Ratto, Rasso, Rago and Rapoto, is popularly known as St Grafrath. His father was count of Diessen and Andechs, and he had one brother who died on a pilgrimage to the Holy Land, and a sister, Halta, who became the mother of St Conrad of Constance. He himself was remarkable for his great stature and for his prowess in all knightly exercises ; he also distinguished himself in battle as leader of the Bavarians against the Hungarians. Peace having been restored, about 948 he laid aside his weapons to undertake pilgrimages to Rome and to the Holy Land from which he brought back numerous relics, the greater part of which are now at Andechs. On what was then an island in the Amper, under the shadow of the height crowned by the castle afterwards known as the Rassoburg, he built a monastery for Benedictine monks to which he gave the name of Wörth. The church was consecrated by St Ulric on May 1, 951. The following year Ratho assumed the habit at Wörth and in 953 he died there. Although shortly after his death the monastery and church were destroyed by the Hungarians, the relics of Bd Ratho were saved, and his tomb escaped the ravages of that period.

It is very difficult to decide what historical value attaches to the narrative compiled by I. Keferlocher from earlier materials. There has been of late a reaction against the complete discredit into which all the Andechs story had fallen. The text is in the *Acta Sanctorum* (for June 19). See also Rader, *Bavaria Sancta*, vol. i, pp. 161–165 ; Blattmann, *Der hl. Rasso* (1892) ; R. Bauerreiss, *Fuss-Wallfahrt zum hl. Berg Andechs* (1927).

ST BRUNO, BISHOP OF WÜRZBURG   (A.D. 1045)

ST BRUNO of Würzburg was the son of Conrad, Duke of Carinthia, and of Baroness Matilda, niece of St Bruno Boniface of Querfurt, the second apostle of Prussia, after whom his great-nephew was named. Having entered the ecclesiastical state, the younger Bruno became bishop of Würzburg in 1033 and ruled his diocese successfully for eleven years. The whole of his patrimony he spent in building the magnificent cathedral of St Kilian and in restoring other churches under his rule. A wise man and a profound scholar, he became the counsellor of two emperors and wrote various books, including commentaries on the Holy Scriptures, the Lord's Prayer, the Apostles' Creed and the Creed of St Athanasius. He accompanied his kinsman, Conrad II, to Italy, and is said to have persuaded him to abandon the siege of Milan and to make terms with its inhabitants, as the result of a warning he received in a vision from the great St Ambrose of Milan. When the Emperor Henry III, " the Black ", marched against the Hungarians in 1045, he took St Bruno with him. On their way through Pannonia the royal party put up for a night at the castle of Bosenburg, or Porsenberg, on the Danube, opposite the present town of Ips in Upper Austria. The building seems to have been in a dilapidated condition, for, while the court was at dinner, the banqueting gallery suddenly collapsed. By grasping at a window the emperor escaped disaster, but all the rest were more or less injured, several of them being killed outright. St Bruno, though dying, lingered on for seven days. His body was taken back to Würzburg, where it was buried in the basilica he had erected.

There seems to be no proper biography, but there is a notice in the *Acta Sanctorum*, May, vol. iv. See also H. Bresslau, *Jahrbücher der deutsche Geschichte unter Konrad II* (1884) ; and J. Baier, *Der hl. Bruno von Würzburg* (1893).

BD ANDREW ABELLON (A.D. 1450)

THE birthplace of Bd Andrew Abellon was Saint-Maximin, the ancient Provençal town which for the last seven hundred years has claimed to possess the relics of St Mary Magdalen and has been visited by countless pilgrims. Andrew received the Dominican habit in his native town and became prior of the royal monastery of St Mary Magdalen at a time when the great church which is supposed to enshrine the head of its holy patroness was slowly approaching completion : it was begun in 1295, but not finished until 1480. Bd Andrew was distinguished for his piety and the zeal with which he enforced regular observance. In addition to labouring as a missioner, he exercised his talents as an artist in many of the Dominican churches of the south of France. He died in 1450.

Not much seems to be known about the life of Bd Andrew. The decree of confirmation of *cultus* is printed with some other matter in the *Analecta Ecclesiastica*, vol. x (1902), pp. 443–448 ; but most of this space is taken up with the proof that the *beatus* after his death was held in great veneration. There is also an account of Bd Andrew by Father H. Cormier (1903), and sundry references in Fr Mortier's *Histoire des Maîtres Généraux O.P.*, vol. iv. It need hardly be pointed out that the sanctity of Bd Andrew is in no way prejudiced by the fact that historical evidence is lacking to establish the genuineness of the relics in which he so devoutly believed. On this question of the authenticity of the St Mary Magdalen legend, see herein under July 22.

18 : ST VENANTIUS, MARTYR (A.D. 257 ?)

I T is necessary to devote a notice to St Venantius because he is commemorated on this day with Mass and office throughout the Western church. Moreover, the fictitious history of this youth of seventeen is narrated in three long lessons in the Breviary and emphasized by a set of hymns written expressly for the feast. The honour thus paid to the martyr of Camerino is due to the personal action of Pope Clement X, who after having held the seé of Camerino for close on forty years was elected pope at the age of eighty (1670–1676).

There is but the slenderest evidence of any *cultus* of this martyr. The fact that the name of Venantius appears in church dedications, or was attached to relics, proves little, because there was an authentic St Venantius who was the first bishop of Salona in Dalmatia, on the shore of the Adriatic. The apocryphal " acts " of the martyr of Camerino narrate that this youth came before the judge to profess himself a Christian, that he was scourged, seared with torches, suspended head downward over fire and smoke, had his teeth knocked out and his jaw broken, was thrown to the lions who only licked his feet, was precipitated without suffering any injury from a high cliff, and finally had his head cut off, with a number of other martyrs who had declared themselves Christians after witnessing the spectacle of his constancy. All this was attended with supernatural apparitions, with the death of two judges who successively presided over the tribunal before which he appeared, and finally with earthquakes and a portentous storm of thunder and lightning.

The text in which all these things are recorded is printed in the *Acta Sanctorum*, May, vol. iv (see also May, vol. vii, appendix), but with a commentary emphasizing its unhistorical character. It seems, in fact, to be of no earlier date than the twelfth century and to be a mere imitation of the equally spurious " acts " of St Agapitus of Praeneste. It is possible that some earlier fiction which grew up round the authentic martyr, St Venantius of Salona, may have influenced both. See Karl Bihlmeyer in the *Kirchliches Handlexikon*, vol. ii, c. 2563.

SS. THEODOTUS, THECUSA AND THEIR COMPANIONS, MARTYRS (A.D. 304 ?)

LIKE many other narratives which have found more or less authoritative acceptance both in the Eastern and Western church, the story of SS. Theodotus, Thecusa and their companions is not historical fact but a pious romance. Shorn of many picturesque details, the tale runs as follows : Theodotus was a charitable and devout Christian who had been brought up by a maiden called Thecusa ; he plied the trade of an innkeeper at Ancyra in Galatia. The faithful in this province, during the persecution of Diocletian, suffered terribly at the hands of a particularly cruel governor. Theodotus fearlessly assisted the imprisoned Christians and buried the martyrs at the risk of his life. He was bearing back the relics of St Valens, which he had rescued from the river Halys, when he encountered, near the town of Malus, a party of Christians who had recently regained their liberty through his exertions. They were overjoyed at the meeting, and sat down to an *alfresco* meal, to which they invited Fronto, the local Christian priest. In the course of conversation, Theodotus remarked that the place would be an ideal site for a *confessio* or chapel for relics. " Yes ", was the priest's reply, " but you must first have the relics". " Build the church ", said Theodotus, " and I will provide the relics." With these words he gave Fronto his ring as a pledge.

Soon afterwards there occurred in Ancyra an annual feast to Artemis and Athene, during the course of which statues of the goddesses were washed at a pond, in which women consecrated to their service bathed in view of the public. There happened to be at that time imprisoned in the town seven Christian maidens, amongst whom was Thecusa. The governor, who had been unable to shake their constancy, condemned them to be stripped, to be carried naked in an open chariot after the idols, and then to be drowned in the pond, unless they consented to wear the garlands and robes of the priestesses. As they indignantly refused to do this, the sentence was carried out, stones having been attached to the necks of the martyrs to prevent their bodies from rising. However, Theodotus recovered them one tempestuous night while the guards were sheltering from the storm, and gave them Christian burial. The secret was betrayed by an apostate, and Theodotus, after being subjected to appalling tortures, was decapitated.

Now it came to pass on the day of his friend's death that the priest Fronto had occasion to come to Ancyra with his ass to sell wine. Night had fallen when he arrived, and as the gates were closed he gladly accepted the hospitality of a little band of soldiers encamped outside the city. In the course of conversation he discovered that they were guarding the pyre on which the body of the dead

Theodotus was to be burnt on the morrow. Thereupon he plied them with his wine till they were completely intoxicated and, after replacing the ring on its former owner's finger, he laid the body of Theodotus across the back of his ass which he set at liberty, well knowing that it would return home. In the morning he loudly bewailed the theft of the ass and thus escaped suspicion. The animal, as he had anticipated, bore its burden back to Malus, and there the *confessio* which Theodotus had desired was built to enshrine his own remains.

It might be said without exaggeration that the attitude adopted by modern scholars towards the story of Theodotus is typical of the change which has come over the whole science of hagiography. Alban Butler, following the footsteps of such generally sound authorities as Ruinart, the early Bollandists and Tillemont, believed that this narrative was written by one Nilus, " who had lived with the martyr, had been his fellow prisoner and was an eye-witness of what he relates ". But there are grave reasons for believing that Nilus has merely been invented by an artifice common to all fiction, and that the story, with its reminiscences of a tale occurring in Herodotus, must be treated as a romance written by an author possessing rather more literary skill than we commonly find in such cases. See Delehaye in the *Analecta Bollandiana*, vol. xxii (1903), pp. 320–328 ; and vol. xxiii (1904), pp. 478–479. The texts are best given in P. Franchi de' Cavalieri, *Studi e Testi*, no. 6 (1901), and no. 33 (1920). See also the *Acta Sanctorum*, May, vol. iv, and the *Revue des Questions historiques*, vol. xviii (1904), pp. 288–291.

ST POTAMON, Bishop of Heraclea, Martyr   (c. A.D. 340)

St Potamon (Potamion) was bishop of Heraclea in Egypt. St Athanasius says that he was doubly a martyr, inasmuch as he suffered cruel persecution first for vindicating the Catholic faith before the heathen and then for defending the divinity of our Lord before the Arians. When Maximinus Daia persecuted the Christians in 310, St Potamon made a bold confession, and was subjected to savage tortures which entailed permanent lameness as well as the loss of an eye. These marks of his sufferings rendered him a conspicuous figure at the Council of Nicaea in 325, where he took a vigorous part. Ten years later he accompanied St Athanasius to the Council of Tyre and nobly defended that champion of the faith. Under the Arian Emperor Constantius, the prefect of Egypt, Philagrius, and the heretical priest Gregory who had usurped the see of Athanasius, travelled over all Egypt, tormenting and banishing the orthodox. Foremost among their victims was St Potamon, whose uncompromising attitude had specially incurred their animosity. By their order he was arrested and beaten with clubs until he was left for dead. The tender care of those who rescued him enabled him to make a partial recovery, but he died soon afterwards as the result of the ill-treatment he had received.

The available information, gathered almost entirely from SS. Epiphanius and Athanasius, is set out in the *Acta Sanctorum*, May, vol. iv. See also Hefele-Leclercq, *Conciles*, vol. i, pp. 658–659.

ST ERIC OF SWEDEN, Martyr   (A.D. 1161)

St Eric was acknowledged king in most parts of Sweden in 1150, and his line subsisted for a hundred years. He did much to establish Christianity in Upper Sweden and built or completed at Old Uppsala the first large church to be erected in his country. It is said that the ancient laws and constitutions of the kingdom were by his orders collected into one volume, which became known as King Eric's Law or the Code of Uppland. The king soon had to take up arms against the heathen Finns, who were making descents upon his territories and pillaging the country.   He vanquished them in battle, and at his desire, St Henry, Bishop of Uppsala, an Englishman, who had accompanied him on the expedition, remained in Finland to evangelize the people.

The king's zeal for the faith was far from pleasing to some of his nobles, and we are told that they entered into a conspiracy with Magnus, the son of the king of Denmark.   St Eric was hearing Mass on the day after the feast of the Ascension when news was brought that a Danish army, swollen with Swedish rebels, was marching against him and was close at hand.   He answered calmly, " Let us at least finish the sacrifice : the rest of the feast I shall keep elsewhere ".   After Mass was over, he recommended his soul to God, and marched forth in advance of his guards.   The conspirators rushed upon him, beat him down from his horse, and cut off his head.   His death occurred on May 18, 1161.

Although St Eric was never formally canonized, he was regarded as the principal patron of Sweden until the Protestant Reformation.   His banner, which was always carried in battle, has played a great part in Swedish history and was regarded as a portent of victory.   The king's relics are preserved in the cathedral of Uppsala, and his effigy appears in the arms of Stockholm.

The principal source for the life of St Eric is the biography written more than a century and a half after his death by the Dominican Israel Erlandson, little enough of which is confirmed by other sources.   It is printed with annotations in the *Acta Sanctorum*, May, vol. iv.   In the *Lexikon für Theologie und Kirche*, vol. iii, c. 753, references are given to some more modern authorities in Swedish who deal with the events of St Eric's reign.   See *Analecta Bollandiana*, vol. lx, p. 267.

BD WILLIAM OF TOULOUSE   (A.D. 1369)

AT a very early age Bd William de Naurose joined the Hermits of St Augustine in his native city of Toulouse.   Young though he was, he had already begun to tread the path of perfection, and with the triple promise he made at his profession he dedicated himself to the Holy Trinity.   With the vow of obedience he offered himself to the Father under whom all things are in subjection, with the vow of poverty to the Son who for our sake became poor, and with the vow of chastity to the Holy Ghost, the spouse of our Lady and all pure souls.   After his ordination he was sent to pursue higher studies at the University of Paris, then the educational centre of Christendom.   His course completed, he was entrusted with mission work and soon became celebrated as a preacher and as a director of souls. A great promoter of prayer for the holy souls in Purgatory, he was once visited by a wealthy woman who gave him gold, requesting his prayers for her deceased relations. Bd William at once said alond, " Eternal rest give to them, O Lord ; and let perpetual light shine upon them.   May they rest in peace," and stopped short— much to the disappointment of his visitor, who plainly intimated that she expected more prayers for her money.   The holy priest replied by bidding her write down his prayer and weigh it in a balance with her bag of gold.   She did so, and lo ! it was the money which kicked the beam, while down came the scale with the prayer. Bd William had a reputation for delivering those possessed by devils, but was himself said to be troubled by evil spirits, who sometimes appeared to him in visible form and tried to do him bodily harm.   He died on May 18, 1369, and his cult was confirmed in 1893.

The short life by Nicholas Bertrand which is printed in the *Acta Sanctorum*, May, vol. iv, was written a century and a half after the death of Bd William.   There is also a brief historical summary in the decree approving the cult ; and a compendious account of the *beatus* by N. Mattioli, in Italian, was published in 1894.

ST FELIX OF CANTALICE (A.D. 1587)

ST FELIX was born at Cantalice, near Città Ducale in Apulia.   His parents were devout peasants and he himself early evinced such piety that his little companions when they saw him approach would cry out, " Here comes Felix the saint ! "   As a child he acted as cowherd and often, after driving his cattle to some quiet pasturage, he would spend much time praying at the foot of a tree in the bark of which he had cut a cross.   At the age of twelve he was hired out, first as a shepherd and afterwards as a ploughman, to a well-to-do landowner of Città Ducale, named Mark Tully Pichi or Picarelli.   When still quite young, Felix taught himself to meditate during his work, and he soon attained to a high degree of contemplation.   In God, in himself, and in all creatures round him, he found a perpetual fund of religious thoughts and affections.   In his later life a religious once asked him how he contrived to keep himself constantly in the presence of God amid the bustle of daily cares and the multiplicity of distractions.   " All earthly creatures can lift us up to God ", he replied, " if we know how to look at them with an eye that is single." He loved to dwell upon the sufferings of our Lord, and he was never weary of contemplating that great mystery.   Always cheerful, always humble, he never resented an insult or an injury.   If anyone reviled him he would only say, " I pray God that you may become a saint ".   An account he heard read of the fathers in the desert attracted him to the life of a hermit, but he decided that it might prove to be a dangerous one for him.

He was still in doubt as to his future vocation when the question was decided for him through an accident.   He was ploughing one day with two fresh young bullocks when his master unexpectedly entered the field.   His sudden appearance or something else scared the animals and they bolted, knocking down Felix as he tried to hold them in.   He was trampled upon ; the plough passed over his body, but in spite of this he arose unhurt.   In gratitude for this deliverance he promptly betook himself to the Capuchin monastery of Città Ducale, where he asked to be received as a lay-brother.   The father guardian, after warning him of the austerity of the life, led him before a crucifix, saying, " See what Jesus Christ has suffered for us ! "   Felix burst into tears, and impressed the superior with the conviction that a soul which felt so deeply must be drawn by God.

During the noviciate, which he passed at Anticoli, Felix appeared already filled with the spirit of his order, with a love of poverty, humiliations and crosses.   Often he would beg the novice-master to double his penances and mortifications and to treat him with greater severity than the rest who, he declared, were more docile and naturally more inclined to virtue.   Although he thought everyone in the house better than himself, his fellow religious, like the children of Cantalice, spoke of him amongst themselves as " The saint ".   In 1545, when he was about thirty, he made his solemn vows.   Four years later he was sent to Rome where for forty years, practically until his death, he filled the post of questor, with the daily duty to go round begging for food and alms for the sustenance of the community.   The post was a trying one, but Felix delighted in it because it entailed humiliations, fatigue, and discomforts, and his spirit of recollection was never interrupted.   With the sanction of his superiors, who placed entire confidence in his discretion, he assisted the poor liberally out of the alms he collected ; and he loved to visit the sick, tending them with his own hands, and consoling the dying.   St Philip Neri held him in great regard and delighted in conversing with him : the two men, as a greeting, would wish each other sufferings for Christ's sake.   When St Charles Borromeo sent to St Philip the rules he had drawn up for his Oblates with a request that he would revise them, St Philip excused himself but referred them to the Capuchin lay-brother.   In vain did St Felix protest that he was illiterate : the rules were read to him and he was commanded to give his opinion about them.   He advised the omission of certain regulations which struck him as being too difficult.   These emendations were accepted by St Charles, who expressed great admiration for the judgement that had prompted them.

St Felix chastised himself with almost incredible severity and invariably went barefoot, without sandals.   He wore a shirt of iron links and plates studded with iron spikes.   When he could do so without singularity, he fasted on bread and water, picking out of the basket for his own dinner the crusts left by others.   He tried to conceal from notice the remarkable spiritual favours he received, but often when he was serving Mass he was so transported in ecstasy that he could not make the responses.   For everything that he saw, for all that befell him, he gave thanks to God, and the words " Deo gratias " were so constantly on his lips that the Roman street-urchins called him Brother Deogratias.   When he was old and was suffering from a painful complaint, their cardinal protector, who loved him greatly, told his superiors that he ought to be relieved of his wearisome office.   But Felix asked to be allowed to continue his rounds, on the ground that the soul grows sluggish if the body is pampered.   He died at the age of seventy-two, after being consoled on his death-bed by a vision of our Lady.   There is record of a great number of miracles worked after his death, and he was canonized in 1709.

The Bollandists, in the *Acta Sanctorum*, May, vol. iv, have published a considerable selection of materials presented in the beatification process, a process which was begun only a short time after Brother Felix's death, when witnesses were still available who had lived with him and had been the spectators of his virtues.   There is no lack of other biographies, but they are mostly based on the same materials, *e.g.* those by John Baptist of Perugia, Maximus of Valenza, Angelo Rossi, etc.   Lady Amabel Kerr published in 1900 a very acceptable sketch entitled *A Son of St Francis*.   See also Léon, *Auréole Séraphique* (Eng. trans.), vol. ii, pp. 198–213, and *Études franciscaines*, t. xxxiii, pp. 97–109.

19 : ST CELESTINE V, POPE   (A.D. 1296)

IN all papal history no figure is more pathetic than that of Peter di Morone, the aged hermit who, after a pontificate of five short months, voluntarily abdicated, and died virtually a prisoner in the hands of his successor.   His unprecedented act of resignation has been variously judged : it has been lauded by some as a proof of humility, while it has been severely condemned by others— notably by Dante, who placed the pathetic old man in the vestibule of his *Inferno* for having basely made " the great refusal ".*   The Church of Christ has judged differently : she canonized him in 1313, and his feast is kept in all the Western church.

Peter, who was the eleventh of twelve children, was born of peasant parents about the year 1210 at Isernia, in the Abruzzi.   Because he showed unusual promise, his mother, though she was early left a widow, sent him to school—against

* *L'Inferno*, iii, 58–61.   But it is not certain that this refers to Celestine.

the advice of her relations. Even as a boy Peter was " different ", and when he was twenty he left the world to live as a hermit on a solitary mountain where he made himself a cell so circumscribed that he could scarcely stand upright or lie down in it. In spite of his desire to remain hidden, he had occasional visitors, some of whom persuaded him to seek holy orders. He accordingly went to Rome and was ordained priest, but in 1246 he returned to the Abruzzi. On the way back he received the Benedictine habit from the Abbot of Faizola, by whom he was permitted to resume his solitary life. For five years he dwelt on Mount Morone, near Sulmona, but in 1251 the wood was cut on the mountain, and Peter, finding his privacy too much invaded, took refuge with two companions in the fastnesses of Monte Majella. His disciples, however, tracked him thither. So, after two further ineffectual attempts to live in solitude, he resigned himself to the inevitable and, returning to Monte Morone, became the head of a community of hermits who lived at first in scattered cells, but afterwards in a monastery. He gave his disciples a strict rule based on that of St Benedict and in 1274 he obtained from Pope Gregory X the approbation of his order, the members of which were afterwards known as Celestines.*

After the death of Nicholas IV, the chair of St Peter remained vacant for over two years owing to the rivalry between two parties, neither of which would give way. To the cardinals assembled at Perugia came a message, it is said, from the hermit of Monte Morone threatening them with the wrath of God if they continued to delay. In any case, to bring the deadlock to an end, the conclave chose the hermit himself to become Christ's vicar upon earth. The five envoys who climbed the steeps of Morone to bear the official notification found the old man (he was eighty-four) red-eyed with weeping and appalled at the tidings of his election which had already reached him. Boundless enthusiasm prevailed at the choice of a pope so holy and so unworldly, while to many it seemed an inauguration of the new era foretold by Joachim del Fiore—the reign of the Holy Ghost, when the religious orders would rule the world in peace and love. Two hundred thousand persons are said to have been assembled in Aquila to acclaim the new pope as he rode to the cathedral on a donkey, its bridle held on the one side by the King of Hungary and on the other by Charles of Anjou, King of Naples.

Scarcely, however, were the consecration and coronation over than it became evident that Celestine V, as he was now called, was quite unequal to the task of ruling the Church. In his utter simplicity he became unwittingly a tool in the hands of King Charles, who used him for the furtherance of his schemes and induced him to live in Naples. He gave great offence to the Italian cardinals by refusing to go to Rome and by creating thirteen new cardinals, nearly all in the Franco-Neapolitan interest. Knowing little Latin and no canon law, his want of experience led him into mistakes of all kinds. To the rigorist *Spirituali* movement he was a pope sent direct from Heaven ; to the place-hunters and the ruck he was a windfall : he gave to anybody anything they asked, and in his innocence would grant the same benefice several times over. Everything fell into hopeless confusion.

Miserable and frightened in these bewildering surroundings, he asked for himself only that a cell should be made in the palace, to which as Advent approached he proposed withdrawing into complete solitude and silence, leaving three cardinals to govern in his place ; but he was warned that by so doing he was practically

* Not to be confused with the " Celestine " Franciscans. The congregation of hermit monks spread in Europe, and in France came to an end only at the Revolution.

creating three rival popes. Conscious of failure, discouraged, and utterly weary, Celestine began to consider how he might lay down a burden he felt unable to bear. It was an unprecedented thing for a pope to abdicate; but Cardinal Gaëtani and other learned men whom he consulted decided that it was permissible, and even advisable in certain circumstances. Although the King of Naples and others strongly opposed, nevertheless on December 13, 1294, at a consistory of cardinals held in Naples, St Celestine read a solemn declaration of abdication, in which he pleaded his age, his ignorance, his incapacity, and his rough manners and speech. He then laid aside his pontifical robes and resumed a religious habit; and he cast himself at the feet of the assembly, begging pardon for his many errors and exhorting the cardinals to repair them as well as they could by choosing a worthy successor to St Peter. The assembly, deeply moved, accepted his resignation, and the old man joyfully returned to a house of his monks at Sulmona.

He was not, however, destined to remain there in peace. Cardinal Gaëtani, who as Boniface VIII had been chosen pope in his place, found himself opposed by a bitterly hostile party and requested the King of Naples to send his too popular predecessor back to Rome, lest he should be used by his opponents. Celestine, duly warned, hoped to escape across the Adriatic; but after several months of wandering among the woods and mountains he was captured. Boniface shut him up in a small room in the castle of Fumone, near Anagni, and there after ten months of hardship he died, on May 19, 1296. " I wanted nothing in the world but a cell ", he said, " and a cell they have given me."

The body of Pope St Celestine V rests in the church of Santa Maria del Colle at Aquila in the Abruzzi, the place where he was consecrated to the episcopate and the papacy.

So excellent an acount of St Celestine's whole history has been given by Mgr Mann in vol. xvii of his *Lives of the Popes in the Middle Ages*, pp. 247–341, that other references seem hardly necessary. Mgr Mann points out that apart from a rather slender collection of papal documents—the official *Registrum* is lost—Cardinal James Gaëtani de' Stefaneschi, in his *Opus Metricum*, and the biographical materials printed by the modern Bollandists in their *Analecta Bollandiana*, vols. ix, x, xvi and xviii, must be regarded as our principal authorities. See also F. X. Seppelt, *Monumenta Celestiniana* (1921); B. Cantera, *S. Pier Celestino* (1892); G. Celidonio, *Vita di S. Pietro del Morrone* (1896); and J. Hollnsteiner, " Die Autobiographie Celestins V " in the *Römische Quartalschrift*, vol. xxxi (1923), pp. 29–40. The novel *San Celestino*, by John Ayscough (Mgr Bickerstaffe-Drew) is a sensitive study of the unfortunate pope.

SS. PUDENTIANA AND PUDENS, MARTYRS   (FIRST OR SECOND CENTURY ?)

IN the Roman Martyrology for May 19 we read : " At Rome (the commemoration) of St Pudentiana, virgin, who after innumerable contests, after caring reverently for the burial of many of the martyrs, and distributing all her goods to the poor, at length passed from earth to heaven. In the same city of St Pudens, a senator, father of the aforesaid maiden, who was by the Apostles adorned for Christ in baptism, and guarded his vesture unspotted unto a crown of life." Opinions are divided as to whether this Pudens is to be identified with the Pudens mentioned in 2 Tim. iv 21. But there can be no reasonable doubt that at an early date there was a Christian so named in Rome who gave a plot of ground with which was subsequently connected a church and " title ". It was first known as the *ecclesia Pudentiana* or *titulus Pudentis* ; but by a later confusion people came to speak of the *ecclesia Sanctae Pudentianae*, and this supposed patroness was honoured as a martyr and a daughter of Pudens. Owing to a slurred pronunciation the name was also often written Potentiana. After the close of the eighth century a story was fabricated purporting to be the Acts of SS. Pudentiana and Praxedes, in which the two maidens were described as sisters (Pudentiana being only sixteen years old) and the daughters of Pudens. They were probably associated in the story because Praxedes and Pudentiana stand together first in the list of the virgins whose bodies were transferred from the catacombs to the church of Praxedes by Pope Paschal I (817–824).

The Acts of St Pudentiana are printed by the Bollandists in their fourth volume for May. A commission appointed by Pope Benedict XIV to revise the Breviary declared them to be fabulous and unworthy of credit. Many points connected with Pudens, Pudentiana and Praxedes still remain matters of controversy, but all the material issues are summed up by Fr Delehaye, in CMH., p. 263, where references are also given to other authorities. Add also Marucchi in the *Nuovo Bullettino di arch. crist.*, vol. xiv (1908), pp. 5–125.

SS. CALOCERUS AND PARTHENIUS, MARTYRS   (A.D. 304)

THE two brothers Calocerus and Parthenius, whom the Church honours together on this day, are said to have been eunuchs occupying the post of *praepositus cubiculi* and *primicerius* in the household of Tryphonia, the wife of the Emperor Decius. They were professing Christians and, on the outbreak of persecution, they suffered martyrdom rather than offer sacrifice to the gods. According to their reputed acts, which are quite untrustworthy, they were Armenians who had come from the East with a consul called Aemilian. Their patron died, leaving them in charge of his daughter Callista or Anatolia as well as of his property, part of which was to be distributed to the poor. They were summoned before Decius on the double charge of being Christians and of dissipating the heritage of Anatolia. After making a bold defence and confession of faith they were condemned to be burnt alive. They emerged unscathed from the flames and were then beaten on the head with lighted stakes until they died. Their bodies were buried by Anatolia in the cemetery of Callistus.

Two texts of the supposed " acts " are known. One is printed in the *Acta Sanctorum*, May, vol. iv, the other in the *Analecta Bollandiana*, vol. xvi (1897), pp. 240–241. De Rossi attaches some importance to this latter recension, and argues from it in favour of the date 250 ; but Delehaye has returned a very sufficient answer in the *Analecta Bollandiana*, vol. xlvi (1928), pp. 50–55, and see further his CMH., pp. 261–262.

BD ALCUIN, ABBOT   (A.D. 804)

ALCUIN is often called Blessed and his name appears in the Benedictine Martyrology and in some old calendars ; this *cultus* has never been officially confirmed, but so significant a figure requires notice, however short. He was born, probably at York about 730, into the noble family to which St Willibrord belonged, and in 767 succeeded to the direction of the cathedral school of that city, where he had himself been educated. He was not a man of great originating mind ; rather was he a conserver and spreader of learning, and he attracted numerous students, outstanding among them being St Ludger, the apostle of Saxony. He was especially careful for the management and building-up of the library, and under him the York school entered into the company of those of Jarrow and Canterbury.

During this period Alcuin visited Rome three times, and in 781 accepted an invitation to take up his residence at the court of Charlemagne, whose educational and ecclesiastical adviser he became. After two visits to England, in 786 and 790, he settled permanently in France, finally in the abbey of St Martin at Tours, of which Charlemagne had made him abbot. It is not altogether certain, however, that Alcuin was ever a monk, nor was he ordained beyond the order of deacon ; but royal favour made him a pluralist, for he also held the abbeys of Ferrières, Troyes and Cormery. As head of the palace school at Aachen and elsewhere, where he was joined by some of his English pupils, he did more than anyone else to make the Frankish court a centre of culture and to encourage Charlemagne's educational enterprises throughout his realm ; so too at Tours he made his monastery a home of learning famous all over western Europe. It was here that he died on May 19, 804.

Alcuin made his mark as a theologian, against the heresy of Adoptionism (that our Lord as man is only the adopted son of God) and in biblical commentaries ; and as a liturgist—his work had a strong influence on the Roman liturgy as we have it to-day. But it was as an educator that his fame has been enduring, for he was the main channel between the English scholarship of St Bede's era and the revival of western learning under Charlemagne : he was " the schoolmaster of his age " ; and like a good schoolmaster a primary activity was to spread enthusiasm for learning. Some of his works seem to have been intended for use as text-books (not very good ones). Of all his writings, however, the best-known now are his letters, some 300 of which have survived, many of them addressed to Charlemagne and to friends in England : they are valuable evidence of the simplicity and moderation of his own character as well as a source for contemporary history.

A life derived from information of Alcuin's disciple Sigulf is printed in *Acta Sanctorum*, May, vol. iv, pp. 335–344, and elsewhere. Later works are numerous. Consult Stubbs in DCB., Vernet in DTC., W. Levison, *England and the Continent in the Eighth Century* (1946) ; see also A. T. Drane, *Christian Schools and Scholars* (1867) ; C. J. B. Gaskoin, *Alcuin* (1904) ; E. M. Wilmot-Buxton, *Alcuin* (1922) ; and E. S. Duckett, *Alcuin* (1951). His works are in Migne, PL, vols. c and ci ; the best edition of the letters is in *Monumenta Alcuiniana*, ed. Jaffé *et al.* (1873).

ST DUNSTAN, ARCHBISHOP OF CANTERBURY (A.D. 988)

ST DUNSTAN, the most famous of all the Anglo-Saxon saints, was born (*c*. A.D. 910) near Glastonbury (at Baltonsborough it is said) of a noble family closely allied to the ruling house. He received his early education from some Irish scholars and others at Glastonbury, and then, while still a lad, he was sent to the court of King Athelstan. There he incurred the ill-will of some : they accused him of practising incantations—he was a very studious youth—and obtained his expulsion. As he was leaving, they further vented their spite by throwing him into a pond of mire, which was probably a cesspool. He had already received the tonsure, and his uncle, St Alphege the Bald, Bishop of Winchester, to whom he now betook himself, urged him to embrace the religious life. Dunstan demurred for a time, but after his recovery from a skin trouble which he took to be leprosy he hesitated no longer, receiving the habit and subsequently holy orders at the hands of his saintly kinsman. Returning to Glastonbury, he is said to have built himself a small cell adjoining the old church. There he divided his time between prayer, study, and manual labour which took the form of making bells and sacred vessels for the church and of copying or illuminating books. He also played the harp, for he was very musical. Indeed we probably possess the actual music of one or more of St Dunstan's compositions, as the late Abbot Cuthbert Butler contended in the article he wrote in 1886 in the *Downside Review*. The chant known as the *Kyrie Rex splendens* is especially famous.

Athelstan's successor, Edmund, recalled St Dunstan to court and in 943 appointed him abbot of Glastonbury, in consequence of an escape from death while hunting at Cheddar, the king having previously listened to those who wanted Dunstan dismissed. This began the revival of monastic life in England, and has been called a turning point of our religious history. At once the new abbot set about reconstructing the monastic buildings and restoring the church of St Peter. By introducing monks amongst the clerks already in residence, he was able without too much friction to enforce regular discipline. Moreover, he made of the abbey a great school of learning. Other monasteries were revived from Glastonbury, and the work was carried on as well by St Ethelwold from Abingdon and St Oswald from Westbury.

The murder of King Edmund after a reign of six and a half years was followed by the accession of his brother Edred. The new monarch made Dunstan practically his chief adviser. The policy which the saint then initiated and which continued to be his throughout his career was vigorous and far-seeing : he stood out for reform—especially in morals—for the spread of regular observance to counteract the laxity of the secular clergy, and for the unification of the country by conciliating the Danish element. He became the acknowledged leader of a party which found its chief support in East Anglia and in the north, but he made bitter enemies amongst those whose vices he opposed and amongst the mass of West Saxon nobles who were reactionary in their views. Edred died in 955 and was succeeded by his nephew Edwy, a boy of sixteen, who on the very day of his coronation left the royal banquet to seek the society of a girl called Elgiva and her mother, and was sternly rebuked by St Dunstan for his unseemly conduct. This reproof the young prince bitterly resented. With the support of the opposition party St Dunstan was disgraced, his property confiscated, and he was driven into exile. He found a refuge in Flanders, where he came into contact for the first time with continental monasticism, then in the fulness of its renewed vigour ; it gave him a vision of Benedictine perfection which was to be an inspiration to him in all his after labours. His banishment, however, did not last long. A rebellion broke out in England, and the north and east, throwing off Edwy's yoke, chose for their ruler his brother Edgar.

The new monarch immediately recalled St Dunstan, upon whom he bestowed first the see of Worcester and afterwards that of London. Upon Edwy's death in 959 the kingdom was reunited under Edgar, and St Dunstan became archbishop of Canterbury. Upon going to Rome to receive the pallium he was appointed by Pope John XII a legate of the Holy See. Armed with this authority the saint set himself energetically to re-establish ecclesiastical discipline, being powerfully protected by King Edgar and ably assisted by St Ethelwold, Bishop of Winchester, and St Oswald, Bishop of Worcester and Archbishop of York. These three prelates restored most of the great monasteries which had been destroyed during the Danish incursions and founded new ones. They were no less zealous in reforming the clergy, many of whom were leading worldly or scandalous lives, openly disregarding the canonical law binding them to celibacy. Where the seculars proved recalcitrant they were ejected, their places being supplied by monks. Laymen in high places were also brought under discipline, for no motives of human respect ever daunted the saintly archbishop. Even King Edgar himself was subjected to a lengthy and humiliating penance for an atrocious crime. Throughout the sixteen years' reign of Edgar, St Dunstan remained his chief adviser and he continued to direct the state during the short reign of the next king, Edward the Martyr. The death of the young prince was a grievous blow to his ecclesiastical prime minister, who when he crowned Edward's half-brother Ethelred in 970 foretold the calamities which were to mark his reign.

The archbishop's political career was now over. He took no further part in state matters, but retired to Canterbury. He had always been a great patron of education, and in his old age he loved to teach the scholars attached to his cathedral and to tell them stories. One of them, afterwards a priest, but only known to us by the initial of his name as " B ", became his first biographer. The saint's memory did not readily fade, and long years after his death the boys used to invoke the aid of their " sweet Father Dunstan " to obtain a mitigation of the savage corporal punishment then in vogue. On the feast of the Ascension, 988, the archbishop, though ill, celebrated Mass and preached thrice to his people, to whom he announced his impending death. In the afternoon he went again to the cathedral and chose a place for his burial. Two days later he died peacefully.

St Dunstan has always been honoured as the patron of goldsmiths, jewellers and locksmiths. His dexterity as a metal-worker seized upon the popular imagination and, in the eleventh century, gave rise to the popular legend that he once, with a pair of blacksmith's pincers, seized the nose of the Devil who was trying to tempt him ; a story which, as Dr Armitage Robinson used to say, has been " the ruin of Dunstan's reputation ", for it has tended to make people forget he was " one of the makers of England ". His feast is kept in several English dioceses and by the English Benedictines.

The outstanding sources for the life of St Dunstan have been painstakingly edited by Bishop Stubbs in a volume of the Rolls Series, *Memorials of St Dunstan* (1874). (There is good reason, however, to believe that Stubbs was mistaken in assigning Dunstan's birth to 924. See on this E. Bishop and L. Toke in *The Bosworth Psalter* (1908), pp. 126–143.) Consult further Dom D. Pontifex, " The First Life of Dunstan ", in *The Downside Review*, vol. 51 (1933), pp. 20–40 and 309–325, and Dean Armitage Robinson, *The Times of St Dunstan* (1923). Besides such obvious sources as the *Acta Sanctorum*, Lingard's *History of England*, Stenton's *Anglo-Saxon England*, etc., much useful information may be gathered from the series of articles on monastic observances published at intervals by Dom T. Symons in the *Downside Review*, from 1921. And see D. Knowles, *The Monastic Order in England* (1949), pp. 31–56 and *passim* ; and T. Symons, *Regularis Concordia* (1954). There is evidence from charters that Dunstan's retirement, referred to above, did not take place or was not complete.

ST IVO OF KERMARTIN   (A.D. 1303)

THE patron of lawyers, St Ivo Hélory, was born near Tréguier in Brittany at Kermartin, where his father was lord of the manor. At the age of fourteen he was sent to Paris, and before the end of a ten years' stay in its famous schools he had gained great distinction in philosophy, theology and canon law. He then passed on to Orleans to study civil law under the celebrated jurist Peter de la Chapelle. In his student days he began to practise austerities which he continued and increased throughout his life. He wore a hair shirt, abstained from meat and wine, fasted during Advent and Lent (as well as at other times) on bread and water, and took his rest—which was always short—lying on a straw mat with a book or a stone by way of a pillow.   Upon his return to Brittany after the completion of his education, he was appointed by the archdeacon of Rennes diocesan " official ", in other words, judge of the cases that came before the ecclesiastical court.   In this capacity he protected orphans, defended the poor and administered justice with an impartiality and kindliness which gained him the goodwill even of the losing side.

Before very long, however, his own diocesan claimed him, and he returned to his native district as official to Alan de Bruc, Bishop of Tréguier.   Here his championship of the downtrodden won for him the name of " the poor man's advocate ". Not content with dealing out justice to the helpless in his own court, he would personally plead for them in other courts, often paying their expenses, and visiting them when they were in prison.   Never would he accept the presents or bribes which had become so customary as to be regarded as a lawyer's perquisite.   He always strove if possible to reconcile people who were at enmity, and to induce them to settle their quarrels out of court.   In this manner he prevented many of those who came to him from embarking on costly and unnecessary lawsuits.*   St Ivo had received minor orders when he was made official at Rennes, and in 1284 he was ordained priest and given the living of Trédrez.   Three years later he resigned his legal office and devoted the last fifteen years of his life to his parishioners—first at Trédrez, and afterwards in the larger parish of Lovannec.

St Ivo built a hospital in which he tended the sick with his own hands.   He would often give the clothes off his back to beggars, and once, when he discovered that a tramp had passed the night on his doorstep, he made the man occupy his bed the following night, whilst he himself slept on the doorstep.   He was as solicitous about the spiritual welfare of the people as about their temporal needs, losing no opportunity of instructing them.   In great demand as a preacher, he would deliver sermons in other churches besides his own, giving his addresses sometimes in Latin, sometimes in French, and sometimes in Breton.   All differences were referred to him, and his arbitration was nearly always accepted.   He used to distribute his corn, or the value of it, to the poor directly after the harvest.   When it was suggested that he should keep it for a time so as to obtain a better price for it, he replied, " I cannot count upon being alive then to have the disposal of it ". From the beginning of Lent, 1303, his health failed visibly, but he would not abate his accustomed austerities.   On Ascension eve he preached and celebrated Mass, although he was so weak that he had to be supported.   He then lay down on his bed, which was a hurdle, and received the last sacraments.   He died on May 19, 1303, in the fiftieth year of his age, and was canonized in 1347.

We are particularly well informed regarding the life of St Ivo Hélory.   In the *Acta Sanctorum*, May, vol. iv, the Bollandists have reprinted a great part of the documents collected twenty-eight years after his death for the process of canonization.   These have been edited again with supplementary matter by A. de La Borderie, *Monuments Originaux de l'Histoire de S. Yves* (1887).   Some further biographical material will be found in the *Analecta*

*Hence the verse :

Sanctus Ivo erat Brito,
Advocatus, et non latro,
Res miranda populo.

" St Ivo was a Breton and a lawyer, but not dishonest—an astonishing thing in people's eyes ! "   Lawyers have opportunities for dishonesty denied to other men ; it would be hard to prove that those opportunities are taken advantage of disproportionately.

Bollandiana, vol. ii and vol. viii.   For details see BHG., nn. 4625–4637.   There are a number of small popular lives, notably that by C. de La Roncière (1925) in the series " Les Saints ". See A. Masseron, *S. Yves d'après les témoins de sa vie* (1952).

BD AUGUSTINE NOVELLO   (A.D. 1309)

AUGUSTINE NOVELLO was the name adopted in religion by Matthew of Termini, otherwise Taormina, in Sicily.   After a brilliant career at Bologna where he studied and taught law, he became chancellor to King Manfred.   Wounded and abandoned for dead at the battle of Benevento in which his royal master perished, Matthew vowed that if he recovered, he would devote himself to God's service.   In accomplishment of this promise he entered the Order of the Hermits of St Augustine as a lay-brother, concealing his identity.   When the community found itself involved in a very complicated lawsuit, Bd Augustine offered to set forth their case, and produced a statement so clear, terse and convincing, that the advocate of the opposition is said to have exclaimed : " This must be the work of an angel or of the Devil—or of Matthew de Termini—but he perished at Benevento."   Confronted at his own request with the author of the statement, the lawyer recognized him at once and congratulated the superior upon possessing among his subjects so great a legal luminary.   Augustine Novello accompanied Bd Clement of Osimo to Rome, where they drew up together the new constitutions of their order.   Pope Nicholas IV appointed him penitentiary to the papal court, and Boniface VIII sent him as legate to Siena.   In 1298 Bd Augustine was elected prior general, but he resigned the office two years later to retire into the hermitage of St Leonard which he had built near Siena.   He died there on May 19, 1309.

A short life which purports to have been written by a contemporary is in the *Acta Sanctorum,* May, vol. iv.   See also the *Analecta Augustiniana,* vol. iv (1908), pp. 326 *seq.,* and vol. iv (1910), pp. 120–133.   There are a number also of short popular lives, *e.g.* that of P. Sanfilippo (1835).

BD PETER WRIGHT, MARTYR   (A.D. 1651)

THE parents of Bd Peter Wright were Catholics who lived at Slipton in Northamptonshire.   Obliged by poverty to enter service when very young, Peter, in Protestant surroundings, temporarily lost his faith, but on reaching manhood he recovered it, and went over to Liège, where he was reconciled to the Church by the English Jesuit fathers in that city.   He entered the Society of Jesus, and was sent on a mission to the English soldiers in Flanders—a congenial task which he accomplished with conspicuous success.   So greatly did he endear himself to their colonel, Sir Henry Gage, that he made the priest his constant companion in the Netherlands and in England.   After Sir Henry had died fighting for the King in 1644, Bd Peter lived mainly with the Marquis of Winchester, upon the roof of whose house he was arrested by priest-catchers, on Candlemas day, 1650.   At his trial before the Lord Chief Justice, he was condemned mainly on the testimony of an apostate, Sir Henry Gage's younger brother.   After being strung up he was allowed to hang until he was dead, and his friends were suffered to carry away his head and other parts of his body when the usual horrible butchery had been consummated.   Father Wright's deportment on the scaffold profoundly impressed many of the spectators and led to several conversions.

See Challoner, MMP., pp. 499–504 ; and Foley, REPSJ., vol. ii, pp. 506–566.

20 : ST BERNARDINO OF SIENA   (A.D. 1444)

ST BERNARDINO was born in the Tuscan town of Massa Marittima, in which his father, a member of the noble Sienese family of the Albizeschi, occupied the post of governor.   The little boy lost both his parents before he was seven and was entrusted to the care of a maternal aunt and her daughter— both excellent women, who gave him a religious training and loved him as though he had been their own child.   Upon reaching the age of eleven or twelve he was placed by his uncles at school in Siena, where he passed with great credit through the course of studies deemed requisite for a boy of his rank.   He grew up a good-looking lad, so merry and entertaining that it was impossible to be dull in his company ; but a coarse or blasphemous remark would always bring a blush to his cheek and generally a remonstrance to his lips.   Once when a man of position sought to lead him into vice, Bernardino struck him in the face with his fists, and on a second and similar occasion he incited his comrades to join him in pelting the tempter with mud and stones.   Except when thus moved by righteous indignation, Bernardino was singularly sweet-tempered ; indeed, throughout his life he was noted for his unfailing affability, patience and courtesy.

At the age of seventeen he enrolled himself in a confraternity of our Lady, the members of which pledged themselves to certain devotional practices as well as to the relief of the sick ; and he at once embarked upon a course of severe bodily mortification.   In 1400 Siena was visited by the plague in a virulent form.   So serious was its toll that from twelve to twenty persons died daily in the famous hospital of Santa Maria della Scala, which found itself bereft of almost all who tended the sick.   In this extremity Bernardino offered to take entire charge of the establishment, with the help of some other young men whom he had fired with the determination to sacrifice their lives if necessary to aid the sufferers.   Their services were accepted, and for four months the noble band worked tirelessly, day and night, under the direction of Bernardino, who, besides nursing the patients and preparing them for death, saw to everything and brought order as well as cleanliness into the hospital.   Though several of his companions died, Bernardino escaped the contagion and returned home after the epidemic was over.   He was, however, so exhausted by his labours that he fell an easy prey to a fever which laid him low for several months.

Upon his recovery he found that his immediate duty lay close at hand.   An aunt named Bartolomea, to whom he was much attached, had become blind as well as bedridden, and to her he devoted himself as he had done to the plague-stricken in the hospital.   When, fourteen months later, God called the invalid to Himself, it was in the arms of her nephew that she breathed her last.   Free now from all earthly ties, Bernardino set himself by prayer and fasting to learn God's will as to his future.   By this means he was led to enter the Franciscan Order, the habit of which he received shortly afterwards in Siena.   The house, however, proved too accessible to the novice's many friends and relations, and with the consent of his superiors he retired to the convent of Colombaio outside the city, where the rule of St Francis was strictly observed.   Here in 1403 he was professed and here he was ordained priest—exactly a year later, on the feast of the Birthday of our Lady which was his birthday and the anniversary of his baptism and of his clothing.

History has little to tell us about the saint during the next twelve years : he preached occasionally, but his life was mainly spent in retirement. Gradually he was being prepared by God for the twofold mission of apostle and reformer. When at last his hour had come, the way was made clear in a singular manner. A novice in the convent at Fiesole in which the saint was staying startled the community on three consecutive nights after Matins by exclaiming, " Brother Bernardino ! Hide no longer the gift that is in you. Go to Lombardy, for all are awaiting you there ! " Reprimanded and questioned as to why he had thus spoken, he replied, " Because I could not help it ! " To Bernardino and his superiors this seemed to be a call from on high, and he obeyed. He opened his apostolic career at Milan to which he went as a complete stranger towards the end of 1417, but soon his eloquence and zeal began to attract enormous congregations. At the close of a course of Lenten sermons, before he was allowed to leave the city to preach elsewhere in Lombardy, he was obliged to promise that he would return the following year. At first he was hampered in his delivery by hoarseness and inability to make himself heard, but afterwards, as the result, he firmly believed, of fervent prayer to our Lady, his voice became singularly clear and penetrating.

It is impossible to follow him on his missionary journeys, for in them he covered nearly the whole of Italy with the exception of the kingdom of Naples. He travelled always on foot, preached sometimes for three or four consecutive hours and often delivered several sermons on the same day. In large cities he frequently had to speak from an open-air pulpit because no church could contain the multitudes who crowded to hear him. Everywhere he preached penance, denounced the prevalent vices and kindled popular fervour by spreading devotion to the Holy Name. At the end of every sermon he would hold up for veneration a tablet upon which he had written the letters I.H.S., surrounded by rays, and after telling the people to implore God's mercy and to live in peace he would give them a blessing with the Holy Name. In cities torn by faction he would heal deadly feuds and would persuade men to substitute the sacred monogram for the Guelf or Ghibelline emblems that too often surmounted their front doors. In Bologna, which was overmuch addicted to games of hazard, he preached with such effect that the citizens gave up gambling and brought their cards and dice to be burnt in a public bonfire. A card-manufacturer who complained that he was deprived of his only means of livelihood was told by St Bernardino to manufacture tablets inscribed with the I.H.S., and so great was the demand for them that they brought in more money than the playing-cards had ever done. All over Italy men spoke of the wonderful fruit of St Bernardino's missions—the numerous conversions, the restoration of ill-gotten goods, the reparation of injuries and the reform of morals. Nevertheless there were some who took exception to his teaching and accused him of encouraging superstitious practices. They went so far as to denounce him to Pope Martin V, who for a time commanded him to keep silence. However, an examination of his doctrine and conduct led to a complete vindication and he received permission to preach wherever he liked. The same pope, in 1427, urged him to accept the bishopric of Siena, but he refused it, as he afterwards declined the sees of Ferrara and of Urbino. His excuse was that if he were confined to one diocese he could no longer minister to so many souls.

In 1430, nevertheless, he was obliged to give up missionary work to become vicar general of the friars of the Strict Observance. This movement within the

Franciscan Order had originated about the middle of the fourteenth century in the convent of Brogliano between Camerino and Assisi and had only maintained a struggling existence until the coming of St Bernardino, who became its organizer and its second founder. When he received the habit there were only three hundred friars of the Observance in all Italy; when he died there were four thousand. Wherever he went on his missionary tours, fervent young men were drawn to the order with which he was identified, and pious persons desirous of founding convents offered to bestow them upon the Observants. It was therefore right and fitting that he should be officially empowered to consolidate and regulate the reform. He accomplished this task with so much wisdom and tact that many convents passed voluntarily and without friction from the Conventual to the Observant rule. The original Observants had shunned scholarship as they had shunned riches, but St Bernardino was aware of the danger of ignorance, especially in face of the ever-increasing demand for Observant friars to act as confessors. He therefore insisted upon instruction in theology and canon law as part of the regular curriculum. He was himself a learned man, as may be judged from a series of Latin sermons which he wrote at Capriola and which are still extant, and also by the fact that at the Council of Florence, St Bernardino was able to address the Greek delegates in their own tongue.

Important as was the work with which he was now entrusted, the saint longed to return to his apostolic labours which he regarded as his only vocation, and in 1442 he obtained permission from the pope to resign his office as vicar general. He then resumed his missionary journeys, which led him through the Romagna, Ferrara and Lombardy. He was by this time in failing health, and so emaciated that he looked like a skeleton, but the only concession he would allow himself was the use of a donkey to convey him from one place to another. At Massa Marittima in 1444 he preached on fifty consecutive days a course of Lenten sermons, which he wound up by exhorting the inhabitants to preserve harmony among themselves and by bidding a pathetic farewell to his native town. Though obviously dying, he still continued his apostolic work and set out for Naples, preaching as he went. He succeeded in reaching Aquila, but there his strength gave out and he died on the eve of the Ascension, May 20, 1444, in the monastery of the Conventuals. He had almost reached the age of sixty-four years, forty-two of which he had spent as a religious. His tomb at Aquila was honoured by many miracles and he was canonized within six years of his death.

The number of early Latin biographies of St Bernardino is considerable, and it must suffice to note that a detailed enumeration is supplied in BHL., nn. 1188–1201. Some are given in full and extracts made from others in the *Acta Sanctorum*, May, vol. v. Excellent modern studies of the life and apostolate of the saint are numerous. The first edition of that by P. Thureau-Dangin was published in 1896 (Eng. trans., 1911). Others which deserve special notice are written by Dr K. Hefele, in German (1912); by A. G. Ferrers Howell, in English (1913); by Father V. Facchinetti (1933) and by Piero Bargellini (1933), both in Italian, but the number of such works is great. A considerable amount of fresh material has been brought to light and printed in modern times, for most of which see the *Archivum Franciscanum Historicum*, more especially vols. vi, viii, xi, xii, xv, etc. For a fuller bibliography consult B. Stasiewski, *Der hl. Bernardin von Siena* (1931), and V. Facchinetti, *Bollettino Bibliografico* (1930). A very pleasant English sketch is that of M. Ward, *St Bernardino, the People's Preacher* (1914). The fifth centenary of the saint's death (1944) produced a number of new books, mostly in Italian. See the life printed in *Analecta Bollandiana*, vol. lxxi (1953), pp. 282–322.

ST THALELAEUS, Martyr   (A.D. 284 ?)

On the ground that St Thalelaeus was a physician who gave his services gratis, the Greeks call him " the Merciful ", and reckon him amongst their so-called " Moneyless " or disinterested saints.   In the Roman Martyrology he is entered as having suffered at Edessa in Syria, but this is a mistake : the actual scene of his martyrdom was Aegae in Cilicia.   Said to have been a native of the Lebanon and the son of a Roman general, he practised at Anazarbus.   When persecution broke out during the reign of the Emperor Numerian, he escaped to an olive grove where he was captured.   After being conveyed to the coast town of Aegae, he was strung up on a rope and cast into the sea.   He managed to swim to shore and was beheaded. This, at least, is the story told in his quite unreliable Greek " acts ".   With him are associated a number of other martyrs, including Alexander and Asterius, who were either officials charged with his execution but converted by his fortitude, or else sympathizing bystanders.

Two Greek texts have been printed in the *Acta Sanctorum*, May, vol. v, and there is also an Armenian rendering, which F. C. Conybeare translated into English in his *Apology and Acts of Apollonius* . . . (1894).   Delehaye (*Origines du Culte des Martyrs*, p. 165) shows that there is no reason to question the fact of the martyrdom of St Thalelaeus, and that there was a considerable *cultus*.

ST BASILLA, or BASILISSA, Virgin and Martyr   (A.D. 304)

According to the Roman Martyrology St Basilla was a maiden related to the imperial family who suffered in Rome about the middle of the third century. Affianced in her childhood to a patrician named Pompeius, she refused after her conversion to Christianity to carry out the contract, because she had consecrated herself to our Lord at the time of her baptism.   Pompeius denounced her to the Emperor Gallienus, who left her free to choose between marriage and death by the sword.   She preferred the second, and was beheaded on the Salarian Way.   These details, and in particular the mention of Gallienus in the third century, are probably wholly erroneous.   In 1654 in the Catacomb of St Cyriacus a tomb was discovered which bore the inscription " Basilla ", together with a palm branch and a dove— the symbols of a virgin martyr.   The bones found within were translated with great pomp to the Hôtel-Dieu at Bayeux in Normandy as being those of our third-century saint, but this identification is now generally discredited, and the Bayeux relics are regarded as being those of an unknown martyr.

Though we have no detailed " acts " of Basilla, but only a passing reference in the quite untrustworthy Passion of St Eugenia, there can be no question that Basilla was an authentic martyr.   Her name is entered with a date (= A.D. 304) in the Roman *Depositio Martyrum*. Inscriptions invoking her have been found in the catacombs, and there is mention of her in the *Hieronymianum* on this day.   The only difficulty is that the *Depositio Martyrum* assigns her martyrdom to September 22.

ST BAUDELIUS, Martyr   (A.D. 380 ?)

It is certain that a large number of churches in France and Spain have been dedicated in honour of St Baudelius, whose tomb was formerly one of the most venerated shrines in Provence, but little is actually known of his history except that he perished for the faith at Nîmes.   Even the date of his martyrdom is uncertain : some authorities give it as 187, others as 297, and others place it as late as the close of the fourth century.   If we may put any trust in his fabulous " acts ", he was a married man who came with his wife from a foreign land to evangelize southern Gaul.   He arrived at Nîmes one day when a feast was being celebrated in honour of Jupiter, and was moved to harangue the people on the truths of Christianity and the errors of paganism.   He was arrested, and his head was struck off with an axe. St Gregory of Tours, who wrote in the sixth century, mentions the numerous miracles wrought at the tomb of St Baudelius, adding that his cult had spread all over the Christian world.   He is the principal patron of Nîmes, where he is called Baudille.

See the *Acta Sanctorum*, May, vol. v ; there are other Latin texts enumerated in BHL., nn. 1043–1047.   St Baudelius is commemorated on this day in the *Hieronymianum* and Delehaye's commentary thereon furnishes references to the evidence for early *cultus*.

ST AUSTREGISILUS, OR OUTRIL, BISHOP OF BOURGES   (A.D. 624)

AT the court of King Guntramnus at Chalon-sur-Saône, the youth Austregisilus, who was the son of an impoverished nobleman of Bourges, bore a high reputation. He did not, however, escape the tongue of calumny, and was sentenced to face his accuser in ordeal by battle in order to clear himself of a serious charge.   The death of his opponent by a fall from his horse just before the fight was regarded as a special intervention of Providence.   It confirmed Austregisilus in an intention which he had previously formed of retiring from the world ; for when the king urged him to marry he had replied, " If I had a good wife I should be afraid of losing her ; if a bad one, I should be better with none ".   Austregisilus was ordained priest by his friend St Aetherius, who also nominated him abbot of Saint-Nizier at Lyons.   As a superior he gained a reputation for wisdom and miracles. In 612 he was elected bishop of Bourges and presided in this his native city until his death, twelve years later.   Amongst his disciples was St Amandus, who as a young man came to Bourges and lived in a cell near the cathedral under the direction of the bishop.

The life printed in the *Acta Sanctorum*, May, vol. v, has also been critically edited in MGH., *Scriptores Merov.*, vol. iv, pp. 188–208.   B. Krusch considers that the writer's claim to be a contemporary is fictitious, and that the text was really compiled a couple of centuries later.   See also Duchesne, *Fastes Épiscopaux*, vol. i, p. 29.

ST ETHELBERT, MARTYR   (A.D. 794)

THE cathedral church of Hereford is dedicated in honour of St Mary and St Ethelbert, and this Ethelbert, who was venerated, apparently for no sufficient reason, as a martyr, was the son and successor of Ethelred as king of the East Angles.   The young king, desiring to perpetuate his line, presented himself before his powerful neighbour, King Offa of the Mercians, at Sutton Walls in Hereford-shire, intending to ask the hand of his daughter, Alfreda, in marriage.

According to the story, Ethelbert was received with outward courtesy, but after a few days was treacherously murdered for " reasons of state " ; the Saint Albans chroniclers, anxious to save the good name of their reputed founder, put all the blame for this assassination on the machinations of Offa's wife, Cynethryth. Ethelbert's body was roughly buried on the bank of the river Lugg at Marden, his severed head being contemptuously kicked about.   In consequence of a vision, the remains were afterwards taken up and buried in a " fair church " at Hereford, and the ill-used head is said eventually to have found a resting-place in Westminster Abbey.

Among the miracles reported at the victim's intercession was one at " Bellus Campus ", no doubt Belchamp-Otten, in Essex, where the parish church is dedicated in honour of St Ethelbert and All Saints. His feast, as a martyr, is still observed in the dioceses of Cardiff (which includes Herefordshire) and Northampton.*

It must be confessed that John Brompton, whose account is printed in the *Acta Sanctorum*, May, vol. v, is not a very satisfactory authority, but the Bollandists apparently had also before them a transcript of a manuscript account by Giraldus Cambrensis, which was hopelessly damaged in the Cottonian fire of 1731. There is, however, a later manuscript text of this life in the library of Trinity College, Cambridge (B. II. 16), which is printed in the *English Historical Review*, vol. xxxii (1917), pp. 222–236 ; there also M. R. James prints an anonymous *passio* from Corpus Christi College, Cambridge, MS. 308, probably " the oldest form of the Hereford story of St Ethelbert that has yet been produced ". For a description of these and other sources, see James, *loc. cit.*, pp. 214–221. From Edmund Bishop's notes on the English calendar in Stanton's *Menology* it is clear that St Ethelbert had a considerable *cultus* as a martyr ; he was represented in the paintings at the English College in Rome. Consult further the account furnished in that undeservedly neglected work, W. B. MacCabe's *A Catholic History of England*, vol. i, pp. 683–697, and the appendix to A. T. Bannister, *The Cathedral Church of Hereford*, pp. 109–114. See also R. M. Wilson, *The Lost Literature of Medieval England* (1952), pp. 106–108.

BD COLUMBA OF RIETI, Virgin (A.D. 1501)

In the chronicles of Perugia we find many references to Bd Columba, a Dominican tertiary who, by virtue of her sanctity and spiritual gifts, became whilst yet living so completely the city's patroness that her mediation was officially sought by the magistrates in times of danger and perplexity. She was a native, not of Perugia, but of Rieti, where her father and mother earned a modest livelihood as weavers and tailors. Although her angelic looks as a baby led her parents to choose for her the name of Angiolella, she was always called Columba, in allusion to a dove which made its appearance during her baptism and alighted on her head. As she grew in years so she grew in beauty of soul and body. From the Dominican nuns who taught her to read she acquired a great veneration for St Dominic and St Catherine of Siena, and during her life they often appeared in visions to encourage or direct her. At the age of ten she secretly dedicated herself to God, and when her parents urged that she should be betrothed to a wealthy young man, she cut off her hair, declaring that her whole heart belonged to Jesus Christ. She now gave herself up to austerities, hidden as far as possible from the eyes of men, and she strove to tread in the footsteps of St Catherine. On one occasion, after a cataleptic trance in which she had lain as though dead for five days, she described the holy places of Palestine which she had been visiting in spirit. But it was at the age of nineteen, when she had been invested with the Dominican tertiary habit which she had long desired, that she emerged from her retirement and entered upon what may almost be described as her public life.

A resident of Rieti lay under sentence of death for murder, and Columba's prayers were asked on his behalf. She visited him in prison, brought him to repentance and, after he had made a good confession, assured him that his execution

* It is difficult to forbear wondering on what principles some of the saints included in the propers of English dioceses were chosen during the last century.

would not take place. Her prophecy was fulfilled when at the eleventh hour a reprieve arrived. Her reputation was further enhanced by miracles and by her almost complete abstention from food. At Viterbo, where she cured a demoniac, and also at Narni, the inhabitants sought to detain her by force, but she eluded them. She was not, however, to remain long at Rieti. It was revealed to her that her mission lay elsewhere, and accordingly early one morning she slipped out of the house in secular clothes—bound she knew not whither. Upon her arrival at Foligno she was arrested on suspicion that she was a fugitive for whom the authorities were searching, and her relations were communicated with. Joined by her father, her brother, and an elderly matron, she was then able to pursue her mysterious journey which led finally to the gates of Perugia—perhaps the most turbulent city in Italy. She was received in a humble dwelling already occupied by several tertiaries, and immediately seems to have been made the object of a popular demonstration. Her fame, no doubt, had preceded her. Not only the poor, but many of the rich, including the ladies of the Baglioni family then in power, welcomed her with open arms. On the other hand, certain excellent persons—notably the Franciscan and Dominican friars—were openly suspicious of a young woman who was said to subsist on a few berries and who was constantly falling into ecstasies. Amongst them was Father Sebastian Angeli, afterwards her confessor and biographer. In his book he confesses his early doubts and the incredulity with which he received the information that she had resuscitated a child. " Wait for ten years ", he said to young Cesare Borgia, who suggested ringing the city bells, " and then if her conduct has not belied her reputation we can reckon her a saint." The citizens generally, however, had no such doubts, and they offered to provide her with a convent. On January 1, 1490, Columba with a few companions took the vows of a Dominican religious of the third order. A few years later, on the outbreak of plague, her position was so well established that the magistrates applied to her for advice and adopted her suggestion of penitential processions. Many of the sick were healed by her touch, some in her convent where they were tended by her nuns, some outside. She had offered herself to God as a victim ; and when in answer to her prayers the plague abated, she contracted it in a virulent form. Her recovery she attributed to St Catherine, in whose honour the magistrates decreed an annual procession which was continued for a hundred years. In the bitter quarrels that rent the city Columba invariably acted as an angel of peace, and once she warned the rulers of a projected attack from outside which they were consequently able to frustrate.

Pope Alexander VI when he came to Perugia asked specially to see her, and was so impressed that at a later date he sent his treasurer to consult her on certain secret projects—only to receive reproaches and warnings the details of which were never made public. But if the pontiff himself was favourably disposed, it was otherwise with his daughter, Lucrezia Borgia, whom Columba had refused to meet and who, it is said, became her bitter enemy. Apparently as the result of her hostile influence, Bd Columba was subjected to a period of persecution, when a decree issued from Rome accused her of magic and deprived her of her confessor. She uttered no complaint and bore all in patience until the attack passed. Towards the end of her life she suffered much bodily pain, but her interest in Perugia continued to the end. To the city fathers who came to visit her in her last illness she gave an exhortation to observe Christian charity and to do justice to the poor. She died at the age of thirty-four, early in the morning on the feast of the Ascension,

1501. The magistrates contributed to provide for her a public funeral, which was attended by the whole city.

In the *Acta Sanctorum*, May, vol. v, the Bollandists have published a Latin biography of Bd Columba which was written by her confessor, Father Sebastian degli Angeli, a Dominican friar of Perugia. Very little other material seems to have been available from Dominican sources, and Father Leander Alberti, who produced an Italian life in 1521, did little more than translate the Latin text of Father Sebastian. It must be confessed that there are many points in his rather surprising narrative which one would have liked to see presented from another angle. Bd Columba has never been canonized, but her cult was formally confirmed in 1627. In view of this confirmation, or of the continuation of the cause, a summary statement with a brief catalogue of miracles was presented to the Congregation of Rites, and this also may be found in the same volume of the Bollandists. The Dominican Father D. Viretti, using these sources, compiled in 1777 a *Vita della B. Colomba da Rieti*, which was translated into English for the Oratorian Series and edited by Father Faber in 1847. The best modern biography of this interesting *beata* seems to be that of Ettore Ricci, *Storia della B. Colomba da Rieti* (1901) ; but see also M. C. de Ganay, *Les Bienheureuses Dominicaines* (1913), pp. 305–354. A short sketch in English will be found in Procter, *Dominican Saints*, pp. 133–136.

21 : ST GODRIC (A.D. 1170)

ST GODRIC was born of very poor parents at Walpole in Norfolk, and in his youth earned a living by peddling in the neighbouring villages. As he improved his stock he was able to go farther afield to the great fairs and cities. Then the spirit of adventure seized him, and he took to a seafaring life which he pursued for sixteen years. He made voyages to Scotland, Flanders and Scandinavia, and probably traded in the ports he visited, for he was able to purchase a half-share in one merchant vessel and a quarter-share in another. The life was a rough one with many temptations, and one chronicler refers to him as a pirate ; but on a visit which he paid to Lindisfarne he was deeply impressed by the account given him of the life of St Cuthbert, whom he ever afterwards regarded with special veneration. He undertook a pilgrimage to Jerusalem, which had lately been captured by the Crusaders, and on the homeward journey he visited Compostela.* After his return to England he became house-steward to a wealthy Norfolk landowner, but the retainers plundered the poorer neighbours unmercifully and Godric gave up the post, partly because he could not induce the master to check this pillaging, partly because he himself had—knowingly or unknowingly—partaken of the booty. He then set out on two more pilgrimages, the one to the shrine of St Giles in Provence and the other to Rome in the company of his mother who, we are told, made the whole journey barefoot.

We hear of him next in Cumberland, where he acquired a psalter, which he learnt by heart and which became his most treasured possession. Having made his way eastward into the wilds of Durham, he fell in at Wolsingham with a recluse called Aelric. Godric was permitted to join this aged hermit, in whose company he spent two happy and fruitful years. Then Aelric died, and Godric made a second pilgrimage to Jerusalem. It was the last of his foreign journeys, for St Cuthbert in a vision had promised him a hermitage in England. After a sojourn

* For the service rendered by " Gudericus pirata de regno Angliae " to King Baldwin I of Jerusalem, see S. Runciman, *History of the Crusades*, vol. ii (1953), p. 79 (Albert of Aix, *Chronicon*, ix).

at Eskdale and another in Durham, where he acted for a time as sacristan, he discovered the place of his dream in the midst of Bishop Flambard's hunting-park on the river Wear, three miles from Durham. There, at Finchale, in a forest which teemed with big and small game, he spent the remaining years of his life, practising mortifications which would have killed any but a very robust man. Shy creatures such as stags, hares and birds were not afraid of him, nor did he fear wolves or snakes. All wild animals were his friends, disporting themselves in his company and fleeing to him from danger. He constructed first a wattle oratory and then a little church. As far as possible he lived in silence and seclusion, but he was under the direction of the prior of Durham who, besides supplying him with a priest to say Mass in his chapel, would often send strangers to be edified by his conversation. Among his visitors were St Aelred and St Robert of Newminster, and a monk called Reginald, who obtained from him, though with difficulty, the story of his early years and wrote a biography which is still extant.

St Godric was endowed with extraordinary powers—notably with the gifts of prophecy and a knowledge of distant events. He foretold the death of Bishop William of Durham, and the exile, return and martyrdom of St Thomas Becket, whom he had never seen. He often beheld scenes that were being enacted far away, breaking off a conversation to pray for vessels in imminent danger of shipwreck. He also knew beforehand the date of his own death which occurred on May 21, 1170, after he had spent some sixty years in his hermitage. At a later period there was built at Finchale a monastery, the ruins of which survive. St Godric is the co-titular of a Catholic church in Durham.

The monk Reginald records not only the words but also the airs of four sacred songs, which he took down from the hermit's lips. Godric claimed that they had been taught him in visions, of our Lady, of his dead sister, and of others. They are in any case of great interest as being the oldest pieces of English verse of which the musical setting has survived, and among the oldest to show rhyme and measure instead of alliteration.

We have two distinct accounts of St Godric, one written by Reginald of Durham who had visited the hermit. This, which is preserved in different recensions, was printed by the Surtees Society in 1845, edited by Fr J. Stevenson. The second, by Galfrid, is also the work of one who had himself seen him, and who had before him the memoir of Prior German who had been St Godric's confessor. This is printed in the *Acta Sanctorum*, May, vol. v. See also DNB., vol. xxii, pp. 47–49 ; and for the songs, J. B. Trend in *Music and Letters*, vol. ix, pp. 111–128. There is a delightful essay on St Godric in Fr J. Brodrick's *Procession of Saints* (1949), and cf. R. M. Wilson, *The Lost Literature of Medieval England* (1952).

BD BENVENUTO OF RECANATI (A.D. 1289)

FEW incidents marked the life of Bd Benvenuto Mareni. He was born at Recanati, a hill-town in the Marches of Ancona at a short distance from Loreto, and entered as a lay-brother amongst the Franciscan Conventuals of his native city. He was remarkable for his piety and for his humility, which made him always desirous of the lowliest offices. Often during Mass, and especially when he had received holy communion, he would fall into an ecstasy, his body at such times appearing to be completely insensible. From one of these trances he awoke to realize that it was long past the hour for him to begin to prepare the brethren's meal. Hastily he made his way to the kitchen, where he was greeted by an angelic deputy who had been doing his work.   All who partook of the repast that day agreed that they had never tasted better food.   Bd Benvenuto had many other supernatural experiences and was, it is said, once permitted to hold the Infant Saviour in his arms.   The saintly friar died on May 5, 1289.   Pope Pius VII confirmed his *cultus.*

In the account which Fr Léon, *Auréole Séraphique* (Eng. trans.), vol. ii, pp. 175–176, gives of this *beatus* he remarks that the annalists of the order have left few details of his life. This observation seems to be thoroughly borne out by an inspection of such chroniclers as Mazzara or Mark of Lisbon.

ST ANDREW BOBOLA, MARTYR   (A.D. 1657)

ST ANDREW BOBOLA came of an aristocratic Polish family and was born in the palatinate of Sandomir in 1591.   He entered in 1609 the Jesuit noviciate at Vilna in Lithuania, which had become united with Poland in 1391 through the marriage of Queen Hedwig with Duke Jagiello.   After he had been raised to the priesthood, Andrew was appointed preacher in the church of St Casimir at Vilna, where his apostolic zeal made a great impression upon the people.   At a later date he was chosen superior of the Jesuit house at Bobrinsk and, during his term of office, distinguished himself by his devotion to the sick and dying when a terrible epidemic was raging.

As soon as he was relieved of his charge, he resumed the missionary career which he had pursued for more than twenty years, travelling the country and bringing whole villages of separated Orthodox back to communion with the Holy See, besides converting numerous lax Catholics.   His success brought upon him hatred and opposition.   One form of petty persecution he found particularly trying. For several years, whenever he entered a village with a sufficiently large anti-Catholic population, he was met by an organized band of children who, in accordance with instructions from their elders, followed him about, hurling abusive epithets at him and trying to shout him down.   He never lost patience with them, nor was he daunted or discouraged by threats or opposition.   Poland at this time had become the scene of a sanguinary conflict in which the revolted Cossacks took a prominent part.   The Jesuit missionaries were driven from their churches and colleges by these relentless foes, and they took refuge in a district of swamps, lakes and marshland formed by branches of the Pripet and Berezina and known as Podlesia.   Thither Prince Radziwill invited the Jesuits, to whom he offered one of his residences at Pinsk in 1652.   St Andrew accepted the invitation although he fully anticipated the fate that was in store for him.

In May 1657 some Cossacks made a sudden attack on Pinsk.   Father Bobola was seized near Janow, and made to run back thither at the heels of a Cossack's horse.   He was invited to abjure Catholicism, and on his refusal was mercilessly beaten.   He was then interrogated, and his firm answers so infuriated the officer that he slashed at him with his sword and nearly severed one of the priest's hands. He was then put to a slow death with the most revolting barbarity.   In the public slaughterhouse he was stripped of his clothes, scorched all over like a dead pig, half flayed, his nose and lips cut off, and his tongue torn out through his neck with pincers.   His prayers to Christ and His mother seemed only to increase his tormentors' savagery.   At last his head was struck off, and the mutilated body cast on a dungheap.

When the remains of St. Andrew Bobola were medically examined in 1730 they were found inexplicably incorrupt—a specially remarkable circumstance in view of the respect for this phenomenon popularly shown among the dissident Orthodox. And the doctors were able to confirm the horrible details of his death. He was canonized in 1938.

See L. Rocci, *Vita del B. Andrea Bobola* (1924); H. Beylard, *Vie . . . de St André Bobola* (1938); Fr Thurston in *Studies*, September 1938, pp. 381–393; and the life by Mareschini, adapted into English by L. J. Gallagher and P. V. Donovan (Boston, 1939). The extraordinary history of the conveyance to Rome in 1922 of the body of the saint, which had been carried off to Moscow by the bolsheviks, is told by Fr L. J. Gallagher in *The Month*, February, 1924.

ST THEOPHILUS OF CORTE   (A.D. 1740)

THE little town of Corte in Corsica was the birthplace of this Theophilus, or, to give him his baptismal and family names, Blasius de' Signori. He was the only child of aristocratic parents who fostered, up to a certain point, the boy's early piety. They encouraged him to invite his schoolfellows on Sundays to his home, where he would say prayers with them and repeat the morning's sermon. But when, at the age of fifteen, he ran away to enter a Capuchin monastery, he was not permitted to remain there. Nevertheless, as he continued to show a marked vocation for the religious life, his father and mother allowed him two years later to take the Franciscan habit in his native town. After studying philosophy and theology at Corte, in Rome and at Naples he was ordained in 1700. In the retreat-house of Civitella, to which he was appointed lector in theology, he formed an intimate friendship with Bd Thomas of Cori. In 1705, while still at Civitella, he was chosen for mission preaching and, overcoming a natural shrinking from publicity, he went forth as an evangelist among the people.

At once it became evident that St Theophilus had great oratorical gifts, which enabled him to touch the hearts not only of careless Christians but also of hardened sinners. The influence exerted by his eloquent words was enhanced by the holiness of his life and by miracles. At Civitella, of which he became guardian, he won the love and veneration of the whole community. In 1730 his superiors sent him back to Corsica in order that he might form one or more houses there on the lines of Civitella. He found himself confronted by many difficulties, but he succeeded in establishing a retreat at Luani, where the rule of Civitella was followed in all its poverty and austerity. Four years later he was recalled to Italy to do similar work in Tuscany, and at Fucecchio, some twenty English miles from Florence, he made his second foundation. That same year he was summoned to Rome to give evidence for the beatification of Thomas of Cori. So great was the impression he then made upon the bishop of Nicotera, who was in charge of the case, that the prelate afterwards exclaimed, " I have been questioning one saint about another saint ". Theophilus died at Fucecchio on May 20, 1740. As his body lay awaiting burial in the church, immense crowds gathered round to venerate it. They kissed his hands and feet and tore so many pieces from his clothing that it became necessary to dress the body in a new habit. St Theophilus was canonized in 1930.

The brief of beatification, which includes a biographical summary, may be read in the *Analecta Ecclesiastica*, vol. iv (1896), pp. 5–7. There is an excellent account in French by the Abbé Abeau, *Vie du B. Théophile de Corte* (1896)—it runs to more than 400 pages—and an almost equally lengthy Italian life, in which the archives of the Franciscans of the Observance have been utilized, by Father Dominichelli, *Vita del B. Teofilo da Corte* (1896). Another full life in Italian is by A. M. Paiotti (1930), and there is a shorter account by M. P. Anglade, *Une page d'histoire franciscaine* (1931).

BD CRISPIN OF VITERBO   (A.D. 1750)

THE Romans have a great devotion to Bd Crispin of Viterbo, whose relics rest under a side altar in the church of the Immaculate Conception in the City.   At an early date he learnt from his mother the deep veneration to our Blessed Lady which characterized him throughout his life.   After he had received a little schooling at the Jesuit College, Peter—as he was named in baptism—served his apprenticeship with an uncle, from whom he learnt the trade of a shoemaker.   The Franciscan Order attracted him greatly, and when he was about twenty-five he obtained admission to the Capuchin convent at Viterbo, choosing the name of Crispin because of his trade.   In the novice house at Paranzana the father guardian hesitated to receive him because he looked so delicate and was diminutive in stature ; but the minister provincial, who had previously admitted him, overruled all objections. As it turned out, Brother Crispin proved equal to the heaviest tasks, and loved to call himself the Capuchin ass, deeming himself unfit to be regarded as anything more than a beast of burden.   At Viterbo he dug the garden and acted as cook, and at Tolfa, where he was infirmarian during an epidemic, he effected some wonderful cures.

A short residence in Rome was followed by a stay at Albano and another at Bracciano, where he again nursed the sick during an epidemic and seems to have healed many of them miraculously.   At Orvieto, where he was questor—charged with soliciting alms—he was so greatly beloved that the citizens were determined to keep him.   When the time came for his departure the housewives with one consent decided to close their doors to his successor, and as the convent depended on the charity of the faithful, the guardian was compelled to re-appoint Brother Crispin rather than allow the brethren to starve.   The holy friar's last years, however, were spent in Rome.   He was then noted for his prophecies, his miracles of multiplication of food, and his wise sayings, some of which have been preserved.   He died in his eighty-second year on May 19, 1750, and was beatified in 1806.

There is an anonymous *Vita del B. Crispino da Viterbo* printed at the time of the beati- fication, and there have been many others since, notably two in French, by Ildephonse de Bard (1889) and by Pie de Langogne (1901), and two in Italian, by P. Pacilli (1908) and by Paolo di Campello (1923).   See also Léon, *Auréole Séraphique* (Eng. trans.), vol. ii, pp. 280–285.

22 : SS. CASTUS AND AEMILIUS, MARTYRS   (A.D. 250)

IN a book which he wrote upon " The Lapsed ", St Cyprian mentions with sympathy the case of two African Christians, Castus and Aemilius by name, who at the time of the great persecution of Decius gave way under the stress of severe torture but afterwards repented, and gained the crown of martyrdom by confessing their faith and boldly facing death by fire.   Nothing further is known about their life or the circumstances of their passion.   Their names occur in several old martyrologies, and St Augustine, in a sermon preached on the occasion of their festival, says that they fell like St Peter, through presuming too much on their own strength.

The names are entered on this day in the Calendar of Carthage, a document which can hardly be dated later than the middle of the fifth century.   See also the *Acta Sanctorum,* May, vol. v, and CMH.

ST QUITERIA, Virgin and Martyr   (Fifth Century ?)

Many churches in southern France and northern Spain have been dedicated under the name of the virgin martyr St Quiteria, who still enjoys a wide *cultus*, especially at Aire in Gascony, where her reputed relics were preserved until they were scattered by the Huguenots.   On the other hand, though her name appears in the Roman Martyrology, no mention of her is made in any of the ancient calendars. She is popularly supposed to have been the daughter of a Galician prince, who fled from home because her father wished to force her to marry and to abjure the Christian religion.   She was tracked to Aire by emissaries from her father, by whose orders she was beheaded.   Most of the details of the story, in the form in which it was most widely circulated, are fabulous, having been borrowed from the well-known legend of King Catillius and Queen Calsia, and nothing is certain about Quiteria except her name and her *cultus*.   Because she is invoked against the bite of mad dogs, she is always depicted with a dog on a lead.   It seems that Portugal is equally devout to St Quiteria, but tells a different story of her martyrdom and claims to possess her relics.

The modern Bollandists seem inclined to put faith in the Aire tradition, being influenced mainly by the researches of Abbé A. Degert, who in the *Revue de Gascogne*, vol. xlviii (1907), pp. 463–469, has printed the most ancient texts of the life of this martyr.   See also the same *Revue*, vol. xlvi (1905), pp. 333–337, and vol. xliv (1903), pp. 293–309, with the *Analecta Bollandiana*, vol. xxvii (1908), p. 457.   The more commonly received account of St Quiteria may be gathered from A. Breuils, *Les légendes de Sainte Quitterie* (1892).

ST ROMANUS   (*c.* A.D. 550)

When the youthful St Benedict had abandoned the world and was wandering about on the rocky height of Monte Subiaco, he came face to face with a holy monk called Romanus who belonged to a neighbouring monastery.   They entered into conversation, and St Benedict opened his heart to the older man and told him he desired to live as a hermit.   Romanus not only encouraged him, but showed him a cave, very difficult of access, which would make him a suitable cell.   For three years the monk was the only connection the young recluse had with the outside world and kept his presence a secret.   Every day he saved part of his portion of food, which he let down by a rope over a cliff to St Benedict.   According to the legend, St Romanus left Italy when it was being overrun by the Vandals and betook himself to the neighbourhood of Auxerre in France, where he founded the monastery of Fontrouge and where he died.   Auxerre, Sens and Vareilles claim to possess some of his relics.

St Romanus is honoured with an elogium on this day in the Roman Martyrology and there is consequently a notice of him in the *Acta Sanctorum,* May, vol. v, which reprints a long and mainly fictitious account of his life and miracles compiled by Gislebert of Vareilles

in the middle of the eleventh century.   Consult further C. Leclerc, *Vie de S. Romain* (1893)
which, though quite uncritical in the matter of his life, supplies some useful information
regarding his *cultus* in Gaul.

ST JULIA, Martyr   (Sixth Century ?)

THE name of St Julia appears in many ancient Western martyrologies and she is
described as a martyr of Corsica.   In the opinion of the Bollandists she suffered
in the sixth or seventh century at the hands of Saracen pirates.   Her legend, as
related in her so-called " acts ", is confessedly based on a late tradition and has
been freely embellished with imaginative detail.   It runs as follows : Julia was a
noble maiden of Carthage who, when the city was taken by Genseric in 439, was
sold as a slave to a pagan merchant of Syria called Eusebius.   She lived an exemplary life and became so valuable a servant to her master that he took her with him
on a journey he was making to Gaul as an importer of Eastern goods.   Having
reached the northern part of Corsica, now known as Cape Corso, their ship cast
anchor.   Eusebius went on shore to take part in a local heathen festival, whilst Julia
remained behind, refusing to assist at the ceremonies, which she openly denounced.
Questioned by Felix, the governor of the island, regarding this woman who had
dared to insult the gods, Eusebius admitted that she was a Christian and his slave,
but declared that he could not bring himself to part with so faithful and efficient a
servant.   When the governor offered four of his best female slaves in exchange for
her, Eusebius replied, " If you were to offer me all your possessions, they could not
equal the value of her services ! "   However, when Eusebius was in a drunken
sleep, the governor took it upon himself to induce her to sacrifice to the gods.   He
offered to obtain her freedom if she would comply, but she indignantly refused,
protesting that all the liberty she desired was freedom to continue serving her
Lord, Jesus Christ.   Her boldness enraged the governor, who gave orders that she
should be beaten on the face and her hair torn out by the roots.   She finally
died by crucifixion.   Monks, we are told, from the island of Giraglia rescued
her body and kept it until 763, when it was translated to Brescia.   St Julia
is patroness of Corsica and of Leghorn, which claims to possess some of her
relics.

There are two texts of the *passio* of this martyr, one of which is printed in full in the
Acta Sanctorum, May, vol. v.   The insertion of her name on this day in the *Hieronymianum*
affords strong presumption of her historical existence, as Delehaye notes in his commentary.
See also particularly Mgr Lanzoni, both in his *Diocesi d'Italia*, pp. 685–686, and in the
Rivista Storico-Critica, vol. vi (1910), pp. 446–543.

ST AIGULF, OR AYOUL, BISHOP OF BOURGES   (A.D. 836)

AFTER the death of his parents, when he was still a young man, St Aigulf left his
native city of Bourges to live as a solitary in a neighbouring forest.   There he led
a most austere life and acquired so great a reputation for sanctity that when the see
of Bourges fell vacant, about the year 811, the clergy and people unanimously chose
him for their bishop.   Although he only accepted office with reluctance, yet he
ruled the diocese wisely and successfully for twenty-four years.   He was one of the
signatories at the Council of Toulouse in 829 and one of the judges selected to
examine the case of Ebbo, archbishop of Rheims, and two other prelates who had
been deposed for joining the sons of Louis the Debonair in their rebellion against
their father.   When he felt that his last hour was approaching, St Aigulf retired

to his old hermitage, where he died and was buried. Over his tomb a church was afterwards built. On the occasion of an elevation or of a translation of his body, the word " Martyr " was added to the inscription on his tomb, but this was a mistake, due probably to confusion with St Aigulf, abbot of Lérins, who was a martyr.

Little is known of St Aigulf beyond what can be gleaned from the poem which St Theodulf, bishop of Orleans, addressed to him. It is printed with some other fragments of information in the *Acta Sanctorum*, May, vol. v. See also DHG., vol. i, cc. 1142–1143.

ST HUMILITY, WIDOW (A.D. 1310)

THE foundress of the Vallombrosan nuns was born at Faenza in the Romagna in the year 1226. Her parents, who were people of high rank and considerable wealth, called her after the town of Rosana, with which they were in some way connected, but she has always been known by the name of Humility, which she adopted when she entered religion. Her parents practically compelled her when she was about fifteen to marry a local nobleman called Ugoletto, a young man as frivolous as his bride was earnest and devout. She had the misfortune to lose both her sons shortly after their baptism, and for nine years she strove, apparently in vain, to appeal to her husband's better nature. A dangerous illness, however, then brought him to death's door and upon his recovery he was induced by his doctors to consent for his own benefit to his wife's request that they should from thenceforth live as brother and sister. Soon afterwards they both joined the double monastery of St Perpetua, just outside Faenza, he becoming a lay-brother and she a choir nun.

Humility was then twenty-four years of age. She discovered before long that the rule afforded her insufficient opportunity for solitude and austerity, and she withdrew first to a house of Poor Clares and then to a cell, which was constructed for her by a kinsman whom she had cured of a painful infirmity of the feet. It adjoined the church of St Apollinaris, and into this there was an opening—what archaeologists call a " squint "—which enabled her to follow Mass and to receive holy communion. The church seems to have been served by religious from a priory dependent on the Vallombrosan abbey of St Crispin, the abbot of which, following the ceremonial provided for in such cases, solemnly enclosed her in her cell. Her life was now one of heroic mortification : she subsisted on a little bread and water with occasionally some vegetables ; she wore a *cilicium* of bristles, and the short snatches of sleep she allowed herself were taken on her knees with her head leaning against a wall. She had never consented to see her husband after she had left the world, but he could not forget her ; and in order that he might keep in touch with her, he left St Perpetua's to become a monk at St Crispin's, where he died three years later. After Humility had lived twelve years as a recluse, the Vallombrosan abbot general persuaded her to emerge from her retirement to organize a foundation for women. At a place called Malta, outside the walls of Faenza, she established the first Vallombrosan nunnery, of which she became abbess and which was known as Santa Maria Novella alla Malta. Long years afterwards, actually in 1501, the convent was removed for safety into the city and occupied the site once covered by the monastery of St Perpetua. Before her death St Humility founded in Florence a second house, of which she was also abbess and where she died at the age of eighty on May 22, 1310.

Tradition credits St Humility with the authorship of several treatises—she is said to have dictated them in Latin, a language she had never studied. One of these deals with the angels and in it she speaks of living in constant communion with two heavenly beings, one of whom was her guardian angel.

A contemporary life is printed in the *Acta Sanctorum*, May, vol. v, from a manuscript notarially attested in 1332 to be an exact copy. There is a modern biography by M. Ercolani (1910), and a shorter one by Dame M. E. Pietromarchi, *S. Umiltà Negusanti* (1935). The Latin tractates of St Humility were edited by Torello Sala at Florence in 1884 ; they are said to be very obscure and the Latin to be stiff and artificial.

ST RITA OF CASCIA, WIDOW   (A.D. 1457)

IN the year 1381 there was born in a peasant home at Roccaporena in the central Apennines a little girl who, as an exemplary daughter, wife and religious, was destined to attain to great heights of holiness in this life, and afterwards to merit from countless grateful souls by her intercession in Heaven the title of " the saint of the impossible and the advocate of desperate cases ".

The child of her parents' old age, Rita—as she was named—showed from her earliest years extraordinary piety and love of prayer. She had set her heart upon dedicating herself to God in the Augustinian convent at Cascia, but when her father and mother decreed that she should marry, she sorrowfully submitted, deeming that in obeying them she was fulfilling God's will. Her parents' choice was an unfortunate one. Her husband proved to be brutal, dissolute and so violent that his temper was the terror of the neighbourhood. For eighteen years with unflinching patience and gentleness Rita bore with his insults and infidelities. As with a breaking heart she watched her two sons fall more and more under their father's evil influence, she shed many tears in secret and prayed for them without ceasing. Eventually there came a day when her husband's conscience was touched, so that he begged her forgiveness for all the suffering he had caused her : but shortly afterwards he was carried home dead, covered with wounds. Whether he had been the aggressor or the victim of a vendetta she never knew. Poignancy was added to her grief by the discovery that her sons had vowed to avenge their father's death, and in an agony of sorrow she prayed that they might die rather than commit murder. Her prayer was answered. Before they had carried out their purpose they contracted an illness which proved fatal. Their mother nursed them tenderly and succeeded in bringing them to a better mind, so that they died forgiving and forgiven.

Left alone in the world, Rita's longing for the religious life returned, and she tried to enter the convent at Cascia. She was informed, however, to her dismay that the constitutions forbade the reception of any but virgins. Three times she made application, begging to be admitted in any capacity, and three times the prioress reluctantly refused her. Nevertheless her persistence triumphed : the rules were relaxed in her favour and she received the habit in the year 1413.

In the convent St Rita displayed the same submission to authority which she had shown as a daughter and wife. No fault could be found with her observance of the rule, and when her superior, to try her, bade her water a dead vine in the garden, she not only complied without a word, but continued day after day to tend the old stump. On the other hand, where latitude was allowed by the rule—as in the matter of extra austerities—she was pitiless to herself. Her charity to her neighbour expressed itself especially in her care for her fellow religious during illness and for the conversion of negligent Christians, many of whom were brought to repentance by her prayers and persuasion.   All that she said or did was prompted primarily by her fervent love of God, the ruling passion of her life.   From childhood she had had a special devotion to the sufferings of our Lord, the contemplation of which would sometimes send her into an ecstasy, and when in 1441 she heard an eloquent sermon on the crown of thorns from St James della Marca, a strange physical reaction seems to have followed.   While she knelt, absorbed in prayer, she became acutely conscious of pain—as of a thorn which had detached itself from the crucifix and embedded itself in her forehead.   It developed into an open wound which suppurated and became so offensive that she had to be secluded from the rest.   We read that the wound was healed for a season, in answer to her prayers, to enable her to accompany her sisters on a pilgrimage to Rome during the year of the jubilee, 1450, but it was renewed after her return and remained with her until her death, obliging her to live practically as a recluse.

During her later years St Rita was afflicted also by a wasting disease, which she bore with perfect resignation.   She would never relax any of her austerities or sleep on anything softer than rough straw.   She died on May 22, 1457, and her body has remained incorrupt until modern times.   The roses which are St Rita's emblem and which are blessed in Augustinian churches on her festival refer to an old tradition.   It is said that when the saint was nearing her death she asked a visitor from Roccaporena to go to her old garden and bring her a rose.   It was early in the season and the friend had little expectation of being able to gratify what she took to be a sick woman's fancy.   To her great surprise, on entering the garden, she saw on a bush a rose in full bloom.   Having given it to St Rita she asked if she could do anything more for her.   " Yes ", was the reply.   " Bring me two figs from the garden."   The visitor hastened back and discovered two ripe figs on a leafless tree.

The evidence upon which rests the story of St Rita as it is popularly presented cannot be described as altogether satisfactory.   The saint died in 1457, but the first biography of which anything is known, written by John George de Amicis, only saw the light in 1600 and we can learn little or nothing of the sources from which it was compiled.   A considerable number of lives have appeared in modern times, but in spite of the diligence of their various authors they add hardly anything in the way of historical fact to the slender sketch which may be read in the *Acta Sanctorum* (May, vol. v), which is derived mainly from the seventeenth century life by Cavallucci.   There are also many chronological problems, which, *pace* Father Vannutelli, still remain unsettled.   In English we have a *Life of St Rita of Cascia*, by R. Conolly (1903), and *Our Own Saint Rita*, by M. J. Corcoran (1919).   Of the numerous Italian biographies those by P. Marabottini (1923) and by L. Vannutelli (1925) seem most in favour.

BD JOHN FOREST, Martyr   (A.D. 1538)

At the age of seventeen John Forest entered the Franciscan convent of the Strict Observance at Greenwich, and nine years later he was sent to Oxford to study theology.   His studies completed, he seems to have returned to his friary with a great reputation for learning and wisdom.   Not only was he invited to preach at St Paul's Cross, but he was also chosen to be Queen Catherine's confessor when the court was in residence at Greenwich.   The close relations into which he was brought with the king and queen and the uncompromising attitude taken up by the Observants with regard to Henry VIII's schemes for divorcing Catherine, rendered his position a delicate one.   At a chapter in 1525 he told his brethren that the king was so incensed against them that he had contemplated suppressing them, but that he, John, had succeeded in dissuading him.   The relief, however, was only temporary.   In 1534, after the pope's decision had been made known, Henry ordered that all Observant convents in England should be dissolved and that the friars should pass to other communities.   Captivity was the punishment for such as proved refractory and we know from a legal report that Bd John was imprisoned in London in the year 1534.

How long he remained there is uncertain as we have no record of the next four years.   According to the testimony of his enemies he admitted to having made an act of submission " with his mouth but not with his mind ", which would appear to have gained him his liberty.   On the other hand in 1538 we find him living in the house of the Conventual Grey Friars at Newgate, under the supervision of a superior who was a nominee of the crown, in a state of semi-captivity but able to minister to those who resorted to him.   Because he was thought to have denounced the oath of supremacy to Lord Mordaunt and other penitents, he was arrested and brought to trial, when he was inveigled or browbeaten into giving his assent to some articles propounded to him ; but when they were submitted to him afterwards for him to read and sign, and he realized that one of them would have amounted to apostasy, he repudiated them altogether.   He was thereupon condemned to the stake.   He was dragged on a hurdle to Smithfield and almost to the last he was offered a pardon if he would conform, but he remained unshaken.   Asked if he had anything to say, he protested that if an angel should come down from Heaven and should show him anything other than that which he had believed all his life, and that if he should be cut joint after joint and member after member—burnt, hanged, or whatever pains soever might be done to his body—he would never turn from his " old sect [*i.e.* profession] of this Bishop of Rome ".   Owing to the wind the flames took a long time in reaching a vital part, but the martyr bore his sufferings with unflinching fortitude.   With him was burnt a wooden statue of St Derfel Gadarn, much venerated in Wales, concerning which it had once been predicted that it would set a *forest* on fire (see April 5).

The best documented account of this martyr is that by J. H. Pollen, contained in LEM., edited by Dom Bede Camm, vol. i (1904), pp. 274–326.   See also Father Thaddeus, *Life of Blessed John Forest.*

ST JOACHIMA DE MAS Y DE VEDRUNA, WIDOW, FOUNDRESS
OF THE CARMELITES OF CHARITY   (A.D. 1854)

AT the end of the eighteenth century the noble family of Vedruna, well-known and respected in Catalonia, was represented in Barcelona by Lawrence de Vedruna, who had married Teresa Vidal.   They had eight children, of whom the fifth, Joachima (Joaquina), was born in 1783.   Her childhood and adolescence—earlier in Spain then farther north—seem to have been uneventful and not marked by anything out of the way.   She was evidently a devout, serious and intelligent child, among the traits her biographers mention being that she always liked to be doing something, especially such useful work as knitting stockings ; but the abounding energy of childhood has manifested itself usefully in numberless children who did not grow up to be saints.   Nor was her attraction towards the life of the cloister any more unusual—though it is not every twelve-year-old girl with that idea who presents herself at the door of a Carmelite convent and demands to be admitted to the community, as Joachima de Vedruna did.

However, in 1798 she met the man who was to be her husband, when he was a witness at the wedding of her sister Josephine. He was a young lawyer of good family in Barcelona, Theodore de Mas, and he too had seriously thought of offering himself as a religious to the Franciscans. It is permissible to think that the biographers of Bd Joachima may have over-stressed the element of parental wishes on both sides overriding an inclination to self-dedication to the religious life in these young people. Certainly it would seem that Theodore de Mas went about his courting with careful deliberation. One of his granddaughters, a Visitation nun at Madrid, tells us that he was uncertain which of the Vedruna girls to marry, whether Teresa or Frances or Joachima. So, she says, he called on them armed with a box of sugared almonds. Teresa and Frances turned up their noses at such a gift—" Does he think we are children ? " But Joachima exclaimed delightedly, " Oh, I should like them ! " And Theodore made his choice accordingly.

On the other hand, a few days after their marriage (in 1799, when she was sixteen), Joachima was very cast down because she felt she had betrayed her true vocation. Her husband comforted her, and ended by saying that should they have children they would bring them up and launch them in life and then, if she wished, she could retire to a convent and so would he. " And so ", Joachima told her confidant years afterwards, " we consoled one another ". And children they had, eight of them. The first, Anne, was born in 1800, then Joseph in 1801, followed by Francis and Agnes, three years after the birth of whom Napoleon I invaded Spain. For greater safety—as he hoped—Theodore de Mas moved his family from Barcelona to Vich, his birthplace, and then joined the army. But when the French troops had crossed the Pyrenees and were approaching Vich, the inhabitants fled, and Joachima set out with the children for a place called Montseny, accompanied by two servants and a boy. They were going to spend the night in the plain of La Calma, but a woman with a donkey suddenly appeared and warned Joachima on no account to do so ; she led them some way farther to a house where they were hospitably received, and then their guide disappeared. That night French troops bivouacked in the plain of La Calma. Nobody could identify the mysterious woman with the donkey, and Joachima always believed it was our Lady herself who had appeared to warn her.

It was during this troubled time that the fifth child, Carlotta, was born and died, and the second son, Francis, also died soon after. Then they were able to return to Vich, where in 1810 Theodora was born and in 1813 Teresa. In the same year Theodore de Mas resigned his military commission and took his family back to Barcelona, where two years later their last child, another daughter, Carmen, was born. Whatever doubts Joachima may have had about her matrimonial vocation, there is no doubt that she was a beloved wife and a devoted mother. And it is interesting to note that when the second daughter, Agnes, wanted to be a nun, Joachima said firmly, " No. God wants you to marry. Two of your sisters will be nuns." And so it was ; but Theodora was able to become a Cistercian nun only after a disappointed young man had brought—and lost—a breach of promise of marriage action against her in the episcopal court of Tarragona. There were other legal proceedings that brought great distress and loss to the Mas family, instituted by Theodore's own brothers and other relatives. Some members of her husband's family were not the least of Joachima's crosses.

One day in September 1815, while Theodore and his wife were sitting at table with their children around them, suddenly and without any warning Joachima had a vivid vision of her husband lying dead, and a voice seemed to say to her, " This will happen in a few months. You will be a widow." She said nothing of this to Theodore or anybody else, and alternately resigned herself to God's will and tried to put the experience aside as meaningless. In the following January she was in Vich, where Theodore wrote her loving letters and seemed perfectly well. Two months later he was dead, at forty-two years old. His wife was then thirty-three.

For the first seven years of her widowhood Joachima lived in the big house at Vich, Manso del Escorial, devoting her time to her children, to prayer, and to waiting on the sick in the local hospital. She " hauled down her flag " (as Francis de Sales said to St Jane de Chantal), even so far as to dress in the Franciscan tertiary habit, and lived a life of the utmost mortification and poverty. " Poor thing " said her neighbours, " her husband's death has driven her crazy." In 1823 two of the children, Joseph and Agnes, got married, and shortly afterwards Joseph and his wife took the two youngest, Teresa and Carmen, into their home at Igualada. " Jesu ", wrote Joachima, " You know what I want for my dear ones. Don't be surprised at the weakness of my heart : I am their mother—and that is why I beseech your goodness." In the years of toil for Christ and His poor that were to follow, she never lost touch with her children ; some of the birthday letters she wrote them are extant.

In 1820, in somewhat remarkable circumstances, Joachima had met the well-known Capuchin, Father Stephen (Fabregas) of Olot, who told her she must not go into any existing convent as she was destined to belong to a new congregation with the double task of teaching the young and nursing the sick. Six years later she was clothed with the religious habit by the bishop of Vich, Mgr Paul Corcuera ; he had approved the formation of a community with those objects, and put it under the invocation of our Lady of Mount Carmel (this was disappointing to Father Stephen of Olot, who had hoped it would be affiliated to his own order). The interest had also been roused of an influential layman, Joseph Estrada, who to the end of his days was a devoted friend of the Carmelites of Charity, as the new sisters were to be called. Father Stephen drew up a rule, and the community started in the Manso del Escorial with six members. They were extremely poor in material resources, and their reception was not always sympathetic. When one day the noble widow de Mas asked an alms from the Marchioness Portanuova, that lady replied, " How could you be so stupid as to get involved in this absurd under-taking ! " Yet within a few months a hospital had been opened at Tarrega.

From then on the new congregation continued to spread throughout Catalonia (all the foundations made during the lifetime of the foundress were in that province of Spain). Even the Carlist wars and the anti-religious activity of the so-called liberal government brought only a temporary set-back. But, after caring for the sick and wounded of both sides, some of the Carmelites of Charity had to take refuge in France. As on a previous occasion, while crossing the Pyrenees, Mother Joachima was aided in a remarkable way, this time by a mysterious young man whom she believed to be a vision of the Archangel Michael. The exile in Perpignan lasted three years, and it was not till the autumn of 1843 that the sisters were able to return to Spain, when there began the most active and fruitful period of Bd Joachima's extension of her congregation.

Early in the following year the foundress and the senior nuns made their final profession. The delegate to receive their vows on behalf of the Church was St Antony Claret, who had an important part in the history of the Carmelites of Charity during these years of St Joachima's life. About 1850 she felt the first warnings of the paralysis that was to strike her down. In the circumstances she was persuaded by Mgr Casadevall, vicar capitular of Vich, that it would be wise for her to resign the leadership of her congregation, and from 1851 its direction was in the hands of a priest, Father Stephen Sala; later on his place was taken by a Benedictine monk, Dom Bernard Sala. Her faculties were completely unimpaired, but the foundress accepted her relegation to the rank of a simple sister humbly and with equanimity. Father Sala was a man of fine quality, and he declared that she was still " the soul, the head, the heart of the congregation, its very self ".

For four weary years Mother Joachima was dying by inches, a complete paralysis creeping over her body. For the last few months she could neither move nor speak, and her spirit too seemed inanimate, except when holy communion was brought to her. But it was an attack of cholera that finally brought her earthly life to an end, on August 28, 1854. Her body was eventually translated to the chapel of the mother house of the Carmelites of Charity at Vich, and in 1940 she was solemnly declared blessed.*

St Joachima was married for seventeen years, and was thirty-three years old, with six children living, when her husband died, she was forty-two before the Carmelites of Charity were instituted, and she died at seventy-one after founding convents with their schools and hospitals all over Catalonia. These facts alone are enough to draw attention to her as a most remarkable woman, and to suggest the strength of her spirit of faith and love. To her have been applied Bossuet's words about the Princess Palatine : " She buried herself in her husband's grave, leaving human ties with his ashes, and gave herself to ceaseless prayer, pouring out all her love to the one bridegroom, Jesus Christ ". Several times when at prayer in the chapel the sisters saw her lifted from the floor in ecstasy, her head ringed with light ; and it was this height of prayer, trust and selflessness that informed all her work. St Joachima de Mas y de Vedruna was a worthy successor of the great women of the past, who in widowhood gave themselves to the dedicated life, of such as Paula, Bridget of Sweden and Elizabeth of Hungary, Frances Romana, Jane de Chantal and Barbara Acarie.

Among the writers on St Joachima de Vedruna have been Cardinal Benedict Sanz y Fores and Dom Bernard Sala ; but *Vida y Virtudes de la Ven. M. Joaquina* (1905) by Fr James Nonell, in two volumes, is outstanding for its detail. The fourth edition of a useful short account of her, *Vida y Obra de . . . Joaquina de Vedruna de Mas*, by Fr Ignatius of Pamplona was published in 1946. The official Italian biography is *La Beata Gioacchina de Vedruna v. de Mas*, by Don Emidio Federici (1940) ; whereas the first-named books were intended primarily for the members of Mother Joachima's congregation, this last, in which full use is made of the documents of the beatification process, is for a wider public.

23 : ST DESIDERIUS, OR DIDIER, BISHOP OF VIENNE, MARTYR (A.D. 607)

AT the time when Queen Brunhildis was exercising her baleful influence over the courts of her grandsons Theodebert, king of Austrasia, and Theodoric, king of Burgundy, the diocese of Vienne was administered by a holy and learned bishop named Desiderius. He was one of the French prelates to whom St Gregory the Great specially commended St Augustine and his companion mission-

* Descendants of Bd Joachima and twenty-five Carmelites of Charity were among the victims of secularist terrorism in Spain in 1936.

aries on their way to evangelize England. The zeal of St Desiderius in enforcing clerical discipline, in repressing simony, and in denouncing the profligacy of the court made him many enemies, the chief of whom was Brunhildis herself. Attempts were made to discredit him with the pope by accusing him of paganism on the ground of his liking for reading the great Latin classics, but St Gregory, after receiving his apologia, completely exonerated him. Brunhildis then persuaded a servile council at Chalon to banish the good bishop on charges trumped up by false witnesses. Recalled after four years, St Desiderius found himself hampered in the exercise of his duties by the governor of Vienne and other old opponents, but he did not scruple boldly to rebuke King Theodoric for his shameless wickedness. On the way home from the court he was set upon by three hired men who, probably exceeding their orders, killed him, at the place where now stands the town of Saint-Didier-sur-Chalaronne.

The *passio*, which was edited in the *Analecta Bollandiana*, vol. ix (1890), pp. 250–262, seems to be a trustworthy document and to be the work of a contemporary. Another account attributed to Sisebut, the Visigothic king, is also probably authentic, but tells us little. Both are included by B. Krusch in his third volume of *Scriptores Merov.*, in MGH., pp. 620–648. See also Duchesne, *Fastes Épiscopaux*, vol. i, pp. 207–208.

ST GUIBERT   (A.D. 962)

GEMBLOUX in Brabant, which is now a centre for agriculture and the manufacture of cutlery, covers the site once occupied by a celebrated Benedictine monastery. It was founded by St Guibert, or Wibert, who, about the year 936, gave his estate of Gembloux for that purpose. He came of one of the most illustrious families of Lotharingia and had served with distinction in warlike campaigns, when he was moved to abandon the world and to make trial of the solitary life on one of his estates. It was whilst he was living as a hermit that he conceived the idea of establishing a religious house where men, drawn from worldly affairs, would honour God unceasingly by singing His praises. St Guibert's grandmother Gisla helped to endow the new foundation, over which he placed a holy man called Herluin to be the first abbot. He himself, as soon as the new monastery was well launched, retired to the abbey of Gorze, where he received the habit. This step he took from humility, to avoid the respect with which he was regarded at Gembloux and the complacency he might feel in his own foundation. At Gorze he hoped to live in obscurity as a simple monk. He soon discovered, however, that he could not thus easily sever his connection with Gembloux. The land he had given to the new abbey appears to have been an imperial fief, and busybodies represented to the Emperor Otto I that the saint was not entitled thus to dispose of it. The monarch summoned him to plead his cause. Guibert defended his action and his rights so successfully that Otto confirmed the establishment of the abbey by charter and subsequently granted to it great privileges.

Nevertheless, in spite of the emperor's letters, the monks of Gembloux were not left in peaceful possession. The count of Namur, St Guibert's brother-in-law, claimed it on behalf of his wife and seized the revenues of the abbey ; so St Guibert was obliged for a time to return to Gembloux to assert his own claims and to protect the community he had founded. At the same time he did missionary work, and succeeded in converting a number of pagans, Hungarian and Slav settlers who had remained in the country after the invasion of 954. St Guibert's last years, which he spent at Gorze, were troubled by a long and painful illness.   He died on May 23, 962, in his seventieth year, and his tomb was afterwards celebrated for the miracles wrought there.

There is a life written in some detail by the chronicler Sigebert of Gembloux, who lived a century later.   It is printed in the *Acta Sanctorum*, May, vol. v, and elsewhere.   A good deal of attention has been paid by various writers to the foundation of Gembloux.   See especially U. Berlière, *Monasticon Belge*, vol. i, pp. 15–26, and also the *Revue Bénédictine*, vol. iv (1887), pp. 303–307.

ST LEONTIUS, Bishop of Rostov, Martyr   (A.D. 1077)

THIS Leontius, who was a Greek from Constantinople, was the first monk of the Caves of Kiev to become a bishop, when soon after the year 1051 he was given charge of the eparchy of Rostov.   He was one of a line of remarkable missionary bishops of this see, and though he received much persecution at the hands of the heathen he was reputed to be more successful in their conversion than any of his predecessors.   Helped by the gift of miracles, he is said to have brought paganism to an end around Rostov, but in view of the mission of St Abraham fifty years later this can hardly be the case (unless St Abraham has been wrongly dated).

St Leontius died in or about 1077, and because of the ill-treatment he suffered from the heathen he has ever been venerated as a martyr.   It is said that two laymen, Varangians, were the first to die for the Christian faith in Russia, in the time of St Vladimir the Great, and St Leontius was distinguished as " the hiero-martyr ", that is, the martyr who was a priest.   Russian usage commemorates him at the preparation of the holy things in the Byzantine Mass.

From Martynov's *Annus ecclesiasticus Graeco-Slavicus* in *Acta Sanctorum*, October, xi. *Cf.* St Sergius, September 25, and bibliography.

ST IVO, Bishop of Chartres   (A.D. 1116)

To the order of Canons Regular of St Augustine the Church in the eleventh century was indebted for one of the most venerated of her episcopal rulers.   Ivo, bishop of Chartres, was born in the territory of Beauvais and studied theology under the celebrated Lanfranc in the abbey of Bec.   After occupying a canonry at Nesles in Picardy, he took the habit at the monastery of Saint-Quentin, a house of regular canons, where he was appointed to lecture on theology, canon law and the Holy Scriptures.   Afterwards Ivo ruled as superior for fourteen years, during the course of which he raised the house to a high pitch of discipline and learning, so that he was constantly being called upon by bishops and princes to send his canons to other places either to reform ancient chapters or to found new ones.   The observances of Saint-Quentin were adopted by St Botulf's at Colchester, the first Augustinian house in England.

When, in the year 1091, Geoffrey, bishop of Chartres, was deposed for simony and other misdemeanours, the clergy and people demanded Ivo for their bishop. He was very unwilling to emerge from his retirement, but Bd Urban II confirmed his election and Ivo set out for Capua, where he was consecrated by the pope, who subsequently checked the endeavours of Richerius, archbishop of Sens, to reinstate Geoffrey.   Scarcely was St Ivo firmly established in his see than he found himself faced with the necessity of opposing the will of his sovereign.   King Philip I had become so greatly enamoured of Bertrada, the third wife of Fulk, Count of Anjou, that he had determined to marry her and to divorce his queen Bertha, in spite of the fact that she had borne him two children. Ivo did his utmost to dissuade the king from proceeding further, but when he found his remonstrances unavailing he declared openly that he would prefer to be cast into the sea with a mill-stone round his neck rather than countenance such a scandal; and he absented himself from the wedding ceremony at which the bishop of Senlis connived. Philip in revenge had him put in prison, seized his revenues and sent officers to plunder his lands. Strong representations, however, were made by the pope, by other influential personages and by the citizens of Chartres, and he was released. Philip indeed could scarcely fail to realize that the bishop was amongst his most loyal subjects, for St Ivo, while actually in custody, nipped in the bud a conspiracy of nobles against their sovereign; and, when the affair had dragged on for years, he exerted himself to reconcile Philip to the Holy See and at the Council of Beaugency in 1104 recommended the absolution of the king, whose real wife had in the meantime died. Though he was devoted to the Holy See, St Ivo maintained a sufficiently independent attitude to enable him to act as mediator in the dispute over investitures and to protest openly against the greed of certain Roman legates and the simony of members of the papal court.

St Ivo died on December 23, 1116, after having governed his see for twenty-three years. He was a voluminous writer and many of his works have survived. His most famous literary undertaking was a collection of decrees drawn from papal and conciliar letters and canons accepted by the fathers. This is preserved to us in two, if not three, independent compilations. We have also 24 sermons and 288 letters which shed an interesting light on contemporary history and ecclesiastical discipline.

Although no formal early biography of St Ivo of Chartres is preserved to us, we have a great deal of information supplied by his letters and by references in contemporary chronicles and correspondence. See the *Acta Sanctorum*, May, vol. v. Ivo has been much studied recently, especially from the point of view of his work as a canonist. A most valuable contribution to this aspect of the subject may be found in the treatise of P. Fournier and G. Le Bras, *Histoire des Collections canoniques en Occident depuis les Fausses Décrétales, etc.*, vol. ii (1932), pp. 55–114. St Ivo's views as to the superiority of the cenobitical life to that of hermits and solitaries are discussed by G. Morin in the *Revue Bénédictine*, vol. xl (1928), pp. 99–115. See also Fliche and Martin, *Histoire de l'Église*, t. viii.

ST EUPHROSYNE OF POLOTSK, Virgin   (A.D. 1173)

WHEN Russia received the Christian faith from Constantinople at the end of the tenth century the Byzantine liturgy of worship also was adopted, including the calendar with its commemorations of numerous Greek and other saints. As time went by Russian holy ones were added to the *sanctorale*; but in this connection there were two rather curious modifications of Greek and Western practice. The first was the very secondary place given to martyrs for the faith as compared with great ascetics or such "sufferers" as SS. Boris and Gleb. The second was the lack of veneration for holy maidens (the All-Holy Mother of God of course excepted). Early Russian iconography ignored the virgin saints of the Greek calendar almost completely; and only twelve women have been canonized by the Russian Church, and of these, eleven have been married. The exception was St Euphrosyne of Polotsk.

She was the daughter of Prince Svyatoslav of Polotsk, and she became a nun in her native town when she was twelve years old, and took up a solitary life in a cell at the cathedral church of the Holy Wisdom. For the most part she spent her time copying books, which she sold in order that she might devote the proceeds to the relief of the sick and needy. But like some other recluses St Euphrosyne travelled about a good bit : she founded a monastery for women at Seltse, she visited Constantinople, where she was received by the Emperor Manuel I and was given by the Patriarch Michael III the *eikon* of our Lady of Korsun, and in her last years she went to the Holy Land. These were the days of the Latin crusading kingdom of Jerusalem, and St Euphrosyne was received by King Amaury I and by the Frankish patriarch, Amaury ; she also visited the famous monastery of Mar Saba, still in existence and occupied, in the wilderness halfway between Jerusalem and the Dead Sea. It was there in Jerusalem that she died, and her body was brought back to Kiev for burial. St Euphrosyne is honoured by the Ruthenians and Lithuanians as well as by the Russians.

See I. Martynov, *Annus ecclesiasticus Graeco-Slavicus*, in the *Acta Sanctorum*, October, vol. xi, and A. Maltsev, *Menologium der Orthodox-Katholischen Kirche des Morgenlandes* (1900) ; and also the account of Euphrosyne's pilgrimage translated in *Revue de l'Orient latin*, vol. iii (1895), pp. 32–35.

ST WILLIAM OF ROCHESTER, Martyr (A.D. 1201)

THE story of this William is that he was a holy and charitable burgher of Perth, who set out from Scotland to make a pilgrimage to Jerusalem. He took with him one David, a foundling whom he had adopted. In the neighbourhood of Rochester this lad murdered his benefactor. The body was found by a poor woman who roamed about the country crazy and half-naked ; she made a garland of honeysuckle and laid it on the corpse. Afterwards, putting the wreath on her own head, she was restored to her right mind and gave notice to the people of Rochester. They came out and honourably buried the victim of this crime. Miracles followed, and it is even alleged that William was canonized by Pope Alexander IV in 1256. What is certain is that before this time there was already a shrine of " St William " in Rochester Cathedral, which was a notable centre of popular devotion.

Father T. E. Bridgett discussed the case at length in *The Month* for August 1891, pp. 501–508. But see also the *Acta Sanctorum*, May, vol. v ; and W. St John Hope, *The Cathedral and Monastery of St Andrew at Rochester* (1900), pp. 37, 127–128, etc. There is no trace of any bull of canonization, and the statement that Bishop Laurence going to Rome *impetravit canonizationem beati Willelmi martyris* probably means no more than that leave was granted to maintain the cult already in existence. We know that King Edward I in 1299 made an offering at the shrine.

BD GERARD OF VILLAMAGNA (A.D. 1245)

THE origins of the Franciscan third order for lay-folk are involved in great obscurity, and it is curious to notice how little evidence is forthcoming to support the claim that certain holy people in the early part of the thirteenth century were admitted as tertiaries by St Francis himself. Something has already been said of the case of Bd Luchesius (April 28) ; and here again when we ask for proof that Gerard of Villamagna was received into the third order by the Saint of Assisi, we are told that all early documents have perished. Gerard was a solitary who occupied a hermitage near his native village of Villamagna in Tuscany. He led a very austere life, absorbed for the most part in contemplation, but also giving direction at times to many struggling souls who came to consult him. We are told that he had been left an orphan at the age of twelve, had been brought up as a kind of page-boy in the household of some wealthy Florentine, had attended his master as a body-servant when he joined the third crusade, had been captured by the Saracens and afterwards ransomed, that he had again returned to the Holy Land with another crusader, and had himself eventually been admitted as a knight of the Holy Sepulchre. Wearied of the world, it is stated that he came back to Italy to lead the life of a hermit, that he received the cord of the third order from St Francis himself, and that he died some twenty years later famous for his miracles and prophecies. His cult was confirmed in 1833.

The Bollandists could find no better materials to print in the *Acta Sanctorum* (May, vol. iii) than an account compiled after the year 1550 by the parish priest of Villamagna. See also Wadding, *Annales*, vol. v, p. 19.

BD BARTHOLOMEW OF MONTEPULCIANO (A.D. 1330)

AMONGST the numerous persons of all ranks who were led by the example of the early Franciscans to abandon all things in order to embrace holy poverty was a prominent citizen of Montepulciano named Bartholomew Pucci-Franceschi. He was a married man and had lived an exemplary Christian life with his family for many years when the call came to him to serve God in complete renunciation of the world. With the consent of his wife, who herself took the vow of chastity, he entered the Franciscan Order. Soon he surpassed all his brethren in piety, and was induced, though against his wish, to receive holy orders. He had frequent visions of our Lady and of angels, and performed many miracles, particularly in the multiplication of food. To avoid human respect he tried to become a " fool for Christ's sake ", behaving at times in such a manner as to be ridiculed and pelted by children in the streets. He lived to be very old, and died at Montepulciano on May 6, 1330.

See Ausserer, *Seraphisches Martyrologium* (1889) ; Léon, *Auréole Séraphique* (Eng. trans.), vol. ii, pp. 375–376.

ST JOHN BAPTIST ROSSI (A.D. 1764)

THIS holy priest was born in 1698 at the village of Voltaggio in the diocese of Genoa, and was one of the four children of an excellent and highly respected couple. When he was ten, a nobleman and his wife who were spending the summer at Voltaggio obtained permission from his parents to take him back with them to Genoa to be trained in their house. He remained with them three years, winning golden opinions from all, notably from two Capuchin friars who came to his patron's home. They carried such a favourable report of the boy to his uncle, who was then minister provincial of the Capuchins, that a cousin, Lorenzo Rossi, a canon of Santa Maria in Cosmedin, invited him to come to Rome. The offer was accepted, and John Baptist entered the Roman College at the age of thirteen. Popular with his teachers and with his fellow pupils, he had completed the classical course with distinction when the reading of an ascetical book led him to embark on excessive mortifications. The strain on his strength at a time when he was working hard led to a complete breakdown, which obliged him to leave the Roman College. He recovered sufficiently to complete his training at the Minerva, but he never was again really robust. Indeed, his subsequent labours were performed under the handicap of almost constant suffering.

On March 8, 1721, at the age of twenty-three, John Baptist was ordained, and his first Mass was celebrated in the Roman College at the altar of St Aloysius

Gonzaga, to whom he always had a special devotion. Even in his student days he had been in the habit of visiting the hospitals, often in the company of his fellow pupils, over whom he exercised the same influence that he had wielded over the children of Voltaggio. Now, as a priest, he could do far more for the patients. Very particularly did he love the hospice of St Galla, a night refuge for paupers which had been founded by Pope Celestine III. For forty years he laboured amongst the inmates, consoling and instructing them. The hospital of the Trinità dei Pellegrini was also a field of his labours. But there were other poor people for whom, as he discovered, no provision had hitherto been made ; these called for his special sympathy and efforts. First and foremost there were the cattle-drovers and teamsters who came up regularly from the country to sell their beasts at the market then held in the Roman Forum. In the early morning and late evening he would go amongst them, winning their confidence, instructing them and preparing them for the sacraments. Another class to whom his pity was extended comprised the homeless women and girls who wandered about begging, or who haunted the streets by night. He had absolutely no money except the little that came as Mass stipends, but with the help of 500 scudi from a charitable person and of 400 scudi from the pope, he hired a house behind the hospice of St Galla and made of it a refuge which he placed under the protection of St Aloysius Gonzaga.

For the first few years after his ordination his diffidence made him shrink from undertaking the work of a confessor. It was not until he had gone to convalesce after an illness to the house of Bishop Tenderini of Civita Castellana that he was persuaded by his friend to make a beginning in his diocese. At once he and his penitents realized that he had found his true vocation, and he followed it up upon his return to Rome. " I used often to wonder what was the shortest road to Heaven ", he remarked to another friend. " It lies in guiding others thither through the confessional. . . . What a power for good that can be ! "

In the year 1731, Canon Rossi obtained for his kinsman the post of assistant priest at Sta Maria in Cosmedin. The church, partly owing to its position, had been poorly attended, but it soon began to fill with penitents of all classes who flocked to St John Baptist's confessional. So much of his time came to be spent there that, at a later date, two successive popes, Clement XII and Benedict XIV, dispensed him from the obligation to say the choir offices when he was on duty in the confessional.

Upon the death of Canon Lorenzo Rossi in 1736 his canonry was conferred upon his cousin, who accepted it but gave up its emoluments to provide the church with an organ and the stipend of an organist. Even the house which he inherited from Canon Lorenzo he presented to the chapter, whilst he himself went to live in a miserable attic. His personal wants were very few : his food was frugal in the extreme, and his dress, although always scrupulously neat, was of the plainest material. One very congenial task was undertaken at the request of Pope Benedict XIV, who inaugurated courses of instruction for prison officials and other state servants and selected this young priest to deliver them. Amongst his penitents was the public hangman. Once he was called in to settle a serious quarrel between that official and a younger subordinate : " To-day I have brought a great affair of state to a happy conclusion ", he afterwards remarked.

As a preacher the saint was in great demand for missions and for giving addresses in religious houses of both men and women. The Brothers of St. John of God, in whose hospitals he often ministered, held him in such high esteem that they chose him to be their own confessor-in-ordinary. Failing health obliged him in 1763 to take up his residence in the Trinità dei Pellegrini, and in the December of that year he had a stroke and received the last sacraments. He rallied sufficiently to resume celebrating Mass, but he suffered greatly and on May 23, 1764, he succumbed to another apoplectic seizure. He was sixty-six years of age. He left so little money that the hospital of the Trinità had to undertake to pay for his burial. As it turned out, however, he was accorded a magnificent funeral : two hundred and sixty priests, many religious, and innumerable lay persons took part in the procession ; Archbishop Lercari of Adrianople pontificated at the requiem in the church of the Trinità, whilst the papal choir provided the music. During his life the saint had been endowed with supernatural gifts, and numerous miracles followed his death. The process of his beatification, begun in 1781, was completed by the bull of canonization in 1881.

There are a number of excellent modern lives, notably that by Fr Cormier, in French (1901), and that in Italian by E. Mougeot (1881), which was translated into English by Lady Herbert, with a preface by Cardinal Vaughan (1906). A contemporary biography was published by one of Rossi's friends, J. M. Toietti, in 1768, and another in the same year by Fr Tavani.

24 : SS. DONATIAN and ROGATIAN, Martyrs (A.D. 289 or 304)

DURING the reign of the Emperor Maximian there was living at Nantes in Brittany a young man called Donatian who belonged to a prominent Romano-Gallic family and was a zealous Christian. After the outbreak of persecution his elder brother Rogatian was moved by his example and piety to desire baptism, but the sacrament was deferred because the bishop was in hiding. The emperor had issued an edict directing that all who refused to sacrifice to Jupiter and Apollo should be put to death. Upon the arrival of the prefect at Nantes, Donatian was brought before him on the charge of professing Christianity and of withdrawing others—notably his brother—from the worship of the gods. He made a bold confession and was cast into prison, where he was soon joined by Rogatian who, in the face of cajolery and threats, had remained constant to his newly-found faith. He only grieved that he had not been baptized, but he prayed that the kiss of peace which he had received from his brother might supply the necessary grace. He was destined to receive the baptism of blood. They spent the night together in fervent prayer and were brought up again the following day before the prefect, to whom they expressed their willingness to suffer for the name of Christ whatever torments might be in store for them. By his order they were tortured on the rack, their heads were pierced with lances, and they were finally decapitated. The two martyrs are greatly venerated at Nantes where they are popularly known as " Les Enfants Nantais ". A few of their reputed relics are preserved in a church dedicated in their honour.

The comparatively sober *passio* of these martyrs has been included in the *Acta Sincera* of Ruinart. This may be read also in the *Acta Sanctorum*, May, vol. v, and another redaction has been printed in the *Analecta Bollandiana*, vol. viii (1889), pp. 163–164. Though it is impossible to regard the text as the report of a contemporary, still it cannot be treated as a mere romance. Mgr Duchesne, who touches upon the matter in his *Fastes Épiscopaux* (vol. ii, pp. 359–361), remarks that in the whole of western Gaul these are the only martyrs whose death can confidently be assigned to the Roman persecutions. See further A. de la Borderie, *Histoire de Bretagne*, vol. i, pp. 187–194; Delanoue, *S. Donatien et S. Rogatien* (1904); G. Mollat in *Annales de Bretagne*, vol. xxii (1907), pp. 205–213; and J. B. Russon, *La passion des Enfants nantais* (1945). H. Leclercq also discussed the question at some length in DAC., vol. xii (1935), cc. 628–634, giving abundant bibliographical references.

ST VINCENT OF LÉRINS   (c. A.D. 445)

St VINCENT of Lérins is described by St Eucherius in his *Instructiones* and in his letter *De Laude Eremi* as a man " pre-eminent in eloquence and learning "· He is supposed to have been the brother of St Lupus of Troyes, and he would seem to have been a soldier before he took the religious habit at the abbey of Lérins on the island off the coast of Cannes now called Saint-Honorat, after the founder of the monastery.   St Vincent was living there as a monk and a priest when, in the year 434—nearly three years after the close of the Council of Ephesus—he composed the book upon which his fame rests, his so-called *Commonitorium* against heresies.   In this book he speaks of himself as a stranger and pilgrim who had fled from the service of this world with all its empty vanities and passing pleasures in order to enter the service of Christ as one of His lowliest servants in the seclusion of the cloister.   He explains that, in the course of his reading, he had gathered from the fathers certain principles or rules for distinguishing Christian truth from falsehood, and that he had jotted them down primarily for his own use, to aid his poor memory.   These notes he expanded into a treatise in two parts, the second of which dealt with the recent Council of Ephesus.   This latter portion, however, was lost or stolen, and St Vincent contented himself with adding to the first part a general summary or recapitulation of the whole.   In this book of forty-two short chapters, which St Robert Bellarmine described as being " small in bulk but very great in value ", we find enunciated for the first time the axiom that for a dogma to be regarded as Catholic truth it must have been held always, everywhere, and by all the faithful—" quod ubique, quod semper, quod ab omnibus creditum est ". Doubtful points must be settled by this test of universality, antiquity and consent, *i.e.* the agreement of all or nearly all bishops and doctors.   The Bible cannot be regarded as the sole test of truth, because it is subject to different interpretations and is quoted as much in the interests of heterodoxy as of orthodoxy ; it must be interpreted according to the tradition of the Church, which alone has the right to expound it.   If a new doctrine is advanced, it must be confronted with the universal teaching of the Church and, where the universality test appears to be defective by reason of widespread apostasy at any period, appeal must be made to the teaching of the primitive Church.   If the error is one which had its counterpart in primitive times, then the final court of appeal would be the faith of the majority.   Progress indeed there must be, but it must be like the growth of the acorn, or the development of the child into a man : it must preserve identity and all essential characteristics.   The chief work of the councils has been to elucidate, define and emphasize that which had already been widely taught, believed and practised.   And behind all the testimony of the fathers, the doctors and the councils, stands the authority of the Apostolic See.

An immense body of literature has been provoked by his treatise and it has been very variously judged.   It appeared at a time when the controversy over grace and free-will was raging, especially in the south of France, and many authorities regard the book as a thinly-veiled attack upon the extreme Augustinian doctrine of predestination.   In support of this view they point to the fact that at the time when the *Commonitorium* was written, the abbot of Lérins and many of the monks were semi-Pelagians ; that in many passages St Vincent uses semi-Pelagian terms ; and that a celebrated vindication of Augustinianism by St Prosper of Aquitaine purported to be a refutation of a book of objections composed by a certain Vincent, whom they identify with St Vincent of Lérins.   On the other hand it is beyond question that Vincent was a very common name and also that, if semi-Pelagian ideas appear in the *Commonitorium*, it has other passages which are so similar to clauses of the Athanasian Creed, that St Vincent has sometimes been credited with the authorship of that most orthodox confession of faith.   In any case the semi-Pelagian controversy had not then been authoritatively settled, and if St Vincent erred in that direction he erred in company with many other holy men.   The exact date of his death is not certain, but it seems to have been about the year 445.

We know very little in detail regarding the life of St Vincent of Lérins.   The brief account in the *Acta Sanctorum* (May, vol. v) is mainly derived from the *De viris illustribus* of Gennadius of Marseilles.   See also DCB., vol. iv, pp. 1154–1158, the *Dictionnaire Apologétique*, vol. iv, cc. 1747–1754, and the *Historisches Jahrbuch*, vol. xxix (1908), pp. 583 *seq.*   There is an excellent translation of the *Commonitorium* in French (1906) by de Labriolle and H. Brunetière.

BD LANFRANC, Archbishop of Canterbury   (A.D. 1089)

LIKE Bd Herluin (August 26) Lanfranc seems to have received no public *cultus*, but he has very commonly been called Blessed, and so is given a bare reference here.

He was born at Pavia *c.* 1005 and when about thirty-five became a monk of Bec, where he founded the school that was to be that abbey's glory.   In 1062 William of Normandy appointed him abbot of Caen, and in 1070 archbishop of Canterbury.   Lanfranc was a great ecclesiastical statesman, and on the administrative side no primate after St Theodore had a deeper effect on the Church in England.   But as a theological writer and in spiritual things he was a far lesser man than his fellow at Bec and successor at Canterbury, St Anselm.   Lanfranc was a critic of the *cultus* of some of the old English saints, of whose worth he was not convinced, and he had trouble with the monks of Christ Church on this account.

There is an excellent life of Lanfranc by A. J. M. Macdonald (1926).   For his calendar revision see Gasquet and Bishop, *The Bosworth Psalter.*

ST DAVID I OF SCOTLAND   (A.D. 1153)

THE name of this king occurs in several old Scottish calendars and more than one modern Catholic church is dedicated in his honour ; he belongs to the category of popularly canonized national heroes, the particulars of whose life belong mainly to secular history.   He was born about 1080, the youngest of the six sons of King Malcolm Canmore and his queen, St Margaret.   In 1093 he was sent to the Norman court in England, where he remained for some years.   When his brother Alexander succeeded to the Scottish throne in 1107, David became prince of Cumbria (roughly the Lowlands), and by his marriage in 1113 to Matilda, widow of the earl of Northampton, he became earl of Huntingdon.   In 1124 he succeeded his brother as King David I.

St Aelred of Rievaulx was in his earlier years master of the household to David, with whom he kept up a close friendship, and after the king's death he wrote an account of him. In it he speaks of David's reluctance to accept the crown, of the justice of his rule, of his almsdeeds and his accessibility to all, of his efforts to maintain concord among the clergy, of his personal piety, and in general of the great work he did for the consolidation of the kingdom of Scotland. Aelred's only criticism was of his failure to control the savagery and rapacity of his troops when he invaded England, on behalf of his niece Matilda against Stephen. For this David was very contrite, and is said to have looked on his defeat at the Battle of the Standard and elsewhere and the early death of his only son as just retribution therefor.

It was afterwards complained that King David's benefactions to the Church impoverished the crown, among the critics being his fifteenth-century successor, James I. For not only did he found the royal burghs of Edinburgh, Berwick, Roxburgh, Stirling and perhaps Perth, but he also established the bishoprics of Brechin, Dunblane, Caithness, Ross and Aberdeen and founded numerous monasteries. Among them were the Cistercian houses of Melrose, Kinloss, Newbattle and Dundrennan, and Holyrood itself for Augustinian canons.

St Aelred gives a circumstantial account of David's death at Carlisle on May 24, 1153. On the Friday he was anointed and given viaticum, and then spent much time in praying psalms with his attendants. On Saturday they urged him to rest, but he replied, " Let me rather think about the things of God, so that my spirit may set out strengthened on its journey from exile to home. When I stand before God's tremendous judgement-seat you will not be able to answer for me or defend me ; no one will be able to deliver me from His hand ". And so he continued to pray ; and at dawn of Sunday he passed away peacefully as if he slept.

St David had helped to endow Dunfermline Abbey, founded by his father and mother, and he had peopled it with Benedictine monks from Canterbury. There he was buried, and at his shrine his memory was venerated until the Reformation.

For the reign of one of the greatest Scottish kings consult standard histories of that kingdom. Bishop Forbes summarizes St Aelred's panegyric in his *Kalendars of Scottish Saints*, and gives references to Robertson, *Scotland under her Early Kings*, vol. i (Edinburgh, 1862) and to Pinkerton's *Vitae Antiquae Sanctorum Scotiae*. See also Bellesheim's *History of the Catholic Church in Scotland*, vol. i, and A. H. Dunbar, *Scottish Kings* (1906). The *cultus* of St David was recognized after the Reformation among Protestants by the insertion of his name in the calendar of Laud's Prayer-book for Scotland, 1637.

ST NICETAS OF PEREASLAV, Martyr (A.D. 1186)

IN the earlier years of his manhood this Nicetas was a collector of taxes at Pereaslav, in the neighbourhood of Rostov, and he was disliked by everybody because of the viciousness of his life in general and his ferocious oppressiveness in his business in particular. But the hand of the Lord touched him. He heard the words of the prophet Isaias (i 16), " Wash you, make you clean . . . Cease to do evil . . . Learn to do well," and they struck him to the heart. He left his wife and family and possessions, and withdrew to a monastery where he gave himself to extreme works of penance. He wore a shirt of metal links next his skin, and lived on a pillar in the manner of the stylites or pillar-saints.

It is not known how long this lasted, but it was long enough for the iron links of the shirt to be polished by wear till they shone like silver—and this caused the death of Nicetas. For robbers, deceived by the shining, set upon and killed him for the sake of this treasure. Because of this unjust death St Nicetas is celebrated as a martyr ; but his veneration was due rather to his miracles of healing, which both in life and after death caused him to be known as " the Wonder-Worker ".

From Martynov's *Annus ecclesiasticus Graeco-Slavicus* in *Acta Sanctorum*, October, xi. *Cf.* St Sergius on September 25, and bibliography.

BD JOHN OF PRADO, Martyr   (A.D. 1613)

AMONGST the heroes of the Friars Minor of the Observance, great honour is paid to Bd John of Prado, who won the crown of martyrdom in Morocco in the seventeenth century even as the Franciscan pioneers, Bd Berard and his companions, had won it there in the thirteenth. He was born of a noble Spanish family at Morgobejo in Leon, and, after being educated at Salamanca University, received the habit as a Franciscan in the year 1584. From the day of his ordination to the priesthood he desired to go as a missionary to the pagans, but his aspirations could not be realized for some time. His superiors set him to preach in his own country and he also filled the offices of novice-master and guardian in several convents. Though one of the holiest and humblest of men he became the victim of cruel calumny, and his provincial removed him from his post of superior. He accepted the disgrace with resignation. " God wills that I should suffer," he said. " May His will be done. The only thing that grieves me is the discredit it may bring upon our order and the scandal it may cause to the weak." His innocence was, however, afterwards completely vindicated and in 1610 he was made minister of the newly formed province of San Diego.

Three years later a widespread epidemic of plague carried off all the Franciscans who were labouring in the Moroccan mission. Bd John's term of office had just expired and he begged to be sent to the relief of the Christians. Pope Urban VIII accordingly named him missionary apostolic with special powers. Accompanied by Father Matthias and Brother Genesius, he arrived in Morocco and immediately embarked upon the work of ministering to the Christian slaves. Though ordered to leave they continued their labours, administering the sacraments to the faithful and reconciling those who had apostatized. They were consequently arrested in Marakesh, cast into prison, and set to grind saltpetre for gunpowder. After a while they were brought into the sultan's presence, but when they still boldly explained Christianity, they were scourged and ordered back to their dungeon. On the occasion of a second public examination, Bd John ignored the sultan and addressed himself to some apostates who were standing by. Whereupon Muley al-Walid struck the old man to the ground, and he was pierced by two arrows. He was taken away to be burned alive ; as the flames mounted he urged his tormentors to follow Christ, till one of them crushed his head with a stone. Bd John of Prado was beatified in 1728, and he is one of the few *beati* named in the Roman Martyrology.

See P. P. Ausserer, *Seraphisches Martyrologium* (1880) ; Léon, *Auréole Séraphique* (Eng. trans.), vol. ii, pp. 292–296 ; F. Fernandez y Romeral, *Los Franciscanos en Marruecos* (1921) ; and H. Koehler, *L'Église chrétienne du Maroc* . . . (1934), pp. 65–83.

25 : ST GREGORY VII, POPE (A.D. 1085)

THE Bollandist compilers of the *Acta Sanctorum* remark by way of a preface to the life of Gregory VII that he suffered much from persecutions during his lifetime and from calumnies after his death. It is, however, satisfactory to note that, whereas it was once the fashion to depict this great pope as an ecclesiastical tyrant, modern historians are agreed in recognizing his whole policy to have been inspired, not by ambition, but by an unquenchable thirst for justice—the establishment of righteousness upon the earth.

St Gregory was born in the hamlet of Rovaco, near Saona in Tuscany, and received at baptism the name of Hildebrand. Nothing is known of his parentage, but he was sent when young to Rome, to the care of an uncle who was superior of the monastery of St Mary on the Aventine. From there he attended the Lateran school where one of his masters, John Gratian, formed so high an opinion of him that, upon being raised to the papacy as Gregory VI, he chose his former pupil as his secretary. After Gregory's death in Germany, Hildebrand retired into a monastery which—if we accept the tradition—was the great abbey of Cluny, then ruled over by St Odilo as abbot and St Hugh as prior. Gladly would Hildebrand have spent the rest of his life in the cloister, but Bruno, bishop of Toul, who was chosen to fill the chair of St Peter, persuaded him to return with him to Rome. There, as *economus* to Pope St Leo IX, he restored financial stability to the treasury and order to the city, besides co-operating with all that pontiff's attempted reforms. Under St Leo's four successors he continued to act as chief counsellor, and indeed was regarded by many as the "power behind the throne". Nobody then was surprised when, at the death of Alexander II in 1073, Cardinal Archdeacon Hildebrand was elected pope by acclamation. He took the name of Gregory VII.

He had reason to be appalled at the magnitude of the task which lay before him. It was one thing to denounce the abuses which were corrupting the Church, as his friend St Peter Damian was doing, or even to wield the sword of justice in the service of other popes as he himself had done. It was quite another thing to feel directly responsible to God as Christ's vicar on earth for the suppression of those abuses. No man was better qualified for the task. "On you, who have reached the summit of dignity, are fixed the eyes of all men", wrote William of Metz. "They know the glorious combats you have sustained in a lower station, and one and all now long to hear great things of you". They were not disappointed.

To aid him in the reforms he was about to undertake Gregory could expect little help from those in authority. Of the great rulers, the best was William the Conqueror, ruthless and cruel though he showed himself at times. Germany was governed by Henry IV, a young man of twenty-three, dissolute, greedy of gold, tyrannical ; whilst of Philip I, king of France, it has been said, " His reign was the longest and most discreditable which the annals of France have known ". The leaders of the Church were as corrupt as the rulers of the state, to whom indeed they had become subservient, bishoprics and abbeys being sold by kings and nobles to the highest bidder or bestowed on favourites. Simony was general, while clerical celibacy was so little regarded that in many districts priests openly lived as married men, squandered the tithes and offerings of the faithful on their families, and even in some cases bequeathed their livings to their children. The rest of

Gregory's life was to be spent in heroic efforts to free and purify the Church by putting down simony and clerical incontinency, and by abolishing the whole system of investitures, *i.e.* the bestowal of church preferments by laymen and their symbolical conveyance by presentation of the crozier and the ring.*

Shortly after his accession Gregory deposed Godfrey, archbishop of Milan, who had obtained his office by bribery, and in his very first Roman synod he enacted stringent decrees against simoniacal and married priests. Not only were they disqualified from exercising ecclesiastical jurisdiction or holding any benefice, but the faithful were warned not to avail themselves of their ministrations. These decrees roused great hostility, especially in France and Germany: a council assembled in Paris declared them intolerable, irrational, and calculated to make the validity of a sacrament dependent on the character of the celebrant. St Gregory, however, was not one to be daunted by opposition or deflected from pursuing the right course. A second synod held in Rome the following year went still further, and abrogated the whole system of lay investiture. It pronounced the excommunication of "any person, even if he were emperor or king, who should confer an investiture in connexion with any ecclesiastical office ". To publish and enforce his decrees he made use of legates, for he could not trust the bishops. These representatives, who were nearly all monks whom he had known and tested, served him courageously and well in these times of exceptional difficulty.

In England, William the Conqueror refused to give up investiture or to do fealty (several Christian princes had at one time or another put their realms under the protection of the Holy See) ; but he accepted the other decrees, and Gregory, who seems to have trusted him, did not press the matter of investiture. In France the reforms were eventually carried through, that is, they were accepted in principle and gradually in practice, through the energy of the legate, Hugh of Die ; but it was a long struggle, and most of the bishops had to be deposed before it was over. But it was from the Emperor Henry IV that the worst trouble came ; eventually he raised the restive clergy of Germany and northern Italy and the anti-papal Roman nobles against the pope. While singing the midnight Mass of Christmas in St Mary Major's, Gregory was carried off and held captive for several hours until rescued by the people. Shortly after, a meeting of German bishops at Worms denounced the pope, the bishops of Lombardy refused him obedience, and Henry sent an envoy to Rome who informed the cardinals that Gregory was a usurper whom the emperor was going to replace. The next day Gregory excommunicated Henry with special solemnity, releasing his subjects from their allegiance to him. It was a moment of deep significance in the history of the papacy.

It was also an opportunity for those German nobles who wished to get rid of their king. In October 1076 these met, and agreed that Henry should forfeit his crown unless he had received absolution from the pope within a year of his excommunication and had appeared for judgement before a council which Gregory should preside over at Augsburg in the following February. Henry resolved to save himself by an appearance of submission. With his wife and baby and one attendant

* The pope's aim, of course, was to keep civil rulers " in their place " vis-à-vis the Church. On the other hand, the large landed properties of bishoprics and abbacies made their holders barons of great power, and sovereigns wanted to keep a feudal relation with and due control over them. To this extent—and it was a most important consideration—the sovereigns were justified, The distinction between the conferring of the episcopal office and the grant of its temporalities was not yet clear in people's minds.

he crossed the Alps in most severe weather, and came up with the pope at the castle of Canossa, between Modena and Parma.   He demanded admission, was refused, and spent three days, dressed as a penitent, at the castle gate.   This has sometimes been called arrogant and cruel conduct on Gregory's part, but he was probably making up his mind what to do.   However, he had little alternative : Henry had come as a private penitent and, though the pope might well suspect him of bad faith, he had no evidence of it.   Accordingly, Henry was at length admitted, accused himself, and was absolved.

In the phrase " Go to Canossa " this incident has become symbolical of the triumph of church over state.   In fact it was a triumph for Henry's political wiliness ;   there is no evidence that he ever seriously gave up his claim to confer investiture, and subsequent events led to something very like downfall for Gregory VII.

In spite of Henry's reinstatement some of the nobles elected his brother-in-law, Rudolf of Swabia, in his place in 1077.   Though for a time St Gregory tried to remain neutral, he found himself compelled to renew the excommunication and declared in favour of Rudolf who, however, was slain in battle.   Henry on his part promoted the election of Guibert, archbishop of Ravenna, as antipope and, as soon as death had freed him of his rival, marched an army into Italy.   For two years he unsuccessfully besieged Rome, but the third year he succeeded in taking it.   St Gregory retired into the castle of Sant' Angelo, where he remained until he was rescued by an army under Robert Guiscard, the Norman duke of Calabria.   The excesses of Guiscard's followers, however, roused the Romans to fury, and St Gregory, because he had summoned the Normans to his aid, shared their unpopularity.   As a consequence he retired first to Monte Cassino and then to Salerno, humiliated and in failing health, deserted by thirteen of his cardinals.

Gregory made a last appeal to all who believed that " the blessed Peter is father of all Christians, their chief shepherd under Christ, that the holy Roman church is the mother and mistress of all the churches " ;   and in the following year he died, on May 25, 1085.   On his death-bed he expressed his forgiveness of all his enemies and raised all the excommunications he had pronounced, except those against Henry IV and Guibert of Ravenna.   " I have loved righteousness and hated iniquity ", he declared with his last breath, " that is why I die in exile."

St Gregory VII was certainly one of the greatest men among the popes, though far from being faultless ;   his faults were those of his time, and to many they make him an unsympathetic character.   But ambitious in any worldly sense he was not : his life was devoted to the cleansing and fortifying of the Church, because it was God's Church and should be the abode of charity and justice upon earth.   His name was added to the Roman Martyrology (wherein he is called not *Sanctus* but *Beatus*) by Cardinal Baronius, and his feast was given to all the Western church by Pope Benedict XIII in 1728—much to the indignation of Gallican churchmen in France.

The Bollandists in the *Acta Sanctorum*, May, vol. vi, print with other material three documents which to some extent help us to appreciate Hildebrand as a man and a saint. The first is a formal biography by Paul Bernried, completed only in 1128, but founded on the recollections of those who knew Gregory VII and upon a study of his Registers.   The second is a memoir of which Pandulf is the probable author ;   the third an adaptation by Cardinal Boso, the Englishman, of Bonizo's *Liber ad Amicum*, which was written in Gregory's lifetime.   But the pope belongs to all history, and official documents such as the *Regesta*, at least what is left of them, do in this case very much help to elucidate his character.   From

Mgr Mann's *Lives of the Popes*, vol. vii (1910), pp. 1–217, a full and satisfactory account of the pontificate, especially in its external aspects, may be obtained. There is also a good bibliography, in which Mgr Mann judiciously goes out of his way to commend J. W. Bowden's *Life and Pontificate of Gregory VII*, though it was published as far back as 1840. The literature of the subject is vast and has grown immensely since Mann wrote in 1910. Mention may be made of the studies by Mgr Batiffol (1928) and H. X. Arquillière (1934) ; an admirable sketch, based on more profound but scattered studies published elsewhere, is that of A. Fliche in the series " *Les Saints* " (1920), and V. Fliche has since published a more exhaustive work, *La Réforme grégorienne* (1925), on which *cf.* the *Analecta Bollandiana*, vol. xliv (1926), pp. 425–433. See also W. Wühr, *Studien zu Gregors VII Kirchenreform* (1930); Fliche and Martin, *Histoire de l'Église*, vol. viii ; and on the problem of Gregory's *Regesta* consult the studies of W. M. Peitz and of E. Caspar. An English translation of Gregory's correspondence, by E. Emerton, appeared in 1932, and at Rome *Studi Gregoriani*, ed. G. B. Borino, began publication in 1947.

ST URBAN I, Pope and Martyr   (c. A.D. 230)

THE notice in the Roman Martyrology reads : " At Rome on the Via Nomentana, the birthday of Blessed Urban, Pope and Martyr, by whose exhortation and teaching many persons, including Tiburtius and Valerian, received the faith of Christ, and underwent martyrdom therefor ; he himself also suffered much for God's Church in the persecution of Alexander Severus and at length was crowned with martyrdom, being beheaded." It is to be feared that even this short notice is mainly apocryphal. The reference to Tiburtius and Valerian is derived from the very unsatisfactory Acts of St Cecilia, from which also the account of Urban in the *Liber Pontificalis* has borrowed. It is quite certain in any case that Pope Urban was not buried on the Via Nomentana, but in the cemetery of St Callistus, on the Via Appia, where a portion of his sepulchral slab, bearing his name, has been found in modern times. Not far from the cemetery of Callistus on the same main road was the cemetery of Praetextatus, and there another Urban, a martyr, had been buried. Confusion arose between the two, and an old building close beside the Praetextatus catacomb was converted into a small church, afterwards known as St Urbano alla Caffarella.

The confusion of the two Urbans and the muddle hence resulting in the notices of the *Hieronymianum* are points full of interest, but too complicated to be discussed here. See CMH., pp. 262 and 273 ; Duchesne, *Liber Pontificalis*, pp. xlvii, xciii and 143 ; De Rossi, *Roma Sotterranea*, vol. ii, pp. xxii–xxv, 53, 151. Besides the *passio* of Pope Urban in the *Acta Sanctorum*, May, vol. vi, several other texts have been printed in the Bollandist catalogues of Latin manuscripts ; see BHL., nn. 8372–8392.

ST DIONYSIUS, Bishop of Milan   (c. A.D. 360)

AMONGST the few faithful bishops who upheld the cause of St Athanasius when the whole world seemed to have turned against him, a place of honour must be accorded to St Dionysius, who succeeded Protasius in 351 as metropolitan of Milan. An ardent champion of the Catholic faith, he found himself summoned in 355 to attend, in his own episcopal city but at the imperial palace, a synod which the Arian Emperor Constantius had convoked to pronounce the condemnation of Athanasius. Although nearly all the prelates present were overawed into signing the decree, St Dionysius, St Eusebius of Vercelli, and Lucifer of Cagliari refused to do so. They were accordingly banished, and St Dionysius retired into Cappadocia, where he died about the year 360, probably shortly before the Emperor Julian sanctioned the return of the exiles to their churches. A point of interest is the fact that the remains of the saint were sent back to Milan all the way from Cappadocia by

St Basil. The letter in which Basil describes to St Ambrose the care taken to authenticate the relics is still preserved.

In the *Acta Sanctorum*, May, vol. vi, a life of St Dionysius is given. It is of little historical value, as the document, or possibly some earlier text upon which it is based, was probably, as Father Savio has shown, compiled by the unscrupulous chronicler Landulf at the end of the eleventh century. Father Savio's comments will be found in his book, *Gli Antichi Vescovi d'Italia, La Lombardia*, pp. 114 *seq.* and 753 *seq.* See also Lanzoni, *Le Diocesi d'Italia*, vol. ii (1927), p. 1014, and especially CMH., pp. 81 and 271, with Hefele-Leclercq's *Conciles*, vol. i, pp. 873–877. For St Basil's letter, see Migne, PG., vol. xxxii, cc. 712–713.

ST ZENOBIUS, BISHOP OF FLORENCE   (*c.* A.D. 390 ?)

FACT and fiction are intermingled in the traditional history of St Zenobius, the principal patron of Florence, and there are no contemporary records from which to reconstruct a reliable biography. A member of the Geronimo family of Florence, he is said to have been baptized at the age of twenty-one by Bishop Theodore, who afterwards ordained him and made him his archdeacon. The virtues and learning of Zenobius won him the friendship of St Ambrose of Milan, by whose advice he was called to Rome by Pope St Damasus. After carrying out successfully a mission from the Holy See to Constantinople, he returned to Italy. Upon the death of Theodore he was chosen bishop of Florence, and edified all men by his eloquence, his miracles and the holy life he led with his deacon St Eugenius and his subdeacon St Crescentius. Five dead persons, we are told, were resuscitated by him, including a child who was run over by a cart as he played before the cathedral. St Zenobius died at the age of eighty and was buried at first in San Lorenzo and then in the cathedral. Scenes from the life of St Zenobius form the subject of many pictures by old masters in the Florentine galleries.

The text of several short lives is printed in *Acta Sanctorum*, May, vol. vi, but no one of them can be dated earlier than the eleventh century. The existence of Bishop Theodore is doubtful. See especially Davidsohn, *Forschungen zur älteren Geschichte von Florenz*, vol. i, and with regard to the reputed relics of the saint, Cocchi, *Ricognizioni . . . delle Reliquie di S. Zenobio.*

ST LEO, OR LYÉ, ABBOT   (*c.* A.D. 550)

AT Mantenay, a village in the diocese of Troyes, St Leo's whole life was passed : there he was born and there he entered a monastery which had been built not very many years earlier by St Romanus, afterwards bishop of Rheims. First as a simple monk, afterwards as abbot in succession to Romanus, Leo led an edifying and uneventful existence. One night when he lay, as was his custom, on the baptistery floor, St Hilary, St Martin of Tours and St Anastasius of Orleans appeared to announce his death which, they told him, was to take place in three days. St Leo asked for a three days' respite to enable him to obtain a mortuary habit which a good woman had promised him. The delay was granted and a messenger was despatched from the abbey to ask for the garment. The lady acknowledged that she had not yet made it as the father abbot seemed hale and hearty, but said he should have it in three days. The promise was kept : the habit was duly sent : and St Leo at the appointed time passed to his reward.

A short account of St Leo is given both in Mabillon and the *Acta Sanctorum*, May, vol. vi, but the materials merit little confidence. His name, however, has been included in certain later recensions of the *Hieronymianum.*

ST ALDHELM, Bishop of Sherborne   (A.D. 709)

The first Englishman to attain distinction as a scholar in his native land and across the seas was St Aldhelm or Ealdhelm. Sufficient is preserved of his Latin writings in prose and in verse to give an idea of his obscure and surprising style. A relation to Ine, King of the West Saxons, he was born about the year 639, and received his early education at Malmesbury under an Irish teacher named Maildub. It is not clear where he spent his first years of manhood, but when he was between thirty and forty we find him at Canterbury, which had become a great centre of religious and secular learning under Archbishop St Theodore and St Adrian. It was to Abbot Adrian that St Aldhelm attributed the literary proficiency he afterwards developed. While he was at Canterbury, or perhaps earlier, he received the tonsure and took the habit. Upon the death or retirement of Maildub, St Aldhelm returned to Malmesbury to take charge of the school, and about the year 683 he was appointed abbot.

He did much to foster religion and education in Wessex, especially after the accession of King Ine, whose counsellor he became. For the edification and instruction of the poor, whose spiritual needs he had so much at heart, he composed verses and songs in English, for he was a skilled musician. King Alfred dearly loved St Aldhelm's English hymns, and the holy man's ballads were popular down to a much later date, but unfortunately they are not now extant. He founded subsidiary monasteries at Frome and Bradford-on-Avon, besides building several churches; one at Bradford-on-Avon dedicated by him to St Laurence is standing to this day, the loveliest remaining piece of Saxon building. At the request of a synod summoned by King Ine, he addressed a letter to Geraint, king of Dumnonia (Cornwall and Devon), which proved the means of reconciling to the Roman use a number of ecclesiastics who had till then adhered to the Celtic tradition in such matters as the date of keeping Easter. St Aldhelm is said to have made a journey to Rome, but of this visit we have no satisfactory evidence.

When, after the death of St Hedda in 705, Wessex was divided into two dioceses, the more westerly was bestowed upon Aldhelm, who fixed his episcopal seat at Sherborne. Four years later he died, while on a visitation to Doulting, near Westbury. His body was conveyed back to Malmesbury with great solemnity, crosses being set up at the places where the body had rested on the way. The best known of St Aldhelm's writings is a treatise on virginity dedicated to the nuns of Barking; there are also a number of Latin poems and a book on prosody containing as illustrations some metrical riddles—it has been remarked that Aldhelm would have appreciated the crossword-puzzles of a later age. His feast is now kept in the dioceses of Clifton, Plymouth and (on May 28) Southwark.

The accounts of St Aldhelm furnished by Faricius of Abingdon and by William of Malmesbury (both printed in the *Acta Sanctorum*, May, vol. vi) are not very trustworthy, as coming from twelfth-century writers. Bede refers to him in respectful terms, but does not tell us very much. The best edition of Aldhelm's works is that edited by Ehwald in MGH., *Auctores Antiquissimi*, vol. xv. See also the *Cambridge History of English Literature*, vol. i, pp. 72–79; Father Thurston in the *Catholic Encyclopaedia*, vol. i, pp. 280–281; and E. S. Duckett, *Anglo-Saxon Saints and Scholars* (1947). The existing Bradford church is probably the successor of Aldhelm's *ecclesiola*.

ST GENNADIUS, Bishop of Astorga   (A.D. 936)

St Gennadius, whom the Spaniards invoke against fever, was trained as a monk from an early age. He was afterwards the abbot and restorer of San Pedro de

Montes, which St Fructuosus had founded at Vierzo in the Cantabrian Mountains. About the year 895, or possibly later, he was chosen bishop of Astorga and during his episcopate he built and restored several religious houses.   Five years before his death he resigned his office to resume the life of a monk or hermit in a mountain desert.   He died about the year 936 and was buried in his monastery of St Peter at Peñalba.   He is described as a man of the deepest piety whose only preoccupation was the honour of God and the salvation of souls.

There is an account pieced together by Mabillon from various materials in *Acta Sanctorum, O.S.B.*, vol. v, pp. 33–38.   Consult also Yepez, *Coronica General de la Orden de San Benito*, vol. iv, folios 266 *seq.* ; Florez, *España Sagrada*, vol. xvi, pp. 129–147 ; V. de la Fuente, *Historia ecclesiastica de España*, vol. iii, pp. 239 *seq.*   The very interesting renunciation, or testament, of St Gennadius is printed in Mabillon and elsewhere.

BD CLARITUS   (A.D. 1348)

THERE stood in old Florence for two centuries and more a convent of Augustinian nuns which was popularly known as " Il Chiarito ".   It was founded in 1342 by Bd Claritus or Chiarito, the last male of the Voglia family, and was dedicated by him in honour of our Lady.   His wife Nicolasia having taken the veil in the new foundation, he himself joined it as servant to the nuns.   In that humble capacity he remained until he was carried off by an epidemic of the plague which decimated the city in 1348.   His shrine was held in great veneration in the convent church and was credited with the property of emitting a peculiar odour whenever one of the nuns was about to die.

There is the dearth of reliable evidence which seems characteristic of saints of the Augustinian Order.   The Bollandists could find no better materials than a life written nearly three centuries after the event by A. M. V. Racconisi.   It is printed in a Latin translation in the *Acta Sanctorum*, May, vol. vi.   See, however, the *Bollettino Storico Agostiniano*, vol. i (1924), pp. 15–20.

ST MADELEINE SOPHIE BARAT, Virgin, Foundress of the Society of the Sacred Heart   (A.D. 1865)

MADELEINE SOPHIE BARAT was born on December 12, 1779, in the Burgundian town of Joigny, where her father was a cooper and the owner of a small vineyard. At her baptism, a brother eleven years her senior stood godfather.   Louis was intended for the priesthood, and when, after completing his course at Sens, he returned as a deacon to take up a post as master in the college of his native city, he found his godchild a sprightly intelligent little girl of ten.   Almost immediately the conviction forced itself upon him that she was destined by God to accomplish some great work for which it was his duty to fit her.   This he proceeded to do by imparting to her an education similar to that which his boy pupils received, coupled with a discipline calculated to teach her to restrain her emotions and control her will.   All day long, without companionship and almost without relaxation, she had to study in her little garret to acquire a grounding in Latin, Greek, history, physics and mathematics under the direction of a stern young taskmaster whose policy it was frequently to blame and punish, but never to praise.   It was fortunate for her that she developed a great love of learning, seeing that the only reward she ever received was instruction in a fresh subject.   Human emotion of any kind was severely repressed ; so much so that once, when she offered a little present to her brother, it was thrown into the fire.   The system, harsh as it was, worked well in this case and Madeleine Sophie was making remarkable progress when she was suddenly deprived of her teacher.

In the year 1793, which saw the execution of Louis XVI and the inauguration of the Reign of Terror, Louis Barat, who had openly withdrawn his adherence to the civil constitution of the clergy as soon as it had been condemned by the pope, fled from Joigny to escape prosecution, but it was only to be arrested in Paris and to remain for two years a prisoner in constant expectation of death. Sophie in the meantime had grown up a charming and vivacious girl, the idol of her parents and the centre of an admiring circle of friends. To Louis, when he revisited Joigny as a priest after his liberation, there seemed real danger that she might lose that sense of vocation to the religious life which she had formerly evinced, and he never rested until he had transplanted her to Paris, where he was living and where he could resume his course of training. To the repressive discipline of her childhood were now added bodily penances and constant self-examination, whilst the classics were replaced by the study of the Bible, the Fathers, and theological treatises. She submitted with cheerful resignation, little anticipating the great future which in God's providence lay before her.

As soon as the first fury of the French Revolution had spent itself, thoughtful men were confronted with the problem of providing education for the younger generation, seeing that all Christian schools had been swept away. Amongst those who took a deep interest in this was a group of young priests who had formed an association pledged to work for the restoration of the Society of Jesus, suppressed by Pope Clement XIV thirty years earlier. Their superior, Father Varin, had for some time been desirous of forming an institute of consecrated women for the training of girls, and when he heard from the Abbé Barat of his sister's abilities and training, he sent for her and questioned her. After a very short acquaintance he satisfied himself that the simple Burgundian girl possessed all the qualifications he required. In reply to her timid admission that she hoped to become a Carmelite lay-sister, he said bluntly, " No, that is not your vocation. The gifts God has given you and your education point elsewhere." He then expounded to her his ideal of a great educational work for girls, a work deriving its inspiration from devotion to the Sacred Heart of Jesus. Humbly and diffidently she responded to the call. " I knew nothing : I foresaw nothing : I accepted all that was given me ", she said long afterwards, referring to that time.

On November 21, 1800, Madeleine Sophie and three other postulants began their religious life, and the following year she was sent to Amiens to teach in a school which had been taken over and which was the first convent of the new order. Soon a second school—a free one for poor children—was opened. More postulants came to the little community, but their first superior left them after two years, having proved herself devoid of ability to govern and lacking a true vocation. To her dismay Madeleine Sophie was appointed superior by Father Varin although she was only twenty-three and the youngest of all. She was to retain that office for sixty-three years.

The success of their educational ventures in Amiens led to requests for other foundations, and in 1804 Mother Barat travelled to Grenoble to take over the derelict convent of Sainte Marie-d'en-Haut as well as to receive into her institute the remnant of a community of Visitation nuns which it had sheltered. Foremost amongst these was Bd Philippine Duchesne, who was destined later on to introduce the Society of the Sacred Heart into America. The next settlement was at Poitiers, where an ancient Cistercian house, the abbey of the Feuillants, had been offered as a gift. St Madeleine Sophie made it the novitiate, and it became her headquarters for two years, which were perhaps the happiest of her life. There she trained her novices and from there she made occasional journeys across France and into Flanders to open fresh houses at Belley, Niort, Ghent and Cugnières. Everything seemed to be going well when the saint was faced with one of those fierce trials which seem almost invariably to beset the founder of a new religious order. During her absence from Amiens a number of important changes had been made without consulting her by the local superior, Madame Baudemont, in conjunction with M. de Saint-Estève, an ambitious young priest who had succeeded Father Varin as chaplain. For eight years these two carried on a persistent campaign, striving, it seemed, to supersede the superior general, to undermine her influence, and to mould the society according to their own ideas. Patience and prayer were the weapons with which Mother Barat met their attacks, and they mistook her strength for weakness. M. de Saint-Estève went so far as to draw up for the order constitutions of his own which would have changed its nature and transformed its very name. However, just when his success seemed assured, he over-reached himself, and the constitutions as passed by the general congregation of 1815 were not his, but a code which had been framed by Mother Barat and Father Varin, now a Jesuit.

The collapse of the opposition was followed by a period of great expansion, and in 1818 Mother Duchesne was sent with four companions to North America. Two years later Mother Barat summoned all the available local superiors to Paris—now the headquarters of the order—to draw up a general plan of study for the schools. Certain definite principles were laid down, but with characteristic clear-sightedness she insisted from the first that there should be facilities for development and adaptation. Indeed, when she arranged that the general council should meet every six years, one of her reasons was the opportunity that would be afforded to its members of revising the curriculum in order to keep abreast of the educational needs and systems of the day. Under her inspiration, the Paris boarding-schools attained a reputation which brought applications from all sides for similar establishments.

It is difficult for us in these days of easy communication to realize the arduous nature of St Madeleine Sophie's labours in the foundation of no less than one hundred and five houses. To establish and maintain them she many times traversed the length and breadth of France, thrice she visited Rome, once she went to Switzerland to make a home for the novitiate driven out of France in 1830 by the July Revolution, in 1844 she came to England and twelve years later she travelled to Austria. " I am always on the road ", she once remarked, and her journeys often entailed great discomforts and even hardships on one who had never been robust.

In her great love for children she tried, wherever it was possible, to provide for the opening of a day-school for poor girls as well as a boarding-school for the daughters of well-to-do parents. With those foundations which she could not personally visit she kept in touch by correspondence, which necessitated the writing of innumerable letters. Even when she was living at the mother-house she was ceaselessly employed, either in administrative work or in giving interviews to the many persons who sought her advice. Words which she addressed to one of her daughters were singularly applicable to herself : " Too much work is a danger for an imperfect soul . . . but for one who loves our Lord . . . it is an abundant harvest."

In the December of 1826, in response to a memorandum drawn up by St Madeleine Sophie and presented by her to Pope Leo XII, the Society of the Sacred Heart received formal approbation. This must have seemed to set the seal of stability on the new order, but thirteen years later a crisis arose which might easily have led to disruption. At the general congregation of 1839 certain fundamental alterations in the constitutions were proposed and carried in spite of Mother Barat's disapproval. It was characteristic of her tact and fairness that, instead of exercising her veto, she consented to allow them to be tried for three years. Time proved her to have been right; the new regulations did not work well: Pope Gregory XVI refused to sanction them, and they were reversed by the next general congregation. Once more prayer and patience had prevailed and those who had promoted the changes were the first to acknowledge their mistake.

Within narrow limits it is not possible to deal with the activities of the saint's later years : they form part of the history of her order. She lived to see her daughters firmly established in twelve countries of two continents. In 1864, when eighty-five years of age, she begged the general congregation to allow her to lay down her office, but all she could obtain was permission to choose a vicaress to assist her. The following year on May 21 she was stricken with paralysis and four days later, on the feast of the Ascension, her soul went to God. She was canonized in 1925.

St Madeleine Sophie has been privileged in her biographers. The admirable *Histoire de la Vén. Mère Madeleine-Sophie Barat*, written by Mgr Baunard, was excellently translated into English by Lady Georgiana Fullerton. Another satisfactory presentment, in two volumes, was that of one of her own religious, Mother Cahier (1884). A short sketch is provided in the series " Les Saints ", by Geoffroy de Grandmaison (1909). For English readers, the first place in order of merit must be accorded to the work of Mother Maud Monahan, *Saint Madeleine Sophie* (1925) ; a good short life by M. K. Richardson has the catchpenny title *Heaven on Thursday* (1948).

26*: ST PHILIP NERI   (A.D. 1595)

ST PHILIP NERI was born in Florence in the year 1515 and was one of the four children of a notary called Francis Neri. Their mother died while they were very young, but her place was well supplied by an excellent stepmother. From infancy Philip was remarkable for his docility and sweet disposition, which caused him to be spoken of as " Pippo buono "—" good little Phil." Indeed, the only time he ever merited and received a reprimand from his elders was when he once pushed away his elder sister because she persisted in interrupting him and his little sister while they were reciting some of the psalms. His first religious teachers were the Dominicans of San Marco, whose instructions and example made a deep and permanent impression. He grew up a pious, attractive, cheerful lad— very popular with all who came in contact with him. When he was eighteen he was sent to San Germano, to a childless kinsman who was supposed to have a flourishing business and who was likely to make him his heir. Philip, however, did not stay there long. Soon after his arrival he passed through a mystical experience which in after years he spoke of as " conversion ", and from thenceforth worldly affairs had no more attraction for him. The atmosphere in which he was

* To-day is the feast of St Augustine of Canterbury in England and Wales ; see May 28, his date in the general calendar.

living became uncongenial, and he set out for Rome, without money and without plans, trusting entirely to the guidance of divine providence. In Rome he found shelter under the roof of Galeotto Caccia, a Florentine customs-official, who provided him with an attic and the bare necessaries of life. It was little enough that Philip needed. His entire fare consisted of bread, water and a few olives or vegetables, which he usually took once a day : and his room was practically bare except for a bed, a chair, some books, and a line on which he hung his clothes. In return for his hospitality Philip gave lessons to his host's two small sons who, if we may accept the testimony of their mother and their aunt, became veritable little angels under his direction.

Except for the hours he devoted to his charges, St Philip seems to have spent the first two years of his residence in Rome almost like a recluse, giving up whole days and nights to prayer in his garret. It proved to be a period of inward preparation, at the close of which he emerged from his retreat, with his spiritual life strengthened and his determination to live for God confirmed, while he proceeded to take up courses of philosophy and theology at the Sapienza and at Sant' Agostino. For three years he worked with diligence and with such success that he was regarded as a promising scholar. Then, quite suddenly—perhaps in response to some intuition or intimation—he threw up his studies, sold most of his books and embarked upon an apostolate amongst the people. Religion at that time was at a low ebb in Rome, which was very slowly recovering from the effects of the sacking in 1527. There were several contributory causes. Grave abuses had crept into the Church : they had long been generally recognized, but nothing was being done to remove them. Elections to the Sacred College had been controlled by the Medici, with the result that the cardinals, with few exceptions, were princes of the state rather than of the Church. The enthusiasm for classical authors fostered by the Renaissance had gradually substituted pagan for Christian ideals, thereby lowering the moral standard and weakening faith. Indifference, if not corruption, was rife amongst the clergy, many of whom seldom celebrated Mass, let their churches fall into disrepair and neglected their flocks. It was small wonder that the people were lapsing into semi-godlessness. To re-evangelize Rome was to be St Philip's life-work, and he accomplished it with such success as to earn from posterity the title of " the Apostle of Rome ".

He began in a small way. He would stand about the street-corners and market place, entering into conversation with all sorts of people—especially with the young Florentines employed in the banks and shops of the Sant' Angelo quarter. He had an attractive personality with a notable sense of humour, and he readily won a hearing. Then he would put in a word in season or speak to his audience about the love of God and the state of their souls. In this manner he gradually prevailed upon many to give up evil practices and to reform their lives. His customary greeting, " Well, brothers, when shall we begin to do good ? " found them willing enough to respond provided he would show them the way. So he took them with him to wait upon the sick in the hospitals and to visit the Seven Churches—a favourite devotion of his own. His days were given up to men ; but towards evening he would retire into solitude, sometimes spending the night in a church porch, sometimes in the catacombs of St Sebastian beside the Appian Way. Here, in the *grotte* as they were then called, he was fervently praying for the gifts of the Holy Spirit on the eve of Pentecost 1544, when there appeared to him as it were a globe of fire which entered his mouth and which he afterwards felt dilating his breast. Immediately he was filled with such paroxysms of divine love that he rolled upon the ground exclaiming, " Enough, enough, Lord, I can bear no more ! " When he had risen and was more composed, on putting his hand to his heart he discovered a swelling as big as a man's fist, but neither then nor subsequently did it give him pain. From that day, under the stress of spiritual emotion he was apt to be seized with violent palpitations, which caused his whole body to tremble and sometimes the chair or the bed on which he rested to be violently shaken. The fervour which consumed him often obliged him to bare his breast to relieve the heat within and he would ask God to mitigate His consolations lest he should die with love. After his death it was discovered that two of the saint's ribs were broken and had formed an arch which added to the normal space for the beating of his heart.

In the year 1548, with the help of his confessor, Father Persiano Rossa, who lived at San Girolamo della Carità, St Philip founded a confraternity of poor laymen who met for spiritual exercises in the church of San Salvatore in Campo. With their aid he popularized in Rome the devotion of the forty hours and under-took the care of needy pilgrims. This work was greatly blessed and developed into the celebrated hospital of Santa Trinità dei Pellegrini, which in the year of jubilee 1575 assisted no less than 145,000 pilgrims, and afterwards undertook the charge of poor convalescents. Thus by the time he was thirty-four, St Philip Neri had accomplished much ; but his confessor was convinced that he could do still more as a priest. Though the saint's humility made him shrink from the idea of taking holy orders, he eventually deferred to his director's wishes. He was ordained on May 23, 1551, and went to live with Father Rossa and other priests at San Girolamo della Carità. His apostolate was now exercised mainly through the confessional. From before daybreak until nearly midday and often again in the afternoon he sat in the tribunal of penance, to which flocked a host of penitents of all ages and ranks. He had a wonderful power of reading the thoughts of those who resorted to him and effected an enormous number of conversions. For the benefit of these peni-tents he would hold informal spiritual conferences and discussions, followed by visits to churches or attendance at Vespers and Complin. Often they would read aloud the lives of martyrs and missionaries. The account of the heroic career and death of St Francis Xavier so inspired St Philip himself that he was tempted to volunteer for the foreign mission field. However, a Cistercian whom he consulted assured him that Rome was to be his Indies, and the saint accepted the decision.

A large room was built over the nave of San Girolamo to accommodate the increasing numbers of those who attended the conferences, in the direction of which St Philip was aided by several other priests. The people called them Oratorians, because they rang a little bell to summon the faithful to prayers in their oratory, but the real foundation of the congregation so-named was laid a few years later, when St Philip presented five of his young disciples for ordination and sent them to serve the church of San Giovanni, the charge of which had been entrusted to him by his fellow Florentines in Rome. For these young priests, amongst whom was Cesare Baronius, the future historian, he drew up some simple rules of life. They shared a common table and spiritual exercises under his obedience, but he forbade them to bind themselves to this state by vows or to renounce their property if they had any. Others joined them and their organization and work developed rapidly— the more so, perhaps, because it met with opposition and even persecution in certain quarters. However, in 1575, the new society received the formal approbation of

Pope Gregory XIII, who afterwards gave to it the ancient church of Sta Maria in Vallicella. The edifice, besides being in a ruinous condition, was far too small, and St Philip decided to demolish it and to rebuild it on a large scale. He had no money, but contributions came in from rich and poor. The pope and St Charles Borromeo were generous in their donations, as were many of the most prominent men in Rome. Cardinals and princes were amongst his disciples, though he not infrequently disconcerted them by the strange things he did and said—sometimes spontaneously, for he was the most unconventional of saints, but often deliberately in order to conceal his spiritual emotion or to lower himself in the esteem of on-lookers. Humility was the virtue which, of all others, he strove to practise himself and to instil into his penitents. He could not succeed, however, in blinding others to his own sanctity or in wholly concealing from them the extraordinary gifts and graces with which he was endowed.

Always a delicate man, he was once cured of a severe attack of stone by our Lady, who appeared to him in a vision. He had been lying in a state of exhaustion when he suddenly rose with outstretched arms exclaiming, " Oh, my beautiful Madonna ! Oh, my holy Madonna ! " A doctor who was present took him by the arm, but St Philip entreated him to let him be. " Would you not have me embrace my holy Mother who has come to visit me ? " he asked. Then, realizing the presence of two physicians at his side, he hid his head in the bedclothes like a bashful child. Many sick persons were restored by him to health, and on several occasions he prophesied future events—all of which came to pass. He lived in such constant touch with the supernatural that sometimes it was with the greatest difficulty that he could pursue his worldly avocations. He would fall into an ecstasy when saying his office, when offering Mass, or even while he was dressing. Men looking upon his face declared that it glowed with celestial radiance.

By April 1577, work on the Chiesa Nuova, as it was called, had advanced sufficiently for the Congregation of the Oratory to be transferred to the Vallicella, but their superior went on living at San Girolamo as before. He had become attached to the room he had occupied for thirty-three years, and it was not until 1584 that he took up residence at the Chiesa Nuova, in compliance with the pope's expressed wish. Even then he continued to live and have his meals apart from the community, although his spiritual sons had free access to him. So far, indeed, was he from leading the life of a solitary that his room was constantly crowded by visitors of all descriptions. The Roman people in his later years held him in extraordinary veneration : the whole college of cardinals resorted to him for counsel and spiritual refreshment ; and so great was his reputation that foreigners coming to Rome were eager to obtain an introduction. It was thus, in his own room, that he continued his apostolate when increasing age and infirmities precluded him from going about freely. Rich and poor mounted the steep steps that led to his apart-ment at the top of the house, with its *loggia* looking out above and beyond the roofs —the holy man always loved open spaces—and to each person he gave advice suited to his special needs.

Towards the close of his life St Philip had several dangerous attacks of illness from which he rallied wonderfully after being anointed. Two years before the end he succeeded in laying down his office of superior in favour of his disciple Baronius. He also obtained permission to celebrate Mass daily in a little oratory adjoining his room. So enraptured did he become when offering the Holy Sacrifice that it became the practice for those who attended his Mass to retire at the *Agnus Dei*.

Even the server would leave the chapel after extinguishing the candles, lighting a little lamp and placing outside the door a notice to give warning that the Father was saying Mass. Two hours later he would return, relight the candles and the Mass would be continued. On the feast of Corpus Christi, May 25, 1595, the saint appeared to be in a radiantly happy mood, bordering on exultation, and his physician told him he had not looked so well for ten years. St Philip alone realized that his hour had come. All day long he heard confessions and saw visitors as usual, but before retiring he said, " Last of all, we must die ". About midnight he was seized with an attack of haemorrhage so severe that the fathers were called. He was obviously dying, and Baronius, who read the commendatory prayers, besought him to say a parting word, or at least to bless his sons. Though St Philip was past speaking, he raised his hand, and in bestowing his blessing passed to his eternal reward. He was eighty years of age and his work was done. His body rests in the Chiesa Nuova, which the Oratorians serve to this day. St Philip Neri was canonized in 1622.

Abbé Louis Ponnelle and Abbé Louis Bordet, in the best documented and most painstaking life of St Philip which has yet been published (*St Philip Neri and the Roman Society of his Times*, translated by Father R. F. Kerr, 1932), devote a preliminary chapter to an exhaustive review of the sources. It is therefore only necessary here to indicate a few of those earlier publications by which Catholics, and more particularly those of English speech, have become familiarized with the lovable personality of the Apostle of Rome. The earliest biography is that of the Oratorian Father Gallonio, written in Latin and published in 1600. It is reproduced in the *Acta Sanctorum*, May, vol. vi, together with another by Father Bernabei, probably chosen because it amounts to little more than a summary of the beatification process. The life by Bacci appeared in Italian in 1622, and it was supplemented by G. Ricci in 1678. This standard work was translated into English as part of the Oratorian Series, edited by Father Faber (1847). Another edition, revised by Father Antrobus, was issued in 1902. The life by Cardinal Capecelatro, written in Italian, has also been twice printed in English, in 1882 and 1926. Finally may be mentioned an excellent sketch, in much more compendious form, published by Father V. J. Matthews in 1934 ; A. Baudrillart's book in the series " Les Saints " (1939) ; and T. Maynard's good popular life, *Mystic in Motley* (1946)—a bad example of American " striking " titles.

ST QUADRATUS, BISHOP OF ATHENS   (c. A.D. 129)

THE first of the great line of Christian apologists was St Quadratus or Codratus who, as some suppose, became bishop of Athens after the death of St Publius. Eusebius and other ecclesiastical writers speak of a certain Quadratus (who may or may not be identical with the apologist) with special respect, as a prophet and as a holy man who had been the disciple of the Apostles. When the Emperor Hadrian came to Athens to be present at the Eleusinian games, St Quadratus addressed to him a written treatise in defence of the Christians, which had the effect of checking the persecution, or at least of preventing the promulgation of any fresh decrees against them. The apology was known to Eusebius and possibly to St Jerome, but it has now unfortunately been lost. In it he quotes our Lord's miracles as an evidence of the truth of His teaching, and mentions the fact that he himself had actually known persons who had been healed or raised to life by Jesus Christ. The date of his death is uncertain : it probably occurred about the year 129 or a little later.

The passages from Eusebius and St Jerome upon which we depend for all our knowledge of St Quadratus are quoted in the *Acta Sanctorum*, May, vol. vi. Quadratus was not an uncommon name, and it is very doubtful whether the apologist, the bishop of Athens, and the prophet in Asia Minor were one and the same person. See Bardenhewer, *Geschichte der altkirchlichen Literatur*, vol. i, pp. 168–169 ; Harnack in *Texte und Untersuchungen*, vol. i, part 1, pp. 100 *seq.* ; Harnack, *Chronologie der altchristlichen Literatur*, vol. i, pp. 269–271 ; and DTC., vol. xiii, cc. 1429–1431.

SS. PRISCUS, OR PRIX, AND HIS COMPANIONS, MARTYRS (c. A.D. 272)

THE persecution initiated under the Emperor Aurelian was carried on with peculiar ferocity in Roman Gaul, notably in the town of Besançon. Mindful of the precept " When they persecute you in one city, flee to another ", two prominent citizens, Priscus and Cottus, went with a number of other Christians to Auxerre, which was surrounded by forests. They were, however, hunted down and slain by the sword. The bodies of the saints were discovered in the first half of the fifth century by St Germanus, who built two churches in their honour and who propagated a *cultus* of these martyrs of Auxerre which became very general. Besançon and Sens still celebrate the feast of St Priscus.

Although the legend of these martyrs printed in the *Acta Sanctorum*, May, vol. vi, is comparatively free from extravagance, it cannot be regarded as trustworthy. On the other hand, the insertion of the name of Priscus in the *Hieronymianum* points to the existence of a genuine and early *cultus*.

ST LAMBERT, BISHOP OF VENCE (A.D. 1154)

ST LAMBERT was born at Bauduen, in the diocese of Riez, and became a monk in the abbey of Lérins, where he had lived from his childhood. Though kindly to all and popular with his brethren, he was so great a lover of solitude and study that he never left his cell except when obedience required him to do so. Much against his will he was made bishop of Vence in 1114. For forty years he ruled his diocese, instructing the people and healing many sick persons by prayer and the laying-on of hands. He was famous for his learning and for his miracles. Beloved of all, he died in the year 1154, and was buried in his cathedral church.

The life printed in the *Acta Sanctorum*, May, vol. vi, seems to have been written within ten years of St Lambert's death, but its dullness is only relieved by the narration of some very dubious miracles. A copy of his epitaph has been published in the *Revue des Sociétés savantes*, vol. iv (1876), p. 196.

BD EVA OF LIÈGE, VIRGIN (c. A.D. 1265)

WHEN Bd Juliana was prioress of Mount Cornillon, one of her closest friends was a holy recluse, Eva, or Heva, of Liège, whom she inspired with her own enthusiastic purpose to obtain the institution of a feast in honour of the Blessed Sacrament. It was in Eva's cell near the church of St Martin that Juliana found refuge when she was driven for the first time from Cornillon, and it was Eva who took up her mission after she died. The accession of Pope Urban IV raised her hopes, for he had formerly shown himself sympathetic when, as Archdeacon James Pantaleon, he had been approached on the subject by Bd Juliana. Eva's hopes were fulfilled. Not only did he institute the festival of Corpus Christi, but he sent to her the bull of authorization as well as the special office for the day which St Thomas Aquinas had compiled at his desire. The *cultus* of Bd Eva was confirmed in 1902.

The brief authorizing the *cultus* may be read in the *Analecta Ecclesiastica*, vol. x (1902), p. 245. See also Demarteau, *La première auteur wallonne, Eve de Saint-Martin* (1898) ; *Analecta Bollandiana*, vol. xvi (1897), pp. 531–532 ; and *cf.* the bibliography given under Bd Juliana on April 5.

ST MARIANA OF QUITO, VIRGIN (A.D. 1645)

THE present capital of Ecuador was a Peruvian town in 1618, the year which saw the birth of its famous citizen, Mariana Paredes y Flores, " the Lily of Quito ". Her parents, who came of noble Spanish stock, died when she was very young, leaving her to the care of an elder sister and brother-in-law, who loved her as they did their own daughters. She was remarkable for her piety almost from infancy and, when a mere child, liked to engage her nieces, still younger than herself, in saying the rosary or making the stations of the cross, and she would manufacture disciplines for her own use from thorn bushes or prickly leaves. So precocious did she appear that her sister obtained permission for her to make her first communion at the then unusually early age of seven. When she was twelve she decided to start off with a few companions to convert the Japanese, and after that scheme had been frustrated she inspired them with the idea of living as hermits on a mountain near Quito. Somewhat perturbed at the adventurous turn her piety was taking, her relations proposed placing her in a convent to try her vocation. But although on two occasions all preparations were made, her departure was prevented at the last moment by what appeared to be some special interposition of Providence. Mariana accordingly remained at home, and, under the direction of her Jesuit confessor, entered upon the life of a solitary in her brother-in-law's house, which she never again left except to go to church.

Gradually she embarked upon a succession of austerities which can only be regarded as horrifying when practised by a frail young girl delicately reared, and one cannot but ask why her spiritual adviser did not restrain her. She kept a coffin, in which she spent each Friday night : at other times it contained the semblance of a corpse, as a constant reminder of death. Chains bound her arms and legs, and besides a wire girdle, she wore a hair shirt. Every Friday she put on two crowns, the one of thorns and the other of spiked iron, followed by other practices whose recital hardly tends to edification. She is said never to have slept more than three hours, the rest of her time being employed in religious exercises, according to a detailed time-table which was found after her death. Little by little she reduced her food until she came to subsist on a small portion of bread taken once a day. Towards the end of her life she deprived herself of drink in order the better to realize our Lord's thirst on the cross ; to add to her sufferings she would raise a glass of water to her parched lips in very hot weather and would then withdraw it untasted. She was, we are told, the recipient of many spiritual favours and was endowed with the gifts of prophecy and miracles.

In 1645 Quito was visited by earthquakes, followed by an epidemic which swept away many of the inhabitants. On the fourth Sunday in Lent Mariana, after listening to an eloquent sermon preached by her confessor in the Jesuit church, was moved to offer herself publicly as a victim for the sins of the people. We read that the earthquakes ceased immediately, but that as soon as the epidemic began to abate, Mariana was seized with a complication of maladies which soon brought her to the grave. She died on May 26, 1645, at the age of twenty-six. The whole city mourned for one whom they regarded as their saviour. St Mariana was canonized in 1950, ninety-six years after her beatification.

There is a life in Italian and in French by Father Boero (1854), and in Spanish others by J. Moràn de Bertròn (1854) and A. Bruchez (1908).

BB. PETER SANZ, Bishop, and his Companions, Martyrs   (A.D. 1747 and 1748)

IT is one of the glories of the Church of Christ that so many of her sons in the prime of life have always been eager to surrender all that the world prizes in order to risk persecution and death on the foreign mission field.   Amongst the number must be reckoned the five Dominican priests who were martyred in the Chinese province of Fu-kien in the years 1747 and 1748.   Their names were PETER MARTYR SANZ, FRANCIS SERRANO, JOACHIM ROYO, JOHN ALCOBER and FRANCIS DIAZ : all five were Spaniards ; and all five from early youth were inflamed with the desire to spread the gospel of Christ amongst the heathen.   Their future leader, Peter Sanz, a native of Asco in Catalonia, was sent in 1714 to the Chinese province of Fu-kien, where he laboured successfully until 1730 when he was named bishop of Mauricastro *i.p.i.* and vicar apostolic of Fu-kien, with the general supervision of the whole mission.

The previous year persecution had broken out against the Christians and it had required great circumspection on the part of the bishop to escape capture.   The storm had died down, but in 1746 it began again on a much greater scale.   A man at Fogan, who had applied to the bishop for money and been refused, drew up a formal indictment of the European missionaries who, as he complained, were infringing the laws and winning thousands in the city to the Catholic faith.   The case came before the viceroy, a bitter enemy to Christianity, and stern measures were adopted.   Bishop Peter, Father Royo and Father Alcober were imprisoned. After some time they were transferred, loaded with chains and emaciated by hunger, to the city of Foochow, where their patience under barbarous ill-treatment won the admiration even of their enemies.   For a year they languished in prison under appalling conditions, and then Bd Peter was beheaded.   His last words to his companions were : " Be of good courage : must we not rejoice that we are to die for the law of our God ? "

The other four captives—Father Serrano and Father Diaz had by now joined their brethren in prison—had not very long to wait.   The arrival of a document appointing Father Francis Serrano coadjutor to Bishop Sanz, the news of whose death had not yet reached Rome, sealed their fate.   Father Serrano—bishop elect of Tipasa *i.p.i.*—Father Royo, Father Alcober and Father Diaz were cruelly executed in prison.   They were all beatified in 1893.

See M. J. Savignol, *Les Martyrs Dominicains de la Chine au XVIIIe siècle* (1894) ;   A. Marie, *Missions Dominicaines dans l'Extrême Orient* (1865) ; *Monumenta O. P. historica*, vol. xiv, pp. 128 *seq. ;* Wehofer, *Die Apostel Chinas* (1894).

27 : ST BEDE THE VENERABLE, Doctor of the Church   (A.D. 735)

ALMOST all that is known about the life of St Bede is derived from a short account he has given of himself and from a touching description of his last hours written by one of his disciples, a monk called Cuthbert.   In the closing chapter of his famous work, the *Ecclesiastical History of the English People*, the Venerable Bede says : " Thus much concerning the ecclesiastical history of

Britain and especially of the English nation, I, Bede, a servant of Christ and priest of the monastery of the Blessed Apostles St Peter and St Paul, which is at Wearmouth and at Jarrow, have with the Lord's help composed so far as I could gather it either from ancient documents or from the traditions of our forefathers or from my own knowledge. I was born in the territory of the said monastery and at the age of seven I was, by the care of my relations, given to the most reverend Abbot Benedict [St Benedict Biscop] and afterwards to Ceolfrid to be educated. From that time I have spent my whole life in that monastery, devoting all my efforts to the study of the Scriptures, and amid the observance of monastic discipline and the daily charge of singing in the church it has ever been my delight to learn or teach or write. In my nineteenth year I was admitted to the diaconate and in my thirtieth to the priesthood—both by the hands of the most reverend Bishop John [St John of Beverley] and at the bidding of Abbot Ceolfrid. From the time of my ordination up till my present fifty-ninth year I have endeavoured, for my own use and that of the brethren, to make brief notes upon the Holy Scriptures either out of the works of the venerable fathers or in conformity with their meaning and interpretation." He goes on to give a list of his writings and concludes with the words : " And I pray thee, loving Jesus, that as thou hast graciously given me to drink in with delight the words of thy knowledge, so thou wouldst mercifully grant me to attain one day to thee, the fountain of all wisdom, and to appear for ever before thy face."

That Bede sometimes visited friends in other monasteries has been inferred from the fact that in 733 he stayed for a few days in York with Archbishop Egbert ; but except for such brief interludes his life was spent in a round of prayer and praise, of writing and of study. A fortnight before Easter 735 he began to be much troubled by shortness of breath, and all seem to have realized that the end was near. Nevertheless his pupils continued to study by his bedside and to read aloud, their reading often interrupted by tears. He for his part gave thanks to God. During the " Great Forty Days " from Easter to the Ascension, in addition to singing the office and instructing his pupils, he was engaged on a translation of St John's Gospel into English, and a collection of notes from St Isidore ; for, he said, " I will not have my scholars read what is false or labour unprofitably on this after my death." On Rogation Tuesday he began to be much worse, but he passed the day peacefully and dictated in school, saying occasionally : " Go on quickly : I do not know how long I shall hold out and whether my Maker will soon remove me."

After a wakeful night spent in thanksgiving he began to dictate the last chapter of St John. At three in the afternoon he sent for the priests of the monastery, distributed to them some pepper, incense and a little linen which he had in a box and asked for their prayers. They wept much when he said they would see his face on earth no more, but rejoiced that he was about to return to his Creator. In the evening the boy who was acting as his amanuensis said, " There is still one sentence, dear master, which is not written down ", and when that last passage had been supplied and he was told that it was finished, Bede exclaimed, " You have well said . . . all is finished. Take my head in your hands that I may have the comfort of sitting opposite the holy place where I used to pray and that, so sitting, I may call upon my Father." And on the floor of his cell, singing " Glory be to the Father and to the Son and to the Holy Ghost ", he breathed his last.

Several fantastic stories have been invented to account for the title of " Venerable " by which Bede is known ; it was actually a term of respect not infrequently bestowed in days of old upon distinguished members of religious orders. We find it applied to Bede by the Council of Aachen in 836, and the title seems to have struck the public imagination as peculiarly suitable. It has clung to him through the succeeding centuries and, though in 1899 he was authoritatively recognized as saint and doctor of the Church, it remains his special designation to this day.

Bede, the only English doctor of the Church, is the only Englishman who sufficiently impressed Dante to name him in the *Paradiso*. That that one should be Bede is not surprising : the monk who hardly left his monastery became known throughout England and far beyond—his homilies are read in the Divine Office everywhere in the Western church. But for his *Ecclesiastical History*—which is more than ecclesiastical—England's history before 729, " the year of the comets ", would be dark indeed ; through the school of York, founded by his pupil Archbishop Egbert, and by his own writings, he was a power in the scholarship of Carolingian Europe ; and if we know little enough about his personal life, that account of his last hours by the monk Cuthbert is enough—" the death of his saints is precious in the eyes of the Lord ". St Boniface said of Bede that he was " a light of the Church lit by the Holy Ghost " ; and that light has never been quenched, even in this world.

Many books have been written about St Bede and his times, especially by Anglicans. Dr William Bright's *Chapters of Early English Church History* (1878) is in some respects open to objection from a Catholic point of view, but no one has written more eloquently or sympathetically of Bede's own character. *Bede : His Life, Times and Writings*, ed. by A. Hamilton Thompson (1935), is a most valuable collection of essays by non-Catholic scholars. H. M. Gillett's popular biography is excellent, as is the essay in R. W. Chambers's *Man's Unconquerable Mind* (1939), pp. 23–52. In the *Acta Sanctorum*, May, vol. vi, we have little but what purports to be a life by Turgot, really an extract from Simeon of Durham, and an account of the translation of Bede's remains to Durham cathedral. The definitive edition of the *Ecclesiastical History* and other historical works is C. Plummer's (1896), but there are several more popular translated editions ; Stapleton's delightful version (1565) was reprinted in 1930, and modernized by P. Hereford in 1935. For Bede's martyrology, see D. Quentin, *Les martyrologes historiques* (1908). See also T. D. Hardy, *Descriptive Catalogue* (Rolls Series), vol. i, pp. 450–455. " Remember ", writes Cardinal Gasquet, " what the work was upon which St Bede was engaged upon his deathbed—the translation of the gospels into English . . ." But of this work " to break the word to the poor and unlearned " nothing is now extant.

ST RESTITUTA OF SORA, Virgin and Martyr   (A.D. 271 ?)

St Restituta was a Roman maiden of patrician rank who is said to have suffered martyrdom about the year 271 in the town of Sora, in Italy, of which she is the principal patroness and which claims to possess her relics. Her so-called " acts " are altogether fabulous. According to this legend, she was told by our Lord to go to Sora and an angel transported her there. She lodged in the house of a widow whose son she cured of leprosy. Thereupon the young man, his mother and thirty-nine other persons were converted to Christianity. The proconsul Agathius, when he was informed of her activities, cast her into prison. As she refused to sacrifice to the gods she was scourged and sent back to her dungeon, where she was left without food or drink for seven days, heavy chains having been bound round her. Upon the appearance of an angel in the prison the chains melted like wax, her wounds were healed, and she felt neither hunger nor thirst. This miracle converted several of her guards, who suffered martyrdom for the Christian faith. St Restituta herself, the priest Cyril, whom she had converted, and two other

Christians were decapitated, their bodies being cast into the River Liri from whence they were afterwards recovered.

In the *Acta Sanctorum*, May, vol. vi, these fabulous acts are printed in full, together with the report of a number of miracles said to have been worked by her intercession, and also the description of the recovery of her relics in the seventeenth century after they had long been lost. The miracles, real or supposed, seem to have resulted in a considerable local *cultus*. Although we know little about either, this Roman saint would seem to be entirely different from the African Restituta commemorated on May 17 in the Roman Martyrology, whose relics are said to be in Naples cathedral.

SS. JULIUS AND HIS COMPANIONS, MARTYRS   (A.D. 302 ?)

ST JULIUS was a veteran soldier and was arraigned by his officers for the Christian faith before Maximus, governor of Lower Moesia, at Durostorum, now Silistria in Bulgaria. Pasicrates and Valentio, men belonging to the same legion, had received the crown of martyrdom a short time before. The judge used threats and promises, but Julius declared that he desired nothing more than to die for Christ in order to live eternally with Him. Thereupon he was sentenced to be beheaded, and was led forth to the place of execution. As he went, Hesychius, a Christian soldier who was also a prisoner and suffered martyrdom a few days after him, said, " Go with courage, and remember me who am about to follow you. Commend me to the servants of God, Pasicrates and Valentio who, for confessing the holy name of Jesus, are gone before us." Julius, embracing Hesychius, replied, " Dear brother, make haste to come to us : those whom you salute have already heard you ". Julius bound his eyes with a handkerchief and, as he presented his neck to the executioner, said, " Lord Jesus, for whose name I suffer death, vouchsafe to receive my soul in the number of thy saints ". His martyrdom took place on May 27, two days after the execution of St Pasicrates, at Durostorum, probably about the year 302.

In the Roman Martyrology Pasicrates and Valentio are commemorated separately on May 25 ; but the story is all one piece, and the historical value of these Acts, as Delehaye points out (*Analecta Bollandiana*, vol. xxxi, 1912, pp. 268–269), has never been called in question. The portion relating to Pasicrates and his companion has only been preserved to us in the summary of the Greek synaxaries, but the section which deals primarily with St Julius is extant and has been printed in Ruinart, *Acta Sincera*, and in the *Acta Sanctorum*, May, vol. vi. See P. Franchi de' Cavalieri in the *Nuovo Bullettino di arch. crist.*, vol. x (1904), pp. 22–26, and especially CMH., p. 272, where it is pointed out that Pasicrates is probably to be recognized in a mention of " Polycarp " in the early Syriac *breviarium* ; " Policratus ", which appears in the Epternach text, suggests how the confusion has arisen. The word " coronatorum " in the same notice has been transformed into the name of a town, Gortyna in Crete.

ST EUTROPIUS, BISHOP OF ORANGE   (c. A.D. 476)

ALTHOUGH Eutropius, a native of Marseilles, seems to have led a careless life at the beginning of his career in that city, still he sobered down after marriage, and when his wife died, he was induced by Bishop Eustachius to enter the ranks of the clergy. His conversion, aided, we are told, by heavenly favours, was very thorough. He gave himself up to prayer and fasting, and when Justus, the bishop of Orange, departed this life, Eutropius was chosen as his successor. The see of Orange had just been ravaged by the Visigoths, and the material and moral desolation of the people was such that Eutropius, losing heart at the sight of the burden imposed upon him, meditated taking refuge in flight. But a holy man whom he consulted showed him where his duty lay, and from that time forth the new bishop set an admirable example. The terms in which he is addressed by St Sidonius Apollinaris in a letter still preserved plainly indicate the repute for piety and learning in which he was held.

A fragmentary biography by Verus, his successor in the see of Orange, is printed in the *Acta Sanctorum*, May, vol. vi. A sepulchral inscription described him as *innocentissimus*, meaning, probably, that his conduct as a bishop was faultless, and his name is commemorated in the *Hieronymianum*. See also Duchesne, *Fastes Épiscopaux*, vol. i, pp. 265–266.

ST JOHN I, POPE AND MARTYR   (A.D. 526)

A TUSCAN by birth, John I joined the Roman clergy while still young and was archdeacon when, after the death of St Hormisdas in 523, he was chosen pope. Italy had been for some thirty years ruled by Theodoric the Goth who, though an Arian by birth and by conviction, treated his Catholic subjects with toleration and even with favour during the greater part of his reign. About this time, however, his policy changed—partly as the result of what he regarded as treasonable correspondence between leading members of the Roman Senate and Constantinople, partly in consequence of severe measures against Arians enacted by the Emperor Justin I. Appealed to by his co-religionists in the East, Theodoric decided to send an embassy to negotiate with the emperor. Much against his own wishes, John was made head of this mission, and his arrival in Constantinople was greeted with enthusiasm : all the inhabitants went out to meet him, headed by Justin, and on Easter day he pontificated in the cathedral. Accounts vary as to the exact nature of the message he bore and the manner in which he carried out his mission, but he appears to have induced the emperor to moderate his measures against the Arians lest reprisals should be made at the cost of the orthodox in Italy. But Theodoric's suspicions had been growing. During the absence of the embassy he had ordered the execution of the philosopher St Severinus Boethius and his father-in-law Symmachus on a charge of high treason, and he seems to have regarded the friendly relations between the pope and the emperor as part of a great conspiracy against him. No sooner had the mission reached Ravenna, Theodoric's capital, than Pope John was cast into prison, where he died not many days later from the treatment he received.

The text and notes of Duchesne's edition of the *Liber Pontificalis*, vol. i, pp. 275–278, tell us almost all that is known of Pope John I ; *cf.* however, what is said in the *Acta Sanctorum*, May, vol. vi, and in Hartmann, *Geschichte Italiens im Mittelalter*, vol. i, pp. 220–224. Pope John's title to be regarded as a martyr has been contested by G. Pfeilschifter, *Theodorich der Grosse*, etc. (1896), pp. 184–203, and defended by Fr Grisar, *Geschichte Roms und der Päpste*, vol. i, pp. 481–483. See also F. X. Seppelt, *Der Aufstieg des Papsttums* (1931), pp.274–276.

ST MELANGELL, OR MONACELLA, VIRGIN   (DATE UNKNOWN)

ST MELANGELL (whose name has been latinized as Monacella) is interesting because the incident for which she is known is a Welsh version of one that is known in various forms in several European countries. She appears in the pedigrees as a descendant of Macsen Wledig (the usurping Roman emperor Magnus Maximus), and according to her legend her father was an Irish king (probably Scottish, in its later meaning, is intended). She vowed herself to God, and when pressed to marry fled to the part of central Wales called Powys, where she remained hidden for fifteen years. Then one day the prince of Powys, Brochwel Ysgythrog, came hunting in her neighbourhood, and pursued a hare into a clearing of the forest where Melangell was at prayer. The hare ran for the shelter of her garments, and turned to face its pursuers from a fold of her skirt. Brochwel urged on his hounds, but they drew off, howling ; the huntsman tried to wind his horn, but it stuck mute to his lips ; and Brochwel approached the girl for an explanation When he had heard Melangell's story of herself, he made her a present of the land on which they were standing as a " perpetual refuge and place of sanctuary ", in recognition of God's protection of the " little wild hare " in the shadow of His servant Melangell.

Accordingly she lived the rest of her life there, another thirty-seven years, gathering a community round her which she directed as abbess. But it was also a meeting-place for hares, who never showed any fear of their protectress, so that they came to be called " Melangell's lambs ".

The church of Pennant Melangell in Montgomeryshire claims to stand on the site of this happening, and it formerly contained St Melangell's shrine. It still has some medieval carving relating the story of the hare, and the shrine chapel at the east end.

The extant *Historia Divae Monacellae* cannot be traced further back than a manuscript of the early sixteenth century (*Archaeologia Cambrensis*, 1848). See Pennant's *Tours in Wales*, cap. iii, and Gould and Fisher, LBS., vol. iii, who give examples from Pennant Melangell and elsewhere of the continuing reverence for the hare shown in Celtic folk lore. There is a more extended treatment of hare mythology in Dr John Layard's *The Lady of the Hare* (1944), but he does not mention the Melangell story.

28 : ST AUGUSTINE, OR AUSTIN, ARCHBISHOP OF CANTERBURY (*c.* A.D. 605)

WHEN Pope St Gregory the Great decided that the time had come for the evangelization of Anglo-Saxon England, he chose as missionaries some thirty or more monks from his monastery of St Andrew on the Coelian Hill. As their leader he gave them their own prior, Augustine, whom St Gregory must have esteemed highly to have made him responsible for a scheme so dear to his heart. The party set out from Rome in the year 596 ; but no sooner had they arrived in Provence than they were assailed with warnings about the ferocity of the Anglo-Saxons and the dangers of the Channel. Greatly discouraged, they persuaded Augustine to return to Rome and obtain leave to abandon the enterprise. St Gregory, however, had received definite assurance that the English were well disposed towards the Christian faith ; he therefore sent Augustine back to his brethren with words of encouragement which gave them heart to proceed on their way. They landed in the Isle of Thanet in the territory of Ethelbert, king of Kent. How the missionaries sent messengers to Ethelbert, how he received them sitting under an oak and listened to their words, how he made over to them a dwelling-place in Canterbury with the use of the old church of St Martin, and how he gave them leave to preach among his subjects, has been already described on February 25, under the article on St. Ethelbert.

The king was baptized at Pentecost 597, and almost immediately afterwards St Augustine paid a visit to France, where he was consecrated bishop of the English by St Virgilius, metropolitan of Arles. At Christmas of that same year, many of

Ethelbert's subjects were baptized in the Swale, as St Gregory joyfully related in a letter to Eulogius, the patriarch of Alexandria. Augustine sent two of his monks, Laurence and Peter, to Rome to give a full report of his mission, to ask for more helpers and obtain advice on various points. They came back bringing the pallium for Augustine and accompanied by a fresh band of missionaries, amongst whom were St Mellitus, St Justus and St Paulinus. With these " ministers of the word ", says Bede, " the pope sent all things needed in general for divine worship and the service of the Church, sacred vessels, altar cloths, furniture for churches, and vestments for clergy, relics, and also many books." Gregory outlined for Augustine the course he should take to develop a hierarchy for the whole country, and both to him and to Mellitus gave very practical instructions on other points. Pagan temples were not to be destroyed, but were to be purified and consecrated for Christian worship. Local customs were as far as possible to be retained, days of dedication and feasts of martyrs being substituted for heathen festivals since, as St Gregory wrote, " he who would climb to a lofty height must go by steps, not leaps ".

In Canterbury itself St Augustine rebuilt an ancient church which, with an old wooden house, formed the nucleus for his metropolitan basilica and for the later monastery of Christ Church. These buildings stood on the site of the present cathedral begun by Lanfranc in 1070. Outside the walls of Canterbury he made a monastic foundation, which he dedicated in honour of St Peter and St Paul. After his death this abbey became known as St Augustine's, and was the burial place of the early archbishops.

The evangelization of Kent was proceeding apace, and Augustine turned his attention to the bishops of the ancient British church which had been driven by the Saxon conquerors into the fastnesses of Wales and Cornwall. Cut off from much communication with the outside world, the British church, though sound in doctrine, clung to certain usages at variance with those of the Roman tradition. St Augustine invited the leading ecclesiastics to meet him at some place just on the confines of Wessex, still known in Bede's day as Augustine's Oak. There he urged them to comply with the practices of the rest of Western Christendom, and more especially to co-operate with him in evangelizing the Anglo-Saxons. Fidelity to their local traditions, however, and bitterness against their conquerors made them unwilling, even though he wrought a miracle of healing in their presence to demonstrate his authority. A second conference proved a sad failure. Because St Augustine failed to rise when they arrived, the British bishops decided that he was lacking in humility and would neither listen to him nor acknowledge him as their metropolitan. Whereupon it is said that Augustine, most unfortunately, threatened them that " if they would not accept peace with their brethren, they should have war with their enemies ". Some claimed that this prediction was fulfilled, about ten years after Augustine's death, when King Ethelfrith of Northumbria attacked and defeated the Britons at Chester, after massacring the monks who had come from Bangor Iscoed to pray for victory.

The saint's last years were spent in spreading and consolidating the faith throughout Ethelbert's realm, and episcopal sees were established at London and Rochester. About seven years after his arrival in England, St Augustine passed to his reward, on May 26, *c.* 605. His feast is observed on this date in England and Wales, but elsewhere on May 28.

St Augustine wrote frequently to Pope St Gregory, consulting him in the least difficulties which occurred in his ministry. This shows the tenderness of his conscience : for in many things which he might have decided by his own learning and prudence he desired to render his conscience more secure by the advice and decision of the chief pastor.   On one occasion Gregory wrote exhorting Augustine to beware of pride and vainglory in the miracles God wrought through him : " You must needs rejoice with fear, and fear with joy concerning that heavenly gift.   You will rejoice because the souls of the English are by outward miracles drawn to inward grace : but you will fear lest, amidst the wonders that are done, the weak mind may be puffed up by self-esteem ; and so the thing whereby it is outwardly raised to honour cause it to fall through vainglory. . . . All the elect do not work miracles, and yet the names of all are written in Heaven.   Those who are the disciples of truth ought not to rejoice save for that good thing which all enjoy as well as they, in which their joy shall be without end."

The text and notes of Plummer's edition of Bede's *Historia Ecclesiastica* supply almost all that can be regarded as trustworthy material for the life of St Augustine.   Such later biographers and chroniclers as Goscelin (in the *Acta Sanctorum*, May, vol. vi), William of Malmesbury, Thomas of Elmham and John Brompton add nothing of value.   The Welsh sources are equally late and unreliable.   There is an excellent account of *St. Augustine of Canterbury and his Companions* (Eng. trans., 1897), by Fr A. Brou.   The longest contribution to Newman's *Lives of the English Saints*, that devoted to St Augustine by Canon F. Oakeley, is thorough and sympathetic ; it was written, of course, in his Anglican days.   See also F. A. Gasquet, *The Mission of St Augustine* (1925) ; F. M. Stenton, *Anglo-Saxon England* (1943), pp. 104–112 ; A. W. Wade-Evans, *Welsh Christian Origins* (1934), for a sensible discussion of the " British trouble " ; and an important work by S. Brechter, *Die Quellen zur Angelsachsenmission Gregors der Grossen* (1941), reviewed in *Analecta Bollandiana*, vol. lx (1942) ; cf. W. Levison, *England and the Continent* . . . (1946), p. 17, and St. Nothelm herein, October, 17.

ST SENATOR, BISHOP OF MILAN   (A.D. 475)

WHEN the Church in the East was threatened with schism or lapse into heresy as the result of the vindication of the monophysite Eutyches and the condemnation of St Flavian by the so-called " Robber Synod ", St Leo the Great decided to send legates to Constantinople to urge upon the Emperor Theodosius II the calling of a general council at which the true doctrine of our Lord's two natures should be definitely and decisively enunciated.   For this mission men of learning, tact and integrity were required, and the pope chose St Abundius, bishop of Como, and a distinguished priest called Senator as being suitable representatives.   By the time these envoys reached Constantinople, Theodosius was dead, but their mission resulted in the summoning of the Council of Chalcedon under the Emperor Marcian.   The year after his return to Italy, St Senator attended a synod at Milan in the same capacity of papal legate.   Upon the death of St Benignus he succeeded to the bishopric of Milan, which he ruled for three years, dying probably in 475.

The fragmentary materials for the history of St Senator have been brought together in the *Acta Sanctorum*, May, vol. vi.   The laudatory reference to him in the verses of Ennodius on the bishops of Milan will be found in MGH., *Auctores Antiquissimi*, vol. vii, p. 166.   But see especially Father Savio, *Gli antichi Vescovi d'Italia, Milano*, vol. i, pp. 197–199.

ST JUSTUS, BISHOP OF URGEL   (c. A.D. 550)

THE Spanish bishopric of Urgel seems to have been founded in the first quarter of the sixth century, and its earliest recorded ruler is St Justus, whose three brothers were Justinian, bishop of Valencia, Nebridius, bishop of Egara, and Elpidius of

Huesca, also a bishop. St Justus took part in the Councils of Toledo and Lerida in the years 527 and 546 respectively. He was the author of a short mystical exposition of the Canticle of Canticles which he dedicated to his metropolitan, Archbishop Sergius of Tarragona. The tone of this treatise and of its dedication leaves a very favourable impression of the writer's intelligence and piety.

Almost all the little we know of St Justus is due to a paragraph in the *De viris illustribus* of St Isidore of Seville, quoted in the brief notice of the *Acta Sanctorum*, May, vol. vi. See also Florez, *España Sagrada*, vol. xlii, pp. 75 and 187 ; but especially H. Quentin in the *Revue Bénédictine*, vol. xxiii (1906), pp. 257–260 and 487–488.

ST GERMANUS, Bishop of Paris   (A.D. 576)

St Germanus (Germain), one of the chief glories of France in the sixth century, was born near Autun about the year 496. After a careful training he was ordained priest by St Agrippinus, and was subsequently chosen abbot of St Symphorian in one of the suburbs of Autun. Happening to be in Paris when that see became vacant, he was nominated by King Childebert I to fill the chair. His promotion made no change in the austerity of his life : he retained his simplicity of dress and food, but his house was always crowded by a throng of beggars whom he entertained at his own table. Through his eloquence and example he brought many sinners and careless Christians to repentance, including the king himself who, from being entirely absorbed in worldly interests, became a generous benefactor to the poor and the founder of religious establishments. When Childebert fell ill at his palace of Celles, near Melun, the saint visited him, and we are told that on hearing that he had been given up by the physicians, he spent the whole night in prayer for his recovery. In the morning he cured the royal patient by the imposition of his hands. The king is said to have related this miracle himself in letters patent in which he declared that, out of gratitude to God, he bestowed upon the church of Paris and Bishop Germanus the land of Celles where he had received this favour. Unfortunately, however, the authenticity of this charter is more than doubtful.

Among Childebert's foundations was a church in Paris which, with the adjoining monastery, was dedicated to God in honour of the Holy Cross and St Vincent ; it was consecrated by St Germanus, who added to it the chapel of St Symphorian, which eventually contained his tomb. After his death the church was renamed Saint-Germain-des-Prés and became for several generations the burial-place of the royal family. Throughout his episcopate St Germanus strove to check the licentiousness of the nobles. He did not scruple to reprove and even to excommunicate King Charibert for his shameless wickedness. During the fratricidal wars in which the nephews of Childebert became involved, he made every effort to induce them to suspend their hostilities, even writing to Queen Brunhildis in the hope of enlisting her influence with her husband to that end. All his remonstrances and appeals, however, were ineffectual. The saint died on May 28, 576, at the age of eighty, mourned by all the people ; King Chilperic himself is said to have composed his epitaph in which he extolled the holy bishop's virtues, his miracles and his zeal for the salvation of souls.

One point of special interest in connection with St Germanus is the fact that the two letters on liturgical observances which were formerly attributed to him and which were believed to furnish a detailed and trustworthy description of the so-called " Gallican " liturgy in the middle of the sixth century, have been shown to be a century or more later in date.

The principal source for the history of St Germanus is the life by Venantius Fortunatus, a contemporary. From a biographical point of view it leaves much to be desired and it is mainly a record of rather dubious miracles. It has been printed many times (*e.g.* in the *Acta Sanctorum*, May, vol. vi), but the most critical text is that of B. Krusch in MGH., *Scriptores Merov.*, vol. vii (1920), pp. 337–428, with a valuable preface, notes and supplementary matter. There are satisfactory articles on St Germanus in the *Kirchenlexikon* and DCB. For the letters on liturgy, see the convincing article of A. Wilmart in DAC., vol. vi, cc. 1049 to 1102. There follows in the same volume a very full discussion by H. Leclercq of the history of Saint-Germain-des-Prés.

ST WILLIAM OF GELLONE   (A.D. 812)

In the time of Pepin the Short, the wife of Thierry, count of Toulouse, gave birth to a son to whom they gave the name of William. Upon attaining manhood William went to court, where he soon became a favourite with Charlemagne, who by this time had succeeded to his father's throne. He filled various offices to the monarch's satisfaction and then was sent by him against the Saracens who were threatening France. At the same time he was created duke of Aquitaine. William vanquished the Saracens, and raised the prestige of Christianity amongst the Moslems by his bravery, justice and piety. Amongst those of his own faith also he came to be regarded as the ideal Christian knight, and he figures as the principal character in several *chansons de geste*, such as *La prise d'Orange* and *Aliscans*. He could not, however, rest satisfied with serving his king ; he desired to place himself at the disposal of the King of kings. With this object in view he sought for a suitable site on which to build a monastery, and discovered it at Gellone, at about an hour's distance from the celebrated abbey of Aniane. There he founded his monastery, which he peopled with monks from the neighbouring religious houses, especially from Aniane. He also built in the vicinity a convent for women, in which his sisters took the veil.

For some time William continued to live in the world, attending the royal court, where he was regarded with great favour, but the call to abandon all came to him as it had done to his sisters. He obtained the requisite permission from Charlemagne, and then made his way to Brioude in the Auvergne, where he hung up his weapons in the church of St Julian after he had laid an offering on the altar. From thence he went to Gellone, where he received the habit from St Benedict of Aniane, who became from that time his director and spiritual guide. Perfect as had been St William's conduct as a layman, it was equally perfect as a monk. He died on May 28, 812, and was buried in his own monastery, which was afterwards renamed St William in the Wilderness.

The life printed in the *Acta Sanctorum*, May, vol. vi, cannot be the work of a contemporary, as it purports to be, but it is relatively sober. See " L. Clarus " (W. Volk), *Herzog Wilhelm von Aquitanien* (1865) ; G. Morin in the *Revue Charlemagne*, vol. ii (1913), pp. 116–126 ; A. Becker, *Die alt-französische Wilhelm-sage* (1896) ; Bédier, *Les Légendes épiques* (1926), t. i.

ST BERNARD OF MONTJOUX   (A.D. 1081 ?)

The founder of the two celebrated hospices of the Great and Little St Bernard which have saved the lives of so many Alpine travellers has a claim to the grateful recognition of posterity and it is strange that until comparatively recent years no attempt was made to deal critically with the matter contained in the obviously highly coloured biographies of St Bernard. He is often referred to as Bernard of Menthon because of his alleged birth in Savoy, son of Count Richard of Menthon and his wife of the Duyn family. He was in fact probably of Italian birth, and his parentage is unknown ; and the story of his projected marriage and flight therefrom seems to be pure invention. We are told that after his ordination Bernard eventually was appointed vicar general in the diocese of Aosta ; and that for forty-two years he travelled up and down the country, visiting the most remote Alpine valleys where the remnants of heathen superstition still lingered, extending his missionary labours even beyond his own jurisdiction into the neighbouring dioceses of Novara, Tarantaise and Geneva. In the territory under his immediate control he founded schools, restored clerical discipline, and insisted that the churches should be well kept. His solicitude went out to all those in need, but especially to the travellers —often French or German pilgrims on their way to Rome—who attempted the crossing of the Alps by the two mountain passes which led into the territory of Aosta. Some lost their way and were frozen to death, some wandered into snow-drifts, whilst others who could face the severity of the climate were plundered or held to ransom by brigands. With the help of the bishop and other generous donors, St Bernard built hospices on the summit of the two passes which were renamed after him the Great and the Little St Bernard.

Actually, his was not the first venture of the kind in those regions. Some sort of hospice under clerical auspices is known to have existed in the ninth century on the Mons Jovis (Montjoux), as it was then called, but the enterprise had lapsed long before the days of St Bernard. The rest-houses which he constructed were new foundations. Provision was made in them for the reception of all travellers indiscriminately, and the hospices were placed under the care of clerics and laymen, who eventually became Augustinian canons regular, for whom a monastery was built close at hand. The same order has continued to direct them to the present day. The boon thus conferred on travellers soon made St Bernard's name famous, and great men were eager to visit the hospices and contribute to their endowment. At some time St Bernard went to Rome, where he is said to have received from the then pope the formal approbation of the hospices together with the privilege of receiving novices to perpetuate his congregation. The saint lived to the age of eighty-five and died probably on May 28, 1081, in the monastery of St Laurence at Novara.

In the *Acta Sanctorum*, June, vol. iii, a life is printed which purports to have been written by a contemporary, Richard, archdeacon of Aosta, as well as some other texts. All these documents are certainly of much later date, and no confidence at all can be placed in the legends which they recount ; the pseudo-Richard in particular is a cento put together in the interest of the Savoyard as opposed to the Italian tradition. It seems to have been clearly demonstrated that St Bernard died, not in 1008, but in 1081. See the article of A. Lütolf in the *Theologische Quartalschrift*, vol. 61 (1879), pp. 179–207. This conclusion is supported by a text printed in the *Biblioteca de la Società Storica Subalpina*, vol. xvii (1903), pp. 291–312, which is probably the oldest known account of the saint, and which records a meeting of Bernard with the Emperor Henry IV at Pavia in 1081. See also Mgr Duc in *Miscellanea di Storia Italiana*, vol. xxxi (1894), pp. 341–388. Other dates have also been suggested, as, for example, by Gonthier, *Œuvres historiques*, vol. iii, who holds that the saint died in 1086. The legend of St Bernard in its older form, after having been presented in the middle ages as a mystery play, was revived by Henri Ghéon in his drama *La merveilleuse histoire du jeune Bernard de Menthon* (English trans. by Barry Jackson). In 1923 Pope Pius XI, in a Latin letter of singular eloquence, proclaimed St Bernard patron of all Alpinists and mountain climbers ; the text is in the *Acta Apostolicae Sedis*, vol. xv (1923), pp. 437–442. For more recent research, see *Analecta Bollandiana*, vol. xxvi (1907), pp. 135–136, and vol. lxiii (1945), pp. 269–270, with references therein, and DHG., t. viii, cc. 690–696.

ST IGNATIUS, BISHOP OF ROSTOV   (A.D. 1288)

FROM being archimandrite of the monastery of the Theophany at Rostov, this Ignatius was raised to the bishopric of that city in 1262.   He was a most faithful shepherd of his flock at a time of great difficulty, for he had to defend his people against the oppression of the Tartars and mediate between the quarrelling nobles of Rostov.   Moreover, false accusations were made against him to the metropolitan of Kiev, and he was for a time removed from office.   It was during the episcopate of Ignatius, in 1274, that a synod of the Russian Church was held at Vladimir, at which he attended.   Words used by this gathering show the sort of thing that the Russian clergy still, and for centuries after almost down to our own day, had sometimes to contend with : " People still follow the customs of the thrice-accursed heathen : they celebrate sacred feast-days with devilish observances, whistling, yelling and howling ; low drunken fellows get together and beat one another with sticks, till some are killed, and these they strip of their clothes ".

St Ignatius was called to the better life on May 28, 1288, and his death was at once followed by reports of miracles, of which the most surprising was that when his body was borne to burial he rose in his coffin and blessed the crowds of by-standers.   Unless they have been destroyed in the events of the past thirty years, the relics of St Ignatius are still in the church of the Assumption at Rostov.

From Martynov's *Annus ecclesiasticus Graeco-Slavicus* in *Acta Sanctorum*, October, xi. *Cf.* St Sergius on September 25, and bibliography.

BD MARGARET POLE, WIDOW AND MARTYR   (A.D. 1541)

NIECE to two English kings, Edward IV and Richard III, Margaret Plantagenet was the child of their brother the duke of Clarence by Isabel, daughter of Warwick the Kingmaker.   Henry VII, whose wife was her first cousin, gave her in marriage to Sir Reginald Pole, a Buckinghamshire gentleman who did him good service in the Scottish campaign and elsewhere.   At the time of Henry VIII's accession, Margaret was a widow with five children, and the young monarch, who described her as the saintliest woman in England, gave her back her brother's estates which had been forfeited by attainder in the previous reign, creating her also countess of Salisbury in her own right.   Upon the birth of Princess Mary she was appointed governess to the royal infant, but her disapproval of Henry's marriage to Anne Boleyn led to her retirement from court with the consequent loss of her post and of the king's favour.   A treatise which her fourth son, Reginald—afterwards Cardinal Pole—wrote against the royal claim to ecclesiastical supremacy still further incensed Henry, who told the French ambassador that he meant to get rid of the whole family.   After Sir Henry Neville's rising in the north, emissaries were sent to examine Margaret in the hope of incriminating her as privy to the conspiracy ; but though they questioned her from the forenoon till the evening they could obtain from her no damaging admission.   They had to own that the tall, dignified woman had the brains as well as the stature of a man.   She was nevertheless taken into custody and was imprisoned, first in Lord Southampton's house at Cowdray and afterwards in the Tower, where she suffered greatly during the winter from lack of firing and from insufficient clothing. She was never brought to trial: it was thought that no jury would convict her; but a servile Parliament passed an act of attainder against her. On May 28, 1541, she was led out into the square to be beheaded. It is said by Lord Herbert that she refused to kneel down and lay her head on the block, saying she was no traitor, and that the executioner, who was a novice, struck at her several times unsteadily with the axe before he felled her. This, however, is contradicted by the French ambassador's account, in which we are told that, the regular executioner being absent, his understudy, as she knelt, hacked at her neck very clumsily. The most weighty authorities reject Lord Herbert's story as improbable. She was seventy years of age when she suffered. An interesting portrait of Bd Margaret Pole is in the National Portrait Gallery, and her feast is observed in several English dioceses.

A full and well documented account of Bd Margaret is given by Father E. S. Keogh in Camm, LEM., vol. i, pp. 502–540. The *Letters and Papers, Foreign and Domestic*, of Henry VIII are our principal source of information, and Bd Margaret's fate is, of course, treated in some detail by Lingard, Gairdner and other historians of the reign.

BD MARY BARTHOLOMEA OF FLORENCE, Virgin (A.D. 1577)

The history of Bd Mary Bartholomea de Bagnesiis is practically the record of a life of suffering heroically borne. Though she came of a noble and wealthy Florentine family, her health was so greatly undermined in infancy by the starvation to which she was subjected by a foster-mother in whose care she had been left, that she was never able in after life to eat a normal meal. A pious child, she had decided even then to devote herself to the religious life as two of her elder sisters had already done, but the death of her mother when she was seventeen placed her in charge of her father's household. It does not seem to have occurred to her that she would be expected to marry, and when her father told her that he had actually chosen a bridegroom for her the shock was so great that she had a complete breakdown, which not only precluded all possibility of marriage but even made her a bedridden invalid. Various grave complications supervened, all of which she bore with unfailing resignation, just as she submitted to the often revolting and most painful remedies prescribed for her by the charlatans her father called in. From her bed she exercised a wonderful influence over the numerous persons who visited her. Enemies were reconciled, the sorrowful consoled, sinners converted and the sick healed by one who forgot her own sufferings in her sympathy for others. When she was thirty-two she was clothed as a Dominican tertiary, and for a short time regained strength enough to get up and go to church, but the improvement was only temporary and she had to take to her bed once more. Her sufferings were intense, and we are told that on eight occasions she received extreme unction. She had the privilege granted her of having Mass said in her room and of receiving holy communion frequently. At times she was rapt in ecstasy, but humility made her loth to speak of her spiritual experiences on these occasions, even to her director. She died after being an invalid for forty-five years and was buried by her own wish in the Carmelite church of St Mary of the Angels.

A full account translated from the Italian life written by her domestic chaplain will be found in the *Acta Sanctorum*, May, vol. vi, Appendix.

THE LONDON MARTYRS OF 1582

ON May 28, 1582, three priests, THOMAS FORD, JOHN SHERT, and ROBERT JOHNSON, were hanged, drawn and quartered at Tyburn—actually for exercising their sacerdotal functions and for denying that Elizabeth was head of the Church, but professedly for participation in a fictitious conspiracy against the queen, known as the plot of Rome and Rheims.

Thomas Ford was a Devonshire man who had taken his M.A. at Oxford and had become a fellow of Trinity. Religious scruples having compelled him to leave the university, he went to the English College at Douai where he was raised to the priesthood—being one of the first batch of its students to be presented for holy orders. About the year 1576 he was sent upon the English mission and laboured successfully until, in 1581, he was arrested with Bd Edmund Campion at the house of Mr. Yates at Lyford in Berkshire. He was committed to the Tower and was condemned to death on the evidence of informers, who had never seen him or his fellow martyrs before their imprisonment. In the cart, as he was being taken to execution, he declared : " I am a Catholic and do die in that religion ". With regard to the queen, he stated on the scaffold that he acknowledged her for his sovereign and queen and had never in his life offended her.

John Shert was also an Oxford man, a student of Brasenose, and a native of Cheshire. For some time after he had left the university he was a schoolmaster in London. Like Ford, however, he became dissatisfied with the established religion, crossed over to Douai to study for the priesthood, and received ordination in Rome. In 1579 he was sent to England, where he worked for two years. He was arrested on July 14, 1581. Though no real evidence could be adduced against him, he was condemned to be hanged. On the scaffold at Tyburn he was made to watch the execution and disembowelling of Thomas Ford. Far from being dismayed, he cried out : " O blessed soul, happy art thou : pray for me ! " He could have saved himself at the last moment by asking pardon and by affirming that Elizabeth was the head of the Church in England, but he stoutly declared : " She is not, nor cannot be, nor any other but only the supreme pastor ".

Robert Johnson, sometimes confused with Laurence Richardson (below), came from Shropshire. After being a manservant in a private family, he went to Douai, became a priest in 1576, and was sent to the English mission. Some four years later he was committed to the Tower, where he was cruelly racked three times. In November 1581 he was sentenced to death on the same charge as his two brother martyrs and suffered in the same place on the same day. As the rope was placed about his neck he prayed aloud in Latin. Bidden rather to pray in English, he replied, " I pray that prayer which Christ taught in a tongue I well understand ". " Pray as Christ taught ", exclaimed one of the ministers present. To which the martyr spiritedly retorted, " What ! do you think Christ taught in English ? " He was still praying in Latin when the cart was drawn away from under him.

Two days after the martyrdom of the above, four other Catholic priests were executed at Tyburn. Their names were WILLIAM FILBY, LUKE KIRBY, LAURENCE RICHARDSON, *vere* Johnson, and THOMAS COTTAM. All four had been educated at English universities before going abroad to be trained for the Catholic ministry, and all had been tried the previous November with Bd Edmund Campion and condemned—nominally for being concerned in the bogus plot of Rheims and Rome, but practically for coming as Catholic priests to minister to the queen's subjects.

The six months between their condemnation and their execution they spent as prisoners in the Tower.

William Filby, a native of Oxford, had been a student at Lincoln College. Religious scruples led him to leave the university and he soon afterwards entered the English seminary at Rheims. Ordained priest in 1581, he was sent to England where he was promptly arrested with Bd Edmund Campion. From July 1581 he was imprisoned in the Tower and after his trial—for six whole months—he was loaded with manacles. Together with his three companions he was taken at seven in the morning of May 30, 1582, to Tyburn, where he was the first to suffer. He was only twenty-seven years of age.

Luke Kirby was from Durham or Yorkshire and a master of arts. He joined the Douai College in 1576 and was ordained the following year. After a short stay in England he went to the English College in Rome to pursue further studies. Returning to England he was soon arrested and imprisoned.

Laurence Richardson, who was born in Lancashire and whose true name was Johnson, quitted Brasenose College, Oxford, to embrace the Catholic faith. After studying at Douai and being raised to the priesthood he laboured with great zeal in his native county, but was apprehended in the early part of 1581. Offered mercy on the scaffold if he would confess his treason and renounce the pope, he answered, " I thank her Majesty for her mercy ; but I must not confess an untruth or renounce my faith ".

Thomas Cottam was also a native of Lancashire and a graduate of Brasenose. On becoming a Catholic he went abroad, first to the Douai College and then to Rome, where he entered the Society of Jesus. Persistent ill-health prevented his completing his noviceship, but he was ordained a priest at Rheims and, at his own earnest entreaty, was sent on the English mission. The authorities had been furnished with an exact description of him by a notorious informer called Sledd who had feigned to be his friend. By this means he was identified upon landing at Dover. One of his fellow-travellers, a Douai professor, Dr Ely, escaped detection and was actually instructed to deliver Mr Cottam up to Lord Cobham. He acquiesced, not intending to carry out the order. After their arrival in London he succeeded, though not without difficulty, in persuading his companion to proceed on his way. As soon, however, as the authorities began to press Dr Ely, Cottam voluntarily gave himself up. He was imprisoned first in the Marshalsea and afterwards in the Tower where he and Luke Kirby were subjected to the instrument of torture known as the Scavenger's Daughter. He was the last of the four to be executed, and was compelled to watch the dismemberment of his fellow martyrs.

Full details of the history, capture and imprisonment of all seven martyrs will be found in Camm, LEM., vol. ii, pp. 443–563. The account in Challoner, MMP., pp. 44–66, is less complete.

29 : ST MARY MAGDALEN DEI PAZZI, Virgin (A.D. 1607)

THE family of the Pazzi was one of the most illustrious in Florence and was closely allied to the Medici, the ruling house : it gave to the state a long line of eminent politicians, governors and soldiers ; and to the world one great woman who in fame has eclipsed them all. The father of St Mary Magdalen dei Pazzi, Camillo Geri by name, had married Mary Buondelmonte, the descendant of a family as distinguished as his own.   The saint was born in Florence in 1566, and in honour of St Catherine of Siena received her name in baptism.   Almost from infancy she began to display an intense attraction for religion and good works, and she made her first communion with wonderful fervour when she was ten.   Her father having been appointed governor of Cortona, she was placed at the age of fourteen as a boarder in the convent of St John in Florence.   There she could give full scope to her devotion and learnt to love the atmosphere of a religious house. Fifteen months later her father took her home with a view to arranging a marriage for her.   Several desirable suitors were proposed, but her heart was so strongly set upon the religious life that her parents after some opposition reluctantly gave way to her desire.   She chose the Carmelite convent of her native town because its members made their communion almost every day.   On the eve of the Assumption, 1582, she entered the convent of St Mary of the Angels upon the understanding that she should continue to wear her secular clothes until she had had full experience of the rule.   She had only been there fifteen days when her parents fetched her home—hoping, no doubt, that she would reconsider her decision.   Her resolution, however, was unbroken, and three months later she re-entered the convent with their approbation and blessing.

On January 30, 1583, she received the habit, and took the name of Mary Magdalen.   When the priest placed the crucifix in her hands with the words, " God forbid that I should glory save in the cross of our Lord Jesus Christ ", her face was suffused with an almost unearthly radiance and her heart was filled with an ardent desire to suffer during the rest of her life for her Saviour.   That desire was never to leave her.   After a most fervent noviciate she was allowed to take her vows unusually early, because she was dangerously ill.   As her sufferings were obviously very severe, one of the sisters asked her how she could bear so much pain without a murmur.   The saint pointed to the crucifix and said, " See what the infinite love of God has suffered for my salvation.   That same love sees my weakness and gives me courage.   Those who call to mind the sufferings of Christ and who offer up their own to God through His passion find their pains sweet and pleasant."   When she was conveyed back to the infirmary after her profession she sank into an ecstasy which lasted over an hour ; and for forty days she enjoyed heavenly consolations in addition to frequent raptures.   It has often been noticed by writers on the spiritual life that God is wont thus to visit elect souls with special consolations after their first act of complete self-surrender.   He does it in order to brace them for the trials which never fail to ensue.   To crucify in them all self-seeking, to teach them to know themselves, and to prepare them to be vessels of His pure love, He refines them in the crucible of internal tribulation.   Usually the higher the degree of sanctity to which they are to rise, the fiercer are the cleansing fires.   This we find exemplified in the state of desolation into which this saint fell after her first transports of spiritual joy.   But she did not desire spiritual consolations.   Her aspiration was to suffer for her Saviour's sake.

Fearing that she might have offended God by over-eagerness to be professed, Mary dei Pazzi asked and obtained permission to live as a novice two years after she had made her vows.   At the expiration of that time she was appointed second directress of the extern girls, and three years later she was set to instruct young nuns.   She was now being tried by the most severe interior trials.   Although she fasted always on bread and water, except on Sundays and holidays, she was assaulted with violent temptations to gluttony and impurity.   To resist them she chastised her body with disciplines, while she never ceased to implore the help of her heavenly Spouse and of our Blessed Lady. She seemed to be plunged into a state of darkness in which she saw nothing but what was horrible in herself and in all around her. For five whole years she remained in this state of desolation and spiritual dryness, and then God restored to her soul His holy peace together with the comfort of His divine presence. In 1590, on Whitsunday at Matins when the *Te Deum* was intoned, she fell into a rapture. On emerging from it, she pressed the hands of the prioress and the novice-mistress, exclaiming, " Rejoice with me, for my winter is at an end ! Help me to thank and glorify my good Creator." From this time onwards God was pleased to manifest His graces in her.

Mary Magdalen dei Pazzi read the thoughts of others and predicted future events. To Alexander dei Medici she foretold that he would one day be pope. Repeating the prophecy on a subsequent occasion she added that his reign would be a short one : it actually lasted twenty-six days. During her lifetime she appeared to several persons in distant places and she cured a number of sick people. As time went on, her ecstasies became more and more frequent. Sometimes in that state she would appear rigid and lifeless, sometimes she would carry on her customary duties while remaining entranced. Occasionally from her words and gestures it was evident that she was in some way participating in the passion of our Lord or conversing with her divine Spouse and the denizens of Heaven. So edifying were the words that fell from her lips that a record was kept of them by her sisters, who collected them after her death into a book. Her union with God seemed unbroken : she would call upon all created things to glorify their Creator and longed for all mankind to love Him as she did. She would pray with tears for the conversion of the heathen, of unbelievers, of heretics, of sinners. She would cry out, " O Love, love is not loved, not known by His own creatures. O my Jesus ! If I had a voice sufficiently loud and strong to be heard in every part of the world, I would cry out to make this Love known, loved and honoured by all men as the one immeasurable good."

In 1604 St Mary Magdalen became bedridden. She was now subject to violent headaches, and she lost all power in her limbs although she suffered agonies if touched. Besides being in constant pain she experienced much spiritual dryness. Nevertheless, the greater her suffering the greater grew her desire for it. " O Lord ", she prayed, " let me suffer or let me die—or rather—let me live on, that I may suffer more ! " She even rejoiced if her prayers were not granted because it meant that God's will was being done, not hers. When she knew that her last hour was approaching, she gave a parting injunction to the nuns assembled round her. " Reverend mother and dear sisters ", she said, " I am about to leave you ; and the last thing I ask of you—and I ask it in the name of our Lord Jesus Christ— is that you love Him alone, that you trust implicitly in Him and that you encourage one another continually to suffer for the love of Him." On May 25, 1607, she went to her eternal reward at the age of forty-one years. Her body, which was untouched by corruption, still lies in a shrine in the church attached to her convent in Florence, and in 1669 she was canonized.

In the *Acta Sanctorum*, May, vol. vi, the Bollandists print a Latin translation of the two earliest lives of St Mary Magdalen dei Pazzi. The first appeared in 1611, written by Vincent Puccini, the saint's confessor in her last years. The narrative portion is comparatively brief, but it is accompanied by a supplement of some 700 pages consisting of extracts from her visions and letters. Father Cepari, who had also acted as her confessor, had likewise a biography in preparation, but he withheld it out of consideration for Puccini.   It appeared, however, in 1669 with additions borrowed from the process of canonization.   These two works, combined with her letters and five manuscript volumes of notes of her revelations and dialogues in ecstasy, taken down by her fellow nuns, constitute our sources.   A new selection of her utterances, *Extases et lettres*, was presented in 1945 (in Italian, 1924) by Maurice Vaussard, who has further contributed a short life to the series " Les Saints " (1925).   The life by Cepari was translated into English for the Oratorian Series and was printed in 1849, and there is a full biography in French by the Viscountess de Beausire-Seyssel (1913).   See Fr E. E. Larkin's paper on " The Ecstasies of the Forty Days of St Mary M. de' Pazzi " in *Carmelus*, vol. i (1954), pp. 29–71.

ST CYRIL OF CAESAREA, MARTYR   (A.D. 251 ?)

OF this boy martyr we are told that without the knowledge of his pagan father he had become a Christian.   The father, discovering that the child refused to pay any mark of respect to the idols, turned him out of doors.   This happened at Caesarea in Cappadocia, and the governor of the city gave orders that Cyril should be brought before him.   Cajoleries and threats proved equally ineffectual to shake the boy's resolution.   Then the governor ordered him off as if to execution ; but he gave directions that after the youth had seen the blazing pyre into which he might be thrown, he was to be brought back to the court.   On his return Cyril only complained that the sentence had not been carried out, and the governor, infuriated, had him put to death by the sword.

The so-called *passio*, which exists only in Latin, looks more like a fragment of a panegyric than a historical document.   It is printed in the *Acta Sanctorum*, May, vol. vii, and in Ruinart.   The real interest of the case lies in the fact that Cyril's name, with a mention of Caesarea in Cappadocia, was included already in the Syriac *breviarium* of the early fifth century under May 28, and that the same entry also appears on May 29 in the *Hieronymianum*, revised in Gaul a century or two later.

ST MAXIMINUS, BISHOP OF TRIER   (*c.* A.D. 347)

ST MAXIMINUS, who was perhaps a native of Poitiers, left his home in early youth for Trier, possibly attracted thither by the reputation of its bishop, St Agritius. There he completed his education and there he was raised to the episcopate to become the successor of St Agritius.   When St Athanasius went to Trier as an exile in 336, St Maximinus received him with honour, deeming it a privilege to be able to entertain so illustrious a servant of God.   St Athanasius stayed with him two years ; and his writings emphasize the courage, vigilance and noble qualities of his host who was, moreover, already famous for his miracles.   St Paul, bishop of Constantinople, when banished by Constantius, likewise found a retreat at Trier and a powerful protector in its bishop.   St Maximinus convened the synod of Cologne which condemned Euphratas as a heretic, depriving him of his see.   He warned the Emperor Constans, whose favourite residence was at Trier, against the errors of the Arians and he himself opposed them on every possible occasion : so that his name was coupled with that of St Athanasius in the excommunication which the Arians afterwards launched against their opponents from Philippopolis.   The date of his death is uncertain : but we are told that it cannot have been later than 347 because his successor Paulinus is known to have been in possession of the see of Trier in that same year.   Although St Maximinus seems to have written much, none of his works have survived.

A life of Maximinus is printed in the *Acta Sanctorum*, May, vol. vii, but the biography written by Servatus Lupus in the ninth century is probably preferable.   It has been edited by B. Krusch in MGH., *Scriptores Merov.*, vol. iii, pp. 71–82. The question of the Council of Cologne in 346 has been much debated. Mgr Duchesne denied the existence of any such council ; see *Revue d'Histoire ecclésiastique*, vol. iii (1902), pp. 16–29 ; but consult H. Quentin in *Revue Bénédictine*, vol. xxiii (1906), pp. 477–486, and Hefele-Leclercq, *Histoire des Conciles*, vol. i, pp. 830–836. On Maximinus, *cf.* Duchesne, *Fastes Épiscopaux*, vol. iii, p. 35, and the summary account by J. Hau, *Sankt Maximinus* (1935).

SS. SISINNIUS, MARTYRIUS and ALEXANDER, Martyrs (A.D. 397)

AMONGST the many strangers who came to sojourn in Milan during the reign of Theodosius the Great were three natives of Cappadocia, Sisinnius and the two brothers Martyrius and Alexander. St Ambrose esteemed them so highly that he commended them to St Vigilius, bishop of Trent, who was in great need of missionaries. Sisinnius having been ordained deacon and Martyrius lector, the three were commissioned to preach the gospel in the Tyrolese Alps where Christianity had made but little way. They laboured especially in the valley of Anaunia (Val di Non). There, in spite of opposition and ill-treatment, they gained a great number of souls and Sisinnius built a church in the village of Methon or Medol, where he assembled his converts to complete their instruction. The pagans, enraged at the success of the missionaries, resolved to force the newly-baptized Christians to take part in one of their festivals. Sisinnius and his companions did their best to keep their converts away, and their opponents thereupon attacked the missionaries in their own church, beating them so severely that Sisinnius died within a few hours. Martyrius managed to creep away into a garden, but his enemies found him the following day, and dragged him by the legs over sharp stones till he died under this brutal treatment. Alexander also fell into their hands. They tried by threats to make him renounce his faith as they were burning the bodies of his companions. Finding their efforts unavailing, they cast him alive into the same fire. The ashes of the saints were collected by the faithful and taken to Trent. Afterwards St Vigilius erected a church on the spot where they had suffered.

Though the details supplied in the supposed " Acts " of Sisinnius, in the Bollandists, May, vol. vii, are of little account, the fact of the martyrdom is certain. We possess the letters written by Vigilius himself to the bishop of Milan and to St John Chrysostom. St Augustine also speaks of them, as does St Maximus of Turin. See further the references given in CMH., p. 281.

ST THEODOSIA, Virgin and Martyr   (A.D. 745)

THE history of St Theodosia was written in the fourteenth century by Constantine Akropolites, who seems to have drawn upon early written records and oral tradition ; he inhabited a house at Constantinople near the martyr's tomb and was one of her great votaries. According to him she came of a noble family and lost her parents when she was still very young. She afterwards took the veil in the monastery of the Anastasis in Constantinople. She lived in the days of the Emperors Leo the Isaurian and his son, Constantine Copronymus, who strove to abolish the public veneration of sacred images. When the order had gone forth for the destruction of a greatly revered image of our Lord, Theodosia at the head of a band of women shook the ladder which supported the official who was about to cast it down. The man fell and was killed. The women then stoned the palace of the pseudo-patriarch

Anastasius, obliging him to flee. Summary punishment was meted out to the women but especially to Theodosia as their ringleader. She was tortured in prison, her throat was torn out, and she died of the treatment she received. It is not difficult to suggest reasons why the name of this nun is not found in the Roman Martyrology.

A sufficient account is provided in the *Acta Sanctorum*, May, vol. vii. Probably the most reliable text is that of the *Constantinople Synaxary* (ed. Delehaye), cc. 828–829, under July 18. A translation of the " passion " will be found in Dom Leclercq, *Les Martyrs*, vol. iv.

SS. WILLIAM, STEPHEN, RAYMUND AND THEIR COMPANIONS, MARTYRS (A.D. 1242)

THE twelve martyrs who are commemorated together on this day were all directly or indirectly connected with the branch of the Inquisition which had been set up at Toulouse in 1228 to combat the errors of the Albigensians and other false teachers in Languedoc. Pope Gregory IX specially commissioned the Order of Preachers to expound the faith in Toulouse and the neighbouring districts, and to deliver heretics over to the secular arm. The Dominicans encountered great hostility and drew upon themselves the bitter hatred of the Albigensians ; they were driven out of Toulouse, Narbonne and other places by the mob. As they went, the friars, undaunted by the treatment they were receiving, chanted aloud the " Salve Regina " and the Apostles' Creed. At Avignonet, to the south-west of Toulouse, they conducted a preaching mission with the assistance of other priests, and were offered hospitality in the local castle, which belonged to Count Raymund VII of Toulouse but which was then in charge of his bailiff. All unsuspecting, they accepted the invitation. As they were retiring for the night, they were set upon and butchered by a band of soldiers who had been secretly introduced into the building. They uttered no cry, but with their dying breath praised God in the words of the Te Deum. The little company included three Dominicans—William Arnaud and two others—two Friars Minor, Stephen and Raymund, two Benedictines, four other clerics and a layman. Many cures reported at their grave led to a *cultus* that was confirmed more than six hundred years later, in 1856.

A summary compiled from the Chronicle of Toulouse and other sources will be found in the *Acta Sanctorum*, May, vol. vii. See also the *Monumenta O. P. Historica*, vol. i, pp. 231 *seq.* ; Mortier, *Histoire des Maîtres généraux O. P.*, vol. i, pp. 357 *seq.* ; Léon, *Auréole Séraphique* (Eng. trans.), vol. ii, pp. 356–374 ; Procter, *Lives of Dominican Saints*, pp. 152–155.

BD PETER PETRONI (A.D. 1361)

IN the Carthusian Order Peter Petroni of Siena is held in great veneration. Born of a distinguished family in that city, he seems to have manifested from his earliest childhood an extraordinary attraction for the things of God. He loved to go apart and pray, and sought out little ragamuffins in the streets to teach them and relieve their needs, spoiling his rich clothes, so his parents complained, by living in such company. When the Carthusian monastery of Maggiano was built near by through the munificence of one of his relatives, he was eager to enter there, and in spite of opposition he accomplished his purpose at the age of seventeen. His superiors wished him later to be ordained priest, but he so shrank from the responsibilities entailed that, after all his remonstrances had proved fruitless, he chopped off the index finger of his left hand to render himself for ever disqualified for ordination. His life was marked by what might seem an almost fanatical determination to have nothing to do with his own family ; on the other hand he is said to have been favoured by God with marvellous graces and with preternatural knowledge. Shortly before his death he commissioned a devoted *protégé* of his, Gioacchino Ciani, to warn the famous humanist, Boccaccio, that unless he gave up his wanton literary work and mended his life, God would very soon summon him to judgement.   The message was delivered ; Boccaccio demurred, but when Ciani proceeded to remind him of secrets in his past, which were known to no human being, but which he had learnt from Bd Peter's disclosures, the scholar was converted.   Peter died on May 29, 1361, and the wonders reported at his tomb threatened to disrupt the peace of the monastery ; so they ceased.

There is an Italian life of Bd Peter, written at least in part by his disciple, Bd John Colombini, which has been translated into Latin in the *Acta Sanctorum*, May, vol. vii.   See also the *Annales Ordinis Cartusiensis*, by Dom Le Couteulx, vols. v, vi and vii.   The conversion of Boccaccio is confirmed by his correspondence with Petrarch.

BD RICHARD THIRKELD, Martyr   (A.D. 1583)

Richard Thirkeld was already an old man when he was ordained a priest in 1579, after having studied at Douai and Rheims.   He had been a student, probably a " scholar ", at Queen's College, Oxford.   He was born in the diocese of Durham, and for eight years he had prayed daily to be allowed to suffer death for the faith. He was sent upon the English mission, where he exercised his ministry chiefly at York and in the neighbouring districts.   A night visit to a Catholic prisoner aroused suspicion, and nine days after the execution of Bd William Hart he was arrested on the charge of being a priest.   He at once acknowledged his priesthood, explaining the purpose for which he had come to England, and he was accordingly imprisoned in the Kidcote prison at York.   Two months later he was tried by a jury which pronounced him guilty of treason, mainly on the score of his admission that he had absolved and had reconciled to the Church of Rome some of the Queen's subjects.   Remitted to the condemned cell, he spent the whole night instructing some of the criminals by whom he was surrounded and preparing them for death.   The following day he came up again before the court, and was condemned to die with the usual barbarities : he fell upon his knees and gave thanks to God, saying, " This is the day which the Lord hath made : let us be glad and rejoice therein."   The sentence was duly carried out, but no details are available because extraordinary pains were taken by the authorities to prevent the public in general from being present, so universal was the admiration and sympathy felt for the holy and venerable-looking old priest.

An account is printed in Challoner, MMP., pp. 79–83, but more fully in Camm, LEM., vol. ii, pp. 635–653.

30 : ST FELIX I, Pope   (A.D. 274)

ACCORDING to the Roman Martyrology and the *Liber Pontificalis*, Felix I (a Roman by birth) ended his life as a martyr.   This is almost certainly a mistake due to confusion with a certain Felix, a martyr who was buried on the Via Aurelia.   The same confusion has led to the undoubtedly incorrect statement in the *Liber Pontificalis* (second edition) that Pope Felix " built a church on the Via Aurelia where he was also buried ".   Very little is known of Felix, though he seems to have sent some reply to the report of the Synod of Antioch—announcing the deposition of Paul of Samosata—which had been brought to Rome in the time of his predecessor, Pope St Dionysius.   On the other hand the quotation from what purported to be Felix's letter which was read at the Council of Ephesus is declared by such scholars as Duchesne, Bardenhewer, Harnack and others to have been an Apollinarian forgery.   The statement that Pope Felix " decreed that Masses should be celebrated on the tombs of the martyrs " may possibly refer to some practice initiated by him of placing an obstruction to block the hollow space (*arcosolia*) left above the tombs in the catacombs, exception only being made for tombs which were known to be those of martyrs.   Thus the decree would mean that the Mysteries should be celebrated (only) on the tombs of martyrs.   The true date of his death was December 30 (III *kal. jan.*), but a misreading of *jun.* for *jan.* has led to its being assigned to May 30.   The *Depositio Episcoporum* which reveals this error also informs us that Felix was buried in the cemetery of Callistus.

See J. P. Kirsch in the *Catholic Encyclopedia*, vol. vi, pp. 29–30 ; Duchesne in *Liber Pontificalis*, vol. i, p. 158 ; CMH., pp. 14–16 ; Bardenhewer, *Geschichte der altkirchlichen Literatur*, vol. ii, pp. 645–647.

ST ELEUTHERIUS, Pope   (*c.* A.D. 189)

As in the case of all the other early Roman pontiffs, we have very little reliable information concerning Pope Eleutherius.   It is stated that he was a Greek by origin.   In his time Montanism was causing uneasiness in both West and East, and St Irenaeus came to Rome with a letter about it from the Christians of Lyons ; but it is not clear what action the pope took.

Eleutherius is now chiefly remembered from his supposed correspondence with the British king, Lucius, who was believed to have written to ask his warranty to be admitted into the Christian fold, thus bringing about the first preaching of Christianity in Britain (see St Lucius, December 3).   This legend is no longer credited, but on the strength of it a feast of St Eleutherius is observed in the dioceses of Westminster and Portsmouth on May 30.

See the *Liber Pontificalis*, ed. Duchesne, vol. i, pp. cii–civ, 58 and 136 ; and J. P. Kirsch in the *Catholic Encyclopedia*, vol. v, pp. 378–379.

ST ISAAC OF CONSTANTINOPLE, Abbot   (*c.* A.D. 410)

When the Arian Emperor Valens was persecuting his Catholic subjects, a hermit named Isaac was inspired to leave his solitude in order to remonstrate with the monarch.   Coming to Constantinople he warned the emperor several times that unless he ceased his oppression and restored to the Catholics the churches which he had given to the Arians, a great disaster awaited him and a miserable end.   Valens treated these warnings with scorn and on one occasion when the hermit seized the bridle of his horse as he was riding out of the city, he gave orders that the prophet should be thrown into a neighbouring swamp.   Isaac escaped— miraculously as it seemed—but on repeating his prophecy he was put in prison.   His words were fulfilled shortly afterwards, for the emperor was defeated and killed at the battle of Adrianople.   St Isaac was released by the successor of Valens, Theodosius, who always held him in great veneration.   The holy man attempted to resume the solitary life, but soon found himself surrounded by disciples who refused to leave him. For them he founded a monastery which is said to have been the oldest in Constantinople. From St Dalmatus, one of St Isaac's disciples and his successor, it was afterwards called the Dalmatian monastery. St Isaac took part in the first Council of Constantinople—usually described as the second ecumenical council of the Church ; and he died at an advanced age.

A Greek life of St Isaac is printed in the seventh volume for May of the *Acta Sanctorum*, from the last paragraph of which it has been inferred that the saint died in 383. This, however, is a mistake, as J. Pargoire has shown in *Échos d'Orient*, vol. ii (1899), pp. 138–145 ; the one reliable life of St Dalmatus proves that Isaac must have lived at least until 406. See the *Analecta Bollandiana*, vol. xviii (1899), pp. 430–431.

ST EXSUPERANTIUS, Bishop of Ravenna (A.D. 418)

The successor of St Ursus as metropolitan of Ravenna was St Exsuperantius, or Superantius—a holy man who did much to promote the temporal as well as the spiritual welfare of his flock. He lived during the reign of the Emperor Honorius, and when Stilicho invested Ravenna with his army, St Exsuperantius prevailed upon him to restrain his soldiers from desecrating and looting the cathedral. The bishop built the town of Argenta—so-called because it paid a tribute in silver to the church of Ravenna. After a peaceful and uneventful episcopate of twenty years St Exsuperantius died in 418 and was buried in the church of St Agnes. His relics now rest in the cathedral of Ravenna.

There is a short account in the *Acta Sanctorum*, May, vol. vii, but the ultimate authority seems to be the not very trustworthy *Liber pontificalis seu vitae pontificum Ravennatum* of Andreas Agnellus. This may conveniently be consulted in Migne, PL., vol. 106, cc. 525–528, but a better text is provided by Holder-Egger in MGH., *Scriptores Rerum Langobardicarum*, pp. 265 *seq.*

ST MADELGISILUS, or MAUGUILLE (*c.* A.D. 655)

St Madelgisilus, or Mauguille, is said to have been an Irishman and the companion of St Fursey, with whom he went to England and afterwards to Gaul. After the death of St Fursey, Madelgisilus joined the monks of Saint-Riquier or Centula. Dismayed at finding himself regarded with veneration by his brethren, he obtained leave from the abbot to retire into the solitude of Monstrelet, on the river Authie. Here he lived an austere life of contemplation alone until he was visited by a holy English recluse named Vulgan who, finding him very ill, nursed him back to health. A great friendship sprang up between them and they continued to practise the eremitic life side by side until Vulgan's death. St Madelgisilus did not long survive his friend. He was buried in the hermitage chapel, but his relics were afterwards removed to a church of his name built near Saint-Riquier.

A life by Hariulphus, who, though he wrote as late as the beginning of the twelfth century, was a painstaking compiler, is printed in the *Acta Sanctorum*, May, vol. vii. See also Corblet, *Hagiographie du diocèse d'Amiens*, vol. iii, pp. 226 *seq.*, and *cf.* Gougaud, *Gaelic Pioneers of Christianity*, pp. 19 and 134.

ST WALSTAN (A.D. 1016)

Not much can be stated with any certainty regarding St Walstan. There is no notice of him in the *Dictionary of National Biography*, and Sir T. D. Hardy in his *Materials relating to the History of Great Britain and Ireland* refers only to the account given in Capgrave, *Nova Legenda Angliae*.   But it is possible that Alban Butler had before him a copy of some manuscript materials which have now perished, perhaps in the fire which so seriously damaged the Cottonian collection.   He wrote at any rate of St Walstan as follows, appealing, besides Capgrave and Blomfield's *History of Norfolk*, to " an old manuscript Life " :

" St Walstan was formerly much honoured at Cossey and Bawburgh, commonly called Baber, two villages four miles from Norwich.   He was born at Baber, and of a rich and honourable family.   The name of his father was Benedict, that of his mother Blida.   By their example and good instructions he, from his infancy, conceived an ardent desire to devote himself to God, with the greatest perfection possible.   In this view, at twelve years of age, he renounced his patrimony, left his father's house, and entered as a poor servant at Taverham, a village adjoining to Cossey.   He was so charitable that he gave his own victuals to the poor, and sometimes even his shoes, going himself barefoot.   He applied himself to the meanest and most painful country labour in a perfect spirit of penance and humility ; fasted much, and sanctified his soul and all his actions by assiduous, fervent prayer, and the constant union of his heart with God.   He made a vow of celibacy, but never embraced a monastic state.

" God honoured his humility before men by many miracles.   He died in the midst of a meadow where he was at work, on the 30th of May in 1016.   His body was interred at Baber : it was carried thither through Cossey or Costessey, where a well still bears his name, as does another which was more famous at Baber, a little below the church.   These places were much resorted to by pilgrims, especially to implore the intercession of this saint for the cure of fevers, palsies, lameness and blindness.   His body was enshrined in the north chapel of that church, which chapel was on that account pulled down in the reign of Henry VIII though the church is still standing.   All the mowers and husbandmen in these parts constantly visited it once a year, and innumerable other pilgrims resorted to it, not only from all parts of England, but also from beyond the seas.   The church is sacred to the memory of the Blessed Virgin and of St Walstan."

Father Joseph Stevenson, s.j., in certain manuscript notes he has left concerning the English saints, adds these details : " St Walstan, after giving away his shoes, loaded thorns in a cart without suffering any injury.   His master offered to adopt him, but he refused, accepting, however, the gift of a cow, which produced two calves at one birth.   When his approaching death was notified to him in a vision, he ordered his body to be placed on a cart drawn by two oxen who should be suffered to go on until they stopped of their own accord.   They proceeded towards Costesheya (Cossey), and, though they passed through some water, the wheel-tracks then made are said to remain to the present day.   The oxen came to a stop at Bawburgh, and there his body is buried."

In the British Martyrology, compiled by Bishop Challoner with the title, *A Memorial of Ancient British Piety* (1761), there is a brief mention of St Walstan under May 30.   On the other hand, the name is apparently not to be found in any surviving pre-Reformation calendar, nor does it figure in the " Martiloge " of R. Whitford (1526) nor in that of Father Wilson (1608 and 1640).   The Bollandists, writing in the seventeenth century, would seem never to have heard of St Walstan, for he is not mentioned even among the " Praetermissi " of May 30.   Fr Paul Grosjean, Bollandist, suggests that the old life of the saint known to Butler may be identified with the English life in 75 stanzas now at Lambeth ; see *Proceedings of the Norfolk and Norwich Arch. Soc.*, vol. xix, p. 250.   It is a transcript from a parchment affixed to a triptych at the saint's shrine in Bawburgh church.

ST FERDINAND III OF CASTILE   (A.D. 1252)

THE father of Ferdinand III was Alfonso IX, king of Leon, and his mother was Berengaria, who was the elder daughter of Alfonso III, king of Castile : her mother was a daughter of Henry II of England, and her sister Blanche became the mother of St Louis of France.   The death of her brother Henry in 1217 left Berengaria heiress to the throne of Castile, but she resigned her rights in favour of her eighteen-year-old son Ferdinand.   Two years later he married Beatrice, daughter of King Philip of Swabia, and they had seven sons and three daughters.

Ferdinand was severe in the administration of justice, but readily forgave personal injuries.   His wisdom showed itself particularly in the choice he made of governors, magistrates and generals ; the archbishop of Toledo, Rodrigo Ximenes, was chancellor of Castile and his principal adviser for many years.   In 1230, on the death of his father, Ferdinand became king also of Leon, but not without strife, for there were those who supported the claim of his two half-sisters.

King Ferdinand was the real founder of the great University of Salamanca ; but it is as the tireless and successful campaigner against the Moors that he impressed himself on the minds and hearts of Spaniards.   For twenty-seven years he was engaged in almost uninterrupted warfare with the oppressors.   He drove them out of Ubeda in 1234, Cordova (1236), Murcia, Jaen, Cadiz and finally Seville itself (1249).   It was at the battle of Xeres, when only ten Spanish lives were lost, that St James was said to have been seen leading the host on a white horse.   In thanksgiving for his victories, Ferdinand rebuilt the cathedral of Burgos and turned the great mosque of Seville into a church.   Unlike some warriors he was a forbearing ruler : it is remembered of him that he said that he " feared the curse of one old woman more than a whole army of Moors " ; and he fought primarily not to extend his territories but to rescue Christian people from the dominion of infidels.

On the death of Queen Beatrice, Ferdinand married Joan of Ponthieu, who bore him two sons and a daughter : that daughter was Eleanor, who became the wife of Edward I of England.   He himself died on May 30, 1252, and was buried in the cathedral of Seville in the habit of the Friars Minor.   Ferdinand was declared a saint by Pope Clement X in 1671.

The Bollandists in the *Acta Sanctorum*, May, vol. vii, have translated into Latin those portions of the chronicle of Rodrigo Ximenes, archbishop of Toledo (referred to above), which refer to St Ferdinand.   With this we have also the summary account of Luke, bishop of Tuy, who was likewise a contemporary, and other miscellaneous documents.   Further, there is preserved a narrative by the Franciscan, Giles of Zamora (*c.* A.D. 1300).   This will be found in the *Boletin de la real Academia de la Historia*, vol. v (1884), pp. 308–321.   St Ferdinand, of course, plays a conspicuous part in all Spanish histories which cover this period.   Among modern biographies may be mentioned those by J. Laurentie in French (1910), F. Maccono in Italian (1924), and a popular life in Spanish by J. R. Coloma (1928).

BD ANDREW, BISHOP OF PISTOIA   (A.D. 1401)

BD ANDREW was a member of the noble family of the Franchi Boccagni of Pistoia, his native city, and early entered the Dominican Order.   A great preacher, he was also endowed with administrative powers which led to his being made prior of three convents in Italy.   In 1378 he was appointed bishop of Pistoia.   For twenty-three years he ruled his diocese wisely and well, promoting peace and spending his revenues on the restoration of churches and the relief of the poor.   As a bishop he led a life of extreme simplicity, striving as far as possible to observe the rule to which he had been bound as a simple friar.   A year before his death he resigned his office and retired to his old convent in Pistoia, where he prepared himself for the end.   He died on May 26, 1401.   In 1921 Pope Benedict XV sanctioned his *cultus* for the Dominicans and for the diocese of Pistoia.

In the decree confirming the *cultus* (see the *Acta Apostolicae Sedis*, vol. xiv, 1922, pp. 16–19) there is a short biographical summary.   A longer account will be found in the *Année Dominicaine*, vol. v (1891), pp. 689–693 ; and in 1922 Fr Taurisano published a brief life in Italian.

ST JOAN OF ARC, Virgin   (A.D. 1431)

St Jeanne la Pucelle, or Joan of Arc as she has always been called in England, was born on the feast of the Epiphany 1412, at Domrémy, a little village of Champagne on the bank of the Meuse.   Her father, Jacques d'Arc, was a peasant farmer of some local standing, a worthy man, frugal and rather morose ; but his wife was a gentle affectionate mother to their five children.   From her the two girls of the family received a good training in household duties.   " In sewing and spinning I fear no woman ", Joan afterwards declared ; reading and writing, however, she never learnt.   Impressive and often touching testimony to her piety and exemplary conduct appears in the sworn depositions of her former neighbours presented in the process for her rehabilitation.   Priests and former playmates amongst others recalled her love of prayer and church, her frequent reception of the sacraments, her care of the sick, and her sympathy with poor wayfarers to whom she often gave up her own bed.   " She was so good ", it was stated, " that all the village loved her."   A happy childhood hers seems to have been, though clouded by the disasters of her country as well as by the dangers of attack to which a frontier town like Domrémy, bordering on Lorraine, was specially exposed.   On one occasion at least before she began her great undertaking Joan had been obliged to flee with her parents to the town of Neufchatel, at eight miles distance, to escape a raid of Burgundian freebooters who sacked Domrémy.

She had been but a very young child when Henry V of England invaded France, overran Normandy and claimed the crown of the insane king, Charles VI.   France, in the throes of civil war between the contending parties of the Dukes of Burgundy and Orleans, had been in no condition from the first to put up an adequate resistance, and after the Duke of Burgundy had been treacherously murdered by the Dauphin's servants the Burgundians threw in their lot with the English, who supported their claims.   The death of the rival kings in 1422 brought no relief to France.   The Duke of Bedford, as regent for the infant King of England, prosecuted the war with vigour, one fortified town after another falling into the hands of the allies, while Charles VII, or the Dauphin as he was still called, seems to have regarded the position as hopeless and spent his time in frivolous pastimes with his court.

St Joan was in her fourteenth year when she experienced the earliest of those supernatural manifestations which were to lead her through the path of patriotism to death at the stake.   At first it was a single voice addressing her apparently from near by, and accompanied by a blaze of light : afterwards, as the voices increased in number, she was able to see her interlocutors whom she identified as St Michael, St Catherine, St Margaret and others.   Only very gradually did they unfold her mission : it was a mission which might well appal her : she, a simple peasant girl, was to save France !   She never spoke about these Voices in Domrémy ;

she was too much afraid of her stern father. By May 1428 they had become insistent and explicit. She must present herself at once to Robert Baudricourt, who commanded the king's forces in the neighbouring town of Vaucouleurs. Joan succeeded in persuading an uncle who lived near Vaucouleurs to take her to him, but Baudricourt only laughed and dismissed her, saying that her father ought to give her a good hiding.

At this time the military position was well-nigh desperate, for Orleans, the last remaining stronghold, had been invested by the English and was in danger of falling. After Joan's return to Domrémy her Voices gave her no rest. When she protested that she was a poor girl who could neither ride nor fight, they replied ; " It is God who commands it ". Unable to resist such a call she secretly left home and went back to Vaucouleurs. Baudricourt's scepticism as to her mission was somewhat shaken when official confirmation reached him of a serious defeat of the French which Joan had previously announced to him. He now not only consented to send her to the king but gave her an escort of three men-at-arms. At her own request she travelled in male dress to protect herself. Although the little party reached Chinon, where the king was residing, on March 6, 1429, it was not till two days later that Joan was admitted to his presence. Charles had purposely disguised himself, but she identified him at once and, by a secret sign communicated to her by her Voices and imparted by her to him alone, she obliged him to believe in the supernatural nature of her mission. She then asked him for soldiers whom she might lead to the relief of Orleans. This request was opposed by La Trémouille, the king's favourite, and by a large section of the court, who regarded the girl as a crazy visionary or a scheming impostor. To settle the matter it was decided to send her to be examined by a learned body of theologians at Poitiers.

After a searching interrogatory extending over three weeks this council decided that they found nothing to disapprove of, and advised Charles to make prudent use of her services. Accordingly after her return to Chinon arrangements were pushed forward to equip her to lead an expeditionary force. A special standard was made for her bearing the words " Jesus : Maria ", together with a representation of the Eternal Father to whom two kneeling angels were presenting a fleur-de-lis. On April 27 the army left Blois with Joan at its head clad in white armour, and in spite of some contretemps she entered Orleans on April 29. Her presence in the beleaguered city wrought marvels. By May 8, the English forts which surrounded Orleans had been captured and the siege raised, after she herself had been wounded in the breast by an arrow. All these events with their approximate dates she had prophesied before starting the campaign. She would fain have followed up these successes, for her Voices had told her that she would not last for long ; but La Trémouille and the archbishop of Rheims were in favour of negotiating with the enemy. They persisted in regarding the relief of Orleans merely as a piece of good luck. However, the Maid was allowed to undertake a short campaign on the Loire with the Duc d'Alençon, one of her best friends. It was completely successful and ended with a victory at Patay in which the English forces under Sir John Fastolf suffered a crushing defeat. Joan now pressed for the immediate coronation of the Dauphin. The road to Rheims had practically been cleared and the last obstacle was removed by the unexpected surrender of Troyes.

But the French leaders dallied, and only very reluctantly did they consent to follow her to Rheims where, on July 17, 1429, Charles VII was solemnly crowned, Joan standing at his side with her standard. That event, which completed the mission originally entrusted to her by her Voices, marked also the close of her military successes. A boldly planned attack on Paris failed, mainly for lack of Charles's promised support and presence. During the action Joan was wounded in the thigh by an arrow and had to be almost dragged into safety by Alençon. Then followed a truce which entailed on the Maid a winter of inaction spent for the most part in the entourage of a worldly court, where she was regarded with thinly veiled suspicion. Upon the resumption of hostilities she hurried to the relief of Compiègne which was holding out against the Burgundians. She entered the city at sunrise on May 23, 1430, and that same day led an unsuccessful sortie. Through panic or some miscalculation on the part of the governor, the drawbridge over which her company was retiring was raised too soon, leaving Joan and some of her men outside at the mercy of the enemy. She was dragged from her horse with howls of execration, and led to the quarters of John of Luxembourg, one of whose soldiers had been her captor. From that time until the late autumn she remained the prisoner of the Duke of Burgundy. Never during that period or afterwards was the slightest effort made on her behalf by King Charles or any of his subjects. With the basest ingratitude they were content to leave her to her fate. But the English leaders desired to have her if the French did not : and on November 21 she was sold to them for a sum equivalent to about £23,000 in modern money. Once in their hands her execution was a foregone conclusion. Though they could not condemn her to death for defeating them in open warfare, they could have her sentenced as a sorceress and a heretic. In an age when fear of witchcraft was general the charge would not seem preposterous, and already the English and Burgundian soldiers attributed their reverses to her spells.

In the castle of Rouen to which she was transferred two days before Christmas Joan was confined at first—we are told, but this is doubtful—in an iron cage, for she had twice tried to escape. Afterwards she lay in a cell where, though chained to a plank bed, she was watched day and night by soldiers. On February 21, 1431, she appeared for the first time before a tribunal presided over by Peter Cauchon, bishop of Beauvais, an unscrupulous man who hoped through English influence to become archbishop of Rouen. The judges were composed of dignitaries and doctors carefully selected by Cauchon, as well as of the ordinary officials of an ecclesiastical court. During the course of six public and nine private sessions the prisoner was examined and cross-examined as to her visions and " voices ", her assumption of male attire, her faith and her willingness to submit to the Church. Alone and undefended she bore herself fearlessly, her shrewd answers and accurate memory astonishing and frequently embarrassing her questioners. Only very occasionally was she betrayed into making damaging replies, through her ignorance of theological terms and lack of education. Nevertheless, at the conclusion of the sittings a grossly unfair summing-up of her statements was drawn up and submitted first to the judges, who on the strength of it declared her revelations to have been diabolical, and then to the University of Paris, which denounced her in violent terms.

In a final deliberation the tribunal decided that she must be handed over to the secular arm as a heretic if she refused to retract. This she declined to do, though threatened with torture. Only when she was brought into the cemetery of St Ouen before a huge crowd, to be finally admonished and sentenced, was she intimidated into making some sort of retractation. The actual terms of this retractation are uncertain and have been the occasion of much controversy. She was led back to prison but her respite was a short one.   Either as the result of a trick played by those who thirsted for her blood or else deliberately of her own free-will, she resumed the male dress which she had consented to discard ; and when Cauchon with some of his satellites visited her in her cell to question her concerning what they chose to regard as a relapse, they found that she had recovered from her weakness.   Once again she declared that God had truly sent her and that her voices came from God.   " Be of good cheer ! " Cauchon is reported as having exclaimed exultingly to the Earl of Warwick as he left the castle, " we shall get her again." On Tuesday, May 29, 1431, the judges after hearing Cauchon's report condemned her as a relapsed heretic to be delivered over to the secular arm, and the following morning at eight o'clock Joan was led out into the market-place of Rouen to be burned at the stake.   Joan's demeanour on that occasion was such as to move even the most hardened to tears.   When the faggots had been lighted, a Dominican friar at her request held up a cross before her eyes, and as the flames leaped up she was heard to call upon the name of Jesus before surrendering her soul to God.

She was not yet twenty years old.   After her death her ashes were contemptuously cast into the Seine, but there must have been many amongst the spectators to echo the remorseful exclamation of John Tressart, one of King Henry's secretaries : " We are lost : we have burned a saint ! "   Twenty-three years later Joan's mother and her two brothers appealed for a reopening of the case, and Pope Callistus III appointed a commission for the purpose.   Its labours resulted, on July 7, 1456, in the quashing of the trial and verdict and the complete rehabilitation of the Maid.   Over four hundred and fifty years later, on May 16, 1920, she was canonized with all the solemnity of the Church.

This canonization was the occasion in England, as elsewhere, of a renewed and widespread interest in Joan of Arc ; and there has been, almost inevitably, a tendency for various " Joan-legends " to grow up.   There is the " Joan the Protestant " legend, popularized by George Bernard Shaw.   Granted an inadequate understanding of Catholicism, this mistake is understandable : it is nevertheless a mistake.   As an accidental by-product of the same, there is the " theatre St Joan " legend, stereotyped as a pert Lancashire mill-girl with experience of festival religious drama : a figure partly attractive, partly tiresome, wholly untrue.   Then there is " Joan the nationalist ".   A great patriot she certainly was ; but when she said " France " can her supernatural Voices have meant anything else but Justice ? There is " Joan the feminist ", in some ways the most foolish of these legends, both historically and in sentiment ; and, of course, there is the Joan of the repositories, who may fitly be typified by the statue in Winchester cathedral.   Moreover, there is the common error that the Church venerates her as a martyr.

What then *was* St Joan ?   Quite simply, a peasant girl, full of natural ability, good sense, and the grace of God ; who knew, amongst other things, the story of the Annunciation, and when the will of God was made known to her, astounding as it was (though less so to her simplicity than to our sophistication), she faced it intelligently, welcomed it and submitted to it.   That is what emerges from every page of the text of the original documents of her trial.

Other things as well can be learned from them, some of them little gratifying to Catholics ; for though the tribunal that condemned her was not the Church, nevertheless it, and the ecclesiastics who upheld its decisions, included some honest and representative churchmen.   It also included others who were not.   The dealings with the Maid are an ineffaceable blot on the history of England. But the Englishmen concerned were not the only people who earned disgrace.

No adequate bibliography of St Jeanne d'Arc is possible within these narrow limits. The list made in 1906 by Canon U. Chevalier contains some 1500 entries, and this was before she was even beatified. Innumerable books and articles have been written since then. The most important sources were first published in Quicherat's *Procès de Condamnation et Réhabilitation*, 5 vols. (1841–1849) ; these are in Latin, but may be read in translations, *e.g.* by P. Champion in French and T. D. Murray in English, and the record of the trial only, by W. P. Barrett (1931). There is also a vast collection of materials, mostly translated, in the five volumes of Fr Ayroles, *La Vraie Jeanne d'Arc* (1890–1901), but it is unfortunate that the polemical note is here so much emphasized. The same exception may also be taken to the otherwise excellent books of Canon Dunand, *Histoire complète de Jeanne d'Arc*, 4 vols. (1912) ; and *Études Critiques*, 4 vols. (1909). Consult further Denifle's *Chartularium Universitatis Parisiensis*, with its supplement ; and C. Lemire, *Le Procès de Jeanne d'Arc* ; and for bibliographies see the *Cambridge Medieval History*, vol. viii, pp. 871 *seq.*, and J. Calmette, *La France et l'Angleterre en Conflit* (1937), pp. 405 *seq.* The following biographies and studies in French may be mentioned : by L. H. Petitot (1921) ; M. Gasquet (1929) ; P. Champion (1934) ; Funck-Brentano (1943) ; J. Cordier (1948). No one has written more convincingly on the subject in English than Andrew Lang, *The Maid of France* (1908), especially in his criticism of Anatole France's misleading *Vie*. Other English works are by Hilaire Belloc (1930), C. F. Oddie (1931) and V. Sackville West (1937). For a consideration of Bernard Shaw's *Saint Joan*, see Fr Bede Jarrett in *Blackfriars*, May 1924, pp. 67 *seq.*, and cf. E. Robo, *St. Joan* (1948), which includes a letter from Shaw. Fr Paul Doncœur's *La minute française des interrogatoires de Jeanne la Pucelle* (1952) is important. There is a highly recommended assessment of evidence, literature and general judgement on St Joan in *La Vie Spirituelle*, January 1954, pp. 84–98.

BD JAMES BERTONI   (A.D. 1483)

AT the age of nine, Bd James Philip Bertoni was placed in the Servite priory of Faenza in fulfilment of a vow which his father had made during a dangerous illness, and in later years as a professed Servite he proved himself a most holy religious. So great was his horror of sin that he made his confession every day. In appearance he was tall, thin and very pallid. After his ordination be became procurator of the priory of Faenza and held other responsible offices. He died on May 25, 1483, at the age of thirty-nine. Miracles wrought at his tomb in the church of St John at Faenza led to a popular *cultus*, which was formally approved in 1766. Soon after his death, in recognition of his son's sanctity, his father was declared a burgher of Faenza and was granted exemption from all taxes.

A short Latin life written by Nicholas Borghesi was printed in the *Acta Sanctorum*, May, vol. vi, as also in the *Monumenta Ordinis Servorum B.V.M.*, vol. iv (1901), pp. 63–67. There is also a modern sketch by L. Trebbi (1867).

BB. WILLIAM SCOTT AND RICHARD NEWPORT, MARTYRS (A.D. 1612)

WILLIAM SCOTT, of Chigwell, was studying law at Trinity Hall, Cambridge, when he was converted by reading Catholic literature. He went abroad, and took the Benedictine habit in the abbey of St Facundus, assuming in religion the name of Maurus. After his ordination he was sent on the English mission. As he entered London he saw Bd John Roberts, the monk who had received him into the Church, being hurried to execution, and three days later he was himself arrested and cast into prison where he remained a year. He was then deported, but soon made his way back to England. According to a contemporary he was imprisoned and exiled more than once and on each occasion he returned.   After his final arrest, as he was being conveyed by boat from Gravesend to London he threw into the river a bag containing his breviary, his faculties and some medals and crosses.   The bag was caught in a fisherman's net and figured at the trial.   In prison he had as his companion a secular priest called Richard Newport, a Northamptonshire man by birth, who after having been trained in Rome, had laboured very successfully in England. He also had been several times imprisoned and twice banished.   The two prisoners were brought up at the Old Bailey before the Lord Mayor, the Bishop of London, the Lord Chief Justice, and other magistrates.   They made a bold defence, but their condemnation was a foregone conclusion and they were sentenced to death as traitors.   They suffered at Tyburn with great fortitude on May 30, 1612.

See Challoner, MMP., pp. 323–329, and B. Camm, *Nine Martyr Monks* (1931), pp. 180–237.

31 : ST MARY THE QUEEN

ST ANGELA MERICI, VIRGIN, FOUNDRESS OF THE COMPANY OF ST URSULA   (A.D. 1540) *(Transferred to June 1)*

THE foundress of the Ursulines—the first teaching order of women to be established in the Church—was born on March 21, 1470 or 1474, at the little town of Desenzano, on the south-western shore of Lake Garda in Lombardy.   She received a good early training from her parents, a pious couple not overburdened with this world's goods.   They both died when Angela was ten years old, leaving their two daughters and a son to the care of a well-to-do uncle living at Salo.   The death of her elder sister came as a great shock to Angela when she was thirteen.   To her natural grief at being separated from one who was almost a second self was added apprehension as to her actual condition ; for the young girl, although she had lived an almost angelic life, had passed away before she could receive the last sacraments.   Angela's first vision—she was to have many in after years—seems to have been granted to her at this time, in order to set her mind completely at rest as to her sister's salvation.   In overflowing gratitude she consecrated herself more completely to God and soon afterwards was admitted as a Franciscan tertiary.   Her life became one of extreme austerity.   Striving to emulate St Francis, she wished to possess nothing of her own—not even a bed— and lived almost entirely on bread, water and a few vegetables.

After the death of her uncle when she was about twenty-two, Angela returned to Desenzano.   There, as she went about amongst her neighbours, she was appalled by the ignorance which prevailed amongst the poorer children whose parents could not or would not teach them the simplest elements of religion.   Gradually it was borne in upon her that she was called to do something to remedy this state of things, and she talked the matter over with her friends.   They were mostly fellow tertiaries or young women of her own class with little money and less influence, but they were eager to help her if she would show them the way.   Though very small of stature, Angela had all the necessary qualifications for leadership, including charm of manner and good looks.   At her suggestion they set to work to gather together the little girls of the neighbourhood, to whom they gave regular and systematic instruction.   The work so humbly begun prospered and developed.   Angela was invited to go to Brescia to begin a similar school in that city.   She consented, and was cordially welcomed into the household of a noble couple whom she had consoled when they were in distress. Through her hosts she was brought into touch with the leading families of Brescia and became the centre of a circle of devout women and men whom she inspired with her great ideals. From time to time we find her making pilgrimages to various shrines. Thus she visited the tomb of Bd Osanna at Mantua and eagerly seized an opportunity which presented itself of going to the Holy Land with a young relative, sailing under the protection of Antonio de Romanis, an elderly merchant. They had travelled as far as Crete on the outward journey when St Angela was suddenly overtaken with complete blindness. Her companions proposed abandoning their purpose, but she would not hear of their doing so. With them she visited the holy places in Palestine with as much devotion as if she could have beheld them with her bodily eyes. On the return journey, as she was praying before a crucifix, her sight was restored in the very place where she had lost it a few weeks previously.

In the holy year of 1525 Angela went to Rome to obtain the jubilee indulgence, and had the privilege of at least one private audience with the pope. Clement VII suggested that she should stay in Rome to take charge of a congregation of nursing sisters, but a sense of her true vocation as well as a shrinking from publicity led her to decline the offer. She accordingly returned to Brescia from whence, however, she was soon obliged to withdraw, for war had broken out again in Italy, and when Charles V was on the point of making himself master of Brescia it became essential that as many non-combatants as possible should leave the city. St Angela with some of her friends went to Cremona, where they remained until peace was concluded. Her return to Brescia was greeted with joy by the citizens who, besides appreciating her charity, venerated her as a prophetess and a saint. We read that as she was assisting at Mass shortly afterwards she fell into a prolonged ecstasy and was seen by a great number of persons to be upraised from the ground.

Years earlier, as a young woman at Desenzano, St Angela had seen in a vision a concourse of maidens ascending to Heaven on a ladder of light and a voice had said : " Take heart, Angela : before you die you will found at Brescia a company of maidens similar to those you have just seen ". And now the time was at hand for the fulfilment of that prophecy. About the year 1533 she seems to have begun to train a select few of her companions in a kind of informal noviciate. Twelve of them came to live with her in a house she took near the church of St Afra, but the greater number continued to live with parents or other relations. Two years later twenty-eight young women consecrated themselves with her to the service of God. She placed them under the protection of St Ursula, the patroness of medieval universities who was popularly venerated as a leader of women : hence the name of Ursulines which her daughters have always borne. This date—November 25, 1535—is reckoned as that of the foundation of the Ursuline Order. It was, however, during the lifetime of its foundress more in the nature of an association ; no habit was worn, although a black dress was recommended ; no vows were taken, and the sisters were not enclosed, nor did they lead a community life. They met together for classes and worship, carried out such duties as were allotted to them, and lived a holy life in the midst of their families. The idea of a teaching order of women was so novel that time was required in which to let it develop.

Yet, although many changes and modifications have taken place, the Ursulines from the period of their foundation until the present day have never lost sight of the object for which they were instituted—the religious education of girls, especially of the poorer classes. At the first election St Angela was unanimously chosen superioress, and she continued to fill that office for the last five years of her life. She was taken ill early in January 1540 and died on the twenty-seventh of the same month. In 1544 Pope Paul III issued a bull confirming the Company of St Ursula and declaring it to be a recognized congregation, and in 1807 its foundress was canonized.

The sources for the history of St Angela are very fully set out in English in the pains-taking work of Sister M. Monica, *Angela Merici and Her Teaching Idea* (1927). The saint's rule, her " testament ", and her counsels were taken down in writing by her secretary, the priest Cozzano. The first sketch of her life was compiled by a notary, G. B. Nazari, in 1560 and is printed as an appendix to the volume of Giuditta Bertolotti, *Storia di S. Angela Merici* (1923). The earliest printed biography seems to have been that of Ottavio Gondi (1600), but it is full of legendary material ; that of Carlo Doneda, compiled with a view to the process of canonization, appeared in 1768, and owing to its relatively critical treatment is more reliable. See the work of the Abbé Postel (1878), in two volumes, that of W. E. Hubert in German, and that entitled *Sainte Angèle Merici et l'Ordre des Ursulines* (2 vols., 1922) ; also M. Aron's *Les Ursulines* (1937), and G. Bernoville's biography (1947). There is an earlier life in English by Bernard O'Reilly, *St Angela Merici and the Ursulines* (1880) ; and a recent popular work by Mother Francis, *St Angela of the Ursulines*. Sister M. Monica's book is no doubt the least unsatisfactory, but it must be confessed that the appendix on St Ursula, which appeals to J. H. Kessel's monograph published in 1863 as a reliable authority on the problem of the 11,000 virgins, is not a little disconcerting. A reference to the article "Ursula" in the *Catholic Encyclopedia* would have been more to the point (*cf.* October 21 herein).

ST PETRONILLA, Virgin and Martyr   (A.D. 251 ?)

The Roman Martyrology for this day has the following entry : " At Rome, [the commemoration of] St Petronilla, Virgin, daughter of the blessed Apostle Peter, who refused to wed Flaccus, a nobleman, and accepting three days' delay for deliberation, spent them in fasting and prayer, and on the third day, after receiving the Sacrament of Christ, gave up the ghost ". It is quite certain that Petronilla was not the daughter of St Peter. The idea that St Peter had a daughter seems to have been derived from certain apocryphal publications of gnostic origin, and her identification with the St Petronilla venerated in Rome was imported into the legends concerning her which were current in the sixth century or earlier. On the other hand, in the cemetery of Domitilla a fresco has been discovered, dating from the middle of the fourth century, which quite unmistakably represents Petronilla as a martyr. Despite De Rossi's adverse view, the opinion that Petronilla was beyond doubt a martyr has prevailed. The legend which survives in the notice just quoted from the Roman Martyrology, according to which the saint died in her bed, has no better authority than the quite worthless Acts of Nereus and Achilleus ; see above on May 12.

H. Delehaye, in his publication *Sanctus* (1927), pp. 118–120, puts the question in its true light, and see further the references in his CMH., pp. 285–286. There is also an excellent, if disproportionately long, article on St Petronilla by Mgr J. P. Kirsch in the *Catholic Encyclopedia*, vol. xi, pp. 781–782.

SS. CANTIUS, CANTIANUS and CANTIANELLA, Martyrs   (A.D. 304 ?)

According to their " acts " preserved in several recensions, the two brothers Cantius and Cantianus with their sister Cantianella were members of the illustrious Roman family of the Anicii. Left orphans, they were brought up in their own mansion in Rome by a Christian tutor and guardian called Protus, by whom they were instructed in the faith. When the persecution of Diocletian began, they liberated their slaves, sold their possessions, the proceeds of which they distribued to the poor, and went to Aquileia. Even there, however, the cruel edict was being rigorously enforced. No sooner were the authorities informed of the arrival of the young nobles than they cited them to appear and to sacrifice to the gods. At the same time a messenger was despatched to Diocletian for instructions, and the emperor, who wished to be rid of them as much for political as for religious motives, sent word that they were to be beheaded unless they consented to sacrifice to the gods. The martyrs had left Aquileia in a chariot drawn by mules, but were held up by an accident four miles from the town of Aquae Gradatae. Here they were overtaken by their pursuers and when called upon to obey the emperor's behest, they replied that nothing should make them unfaithful to the only true God. They were accordingly beheaded, together with their tutor Protus, in the year 304.

As to the accuracy of these details we have no certainty. The story, with variations, is preserved in many texts, one is printed in the *Acta Sanctorum*, May, vol. vii, and the others are catalogued in the BHL., nn. 1543–1549. A sermon in honour of these martyrs attributed to St Ambrose is not genuine, but it may possibly be the composition of St Maximus of Turin. On the other hand there is much evidence which establishes the early cult of St Cantius and his companions at Aquileia. The casket of Grado on which their names are engraved (it is figured in Leclercq, DAC., vol. vi, cc. 1449–1453) may be as old as the early seventh century ; but before this we have mention of them in the verses of Venantius Fortunatus, and in the earliest text of the *Hieronymianum*. See Delehaye's commentary on this last, p. 284, and his *Origines du Culte des Martyrs*, p. 331.

ST MECHTILDIS OF EDELSTETTEN, Virgin   (A.D. 1160)

THIS Mechtildis was only five years old when she was placed by her parents, Count Berthold of Andechs and his wife Sophia, in the double monastery they had founded on their own estate at Diessen, on the Ammersee in Bavaria. Trained by the nuns, Mechtildis grew up a devout and exemplary maiden, much given to prayer and austerities. Her one weakness in youth was a somewhat quick temper which occasionally betrayed her into hasty speech, but over this she obtained complete control. Indeed, in later life she was remarkable for her silence, and it was said of her by the Cistercian monk Engelhard that on the rare occasions when she opened her lips to speak her words were as those of an angel. After she had received the habit, she made still further advance along the path of perfection. Upon the death of the superior, she was elected abbess, in which capacity she raised the whole community to a high pitch of virtue. This she effected far more by her example than by the strictness of her rule.

So highly was she esteemed by the Bishop of Augsburg that he requested her to undertake the charge of the convent of Edelstetten which stood in great need of reform. Mechtildis shrank from the task : she was only twenty-eight, and felt incapable of coping with the difficulties of the situation. Nevertheless, in compliance with an injunction from Pope Anastasius IV, who reminded her that obedience is better than sacrifice, she allowed herself to be installed abbess of Edelstetten. At first she was well received, for her youth and noble rank commended her to her new daughters. But when she proceeded to enforce the rule, to insist upon enclosure and generally to tighten the reins of discipline she met with opposition. It finally became necessary for the bishop to order the expulsion of the chief malcontents. The rest of the nuns were won over by the holy life of their superior, enhanced as it was by the extraordinary gifts and graces which, from this period onwards, became manifest to all. She healed the sick, restored speech to the dumb, and the sight of an eye to one of the nuns. Very often she was rapt in ecstasies which lasted for a long period. Her fame spread far and wide, and the Emperor Frederick I was proud to claim her as a kinswoman. Shortly before her death she had a premonition that her end was near ; she thereupon laid down her office and returned to Diessen, where she died on May 31, 1160.

Her life, written in some detail by Engelhard, abbot of the Cistercian monastery of Langheim (*c.* A.D. 1200), is printed in the *Acta Sanctorum*, May, vol. vii. See also Rader, *Bavaria Sancta*, vol. i, pp. 241–244. This Mechtildis is, of course, to be carefully distinguished from St Mechtildis of Hackeborn, younger sister of Abbess Gertrude of Helfta. Even Canon Chevalier, in the references he enumerates in his *Bio-bibliographie*, has occasionally confused them.

BD JAMES THE VENETIAN (A.D. 1314)

JAMES SALOMONIUS was born of a noble family at Venice in 1231. His father having died when he was very young, he was brought up partly by his mother who, however, retired after a few years into a Cistercian convent, partly by a grandmother. James was devout almost from infancy, and at the age of seventeen he distributed all his property to the poor and joined the Dominicans. Very much against his will he was chosen to fill the office of prior at Forlì, Faenza, San Severino and Ravenna, but he was finally allowed to settle down at Forlì, where he led a life of great austerity, devoting himself especially to prayer, to reading and to charity towards the sick poor, for whom he had a great affection. In addition to the Bible he regularly studied the martyrology which, as he was wont to aver, provided him with constant food for meditation. The holy friar had many ecstasies, was endowed with the gift of prophecy, and miraculously healed a number of paralytics and other sick persons. Although he suffered for four years from cancer, he never complained, appearing always to be cheerful and calm. The cancer is said to have been healed shortly before his death, which took place on May 31, 1314, when he was eighty-two years of age. Many miracles were wrought at his intercession, and the year after he died a brotherhood was formed to promote his veneration. His *cultus* was sanctioned for Forlì in 1526, for Venice by Pope Paul V, and for the Dominicans by Gregory XV.

The Bollandists, in the *Acta Sanctorum*, May, vol. vii, print from MS. sources a copious life by an anonymous contemporary. See also Procter, *Lives of Dominican Saints*, pp. 155–159.

JUNE

1 : ST ANGELA MERICI   *(Transferred from May 31. See page 432)*

ST PAMPHILUS AND HIS COMPANIONS, MARTYRS   (A.D. 309)

IN the section of his *Ecclesiastical History* devoted to the Palestinian confessors, Eusebius describes his master Pamphilus as " the most illustrious martyr of his day for philosophical learning and for every virtue ". This is not mere conventional panegyric. There is an unmistakable note of sincerity in the phrases which the historian uses when he speaks of " my lord Pamphilus ", for he adds, " it is not meet that I should mention the name of that holy and blessed man without entitling him ' my lord ' ". In grateful veneration he had himself assumed what he calls " that name thrice dear to me ", styling himself Eusebius Pamphili, and he had written his hero's biography in three volumes which were known to St Jerome but which are now no longer extant. Pamphilus, who came of a rich and honourable family, was born at Berytus (Bairut) in Phoenicia. After distinguishing himself in all branches of secular knowledge in his native city, itself renowned as a centre of learning, he went to Alexandria where he studied in the great catechetical school and came under the influence of Origen's disciple Pierius. The remainder of his life was spent at Caesarea, at that time the capital city of Palestine. There he was ordained priest ; there also he collected a splendid library which survived until the seventh century, when it was destroyed by the Arabs. He was the greatest biblical scholar of his age, and the founder of a school of sacred literature. With infinite pains and after examining and correcting many manuscripts he produced a more correct version of the Holy Scriptures than any of those then current.

This he transcribed with his own hand, and disseminated by means of copies made in his school which he bestowed upon worthy recipients, in many cases gratis —for, besides being the most generous of men, he was always anxious to encourage sacred study. An indefatigable worker, he lived a most austere, self-denying life and was remarkable for his humility. He treated his slaves and dependants as brothers and distributed to his relatives, his friends and the poor the wealth which came to him from his father. So exemplary a life found a fitting culmination in a martyr's death. In the year 308 Urban, the governor of Palestine, caused him to be apprehended, cruelly tortured and imprisoned for refusing to sacrifice to the gods. During his captivity he collaborated with Eusebius, who may have been his fellow prisoner, in writing an Apology for Origen, whose works he had greatly admired and had copied. Two years after his arrest, he was brought before Firmilian, the successor of Urban, for examination and judgement, together with Paul of Jamnia, a man of great fervour, and Valens, an aged deacon of Jerusalem, who was credited with having committed the whole of the Bible to memory. Finding them staunch in the faith, Firmilian passed upon them the sentence of death. As soon as the verdict had been pronounced, Porphyrius, a gifted young scholar whom Pamphilus had cherished as a son, boldly asked the judge for permission to bury his master's body.

Firmilian inquired if he were also a Christian, and upon receiving an answer in the affirmative directed that he should be delivered to the torturers. Although his flesh was torn to the bone and his vital organs were exposed, the youth never uttered a groan. He ended his martyrdom by slow fire, invoking the name of Jesus. After him a Cappadocian named Seleucus, who brought news of the triumph of Porphyrius and applauded his constancy, was condemned to be decapitated with the rest. So infuriated was the tyrant that even his own household was not spared ; for, having been informed that his favourite servant, the aged Theodulus, was a Christian and had embraced one of the martyrs, he had him crucified forthwith. That same evening, for a similar offence, a catechumen named Julian was burnt at a slow fire. The other confessors, Pamphilus, Paul, Valens and Seleucus, were beheaded. Their bodies, which were thrown out but left untouched by the wild beasts, were afterwards rescued and buried by the Christians.

The principal source is Eusebius, *De Martyribus Palaestinae.* The Greek text of the later and fuller recension was first edited in the *Analecta Bollandiana,* vol. xvi (1897), pp. 113–139 ; but *cf.* also vol. xxv (1906), pp. 449–502. See also Violet, in *Texte und Untersuchungen,* vol. xiv, part 4 (1895) ; Harnack and Preuschen, *Altchrist. Literaturgeschichte,* vol. i, pp. 543–550, and ii, pp. 103–105 ; DCB., vol. iv, pp. 178–179. Pamphilus is commemorated both in the early Syriac *Breviarium* and in the *Hieronymianum* (pp. 100–101, in Delehaye's commentary). The proper day is February 16, and as the two years' imprisonment spoken of by Eusebius would not have expired in 309, some authorities assign the martyrdom to the following year, but Harnack and others hold fast to 309. Compare also Bardenhewer, *Altkirchliche Literatur,* vol. ii, pp. 287–292.

ST WITE, or CANDIDA   (Date Unknown)

This unknown saint is included herein for the same reason as St Afan (November 16), namely, the contemporary existence in Great Britain of a tomb bearing the name.

The village of Whitchurch Canonicorum in Dorset, mentioned in the will of King Alfred as Hwitan Cyrcian, presumably takes its name from St Wite, and its church is dedicated in her honour (the Latin form Candida is not recorded before the sixteenth century). In the north transept of the church is her shrine. On a thirteenth-century base with three openings there rests a fourteenth-century coffin, covered by a slab of Purbeck marble : the whole is plain and without inscription, but has always been called locally the shrine of the titular saint. While repairs to the transept were being carried out in 1900 the coffin was opened at the end, and within, beside odd pieces of bone, teeth, wood and lead, was found a large leaden casket. On it, in twelfth/thirteenth-century raised letters, was the inscription *Hic Reqesct Reliqe Sce Wite ;* inside was a considerable number of bones, which the finders with commendable piety did not disturb. The coffin was cleaned out, all returned to its place, and the end sealed up.

Who was St Wite, who (if the relics be really hers) shares with St Edward the Confessor the distinction of still resting in her shrine, undisturbed by the storms of the Protestant Reformation ? It is not known, and there are no solid grounds for speculation. It is usually assumed that she was some West Saxon woman of whom all other records have perished. Another suggestion is that when in 919–920 some Bretons fled to England, bringing saints' relics with them, and King Athelstan gave the relics of some Breton saints to various churches in Wessex, he gave those of a certain St Gwen (*i.e.* White) Teirbron to Whitchurch, which his grandfather Alfred had founded. Were this surmise true it would raise a fresh problem : for who then was the saint in whose honour Alfred's church was founded ? Or did he call it " white " for some other reason ?

A third suggestion makes St Wite a man (William of Worcester was confused about the saint's sex), and identifies him with St Witta (Albinus), an Anglo-Saxon monk who died bishop of Buraburg in Hesse *c.* 760. Local place-names are invoked, connecting the neighbouring St Reyne's hill and farm with Witta's contemporary, Reginfred or Reinfred, bishop of Cologne. This theory is based partly on the mistaken idea that Witta and Reginfred were martyred with St Boniface. It is suggested that their bodies were brought home to Wessex for burial.

Though it has been used in support of the Witta theory (*cf.* Haddan and Stubbs, *Councils*, vol. iii, p. 391), it may not be without other significance that the patronal feast of St Wite's church was formerly on or about Whitsunday.

See William of Worcester's *Itinerary*, pp. 90–91 of the 1778 edition ; Dr Hugh Norris in the *Proceedings* of the Somerset Archaeological Society, vol. xxxvii (1891), pp. 44–59 ; a booklet on the church of St Wite by the Rev. E. H. H. Lee (*c.* 1928) ; and LBS., vol. iii, pp. 169–171. There is an interesting reference to the relics of " St Vita " in John Gerard's autobiography, 1951 edn., p. 50.

ST PROCULUS, "THE SOLDIER", AND ST PROCULUS, BISHOP OF BOLOGNA, MARTYRS   (A.D. *c.* 304 and 542)

POPULAR veneration to the " soldier ", St Proculus of Bologna, goes back to a very early date, and he was formerly regarded as the principal patron of that city. He suffered martyrdom for the faith—probably about the year 304. According to one tradition he was beheaded, but St Paulinus of Nola, in one of his poems, states that he was crucified. He is generally held to have been an officer in Diocletian's army, and to have suffered under Diocletian's colleague Maximian. Nothing, however, is actually known of his history. Nearly two hundred and fifty years after the death of the " soldier " saint, a second Proculus was martyred in Bologna. He was a native of the town, who was raised to the bishopric in 540. Two years later he was put to death, with numerous other Catholics, by order of Totila the Goth. When the Benedictines at the end of the fourteenth century built a church upon the site of the subterranean chapel of St Sixtus, their Abbot John caused the relics of the two saints to be translated to the new basilica, which received the name of St Proculus, or San Proclo. Both bodies were placed in the same tomb. In 1536 they were enshrined anew, and in 1584 Pope Gregory XIII sanctioned the keeping, on June 1, of an annual feast in honour of the translation.

The *cultus* of St Proculus spread to other Italian cities, and Father Delehaye suggests that St Proculus of Pozzuoli and St Proculus of Ravenna may perhaps be identified with St Proculus the soldier-saint of Bologna, while St Proculus, bishop of Terni, who is said also to have been put to death by King Totila, may quite possibly be none other than St Proculus, bishop of Bologna.

In the *Acta Sanctorum*, June, vol. i, will be found collected what little information is obtainable regarding these saints, and the matter is treated still more at length in the pre-liminary dissertation to the first volume for July (see pp. 47–65 in the original edition of 1719). Delehaye deals with the question in his *Origines du Culte des Martyrs*, pp. 300–301, 316, 328, and also in his CMH., pp. 482, 563.

ST CAPRASIUS, OR CAPRAIS (A.D. 430)

THE spiritual master and guide of St Honoratus of Lérins was a gifted and learned man named Caprasius, who had given up great worldly prospects to lead the life of a solitary in Provence. Honoratus and his brother Venantius, then very young men, were amongst those who visited him, to learn from him the way of perfection. Becoming convinced that they were called, like Abraham, to abandon their home and country, they resolved to go to the East, and Caprasius consented to accompany them. They accordingly set forth, but their health was seriously affected by the hardships and privations they had to bear. At Modon in Greece, Venantius succumbed, and after his death his companions returned to Gaul. In the deserted island of Lérins they embarked upon a mode of life which rivalled that of the fathers in the desert. Disciples came, and for them St Honoratus founded the monastery and rule which afterwards became famous throughout Christendom. St Caprasius is commonly reckoned among the abbots of Lérins—presumably because he continued to be the director of St Honoratus, and thus indirectly of the community. He does not seem actually ever to have been superior, for St Honoratus, the first ruler, was succeeded by St Maximus, who was still abbot when St Caprasius died in 430. His sanctity was extolled by St Eucherius, bishop of Lyons, and by St Hilary of Arles who had been present at his deathbed and who, in a panegyric he delivered on St Honoratus, spoke of St Caprasius as being already a saint in Heaven.

St Caprasius has already been mentioned in the account given of St Honoratus (January 16). All we know about him is derived from the *laudatio* of St Hilary of Arles ; but see the *Acta Sanctorum*, June, vol. i ; H. Moris, *L'Abbaye de Lérins* (1909) ; A. C. Cooper-Marsdin, *History of the Islands of the Lérins* (1913).

ST WISTAN (A.D. 849)

ST WISTAN is named in a calendar of the medieval abbey of Evesham, where he was eventually buried. He was a grandson of King Wiglaf of Mercia, and according to the Evesham tradition was assassinated for opposing marriage between his godfather and his widowed mother on account of their spiritual relationship. But others allege dynastic reasons.

A very extravagant miracle was believed to take place every year at Wistanstow in Shropshire on the spot where he was murdered. Immediately after his death, a shaft of light penetrating to the heavens was observed for thirty days to proceed from the place where he had been struck down. But more wonderful still, on every first day of June for centuries afterwards a crop of human hair, in commemoration apparently of the manner in which the martyr had been scalped, grew up among the grass surrounding the spot. It was visible for an hour only, and then disappeared. The case is interesting because we have what purports to be a contemporary account of the verification of the miracle. Thomas Marleberge, abbot of Evesham and reputed a man of credit, reports that Baldwin, archbishop of Canterbury, wishing to know the truth, sent two deputies to Wistanstow, Paul, abbot of Leicester, and a relative of his own who was prior of Kirkby. They waited there three days with fasting and prayer, and after this they saw the hair, felt it with their hands and kissed it. This they reported to the archbishop of Canterbury and his clergy, who made great rejoicings over the wonderful manifestation with which God continued to honour the martyr !

The principal source available is the short legend just quoted, written at the beginning of the thirteenth century by Thomas Marleberge. The " martyr's " body was at Evesham, having been transferred thither from Repton at the command of King Canute. The text is printed in the *Chronicon Abbatiae de Evesham*, in the Rolls Series, pp. 325–337. A somewhat earlier notice is provided by William of Malmesbury, *Gesta Pontificum* (Rolls Series), pp. 297–298, and by Florence of Worcester, *s.a.* 850. See also the *Acta Sanctorum*, June, vol. i, and an important paper by D. J. Bott, " The Murder of St Wistan ", in *Transactions of the Leicestershire Arch. Soc.*, vol. xxix (1953).

ST SIMEON OF SYRACUSE (A.D. 1035)

THE history of St Simeon reads like a tale of adventure, but it rests on excellent authority, for it was written within a short time of his death by his friend Eberwin, abbot of Tholey and St Martin's at Trier, at the request of Poppo, archbishop of Trier, who was engaged in promoting his cause at Rome. St Simeon was born at Syracuse in Sicily, of a Greek father, who took him when he was seven to Constantinople to be educated. Upon reaching manhood he went on a pilgrimage to the Holy Land, where he decided to settle. At first he lived with a hermit by the Jordan ; then he took the monastic habit at Bethlehem, and from thence he passed to a monastery at the foot of Mount Sinai. With the abbot's permission, he spent two years as a solitary in a little cave near the Red Sea, and later on he withdrew for some time to a hermitage on the top of Mount Sinai. After his return to the monastery he was charged with a task which he accepted very reluctantly. He was to go with another monk to Normandy to collect from Duke Richard II a promised tribute urgently needed for the support of the community. They set out, but their ship was captured by pirates, who murdered the passengers as well as the crew. Simeon jumped into the sea and swam to shore. On foot he made his way to Antioch. There he met Richard, abbot of Verdun, and Eberwin, abbot of St Martin's, both on the way home from Palestine ; a warm friendship ensued and they agreed to travel together.

At Belgrade, however, they had to separate, for Simeon and a monk called Cosmas, who had joined him at Antioch, were arrested by the governor, who would not suffer them to proceed with the French pilgrims. As soon as they were set free, the two religious attempted to retrace their steps in the direction of the sea, encountering robbers and many other perils before they succeeded in finding a ship which took them safely to Italy. From Rome they passed to the south of France, where Cosmas died. Simeon made his way alone to Rouen—only to discover that Duke Richard was dead and that his successor refused to continue the tribute. Loth to go back to the monastery empty-handed, Simeon went to visit Abbot Richard of Verdun, and Abbot Eberwin of Trier. Here he became acquainted with Archbishop Poppo, who persuaded him to accompany him as his guest and companion on a pilgrimage to Palestine. Doubtless the prelate foresaw in him an admirable cicerone. After their return to Trier, St Simeon felt once more the call to a solitary life. He chose for his retreat a tower near the Porta Nigra—afterwards known as St Simeon's Gate—and the archbishop carried out the enclosure. The rest of the saint's life was spent in prayer, penance and contemplation, though he had to endure assaults from the Devil and from men. The rumour that he was a magician practising the black art led the populace at one time to attack his tower with stones and missiles ; but, long before his death, he was venerated as a saint and a wonder-worker. His eyes were closed by Abbot Eberwin, and his funeral was attended by the entire population. He was raised to the altars of the Church seven years after his death, being the second recorded solemn papal canonization—if we regard that of St Ulric, bishop of Augsburg, as having been the first.

The Latin biography by Abbot Eberwin has been printed by Mabillon and by the Bollandists in the *Acta Sanctorum*, June, vol. i.   Consult also Hauck, *Kirchengeschichte Deutschlands*, vol. iii, and Levison's contribution on Tholey in the *Historische Aufsätze Aloys Schulte gewidmet* (1927).   There is also some discussion of his relics and other memorials at Trier, in E. Beitz, *Deutsche Kunstführer an Rhein und Mosel*, vol. ix (1928).   For Simeon's canonization, see E. W. Kemp, *Canonization and Authority* (1948), pp. 60–61. See also an important paper by Fr Maurice Coens in *Analecta Bollandiana*, vol. lxviii (1950), pp. 181–196.

ST ENECO, OR IÑIGO, ABBOT   (A.D. 1057)

ABOUT the year 1010 Sancho, Count of Castile, founded a religious house at Oña, which he placed under the rule of his daughter Tigrida, who is venerated as a saint. It was probably a double monastery, but we only hear about the nuns.   It seems that after a time they fell into lax observance and King Sancho the Great determined to restore discipline in his father-in-law's foundation.   He was an ardent supporter of the Cluniac reform, which he had introduced into his dominions.   From the abbey of San Juan de Peña, the first monastery to accept the revised rule, he drafted monks to Oña to replace the nuns, about the year 1029.   Over them he appointed a disciple of St Odilo's called Garcia who, however, died before he had consolidated his work.   It was therefore essential that a suitable successor should be found. There was living at the time in the mountains of Aragon a saintly hermit named Eneco, or Iñigo, who had a great reputation for austerity and the working of miracles.   Said to have been a native of Calatayud in the province of Bilbao, he had taken the habit at San Juan de Peña.   According to one account he had risen to be prior, when the call came to him to resume the solitary life which he had practised in his pre-monastic days.   King Sancho decided that he had all the necessary qualifications, but the efforts he made through envoys to induce Eneco to leave his retreat were unavailing.   Only when he himself visited the saint did he succeed in persuading him to take up the charge.

The choice proved an excellent one.   The abbey under his government increased rapidly in sanctity as well as in numbers and Sancho, well pleased by these results, showered gifts and privileges upon this favoured foundation.   St Eneco's influence extended far beyond the walls of the monastery.   He made peace between communities and individuals who had long been at bitter variance and he tamed men of violent passions.   When a severe drought threatened a total failure of the crops, St Eneco prayed, and rain fell in abundance.   On another occasion he is said to have fed a great multitude with three loaves.   He was two leagues from the abbey when he was seized with the malady which was to prove fatal.   He was carried home, and upon his arrival he asked that refreshment should be given to the boys who had escorted the party with torches.   As no one else had seen the boys, it was concluded that they must have been angels.   He passed away on June 1, 1057, deeply lamented even by Jews and Moors.   St Eneco seems to have been canonized by Pope Alexander III about a century later.

There is a short Latin life of St Eneco which has been printed by Mabillon and by the Bollandists in the *Acta Sanctorum*, June, vol. i, but by far the most reliable information concerning him is that furnished by Fr Fidel Fita, in two contributions to the *Boletin de la real Academia de la Historia*, Madrid, vol. xxvii (1895), pp. 76–136, and vol. xxxviii (1901), pp. 206–213.   In these articles we find evidence of a full liturgical *cultus* at an early date.

See also Florez, *España Sagrada*, vol. xxvii, pp. 284–350.   There is some obscurity regarding the manner and time of the canonization, but it is certain that in 1259 Pope Alexander IV granted an indulgence to those who visited the church of Oña " on the feast of Blessed Eneco, confessor, formerly abbot of the said monastery " ; see further E. W. Kemp, *Canonization and Authority* (1948), pp. 83–85.   It would seem to have been out of devotion to the organizing genius who made Oña famous that St Ignatius Loyola received in baptism the name of Iñigo.   Several early signatures of his are preserved in this form.   See the *Analecta Bollandiana*, vol. lii (1934), p. 448, and vol. lxix (1951), pp. 295–301.

ST THEOBALD OF ALBA   (A.D. 1150)

HONOURED throughout Piedmont as the patron of cobblers and porters, St Theobald Roggeri is specially venerated at his birthplace, Vico, near Mondovi, and at Alba, where he spent the greater part of his life.   His parents were well-to-do people who gave him a good education, but the respect in which his family was held seemed to Theobald incompatible with the lowly estate to which a Christian is called.   Forsaking his home, he went to Alba, where he placed himself under a shoemaker to learn the trade.   So reliable and proficient did he prove himself that his master on his death-bed suggested his marrying the daughter of the house and taking over the business.   Not wishing to grieve an old man whose days were numbered, Theobald returned an evasive answer.   He had, however, vowed himself to celibacy and, as soon as his master was buried, he took leave of the widow to whom he handed all his earnings for distribution to the poor.   Penniless, he then set forth on a pilgrimage to Compostela.   Upon his return to Alba, instead of resuming his trade, he hired himself out to carry sacks of corn and other merchandise.   As he made his way through the streets and alleys he came into contact with sufferers of all kinds, to whom he proved a ministering angel ; two-thirds of his earnings he always gave to the poor.   In spite of the strenuous character of his work he undertook severe fasts and practised other austerities.   Until the day of his death he took his rest upon the bare ground.   To expiate a malediction he had uttered under provocation, he undertook for the remainder of his life to sweep out the cathedral church of St Laurence and tend the lamps.   A number of miracles are reported to have taken place at his tomb and led to a great development of his *cultus*.

In spite of a still surviving veneration in the diocese of Alba, it must be confessed that we have no reliable materials for the life of St Theobald.   The Bollandists in the *Acta Sanctorum*, June, vol. i, were reduced to the necessity of printing a Latin translation of an account compiled in Italian as late as 1626 by D. Passoni.   He professed to have had access to authentic documents, but as these in some mysterious way perished in that very year or shortly afterwards, it is impossible not to regard his narrative with considerable suspicion. There are a number of small devotional booklets of more recent date, but they all depend for their facts upon the story as told by Passoni.

BD JOHN PELINGOTTO   (A.D. 1304)

JOHN PELINGOTTO was the son of a prosperous merchant of Urbino, but he himself from childhood cared nothing for the things of this world.   He became a Franciscan tertiary and would have retired into a hermitage had it not been for the determined opposition of his parents ; out of regard for their wishes he remained at home, where he lived a life of prayer and austerity.   For a time he shut himself up and never went out except to church.   Then, in obedience to a call to serve our Lord in His suffering members, he emerged from his retreat.   During the rest of his life he went about tending the sick and seeking out the destitute poor to whom he gave the greater portion of his own food and the clothes off his back.   To the mortification of his family he would sally forth in a garment made of sacking and old pieces. Regarding himself as the vilest of creatures he used odd means of attracting the contempt of his fellow men.   Once on Passion Sunday he went to the cathedral with a rope tied round his neck, like a criminal, but, as he knelt in prayer in the Lady chapel he fell into an ecstasy which lasted many hours, and from which he was roused with difficulty.   On another occasion, when it was bitterly cold, he made his way to the market-place and spent the day amid a crowd of beggars and rogues, exposed to public derision, until at last, more dead than alive, he was discovered and rescued by his parents.   In spite of all his efforts, John came to be venerated in his own city as a holy man who was also a prophet and a wonder-worker, and when, four years before his death, he went to Rome for the jubilee with two fellow tertiaries, he was saluted by a complete stranger as " the saint from Urbino ".

There is a life by a contemporary, which has been printed in the *Acta Sanctorum*, June, vol. i ; but see also the *Acta Ordinis Fratrum Minorum* for 1918 and 1919, and Wadding, *Annales Ord. Min.*, vol. vi, pp. 38–42.   The *cultus* of Bd John Pelingotto was confirmed in 1918.   The official decree, which contains a biographical summary, will be found in the *Acta Apostolicae Sedis*, vol. x (1918), pp. 513–516.

BD HERCULANUS OF PIEGARO   (A.D. 1451)

ONE of the foremost preachers of the fifteenth century was Bd Herculanus, a native of Piegaro in Emilia.   He entered the Franciscan convent of the strict observance at Sarteano, and for a time led a life of retirement and prayer.   After his ordination, however, he was sent forth to preach, and at once displayed extraordinary powers in winning souls to God.   Wherever he went he spoke of the sufferings of our Lord, frequently by his eloquence reducing his hearers to tears, and by his personal holiness inspiring them to reform their lives.   At Lucca, he was preaching during Lent whilst the city was being besieged by the Florentines.   When provisions began to fail and the inhabitants contemplated surrender, Bd Herculanus bade them hold out, promising them relief after Easter if they would do penance and reform their lives.   His prophecy was fulfilled ; the Florentines raised the siege and the city was delivered.   If he urged penance on others he set the example himself by his own great austerity.   He would go without food for days, and when he ate, he confined himself to a little bread and vegetables.   He died in the convent at Castronovo, which he himself had founded, in Tuscany.   Five years after his death his body was found to be incorrupt, although it had been buried in a damp place. Pope Pius IX beatified the holy friar in 1860.

There is a short notice of Bd Herculanus in the *Acta Sanctorum* in vol. vi, May ; and a fuller account in the *Analecta Juris Pontificii*, vol. v (1861), pp. 134–139.   All our information seems to be derived from the chronicle of Mariano of Florence, from whom S. Razzi, Luke Wadding, and other later writers have borrowed.   See also Léon, *Auréole Séraphique* (Eng. trans.), vol. ii, pp. 297–300.

BD JOHN STOREY, MARTYR   (A.D. 1571)

THE life of Bd John Storey recalls in some respects the career of his more famous contemporary St Thomas More, but perhaps the contrast is even more striking than the resemblance.   Born about 1504 and educated at Oxford for the law, Storey was selected to fill one of the lectureships founded by Henry VIII's commissioners on the ground that he was " the most noted civilian and canonist of his time ".

He thus became Oxford's first Regius professor of civil law.   He was also for two years principal of Broadgates Hall, now Pembroke College.   This post he resigned in 1537 to be admitted to Doctors' Commons, and to practise as an advocate.   He married and entered Parliament for Hindon in Wiltshire.   He had taken the oath of supremacy in the reign of Henry VIII, but in the first parliament of Edward VI he boldly opposed the Act of Uniformity, as well as the new liturgy.   In an impassioned speech he exclaimed, " Woe to thee, O land, whose king is a child ", and the House of Commons was so greatly incensed that he was committed to the Tower for three months.   Soon after his liberation he retired with his family to Louvain, where he could freely practise his religion, but Mary's accession brought him back to England, and he was made chancellor of the dioceses of Oxford and London, and dean of Arches.   In his capacity of chancellor he took a prominent part under Bishop Bonner in enforcing the queen's stern measures against Protestants ; he was also her proctor at Cranmer's trial.

The beginning of Elizabeth's reign found him still in England, and he was the foremost opponent of the Bill of Supremacy in the new Parliament.   But he was soon arrested and suffered imprisonment, first in the Fleet and afterwards in the Marshalsea.   On the eve of being brought to trial he effected his escape, finding his way once more to Louvain.   In his exile he and his dependants were so impoverished that he was reduced to becoming a pensioner of the king of Spain, and to accepting the office of searcher for heretical books and other contraband in English ships stationed at Antwerp.   This post furnished his enemies with the means of capturing him.   Storey was inveigled into a ship secretly bound for England and, as soon as he was in the hold examining the cargo, the hatches were closed, the anchor raised and he found himself trapped.   At Yarmouth he was delivered to the authorities.   During his trial for treason he refused to plead, asserting that he was no longer an English citizen, but a subject of the king of Spain.   He was condemned to death and his execution at Tyburn was carried out with even greater barbarity than was usual.

Though Storey has been accused by Foxe, the martyrologist, and in modern times by A. F. Pollard, of being " the most active of all Queen Mary's agents in bringing heretics to trial and the stake ", he was able, when this point was pressed against him before his judges, to present a very convincing defence.   He said, for example : " when at one time twenty-eight were condemned to the fire . . . Mr Fecknam [the last abbot of Westminster] and I laboured to the Lord Cardinal Poole, showing that they were *nescientes quid fecerint.*   The cardinal and we did sue together to the queen . . . and so we obtained pardon for them all, saving an old woman that dwelt about Paul's Churchyard ; she would not convert and therefore was burned.   The rest of them received absolution and that with all reverence.   Search the register and you shall find it.   Yea and it was my procurement that there should be no more burnt in London ; for I saw well that it would not prevail, and therefore we sent them into odd corners, into the country."

The best account, based on contemporary records, of John Storey, is that contained in Camm, LEM., vol. ii, pp. 14–110.   See also on the general situation in England, J. H. Pollen, *The English Catholics in the Reign of Elizabeth* (1920).

THE MARTYRS OF JAPAN, II   (A.D. 1617-1632)

IN the year 1614 a terrible era of persecution began in Japan, heralded by the decree of the former *shōgun*, Ieyasu (still the real ruler), banishing all Christian teachers from the country. Measures taken became more and more severe, and, while there were many glorious exceptions, the number of flagrant apostasies in the families of the Christian *daimyōs* had given terrible scandal. Hidetada, the son and successor of Ieyasu, launched edict after edict, each one more relentless than the preceding. On pain of being burned alive, all Japanese were forbidden to have the slightest relations with priests. The same punishment was extended to the women and children, and even to the neighbours of those who had rendered themselves guilty of an infraction of the law. The *daimyōs* were rendered responsible for the Christians who were discovered in the territories they ruled.

One of the more prominent *daimyōs* in the early part of the seventeenth century was Date Masamune, of Sendai. Some of the missionaries believed him to be a fervent catechumen, but though he had favoured the Christians he never went so far as to receive baptism. He had, however, become very friendly with the Spanish Franciscan, Louis Sotelo, who afterwards died a martyr's death, and Sotelo, writing at a later date to Pope Gregory XV, even then describes Date as eager to have the Christian faith preached in his dominions. How far Date was sincere is an extremely doubtful matter, but in 1613, either of his own initiative or yielding to Sotelo's instances, he sent an embassy to the king of Spain and the pope. Father Sotelo himself and Hasekura Rokuyemon, Date's most trusted henchman, were the leaders, and this deputation of some 250 Japanese, who were vaguely regarded as representing the " King " of Japan, made a considerable impression both at the Spanish court and in Rome. But before the ambassadors arrived in Europe, the era of persecution had begun in their own country. When the news of this deputation overseas, about which he had not been consulted, reached Ieyasu, that crafty and extremely capable ruler, whose life-work it had been to break the feudal power of the *daimyōs*, allowed Date Masamune to feel the full weight of his displeasure. Probably he discerned in this embassy the germ of a design on Date's part to strengthen himself against the authority of the *shōgun* by forming a European alliance. In any case he was determined that this audacious vassal should not in future carry out a policy of toleration for Christian missionary work, and he made his will known very clearly to that effect.

As soon, then, as the ambassadors (without Sotelo, who was detained in Mexico for many months) returned to Japan in the year 1620, it seems that under Date's orders Hasekura, who had been baptized at Madrid in the presence of the king of Spain, incontinently apostasized with all the members of the embassy. Moreover, in the course of the next few years a systematic attempt to round up the Christians was carried out in Masamune's territory.

The imposing band of two hundred and five martyrs of this persecution, each separately mentioned by name, who were beatified by Pope Pius IX on July 7, 1867, included many Dominicans. Foremost among these was the Spaniard, BD ALPHONSUS NAVARETTE, who left the Philippines in 1611 for the much more dangerous mission-field of Japan. At Nagasaki, in co-operation with members of other religious orders, Father Alphonsus, amid many other good works, organized confraternities for tending the sick and for the rescue of infants exposed to death by their heartless parents. The good Dominican's fervour often led him to court danger without thought of the consequences. On one occasion he boldly faced and upbraided a hostile crowd of Japanese who had laid hands upon some poor Christian women. When a new development of persecution was reported at Omura, it is said that, in the course of an ecstasy in which he was seen raised from the ground, Father Alphonsus was inspired to go thither to confirm the faith of the suffering Christians. Crowds sought his ministrations, as well as those of an Augustinian friar BD FERDINAND AYALÀ. The sensation thus caused drew the attention of the governor, and they were taken into custody. At first they were treated with a show of consideration, but when the Christians of the neighbourhood, including some highly-placed ladies, still continued to haunt the locality of their confinement, order was given for their execution. They were accordingly beheaded, in company with a Japanese catechist, on June 1, 1617.

There were many other heroic Dominicans who suffered in Japan, particularly on September 10, 1622, when five priests of that order, together with four scholastics, were put to death at Nagasaki by the torment of a slow fire. The victims of this refinement of cruelty numbered twenty-two in all, including many Franciscans and Jesuits, while thirty others, mostly Japanese converts, with women and children, were beheaded on the same occasion. Some account of the scene, perhaps the most dramatic in all the annals of martyrdom, which was witnessed by more than thirty thousand spectators, will be found under September 10, upon which day the Franciscan and Jesuit martyrs are commemorated.

When BD JOHN BAPTIST MACHADO as a little boy heard his elders talking about Japan, he made up his mind that some day he would go there as a missionary, and that determination never left him. He was of Portuguese origin, having been born in the Azores. His wish was fulfilled when in 1609 he was sent as a Jesuit to the Japanese mission. After working for eight years at Nagasaki, he was called to the Goto islands, but was arrested immediately after landing. He was taken back to Japan and imprisoned at Omura. The conditions were dreadful. But he had with him a Spanish Franciscan, BD PETER OF CUERVA, who had distinguished himself by the extraordinary speed with which he learned the language when preparing for the Japanese mission a dozen years earlier; and the two were able to offer Mass daily until the day appointed for their execution. On that day the two priests heard one another's confession and said the litany of the saints together, and then walked, crucifix in hand and followed by a large crowd, to the place of execution between Omura and Nagasaki. After Bd Peter had addressed the people, the martyrs embraced each other and cheerfully laid their heads upon the block. With them perished a Japanese youth called Leo, who had been Bd John Baptist's server. It was May 22, 1617: they were the first martyrs of the second great Japanese persecution.

The circumstances in which BD LEONARD KIMURA and his four companions gave final testimony of their constancy recall the scenes which must have occurred when the early Roman martyrs laid down their lives in the arena. Twenty thousand people, we are told, from Nagasaki and the neighbourhood had assembled to witness the spectacle, many of them being Christians. The five victims were burnt at five stakes on an eminence beside the sea-front. There were three Japanese, a Korean and a Portuguese, but they had no priest among them. Leonard Kimura was a Jesuit lay-brother who, though of good family and education, had refused ordination out of humility. It is stated that he was a collateral descendant of another Kimura, who had been among the first to befriend St Francis Xavier on his arrival in Japan three-quarters of a century earlier. The martyr, who in 1619 was forty-five years old, had been busy since early manhood in instructing and catechizing his heathen fellow countrymen. Even during the two and half years in which he had lain in prison he had found means to baptize ninety-six of those who shared his confinement or had been able to visit him there. His four fellow martyrs were laymen who had been arrested for harbouring or aiding Father Charles Spinola and other priests. During a long imprisonment threats and promises were powerless to shake their constancy, and the gruesome sentence that they were to be burnt alive was received by them with demonstrations of joy. It is stated that even amid the flames they betrayed no sign of anguish. Their charred remains were thrown into the sea, but the Christians secured some fragments, though without being able to tell to which particular martyr each relic belonged. The day of their passion was November 18, 1619.

On his second, and successful, attempt to reach Japan in the opening years of the seventeenth century, Bd Charles Spinola was accompanied by BD JEROME DE ANGELIS, S.J. He was a Sicilian who, giving up the law, joined the society and was ordained priest in Lisbon. He was a successful missionary for twenty years in Japan, chiefly in the central island, Hondo. At the height of the persecution of Hidetada, in 1623, he was at Yedo (Tokyo), where he was denounced and thrown into prison, together with BD FRANCIS GALVEZ, O.F.M., and many others. Fr Francis was a Castilian ; while pursuing his studies at Valencia he offered himself to the Franciscans, and in due course he was sent to the Philippine Islands, where he learnt Japanese, and three years later went to Japan. In the course of his mission he translated several religious works into Japanese, but he was soon exiled to Manila. After a time he was given permission to return to Japan if he could get there, and eventually succeeded from Macao in 1618, by disguising himself as a Negro and working his passage. He ministered secretly and in the greatest danger for five years before he was captured.

On December 4, 1623, fifty Christians were taken out of Yedo to be burnt alive at slow fires on a neighbouring hill. They were led by the two priests. It is related that a Japanese nobleman riding by asked who these noble-looking criminals were, and on being told, exclaimed that he also was a Christian and ought to be among them. His example fired a number of other Christians among the bystanders to fall on their knees and make their profession of faith, so that the officers were in fear of a riot and hurried on the execution. Of these fifty martyrs Bd Jerome and Bd Francis were beatified in the decree of July, 1867, and with them was joined BD SIMON YEMPO, who suffered on the same occasion. He was one of a number of Japanese inmates of a Buddhist monastery who received baptism, and he became a catechist for the Jesuit missionaries.

There were two beatified Jesuit martyrs named Carvalho who were put to death in Japan in the year 1624 (and an Augustinian friar of the same name in 1632). They were both Portuguese, but apparently not related. The places where they suffered were many hundred miles apart, and while one died in February from cold and exposure, the other in August was burnt alive by a slow fire. BD JAMES CARVALHO (called Diogo in Portuguese, Diego in Spanish, and often Didacus in Latin) was born at Coimbra in 1578. He left Portugal for the East in 1600, was ordained priest at Macao, and laboured for five years in the neighbourhood of Kyôto, or, as it was then called, " Miyako " (*i.e.* capital), until the terrible persecution broke out in 1614. Whether Father Diogo was deported or simply withdrew in obedience to the order of his superiors is not clear, but we know that at the close of 1614 he went from Macao with Father Buzomi to begin a mission in Cochin-China. Returning to Japan in 1617, he spent the rest of his days under very arduous conditions in the more northern districts of the central island. On two occasions at least, he crossed over to Yezo (now called Hokkaido) where he was the first Christian priest to offer the holy sacrifice of the Mass, and where he came into contact with the Ainos, of whom he left an interesting description in one of his letters.

The persecution came to a crisis in the winter of 1623-24. Father Diogo who, with a band of fugitive Christians, had hidden himself in a remote valley among the hills, was tracked by the footsteps of the party in the snow. We have a terrible account of the barbarity with which they were treated after their capture. In spite of the fact that a blizzard was raging and that the cold was intense, they were stripped almost naked and left to wait for many hours in the open, without shelter of any kind. Eventually they were fettered and compelled to travel on foot several days' journey to Sendai. Two of the band, unable to keep up, were beheaded on the spot, and the escort tested the keenness of their blades by cutting to pieces the naked bodies.

When they reached Sendai the weather still remained exceptionally severe, and on February 18 Father Diogo and some nine others, Japanese, were stripped of their clothing, tied to stakes, and compelled to stand and sit alternately, each in a shallow pit of freezing water which reached above their knees. After three hours they were taken out and invited to apostatize. Two of them, utterly incapable of movement, died shortly afterwards on the sand on which they had thrown themselves in helpless agony. Father Diogo, owing perhaps to the fact that a certain consideration had been shown him during the journey, gave proof of greater vitality than the rest. He sat down on his heels in Japanese fashion and recollected himself in prayer. During an interval of four days fresh attempts were made to persuade them to renounce Christianity, but without result; and on February 22 the same torment was repeated. Seven of them died in the course of the afternoon, praying aloud as long as strength remained, and encouraged by the priest with comforting words until the last. At sunset Bd Diogo alone survived, and from some faithful Christians who hung about the piteous scene it was learnt that he expired just before midnight.* In the morning the bodies of the victims were hacked to pieces and thrown into the river, but the head of Father Carvalho and those of four others were recovered and preserved as relics.

BD MICHAEL CARVALHO was born at Braga in Portugal in 1577, entered the Jesuit novitiate in 1597, and was sent at his own request to India in 1602. There, in the College of Goa, he was found so useful as a teacher that obedience detained him for fifteen years, preparing others for the active missionary work for which his own soul thirsted. At last his desire was gratified, and after an incredibly toilsome journey (in the course of which he was shipwrecked at Malacca, made his way to Macao, and was thence recalled to Manila in the Philippines), he succeeded in getting to Japan in the disguise of a soldier. For two years, despite the persecution, he ministered to the Christians in the island of Amakusa, opposite Nagasaki. Having been summoned to hear confessions in another province, he was betrayed by a spy and captured. For more than twelve months he was kept a prisoner in irons, but managed to get letters out of prison, several of which, still preserved to

---

* An examination of the map shows that Sendai is in approximately the same latitude as Cordova, Messina and San Francisco. Moreover, being on the coast, it can be at no great elevation above sea-level. There is consequently no reason to suppose the existence of any extremely low temperature in February, but it was freezing, for the witnesses speak of ice forming on the water. For those already exhausted by exposure a greater cold would have meant a quicker and more merciful death.

us, manifest an extraordinary desire to give his life for the faith by any form of torment the persecutors might devise.

His imprisonment was shared by a Spanish Dominican priest, BD PETER VASQUEZ, and by three Franciscans, all named Louis.   BD LOUIS SOTELO, also a Spaniard, is mentioned elsewhere in this notice.   The Japanese BD LOUIS SASANDA (whose father Michael also was a martyr) became a friar minor in Mexico, and was ordained in Manila in 1622.   BD LOUIS BABA was a Japanese catechist, who had been in Europe with Father Sotelo.   He was clothed as a Franciscan in prison. These five were all put to death by being roasted at a slow fire, on August 25, 1624.

On June 20, 1626, a group of nine martyrs, members of the Society of Jesus or associated with it, were burned alive at Nagasaki.   Their leader, BD FRANCIS PACHFCO, was a native of Portugal.   From an early age he had cherished visions of attaining the crown of martyrdom in the mission field, and in 1584 he became a Jesuit.   After a short stay in Japan he was recalled ; but when Father Louis Cerquiera was named bishop there he took Father Pacheco with him as his vicar general.   After the bishop's death in 1614 and the banishment of Christian clergy, Father Pacheco came back again disguised as a merchant.   For eleven years he continued his labours, in constant danger of his life, enduring great hardships and being compelled frequently to change his abode.   Shortly before his arrest he received a papal mandate to act as episcopal administrator for the whole of the Church in Japan.   Father Pacheco's companions in martyrdom were BD BALTHASAR DE TORRES and BD JOHN BAPTIST ZOLA, a Spanish and Italian Jesuit respectively, together with a Korean catechist, BD VINCENT CAUN, two Japanese Jesuits (one a novice), BD JOHN KINSACO and BD CASPAR SADAMAZU, and three Japanese catechists, BB. PETER RINXEI, PAUL XINSUKI and MICHAEL TOZO.

September 6, 1627, saw the martyrdom of another Jesuit, BD THOMAS TZUGI, a Japanese of noble family in the Umura province, who had been a Christian from his boyhood.   During the persecution he carried on his work, disguised as a porter, but at one moment lost his nerve and asked to be released from his vows—but within twenty-four hours he had recovered himself.   In the end Bd Thomas was betrayed by an apostate, and after a cruel imprisonment of more than a year he was sentenced to be burnt alive at Nagasaki.   He refused to let his family buy his reprieve with bribes ; and the courage with which he met his death, singing " Laudate Dominum, omnes gentes " amidst the flames, produced a great impression.   With him suffered BD LOUIS MAKI, a Japanese in whose house he had celebrated the holy Mysteries.

BD LOUIS SOTELO, burnt at Simabura on August 25, 1624, was a remarkable man and a very able missionary, who went to Japan in 1603.   After he had preached there for ten years, making a large number of conversions and breaking entirely fresh ground, he was, as we have seen, sent with Hasekura Rokuyemon and a large suite on an embassy to Pope Paul V and the king of Spain by Date Masamune. They travelled *via* Mexico, where on Holy Saturday 1614, seventy-eight members of the embassy were baptized (they all afterwards apostatized).   Bd Louis accompanied the ambassador throughout his peregrinations in Spain and Italy, an office which required much tact and earned some obloquy for the Franciscan, for behind the embassy lay considerations of both ecclesiastical and secular politics (the last named *vis-à-vis* the Dutch in the Far East).   Bd Louis landed in Japan again in 1622, at the height of the persecution ; two years later he gained his crown.   Of another Franciscan, BD ANTONY OF TUY, the commissary general in Japan wrote :

" He was a tireless worker and gained very many souls for God. He worked night and day, hearing confessions, baptizing, catechizing, raising those who had fallen through fear. Within a short time he thus reconciled more than two thousand, and many of them persevered unto martyrdom. In these difficult days when Christianity was everywhere reviled and suppressed he baptized more than a thousand pagans. For the ten years of his ministry nothing could check his zeal." Bd Antony was burned at Nagasaki on September 8, 1628, after being in prison for many months. Among the secular tertiaries included in these *beati* are some who are claimed equally by the Friars Minor and by the Friars Preachers, such as BB. JOHN TOMAKI and his four sons, all under sixteen ; BB. LOUIS NIFAKI and his sons, aged five and two ; and BD LOUISA, an aged woman who was burnt with her husband and daughter.

The last in order of time of the martyrs in Japan beatified in 1867 were BD ANTONY IXIDA and his companions. Antony was a native of Japan, born there in 1569. After his ordination to the priesthood as a Jesuit, he played a big part by his eloquence, energy and knowledge of his people, in reconciling apostates and making new conversions after the persecution of 1597. During the persecution that began in 1614 he continued to work among its victims in the province of Arima until the end of 1629, when, going on a sick-call to Nagasaki, he was there captured.

He was sent to Omura, but was then apparently forgotten, for he remained in gaol for two years. At the end of that time he was taken back with some companions to Nagasaki, and it was then decided to make a determined effort to induce these men to apostatize by the application of a quite ferocious form of torture. There lies between Nagasaki and Simabara a volcanic mountain called Unsen, water from the sulphurous hot springs of which produces ulceration of the human flesh. The bodies of the confessors were sprinkled with this corrosive fluid until they were covered with virulent sores, and they were then laid on beds of prickly straw. When they remained firm, the ulcers were carefully dressed by physicians, and when they had gained some degree of ease their flesh was again sprinkled. And so on. This went on for thirty-three days, until, in despair of bringing about apostasy, the persecutors slew their victims by burning on September 3, 1632. The five blessed companions of Bd Antony were three Augustinians, BB. BARTHOLO-MEW GUTIERREZ (a Mexicàn), FRANCIS ORTEGA and VINCENT CARVALHO, and two Franciscans, a priest tertiary, the Japanese BD JEROME, and a lay-brother, BD GABRIEL OF FONSECA.

The object of the persecutors who perpetrated these crimes was to destroy Christianity, not Christians. And therefore, as in some other persecutions, every effort was made by the infliction of physical and moral suffering to induce apostasy ; the ingenious tortures which were sometimes inflicted with this object are sickening to read, and justly deserve the epithet diabolical. Many broke down under them Many more, priests, religious, men and women, boys and girls in their 'teens, even small children, were faithful to the terrible and glorious end. For other martyrs in Japan, see under February 5 and September 10.

See G. Boero, *Relazione della gloriosa Morte di* 205 *B. Martiri nel Giappone* (1867) ; French translation, *Les* 205 *Martyrs du Japon*, 1868 ; L. Delplace, *Le Catholicisme au Japon* (1869, 2 vols.) ; L. C. Profillet, *Le Martyrologe de l'Église du Japon* (1897, 3 vols.) ; L. Pagès, *Histoire de la religion chrétienne au Japon* (1869, 2 vols.). For Navarette, see Procter, *Lives of the Dominican Saints*, pp. 159–162 ; for Machado, Broeckaert's *Vie du B. Charles Spinola*, pp. 133, 225–226 ; and for M. Carvalho, Guilhermy's *Ménologe de l'Assistance de Portugal*, vol. ii, pp. 172–174. See also C. R. Boxer, *The Christian Century in Japan* (1951).

BD FELIX OF NICOSIA   (A.D. 1787)

BD FELIX was born in the Sicilian town of Nicosia, where his father was a poor cobbler.   Both his parents were very devout, and the child, who seemed to have imbibed piety with his mother's milk, had from his earliest years a horror of the least shadow of sin.   In the shoemaker's shop to which he was sent at the age of six, he suffered so acutely from the foul language prevalent that he would sometimes stop his ears with wool in order not to hear.   A complete reform in that respect is said to have been effected as the result of a miracle which God wrought through the innocent lad.   One of the workmen, who had accidentally made a cut across the leather of the upper of a shoe, swore a horrible oath.   The shrinking apprentice beside him winced as though struck by a blow.   Then, quickly recovering himself, he seized the shoe, passed his finger moistened with saliva across the slit, and re-turned the shoe undamaged and unmarked to the offender in the presence of his amazed fellow workmen.   After his parents' death, when he was about twenty, James—to give him his baptismal name—applied to the Capuchins for admission, but was refused.   Disappointed but undaunted, the young man held on, working, praying, mortifying himself and periodically renewing his application.   At the end of seven years he was accepted at the convent of Mistreta, where he received the habit together with the name of Felix.

Upon his profession a year later he was recalled to Nicosia, to assist the questing brother on his mendicant rounds.   In private, Felix practised great austerities ; in public his love of God expressed itself in charity towards his neighbours.   He was endowed with the gift of healing temporal and spiritual diseases, and he delighted in tending the sick.   Numberless sinners were reclaimed through his efforts, including poor prisoners to whom he ministered food and consolation.   Wherever he went he did good ; he worked, he prayed, he offered up his penances for all without distinction.   When a malignant epidemic was decimating Cerami in March 1777, the local superiors of the order, anxious to relieve the sufferers, applied for Brother Felix.   He was then over sixty, but he responded eagerly to the call. Fearlessly and indefatigably he went about ministering to the sick, and his labours were crowned with abundant success.   " So be it for the love of God " were the words with which he accompanied his miracles of healing, and for the love of God he may be said to have lived his whole life.   Second only to love came obedience. He never did anything without permission, and when he was overtaken by his last illness he asked the guardian to give him leave to die.   He passed away on May 31, 1787, at the age of seventy-two.

A brief account of Felix of Nicosia is given in P. Seeböck, *Die Herrlichkeit der Katholischen Kirche in ihren Heiligen und Seligen des* 19 *Jahrhunderts* (1900), pp. 330 *seq.* He was beatified in 1888, on which occasion a somewhat fuller biography was published by Fr Gesualdo da Bronte.

2 : SS. MARCELLINUS AND PETER, Martyrs   (A.D. 304)

SS. MARCELLINUS and Peter are amongst the Roman saints who are commemorated daily in the canon of the Mass.   Marcellinus was a prominent priest in the City during the reign of Diocletian, and Peter is said to have been an exorcist.   From a misreading of the *Hieronymianum* it has been inferred that other martyrs perished with them, numbering forty-four in all, but for this there is no evidence.   Their quite unreliable *passio* states that they were apprehended and cast into prison, where Marcellinus and Peter were zealous in strengthening the faithful and in making new converts, amongst whom were the jailer Arthemius with his wife and daughter.   According to the same authority, all were condemned to death by Serenus, or Severus, the magistrate.   Marcellinus and Peter were privately conveyed to a wood called the Silva Nigra, and there beheaded, in order that their place of burial should not be known.   The secret, however, was divulged, possibly by the executioner, who subsequently became a Christian.   Two devout women, Lucilla and Firmina, rescued their relics and interred them honourably in the Catacomb of St Tiburtius on the Via Lavicana.   Pope Damasus, who composed an epitaph for the tomb of these two martyrs, stated that he learnt the particulars of their execution when a boy from the lips of their executioner.   Over their tomb Constantine built a church, in which he caused his mother, St Helen, to be buried. The bodies of the saints were sent in 827 by Pope Gregory IV to Eginhard, Charlemagne's former secretary, to enrich the monasteries he had built or restored, and were eventually deposited at Seligenstadt, fourteen miles from Frankfort-on-the-Main.   Accounts are preserved to us recording every detail of the miracles which attended this very famous translation.   That there was an active *cultus* of these two martyrs in Rome is proved by such inscriptions as, " Sancte Petr(e) Marcelline, suscipite vestrum alumnum ".

The legendary *passio*, with other matter, is printed in the *Acta Sanctorum*, June, vol. i. Consult especially J. P. Kirsch, *Die Märtyrer der Katakombe " ad duas Lauros "* (1920), pp. 2–5 ; Marucchi, in the *Nuovo Bullettino*, 1898, pp. 137–193 ; Wilpert in the *Römische Quartalschrift*, 1908, pp. 73–91.   On the translation, M. Bondois can only be read with extreme caution ; see *Analecta Bollandiana*, vol. xxvi (1907), pp. 478–481.   A better study of this question is that of K. Esselborn, *Die Übertragung*, etc. (1925).   An English version of the story of the translation has been published by B. Wendell (1926).

ST ERASMUS, Bishop and Martyr   (A.D. 303 ?)

St Erasmus, or St Elmo, formerly widely venerated as the patron of sailors and as one of the Fourteen Holy Helpers, is joined with the above martyrs in the Mass and Office of the Western church to-day.   In the *Acta Sanctorum* he is described as bishop of Formiae, in the Campagna, and we know from St Gregory the Great that his relics were preserved in the cathedral of that town in the sixth century. When Formiae was destroyed by the Saracens in 842, the body of St Erasmus was translated to Gaëta, of which city he still remains a principal patron.   Nothing is actually known of his history, his so-called " acts " being late compilations based on legends which confuse him with a namesake, a martyr bishop of Antioch. According to the oldest of these spurious biographies, St Erasmus of Formiae was a Syrian bishop who, during the persecution under Diocletian, fled to Mount Lebanon, where he lived as a solitary and was fed by a raven.   He was discovered, haled before the emperor, beaten with whips and lead-loaded clubs, and rolled in pitch which was then ignited.   As he remained unhurt he was cast into prison to be starved to death.   An angel, however, released him and conveyed him to the Roman province of Illyricum.   There he effected numerous conversions, but was subjected to other tortures, including the iron chair and a red-hot cuirass.   The angel again saved him and brought him to Formiae, where he died of his wounds.

In Belgium, France and elsewhere St Erasmus is popularly represented with a large aperture in his body through which his intestines have been wound, or are being wound, round a windlass which stands beside him. He is accordingly invoked against cramp and colic, especially in children. There is nothing in the legendary history of St Erasmus of Formiae to connect him with that particular form of torture. The blue lights sometimes seen at mastheads before and after storms were reckoned by Neapolitan seamen as signs of their patron's protection and were called by them " St Elmo's Fire ".

There is no reasonable doubt that the appellation St Elmo or St Telmo is etymologically derived from St Erasmus, which became Eramus, then Ermus and finally Ermo. From this we get Elmo, just as Catalina comes from Catharina. Now the blue electrical discharges which under certain atmospheric conditions are seen on the masts or rigging of ships were formerly called St Elmo's lights, because St Erasmus, honoured at first as the patron of mariners, was believed to manifest his protection in this manner after the storm had passed. But when Portuguese sailors adopted Bd Peter Gonzalez as their patron, the St Elmo lights became Peter's lights, and to the sailors of that nation he became the true St Elmo.

The parish church of the little port of Faversham in Kent had before the Reformation an altar of St Erasmus ; and it is said that "no one died who had anything to give, but he left a legacy to maintain the lights which burnt about it ".

The most widely circulated text of the legendary story of St Erasmus is printed, with other materials, in the *Acta Sanctorum*, June, vol. i.   A more complete list of the various recensions of this mythical narrative is furnished in BHL., nn. 2578–2585.   See also F. Lanzoni, *Le Diocesi d' Italia*, pp. 163–164 ; R. Flahault, *S. Erasme* (1895) ; E. Dümmler, in *Neues Archiv*, vol. v (1880), pp. 429–431 ; and M. R. James, *Illustrations to the Life of St Alban* (1924), pp. 23 and 27.   The subject in art is dealt with in Künstle, *Ikonographie*, vol. ii, pp. 210–213, and the folk-lore aspects are discussed by Bächtold-Stäubli, *Handwörterbuch des deutschen Aberglaubens*, vol. ii, cols. 791, 866.   Confusion has arisen from the identification at a later period of the sailor's patron, St Elmo, with the Dominican, Bd Peter Gonzalez ; see April 14.   There can be little doubt that St Erasmus really existed, however improbable the legends which subsequently were recounted concerning him.   His name is commemorated in the *Hieronymianum*, as also in the *Félire* of Oengus, and his story is told in the Old English Martyrology of the ninth century.   For the confusion between St Erasmus and St Agapitus of Praeneste, under the name "Agrappart" or "Agrapau", see the paper in *Etudes d'Histoire et d'Archéologie Namuroises*, dédiées à Ferdinand Courtoy (1952), by Fr B. de Gaiffier, who kindly supplied this editor with an off-print.

SS. POTHINUS AND HIS COMPANIONS, THE MARTYRS OF LYONS AND VIENNE   (A.D. 177)

THE letter which records the sufferings of the martyrs of Vienne and Lyons in the terrible persecution under Marcus Aurelius in the year 177 has been described by an eminent French writer as " the pearl of the Christian literature of the second century ".   It was addressed by the survivors to the churches of Asia and Phrygia, and has been preserved to posterity in the pages of Eusebius of Caesarea.   Its merit lies in its unquestionable authenticity, in its intrinstic interest, and in the lofty Christian spirit which pervades it throughout.   Moreover it furnishes the earliest evidence of the existence in Gaul of an organized community of the Catholic Church.   Lyons, on the right bank of the Rhône, and Vienne, on the left, formed the western terminus of the trade route to the East, and their Christian congregations comprised many Greeks and Levantines, including their bishop Pothinus, who was probably the elder of whom his successor, St Irenaeus, stated that he had "listened to those who had seen the Apostles ".

" It is impossible to convey to you in words or in writing ", says the preamble to the letter, " the magnitude of the tribulation, the fury of the heathen against the saints, and all that the blessed martyrs endured." The persecution began unofficially with social ostracism—" we were excluded from houses, from the baths, and from the market " ; and with popular violence—stoning, plunderiug, blows, insults " and everything that an infuriated crowd loves to do to those it hates ". Then it was taken up officially. Representative Christians were led into the forum, publicly questioned and consigned to prison. The unfair treatment to which they were subjected by the magistrate when they were brought before him roused the indignation of a young Christian in the audience named Vettius Epagathus. Boldly he pleaded that he might be allowed to defend his brethren from the charges of impiety and treason. The judge asked if he too was a Christian, for he was a well-known man. He answered in the affirmative, with this result, that he was himself promoted to take his place among the ranks of the martyrs. After that ensued a time of crisis which tried the steadfastness of all, and checked the zeal of some who had hitherto ministered to the prisoners. About ten of the confessors, unable to bear the strain, abjured. " Then we were all greatly distraught," proceeds the letter, " not from fear of the torments that were to come upon us, but from looking to the end and dreading lest others should fall away. However, day by day there were taken up those who were worthy to fill up their number, until there had been gathered from the two churches all their most earnest and active members."

" As the governor had given orders to let none of us escape, certain pagan servants of ours were also arrested. These slaves, afraid lest they might have to undergo the tortures they saw inflicted on the saints, and instigated by Satan and by the soldiers, accused us of feeding on human flesh like Thyestes and of committing incest like Oedipus, as well as other abominations which it is unlawful for us even to think of, and which we can scarcely believe ever to have been perpetrated by men. When these things were made public, all were exasperated against us, including some who had formerly shown friendliness. . . . The fury of the mob, the governor, and the soldiers fell most heavily upon Sanctus, a deacon from Vienne, on Maturus, newly baptized but a noble combatant, on Attalus, a native of Pergamos, who had always been a pillar and support of the Church, and on Blandina "—a slave " in whom Christ made manifest that the things that appear mean and contemptible among men are esteemed of great glory with God on account of that love of Him which is shown in truth and not in appearances. When we were all in fear, and her mistress according to the flesh, who was herself an athlete among the martyrs, was apprehensive lest Blandina should not be able from bodily weakness to make her confession boldly, she was endued with so much power that even those who in relays tortured her from morning till evening grew faint and weary." All marvelled how she could possibly survive, so torn and broken was her body. But in the midst of her sufferings she seemed to derive refreshment and peace from continually repeating the words, " I am a Christian, and nothing vile is done amongst us ".

The deacon Sanctus also endured cruel torments with unflinching courage. To all questions that were put to him, he only replied, " I am a Christian ". When all the ordinary forms of torture had been exhausted, red-hot plates were applied to the tenderest parts of his body until he appeared a shapeless mass of swollen flesh. Three days later, when he had revived, the same treatment was repeated.

Amongst the lapsed, who had been retained in prison in the hope that they would give evidence against their former associates, was a woman named Biblias, who was known to be frail and timid. Subjected to torture, however, she " woke as it were from a deep sleep, and directly contradicted the blasphemers, saying, ' How can those eat children who are forbidden to taste the blood even of brute beasts ? ' From that moment she confessed herself a Christian and was added to the company of the martyrs."

Many of the prisoners, especially the young and untried, died in prison from torture, from the foul atmosphere and from the brutality of their gaolers, but some who had already suffered terribly and seemed at the last gasp, lingered on, confirming the rest. Bishop Pothinus, in spite of his ninety years and manifold infirmities, was dragged before the tribunal amid the railing of the populace. Upon being asked by the governor, Who was the God of the Christians, he replied, " If you are worthy, you shall know ". Thereupon he was beaten, kicked, and pelted until he was nearly insensible. Two days later he died in prison.

The martyrdom of the rest took various forms. In the beautiful words of the letter : " They offered up to the Father a single wreath, but it was woven of divers colours and of flowers of all kinds. It was meet that the noble athletes should endure a varied conflict, and win a great victory that they might be entitled in the end to receive the crown supreme of life everlasting."

Maturus, Sanctus, Blandina and Attalus were exposed to the beasts in the amphitheatre ; Maturus and Sanctus ran the gauntlet of whips, endured mauling by beasts, and bore everything else that was done to them at the suggestion of the people. Finally, they were placed on the iron chair and roasted until the odour of their scorched flesh filled the nostrils of the crowd. But their courage never faltered, nor could Sanctus be induced to utter a word except the confession he had made from the beginning. After they had throughout that day supplied not merely the varied entertainment demanded in the games, but a spectacle to the world, they were offered up at last in the sacrifice of their lives. But for Blandina the end had not come yet. She was hung from a stake, to be the prey of the beasts let loose upon her. The sight of her as she hung with outstretched arms like one crucified and the fervour of her prayers put heart into the other combatants. None of the animals would touch her ; so she was taken back to prison to await a further contest. Attalus, a man of note, was loudly called for by the crowd and was led round the amphitheatre with a tablet borne before him on which was written " This is Attalus the Christian ". The governor, however, having been informed that he was a Roman citizen, ordered him to be remanded until the emperor's wishes could be ascertained.

From the outset the confessors had given extraordinary evidence of their charity and humility. Though ready to give an explanation of their faith to all, they accused none, but prayed for their persecutors like St Stephen, as well as for their lapsed brethren. Far from taking up an attitude of superiority, they besought the prayers of their fellow Christians that they themselves might remain faithful, and they remonstrated with those who called them martyrs. In the end their loving concern for their weaker brethren was rewarded. In the words of the letter, " Through the living the dead were brought to life, and those who were martyrs reconciled those who had failed to be martyrs ". When the emperor's rescript arrived, condemning convicted Christians to death, but ordering the release of such as had abjured, those who had formerly denied now boldly confessed Christ and were added to the sacred order of those who bore witness. Only those few remained outside who had never been Christians at heart. A physician named Alexander, a Phrygian by birth, was present while they were under examination. He had lived many years in Gaul and was well known for his love of God and for his boldness in spreading the Gospel. Standing close to the dock, he so openly encouraged the prisoners that no one could fail to notice him. The crowd, incensed at the profession of Christianity by those who had previously abjured, raised an outcry against Alexander as the instigator of the change, and the governor asked him who and what he was. " A Christian ", was the reply. He was summarily condemned to be thrown to the beasts. The next day he appeared in the arena with Attalus whom the governor delivered up for the second time in order to gratify the mob. They were subjected to all the tortures used in the amphitheatre, and were at last sacrificed. Attalus, when he was being roasted in the iron chair, exclaimed, " This is in truth a consuming of human flesh—and it is you who do it. We neither eat men nor commit any other enormity ! "

" After all these ", continues the letter, " on the last day of the single combats, Blandina was again brought into the amphitheatre with Ponticus, a boy of about fifteen. They had been compelled day after day to watch the torture of the rest, and were now urged to swear by the idols. Because they refused and set them at naught, the multitude pitied neither the age of the boy nor the sex of the woman. They exposed them to all the torments, endeavouring unsuccessfully from time to time to induce them to swear. Ponticus, encouraged, as the heathen could see, by the exhortations of his sister, nobly endured every torment and then gave up the ghost. The blessed Blandina last of all, like a mother of high degree, after encouraging her children and sending them on before as victors to the King, hastened to join them—rejoicing and triumphing over her departure as if she had been summoned to a marriage-feast instead of being cast to the beasts. After the scourges, after the wild animals, after the frying-pan, she was thrown at last into a net and exposed to a bull. When she had been tossed for a time by the beast, and was completely upheld by her faith and her communing with Christ as to have become insensible to what was being done to her, she too was immolated, the heathen themselves confessing that they had never known a woman to show such endurance."

The bodies of the martyrs were cast into the Rhône that no relic or memory of them might remain on earth. But the record of their glorious victory over death was quickly borne over the sea to the East, and has been handed on by the Church throughout the ages. To quote once more the words of the epistle : " They asked for life and He gave it them : they shared it with their neighbours, and departed to God in every way victorious. Having always loved peace and having ever commended peace to us, they went in peace to God, leaving no sorrow to their Mother, nor strife nor conflict to their brethren, but joy and peace and concord and love."

The personification of the Christian Church under the term " Mother " affords an interesting illustration of that use of symbols by the faithful which was so widespread in the early centuries and which was fostered by the *disciplina arcani*. Earlier in the same letter occurs the sentence : " There was much joy in the heart of the Virgin Mother [*i.e.* the Church] in recovering alive those untimely births she had cast forth as dead." Such language enables us to understand how the

phrases used in the Abercius inscription and the representations of the Good
Shepherd which recur in the catacombs were full of meaning for the Christian
believer in those times.

The whole account depends primarily on the *Ecclesiastical History* of Eusebius, bk v,
ch. i. For the names of the martyrs see H. Quentin in *Analecta Bollandiana*, vol. xxxix
(1921), pp. 113–138, and *cf.* CMH., pp. 297–298. Consult also Hirschfeld in *Sitzungsberichte der Berliner Akademie*, 1895, pp. 38–409. There seem to have been forty-eight
martyrs in all, whose names are preserved. See also A. Chagny, *Les martyrs de Lyon* (1936),
and for a translation of the letter, E. C. E. Owen, *Some Authentic Acts . . .* (1927).
There has been a controversy about the date; see mainly H. I. Marrou in *Analecta
Bollandiana*, vol. lxxi (1953), pp. 5–20.

ST EUGENIUS I, POPE   (A.D. 657)

THIS Eugenius was a Roman, who had been brought up in the service of the
Church; he was, we are told, distinguished for his goodness, generosity and
gentleness. A year or so after Pope St Martin I was carried off from Rome, but
while he was still living, Eugenius was appointed in his place, and Martin approved
the appointment before he died. It is said that Eugenius was a nominee of the
monothelite Emperor Constans II, but if this be true the emperor was disappointed
in his protégé. On his election Eugenius sent legates to Constantinople, who came
back with a request from Constans that the new pope would declare himself in
communion with the Byzantine patriarch Peter, and bearing a theologically ambiguous letter from that hierarch. This letter was publicly discussed in the church
of St Mary Major, and so angered the assembled clergy and people that they
would not let Eugenius begin Mass until he had promised to send its rejection to
Constans—thereby making up for having tamely accepted Eugenius at the emperor's bidding—if they did. Eugenius would probably have suffered a like fate
to his predecessor's had not the emperor's hands been full with a campaign against
the Arabs. It was probably this pope who received St Wilfrid from England on
his first visit to Rome as a young man.

See the *Acta Sanctorum*, June, vol. i; Duchesne, *Liber Pontificalis*, vol. i, p. 341; and
A. Clerval in DTC., *s.v.* Eugène I.

ST STEPHEN, BISHOP IN SWEDEN, MARTYR   (A.D. 1075 ?)

NOTHING is known of the birthplace, parentage and early life of St Stephen,
" Apostle of the Helsings "; in fact, very little is known about him at all. He was
a monk of New Corbie, in Saxony, and was ordained and sent, it has been said,
as a regionary bishop to Sweden either by St Anskar or by St Adalgar of Bremen.
This, however, is all very questionable and it is much more probable that there was
only one St Stephen who was bishop in Sweden and that he lived two centuries
later than the time of St Anskar. He is said to have been very successful in his
missionary efforts, and he was the first to plant the Christian faith on the shores of
the Sound. As he was very energetic in suppressing the worship of Woden, he
was martyred by the pagans, either during a missionary visit to Uppsala, or else
at Norrala in Helsingland. His story may possibly have been confused with that
of another Bishop Stephen, who took part in the revival of Christianity in Sweden
in an earlier century, and who also died a martyr. In any case the first attempted
evangelization of the country produced no permanent effect. The tomb of one
St Stephen was venerated at Norrala until the Reformation.

See the *Acta Sanctorum*, June, vol. i, and Adam of Bremen, in Pertz, MGH., *Scriptores*, vol. vii, pp. 366 and 378.   Consult also Ihre, *Dissertatio de S. Stephano* (1748) ; and Strunck, *Westfalia sancta*, vol. i (1854), pp. 98–102.

ST NICHOLAS THE PILGRIM   (A.D. 1094)

THE traditional histories of St Nicholas Peregrinus are untrustworthy, and nearly everything they profess to tell us of his early life is probably fabulous.   All that can be positively stated about him is that he was a pious and simple-minded young Greek who landed in Italy as a perfect stranger.   There, after remaining for a time at Otranto and wandering from one place to another in Apulia, he fell ill and eventually died at Trani.   Clad in a single garment which reached only to his knees, he had gone about bearing a cross in his right hand and crying aloud wherever he went, " Kyrie eleison ! "   In a wallet he carried apples and other things with which he would please the children who flocked round him and echoed his chant. Often he was roughly handled as a vagrant or a madman, but after his death he came to be venerated because of the miracles believed to be worked by his inter- cession.   On the strength of the cures reported at his grave, he was canonized by Pope Urban II.

Such legendary materials as are available have been printed by the Bollandists in the *Acta Sanctorum*, June, vol. i, as also by Ughelli, *Italia Sacra*, vol. vii, pp. 894–906. See, further, A. di Jorio, *Della Vita di S. Nicolao Pellegrino* (1879), and H. Günter, *Die christliche Legende des Abendlandes* (1910), pp. 15–22. For his canonization, see E. W. Kemp, *Canoniza- tion and Authority* (1948), pp. 67–68 and 163–165.

BB. SADOC AND HIS COMPANIONS, MARTYRS   (A.D. 1260)

IN the year 1221, at the second general chapter of his order, which was held at Bologna, St Dominic charged his sons to go forth into the world to preach the Gospel.   One band of missionaries was sent to Hungary and the land of the Tartars—a region which St Dominic himself had greatly desired to evangelize in person.   They were under the leadership of a Hungarian friar named Paul, who was to found the first Dominican province in his native land.   Amongst the most zealous and successful of the missionaries was a young man named Sadoc, probably also a Hungarian.   After he had preached in Hungary, he passed on to Sandomir in Poland where, while continuing to preach, he founded a Dominican priory, of which he became the superior.   In 1260 the Tartars besieged and captured Sandomir.   As the brethren were sitting in the refectory, the lector was inspired to announce, as from the martyrology, " At Sandomir, forty-nine martyrs ".   That was the number of the community.   The prior, regarding this as a warning from on high, bade all prepare for death, and the following day the whole community was butchered while singing the " Salve Regina".

It would seem that such materials as the Bollandists in the *Acta Sanctorum*, June, vol. i, were able to consult regarding this wholesale martyrdom, tend to throw a certain doubt both upon the date and even the fact.   A grant of indulgence conceded by Pope Boniface VIII in 1295 speaks only of a general massacre at Sandomir, without making any particular refer- ence to the Dominicans.   As, however, the *cultus* of Bd Sadoc and Companions was con- firmed by Pope Pius VII, it may be assumed that evidence was presented which met the difficulties raised.   See Mortier, *Histoire des maîtres généraux O.P.* (1903), t. i, pp. 529–530 ; the *Année Dominicaine* ; and Procter, *Lives of Dominican Saints*, pp. 163–166.   See also Prileszky, *Acta Sanctorum Hungariae* (1744), vol. ii, Appendix, pp. 50–53.

3 : ST CECILIUS   (*c.* A.D. 248 ?)

IN the Roman Martyrology St Cecilius is commemorated on this day as " a priest of Carthage who brought St Cyprian to the faith of Christ ".   Nearly ten pages are devoted to the saint by Alban Butler, but he proceeds upon the very questionable assumption that this Cecilius is identical with the Cecilius whose conversion to Christianity is described by Minucius Felix in the apologetical treatise which is known to us as the *Octavius*.   In this book a discussion about the Christian religion is carried on in dialogue form, the interlocutors being Minucius himself, his friend Octavius, and the still pagan Cecilius.   The argument ends happily by convincing the last-named of the truth of Christianity.   That this Cecilius Natalis may have been a historical personage who was chief magistrate of Cirta in Africa in A.D. 210 is probable enough, but there are reasons which would prevent us from identifying him with the Cecilius who was instrumental in bringing about the conversion of St Cyprian.

Despite the form adopted in the Roman Martyrology, which is borrowed from *De Viris Illustribus* of St Jerome, there is good evidence, drawn from the best manuscripts of the biography of St Cyprian by his deacon Pontius, that Cecilianus, and not Cecilius, was the name of the Christian teacher who won over Cyprian by his argument and example.   It seems certain that he was a man advanced in years, and that St Cyprian, who had probably lived in his house for some time after his conversion, reverenced him greatly as " the father of his new life ".   On the other hand, Pontius tells us that when Cecilianus was dying he commended his wife and children to the pious care of his beloved convert.   Alban Butler, though probably mistaken in his view that the *Octavius* of Minucius Felix had anything to do with the subject of this notice, concludes his account with some reflections which deserve the very careful consideration of all who engage in controversy.

It is a great proof of sincere virtue, he says, a great but rare victory over pride, for a learned man to own himself vanquished by truth in a disputation.   Pride recoils at opposition, and however much the understanding may be convinced, the will is thereby apt to become more averse and more obstinately fixed in error.   On this account he who would bring another over to the truth ought to be careful not to alarm or awaken so dangerous an enemy, but to insinuate virtue by such indirect means that the opponent may almost seem to be his own instructor.   Our three disputants [in the *Octavius*] all vanquished because they were all armed with docility, charity and humility ; not like those vain combatants in the schools who love opinions, not for the sake of truth, but because, as St Augustine complains, the opinions are their own.   In this happy company, though all could boast of a conquest, yet none had reason to prize his victory higher than Cecilius.   He, overcoming both pride and errors, had achieved a triumph beyond compare.   According to the maxim of a great man, " It is then we vanquish when we consent to welcome the truth ".

See the *Acta Sanctorum*, June, vol. i ; and DCB., vol. i, pp. 366–367 (*cf. ibid.*, vol. iii, p. 924).   Consult also the article of Dessau in *Hermes*, 1880, p. 471.

SS. PERGENTINUS AND LAURENTINUS, MARTYRS   (A.D. 251)

THE persecution which arose in the middle of the third century was the greatest and most general attack Christianity had yet had to face, for the Emperor Decius had come to the throne determined to extirpate it.   Amongst a number of victims who are said to have perished at Arezzo in Umbria, the brothers Pergentinus and Laurentinus are specially venerated to this day as patrons of the city. According to the legend they were of noble birth and were still students attending the schools when they were arrested and brought before the consul Tiburtius on the charge of being Christians and of proselytizing. Although they pleaded guilty the magistrate dismissed them on the score of their noble lineage—perhaps also of their youth. He bade them relinquish their faith and threatened to have them tortured if he heard further complaints against them. Far from being daunted the two young men redoubled their activities. The *passio* speaks of numerous conversions caused by their preaching and miracles. Apprehended once more, they refused to sacrifice and were beheaded. The " acts " of these martyrs are a compilation from older hagiographical fictions and can claim no historical value of any kind. They contain many improbable details and the existence of any such martyrs is quite uncertain.

The one fragment of anything like evidence of early *cultus* consists of an entry in the *Hieronymianum*, " apud Arecium civitatem Tusciae Laurenti diaconi ". Delehaye and others think that the whole has grown out of the dedication on this day at Arezzo of a church in honour of St Laurence, the deacon martyr, the name Laurentinus having been misread as Laurentinus, and Pergentinus having been supplied by an " Expergenti ", whose name occurs next day. See CMH., p. 300, and also Mgr Lanzoni, *Diocesi d' Italia*, pp. 567–568 ; H. Quentin, *Les Martyrologes historiques*, p. 273, and Dufourcq, *Étude sur les Gesta Martyrum romains*, vol. iii, pp. 172–175. The text of the short *passio* will be found in the *Acta Sanctorum*, June, vol. i.

SS. LUCILLIAN and his Companions, Martyrs   (A.D. 273)

ACCORDING to the Menology of the Emperor Basil, St Lucillian was a Christian martyr who had been a pagan priest of Nicomedia before he was converted at an advanced age. He was arrested in the reign of the Emperor Aurelian, and was brought before the magistrate Silvanus. Because he refused to deny Christ his face was bruised with stones, he was beaten with whips, and he was hung up by the neck. In the prison to which he was afterwards committed, he found four Christian youths, Claudius, Hypatius, Paul and Dionysius, whom he strengthened in the faith so that when they came up again for trial they made a bold confession. St Lucillian was then shut up in a hot oven from which, however, he emerged unscathed. All five were finally sent in chains to Byzantium, where Lucillian was crucified and the others were decapitated.

Paula was a Christian woman who fed the martyrs in prison and tended their wounds. She also was apprehended, tortured, placed in the oven, and finally beheaded. The people of Constantinople had a great devotion to these saints, and several versions of their story survive. Thus we find St Lucillian represented as a Christian priest, as the husband of Paula, and as the father of his young fellow prisoners. Another legend makes them natives and martyrs of Egypt. As a matter of fact, it is most unlikely that St Lucillian and his companions were martyred at Byzantium at all. Their *cultus* at Constantinople is due to the fact that their relics were translated thither—perhaps from some other Thracian town, but more probably from Nicomedia, which may well have been the scene of their martyrdom.

The Bollandists in the *Acta Sanctorum* (June, vol. i) printed the Greek text of a panegyric of Lucillian, written by a certain Photius. Delehaye in the *Analecta Bollandiana*, vol. xxxi (1912), has edited a Greek *passio* of the same martyrs ; see pp. 187–192, and the editor's comments, pp. 232–235. The story cannot be regarded as anything better than a pious romance.

461

ST CLOTILDA, WIDOW   (A.D. 545)

ST CLOTILDA, a Burgundian, was the wife of Clovis, king of the Salian Franks, who at the time of their marriage, in 492 or 493, was still a heathen. From the outset Clotilda exercised great influence over her husband and made earnest efforts to win him to Christ's religion. "You have heard from your grandmother, Clotilda of happy memory," wrote St Nicetius of Trier to the French princess Clodoswind, "how she drew to the faith her royal husband and how he, a man of keen intelligence, would not yield until he was convinced of the truth." He permitted the baptism of their first-born son, who died in infancy, and of their second boy, Clodomir, but he still hesitated to declare himself a Christian. His decision was made in the heat of battle. He was fighting the Alemanni, and his troops were yielding to the enemy when he appealed for help to "Clotilda's God", vowing that if he was granted victory he would accept the Christian faith. He won the day, and on Christmas morning, 496, he was baptized by St Remigius in Rheims cathedral. History has little more to tell us about St Clotilda's further married life ; together they founded in Paris the church of the Apostles Peter and Paul, which was afterwards renamed St Geneviève. There she buried Clovis, who died in 511.

Clotilda's after life was saddened by the family feuds and fratricidal struggles in which her three sons, Clodomir, Childebert and Clotaire, became involved, and by the misfortunes of her daughter (who bore her own name), so cruelly treated by her Visigothic husband Amalaric. Clodomir attacked his cousin St Sigismund, captured him and put him to death with his wife and children, but was himself overcome and slain by Sigismund's brother. Queen Clotilda then adopted Clodomir's three little sons, intending to bring them up as her own children. Childebert and Clotaire, however, were determined to remain in undisputed possession of Clodomir's inheritance. They induced their mother to send the children to them—and Clotaire with his own hand killed his two elder nephews, aged ten and seven. Clodoald, the youngest, was saved and afterwards became a monk in the monastery of Nogent, near Paris, which was afterwards renamed St Cloud in his honour.

Broken-hearted, St Clotilda left Paris and took up her abode at Tours, where she spent the rest of her life in relieving the poor and suffering. There she learnt that her two surviving sons had turned their arms against each other and were actually on the verge of battle. In her anguish she spent the whole night in prayer before St Martin's shrine entreating God to put an end to this unnatural conflict. The answer, St Gregory of Tours tells us, was not long delayed. The very next day, as the armies were about to engage, there arose so terrible a tempest that all military operations had to be abandoned.

But Clotilda's trials were at an end. She died a month later, after having been a widow for thirty-four years, and her sons, who had caused her so much suffering, buried her beside her husband and elder children. Recent historical research has relegated to the realm of fiction many picturesque incidents in connection with St Clotilda, which successive generations of chroniclers have been content to accept unquestioningly from the uncritical pages of St Gregory of Tours and similar sources, and in so doing it has vindicated the queen from charges of ferocity and vindictiveness, little in keeping with her saintly character. In these legends she plays the part of a fury, goading her husband and sons to avenge on her uncle Gundebald and his son, St Sigismund, the murder by the former of her two parents.

It is now established with reasonable certainty that Gundebald, far from causing Chilperic's death, sincerely lamented his loss and that Caretana did not perish in the Seine with a stone tied round her neck, but survived her husband for many years and died a peaceful, natural death in 506.

The only ancient biography of St Clotilda is of no great value as a historical source, for it was not compiled before the tenth century. It has been edited by Bruno Krusch in the second volume of MGH., *Scriptores Merov.*, but it is largely dependent upon the document known as the *Gesta regum Francorum*, or *Liber Historiae*, which was written by a monk of Saint-Denis, a couple of centuries earlier. The story of St Clotilda has to be pieced together from such authors as Gregory of Tours, Fredegarius, and certain lives of saints. By far the most reliable account of this sadly tried mother is that furnished by Godefroid Kurth, in his book *Clovis*, or more concisely in the little volume, *Sainte Clotilde* (Eng. trans., 1898), contributed by him to the series " Les Saints ". See also the bibliography appended to the notice of St Remigius, October 1. There are French lives by Archbishop Darboy, V. de Soucy, G. Rouquette, and others, but most of them, being earlier in date than Kurth's critical discussion of the subject, are unsatisfactory.

SS. LIPHARDUS AND URBICIUS, ABBOTS   (SIXTH CENTURY)

ST LIFARD, Liéfard, or Liphardus, was a lawyer with a great reputation for probity who was occupying one of the highest judicial posts at Orleans when, at the age of forty, he decided to take the habit of a monk. He may have been (as some writers have maintained) brother to St Maximin, abbot of Micy, and nephew to St Euspicius, who founded that monastery, or he may have been the brother of St Leonard of Vandoeuvre, but he was certainly not the brother of St Leonard of Limoges, as is sometimes stated. From Orleans St Lifard went first to visit the abbey of St Mesmin at Micy. Before long, however, the desire for greater solitude led him to retire with one companion, St Urbicius, to an unfrequented place where, in the ruins of an old castle, they built themselves huts. Their food was a little barley bread, their drink water, taken every third day. Very soon disciples began to gather round them, and the bishop of Orleans, who had a great regard for Lifard, not only gave him permission to form a religious community, but ordained him priest and built him a church. A flourishing monastery arose on a site now covered by the town of Meung-sur-Loire. St Lifard died about the year 550 at the age of seventy-three, after having nominated St Urbicius as his successor.

In the very valuable article of A. Poncelet, " Les Saints de Micy " (*Analecta Bollandiana*, vol. xxiv, 1905, pp. 1–97), he points out that the whole group of biographies connected with Micy are extremely unreliable. That of St Lifard is no exception, and cannot have been composed before the ninth century. It has been printed by Mabillon, and in the *Acta Sanctorum*, June, vol. i. On the other hand, the fact that there was an almost contemporary *cultus* of St Lifard in his abbey of Meung-sur-Loire is attested by the inclusion of his name on this day in the *Hieronymianum*.

ST KEVIN, OR COEMGEN, ABBOT OF GLENDALOUGH   (A.D. 618 ?)

IN the forefront of the great company of saints who made Ireland glorious in the sixth century stands St Kevin, one of the principal patrons of Dublin. He it was who founded the celebrated abbey of Glendalough, which became one of the four principal pilgrimage-places of Ireland, seven visits to Glendalough being reckoned as equivalent to one pilgrimage to Rome. St Kevin's traditional history is to be found in several Latin and Irish versions, none of them ancient; how much of real fact underlies the picturesque legends and curious folk-lore they embody can only be conjectured. The saint, we are told, was of royal descent and was born in Leinster at the Fort of the White Fountain. At his baptism by St Cronan he received the name of Coemgen, anglicized as Kevin, " the Well-begotten ". When he was seven his parents sent him to be educated by monks, under whose care he remained until he was grown up. After his ordination he was moved to withdraw into solitude, and an angel led him to the upper reaches of Glendalough, the Valley of the Two Lakes. In that wild lovely district he lived for seven years, clad in skins, sleeping on the stones by the water-side and nourished only by the nettles and sorrel, which for his sake remained green all the year round.

While he was living so austerely, " the branches and leaves of the trees sometimes sang sweet songs to him, and heavenly music alleviated the severity of his life ". At last he was discovered in a cave by a cattle-farmer called Dima, who persuaded him to leave his solitude. The good man and his children " out of respect and honour " made a litter upon which they bore the saint through the thick wood. The trees lay down to make a pathway for them, and when the litter had passed they all rose up again. At Disert-Coemgen, where Refert church now stands, St Kevin made a settlement for the disciples who gathered round him. For a long time—says the legend—a kindly otter brought a salmon every day to supply them with nourishment. But one day " it occurred to Cellach ", son of Dima, " that a fine splendid glove might be made of the otter's skin. The otter, though a brute beast, understood his thought and from that time ceased to perform his service to the monks." Perhaps in consequence of a shortage of food, St Kevin removed his community farther up the glen to the place " where two sparkling rivers meet ". Here at Glendalough he made his permanent foundation, to which numerous disciples soon flocked. To beg a blessing on himself and on them he made (we are told) a pilgrimage to Rome, and " because of the holy relics and mould which he brought back, no single saint in Erin ever obtained more from God than Coemgen, save Patrick only ".

King Colman of Ui Faelain sent his infant son to be fostered by St Kevin, after all his other sons had been " destroyed by the bright people of the fairy courts ". As there were " no cows or boolies* in the glen " the saint commanded a doe he saw with her fawn to give half her milk to his foster-child. " But a wolf came to the doe and killed her fawn. Then Coemgen wrought great miracles. He commanded the wild wolf to take the place of the fawn with the doe," and the beast obeyed him. " In this way was Faelan nourished by the wonderful works of God and Coemgen." In the Félire of Oengus, Kevin is referred to in a quatrain as " A soldier of Christ into the land of Ireland, a high name over the sea's wave : Coemgen the pure, bright warrior, in the glen of the two broad lakes."

The holy abbot was on intimate terms with St Kieran of Clonmacnois, and went to visit him on his death-bed. St Kieran was actually dead or unconscious when St Kevin arrived, but he came back to life for sufficiently long to hold sweet converse with his soul-friend, to whom he presented his bell as a parting gift. In his old age he contemplated making another pilgrimage, but was dissuaded by a wise man whom he consulted : " Birds do not hatch their eggs when they are on the wing ", said his adviser, and St Kevin remained at home. He is said to have died at the age of 120. His feast is kept in all Ireland.

* " Boolies " is a word recognized by the O.E.D. It is of Irish derivation and hardly known outside Ireland. It seems to mean a particular kind of enclosure for keeping cattle in the open.

There are five versions of the life of St Coemgen : three in Irish (for which, see C. Plummer's edition in his *Bethada Náem nÉrenn*, vol. i, pp. 125–167, with the preface and translation) ; and two in Latin. The more important of these last was also edited by Plummer in VSH., vol. i, pp. 234–257, and the other is in the *Codex Salmanticensis*, which was printed by Fr De Smedt in 1888. It would seem that, even to the most ancient of these, no earlier date can be assigned than the tenth or eleventh century. " The texts ", says Dr J. F. Kenney (*The Sources for the Early History of Ireland*, i, p. 404), " have little historical value . . . they illustrate the development of extreme ideas in asceticism, if not in the 6th and 7th, then in the 10th and later centuries ". See also Gougaud, *Christianity in Celtic Lands, passim ;* and Ryan, *Irish Monasticism*, p. 130.

ST GENESIUS, Bishop of Clermont   (*c.* A.D. 660)

The twenty-first bishop of Clermont (or Auvergne) was St Genesius, better known in France as Genet and Genès. He was born at Clermont, of a senatorial family, and became archdeacon. Learned, virtuous and benevolent, he was beloved by young and old, rich and poor. When the bishopric fell vacant at the death of St Proculus he was chosen unanimously by clergy and people to fill the see, but he would only accept office after a three-days' delay had proved that they would elect no one else. Five years later, on the hope of obtaining leave to lay down his charge and retire into solitude, he went as a pilgrim to Rome, but his people sent after him and he was obliged to return. As he drew near to Clermont, the population came to meet him, headed by the clergy carrying candles and singing ; the sick were also brought out into the street for him to heal. The rest of his episcopate seems to have been uneventful and prosperous. He ruled his people like a wise father, built a church dedicated to St Symphorian in a suburb of Clermont, a hospice near one of the city gates, and a monastery called Manlieu, or Grandlieu. Amongst his trusted advisers was a priest destined eventually to occupy the same see, *viz.* St Praejectus (Prix) who had been committed to his charge as a child. St Genesius died *c.* 660, and was buried in his church of St Symphorian, which afterwards bore his name.

There is a short medieval life, which has been printed in the *Acta Sanctorum* (June, vol. i), and some further details are furnished by the lives of St Praejectus on January 25. See also the *Gallia Christiana*, vol. ii, p. 245 ; Duchesne, *Fastes Épiscopaux*, vol. ii, p. 37 ; and DCB., vol. ii, p. 627.

ST ISAAC OF CORDOVA, Martyr   (A.D. 852)

Amongst the martyrs of Cordova, the foremost place is given in the old Spanish martyrologies to St Isaac, who, although he was a devout Christian, had made himself so proficient in Arabic that he obtained an appointment as a notary under the Moorish government. He did not occupy it for long, but withdrew to a refuge monastery where he lived for some years with his relative Abbot Martin. He was then moved to go back to the city and to challenge the chief magistrate to a religious discussion. The invitation was accepted, but during the course of the debate a panegyric upon Mohammed drew from Isaac an outspoken denunciation of the false prophet. His opponents, roused to fury, arrested him. He was tried, tortured and sentenced to death. After his execution he was impaled, and the stake with his body head downwards was set up in a conspicuous position on the far side of the river Guadalquivir.

Almost all we know of St Isaac is derived from the *Memoriale Sanctorum* of St Eulogius, who was his fellow citizen and a contemporary. The Bollandists in the *Acta Sanctorum*,

June, vol. i, have extracted all that Eulogius has left on record concerning the martyr.   See also Sanchez de Feria, *Santos de Córdoba*, vol. ii, pp. 1–24 ; and *cf.* F. J. Simonet, *Historia de los Mozárabes de España ;* and J. Pérez de Urbel, *San Eulogio de Córdoba* (1928).

ST MORAND   (*c.* A.D. 1115)

THE parents of St Morand appear to have been nobles living in the Rhine valley near Worms, and he was educated in the cathedral school of that city.   After his ordination to the priesthood, he undertook a pilgrimage to Compostela.   On the way there he stayed at Cluny where he was so deeply impressed by the life of the monks that on his return he took the habit at the hands of St Hugh ; he continued to advance in the path of perfection until he had outstripped most of his brethren in sanctity and in fidelity to the rule.   His earlier years as a religious were spent in one or other of the Cluniac houses in Auvergne, but he was not destined to remain in France.   At the opening of the twelfth century Count Frederick Pferz, the principal magnate of the Sundgau, or lower Alsace, rebuilt or restored on a larger scale the church of St Christopher which his ancestors had built close to the site upon which stands the present town of Altkirch.   He then applied to St Hugh for some of his sons to serve the church and the neighbourhood.   Several monks were sent, but their abbot Constantius almost immediately realized that a knowledge of German was essential if they were to do missionary work.   In answer to his representations Morand was despatched, as being equally proficient in French and in German.

The choice proved an excellent one, for Morand had the true missionary spirit and the people heard him gladly.   Regardless of snow or rain he would travel about the countryside, bareheaded and with a pilgrim's staff in his hand, to search out sinners and bring them to repentance.   His sanctity and eloquence were enhanced by his reputation as a wonder-worker.   Count Frederick, after having been cured by him of facial paralysis, would do nothing without consulting him. With the sign of the cross he extinguished a fire which threatened to destroy the monastery, and restored many sick persons to health.   Every Friday he visited the shrine of our Lady at Gildwiller—said to be the oldest sanctuary in Alsace— and the country people gave his name to a spring, beside which he used to rest after his weekly pilgrimage.   He died about the year 1115.   Perhaps on account of the tradition that he fasted throughout one Lent with only a bunch of grapes to sustain him, St Morand is regarded as the patron of vine-growers.

The medieval life of St Morand, which is printed in the *Acta Sanctorum*, June, vol. i, is an altogether favourable specimen of its class.   It must have been written less than half a century after the death of the saint.   Popular devotion to him has by no means died out in Alsace.   There is a considerable literature concerning both the devotional and archaeological aspects of his *cultus*.   See especially J. Clauss, *Historisch-topographisches Wörterbuch des Elsass*, pp. 974 *seq. ;* and the same writer's smaller work, *Die Heiligen des Elsass . . .* (1935). Consult also J. Levy, *Wallfahrten der Heiligen in Elsass* (1926), pp. 203–210 ; Grandidier-Ingold, *Alsatia Sacra*, vol. i (1899), pp. 325–335 ; and F. Fues, *Vie de S. Morand* (1840). The representations in art are discussed by Künstle, *Ikonographie*, vol. ii, p. 455 ; the folklore aspects in *Archives Suisses des Traditions populaires*, vol. viii (1904), p. 220 *seq.*

BD ANDREW OF SPELLO   (A.D. 1254)

BD ANDREW CACCIOLI was a man of means who in his early manhood served as a priest in the diocese of Spoleto.   At the age of about twenty-nine, after the death of his mother and sister, he gave his property to the Church and to the poor, resigned his living, and took the habit at the hands of St Francis of Assisi. He was one of the seventy-two disciples of the Seraphic Father, and Bd Andrew was privileged to watch by his death-bed and receive his last blessing. He was in Spain in 1223 when he was summoned to a special chapter in Italy. The country was then suffering from a prolonged drought which threatened to ruin the crops. Bd Andrew from the pulpit appealed to his brethren and to his other hearers to join him in fervent prayers for deliverance from famine. In response to their petition rain fell in such abundance that the harvest was saved and proved to be an exceptionally good one. The people in their gratitude called him Andrew of the Waters.

After his return to Italy the holy friar laboured with great success as a missioner in various parts of Lombardy. At a later date he was involved in the struggle carried on by the " Spirituals " to maintain the strict rule of St Francis. He was subjected in consequence to much persecution, including imprisonment on two occasions. Having been charged with the direction of the Poor Clares of Spello, he was instrumental in obtaining for them as abbess Bd Pacifica Guelfoccio, St Clare's aunt, who inspired them with such devotion that they became one of the order's most fervent communities. Towards the close of his life, Bd Andrew made a long stay at the friary of the Carceri, near Assisi, where he spent much time in contemplation. One day our Lord appeared to him in the form of a child and talked with him ; and in the midst of their discourse the bell rang for Vespers. Bd Andrew in obedience to the rule immediately repaired to the chapel. On returning to his cell he found himself once more in the presence of his Divine Guest, who greeted him, saying, " You did well in thus obeying the first summons. If you had not gone, I should not have stayed. But now I will reward you shortly." He in fact died that same year. His body was buried in the convent at Spello which he had himself founded, and his relics are preserved there to this day.

The account printed in the *Acta Sanctorum* (June, vol. i), which includes a valuable summary made from an early life of Bd Andrew once preserved at Spello, corrects several errors into which Wadding, through lack of materials, had inadvertently fallen. See also *Analecta Frànciscana*, vol. iii, pp. 210 *seq.* In Léon, *Auréole Séraphique* (Eng. trans.), vol. ii, pp. 349–351, some of Wadding's errors are still repeated. The *cultus* was approved by Pope Benedict XIV.

BD JOHN "THE SINNER" (A.D. 1600)

JOHN GRANDE was born at the little Andalusian town of Carmona in 1546. His father having died when he was fifteen, he was sent to Seville to a relation engaged in the linen trade, and afterwards was set up in business at Carmona. The things of this world, however, had no attraction for him. At the age of twenty-two he distributed his possessions to the poor and retired into a hermitage near Marcena. Although he had led an irreproachable life from childhood, he regarded himself as the basest of men. Partly from a sense of his own unworthiness, partly because he fancied that he was regarded as a hypocrite, he substituted for his surname Grande the nickname El Grande Pecador, and it is as Bd John the Sinner that he is now honoured in Andalusia. One day he saw two sick tramps lying by the roadside. Filled with pity he carried them to his hut, nursed them and solicited alms on their behalf. Soon other similar cases presented themselves, and it was revealed to him that he was called to serve God, not in solitude, but in ministering to Him in the persons of the afflicted and destitute. Abandoning his retreat he went to Xeres, where he obtained leave to serve the prisoners.   For three years he lived and laboured under dreadful conditions amongst the dregs of humanity, assisting them, nursing them, begging on their behalf and trying to soften the hearts of hardened criminals.   With wonderful patience he bore with insults, ingratitude and even ill-treatment.

He then transferred his services to the hospital.   There he had to undergo persecution from officials and menials who resented his devotion to the sick as a standing reproach to themselves for their negligence and harshness.   Unprejudiced observers, however, were attracted and impressed ; so much so that a wealthy couple founded a hospital which they entrusted to his care.   It promptly filled with patients, and there gathered round him a band of young men, fired by his example and eager to assist him.   To ensure the continuance of his work he affiliated the hospital to, and was himself enrolled in, the Order of Hospitallers the founder of which, St John of God, had died at Seville when he—John Grande—was a child of four.

Although the sick were his primary care, his help and sympathy were extended. to all in distress.   He would gather neglected waifs around him and would provide them with nourishment for their bodies and guidance for their souls ; he would also collect money to give marriage-portions to poor girls.   He never lost interest in prisoners, and when, after the storming of Cadiz by the English, three hundred fugitive Spanish soldiers came to Xeres, he cared for them, nursed the wounded, and provided them all with food and clothing—miraculously as it seemed to the men themselves.   His active life did not prevent him from attaining to great spiritual heights.   Often he was rapt in ecstasy—sometimes when he was on his errands of mercy.   If on regaining consciousness he found himself surrounded by strangers who jeered at him or upbraided him as a drunken fool, he would beg their pardon and proceed on his way with bowed head.   He was also a prophet of whom it is recorded that he foretold the destruction of the Spanish Armada.   It was from plague contracted while nursing the sick during a terrible epidemic in Xeres that John Grande died in the year 1600, at the age of fifty-four.   He was beatified in 1853.

A *Vie abrégée du B. Jean Grandé* was published at the time of the beatification, and another anonymous life in Italian, *Vita del Ven. Fra Giovanni Peccatore*, appeared at Milan in 1727.   See also Seeböck, *Die Herrlichkeit der Kat. Kirche* (1900), and the *Acta Apostolicae Sedis*, vol. xxiii (1931), pp. 18–19.

SS. CHARLES LWANGA, JOSEPH MKASA AND THEIR COMPANIONS, THE MARTYRS OF UGANDA   (A.D. 1886)

THE story of the martyrs of Uganda is one which may well give encouragement to all Christian hearts, revealing as it does the power of God's grace and that the miracles of constancy which stagger us when we read of them in the first ages of persecution have been renewed in our own time among the uncultured peoples of the interior of central Africa, where the first Catholic missions were established by Cardinal Lavigerie's White Fathers in 1879.   In Uganda some progress was made under the not unfriendly local ruler, Mtesa ; but his successor, Mwanga, determined to root out Christianity among his people, especially after a Catholic subject, St JOSEPH MKASA, reproached him for his debauchery and for his massacre of the Protestant missionary James Hannington and his caravan.   Mwanga was addicted to unnatural vice (a crime introduced among these relatively decent Africans by the Arabs), and in what followed his anger against Christianity, already kindled by ambitious officers who played on his fears, was kept alight by the refusal of Christian boys in his service to minister to his wickedness.

Joseph Mkasa himself was the first victim : Mwanga seized on a trifling pretext and on November 15, 1885, had him beheaded. To the chieftain's astonishment the Christians were not cowed by this sudden outrage, and in May of the following year the storm burst. When he called for a young " page " called Mwafu, Mwanga learned that he had been receiving religious instruction from another page, St DENIS SEBUGGWAWO ; Denis was sent for, and the king thrust a spear through his throat. That night guards were posted round the royal residence to prevent anyone from escaping, sorcerers were summoned, and war-drums beat to assemble the numerous professional executioners. Meanwhile in a room secretly St CHARLES LWANGA, who had succeeded Joseph Mkasa in charge of the " pages ", baptized four of them who were catechumens ; among them ST KIZITO, a boy of thirteen whom Lwanga had repeatedly saved from the designs of the king. Next morning the pages were all drawn up before Mwanga, and Christians were ordered to separate themselves from the rest : led by Lwanga and Kizito, the oldest and youngest, they did so—fifteen young men, all under twenty-five years of age. They were joined by two others already under arrest and by two soldiers. Mwanga asked them if they intended to remain Christians. " Till death ! " came the response. " Then put them to death ! "

The appointed place of execution, Namugongo, was thirty-seven miles away, and the convoy set out at once. " The heroic little band passed within a few feet of me ", wrote Father Lourdel, W.F., the superior of the mission. " Little Kizito was laughing and chattering. . . . I was so overcome that I had to support myself against the palisade. . . . I was not allowed to say a word to them and had to content myself with seeing on their faces the resignation, happiness and courage of their hearts ". Three of the youths were killed on the road ; the others underwent a cruel imprisonment of seven days at Namugongo while a huge pyre was prepared. Then on Ascension day, June 3, 1886, they were brought out, stripped of their clothing, bound, and each wrapped in a mat of reed :* the living faggots were laid on the pyre (one boy, ST MBAGA, was first killed by a blow on the neck by order of his father who was the chief executioner), and it was set alight. Above the ritual chants of the executioners were heard the voices of the burnt-offerings, calling on the name of Jesus.

The persecution spread and Protestants as well as Catholics gave their lives rather than deny Christ. A leader among the confessors was St MATTHIAS MURUMBA, who was put to death with revolting cruelty ; he was a middle-aged man, assistant judge to the provincial chief, who first heard of Jesus Christ from Protestant missionaries and later was baptized by Father Livinhac, W.F. Another older victim, who was beheaded, was St ANDREW KAGWA, chief of Kigowa, who had been the instrument of his wife's conversion and had gathered a large body of catechumens round him. This Andrew together with Charles Lwanga and Matthias Murumba and nineteen others (seventeen of the total being young royal servants) were solemnly beatified in 1920. Once again the often quoted words of the African Tertullian, " The blood of martyrs is the seed of Christians ", were exemplified : within a year of the death of St Charles Lwanga and his

---

* We are reminded of what Julius Caesar records of the human sacrifices of the Gauls, who enclosed their victims in baskets of osier before burning them (*Gallic War*, vi).

fellows the number of baptized among the Baganda had risen from barely two hundred to over five hundred, and of catechumens from eight hundred to three thousand. These martyrs were canonized in 1964.

The apostolic letter of Pope Benedict XV, which includes a detailed statement of the names and of the more outrageous barbarities of which the martyrs were victims, may be read in the *Acta Apostolicae Sedis*, vol. xii (1920), pp. 272-281. See Mgr C. Salotti, *I martiri dell' Uganda* (1921) ; M. Hallfell, *Uganda, eine Edelfrucht* . . . (1921) ; Mgr H. Streicher, *The Blessed Martyrs of Uganda* (1928) ; J. P. Thoonen, *Black Martyrs* (1941) ; and A. E. Howell, *The Fires of Namugongo* (1948) ; and J. F. Faupel, *African Holocaust* (1962).

4 : ST FRANCIS CARACCIOLO, FOUNDER OF THE MINOR CLERKS REGULAR (A.D. 1608)

THE saint whom the Church specially honours on this day was born on October 13, 1563, at Villa Santa Maria, in the Abruzzi. His father belonged to the Pisquizio branch of the Neapolitan princes of Caraccioli, and his mother's family could claim relationship with St Thomas Aquinas. In his baptism he received the name of Ascanio. Well trained by pious parents, he grew up fulfilling their highest hopes, a devout and charitable young man. In other respects he lived the usual life of a young nobleman in the country, being addicted to sport, especially hunting. When he was twenty-two, he developed a skin disease which seemed akin to leprosy and it soon assumed so virulent a form that his case was considered hopeless. With death staring him in the face, he vowed that if he regained his health he would devote the rest of his life to God and to the service of his fellow men. He recovered so speedily that the cure was held to be miraculous. Eager to carry out his promise, he went to Naples to study for the priesthood. After his ordination he joined a confraternity called the *Bianchi della Giustizia*, the members of which were specially concerned with caring for prisoners and with preparing condemned criminals to die a holy death. It was a fitting prelude to the career which was about to disclose itself to the young priest.

In the year 1588, John Augustine Adorno, a Genoese patrician who had taken holy orders, was inspired with the idea of founding an association of priests pledged to combine the active with the contemplative life. He consulted Fabriccio Caracciolo, the dean of the collegiate church of Santa Maria Maggiore in Naples, and a letter inviting the co-operation of another Ascanio Caracciolo—a distant kinsman— was by mistake delivered to our saint. So entirely, however, did Adorno's aspirations coincide with his own, that the recipient at once recognized in the apparent error the finger of God, and hastened to associate himself with Adorno. By way of preparation they made a forty-days' retreat in the Camaldolese settlement near Naples where, after a strict fast and earnest prayer, they drew up rules for the proposed order. Then, as soon as their company numbered twelve, Caracciolo and Adorno went to Rome to obtain the approval of the sovereign pontiff. On June 1, 1588, Sixtus V solemnly ratified their new society, under the title of the Minor Clerks Regular, and on April 9 of the following year, the two founders made their solemn profession, Caracciolo taking the name of Francis, out of devotion to the great saint of Assisi. In addition to the usual three vows, the members of the new association took a fourth, *viz.* never to seek any office of dignity either within the order or outside it. To ensure unceasing penance, it was decided that each day one brother should fast on bread and water, another should take the discipline, and a third should wear the hair shirt.   In the same manner, St Francis, either at this period or when he became superior, decreed that everyone should spend an hour a day in prayer before the Blessed Sacrament.

No sooner had Francis and Adorno settled their companions in a house in a suburb of Naples than the two set off for Spain in compliance with the pope's desire that they should establish themselves there, seeing that it was a country with which Adorno was well acquainted.   However, the time was not yet ripe : the court of Madrid would not allow them to found a house, and they had to return without attaining their object.   On the way home they were shipwrecked, but when they reached Naples they discovered that their new foundation had not been allowed to suffer in their absence.   Indeed, the house could not contain all who wished to enter and soon afterwards they were invited to take over Santa Maria Maggiore, the former superior of which, Fabriccio Caracciolo, had become one of their number.   The Minor Clerks Regular worked mainly as missioners, but some of them devoted themselves to priestly work in hospitals and prisons.   They also had places which they called hermitages for those who felt called to a life of contemplation.

St Francis contracted a serious illness, from which he had scarcely recovered when he had the great grief of losing his friend Adorno, who died at the age of forty, shortly after his return from a visit to Rome in connection with the affairs of the institute of which he was superior.   Very much against his wishes, Francis was chosen to take his place ; he thought himself unworthy of holding office, and habitually signed his letters Franciscus Peccator.   He insisted on taking his turn with the others in sweeping rooms, making beds and washing up in the kitchen, and the few hours he gave to sleep were passed on a table or on one of the altar-steps. The poor, whom he loved, knew that they could find him every morning in his confessional.   For them he would beg in the streets, with them he would share the greater part of his scanty meals, and sometimes in winter he would even give away his outer garments.   In the interest of his society he paid a second and a third visit to Spain in the years 1595 and 1598, and succeeded in founding houses in Madrid, Valladolid and Alcalá.

For seven years Francis was obliged to retain the position of general superior, though it was a severe strain upon him, not only because he was a delicate man, but because in establishing and extending the order he found himself and his brethren faced by opposition, misrepresentation, and sometimes by malicious calumnies.   At last he obtained permission from Pope Clement VIII to resign, and then he became prior of Santa Maria Maggiore and novice-master.   He still carried on his apostolic work in the confessional and in the pulpit, discoursing so constantly and movingly on the divine goodness to man that he was called " The Preacher of the Love of God ".   We are also told that with the sign of the cross he restored health to many sick persons.

In 1607 he was relieved of all administrative duties and was allowed to give himself to contemplation and to preparing for death.   He chose as his cell a recess under the staircase of the Neapolitan house and was often found lying there in ecstasy with outstretched arms.   It was in vain that the pope offered him bishoprics ; he had never desired dignities and now his eyes and heart were directed only towards Heaven.   But he was not destined to die in Naples.   St Philip Neri had offered the Minor Clerks Regular a house at Agnone, in the Abruzzi, as a novitiate,

and it was thought desirable that St Francis should go to help with the new foundation.   On his way he visited Loreto, where he was granted the favour of spending
the night in prayer in the chapel of the Holy House.   As he was invoking our
Lady's help on behalf of his brethren, Adorno appeared to him in a dream or vision,
and announced his approaching death.   He arrived at Agnone apparently in his
usual health, but he himself was under no illusion.   On the first day of June he
was seized with a fever which rapidly increased, and he dictated a fervent letter in
which he urged the members of the society to remain faithful to the rule.   He then
seemed absorbed in meditation until an hour before sunset when he suddenly cried
out, " Let us go ! Let us go ! "   " And where do you want to go, Brother Francis ?"
inquired one of the watchers.   " To Heaven ! To Heaven ! " came the answer
in clear and triumphant accents.   Scarcely had the words been uttered when the
wish was realized, and the speaker passed to his reward.   He was forty-four years
of age.

St Francis was canonized in 1807.   His order of Minor Clerks Regular was at
one time a very flourishing body, but to-day it is hardly known outside of Italy,
where there are a few small communities.

A considerable number of lives of St Francis Caracciolo were published in the seventeenth
and eighteenth centuries ; for example, those by Vives (1654), Pistelli (1701), and Cencelli
(1769).   In more modern times we have a biography by Ferrante (1862), and in 1908 a book
entitled *Terzo Centenario di S. Francesco Caracciolo*, by G. Taglialatela.   A good account
of the rise and development of the Minor Clerks Regular is given in M. Heimbucher's *Orden
und Kongregationen . . .*, third edition.

ST QUIRINUS, BISHOP OF SISCIA, MARTYR   (A.D. 308)

OF the many martyrs who suffered in the Danubian provinces during the reign of
Diocletian, one of the most celebrated was Quirinus whose praises have been
sounded by St Jerome, by Prudentius and by Fortunatus.   The " acts " which
record his trial, sufferings and death are substantially genuine, although they have
undergone amplification and interpolations at the hands of later copyists.   He was
bishop of Siscia, now Sisak in Croatia.   As he had been informed that orders were
out for his arrest, he left the city, but was pursued, captured and brought before
the magistrate Maximus.   Questioned with regard to his attempted escape he
replied that he was only obeying his Master, Jesus Christ, the true God, who had
said : " When they persecute you in one city, fly to another."   " Do you not know
that the emperor's orders would find you anywhere ? " asked the magistrate.   " He
whom you call the true God cannot help you when you are caught—as you must
now realize to your cost."   " God is always with us and can help us," declared the
bishop.   " He was with me when I was taken and He is with me now.   He it is
who strengthens me and speaks through my lips."   " You talk a great deal ",
observed Maximus, " and by talking you postpone obeying the commands of our
sovereigns : read the edicts and do as they bid you ! "   Quirinus protested that
he could not consent to do what would be sacrilege : " The gods whom you serve
are nothing ! " he exclaimed.   " My God, whom I serve, is in Heaven and earth,
and in the sea and everywhere, but He is higher than all, because He contains all
things in Himself : all things were created by Him, and by Him alone they subsist."   " You must be in your second childhood to believe such fables ! " declared
the judge.   " See, they are offering you incense : sacrifice and you shall be well
rewarded ; refuse and you will be tortured and put to a horrible death."

Quirinus replied that the threatened pains would be glory to him, and Maximus ordered him to be beaten. Even while the sentence was being carried out, he was urged to sacrifice and was told that if he did so he would be made a priest of Jupiter. " I am exercising my priesthood here and now by offering myself up to God ", cried the martyr undaunted. " I am glad to be beaten ; it does not hurt me. I would willingly endure far worse treatment to encourage those over whom I have presided to follow me by a short road to eternal life." As Maximus had not the authority to pronounce a death-sentence, he arranged to send Quirinus to Amantius, the governor of Pannonia Prima. The bishop was taken through various towns on the Danube until he reached the town of Sabaria (now Szombathely in Hungary), destined a very few years later to be the birthplace of St Martin. Here he was brought up before Amantius who, after reading the report of the previous trial, asked him if it was correct. The saint answered in the affirmative and said, " I have confessed the true God at Siscia, I have never worshipped any other. Him I carry in my heart, and no man on earth shall succeed in separating me from Him." Amantius declared himself unwilling to torture and destroy one of his venerable age, and urged him to fulfil the conditions which would enable him to end his days in peace. Neither promises nor threats, however, could move the saint. The governor therefore had no option but to condemn him.

Quirinus was sentenced to death, and thrown into the river Raab, with a stone round his neck. He did not immediately sink and was heard to utter words of prayer or of exhortation before he disappeared from sight. His body, carried a little way down the stream, was rescued by Christians. In the early fifth century, refugees driven from Pannonia by the barbarians bore the relics to Rome, where they rested in the Catacomb of St Sebastian, until in 1140 they were translated to Santa Maria in Trastevere.

The text of the *passio* is printed by Ruinart, and in the *Acta Sanctorum*, June, vol. i. Much interest has been taken in this St Quirinus since the researches of Mgr de Waal in the Platonia and its surroundings revealed the existence of a fragment of a great inscription engraved there in honour of the saint. See de Waal's monograph, *Die Apostelgruft " ad Catacumbas "*, printed as a " Supplementheft " to the *Römische Quartalschrift* (1894) ; and also Duchesne, " La Memoria Apostolorum de la Via Appia ", in *Memorie della pontificia Accademia romana di Archeol.*, vol. i (1923), pp. 8–10 ; with CMH., p. 303.

ST METROPHANES, BISHOP OF BYZANTIUM (*c.* A.D. 325)

NEXT to nothing is actually known about St Metrophanes, who was bishop of Byzantium in the days of Constantine ; he was probably its first bishop, for the town had previously been included in the diocese of Heraclea. He had a great reputation for sanctity throughout eastern Christendom. A church was built in his honour soon after the death of Constantine, and when it was falling into ruin in the sixth century it was restored by Justinian. The Greek Synaxaries and the Menaia—never a very reliable authority—give his story as follows : Metrophanes was the son of Dometius, brother to the Emperor Probus. Dometius was converted to Christianity and went to live at Byzantium, where he contracted a close friendship with its Bishop Titus, by whom he was ordained, being himself invested at his death with the same dignity. Dometius in his turn was succeeded first by his two sons, Probus, who ruled the see twelve years, and then Metrophanes. The holy life of Bishop Metrophanes, it is alleged, weighed as much with Constantine in his choice of Byzantium for his capital as did the exceptionally favourable position of the city. Old age and infirmity prevented Metrophanes from attending the Council of Nicaea, but he sent his chief presbyter Alexander to represent him. Upon the return of the emperor and the clergy who had attended the council, Metrophanes was inspired to announce to them that Alexander would be his successor and that the boy reader Paul would eventually follow Alexander as bishop. His death took place a few days later.

The text of a late and quite untrustworthy life of Metrophanes has been printed by L. Gedeon, in vol. xx (1900) of *Ἐκκλησιαστικὴ Ἀλήθεια* and there is also another text noticed in BHG. See, further, the notice in the *Acta Sanctorum*, June, vol. i, and in Nilles, *Kalendarium Utriusque Ecclesiae*, vol. i, p. 172. *Cf.* also *Texte und Untersuchungen*, vol. xxxi, part 3 (1903), pp. 188 *seq.* Metrophanes is commemorated in the Roman Martyrology, where he is described as *confessor insignis*.

ST OPTATUS, Bishop of Milevis   (*c.* A.D. 387)

ONE of the most illustrious champions of the Church during the fourth century was St Optatus, a bishop of Milevis in Numidia. St Augustine styles him a prelate of venerable memory who was by his virtue an ornament to the Catholic Church, and in another passage he couples him with St Cyprian and St Hilary, converts like Optatus from paganism. St Fulgentius not only honours him with the title of saint, but places him in the same rank as St Ambrose and St Augustine. He was the first bishop to attempt in his writings to refute the errors of the Donatists, who were rending the Church in Africa by their schism, setting up a rival hierarchy, repudiating the validity of the orders as well as of the sacraments of Catholics, and declaring that they alone were the true Church of Christ. Their claims were set forth and published in a treatise written by one of their bishops, a man of ability named Parmenian. To expose the fallacy of these claims, St Optatus, about the year 370, brought out a book, to which he added some fifteen years later, when he appears to have revised his earlier work. The treatise of Parmenian has long since perished, but that of St Optatus is extant. Written in vigorous and spirited terms, it breathes a conciliatory spirit, for the bishop, though he denounces schism as a greater sin than parricide, is primarily concerned with winning over his opponents.

Throughout he makes a clear distinction between heretics, " deserters or falsifiers of the creed ", who have no true sacraments or worship, and schismatics, rebellious Christians who have true sacraments derived from a common source. Whilst agreeing with Parmenian that there is only one church, he points out that one of its essential marks is universality, or catholicity in extension. He asks how the Donatists can claim to be The Church—cooped up as they are in one corner of Africa and in one very small colony in Rome. Another of the Church's prerogatives is the chair of Peter " which ", says he, " is ours ". " Peter sat first in this chair and was succeeded by Linus." He then gives a list of popes (incorrect) from the earliest times to the reigning pontiff Siricius, " with whom ", he says, " we and the world are united. . . . It was to Peter that Jesus Christ declared : ' I will give thee the keys of the kingdom of Heaven and the gates of hell shall not prevail against thee.' By what right do you claim the keys—you who presume to contend against Peter's chair ? You cannot deny that the episcopal chair was originally given to Peter in the city of Rome ; that he sat there first as head of the Apostles : that this chair was one—unity being maintained through union with it : that the other apostles did not claim rival chairs and that only schismatics have ever ventured to do so." In opposition to the teaching of the Donatists he sets forth the Catholic doctrine that sacraments are holy in themselves and that their operation is not dependent on the character of those who administer them. As regards the connection between church and state, he declares that the state is not in the Church, but the Church is in the state, *i.e.* the Roman Empire. In treating of original sin and the necessity for baptismal regeneration, he alludes to the exorcism and anointing which took place at baptisms. He also describes the ceremonies used at Mass, which he speaks of as a sacrifice, and he mentions the penances which the Church exacted in his day and the veneration then paid to relics. Nothing further is known of the history of St Optatus : he was living in 384, but the date of his death is not recorded. His name was added to the Roman Martyrology by Baronius.

There is a short notice of St Optatus in the *Acta Sanctorum*, June, vol. i, but little information was obtainable regarding his personal history. His writings, however, present many points of interest, which have been discussed by scholars in recent times. See, for example, O. R. Vassall-Phillips, *The Work of St Optatus against the Donatists* (1911) ; L. Duchesne, in *Mélanges d'Archéologie et d'Histoire* (1890), pp. 589–650 ; N. H. Baynes, in *Journal of Theological Studies* (1924), pp. 37–44, and (1925), pp. 404–406 ; P. Monceaux, *Histoire littéraire de l'Afrique chrétienne*, vol. v ; and *cf.* A. Wilmart in *Recherches* (1922), pp. 271–302, and in *Revue Bénédictine*, vol. xli (1929), pp. 197–203 ; Gebhardt, *Acta Martyrum Selecta* (1902), pp. 187 *seq.* ; and Abbot Chapman in the *Catholic Encyclopaedia*, vol. xi.

ST PETROC, ABBOT   (SIXTH CENTURY)

THE numerous churches in Devon and several in Cornwall dedicated to God in honour of St Petroc show in how great esteem this saint was formerly held in Dumnonia. A Welshman by birth, he came south with some of his followers during the sixth century, and made his headquarters in the monastic buildings of Lanwethinoc, founded by the holy bishop Wethinoc. Afterwards, when the *cultus* of St Petroc displaced that of Wethinoc, Lanwethinoc became Padristowe, and ultimately Padstow. Some time before the eleventh century the monks moved to Bodmin, taking St Petroc's body with them, and the centre of his *cultus* was henceforward there. In 1177 the relics were stolen by one of the canons of Bodmin priory, who gave them to the abbey of Saint-Méen in Brittany, but King Henry II, to whom the prior of Bodmin appealed, obliged this community to restore them. Thereupon, according to the Chronicles of Roger of Hoveden and Benedict of Peterborough, " the above-named prior of Bodmin, returning to England with joy, brought back the body of blessed Petroc in an ivory shrine ".* This shrine or reliquary was the gift of Walter of Coutances, and there were put therein the skull and other adjacent bones, the rest being enclosed in a wooden coffin. In the eighteenth century this reliquary was discovered in the room over the south porch of Bodmin church, where it had been hidden at the Reformation. It has now found a safe but incongruous resting-place in a local bank. The medieval life of St Petroc written at Saint-Méen seems to be simply a copy of one composed probably at Bodmin priory—a collection of legends compiled from an earlier biography, embodying a certain amount of Cornish folklore.

According to this composition St Petroc was the son of a Welsh " king ", the grandfather of St Cadoc. He and some of his friends became monks and repaired to Ireland, where they studied for some years. They then took ship to Cornwall,

* The annual " riding " custom at Bodmin was apparently in commemoration of this restoration. See A. K. Hamilton Jenkin, *Cornwall and Its People* (1945), pp. 466–469.

to the estuary of the river Camel, where St Petroc proceeded to visit first the holy hermit Samson (perhaps *the* St Samson) and then St Wethinoc, who yielded up his residence to him and his companions.   After living a most austere life in that place for thirty years, St Petroc is said to have made a pilgrimage to Rome and Jerusalem, and even to have reached the Indian ocean, where he spent some time on a tiny island.   After his return to Cornwall he spent his time in prayer and in deeds of charity to man and beast.   Thus we read that he healed many sick persons, tamed a terrible and destructive monster, prescribed successfully for a poor dragon which came to him with a splinter in its eye, and not only saved the life of a stag, which took refuge with him from its pursuers, but also converted the hunter and his attendants.   Another story tells that once when Petroc and Wethinoc were " conversing sweetly together about heavenly things " a handsome cloak fell between them from Heaven.   And when, " ' eager to give one another precedence ', each offered it to the other and in holy contention piled reason upon reason why the other should have it, straightway it was taken away before their eyes.   And at once two cloaks appeared, one for each ".

Further particulars, some of them more convincing, can be extracted from a version of the Saint-Méen life made by a canon at Bodmin, included in a fourteenth-century manuscript found at Gotha in Germany in 1937.   According to this, Petroc built a chapel and a mill at Little Petherick, near Padstow, at a spot afterwards known as Nanceventon.   After his return from the East he established himself here with some of his brethren.   Later he withdrew to the recesses of Bodmin Moor, where a hermit named Wronus (Guron) gave up his cell to him, and here he was again joined by some brethren.   When he foresaw his end was at hand, Petroc went to say farewell to the communities at Nanceventon and Lanwethinoc ; between the two places his strength failed and he turned into the house of one Rovel, where he died.   The present farmhouse called Treravel must be close to the spot.

There is a considerable literature connected with St Petroc, as the references in DNB. (under Pedrog), DCB. and LBS. alone suffice to show.   By far the best and most critical account of the unpromising materials is Canon Doble's *St Petroc*, the 3rd edition of which (1938) takes account of the *vita* in the Gotha MS.   See also " Grimspound, a Dartmoor Laura ", by Abbot Vonier, in *The Month*, March, 1928, pp. 193–200, and " St Petroc's Cell on Bodmin Moor ", by Dom J. Stonor, in the *Downside Review*, no. 203 (1948), pp. 64–74.   The medieval priory at Bodmin housed Austin canons regular, so it is fitting that the same canons should have their English novitiate there to-day.   The Catholic churches at Padstow and Bodmin bear St Petroc's name.   The long account in the Gotha MS. of the theft and return of the saint's relics is translated in G. H. Doble's *The Relics of St Petroc*, reprinted from *Antiquity*, December 1939, pp. 403–415.   The text is to be printed in *Analecta Bollandiana*.

ST VINCENTIA GEROSA, Virgin, Co-Foundress of the Sisters of Charity of Lovere   (A.D. 1847)

Under July 26 herein will be found an account of St Bartholomea Capitanio, foundress of the " Suore della Carità " of Lovere—an institute closely resembling both in its spirit and its activities the world-famous Sisters of Charity of St Vincent de Paul.   In the work of giving life to this project Bartholomea was assisted from the first by a companion much older than herself, who was also a native of Lovere. Catherine Gerosa—the name Vincentia only came to her when she assumed the habit of a nun—had been born in 1784 and for forty years had led a most holy life, devoted almost entirely to works of charity and the domestic duties which had devolved upon her after the early death of her parents. It seems to have been in 1823 or 1824 that she was brought into intimate contact with Bartholomea Capitanio, both of them having been deeply moved by an appeal of Mgr Nava, bishop of Brescia, who called for volunteers to help in rescue work, especially through the education of the young. This was at the time sadly neglected in that part of Italy under Austrian rule. Though Catherine Gerosa's *attrait* was rather in the direction of the service of the sick and poor, she was persuaded to join forces with her younger friend who felt specially called to the work of instructing children.

In the end both aims were combined in the institute which they planned in close dependence upon the rule of the Sisters of Charity of St Vincent de Paul. They would gladly have affiliated themselves to the great French order, but the political theories of the then government refused recognition of any organization which depended upon foreign control. The work prospered astonishingly, despite the lack of all resources and despite the death in 1833 of the more active of its foundresses at the early age of twenty-six. But Vincentia, though she had to carry on alone, was truly possessed by the spirit of God. She seems also to have been an admirable organizer and under her rule recruits and new foundations continued to multiply. She herself was the humblest of creatures and found the marks of respect paid to her a great trial. She turned continually to the remembrance of our Lord's sufferings on the cross for strength and guidance. Hence she used to say, " He who has not learnt what the crucifix means knows nothing, and he who knows his crucifix has nothing more to learn ". After a long illness most patiently borne, Mother Vincentia died on June 29, 1847. She was canonized in 1950.

Fr Luigi Mazza, S.J., who published in 1905 a full account of Bd Bartholomea Capitanio and her institute, supplemented this in 1910 with a *Life of Mother Vincenza Gerosa*. The decree of beatification (in *Acta Apostolicae Sedis*, vol. xxv, 1933, pp. 300–303) includes a biographical summary. See also Kempf, *The Holiness of the Church in the Ninteeenth Century*, pp. 204–207.

5 : ST BONIFACE, Archbishop of Mainz, Martyr (A.D. 754)

THE title of Apostle of Germany belongs pre-eminently to St Boniface, for although the Rhineland and Bavaria had accepted the Christian faith before his time and isolated missionaries had penetrated into other parts of the country, especially into Thuringia, to him belongs the credit of systematically evangelizing and civilizing the great regions of central Germany, of founding an organized church and of creating a hierarchy under the direct commission of the Holy See. Second only in importance, though less generally recognized, was the saint's other great achievement—the regeneration of the Frankish church.

Boniface, or Winfrid—to give him his baptismal name—was born about the year 680, probably at Crediton in Devonshire. At the age of five, after listening to the conversation of some monastic visitors to his home, he determined to be a monk, and when he was seven he was sent to school to a monastery near Exeter. Some seven years later he went to the abbey of Nursling, in the diocese of Winchester. There he became the apt pupil of its learned abbot, Winbert, and after completing his own studies, he was made director of the school. His skill in teaching and his personal popularity attracted many scholars, for whose benefit he wrote the first Latin grammar known to have been compiled in England. His pupils were not confined to the schools ; notes taken at his classes were copied, circulated and eagerly studied.   At the age of thirty he was ordained to the priesthood, and found further scope for his talents in sermons and instructions—all based on the Bible, which was his study and delight throughout life.

Teaching and preaching, however, did not exhaust his activities, and when high preferment in his native land seemed assured, God revealed to him that his vocation was to the foreign mission-field.   The whole of north and the greater part of central Europe lay still in heathen darkness, and in Friesland St Willibrord had long been striving against great odds to bring the truths of the Gospel home to the people.   Here seemed to Winfrid the place to which he was specially called. Having wrung a reluctant consent from his abbot, he set forth and landed with two companions at Duurstede in the spring of 716.   The time was, however, inauspicious, and Winfrid, realizing that it was useless to stay, returned to England in the autumn.   His brethren at Nursling, delighted to welcome him back, tried to retain him by electing him abbot upon the death of Winbert, but he was not to be deflected from his call.   His first attempt had convinced him that if he was to succeed he must have a direct commission from the Pope ; and in 718 he presented himself before St Gregory II in Rome.   The pontiff in due course despatched him with a general commission to preach the word of God to the heathen.   He also changed his name Winfrid to that of Boniface.   Without loss of time, the saint took the road to Germany, crossed the lower Alps, and travelled through Bavaria into Hesse.

Scarcely had he embarked upon his new work when he was informed of the death of the pagan ruler Radbod, and of the hopeful prospect opened up through the accession of a friendly successor.   In obedience to what appeared like a recall to his original mission, St Boniface returned to Friesland, where for three years he laboured energetically under St Willibrord.   But when St Willibrord, now a very old man, would have made him his coadjutor and successor, St Boniface declined, alleging that his commission had been a general one, not confined to any one diocese. Then, fearing lest he might be forced to consent, he returned to Hesse.   The dialects of the various Teutonic tribes of north-western Europe so closely resembled the language spoken in England at this period that Boniface seems to have experienced no difficulty in making himself understood, and in spite of many difficulties the mission made wonderful progress.   Boniface was able to make such a satisfactory report to the Holy See that the pope summoned him to Rome with a view to raising him to the episcopate.

Accordingly, on St Andrew's day, 722, he was consecrated a regionary bishop with a general jurisdiction over Germany ; and Gregory gave him a special letter to the powerful Charles Martel.   This letter, which the newly ordained bishop presented in person on his way back to Germany obtained for him the valuable concession of a sealed pledge of protection.   Armed in this way with authority from church and state, Boniface, on his return to Hesse, made a bold attempt to strike at the root of the pagan superstitions which constituted the chief hindrance to the progress of the Gospel as well as to the stability of the recent converts.   On a day which had been publicly announced, and in the midst of an awestruck crowd, he attacked with an axe one of the chief objects of popular veneration, Donar's sacred oak, which stood on the summit of Mount Gudenberg at Geismar, near Fritzlar. Almost as the first blows fell upon it, the huge tree crashed, splitting into four parts, and the people who had expected a judgement to descend upon the perpetrators of such an outrage acknowledged that their gods were powerless to protect their own sanctuaries. From that time the work of evangelization advanced steadily, but success in one field only spurred St Boniface to further efforts, and as soon as he felt that he could safely leave his Hessian converts for a time, he passed on into Thuringia.

Here he found a sprinkling of Christians, including a few Celtic and Frankish priests, but they tended to be more of a hindrance than a help. At Ohrdruf, near Gotha, he established his second monastery, to serve as a missionary centre for Thuringia. Everywhere he found the people ready to listen ; it was the teachers who were lacking. To obtain them he applied to the English monasteries, with which he had continued to keep up a regular correspondence. The lapse of time had not dulled their keen interest in his work. Throughout his life he seems to have been able to fire others with some of his own enthusiasm, but the response to this appeal must have surpassed his most ardent hopes. For several years in succession parties of monks and nuns—the noblest representatives of the religious houses of Wessex—continued to cross the sea and to place themselves at his disposal to assist in preaching the Gospel to the heathen. The two existing monasteries were enlarged, and many new ones founded. Foremost among the English missionaries were St Lull, who was to succeed St Boniface at Mainz, St Eoban, who was to share his martyrdom, St Burchard and St Wigbert ; whilst the women included St Thecla, St Walburga, and Boniface's beautiful and learned young cousin, St Lioba.

In 731 Pope Gregory II died, and his successor, Gregory III, to whom St Boniface had written, sent him the pallium and constituted him metropolitan of Germany beyond the Rhine, with authority to found bishoprics wherever he thought fit. Several years later the saint went to Rome for the third time, in order to confer about the churches he had founded. He was then appointed legate of the Apostolic See ; and at Monte Cassino he obtained another missionary for Germany in the person of St Walburga's brother, St Willibald. In his capacity of legate he then went to Bavaria, where he organized its hierarchy, besides deposing unworthy priests and remedying abuses. From Bavaria he returned to his mission-fields. There he proceeded to found other bishoprics—Erfurt for Thuringia, Buraburg for Hesse, and Würzburg for Franconia. At a later date he established an episcopal seat also in the Nordgau—at Eichstätt. In charge of each diocese he placed one of his English disciples. To the year 741 belongs the commencement of the abbey of Fulda, of which he and his young disciple, St Sturmi, are reckoned as the joint founders. It was destined in after days to become—what St Boniface must surely have intended it to be—the German Monte Cassino.

Whilst the evangelization of Germany was thus proceeding apace, the condition of the Church in France under its last Merovingian kings was going from bad to worse. Ecclesiastical offices were kept vacant or sold to the highest bidder, the clergy were not only ignorant, but also often heretical or evil-living, and no church council had been held for eighty-four years. The mayor of the palace, Charles Martel, regarded himself as the champion of the Church, yet he persistently plundered it to obtain funds for his wars and did nothing to help on reform. His death, however, in 741, and the accession of his sons, Pepin and Carloman, provided an opportunity which St Boniface was not slow to seize. Carloman was earnestly devout ; it was, therefore, a comparatively easy matter for St Boniface, whom he greatly venerated, to persuade him to call a synod to deal with abuses. The first assembly was followed by a second in 743. Not to be outdone, Pepin, the next year, summoned a synod for Gaul, which was succeeded in 745 by a general council for the two provinces. St Boniface presided over them all, and succeeded in carrying all the reforms he had most at heart. Fresh vigour was infused into the Church, and as the result of five years' work Boniface had restored the Church of Gaul to her former greatness. The date of the fifth Frankish council, 747, was in other respects a memorable one for Boniface. Until then he had held a general commission ; the time had come for him to have a fixed metropolitan see. Mainz was chosen, and Pope St Zachary created him primate of Germany as well as apostolic legate for Germany and Gaul.

No sooner had this matter been arranged than Boniface lost his ally Carloman, who decided to retire into a monastery. However, Pepin, who then united France under one rule, though a man of very different calibre, continued to give him the general support he still needed. " Without the patronage of the Frankish chiefs ", he wrote to one of his English correspondents, " I cannot govern the people or exercise discipline over the clergy and monks, or check the practices of paganism." As papal legate it was he who crowned Pepin at Soissons ; but there is absolutely no evidence to support the theory that Pepin's assumption of the nominal as well as of the virtual sovereignty was in any way prompted by him.

Boniface was now growing old, and he realized that the administration of his vast fold required the vigour of a younger man. He obtained the appointment of his disciple Lull to be his successor ; but in laying down his office he had no thought of taking rest. The missionary zeal burned within him as ardently as ever, and he was resolved to spend his last years amongst his first converts, the Frieslanders, who since the death of St Willibrord were relapsing once more into paganism. Now a man of about seventy-three, he embarked with some companions to sail down the Rhine. At Utrecht they were joined by Bishop Eoban. At first they worked to reclaim the lapsed in that part of the country which had been previously evangelized, but in early spring of the following year they crossed the lake which then divided Friesland into two parts, and bore their message to the wholly unevangelized tribes of north-east Friesland. Their efforts seemed crowned with success and large numbers were baptized. St Boniface arranged to hold a confirmation on Whitsun eve in the open fields on the plain of Dokkum, near the banks of the little river Borne.

He was quietly reading in his tent while awaiting the arrival of the new converts, when a hostile band suddenly descended upon the encampment. The attendants would have defended the saint, but he would not allow them. As he was exhorting them to trust in God and to welcome the prospect of dying for the faith, they were attacked—St Boniface being one of the first to fall. His companions shared his fate. The body of Boniface was taken finally to Fulda, where it still rests. There also is treasured the book the saint had been reading, and which he is said to have raised above his head to save it when he was being attacked. It is dented with sword-cuts, and on its wooden cover are marks reputed to be stains of the martyr's blood.

Christopher Dawson's judgement that Boniface " had a deeper influence on the history of Europe than any Englishman who has ever lived " (*The Making of Europe*, 1946, p. 166) is hard to gainsay. And to his outstanding holiness, to his tremendous power and foresight as missionary and reformer, to his glory as a martyr must be added the personal loveableness and simplicity to which his letters in particular bear witness. Already his contemporary, Archbishop Cuthbert of Canterbury, could write that, " We in England lovingly count him one of the best and greatest teachers of the true faith ", and add that his feast is to be celebrated every year as England's patron equally with St Gregory the Great and St Austin.

There are a number of more or less early lives of St Boniface, the most important being that by Willibald ; most of them are accessible in the *Acta Sanctorum*, June, vol. i, but a better critical text is available in MGH., and especially in the volume edited by W. Levison, *Vitae sancti Bonifacii epis. Moguntini* (Eng. trans., Harvard, 1916). A very considerable literature, mostly of German origin, centres round St Boniface, too big to be discussed here. A source of supreme importance are the letters of Boniface himself ; they have been best edited by Tangl, in MGH., *Epistolae Selectae*, vol. i, and translated into English by E. Emerton (New York, 1940) ; *English Correspondence*, translated by E. Kylie (1924). The best German biographies are those by G. Schnürer (1909) and J. J. Laux (1922) ; and there is an excellent book on his mission work by F. Flaskamp (1929). An admirable study in French is that by G. Kurth (Eng. trans., Milwaukee, 1935), and there is a good life by the Anglican Bishop G. F. Browne, *Boniface of Crediton* (1910). See also W. Levison, *England and the Continent in the Eighth Century* (1946) ; E. S. Duckett, *Anglo-Saxon Saints and Scholars* (1947). There is a translation of the life by Willibald in C. H. Talbot's *Anglo-Saxon Missionaries in Germany* (1954) ; the writer was not Willibald the saint.

ST DOROTHEUS OF TYRE, Martyr   (A.D. 362 ?)

THE martyr St Dorotheus, commemorated on June 5 in the Roman Martyrology, was a priest of Tyre, and, according to some authorities, bishop of the diocese. In the reign of Diocletian, after suffering much for the faith in his own city, he was driven into exile. A lull in the persecution enabled him to return to his flock and he attended the Council of Nicaea in 325. A man of learning, well versed in Greek and Latin, he is reported to have been the author of several books. The accession of Julian the Apostate brought a renewal of persecution, and he withdrew once more to Odyssopolis in Thrace, the present Bulgarian port of Varna. Even there he was not left in peace. He was arrested and so cruelly beaten that he died of his injuries at the age, it is said, of 107. He is not to be identified with his namesake, Dorotheus, superintendent of the Tyrian dye-works, who was martyred during the reign of Diocletian, and whose feast falls, in the Roman Martyrology, on September 9.

As a matter of fact, Dorotheus was a common appellation, and the Greeks honour several holy men of the name, though they seem to have confused their history. Of these no less than three, besides the subject of the above memoir, discussed·by the Bollandists, are assigned to June 5, though none of them seem to have any association with this date. Two of them, moreover, seem never to have had any *cultus*. These are Dorotheus the Theban, of whom Palladius gives an account in the second chapter of his *Lausiac History ;* and the Archimandrite Dorotheus, a monk of Gaza (*cf.* St Dositheus, February 23), whose ascetical writings were so highly esteemed by Abbot de Rancé that he had them translated into French for his Trappists. The fourth Dorotheus is noticed herein on January 5, the day on which he is celebrated by the Greeks.

This is the only Dorotheus commemorated on this day in the Roman Martyrology. Though his story is to be found in Theophanes, *Chronographia*, it would seem to be entirely apocryphal. It may possibly have been suggested to some fabricator by the references in Eusebius (*Hist. Eccl.*, bk vii, ch. xxxii ; bk viii, ch. vi) to a learned Dorotheus who was living in Syria in his time, and who had been made superintendent of the Tyrian dye-works. But the whole matter of identification is quite hopeless. Under the name of this supposed Dorotheus of Tyre, certain writings were current concerning the Prophets, Apostles, and the seventy-two Disciples.   See DTC., vol. iv (1911), cc. 1786–1788 ; and T. Schermann, *Propheten-und Apostellegenden.*   For the Theban, see Abbot Butler, *Lausiac History* (1904), vol. ii ; and for the Archimandrite, *Echos d'Orient*, vol. iv (1901), pp. 359–363, and the *Byzantinische Zeitschrift*, vol. xiii (1904), pp. 423 *seq.*

ST SANCTIUS, OR SANCHO, MARTYR   (A.D. 851)

ST SANCTIUS, or Sancho, was born at Albi in the south of France, but was captured as a boy by the Moors and conveyed by them as a prisoner of war to Cordova. There he was enrolled amongst the young cadets who were trained to arms as *doncellos*, or janissaries.   Fired, as it seems, by the example of St Isaac, Sanctius openly declared himself to be a Christian and refused the prophet Mohammed. He was tried and condemned to death.   Several other Christians suffered at the same time and for the same cause, but Sanctius alone appears to have undergone the terrible ordeal of being extended on the ground and impaled while still alive— this torment being doubtless meant as a warning to those who had been his comrades.   His corpse, like that of St Isaac, was afterwards exposed for several days. It was then burnt to ashes which were scattered in the river.

Here, again, as in the case of St Isaac on June 3, all our information is derived from Eulogius.   See the bibliographical note there.   Other martyrs of this persecution are commemorated in the Roman Martyrology on the 7, 13, 14 and 28 of this month.

BD MEINWERK, BISHOP OF PADERBORN   (A.D. 1036)

ALTHOUGH his *cultus* appears never to have been formally confirmed, Bd Meinwerk was undoubtedly one of the greatest and most high-minded churchmen of his age. Of noble Saxon birth, he was educated for the priesthood, first at Halberstadt and afterwards in the cathedral school of Hildesheim, where he formed what was to prove a life-long friendship with his kinsman, the future sainted Emperor Henry II. Upon the death of Ratherius, bishop of Paderborn, Meinwerk was appointed to succeed him and was consecrated by St Willigis, archbishop of Mainz, on March 13, 1009.   He did so much for his episcopal city that he has been called the second founder of Paderborn.   He rebuilt the cathedral which had been destroyed by fire, he erected an episcopal residence, he founded a monastery for Cluniac monks at Abdinghof, and another religious house in Paderborn, he constructed the city walls, strengthened the fortifications and restored dilapidated buildings in all parts of his diocese.   A great patron of art and learning, he made the cathedral school of Paderborn famous all over Germany.   The discipline was stern—even for those days.   According to a letter written in 1050 by his nephew Bishop Imad, a former pupil, the boys lived in the school like little monks and might never speak in private even to their own fathers, because, as he had often heard his " dear uncle, Dominus Meinwerk ", say, children and boys ought to be strictly kept down—pampering only made them forward and rude.

The good bishop's enterprises were costly, and when he had exhausted his own resources (which were considerable) he did not scruple to importune his wealthy friends, especially the emperor.   So frequent, indeed, and sometimes unreasonable, were his visits for this purpose that the monarch would resort to stratagem to elude him.   On the other hand St Henry well knew that he had no truer friend or more reliable adviser : he summoned him to all his councils and took him with him on his journeys.   These expeditions enabled the bishop to satisfy a passion for relic collecting, in which he found Pope Benedict VIII specially generous.

In 1015 the new cathedral was consecrated, and in 1024 St Henry died, to the great grief of his faithful friend. The accession of a new emperor, however, in no way affected Meinwerk's status at court. Indeed it was said that Conrad II could refuse him nothing. With Conrad he paid his last visit to Italy in 1031, and from Aquileia he brought back to Abdinghof the relics of a St Felix. His last work was the building of a church after the pattern of the church of the Holy Sepulchre, to contain relics which an abbot called Wino had brought from Jerusalem. Its completion was hurried on because Bd Meinwerk felt that his life was drawing to an end. The basilica was dedicated in 1036, and later that same year, at Whitsuntide, its founder passed away.

A twelfth-century life, written by a monk of Abdinghof, has been printed in the *Acta Sanctorum*, June, vol. i. The best text is that edited by F. Tenckhoff (1921). A good German life was published by F. X. Schrader in 1895, but many special points have been discussed since. See, especially, F. Tenckhoff, *Vita Meinwerci* (1921) ; J. Bauermann, in *Westfal. Lebensbilder*, vol. i (1930), pp. 18–31 ; H. Deppe, in *Westfal. Zeitschrift*, vol xc (1934), pp. 171–192. See also A. Stonner, *Heilige der deutschen Frühzeit* (1935), vol. ii.

BD FERDINAND OF PORTUGAL   (A.D. 1443)

IT is as the hero of one of the finest plays of the great Spanish dramatist Calderon that Prince Ferdinand the Constant is best known to the world to-day. He was born at Santarem on September 29, 1402. His father was King John I of Portugal, and his mother was Philippa, daughter of John of Gaunt ; he was therefore a great-grandson of King Edward III of England. Even as a child he was devout, and although he was delicate and often prostrated by illness, he always led an austere disciplined life. From the age of fourteen, he regularly recited the canonical hours, according to the Use of Sarum—a practice he must have learnt from his English mother—and he was untouched by the temptations and dissipations of court life.

The death of his father left him so ill-provided that his eldest brother Edward (Duarte) conferred on him the grand-mastership of the Knights of Aviz, an order which had originally been formed under the name of the New Militia to fight the Moors. The pope had granted a dispensation to the Portuguese princes allowing them, though laymen, to occupy the post, but the office was primarily an ecclesiastical one, and Ferdinand only accepted it with reluctance. At one time he wanted to settle in England where he was assured of a welcome from his Lancastrian cousins ; King Edward, however, refused to allow his brother to leave Portugal. Soon afterwards Pope Eugenius IV sent a legate to offer the prince the cardinal's hat, but again Ferdinand's scruples stood in the way, and he declined the honour, on the plea that he could not take that burden upon his conscience.

It was perhaps largely at Ferdinand's persuasion and in opposition to the advice both of their brother, Dom Pedro, and of Pope Eugenius, that King Edward determined to send an expedition against the Moors in Africa under the leadership of his two brothers, Henry the Navigator and Ferdinand. Although the latter was ill when they embarked, he made light of it for fear of delay. They arrived at Ceuta with less than half the forces the king had ordered, but they would not wait for reinforcements. Their object was to take Tangier, and they attacked with reckless courage. The result was disastrous. The Portuguese could only save themselves by accepting humiliating terms, leaving Ferdinand as a hostage in the hands of the enemy. With twelve others, one of whom was his secretary and future biographer

Alvarez, he was conveyed to Arzilla where he was laid low by illness for seven months. At first he does not appear to have been very badly treated. When, however, it became known that the Portuguese would not ratify the treaty which required the surrender of Ceuta, the Moors vented their indignation upon their hostage.

In May, 1438, he was removed from Arzilla and taken to Fez, where his lot became a pitiable one. Loaded with chains and constantly threatened with death, he spent his days doing heavy menial work in stables and gardens, and his nights in a verminous prison. Yet he never complained, nor did he ever speak a harsh word against the Moors. He was far more concerned for his followers than for himself, and refused to attempt escape because it would mean leaving them and rendering them liable to worse treatment. Great efforts were made by his brothers to ransom him, but the Moors refused to release him except in exchange for Ceuta.

During the last fifteen months of his life he had still harder trials to face. He was separated from his attendants and thrown into a bare and airless dungeon. Towards the sixth year of his captivity, it became evident that he had not long to live. He was still kept in prison, but a doctor, a priest, and a few other Christians were allowed, one at a time, to visit him. Shortly before his death he was strengthened by a vision of our Lady, the Archangel Michael and St John the Evangelist. He passed from prison darkness to everlasting light on June 5, 1443. After his death his body was exposed head downwards on the city wall. When Alvarez, in 1451, regained his freedom, he carried his master's heart back to Portugal, and in 1463 the prince's bones were also brought to his native land, where they were deposited in the church of our Lady at Batalha, in the diocese of Leira. Bd Ferdinand's *cultus* was allowed by the Holy See in 1470.

There is a Portuguese life by his devoted follower, John Alvarez : *Chronica dos feitos, vida e morte do Iffante D. Fernando* (Lisbõa, 1577) : a Latin translation is printed in the *Acta Sanctorum*, June, vol. i. See also the biography by M. Gloning (1916) ; and A. Sanchez Moguel, in the *Boletin de la real Academia de la Historia*, Madrid, vol. xx (1892), pp. 332 *seq.* Some further information may be gleaned from the lives of Prince Henry the Navigator, *e.g.* those by R. H. Major (1868), and J. P. Oliveira Martins (Eng. trans., 1914).

6 : ST NORBERT, Archbishop of Magdeburg, Founder of the Canons Regular of Prémontré   (A.D. 1134)

XANTEN, in the duchy of Cleves, was the birthplace of St Norbert. His father, Heribert, Count of Gennep, was related to the emperor, and his mother, Hedwig of Guise, derived her pedigree from the house of Lorraine. Although he appeared to cherish no higher ambition than to lead a life of pleasure, he received minor orders, including the subdiaconate, and was presented to a canonry in the church of St Victor at Xanten, as well as to other benefices. At the court of the Emperor Henry V, who appointed him his almoner, Norbert joined in all the diversions, though not without signs of more serious preoccupations ; and one day, when he was riding near the Westphalian village of Wreden, he was overtaken in open country by a violent thunderstorm. His horse, frightened by a flash of lightning, threw its rider, who lay on the ground as though dead for nearly an hour. His first words on regaining consciousness were those of Saul on the road to Damascus : " Lord, what wilt thou have me to do ? " To which an inner voice replied : " Turn from evil and do good : seek after peace and pursue it."

This conversion was as sudden and complete as that of the great Apostle of the Gentiles. He retired to Xanten, where he gave himself up to prayer, fasting, meditation and a review of his past life. He then made a retreat at the abbey of Siegburg, near Cologne, where he came under the influence of its Abbot Conon. He was now preparing himself for ordination as a priest, from which, in spite of his canonry, he had formerly shrunk, and Frederick, archbishop of Cologne, conferred on him the diaconate and the priesthood in 1115. He appeared on this occasion clad in a lambskin garment with a rope for a girdle, as a public expression of his determination to renounce worldly vanities. After another forty days' retreat he returned to Xanten determined to lead " an evangelical and apostolic life " ; but the vigour of his exhortations, joined apparently with a certain eccentricity of behaviour, made enemies for him, and at the Council of Fritzlar in 1118 he found himself denounced to the papal legate as a hypocrite and an innovator, and charged with preaching without a licence or commission. Any doubt as to his sincerity must have been dispelled by his next step. He sold all his estates and gave all he possessed to the poor, reserving only forty silver marks, a mule (which soon died), a missal, a few vestments, a chalice, and a paten. Then, accompanied by two attendants who refused to leave him, he travelled barefoot to Saint-Gilles in Languedoc, where Pope Gelasius II was residing in exile. At the feet of the vicar of Christ he made a general confession of his misdeeds and irregularities, and offered himself for any penance that might be laid upon him. In response to his petition the pope granted him leave to preach the Gospel wherever he chose.

Armed with this permission St Norbert started forth again, barefoot in the snow —for it was mid-winter—and seemingly insensible to the inclemency of the weather. At Valenciennes his companions fell ill and died. But he was not destined to remain long alone. He was still at Valenciennes when he received a visit from Burchard, archbishop of Cambrai, and his young chaplain Bd Hugh of Fosses. The bishop was amazed at the change in one whom he had formerly known as a frivolous courtier, whilst Hugh was so impressed that he elected to follow him. He became St Norbert's most trusted follower, and eventually succeeded him as head of his order. Pope Callistus II having succeeded Gelasius II in 1119, St Norbert, with a view to obtaining a renewal of the sanction he had received from Gelasius, went to Rheims, where the pontiff was holding a council. Although the saint does not seem to have achieved his main purpose, Bartholomew, bishop of Laon, received permission to retain the missioner in his diocese to assist him in reforming the canons regular of St Martin's at Laon. But as the canons could not be induced to accept St Norbert's strict regulations, the bishop offered the holy man his choice of several places in which to found a community of his own. Norbert chose a lonely valley called Prémontré in the forest of Coucy, which had been abandoned by the monks of St Vincent at Laon because of the poverty of the soil. There a beginning was made with thirteen disciples. Their number soon increased to forty, who made their profession on Christmas day, 1121. They wore a white habit and kept the rule of St Augustine with certain additional regulations. Their manner of life was extremely austere, but their institute was not so much a new religious order as a reform of the regular canons. It soon spread to other countries, and distinguished persons of both sexes offered themselves as postulants and made gifts of property for new foundations. Amongst these recruits were Bd Godfrey of Kappenberg, Bd Evermod and Bd Waltman.

When the new organization could number eight abbeys as well as one or two nunneries, St Norbert became desirous of securing a more formal approbation for its constitutions. With that object in view he in 1125 undertook a journey to Rome, where he obtained from Pope Honorius II all that he asked for. The canons of St Martin's, Laon, who had formerly refused to submit to his rule, now voluntarily placed themselves under his obedience, as did also the abbey of Vervins.

Another magnate, Theobald, Count of Champagne, aspired to enter the order, but St Norbert, who recognized his lack of vocation, dissuaded him, urging him rather to carry out the duties of his station and to marry. At the same time he gave him a small white scapular to wear under his outer garments, and prescribed certain rules and devotions for his use. This seems to have been the first known case of the affiliation of a layman living in the world to a recognized religious order, and from the Premonstratensians St Dominic is thought to have derived the idea of secular tertiaries. When the count went to Germany to conclude a marriage treaty in 1126, he took the saint with him. On their way they visited Speyer, where the Emperor Lothair was holding a diet, and at the same time there arrived deputies from Magdeburg to ask the monarch to nominate a bishop to their vacant see.

Lothair chose St Norbert. The deputies led him back to Magdeburg, where he entered the city barefoot, and so meanly clad that the porter at his episcopal residence is said to have denied him admission, bidding him go and join the other beggars. " But he is our bishop ! " shouted the crowd. " Never mind, dear brother," said the saint to the startled servant. " You judge me more truly than those who brought me here ! " In his new station he still practised the austerity of a monk, whilst his residence came to resemble a cloister. But though personally humble and requiring for himself only the bare necessaries of life, he was unflinching in his determination to resist all attempts to deprive the Church of her rights. Under the weak rule of his predecessors, laymen, sometimes local magnates, had alienated much ecclesiastical property. St Norbert did not hesitate to take action against them, for he regarded them as little better than robbers. Many of the clergy were leading careless—sometimes scandalous—lives, neglecting their parishes and disregarding the obligations of celibacy. Where they would not listen to reason the bishop resorted to compulsion, punishing some, dispossessing others, and occasionally replacing them by his own Premonstratensian canons.

His reforms met with much opposition, his enemies joining forces to discredit him and to instigate the people to active resistance. On two or three occasions he narrowly escaped assassination, and once the rabble broke in upon him as he was ministering in his cathedral. So rebellious was their attitude that Norbert at last decided to retire from the city for a time and leave the people to their own devices. The step proved a wise one. For the citizens, finding themselves under ecclesiastical censure and fearing the emperor's displeasure, soon sent to beg him to return, promising to be more submissive for the future. Before the end of St Norbert's life he had successfully carried through the greater part of his projected reforms. All this time he was also directing his Premonstratensian houses through his lieutenant Bd Hugh, and for several years before his death he was taking an important part in the politics of the papacy and the empire.

After the death of Pope Honorius II, an unhappy schism divided the Church. One section of cardinals had elected Cardinal Gregory Papareschi, who adopted the name of Innocent II, whilst the rest chose Cardinal Pierleone. The latter, who called himself " Anacletus II ", was the favourite in Rome, and Innocent found himself obliged to escape to France. There he was accepted as the lawful pontiff, largely through the efforts of St Bernard and of St Hugh of Grenoble. A council which he held at Rheims was attended by St Norbert, who embraced his cause and won favour for it in Germany as St Bernard had done in France. He it was who persuaded the emperor to declare himself for Innocent. Furthermore, when it became evident that although France, Germany, England and Spain had acknowledged Innocent, he could only enter Rome with the help of armed forces, it was mainly through the influence of St Norbert that Lothair consented to lead an army into Italy. In March 1133, the emperor and the pope entered the Holy City accompanied by St Norbert and St Bernard.

In recognition of his outstanding services St Norbert was invested with the pallium, but his activities were nearly at an end. Although after their return from Italy the emperor insisted upon making him his chancellor, it was evident that his health was failing fast. Into the twenty years which had elapsed since his ordination he had crowded the work of a lifetime, and it was as a-dying man that he was borne back to Magdeburg. He expired on June 6, 1134, in the fifty-third year of his life. His relics were translated in 1627 by the Emperor Ferdinand II to the Premonstratensian abbey of Strahov in Bohemia ; he was formally recognized as a saint by Pope Gregory XIII in 1582.

The medieval life of St Norbert, printed in the *Acta Sanctorum*, June, vol. i, is less reliable than an older redaction which was edited by R. Wilmans in MGH., *Scriptores*, vol. xii, pp. 663–703. The modern lives are numerous, especially in German and Flemish ; the best is perhaps that by A. Žak, *Der heilige Norbert* (1930). In French, there are biographies by E. Maire (1922) and G. Madelaine (1930). See also C. J. Kirkfleet, *History of St Norbert* (1916) ; F. Petit, *La spiritualité des Prémontrés aux XII et XIII siècles* (1947) ; and an important article on the origins of Prémontré by C. Dereine, in *Revue d'histoire ecclésiastique*, vol. xli, pp. 352 *seq. Cf.* H. M. Colvin, *The White Canons in England* (1951), pp. 1–25.

ST PHILIP THE DEACON   (FIRST CENTURY)

ALL that is actually known about St Philip is to be found in the Acts of the Apostles. His name suggests that he was of Greek origin, but St Isidore of Pelusium asserts that he was born at Caesarea. He stands second in the list of the seven·deacons specially set aside in the early days of the Church to look after its needy members, in order that the Apostles might be free to devote themselves exclusively to the ministry of the word. The work of the deacons, however, soon developed, and we find them ministering to the priest at the Eucharist, baptizing in the absence of a priest, and preaching the Gospel. St Philip in particular was so zealous in spreading the faith that he was surnamed the Evangelist. When the disciples dispersed after the martyrdom of St Stephen he carried the light of the Gospel to Samaria. His great success induced the Apostles at Jerusalem to send St Peter and St John to confirm his converts. Simon Magus, whom he had baptized, was amongst his adherents. St Philip was probably still in Samaria when an angel directed him to go south to the road that led from Jerusalem to Gaza. There he came upon one of the chief officials of Queen Candace of Ethiopia. The man, who was presumably an African proselyte of the Jews, was returning from a religious visit to the temple at Jerusalem, and was sitting in his chariot studying with some perplexity the prophecies of Isaias. St. Philip joined him, and explained that the prophecies had found their meaning and fulfilment in the incarnation and death of Jesus Christ. The eunuch believed and was baptized. St Philip was then led by the Spirit to

Azotus, where he preached, as he continued to do in all the cities through which he passed until he reached Caesarea, perhaps his ordinary place of residence. Some twenty-four years later, when St Paul came to Caesarea, he lodged in the house where St Philip lived with his four unmarried daughters, who were prophetesses. According to a later Greek tradition St Philip afterwards became bishop of Tralles, in Lydia.

See the *Acta Sanctorum*, June, vol. i, and *cf.* what is said under St Philip the Apostle, May 1. The commemoration of the Deacon Philip on this day seems to be due to a blunder of the martyrologist Ado, who identified another martyr, Philip of Noviodunum in Moesia, whose name occurs in the *Hieronymianum*, with the Deacon of the New Testament.

ST CERATIUS, or CÉRASE, Bishop of Grenoble   (*c.* A.D. 455)

THE accounts in which Bishop Ceratius is mentioned are meagre and apparently conflicting. But we have definite data which prove his existence as bishop of Grenoble in the middle of the fifth century and also that he was honoured in that city a century or so later on June 6. We know that he was present at the Council of Orange in 441, also that he with two other Gaulish bishops wrote to Pope St Leo the Great in 450, and finally there is mention of him in a letter written to the same pope by Eusebius of Milan. On the other hand, the Gascons claim a Ceratius, or Cerasius, as the founder and first occupant of the see of Eauze, later the diocese of Auch. His relics are said to be preserved in the abbey of Simorre, near Lombez. Theories have been broached that the saint was driven from Grenoble by the persecution of the Burgundian Arians and then migrated to Aquitaine to found what is now the see of Auch. There is, however, no historical evidence to support these conjectures. The *cultus* of St Ceratius of Grenoble was confirmed in 1903.

The Bollandists in the *Acta Sanctorum*, June, vol. i, 708–710, and vol. ii, p. lxxxviii, endeavoured without success to find an acceptable solution of the difficulty. See Delehaye's commentary on the *Hieronymianum*, where St Ceratius's name is entered on June 6 as bishop of Grenoble, and also Duchesne, *Fastes Épiscopaux*, vol. i, p. 231.

ST EUSTORGIUS II, Bishop of Milan   (A.D. 518)

IT is the proud, if somewhat misleading, boast of the diocese of Milan that no less than thirty-six of her archbishops and bishops are reckoned among the saints.* Of these, two were called Eustorgius. The second bearer of the name succeeded in 512 and ruled the see for nearly seven years ; he is said by some writers to have been, like Eustorgius I, of Greek origin, and to have lived in Rome during the reigns of Popes Gelasius, Symmachus and Hormisdas. His episcopate seems to have been uneventful ; he is described as having been a man of great virtue, an excellent shepherd of his people and a defender of the patrimony of the Church. He also beautified and perhaps enlarged the baptistery his predecessor had built. He received into his house, instructed, baptized and ordained a young native of Pannonia called Florian, who afterwards preached the Gospel in Berry and, under the name of St Laurien, is venerated by the French as having been martyred by Arians near Vatan, and by the Spanish as having become bishop of Seville. St

* This does not mean that they have all been canonized by any formal process, but only that the names of many early occupants of the see appear in the episcopal lists with the prefix *sanctus*. We know nothing of the compilers of these lists, or of their competence to pronounce judgement.

Eustorgius was buried in the church of St Lawrence, in Milan, where his relics are still preserved.

In the short notice devoted to this Eustorgius II in the *Acta Sanctorum*, June, vol. i, two documents are quoted from Cassiodorus which show that King Theodoric the Great regarded the holy bishop with much respect. We also have a letter addressed to him by St Avitus of Vienne, but, except for some short Breviary lessons, this is almost all we know about him. See, further, Savio, *Gli antichi Vescovi d'Italia ; La Lombardia* (1913), pp. 6–10, 108–114, 217–221.

ST JARLATH, BISHOP OF TUAM   (*c.* A.D. 550)

THE archdiocese of Tuam in Galway venerates St Jarlath as its principal patron and as the founder of its ancient episcopal seat. This saint is not to be identified with his earlier namesake, one of St Patrick's disciples, who became bishop of Armagh, and whose festival is kept on February 11. St Jarlath of Tuam ranks with the second class of Irish saints, *viz.* those whose activities belong rather to the sixth than to the fifth century. No traditional " acts " are available for the reconstruction of the saint's history : only a bare outline of his career can be derived from allusions to him in glosses of late date—allusions which are often puzzling and do not always agree. His father is said to have belonged to the noble Conmaicne family which dominated a large district in Galway, and his mother, called Mongfinn, or the Lady of the Fair Tresses, was the daughter of Cirdubhan of the Cenneans. The date of his birth is quite unknown. In early youth he was sent to be trained by a holy man, who eventually ordained him and his cousin Caillin, or perhaps presented them for ordination. St Benignus is quoted by some writers as having been that master, but Benignus died about the year 469, when Jarlath could scarcely have been old enough for the priesthood. It seems probable that the writers were confusing him with the other Jarlath, who succeeded St Benignus in the see of Armagh. As a priest St Jarlath is supposed to have returned to his native district, where he founded a monastery at Cluain Fois—the meadow of rest—a short distance from the present town of Tuam. Over this community he ruled as abbot-bishop, honoured by all for his piety and learning. In connection with the monastery he opened a school which attained great renown. Among his pupils were St Brendan of Clonfert, and St Colman son of Léníne, the " royal bard of Munster ", who went to study at Cluain Fois after he had been induced by St Brendan and St Ita to renounce his worldly career. St Jarlath appears to have died about the middle of the sixth century. His feast is kept throughout Ireland.

The whole matter is very uncertain, though Colgan, *Acta Sanctorum Hiberniae*, vol. i, pp. 307–308, professes to give some account of this saint. There are references to him in Healy, *Ireland's Ancient Schools and Scholars* ; J. Ryan, *Irish Monasticism* ; and O'Hanlon, LIS. And see *Acta Sanctorum*, November, vol. iv, pp. 147–186.

ST GUDWAL, OR GURVAL   (SIXTH CENTURY ?)

ST GUDWAL, whom the most recent historical research identifies with St Gurval, was probably one of the earliest of the missionaries who evangelized Brittany. His name figures prominently in the ancient Armorican litanies, notably in that of the Missal of S.-Vougay where he comes third in the list of the seven pioneer saints of Brittany, St Samson being first and St Malo second. That he was, as tradition states, a native of Britain is likely but not certain. On the inland sea of Etel he founded the monastery of " Plecit " near the island called after him, Locoal, which still remains the centre of his *cultus*. He made other settlements on the mainland in the vicinity and a more distant one at Guer, which annually celebrates his feast with a procession to St Gurval's holy well. Moreover, the chapel of St Stephen in the parish of Guer, which is described as the oldest religious monument in the department of Morbihan, is regarded by at least one modern archaeologist as having been St Gurval's hermitage.

We have, unfortunately, no trustworthy account of the saint's activities. He appears to have died in one of his monasteries which stood in a wood, but his body was taken back to Locoal after his death. When the Northmen invaded Brittany in the tenth century the relics of St Gudwal were removed for safety, first to Picardy and then to Ghent, in the abbey of St Peter. Long years afterwards a monk compiled a Latin life of the saint, ultimately based on such scanty oral or written tradition as had survived, but so much amplified by fictitious details as to be quite unreliable. Even less worthy of credence is a late tradition from Saint-Malo which claims St Gurval or Gudwal as one of its bishops. He may have been a regionary bishop, but he was never bishop of Saint-Malo. As Canon Doble points out, the *cultus* of St Gudwal was probably introduced into that region from Guer which, though in the south of Brittany and geographically belonging to the diocese of Vannes, actually was in the middle ages under the jurisdiction of the bishops of Saint-Malo.

The parish of Gulval, near Penzance, takes its name from St Gulval, Gwelvel, or Welvela, but it is not known what connection, if any, there was between the Breton saint and the Celtic founder of that remote parish.

By far the most thorough investigation of the problems presented by the history of St Gudwal is that of Canon Doble in his collection of " Cornish Saints " (1933). With the exception of a brief reference in the Abbé Duine's *Memento* (p. 147), the account given by most earlier writers such as Baring-Gould and Fisher, LBS., vol. iii, pp. 150 and 161, needs revision. The subject finds a place in several collections such as DNB. and Stanton's *Menology*.

ST CLAUD, Bishop of Besançon   (c. A.D. 699)

St Claud is said to have been born in Franche-Comté, of a senatorial family, and after his ordination he became one of the clergy of Besançon. According to the generally accepted tradition, he retired twelve years later to the monastery of Condate, or, as it is now called, Saint-Claude, in the Jura Mountains, where he lived a most holy and austere life. Raised to the position of abbot, he introduced or enforced the Rule of St Benedict and restored the monastic buildings. In 685 he was chosen bishop of Besançon. He was, by all accounts, already an old man and most unwilling to accept the dignity. Nevertheless he ruled the diocese wisely and well for seven years. He then resigned and went back to Condate, the direction of which he had retained during his episcopate. He died in 699, at a very advanced age. Another tradition represents St Claud as having remained a secular priest until his elevation to the episcopate, and only to have retired to the monastery after vacating his office.

The *cultus* of St Claud became widespread in the twelfth century when his body was discovered to be incorrupt. His burial-place was for centuries a favourite place of pilgrimage at which miraculous cures took place.

There are two medieval texts of relatively late date which profess to tell the story of St Claud. One is printed in the *Acta Sanctorum*, June, vol. i. It is not very clear whether the abbot of Condate was identical with the bishop of Besançon. There was a Claudius, bishop of Besançon, who took part in the council of Epaon in 517 and in that of Lyons in 529 ; this, of course, cannot have been the abbot of Condate, if the latter died in the seventh century ; but the existence of such a bishop may have given rise to confusion. See also Duchesne, *Fastes Épiscopaux*, vol. iii, p. 212, and G. Gros, *Louis XI, pèlerin à Saint-Claude* (1946).

BD GERARD OF MONZA (A.D. 1207)

MONZA, the ancient capital of Lombardy, venerates one of its own citizens, Gerard Tintorio, as its principal patron. More than two and a half centuries after his death his *cultus* was revived by St Charles Borromeo, who promoted his cause and obtained its confirmation in 1582. He is honoured not only in his native city, but throughout the dioceses of Milan and Como. The saint, who came of a well-to-do burgher family, lost his parents in early youth. On reaching manhood he spent his patrimony in building a hospital for the sick poor, and to their care he devoted the whole of his life. He would go about in search of them and carry them to the hospital ; he washed the lepers with his own hands, and greeted each newcomer with the kiss of peace. No service he could render them was too unpleasant or menial. Small wonder that many of them recovered, thanks to the holy man's tender care or to his miraculous power. He placed his institution under the protection of the cathedral canons, and drew up wise and business-like rules for its management, which are still to be seen in a copy of the original charter. At a later date the staff consisted chiefly or entirely of Franciscan tertiaries.

The sick were not the only objects of his charity. No beggar who applied for alms or assistance was turned away empty-handed. Once during a famine the appeals were so numerous that the steward came to Gerard in despair, saying that the stores were exhausted and that starvation stared them in the face. The holy man betook himself to prayer. When the steward next went to the store-rooms he found the granary so full of corn that he could scarcely open the door, and the cellar well stocked with good wine. Another miracle attributed to Bd Gerard accounts for the bunch of cherries which in pictures of the saint he is represented as carrying in his hand. Once in mid-winter he asked permission to spend the night in prayer in the church of St John Baptist. The doorkeepers demurred, but one of them said that he might stay if he would undertake to get them some cherries. He accepted the condition and the following day, we are told, presented each of them with a bunch of fresh ripe cherries. Bd Gerard died on June 6, 1207.

There does not seem to be much information about Bd Gerard available from contemporary sources. The Bollandists published in the *Acta Sanctorum*, June, vol. i, an account derived from manuscript materials collected by St Charles Borromeo in view of the confirmation of the *cultus*. See also Frisi, *Memorie Storiche di Monza* (1841), pp. 292–304 ; A. Lesmi, *La Vita del V. Gherardo di Monza* (1647) ; F. Meda, *S. Girardo Tintore* (1896).

BD LAURENCE OF VILLAMAGNA (A.D. 1535)

BD LAURENCE, who belonged to the noble family of the Mascoli, was born at Villamagna in the Abruzzi on May 15, 1476. He entered the Franciscan convent of Santa Maria delle Grazie, near Ortona, and after his ordination became one of the greatest preachers of the age. He appeared in almost every important pulpit in Italy. He would scourge himself severely before delivering his sermons, which were so impassioned that often he and his whole congregation were reduced to tears. There is recounted of him a story of ripe cherries in January, very similar to the miracle mentioned above in the notice of Bd Gerard of Monza.   His death took place at Ortona on June 6, 1535, and his *cultus* was confirmed in 1923.

Not very much seems to be known about Laurence of Villamagna.   The *Vita del Beato Lorenzo da Villamagna*, by Fr Giacinto d'Agostino (1923), contains extraordinarily little in the way of historical fact.   See also Mazzara, *Leggendario Francescano* (1676), vol. i, p. 679 ; *Acta Ordinis Fratrum Minorum*, 1906, pp. 127–130 ; 1924, pp. 21–24 ; and the decree of *confirmatio cultus* in the *Acta Apostolicae Sedis*, vol. xv (1923), pp. 170–173.

7 : ST PAUL I, BISHOP OF CONSTANTINOPLE   (A.D. 350 OR 351)

ST PAUL was a native of Thessalonica, but from his boyhood he had been secretary to Bishop Alexander by whom he was afterwards promoted to be a deacon in the church of Constantinople.   When the aged hierarch lay on his death-bed—apparently in the year 336—he recommended St Paul as his successor and the electors endorsed his choice.   Paul was accordingly consecrated by several orthodox bishops, and practically all that is known of himself and his life is the record of an episcopate made stormy by the heretical Arians, who had supported the candidature of an older deacon called Macedonius.   At their instigation the Emperor Constantius summoned a council of Arian bishops, by whom Paul was deposed and banished.   The vacant see was bestowed, not upon Macedonius, but upon the neighbouring metropolitan Eusebius of Nicomedia.   St Paul took shelter in the west, and could not regain possession of the see until after the death of his powerful antagonist, which, however, took place soon afterwards.   He was then reinstated amid popular rejoicings.   The Arians, who still refused to acknowledge him, set up a rival bishop in the person of Macedonius, and soon the opposing factions came into open conflict and the city became a prey to violence and tumult. Constantius therefore ordered his general Hermogenes to eject Paul from Constantinople.   But the populace, infuriated at the prospect of losing their bishop, set fire to the general's house, killed him, and dragged his body through the streets. This outrage brought Constantius himself to Constantinople.   He pardoned the people, but he sent St Paul into exile.   On the other hand he refused to confirm the election of Macedonius which, like that of his rival, had taken place without the imperial sanction.

We find St Paul once more at Constantinople in 344, and Constantius then consented to re-establish him for fear of incurring the hostility of his brother Constans, who with Pope St Julius I supported Paul.   But on the death of the Western emperor in 350 Constantius sent the praetorian prefect Philip to Constantinople with instructions to expel Paul and to instal Macedonius in his place. Too astute to risk incurring the fate of Hermogenes, Philip had recourse to a stratagem.   He invited St Paul to meet him at the public baths of Zeuxippus and, whilst the people, suspicious of his designs, were gathered outside, he hustled Paul out of a side window and got him away by sea.   The unfortunate bishop was exiled to Singara, in Mesopotamia, and from thence was removed to Emesa in Syria and finally to Cucusus in Armenia.*   There he was left for six days and nights without food in a gloomy dungeon, and then strangled.   This, at any rate, was the account given by Philagrius, an official who was stationed at Cucusus at the time.

* Fifty-four years later another bishop of Constantinople, St. John Chrysostom, was banished to the same place.

The career of St Paul I of Constantinople belongs to general ecclesiastical history, and such works as Hefele-Leclercq, *Histoire des Conciles*, L. Duchesne, *History of the Early Church*, and Fliche and Martin, *Histoire de l'Eglise*, must be consulted to view the incidents in their proper setting. Of St Paul's private life as a man or as a pastor of souls we know little or nothing, though there are two late Greek biographies printed in Migne, PG (see BHG., nos. 1472, 1473). The Bollandists in the *Acta Sanctorum*, June, vol. ii, have gathered up such references as could be found in early Christian literature. They give him, it may be noticed, the title Martyr, which is not explicitly conferred in the Roman Martyrology ; but in the Oriental churches he is honoured as a martyr, his feast among the Greeks and Armenians being kept on November 6, among the Copts on October 5. It is remarkable that St Paul is commemorated in the *Hieronymianum*, and his name has passed from thence into the *Félire* of Oengus. See also DCB., vol. iv, pp. 256–257 ; and also vol. iii, pp. 775–777, under Macedonius.

ST MERIADOC, BISHOP   (SIXTH CENTURY ?)

ST MERIADOC, or Meriadec, is venerated in Brittany, and was formerly honoured also in Cornwall, where the parish church of Camborne was originally dedicated in his honour. His legend in Cornish, *Beunans Meriasek*, is the only complete miracle-play founded on the story of a saint and written in the vernacular in our own country which has survived to this day. No reliance can be placed on the popular biographies or other accounts of the saint (*e.g.* the breviary lessons used in the diocese of Vannes) ; all are based on a life compiled in the twelfth century, one object of which was to glorify the Rohan family by inventing a descent from the " royal " family of St Meriadoc.

Nothing is actually known of Meriadoc's history, but a conjectural outline of his career based on topographical data was suggested in a very learned investigation by Canon G. H. Doble.* The point that the name is Welsh confirms the assumption that Meriadoc was a Welshman. From Wales he seems to have passed first to Cornwall, where he founded one or more churches, and then to Brittany. The circumstance that the parish of Camborne, with which he is associated, is adjacent to that of Gwinear, coupled with the fact that St Meriadoc and St Gwinear are both venerated in the Breton parish of Pluvigny, *i.e.* St Gwinear, suggests the hypothesis that the two holy men, both of whom have Welsh names, were companions who went together to Cornwall and Brittany. He may have been a regionary bishop, but he never was bishop of Vannes, although his name appears in the official list.

Canon Doble's contribution is no. 34 in his Cornish Saints series (1935). A text and translation of *Beunans Meriasek* was published by Whitley Stokes (1872) ; and an extract in handy form, by R. Morton Nance and A. S. D. Smith, was printed at Camborne in 1949. Little profit can be derived from the legendary materials accumulated by Albert Le Grand and André du Saussay, to which the Bollandists in 1698 were forced to have recourse for want of better sources. See, however, Duine, *Memento*, p. 71.

ST COLMAN OF DROMORE, BISHOP   (SIXTH CENTURY)

THE first bishop of Dromore (Druim Mór), in County Down, was this St Colman, who founded a monastery there, probably about the year 514. He was venerated from early times in Scotland as well as in Ireland, and under the date of June 7 we find him mentioned in several of the ancient calendars of both countries—

* In Wales, Cornwall and Brittany " it is not the Lives of the Saints that tell us most about the existence of the saints and the national organization of religion, but the *names of places* " (Joseph Loth). " Place-names ", says M. Largillière, " are documents of indisputable truthfulness."

sometimes as Mocholmoc, or Mocholmog—" my dear little Colum ". The *Félire* of Oengus describes him as " the great descendant of Artae ", but nothing is actually known of his parentage and of his career, the manuscripts of a much later date which profess to relate his life being full of anachronisms and extravagant stories. As there are over two hundred Irish saints of the name of Colman, it is scarcely to be wondered at if their histories have become confused.

According to tradition, St Colman of Dromore was born in Dalriada (Argyllshire). After receiving his early training at Nendrum, or Mahee Island, from St Coelan, he became a disciple of St Ailbe of Emly. Amongst his friends was St Macanisius, whose advice he sought as to his future career. " It is the will of God that you erect a monastery within the bounds of Coba plain ", was the answer he received. He accordingly set to work and established his community by the river Lagan which passes through Dromore. The most famous of his pupils was St Finnian of Moville. St Colman seems to have died about the middle of the sixth century or rather earlier, and was probably interred at Dromore, though the Breviary of Aberdeen gives Inchmacome as his place of burial. His feast is kept in all dioceses of Ireland.

There is a Latin life of St Colman, mutilated at the end, which has been printed by the Bollandists in the *Acta Sanctorum*, June, vol. ii, from the *Codex Salmanticensis*. Besides this, we have only the lessons in the *Aberdeen Breviary*. Some references to the same saint occur in Fr J. Ryan's *Irish Monasticism*. See also Forbes, KSS., pp. 304–305.

ST VULFLAGIUS, OR WULPHY   (*c.* A.D. 643)

IN his early youth, St Vulflagius married and settled down in his native town of Rue, a little place near Abbeville. There he led so exemplary a life with his wife and three daughters that his fellow citizens upon the death of their priest elected him to be their pastor. Accordingly, with the consent of his wife, Vulflagius received ordination from St Richarius (Riquier). After a time, however, acting against his conscience, he resumed relations with his wife, to whom he was greatly attached.* This he soon regretted and as part of his expiation undertook a pilgrimage to the Holy Land. When he returned he still regarded himself as unworthy to act as a shepherd to others. Accordingly he withdrew to a lonely place where he lived as a hermit. He was greatly tempted to abandon his solitude, but stood firm and was rewarded by the gifts of wisdom and of miracles. Men resorted to him from near and far to profit by his instructions and to be healed of their diseases. He died probably about 643. His relics were translated in the ninth century to Montreuil-sur-Mer and are still venerated there.

There is very little serious evidence for the story of St Wulphy (whose name is written in many different ways), but there can be no question that a vigorous cult was paid to him at Montreuil. The old legend will be found recounted in the *Acta Sanctorum*, June, vol. ii. See Braquehay, *Le Culte de S. Wulphy* (1896), and Corblet, *Hagiographie d'Amiens* (1874), vol. iv, pp. 96–106. Wulphy seems to be identical with, or to have been confused with, St Walfroy. See *Analecta Bollandiana*, vol. xvii (1898), p. 307, and xxi, p. 43.

ST WILLIBALD, BISHOP OF EICHSTÄTT   (A.D. 786)

WILLIBALD was born about the year 700, in the kingdom of the West Saxons, the son of St Richard (February 7) and so brother of SS. Winebald and Walburga.

* It must be remembered that at this date celibacy in the priesthood, though recommended, was not of general obligation.

When he was three years old his life was despaired of in a violent sickness. When all natural remedies proved unsuccessful, his parents laid him at the foot of a great cross which was erected in a public place near their house. There they made a promise to God that if the child recovered they would consecrate him to the divine service, and he was immediately restored to health. Richard put him under the abbot of the monastery of Waltham in Hampshire. Willibald left here about the year 720 to accompany his father and brother on a pilgrimage, as is narrated in the life of St Richard on February 7.

After staying for a time in Rome, where he suffered from malaria, Willibald set out with two companions to visit the holy places which Christ had sanctified by His presence on earth. They sailed first to Cyprus and thence into Syria. At Emesa (Homs) St Willibald was taken by the Saracens for a spy, and was imprisoned with his companions, but after a short time they were released. When first the prisoners were arraigned, the magistrate said, " I have often seen men of the parts of the earth whence these come travelling hither. They mean no harm, wishing but to fulfil their law." They then went to Damascus, Nazareth, Cana, Mount Tabor, Tiberias, Magdala, Capharnaum, the source of the Jordan (where Willibald noticed that the cattle differed from those of Wessex, having " a long back, short legs, large upright horns, and all of one colour "), the desert of the Temptation, Galgal, Jericho, and so to Jerusalem. Here he spent some time, worshipping Christ in the places where He wrought so many great mysteries, and seeing marvels that are still shown to the pious pilgrim to-day. He likewise visited famous monasteries, lauras and hermitages in that country, with a desire of learning and imitating the practices of the religious life, and whatever might seem most conducive to the sanctification of his soul. After visiting Bethlehem and the south, the coast towns, Samaria and Damascus, and Jerusalem several times again, he eventually took ship at Tyre and, after a long stay in Constantinople, reached Italy before the end of the year 730. Willibald was the first recorded English pilgrim to the Holy Land, and his *vita* the earliest travel book by an English writer.

The celebrated monastery of Monte Cassino having been lately repaired by Pope St Gregory II, Willibald chose that house for his residence, and his example contributed to settle it in the primitive spirit of its holy rule during the ten years that he lived there : indeed he seems to have had an important part in the restoration of observance there. At the end of that time. coming on a visit to Rome, he was received by Pope St Gregory III, who, being interested in his travels and attracted by his character, eventually instructed Willibald to go into Germany and join the mission of his kinsman Boniface. Accordingly he set out for Thuringia, where St Boniface then was, by whom he was ordained priest. His labours in the country about Eichstätt, in Franconia, were crowned with great success, and he was no less powerful in words than in works.

Very shortly afterwards he was consecrated bishop by Boniface and given charge of a new diocese of which Eichstätt was made the see. The cultivation of so rough a vineyard was a laborious and painful task ; but his patience and energy overcame all difficulties. He set about founding, at Heidenheim, a double monastery, whose discipline was that of Monte Cassino, wherein his brother, St Winebald, ruled the monks, and his sister, St Walburga, the nuns. From this monastery the care and evangelization of his diocese was organized and conducted, and in it the bishop found a congenial refuge from the cares of his office. But his love of solitude did not diminish his pastoral solicitude for his flock. He was attentive to all their spiritual necessities, he often visited every part of his charge, and instructed his people with indefatigable zeal and charity, so that " the field which had been so arid and barren soon flourished as a very vineyard of the Lord ". Willibald outlived both his brother and sister and shepherded his flock for some forty-five years before God called him to Himself. He was honoured with many miracles and his body enshrined in his cathedral, where it still lies. St Willibald's feast is kept in the diocese of Plymouth on this day, but the Roman Martyrology names him on July 7.

The materials for St Willibald's life are unusually abundant and reliable. We have in particular the account of his early history and travels (the " Hodoeporicon ") taken down by a nun of Heidenheim, Hugeburc, an Englishwoman by birth and a relative of the saint. The best text is in Pertz, MGH., *Scriptores*, vol. xv. Besides this there are several minor biographies and references in letters, etc. All that is most important will be found both in Mabillon, vol. iii, and in the Bollandist *Acta Sanctorum*, July, vol. ii. For English readers a translation of the " Hodoeporicon " will be found in C. H. Talbot, *Anglo-Saxon Missionaries in Germany* (1954), and in the publications of the Palestine Pilgrims' Text Society (1891). There has been much debate over obscure questions of chronology. See also Hauck, *Kirchengeschichte Deutschlands*, vol. i ; H. Timerding, *Die christliche Frühzeit Deutschlands*, part ii (1929) ; *Analecta Bollandiana*, vol. xlix (1931), pp. 353–397 ; Abbot Chapman in *Revue Bénédictine*, vol. xxi (1904), pp. 74–80, and *St Benedict and the Sixth Century* (1929), p. 131 ; and W. Levison, *England and the Continent in the Eighth Century* (1946).

ST GOTTSCHALK, MARTYR   (A.D. 1066)

GOTTSCHALK was a Wendish prince who repudiated Christianity when his father was murdered by a Christian Saxon. He fought in the service of Canute of Denmark, came to England with Sweyn, whose daughter he married, and returned to Christianity. Later he recovered his own territories, and sought to convert his people, introducing Saxon missionaries and establishing monasteries. But in 1066 his brother-in-law raised an anti-Christian and anti-Saxon revolt, in which many were killed. Gottschalk himself was one of the first, being attacked and slain at Lenzen on the Elbe.

In the past there seems to have been a sporadic *cultus* of Gottschalk, but no solid reason appears for regarding him as either a saint or a martyr.

There is no medieval life of Gottschalk, and his history has to be gathered, as in the *Acta Sanctorum*, June, vol. ii, pp. 39 *seq.*, from the chroniclers, notably Adam of Bremen. For his services to the Church, see E. Kreusch, *Kirchengeschichte der Wendenlande* (1902), pp. 28 *seq.*, and A. Hauck's *Kirchengeschichte Deutschlands*, vol. iii, p. 654, with the *Cambridge Medieval History*, vol. iii, pp. 305–306.

ST ROBERT, ABBOT OF NEWMINSTER   (A.D. 1159)

GARGRAVE, in the Craven district of Yorkshire, was the birthplace of St Robert, and the name by which he is known to us comes not from his native town but from the abbey over which he ruled. Ordained to the priesthood, he ministered for a time as rector of Gargrave and then took the Benedictine habit at Whitby. Afterwards he obtained his abbot's permission to join a band of monks from St Mary's abbey, York, who, with the sanction of Archbishop Thurston and on land granted by him, proposed to revive the strict Benedictine rule. Making a beginning in the depth of winter under conditions of extreme poverty, they had settled in the desert valley of Skeldale, and founded the celebrated monastery which was known as Fountains Abbey on account of certain springs within its precincts. At their own request the monks were affiliated to the Cistercian reform, and Fountains became one of the most fervent houses of the order.   The spirit of holy joy pervaded their life of devotional exercises, alternating with hard manual work.   Pre-eminent amongst them stood St Robert by reason of his sanctity, his austerity, and the sweetness of his disposition.   " He was modest of demeanour ", says the Fountains Chronicle, " gentle in companionship, merciful in judgement and exemplary in his holy conversation."

Ralph de Merly, lord of Morpeth, who visited the abbey five years after its foundation, in 1138, was so impressed by the brethren that he decided to build a Cistercian monastery on his own territory.   To people the house, which became known as the abbey of Newminster, he obtained from Fountains twelve monks over whom St Robert was appointed abbot.   He retained that office until his death and made the abbey so flourishing that he was able to establish a second house at Pipe-well in Northamptonshire in 1143, and two others later on at Sawley and Roche.

A great man of prayer, Robert wrote a commentary on the psalms, which has not survived.   He was endowed with supernatural gifts and had power over evil spirits.   A story illustrates his spirit of mortification.   He fasted so rigorously during Lent that when Easter came one year he had entirely lost his appetite.   "Oh, father ! why will you not eat ? " asked the refectory brother in distress.   " I think I could eat some buttered oatcake ", replied the abbot.   But when it was brought he was afraid of yielding to what he regarded as greediness, and ordered the food to be given to the poor.   A beautiful young stranger at the gate received it and then disappeared—dish and all.   When the brother was relating the loss of the platter, the dish suddenly reappeared on the table in front of the abbot.   The stranger, it was believed, must surely have been an angel.   We are told that St Robert in his youth had studied at Paris, and there is record of a second journey of his across the seas when, being slandered by some of his monks, upon some false report of maladministration of his abbey, he went to St Bernard to give an account of himself ; but Bernard knew his man and decided that no defence was needed to meet the charge which had been made.   This visit must have taken place in 1147 or 1148, for Robert had an interview with Pope Eugenius III before he returned.   The abbot of Newminster often visited the hermit St Godric, to whom he was much attached, and the night St Robert died his friend saw his soul ascending to Heaven like a ball of fire.   This was on June 7, 1159.   His feast is kept in the diocese of Hexham.

The account, borrowed from Capgrave's *Nova Legenda Angliae*, which the Bollandists printed in the *Acta Sanctorum*, June, vol. ii, is itself a summary of a longer life preserved in Lansdowne MS. 436, at the British Museum.   Dalgairns, when compiling a life of St Robert for the series of English Saints edited by Newman, used this manuscript, and was able to add details to pre-existing accounts.   The manuscript was printed, with notes by Fr P. Grosjean, in *Analecta Bollandiana*, vol. lvi (1938), pp. 334–360.   For a summary, see W. Williams in the *Downside Review*, vol. lvii (1939), pp. 137–149.

BD BAPTISTA VARANI, Virgin   (A.D. 1527)

LITTLE Camilla Varani, only daughter of the lord of Camerino, was eight or ten years old when she was taken to hear Bd Mark of Montegallo preach.   Writing to him many years later, she says it will surprise him to learn that his sermon that day was the foundation of her whole spiritual life.   He had preached on the Passion, and concluded by entreating his congregation to meditate every Friday on our Lord's sufferings, or at any rate to bewail them.   Soon afterwards the little girl made a vow to shed at least one tear every Friday out of love for our Saviour, and that vow she kept, although she sometimes found it exceedingly difficult. Her father, who anticipated that she would make a brilliant marriage, gave her an excellent education which included general literature and the Latin language as well as more frivolous accomplishments. While she was growing up she endeavoured to lead a devout and even, spasmodically, a penitential life, but once she had made her entry into society she became wholly absorbed in pleasure. " Except for the time I gave to meditation on the Passion ", she writes, " all my life was spent in music, dancing, driving, dress and other worldly amusements : I felt a great repugnance to piety, and my aversion from monks and nuns was such that I could not bear the sight of them." This phase lasted for three years. She was then roused to a sense of her danger and overwhelmed with shame by a sermon preached by another Franciscan on the text : " Fear God ". She made a general confession and abandoned her former frivolities.

Gradually she began to realize that God was calling her to the religious life. After a hard struggle she surrendered herself to the divine will, and, to use her own words, God then gave her three lilies—a hatred of the world, a sense of her own unworthiness, and so ardent a craving for suffering that if God had permitted her to attain to Heaven without pain she would not herself have wished it. An infirmity which attacked her about that time and which lasted for many years she regarded as a fulfilment of her desire. By that time she had overcome herself ; it remained for her to overcome her father's opposition, and it took her over two years to do it.

On November 14, 1481, she received the habit at the convent of Poor Clares in Urbino, assuming the name of Baptista. Immediately afterwards she began to have mystical revelations on the Passion—revelations which under obedience she embodied in a book entitled *The Sufferings of the Agonizing Heart of Jesus*. " During the two years I spent at Urbino ", she writes, " a wonderful grace of the Holy Spirit led me into the depths of the heart of Jesus—an unfathomable sea of bitterness in which I should have been drowned had not God supported me." It was made known to her that meditation on our Lord's interior sufferings was even more profitable than contemplation of His physical torments. After her profession she was obliged to leave Urbino, for her father, determined to have her near him, built at Camerino a convent for Poor Clares to which he succeeded in having her transferred, together with several other nuns of the Varani family.

Bd Peter of Mogliano now became her director, and for three years she was the recipient of extraordinary favours. For a fortnight she rejoiced in the constant presence of St Clare : for two months she remained in spirit at the foot of the Cross, and for three months she seemed as though consumed with the fire of seraphic love. Her soul was drawn to contemplate in a vast sea of light God's love for His creatures, and she had great interior peace. This period of spiritual joy was followed by a long series of trials. At first they took the form of delusive apparitions : afterwards came assaults from the unseen powers of darkness, with spiritual desolation which she had to endure almost without assistance. Bd Peter, her former director, was no longer at hand, and although in 1490, to her great joy, he was reappointed minister provincial of the Marches, he died within a few months of his return to Camerino. Shortly afterwards she was moved to write the history of her spiritual life in the form of a letter which she sent to Bd Mark of Montegallo. Eight years later, for the benefit of a Spanish priest who regarded her as his spiritual mother, she drew up a series of instructions upon how to attain perfection. They exhibit that shrewd common sense not unmixed with humour which characterizes some of the great mystics. Though written for a fifteenth-century monk, they would form an excellent rule of life for any devout twentieth-century Catholic. History has little more to tell us about Bd Baptista, although she survived till 1527. She had the grief of losing her father and three elder brothers under tragic circumstances, for they were murdered in an insurrection of their subjects provoked by Caesar Borgia. Camerino was afterwards restored to her only surviving brother by Pope Julius II. The same pontiff commissioned Baptista to establish a new house of her order at Fermo. She remained there a year, and then returned to the convent at Camerino, which she continued to rule until her death. During her life she had insisted on maintaining herself and her community in proper poverty, but after she was dead her brother accorded her a most magnificent funeral. Her *cultus* was formally approved in 1843.

Most of our information concerning Bd Baptista is derived from her own writings. The Bollandists in the *Acta Sanctorum*, May, vol. vii, print much of these in a Latin translation, as also a translation of considerable portions of the Italian life by Fr Pascucci, which appeared in 1680. A large number of biographies or studies of the spirit of Bd Baptista have seen the light since then. It will be sufficient to mention that of the Countess de Rambuteau in French (1906); and those of Marini (1882), Puliti (1915), Jörgensen (1919), and Aringoli (1928). Her works have been edited in the original Italian by Santoni, *Le opere spirituali della ba. Battista Varani* (1894); and by Venanzio della Vergiliana, *Beata Battista Varano* (1926). Among her writings special interest attaches to that headed *I Dolori mentali di Gesù*, for it directs attention very explicitly to the interior sufferings of the heart of Jesus. It was written in 1488, published in 1490, and repeatedly afterwards, often as an appendix to that widely-popular book, the *Spiritual Combat* of Scupoli. The general diffusion of this little tractate must have contributed much to pave the way for an explicit recognition of devotion to the Sacred Heart. See on this, J. Heerinck, *Devotio SS. Cordis in scriptis B. Baptistae Varani* in the periodical *Antonianum*, 1935, January to April. There is a full account also of Bd Baptista in Léon, *Auréole Séraphique* (Eng. trans.), vol. ii, pp. 315-348.

BD ANNE OF ST BARTHOLOMEW, Virgin   (A.D. 1626)

In the writings of St Teresa of Avila we find various allusions to a young lay-sister, Anne-of-St-Bartholomew, whom she made her special companion and whom she once described as a great servant of God. Anne was the child of Ferdinand Garcia and Catherine Mançanas, peasants living at Almendral, four miles from Avila. Until the age of twenty she was employed as a shepherdess, but she then obtained admission to the Carmelite convent of St Joseph at Avila. During the last seven years of her life St Teresa took Anne on nearly all her journeys, declaring that in her work of foundations and reforms she found her more useful than anyone else. Several times she proposed that Anne should receive the black veil, but Anne always refused, preferring to remain a lay-sister. Anne has left a graphic description of their journey from Medina to Alba and of the saint's death, pathetically recording the consolation she herself derived from being able to gratify the holy Mother's love of neatness up to the very end. " The day she died she could not speak. I changed all her linen, headdress and sleeves. She looked at herself quite satisfied to see herself so clean : then, turning her eyes on me, she looked at me smilingly and showed her gratitude by signs." It was in Anne's arms that St Teresa breathed her last.

For six years more Anne remained on quietly at Avila, and then a great change came into her life. Important personages in Paris—notably Madame Acarie and Peter de Bérulle—had for some time been anxious to introduce the Barefooted Carmelites into France. They now applied for some Spanish nuns to help in making a foundation, and Teresa's successor, Anne-of-Jesus, set out with five nuns, of whom Bd Anne-of-St-Bartholomew was one. Upon their arrival in Paris, whilst the rest were being welcomed by Princess de Longueville and ladies of the court, Anne slipped into the kitchen to prepare a meal for the community. Her superiors, however, had decided that St Teresa's chosen companion was fitted for higher work, and shortly afterwards Anne unwillingly found herself promoted to be a choir sister. She had signed her own profession with a simple cross, but according to the best authorities she had acted long before this as secretary to St Teresa : according to others, she now found herself miraculously able to write. It may be that the gift of letters was bestowed upon her with other wisdom when she was about to be faced with new responsibilities. Difficulties of various kinds attended the establishment of Carmel in France, and five of the six Spanish nuns went to the Netherlands. Anne, who remained in France, was appointed prioress at Pontoise and then at Tours. The prospect of being set to govern others at first distressed her greatly, and in fervent prayer she pleaded her incompetence, comparing herself to a weak straw. The answer she received reassured her : " It is with straws I light my fire ", our Lord had replied.

A few years later Carmelite houses were opened in the Netherlands. Bd Anne was sent to Mons, where she remained a year. In 1612 she made a foundation of her own at Antwerp. It was soon filled with the daughters of the noblest families in the Low Countries,* all eager to tread the path of perfection under the guidance of one who already in her lifetime was regarded as a saint and was known to be a prophet and a wonder-worker. On two occasions, when Antwerp was besieged by the Prince of Orange and was on the point of capture, Anne prayed all night ; the city was saved, and she was acclaimed the protectress and defender of Antwerp. Her death in 1626 was the occasion for extraordinary demonstrations, when twenty thousand persons touched her body with rosaries and other things as it lay exposed before burial. For many years afterwards the city continued to venerate her memory by an annual procession in which the members of the municipality, candle in hand, led the way to her convent. Bd Anne was beatified in 1917.

The apostolic letter pronouncing the decree of beatification is printed in the *Acta Apostolicae Sedis*, vol. ix (1917), pp. 257–261, and it contains the usual biographical summary. Bd Anne wrote an autobiography at the command of her superiors ; the account is carried down to the first years of her residence in Antwerp, and the original document is preserved in the Carmelite convent there. An incomplete French translation was published in 1646, and Fr Bouix makes limited use of the autobiography in his life, " purement édifiante ", of the *beata* (1872) ; see also Fr Bruno's *La belle Acarie* (1942). C. Henriquez published a life in Spanish in 1632, and a modern account in the same language, by Florencio del Niño Jesus, appeared in 1917 : this was adapted into French by Abbé L. Aubert (1918). See also H. Bremond, *Histoire littéraire . . .*, t. ii, pp. 299–319 (there is an English translation of this volume).

ST ANTONY GIANELLI, BISHOP OF BOBBIO, FOUNDER OF THE MISSIONERS OF ST ALPHONSUS AND THE SISTERS OF ST MARY DELL' ORTO (A.D. 1846)

ANTONY GIANELLI was born in the diocese of Genoa in 1789 of a middle-class family. As a youth he was conspicuous for his gentle docility and industry and

---

* Among them was Anne Worsley (Anne-of-the-Ascension), the first English Teresian Carmelite. It was she who in 1619 established the English community at Antwerp, now at Lanherne in Cornwall. See Sr A. Hardman, *English Carmelites in Penal Times* (1936).

for the promise of more than ordinary intellectual gifts.   A generous benefactress made it possible for him to pursue his studies at Genoa, and there, entering the ecclesiastical seminary, he so distinguished himself that when still only a subdeacon he was allowed to preach and attracted great crowds by his eloquence.   By special dispensation he was ordained priest in 1812 before he had reached the canonical age.

Though employed in important educational work he still found time to deliver sermons and give missions resulting in a great harvest of souls, as well as to discharge the functions of an ordinary parish priest, his confessional being at all times besieged by penitents.   Before he was forty he had organized two religious congregations, the one of priests who were known as the Missioners of St Alphonsus Liguori, the other of women living under rule whose activities in teaching poor children and nursing the sick were dedicated in honour of Santa Maria dell' Orto (" of the Garden ").   These sisters are now well known in Italy and they have houses in other parts of Europe as well as in America and Asia.   Meanwhile, in the year 1838, St Antony was appointed bishop of Bobbio, and in that office he gave an extraordinary example of virtue, prudence and firm government.   He died, all too soon, in 1846, and he was canonized in 1951.

There are Italian biographies by L. Bodino (1924) and L. Sanguinetti (1925) ; this last is an illustrated volume of nearly six hundred pages.   The decree of beatification is printed in the *Acta Apostolicae Sedis*, vol. xvii (1925), pp. 176–179.   The saint's canonization was the occasion of further biographies.

8 : ST MAXIMINUS OF AIX   (FIFTH CENTURY ?)

HISTORICAL research has hitherto failed to yield any reliable information respecting St Maximinus of Aix whom the Roman Martyrology commemorates upon this day, but whose *cultus* can be traced in no early document. It is even uncertain in what century he lived.   On the other hand he figures largely in the Provençal legend of the coming of the Three Maries and their companions— a tradition which was regarded as genuine in the later middle ages, but which appears to have been unknown in Provence before the eleventh century.   In our own days it has furnished the poet Mistral with the subject matter of some of the most charming passages in *Mireio* and *Mes Origines*.   According to the legend, Maximinus, one of our Lord's seventy-two disciples, left Palestine after the Ascension with St Mary Magdalen, St Martha, St Lazarus, St Mary Cleophas, St Mary Salome and other holy persons and came to evangelize Provence.   Maximinus made his headquarters at Aix, of which he became the first bishop.   When St Mary Magdalen was dying she was carried from the cave at the Sainte-Baume in which she had lived to a spot now called Le Saint Pilon, where she received viaticum from St Maximinus. At a short distance from Le Saint Pilon stands the church of Saint-Maximin, which was built to replace an older church with the same dedication and to enshrine the reputed relics of these two saints.   The body of St Maximinus was translated in 1820 to Aix, of which city he is the principal patron ; but the head of St Mary Magdalen is still supposed to be preserved in the ancient crypt of Saint-Maximin.

An account of the legend of St Mary Magdalen's and of St Martha's presence in Provence will be found under July 22 and 29.   For the shrine at Saint-Maximin, the reader may be referred to H. Leclercq's article in DAC., vol. x (1932), cc. 2798–2819.   The legend of

Maximin and Sidonius seems to have been originally suggested by the bringing to Provence of certain relics from Aydat, near Billom in Auvergne.   See also Duchesne, *Fastes Épiscopaux*, vol. i, pp. 321–362.

ST MEDARD, BISHOP OF VERMANDOIS   (*c.* A.D. 560)

ST MEDARD is a favourite with the peasants of northern France, and his *cultus* goes back to his death in the sixth century ; it has been enhanced by the legends that have grown up round his name, as well as by his veneration as the patron of the corn harvest and the vintage.   He was born at Salency in Picardy, perhaps about the year 470, his father being a Frankish nobleman and his mother a Gallo-Roman. They sent their son to be educated first at the place now called Saint-Quentin and for some time he remained a layman, but he was ordained priest when he was thirty-three.   Medard's powers as a preacher and missionary were such that on the death of Bishop Alomer he was chosen to succeed him.   The consecration is stated, but on no reliable authority, to have been carried out by St Remigius of Rheims, who was then extremely old.   St Medard himself appears to have been well advanced in years, but his energy was that of a man in the prime of life ; and though his diocese was very large, he went wherever he saw an opportunity of furthering the glory of God and getting rid of idolatry.

The rest of St Medard's story is probably pure invention.   According to it he moved his see from Saint-Quentin to Noyon in consequence of a raid by Huns and Vandals, and eventually was given charge of the diocese of Tournai as well.   And it is alleged that for more than five hundred years from that time Noyon and Tournai remained united under one bishop.   One thing at least is historical : he gave the veil to Queen St Radegund and blessed her as a deaconess, in the circumstances related herein under date August 13.   St Medard's death, the exact date of which is uncertain, was lamented by all, for he was looked on as a true father in God ; we know from Fortunatus and from St Gregory of Tours that his feast was celebrated in their days with great solemnity.

Popular tradition in the saint's native town of Salency attributes to him the institution of the old local observance of the Rosière.   Annually on the feast of St Medard the maiden who has been judged to be the most exemplary in the district is escorted by twelve boys and twelve girls to the church, where she is crowned with roses and rewarded with a small gift of money.   St Medard sometimes is depicted with a spread eagle above his head, in allusion to the tradition that once in his childhood an eagle extended its wings over his head to shelter him from the rain.   This story may account for his supposed connection with the weather.   The peasants say that if it rains on St Medard's feast the forty ensuing days will be wet, and that if, on the other hand, the eighth of June is fine, a spell of forty fine days is to be expected, just like our English St Swithun.   Occasionally the saint is represented with St Gildard, who is erroneously described as his twin brother, and who as such is commemorated with him in the Roman Martyrology.   St Medard for some reason was sometimes depicted in the middle ages laughing inanely with his mouth wide open (" *le ris de St Médard* "), and he was invoked to cure the toothache.   Whether his association with dental troubles was the consequence or the cause of this representation, it is hard to say.

To judge by the number of entries, nn. 5863 to 5874, in BHL., one would be disposed to think that materials for a life of St Medard were abundant.   But most of these sources are very unsatisfactory.   The poem of Venantius Fortunatus, though he was a friend of St

Radegund and himself of contemporary date, tells us but little : it is largely taken up with recounting some rather trivial and improbable miracles. The early prose life (*c.* A.D. 600), at one time also attributed to Venantius, is not by him, but it seems reliable. The best text of this is that edited by Bruno Krusch in MGH., *Auctores Antiquissimi*, vol. iv, part ii, pp. 67–73. Another anonymous life of the ninth century adds relatively little to our knowledge. On the other hand, a biography by Radbod, written about 1080, is full of information, but it is information of a most suspicious kind. He himself was bishop of the united sees of Noyon and Tournai, and there is grave reason to think that, being faced by a strong party who were opposed to this union of dioceses, he hoped to secure himself in his position by claiming that the arrangement was centuries old, and was based upon a precedent set by the deeply venerated St Medard. It seems incredible that, if the saint had really become bishop of Tournai, Gregory of Tours, Venantius and all other early writers could have failed to mention the fact. It is not even certain that the transfer of the see to Noyon took place in St Medard's time. There is a convenient summary of the case by H. Leclercq in DAC., vol. xi, cc. 102–107 ; and see Duchesne, *Fastes Épiscopaux*, vol. iii, p. 102 ; and R. Hanon de Louvet, *Histoire de la ville de Jodoigne* (1941), cap. vii.

ST CLODULF, OR CLOUD, BISHOP OF METZ   (*c.* A.D. 692)

ST CLODULF and Ansegis were the sons of St Arnoul, bishop of Metz, and his wife Doda, who took the veil when her husband became a priest. Like their father, the two brothers held important offices at the court of the kings of Austrasia. Ansegis married Begga, a daughter of Pepin of Landen, and became the ancestor of the Carlovingian kings of France, but Clodulf, after the death in 656 of St Godo, bishop of Metz, was chosen to fill the episcopal seat formerly occupied by his father. As a layman he had lived a devout, edifying life, and as a priest and bishop he proved a model pastor, ruling his diocese wisely, giving alms liberally and ever advancing in the path of holiness. To illustrate his humility it is recorded that when, at his desire, a biography of his father was being compiled, he insisted upon mention being made of an episode which the writer would fain have omitted. It happened on one occasion that St Arnoul, after he had exhausted his own purse in charities, applied to his sons for more money to spend on the poor. Clodulf, whom he approached first, was ungracious and made no more than a niggardly response, but Ansegis generously placed all that was required at St Arnoul's disposal.

St Clodulf ruled the church of Metz for forty years and died a very old man in 692 or 696.

The life printed in the *Acta Sanctorum*, June, vol. ii, is of the usual legendary type, written long after the events described. Rather better material is furnished by Paulus Diaconus in his *Gesta Episcoporum Mettensium* (edited in Pertz, MGH., *Scriptores*, vol. ii). See also Weyland, *Vies des Saints du diocèse de Metz*, vol. iii (1909), pp. 322–347 ; J. Depoin, in the *Revue Mabillon*, 1921-1922 ; and Duchesne, *Fastes Épiscopaux*, vol. iii, p. 56.

ST WILLIAM, ARCHBISHOP OF YORK   (A.D. 1154)

ST WILLIAM FITZHERBERT, also known as William of Thwayt, is stated to have been the son of King Stephen's half-sister Emma and of Count Herbert, treasurer to Henry I, and while yet young William himself was appointed treasurer of the church of York. He appears to have been somewhat indolent, but he was personally popular and, on the death of Archbishop Thurston of York in 1140, he was chosen to fill the vacancy. The validity of the election, however, was contested by Archdeacon Walter of York, together with a number of Cistercian abbots and Augustinian priors, who alleged unchastity and simony on the part of William and

undue influence on the part of the king.   Stephen invested him with the temporalities of the see, but the archbishop of Canterbury, Theobald, hesitated to consecrate
him, and the parties carried their case to Rome, where the objectors relied chiefly
on the charge of intrusion into the see.   Pope Innocent decided that the election
might be regarded as valid provided the dean of York, also called William, should
appear before a court to be held by Henry of Blois,who was bishop of Winchester and
papal legate, and there swear that the chapter had received no mandate from the king.
    Dean William, who just at this time was made bishop of Durham, did not take
that oath—it is possible that he could not without committing perjury.   But in
consequence of another papal letter, whose origins are uncertain and not altogether
above suspicion, William Fitzherbert was able to satisfy Henry of Winchester, who
duly consecrated him, and he was warmly welcomed by the clergy and people of
York.   He governed his diocese well, promoting peace so far as in him lay.   But
his opponents had abated none of their energy ; and William, through, says a
chronicler, his easy-goingness and tendency to procrastination, made a mistake
that played into their hands.   He failed to make arrangements for receiving the
pallium which Pope Lucius II had sent by the hands of his legate, Cardinal Imar
of Tusculum.   Lucius died while the pallium was yet unconferred, and Imar took
it back to Rome.   To sue for it William was obliged to go again to Rome, selling
or pledging some of the treasures of York to pay his expenses.   But the new pope,
Eugenius III, was a Cistercian and completely under the influence of St Bernard
of Clairvaux, who had all along vigorously supported the cause of William's
opponents.   Though the majority of the cardinals were in his favour, William was
suspended on the ground that the bishop of Durham had not taken the oath
prescribed by Innocent II.   Thereupon the archbishop retired to the hospitality
of his relative King Roger of Sicily.   But his supporters in England, directly the
news of the papal decision reached York, made an attack on Fountains Abbey, of
which Henry Murdac, formerly a monk with Pope Eugenius, was abbot, and burnt
its farms ; they also seized and mutilated Archdeacon Walter.   This criminality
still further prejudiced William's cause, and in 1147 the pope deposed him.   Soon
after Henry Murdac was nominated to be archbishop of York in his stead.
    Upon his return to England William took refuge with his uncle, Henry of
Winchester, who treated him with honour ; but the deposed prelate was chastened
by his misfortunes ; he now shunned the luxury to which he had been accustomed,
and elected to lead a penitential and austere life in the cathedral monastery.   He
remained thus in Winchester for six years, when in 1153 Pope Eugenius, St
Bernard and Murdac all died within three months of one another : whereupon
William went to Rome to plead for the restoration of his see with Pope Anastasius
IV.   The new pontiff granted his petition, and conferred the pallium on him
before he returned home.
    St William re-entered York in May 1154 amid popular demonstrations of joy.
Under the weight of the crowds gathered to welcome him, the wooden bridge over
the Ouse broke down, throwing many into the river.   The rescue of these unfor-
tunates, not one of whom sustained injury, was attributed by the citizens to the
prayers of their restored archbishop.   William showed no resentment towards his
adversaries and almost at once visited Fountains Abbey, to which he promised
restitution for the damage it had received from his violent relatives.   But he did
not live to carry out his projects for the benefit of his province.   A month after
his return to York he was taken with violent pain after celebrating a solemn Mass,

and within a few days, on June 8, he was dead. The new archdeacon of York, Osbert, was haled before the king's court on a charge of having poisoned the archbishop. The case was removed to the Holy See, but there is no record of any judgement having been given : the guilt or innocence of Osbert remains uncertain.

St William's body was in 1284 translated from a chapel of the cathedral to the nave, in the presence of King Edward I and Queen Eleanor ; but though the relics escaped destruction at the time of the Reformation and appear to have been preserved until the eighteenth century, they have now disappeared. His chief memorial in his cathedral is the great window which was put up in 1421 and is one of York's three celebrated " walls of glass " ; in its many lights there are depicted scenes from William's life and miracles, supplemented by a few which properly belong to St John of Beverley and St John of Bridlington. Pope Honorius III canonized St William in 1227, after inquiry into the many wonders reported to have taken place at his tomb, and his feast is still observed in the dioceses of the north of England.

See John of Hexham's continuation of Symeon of Durham's *Historia Regum* and William of Newburgh's *Historia Regum* (both in the Rolls Series) ; the " Narratio fundationis " in *Memorials of Fountains*, vol. i (ed. J. Walbran, 1863) ; Walter Daniel's Life of St Aelred (ed. F. M. Powicke, 1950) ; and St Bernard's letters in Migne, PL, vols. clxxxii–clxxxv. An anonymous Life of St William, jejune and mostly untrustworthy, is printed in J. Raine's *Historians of the Church of York*, vol. ii. Among modern accounts, see that of T. F. Tout in DNB., vol. xix ; more recent are those of R. L. Poole in the *English Historical Review*, 1930, pp. 273–281, and D. Knowles in the *Cambridge Historical Journal*, 1936, pp. 162–177 and 212–214 (bibliography and notes). It is curious that in a thirteenth-century calendar painted on the walls of the church of the Quattro Coronati at Rome the name of St William of York occurs on February 4.

BD JOHN RAINUZZI (A.D. 1330 ?)

IT was formerly the custom at Todi in Italy for those regarded as being possessed by evil spirits to be taken to the church of St Margaret, where an office of exorcism was pronounced over them by a priest in a crypt under the high altar. Whilst this service was being held one day in 1568, the demoniac suddenly cried out, " Here rests the body of Blessed John the Almsgiver ! " There had already been a tradition that some saint lay buried in the chapel, and investigations were accordingly made. They resulted in the discovery of a marble tomb containing bones, and bearing the inscription : " This is the body of Blessed John Raynutius of Todi, buried in the monastery of St Margaret of Todi, who passed from this world to the Father in the year 1330 on the eighth day of June ". It was no unusual thing in the fourteenth century for the words " blessed " and " saint " to be inserted without ecclesiastical sanction in epitaphs on tombs. In this case, however, a local missal seems to have been found which contained a notice of Bd John of Todi, who died and was buried in the monastery of St Margaret in 1330. This was accepted as sufficient proof of an ancient *cultus* by the bishop of Todi, who exposed the relics to the veneration of the faithful on September 3, 1568, and then caused them to be replaced in the marble tomb. Afterwards in the church of St Margaret an image was set up of Bd John Raynutius, or Rainuzzi, clad in a Benedictine habit and carrying on his shoulders seven bags—presumably filled with alms for the poor.

A brief account of this rather unsatisfactory case is given in the *Acta Sanctorum*, June, vol. ii. It is mainly derived from J. B. Possevinus, *De Sanctis et Beatis Tudertibus* (Perugia, 1597).

BD PACIFICO OF CERANO   (A.D. 1482)

BD PACIFICO RAMOTA was born at Novara in Piedmont in the year 1424. His parents died when he was very young, and he was educated in the Benedictine abbey of his native city. He then took the habit in the Franciscan convent of the strict observance, being about twenty-one years of age, and he became one of the most learned ecclesiastics of his time. After his ordination he laboured chiefly as a preacher in Italy, conducting many successful missions between the years 1452 and 1471. His evangelistic work was interrupted by a visit to Sardinia, where he went with a commission from Pope Sixtus IV to redress certain disorders and irregularities that had crept into the church. He was induced to write a treatise on moral theology, which was published in Milan in 1475 and was long regarded as the standard work on that subject, though aiming at simple explanations, intelligible to all. He entitled it *Sommetta di Pacifica Coscienza*, but it was commonly known as *Somma Pacifica*. He resumed his mission work, labouring chiefly in the north of Italy and using as his headquarters the convent of Vigevano which he had founded in the diocese of Novara.

In 1480 came another summons to go to Sardinia, this time as visitor and commissary general for the convents of the strict observance, and also as apostolic nuncio charged by Pope Sixtus IV to proclaim a crusade against Mohammed II. The order arrived when he was preaching at Cerano. He knew that he had not long to live, and in his farewell address he said : " I ask you to do me this favour—that when you hear of my death, you will have my poor wretched remains brought back to my native land, so that I may be buried in this dear church which I have built in honour of the Blessed Virgin." He went to Sardinia, but had scarcely begun to preach the crusade when he was taken ill. He died at Sassari on June 4, 1482. In compliance with his request his body was taken back to Cerano, where a church was afterwards built in his honour. The cult of Bd Pacifico was confirmed in 1745.

An account of Bd Pacifico is furnished in an appendix to the June volume i of the *Acta Sanctorum*. He is also prominent in Wadding's *Scriptores*, and in the *Annales Ordinis Minorum*, vol. xiv. See further, the *Miscellanea Franciscana*, vols. iii and vii, and Léon's *Auréole Séraphique* (Eng. trans.), vol. ii, pp. 352–355. Small separate lives have been published by M. Cazzola and by another writer, who remains anonymous.

9 : ST COLUMBA, OR COLMCILLE, ABBOT OF IONA *   (A.D. 597)

THE most famous of Scottish saints, Columba, was actually an Irishman of the Uí Néill of the North and was born, probably about the year 521, at Gartan in County Donegal. On both sides he was of royal lineage, for his father Fedhlimidh, or Phelim, was great-grandson to Niall of the Nine Hostages, overlord of Ireland, whilst his mother Eithne, besides being related to the princes of Scottish Dalriada, was herself descended from a king of Leinster. At his baptism, which was administered by his foster father the priest Cruithnechan, the little boy received the name of Colm, Colum or Columba. In later life he was commonly called Colmcille—a designation which Bede derives from *cella et Columba*, and

* Since the feast of St Columba is observed throughout Scotland (with a proper Mass), Ireland, Australia and New Zealand he is put first herein on this day.

which almost certainly refers to the many cells or religious foundations he established. As soon as he was considered old enough, he was removed from the care of his priest guardian at Temple Douglas to St Finnian's great school at Moville. There he must have spent a number of years, for he was a deacon when he left. From Moville he went to study in Leinster under an aged bard called Master Gemman. The bards preserved the records of Irish history and literature, and Columba himself was a poet of no mean order. He afterwards passed on to another famous monastic school, that of Clonard, presided over by another Finnian, who was called the tutor of Erin's saints. Columba was one of that distinguished band of his disciples who are reckoned as the Twelve Apostles of Erin. It was probably while he was at Clonard that he was ordained priest, but it may have been a little later when he was living at Glasnevin, with St Comgall, St Kieran and St Canice, under their former fellow student St Mobhi. In 543 an outbreak of plague compelled Mobhi to break up his flourishing school and Columba, now twenty-five years of age and fully trained, returned to his native Ulster.

A striking figure of great stature and of athletic build, with a voice "so loud and melodious it could be heard a mile off ", Columba spent the next fifteen years going about Ireland preaching and founding monasteries of which the chief were those of Derry, Durrow and Kells. Like the true scholar that he was, Columba dearly loved books and spared no pains to obtain them. Amongst the many precious manuscripts his former master, St Finnian, had obtained in Rome was the first copy of St Jerome's psalter to reach Ireland. St Columba borrowed the book of which he surreptitiously made a copy for his own use. St Finnian, however, on being told what he had done, laid claim to the transcript. Columba refused to give it up, and the case was laid before King Diarmaid, overlord of Ireland. The verdict went against Columba. " To every cow her calf ", said the judge, " and to every book its son-book. Therefore the copy which you have made, Colmcille, belongs to Finnian."

This sentence Columba bitterly resented, but he was soon to have a much more serious grievance against the king. For when Curnan of Connaught, after fatally injuring an opponent in a hurling match, took refuge with Columba, he was dragged from his protector's arms and slain by Diarmaid's men in defiance of the rights of sanctuary. The war which broke out shortly afterwards between Columba's clan and Diarmaid's followers is stated in most of the Irish *Lives* to have been instigated by Columba, and after the battle of Cuil Dremne in which 3000 were slain he was accused of being morally responsible for their death. The synod of Telltown in Meath passed upon him a censure which would have been followed by an excommunication but for the intervention of St Brendan. Columba's own conscience was uneasy, and by the advice of St Molaise he determined to expiate his offence by exiling himself from his own country and by attempting to win for Christ as many souls as had perished in the battle of Cuil Dremne.

This is the traditional account of the events which led to Columba's departure from Ireland, and it is probably correct in the main. At the same time it must be admitted that missionary zeal and love of Christ are the only motives ascribed to him by his earliest biographers or by St Adamnan, who is our chief authority for his subsequent history. In the year 563 Columba embarked with twelve companions—all of them his blood relations—in a wicker coracle covered with leather, and on the eve of Pentecost he landed in the island of I, or Iona. He was in his forty-second year. His first work was the building of the monastery which was to be his home for the rest of his life and which was to be famous throughout western Christendom for centuries. The land was made over to him by his kinsman Conall, king of Scottish Dalriada, at whose invitation he may have come to Scotland. Situated opposite the border between the Picts of the north and the Scots of the south, Iona formed an ideal centre for missions to both peoples. At first Columba appears to have devoted his missionary effort to teaching the imperfectly instructed Christians of Dalriada—most of whom were of Irish descent—but after about two years he turned his attention to the evangelization of the Scotland Picts. Accompanied by St Comgall and St Canice he made his way to the castle of the redoubtable King Brude at Inverness.

That pagan monarch had given orders that they were not to be admitted, but when St Columba upraised his arm to make the sign of the cross, bolts were withdrawn, gates fell open, and the strangers entered unhindered. Impressed by their supernatural powers the king listened to their words and ever afterwards held Columba in high honour. He also, as overlord, confirmed him in the possession of Iona. We know from St Adamnan that two or three times the saint crossed the mountain range which divides the west of Scotland from the east and that his missionary zeal took him to Ardnamurchan, to Skye, to Kintyre, to Loch Ness and to Lochaber, and perhaps to Morven. He is commonly credited, furthermore, with having planted the Church in Aberdeenshire and with having evangelized practically the whole of Pictland, but this has been contested on various grounds. When the descendants of the Dalriada kings became the rulers of Scotland they were naturally eager to magnify St Columba and a tendency may well have arisen to bestow upon him the laurels won by other missionaries from Iona and elsewhere.

Columba never lost touch with Ireland. In 575 he attended the synod of Drumceat in Meath in company with Conall's successor Aidan, and there he was successful in defending the status and privileges of his Dalriada kinsfolk, in vetoing the proposed abolition of the order of bards, and in securing for women exemption from all military service. He was in Ireland again ten years later, and in 587 he seems to have been regarded as in some way responsible for another battle—this time at Cuil Feda, near Clonard. When not engaged on missionary or diplomatic expeditions his headquarters continued to be at Iona, where he was visited by persons of all conditions, some desiring spiritual or bodily help, some attracted by his reputation for sanctity, his miracles and his prophecies. His manner of life was most austere ; and in his earlier life he was apt to be no less hard with others. Montalembert remarked that, " Of all qualities, gentleness was precisely the one in which Columba failed the most '. But with the passage of time his character mellowed and the picture painted by St Adamnan of his serene old age shows him in a singularly attractive light, a lover of man and beast. Four years before his death he had an illness which threatened to prove fatal, but his life was prolonged in answer to the prayers of the community. As his strength began to fail he spent much time transcribing books. On the day before his death he was copying the Psalter, and had written, " They that love the Lord shall lack no good thing ", when he paused and said, " Here I must stop : let Baithin do the rest ". Baithin was his cousin whom he had nominated as his successor.

That night when the monks came to the church for Matins, they found their beloved abbot outstretched helpless and dying before the altar. As his faithful attendant Diarmaid gently upraised him he made a feeble effort to bless his brethren and then immediately breathed his last. Columba was indeed dead, but his influence lasted on, extended until it came to dominate the churches of Scotland, Ireland and Northumbria. For three-quarters of a century and more, Celtic Christians in those lands upheld Columban traditions in certain matters of order and ritual in opposition to those of Rome itself, and the rule Columba had drawn up for his monks was followed in many of the monásteries of western Europe until it was superseded by the milder ordinances of St Benedict.

Adamnan, St Columba's biographer, had not personally known him, for he was born at least thirty years after his death, but as his kinsman by blood and a successor in the office of abbot at Iona itself, he must have been steeped in the traditions which such a personality could not fail to have created for those who followed in his footsteps. The portrait of Columba left by Adamnan in any case deserves to be quoted. " He had the face of an angel ; he was of an excellent nature, polished in speech, holy in deed, great in counsel. He never let a single hour pass without engaging in prayer or reading or writing or some other occupation. He endured the hardships of fasting and vigils without intermission by day and night, the burden of a single one of his labours would seem beyond the powers of man. And, in the midst of all his toils, he appeared loving unto all, serene and holy, rejoicing in the joy of the Holy Spirit in his inmost heart." And Columba's prophetical last blessing of the Isle of Iona came true : " Unto this place, small and mean though it be, great homage shall yet be paid, not only by the kings and peoples of the Scots, but by the rulers of barbarous and distant nations with their peoples. The saints, also, of other churches shall regard it with no common reverence."

The most important source, but not nearest in point of time, is undoubtedly Adamnan. J. T. Fowler's revised edition of 1920 supplies the best text, but Reeves's text and notes are also valuable, and there is a translation by Wentworth Huyshe (1939). Two Latin lives of Irish origin, neither of them complete, are in the *Codex Salmanticensis*. They have been printed by the Bollandists, and besides these there are three Irish lives, all of which are described with references by C. Plummer, in *Miscellanea Hagiographica Hibernica*. Another valuable source is the *Ecclesiastical History* of Bede. But for a general view of the materials J. F. Kenney's *Sources for the Early History of Ireland* should above all be consulted, and also his article in the *Catholic Historical Review* (Washington, D.C., 1926), pp. 636–644. A notable increase in the number of books and articles devoted to St Columba was no doubt due to the writings of Dr W. D. Simpson (notably *The Historical St Columba*, 1927, and *The Celtic Church in Scotland*, 1935), who threw doubt upon the claim made for Columba that he was the true apostle of the north of Scotland. Dr Simpson's views roused active opposition, on which see P. Grosjean in the *Analecta Bollandiana*, vol. xlvi (1928), pp. 197–199 and vol. liv (1936), pp. 408–412 ; L. Gougaud in *Scottish Gaelic Studies*, vol. ii (1927), pp. 106–108, and J. Ryan in *The Month*, October, 1927, pp. 314–320. *Cf.* Leclercq under " Iona ", in DAC., vol. vii, cc. 1425 *seq.* and *Analecta Bollandiana*, vol. lv (1937), pp. 96–108 ; and for how the name I, Y or Hi, became Iona, see Plummer's *Bede*, vol. ii, p. 127.

SS. PRIMUS AND FELICIAN, MARTYRS   (c. A.D. 297)

THE brothers Primus and Felician were Roman patricians who embraced Christianity and devoted themselves to works of charity, especially to visiting the confessors in prison. In spite of their zeal they escaped persecution for many years, but about the year 297, in the reign of Emperors Diocletian and Maximian, they were arrested. They refused to sacrifice, were imprisoned, and scourged. Afterwards they were conveyed to Nomentum, a town twelve miles from Rome, where they were tried by a magistrate named Promotus. As they remained steadfast they were again tortured. Both were then sentenced to be beheaded. After Primus, who was eighty years of age, had been executed, the judge tried to overcome the constancy of Felician by pretending that his brother had yielded. The confessor, however, was not to be deceived and cheerfully faced death on the same day. Over the burial-place of the two martyrs in the Via Nomentana a church was afterwards built. In 640 Pope Theodore caused their relics to be brought to San Stefano Rotondo, and this translation is said to have been the first instance of the removal of the bodies of martyrs from a church dedicated to them outside the walls of Rome to a basilica within the city.

The *passio* of these martyrs, printed in the *Acta Sanctorum*, June, vol. ii, is of the usual legendary character, but they were unquestionably put to death, and buried by their fellow Christians in the place indicated. Their feast is honoured in the earliest text of the Gelasian Sacramentary. When the bodies were translated to Rome by Pope Theodore, a representation of the two saints in mosaic, which is still in existence, was set up behind the spot where their relics were venerated. See CMH., p. 311, and also J. P. Kirsch, *Der Stadtrömische christliche Festkalender* (1924), pp. 59–60.

ST VINCENT OF AGEN, Martyr   (*c.* A.D. 300 ?)

St Vincent was a deacon who lived in Gascony, probably towards the end of the third century. Apparently because he interrupted a pagan ceremony, which may have been a druidical feast, he was arrested at Agen and brought before the governor. He was laid flat with his limbs extended, fixed to the ground by four stakes. In that position he was cruelly scourged and then beheaded. His relics were buried at Mas d'Agenais ; St Gregory of Tours and Fortunatus of Poitiers testify that in the sixth and seventh centuries many flocked from all parts of Europe in pilgrimage to his tomb.

The facts regarding the martyrdom are quite uncertain, and Father Delehaye is not satisfied that the alleged tragedy at Agen ever occurred. He thinks it possible that the story was elaborated out of some special cult of the great Spanish martyr St Vincent, the nature and origin of which was forgotten. Still the references to the martyr in St Gregory of Tours and Venantius Fortunatus are relatively early. The matter is too intricate to be discussed here.

There are several texts of the *passio*, for which see the *Acta Sanctorum*, June, vol. ii ; and the BHL., nn. 8621–8625. See for fuller details Delehaye's CMH., p. 312 ; L. Saltet, " Étude critique de la Passio S. Vincentii Aginensis ", in the *Revue de Gascogne*, 1901, pp. 97–113 ; Duchesne, *Fastes Épiscopaux*, vol. ii, pp. 142–144 ; and the Marchioness de Maillé, *Vincent d'Agen et Vincent de Saragosse* (1949). See especially Fr B. de Gaiffier in *Analecta Bollandiana*, vol. lxx (1952), pp. 160–181.

ST PELAGIA OF ANTIOCH, Virgin and Martyr   (*c.* A.D. 311)

The name of St Pelagia stands in the canon of the Ambrosian Mass of Milan, and her praises have been sung by St Ambrose and by St John Chrysostom, who made her the subject of one, or possibly two, of his homilies. Pelagia was a young Christian girl of fifteen, a native of Antioch and probably a disciple of St Lucian. She was alone in the house when it was surrounded by soldiers sent to arrest her. Well aware that her ultimate fate—whatever it might be—would be preceded by dishonour, she asked leave to withdraw for a little, in order to put on suitable clothing. The permission having been granted, she went upstairs and threw herself from the top of the house. She was killed on the spot ; but she had preserved her chastity, which she valued more than her life. St John Chrysostom asserts that she acted under the inspiration of our Lord within her, exhorting her, strengthening her, and casting out her fear.

This is the historical St Pelagia, whose name has been borrowed by later hagiographers, or more truly romance-writers, to graft upon it two entirely different stories. Upon this, see Delehaye, *Légendes Hagiographiques* (ed. 1927), pp. 186–195. The reality of Pelagia's fate is attested not only by the homily of St John Chrysostom, but also by an entry in the early Syriac *Breviarium* under October 8. It is on this day also that Pelagia is commemorated in the *Hieronymianum*, on which consult Delehaye's commentary, p. 546. A second homily on St Pelagia has been attributed to St John Chrysostom, but this is probably not his genuine work ; see Franchi de' Cavalieri in *Studi e Testi*, vol. lxv, pp. 281–303, who has edited the text.

ST RICHARD, Bishop of Andria   (Twelfth Century ?)

ALL the records agree that the St Richard who is commemorated on June 9 was an Englishman and that he was the first bishop of Andria in Apulia. His reputed " acts ", however, are spurious and the very period at which he flourished is uncertain. Local tradition asserts that he came from Rome to Andria in 453, when Attila was ravaging Italy, that he was elected bishop and that he was one of the three prelates commissioned by Pope St Gelasius I to dedicate the sanctuary on Monte Gargano after the famous vision of St Michael. On the other hand, there is no evidence of the existence of a bishopric at Andria before 1118 and it is certain that the English (Britons ?) were still, for the most part, heathen in the fifth century. It seems more reasonable to identify to-day's saint with the Bishop Richard of Andria who attended the third Council of the Lateran in 1179 and who translated the relics of SS. Erasmus and Pontian from Civitella to Andria in 1196. He may possibly have owed his elevation to the episcopate to Pope Adrian IV, himself an Englishman. The remains of St Richard, which had been long lost, were discovered in 1434 with documents testifying to his ancient *cultus*, and Eugenius IV consented to its revival and continuance. St Richard, or Riccardo, is the principal patron of Andria.

The so-called life of St Richard has been printed by Ughelli, *Italia Sacra*, vol. vii, cc. 1248–1255 ; and see also the *Acta Sanctorum*, June, vol. ii. In comparatively recent years the whole subject has been soberly discussed by R. Zagaria, *San Ricardo nella legenda, nella storia* . . . (1929) ; and *cf.* the *Analecta Bollandiana*, vol. l (1932), pp. 206–207.

BB. DIANA, CECILIA and AMATA, Virgins   (A.D. 1236 and 1290)

WHEN St Dominic sought a wider field for the activities of his order in Italy, he made special choice of Bologna because he foresaw that its famous university would provide him with the kind of recruits he desired. A suitable site for a priory was found, but strong opposition was encountered from the powerful d'Andalo family who owned the land. Eventually they yielded to the earnest entreaties of Andalo's only daughter Diana, who from the first coming of the friars had listened eagerly to their preaching. St Dominic privately received her vow of virginity, together with an undertaking that she would enter the religious life as soon as possible. For some time she continued to live at home, rising very early for her devotions and practising penance. She had anticipated being able to persuade her family to found a convent for Dominican nuns which she could enter, but when she broached the subject her father absolutely refused to consider it or to allow her to become a religious. She then took the law into her own hands. On the pretext of paying them a visit she went to the Augustinian canonesses at Roxana and induced them to give her the veil. As soon as this became known, her family went in force to fetch her, so much violence being employed that one of her ribs was broken in the scuffle. She was taken home and kept in close confinement, but after she had recovered she managed to escape and to return to Roxana. No further attempts seem to have been made to interfere with her. Indeed, Bd Jordan of Saxony so completely won over Andalo and his sons that they helped him to found a small convent for Dominican nuns ; and there in 1222, Diana and four companions were installed. As they were quite inexperienced in the religious life, four nuns were obtained from the convent of San Sisto in Rome. Two of these, Cecilia and Amata, are always associated with Diana : they were buried in her tomb and were beatified with her in 1891.

Nothing else is known of Amata, but Cecilia was a member of the noble Roman family of the Cesarini and was a remarkable woman. When she was a girl of seventeen in the convent at the Trastevere before its removal to San Sisto, she had been the first of the nuns to respond to St Dominic's efforts to reform them, and she it was who persuaded the abbess and the other sisters to submit to his rule. Having been the first woman—so, at least, it is said—to receive the Dominican habit, she was well fitted to govern the convent of St Agnes at Bologna in its early days. Bd Jordan had a special affection for the little community and kept up an active correspondence with Diana. Frequently in his letters he attributes the progress of the order in a great measure to their prayers ; his one apprehension is that they may be overtaxing their strength by their austerities. Bd Diana died on January 9, 1236, at about the age of thirty-five. Cecilia survived her by many years and as an old woman dictated her reminiscences of St Dominic. They contain a simple and graphic pen portrait of the holy founder himself.

There is a Latin biography of Bd Diana which will be found printed in the volume of H. M. Cormier, *La bse Diane d'Andalo* (1892). Bd Jordan's letters were re-edited in 1925 by B. Altaner, *Die Briefe Jordans von Sachsen*, and there is a French translation of the letters written to Bd Diana, produced by M. Aron in 1924. See also M. C. de Ganay, *Les Bien-heureuses Dominicaines* (1913), pp. 23–48 ; Procter, *Lives of the Dominican Saints*, pp. 168–170; and N. Georges, *Bd Diana and Bd Jordan* (1933).

BD SILVESTER OF VALDISEVE (A.D. 1348)

A CARDER and bleacher of wool by trade, Bd Silvester (whose baptismal name was Ventura) was born near Florence. In middle life he came under the influence of a certain Brother Jordan, and at the age of forty he entered the Camaldolese monastery of St Mary in Florence as a lay-brother. There he was cook. Although he was totally uneducated, he was so liberally endowed with infused wisdom that he was often consulted by learned men, notably by Bd Simon of Cascia, who stated that he had been enlightened by him on at least one hundred abstruse theological points. The prior would frequently seek his advice, as did also the monks, who treasured up many of his wise sayings. He used to dissuade them from under-taking extraordinary and prolonged penitential exercises as tending to pride ; the discipline, he declared, should be taken with moderation, humility and devotion. When a monk told him that he was troubled with carnal thoughts, the holy man made light of it and remarked that it was only what was to be expected ; but when another brother acknowledged that he had been murmuring, Silvester took the matter very seriously. He asked how he, a servant of Almighty God, could do such a thing and entreated him to cure himself of that vice in this life, that he might not have to atone for it in eternity. He never learnt to read ; but Silvester had so great a devotion to the Divine Office—which he could hear—that he expressed wonder that the hearts of men could remain unbroken at the sound of words so sweet and so sublime. In accordance with his own prediction, the good lay-brother passed away on the day that a beloved sister of the name of Paula died in the neighbouring convent of St Margaret. He was seventy years of age.

In the *Acta Sanctorum*, June, vol. ii, will be found a short life of Bd Silvester, translated from the Italian of Fr Zenobius, and also an interesting poem in the original Italian, recounting the more striking features of Bd Silvester's character and history.

BD HENRY THE SHOEMAKER   (A.D. 1666)

HENRY MICHAEL BUCHE—" Good Henry "—has never been beatified nor apparently the object of *cultus*, but he is commonly referred to as Blessed or Saint. He was a shoemaker by trade at Arlon in Luxembourg, where he formed a religious society for his fellow tradesmen under the traditional patronage of SS. Crispin and Crispinian.

Afterwards, in 1645, when he had migrated to Paris, Henry formed there a similar association the members of which were known as the " Frères Cordonniers". Baron de Renty, who took great interest in it, obtained for him the rights of citizenship and recognition as a master-shoemaker in order that he might be able to accept apprentices and journeymen who wished to follow his rule. It was a strict one. The members rose at five, had prayer in common at stated hours, attended Mass daily, visited prisons and hospitals, and attended an annual retreat. The association grew and prospered : branches were started in other cities, and the tailors established a society for themselves on parallel lines. It would be difficult to overestimate the influence Henry was thus able to exert, both directly and indirectly, over people for whom comparatively little had been done in the past. He died in Paris, on June 9, 1666, and was buried in the cemetery attached to the Hospital of St Gervais in which he had often tended the patients.

The best available account will be found in Hélyot, *Histoire des Ordres Monastiques* (ed. 1721), vol. viii, pp. 175–184, which quotes an earlier work, J. A. Le Vachet, *L'Artisan chrétien, ou la Vie du bon Henri* (1670). There is also a notice of Henri Buche in the *Bio-graphie nationale* (Brussels, 1872), vol. iii, pp. 143–144. It would seem that the Baron de Renty had much to do with drafting the rules of the association which Henry founded.

BD ANNE MARY TAIGI, MATRON   (A.D. 1837)

THERE can have been no more remarkable woman in the Rome of the early nineteenth century than Anne Mary Taigi, the hard-working wife of a domestic servant and the exemplary mother of a large family, who was honoured by three successive popes with their special esteem and whose humble home was the resort of some of the highest personages in church and state—desirous to enlist her intercession, to obtain her advice or to seek enlightenment in the things of God. Anne Mary Antonia Gesualda was born on May 29, 1769, at Siena, where her father carried on business as an apothecary. Reduced to poverty, the family migrated to Rome, and Anne's parents entered private domestic service, whilst she herself was sent to a community of women who undertook the education of poor children. At the age of thirteen the little girl also became a breadwinner. After working for a short time in silk factories, she became a housemaid in the palace of a noble lady.   As she grew to womanhood she developed a love of dress and a thirst for admiration which occasionally led her into peril ; that she did not fall into grave sin was due to her good upbringing, and to her marriage in 1790 to Dominic Taigi, a servant in the Chigi palace.   Even then the things of the world continued to engross her, but gradually grace began to stir in her heart, she felt the pricks of conscience, and was moved to make a general confession.   Her first attempt to open her heart to a priest met with a severe rebuff ; but a second was more successful.

She found the spiritual guide she needed in a Servite friar, Father Angelo, who was to continue to be her confessor for many years.   He realized from the first that he was dealing with an elect soul, and she on her part always regarded the hour she first met him as the date of her conversion.   From that time she renounced all vanities, contenting herself with the plainest of clothes, and took no part in worldly amusements unless by her husband's special desire.   In prayer she found her chief solace, and her generous desire for external mortifications had to be limited by her confessor to such as were compatible with her duties in life.   Her husband was a good man, but narrow and rather cantankerous, and whilst he fully appreciated his wife's good qualities, as far as they affected him and the family, he never understood her heroic efforts to reach a high ideal of renunciation or the divine graces with which they were rewarded.   His testimony to her fulfilment of everyday duties is therefore all the more convincing.

Referring to the time when she was already well known Dominic said : " It often happened that upon my return home I found the house full of people.   At once she would leave anyone who was there—a great lady, maybe, or a prelate—and would hasten to wait upon me affectionately and attentively.   One could see that she did it with all her heart : she would have taken off my shoes if I would have allowed it.   In short, she was my comfort and the consolation of all. . . . Through her wonderful tact she was able to maintain a heavenly peace though we were a great houseful and of very different temperaments—especially when my eldest son Camillus was living with us in his early married days.   My daughter-in-law was a disturbing element and always wanted to play the mistress, but the servant of God knew how to keep everyone in his place and she did it with a graciousness that I cannot describe.   I often came home tired, moody and cross, but she always succeeded in soothing and cheering me."   The family Anne had to look after consisted of her seven children, five of whom lived to grow up, and also of her parents.   Every morning she gathered them all together for prayers ; those who could do so attended Mass, and in the evening all met together again for spiritual reading and for night prayers.   She took extraordinary care over the upbringing of her children.

Bd Anne also worked with her needle, sometimes to supplement her husband's earnings, sometimes to be able to assist those poorer than herself, for she was always exceedingly generous and she trained her children to be generous too.   It might seem as though domestic cares such as those mentioned above would mono-polize the energies of any woman ; and yet her family duties did not preclude absorption in mystical experiences of a very high order.   Some idea of these can be gleaned from a memoir written after her death by Cardinal Pedicini, to whom she had originally been introduced by her confessor, and who shared with him the responsibility of her spiritual direction for thirty years.   It was probably also through him that her virtues and supernatural gifts became known, even during her lifetime. From the time of her conversion God gave her wonderful intimations about His intentions with regard to the dangers that threatened the Church, about future events, and about the hidden things of the faith. They were revealed to her in a " mystical sun ", which hovered before her eyes and in which she also saw the iniquity man was continually committing against God : she felt it to be her task to make satisfaction for it and to offer herself as a victim.

Anne would endure agonies of mind and body when wrestling in prayer for the conversion of some hardened sinner. She often read the thoughts and motives of those who visited her, and was thus able to help them in what appeared to be a supernatural way. Amongst others with whom she was in touch may be mentioned St Vincent Strambi, the date of whose death she foretold. In the early years after her conversion Bd Anne Mary had many spiritual consolations and ecstasies, but later, and especially during her last years, she suffered much from the assaults of Satan and spiritual desolation. All these trials, as well as ill-health and calumny, she bore with cheerfulness. She died on June 9, 1837, after seven months of acute suffering, at the age of sixty-eight ; and she was beatified in 1920. Her shrine is in the church of St Chrysogonus of the Trinitarians, of which order she was a tertiary member.

The depositions of the witnesses in the process of beatification—of whom her ninety-two year old husband was one—are particularly interesting and valuable as biographical material. Biographies are numerous. One of the earliest was that by Luquet (1854) ; that written by Fr Callistus (Eng. trans. 1875) was widely circulated, as also was another French life by Fr G. Bouffier. Perhaps the fullest and most satisfactory is that published in Italian by Mgr C. Salotti in 1922, and since translated into German ; A. Bessières's French biography, Eng. tr., *Wife, Mother and Mystic* (1953), is exaggerated and without discrimination. It may be noticed that the prophecies attributed to Anne Mary by earlier writers, particularly that regarding " the three days' darkness " which was to come upon the world, seem to rest upon very insufficient evidence.

10 : ST MARGARET OF SCOTLAND, Matron *   (A.D. 1093)

MARGARET was a daughter of Edward d'Outremer (" The Exile "), next of kin to Edward the Confessor, and sister to Edgar the Atheling, who took refuge from William the Conqueror at the court of King Malcolm Canmore in Scotland. There Margaret, as beautiful as she was good and accomplished, captivated Malcolm, and they were married at the castle of Dunfermline in the year 1070, she being then twenty-four years of age. This marriage was fraught with great blessings for Malcolm and for Scotland. He was rough and uncultured but his disposition was good, and Margaret, through the great influence she acquired over him, softened his temper, polished his manners, and rendered him one of the most virtuous kings who have ever occupied the Scottish throne. To maintain justice, to establish religion, and to make their subjects happy appeared to be their chief object in life. " She incited the king to works of justice, mercy, charity and other virtues ", writes an ancient author, " in all which by divine grace she induced him to carry out her pious wishes. For he, perceiving that Christ dwelt in the heart of his queen, was always ready to follow her advice." Indeed, he not only left to her the whole management of his domestic affairs, but also consulted her in state matters.

* In Scotland the feast of St Margaret is observed on the anniversary of her death, November 16.

What she did for her husband Margaret also did in a great measure for her adopted country, promoting the arts of civilization and encouraging education and religion.   She found Scotland a prey to ignorance and to many grave abuses, both among priests and people.   At her instigation synods were held which passed enactments to meet these evils.   She herself was present at these meetings, taking part in the discussions.   The due observance of Sundays, festivals and fasts was made obligatory, Easter communion was enjoined upon all, and many scandalous practices, such as simony, usury and incestuous marriages, were strictly prohibited. St Margaret made it her constant effort to obtain good priests and teachers for all parts of the country, and formed a kind of embroidery guild among the ladies of the court to provide vestments and church furniture.   With her husband she founded several churches, notably that of the Holy Trinity at Dunfermline.

God blessed the couple with a family of six sons and two daughters, and their mother brought them up with the utmost care, herself instructing them in the Christian faith and superintending their studies.   The daughter Matilda afterwards married Henry I of England and was known as Good Queen Maud,* whilst three of the sons, Edgar, Alexander and David, successively occupied the Scottish throne, the last named being revered as a saint.   St Margaret's care and attention was extended to her servants and household as well as to her own family ; yet in spite of all the state affairs and domestic duties which devolved upon her, she kept her heart disengaged from the world and recollected in God.   Her private life was most austere :   she ate sparingly, and in order to obtain time for her devotions she permitted herself very little sleep.   Every year she kept two Lents, the one at the usual season, the other before Christmas.   At these times she always rose at midnight and went to the church for Matins, the king often sharing her vigil.   On her return she washed the feet of six poor persons and gave them alms.

She also had stated times during the day for prayer and reading the Holy Scriptures.   Her own copy of the Gospels was on one occasion inadvertently dropped into a river, but sustained no damage beyond a small watermark on the cover :   that book is now preserved amongst the treasures of the Bodleian Library at Oxford.   Perhaps St Margaret's most outstanding virtue was her love of the poor.   She often visited the sick and tended them with her own hands.   She erected hostels for strangers and ransomed many captives—preferably those of English nationality.   When she appeared outside in public she was invariably surrounded by beggars, none of whom went away unrelieved, and she never sat down at table without first having fed nine little orphans and twenty-four adults. Often—especially during Advent and Lent—the king and queen would entertain three hundred poor persons, serving them on their knees with dishes similar to those provided for their own table.

In 1093 King William Rufus surprised Alnwick castle, putting its garrison to the sword.   King Malcolm in the ensuing hostilities was killed by treachery, and his son Edward was also slain.   St Margaret at this time was lying on her death-bed. The day her husband was killed she was overcome with sadness and said to her attendants, " Perhaps this day a greater evil hath befallen Scotland than any this long time."   When her son Edgar arrived back from Alnwick she asked how his father and brother were.   Afraid of the effect the news might have upon her in her weak state, he replied that they were well.   She exclaimed, " I know how it is ! "

* Through this marriage the present British royal house is descended from the pre-Conquest kings of Wessex and England.

Then raising her hands towards Heaven she said, " I thank thee, Almighty God, that in sending me so great an affliction in the last hour of my life, thou wouldst purify me from my sins, as I hope, by thy mercy." Soon afterwards she repeated the words, " O Lord Jesus Christ who by thy death hast given life to the world, deliver me from all evil ! " and breathed her last. She died four days after her husband, on November 16, 1093, being in her forty-seventh year, and was buried in the church of the abbey of Dunfermline which she and her husband had founded. St Margaret was canonized in 1250 and was named patroness of Scotland in 1673.

The beautiful memoir of St Margaret which we probably owe to Turgot, prior of Durham and afterwards bishop of St Andrews, a man who knew her well and had heard the confession of her whole life, leaves a wonderfully inspiring picture of the influence she exercised over the rude Scottish court. Speaking of the care she took to provide suitable vestments and altar linen for the service of God, he goes on :

These works were entrusted to certain women of noble birth and approved gravity of manners who were thought worthy of a part in the queen's service. No men were admitted among them, with the sole exception of such as she permitted to enter along with herself when she paid the women an occasional visit. There was no giddy pertness among them, no light familiarity between them and the men ; for the queen united so much strictness with her sweetness of temper, so pleasant was she even in her severity, that all who waited upon her, men as well as women, loved her while they feared her, and in fearing loved her. Thus it came to pass that while she was present no one ventured to utter even one unseemly word, much less to do aught that was objectionable. There was a gravity in her very joy, and something stately in her anger. With her, mirth never expressed itself in fits of laughter, nor did displeasure kindle into fury. Sometimes she chid the faults of others—her own always—with that commendable severity tempered with justice which the Psalmist directs us unceasingly to employ, when he says " Be ye angry and sin not ". Every action of her life was regulated by the balance of the nicest discretion, which impressed its own distinctive character upon each single virtue. When she spoke, her conversation was seasoned with the salt of wisdom ; when she was silent, her silence was filled with good thoughts. So thoroughly did her outward bearing correspond with the staidness of her character that it seemed as if she had been born the pattern of a virtuous life. I may say, in short, every word that she uttered, every act that she performed, showed that she was meditating on the things of Heaven.

By far the most valuable source for the story of St Margaret's life is the account from which the above quotation is taken, which was almost certainly written by Turgot who, in spite of his foreign-sounding name, was a Lincolnshire man of an old Saxon family. The Latin text is in the *Acta Sanctorum*, June, vol. ii, and elsewhere ; there is an excellent English translation by Fr W. Forbes-Leith (1884). Other materials are furnished by such chroniclers as William of Malmesbury and Simeon of Durham ; most of these have been turned to profit in Freeman's *Norman Conquest*. An interesting account of the history of her relics will be found in DNB., vol. xxxvi. There are modern lives of St Margaret by S. Cowan (1911), L. Menzies (1925), J. R. Barnett (1926) and others. For the date of her feast, see the *Acta Sanctorum, Decembris Propylaeum*, p. 230.

SS. GETULIUS AND HIS COMPANIONS, MARTYRS (*c.* A.D. 120)

GETULIUS, the husband of St Symphorosa, had been an officer in the Roman army under Trajan and Hadrian : but after his conversion to the Christian faith he resigned his commission and withdrew to his estate in the Sabine Hills, near Tivoli. Here he lived in retirement, surrounded by a little band of Christians whom he taught and supported. He was one day engaged in instructing some of his people when he was surprised by a visit from Cerealis, the imperial vicar, who had been sent to arrest him. But Cerealis himself was won over to Christianity as the result of conversations with Getulius and with his brother Amantius who, though an ardent believer, still remained a tribune in the Roman army. As soon as the emperor had been informed of the conversion and baptism of Cerealis, he ordered the consul Licinius to apprehend the three men and to condemn them to death unless they consented to abjure their faith. All made a bold confession, and after suffering imprisonment for twenty-seven days, at Tivoli, with divers tortures, they were beheaded or burnt at the stake on the Via Salaria. With them perished another Christian, of the name of Primitivus. The relics of the saints were buried by St Symphorosa in an *arenarium* upon her estate.

St Getulius is honoured with an unusually long *elogium* in the Roman Martyrology, but his *passio*, printed in the *Acta Sanctorum*, June, vol. ii, is of the legendary type, and his name is lacking in the *Depositio Martyrum*, and other early records. There are also conflicting statements as to his resting-place. It is possible, however, that the early date of the martyrdom may in part explain these difficulties. See also Dufourcq, *Étude sur les Gesta Martyrum romains*, vol. i, pp. 197–199 and 227 ; H. Quentin, *Martyrologes historiques*, p. 542 ; F. Scavini, *Septem Dioeceses Aprutienses* (1914), where see the index.

ST ITHAMAR, Bishop of Rochester   (*c.* A.D. 656)

St Ithamar has a special claim upon our interest, because he was the first Englishman to occupy an English bishopric. Unfortunately, we know very little about him. St Honorius, archbishop of Canterbury, consecrated him to the see of Rochester after the death of St Paulinus, and Bede tells us that " though he was a man of Kent ", yet in piety as well as in learning he was the equal of his predecessors, St Justus and St Paulinus, both of whom had been Italian missionaries under St Augustine. In 655 St Ithamar consecrated a fellow-countryman— Frithona or Deusdedit—to be archbishop of Canterbury. His death appears to have taken place the following year. On account of his reputation for miracles, several churches were dedicated in his honour, and his relics were enshrined in 1100.

The very little we know about St Ithamar is derived almost wholly from Bede's *Ecclesiastical History ;* see C. Plummer's edition, and the notes. There is a considerable catalogue (compiled in the twelfth century) of miracles wrought at his shrine ; the full text has never been edited, but the Bollandists, in *Acta Sanctorum*, June, vol. ii, have printed a compendium which had been incorporated by Capgrave. See T. D. Hardy, *Catalogue of Materials for British History* (Rolls Series), vol. i, pp. 251–252.

ST LANDERICUS, or LANDRY, Bishop of Paris   (*c.* A.D. 660)

During the reign of Clovis II and in the year 650 St Landericus became bishop of Paris. He was a very earnest and devout man, distinguished especially by his great love of the poor ; to relieve them, during a time of famine, he sold not only his personal possessions, but also some of the vessels and furniture of the church. Before his day the only facilities for the care of the sick poor of Paris were provided by a few little hostels, *matriculae*, dependent for their upkeep from day to day on casual alms. To St Landericus is attributed the foundation of the city's first real hospital, near Notre-Dame, and dedicated under the name of St Christopher. It subsequently developed into the great institution which was famous in later ages as the Hôtel-Dieu. In 653 Landericus signed an exemption of the newly established abbey of St Denis from episcopal jurisdiction. The date of the death of St Landericus is uncertain, but it cannot have taken place earlier than 660, for in that year a monk named Marculf dedicated to him a collection of ecclesiastical formulae which he had compiled under his instructions.

Not much information is available concerning St Landry, but the Bollandists, in the *Acta Sanctorum*, June, vol. ii, have pieced together an account mainly derived from breviary lessons of much later date. On the beginnings of Saint-Denis, see J. Havet, in the *Bibl. de l'École des Chartes*, vol. li (1890), pp. 5–62. *Cf.* also Duchesne, *Fastes Épiscopaux*, vol. ii, p. 472.

BD OLIVE OF PALERMO, Virgin and Martyr (Ninth Century ?)

The story of Bd Olive, or St Olive as she is generally styled, belongs to the realm of pious fiction, and it is through the religious drama that her *cultus* seems to have been propagated in Italy. Her feast, however, is observed to this day in the diocese of Carthage, as well as in Palermo. In a fifteenth-century codex in the library of the cathedral of Palermo, her legend is given in nine lessons. A beautiful Christian maiden of thirteen, she was carried off from her home in Palermo by the Saracens, who conveyed her to Tunis. At first, in consideration of her noble lineage, she was allowed to live in a cave near the city ; there she effected a number of cures. But when it came to light that Mohammedans were being converted by her to the Christian faith, she was arrested and subjected to various tortures. She was shut up in a dungeon without light or food ; she was scourged until her flesh was cut to the bone ; she was extended on the rack and torn with the iron comb ; she was plunged into boiling oil. As she emerged from her steaming bath, unhurt but saturated with oil, she was stretched again upon the rack and executioners were directed to set light to her with torches ; the burning brands fell from the hands of the men, who were instantaneously converted. Finally, Olive was beheaded, and her soul was seen to escape from her body in the form of a dove, which soared up to Heaven.

This is the fantastic story which the Bollandists have summarized mainly from Cajetan, *De Vitis Sanctorum Siculorum*, who professes to have drawn his materials from earlier manuscript sources. There is, however, a text of the supposed *passio* printed in *Analecta Bollandiana*, vol. iv (1885), pp. 5–10. It is curious that Bd Olive seems to be held in veneration by the Mohammedans of Tunis ; the great mosque in that city bears the name of Jama as-Zituna, *i.e.* the mosque of Olive, and it seems to be a popular belief among the Arabs of that region that those who speak ill of her are always visited by calamity. See S. Romano in the *Archivio Storico Siciliano*, vol. xxvi (1901), pp. 11–21. There are several small popular accounts of Bd Olive which have been published in Sicily and elsewhere. See also A. d'Ancona, *Origini del Teatro italiano*, vol. i, pp. 436–437, and C. Courtois in *Miscellanées G. de Jerphanion* (1947), t. i, pp. 63–68.

ST BOGUMILUS, Archbishop of Gniezno (A.D. 1182)

Bogumilus and Boguphalus are said to have been the twin sons of noble Polish parents. The brothers, who were born near Dobrow, on the Werthe, received an excellent education, completing their studies at Paris. Boguphalus then received the habit in a Cistercian monastery, and Bogumilus built at Dobrow a church which he dedicated to the Holy Trinity. Having been raised to the priesthood he took charge of the parish himself. His uncle John, who was archbishop of Gniezno, appointed him his chancellor and nominated him his successor ; and in 1167, after his uncle's death, he was accordingly consecrated and ruled the archdiocese for nearly five years. He founded the Cistercian monastery of Coronowa, and endowed it with some of his family estates. Though a wise and zealous pastor, he proved quite unable to enforce discipline upon his clergy. Unwilling to countenance abuses which he was unable to remedy, he asked and obtained permission to resign his office. He subsequently entered the Camaldolese Order and spent the remainder of his life in one of its hermitages at Uniow. He died there in 1182, but his body was afterwards translated to the church at Dobrow which he had founded.

The Bollandists in the *Acta Sanctorum*, June, vol. ii, have reprinted in a contracted form a Latin life which was written by Stephen Damalewicz and published by him at Warsaw in 1649. The *cultus* was formally approved by the Holy See in 1925, for which see the *Acta Apostolicae Sedis*, vol. xvii (1925), pp. 384–387. " Bogomil " means " friend of God ", or " loved of God ", *i.e.* Theophilus.

BD HENRY OF TREVISO (A.D. 1315)

HENRY of Treviso, or San Rigo as he is often called in Italy, was born at Bolzano in the Trentino. His parents were very poor, and he never learnt to read or write. He went as a young man to Treviso, where he supported himself as a day labourer, secretly giving away to the poor whatever he could save from his scanty wages. Throughout his whole life his one object was the service of God. He heard Mass daily, frequently making his communion, and every day he went to confession—not from scrupulosity, but to preserve the utmost purity of conscience. All the time that was not employed in labour and in necessary duties he spent in devotion, either at church or in private ; the penitential instruments he used for the discipline of his body were preserved after his death in the cathedral. Men marvelled at his extraordinary equanimity, which nothing could ever ruffle. Foolish people and children sometimes mocked or molested the shabby, thick-set little man, with his sunken eyes, long nose, and crooked mouth, but he never resented their treatment or replied to it, except to pray for them.

When he could no longer work, a citizen called James Castagnolis gave him a room in his house and, when necessary, food. Usually, however, Bd Henry subsisted on the alms of the charitable, which he shared with beggars, never holding anything over from one day to the next. Even extreme bodily weakness in advancing age could not keep him from God's house and from visiting all the churches within walking distance of Treviso. He died on June 10, 1315. His little room was immediately thronged with visitors eager to venerate him and to secure some fragment of his possessions, which consisted of a hair-shirt, a wooden log which had been his pillow, and some cords and straw that had served as his bed. Extraordinary scenes were witnessed after his body had been removed to the cathedral. The people broke into the basilica at night, and the bishop and the *podestà*, roused from their sleep, were obliged to go and protect the body by putting a wooden palisade round it. No fewer than 276 miracles, said to have been wrought by his relics, were recorded within a few days of Bd Henry's death by the notaries appointed by the magistrates : they occupy thirty-two closely printed columns of the *Acta Sanctorum*. The *cultus* of Bd Henry was confirmed by Pope Benedict XIV.

A life of Bd Henry, by his contemporary Bishop Pierdomenico de Baone, has been printed by the Bollandists, June, vol. ii.   See also R. degli Azzoni Avogaro, *Memorie del Beato Enrico* (2 vols., 1760) ; A. Tschöll (1887) ; *Austria Sancta, Die Heiligen und Seligen Tirols*, vol. ii (1910), pp. 41 *seq.* ; and *Il B. Enrico* . . . (Treviso, 1915).

BD BONAVENTURE OF PERAGA, CARDINAL OF THE HOLY ROMAN CHURCH   (A.D. 1386)

THE first member of the Augustinian Order of Hermits to be raised to the dignity of a cardinal was Bonaventure Baduario.   He belonged to one of the leading families of Padua, and was born at Peraga at a short distance from the city.   Having received the Augustinian habit at an early age, he was sent to the University of Paris, and when Pope Innocent VI established a theological faculty at the University of Bologna, Bonaventure was one of the earliest occupants of a chair.   In addition to his teaching he wrote a number of treatises and commentaries, and he was interested in profane as well as in sacred literature.   Community of tastes and mutual attraction led him to form a close friendship with the poet Petrarch, whose funeral oration he preached.   In 1377 he was chosen prior general of his order : the following year he was created cardinal of St Cecilia.   On several occasions he acted as ambassador for Pope Urban VI during the Schism.   He always stoutly defended the rights of the Church, and in so doing came into conflict with his kinsman, Francis, Prince of Carrara, who was the ruler of Padua.   On the occasion of a visit to Rome, as Bonaventure was crossing the Tiber to visit the Vatican, he was struck by an arrow and killed.   The perpetrator of the deed was never identified, but it was generally believed that the murder had been committed by order of the Prince of Carrara.

Cardinal Bonaventure's claim to the title Blessed seems a little doubtful, though his own order venerated him as a martyr shortly after his death.   The Bollandists, in the *Acta Sanctorum*, June, vol. ii, have compiled an account based mainly on T. de Ferrera's *Alphabetum Augustinianum*.   In modern times, D. A. Perini has published a small volume, *Il b. Bonaventura Baduario-Peraga* (1912).

BD JOHN DOMINICI, ARCHBISHOP OF RAGUSA AND CARDINAL (A.D. 1419)

AMONGST the almost contemporary records of Bd John Dominici which have come down to us are a short biography written by one of his most famous sons— St Antoninus, archbishop of Florence—and a portrait painted by another—Fra Angelico—on the walls of San Marco.   A Florentine of humble parentage, born in 1376, John received the Dominican habit at the age of eighteen in the priory of Santa Maria Novella, in spite of some opposition caused by his lack of education and a tendency to stammer.   An unusually retentive memory and great perseverance enabled him soon to remedy these defects and he became one of the leading theologians of his day as well as an eloquent preacher.   In addition to commentaries on the Holy Scriptures and one or two treatises, he wrote *laudi* or hymns in the vernacular.   For twelve years after completing his studies at the University of Paris he taught and preached in Venice.   He was then prior of Santa Maria Novella and elsewhere.   At Fiesole and in Venice he founded new houses for men— and in the latter city he established the convent of Corpus Christi for Dominican nuns.   He it was who contributed most to the reform movement in Italy, introducing or restoring the strict rule of St Dominic in several priories, with the approval of the master general, Bd Raymund of Capua. It should be further noticed that he took the keenest interest in the Christian education of the young and that he was one of the first to detect and resist the pernicious tendencies of the new paganism that was growing up with the humanists. In 1406 he attended the conclave which elected Pope Gregory XII, and he afterwards became confessor and adviser to that pope, who created him archbishop of Ragusa and cardinal of San Sisto.

By encouraging Pope Gregory to resign—as the only possible means of inducing the antipopes likewise to forego their claims—Bd John was instrumental in helping to end the great schism, and it was he who conveyed Gregory's resignation to the Council of Constance. The next pope, Martin V, appointed him legate to Bohemia and Hungary, charged especially with the duty of counteracting the influence of the Hussites. He found Bohemia in a turmoil : public opinion had been roused to the verge of frenzy by the execution of John Huss ; and King Wenceslaus would not take the repressive measures advocated by the nuncio. As he could do nothing there, Dominici passed on to Hungary, but he caught fever soon after his arrival and died at Buda on June 10, 1419. His *cultus* was confirmed in 1832.

In the *Acta Sanctorum*, two lives are printed : one, a short memoir by St Antoninus of Florence ; the other, of much greater length, by John Caroli. Unfortunately this last is not very accurate or reliable. But a good deal has been written otherwise concerning Bd John's life and work, particularly in relation to the later phases of the great schism. See especially the articles of J. Hollerbach in the *Römische Quartalschrift* for 1909 and 1910, and H. Finke's *Acta Concilii Constantiensis*. Bd John's two works on education, *Lucula Noctis* (new ed. by E. Hunt, U.S.A., 1940) and *Regola del governo di cura familiare*, are of notable importance in the history of pedagogy. He also wrote a very edifying tractate of an ascetical character, *Il Libro d'amore di carità*. Consult further the preface of Fr Coulon to his edition of the *Lucula Noctis* (1908), and Fr Mortier's *Histoire des Maîtres Généraux O.P.*, vols. iii and iv ; with Taurisano's *Catalogus Hagiographicus O.P.*

11 : ST BARNABAS, Apostle (First Century)

ALTHOUGH St Barnabas was not one of the twelve chosen by our Lord, yet he is styled an apostle by the early fathers and by St Luke himself on account of the special commission he received from the Holy Ghost and the great part he took in apostolic work. He was a Jew of the tribe of Levi, but was born in Cyprus ; his name was originally Joseph, but the apostles changed it to Barnabas—which word St Luke interprets as meaning " man of encouragement ". The first mention we find of him in the Holy Scriptures is in the fourth chapter of the Acts of the Apostles, where it is stated that the primitive converts at Jerusalem lived in common and that as many as were owners of lands or houses sold them and laid the proceeds at the feet of the apostles for distribution. St Barnabas's sale of his estate is singled out for mention on this occasion. When St Paul came to Jerusalem three years after his conversion the faithful were suspicious of the genuineness of this conversion, and avoided him. Barnabas it was who then " took him by the hand " and vouched for him among the other apostles.

Some time later, certain disciples having preached the Gospel with success at Antioch, it was thought desirable that someone should be sent by the Church in Jerusalem to guide and confirm the neophytes. The man selected was St Barnabas —" a good man, full of the Holy Ghost and of faith," as we read in the Acts of the Apostles.   Upon his arrival he rejoiced exceedingly at the progress the Gospel had made and by his preaching added greatly to the number of converts.   Finding himself in need of an able assistant he went to Tarsus to enlist the co-operation of St Paul, who accompanied him back and spent a whole year at Antioch.   Their labours were crowned with success, and it was in that same city and at this period that the name Christians was first given to the followers of our Lord.

A little later the flourishing church of Antioch raised money for the relief of the poor brethren in Judaea during a famine.   This they sent to the heads of the church of Jerusalem by the hands of Paul and Barnabas, who returned accompanied by John Mark.   Antioch was by this time well supplied with teachers and prophets, amongst whom were Simeon called Niger, Lucius of Cyrene, and Herod's foster-brother Manahen.   As they were worshipping God, the Holy Ghost said to them by some of these prophets, " Separate me Paul and Barnabas for the work whereunto I have taken them ".   Accordingly, after all had fasted and prayed, Paul and Barnabas received their commission by the laying on of hands and set forth on their first missionary journey.   Taking with them John Mark, they went first to Seleucia and then to Salamis in Cyprus.   After they had preached Christ there in the synagogues they proceeded to Paphos, where they converted Sergius Paulus, the Roman proconsul.   Embarking again at Paphos, they sailed to Perga in Pamphylia.   At this stage John Mark left them to return by himself to Jerusalem.   Paul and Barnabas then travelled north to Antioch in Pisidia ;   they addressed themselves first to the Jews, but finding them bitterly hostile they now openly declared that henceforth they would preach the Gospel to the Gentiles.

At Iconium, the capital of Lycaonia, they narrowly escaped stoning at the hands of the mob whom the rulers had stirred up against them.   A miraculous cure wrought by St Paul upon a cripple at Lystra led the pagan inhabitants to conclude that the gods were come amongst them.   They hailed St Paul as Hermes or Mercury because he was the chief speaker, and St Barnabas as Zeus or Jupiter— perhaps because of a handsome appearance—and were with difficulty restrained from offering sacrifices to them.   But, with the proverbial fickleness of the mob, they soon rushed to the other extreme and stoned St Paul, severely wounding him.   After a stay at Derbe, where they made many converts, the two apostles retraced their steps, passing through the cities they had previously visited in order to confirm the converts and to ordain presbyters.   Their first missionary journey thus completed, they returned to Antioch in Syria well satisfied with the result of their efforts.

Shortly afterwards a dispute arose in the church of Antioch with regard to the observance of Jewish rites, some of the Jewish Christians maintaining in opposition to the opinion of St Paul and St Barnabas that pagans entering the Church must be circumcised as well as baptized.   This led to the calling of a council at Jerusalem, and in the presence of this assembly St Paul and St Barnabas gave a full account of their labours among the Gentiles and received approbation of their mission.   The council, moreover, emphatically declared that Gentile converts were exempt from the obligation to be circumcised.   Nevertheless, there continued to be such a marked division between Jewish and Gentile converts that St Peter, when on a visit to Antioch, refrained from eating with the Gentiles out of deference for the susceptibilities of the Jews—an example which St Barnabas followed.   St Paul upbraided them both, and his expostulations carried the day.   Another difference, however, arose between him and St Barnabas on the eve of their departure on a visitation to the churches they had founded, for St Barnabas wished to take John

Mark, and St Paul demurred in view of the young man's previous defection. The contention between them became so sharp that they separated, St Paul proceeding on his projected tour with Silas, whilst St Barnabas sailed to Cyprus with John Mark. Here the Acts leave him without further mention. It seems clear, from the allusion to Barnabas in 1 Corinthians ix, 5 and 6 that he was living and working in A.D. 56 or 57, but St Paul's subsequent invitation to John Mark to join him when he was a prisoner in Rome leads us to infer that by A.D. 60 or 61 St Barnabas must have been dead : he is said to have been stoned to death at Salamis. Other traditions represent him as having preached in Alexandria and Rome, and as having been the first bishop of Milan. Tertullian attributes to him the authorship of the Epistle to the Hebrews, whilst other writers—not less erroneously—believe him to have been the writer of the Alexandrian work known as the Epistle of Barnabas. Actually nothing is known of him beyond what is to be found in the New Testament.

The Bollandists in the *Acta Sanctorum*, June, vol. ii, have gathered up all the references to St Barnabas which were available at the beginning of the eighteenth century. Not much has been added to our knowledge since then, except perhaps what is due to a fuller acquaintance with early apocryphal literature. The text there printed of the so-called *Acts of Barnabas* has been critically edited from better manuscripts by Max Bonnet (1903) in continuation of R. H. Lipsius's *Acta Apostolorum Apocrypha*. This document purports to be the work of John Mark, but it was actually written at the end of the fifth century. It is a history of the whole career of St Barnabas, describing his martyrdom in Cyprus and the miracles wrought afterwards at his tomb. A very much earlier apocryphal document is the so-called *Epistle of Barnabas*, which dates from the first half of the second century, probably after A.D. 135. For many centuries no one doubted that it was really the composition of St Barnabas. It was even reckoned by some of the early fathers as forming part of the canon of Holy Scripture ; and those who rejected it and called it " spurious ", only meant that it was not to be received as the inspired word of God. They did not doubt that St Barnabas wrote it. At the present day, however, it is generally recognized that it can have had no connection with him : it probably was the composition of a Jewish Christian of Alexandria. No serious argument can be urged for the belief that St Barnabas became the first bishop of Milan ; see on this, Duchesne in *Mélanges G. B. de Rossi* (1892), pp. 41–71, and also Savio, *Gli antichi vescovi d'Italia ; Milano*, vol. i. The latter gives good reason for thinking that the claim of Milan to have had Barnabas for its first bishop originated in a fabrication by Landulf in the eleventh century. There is also a work, at one time current among the Mohammedans, under the name of the *Gospel of Barnabas ;* on this see W. Axon, in *Journal of Theological Studies*, April, 1902, pp. 441–451.

SS. FELIX AND FORTUNATUS, MARTYRS   (A.D. 296 ?)

THE Roman Martyrology on this day commemorates the martyrs Felix and Fortunatus in these terms : " At Aquileia the passion of SS. Felix and Fortunatus, brothers, who were racked in the persecution of Diocletian and Maximian. Lighted torches were applied to their sides, but by the power of God they were extinguished : boiling oil was poured into them, and since they persisted in confessing Christ, they were at last beheaded." On April 23 the same calendar does honour to the martyrs Felix, Fortunatus and Achilleus, but the time, place and manner of suffering there indicated are widely different from what we read here. That the Fortunatus now in question was an authentic martyr can hardly be doubted. Not only is he quite clearly located at Aquileia in the *Hieronymianum*, but the poet Venantius Fortunatus (*c.* 590) refers to both martyrs in some verses of his in these terms :

Felicem meritis Vicetia laeta refundit
Et Fortunatum fert Aquileia suum.

Further, at Vicetia (Vicenza) an ancient inscription has been discovered with the words : " Beati martyres Felix et Fortunatus ". According to their " acts " both brothers were natives of Vicenza, but they suffered at Aquileia. The Christians of Aquileia recovered their bodies and buried them honourably, but their brethren of Vicenza came over to claim them, and to settle the dispute a compromise was arrived at by which the relics of Fortunatus remained at Aquileia, while those of Felix were transferred to their native town.

The short *passio* will be found in the *Acta Sanctorum*, June, vol. ii. The difficulties caused by the various entries in the *Hieronymianum* are discussed by Delehaye in his commentary, and also in his *Origines du Culte des Martyrs*, pp. 331–332. See also Quentin, *Martyrologes historiques*, pp. 532–533 and 335.

ST PARISIO   (A.D. 1267)

BOLOGNA and Treviso both claim to have been the birthplace of St Parisio, and the Roman Martyrology assigns him to Bologna. The researches of the Bollandists, however, render it almost certain that he was a native of Treviso, where nearly the whole of his long life was spent. Parisio almost from infancy showed so evident a vocation for the religious life that he was allowed to receive the Camaldolese habit at the age of twelve. Young though he was, the lad immediately entered fully into this cloistered life, and soon became a model of fervour and of obedience to the rule. Having been ordained to the priesthood, he was appointed in 1190, at the age of thirty, to be spiritual director of the nuns of St Christina ; this office he is said to have exercised, with wonderful fruit to the community, for seventy-seven years. The life of the saint seems to have been uneventful, and would probably have been forgotten had it not been for his prophecies and for the miracles which took place during his life and after his death. He appears to have survived to the age of one hundred and seven. His body was laid to rest in the church of the convent he had served so long, and his popular *cultus* began with his death ; his penitent, Bishop Albert of Treviso, did much to foster devotion to him.

The Bollandists, writing in the year 1698, complained that they could obtain no satisfactory information from the Camaldolese authorities regarding this saint or concerning the *processus* which was said to have been drawn up for his beatification. They had to fall back upon the jejune account printed in the *Historiae Camaldulenses* (1575) of A. Florentinus. Not much more detail seems to be furnished by G. B. Mittarelli in his *Memorie della Vita di San Parisio* (1748).

BD PAULA FRASSINETTI, VIRGIN, FOUNDRESS OF THE SISTERS OF ST DOROTHY   (A.D. 1882)

AFTER the French Revolution and the flood of impiety it had let loose over Europe, the need of Christian education became everywhere more clearly understood by those who had the cause of God at heart. We find then a considerable number of religious institutes devoted to this work growing up everywhere during the first half of the nineteenth century, many of them being founded by earnest and saintly souls who seem to have been divinely guided in their efforts to meet a most crying need. Such a valiant woman was Paula Frassinetti, the sister of a priest well known as the author of a number of devotional books and himself a very ardent apostolic worker. Paula was born at Genoa on March 3, 1809. Her health in early life was very frail and in the hope that a change of air would prove beneficial, she joined her brother who was then parish priest of Quinto.

There she undertook to instruct poor children and in a short time it was apparent that she had found her true vocation.   She felt inspired to gather others round her and to found an institute which should be devoted entirely to such work.   She had many difficulties to encounter, complete lack of resources being not the least of the obstacles in her path.   But her tact, self-sacrifice and ardent devotion—she often spent the best part of the night in prayer—triumphed in the end.   The Sisters of St Dorothy—for this was the name by which the congregation was known—spread and multiplied not only in many parts of Italy, but also beyond seas in Portugal and in Brazil.   The institute was formally approved by the Holy See in 1863.   Bd Paula was credited with a wonderful insight into character and with a knowledge of the secrets of hearts.   After a series of strokes and worn out with incessant labours, she died very peacefully in the Lord on June 11, 1882.

See the decree of beatification in the *Acta Apostolicae Sedis*, vol. xxii (1930), pp. 316–319, and also the *Analecta Ecclesiastica* for 1907.   There is an Italian life, by A. Capecelatro (1901), and one in English by J. Unfreville, published in U.S.A. *c.* 1944, called *A Foundress in the Nineteenth Century.*

12 : ST JOHN OF SAHAGUN   (A.D. 1479)

THERE was an early Spanish martyr named Facundus, and he seems to have been adopted as patron by the abbey of Sahagun or San Fagondez in the kingdom of Leon.   This locality was the birthplace of this John, and from it he derives his distinctive surname.   His early education he received from the monks in the Benedictine monastery just mentioned.   While he was yet a boy, his father, Don Juan Gonzalez de Castrillo, procured for him a small benefice, and when he was twenty the bishop of Burgos gave him a canonry in his cathedral, although the abbot of San Fagondez had already presented him with three other livings.   Pluralism was one of the chief abuses of the age, but was leniently regarded in many quarters as being a necessary evil in view of the alleged meagreness of many stipends.   John from his early youth led a moral, upright life—exemplary in the eyes of ordinary Christians—but as he grew older he was led by divine grace to see much that was imperfect in his conduct and to set himself seriously to amend. He had received the priesthood in 1445, and his conscience reproached him for disobeying the Church's ordinances against pluralities.   He accordingly resigned all his benefices except the chapel of St Agatha in Burgos.   There he daily celebrated Mass, frequently catechized the ignorant, and preached, leading the while a very mortified life in evangelical poverty.   Realizing the necessity for a sounder knowledge of theology, he then obtained the bishop's permission to go to Salamanca University, where he studied for four years.

His course completed, he soon won a great reputation as a preacher and director of souls in the parish of St Sebastian, Salamanca, which he seems to have worked while holding one of the chaplaincies in the College of St Bartholomew.   Nine years were thus spent, and then St John, faced with the ordeal of a severe operation, vowed that if his life were spared he would receive the religious habit.   The operation having proved successful, he made his application to the superior of the local community of Augustinian friars, who admitted him with alacrity, for his merits were known to all.   A year later, on August 28, 1464, he was professed.   He had already so fully acquired the spirit of his rule that no one in the convent was more mortified, more obedient, more humble or more detached than he.   He spoke with such eloquence and fervour that his sermons, coupled with his private exhortations, produced a complete reformation of manners in Salamanca.   He had a wonderful gift for healing dissensions and succeeded in ending many of the feuds which were the bane of society, especially amongst the young nobles.   Not only did he induce his penitents to forgive injuries and to forego revenge, but he led many of them to return good for evil.

Soon after his profession St John was appointed novice-master, an office he discharged with great wisdom.   Seven times in succession he was definitor and he also became prior of Salamanca.   It was a house which was famous for its discipline, and that discipline St John maintained far more by his example than by severity, for the high opinion everyone had of his sanctity lent the greatest weight to his advice and admonitions.   He was, moreover, endowed with a judicious discernment and with a remarkable gift for reading the thoughts of his penitents.   He heard the confessions of all who presented themselves, but was rigid in refusing, or at least deferring, absolution in the case of habitual sinners, or of ecclesiastics who did not live in accordance with the spirit of their profession.   His fervour in offering the divine sacrifice edified all present, although his superior sometimes reproved him for the length of time he took in celebrating Mass.   We are also told that he was one of those to whom it has been granted to behold with bodily eyes the human form of our Lord at the moment of consecration.   The graces he received in his prayers and communions also gave him courage and eloquence in the pulpit. Without respect of persons he reproved vice in high places with a vigour which sometimes drew upon him persecution and even physical violence.

A sermon at Alba, in the course of which he sternly denounced rich landlords who oppressed their poor tenants, so enraged the Duke of Alba that he sent two assassins to kill the bold preacher.   In the presence of their intended victim, however, the men were struck with remorse, confessed their errand and humbly implored his forgiveness.   On another occasion certain women of the city whose loose life he had reproved attempted to stone him, and were only prevented from causing him grievous injury by the appearance of a patrol of archers.   A prominent personage whose unblushing association with a woman not his wife was causing grave scandal in Salamanca was induced by St John to sever the connection entirely. The woman vowed vengeance on the holy man and it was generally believed that the disorder of which he died was occasioned by poison administered at her instigation.   He passed away on June 11, 1479.   He was glorified by many miracles, both before and after his death, and was canonized in 1690.

The most reliable source for the life of St John of Sahagun is an account written by John of Seville in the form of letters addressed to Duke Gonsalvo of Cordova.   They have been translated into Latin from the original Spanish, and are printed in the *Acta Sanctorum*, June, vol. iii.   The Bollandists have also collected a certain amount of information from other later writers.   There is also a summary written about a hundred years after the death of St John by his fellow Augustinian, the famous preacher, Bd Alphonsus d'Orozco.   It will be found printed in M. Vidal, *Agustinos de Salamanca*, vol. i (1751), pp. 51 *seq.*   The best modern life seems to be that by T. Camara (1891) in Spanish.   Seventeenth-century lives in Spanish and French are numerous ; several are mentioned in U. Chevalier's *Bio-Bibliographie*.

SS. BASILIDES and his Companions, Martyrs   (End of Third Century ?)

SEEING that SS. Basilides, Quirinus (or Cyrinus), Nabor and Nazarius are commemorated this day in the Roman calendar as well as in the martyrology, and that collects in their honour form part of the liturgy of the Mass wherever the Roman rite is followed, they cannot be passed over in silence in such a work as the present. But the reputed " acts " of this group of four are altogether spurious. The Cyrinus is probably no other than the Quirinus who has already been discussed on June 4. The whole story seems to have arisen out of a confusion of names in the *Hieronymianum*, and to have been invented afterwards to explain the occurrence of these names together. The combination is also found in certain early manuscripts of the *Sacramentarium Gelasianum*, and in the calendar of Fronto. Three different " passions " exist, in one of which Basilides appears alone, and so far as the fact of his martyrdom is concerned, and his burial near the fourth milestone on the Via Aurelia, we are probably on safe ground. If the mention of Nabor and Nazarius has any reference to the cult of genuine martyrs, these probably belong to Milan : but the whole tangle is too intricate to admit of any certain solution.

Three separate sets of alleged " acts " of St Basilides and companions have been printed by the Bollandists in the third volume for June of the *Acta Sanctorum*. The most satisfactory discussion of the problem is probably that of Delehaye, in his CMH., pp. 315–316 ; but see also J. P. Kirsch, *Der stadtrömische christliche Festkalender* (1924), pp. 60–63.

ST ANTONINA, Martyr   (A.D. 304 ?)

THE St Antonina who is commemorated on this day in the Roman Martyrology was a woman who is said to have suffered martyrdom under the governor Priscillian during the persecution of Diocletian. She is thought to be identical with the saint or saints of the same name also honoured in the Roman Martyrology on March 1 and May 4. That she was cruelly tortured seems certain, but the mode of her death is doubtful. According to one account, she was suspended by an arm for three days, then imprisoned, and finally burnt at the stake ; according to another. she was stretched on the iron horse, her sides were torn with combs, and she was slain with the sword ; whilst a third tradition relates that after suffering many torments she was placed in a sack or a cask and thrown into a marsh. Her head is supposed to have been taken to Prague in 1673. Whereas the Greek *Menaion* claims her as a martyr of Nicaea (Cea) in Bithynia, the Spaniards have adopted her as a virgin saint of Ceja in Galicia, and the Aegean islanders as belonging to the island of Cea. Actually she may have suffered at Nicomedia, for that is the city mentioned in the ancient Syriac *Breviarium*, though here we find a man, Antoninus, net Antonina. But the Greek synaxaries are agreed in retaining the feminine form, and they also keep to Nicaea, and to the name Priscillian as that of the governor. It is curious that in the case of a martyr so obscure, for whom no formal *passio* is forthcoming, the *Hieronymianum* supplies an abundance of detail, rarely met with in other entries.

The question is discussed very fully by Delehaye, in his CMH., p. 229. See also the *Analecta Bollandiana*, vol. xxx (1911), p. 165 ; and the Constantinople *Synaxary* (ed. Delehaye), cc. 500 and 746.

ST ONUPHRIUS   (*c.* A.D. 400 ?)

AMONGST the many hermits in the Egyptian desert during the fourth and fifth centuries was a holy man called Onuphrius. The little that is known of him is derived from an account attributed to a certain Abbot Paphnutius of a series of visits paid by him to some of the hermits of the Thebaïd. This account seems to have been committed to writing by one or more of the monks to whom it was related, and several versions of it became current. Obviously the story has lost nothing in the telling.

Paphnutius undertook the pilgrimage in order to study the eremitic life and to discover whether he himself was called to lead it. For sixteen days after leaving his monastery he wandered in the desert, meeting with one or two strange and edifying adventures, but on the seventeenth day he was startled at the sight of what appeared to be an aged man with hair and beard falling to the ground, but covered with fur like an animal and wearing a loincloth of foliage. So alarming was the apparition that he began to run away. The figure, however, called after him, inviting him to return and assuring him that he also was a man and a servant of God. They entered into conversation and Paphnutius learned that the stranger's name was Onuphrius, that he had once been a monk in a monastery of many brethren, but that he had felt a vocation for the solitary life which he had now led for seventy years. In reply to further questions he admitted that he had suffered severely from hunger and thirst, from extremes of temperature, and from violent temptations. Nevertheless God had given him consolation and had nourished him with the dates that grew on a palm-tree beside his cell. He then conducted Paphnutius to his cave, where they spent the rest of the day discoursing of heavenly things. At sunset some bread and water suddenly appeared before them and they were wonderfully refreshed after partaking of this food. All that night they prayed together.

In the morning Paphnutius was distressed to see that a great change had come over his host, who was evidently at the point of death. But Onuphrius said, " Fear not, brother Paphnutius, for the Lord of His infinite mercy has sent you here to bury me." To a suggestion made by Paphnutius that he should remain on in the cell after his host's death, the aged hermit replied that God willed it otherwise. He then asked to be commended to the prayers and oblations of the faithful for whom he promised to intercede, and after having blessed Paphnutius he prostrated himself to the ground and gave up the ghost. His visitor made a shroud for him with half his tunic which he rent asunder. He then buried the old man in a cleft of the rock which he covered with stones. No sooner was this done than the cave crumbled and the date palm faded away, thus clearly indicating to Paphnutius that he was not intended to linger in that place.

It would not be difficult to compile a long bibliography of St Onuphrius. The Greek and Latin texts are indicated in BHG., nn. 1378–1382, and BHL., nn. 6334–6338, but a sufficient selection may be found in the *Acta Sanctorum*, June, vol. iii. There are also other oriental versions, notably in Coptic and Ethiopic. See, in particular, W. Till, *Koptische Heiligen- und Märtyrer-legenden* (1935), pp. 14–19 ; E. A. Wallis Budge, *Miscellaneous Coptic Texts* (1915) ; W. E. Crum, " Discours de Pisenthios " in *Revue de l'Orient chrétien*, vol. x (1916), pp. 38–67. Although Pisenthios tells us nothing new about Onuphrius, his sermon shows that already, about A.D. 600, the feast was celebrated with solemnity. St Onuphrius has also been discussed at length in the essay of C. A. Williams, *Oriental Affinities of the Legend of the Hairy Anchorite* (Illinois Studies, vols. x and xi, 1926), but see the criticism in *Analecta Bollandiana*, vol. xlvii (1929), pp. 138–141. It does not seem that the popularity of the names Onfroi, Humfrey, and their derivatives in medieval France and England was due to a cult of St Onuphrius introduced by crusaders : cf. E. G. Withycombe, *Oxford Dictionary of English Christian Names* (1950).

ST TERNAN, Bishop   (Fifth or Sixth Century)

It is tolerably certain that St Ternan was actively employed in the conversion of the Picts and was one of their earliest bishops, but the accounts of him that have come down to us are so confused and conflicting that it is hopeless to attempt to reconstruct his history. Even his date and nationality are disputed. According to one tradition, he had been for many years a monk in the monastery of Culross, whilst the Aberdeen Breviary states that he was a native of the Scottish province of the Mearns, and that he received baptism from St Palladius, whose disciple he was. A gloss upon the *Félire* of Oengus declares indeed that he was identical with Palladius. Perhaps he was consecrated a bishop in succession to St Ninian by Palladius in 432, or he may have received his commission directly from Rome, which he is said to have visited. He appears to have had his headquarters at Abernethy—the capital of the Pictish kings—and to have died there. His body, however, was buried and venerated at Liconium, or Banchory Ternan as it came to be called. About the year 1530 the compiler of the Aberdeen Breviary saw St Ternan's skull at Banchory. A bell which is supposed miraculously to have followed the saint from Rome was also preserved there until the Reformation. Some of the saint's relics were venerated in Aberdeen cathedral, which is thought to have been originally dedicated to him ; several churches and chapels in that part of Scotland actually bore or bear his name. His *cultus* spread to Ireland and his name appears on this day in the *Félire* of Oengus and in other old Irish calendars, but there is no reliable evidence of his having even visited the island.

An account of St Ternan is given in the *Acta Sanctorum*, June, vol. iii, but it is not wonderful that Father Papebroch, with the limited sources at his disposal, was unable to arrive at any satisfactory conclusion. Things are not much better even now, but the reader should consult Forbes, KSS., pp. 450–451, and also W. Douglas Simpson's booklets, *The Origins of Christianity in Aberdeenshire* (1925), *The Historical St Columba* (1927) and *On Certain Saints and Professor Watson* (1928).

ST PETER OF MOUNT ATHOS   (EIGHTH CENTURY ?)

MANY years before any monastery had been built on Mount Athos in Macedonia a holy man named Peter lived as a solitary on its slopes. He is said to have been the first Christian hermit to settle in that district, but nothing is actually known of his history. His relics were taken after his death to the monastery of St Clement and from thence, in the tenth century, to Thrace, where his *cultus* was fostered. His legend as given by Gregory Palamas, archbishop of Thessalonica, resembles many other stories related in the Greek *Menaia* : it may be regarded as being of the nature of edifying fiction. In his youth, we read, Peter took up arms against the Saracens and was captured and imprisoned. But St Nicholas and St Simeon, to whom he appealed in his distress, came to his assistance : Simeon set him free, whilst Nicholas directed him on his way. Having thus regained his liberty he went to Rome, where St Nicholas introduced him to the pope, who gave him the monastic habit. He then embarked in a ship bound for Asia. Soon after they had started our Lady appeared to him in a vision and bade him spend the remainder of his life as a hermit on Mount Athos.

Accordingly, when they had left Crete the captain landed him near his objective and he entered upon a penitential life. Besides enduring many hardships he had to meet diabolical attacks. First he was assailed by legions of devils who mocked him, shot at him with arrows and pelted him with stones. He repelled them by the power of prayer. Afterwards they assumed the form of snakes which struck terror into his soul. But he prayed yet more fervently and they disappeared. Then Satan took the form of one of his former servants and begged him to return to the world, representing to him how greatly he was missed and how much good he might do to his neighbours.   Greatly perturbed, Peter called upon our Lady, who responded by obliging the tempter to show himself in his true form and then to vanish.   Finally the Evil One returned as an angel of light.   Peter, however, overcame him by his humility.   He said that he was unworthy to mix with his fellow men : much less could he expect to be visited by a celestial being.   Consequently he refused to listen to the suggestion made to him by his supernatural guest. For fifty years he had lived on Mount Athos without seeing a human creature when at last he was discovered by a huntsman.   To him the hermit told his story. Though the man wished to stay with him, Peter sent him back to his home, requesting him to return in a year's time.   When the hunter, accompanied by a friend, kept the appointment twelve months later they found Peter's dead body.

This is another example of a familiar type of pious fiction to which the legend of St Onuphrius (see above) also belongs.   There are two Greek texts preserved to us (see BHG., nn. 1505–1506).   But it would probably be going too far to treat Peter as an imaginary person who has never existed.   C. A. Williams's essay (in *University of Illinois Studies*, vol. xi, pp. 427–509) on " Oriental Affinities of the Legend of the Hairy Anchorite ", shows that he is very imperfectly grounded in Christian hagiography.   A more reliable discussion of the story of Peter the Athonite is to be found in Kirsopp Lake, *Early Days of Monasticism on Mount Athos* (1909).

ST LEO III, POPE   (A.D. 816)

ON the very day after the death of Pope Adrian I the electors proceeded to appoint his successor.   Their unanimous choice was the cardinal-priest of St Susanna, and on the morrow, December 27, 795, he was consecrated and enthroned as Leo III. But there was in Rome a faction bitterly hostile to the new pope, mostly turbulent young nobles led by Pope Adrian's disappointed nephew and another ambitious official.   In 799 they hatched a plot to render Leo incapable of carrying out his pontifical duties.   As he was riding in the St Mark's day procession a band of these conspirators attacked him outside the church of St Silvester, dragged him from his horse, tried to blind him and to cut out his tongue, and left him nearly senseless. That he should have recovered so quickly and completely from his hurts as he did was regarded as nothing short of a miracle.

For a time Leo took refuge with the king of the Franks, Charlemagne, who was then at Paderborn ; and on his return to Rome, where he was received with great rejoicing, a commission examined the circumstances of the attempt on his person. The promoters of it retorted by making such serious charges against the pope that the commissioners felt bound to refer them to Charlemagne.   And a few months later the king came to Rome.   On December 1 a synod was assembled in the Vatican basilica at which he was present and Leo's accusers were invited to appear. They did not do so ; but in spite of this *nolle prosequi* it was considered desirable that Leo should take an oath of innocence of the charges made.   This he did on December 23 before the same assembly.

On Christmas day, during Mass in St Peter's, Pope Leo solemnly crowned Charlemagne as he knelt before the *confessio* of the Apostle ; the congregation applauded, the choir acclaimed Charles—" Long life and triumph to Charles, the most religious *augustus*, crowned by God, the great and peace-loving emperor of the Romans "—and the pope knelt and did his temporal homage.   Thus was inaugurated the Holy Roman empire of the West, which was hailed by some of the noblest minds of that and later ages as the realization of the ideal set forth by St Augustine in his *De civitate Dei*. This spectacular happening, fraught with such far-reaching results, has been surrounded by a good deal of mystification, some of it unnceessary. But it is a matter of general history, civil and ecclesiastical, and need not be considered here.

To St Leo his alliance with the monarch was of great benefit. Not only did it enable him to regain some of the patrimony of the Roman church and to keep at bay the turbulent elements in the papal states, but it also enabled him to intervene successfully in foreign disputes and to enforce ecclesiastical discipline in more distant lands. But when the emperor attempted to trespass into the field of dogma and pressed him to introduce the clause " And the Son " (*Filioque*) into the Nicene creed, Leo refused. He would not hastily and at the bidding of the secular power admit innovations—however doctrinally true—into the liturgy, and he did not wish to alienate his Byzantine children, whose importance he never underrated.

As long as Charlemagne lived St Leo was able to maintain order, but after the emperor's death in 814 troubles immediately broke out. The Saracens descended on the coasts of Italy, and in Rome there was another plot to murder the pope. By the time order had been restored it was evident that Leo's health had given way ; and on June 12, 816, he died after a pontificate of twenty years. His name was added to the Roman Martyrology in 1673.

The pontificate of St Leo III belongs very largely to general history. There seems to be nothing in the nature of an early biography beyond what may be read in the *Liber Pontificalis* (ed. Duchesne, vol. ii, pp. 1–34). A certain number of the letters of this pope are extant, in particular his more important communications addressed to Charlemagne. There is an account, based upon these materials and upon extracts from the later chroniclers, in the *Acta Sanctorum*, June, vol. iii. But, for the English reader, the most satisfactory source of information is Mgr Mann's *Lives of the Popes*, vol. ii (1906), pp. 1–110, in which will also be found an adequate bibliography. Mgr Duchesne's work, *Les premiers temps de l'état pontifical* (1904), deserves special notice ; and among more recent works see, in particular, K. Heldmann, *Das Kaisertum Karls d. Gr.* (1928), and in the *Rendiconti della Pontificia Accademia Romana di Archeologia*, vol. i (1923), pp. 107–119, an article of C. Huelsen on the Life of Leo III in the *Liber Pontificalis*.

ST ODULF (*c.* A.D. 855)

THE most successful of the missionaries who helped St Frederick to complete the evangelization of Friesland was undoubtedly St Odulf ; churches dedicated to him are still to be found in Holland and Belgium. He was born at Oorschot in North Brabant, and after his ordination he had charge of his native town ; but afterwards he transferred to Utrecht, where he attracted the favourable notice of St Frederick, bishop of the diocese. His eloquence as a preacher as well as his learning induced Frederick to send him to Friesland, the inhabitants of which were only partially converted. There St Odulf spent many years labouring with great fruit. According to the old chronicler he converted his hearers by reiterated instructions —preaching to the people and leading them into the way of truth through frequent admonitions, arguments, and rebukes, " until the men who had formerly been, as it were, ferocious wolves, had been transformed by sound doctrine into peaceable sheep ". Although he worked in all parts of the Zaanland, his headquarters were at Stavoren ; there he had his church, and there he founded a monastery. In spite of invitations to return to his own country, he persevered in his missionary work until he was very old.   He then returned to Utrecht, where he died about the year 855.   His body disappeared from its shrine, probably in a raid by the Northmen, and seems to have been taken to England and to have found a resting-place at Evesham Abbey, in the year 1034.

At the beginning of the thirteenth century, a most unpleasant story was somehow copied into an English manuscript (Rawlinson A 287, in the Bodleian) which contains the Chronicle of Evesham.   It is there narrated that St Odulf when in Friesland, and himself in the act of offering Mass at Eastertide, was admonished by an angel to make all haste and go aboard a ship, because his friend St Frederick had fallen into a terrible sin, but was nevertheless purporting to offer the Holy Sacrifice.   The ship was wafted to Utrecht with inconceivable rapidity, and Odulf was in time to warn his friend, to hear his confession, and to celebrate Mass in his stead.   Then Frederick disappeared for ten years to do strenuous penance, and St Odulf meanwhile took his place as bishop.   At the end of the ten years, Frederick, now a model of every virtue, resumed his episcopal duties and in the end died famous for the miracles he had wrought.   There is not, of course, a shadow of foundation for this in sober history, but the insertion of such a piece of scandal affords a curious illustration of the medieval tendency to cherish every story which chronicled the failings of the great.

The not very reliable life of St Odulf printed in the *Acta Sanctorum*, June, vol. iii, has also been partly edited in Pertz, MGH., *Scriptores*, vol. xv, pp. 356–358.   See also Macray, *Chronicle of Evesham* (Rolls Series), pp. 313–320 ; and Stanton, *English Menology*, pp. 265–267.

ST ESKIL, BISHOP AND MARTYR   (*c.* A.D. 1080)

THE name of St Eskil does not appear in the Roman Martyrology, but until the Reformation he was honoured in northern Europe as one of the most illustrious martyrs of Scandinavia.   He was said to be English, a kinsman of St Sigfrid, whom he accompanied on his mission to reconvert Sweden which had almost entirely lapsed into paganism since the death of St Anskar, its first apostle, in the ninth century.   He was consecrated bishop at Strängnäs, and from that circumstance later writers have described him as bishop of Strängnäs ; but the see was not founded until 1245, and Eskil was probably a regionary bishop.   He laboured with success in Södermanland, making many converts during the reign of King Inge, who encouraged and supported the missionaries.   Inge, however, was murdered, and under Sweyn the Bloody a pagan reaction set in.   A great heathen festival was held at Strängnäs which was attended by many who had professed to be Christians : St Eskil hastened to the assembly and appealed to the people to abandon their pagan rites.   Finding them deaf to his remonstrances he is said to have appealed to God to give a visible sign that He alone was the true God.   Instantly a violent storm arose which destroyed the altar and its sacrifice, while sparing the bishop and his attendants.   The pagans ascribed this wonder to magic and by the king's orders they stoned the saint to death.   The place where his body was laid in 1082 is called after him, Eskilstuna.

There are two medieval lives (neither very satisfactory), both of which may be found in *Scriptores rerum Suecicarum*, vol. ii, part 1, pp. 389–404.   See also the *Acta Sanctorum*, June, vol. iii, and especially S. Lindquist, *Den helige Eskils biskopsdöme* (1915), and Toni Schmid, in *Scandia*, vol. iv (1931), pp. 102–114.   A short English account is in C. J. A. Oppermann, *English Missionaries in Sweden* (1937), pp. 103–111 ; but on this book see *Analecta Bollandiana*, vol. lvii (1939), pp. 162–164.

BD STEPHEN BANDELLI   (A.D. 1450)

ONE of the most successful preachers of the Dominican Order in the first half of the fifteenth century was Friar Stephen Bandelli. He was born in 1369 in northern Italy, and received the Dominican habit at Piacenza. His piety and obedience were an inspiration to his brethren, while his learning obtained for him the degree of doctor of canon law and a professorship in the University of Pavia. But it was in the pulpit and in the confessional that he specially shone. Wherever he preached, in Liguria and elsewhere, crowds assembled to hear him, and innumerable sinners were converted from the error of their ways. He died at the age of eighty-one at Saluzzo, in the diocese of Turin, and was honoured as a saint and a wonder-worker. Thirty-seven years after his death, when Saluzzo was surrounded by a hostile force, strange forms appeared in the sky, which were held to be those of our Lady and Bd Stephen ; the enemy withdrew without laying siege to the town, and the people of Saluzzo, in gratitude to Bd Stephen, instituted an annual procession in his honour. Pope Pius IX confirmed his ancient *cultus* in 1856.

See Seeböck, *Die Herrlichkeit der katholischen Kirche*, pp. 127 *seq.* ; Procter, *Lives of Dominican Saints*, pp. 174-175 ; Taurisano, *Catalogus Hagiographicus O.P.*

13 : ST ANTONY OF PADUA, DOCTOR OF THE CHURCH   (A.D. 1231)

A PORTUGUESE by nationality and a native of Lisbon, St Antony nevertheless derives his surname from the Italian city of Padua where he made his last home and where his relics are still venerated. He was born in 1195 and was baptized Ferdinand, a name which he was to change to that of Antony when he entered the Order of Friars Minor, out of devotion to the great patriarch of monks who was titular saint of the chapel in which he received the Franciscan habit. His parents, young members of the Portuguese nobility, confided his early education to the clergy of the cathedral of Lisbon, but at the age of fifteen he joined the regular canons of St Augustine who were settled near the city. Two years later he obtained leave to be transferred to the priory at Coïmbra—then the capital of Portugal—in order to avoid the distractions caused by the numerous visits of friends. There he devoted himself to prayer and study, acquiring, with the help of an unusually retentive memory, an extraordinary knowledge of the Bible. He had been living at Coïmbra for eight years when Don Pedro of Portugal brought from Morocco in 1220 the relics of the Franciscans who had there lately suffered a glorious martyrdom. Ferdinand was profoundly moved, and conceived an ardent desire to lay down his life for Christ—an aspiration he had little prospect of realizing as a canon regular. To some Franciscans who came to his monastery of Holy Cross to beg, he laid open his heart, and eventually he was admitted to their order in 1221.

Within a very short time he was permitted to embark for Morocco with the intention of preaching the Gospel to the Moors. But hardly had he arrived than he was prostrated by a severe illness which totally incapacitated him for some months and eventually necessitated his return to Europe. The vessel in which he sailed was driven out of its course by contrary winds and he found himself landed at Messina in Sicily. From thence he made his way to Assisi where, as he had learnt from his Sicilian brethren, a general chapter was about to be held. It was the great gathering of 1221—the last chapter open to all members of the order—

and was presided over by Brother Elias as vicar general, with St Francis seated at his feet. It cannot fail to have deeply impressed the young Portuguese friar. At the close the brethren returned to the posts allocated to them, and Antony was appointed to the lonely hermitage of San Paolo near Forli. It is a moot point whether or no he was already a priest at this time. What is certain is that no one suspected the brilliant intellectual and spiritual gifts of the sickly young brother who kept silence about himself. When he was not praying in the chapel or in the little cave which had been made over to him, he was serving the other friars by washing up pots and dishes after the common meal.

But his light was not destined to remain long hidden. It happened that an ordination was held at Forli, on which occasion the Dominican and Franciscan candidates were entertained at the Minorite convent there. Through some misunderstanding none of the Dominicans had come prepared to deliver the customary address at the ceremony, and as no one among the Franciscans seemed capable of filling the breach St Antony, who was present, was told to come forward and speak whatever the Holy Ghost should put into his mouth. Very diffidently he obeyed ; but once he had begun he delivered an address which amazed all who heard it by its eloquence, its fervour, and the learning it displayed. The minister provincial, informed of the talent possessed by the young friar he had brought from Assisi, promptly recalled him from his retreat and sent him to preach in various parts of Romagna, which then comprised the whole of Lombardy. Antony immediately sprang into fame and proved particularly successful in converting the heretics who abounded in northern Italy and who were in many cases men of some education and best reached by arguments based on the Holy Scriptures.

In addition to his commission as a preacher, he was appointed lector in theology to his brethren—the first member of his order to fill such a post. In a letter generally regarded as authentic St Francis confirmed this appointment : " To my dearest brother Antony, brother Francis sends greetings in Jesus Christ. I am well pleased that you should read sacred theology to the friars provided that such study does not quench the spirit of holy prayer and devotion according to our rule." But it became more and more evident that his true mission lay in the pulpit. He had indeed all the qualifications —learning, eloquence, great power of persuasion, a burning zeal for souls and a sonorous voice which carried far. Moreover, he was said to be endowed with the gift of miracles* and, though undersized and inclined to corpulence, he had an attractive, almost magnetic, personality. Sometimes the mere sight of him brought sinners to their knees : he appeared to radiate holiness. Wherever he went crowds flocked to hear him and hardened criminals, careless folk, and heretics alike were converted and brought to confession. Men closed their shops and offices to go to his sermons ; women rose early or remained overnight in church to secure their places. Often the churches could not hold the congregations and he preached to them in the squares and market-places. Shortly after the death of St Francis he was recalled to Italy, apparently to be minister provincial of Emilia or Romagna. With regard to his attitude in the dissensions which arose in the order, modern historians discredit the legend that he headed the opposition to Brother Elias and to any departure from the original rule. They point out that the very lectorship which was created for him had been a signal innovation. He seems rather to have acted as envoy from the chapter

---

* The question whether St Antony worked miracles in his lifetime has given rise to much controversy. See Felder, *Die Antonius Wunder* (1933), p. 156.

general in 1226 to Pope Gregory IX, charged to lay before him for his decision the questions that had arisen. Antony on that occasion obtained from the pope his release from office that he might devote himself to preaching. The pope had the highest opinion of him and once called him " the Ark of the Testament ", because of his singular knowledge of the Holy Scriptures.

From that time St Antony resided at Padua—a city where he had previously laboured, where he was greatly beloved, and where, more than anywhere else, he was privileged to see the great fruit which resulted from his ministry. For not only were his sermons listened to by enormous congregations, but they led to a great and general reformation of conduct. Long-standing quarrels were amicably settled, prisoners were liberated and the owners of ill-gotten goods made restitution, often in public at St Antony's feet. In the interests of the poor he denounced the prevailing vice of usury and induced the state to pass a law exempting from prison such debtors as were willing to part with their possessions in order to pay their creditors. He is also said to have ventured boldly into the presence of the truculent Duke Eccelino to plead for the liberation of certain citizens of Verona the duke had captured. Although his efforts were unsuccessful it says much for the respect he inspired that he was apparently listened to with patience and allowed to depart unmolested.

After preaching a course of sermons in the spring of 1231, St Antony's strength gave out and he retired with two other friars to a woodland retreat at Camposanpiero. It was soon clear that his days were numbered, and he asked to be taken back to Padua. He never reached the city, but only its outskirts. On June 13, 1231, in the apartment reserved for the chaplain of the Poor Clares of Arcella, he received the last rites and passed to his eternal reward. He was only thirty-six. Extraordinary demonstrations of veneration were witnessed at his funeral and the Paduans have always regarded his relics as their most precious possession.

Within a year of his death Antony was canonized ; on that occasion Pope Gregory IX intoned the anthem " O doctor optime " in his honour, thus anticipating the year 1946 when Pope Pius XII declared him a doctor of the Church. It has been impossible in this short account to embark upon any discussion of the miracles wrought by the saint. Whether he did or did not perform wonders in his lifetime, it is the innumerable favours he has obtained for his devotees since his death that have won for him the title of " The Wonder-worker ". Since the seventeenth century St Antony has been usually represented with the Infant Saviour because of a story of late date that once, when he was on a visit, his host, glancing through a window, saw him gazing with rapture on the Holy Child whom he w s holding in his arms. In the earliest pictures we find nothing more distinctive than a book, emblematic of his knowledge of Holy Scripture, or a lily. Occasionally he is accompanied by the mule which, according to the legend, knelt before the Blessed Sacrament upheld in the hands of the saint, and by so doing converted its owner to a belief in the real presence. St Antony is the patron of the poor, and alms specially given to obtain his intercession are called " St Antony's Bread " ; this practice, however, seems only to date from 1890. How he came to be invoked to find lost articles admits of no quite satisfactory explanation, but it may not impossibly be connected with a story recounted among the miracles in the *Chronica XXIV Generalium* (No. 21). A novice ran away and carried off a valuable psalter St Antony was using. He prayed for its recovery and the novice was compelled by an alarming apparition to come back and return it.

The literature which has grown up around St Antony of Padua is only exceeded by that which attests the veneration paid to St Francis himself.   A summary account of the more important sources was published in 1931 by Father Pou y Marti, in the periodical *Antonianum*, vol. vi, pp. 225–252 ; but even this requires to be supplemented, as has been done in the *Analecta Bollandiana*, vol. li (1933), pp. 451–456.   Nevertheless, the positive knowledge we possess regarding the details of St Antony's life amounts to extremely little, and is almost entirely dependent upon the anonymous narrative, known from its first word as the " Assidua ", which was edited originally in the *Portugalliae Monumenta Historica*, vol. i (1856), pp. 116–130.   This may be most conveniently consulted in the edition of L. de Kerval, *S. Antonii de Padua Vitae Duae* (1904).   From this source, developed by various amplifications, come most of the documents catalogued in BHL., nn. 587–602.   The most important of the texts more recently brought to light is probably that by Bishop Jean Rigaud, *Vita B. Antonii ;* it was edited in 1900 by F. M. d'Araules, and it probably does provide some authentic information regarding the saint's preaching in the south of France. The legend known as the *Laurentiana*, published in 1902 by Fr Lemmens, is also worthy of notice, as investigation seems to have proved that it was written in the middle of the thirteenth century.   A useful book is that of F. Conconi (1930), who publishes the best texts of those legends which belong to the earlier period.   There is also a probability that certain sermons attributed to the saint do preserve for us the substance of his discourses and render testimony to the spirit which inspired him.   The lives of St Antony which have been published in modern times are very numerous.   One of the most bulky, but hardly the most critical, is that of D. M. Sparacio, *S. Antonio di Padova taumaturgo* (1923) ; it runs to over one thousand pages in two volumes quarto.   A shorter but acceptable work in Italian is that of N. Dal-Gal, *S. Antonio di Padova; taumaturgo francescano* (1907 ; French trans.). A further treatment of the subject under another title, *Il santo di Padova nella storia*, was issued by Father Dal-Gal in 1933.   There are French biographies by L. de Chérancé (1906), I. Boucard (1897), W. Vian (Eng. trans., 1936), and others.   B. Kleinschmidt's *Antonius von Padua in Leben und Kunst . . .* (1931) is a particularly valuable work for the attention paid to the artistic developments of devotion to St Antony.   In English we have a good translation of Canon A. Lepitre's excellent life in the series " Les Saints ", and also original works by C. M. Antony (1911), E. Gilliat-Smith (1926), R. Maloney (1931), R. M. Huber (1949), and Alice Curtayne (1950).   In 1946 the Conventual friars of Padua issued a commemorative volume of studies.

ST FELICULA, Martyr   (*c*. A.D. 90 ?)

THE *cultus* of St Felicula is closely connected with that of St Petronilla, whose foster-sister she is thought to have been.   Both martyrs lived and suffered in Rome towards the end of the first century.   Their legend asserts that after the death of St Petronilla, her rejected suitor, Count Flaccus, offered St Felicula the choice between marrying him and sacrificing to idols.   As she refused to do either he delivered her over to an official who imprisoned her in a dark dungeon for seven days without food or drink.   She was then consigned to the Vestal Virgins that they might overcome her opposition.   But she would not touch the meals they had prepared, electing rather to starve for another seven days.   At the end of a week she was tortured on the rack and then suffocated in one of the city sewers.   Her body was rescued by St Nicomedes, a priest, and was buried on the Via Ardeatina at the seventh milestone.   Several Roman churches—including those of St Praxedes and St Laurence in Lucina—claim to possess her relics, but it is uncertain where they actually lie.   There were other saints called Felicula in the City itself, and their remains, when discovered, may well have been ascribed to their more famous namesake, the companion of St Petronilla.

The acts of SS. Nereus and Achilleus, to which the account given of St Felicula forms a kind of supplement, are printed in the *Acta Sanctorum*, May, vol. iii.   See also Fr Delehaye's Commentary on the *Hieronymianum*, p. 317, and *cf. ibid.*, p. 306.   Other references will be found in the bibliography to SS. Nereus and Achilleus on May 12.

ST AQUILINA, MARTYR   (END OF THIRD CENTURY ?)

EASTERN Christians in early ages had a great veneration for St Aquilina, and her name appears in nearly all their martyrologies.   St Joseph the Hymnographer composed a special office in her honour with an acrostic hymn, in which the initial letters of the successive lines form an appeal to her, as his spiritual mother, graciously to accept his verses.   She was a native of Byblus in Phoenicia, the child of Christian parents, and was baptized by the local Bishop Euthalius.   At the age of twelve, in the persecution of Diocletian, she was arrested and brought before the magistrate Volusian.   She boldly confessed her faith, and when blandishments and threats failed to shake her constancy she was buffeted, beaten with whips, and decapitated.   Her so-called acts, written in Greek centuries after her death, are quite unreliable, though they may contain a substratum of truth.   According to them, red-hot needles were thrust into her ears, so that she fainted and was thought to be dead.   Her body was cast out, but was rescued by an angel who completely healed her.   The following day she again presented herself before Volusian who, when he had recovered from his surprise at seeing her, ordered her to be cast into prison and beheaded.   She expired before the sentence of execution could be carried out, and when the mutilation was executed upon her dead body, milk streamed forth instead of blood.

A Greek *passio* is printed in the *Acta Sanctorum*, June, vol. iii.

ST TRIPHYLLIUS, BISHOP OF NICOSIA   (*c.* A.D. 370)

THE Church in Cyprus in the fourth century numbered in its hierarchy two very remarkable men : St Spiridion and St Triphyllius (as their names are spelt in the Roman Martyrology).   St Spiridion was originally a shepherd, whereas St Triphyllius, who was intended for the law, received an excellent education at Bairut in Syria.   Changing his mind, however, while still young, he attached himself to St Spiridion, his senior by many years, and became his constant companion and devoted disciple.   Together they attended the Council of Sardica in 347, where they were zealous opponents of the Arian heresy.   It is not known at what date Triphyllius became bishop of Leucosia (Nicosia).   Besides being a learned man, he was a powerful preacher, and appears to have been a voluminous writer.   Referring to him as a speaker and as a writer, St Jerome describes him as " the most eloquent of his age, and the most celebrated during the reign of King Constantius ".   Elsewhere he writes of " Triphyllius the Cretan, who so filled his books with the doctrines and maxims of the philosophers that you did not know which to admire the more—his secular erudition or his knowledge of the Scriptures ".   The good bishop was also something of a poet, and recorded the miracles of his master St Spiridion in iambics.   His death is thought to have taken place about the year 370. The Hodigitria church at Nicosia still venerates his relics.

See the *Acta Sanctorum*, June, vol. iii, where a rather lengthy text is printed from a late MS. of the Constantinople *Synaxary*.   Compare, however, Delehaye's edition of this *Synaxary*, p. 173.   In the Cypriot magazine Ἀπόστολος Βαρνάβας (1934, pp. 181–188), an *akolouthia* is printed in honour of the saint.

BD GERARD OF CLAIRVAUX   (A.D. 1138)

ST BERNARD'S second and favourite brother, Gerard, was not one of the party of young kinsmen and friends who accompanied him to Cîteaux and received the habit with him.   At that time Gerard was too much engrossed in his prospects as a soldier to heed St Bernard's exhortations.   But a severe wound received at the siege of Grancy, followed by a long term of imprisonment, led him to recognize the transitoriness of earthly glory, and after his liberation he came to place himself under his brother's rule.   As a monk he became the right hand of St Bernard, whom he accompanied to Clairvaux.   In the capacity of cellarer he not only conducted with efficiency the domestic affairs of the abbey, but he also developed such remarkable technical skill that the builders, smiths, labourers, shoemakers and weavers all turned to him as to their master for instruction and direction.   These external activities in no way interfered with his spiritual life : he was a pattern of obedience and of religious fervour.   He was on his way to Rome with St Bernard, in 1137, when he became so ill at Viterbo that he appeared to be at the point of death.   St Bernard prayed earnestly that he might be spared to go home, and his petition was granted.   Gerard made a temporary recovery, but fell ill again the following year.   Just before his death he exclaimed with a happy smile, " How good it is of God to be the Father of men, and what glory it is for men that they are the children of God ! "   In a sermon which is still extant, St Bernard paid a most eloquent and touching tribute to the memory of his brother Gerard.

The Bollandists have extracted the relevant passages from the Cistercian *Magnum Exordium*, and printed these in the *Acta Sanctorum*, June, vol. iii.

14 : ST BASIL THE GREAT, Archbishop of Caesarea and Doctor of the Church, Patriarch of Eastern Monks   (A.D. 379)

ST BASIL was born at Caesarea, the capital of Cappadocia in Asia Minor, in the year 329.   One of a family of ten, which included St Gregory of Nyssa, St Macrina the Younger, and St Peter of Sebaste, he was descended on both sides from Christians who had suffered persecution.   His father, St Basil the Elder, and his mother, St Emmelia, were possessed of considerable landed property, and Basil's early years were spent at the country house of his grandmother, St Macrina, whose example and teaching he never forgot.   He studied at Constantinople and completed his education at Athens.   He had there as fellow students St Gregory of Nazianzus who became his inseparable friend, and Julian, the future emperor and apostate.   The two young Cappadocians associated with the most serious-minded of their contemporaries and, according to St Gregory, knew only two streets, those leading to the church and to the schools.   As soon as Basil had learnt all that his masters could teach him, he returned to Caesarea.   For some years he taught rhetoric in the city, but on the very threshold of a brilliant career he was led to abandon the world through the influence of his eldest sister, Macrina, who, after helping to educate and settle her sisters and youngest brother, had retired with her widowed mother and other women to live a community life on one of the family estates at Annesi on the river Iris.

About the same time Basil appears to have been baptized ; and determined from thenceforth to serve God in evangelical poverty, he visited the principal monasteries of Egypt, Palestine, Syria and Mesopotamia to study the religious life.   Upon his return he withdrew to a wild and beautiful spot in Pontus, separated by the river Iris from Annesi, and devoted himself to prayer and study.   With the disciples who soon gathered round him, including his brother Peter, he formed the first monastery in Asia Minor and for them he organized the life and enunciated the principles which have continued through the centuries down to the present day to regulate the lives of monks of the Eastern church. Basil lived the life of a monk in the strict sense for only five years ; but in the history of Christian monachism he ranks in importance with St Benedict himself.*

At this time the Arian heresy was at its height, and heretical emperors were persecuting the orthodox. In 363 Basil was persuaded to be ordained deacon and priest at Caesarea ; but the archbishop, Eusebius, became jealous of his influence, and the saint quietly retired again to Pontus to aid in the foundation and direction of new monasteries. Caesarea, however, could not spare him for long. In 365, St Gregory of Nazianzus, on behalf of the orthodox, fetched Basil from his retreat to assist them in the defence of their faith, their clergy, and their churches. A reconciliation was effected between him and Eusebius, Basil remained on in Caesarea to become the bishop's right hand and actually to rule the church, whilst tactfully giving credit to Eusebius for all that he was really doing himself. During a season of drought followed by famine he not only distributed his maternal inheritance in charity, but he also organized a great system of relief with a soup kitchen in which he could be seen, girt with an apron, dealing out food to the hungry. Eusebius died in 370, and Basil, in spite of considerable opposition, was elected to fill the vacant see on June 14—to the great joy of St Athanasius and the equally great mortification of the Arian emperor, Valens. It was indeed an important post and in Basil's case a difficult one, because as bishop of Caesarea he was exarch of Pontus and metropolitan over fifty suffragans, many of whom had opposed his election and continued to be hostile until by patience and charity he was able to win their confidence and support.

Within twelve months of Basil's accession, the Emperor Valens was in Caesarea, after having conducted in Bithynia and Galatia a ruthless campaign of persecution. He had sent on in advance the prefect Modestus, to induce Basil to submit or at any rate to agree to some compromise. Neither to Modestus, however, nor to the emperor would the holy bishop yield, either to keep silence about Arianism or to admit Arians to communion. Promises and threats were equally useless. " Nothing short of violence can avail against such a man ", was the report of Modestus to his master, and violence Valens was unwilling—perhaps afraid—to attempt. He decided in favour of banishment, but thrice in succession the reed pen with which he was signing the edict split in his hand. A weak man himself, he was overawed and moved to reluctant admiration by Basil's determination, and eventually took his departure, never again to interfere with the ecclesiastical affairs of Caesarea. This contest ended, the saint soon found himself involved in another struggle, owing to the division of Cappadocia into two civil provinces and the consequent claim of Anthimus, Bishop of Tyana, to be metropolitan of New Cappadocia. The dispute was an unfortunate one for Basil, not so much because he was obliged to yield to the division of his archdiocese, as because it led to an estrangement from St Gregory of Nazianzus, whom he insisted on consecrating to the bishopric of Sasima, a miserable town on debatable ground between the two Cappadocias.

Whilst he was thus engaged in defending the church of Caesarea against attacks upon its faith and jurisdiction, St Basil was no less zealously fulfilling his strictly pastoral duties. Even on working days he preached morning and evening to congregations so vast that he himself compared them to the sea. His people were

* St Basil's " new range of ideas " is finely summarized by Abbot Cuthbert Butler in the *Cambridge Medieval History*, vol. i, pp. 528–529.

in the habit of making their communion every Sunday, Wednesday, Friday and Saturday. Amongst other practices which he had observed on his travels and had introduced among his flock, was that of assembling in church before sunrise to sing psalms. For the benefit of the sick poor he organized outside the gate of Caesarea a hospital which St Gregory of Nazianzus described as almost a new city and worthy to be reckoned one of the wonders of the world. It came to be called the Basiliad and continued to be famous long after its founder's death. Away from his own episcopal residence, in spite of chronic ill-health, he made frequent visitations into mountainous districts, and by his vigilant supervision of his clergy and his insistence on the ordination of none but suitable candidates he made of his archdiocese a model of ecclesiastical order and discipline.

He was less successful in his efforts on behalf of the Church outside his own province. Left by the death of St Athanasius the champion of orthodoxy in the East, he strove persistently to rally and unite his fellow Catholics who, crushed by Arian tyranny and rent by schisms and dissensions amongst themselves, seemed threatened with extinction. His advances, however, were ill-received and he found himself misunderstood, misrepresented, and accused of ambition and of heresy. Even appeals which he and his friends made to Pope St Damasus and the Western bishops to intervene in the affairs of the East and to heal the troubles met with little response—apparently because aspersions upon their good faith had been made in Rome itself. " For my sins I seem to be unsuccessful in everything ! " wrote St Basil in a mood of deep discouragement.

Nevertheless, relief was at hand, and that from an unexpected quarter. On August 9, 378, the Emperor Valens was mortally wounded at the battle of Adrianople, and with the accession of his nephew, Gratian, came the end of the Arian ascendancy in the East. When the news reached St Basil he was on his death-bed, but it brought him consolation in his last moments. He died on January 1, 379, at the age of forty-nine, worn out by his austerities, his hard work, and a painful disease. The whole of Caesarea mourned him as a father and protector—pagans, Jews, and strangers joining in the general lamentation. Seventy-two years after his death the Council of Chalcedon described him as " The great Basil, the minister of grace who has expounded the truth to the whole earth ". He was undoubtedly one of the most eloquent orators the Church has ever produced and his writings have entitled him to a high place amongst her doctors. In the Eastern church his chief feast-day is on January 1.

Many details of St Basil's life are found in his letters, of which a large collection has survived. He required exact discipline from clergy and laity alike, and he tells of a troublesome deacon, not sinful but silly, who went around with a troupe of girls who sang hymns and danced ; he dealt with simony in ecclesiastical offices and the reception of unfit persons among the clergy ; he fought the rapacity and oppression of officials, and excommunicated all concerned in the " white-slave traffic ", which was widespread in Cappadocia. He could rebuke with dreadful severity, but preferred the way of gentleness : there is the letter to the girl who had strayed, and the one to an ecclesiastic in a responsible position who was mixing himself up in politics ; and thieves, expecting to be handed over to the magistrates and a stiff sentence, were often sent away free—but with a lively admonishment ringing in their ears. Nor was Basil silent when the well-to-do failed in their duty. " You refuse to give on the pretext that you haven't got enough for your own needs ", he exclaimed in one of his sermons, " But while your tongue makes excuses, your hand convicts you—that ring shining on your finger silently declares you to be a liar ! How many debtors could be released from prison with one of those rings ? How many shivering people could be clothed from only one of your wardrobes ? And yet you turn the poor away empty-handed." But he did not confine the obligation of giving to the rich alone. " You are poor ? But there are others poorer than you. You have enough to keep you alive for ten days—but this man has enough for only one. . . . Don't be afraid to give away the little that you have. Don't put your own interests before the common need. Give your last loaf to the beggar at your door, and trust in God's goodness."

Materials for the life of St Basil the Great are in one sense abundant. His own correspondence, the letters of St Gregory of Nazianzus and other contemporaries, the historians Socrates, Sozomen, and others of later date, the funeral orations of the two Gregories, and the panegyrics of St Ephraem, Amphilochius, etc., together with the theological and ascetical writings of St Basil himself, all help to elucidate his history. The Bollandists, in the *Acta Sanctorum*, June, vol. iii, have devoted to him an article of over 100 pages, and have printed the apocryphal life attributed wrongly to St Amphilochius. There is an English translation of Basil's Letters, by R. J. Deferrari, in the Loeb Classical Library, 3 vols. (1926–1930) ; unfortunately, critical questions of authenticity and date have not always here received adequate attention. On the ascetical teaching of St Basil, and the question of his so-called " Rule ", useful information will be found in P. Humbertclaude, *La Doctrine ascétique de S. Basile* (1932), in M. G. Murphy, *St Basil and Monasticism* (1930), and particularly in F. Laun, " Die beiden Regeln des Basilius ", in *Zeitschrift f. Kirchengeschichte*, vol. xliv (1923), pp. 1–61. See also W. K. L. Clarke, *St Basil the Great* (1913) and *Ascetic Writings of St Basil* (1925), and D. Amand, *L'ascèse monastique de S. Basile* (1949). There is a good article by G. Bardy in DHG., vol. vi (1931), and also in Bardenhewer, *Geschichte der altkirchlichen Literatur*, vol. iii, and in DCB., vol. i, and a valuable study by M. Bessières, *La Correspondance de S. Basile* (1923), which completes the articles published by the same writer in the *Journal of Theological Studies* (1920–1922). There is a short study by P. Allard (" Les Saints " series), and sketches by Dr A. Fortescue in *The Greek Fathers* (1908) and D. Attwater in *Eastern Saints* (1938).

SS. VALERIUS AND RUFINUS, MARTYRS   (*c.* A.D. 287 ?)

NEARLY all the chief martyrologies of the West make mention of SS. Valerius and Rufinus who suffered at or near Soissons towards the close of the third century. According to some accounts they were two of a group of missionaries sent from Rome to evangelize that part of Gaul. According to others, they were local young Gallo-Romans who held the office of keepers of the granaries in one of the imperial palaces situated on the river Vesle. In any case they were Christians and openly practised their religion. When the persecution broke out under Diocletian, Valerius and Rufinus, knowing that they were marked men, fled to a cave in one of the neighbouring woods. They were, however, discovered and arrested. After making a bold confession they were scourged, tortured and beheaded. Over their place of burial a church was built and the town of Bazoches arose.

Two short texts of the supposed *passio* are printed in the *Acta Sanctorum*, June, vol. iii, and there is another, much longer, by Paschasius Radbertus. The fact that the names are entered on this day in the *Hieronymianum* constitutes a presumption for the real existence and early veneration of the two martyrs, but we hear little of them otherwise.

ST DOGMAEL   (SIXTH CENTURY ?)

DOM LOBINEAU in his *Lives of the Saints of Brittany* confesses his inability to identify this saint. It is now, however, generally recognized that he was a Welshman, who flourished in the fifth century, or early in the sixth. He is called the son of Ithel ab Ceredig ab Cunedda Wledig, and his name appears as Dogmael, Dogfael and Dogwel. He must have exerted considerable influence in Pembrokeshire, for at least four churches were dedicated under his name there, besides one in Anglesey. From Wales he seems to have passed to Brittany where, under the names of Dogméel and Toël, he has had a considerable *cultus*, especially in the diocese of Tréguier. He must not be confused with Dogfael, son of Cunedda Wledig. In Brittany, at the present day, mothers are wont to invoke St Toël to help their little children to walk ; nearer home his name is best remembered as the titular of an abbey of Tironian Benedictines near Cardigan, of which Caldey was a cell.

The Bollandists provide a short notice founded upon such materials as were then access- ible to them. In the *Archaeologia Cambrensis*, 6th series, vol. v (1905), p. 166, is a short account of " St Dogmael's Stone ". See LBS., vol. ii, pp. 349–351, and a reference in the *Gemma ecclesiastica* of Giraldus Cambrensis (Rolls Series), vol. ii, p. 216.

ST METHODIUS I, PATRIARCH OF CONSTANTINOPLE   (A.D. 847)

THE Greeks regard St Methodius, Patriarch of Constantinople, with great venera- tion because of the important part he took in the final overthrow of Iconoclasm as well as for his heroic endurance of persecution, and they honour him with the titles of " The Confessor " and " The Great ". He was a Sicilian by birth, and received an excellent education in his native town of Syracuse. He went to Constantinople with the object of obtaining a post at court, but through the influence of a monk he decided to abandon the world for the religious life. He built a monsatery in the island of Chios, from whence he was called to Constantinople by the Patriarch Nicephorus. At the second outbreak of the iconoclastic persecution, under Leo the Armenian in 815, he stood out boldly in favour of the veneration of sacred images. After the deposition and exile of St Nicephorus, however, he went to Rome, apparently charged to inform Pope St Paschal I of the condition of affairs ; and he remained there until the death of Leo V. Great hopes were entertained of the next emperor, Michael the Stammerer, and St Methodius in 821 returned to Constantinople, following upon a letter from Pope Paschal which requested the reinstatement of St Nicephorus. But the emperor after reading the letter de- nounced Methodius as a stirrer-up of sedition and ordered that he should be scourged and deported.

He was confined for seven years in a tomb or mausoleum with two thieves one of whom died, and was left, we are told, to rot in the prison. It should be said, however, that there is a conflict of evidence regarding the place of his detention and the nature of the building. When at last Methodius was liberated he was reduced to a skeleton and scarcely recognizable. His spirit, however, was un- broken. Fresh persecution broke out under the new emperor, Theophilus, and Methodius was summoned before him. Blamed for his past activities and for the letter which he was supposed to have incited the pope to write, he replied boldly, " If an image is so worthless in your eyes, how is it that when you condemn the images of Christ you do not also condemn the veneration paid to representations of yourself ? Far from doing so, you are continually causing them to be multiplied." The death of the emperor in 842 was followed by the proclamation of his widow, Theodora, as regent for her infant son, Michael III, and she now came forward as the champion of images. A cessation of persecution was declared, the exiled clergy were recalled, and within thirty days the sacred images had been replaced in the churches of Constantinople amid great rejoicings. John the Grammarian, an iconoclast, was deposed from the patriarchate, St Methodius being installed in his place.

The chief events that marked the patriarchate of St Methodius were the holding in Constantinople of a synod which endorsed the decrees about eikons of the second Council of Nicaea, the institution of a festival called the feast of Orthodoxy, which is still held on the first Sunday in Lent, and the translation to Constantinople of the body of his predecessor, St Nicephorus. On the other hand, this period of reconciliation was marred by a very unfortunate quarrel with the Studite monks, who had formerly been Methodius's most ardent supporters ; one cause of this difference was apparently the patriarch's condemnation of some of the writings of St Theodore Studites. After ruling for four years, St Methodius died of dropsy on June 14, 847. He was a prolific writer, but of the many poetical, theological and controversial works attributed to him, there are only fragmentary remains which have any claim to be considered authentic. Recent opinion, however, in view of the manuscript evidence now available, is inclined to believe that he was really the author of certain hagiographical writings still preserved, notably the Life of St Theophanes.

The sources available for the history of St Methodius are considerable. We have, to begin with, an anonymous life in Greek, which will be found in the *Acta Sanctorum*, June, vol. iii, and elsewhere. Then there is a good deal to be learnt regarding particular phases of his career from three or four other hagiographical documents : a life of St Michael Syncellus published by the Russian Archaeological Institute at Constantinople in 1906 ; the Acts of SS. David and companions in the *Analecta Bollandiana*, vol. xviii (1899), pp. 211–259 ; and two long lives of St Joannicius printed in the *Acta Sanctorum*, November, vol. ii. There are also a variety of other materials belonging more directly to secular history, especially the continuation of Theophanes. A remarkably full and discerning bibliography is provided in the article on St Methodius, contributed by V. Laurent to DTC., vol. x (1928), cc. 1597–1606. He in particular calls attention to the articles published by Father Pargoire in the *Échos d'Orient*, vol. vi (1902) ; see also therein, in 1935, Fr Grumel on pp. 385–401. See, further, Dobschütz, " Methodius und die Studiten " in the *Byzantinische Zeitschrift*, 1909, pp. 41–105 ; and the *Regestes des Patriarches de Constantinople*, 1935, fascicule 2.

BD CASTORA GABRIELLI, Widow   (A.D. 1391)

A MEMBER of one of the principal families of Gubbio in Umbria, Castora is described as having been very beautiful in her youth, and of a retiring disposition. She married a man of her own rank, a doctor of laws, whose home was at Sant' Angelo in Vado. He proved to be a man of violent temper, from whom she had much to suffer, but she bore her trials with invincible patience. All the time she could spare from her domestic duties were spent in prayer, often in the local church of St Francis, for whom she had a great veneration. Thanks to her training and example, her only child, a son named Odo, grew up to be an upright and religious man. After her husband's death, Bd Castora received the mantle of a Franciscan tertiary, and sold her possessions, the proceeds of which she gave to the poor. The remainder of her life she passed in prayer and austerities.

There is a short account of this servant of God in the *Acta Sanctorum*, June, vol. iii. It is taken for the most part from Jacobilli's *Sancti Umbriae*. See also Stadler's *Heiligen Lexikon*. There seems, however, to be no evidence that the *cultus* of Castora Gabrielli has received any sort of. papal sanction ; her feast is not kept among the Franciscans.

15 : SS. VITUS, MODESTUS AND CRESCENTIA, MARTYRS (*c.* A.D. 300 ?)

THE *cultus* of these three saints goes back to very early times : their names appear in the so-called martyrology of St Jerome or *Hieronymianum*, and it may be taken as certain that they were actually Christians who gave their lives for the faith in the Roman province of Lucania, in southern Italy. Nothing is known of their true history or of the circumstances of their martyrdom ; their very date is a matter of conjecture. It is quite possible that they were natives of Sicily as tradition asserts, but their legends are fantastic compilations of a much later time. The reputed relics of St Vitus were conveyed to Saint-Denis, in Paris, in 775, and from thence were translated to Corvey, or New Corbie, in Saxony in 836. So great was the devotion to him which developed in Germany that he was included among the Fourteen Holy Helpers. He came to be regarded as the special protector of epileptics as well as of those suffering from the nervous affection called after him, St Vitus's Dance, and he is regarded as the patron of dancers and actors. He was also invoked against storms, over-sleeping, the bites of mad dogs, the bites of serpents, and against all injuries that beasts can do to men. Hence he is often represented accompanied by an animal.

The story told in the popular legend may be summarized as follows : Vitus was the only son of a senator of Sicily named Hylas. The boy was converted to Christianity at the age of seven or twelve, and was baptized without the knowledge of his parents. The numerous miracles and conversions he effected, however, attracted the notice of Valerian, the administrator of Sicily, who joined with Hylas in trying to detach him from the faith. But neither promises nor threats nor even torture could shake the boy's constancy. Moved by divine inspiration, Vitus escaped from Sicily with his tutor, Modestus, and his attendant, Crescentia. An angel guided their boat safely to Lucania, where they remained for a time preaching the Gospel to the people and sustained by food brought them by an eagle. They then went to Rome, and St Vitus cured the son of the Emperor Diocletian by expelling the evil spirit which possessed him; but because he would not sacrifice to the gods his powers were attributed to sorcery. He was cast into a cauldron filled with molten lead, pitch and resin, from which he emerged as from a refreshing bath ; a lion to which he was exposed crouched before him and licked his feet. Then Modestus, Crescentia and he were racked on the iron horse until their limbs were dislocated. At this juncture a great storm arose which destroyed many temples, killing a multitude of pagans. An angel now descended from Heaven, set the martyrs free, and led them back to Lucania, where they peacefully expired, worn out by their sufferings.

The various texts of the *acta* of St Vitus and his companions are duly registered in BHL. together with the accounts of the translations of the relics, etc. (nn. 8711–8723). The more important of these documents are printed in the *Acta Sanctorum*, June, vol. iii. A Greek version of the story was also current, and from this it has found its way into the synaxaries. See Delehaye's edition of the *Constantinopolitanum*, c. 751. Everything points to the conclusion that St Vitus was at first honoured alone, and that the names of Modestus and Crescentia were only joined to his after some romance-writer had fabricated the story now current. A good deal has been written on the cult of these martyrs. See for example Lanzoni, *Le Diocesi d'Italia*, pp. 320–322 ; and Huelsen, *Le Chiese di Roma nel medio evo*, pp. 499–500. At Corvey, in particular, owing to the presence there of the alleged relics, great interest has been taken in St Vitus, as may be learnt, *e.g.* from Philippi, *Abhandlungen über Corveyer Geschichtsschreibung* (1906), pp. 49–100, and from K. Thiele, *Die Reichsabtei*

Corvey (1928). In Sicily the people still come to the little church of Regalbuto to solicit St Vitus's help for the cure of mad people, as is proved by a booklet of Mgr Salvatore, *Breve Storia di S. Vito*, published as recently as 1934.

ST HESYCHIUS, MARTYR (A.D. 302 ?)

ALL that we know about St Hesychius is derived from the Acts—admittedly genuine—of St Julius, a martyr of Durostorum in Moesia (the present Silistria in Bulgaria), about the year 302. When St Julius was being led to execution Hesychius said to him, " I pray, Julius, that you may happily complete your sacrifice and receive the crown : and that I may follow you. My warmest greetings to Pasicrates and Valentius." (These were two other Christians of their acquaintance who had been martyred a very short time before.) Julius embraced Hesychius and replied, " Brother, make haste to come. They have already heard your message : I can see them now standing beside me even as I see you." The execution of St Hesychius actually took place soon after that of his friend. St Hesychius, " martyr of Durostorum ", is honoured in the *Hieronymianum* on June 15 and also in the present Roman Martyrology. Father Delehaye identifies him with the St Hesychius whom the Eastern church assigns to Constantinople and venerates, together with some anonymous companions, on May 19. It is highly probable that the remains of St Hesychius were taken to Constantinople, the inhabitants of which (like some other places) were apt to claim as local martyrs any saints whose relics had been translated thither from elsewhere.

See Delehaye, *Les Origines du Culte des Martyrs*, pp. 248–249, and 285–286, as well as his article " Saints de Thrace et de Mésie " in the *Analecta Bollandiana*, vol. xxxi (1912), pp. 161–300. On St Julius, see May 27.

ST TATIAN DULAS, MARTYR (*c.* A.D. 310 ?)

ABOUT the year 310 a prefect of Cilicia named Maximus held an assize on the promontory of Zephyrium. The first prisoner to be brought before him was a well-known local Christian who had been arrested for his faith. Questioned as to his name, he said that it was Tatianus, but that he was commonly called Dulas, and a δοῦλος he was indeed, the servant of Christ. As he refused to worship the gods, the magistrate ordered that he should be beaten to bring him to his senses. While the lashes were being administered, he rejoiced aloud that he was counted worthy to confess Christ's holy name. Afterwards also, under cross-examination, he displayed great spirit, and did not scruple to denounce the heathen deities as wood and stone, the work of men's hands. " Do you call the great god Apollo a work of men's hands ? " demanded the prefect sternly. Dulas in reply cited Apollo's unsuccessful pursuit of Daphne, and scoffingly asked how a being so unchaste and so powerless could possibly be regarded as a god. The indignant judge ordered him to be scourged across the stomach and then roasted on a gridiron. Even these tortures did not daunt the confessor. The following day, when again led to the court, he once more began to deride the gods, and was punished by having hot coals applied to his head and pepper thrust up his nostrils. Although he refused to eat food which had been offered in sacrifice, some of it was forced down his throat. He was then strung up and his flesh was torn with iron rakes. Maximus was that day returning to Tarsus, and had given orders that all the Christian prisoners should be led after him in chains. But Dulas was so completely shattered by his sufferings that he died after the convoy started. His body was cast into a ditch, where it was discovered by a shepherd's dog. The Christians obtained possession of the relics and gave them honourable burial.

This martyr seems to be identical with the " Dulas " who is mentioned as having been put to death at Nicomedia on March 25, an entry found in all the texts of the *Hieronymianum* : see Delehaye's Commentary, p. 160. For this we have the still more reliable testimony of the early Syriac *Breviarium*, again under March 25, and assigning Nicomedia as the place of his suffering. If this identification be accepted it is clear that the Greek *passio*, which the Bollandists in the eighteenth century printed under June 15 in the *Acta Sanctorum* (June, vol. iii), and which has been summarized above, is not, as its editors then declared, of the highest character, but open to grave suspicion. Still, the identity of the martyr of Nicomedia with Tatian Dulas is not proved ; though it is curious that the Constantinople *Synaxary* (see Delehaye's edition, cc. 750–751), while telling the same story, speaks only of Dulas, omitting the name Tatianus.

ST ORSIESIUS, ABBOT   (*c*. A.D. 380)

WHILE St Pachomius was ruling the great communities he had formed at Tabennisi and elsewhere in the Egyptian desert he numbered among his disciples two quite young men of exceptional promise : their names were Orsiesius (Horsi-isi) and Theodore. Pachomius trained them with special care, often made them his travelling companions and even consulted them about the rule he was composing. But when he set Orsiesius over the monastery of Khenoboski some of the older monks murmured at the appointment of so young a man. " Is the kingdom of God then only for the old ? " asked Pachomius, and he went on to prophesy that Orsiesius would one day diffuse the splendour of a golden lamp over the house of God. Petronius, who succeeded Pachomius, only survived his predecessor by fifteen days ; Orsiesius was then chosen to fill his place. To deputations sent from Tabennisi to St Antony and St Athanasius to inform them of the death of Pachomius and the election of Orsiesius, both those great saints spoke in terms of high praise of their new superior. St Orsiesius indeed proved a holy ruler, but after a time his strictness in enforcing the regulations about property provoked discontent in certain monasteries not immediately under his eye. The opposition increased until at length he felt unable to cope with it.

Rather than be the occasion of a cleavage he resigned in favour of St Theodore who, however, accepted office with the utmost reluctance, and would do nothing without consulting St Orsiesius, to whom he was deeply attached. They even took it in turns to make visitations of the various communities. After the death of St Theodore, in 368, Orsiesius again assumed charge, and he continued to rule alone until his death, the exact date of which is uncertain. He left as a legacy to his monks an ascetic treatise in the form of an abridged compendium of the rules and maxims of the religious life. St Jerome at a later date translated it into Latin.

There seems to be no separate biography of St Orsiesius, but in the *Acta Sanctorum*, June, vol. iii, an account has been compiled from what materials were then available concerning St Pachomius and St Theodore. See the bibliography to St Pachomius (May 9). Two letters are extant, addressed by St Athanasius to Orsiesius. See also the *Analecta Bollandiana*, vol. xlvii (1929), pp. 376–377 ; Bardenhewer, *Geschichte der altkirchlichen Literatur*, vol. iii, pp. 85–86 ; and De L. O'Leary, *The Saints of Egypt* (1937), pp. 156–157.

ST LANDELINUS, ABBOT   (*c*. A.D. 686)

As the founder of the great abbeys of Lobbes and Crespin, and of two others less celebrated, St Landelinus was held in honour by succeeding generations, though we do not know much about his life. He was born about the year 625 at Vaux, near Bapaume, of Frankish parents, who entrusted him to St Autbertus, bishop of Cambrai. But at the age of eighteen he broke away from his guardian and fell in with evil companions, by whom he was led into robbery and other crimes. The sudden death of one of his associates roused him to a sense of his danger. A humble penitent, he returned to St Autbertus, and then determined to withdraw to one of the places of his former life, Lobbes, in the hope of atoning in solitude for his past excesses. But he soon found himself surrounded by disciples who wished to imitate his life ; they were the nucleus from which grew the abbey of Lobbes.

St Landelinus constituted his follower St Ursmar its first abbot, for he regarded himself as totally unworthy to rule a religious house, and from Lobbes he went to Aulne and from thence to Wallens, where, according to one biographer, other communities sprang up round him. Still craving for solitude he penetrated, with St Adelinus and St Domitian, into the vast forest which stretched between Mons and Valenciennes. Even here he was followed, and for his new disciples he founded the abbey of Crespin, which he was obliged to govern himself. Nevertheless, he spent much of his time in a cell at some distance from the rest of the community. He is said to have died in 686 or thereabouts.

There are two short biographies of St Landelinus which profess to be of early date, but the earliest of these was written more than a century after his death and cannot be regarded as trustworthy. It has been critically edited in MGH., *Scriptores Merov.*, vol. vi, pp. 433–444. We have perhaps more reliable materials in the metrical life of St Ursmar and in the *Gesta Abbatum Lobbiensium*. On this life of Ursmar there is a useful article by K. Strecker, in the *Neues Archiv* for 1933, pp. 135–158. See also J. Warichez, *L'Abbaye de Lobbes* (1909), pp. 5 *seq.* ; U. Berlière, *Monasticon Belge*, vol. i, pp. 200 *seq.* ; and Van der Essen, *Étude critique sur les Saints mérovingiens* (1907), pp. 126–133.

ST EDBURGA OF WINCHESTER, Virgin   (A.D. 960)

THREE Anglo-Saxon princesses of the name of Edburga are included in the calendars of the saints. The nun who is venerated on this day was the granddaughter of King Alfred, and the daughter of King Edward the Elder, by his third wife, Edgiva. Her parents, who seem to have destined her to the religious life from the cradle, determined to test her vocation when she was only three years old. Her father took her on his knees and, showing her on the one hand a chalice with a book of the Gospels, and on the other a little pile of necklaces and bracelets, asked her to choose which she would have. The little girl eyed the trinkets with obvious aversion, but held out her arms towards the sacred objects. She was placed in the abbey which King Alfred's widow had founded at Winchester, and in due course rose to be abbess. She was famous for her charity, her humility and her miracles. It is recorded that she would sometimes rise during the night while the other nuns were sleeping and would silently remove their sandals, clean them, and replace them beside their beds.

St Edburga, whose name, like other Anglo-Saxon names of this class, is variously spelt, seems to have enjoyed a considerable *cultus* in Worcestershire and the neighbouring region, probably because her relics, or part of them, were preserved at Pershore. See the list of calendar entries in Stanton's *Menology*, p. 271. The account given above is derived almost entirely from William of Malmesbury, but there is also a life, apparently still unprinted, by Malmesbury's contemporary, Osbert of Clare. There is also a life, still unpublished, in the Gotha MS.; see *Analecta Bollandiana*, vol. lviii (1940), p. 100, n. 54. St Edburga's fame rested largely on the miracles her relics were believed to have worked ; a short summary of these is to be found in one of the Harleian manuscripts at the British Museum.

ST BARDO, Archbishop of Mainz   (A.D. 1053)

St Bardo was born about the year 982 at Oppershofen in the Welterau, on the right bank of the Rhine.   His parents, who were related to the Empress Gisela, sent him to be educated in the abbey of Fulda, where he received the habit.   In after days his former fellow students liked to recall how, when they had found him poring over the famous book of St Gregory on the duties of pastors (*Regula Pastoralis*), he had jokingly remarked in reply to their surprise, " Well, perhaps some silly king will make me a bishop some day if no one else can be found for the work ; so I may as well learn how it should be done."   About the year 1029 he was nominated abbot of Kaiserswerth by the Emperor Conrad II, and he subsequently became superior of Horsfeld.   Still higher promotion was in store for him.   In 1031, after the death of Aribo, he was chosen to occupy the important metropolitan see of Mainz.   In his new office he retained all the simplicity and austerity of a monk whilst dispensing alms and hospitality as befitted a bishop.   He was esteemed by all classes, but made himself particularly the champion of the poor, whom he defended from their oppressors and to whom his house was ever open.

Bardo played an important part in two synods of Mainz which met under the presidency of Pope Leo IX to put down simony and to enforce clerical celibacy. The pope took occasion on one of his visits to persuade Bardo to relax some of his austerities which were undermining his health and threatened to shorten his life. Always stern with himself, the good archbishop was extraordinarily merciful to others : insults or wrongs against himself he seemed never to resent.   One day, at his own table, as he was denouncing the vice of intemperance, his eyes fell upon a young man whose mocking expression and tittering clearly indicated that he was making fun of his host.   The archbishop ceased speaking and looked straight at the culprit.   Then, instead of administering the rebuke which all present expected, he took up a dish of food and directed that both the vessel and its contents should be presented to the young man.   Bardo's kind heart also made him a lover of animals.   He had a collection of rare birds, many of which he had tamed and had taught to feed from his hand.   His death took place on June 10, 1053.   He was universally mourned, Jews as well as Christians lamenting his loss.

There is a short life by Fulkold, who was the chaplain of Bardo's successor in the see of Mainz.   It was edited for Pertz, MGH., *Scriptores*, vol. xi, pp. 317–321.   This is a much better source than the longer biography by an anonymous monk of Fulda, which was alone accessible to Mabillon and the Bollandists, but which is mainly filled with hagiographical commonplaces.   See also H. Bresslau in *Jahrbücher des Deutschen Reichs unter Konrad II* (1879), pp. 473–479 ; F. Schneider, *Der hl. Bardo* (1871) ; C. Will, *Regesten zur Gesch. der Mainzer Erzbischöfe*, vol. i (1877), pp. 165–176 ; Strunck and Giefers, *Westfalia Sancta* (1855), pp. 143–153.

ST ALEYDIS, OR ALICE, Virgin   (A.D. 1250)

This is a very simple life but it leaves the impression of an absolutely sincere record, written down by a contemporary who was probably a Cistercian monk and confessor to the community.   Aleydis was a charming and delicate little girl, born at Schaerbeek, near Brussels, who at the age of seven seems of her own choice to have been committed to the care of a community of Cistercian nuns in the neighbouring convent called " Camera Sanctae Mariae ", a name which still survives in the Bois de la Cambre just outside the city. She was, before all else, humble and retiring. There are some simple miracles recorded of her, such as the spontaneous relighting of a candle which had fallen and been extinguished, and she devoted herself in every possible way to the service of her religious sisters. While still very young she contracted leprosy, and to the great sorrow of all the community had to be segregated. This was only the occasion, we are told, of her taking refuge more completely than before in the wounds of Christ. Her one comfort lay in the reception of holy communion. She was not, however, on account of possible contagion from her lips touching the cup, allowed to receive in both kinds, as the others then did, and this was a matter of great distress to her until our Lord Himself assured her that she lost nothing thereby. " Where there is part ", she was told, " there also is the whole." On the feast of St Barnabas, 1249, she suddenly became very ill and was anointed, but it was revealed to her that she would remain on earth yet a year longer. She then lived on in great suffering, losing the sight of both eyes, but offering her pains for the souls in purgatory. Moreover, she was sustained by ecstasies and revelations, which came to her more and more frequently as the end drew near. A year later, on Friday, June 10, she was again anointed, and the next morning Aleydis happily breathed her last at daybreak on the feast of St Barnabas.

The life is printed in the *Acta Sanctorum*, June, vol. iii, and also in Henriquez, *Quinque Prudentes Virgines*. Pope Pius X in 1907 formally authorized her *cultus* under the title of *Saint* Aleydis. Her feast is kept in the Cistercian Order and in the diocese of Malines, on June 15.

BD JOLENTA OF HUNGARY, Widow   (A.D. 1299)

JOLENTA, or Helena as she is called by the Poles, was one of four sisters who are honoured with the title of Blessed. They were the daughters of Bela IV, King of Hungary, the nieces of St Elizabeth, the great-nieces of St Hedwig, and lineal descendants of the Hungarian kings St Stephen and St Ladislaus. When she was five years old, Jolenta was committed to the care of her elder sister, Bd Cunegund, or Kinga, who had married Boleslaus II, King of Poland. Under their fostering care, the little girl grew up a pattern of virtue. She became the wife of Duke Boleslaus of Kalisz, with whom she spent a happy married life. Both of them were addicted to good works, and together they made various religious foundations. Jolenta was beloved by all, but especially by the poor, for whom she had a tender love. After the death of her husband, as soon as she had settled two of her daughters, she retired with the third and with Bd Cunegund, now, like herself, a widow, into the convent of Poor Clares which Cunegund had established at Sandeck. Jolenta's later years, however, were spent at Gnesen as superior of the convent of which she had been the foundress. She died there in 1299.

See J. B. Prileszky, *Acta Sanctorum Hungariae*, vol. ii, Appendix, pp. 54–55 ; Hueber, *Menologium Franciscanum*, p. 918 ; and *cf.* the bibliography attached to Bd Cunegund on July 24.

ST GERMAINE OF PIBRAC, Virgin   (A.D. 1601)

" A SIMPLE maiden, humble, and of lowly birth, but so greatly enlightened by the gifts of divine wisdom and understanding, and so remarkable for her transcendent virtues, that she shone like a star not only in her native France but throughout the Catholic Church." Such is the description of St Germaine Cousin set down in the apostolic brief which numbered her among the Blessed.

She was the daughter of Laurent Cousin, an agricultural labourer, and was born about the year 1579 at Pibrac, a village near Toulouse. Her mother, Marie Laroche, died when her little girl was scarcely out of the cradle. From her birth Germaine suffered from ill-health ; she was scrofulous, and her right hand was powerless and deformed. Her father had no affection for her, whilst his second wife actively disliked her. She treated her stepdaughter most harshly, and after the birth of her own children she kept Germaine away from her healthier step-brothers and sisters. The poor girl was made to sleep in the stable, or under the stairs, was fed on scraps, and as soon as she was old enough was sent out to mind sheep in the pastures. She was destined to remain a shepherdess for the rest of her life.

Germaine accepted the treatment she received as though it were her due, and God made use of it to lead her to great perfection. Out in the fields, alone with nature, she learned to commune with her divine Creator, from whom she learnt directly all that she required to know. He spoke to her soul as He speaks to the humble and clean of heart, and she lived ever consciously in His presence. Nothing could keep her from Mass. If she heard the bell when she was in the fields, she would plant her crook and her distaff in the ground, commend her flock to her angel guardian, and hurry off to church. Never once on her return did she find that a sheep had strayed, or had fallen a prey to the wolves that lurked in the neighbouring forest of Boucône, ever-ready to pounce upon unattended sheep. As often as she could she made her communion, and her fervour was long remembered in the village. Although she took no part in the social life of her neighbours, and never mixed with girls of her own age, yet she would often gather the young children round her to teach them the simple truths of religion, and to lead them to love God. Her neighbours at first accepted the estimate of her family, and were disposed to despise her and to turn her to ridicule. But gradually strange stories began to circulate respecting her. To reach the church from the pastureland, she had to cross a stream which was sometimes swollen by the rain. On one occasion, when it had become a torrent so strong that men feared to cross, people said, " Germaine will not come to Mass to-day ! " But they were mistaken ; and two villagers who had watched her at the stream confidently asserted that the waters had parted to let her cross, just as the Red Sea had parted for the Israelites of old.

It might have been thought that anyone so poor as Germaine would be unable to exercise the corporal works of mercy. Love, however, can always find a way, and the scanty food that was grudgingly doled out to her was shared with beggars. Even this was made a cause for complaint. One cold winter's day her stepmother pursued her with a stick, declaring that she was concealing stolen bread in her apron. To the amazement of the pitying neighbours, who would have protected her, that which fell from the apron was not bread, but summer flowers. Contempt now gave way to veneration, and the inhabitants of Pibrac began to realize that they had a saint in their midst. Even her father and stepmother relented towards her ; they would now have allowed her to take her proper place in their home, but Germaine chose to continue to live as before. It was not for long. Her feeble frame was worn out ; her work on earth was done ; and one morning she was found lying dead on her straw pallet under the stairs. She was twenty-two years old. Her body, which was buried in the church of Pibrac, was accidentally exhumed in 1644, forty-three years after her death, and was found in perfect preservation. It was afterwards enclosed in a leaden coffin, which was placed in the sacristy. Sixteen years later it was still flexible and well preserved. This circumstance, and the numerous miracles which were ascribed to her, encouraged a desire for official sanction of her *cultus*. Owing to the French Revolution, however, and other hindrances, her beatification and canonization were deferred until the pontificate of Pius IX. An annual pilgrimage takes place on June 15 to Pibrac church, where her relics still rest.

A painstaking biography is that of Louis Veuillot, which has been revised for the series " Les Saints ", by his nephew, François Veuillot. See also the attractive sketch of H. Ghéon, *La Bergère au pays des loups* (1923). The most authentic source is D. Bartolini, *Commentarium actorum omnium canonizationis . . . Germanae Cousin . . .* (2 vols., 1868).

16 : SS. FERREOLUS AND FERRUTIO, Martyrs   (*c.* A.D. 212 ?)

ST IRENAEUS, bishop of Lyons, ordained St Ferreolus to be a priest and St Ferrutio (Ferjeux) to be a deacon and sent them forth to evangelize Besançon with the surrounding districts. They may have been Greeks, but more probably they were natives of Gaul who had studied in the East where they had come under Christian influence. (Their legendary history represents them as having been converted by St Polycarp.) After labouring with success for some thirty years on their mission, they were apprehended for their faith, subjected to many tortures, and finally beheaded about the year 212—presumably during the reign of Caracalla. Their relics, which are said to have been discovered in 370 at Besançon, and enshrined by Bishop Anianus, were greatly venerated in the days of St Gregory of Tours, who asserts that his brother-in-law was cured through them of a dangerous malady. St Gregory's sister went to worship at the shrine, and while praying prostrate before it her hand accidentally clasped a leaf of certain herbs which had been strewn there. She thought this providential, and coming home dipped the leaf in water which she gave her husband to drink. By this means he recovered his health. This St Ferreolus is not to be confused with another St Ferreolus, a martyr at Vienne (September 18), who is mentioned more than once by the same St Gregory of Tours. One satisfactory testimony to the actuality of the *cultus* of SS. Ferreolus and Ferrutio is the occurrence in the *Missale Gothicum* (*c.* A.D. 700) of a full " proper " Mass in their honour. As it is inserted just before the birthday of St John the Baptist, it seems likely that June 16 was even then kept as their feast day.

There are two or three short texts of the *passio* (see *e.g.* the *Acta Sanctorum*, June, vol. iv), but none of them have any historical value. Ferreolus and Ferrutio are entered in the *Hieronymianum* as martyrs of Besançon, but under September 5. See also Duchesne, *Fastes Épiscopaux*, vol. i, pp. 48–62 ; W. Meyer in the *Abhandlungen* of the Göttingen Scientific Society, n.s., vol. viii (1904), part 1, pp. 69 *seq.* ; and Quentin, *Martyrologes Historiques*, p. 74, note.

SS. CYRICUS AND JULITTA, Martyrs   (A.D. 304 ?)

WHEN the edicts of Diocletian against the Christians were being enforced with great severity in Lycaonia, Julitta, a widow of Iconium, judged it prudent to withdraw from a district where she occupied a prominent position and to seek safety in obscurity under a more clement rule. With her three-year-old son Cyricus, or Quiricus,* and two maidservants she went first to Seleucia, only to discover that persecution was raging there under Alexander, the governor, and from thence to Tarsus. Her arrival, however, proved ill-timed, for it coincided with that of Alexander, some of whose officials recognized the little party. Almost immediately Julitta found herself under arrest and in prison. Brought up for trial, she appeared before the court leading her child by the hand. She was of noble lineage and had great possessions at Iconium, but in answer to questions as to her name, her position and her country she would give no other reply than that she was a Christian. She was accordingly condemned to be racked and scourged. Before the sentence could be carried out, Cyricus was separated from her in spite of his tears and pro-testations. He is described in the legend as a very attractive child and the governor, we are told, took him upon his knee in a vain attempt to pacify him. The boy had eyes and ears only for his mother. Piteously he held out his hands towards her as she was being racked, and when she exclaimed, " I am a Christian ! " he cried out, " I am a Christian too ! "

Finally, in a desperate struggle to release himself in order to get to her, the child kicked Alexander and scratched his face with his little nails. His action, natural enough in such circumstances, roused Alexander to fury. Seizing the child by the foot, he hurled him down the steps leading to his tribune, fracturing his skull and killing him on the spot. Instead of exhibiting distress, Julitta exultantly gave thanks to God for granting to her child the crown of martyrdom. Her attitude only increased the governor's rage. After her sides had been torn with the hooks, he ordered that she should be beheaded and that her child's body should be cast out of the city with the carcasses of malefactors. After her execution Julitta's body, with that of Cyricus, was rescued by the two maids who interred them privately in a field near the city. When Constantine had given peace to the Church their burial-place was revealed by one of the maids, and the faithful came in crowds to venerate the two martyrs. Reputed relics of St Cyricus are said to have been brought from Antioch in the fourth century by St Amator, bishop of Auxerre, and this translation led to an extensive *cultus* of St Cyricus in France, under the name of St Cyr, but actually there is no evidence to connect the historical SS. Julitta and Cyricus, assuming their real existence, with the city of Antioch. Although they appear to have suffered on July 15—the day on which their festival is observed in the East—the Roman Martyrology commemorates them on June 16.

It is distressing to have to discard a story so piously credited both in the East and the West throughout the middle ages, but the legend, preserved as it is in many varying forms, is certainly a fiction. The " Acts of Cyricus and Julitta " were proscribed in the decree of Pseudo-Gelasius regarding books which ought not to be received, and though this ordinance did not emanate from Pope St Gelasius himself, it comes to us with the authority of high antiquity and general acceptance. Father Delehaye inclines to the opinion that Cyricus was the real martyr and the nucleus upon which the legend was afterwards fabricated. He may have come from Antioch, as stated in the *Hieronymianum*, but what is certain is that his name, not associated with Julitta, recurs in very many church dedications and place-names all over Europe and the Near East.

* The name is spelt in a great variety of ways, Ciricus, Cirycus, Ciriacus. In the Roman Martyrology it is now printed Quiricus. In French he is Cyr or Cirgues.

The number of variant forms in which the legend is preserved to us may be taken as testimony to its popularity.   In the three divisions of the *Bibliotheca Hagiographica* published by the modern Bollandists, the various texts will be found catalogued.   In the *Graeca* there is mention of five such documents (nn. 314–318), in the *Latina* of eight (nn. 1801–1808), and in the *Orientalis* of two (nn. 193–194).   More than one of these texts has been printed in the *Acta Sanctorum*, June, vol. iv.   On the whole question, consult Delehaye, *Origines du Culte des Martyrs*, pp. 167–168, and his CMH., pp. 321 and 254.   See also Dillmann in the *Sitzungsberichte* of the Prussian Academy for 1887, vol. i, pp. 339–352 ; H. Stocks in the *Zeitschrift f. Kirchengeschichte*, 1910, pp. 1–47 ; Wilpert, *Röm. Mosaiken und Malereien* (1924), vol. ii, part II, pp. 685–694, and vol. iv, pp. 179–181.

ST TYCHON, Bishop of Amathus   (Fifth Century ?)

ALL that can be confidently asserted about St Tychon is that he was a very early bishop of Amathus, the site of the modern Limassol in Cyprus, and that he has been for many centuries greatly venerated by the inhabitants of the island, who style him " the Wonder-worker " and regard him as the patron of vine-growers.   The two things his biographer specially emphasizes in his life are : first, that as a boy, being the son of a baker, he used to give away to the poor the bread he was sent out to sell. His father was very angry, but when he opened the granary where he kept his flour, he found that by miracle it was full to overflowing and that his loss had many times over been made good.   Secondly, when Tychon had become a bishop he possessed a small vineyard but had no means to stock it.   He accordingly took one of the cuttings which other vine-growers had thrown away because it was dead, and planted it with a prayer that God would grant four favours, *viz.* that the sap should run in it again, that it should produce abundance of fruit, that the fruit should be sweet, and that it should ripen early.   Ever afterwards the grapes in this vineyard ripened long in advance of all others, and this is the reason why St Tychon's feast and the blessing of the grape harvest take place there on June 16.   Elsewhere in Cyprus the vine-gathering festival could not be celebrated until many weeks later.

Although no credence whatever can be placed in his legendary history, and notwithstanding the attempts made by some recent German writers, notably H. Usener, to identify him with the pagan god Priapus, it may be accepted as certain that he was a real personage and a Christian prelate.   On the strength of a tradition that he once caused the vintage to mature before its season, part of the ceremonial locally observed on his feast-day, June 16, consists of squeezing into a chalice the juice of a bunch of partially ripened grapes.   Before the end of the sixth century St Tychon's tomb was a famous shrine, and during the ninth century St Joseph the Hymnographer composed an office in his honour.

There is a Greek life of St Tychon which was prepared for the press by H. Usener, *Der heilige Tychon* (1907).   This biography was written by St John the Almoner (see January 23), and from a literary point of view it is held a very elegant example of Byzantine Greek composition, but it tells us little that is reliable in the way of historical fact.   An epitome of this text was previously printed in the *Analecta Bollandiana*, vol. xxvi (1907), pp. 229–232 from the MS. Paris, 1488.   See also Delehaye in *Analecta Bollandiana*, vol. xxviii (1909), pp. 119–122 ; A. Brinkmann in *Rheinisches Museum* (1908), pp. 304–310, and the notice of St. Tychon in the *Acta Sanctorum*, June, vol. iv.

ST AURELIAN, Bishop of Arles   (A.D. 551)

ST AURELIAN was raised to the bishopric of Arles in 546, and he received the pallium from Pope Vigilius, as well as an appointment to be papal vicar for Gaul.

Aurelian founded a monastery for men, which he enriched with many relics and for which he composed a rule, and also established at Arles a convent for women. In the interest of sound doctrine he wrote a letter to Pope Vigilius, who was then in Constantinople, asking for an explanation of his qualified condemnation of what were known as the Three Chapters—a condemnation which had been urged upon him by the Emperor Justinian, but which was regarded with apprehension in the West as reflecting on the validity of the Council of Chalcedon.   In return, he received from the pope a letter of reassurance, kindly, but couched in somewhat vague terms.   St Aurelian died in Lyons, where his grave was discovered in 1308.

A short notice is devoted to St Aurelian in the *Acta Sanctorum*, June, vol. iv.   A letter of this saint addressed to King Theodebert is critically edited in MGH., *Epistolae*, vol. iii, p. 124.   On the controversy over the Three Chapters, see Hefele-Leclercq, vol. iii, pp. 1–67. On Aurelian's place in the bishop lists of Arles, consult Duchesne, *Fastes Épiscopaux*, vol. i, pp. 258–259.

ST BENNO, BISHOP OF MEISSEN   (*c.* A.D. 1106)

THE little that contemporary history has to tell us about St Benno, bishop of Meissen, consists of casual references to him in chronicles and archives.   He was one of the canons attached to the imperial collegiate church of Goslar when, in 1066, he was made bishop of Meissen.   Because he sided with the Saxon nobles in their revolt against Henry IV he was imprisoned for a year, although he seems to have taken no active part in the struggle.   After his release he identified himself with the supporters of Pope Gregory, and in 1085 at the synod of Mainz he was deposed from his bishopric by the assembled German prelates, the greater part of whom were entirely subservient to the emperor.   He regained his see, however, three years later, through the good offices of the antipope Guibert, to whom he made submission.   In 1097, when the star of the emperor had waned and that of Pope Urban II was in the ascendant, Benno again changed his allegiance and declared himself an adherent of the true pope.

But if this is all that historians of his own age have to tell us about St Benno, later writers have supplied ample and picturesque biographies based largely on tradition and legend.   According to them he was born in 1010 at Hildesheim, the son of Count Frederick of Bultenburg, who sent him to be educated by his kinsman St Bernward, bishop of Hildesheim.   Eventually he was made bishop of Meissen by St Anno of Cologne.   His biographers wax eloquent over the benefits St Benno conferred upon the diocese.   Meissen had never known such a prelate.   He watched diligently over his flock, enforced discipline on his clergy, preached frequently, made regular visitations, gave liberally to the poor, set the example of a holy ascetic life, restored the public singing of the Divine Offices, and introduced into his church the chants to which he had been accustomed at Hildesheim.   A lover of good music, he was one day disturbed as he was walking in the fields by the harsh croaking of frogs, and silenced them by a peremptory command.   Scarcely had he done so when there flashed into his mind the words of the canticle : *Benedicite, cete, et omnia quae moventur in aquis, Domino*—" Ye whales and all that move in the waters, bless the Lord ! "   Addressing the frogs once more he withdrew his prohibition, bidding them sing on and give glory to God in their own manner.

His beneficent activities were suspended for a time through the imprisonment to which he was subjected by the emperor, but he resumed them as soon as he was liberated.   He exerted himself particularly to combat the shameless simony which, together with the question of investitures, constituted the main grounds for the struggle between Henry IV and Pope Gregory VII. Although summoned with the other German prelates to the Council of Worms which, under imperial pressure, dared to declare the deposition of the pope, he took no part in its deliberations ; realizing at the outset the futility of any attempt at opposition he escaped and made his way to Rome, where he was warmly received. He had previously sent a message to the canons of Meissen instructing them to throw the keys of the cathedral into the Elbe as soon as they should hear of the excommunication which he foresaw would fall on Henry. They obeyed him : but when the storm had abated sufficiently for him to return to his diocese, lo ! the keys, we are told, were found entangled in the gills of a fish which was brought by a fisherman to the bishop's kitchen.

St Benno died about 1106, and was canonized in 1523. This canonization drew from Martin Luther a violent polemical treatise entitled : " Against the New Idol and the Old Devil about to be set up at Meissen." Fifty-three years later, when Meissen had become a Protestant city, the relics of St Benno were translated to Munich, of which he remains the principal patron.

The materials for a biography of St Benno are unfortunately by no means satisfactory. The long life by Jerome Emser, which occupies twenty-four folio pages in the *Acta Sanctorum*, June, vol. iv, was only written early in the sixteenth century, and though it professes to be based on earlier sources it does not inspire confidence. There is also a short epitome of uncertain origin, but again this is a document which lacks adequate confirmation. The question of St Benno's career has perhaps been most carefully investigated by O. Langer in the *Mitteilungen des Vereins f. Geschichte Meissens*. See vol. i, part III (1884), pp. 70–95 ; vol. i, part V (1886), pp. 1–38 ; and vol. ii, part II (1888), pp. 99–144. *Cf.* also *Neues Archiv für sächs. Geschichte*, vol. vii (1886), pp. 131–144 ; and E. Machatschek, *Geschichte der Bischöfe der Hochstifter Meissen* (1884), pp. 65–94 ; and a study by E. Klein (1904). Both these last seem to place somewhat undue reliance on the statements of Emser.

BD GUY OF CORTONA   (*c.* A.D. 1245)

OF the parentage and early years of Guy Vignotelli, nothing is known. He is introduced to our notice as a young citizen of Cortona, living partly upon his patrimony, partly by the work of his hands, and giving away in charity all that he did not actually require for his own use. When St Francis of Assisi with one of his companions paid a first visit to Cortona in 1211, Guy gave them hospitality, and at the close of a meal he asked the Seraphic Father to receive him as a disciple. Upon being told that he must first abandon all things, he went out and sold his possessions, the proceeds of which he and his two guests immediately distributed in alms. The following day, St Francis formally clothed him with the habit. A little friary called Cella was built at or near Cortona, but Guy received permission to occupy a cell on a bridge. Because he was a man of education it was thought desirable that he should be ordained, and he was accordingly raised to the priesthood.

On a subsequent visit to Cortona, St Francis spoke in high terms of Bd Guy to the people who, for their part, had already learnt to appreciate his sanctity, his eloquence and his gifts. Amongst the miracles ascribed to him are many cures, the resuscitation of a girl who had apparently been drowned, and the multiplication of meal in a time of famine. When he was sixty years of age, St Francis appeared to him in a vision and said : " My son, the time has come for you to receive the reward of your labours. In three days, at the hour of None, I will return to lead you, by the grace of God, into Paradise." Bd Guy passed away at the hour predicted, in the convent of Cortona ; the date of his death is given by some authorities as 1245, by others as 1250.

See the *Acta Sanctorum*, June, vol. iii ; Wadding, *Annales Ord. Minorum*, vol. iii, pp. 601–607 ; and Léon, *Auréole Séraphique* (Eng. trans.), vol. ii, pp. 379–381.

ST LUTGARDIS, Virgin   (A.D. 1246)

AMONGST the notable women mystics of the twelfth and thirteenth centuries there is no more sympathetic or lovable figure than that of St Lutgardis. Born in 1182, the daughter of a citizen of Tongres in the Netherlands, she was placed at the age of twelve in the Benedictine convent of St Catherine near Saint-Trond, for no better reason than that the money intended for her marriage-portion had been lost in a business speculation, and that without it she was unlikely to find a suitable husband. She was an attractive girl, fond of pretty clothes and of innocent amusement, without any apparent religious vocation, and she seems to have lived at first as a kind of boarder, free to come and go, as well as to receive visitors of both sexes. One day, however, while she was entertaining a friend, our Lord appeared to her, and, showing her His sacred wounds, bade her love Him and Him only. Accepting Him instantly as her heavenly Bridegroom, she renounced from that moment all earthly concerns. Some of the nuns who observed her sudden fervour prophesied that it would not last ; but it only increased. So vividly did she come to realize God's presence that, when engaged in prayer, she beheld our Lord as with her bodily eyes. She would speak with Him familiarly, and if summoned away to perform some duty she would say, quite simply, " Wait here, Lord Jesus, and I will come back directly I have finished this task." Our Lady frequently appeared to her, and once she had a vision of St Catherine, the patroness of the convent ; on another occasion she saw St John the Evangelist, under the semblance of an eagle. Sometimes during her frequent ecstasies she would be upraised from the ground, or a strange light would be seen above her head.

In her meditations on our Lord's passion she was permitted to have a mystical share in her Saviour's sufferings, and her forehead and hair appeared at such seasons to be bedewed with drops of blood. Her sympathy was extended to all for whom Christ died ; she felt their sorrows and sufferings as though they were her own. Indeed, in the ardour of her intercession for others she would entreat God to blot her name out of the Book of Life rather than withhold His mercy from the soul for whom she was pleading.

Lutgardis had been at St Catherine's twelve years when she was inspired or counselled to place herself under the stricter rule of the Cistercians. Although she would have preferred a German-speaking house, she selected the convent of Aywières, upon the advice of her confessor and of her friend, St Christine the Astonishing, who was then living at St Catherine's. Only French was spoken at Aywières, and St Lutgardis never mastered French. In after years, her ignorance of the language served her as a valid excuse for refusing to hold office at Aywières or elsewhere. Her humility was at all times extraordinary ; she continually bewailed the inadequate response she was making to the graces bestowed upon her. In the vehemence of her prayer that she might at least lay down her life for our Lord, she once burst a blood-vessel, and it was said to be revealed to her that this effusion of blood was accepted as equivalent to martyrdom.

God endowed her with the gifts of healing and prophecy as well as an infused knowledge of the meaning of the Holy Scriptures.　In spite of her imperfect French, she had great success in imparting spiritual consolation, and Bd Mary of Oignies was wont to assert that there was no one whose prayers were so efficacious in obtaining the conversion of sinners and the release of souls from purgatory. Eleven years before her death, she lost her sight, and this affliction she accepted with joy, as a God-sent means of detaching her from the visible world.　It was after she had become blind that she undertook the last of several prolonged fasts. Our Lord appeared to her to warn her of her approaching death, and to bid her prepare for it in three ways.　She was to give praise to God for what she had received ; she was to pray unremittingly for the conversion of sinners ; and she was to rely in all things on God alone, awaiting the time when she would possess Him for ever.　St Lutgardis died, as she had predicted, on the Saturday night after the feast of the Holy Trinity, just as the night office for Sunday was beginning. It was June 16, 1246.

The life of St Lutgardis was written by Thomas of Cantimpré, who died in 1270, and consequently was in part her contemporary.　The text is printed (from a collation of three or four manuscript copies) in the *Acta Sanctorum*, June, vol. iv.　It is a very attractive record, though the author's obvious credulity, as evidenced not only here but in other writings of his, must rather tend to lessen our confidence in the accuracy of his report of supernatural incidents.　Other sources are apparently lacking, but there seems to be a translation of part of this life in the Low-German vernacular, possibly made before the end of the same thirteenth century.　This version has been attributed with some probability to William of Afflighem, abbot of Saint-Trond ; see F. Van Veerdeghem, in the *Bulletin de l'Académie de Belgique*, vol. xxxiv (1897), pp. 1055–1086.　Other modern accounts of St Lutgardis will be found in H. Nimal, *Vies de quelques-unes de nos grandes Saintes au pays de Liége* (1898), and in Jonquet (1906).　See also articles by S. Roisin and others in *Collectanea ordinis Cisterciensium Reformatorum*, nos. 3 and 4 of 1946 ; and the study by Fr L. (Thomas) Merton, *What Are These Wounds ?* (Milwaukee, 1950).

ST JOHN FRANCIS REGIS　(A.D. 1640)

St John Francis Regis was born in 1597 at Fontcouverte, in the diocese of Narbonne, of a family that had recently emerged from the *bourgeoisie* into the ranks of the small landed gentry.　He was educated at the Jesuit college of Béziers, and in 1615 sought admittance into the Society of Jesus.　His conduct from the time he was allowed to begin his noviciate was exemplary : so marked was his severity towards himself and his tenderness towards others that it was said that he vilified himself beyond measure but canonized everyone else.　The first year of noviciate ended, he passed on to follow courses of rhetoric and philosophy at Cahors and Tournon.　Whilst at Tournon, every Sunday and holiday, he accompanied the father who served the little town of Andance, and through the catechetical instructions he gave when the priest was hearing confessions he gained a wonderful influence not only over the children but also over their elders.　He was then only twenty-two years of age.

In 1628 he was sent to Toulouse to begin his theology course.　A companion who shared his room at this time informed the superior that Regis spent the greater part of the night at prayer in the chapel.　The reply he received was prophetic ; " Take care not to disturb his devotions ", said Father Francis Tarbes, " nor to hinder his communion with God.　He is a saint ; and if I am not greatly mistaken, the Society will some day celebrate a feast in his honour."　In 1631 he was ordained, and on Trinity Sunday, June 15, he celebrated his first Mass. His superiors had already destined him for the missionary work that was to occupy the last ten years of his life : beginning in Languedoc, it was to extend throughout the Vivarais, and to end in the Velay, of which Le Puy was the capital. The summers were spent in the towns, but the winter months were to be devoted to the villages and the country-side. He may be said to have initiated his campaign in the autumn of that same year, 1631, by a mission which he conducted in the Jesuit church at Montpellier. Unlike the formal rhetorical sermons of the day, his discourses were plain—even homely—but so eloquently expressive of the fervour that burnt within him that they attracted enormous congregations, drawn from all classes. He addressed himself particularly to the poor : the rich, he was wont to say, never lack confessors. He would himself convey to his humble protégés any comforts he could procure for them, and when warned that he was making himself ridiculous he retorted, " So much the better : we are doubly blest if we can relieve a poor brother at the expense of our dignity." His mornings were spent in the confessional, at the altar and in the pulpit : the afternoons he devoted to prisons and hospitals. Very often he was so busy that he forgot to take his meals. Before he left Montpellier he had converted several Huguenots and many lax Catholics, he had formed a committee of ladies to look after prisoners, and had reclaimed a number of women from a life of sin. To the critics who contended that the penitence of such rescue cases is seldom sincere, he replied, " If my efforts do no more than to hinder one sin I shall consider them well expended." After Montpellier he made his temporary headquarters at Sommières, from whence he penetrated into the most out-of-the-way places, winning the confidence of the people by talking to them and instructing them in their own patois.

His success at Montpellier and Sommières prompted Mgr de la Baume, bishop of Viviers, to apply for the services of Father Regis and of another Jesuit to help him in his diocese. No part of France had suffered more as the result of prolonged civil and religious strife than the wild, mountainous regions of south-eastern France known as the Vivarais and the Velay. Law and order seemed to have disappeared, the poverty-stricken peasantry were lapsing into savagery, and the nobles were often no better than brigands. Absentee prelates and negligent priests had allowed the churches to fall into ruin, whole parishes having been deprived of the sacraments for twenty years or more. A considerable proportion of the inhabitants, indeed, were traditionally Calvinist, but their Protestantism in many cases was a mere party badge, and in laxity of morals and indifference to religion there was little to choose between Catholics and Protestants. With the help of his Jesuit assistants Bishop de la Baume undertook a thorough visitation of his diocese, and Father Regis went everywhere a day or two in advance of him, conducting a kind of mission. It proved the beginning of a three-years' ministry, during the course of which he succeeded in effectively bringing back religious observance, as well as in converting a great number of Protestants.

That such a vigorous campaign should remain unopposed was scarcely to be expected, and in fact there was actually a moment when those who resented his activities were on the point of obtaining his recall. He himself never said a word in his own defence ; but the bishop's eyes were opened in time to the baselessness of the charges that had been made against him. About this time Father Regis made the first of several unsuccessful applications to be sent on the Canadian mission to the North American Indians. His superiors were no doubt satisfied with the work he was doing in France, but he always regarded it as a punishment for his sins that he was not allowed the chance of winning the crown of martyrdom. So instead he extended his missions to the wildest and most desolate part of all that highland district, a region where no man went unarmed, and where the winters were rigorous in the extreme. On one occasion he was held up by a snow-drift for three weeks, with only a little bread to eat and with the bare ground for a bed.

Graphic and touching descriptions of those expeditions are to be found in the depositions for the saint's canonization furnished by those who could still remember them. " After the mission I did not recognize my own parishioners, so completely had he reformed them ", stated the curé of Marlhes. " No cold, no snow-blocked path, no mountains, no rain-swollen torrent could stop him. His fervour inspired others with courage, for wherever he went countless multitudes followed him and came out to bid him welcome, in spite of danger and difficulties. I have seen him stop in the middle of a forest to satisfy a crowd who wished to hear him. I have seen him stand all day on a heap of snow at the top of a mountain instructing and preaching, and then spend the whole night hearing confessions." Another witness had been passing through the district when he noticed a procession winding its way in the distance. " It is the saint ", he was told, " and the people are following." As he entered the town of Saint-André he came upon a huge crowd assembled in front of the church. " We are waiting for the saint ", was the explanation he received. " He is coming to give us a mission." Men and women would walk a dozen leagues or more to seek him, confident that however late they might arrive Father Regis would always be ready to minister to them. He, on his part, would often set off to visit a distant hamlet at three o'clock in the morning with a few apples in his pocket. Never did he fail to keep an appointment. Once he had stumbled and broken his leg : nevertheless, with the help of a stick and the shoulder of his companion, he arrived at his destination and entered the confessional as though nothing had happened. When after his day's work was over he submitted himself to a medical examination, the leg was found to be healed.

The four last years of the saint's life were spent in Velay. All through the summer he worked in Le Puy, where the Jesuit church proved too small for congregations which often numbered four or five thousand. His influence reached all classes and brought about a very real and lasting spiritual revival. He established and organized a complete social service with prison visitors, sick-nurses and guardians of the poor drawn from his women penitents. With the help of money freely given to him by the well-to-do he set up a granary for the poor, and a refuge for women and girls who had been leading sinful lives. This last enterprise involved him in many difficulties. Evil men, robbed of their victims, assaulted him and blackened his character, whilst some of his own brethren questioned his prudence. For a short time his activities were checked by an over-timorous superior, and Father Regis made no attempt to justify himself ; but God, who exalts the humble, was pleased to set the seal of His approval upon His servant by granting him the gift of miracles. Numerous cures were wrought by him, including the restoration of sight to a boy, and to a middle-aged man who had been blind for eight years. In a time of dearth, when many demands upon his granary had to be satisfied, the store of corn was three times miraculously renewed—to the utter bewilderment of the good woman who had been left in charge.

The work went on until the autumn of 1640, when St John Francis seems to have realized that his days were numbered. He had to give a mission at La Louvesc

ST GREGORY BARBARIGO [*June* 17]

towards the end of Advent. Before doing so he made a three-days' retreat at the college of Le Puy and settled a few small debts. On the eve of his departure he was invited to stay on until the semi-annual renewal of vows, but replied : " The Master does not wish it. He wishes me to leave to-morrow," adding, " I shall not be back for the renewal of vows : my companion will." They set out in appalling weather, lost their way, and were overtaken by night in the woods. They were obliged to rest in a ruined house open to the piercing wind, and Father Regis, already completely exhausted, contracted pleurisy. Nevertheless, the next morning he managed to crawl to La Louvesc, where he opened his mission. He preached three times on Christmas day, three times on St Stephen's day, and spent the rest of those days in the tribunal of penance. At the close of the last address when he again entered the confessional he fainted twice. He was carried to the curé's house and was found to be dying. On December 31, during the whole day, he kept his eyes on the crucifix : in the evening he suddenly exclaimed, " Brother ! I see our Lord and His Mother opening Heaven for me ! " Then with the words : " Into Thy hands I commend my spirit ", he passed to his eternal reward. He was forty-three years of age. His body remains to this day at La Louvesc, where he died, and his tomb is annually visited by some fifty thousand pilgrims from every part of France. It was such a pilgrimage to La Louvesc that St John Vianney, the Curé d'Ars, made in 1806 : he ascribed to St Francis Regis the realization of his vocation to the priesthood.

There are many excellent lives of St John Francis Regis (who was canonized in 1737), especially in French. The biography by C. de la Broüe, printed ten years after his death, has a special charm, but much fuller detail is available in more modern works, especially those of de Curley and L. J. M. Cros. An excellent short life is that of J. Vianney in the series " Les Saints ". See also L. Pize, *La perpetuelle mission de St Jean François Regis* (1924) ; the admirable account by Fr Van Ortroy in the *Catholic Encyclopedia*, vol. viii, pp. 464–465, and that by Fr Martindale which forms a chapter of his little book, *In God's Army.*

17 : ST GREGORY BARBARIGO, BISHOP OF PADUA AND CARDINAL
(A.D. 1697)

BORN at Venice in 1625 of an ancient and noble house, Gregory Luigi Barbarigo was educated in his native city. While still in his early twenties he was chosen by the Venetian government to accompany its ambassador, Luigi Contarini, to the famous Congress of Münster, where on October 24, 1648, the plenipotentiaries of Germany, France and Sweden signed the Treaty of Westphalia, and thus brought to an end the Thirty Years' War. At Münster Barbarigo became acquainted with the apostolic nuncio, Fabio Chigi, who was so favourably impressed with him that, after he had been raised to the papal throne as Alexander VII, he showed the young Venetian many tokens of his esteem and became his strong supporter. In 1657 he nominated him to the bishopric of Bergamo, in 1660 he created him a cardinal, and in 1664 he transferred him to the bishopric of Padua.

The zeal with which Bd Gregory carried out his pastoral duties caused him to be hailed as a second Charles Borromeo. He was indeed exemplary in every relation of life. His charities were enormous, and he is known to have distributed in alms eight hundred thousand crowns. Severe only with himself, he was kind to all, especially to those in trouble or distress. In the interest of learning he founded a college, and also a seminary for young priests which attained great renown. He gave it a printing press of its own, and also a fine library particularly well furnished with the writings of the fathers and with works dealing with the Holy Scriptures. He died a peaceful death on June 15, 1697, and was beatified in 1761.

A life of Bd Gregory was written in Latin by A. Ricchini, which was also translated into Italian. His unpublished writings were edited by P. Uccelli in 1877, and the account of his pastoral visitations by A. Coi in 1907. His earnest efforts to bring about a union with the Greeks are described by G. Poletto in three articles in *Bessarione* for 1901–1902. See also the references to him in Pastor, *Geschichte der Päpste*, vol. xiv ; and in P. Bergamaschi's life of his namesake, Marc' Antonio Barbarigo (1919). Nine studies for the biography of Bd Gregory were published by Prof. S. Serena, of Venice, between 1929 and 1940.

SS. NICANDER AND MARCIAN, Martyrs   (Fourth Century)

ALBAN BUTLER, putting his trust in Ruinart, accepted without question the " acts " of these saints as a genuine document. The narrative certainly cannot claim to be regarded as authentic history, but it is a favourable specimen of the art of the hagiographer who made it his business to embellish a kernel of fact with fictional details. Following more or less closely Butler's presentment the story runs thus :

Nicander and Marcian had served some time in the Roman army, but when the edicts were published against Christians they gave up their military career. This was made a crime in them, and they were impeached before Maximus, the governor of the province. The judge informed them of the imperial order that all were commanded to sacrifice to the gods. Nicander replied that the order could not be binding on Christians who looked upon it as unlawful to abandon the immortal God in order to worship wood and stone. Daria, the wife of Nicander, was present and encouraged her husband. Maximus, interrupting her, said, " You wicked woman ; why do you want your husband to die ? " " I do not wish for his death ", she said, " but that he live in God, so as never to die." Maximus insinuated that she desired his death because she wanted another husband. " If you suspect that ", said she, " put me to death first."

Maximus, turning again to Nicander, said, " Take a little time and deliberate with yourself whether you will decide to die or to live ". Nicander answered, " I have already made up my mind that my own safety must come first." The judge took it that he meant that he would save his life by sacrificing to the idols. But Nicander soon undeceived him, for he prayed aloud, expressing his joy that he was to be delivered from the dangers and temptations of the world. " How is this ", asked the governor, " you but just now desired to live, and now you ask to die ? " Nicander replied, " I desire that life which is immortal, not the fleeting life of this world. To you I willingly yield up my body ; do with it what you please : I am a Christian." " And what is your view, Marcian ? " asked the judge, addressing himself to the other. He declared that it was the same as that of his fellow prisoner. Maximus then gave orders that they should be both confined in a dungeon, where they lay twenty days.

After this they were again brought before the governor, who asked them if they would at length obey the edicts of the emperor. Marcian replied, " All you can say will never make us abandon our religion or deny God. By faith we behold

Him present and know whither He calls us. Do not, we beseech you, detain us, but send us quickly to Him that was crucified, whom you fear not to blaspheme, but whom we honour and worship." The governor, excusing himself by the necessity he was under of complying with his orders, condemned them both to be beheaded. The martyrs expressed their gratitude and said, "May peace be with you, most kind judge".

They walked to the place of execution joyful, and praising God as they went. Nicander was followed by his wife, Daria, with his child whom Papinian, brother to the martyr St Pasicrates, carried in his arms. Marcian's wife followed him too, but weeping and making an outcry. She did all in her power to overcome his resolution, drawing his attention to their little child. At the place of execution Marcian kissed his son, and looking up to Heaven said, "Lord, all-powerful God, do thou take this child under thy protection". Then with a rebuke to his wife for her faint-heartedness, he bade her go away in peace, because she would not have the courage to see him die. The wife of Nicander continued by his side, exhorting him to constancy and joy. "Be of good heart, master", said she. "Ten years have I lived at home away from you, never ceasing to pray that I might see you again. Now I have that comfort, and I behold you going to glory and myself the wife of a martyr. Give to God that testimony you owe to His holy truth, that you may also deliver me from eternal death"; meaning that by his sufferings and prayers he might obtain mercy for her. The executioner having bound their eyes with handkerchiefs struck off their heads, the day assigned in this version of the *passio* being June 17.

It may seem a wanton piece of iconoclasm to discredit this very natural and relatively sober tale, but the difficulty is that among a number of differing accounts there is no agreement as to the place where the martyrdom took place, the names of the group of martyrs, for Nicander and Marcian are often grouped with several others, or, what is perhaps most suspicious of all, the date of the celebration. No one has ever doubted that the " acts " have some historical foundation and that Nicander and Marcian really existed as martyrs. But four distinct regions in different countries claim to have been the scene of their passion : Durostorum, in Moesia or Bulgaria ; Tomi, or Constanta, in what is now Rumania ; Alexandria in Egypt ; and Venafro in Italy, where their reputed relics are still venerated. The Bollandist Father Delehaye, however, inclined to the belief that they suffered at Durostorum. In his opinion, Italy merely imported their *cultus*, whilst with regard to the inclusion of their names in a list of Egyptian martyrs in the *Hieronymianum*, he suggests that a careless copyist, seeing the name of Marcian, may quite possibly have interpolated that of Nicander through associating in his mind the two martyrs of Durostorum.

As well as Nicander and Marcian, " at Venafro ", to-day, the Roman Martyrology on June 5 commemorates SS. Marcian, Nicanor and others, " in Egypt ".

The *passio* from which Alban Butler took his account is printed in Ruinart's *Acta Sincera*. There is another version, in Latin and Greek, in the *Acta Sanctorum*, June, vol. iv, and another in vol. i. For other texts, consult BHL., nn. 5260, 6070–6074, and supplement, and BHG., nn. 1194 and 1330 ; with B. Latysev, *Menologii byzantini saeculi X quae supersunt*, vol. ii, pp. 16–17 and 27–30. See also Delehaye in *Analecta Bollandiana*, vol. xxxi (1912), pp. 268–272 and vol. xl (1922), pp. 54–60 ; his *Origines du Culte des Martyrs*, pp. 249–250, etc. ; and his CMH., pp. 305 and 323 ; and P. Franchi de' Cavalieri in *Studi e Testi*, vol. xxiv (1912), pp. 141–157.

ST BESSARION   (FOURTH CENTURY)

BESSARION is greatly venerated in the East, where his name in various forms is sometimes given in baptism ; *e.g.* Joseph Stalin's father was called Vissarion. He was a native of Egypt, and having heard the call to perfection he went into the wilderness, where he was a disciple first of St Antony and then of St Macarius. We are told that rather than live under a roof he wandered about like a bird, observing silence and subduing his flesh by mighty fasting ; he is said to have once gone forty days without food, standing in prayer amid brambles. His neighbourly charity led him to a height of perfection that was manifested by miracles : he made salt water fresh, he several times brought rain during drought, he walked on the Nile, he overcame demons. Like so many other desert fathers, St Bessarion lived to a great age ; and he was compared by his admirers with Moses, Joshua, Elias and John the Baptist.

St Bessarion is named in the Roman Martyrology to-day, but his usual date in the East is June 6.

The above particulars are taken from a panegyric of his namesake written by the great Cardinal Bessarion, the text of which was printed, with an introduction by Peter Joannou, in *Analecta Bollandiana*, vol. lxv (1947), pp. 107–138. The cardinal's sources were the pertinent Greek synaxaries. See also the *Acta Sanctorum*, June, vol. iii. The three Bessarions in DHG., t. viii, cc. 1180–1181, are apparently all the same person.

ST HYPATIUS, ABBOT   (A.D. 446 ?)

IN the suburb of Chalcedon that gave its name—The Oak—to the infamous pseudo-synod by which St John Chrysostom was condemned, a certain consular official called Rufinus built a church dedicated under the names of St Peter and St Paul, together with a monastery alongside to serve it. The community flourished for a time, but after the founder's death the monks dispersed and the derelict fabric soon acquired an unsavoury reputation as the haunt of evil spirits. The building remained unoccupied until a holy ascetic named Hypatius, attended by two companions, Timotheus and Moschion, came upon it in their wanderings through Bithynia in search of a suitable retreat, and took up their residence in the ruins. Disciples gathered round them and a great community was formed over which Hypatius ruled for many years. After his death the monastery was known by his name.

The life of St Hypatius has come down to us in the shape of a biography written by Callinicus, one of his monks, who in his desire to glorify his master sometimes lets his imagination or his credulity run away with him. According to him St Hypatius was born in Phrygia and was educated by his father, a learned scholar who intended that his son should follow in his steps. Hypatius himself, however, always desired monastic life. At the age of eighteen, having been cruelly beaten by his father, he ran away from home, and in obedience to a supernatural admonition proceeded to Thrace. There for a considerable time he acted as a shepherd. A priest who heard him singing to his flock taught him the Psalter and the chant. Hypatius then joined a solitary, an ex-soldier named Jonas, with whom he led a most austere life, abstaining, it is said, from drink of any kind sometimes for forty consecutive days. Hypatius was discovered by his father, and a reconciliation took place.

Afterwards Hypatius and Jonas made their way to Constantinople, where Jonas seems to have remained.   But Hypatius crossed the straits into Asia Minor again, and revived religious life in the ruins of the old Rufinian monastery.   As head of a great body of monks he stood forth as a powerful champion of orthodoxy.   Even before the errors of Nestorius had been denounced by the Church, he had ordered the removal of that hierarch's name from the office books of his church, paying no heed to the remonstrances of Bishop Eulalius of Chalcedon.   He protected and hospitably entertained St Alexander Akimetes and his monks who had fled from Constantinople to Bithynia ; and when a proposal to revive the Olympic games at Chalcedon had met with no opposition from Eulalius, Hypatius defeated the project by the vehemence with which he protested that he and his monks would die rather than permit any such restoration of pagan practices.

The historical accuracy of these stories, it must be said, is discredited by critical commentators.   They question the very existence of Eulalius : no other record can be found of any such bishop of Chalcedon ; his name appears neither amongst the signatories of the Council of Ephesus in 431, nor amongst those of the Latrocinium in 449.   On the other hand, it is certain that a certain Eleutherius was bishop of Chalcedon in 451.   St Hypatius, " the scholar of Christ ", became famous for his reputed miracles and prophecies.   He is said to have died about the middle of the fifth century at the age of eighty.   His name is entered on this day in the Roman Martyrology as belonging to Phrygia.

The long Greek life by Callinicus is printed in the *Acta Sanctorum*, June, vol. iv, but the text is unfortunately incomplete.   It has since been edited critically (1895) from another manuscript which contains the whole, by the pupils of H. Usener.   See also H. Mertel, *Die biograph. Form der griech. Heiligenlegenden* (1909).   Hypatius seems to have been especially invoked in the Greek church as a protector against harmful beasts ; see Franz, *Kirchlichen Benediktionen*, vol. ii, p. 143.

ST AVITUS, ABBOT   (A.D. 530 ?)

AT the close of a scholarly article upon St Avitus and the Saints of Micy in the *Analecta Bollandiana*, the late Father Albert Poncelet, s.j., urged his readers to convince themselves that a wide difference exists between evidence of *cultus* and hagiographical narratives.   " The former ", *i.e.* evidence of *cultus*, " attests the actual existence of the saint and the fact that devotion has been paid to him from early times.   It is a very different matter when we have to deal with lives compiled two or three hundred years after the hero's death, and seldom embodying a wholly reliable collection of traditions.   For the honour of the saints and in the interest of sane hagiography one cannot be too careful not to be led astray by those who, not satisfied with venerating the saints, imagine that respect for them entails a sort of canonization of the stories whereby posterity has sought to enhance their glory, in the compilation of which knowledge of the facts has unfortunately not always been on a level with the piety of the author."

That St Avitus was a real person is unquestionable.   St Gregory of Tours informs us that he was an abbot in that part of France which formed the ancient province of Perche, that he pleaded unsuccessfully with King Clodomir to spare the lives of St Sigismund of Burgundy, his wife and his sons, whom Clodomir had captured, and that he was buried near Orleans, where he was held in great honour. St Gregory had visited the church which was dedicated under his name, and adds, as an instance of his miraculous powers, that a citizen of Orleans, who refused to observe his festival because he wanted to work in his vineyard was punished by a painful affliction from which he was not freed until he visited the saint's church and paid him the respect which was his due.   This is all that is known about St Avitus—despite his so-called biographies, none of which are earlier than the ninth century.   They form part of an attempt made, when the abbey of Micy had taken on a new lease of life under Benedictine rule, to shed lustre on an obscure and inglorious phase of its past history by assigning to it as former abbots a number of saints honoured in the neighbourhood of Orleans and Le Mans, but of whom very little indeed was known.

The legend of St Avitus, which appears with variations in these so-called biographies, represents him as having entered the abbey of Micy as a lay-brother. His ignorance and simplicity caused him to be despised by all except the abbot, St Maximinus, who recognized his sanctity and made him cellarer.   Avitus, however, left the abbey and retired into solitude.   After the death of Maximinus the monks made search for Avitus and elected him abbot.   Again, after a short stay at Micy, he escaped, this time with St Calais (Carilefus), and lived as a recluse on the frontiers of Perche.   Others joining them, St Calais withdrew into a forest in Maine; but King Clotaire built a church and monastery for St Avitus and his companions at the place which is now Châteaudun.   There he died in the year 530 (?).

For one text of the life of St Avitus see the *Acta Sanctorum*, June, vol. iv ; another has been printed entire by the Bollandists in their catalogue of the hagiographical manuscripts of the Brussels Library, vol. i, pp. 57–63.   B. Krusch has re-edited portions of this in MGH., *Scriptores Merov.*, vol. iii, pp. 380–385.   The article of Albert Poncelet referred to above is in the *Analecta Bollandiana*, vol. xxiv (1905), pp. 5–97.

ST NECTAN   (Sixth Century ?)

THE tomb of St Nectan at Hartland in Devonshire was the centre of a *cultus* which seems to have been fostered in the middle ages by the Augustinian canons, who were the custodians of his tomb.   He was also venerated in Cornwall, especially at Launceston, where a fair is still held on his feast-day, June 17.   In the neighbourhood of Lostwithiel and Newlyn chapels were dedicated in his honour under the name of St Nighton, and perhaps also at Tintagel, not far from which famous resort " St Nighton's Kieve " (*i.e.* vat) is still shown.   William of Worcester and some later writers, such as Nicholas Roscarrock, describe the saint as having been the eldest of the twenty-four children of the Welsh king, Brychan, who gave his name to Brecknock.   The saint may possibly have been an Irish missionary who came to England and founded churches in Devon and Cornwall.   Actually nothing is known of his true history.   All that Worcester is able to tell us about him is this : " And the venerable man Nectan, while he was making his way through certain woody districts in order to explore the country, was found by robbers in the place which to this day is called New Town (*i.e.* New Stoke), and there a church is built to his honour.   On the fifteenth day before the kalends of July he was beheaded, and he took up his head in his own hands and carried it about a distance of half a stadium, as far as the fountain where he lived, and there laid it down, besmeared with his blood and sweat, on a certain stone, and blood-stained traces of this murder and miracle still remain on that same stone."   This is a quotation from the saint's Life.

The twelfth-century life of St Nectan, which came to light in the Gotha MS. I. 81 in 1937 and was translated by Canon Doble (see note below), adds little of interest

about the saint, though it gives interesting particulars about his shrine and side-
lights on life at Hartland in the middle ages.

By far the best attempt in English to cope with the incoherencies of the materials is that of
Canon Doble in no. 25 of his " Cornish Saints " series, *St Nectan and the Children of Brychan*
(1930) ; his translation of the *vita* appeared in *A Book of Hartland* (1940), ed. by Miss
I. D. Thornley, and was reprinted separately in the same year.   See also DCB., vol. iv,
pp. 10–11, and LBS., vol. iv, pp. 1–2.   But consult especially *Analecta Bollandiana*, vol. lxxi
(1953).

ST HERVÉ, or HARVEY, Abbot   (Sixth Century)

St Hervé is one of the most popular saints in Brittany, and figures largely in the
folklore and ballads of the country.   At one period his feast was a holiday of
obligation in the diocese of Léon.   His *cultus*, which originally centred in Lanhouarneau, Le Menez-Bré and Porzay, was propagated by a distribution of his
relics in 1002, and is general throughout Brittany.   No name, with the exception
of Yves, is more commonly given to Breton boys than that of Hervé.   Solemn oaths
were taken over his relics until the year 1610, when the *parlement* made it obligatory
for legal declarations to be made only upon the Gospels.   In the absence of any
reliable records it is unfortunately impossible to reconstruct St Hervé's true history,
but the legend, as set forth in a late medieval Latin manuscript, may be summarized
as follows :

In the early years of the reign of King Childebert, there came to the court of
Paris a British bard named Hyvarnion, who had been driven from his country by
the Saxons.   He charmed all who heard him by his music, but worldly applause
had no attraction for him.   After two or three years he retired to Brittany, where
he married a girl called Rivanon, and became the father of a little blind boy, who
received the name of Hervé.   The child, bereft in infancy of his father, was brought
up until he was seven by his mother.   She then confided him to the care of a holy
man called Arthian, and afterwards he joined his uncle, who had founded a little
monastic school at Plouvien, and helped him with his farm and his pupils.   One
day, as Hervé was working in the fields, a wolf came and devoured the ass which
was drawing the plough ; a young child, who was the saint's guide, uttered cries of
distress, but in answer to Hervé's prayers the wolf meekly passed his head into
the ass's collar and finished his work.   During these years his mother Rivanon had
been living in the heart of a dense forest, seeing no human face except that of her
niece, who waited on her.   Now the hour of departure was at hand, and Hervé
sought her out in time to receive her last blessing and to close her eyes.

Soon afterwards he was entrusted with the care of the community of Plouvien
by his uncle, and the monastery continued to flourish ; but after three years he was
inspired to establish it elsewhere.   Surrounded by a band of monks and scholars
he went forth, directing his steps first to Léon.   There he was cordially received
by the bishop, who would have conferred the priesthood on him if the saint's
humility had not precluded him from accepting any higher order than that of
exorcist.   From Léon they made their way westward, and beside the road to
Lesneven may still be seen the fountain of St Hervé, which he caused to spring
forth to quench the thirst of his companions.   They reached their final destination
at the place now known as Lanhouarneau, where St Hervé founded a monastery
which became famous throughout the country.   It was his home for the rest of
his life, although he sometimes left it in order to preach to the people and to

exercise the duties of an exorcist, in which capacity some of his most outstanding miracles were worked. Venerated by all for his sanctity and for his miracles, the blind abbot lived on for many years ; his monks, as they watched beside his death-bed, heard the music of the celestial choirs welcoming the saint to Heaven.

St Hervé is usually represented with the wolf, and with Guiharan, his child guide. He is invoked for eye-trouble of all sorts, and his wolf serves Breton mothers as a bugbear with which to threaten troublesome children.

The so-called life of St Hervé, which in the very competent judgement of A. de la Borderie cannot have been written (at any rate in the form in which it has been preserved to us) earlier than the thirteenth century, was published for the first time by the same distinguished scholar in 1892 in the *Mémoires de la Soc. d'Émulation des Côtes-du-Nord*, vol. xxix, pp. 251–304. There is an account in the *Acta Sanctorum*, June, vol. iv, mainly based on Albert Le Grand. See, further, LBS., vol. iii, pp. 270 *seq. ;* but Canon Doble affirms strongly that there is no ground for connecting Hervé in any way with either Cornwall or Wales ; he had no cult in Britain. *Cf.* Duine, *Memento,* p. 91.

ST BOTULF, OR BOTOLPH, ABBOT, AND ST ADULF (*c.* A.D. 680)

No less than seventy English churches—sixteen of them in Norfolk—are dedicated in honour of St Botulf, but though he seems to have been held in great veneration in Anglo-Saxon England little is actually known of his history. According to a life written by Folcard, abbot of Thorney, in 1068, he and his brother Adulf were the sons of noble Saxon parents and were born early in the seventh century. In the Slesvig Breviary, however, he is said to have been a " Scot ", *i.e.* an Irishman. Brought up Christians, they were sent to complete their education in Germany or in Belgian Gaul, where they received the monastic habit. Adulf is said to have been raised to the episcopate, either at Utrecht or Maestricht. If this statement is correct, he was probably a regionary bishop, for his name does not appear in the list of prelates of either diocese. Botulf in the course of time returned to England, and was favourably received by Ethelmund, a king of the southern Angles, whose sisters he had met abroad.

At his request, Ethelmund (of whom no other record exists) granted him a barren spot, almost surrounded by water, on which to build a monastery. It was called Icanhoh, and is usually identified with Boston. *i.e.* Botulf's stone, in Lincolnshire, but it may have been Iken in Suffolk, or elsewhere. He began to build his abbey in 654, as we learn from the Anglo-Saxon Chronicle, and soon gathered round him a band of disciples. We read that they suffered molestation from the evil spirits who had formerly haunted the district. Otherwise, St Botulf, except for two recorded journeys, appears to have led a peaceful, uneventful life amongst his brethren until his death in 680. It is related of St Ceolfrid, abbot of Wearmouth, that he " once journeyed to the East Angles that he might see the foundation of Abbot Botulf, whom fame had proclaimed far and wide as a man of remarkable life and learning, full of the grace of the Holy Spirit " and that " after having been instructed as far as possible in a short time, he returned home so well grounded that no one could be found better versed than he, either in ecclesiastical or in monastic traditions."

Although Icanhoh and its church were destroyed in one of the Danish invasions, the remains of St Botulf were saved, as well as those of St Adulf, who had been buried with him. In the reign of King Edgar the relics were distributed to the abbeys of Thorney and Ely. The feast of St Botulf is now kept in the dioceses of Brentwood, Northampton and Nottingham.

In the *Acta Sanctorum*, June, vol. iv, the Bollandists have printed such information regarding St Botulf as was accessible to them at the beginning of the eighteenth century. Not very much has been added since ; but it is worth while to consult the notes to Plummer's edition of the *Ecclesiastical History* of Bede, and also the article in the *Dictionary of Christian Biography* vol. i, p. 332. Edmund Bishop's notes on the English calendars in Stanton's *Menology* point to the fact that the observance of some feast in commemoration of St Botulf was widespread in this country. By far the most thorough account which has been written of Botulf is that contributed in 1922 to the *Proceedings of the Suffolk Institute of Archaeology and Natural History* (pp. 29–52) by F. S. Stevenson.

ST MOLING, BISHOP IN LEINSTER   (A.D. 697)

THE *cultus* of St Moling (Mulling, Molingus, Daircheall) goes back to a very early date and has been widespread over Ireland. Giraldus Cambrensis states that the books of SS. Patrick, Columba, Moling and Broccan, whom he characterizes as the four prophets of Ireland, were extant in his time in the Irish language. Unfortunately no accurate record of the history of St Moling, nor any of his writings, have been preserved to us, and we can only arrive at a conjectural outline of his career based on a late tradition. He is said to have been born in the district of Kinsellagh in County Wexford, of a family related to the kings of Leinster. After spending some years at Glendalough, where he received the monastic habit, he founded an abbey at Achad Cainigb, which derived so much glory from his wisdom and example that it was named Tech Moling in his honour. He is said to have lived for a time in a hollow tree, and to have fasted every day during all his later life, except when he was entertaining guests. He succeeded St Aidan as bishop at Ferns, and induced King Finacta, in 693, to remit for the kingdom of Leinster the heavy tribute of oxen, called the Cattle tribute, that had been imposed by King Tuathal Techtmar and had been the cause of many wars. The holy bishop resigned his see several years before his death, which occurred in 697. He was interred in his own monastery of Tech Moling, a site now covered by the town of St Mullins, in County Carlow.

The Bollandists in the *Acta Sanctorum*, June, vol. iv, have printed a Latin life from the *Codex Salmanticensis*, and another has been edited by C. Plummer in VSH., vol. ii, pp. 190–205. There is also an Irish life, which has been printed by Whitley Stokes in the *Revue Celtique*, vol. xxviii (1906), pp. 256–312. See further Kenney, *The Sources for the Early History of Ireland*, vol. i. What is believed to be St Moling's book shrine is preserved as a notable work of art.

ST RAINERIUS OF PISA   (A.D. 1160)

THE relics of the saint who is Pisa's principal patron lie in the chapel of St Rainerius, or Raniero, at the end of the south transept of the cathedral, and eight scenes from his life and some of his miracles are amongst the celebrated fourteenth-century frescoes which adorn the walls of the ancient Campo Santo. His life was written soon after his death by Canon Benincasa, a personal friend who regarded himself as a disciple. Rainerius, sprung from a good Pisan family, frittered away his early manhood in frivolity and dissipation. Through the influence of an aunt or cousin, however, he came into contact with Alberto Leccapecore, a religious from the monastery of San Vito, who made him realize the error of his ways. So overwhelming was his penitence for his sinful life that he refused to eat, and wept unceasingly—to the scornful amusement of his former associates and to the distress of his parents, who thought he was going out of his mind.   At the end of three days he could weep no longer : he was blind.   His mother was in despair, but God restored sight to his body, besides enlightening his soul.

Business as a merchant soon afterwards took him to Palestine, and as he followed in the footsteps of our Lord his spiritual life developed.   Then one day he seemed to see his jewelled money-pouch filled, not with coins, but with pitch and sulphur. It suddenly caught fire and he was unable to extinguish the flames until he had sprinkled it with water from a vessel which he found himself holding in his hand. The meaning of the vision was explained by a voice which said : " The purse is your body : fire, pitch and sulphur are inordinate desires which water alone can wash away."   He had purged himself from past sin by penitential tears, but from that time forth he redoubled his austerities, going barefoot and begging his way, and was rewarded with the gift of miracles.   We read that on the road to Mount Tabor he tamed wild beasts by making the sign of the cross, that he multiplied the bread a charitable woman was distributing to the poor, and that he wrought many other wonders.

Upon his return to Pisa Rainerius made his home for a time with the canons of Santa Maria.   Afterwards, though he never joined an order, he lived a more or less cloistered life, first in the abbey of St Andrew, and later in the monastery of St Vitus, where he died in 1160.   Because he seems sometimes to have preached, it has been inferred that he must have received holy orders, but this is doubtful. His great reputation is primarily due to the numerous cures which were worked by him during his life and after his death.   From the use he made of holy water in his miracles of healing he received the nickname of De Aqua, and his name was inserted in the Roman Martyrology by Cardinal Baronius.

The long biography of Rainerius, much of it taken up with miracles attributed to him before and after his death, seems really to have been compiled by a contemporary.   It is printed in the *Acta Sanctorum*, June, vol. iv.   The devotion of the people of Pisa to St Rainerius is attested by the considerable number of books which have been printed there to do him honour.   See particularly G. M. Sanminiatelli, *Vita di St Ranieri*, first published in 1704, but followed by other editions ; and G. Sainati, *Vita di S. Ranieri Scacceri* (1890).

SS. TERESA AND SANCHIA OF PORTUGAL   (A.D. 1250 AND 1229)

SANCHO I, King of Portugal, had three daughters, Teresa, Sanchia and Mafalda, all of whom are honoured by the Church.   Teresa, the eldest, became the wife of her cousin, Alfonso IX, King of León, by whom she had several children.   The marriage, however, was after some years pronounced invalid, because it had been contracted within prohibited degrees without dispensation.   Teresa was attached to her husband and loth to leave him, but eventually they agreed to part.   Teresa returned to Portugal, and at Lorvão she found on her estate an abbey of Benedictine monks now fallen low in numbers and observance.   These she ejected and replaced by a community of women pledged to the Cistercian rule.   She rebuilt the church, besides restoring and extending the buildings to accommodate 300 nuns.   Although she made her home with them, taking full part in their life, yet she retained the direction of her affairs, the disposal of her property, and the right to come and go as she pleased.

Teresa's sister, Sanchia, who never married, had lived since their father's death on her estates at Alenquer, where she devoted herself to good works. She welcomed the Franciscan and Dominican friars into Portugal, and founded the convent of Cellas, for women under the Augustinian rule. But during a visit to her sister she was so impressed by the life led by the community at Lorvao that she afterwards converted Cellas into a Cistercian abbey, and herself took the veil there. Sanchia died in 1229, at the age of forty-seven ; Teresa surreptitiously smuggled her sister's body out of the choir at Cellas, where it lay on a bier, and conveyed it to Lorvão, where it was buried. The last public appearance of Teresa occurred two or three years later. It was made in response to an earnest entreaty from Berengaria, the widow of her former husband, that she would intervene to settle the quarrels between their respective children over the succession to the kingdom of León. Teresa went, and through her mediation an equitable arrangement was arrived at and peace was restored. Her work in the world, she felt, was now done and she determined never again to leave the convent. It was probably at this time that she actually received the veil. She survived until 1250, and at her death was buried beside St Sanchia. Their *cultus* was approved in 1705.

The life of Teresa by Francis Macedo, though written in the seventeenth century, purports to be based on authentic materials, especially those collected in view of her expected canonization. This biography has been reprinted in the *Acta Sanctorum*, June, vol. iv, and the Bollandists have added certain documents also drawn from the process of canonization, with accounts of miracles attributed to Teresa's intercession. Henriquez in his *Lilia Cistercii* (1633), vol. ii, pp. 131–144, also recounts her history in some detail. J. P. Bayão in his *Portugal glorioso e illustrado* (1727) gives an account of both sisters and of St Mafalda (May 2).

BD PETER OF PISA (A.D. 1435)

THE founder of the Hermits, or Poor Brothers, of St Jerome was born in 1355 at Pisa, while his father, Peter Gambacorta, whose name he bore, was ruling that republic. At the age of twenty-five he secretly left the court in the disguise of a penitent, and retired to the Umbrian solitude of Monte Bello. There he subsisted on alms, which he collected in the nearest village. In 1380 he found means to build an oratory and cells for a dozen companions who had joined him (according to popular tradition they were highwaymen whom he had converted). He prescribed for his community a rule supplemented by certain constitutions gathered from the works of St Jerome, whom he chose as patron of the new congregation. His monks kept four Lents in the year, fasted on all Mondays, Wednesdays and Fridays, and continued in prayer every night for two hours after Matins. As for himself, his whole time was spent in prayer or in penitential exercises. Many miracles were ascribed to him.

When his father and brothers were assassinated in 1393 by Giacomo Appiano, he was sorely tempted to leave his retreat to punish the perpetrator of the outrage ; but he overcame the temptation and, following the example of his sister, Bd Clare Gambacorta (April 17) he freely forgave the murderer. His congregation, approved by Pope Martin V in 1421, soon established itself elsewhere in Italy. Bd Peter survived until 1435, dying in Venice at the age of eighty, and was beatified in 1693. At one time there were forty-six houses of Poor Brothers in the provinces of Ancona and Treviso. Small groups of hermits and tertiaries became affiliated to them, and in 1668 Pope Clement IX united the community of St Jerome of Fiesole, which had been founded by Charles Montegranelli, to Bd Peter's order. But by 1933 its members had become so few that it was suppressed by the Holy See.

An account, founded on rather late materials, is given in the *Acta Sanctorum*, June, vol. iv ; but see further the *Kirchenlexikon*, vol. v, cc. 2016–2017 ; Sajanello, *Hist. Mon. Ord. S. Hieron. Cong. S. Petri de Pisis*, vol. i, pp. 100 seq. ; and Heimbucher, *Orden und Kongregationen*, vol. i, pp. 592–596. The brief of suppression is in *Acta Apostolicae Sedis*, vol. xxv (1933), pp. 147–149.

ST EMILY DE VIALAR, Virgin, Foundress of the Sisters of St Joseph "of the Apparition" (A.D. 1856)

Anne Marguerite Adelaide Emily de Vialar was the eldest child and only daughter of Baron James Augustine de Vialar and his wife Antoinette, daughter of that Baron de Portal who was physician-in-ordinary to Louis XVIII and Charles X of France. She was born at Gaillac in Languedoc in 1797. At the age of fifteen she was removed from school in Paris to be companion to her father, now a widower, at Gaillac ; but unhappily differences arose between them because of Emily's refusal to consider a suitable marriage. On one occasion M. de Vialar threw a decanter at his daughter's head, and she was relegated to a place of no importance in the household. Moreover, things were made more difficult for her by there being no priest or other suitable person in the place to advise and guide her ; " God became my director ", she said in after years : but even so it is not always easy to be certain what is the voice of God and what the voice of self. Of Emily de Vialar's religious experiences at this time a vision of our Lord, His body showing the wounds of His passion, made so deep an impression on her that it is still commemorated daily in the congregation she founded.

Then in 1818, when she was twenty-one, a young curate (afterwards rector), the abbé Mercier, came to Gaillac, and in him Emily found a friend who understood and appreciated her. He set himself to test her religious vocation, and in the meantime she devoted herself to the care of children neglected by their parents and to the help of the poor generally ; this led to further difficulties with her father, who objected to the use of the terrace of his house as a sort of out-patients' department for the sick, the destitute and the sad. For fifteen years Emily was the good angel of Gaillac ; and then, in 1832, occurred the event which decided both her and the abbé Mercier that the time had come for her to launch out on her own : her maternal grandfather, the Baron de Portal, died, and Emily's share of his estate was a quite considerable fortune.

She at once bought a large house at Gaillac, and at Christmas took possession of it with three companions, Victoria Teyssonnière, Rose Mongis and Pauline Gineste. Others joined them, and three months later the archbishop of Albi authorized the abbé Mercier to clothe twelve postulants with the religious habit. They called themselves the Congregation of Sisters of St Joseph of the Apparition, the epithet referring to the appearing (*apparitio*) of the angel to Joseph to reveal the divine incarnation (Matthew i 18–21) ; and their work was to be the care of the needy, especially the sick, and the education of children. They looked not only to France but also to foreign countries and the missions ; and in fact they developed as a primarily missionary congregation. The sisters encountered the usual initial opposition and criticism,* details of which found a lively chronicler in Eugénie de

* A less usual trial was a threat of extirpation by a band of brigands, who were said to have threatened to strangle every one of the sisters.

Guérin : postulants too young and pretty to be exposed to the air, a too-becoming head-dress, " A new order ?   It's a disorder ! "   " That Vialar girl . . .".   But Miss de Guérin opined that Sister Emily would do great things, and the discerning archbishop of Albi, Mgr de Gualy, agreed : in 1835 he received her profession, with that of seventeen other sisters, and gave formal approval to the rule of the congregation.

In the previous year the second foundation was made, at Algiers, whither the sisters were invited at the instance of Emily's brother Augustine, one of the municipal councillors, to take charge of a hospital.   A correspondent of Eugénie de Guérin speaks of " Emily de Vialar's conquest of Algeria "—but it proved to be only a temporary occupation.   From the big establishment at Algiers another foundation was made at Bône, which in turn gave birth to convents in Constantine and Tunis ; Tunis had a filiation in Malta, and from there sprang the houses of the Balkans and the Near East.   The Sisters of St Joseph were the first Catholic nuns in modern times to be established in Jerusalem, whither they were invited by the Franciscan Guardian of the Holy Land ; and when Mgr Dupuch, the first bishop of Algiers, celebrated the Holy Mysteries on the hill of St Augustine's Hippo, Mother Emily and some of her sisters were there.   Unfortunately her relations with this prelate were spoiled by a long disagreement about jurisdiction ; Rome decided in her favour, but Mgr Dupuch had the support of the civil power and the sisters had to give up the Algerian establishments, at great temporal loss to themselves.   It was at this time that Mother Emily turned her attention to Tunisia and then Malta, on which island she landed from a wrecked ship, as St Paul did.

Her friend and helper the abbé Mercier had died in 1845, and on her return to Gaillac in the following year the foundress found her headquarters in a state of confusion, and its finances in a chronic mess owing to the rashness—if not worse— of a trustee.   Consequent lawsuits did nothing to improve matters ; and the upshot was that the mother house was moved to Toulouse, after several of the senior nuns had left the congregation and its very existence was threatened.   " I've had my lesson ", wrote Mother Emily.   " A quiet trust in God is better than trying to safeguard material advantages."   Then she set out for Greece, and founded a convent on the island of Syra.

The visit to Greece was the last of Mother Emily's longer journeys (these fatiguing undertakings provoked unfavourable comments from some highly-placed ecclesiastics) ; but during her lifetime foundations were made much farther away. In 1847 a call from Burma was answered by the dispatch of six sisters thither, and in 1854 the bishop of Perth in Australia visited Mother Emily to ask for help. Accordingly a contingent was sent to Freemantle.   The foundress thus in the course of twenty-two years saw her congregation grow from one to some forty houses, many of which she had founded in person.   Two years before, the mother house had again been moved, this time to Marseilles (where it still is).   Here Mother Emily was warmly welcomed by the famous bishop Mgr de Mazenod, himself the founder of a missionary congregation, the Oblates of Mary Immaculate.

St Emily de Vialar was by nature shrewd, exact, lively but well-balanced, qualities that showed themselves in her face no less than in her life, and her intelligence was controlled and directed by a will of exceptional strength.   Not otherwise could she have done the work that she did, beginning only when she was already thirty-five, and meeting with considerable opposition in the preparatory stages and serious set-backs from time to time afterwards.   She was particularly immovable when the constitutional or canonical integrity of her congregation seemed to be threatened : it was that which led to the breach with Mgr Dupuch, and to the abandonment of Toulouse as headquarters after only five years there. Such difficulties, and the troubles at Gaillac in 1846, seemed not to discourage her ; but her letters show what interior trials and uncertainties she underwent. St Emily's correspondence was necessarily voluminous, and her writing is marked by a vigorous and appealing style, especially when some moral implication added a touch of high eloquence to her pen ; this is well illustrated in the memorial she addressed to Field-Marshal Soult after the Algerian disaster.

St Emily deliberately chose the way of Martha, but she was not excluded from the way of Mary. From the account written at the direction of her confessor we know in how close a state of union with God she lived, and there is as well the testimony of her daughters in religion as to how far she progressed in the path of contemplation. " I have plenty of trials, but God is always there to support me ", she wrote. " How often is the Lord with me in the long night watches. The outpouring of His love is all about me, and I try to follow Him always, even though some new tribulation will come upon me. . . . But as troubles increase, so does my trust in Him. . . ." It has been well said that " Civilization is a matter of the spirit "; and the spirit of St Emily, inspired by a love that Cardinal Granito di Belmonte characterized as " wise, understanding and most considerate ", has through the congregation that she founded " done more in the past hundred years for civilization in Africa, Asia and Australia than conquerors and colonizers could ever do ".

The physical energy and achievements of St Emily de Vialar are the more remarkable in that from her youth she was troubled by hernia, contracted characteristically in doing a deed of charity. From 1850 this became more and more serious, and it hastened her end, which came on August 24, 1856. The burden of her last testament to her daughters was " Love one another ". Her canonization took place in 1951, and her feast is kept on this day.

The standard biography is *La vie militante de la Bse Mère Emilie de Vialar*, by Canon Testas, reissued in 1939. The author made an *Histoire abrégée* from this in 1938. The letters of Eugénie de Guérin (1805–48), to her brother Maurice, referred to above, were published at Paris in the sixties of last century ; a fresh English translation of this " journal ", by Naomi Royde Smith, appeared in *The Idol and the Shrine* (1949). Like Bd Emily, Miss de Guérin was a native of Languedoc. See also G. Bernoville, *Emilie de Vialar* (1953).

18 : ST EPHRAEM, Doctor of the Church   (A.D. 373 ?)

FAMOUS in his lifetime as a great teacher, orator, poet, commentator and defender of the faith, St Ephraem is the only Syrian father who is honoured as a doctor of the Universal Church (since 1920) ; the Syrians, both Catholic and separated, style him " the Harp of the Holy Ghost ", and enrich their liturgies with his homilies and hymns. Steeped in the Holy Scriptures, though not a man of wide scholarship he had a deep insight into the mysteries of God.* St Basil described him as " one conversant with the knowledge of all that is true " ; and St Jerome mentions him in these terms when making a catalogue of the great Christian writers : " Ephraem, deacon of the Church of Edessa, wrote many works

---

* It was the opinion of another doctor of the Church, St Robert Bellarmine, that St Ephraem was " more pious than learned ".

in Syriac, and became so famous that his writings are publicly read in some churches after the Sacred Scriptures. I have read in Greek a volume of his on the Holy Spirit ; though it was only a translation I recognized therein the sublime genius of the man." His chief interest to most people, however, lies in the fact that to him we owe very largely the introduction of sacred songs into the Church's public services as an important feature in her worship and a recognized means of instruction. It soon found its way from Edessa into all the Eastern churches and gradually it spread to the West. " To the hymns on which his fame rests ", writes a modern Anglican commentator, " the Syrian ritual in all its forms owes much of its strength and richness, and to them is largely due the place which hymnody holds throughout the churches everywhere " (Dr John Gwynn in vol. xiii of *Nicene and Post-Nicene Fathers*).

St Ephraem was born about the year 306 at Nisibis in Mesopotamia, then still under Roman rule. That his parents were Christians is asserted in what purport to be his own words. " I was born in the way of truth ", he tells us. " Although my boyhood did not understand the greatness of it, I knew it when trial came." Elsewhere, in the same doubtful source, he is made to say : " I had been early taught about Christ by my parents : they who begat me after the flesh had trained me in the fear of the Lord. . . . My parents were confessors before the judge : yea, I am of the kindred of the martyrs." It is, however, more commonly believed that his father and mother were pagan, and that on his conversion in his boyhood he was turned out of doors by them. He was baptized at the age of eighteen, and attached himself to the famous bishop of Nisibis, St Jacob (or James), whom he is said to have accompanied to the Council of Nicaea in 325. After St Jacob's death, Ephraem remained in close relation with the three succeeding hierarchs, probably as head of their school. He was living at Nisibis through the three sieges laid to it by the Persians, and in some of his Nisibeian hymns are to be found descriptions of the city's perils, of its defences, and of the final repulse of the enemy in 350. But although the Persians failed to capture Nisibis by direct attack, they obtained it thirteen years later as part of the price of the peace the Emperor Jovian was forced to negotiate after the defeat and death of Julian. The Christians abandoned the city, and Ephraem retired finally to a cave in a rocky height overlooking Edessa. Here he led a most austere life, sustained only by a little barley bread and a few vegetables, and here he wrote the greater part of his spiritual works.

His appearance was indeed that of an ascetic : he was of small stature, we are told, bald, beardless, and with skin shrivelled and dried up like a potsherd ; his gown was all patches, the colour of dirt, he wept much and never laughed. Nevertheless, an incident related by all his biographers proves that in spite of his gravity he could appreciate a repartee, even when directed against himself. On the first occasion that he entered the city of Edessa he encountered the bold stare of a woman who was washing clothes in the river and rebuked her sharply, bidding her cast her eyes modestly to the ground. Unabashed, she promptly retorted, " No : it is for you to look down to the ground because out of it you were taken. It is quite right for me to look at you, for from you—as man—I was taken." Ephraem was impressed by her ready wit and exclaimed, " If the women of this city are so wise, how exceedingly wise its men must be ! " Although the cave continued to be his headquarters, he was by no means a recluse, and concerned himself with all questions that affected the Church especially in Edessa, which he called " the city of blessing " and where he exerted great influence. He frequently preached there, and when, with fiery eloquence, he treated of the second coming of Christ and of the last judgement, the sobs of the congregation nearly drowned his words.

What he regarded as his special task was to oppose the false doctrines that were then rampant, and it was through observing the success of Bardesanes in propagating erroneous teaching by means of popular songs set to attractive tunes that St Ephraem was led to recognize the potentialities of sacred song as an adjunct to public worship. He imitated the enemy's tactics and partly no doubt through his personal prestige but largely through the superior merit of his own compositions, which he set to the same tunes and caused to be sung in church by a women's choir, he succeeded in completely supplanting the gnostic hymns by his own. It was not until late in his life that he was raised to the diaconate. Humility had made him shrink from ordination and the fact that he is often designated as St Ephraem the Deacon supports the assertion made by some of his biographers that he never attained to higher rank. On the other hand, there are passages in his own writings which seem to indicate that he held the priestly office.

About the year 370 he undertook a journey from Edessa to Caesarea in Cappadocia in order to visit St Basil, of whom he had heard much. Their meeting is mentioned by St Ephraem himself and also by St Basil's brother, St Gregory of Nyssa, who wrote an encomium on the holy Syrian. A statement to the effect that St Ephraem extended his tour to include Egypt and that he spent several years there rests on no good authority and cannot be reconciled with what we know of the chronology of his life. The last time that he took part in public affairs was in the winter of 372–373, shortly before his death. There was famine in the land and his heart was wrung by the sufferings of the poor. When rich men excused themselves from opening their granaries and their purses on the plea that no one could be trusted to make a fair distribution, he offered his services, which were accepted. He administered the large sums of money and the stores entrusted to him to the satisfaction of all, besides organizing a relief service which included the provision of 300 litters for carrying the sick. In the words of an early biographer, " God gave him this occasion to win the crown in the close of his life." Perhaps he overtaxed his strength, for he only survived his return to the cave for one month. The date of his death is given by the Chronicle of Edessa and the best authorities as 373, but some writers have asserted that he lived until 378 or 379.

St Ephraem was a very prolific writer. Of the works that have come down to us, some are in the original Syriac, others are in Greek, Latin and Armenian translations. They may be grouped as exegetical, polemical, doctrinal and poetical, but practically all except the commentaries are in metrical form. Sozomen states that St Ephraem wrote three myriads of lines. The most interesting of his poems are the Nisibeian hymns (*carmina Nisibena*), of which seventy-two out of seventy-seven are extant, and the canticles for the seasons which are still in use in the Syrian churches. His commentaries included nearly all the Old Testament and a great part of the New. For the gospels he used the only version then current in Syria, the Harmony called the Diatessaron, which now survives only in an Armenian translation, though a small early fragment in Greek has been discovered in Mesopotamia.

Although we know hardly anything of St Ephraem's life, his writings help us not a little to form an idea of the kind of man he was. What impresses the reader most is the realistic and humanly sympathetic spirit in which he discourses of all the great mysteries of man's redemption. He seems to have anticipated that attitude towards our Saviour's physical sufferings which does not notably manifest itself in the West before the period of St Francis of Assisi. A few specimens of St Ephraem's language can hardly be out of place. For example, in one of his hymns or addresses—it is difficult to decide how these metrical compositions should be classed—the poet apostrophizes the upper room of the Last Supper in these terms:

O blessed spot, thy narrow room may be set against all the world. That which is contained in thee, though bounded in so strait a compass, filleth the universe. Blessed is the dwelling-place in which with holy hand the bread was broken. In thee the grape which grew on Mary's vine was crushed in the chalice of salvation.

O blessed spot! No man hath seen nor shall see the things which thou hast seen. In thee the Lord Himself became true altar, priest, and bread and chalice of salvation. He alone sufficeth for all, yet none for Him sufficeth. Altar He is and lamb, victim and sacrificer, priest as well as food.

Or take this description of the scourging at the pillar:

After many vehement outcries against Pilate, the all-mighty One was scourged like the meanest criminal. Surely there must have been commotion and horror at the sight. Let the heavens and earth stand awe-struck to behold Him who swayed the rod of fire, Himself smitten with scourges; to behold Him who spread over the earth the veil of the skies and who set fast the foundations of the mountains, who poised the earth over the waters and sent down the blazing lightning-flash, now beaten by infamous wretches over a stone pillar that His own word had created. They, indeed, stretched out His limbs and outraged Him with mockeries. A man whom He had formed wielded the scourge. He who sustains all creatures with His might submitted His back to their stripes; He who is the Father's right arm yielded His own arms to be extended. The pillar of ignominy was embraced by Him who sustains the heavens and earth in all their splendour. Savage dogs did bark at the Lord who with his thunder shakes the mountains, they sharpened their teeth against the Son of Glory.

An even fuller revelation of the character of the saintly writer is supplied by the document known as the *Testament of St Ephraem*. Though it has probably been subject to interpolations at a later date, Rubens Duval, who speaks authoritatively on such questions, is satisfied that the greater part of the testament is authentic and in particular the passages now to be quoted. St Ephraem appeals to his friends and disciples in such language of profound humility as the following:

Lay me not with sweet spices,
    For this honour avails me not,
Nor yet use incense and perfumes,
    For the honour benefits me not.
Burn ye the incense in the holy place;
    As for me, escort me only with your prayers.
Give ye your incense to God,
    And over me send up hymns.
Instead of perfumes and spices
    Be mindful of me in your intercessions . . .

The decree has gone forth that I can tarry no longer.

Give me, as provision for my journey,
Your prayers, your psalms and your sacrifices.
When the number of thirty days is complete
Then, O my brothers, make remembrance of me,
For the dead truly derive succour
From the sacrifices offered up by the living.

There are several documents, both in Syriac and in Greek, which purport to be lives or biographical notices of St Ephraem. The Greek texts have been printed by J. S. Assemani, in his introduction to the first volume of *S. P. N. Ephraem Syri Opera*, pp. i–xxxiii, and in that of the third volume, pp. xxiii–xxxv. The Syriac texts may be found in Assemani, *Bibliotheca Orientalis*, vol. i, p. 26, and in Lamy, *S. Ephraem Syri Hymni et Sermones*, vol. ii, pp. 5–90. There are also two similar pieces of Nestorian origin which are printed in the *Patrologia Orientalis*, vol. iv, pp. 293–295, and vol. v, pp. 291–299. It is generally agreed that no trust can be placed in any of the information which comes from these sources. To discuss the character or the authenticity of the many works which have been attributed to St Ephraem would be out of place here. The interesting " Testament of St Ephraem " has been critically edited and translated by Rubens Duval in the *Journal Asiatique* for 1901, pp. 234–319. See also C. W. Mitchell, *St Ephraem's Prose Refutations of Mani, Marcion and Bardesanes* (1912–1924) ; and the articles on Ephraem, with bibliographies, in Bardenhewer, *Geschichte der altkirchlichen Literatur*, vol. iv, pp. 342–375 ; DTC., vol. v, cc. 188–193 ; DCB., vol. ii, pp. 137–144 ; *Lexikon f. Theologie und Kirche*, vol. iii (1931), cc. 715–718 ; E. Émerau, *St Éphrem le Syrien* (1919) ; and G. Ricciotti, *Sant' Efrem Siro* (1925).

SS. MARK AND MARCELLIAN, MARTYRS   (*c.* A.D. 287)

INTEREST in SS. Mark and Marcellian has been revived in modern times by the discovery, in that part of the Catacomb of St Balbina which bears their name, of the tombs of the two martyrs, surmounted by a fresco representing the " coronation " of themselves and their companions. They were brothers, deacons of the Roman church, who perished early in the reign of Diocletian. For details of their sufferings and death we have nothing more reliable than the so-called Passion of St Sebastian, a fifth-century collection of traditions and legends. According to this compilation Mark and Marcellian were twins of high birth who had been converted to Christianity in their youth and had married. In the persecution which broke out soon after Diocletian's accession, they were cast into prison and were condemned by Chromatius, lieutenant of the prefect of Rome, to be beheaded. Their friends obtained for them a thirty-days' respite in the hope of being able during that time to persuade them to offer the required sacrifices, and they were removed to the house of Nicostratus, the public registrar. Their wives, their little children, and their heathen parents, Tranquillinus and Martia, sought by tears and entreaties to shake their constancy, but St Sebastian, then an officer in the emperor's household, visited them daily and encouraged them to persevere.

The outcome of the various interviews and discussions which took place was the conversion of the martyrs' relations, of Nicostratus, and shortly afterwards of Chromatius, who set the prisoners free, resigned his post and retired into the country. Although Mark and Marcellian were concealed by a Christian official of the imperial household, they were betrayed by a renegade and recaptured. Fabian, who had succeeded Chromatius, condemned them to be bound to two wooden pillars, to which their feet were then nailed. When they had been thus exposed for twenty-four hours they were pierced by lances. Their relics were translated from the catacombs to the church of SS. Cosmas and Damian, and are now in the basilica of St Praxedes in Rome.

That portion of the *passio* of St Sebastian which relates to SS. Mark and Marcellian has been printed in the *Acta Sanctorum*, June, vol. iv, as well as elsewhere. Upon the question of the crypt in the cemetery of Balbina, much has been written. See especially G. Wilpert in the *Nuovo Bullettino di arch. crist.*, 1903, pp. 43–58 ; Wilpert in the *Römische Quartalschrift*, 1908, pp. 124–164, and 1930, pp. 1–5 ; O. Marucchi, in *Nuovo Bullettino*, 1909, pp. 221–235, and 1910, pp. 120–130 ; J. P. Kirsch, *Der stadtrömische christ. Festkalender* (1924), pp. 155–156 ; Delehaye's CMH., pp. 324–325 ; and Leclercq in DAC., vol. x (1932), cc. 1749–1753.

ST AMANDUS, BISHOP OF BORDEAUX   (*c.* A.D. 431)

WE read in the letters of St Paulinus of Nola that St Amandus served God from his infancy, that he was nurtured in the knowledge of the Holy Scriptures, and that he always remained uncontaminated by carnal sin or by worldly intercourse. Nothing whatever is known of his birth or parentage.   Ordained priest by St Delphinus, bishop of Bordeaux, who retained him to serve in his church, Amandus displayed great zeal for the glory of God.   It was he who gave St Paulinus of Nola the necessary instruction to prepare him for baptism.   This led to a lifelong friendship between them.   St Paulinus wrote him many letters, and we see from those which survive that he had the highest opinion of his piety and wisdom.   Upon the death of St Delphinus, in the year 400, St Amandus was elected to fill the vacant see.   He resigned some years later in favour of St Severinus, after whose death he was prevailed upon to resume his former office.   " If you wish to see bishops worthy of God ", wrote St Gregory of Tours, quoting the words of St Paulinus, " you have only to look at·Exuperius of Toulouse, Simplicius of Vienne, Amandus of Bordeaux . . ."   It is said that to St Amandus is due the preservation of the writings of St Paulinus, but this is very doubtful.   The exact date of his death is uncertain.

We have no materials beyond those indicated above for any biography of St Amandus. There is a short notice in the *Acta Sanctorum*, June, vol iv.   On his relations with St Paulinus of Nola, consult P. Reinelt, *Studien über die Briefe der hl. Paulinus* (1904), pp. 17 *seq.* ; and see also Duchesne, *Fastes Épiscopaux*, vol. ii, p. 59 ; and DHG., vol. ii, c. 938.

ST ELIZABETH OF SCHÖNAU, VIRGIN   (A.D. 1164)

THREE German monasteries have borne the name of Schönau : one, a community of Cistercian monks near Heidelberg ; another, a nunnery in Franconia ; and the third, a double house of Benedictines not far from Bonn, built by Hildelin, who became its first abbot in 1125.   Into the great nunnery of Hildelin's foundation, Elizabeth, a girl of humble extraction, entered at the age of twelve.   Some six years later, in 1147, she was professed.   She threw herself fervently into the religious activities of the convent, and, though suffering from continual ill-health, wore a hair-shirt, girded herself with an iron chain, and practised other austerities. " The lowliest of His poor ", she says of herself in one of her books, " I thank God that from the moment I entered the order until this hour, His hand has pressed down upon me so persistently that I have never ceased to feel His arrows in my body." From her twenty-third year onwards she was subject to extraordinary supernatural manifestations, celestial visions, and diabolic persecutions.   In a letter addressed to her friend St Hildegard, Elizabeth describes how an angel had told her to proclaim a series of judgements that would fall on the people unless they did penance, and how, because she had delayed obeying him, he had beaten her so severely with a whip that she had been ill for three days !

At a later date, when some of her prophecies had failed in their fulfilment, the angel informed her that penance had actually averted the impending doom.   For a time she was assailed by terrible temptations, and worried by the sudden appearance in her cell and elsewhere of demons habited as monks or priests, who mocked, mimicked and threatened her. Once she saw the devil as a black bull, presently metamorphosed into a black fire, from the midst of which there emerged a herd of loathsome goats. But this period of trial was the prelude to great consolations and heavenly visitations. On Sundays and festivals in particular she would fall into ecstasies during the saying of the Office or at Mass. In this condition she would receive, as she believed, admonitions and messages from an angel, or from the saint whose feast was then being kept. She visualized these celestial visitors so distinctly that she could afterwards describe in detail their appearance and attire. Scenes from the passion, resurrection and ascension of our Lord presented themselves similarly as though enacted before her bodily eyes. She recorded some of her visions on wax tablets which, at the bidding of Abbot Hildelin, she sent to her brother Egbert, a canon of Bonn, who subsequently took the habit at Schönau and succeeded Hildelin as abbot. These notes, supplemented by her oral explanations, Egbert embodied in three books of her visions, which he published with a preface of his own and a chronological list of her chief religious experiences.

The first book is written in simple language, such as Elizabeth herself might have used ; but the others are more sophisticated in terminology and in thought, evincing at times a theological training more suggestive of Egbert than of his sister. This is even more evidently the case with another of her works, *viz. The Book of the Ways of God*, written, apparently, in imitation of the *Scivias* of St Hildegard. It sets forth stern warnings addressed to various classes of clergy and laymen, and in its advocacy of the antipope " Victor IV ", whom Egbert's friends supported, and in the terms of its denunciation of the Cathari and of its invectives against worldly prelates and unfaithful priests, it clearly reveals the mind and the hand of Egbert. The last of Elizabeth's books, as well as the most famous, was her contribution to the Ursuline Legend. It has a curious history. Excavations, which had been made on several occasions since the beginning of the twelfth century in a certain district of Cologne, had resulted in the discovery of a great number of human bones. The place came to be known as the " Ager Ursulinus ", and the remains were thought to be those of St Ursula's eleven thousand virgins. Mingled with the rest, however, were the skeletons of men, and a number of tablets—now known to have been forgeries—ostensibly bearing names of the supposed martyrs. Gerlac, abbot of Deutz, who had assisted in translating the alleged relics of St Ursula in 1142, and who had spent nine years searching for the remains of her companions, addressed himself to Egbert in the hope that Elizabeth, through her visions, might be able to throw light on the problem thus presented.

Under strong pressure from her brother, as it would appear, she evolved an elaboration of the already fantastic story of St Ursula, into which she introduced a Pope Cyriacus, who never existed, and all the newly discovered " martyrs ". That this extravagant romance, entirely at variance with easily verifiable historical facts, should have gained immediate and widespread acceptance throws a rather sinister light upon the credulity of the age ; though, on the other hand, it is proof of the esteem in which Elizabeth was held.

She must actually have been a woman of judgement in the affairs of daily life, or she could scarcely have held, as she did, the post of superioress during the last seven years of her life. Her office was second only to that of the abbot, who ruled the double community. She died on June 18, 1164, in her thirty-eighth year. Confusion between the abbeys at Schönau afterwards led to her being regarded as a Cistercian, and entered as such by Molanus in 1568 in a new edition of Usuard.

From Molanus her name was transferred in 1584 to the Roman Martyrology, where it still stands, without any reference to her writings. Elizabeth has never been formally canonized or beatified, and widely divergent views have been entertained as to the nature of her visions. All critics, however, admit that Elizabeth herself, her brother, and those who knew them best, were firmly convinced that they came to her from on high.

What we know of the life of Elizabeth is mainly derived from a memoir which her brother Egbert prefixed to the collection of her visions. This biographical matter, with a letter also of Egbert's, is printed in the *Acta Sanctorum*, June, vol. iv, and elsewhere. The best edition of the visions and the writings which bear her name is that of F. W. E. Roth (1884). Roth also printed in 1886 a copy of what he called the " Prayerbook " (*Gebetbuch*) of Elizabeth ; on this, *cf.* Omont, in vol. xxxviii (1905) of *Notices et Extraits des MSS. de la Bib. Nationale.* The Ursula visions are also printed in the *Acta Sanctorum*, October, vol. viii (pp. 165–173). See further, Nebe in the *Annalen* of the *Nassau Verein f. Alt*, etc., vol. viii (1866), pp. 157–292 ; Preger, *Deutsche Mystik*, vol. i, pp. 37–43 ; and L. Oliger, who in vol. i (1926) of *Antonianum* has shown that certain revelations attributed by Montalembert to St Elizabeth of Hungary are-really taken from the writings of Elizabeth of Schönau. A popular but quite uncritical life with a selection of her visions was brought out by J. Ibach, *Das Leben der hl. Jungfrau Elizabeth von Schönau* (1898). See, also, P. Schmitz, in the *Revue Bénédictine*, vol. xlvii (1935), pp. 181–183 ; and *Analecta Bollandiana*, vol. lxxi (1953), pp. 494–496, where two important studies on false ascriptions are reviewed.

19 : ST JULIANA FALCONIERI, VIRGIN, FOUNDRESS OF THE SERVITE NUNS   (A.D. 1341)

ST JULIANA was one of the two glories of the noble family of the Falconieri, the other being her uncle, St Alexis, one of the Seven Holy Founders of the Servite Order. Her father, Chiarissimo, and her mother, Riguardata, were a devout couple of great wealth who had built at their own cost the magnificent church of the Annunziata in Florence. They were childless and already well advanced in age when, in 1270, Juliana was born—the answer to prayer. After the death of her father, which occurred while she was still quite young, her uncle Alexis shared with Riguardata the direction of her upbringing. She never cared for the amusements and occupations which interested other girls, but loved to spend her time in prayer and in church. Sometimes, indeed, her mother would tell her that if she continually neglected her needle and spinning-wheel she would never find a husband. The threat, however, had no terror for Juliana, and when she found that her relations were trying to arrange a suitable match for her she expressed her determination to consecrate herself to God and to renounce the world. She was then fifteen. After being carefully instructed by her uncle Alexis, she was invested with the Servite habit by St Philip Benizi in the church of the Annunziata, and a year later she was professed a tertiary of the order.

The ritual employed on this occasion appears to have been identical with that used in the profession of a Servite brother. Juliana continued to live at home, and Riguardata, who had originally opposed her profession, ended by placing herself under her daughter's direction. Bereft of her mother in 1304, when she was thirty-four, Juliana moved to another house, where she led a community life with a number of women who devoted themselves to prayer and works of mercy. Their habit resembled that of the men of the Servite Order, but to facilitate their work they wore short sleeves, which caused them to be nicknamed " Mantellate ", a term subsequently applied to women tertiaries in general. With great reluctance Juliana accepted the post of superior at the urgent desire of her companions. For them she drew up a code of regulations which was formally confirmed 120 years later for their successors by Pope Martin V.   Just as the Order of the Servants of Mary is commonly ascribed to St Philip Benizi because he framed their constitutions, so also for the same reason St Juliana is honoured as a foundress by all the women religious of the Servite Order, although she was not the first to be admitted into its ranks.

Those who were her contemporaries and were privileged to live under her guidance testified that she outstripped them all in her zeal, her charity and her austerities.   Her sympathies extended to all with whom she came into contact, nor did she ever let slip an opportunity of helping others, especially when it was a question of reconciling enemies, of reclaiming sinners and of relieving the sick. Her mortifications seriously impaired her health, and towards the close of her life she suffered much from gastric derangement.   She had been in the habit of making her communion three times a week, and it was a source of deep sorrow to her in her last illness that her frequent attacks of sickness precluded her from receiving the sacrament of the altar.   Juliana died in 1341, in her seventy-first year, and she was canonized in 1737.

In the collect appointed for St Juliana's feast reference is made to the eucharistic miracle by which she is said to have been comforted in her last moments.   In memory of this also the members of her order wear upon the left breast of their habit the device of a Host surrounded with rays.   It is stated that a document is still in existence which claims to have been drawn up and witnessed eighteen days later by those who were present at her death-bed.   The original is in Latin, but it may be translated as follows :

" He hath made a memorial of His wonderful works " [Ps. cx 4].   Let it be placed on record how eighteen days ago our Sister Juliana died and flew to heaven with her spouse Jesus ; and it was in this manner.

Being more than seventy years old her stomach had become so weakened from her voluntary sharp penances, from fasts, from chains, from an iron girdle, disciplines, nightly vigils and spare diet, that she was no longer able to take or retain food.   When she knew that because of this she must be deprived of the viaticum of the most sacred Body of Christ, no one could believe how much she grieved and wept, so much so that they were afraid she would die from the vehemence of her sorrow.

She, therefore, most humbly begged Father James de Campo Reggio that at least he would bring the most holy sacrament in a pyx and set it before her, and this was done.   But when the priest appeared carrying the Body of our Lord, she straightway prostrated herself upon the ground in the form of a cross and adored her Master.

Then her face became like the face of an angel.   She desired, since she was not allowed to unite herself to Jesus, at least to kiss Him, but this the priest refused.   She then begged piteously that over the burning furnace of her breast they would spread a veil upon which they might put the Host. This was granted her.   But—O wonderful prodigy !—scarcely had the Host touched this loving heart than it was lost to sight and never more was found. Then Juliana, when the Host had disappeared, with a tender and joyous face, as if she were rapt in ecstasy, died in the kiss of her Lord, to the amazement and admiration of those who were present—to wit, of Sister Joanna, Sister Mary, Sister Elizabeth, Father James and others of the house.

The Sister Joanna whose name is appended to this is the Bd Joan Soderini (September 1) who succeeded the foundress in her office of superior general. What strikes one as curious is the fact that no mention is made of the discovery on St Juliana's left breast of a mark resembling the impression upon the Host, as was averred later. No earlier authority has been adduced for this prodigy than a sentence occurring in a manuscript entitled *Giornale e Ricordi*, written by the Servite Nicholas Mati about the year 1384. In this volume, when he has occasion to refer to Joan Soderini, he remarks : " She was the happy disciple who, sooner than Sister Elizabeth or the others, discovered upon the breast of St Juliana that astounding marvel of the figure of Christ nailed to the cross impressed upon her flesh within a circle like a Host." It must be admitted, however, that Father Mati speaks of the prodigy as a thing which was in his time generally known.

The information obtainable about the life of St Juliana is very scanty. The promoters of the cause of her beatification seem to have contented themselves with producing proof of an immemorial *cultus* and of miracles worked by her relics. The Bollandists had to be satisfied with printing in the *Acta Sanctorum*, June, vol. iv, a short life translated from the Italian of Father Archangelo Giani. There is an English life (1898) translated from the French of Fr Soulier, another in French by Cardinal Lépicier, and in Italian by Poletti (1903), Barbagallo (1912), and Panichelli (1928) ; a popular life in English was published in 1951, by M. Conrayville. A copy of the Latin original of the statement above is printed by Father V. de Buck in the *Acta Sanctorum*, October, vol. xii, pp. 403–404, in a notice he compiled of the life of Bd Joan Soderini.

SS. GERVASE AND PROTASE, MARTYRS   (DATE UNKNOWN)

IN a letter addressed to his sister, Marcellina, St Ambrose describes the circumstances which led to the finding of the relics of SS. Gervase and Protase, who from that time to the present day have been venerated as the first martyrs of Milan. He tells her that he had completed the famous basilica which bears his name, and was preparing for the dedication, when he was asked by some of his people to solemnize it with all the ceremonial that had dignified his recent consecration of a Roman church dedicated in honour of the Apostles and enshrining some of their relics. " I will do so ", he had replied, " if I can find the necessary relics." In order to fulfil his promise—St Augustine says it was as the result of information imparted to him in a vision—he caused excavations to be made in the cemetery church of SS. Nabor and Felix. They revealed the remains of two very tall men buried in close proximity. The heads were severed from the bodies, but the skeletons were otherwise entire. These were identified as being the bones of SS. Gervase and Protase, of whom nothing was remembered except their names and a vague tradition of their martyrdom. The relics were borne on litters, first to the basilica of Faustus, where they were venerated by a great concourse of people, then to the Ambrosian church amid the rejoicings of the whole city. A number of miracles reported as having taken place during the translation were regarded as attesting the genuineness of the relics. St Ambrose, his secretary Paulinus, and St Augustine, who were all three in Milan at the time, particularly mention the case of a blind butcher, Severus, who regained his sight upon touching the fringe of the ornaments that covered the remains. The man made a vow to continue in the service of the church of the saints and was still a servant there in 411, when Paulinus was writing the life of St Ambrose.

No credence can be attached to the so-called acts of these two saints, based as they are on a letter purporting to have emanated from St Ambrose, but now universally admitted to be spurious.   They represent Gervase and Protase as the twin sons of the two martyrs, Vitalis and Valeria, and as having suffered in the days of Nero, ten years after the death of their father.   Gervase is said to have been beaten to death with leaded whips ; Protase was beheaded.

Much controversy has arisen over these two martyrs.   Dr J. Rendel Harris has boldly attempted to identify them with the pagan deities Castor and Pollux, whilst others have contented themselves with denying their existence.   The majority of modern hagiographers, however, regard them as genuine martyrs whose history has perished, but who belonged to the reign of the Emperor Antoninus or even to an earlier period.   The mortal remains of St Ambrose were laid, at his own wish, beside those of St Gervase and St Protase, and one of his successors in the see of Milan, Angilbert II, in the ninth century, placed the three bodies in a porphyry sarcophagus.   It was for some time believed that the bones were removed by the Emperor Frederick Barbarossa, to be subsequently parcelled out to various churches in Germany and France ; but this is quite untrue.   Actually they remained undisturbed under the high altar of Sant' Ambrogio, where they were rediscovered in 1864.   A crypt has since been constructed accessible to worshippers, and there the relics can be viewed behind a panel of glass.   From an early date almost all calendars and martyrologies contain an entry commemorating SS. Gervase and Protase on this day, June 19.

The relevant passages of St Ambrose, St Augustine, Paulinus, etc., will be found quoted in the *Acta Sanctorum*, June, vol. iv, as also the pseudo-Ambrosian letter which professes to narrate the history of the martyrs.   For a general discussion of St Ambrose's discovery of the bodies, see F. Savio, *Gli antichi Vescovi d'Italia*, Milano, pp. 788–810 ; F. Lanzoni, *Diocesi d'Italia*, vol. ii, pp. 1000–1007 ; and CMH., pp. 325–326.   There is a certain difficulty in reconciling the statements of St Ambrose and St Augustine regarding the date and day of the week on which the bodies were found and transferred to Sant' Ambrogio ; on this, Delehaye has written in some detail in the *Analecta Bollandiana*, vol. xlix (1931), pp. 30–34.   The attempted identification of Gervase and Protase with the Dioscuri has been dealt with by P. Franchi de' Cavalieri in the *Nuovo Bullettino di archeologia cristiana*, vol. ix (1903), pp. 109–126, and *cf. Analecta Bollandiana*, vol. xxiii (1904), pp. 427–432.

ST DEODATUS, OR DIÉ, BISHOP OF NEVERS   (A.D. 679 ?)

KNOWN in his native land as Dié and Didier, St Deodatus was formerly widely venerated in France and no less than nine translations of his relics are recorded between 1003 and 1851.   He became bishop of Nevers about 655, and in 657 he attended the Synod of Sens, together with St Amandus of Maestricht, St Eligius of Noyon, St Ouen of Rouen, St Palladius of Auxerre and St Faro of Meaux. After occupying the episcopal chair for several years he resigned, retiring into the Vosges to lead the solitary life.   His story during the ensuing period is largely based on uncertain tradition, and we find his name linked with that of several holy men, not all of whom seem to have been even his contemporaries.   According to his biographers he was driven from his retreat by the enmity of the people of the surrounding country and withdrew to an island near Strasbourg, where a few solitaries were already leading a common life.   St Deodatus became their leader, and with the help of King Childeric built a church.

The growing community was the nucleus from which the abbey of Ebersheim was afterwards to develop.   Finding his temporal duties incompatible with the contemplative life, Deodatus left and sought elsewhere a place where he could serve God undisturbed.   Everywhere, however, he found himself opposed or persecuted.

Eventually he returned to the Vosges, and there, in what he called the Vale of Galilee, now the Vale of Saint-Dié, he settled down. Disciples soon gathered round, and for them was founded a monastery, which was called Jointures because it stood at the junction of the Rothbach and the Meurthe. The rule followed was that of St Columban. Not far from Jointures (now Saint-Dié) was Moyenmoutier, where another retired bishop, St Hidulf of Trier, was ruling another community of hermits. The two saints became close friends, periodically exchanging visits, and it was to St Hidulf, who came to administer the last sacraments to him, that St Deodatus commended his monastery. He was then extremely old, but had retained the direction of the community whilst spending the greater part of his time in a cell near at hand.

The long life written in the tenth century and printed in the *Acta Sanctorum*, June, vol. iv, is of little or no historical value. The part of Deodatus in the founding of Jointures is doubtful. See also Duchesne, *Fastes Épiscopaux*, vol. ii, p. 484.

ST BRUNO, OR BONIFACE, OF QUERFURT, BISHOP AND MARTYR (A.D. 1009)

THIS missionary monk was born about the year 974 of a noble Saxon family at Querfurt, and was baptized Bruno. He was educated in St Adalbert's city of Magdeburg, from whence he went to the court of Otto III, who regarded him with much confidence and affection and made him a court chaplain. When Otto went to Italy in 998, Bruno accompanied him and, like his master, came under the influence of St Romuald. With the memory of St Adalbert of Prague fresh in mind (who had been martyred the previous year) he received the monastic habit at the abbey of SS. Boniface and Alexis in Rome, and about 1000 he joined St Romuald. In the following year the emperor founded a monastery for them at Pereum, near Ravenna.

It was here that there came to Boniface (as he was now named) the call to carry the Christian message to the Veletians and Prussians and thus to continue the work of St Adalbert, whose life he had set himself to write. This scheme met with imperial approval, and two monks were sent in advance to Poland to learn Slavonic, while Boniface went to Rome for a papal commission ; but these two, Benedict and John, with three others, were murdered by robbers on November 10, 1003, at Kazimierz, near Gniezno, before he could join them. These were the Five Martyred Brothers, whose biography Boniface subsequently wrote. With the authorization of Pope Silvester II duly granted, he set out for Germany in the depth of a winter so severe that his boots sometimes froze tight to the stirrups. After interviewing the new emperor, St Henry II, at Regensburg, he was consecrated a missionary bishop by the archbishop of Magdeburg at Merseburg—perhaps " missionary archbishop " would be more accurate, for he had received a pallium from the pope, which has given rise to the suggestion that Boniface was in fact meant to be a metropolitan for eastern Poland. But owing to political difficulties he had to work for a time among the Magyars around the lower Danube ; here he had no great success, and he went on to Kiev where, under the protection of St Vladimir, he preached Christ's gospel among the Pechenegs.

Eventually Boniface made another attempt to reach the Prussians from the Polish territories of Boleslaus the Brave, after writing an eloquent but fruitless letter to the Emperor St Henry, imploring him not to ally himself with the heathen against the Christian Boleslaus. While much is uncertain in his career we can accept without hesitation the statement made by the chronicler Thietmar, bishop of Merseburg, who was related to Boniface. He tells us that his kinsman encountered violent opposition in his efforts to evangelize the borderland people in eastern Masovia ; and that when he persisted in disregarding their warnings he was cruelly slain with eighteen companions on March 14, 1009. The saint's body was purchased by Boleslaus, who removed it to Poland ; and the Prussians afterwards honoured his memory by giving his name to the town of Braunsberg, on the reputed site of his martyrdom. St Boniface was a missionary of large ideas, including the evangelization of the Swedes, to whom he sent two of his helpers, perhaps from Kiev ; but his achievements were, humanly speaking, disappointing.

Because he was sometimes called Bruno and sometimes Boniface, several later historians, including Cardinal Baronius in the Roman Martyrology (June 19 and October 15), have made the mistake of regarding Boniface and Bruno of Querfurt as different persons.

Sources for this life are not copious. There is a passage in the chronicle of Thietmar of Merseburg, another in St Peter Damian's *Life of St Romuald*, a short *passio* attributed to Wibert, who claimed to be a companion of the martyr, and a set of *legendae* in the Halberstadt Breviary. A rather tantalizing document has been published by H. G. Voigt, which, though preserved in a manuscript of very late date, has some pretensions to retain traces of a much older biography. It was first edited in the periodical *Sachsen und Anhalt*, vol. iii (1927), pp. 87–134 ; but it has since been included in Pertz, MGH., *Scriptores*, vol. xxx, part II. See also H. G. Voigt, *Bruno von Querfurt . . .* (1907) and *Bruno als Missionar der Ostens* (1909) ; the *Historisches Jahrbuch*, vol. xiii (1892), 493–500 ; the *Stimmen aus Maria-Laach*, vol. liii (1897), pp. 266 *seq.;* F. Dvornik, *The Making of Central and Eastern Europe* (1949), pp. 196–204 and *passim ;* and the *Cambridge History of Poland*, vol. i (1950), pp. 66–67.

BD ODO, Bishop of Cambrai   (A.D. 1113)

OF the distinguished scholars who taught in the great French schools of the eleventh century one of the most learned and influential was Odo, afterwards bishop of Cambrai. Where he was educated is not known, but he was a native of Orleans and, while still young, wrote a poem on the Trojan War which obtained considerable popularity. He had been teaching for several years at Toul when the canons of Tournai gave him the post of *scholasticus*—actually director—in their cathedral school. There he soon evinced a genius for teaching and a skill in disputation which, combined with a powerful and attractive personality, drew to him young men not only from the neighbouring towns, but also from Normandy, Saxony and Italy. A follower of Boethius and an exponent of realistic philosophy, he contended so successfully against the nominalism taught by Raimbert of Lille that he ended by winning over most of Raimbert's followers. Besides philosophy, rhetoric, and dialectics he also taught astronomy, and was often to be seen seated on the cathedral steps on a starry night demonstrating to his pupils the position of the constellations and the movement of the planets.

Immersed in secular studies Odo had little or no time to spare for theology or the writings of the fathers. He had been at Tournai five years when some lectures he was giving on Boethius led him to consult for the first time St Augustine's book on free will. Almost from the beginning it riveted his attention, and as he read on he was reduced to tears and overwhelmed with a sense of the futility of his past career. It was a case of sudden and complete conversion. At once he restricted his times for instruction, gave away all his money to the poor, began to spend long hours in church, and embarked upon such severe mortifications that he soon resembled a walking skeleton. Obviously, he would not remain satisfied with a secular life, and the bishop and citizens of Tournai, anxious to retain him in their midst, bestowed upon him the disused abbey of St Martin. At first he and a number of his former pupils lived there as canons, but after three years, by the advice of his friend Aimeric, abbot of Anchin, he gave them the Benedictine rule.

Odo had been abbot of St Martin's for thirteen years when, in 1105, he was chosen bishop of Cambrai in the place of Gaucher, whom Pope Paschal II had excommunicated and deposed for simony and for having accepted investiture from Henry IV. The emperor's party, however, was in the ascendant at Cambrai, and not until his death a year later could Odo obtain possession of his see. Even then he was unable to retain it. Within a very short time he was driven into exile because he refused to accept the ring and the cross from Henry V. He found a refuge with Aimeric at Anchin, where he occupied himself in writing books. He appears to have returned to Cambrai for a brief period towards the close of his life, but he died and was buried at Anchin. Amongst his numerous writings may be mentioned an exposition of the canon of the Mass, a treatise on original sin, another on the coming of the Messias, a harmony of the gospels and a polyglot psalter in four languages.

Although no lengthy biography of early date is available we have a letter of Amand de Castello, prior of Anchin, which gives a sketch of Odo's career, and another account attributed to Herman of Tournai. These have been printed in Pertz, MGH., *Scriptores*, vol. xv, pp. 942–945, and vol. xiv, pp. 210–211, and cf. pp. 274–318. See especially *Histoire littéraire de la France*, vol. viii, pp. 399–400 ; Berlière, *Monasticon Belge*, vol. i, pp. 273–275 ; Auger, *Études sur les Mystiques des Pays Bas*, pp. 66–71, and three articles by Labis in the *Revue Catholique de Louvain*, vol. xiv (1856).

BD THOMAS WOODHOUSE, Martyr   (A.D. 1573)

The second priest to suffer martyrdom under Elizabeth was Thomas Woodhouse. Ordained in the days of Queen Mary and appointed rector of a small Lincolnshire parish, he was obliged at the outbreak of persecution after her death to resign the living he had only held for a year and afterwards a post as tutor in Wales. In 1561 he was arrested in the act of saying Mass and was committed to the Fleet : he was destined to remain a prisoner for twelve years. During the early part of his captivity he was allowed considerable freedom : he said his office daily, celebrated Mass in his cell, and even tried to make converts by discussions with his fellow prisoners and by writings which he attached to stones and threw out of the window. When plague broke out in London in 1563, he and other prisoners for religion were removed to the country house of Tyrrell, the warden of the Fleet, who was sympathetic to the Catholics.

About the year 1572, after negotiations had been secretly carried on with the provincial in Paris, he was admitted by letter into membership of the Society of Jesus—and in the first fervour of his reception he wrote a letter to Lord Burleigh, in which he urged him to persuade Queen Elizabeth to submit to Pope Pius V, by whose decree, he pointed out, she was already *de jure* deposed. In a personal interview with Burleigh, and under examination before the Council, he was still more outspoken, his fearlessness causing him to be classed as a dangerous fanatic. At his final trial in the Guildhall, in April, 1573, he challenged not only the authority of the judges, but also the right of a secular court to try a priest. He was found guilty of high treason.   As he stood on the scaffold he was told to ask pardon of God, the queen and the country.   He replied : " Nay, on the part of God I demand of you and of the queen that ye ask pardon of God and of holy mother Church because, contrary to the truth, ye have resisted Christ the Lord, and His vicar upon earth, the pope."

See Camm, LEM., vol. ii, pp. 187–203 ; Foley, REPSJ., vol. viii ; and DNB., vol. lxii, p. 403.

20 : ST SILVERIUS, POPE AND MARTYR   (*c.* A.D. 537)

SILVERIUS, the son of Pope St Hormisdas, was only a subdeacon when, on the death of Pope St Agapitus I at Constantinople on April 22, 536, he was forced as bishop on the Roman church by the Ostrogothic king of Italy, Theodehad, who foresaw the appearance of a Byzantine candidate ; however, after Silverius had been consecrated the clergy of Rome agreed to accept him.   The Empress Theodora wrote asking him to recognize as patriarchs the monophysites Anthimus at Constantinople and Severus at Antioch ; Silverius replied politely with what was in effect a refusal, and he is said to have remarked as he did so that he was signing his own death warrant.   He was right ; Theodora was a woman who would tolerate no opposition : but she could afford to wait.

After the devastation of suburban Rome by the Ostrogothic general Vitiges, the pope and the senate willingly opened the gates of the City to his Byzantine opponent Belisarius—and Theodora had her chance.   An attempt to entrap Silverius by means of a forged letter in a charge of treasonable conspiracy with the Goths having apparently failed, he was kidnapped and carried away to Patara in Lycia in Asia Minor ; and the next day Belisarius—who was acting under pressure from his wife Antonina—proclaimed as pope in his stead the Empress Theodora's nominee, the deacon Vigilius.   A very bad episode in the history of the papacy had begun.

Apparently the Emperor Justinian had been kept in ignorance of what was going on ; and when he was told by the bishop of Patara of what had happened, he ordered that Silverius be sent back to Rome and an inquiry instituted.   But when the pope landed in Italy the supporters of Vigilius intercepted and captured him ; and Antonina, eager to gratify Theodora, prevailed on her husband to let them deal with him as they chose.   Accordingly Silverius was taken under escort to the island of Palmarola in the Tyrrhenian Sea, off Naples.

There, or perhaps in the neighbouring island of Ponza, he ended his days soon afterwards, as the result of the ill-treatment he received.   According to Liberatus, who wrote from hearsay, he died of hunger ; but his contemporary, Procopius, states that he was murdered at the instigation of Antonina, by one of her servants. In any case the feast of St Silverius is kept as that of a martyr.

It is not at all clear how the appointment of Vigilius to the papal see came to be regularized ; but once he was recognized as pope his patroness Theodora experienced disappointment, for he ceased to support her intrigues on behalf of Monophysism and stood forward as the upholder of orthodoxy—which after all is what is expected of a pope.

See the *Liber Pontificalis* (ed. Duchesne), vol. i, pp. 290–295.   Duchesne, in his introduction (pp. xxxvi–xxxviii), points out that there is a curious difference of tone between the earlier and later part of this notice. He concludes that it was compiled by two different writers, the former hostile, the latter friendly to Silverius. The remaining jejune, but, for lack of better material, not negligible, sources are the *Breviarium* of Liberatus ; Procopius, *De Bello Gothico* ; and the documents of Vigilius in Mansi, *Concilia*, vol. ix. See also Grisar, *Geschichte Roms und der Päpste*, vol. i, pp. 502–504 ; Lévêque, *Étude sur le Pape Vigilius* ; DCB., vol. iv, pp. 670–675 ; and E. Amann in DTC., *s.v.* Silvère. Benedict XIV's commission proposed to remove the feast of St Silverius from the general calendar.

ST GOBAN, or GOBAIN, Martyr   (c. A.D. 670)

An Irishman by birth, and a disciple of St Fursey, St Goban accompanied his master to East Anglia, and with St Ultan afterwards passed over to Gaul. After a short stay at Corbie, where as yet there was no abbey, St Goban went to Laon. From thence he made his way to the great forest near the Oise, and constructed a cell near La Fère and Prémontré ; then he built a church dedicated to St Peter, later known as Saint-Gobain. Eventually he fell a victim to barbarians from Germany, who were plundering the district. They cut off his head, either out of hatred for the Christian faith or because they found no treasure in the hermit's cell. The town of Saint-Gobain, famous for its glass-works, stands on the Mont d'Ermitage where the saint is said to have lived and died.

Though the short medieval life of uncertain date which is printed in the *Acta Sanctorum*, June, vol. v, lacks independent confirmation, there can be no doubt of St Goban's real existence. He is mentioned by Bede in book III, chapter xix of his *Ecclesiastical History*, but the matter of this chapter was borrowed by Bede from a still older Life of Fursey. As C. Plummer remarks, in a note to this passage of Bede, Goban was a common Irish name ; there are no less than seven Gobans commemorated in the *Félire* of Gorman. *Cf.* also L. Gougaud, *Les Saints irlandais hors d'Irlande* (1936), p. 112, who mentions Goban, but evidently attaches no weight whatever to the account of his doings in Gaul.

ST BAGNUS, or BAIN, Bishop of Thérouanne   (c. A.D. 710)

Few outstanding events seem to have marked the career of the saint who is the principal patron of the town of Calais. Bagnus, or Bain as the French call him, was a monk in the abbey of Fontenelle, and one of the most ardent of the disciples of St Wandregisilus. About the year 689 he was raised to the bishopric of Thérouanne, a see which owed its foundation to St Audomarus and comprised what is now known as the Pas de Calais. He did much to evangelize those parts of the diocese which bordered upon the Channel, and was particularly successful in the neighbourhood of Calais. From a visit to Pope St Sergius I in Rome he returned with many gifts, including the reputed relics of St Silas, the companion of St Paul, which he placed in his cathedral church. He buried the bodies of SS. Luglius and Luglian, two Irish pilgrims who were murdered by robbers as they were on their way back from the Holy Land. When he had ruled for twelve years he resigned his office, and went back to live as a simple monk at Fontenelle. Three years later, however, he was obliged to accept the post of abbot. The date of St Bain's death is contested : it probably took place in 710. He has given his name to the village of Bainghien, with which he is believed to have been connected.

A short account of St Bagnus is furnished in the *Acta Sanctorum*, June, vol. v. It is derived mainly from the *Gesta Abbatum Fontanellensium*. See also Duchesne, *Fastes Épiscopaux*, vol. iii, p. 134 ; and Lohier and Laporte, *Gesta sanctorum patrum Fontanellensis coenobii* (1936), pp. 14–21.

ST ADALBERT, ARCHBISHOP OF MAGDEBURG (A.D. 981)

MAGDEBURG, the capital of Prussian Saxony, owes its foundation as a town and as an archiepiscopal seat to the Emperor Otto the Great. Recognizing the strategic value of the site, he began the construction of a strongly fortified city calculated to overawe the neighbouring Slavs; and to serve as a centre for Christian missions amongst them he in 937 founded a monastery, with the active co-operation of his first wife, the English princess Edith (she was a sister of King Athelstan and a granddaughter of Alfred the Great). They dedicated the abbey in the names of the apostles St Peter and St Paul, and St Maurice. Political and religious motives combined to make Otto an ardent advocate of the evangelization of the Slavs, the Magyars, and other pagans of eastern Europe. Consequently, when the Russian princess St Olga, after her conversion at Constantinople at the age of seventy, asked him to provide missionaries to evangelize her Russian subjects he willingly acceded to her request. The leader chosen for the little band was Adalbert, a monk of St Maximin at Trier, of whose antecedents nothing is now known, but he would seem even then to have been a man of mark.

In 961 the missionaries went forth, but directly they set foot in Russia they found their mission was futile as Olga had had to hand over her authority to her heathen son Svyatoslav at Kiev. Some of the missionaries lost their lives, but Adalbert managed to escape and to return to his own country. For four years he remained at the imperial court at Mainz, and then he was made abbot of the abbey of Weissenburg. There he did much to foster learning. He also continued, or caused one of his monks to continue, the chronicle of Reginald von Prüm which covers the years between 907 and 967. By this time Magdeburg had become an important city, and Otto greatly desired, for various reasons, to see it raised to archiepiscopal rank. After much opposition from the archbishop of Mainz and others, his request received papal sanction in 962, and Adalbert was nominated the first archbishop of Magdeburg, with a general jurisdiction over the Slavs. A true apostle, he laboured indefatigably for the extension of Christianity amongst the Wends on the opposite bank of the river Elbe, and was strict in enforcing discipline in religious houses. When Otto the Great died, in 973, St Adalbert buried him beside his first wife, Edith, in the church of St Maurice, which had now become the cathedral. The holy archbishop was taken ill and died eight years later, when making a visitation in the diocese of Merseburg.

Our knowledge of the facts of Adalbert's career is mainly derived from Thietmar's Chronicle and from the *Gesta Episcoporum Magdeburgensium*. These can best be consulted in Pertz, MGH., *Scriptores*, vol. i, pp. 613–629; and vol. xiv, pp. 381–386. There is a notice of St Adalbert in the *Acta Sanctorum*, June, vol. v. See also Hauck, *Kirchengeschichte Deutschlands*, vol. iii; and F. Dvornik, *The Making of Central and Eastern Europe* (1949), pp. 60 and 68–70.

ST JOHN OF MATERA, ABBOT OF PULSANO (A.D. 1139)

THE founder of the Benedictine congregation of Pulsano was born at Matera, a town in the Basilicata, part of the kingdom of Naples. While yet a boy John longed to be a hermit, and on reaching manhood he left his father's house and made his way to an island off Taranto, where he joined a monastery in the capacity of shepherd. His austerity, however, and his refusal to join his brethren in any form of recreation, made him unpopular, so he left them and went, first to Calabria, then on to Sicily.   Afterwards, in obedience to what he regarded as a divine admonition, he returned to the mainland, and at Ginosa for two and a half years he maintained unbroken silence, without making his presence known to his parents, whom war had compelled to take refuge in the vicinity.   He now had a vision of St Peter, who bade him rebuild a ruined church dedicated in his honour about a mile from Ginosa.   This task he successfully accomplished with the help of a few companions who rallied round him.   But then he was accused of having discovered and appropriated hidden treasure, and was brought up before the governor of the province, by whom he was committed to prison.

He managed to escape—liberated, it is said, by an angel—and reached Capua. He was not permitted to remain there.   An inward voice bade him return to his own land, and he entered the community of St William of Vercelli on Monte Laceno.   John stayed with them until their dwellings were destroyed by fire.   The rest then moved to Monte Cagno, but John went to Bari, where he preached to the people with wonderful effect.   His very success seems to have aroused jealousy and he found himself once more under accusation—this time on a charge of heresy. He was able, however, to clear himself triumphantly.   He then returned to Ginosa, where he was welcomed by his former disciples, and he conducted in St Peter's church what appears to have been a very fruitful mission.   His wanderings were now nearly at an end.   Still directed by the voice which had led him in the past, he betook himself to Monte Gargano, and at Pulsano, three miles from the spot hallowed by the appearance of St Michael, he built a monastery.   Disciples flocked to join his community, which soon numbered sixty monks, over whom he ruled until his death.   Honoured by all for his wisdom, his miracles and his prophetical gifts, he passed to his reward on June 20, 1139.   Other religious houses were afterwards affiliated to his, and the congregation of Monte Pulsano was at one time a recognized part of the great Benedictine family.   It has long since disappeared.

There is a Latin life in tolerably full detail, which seems to have been written before the end of the twelfth century.   It is printed in the *Acta Sanctorum*, June, vol. v.   A metrical account, of which the Bollandists have only extracted a specimen, may be read in full in G. Giordano, *Chroniche de Monte Vergine* (1640), pp. 520–527.   A life has been published in more recent times (1930) by M. Morelli, and see *Analecta Bollandiana*, vol. lvii (1939), pp. 174–176.

BD MICHELINA OF PESARO, WIDOW   (A.D. 1356)

THE town of Pesaro on the east coast of Italy has a special devotion to this holy widow, who was one of its own citizens.   Born of wealthy and distinguished parents, Michelina Metelli married at the age of twelve a member of the Malatesta family of Rimini.   The union was a happy one, but when the death of her husband left her a widow at twenty, with one little son, she seems to have been by no means disconsolate.   She had always been fond of pleasure, and she continued for some time to lead the same life as before, giving little or no thought to religion.   There was staying in Pesaro at that period a Franciscan tertiary of unknown origin and antecedents who went by the name of Syriaca.   She lived on alms, spent most of her time in prayer, and depended for shelter at night on the casual hospitality of the charitable.   Michelina, who was one of those who opened their doors to the stranger, gradually came under her influence.

An intimacy sprang up between them which ended in Michelina's complete conversion.   Only her boy now bound her to the world, and when he fell a victim to some childish complaint she determined to renounce all things. By Syriaca's advice she took the Franciscan tertiary habit, distributed her possessions to the poor, and begged her bread from door to door. It was by no means a simple thing for one who had always lived in ease and comfort to accustom herself to rejected scraps. Once, in the early days of her new life, she acknowledged to a former associate that she longed for a taste of freshly roasted pork. Eager to give her that small gratification her friend promptly invited her to dinner. But when the joint was dished up and the savoury smell assailed her nostrils, Michelina suddenly recollected herself. Refusing to sit down to table, she withdrew from the company and beat herself with an iron chain until the blood flowed. As each blow fell she apostrophized herself bitterly, exclaiming : " Do you still want pork, Michelina ? Do you want still more ? "

Many other trials she had to bear from within and without. Her relations took strong objection to her conduct and at one time went the length of shutting her up as a lunatic. Her patience and gentleness, however, disarmed them : they concluded that though deluded she was quite harmless and they liberated her. The rest of her life was spent in self-abnegation and good works. She nursed lepers and others afflicted with loathsome diseases, performing for them the most menial offices ; and she is said to have cured several of them by kissing their sores. Towards the close of her life Michelina made a pilgrimage to Rome. There on one occasion she was allowed a mystical participation in the sufferings of our Lord. She died on Trinity Sunday, 1356, at an age which is given as fifty-six. From the moment of her death she was venerated by her fellow citizens who kept a lamp burning day and night before her tomb in the Franciscan church. In 1580 the house she had once occupied at Pesaro was converted into a church, and in 1737 her *cultus* was approved.

There is a short account in the *Acta Sanctorum*, June, vol. iv, and in Wadding, *Annales Ordinis Minorum*, vol. viii, pp. 140–143 ; several lives were also printed in the eighteenth century by Bonucci, Matthaei, Ermanno, Bagnocavallo and others. See also Léon, *Auréole séraphique* (Eng. trans.), vol. ii, pp. 422–426.

BD OSANNA OF MANTUA, VIRGIN   (A.D. 1505)

WHEN we study the internal history of the Italian states in the late middle ages we cannot fail to notice the important part played by certain holy women living in their midst, whose advice and prayers are sought by rulers and people, and who come to be regarded even during their lifetime as the protectors of the community and as mediators with God and man. One such woman was Bd Osanna. Born on January 17, 1449, at Mantua, she was the daughter of Nicholas Andreasi and of Louisa Gonzaga, whose name shows her to have been in some way related to the reigning dukes. Osanna was the eldest of a numerous family, some members of which were to be her almost constant care all her life. She was five when she had her first religious experience. As she was wandering one day beside the river Po at Carbonarola, she heard a voice which said, gently but distinctly, " Child, life and death consist in loving God." Immediately she fell into an ecstasy and was led by an angel to Paradise. There he showed her all creatures praising God after their fashion, and explained that this praise, which will be our chief function in eternity, ought to be our preoccupation and our happiness even in this life. It was a wonderful revelation to be disclosed to a little child ; but she responded by the surrender of her whole being to God.

From that time she began to spend long hours in prayer and penance. She often fell into ecstasies—to the great concern of her parents, who at first attributed her trances to epilepsy. Eager to learn more about her religion, she asked to be taught to read, but her father refused, on the plea that learning was dangerous to women. That she did learn to read and write, her biographers attribute to the direct intervention of our Lady : in view, however, of the ease with which an intelligent girl can assimilate the lessons given to her brothers, a purely natural explanation may be preferred. When she was fourteen she sought permission to join the third order of St Dominic, but again she met with opposition, because her father wished her to marry. He allowed her, nevertheless, a little later on to assume the Dominican habit temporarily as a thanksgiving for recovery from a serious illness ; and when, at the close of the prescribed period, she announced that she had committed herself for life, although he was angry he did not insist.

Strange as it seems, she did not make her profession as a tertiary for another thirty-seven years, remaining a novice and always taking the lowest place at all tertiary gatherings. The reason for the delay is obscure : probably she felt that the obligations entailed were incompatible in some way with the duties in the world which God required her to discharge. She was still young when both her parents died, and she continued to reside in the Andreasi palace, devoting herself to her brothers and their families, never seeking her own will, but serving all as though she were their humblest domestic. Her austerities and devotions were practised as privately as possible.

At the age of eighteen Osanna received another signal favour from on high. In a vision our Lady espoused her to our Lord, and He placed a ring on her finger : she could always feel it, though it remained invisible to others. About this time she seems to have encountered some measure of persecution. In her letters she is reticent and disposed to blame herself, but she appears to have been misjudged by her fellow tertiaries, who questioned her sincerity and the genuineness of the spiritual manifestations, which, in spite of her efforts, she could not always conceal. They went so far as to denounce her to the duke and to threaten her with expulsion from the order. It was some time before the agitation completely died down. Between 1476 and 1481 she had a series of experiences in which she was permitted to participate physically in the mysteries of the Passion—first the crown of thorns, then the wound in the side, and finally the wounds in the hands and feet. They were not apparent, but they caused her intense suffering.

The high regard in which Bd Osanna was held by Duke Frederick of Mantua was evinced in a striking manner in 1478. On the eve of starting to conduct a campaign in Tuscany he sent for her and asked her not only to look after the duchess and their six children, but practically to supply his place in his absence. Osanna at first demurred, pleading her inexperience and her youth, for she was not yet thirty. However, he insisted, and she consented with the simplicity and trust in God that characterized her throughout her life. Though she never ceased to live at home, she now spent a great deal of her time at the palace, dealing so wisely with the various matters that came before her that even after his return Frederick continued to consult her. Indeed, when a visit she had paid to Milan under pressure from her Dominican superiors had been, as he thought, unduly prolonged, he wrote to implore her to return. The whole of his family regarded her as their dearest friend, and when Francis II succeeded his father, he and his young bride, Isabella d'Este, carried on the tradition. In letters which are still extant we find her trusting in their friendship to intercede for every kind of distressed person—sometimes demanding justice for some unfortunate victim, sometimes asking mercy for a prisoner, even at the risk, she on occasion acknowledges, of seeming importunate. In 1501 she at last made her full profession as a tertiary, and during the four remaining years of her life, when she was in failing health, she seemed hardly to belong to this world. She died at the age of fifty-six on June 20, 1505. The duke and Isabella d'Este, who were with her at the end, accorded her a magnificent funeral and exempted the Andreasi family from all taxes for twenty years.

It will not be out of place, if only as a tribute to the memory of a man whom Professor R. W. Chambers described as " that beloved and saintly scholar . . . Edmund Gardner ", to quote somewhat at length from a privately printed essay of his entitled : " A Mystic of the Renaissance : Osanna Andreasi of Mantua ". Speaking of the vision vouchsafed to her in her childhood, Professor Gardner tells how, in her own words, " she feared greatly because of the vision she had had, knowing herself not to be a true and perfect lover of God as she needs must be ", and how her aspirations after this perfect state took articulate form in her simple prayer for divine guidance along the way of love.

This prayer, with other writings and letters, has been preserved to us by a monk friend whose relations with Osanna remind us much of those of the Dominican Peter of Dacia, more than two centuries earlier, with the *stigmatisée* Christina of Stommeln. Professor Gardner refers to this curiously interesting feature of her spiritual development in the following passage :

A peculiar element in Osanna's mystical life is the part played therein by the intense, purely spiritual bond of love of friendship that bound her to a man ten years younger than herself, Girolamo da Monte Oliveto. He tells us how, when a youth of fifteen on his way to attend a lecture, he entered a church and there saw her rapt in contemplation, and ever after had her image impressed upon his heart. So moved was he that he abandoned the world, took the Olivetan habit, and, after much entreaty, prevailed upon her to accept him as a spiritual son. The " spiritual colloquies ", which he published after her death, are the records of the conversations they held together—speaking heart to heart, " with only God between us ", as he says. " O goodness of God ", he cries in one place, " our two hearts were bound together in one will in His sight, such was the innate love between us that I cannot tell it without tears. The virgin loved her beloved son in Christ as her own soul, and he loved his only mother almost more than his soul. O great charity of God, surely inserted into our hearts before there was ever any spiritual conversation between us or we ever knew each other ! " In her visions of the divine union one sees his soul with hers in the presence of God, and her letters to him, when the duties of his order take him from Mantua, have the form of spiritualized love-letters. " I have received a sweet and gentle letter of yours ; and I cannot express in words how delightful it has been to me, and what great consolation it has brought. . . ." " My soul rejoices at every consolation of yours, as though we were one single soul and one same heart, as indeed we are, through the bond and effect of the charity of sweet Jesus."

Or, again, when she hears that her *caro amante in Cristo* has returned to Mantua : " I leave you to think how, when I heard, I was almost bereft of spirit through my great joy and gladness. Father and my only son, conceived in the great fountain of the Divine Goodness, if you had seen your unworthy

mother become transformed in colour : where is so much cordial love ?
I answer that it is only found in the sacred side of our Saviour.   And this
spiritual love has grown so strong that I believe, with the divine aid, that
neither angel nor archangel nor demon nor any creature will be able to sever
it ; but, by means of the grace of God, it will come to perfection in our blessed
and eternal country ."

As for Osanna's relations with the outside world, corrupt as society was for the
most part in her day and permeated with the semi-paganism of the Renaissance,
Professor Gardner held that her thought during her later years was profoundly
coloured by the influence of Savonarola.   It is true that the great reformer's name
occurs nowhere in her letters or conversations, but " I am convinced ", says
Gardner, " that this was due to deliberate suppression on the part of her two
contemporary biographers."

It is recorded that she pored over the *Triumph of the Cross* (Savonarola's most
important work) in the watches of the night.   It was entirely in his spirit that she
had visions of the horror in store for Italy and that she prayed that the thunderbolt
of the divine wrath might not fall upon the land.   " Again and again ", says
Professor Gardner, " we find her foretelling the scourge overhanging Italy for the
sins of her people, unless they repent ; and more particularly in the opening years
of the sixteenth century following with agonized apprehension the career of the
pope, realizing ever more and more the awful corruption of the Church.   Girolamo
tells us that ' she feared greatly for the Church ', and it is clear that prudential
motives prevented him from recording more than the safer portions of her utterances
on the subject." On the other hand, Osanna, while evidently believing in the imminent damnation of vast numbers of unrepentant souls, invariably sees individuals
as saved—and, very frequently, their immediate passing into Paradise.

There is only one exception, and that is the sovereign pontiff, Alexander
VI.   In one of her revelations she tells Girolamo that she has prayed three
times for the salvation of the pope.   The first two times God seemed disposed
to show mercy to him, the third time she received no reply.   " And, my soul
persevering in the demand, there appeared our Lady, the holy Mother of God,
and standing before her Son she began to pray, and to help my soul that she
might be consoled by the salvation of the pope, and by the renovation of Holy
Church.   And thereafter came all the Apostles, standing round the divine
presence, and all prayed that mercy might be shown him.   Alas, wretched
sinner that I am !   God ever kept motionless, with aspect and countenance
of wrath ; and He gave no reply to anyone who prayed ; not to the Madonna,
nor to the Apostles, nor to my soul."

Finally Professor Gardner insists that Osanna was not one of those mystics
who so turn their backs on the world that they are entirely absorbed in their own
spiritual development and progress in perfection.

She was never happy, Girolamo tells us, on any day when she had done no
temporal act of mercy, by visiting the sick, giving alms to the poor, nursing
and consoling the afflicted.   We find her ever protecting the weak and oppressed from the rigour of the law, using her influence to remedy injustice.
High and low alike thronged to her house for advice and comfort, and we have
many amusing passages in Girolamo's book in which their spiritual colloquies
are interrupted by the sudden arrival of Browning's " certain people of importance ".   Her spirit of detachment does not prevent her from caring for

the interests of her brothers, in the court and in the camp, and a charming little letter has been preserved in which on the occasion of a nephew of hers singing his first Mass, she tells the Marquis of Mantua that she is entertaining the friars afterwards, and invites him to form one of the party.

A Latin biography of Bd Osanna, written by her confessor Francis Silvestri, was printed a few months after her death.   The Olivetan monk, Dom Girolamo referred to above, published his notes of their colloquies and of her letters in an Italian volume in 1507.   But by far the most satisfactory materials for her history are to be found in the book of G. Bagolini and L. Ferretti, *La Beata Osanna Andreasi da Mantova* (1905) ; this incorporates the earlier materials just spoken of, and adds a considerable collection of her original letters.   See also M. C. de Ganay, *Les bienheureuses Dominicaines* (1924), pp. 369–412.

THE ENGLISH MARTYRS OF THE OATES PLOT   (A.D. 1678–1680)

DURING the seventeen years which followed the Stuart Restoration in 1660, the Catholics of England suffered little molestation : they had, in the past, given abundant evidence of their loyalty, and King Charles II was known to be well affected towards them.   But in 1678 the pretended revelations of what came to be known as the Popish Plot roused the fears and fury of the nation to fever pitch and caused a renewal of persecution in its bitterest form.

The first victim of the Titus Oates " plot " was BD EDWARD COLEMAN, a gentleman of Suffolk.   He was the son of an Anglican parson, went to Peterhouse, Cambridge, and after his conversion became secretary to the Duchess of York.   He was a man of considerable talent, and a controversy which he carried on with the Anglican dignitaries Stillingfleet and Burnet led to the conversion of Lady Tyrwhit. A contemporary Protestant chronicler refers to him as " A great bigot in his religion, and of a busy head.   This engaged him in many projects for the restoring of Popery here, or at least procuring a liberty of conscience for those of that profession.   He had been engaged in a correspondence with Père la Chaise, the French king's confessor, since the year 1674, in the course of which he was continually entertaining him with schemes and projects for advancing the interest of the French king and the Church of Rome."

This and other foreign correspondence being opportunely discovered, Oates made use of it to add further details to his fabricated papal conspiracy, and Coleman was arrested along with Sir George Wakeman and many others.   He was brought to trial at the Old Bailey on November 28, 1678, charged with consenting to a resolution for the assassination of the king and with invoking the assistance of a foreign power to re-establish Catholicism.   Oates's concocted evidence on the first charge broke down, and Coleman pleaded that his correspondence was intended only to raise money from abroad wherewith to prosecute his efforts to further the cause of his religion by constitutional means.   The Lord Chief Justice (Scroggs) almost ignored the evidence of Oates and his accomplice Bedloe, but construed the prisoner's admissions in such a way as to involve the guilt of conspiring with a foreign power and compassing the king's death : " though he might hope to bring in Popery by procuring a dissolution of the Parliament and a toleration, it was to be supposed other methods would have been taken if these had failed, by his confederates at least, if not by himself . . ." *et cetera*.   He was accordingly convicted and sentenced to be hanged, drawn, and quartered.   At Tyburn on December 3, having denied knowledge of any plot, he declared that as a Catholic he repudiated the doctrine " that kings may be murdered, and the like. I say I abominate it " ; and maintained once more that he was innocent of any illegal action against the state or individuals.

Bd WILLIAM IRELAND (*alias* Ironmonger) was born in Lincolnshire in 1636. He was the eldest son of William Ireland, of Crofton Hall in Yorkshire, of a strongly royalist family, kin to the Giffards and the Pendrells.   William junior was educated at the English college at Saint-Omer, was professed in the Society of Jesus in 1673, and, after being for a time confessor to the Poor Clares at Gravelines, was sent on the mission in 1677.   In the following year Titus Oates exploded his plot, and on September 28, Father Ireland was arrested by Oates himself, at a house in London that lodged a number of Jesuits as well as the Spanish ambassador.   Bd JOHN GROVE, nominal owner of the house, but really manservant to the clergy there, was also taken up.

After nearly three months' brutal imprisonment in Newgate, these two were brought to trial, together with BB. Thomas Whitebread and John Fenwick (below) and THOMAS PICKERING.   The last-named was a Benedictine lay-brother of St Gregory's monastery at Douay, a man of about fifty-eight, who had been sent over in 1665 as procurator to the seven Benedictines who served the chapel of Charles II's queen, Catherine of Braganza, at Somerset House in The Strand ; when the monks were banished ten years later, he was allowed to remain.

These five—three Jesuit priests, a Benedictine lay-brother and a layman—were charged with conspiring to assassinate the king.   For lack of sufficient witnesses Father Whitebread and Father Fenwick were put back for trial at another time— illegally, as their trial had already been begun, and they should have been discharged.   The conspiracy was alleged to have taken place in the rooms of Bd William Harcourt (below), and Oates and Bedloe swore that Grove and Pickering were to do the job, for which the first was to receive £1,500 and the second 30,000 Masses.*   Embroideries on this farrago were that the two accused had hung about St James's Park with pistols, and that on three occasions only a mishap, such as a loose pistol flint, had saved the king's life.   Naturally the charge was strenuously denied, Pickering declaring that he had never fired a pistol in his life.   Father Ireland had not been in London for a fortnight before and three weeks after the date he was supposed to have assisted at devising the conspiracy : he had been in the Midlands and North Wales all the time, and could have produced fifty witnesses to prove it.   But a woman swore away his life, saying she had seen him in Fetter Lane at the pertinent date.   All three were brought in guilty.

Father Ireland and Grove were executed together at Tyburn on January 24, 1679.   The priest spoke first from the scaffold, and the layman summed up what he had said in one brief sentence.   " We are innocent.   We lose our lives wrongfully.   We pray God to forgive them that are the causers of it."

King Charles had made half-hearted attempts to save their lives, for he was satisfied that the plot " was all a fiction, never believing one tittle of it ".   Brother Thomas was in fact reprieved until May 9, when he too suffered at Tyburn.   Just as he was going to be turned off the cart he was called on to confess his guilt by someone in the crowd.   " Pulling up his cap and looking towards them with an innocent, smiling countenance, ' Is this ', said he, ' the countenance of a man that

---

* Presumably stipends for Masses which, as Challoner points out, " at a shilling a Mass amounts to the same sum ".   But as he was not a priest, Brother Thomas could not celebrate Mass anyway.   Or perhaps the benefits of Masses celebrated for him was intended.

dies under so gross a guilt ? ' " It was the face of a man " of all men living the most unlikely and the most unfit for that desperate undertaking of which he was accused ".

Suspicion was particularly directed against members of the Society of Jesus, and on June 20 of the same year, 1679, five of its priests were executed at Tyburn, including the provincial superior, BD THOMAS WHITEBREAD. A man of good birth, a native of Essex, he had studied abroad in the seminary of St Omer and had entered the Jesuit novitiate at Watten in 1635. After he had been raised to the priesthood, he was sent to England, where he laboured with fervour and success for over thirty years, teaching by word of mouth and through controversial pamphlets. A sermon he delivered to his brethren at Liège, shortly before the outbreak of persecution, seemed to indicate foreknowledge of his fate. He had taken for his text the words : " Can you drink the chalice that I am to drink ? " and after enumerating one by one the trials which actually afterwards befell him he repeated several times most solemnly : " *Possumus*—We can." He was apprehended on his return to England and, though ill and very weak, was imprisoned loaded with chains. He languished in gaol for several months before he, with four companions, was brought up for trial at the Old Bailey, on June 13, 1679.

BD WILLIAM HARCOURT, or Waring—whose real name was Barrow—came from Lancashire. He had entered the Society of Jesus at the age of twenty-three, had worked in England for thirty-five years and had prayed daily for twenty years that he might gain the crown of martyrdom : his petition was granted when he was over seventy.

A north countryman from Durham, BD JOHN FENWICK—*alias* Caldwell—was the son of Protestant parents who cast him off when he embraced the Catholic faith. He went for his education to St Omer and joined the Society of Jesus in 1656, when he was twenty-eight. In 1675 he was sent on the English mission. At the time of his arrest a sore from which he suffered was so badly aggravated by the weight of his fetters that amputation of his leg was seriously contemplated. He was fifty years of age when he was condemned to death.

BD JOHN GAVAN, or Gawen, was London born. He was educated at St Omer, and after being admitted to the order at the age of twenty, he continued his studies at Liège and in Rome. He had been working in England for eight years and had made a number of converts when he was apprehended.

Like Father Fenwick, BD ANTONY TURNER was a convert. He was born in Leicestershire, where his father was a Protestant clergyman, and was educated at the University of Cambridge. He became a Catholic after he had taken his B.A. degree and passed on to the English College in Rome. At the age of twenty-four he entered the Jesuit novitiate at Watten. When he had been ordained to the priesthood he was sent to England, where he worked for eighteen years, making his headquarters mainly at Worcester. He was an ardent and successful missioner. He had always longed for martyrdom, and at the outbreak of persecution he gave himself up to a magistrate in London, saying that he was a priest and a Jesuit.

The charge brought against them at their trial was that of conspiring to murder the king, and the accusations rested entirely on the evidence of three unprincipled men—Oates, Bedloe and Dugdale. A number of reliable witnesses appeared for the defence, but the trial was a travesty of justice : its result was a foregone conclusion. Nevertheless, Father Whitebread conducted the defence with great spirit. He denounced the odious accusations levelled against himself and his fellow Jesuits.

With regard to his accusers, he pointed out that Oates had been ignominiously expelled from St Omer as a man of irregular life and was actuated by malice, whilst Dugdale was equally disreputable. The third witness flatly contradicted himself in court and was palpably guilty of perjury. As an onlooker was heard to remark : " If there had been a jury of Turks the prisoners would have been acquitted." Lord Chief Justice Scroggs, however, was so determined to convict them that he practically dictated to the jury the verdict they were to return. He then sentenced them to death as guilty of high treason. On the scaffold, when the ropes were about their necks, they were offered a free pardon if they would acknowledge the conspiracy and reveal what they knew about it. In reply they thanked the king for his clemency, but disclaimed all knowledge of any such plot. After they had been executed they were allowed to hang until they were dead. Their bodies, which were then cut down and quartered, were delivered to their friends who buried them in the churchyard of St Giles in the Fields.

Among those denounced by Titus Oates as being privy and consenting to the bogus plot to kill King Charles was a barrister of the Inner Temple, BD RICHARD LANGHORNE. He came of good families in Bedfordshire and Hertfordshire, and had been called to the bar in 1654 ; he was reputed a lawyer of some distinction, and an upright and religious man. He was under arrest for a time in 1667 after the Great Fire of London (this having of course been fathered on the long-suffering Catholics) ; and when Oates hatched out his " plot " eleven years later, Mr Langhorne was one of the first to be seized, at his house near Temple Bar or his chambers in Middle Temple Lane, and lodged in Newgate. He was kept in solitary confinement for eight months, and brought to trial at the Old Bailey the day after Bd Thomas Whitebread and his companions.

Mr Langhorne had no difficulty in showing that Oates, Bedloe and the rest were perjuring themselves, but that did not save him from being found guilty and condemned to death. But his execution was put off, in order that he might be persuaded by a promise of pardon to disclose particulars of property held for the Jesuit missionaries and to make a false admission of his own guilt. The first he did, and no doubt had been given authority to do so by his fellow prisoner, Father Whitebread, who was the Jesuit provincial superior ; but the second he would not do. Instead he drew up a statement which he handed to the sheriff for publication. In it he again declared his innocence and his loyalty to the king, and said that it was clear to him that he had been charged and condemned solely because of his religion ; and he prayed that his enemies, naming particularly Mr Oates and Mr Bedloe, might repent and receive God's pardon.

Bd Richard Langhorne was executed at Tyburn on July 14, 1679. On the scaffold he freely forgave his executioner, and his last words were, " Blessed Jesus, into thy hands I recommend my soul and spirit ; now at this instant take me into paradise. I am desirous to be with my Jesus. [To the hangman] I am ready, and you need stay no longer for me."

BD JOHN PLESINGTON (or William Pleasington, alias Scarisbrick) was a secular priest who in the panic of the " plot " was condemned for his priesthood, and executed at Chester. He was born at the Dimples, near Garstang in Lancashire, and did his higher studies at the English College at Valladolid. Little else is known of him, except that he ministered at Holywell in Flintshire. His speech to the people from the scaffold is remarkable as a particularly clear statement and denial in the face of death of the charges upon which he was condemned : charges which even nowadays are sometimes made against the Catholic martyrs of the sixteenth and seventeenth centuries, and some of which, if true, would make them not martyrs but common criminals. It also shows the sort of witnesses which were brought against them. The speech, according to a former custom which only went out with public executions, was printed for circulation ; this often enabled a prisoner to make more public than he had time or permission to say aloud. Bd John Plesington's printed speech has been preserved and may be read in Challoner's *Memoirs of Missionary Priests.* He declared that the course of his trial showed that he was condemned only for his priesthood, and that it was not Catholic belief that " the pope hath power to depose or give licence to murder princes " ; and ended, " God bless the king and the royal family, and grant his Majesty a prosperous reign here, and a crown of glory hereafter. God grant peace to the subjects, and that they live and die in true faith, hope and charity. That which remains is that I recommend myself to the mercy of my Jesus, by whose merits I hope for mercy. O Jesus, be to me a Jesus." Which having said, and recommended his departing soul to God, he was turned off and executed. It was July 19, 1679.

BD THOMAS THWING (or Thweng) was a kinsman of the Venerable Edward Thwing (executed at Lancaster in 1600), who was uncle to George Thwing, of Kilton Castle and Heworth Hall, Thomas's father by his wife Anne Gascoigne ; he was a sister of that stout Catholic, Sir Thomas Gascoigne, of Barnborough Hall. Thomas was born at Heworth, in the North Riding of Yorkshire, in 1635, and was sent to his own county as a priest from Douay when he was twenty-nine years old. At first he was chaplain to his cousins, the Stapletons, at Carlton Hall ; then he conducted a school in the Stapleton dower-house, curiously named " Quosque " ; and finally, in 1677, he became chaplain to the nuns of the Institute of Mary at Dolebank, Thwing, where three of his own sisters belonged to the community.

At the time of the Oates " plot ", two men who had been discharged from the service of Sir Thomas Gascoigne, for dishonesty and " divers villainies ", by name Robert Bolron and Laurence Maybury, sought to get their own back by implicating Sir Thomas in the alleged plot. They therefore laid an information that Barnborough Hall had been used by Gascoigne, Sir Miles Stapleton, the Lady Tempest and others as a meeting-place for forwarding the ends of the plot ; and all the persons named, and Mr Thomas Thwing who was not named, were taken off to London for trial. All those accused were duly acquitted (there was a limit to the credulity of juries, even in that mad time) ; but Mr Thwing was kept in custody and sent back to York to stand his trial there.

In spite of his challenging of the panel, he failed to get an impartial jury, and was found guilty on precisely the same evidence which had led to the acquittal of the others. Out of consideration for his gentle birth he was removed from the company of common criminals to hear his sentence, and he replied to it with three words : " Innocens ego sum ", I am innocent. But for a remonstrance from the House of Commons, King Charles would have reprieved him. And so Thomas Thwing was hanged, drawn and quartered at York on October 23, 1680. He was dragged on a hurdle to the scaffold past the house which sheltered his sisters and the other nuns to whom he had ministered ; and before sentence was carried out he spoke to the assembled people, declaring that he had the honour of being a priest and calling God to witness that he was innocent of the charge made against him. " Though I know the affairs of the kingdom are in a bad posture, yet I hope they will be cleared ere long, and then the actors thereof will be more fully known," he concluded. His relatives recovered his mutilated body, and buried it in St Mary's churchyard, Castlegate, in the city of York. It is appropriate that certain relics of him are preserved at The Bar convent of the Institute of Mary in the same city.

Thomas, Earl of Arundel (collector of the "Arundel Marbles"), son and heir of Bd Philip Howard, conformed to the Established Church in 1615, shortly after the birth of his fifth son. This William, though he was educated by the Bishop of Norwich and at St John's College, Cambridge, was brought up a Catholic. He was made a knight of the Bath, when he was fourteen, at the coronation of Charles I, and in 1637 secretly married Mary Stafford, the Catholic sister of the last Baron Stafford. Three years later Charles transferred the barony to Sir William Howard and immediately after raised him to the rank of viscount. Sir William was a trusty and loyal if not distinguished servant of the king, and he was entrusted both by Charles and the Emperor Ferdinand III with responsible commissions on the continent, where he was able to indulge the taste, inherited from his father, for collecting works of art. After the death of the earl in 1646, Lord Stafford was involved in long and bitter disputes and litigation with his eldest surviving brother, Earl Henry Frederick, and then with his nephews, in which, even when right was on his side, he seems to have conducted himself with sufficient "unhandsomeness" to account for the comment of Evelyn, "Lord Stafford was not a man beloved, especially by his own family". He certainly appears to have been litigious—in 1655 he had lawsuits on hand at Douay, Brussels and Amsterdam; but Dom Maurus Corker, his confessor in the Tower, says that he was "ever held to be of a generous disposition, very charitable, devout, addicted to sobriety, inoffensive in his words, and a lover of justice". At the Restoration his sequestered lands were restored to him, and "he lived in peace, plenty, and happiness, being blessed with a most virtuous lady to his wife, and many pious and dutiful children, in which state he remained till the sixty-sixth year of his age ".*

When Titus Oates "revealed" the details of the "Popish Plot" before the House of Commons, in the army which was to invade England in the interests of the pope Lord Stafford had been cast for the part of paymaster general, and warrants were at once issued against him and four other peers. When he heard it, Stafford, who was out of town, immediately returned to London, to be arrested on October 25 and lodged in the King's Bench prison, from whence he was transferred with others to the Tower. Not until two years later, November 30, 1680, was he brought to trial (a clause had been inserted in the Habeas Corpus Act of the previous year making it not retrospective), and then he was the first of the five lords to be dealt with. The trial occupied a week before the House of Lords assembled in Westminster Hall, Lord Chancellor Finch presiding as lord high steward. A dozen legal "managers of the evidence" produced as witnesses such scoundrels as Dugdale, the Irish ex-Dominican Dennis, the apostate priest Smith, Turberville, and Oates himself, and Stafford was too deaf properly to hear all that was said by these perjurers: he had the benefit of counsel only on points of law. Nevertheless, though, as Sir John Reresby wrote in his memoirs, "he was deemed to be weaker than the other lords in the Tower and was purposely brought on first, he deceived them so far as to plead his cause to a miracle". But it was all to no purpose. Had the Lords acquitted, it would have been open acknowledgement that the plot was a

* Stafford County, in Virginia, testifies to his practical interest in colonization by English Catholics.

sham, and when they gave their votes, " upon their honour ", thirty-one said not guilty and fifty-five guilty. * After a speech full of abuse and calumny of Catholics, the lord high steward sentenced the aged prisoner to be hanged, drawn and quartered.   The king disapproved both of the verdict and the sentence, but the most he could do was to alter the manner of execution to beheading.

The three weeks that elapsed before the execution were mostly passed, wrote Dom Maurus Corker, who was able to see Lord Stafford, " in serious reflection and fervent prayers, wherein he seemed to find a daily increase of courage and of comfort, as if the Divine Goodness intended to ripen him for martyrdom and give him a foretaste of Heaven ".   He wrote his testament, of which the seven drafts are extant, wherein he says : " I hold the murder of one's sovereign a greater sin than anything since the passion of our Saviour ", and expresses in moving terms his cheerful willingness to leave his " most deserving wife and most dutiful children " at the call of God : " Receive, therefore, most dear Jesus, this voluntary oblation ". He wrote brief messages to all his children and on St Stephen's day a most loving letter to his wife, and again to her before he dressed on his last morning, December 29, 1680.   A guinea was being given for seats in a very bad position to see this man die on Tower Hill.   At the scaffold he protested his innocence and gave it as his considered opinion that he was charged because of his religion ; then, having prayed aloud in Latin with his friends around him, he said to the crowd, " God bless you all, gentlemen !   God preserve his Majesty !   He is as good a prince as ever governed you.   Obey him as faithfully as I have done."   And many shouted, " We believe you !   God bless you, my Lord ! "   He took off his wig and replaced it by a blue silk cap, made the sign of the cross, and his head was struck off.   The executioner was a hangman, not used to the axe, and he raised and lowered it twice before delivering the stroke.   His name was Jack Ketch.

It is not known where the body of BD WILLIAM HOWARD lies buried.   The attainder that he had incurred was reversed in 1824 in favour of Sir George William Stafford Jerningham, who then became eighth Baron Stafford.

All the above martyrs were beatified by Pope Pius XI in 1929.   Others who suffered in the Oates plot, and were beatified at the same time with so many others, will be found under the dates July 11, 22, and August 22, 27.   Those noticed above are collected under this date of June 20 as that of the largest group, BB. Thomas Whitebread and his fellows.

For Coleman our information is mainly derived from the printed reports of the trials, from contemporary letters and from the martyr's dying speech.   See Challoner, MMP., pp. 515–518 ; Gillow, *Biog. Dict.*, *s.v.* ; and two articles by Fr J. H. Pollen in *The Tablet*, September 2 and 9, 1922 ; M. V. Hay's book (below) gives some curious glimpses of his political activity.   For Ireland and his companions the sources are *The Tryals of William Ireland* . . . (1678) ; *An Exact Abridgment of all the Trials* . . . *relating to the Popish* . . . *Plots* . . . (1690) ; Keynes's *Florus Anglo-Bavaricus.*   See MMP., pp. 519–525 ; Foley, REPSJ., vol. v ; Gillow, *Biog. Dict.*, *s.v.* ; Oliver's *Collections* and B. Camm's *Nine Martyr Monks* (for Pickering).   A summary of the history of Whitebread and his companions is given in MMP., pp. 525–537 ; see further REPSJ., vol. v ; and Cobbett's *State Trials*, vol. vii.   For Langhorne, Challoner's account in MMP. is taken from the printed trial and dying speech (the statement referred to above) and Baker's *Chronicle ;* see also Gillow, *Biog. Dict.*, *s.v.*   For Plesington, see MMP., pp. 541–543.   The government indictment is printed in the documents of the beatification process, and Plesington is mentioned in the

* The lords spiritual, *i.e.* the bishops, had no part in the trial on account of their office. Out of Stafford's five kinsmen, only one, Lord Mowbray, an apostate and one who had had serious differences with him, voted not guilty.

Valladolid College Register (C.R.S. Publications, vol. xxx, p. 169). For Thwing, see Cobbett's *State Trials*, vol. vii ; MMP., pp. 566–568 ; Dodd's *Church History*, vol. iii ; and in the *Downside Review* for July 1909 there is an article on Quosque Hall. An excellent *Life of Sir William Howard, Lord Stafford*, was published in 1929 by S.N.D. ; it is based largely upon family papers and is illustrated by interesting portraits. See also DNB., vol. xxviii, pp. 81–83 (with a copious bibliography) ; Causton, *The Howard Papers ;* MMP., pp. 569–574 ; and Durrant, *Flemish Mystics and English Martyrs*, pp. 264–265. Sir John Pollock's *The Popish Plot*, which aimed at substantiating belief in the reality of some sort of conspiracy by Catholics, was answered by Alfred Marks, *Who Killed Sir Edmund Berry Godfrey?* (1905) ; and Sir John replied in the *Law Quarterly Review*, October 1906. Sir John's book was reissued in 1944, with a new preface in which he refers to Marks's book and gives further references. On this subject see further J. G. Muddiman in *The Month* for July and October 1921, pp. 31–37 and 327–333. Consult also Arthur Bryant, *The Life of Samuel Pepys*, vol. ii, and M. V. Hay, *The Jesuits and the Popish Plot* (1934). The character of Oates, Bedloe and Dugdale is thoroughly exposed in the separate notices accorded to them in DNB. ; for Oates, see further Jane Lane's *Titus Oates* (1949), and for Bedloe, in M. Petherick's *Restoration Rogues* (1951).

21 : ST ALOYSIUS (A.D. 1591)

THE patron of Catholic youth, St Aloysius, or Luigi Gonzaga, was born on March 9, 1568, in the castle of Castiglione delle Stivieri in Lombardy. He was the eldest son of Ferrante, Marquis of Castiglione, and of Marta Tana Santena, lady of honour to the wife of Philip II of Spain, in whose court the marquis also held a high position. His father's one ambition was that his first-born son should become a great soldier. Accordingly, when he was only four, the child was provided with a set of miniature guns and mortars, and a year later he was taken by Don Ferrante to Casalmaggiore, where some three thousand soldiers were being trained for a Spanish expedition against Tunis. During a stay extending over several months Aloysius delighted to take part in parades, walking at the head of a platoon with a pike over his shoulder : once he contrived, unnoticed and unassisted, to load a field piece which he fired off while the camp was at rest—to the general consternation. Through being left constantly in the company of soldiers, he learnt some of their coarse expletives and innocently repeated them on his return home. But when his tutor reproved him, pointing out that such language was not only vulgar, but definitely blasphemous, Aloysius was overcome with shame and sorrow. Indeed, he never ceased to lament what he regarded as a great sin.

He was about seven when he experienced what may perhaps best be described as a spiritual quickening or sudden development of his religious faculties. He had said his morning and evening prayers from babyhood ; now he began every day to recite the Office of our Lady, the seven penitential psalms, and other devotions, which he said on his knees without a cushion. So complete was his self-surrender to God in his childhood, and so permanent did it prove, that, in the opinion of his director, St Robert Bellarmine, and three of his other confessors, he never in his life committed a mortal sin. In 1577 his father took him and his brother, Ridolfo, to Florence, and left them there under the charge of tutors to improve their Latin and to learn to speak the pure Italian of Tuscany. Whatever may have been his progress in those secular subjects, Aloysius made such rapid strides in the science of the saints that he used to call Florence the mother of piety. Obliged by etiquette to appear frequently at the grand-ducal court, he found himself immersed in what has been aptly described as " a society of fraud, dagger, poison and lust of the most hideous kind ". The only result, as far as he was concerned, was to arouse in him an intense zeal for the virtue of chastity. To safeguard himself and others from possible temptation he subjected himself to a discipline moulded, perhaps, upon that of the fathers in the desert : it was scarcely one likely to occur spontaneously to a boy of nine. We are told, for instance, that he would keep his eyes persistently downcast in the presence of women, and that neither his valet nor anyone else was allowed to see so much as his foot uncovered.

The boys had been living in Florence a little more than two years when their father removed them and placed them at the court of the Duke of Mantua, who had lately made him governor of Montserrat. This was in November 1579, when Aloysius was eleven and eight months. Even then he had it in his mind to resign to his brother his right of succession to the marquisate of Castiglione, although he had already received investiture from the emperor. A painful attack of kidney disease furnished him with an adequate excuse for appearing little in public, and he spent most of his time in prayer and in reading the collection of the Lives of the Saints made by Surius. The malady left him with his digestion so seriously impaired that he ever afterwards had difficulty in assimilating ordinary food. Another book he read about this time, describing the experiences of the Jesuit missionaries in India, seems to have suggested the idea of entering the Society of Jesus in order to labour for the conversion of the heathen. As a first step to a future missionary career he set about instructing the poor boys of Castiglione in the catechism, during the summer holidays. At Casale-Monferrato, where the winter was spent, he haunted the churches of the Capuchins and the Barnabites : he also began to practise the austerities of a monk, fasting three days a week on bread and water, scourging himself with his dog-whip and rising at midnight to pray on the stone floor of a room in which he would suffer no fire to be lighted however bitter the weather.

In 1581 Don Ferrante was summoned to attend the Empress Mary of Austria on her journey from Bohemia to Spain. His family accompanied him, and on their arrival in Spain, Aloysius and Ridolfo were appointed pages to Don Diego, Prince of the Asturias. Although, as in duty bound, Aloysius waited on the young *infante* and shared his studies, yet he never omitted or curtailed his devotions. He had prescribed for himself a daily task of an hour's meditation without distraction, and this frequently entailed several hours of attempted concentration. His abnormal gravity and circumspection led the other courtiers sometimes to say that the young Marquis of Castiglione appeared not to be made of flesh and blood like other people. He was now quite resolved to become a Jesuit. His mother, whom he first approached, approved, but when she communicated their son's decision to his father, Don Ferrante was furious. In his passion he threatened to have Aloysius flogged. Disappointment was mingled with a suspicion that he was being made the victim of a scheme to induce him to give up gambling, at which he had recently been losing large sums of money. However, through the mediation of friends, he so far relented as to give a grudging and provisional consent. The death of the *infante* released the young Gonzagas from their court duties, and after a two-years' stay in Spain they returned to Italy in July, 1584.

Upon their arrival at Castiglione the contest broke out again, and Aloysius found his vocation opposed not only by his father but by most of his relations, including the Duke of Mantua. Eminent churchmen and laymen were sent to argue with him, and promises and threats employed by turns as dissuasives. Don Ferrante insisted on sending him to visit all the rulers of northern Italy, and then engaged him in a number of secular commissions in the hope of awakening some new interest, or at least of putting off the evil hour. But nothing could move Aloysius. After giving his consent and retracting it several times, Don Ferrante finally capitulated when the imperial commission arrived transferring the succession to Ridolfo. Shortly afterwards Aloysius set out for Rome, and, on November 25, 1585, he entered the Jesuit novitiate house of Sant' Andrea. He was then in his eighteenth year. As he took possession of his little cell he exclaimed exultingly, " This is my rest for ever and ever : here will I dwell, for I have chosen it " (Ps. cxxxi 14). Six weeks later Don Ferrante died : from the moment his son had left him to enter the Society of Jesus the marquis had completely reformed his mode of life.

There is little to be said about St Aloysius during the next two years except that he proved in all respects an ideal novice. Being under regular discipline he was obliged to take recreation, to eat more, and to distract his mind. Moreover, because of his weak health, he was forbidden to pray or meditate except at stated times : he obeyed, but it cost him the greatest struggle of his life to resist the impulse which urged him to keep his mind always fixed upon heavenly things. He realized that an aristocrat by birth tends to be a stranger to humility, and he would beg to be allowed to serve in the kitchen, to wash dishes and to perform the most menial duties. He was at Milan when one day, during his morning prayers, he had a revelation that he had not long to live. This filled him with joy and weaned his heart still more from the things of the world. Out of consideration for his precarious health he was recalled from Milan to Rome to complete his theological course in the City. Aloysius by some artifice seems to have secured for himself a small dark room over a staircase, with a window in the roof ; the only furniture it contained was a bed, a chair and a stool for his books. Often now in the schools and in the cloister he appeared to be absorbed in contemplation ; sometimes, too, at table or during recreation he would fall into an ecstasy. The attributes of God were the young saint's favourite subject for meditation, and, as he dwelt upon them, he seemed unable to restrain the joy which thrilled him.

In 1591 an epidemic of plague caused great ravages in Rome. The Jesuits opened a hospital of their own, in which the father general himself and many members of the order rendered personal service. Aloysius, at his own entreaty, was one of the number. He instructed and exhorted the patients, washed them, made their beds, and performed with zeal the lowliest offices of the hospital. Several of the fathers fell victims to the disease and Aloysius caught it. He believed that he was dying, and, with a joy which he afterwards feared might have been impatience, he received viaticum and was anointed. Contrary to all expectation he recovered from the plague, but only to fall into a low fever which in three months reduced him to great weakness. As long as he possibly could, he would rise from his bed at night to worship before his crucifix and would kiss his sacred pictures, going from one to another ; then he would kneel in prayer, propped up between the bed and the wall. Very humbly and anxiously he asked his confessor, St Robert Bellarmine, if he thought that anyone could go straight into the presence of God without passing through Purgatory. St Robert replied in the affirmative and, from his knowledge of Aloysius, encouraged him to hope that this grace might be his. Aloysius immediately fell into an ecstasy which lasted throughout the night, and during which he learnt that he would die on the octave of Corpus Christi. On the succeeding days he recited the *Te Deum* in thanksgiving.

Sometimes he cried out, " I rejoiced when they said to me : We will go into the house of the Lord " (Ps. cxxi 1), adding on one occasion, " We are going— gladly, gladly ! " On the octave-day he seemed so much better that the rector spoke of sending him to Frascati. Aloysius, however, maintained that he would die before the morrow and again received viaticum. To the provincial who came in to inquire after him he said, " We are going, father, we are going ! " " Where? " " To Heaven." " Just listen to that young man," exclaimed the provincial. " He talks of going to Heaven as we talk of going to Frascati ! " In the evening, as he was thought to be in no immediate danger, all but two or three watchers were told to retire to rest. Nevertheless, at the request of Aloysius, Father Bellarmine recited the prayers for the departing. Afterwards the patient lay very still, occasionally murmuring, " Into thy hands." Between ten and eleven a change came over him and it was evident that he was sinking. With his eyes fixed on the crucifix and with the name of Jesus upon his lips he died about midnight, between June 20 and 21, 1591. He had attained the age of twenty-three years and eight months. The relics of St Aloysius now lie under the altar in the Lancellotti chapel of the church of St Ignatius in Rome ; he was canonized in 1726.

It must be confessed that the letters of St Aloysius which have been preserved to us do not make very attractive reading. Owing, perhaps, in part to the conditions of strict censorship under which the correspondence of all young religious was then conducted, and also in part to the detachment from home ties which was inculcated as a point of virtue, the saint's communications, even with his mother, strike us as strangely stiff and formal. But there is a definite pathos about one or two of his last epistles, written practically speaking from his death-bed, if only because they show how deeply the realization of the eternal truths had penetrated and become part of his being.

Materials for the life of the saint are abundant and reliable. The biography by Father Virgilio Cepari, his contemporary and associate, was actually written, so far as the earlier portion is concerned, before the death of Aloysius, although it was only printed—after it had passed under the eyes of a number of trustworthy critics, including St Robert Bellarmine, who had known him and dwelt in the same house with him—as late as 1606. Since then, this work of Cepari has been republished in a multitude of editions and translations. From the point of view of completeness and the inclusion of all relevant evidence, the edition of Cepari's life with copious appendices, prepared by Father Frederick Schroeder in 1891, may still probably be regarded as the most reliable source of information ; an English translation was published in the same year. There are, of course, a number of other lives. For the account printed in the *Acta Sanctorum*, June, vol. v, the Bollandists, besides Cepari, had access to the processes of beatification and canonization. Among other works, those by Meschler, Lambrette and Fournier may be recommended, and for English readers no presentment of the saint's character can rival for its freshness and its very needful study of the atmosphere in which he lived, the book of Father C. C. Martindale, *The Vocation of Aloysius Gonzaga* (1927). See also *S. Louis de Gonzague et la renaissance italienne*, by Frs Delpierre and Noché (1945). The letters and spiritual writings of St Aloysius have been collected by E. Rosa, and these also have been several times translated. F. Crispolti in his *San Luigi Gonzaga, Saggio* (1924), has skilfully vindicated St Aloysius from the contemptuous criticism of Gioberti and others. Also it may be noted that the saint's avoidance of women and even of a *tête-à-tête* with his own mother (albeit Cepari's statement has been misrepresented through inaccurate translations) was an attitude probably assumed by Aloysius in devout imitation of what he had read as recorded of his patron, St Louis of Anjou, by Surius —" nolebat sorores suas nec matrem propriam osculari. Omnino colloquia et aspectus mulierum evitabat." See *The Month*, August, 1924, pp. 158–160.

ST EUSEBIUS, Bishop of Samosata   (*c.* A.D. 379)

Nothing is known of the origin and early history of St Eusebius. He first comes before us in 361, when as bishop of Samosata he attended a synod convened at Antioch to select a successor to Bishop Eudoxus. Partly through his efforts the choice fell upon a former bishop of Sebaste, St Meletius, a man highly esteemed for his piety and gentleness. A great proportion of the electors were Arians, and they fondly believed that if they voted for St Meletius he would—at least tacitly—countenance their doctrines. They were promptly undeceived. In the very first discourse which the new bishop of Antioch delivered in the presence of the Emperor Constantius—himself an Arian—he propounded the Catholic doctrine of the Incarnation as set forth in the Nicene Creed. The infuriated Arians forthwith set about procuring his deposition, and Constantius sent an official to demand from St Eusebius the synodal acts of the election which had been entrusted to his keeping. He replied that he could not surrender them without the authorization of all the signatories. Threatened with the loss of his right hand if he persisted in his refusal, he held out the left one also, saying that he would rather lose them both than be guilty of such a breach of trust. The emperor admired his courage and did not insist.

For some time afterwards St Eusebius continued to take part in the councils and conferences of the Arians and semi-Arians in order to uphold the truth and in hope of promoting unity, but he ceased to do so after the Council of Antioch in 363 because he realized that his action shocked some of the orthodox and did no good. Nine years later, at the urgent request of the elder Gregory of Nazianzus, he went to Cappadocia to exert his influence on behalf of St Basil in the election to the vacant see of Caesarea. So outstanding were his services on that occasion that the younger Gregory, in a letter written about this time, describes him as " the pillar of truth, the light of the world, the instrument of the favours of God towards His people and the support and glory of all the orthodox." Between St Basil and St Eusebius there sprang up a warm friendship that was subsequently maintained through correspondence.

After the outbreak of persecution under Valens, St Eusebius, not satisfied with defending his own flock from heresy, made several expeditions into Syria and Palestine in disguise to strengthen the Catholics in the faith, to ordain priests, and to assist orthodox bishops in filling vacant sees with worthy pastors. His zeal aroused the animosity of the Arian party ; and in 374 Valens issued an order condemning him to banishment in Thrace. When the official charged with enforcing this decree presented himself before Eusebius, the bishop warned him not to make his errand public lest the people should rise up and kill him : the holy man wished no man to lose his life on his behalf. Accordingly, after saying the night office as usual, he quietly left his house when all were at rest and with one servant made his way to the Euphrates and there boarded a vessel. In the morning, when his departure became known, search was made and he was overtaken by some of his flock, who implored him not to abandon them. Though deeply moved he explained that he must needs obey the emperor's orders, but he exhorted them to trust in God. They proved staunchly loyal, and during his exile they refused to have any dealings whatever with the two prelates the Arians thrust into his place.

When the death of Valens in 378 put an end to the persecution, St Eusebius was restored to his seat and to his flock. His zeal had been in no degree impaired by his sufferings. Through his efforts Catholic unity was restored throughout his own diocese, and neighbouring sees were filled by orthodox prelates. He was visiting Dolikha to instal a Catholic bishop there when he was struck on the head by a tile thrown on him from a roof by an Arian woman. The wound proved fatal, and he died several days later, after extracting from his friends a promise that they would not seek out or punish his assailant.

The Bollandists in giving an account of St Eusebius of Samosata do not print any formal biography, but are content in the *Acta Sanctorum*, June, vol. v (under June 22), to reproduce certain chapters from the historian Theodoret. There is, however, a Syriac life which has been printed by Bedjan, *Acta Martyrum et Sanctorum*, vol. vi, pp. 343–349. See also DCB., vol. ii, pp. 369–372, and Bardenhewer, *Geschichte der altkirchlichen Literatur*, vol. iv, p. 388.

ST ALBAN, OR ALBINUS, OF MAINZ, MARTYR (FIFTH CENTURY)

IT is no easy matter to disentangle the legendary and, in many details, conflicting accounts of this St Alban that have come down to us. He is said to have been a Greek, or Albanian, priest, who travelled with St Ursus from the island of Naxos to Milan, in the days when St Ambrose was in the throes of his struggle with the Arians. (There seems to be no basis for a tradition which represents Ursus and Alban as the companions of SS. Theomnestus, Thabra and Thabrata, local martyrs of Altino, near Venice.) The great archbishop received the two strangers with his usual courtesy, and after satisfying himself of their orthodoxy encouraged them to proceed as champions of the faith to the Christian lands beyond the Alps—to Gaul or to Germany. They accordingly set forth, but St Ursus was killed in the Val d'Aosta. Alban then made his way to Mainz. He took up his residence there, and ably seconded Bishop St Aureus in his fight against heresy. Eventually he was attacked and beheaded in the village of Hunum, either by some of his Arian opponents, or more probably by the Vandals in one of their raids. The date of his death cannot be determined, but it was certainly before the year 451, when Mainz was destroyed by the barbarians. Catholics regarded him as a martyr for the faith, and churches were soon put under his dedication.

We are told that a ninth-century metrical inscription round an ancient painting of the saint at Mainz stated that he had come " from distant shores " to Mainz in the reign of the Emperor Honorius, during the episcopate of St Aureus, that he had battled courageously against heretics, and that he had been beheaded by them. The inscription went on to say that, after his execution, he had miraculously carried his head in both hands to his resting-place. With regard to this last assertion, it may be pointed out that decapitated martyrs are sometimes conventionally represented in art as holding their heads in their hands. The inscription is interesting, as reflecting the tradition current in Mainz some four hundred years after the saint's death. When Mainz was rebuilt in the latter part of the fifth century the relics of St Alban were removed from outside the old city walls to a hill which had previously borne the names of Mons Martis and Mons Martyrum, but which was afterwards called Albansberg. There a Benedictine abbey was erected towards the end of the eighth century which became very famous.

Whether we can suppose there to be any historical foundation for this improbable story must remain very doubtful. In the *Acta Sanctorum*, June, vol. v, will be found the *passio* compiled by Gozwin in the eleventh century, and another *passio*, in which Theomnestus figures most prominently, will be found in the *Acta Sanctorum*, October, vol. xiii. See also the *Mainzer Zeitschrift*, 1908, pp. 69 *seq.*, and 1909, pp. 34 *seq.* ; and T. D. Hardy, *Materials for British History* (Rolls Series), vol. i, pp. 31–32.

ST MÉEN, OR MEWAN, ABBOT (SIXTH CENTURY ?)

THE holy abbot known as Méen, Main and Mewan (Mevennus) was formerly famous throughout France as the healer of the various skin diseases so prevalent in the middle ages and indeed until comparatively recent times. One particular form of cutaneous trouble was popularly known as St Méen's Evil. The cures were generally attributed to the water of wells and springs dedicated in honour of the saint, but more especially to the fountain which he is said to have caused to flow in the vicinity of his monastery at Gaël in Brittany. Numberless pilgrims—sometimes as many as 5000 in one year—have come from all parts of France to venerate the relics of the saint and to resort to his fountain. In Upper Brittany one variety of scabious is commonly called *l'herbe de St Main* to this day. The reputed history of St Mewan is largely a late compilation of legend and tradition from which, however, a conjectural outline of his life can be formed with the help of place-names. He was born in Gwent in South Wales and was related to St Samson, whose monastery he entered and whom he accompanied, or followed, in the first instance perhaps to Cornwall, afterwards to Brittany. There he established at Gaël a monastery on land given him in that forest of Brocéliande which figures so largely in the Arthurian romances, and it became a great mission centre. Another foundation afterwards developed into the great abbey of Saint-Méen.

Amongst his friends and disciples was his godson, St Austol, who was tenderly attached to him and whom he consoled when he was dying with the assurance that they would only be separated for a week. The relics of the saint, or part of them, are still venerated at Saint-Méen. A great number of places in Brittany, and some in Normandy, bear his name ; a few are to be found in other parts of France. In Cornwall, St Mewan and St Austell are the eponyms of two large adjoining parishes, and possibly his memory is perpetuated in the name of the village of Mevagissey.

There is an account of St Mevennus in the *Acta Sanctorum*, vol. v, based mainly upon the French of Albert Le Grand ; and the Latin text of a late medieval biography is printed in the *Analecta Bollandiana*, vol. iii.(1884), pp. 141–158. See also F. Duine, *Mémento des Sources* etc. (1918), pp. 98–99 ; and Canon Doble, *St Mewan and St Austol.*

ST ENGELMUND (*c.* A.D. 720)

PERHAPS the most successful of all the missionaries who came to the Netherlands in the days of St Willibrord to assist him in his evangelistic work was St Engelmund. An Englishman by birth and education, he had received the monastic habit at a very early age, had been raised to the priesthood, and had acquired a great reputation for sanctity and learning. He was ruling his community as abbot when he was moved to offer himself for missionary work in North Holland or in Friesland, from whence his family had originally migrated to England. His offer was accepted, and for the remainder of his life he laboured there, making his head-quarters at Velsen, north of the present city of Haarlem. Helped, it may be, by familiarity with their speech and customs, he converted and civilized a considerable proportion of the inhabitants, who honoured him as a saint and a wonder-worker. He was eventually stricken down by fever and died a holy death, after giving his blessing to his people. He was buried at Velsen, but at a later date Balderic, bishop of Utrecht, caused his remains to be translated to his cathedral, where they remained until they were desecrated by the Gueux. Pious hands rescued what they could from the pavement upon which they lay scattered, and they are now preserved at Haarlem.

There is a short notice in the *Acta Sanctorum*, June, vol. v, but information is very scanty and is mainly derived from a set of breviary lessons formerly used in the diocese of Haarlem.

ST LEUTFRIDUS, OR LEUFROY, ABBOT   (A.D. 738)

IN the period preceding the conquest of Normandy by the Northmen, the diocese of Évreux, so it was believed, produced quite a little galaxy of saints of whom not the least eminent was St Leutfridus. For the main outlines of his career we have to rely upon a biography compiled by a monk of his community from manuscripts and tradition a considerable time after his death. He came of a Christian family and was born not far from Évreux. His studies were made with the sacristan of St Taurinus's church at Évreux, then at Condat, and finally at Chartres, where he distinguished himself so much as to excite the envy of his fellow pupils. Upon his return home he devoted himself especially to the instruction of boys, but soon decided to abandon the world in order to embark on a life of self-abnegation. Slipping away secretly one night and changing his clothes with a beggar, he made his way to the monastery of Cailly, where for a while he lived under the direction of a hermit. He then moved on to Rouen to submit himself to the guidance of the Irishman, St Sidonius (Saens), from whom he received the religious habit. St Ansbert, archbishop of Rouen, conceived a great regard for him.

After a time Leutfridus went back to his own land. He settled at a place two miles from Évreux, upon the river Eure, where the predecessor of St Ansbert, St Ouen, had set up a cross in consequence of a heavenly vision. Here, about the year 690, St Leutfridus built a monastery and a church which he dedicated in honour of the Holy Cross. The monastery, which was called at first La Croix-S.-Ouen, was afterwards renamed La Croix-S.-Leufroy. Many disciples gathered round the founder, who ruled as abbot for about forty-eight years. So greatly did he value poverty that, as in the story recounted by St Gregory the Great, he once refused Christian burial to a monk who had died with money in his possession. St Leutfridus died in 738.

The life of St Leutfridus, printed in the *Acta Sanctorum*, June, vol. v, was not written until a century or more after the death of the saint and deserves little confidence. A critical text has been edited by W. Levison in MGH., *Scriptores Merov.*, vol. vii, pp. 1–18. A modern account was published by J. B. Mesnel in 1918 upon which see the *Analecta Bollandiana*, vol. xli (1923), pp. 445–446.

ST RALPH, OR RAOUL, ARCHBISHOP OF BOURGES   (A.D. 866)

ST RALPH, whose name appears also as Rodulphus, Radulf and Raoul, was the son of Count Raoul of Cahors, and in his boyhood was entrusted to the care of Bertrand, abbot of Solignac, from whom he seems to have derived a great love for the monastic order, although it is doubtful if he himself ever received the habit. Whether as a religious or not, he certainly held several abbacies, probably including that of Saint-Médard, Soissons, upon which his parents had bestowed donations and privileges. In 840 he was raised to the see of Bourges, and from that time he took a prominent part in ecclesiastical affairs within his diocese and outside. He was regarded as one of the most learned ecclesiastics of his day, and his presence was in great demand at synods. At one of these, that of Meaux in 845, steps were taken to safeguard the incomes of hospices, notably the Scottish (*i.e.* Irish) ones, those who interfered with them being stigmatized as " murderers of the poor ".

All his own means St Ralph expended in making religious foundations for men and women. Chief amongst them were the abbeys of Dèvres in Berri, of Beaulieu-sur-Mémoire and Végennes in the Limousin, and of Sarrazac in Quercy. He died on June 21, 866, and was buried in the church of St Ursinus at Bourges.

Not the least of his services to the Church was a book of Pastoral Instruction which he compiled for his clergy, basing it mainly on the capitularies of Theodulf, bishop of Orleans. His main object was to revive the spirit of the ancient canons and to correct abuses. Precise directions with regard to the tribunal of penance were essential to remedy the errors caused by ignorance and by unauthorized penitentials wrongly attributed to famous saints and teachers. Very wisely, before making these instructions public, St Ralph submitted them to his clergy for their consideration. The book after a time was forgotten and was not rediscovered till the beginning of the seventeenth century. It shows the compiler to have been well versed in the writings of the fathers and in the decrees of the councils.

There seems to have been no formal life of St Ralph written in medieval times. In the *Acta Sanctorum*, June, vol. v, an account has been compiled from various fragmentary sources, including some breviary lessons. See also *Histoire littéraire de la France*, vol. v, pp. 321–324 ; Chavanet, *St Rodolfe, archevêque de Bourges* (1905), and especially A. Gandilhon, *Catalogue des actes des archevêques de Bourges* (1927), pp. 7–13 ; and Duchesne, *Fastes Épiscopaux*, vol. ii, pp. 20 and 122. On the number and importance of the settlements of the Scottish referred to above, see Berlière in *Revue Bénédictine*, vol. xix (1902), pp. 68–70.

BD JOHN RIGBY, Martyr (A.D. 1600)

ALTHOUGH he was the son of a Lancashire gentleman of ancient lineage, the straitened means of his family compelled John Rigby to enter domestic service. As a convinced Catholic living in a Protestant household, he found himself placed in a dilemma by the penal laws and occasionally he so far outwardly conformed as to attend the established church. It was a weakness which he afterwards deeply regretted. He made his confession to a priest imprisoned in the Clink prison, and from that time led an irreproachable life. Moreover, he was the means of winning back several lapsed Catholics, one of whom was his own father. Whilst he was an inmate of the household of Sir Edmund Huddlestone, he was sent to the sessions-house of the Old Bailey to plead illness as the cause of the non-appearance in court of Sir Edmund's daughter, Mrs Fortescue, against whom a summons had been issued on a charge of recusancy. There had been no accusation against Rigby, but one of the commissioners began to question him as to his own religion. He frankly acknowledged that he was a Catholic and that he would not go to church or acknowledge the queen's supremacy. He was summarily committed to Newgate prison.

An interesting account which he wrote of his trials and prison experiences was preserved by a friend. It is clear that some of the judges—notably Mr Justice Gaudy—were very favourably impressed by his bearing and sincerity and would have liked to release him. He was told, in so many words, that if he would go to church the case could be dropped, but he replied : " If that be all the offence I have committed, as I know it is, and if there be no other way but going to church to help it, I would not wish your Lordship to think I have (as I hope) risen this many steps towards Heaven and now will wilfully let my foot slip and fall into the bottomless pit of Hell.   I hope in Jesus He will strengthen me rather to suffer a thousand deaths, if I had so many lives to lose.   Let your law take its course."   Only after much discussion amongst themselves did the judges decide to condemn him.   Mr Justice Gaudy, in pronouncing the death sentence, was deeply affected, but Rigby himself heard it with the utmost composure.   On June 21, when he was told he was to die that day, he said gaily : " *Deo gratias !*   It is the best tidings that ever were brought to me since I was born."   Even as he was being dragged on a hurdle to St Thomas's Watering, the place of execution, he was urged by the Earl of Rutland and Captain Whitlock " to do as the queen would have him and conform ". On the scaffold he gave the executioner a gold piece, saying, " Take this in token that I freely forgive thee and all others that have been accessory to my death."   His execution was carried out with great barbarity, for he was cut down and disembowelled while still quite conscious.   His last words were, " God forgive you : Jesus receive my soul ".   Bd John was about thirty years of age when he suffered.

We possess a particularly interesting and detailed narrative of the circumstances of Bd John Rigby's arrest and martyrdom.   The account which, as mentioned above, he himself wrote of his experiences, came into the hands of Dr Thomas Worthington, the president of Douay College, and by him it was printed abroad in 1601 in a little book entitled, *A Relation of Sixtene Martyrs glorified in England in twelve months*.   Rigby's text, with introductory matter and notes, was admirably edited by Father C. A. Newdigate in a booklet which he called *A Lancashire Man ; the Martyrdom of John Rigby at Southwark* (1928).   See also Challoner, MMP., pp. 238–245.

22 : ST ALBAN, Martyr   (Date Unknown)

S T ALBAN is venerated as the proto- or first martyr of the Island of Britain, and his feast is kept throughout England and Wales on this day (but in the diocese of Brentwood to-morrow).   His story, or legend, as it is set forth in Bede's *Ecclesiastical History*, may be epitomized as follows : Alban was a native, and apparently a prominent citizen of Verulamium, now St Albans in Hertford-shire.   Although he was a pagan, yet, when the persecution broke out under Diocletian and Maximian, he gave shelter to a Christian priest who had sought refuge with him.   So profoundly impressed was he by his guest that he became a convert to Christianity and received baptism.   In the meantime the governor had been informed that the preacher of the Christian religion after whom inquiry had been made lay concealed at Alban's house.   Soldiers were accordingly sent to make search, but the priest was no longer there.   To facilitate his escape Alban had exchanged clothes with him, and it was Alban, wrapped in his guest's long cloak, or *caracalla*, that the soldiers conveyed bound to the judge, who was then standing beside an altar, engaged in offering sacrifice to the gods.

When the cloak which covered the prisoner's head was removed and his identity was established the magistrate was very angry.   Ordering the confessor to be dragged before the images he said, " Since you have chosen to conceal a sacrilegious person and a blasphemer whom you ought to have handed over to the guard whom

I despatched, the punishment due to him shall be meted out to you unless you comply with the worship of our religion." The saint boldly declared that he would do so no more. Asked by the judge to what family he belonged, Alban exclaimed, " Why do you want to know about my family ? If you wish to know my religion —I am a Christian." He was then asked his name. " I am called Alban by my parents ", he replied, " and I worship and serve the living and true God who created all things." The magistrate impatiently urged him to waste no more time, but to offer sacrifice forthwith. Alban retorted, " Your sacrifices are offered to demons who can neither give help nor grant petitions : whoever offers sacrifices to these idols shall receive as his recompense the eternal punishments of Hell."

The judge, still further incensed at these defiant words, caused the prisoner to be scourged : then, seeing that he bore the lashes not merely with resignation but with joy, he sentenced him to be beheaded. The whole population went forth to witness the execution, the judge remaining alone in the city. Now the river which they had to cross was in that part rapid, and if Alban had waited to follow in the wake of the crowds who were thronging the bridge he could scarcely have passed over that evening. So, going down to the water's edge, he upraised his eyes to Heaven and immediately the stream was miraculously divided, the river bed drying up so as to afford an easy passage not only to the martyr, but to a thousand other persons. This marvel brought about the instant conversion of the executioner, who threw down his sword at St Alban's feet and begged to be allowed to die with him or instead of him. The procession then made its way up a pleasant grassy slope, gay with flowers. At the summit, in response to the martyr's prayers, there gushed up beside him a fountain of clear water with which he was able to quench his thirst.* Another executioner carried out the sentence, but, as St Alban's head rolled from the block, the headsman's eyes fell out and lay beside it on the ground. As for the soldier who had been so recently converted, he also was beheaded, thus receiving the baptism of blood.

It is impossible to decide how much truth underlies this story : there is considerable difference of opinion on the subject. Mainly on the ground that the decrees of Diocletian against the Christians were not enforced in Britain, some scholars have been disposed to conclude that no such person as St Alban ever existed. On the other hand, he may well have been the victim of some local persecution ; and the prevalence of an early and widespread *cultus* creates a strong presumption—in the view of many, convincing evidence—of his real existence and of his fate. The earliest known reference to St Alban is by Constantius of Lyons who, in his life of St Germanus of Auxerre, written in the fifth century, states that when on a visit to Britain Germanus visited the tomb of St Alban (he does not say where), and declares that " the intercession of the blessed martyr St Alban procured a smooth passage " for him and his companions on their return to Gaul.

Gildas and Bede relied for their accounts on a *passio Albani* of the earlier part of the sixth century. How popular the story was may be inferred from the number of variants catalogued in Hardy's *Materials for British History* (vol. i, pp. 3–30). It was considerably developed after the translation of the martyr's relics to a new

* This description of the place of martyrdom on Holmhurst Hill is perhaps part of the early tradition. Except that the river Ver is neither deep nor rapid the topographical particulars fit correctly. There was a spring of water (now covered in) near the *foot* of Holmhurst (*cf. Holywell* Hill to-day).

shrine in 1129. A *passio* of St Amphibalus was then composed, a purely fictitious martyr, at least as regards the name, which is derived from Geoffrey of Monmouth's misinterpretation of the word *amphibalus*, which means a cloak. Amphibalus was represented to have been the preacher originally sought for, and to have been afterwards caught and stoned to death at Redbourn, four miles from St Albans. At the same time his " relics " were very conveniently discovered in a heathen Saxon burying-ground at the same place.

We know from Constantius that there was a church and tomb of St Alban in 429 ; Gildas, writing *c.* 540, connects Alban with Verulamium ; and there was a newer church and shrine there in Bede's time (731). The tradition is that Offa of Mercia in 793 built a new church and founded a monastery, which developed into the great Benedictine abbey of St Alban, and the tradition may well be right.

In recent years the Rev. A. W. Wade-Evans has sought to localize the martyrdom of St Alban in the neighbourhood of Caerleon in Monmouthshire, with St Julius and St Aaron (July 3). This hypothesis has received more attention on the continent than in England, and Father P. Grosjean, Bollandist, considers that the passion of these three martyrs at Caerleon " is not without some appearance of probability " (*Analecta Bollandiana*, vol. lvii (1939), pp. 160–161). But Wilhelm Levison firmly rejects the theory : the martyrdom of St Alban, he says, " can be ascribed without hesitation to Verulamium and St Albans, as far as certainty or probability is at all applicable in such traditions ".

The whole subject is fully dealt with by W. Levison, " St Alban and Saint Albans ", in *Antiquity*, vol. xv (1941), pp. 337–359. Bede's account is in the *Ecclesiastical History*, bk. 1, cap. vii (see also caps. xviii and xx, and Plummer's notes) ; Gildas in *De excidio Britanniae*, cap. x, says he *conjectures* that Alban was put to death under Diocletian. For A. W. Wade-Evans's theory, see his *Welsh Christian Origins* (1934), pp. 16–19, and his translation of Nennius (1938), pp. 131–132. St Alban's fame was not confined to Britain, for Venantius Fortunatus, towards the close of the sixth century, commemorates him in the line, *Albanum egregium fecunda Britannia profert* (" Fruitful Britain vaunts great Alban's name "), and a mention of him is found in the *Hieronymianum ;* on which see Delehaye's Commentary. Although certain details occurring in Constantius's Life of St Germanus in its later interpolated form do not belong to the original, as Levison (MGH., *Scriptores Merov.*, vol. vii) has shown, still there is every reason to believe that Germanus did bring back with him to Auxerre relics of this martyr, and built a basilica there in his honour, as Heiricus, the author of the metrical Life of St Germanus, records. See also W. Meyer in the *Abhandlungen* of the Göttingen Scientific Society, vol. viii (1904), no. 1, for the *Passio Albani ;* E. P. Baker, " The Cult of St Alban at Cologne ", in the *Archaeological Journal*, vol. xciv (1938), pp. 207–256 ; M. R. James *et al.*, *Illustrations to the Life of St Alban* (1924) ; and H. Delehaye, *Les Passions des martyrs* (1921), pp. 403–407.

ST NICETAS, BISHOP OF REMESIANA   (*c.* A.D. 414)

THE Roman Martyrology under January 7 has an entry : " In Dacia of St Nicetas, Bishop, who by his preaching made nations mild and gentle that before were barbarous and savage." This undoubtedly describes Nicetas of Remesiana, though Baronius, owing to his erroneous identification of this Nicetas with Nicetas, or Niceas, of Aquileia, transferred the commemoration, when he revised the martyrology, from June 22 to January 7. Nicetas of Remesiana was a close friend of St Paulinus of Nola, and it is principally from him that we learn of Nicetas's marvellous success in taming the wild peoples among whom he resided. The Bessi, in particular, were a race of marauders, as Strabo testifies, but Paulinus congratulates his friend in a poem on having brought them like sheep within Christ's peaceful fold :

> Nam simul terris animisque duri
> Et sua Bessi nive duriores,
> Nunc oves facti, duce te gregantur
> Pacis in aulam.

Remesiana has been identified with a place called Bela Palenka, in Serbia. We know little of Nicetas himself beyond the fact that on at least two occasions he made his way from a country which Paulinus regarded as a wild region of snow and ice to visit his friend at Nola in Campania. St Jerome also speaks very appreciatively of his work in converting the people of Dacia, but of the details of his missionary expeditions, the manner of his promotion to the episcopate, or the date of his death, we know nothing.

On the other hand much interest has centred in Nicetas on account of his writings, some of which, previously attributed to Nicetas of Aquileia or others, have now on fuller investigation been restored to their true author. Dom Germain Morin has been prominent in drawing attention to the importance of his literary work and in particular has gone far to prove that it is to Nicetas, and not to St Ambrose, that we owe the composition of the great hymn of thanksgiving, the *Te Deum*. This view has not found universal acceptance, but it has many adherents among competent scholars.

The Bollandists have twice given some account of Nicetas, so far as information was then available, *viz.* in the *Acta Sanctorum*, January, vol. i, and June, vol. v. But a newer and fuller investigation will be found in A. G. Burn's volume, *Niceta of Remesiana, His Life and Works* (1905), which re-edits the text of his remains. Further, Dr Burn has published a booklet, *The Hymn " Te Deum " and Its Authors* (1926). Dom Morin's articles have appeared principally in the *Revue Bénédictine*, vol. vii (1890), pp. 151 *seq.* ; vol. xi (1894), p. 49, and vol. xv (1898), p. 99. See, further, W. A. Patin, *Niceta Bischof von Remesiana als Schriftsteller und Theolog* (1909), and consult DTC., vol. xi, cc. 477-479. Two of Nicetas's more important dissertations have also been edited and made more intelligible by the care of Professor C. H. Turner : the texts have been rearranged and annotated by him in the *Journal of Theological Studies*, vol. xxii (1921), pp. 305-320 ; and vol. xxiv (1923), pp. 225-252. A volume of translations of Nicetas's writings by Fr G. G. Walsh was published in New York in 1950.

ST PAULINUS, BISHOP OF NOLA (A.D. 431)

ST PAULINUS, more formally designated Pontius Meropius Anicius Paulinus, was one of the most remarkable men of his age, and we find him eulogized in terms of warm appreciation by St Martin, St Sulpicius Severus, St Ambrose, St Augustine, St Jerome, St Eucherius, St Gregory of Tours, Apollinaris, Cassiodorus and other writers. His father, who was prefect of Gaul, had lands in Italy, Aquitaine and Spain, and Paulinus was born at or near Bordeaux. He had for his master in poetry and rhetoric the famous poet Ausonius. Trained under such a teacher, Paulinus more than fulfilled the high hopes that had been entertained of him, and while still quite young made a name for himself at the bar. " Everyone ", says St Jerome, " admired the purity and elegance of his diction, the delicacy and loftiness of his sentiments, the strength and sweetness of his style and the vividness of his imagination." He was entrusted with various public offices, the exact nature of which we do not know, but there is some ground for surmising that he held an appointment in Campania and had also been prefect of New Epirus. His duties, whatever they were, required or permitted him to travel extensively, and during the course of his public life he made many friends in Italy, Gaul and Spain. He married a Spanish lady called Therasia, and after some years he resigned his offices and retired to lead a life of cultured leisure in Aquitaine. He now came into relations with St Delphinus, bishop of Bordeaux, through whose ministrations Paulinus and his brother were brought to receive baptism. Then, about the year 390, he went with his wife to live on her estate in Spain where, after years of childlessness, a son was born to them ; but the boy died at the end of a week. They now determined to live more austerely and charitably, and proceeded to dispossess themselves of much property for the benefit of the needy. This liberality had a result which appears to have come upon them as a surprise. On Christmas day, about 393, in response to a sudden outcry on the part of the people, the bishop of Barcelona in his cathedral conferred upon Paulinus the orders of a priest, although he had not previously been a deacon.*

If the citizens had hoped thereby to retain Paulinus amongst them, they were disappointed. He had already decided to settle at Nola, a small town near Naples, where he had property. As soon as his intentions became known and he attempted to deal with his possessions in Aquitaine, as he had done with those of Therasia in Spain, he found he had to encounter the remonstrances of his friends and the opposition of his relatives. However, he did not allow himself to be deterred, and successfully carried his purpose into effect. He proceeded to Italy, where St Ambrose and other friends gave him a warm welcome. In Rome, on the other hand, he met with a chilly reception from Pope St Siricius and his clergy, who possibly resented the uncanonical nature of his ordination. His stay in the City was accordingly a short one, and he passed on to Nola with his wife. There he took up his residence in a long, two-storied building outside the walls, close to the tomb of St Felix. Although he had parted with so much he was still possessed of considerable means—presumably his Italian property.

This he gradually disposed of to further religious and philanthropic schemes. Thus he built a church for Fondi, gave Nola a much-needed aqueduct, and supported a host of poor debtors, tramps and other necessitous persons, many of whom he lodged in the lower part of his own house. He himself, with a few friends, occupied the upper story, living under semi-monastic rule and reciting the daily office in common ; Therasia presumably was the housekeeper for this establishment. Adjacent was a building with a garden which served as a guest-house for visitors. Amongst those who enjoyed his hospitality may be mentioned St Melania the Elder and the missionary bishop St Nicetas of Remesiana, who stayed with him on two occasions. Very striking is the account preserved in the Life of the younger Melania, which describes the coming to Nola of herself and her husband with other devoted Christians. When St Paulinus went to settle at Nola, there were already three little basilicas and a chapel grouped about the tomb of the former presbyter there, St Felix ; to these he added another, which he caused to be adorned with mosaics of which he has left a description in verse. Three of these churches shared a common outside entrance, and they were probably connected in

---

* It should not be supposed that this conferring of sacred orders in deference to popular clamour is altogether without a parallel. Apart from the well-known case of the raising of St Ambrose to the episcopate, we have a very similar incident occurring to the husband of St Melania the Younger (December 31). Melania and Pinian were not only the contemporaries, but the personal friends of St Paulinus, and like him they had divested themselves of large sums of money to give away in charity.

much the same way as the seven old basilicas which constitute San Stefano in Bologna. Every year for the festival of St Felix, Paulinus rendered him what he described as a tribute of his voluntary service, in the shape of a birthday poem in his honour. Fourteen or fifteen of these poems are still extant.

Upon the death of the bishop of Nola, about the year 409, St Paulinus was chosen as obviously the right person to fill his place. He occupied the episcopal chair until his death. Beyond the fact that he ruled with wisdom and liberality, we have no reliable information about his career as a shepherd of souls. Once a year he went to Rome for the feast of St Peter and St Paul : otherwise he never left Nola. But he was a great letter-writer and kept in touch by correspondence with the leading churchmen of his day—notably with St Jerome and St Augustine, whom he consulted on many subjects, often on the meaning of obscure passages of the Bible. It was in response to a query of his that St Augustine wrote his book *On the Care of the Dead*, in which he emphasizes that pompous funerals and similar honours are only comforts to surviving friends, and of no use to the dead.

St Paulinus survived until the year 431, and the closing scenes of his life are described in the letter of an eye-witness named Uranius. Three days before his death he was visited by two bishops, Symmachus and Acyndinus, with whom at his bedside he celebrated the Divine Mysteries. Then the priest Postumian came to tell him that forty pieces of silver were owing for clothes for the poor. The dying saint replied with a smile that someone would pay the debt of the poor ; and almost immediately afterwards there arrived a messenger bearing a gift of fifty silver pieces. On the last day, at the hour for Vespers, when the lamps were being lighted in the church, the bishop roused himself from a prolonged silence, and, stretching out his hand, said in a low voice, " I have prepared a lamp for my Christ." Some hours later the watchers felt a sudden tremor, as of a slight earthquake, and at that moment St Paulinus yielded up his soul to God. He was buried in the church he had built in honour of St Felix ; and his relics having been translated to Rome, they were restored to Nola by order of St Pius X in 1909.

Of the writings of St Paulinus, which seem to have been numerous, only thirty-two poems, fifty-one letters, and a few short fragments have come down to us. But he is esteemed the best Christian poet of his time after Prudentius, and his epithalamium for Julian, bishop of Eclanum and Ia, is one of the earliest Christian wedding poems that has survived.

There is no proper life of St Paulinus of early date, but we have a letter of Uranius describing his death and a short notice by St Gregory of Tours. But in Paulinus's own correspondence and in the references of contemporaries we have a good deal of biographical material which has been used in the *Acta Sanctorum*, June, vol. v. Another source which has only become available in comparatively recent times is the Life of Melania the Younger, preserved both in a Greek and a Latin text, which may be best consulted in the edition of Cardinal Rampolla, *Santa Melania Giuniore* (1905). There are modern biographies by A. Buse, F. Lagrange and A. Baudrillart, and a good article in DCB., vol. iv, pp. 234–245, as well as in DTC., vol. xii, cc. 68–71. See, further, G. Boissier, *La Fin du Paganisme*, vol. ii, pp. 49–103 ; F. de Labriolle, *La Correspondance d'Ausone et de Paulin* (1910) ; C. Weyman, *Beiträge zur Geschichte der christ.-latein. Poesie* (1926), pp. 92–103 ; P. Fabre, *S. Paulin et l'amitié chrétienne* (1947) ; and P. de Labriolle, *Histoire de la littérature chrétienne* (1947), p. 877.

ST EBERHARD, ARCHBISHOP OF SALZBURG   (A.D. 1164)

ST EBERHARD was the son of a very religious mother of noble family, and was born at Nuremberg between the years 1085 and 1090. After being educated by the

Benedictines, he received a canonry in Bamberg cathedral, which he soon resigned to enter the local abbey of Mount St Michael. The chapter, however, would not allow him to remain there, and the dean insisted upon sending him to Paris to study for a master's degree. He completed the course with distinction and then returned home with his desire for the religious life as strong as ever. Further opposition being useless, Bishop Otto and the canons consented to his entering the monastery of Prüfening, near Regensburg. There he found a spiritual guide after his own heart in the person of Abbot Erbo, whom his contemporaries modestly described as a second Elias and John the Baptist. From Prüfening Eberhard was called to become the superior of a new abbey which his two brothers and his sister had founded at Biburg, between Ingoldstein and Regensburg.

Under his wise rule the young community increased rapidly in numbers and developed a fervent spiritual life. His virtues and ability were so generally recognized that when in 1146 the see of Salzburg fell vacant, he was chosen to fill the archiepiscopal chair. Eberhard began his episcopate by settling a dispute between the chapter and two abbeys, and in the following years he was constantly acting as mediator between contending parties. But the main object to which he devoted his energies was the moral improvement of his people, clergy as well as laity, and in particular he spared no effort to bring about the abolition of certain abuses which had become widespread in the archdiocese. He was so successful that the Emperor Conrad III, when passing through Salzburg, publicly congratulated him upon the result of his reforming ordinances.

The saint held two synods, at one of which he gave expression to his devotion to the Mother of God by enacting that her greater festivals should be honoured with octaves. In the struggle which took place between Frederick Barbarossa and Pope Alexander III, St Eberhard was one of the very few German dignitaries who refused to recognize the antipope " Victor IV ". Frederick was annoyed at his attitude, but so great was the prestige of the holy archbishop that he made no attempt to coerce him or interfere with him in any way. The last of St Eberhard's recorded acts was to undertake a journey as peacemaker between two quarrelsome noblemen. He accomplished his object, but his strength gave out as he was travelling home, and he died at the Cistercian monastery of Rein. It was in the year 1164.

A life of Eberhard was written about the year 1180. It is more accurately edited in Pertz, MGH., *Scriptores*, vol. xi, pp. 78–84, but it is also in the *Acta Sanctorum*, June, vol. v. St Eberhard was an important figure in the political world of his day, and in consequence he figures prominently in the pages of those who discuss the situation created by the anti-papal campaigns of Frederick Barbarossa. See, for example, Hauck, *Kirchengeschichte Deutschlands*, vol. iv, and J. Engel, *Schisma Barbarossas im Bisthum Freising* (1930). It is worth noticing that there is no foundation for the statement that St Eberhard was the author of the tract, *Oratio de Hildebrandi antichristiano Imperio*. The cause of Eberhard's canonization was urgently pressed by Archbishop Burkhard in 1469, but no formal pronouncement was ever reached.

BD INNOCENT V, POPE (A.D. 1277)

THE first Dominican pope, Innocent V, was baptized Peter, and until his elevation to the papacy was commonly known as Peter of Tarentaise, from the name of his birthplace, Tarentaise-en-Forez (Loire).* When still very young he received the

* He must not be confused with the Cistercian abbot and bishop, St Peter of Tarentaise (May 8).

Dominican habit from Bd Jordan of Saxony ; and he became one of the most eminent theologians of his age.   After he had taken his master's degree, he was given a chair in the University of Paris, although, like his friend and fellow lecturer St Thomas Aquinas, he had not yet entered upon his thirtieth year ; and in 1259 he was associated with St Albertus Magnus, St Thomas and two other members of the order in drawing up a curriculum of study for the schools, which still remains the basis of Dominican teaching.   Besides lecturing orally to his students Peter wrote books : some of them—notably his commentaries on the Pauline Epistles and on the Sentences of Peter Lombard—were as highly esteemed by his contemporaries as the writings of the Angelic Doctor himself.

Scholar though he was, Peter of Tarentaise was endowed with remarkable practical qualities which qualified him to be a ruler of men, and at the age of thirty-seven he was appointed prior provincial for France.   Visitations of the fifty houses under his control entailed much travelling, all of which he did on foot ; and in every priory he strove, generally with success, to maintain the discipline of the rule.   In the meantime requests were so continually being made for his return to Paris (where he had been involved in difficulties) that, when St Thomas was summoned to Rome by the pope, the general chapter sent Peter to replace him in the University of Paris.   In 1272 he was appointed archbishop of Lyons by Pope Gregory X, who had formerly attended his lectures in Paris and who held him in great esteem ; and in the very next year Peter was promoted to the cardinal-bishopric of Ostia, but with the duty of administering Lyons, which city the pope had chosen as the meeting-place for the ecumenical council he was about to summon for the purpose of healing the Greek schism.

From the opening of the first session, in May, 1274, Cardinal Peter took a prominent part in its deliberations.   Twice he preached to the delegates, and it was largely through his clear and scholarly enunciation of Catholic dogma that the Greek envoys were led to give their adhesion and assent.   The council broke up amid general rejoicings at its success (which was very short-lived), marred only by the death of St Bonaventure.   His panegyric was preached by Peter of Tarentaise, who chose as his text the words, " I grieve for thee, my brother Jonathan ", and who spoke of the great Franciscan in such affecting terms that many of those present were moved to tears.   With the appointment of a new archbishop Peter's work at Lyons ended, and he was free to return to Italy with the pope and the other cardinals.   Consequently, he was with Bd Gregory X when he died, shortly after their arrival at Arezzo in January, 1276.

In the election which ensued immediately no candidate seems to have been seriously considered but Peter of Tarentaise, and he was thus unanimously chosen. He took the name of Innocent V.   His short pontificate was chiefly remarkable for his efforts to establish peace among the Italian states which were rent by internal and external dissensions, and to implement the reunion with the Byzantines. He was arranging to send envoys to Constantinople to obtain from the Emperor Michael Palaeologus his confirmation of the pact agreed to at Lyons, but the delegates never left Italy.   With tragic suddenness all the high hopes which centred in the new pope were dashed to the ground.   Though a man of splendid physique and of a constitution so robust that neither austerities nor hard work had ever impaired it, he was struck down by a malignant fever which carried him off in a few days.   He died on June 22, 1277, at the age of fifty-one, after having been pope for only five months.   The *cultus* of Bd Innocent was confirmed in 1898, and his name added to the Roman Martyrology as one who " laboured for concord among Christians ".

A very full account with indication of sources is supplied by Mgr Mann in his *History of the Popes*, vol. xvi, pp. 1–22. See also Mortier, *Histoire des Maîtres Généraux O.P.*, vols. i and ii. There are modern lives by J. P. Mothon (1896), Turinaz (1901), and Bourgeois (1899). But the definitive study is by M. H. Laurent, *Le b. Innocent V et son temps* (1947), in the series " Studi e testi " of the Vatican Library.

23 : ST AGRIPPINA, Virgin and Martyr (A.D. 262 ?)

ST AGRIPPINA is a virgin martyr greatly honoured in Sicily and, to a lesser degree, in Greece. Nothing is known of her true history, her reputed acts in the Greek *Menaia* are quite unreliable and no evidence is forthcoming of any *cultus* of early date. She is believed to have been a maiden of high degree who was beheaded or scourged to death in Rome during the reign of Valerian or in the persecution under Diocletian. Three women, Bassa, Paula and Agathonice, afterwards conveyed her body to Mineo, in Sicily, for burial. Through it many miracles were wrought, including the cure of sick persons and demoniacs. The Greeks claim that the saint's relics were translated from Sicily to Constantinople—presumably to save them from profanation by the infidels. St Agrippina is invoked against evil spirits, leprosy and thunderstorms.

The account in the *Acta Sanctorum*, June, vol. v, furnishes little beyond some extracts from the *Menaia*, with a suspicious narrative in Latin of the translation to Sicily. The *Annus Graeco-slavicus* of Martynov bears testimony to her later *cultus*, and there is a short story of her martyrdom in the Synaxary of Constantinople ; see Delehaye's edition, cc. 704–706. From this we learn that she was honoured on June 23, on which day also she is commemorated in the Roman Martyrology.

ST ETHELDREDA, or AUDREY, Abbess of Ely, Widow (A.D. 679)

To judge from the great number of churches dedicated in her honour in England, St Etheldreda (Aethelthryth), otherwise called Audrey, must have been the most popular of all the Anglo-Saxon women saints. She was the daughter of Anna, king of the East Angles, and the sister of St Sexburga, St Ethelburga and St Withburga. The place of her birth was Exning in Suffolk. In compliance with the wishes of her parents she married one Tonbert, with whom, it is said, she lived in perpetual continence. Three years after her marriage she lost her husband. She seems then to have retired to the island of Ely, which she had received as her marriage gift. There, for five years, she led a secluded life of prayer. But her hand was again sought in marriage, and again she yielded to the representations of her relatives. Her second bridegroom was Egfrid, the younger son of Oswy, king of Northumbria. He was a mere boy at the time and seems to have been quite content that they should live as brother and sister. But with the passage of years, when Egfrid was grown to manhood and had become a powerful monarch, he became dissatisfied, and urged that Etheldreda should become his wife in more than name.

She refused, because she had long since vowed her virginity to God. Both parties appealed to St Wilfrid of York, Egfrid going so far as to offer him presents if he would persuade Etheldreda to fall in with his wishes. St Wilfrid, however, was on her side, and by his advice she withdrew to the convent of Coldingham, where she received the veil from Egfrid's aunt, St Ebba. A year later she retired to Ely ; and there, about the year 672 she founded a double monastery, over which she ruled until her death. Her manner of life was very austere : except on great festivals, or when she was ill, she ate only once a day : and instead of the linen worn by women of high degree she dressed in rough woollen clothing. After Matins, which were sung at midnight, she did not retire like the other nuns, but remained in church in prayer until the morning. Endowed with the gift of prophecy, she not only foretold the pestilence of which she was to die, but also the exact number of her religious who would be carried off by it. Etheldreda herself died on June 23, 679, and in accordance with her own instructions she was buried in a simple wooden coffin. Sixteen years later her body was found to be incorrupt.

The shrine of St Etheldreda became a great centre of devotion on account of the many miracles reported to have been wrought by her relics and by linen cloths which had rested on her coffin. Her remains have long since perished, but the empty shrine is still shown in Ely cathedral. The word *tawdry*, a corruption of St Audrey, was originally applied to the cheap necklaces and other trumpery exposed for sale at St Audrey's great annual fair. Her feast is still observed in several English dioceses.

Most of the references made to St Etheldreda in Bede, and by Thomas of Ely in the *Liber Eliensis*, etc., have been printed in the *Acta Sanctorum*, June, vol. v. There are difficulties about the chronology, for which see C. Plummer's notes to his edition of *Bede*, vol. ii, pp. 234–240. Full accounts are also given in DNB., vol. xviii, pp. 19–21, and in DCB., vol. ii, pp. 220–222.

ST LIETBERTUS, OR LIBERT, BISHOP OF CAMBRAI (A.D. 1076)

ST LIETBERTUS, Libert or Liébert came of a noble Brabantine family and was the nephew of Gerard, bishop of Cambrai, by whom he was educated and under whom he afterwards served as archdeacon, provost, and in other capacities. Upon the death of his uncle in 1051, he was elected his successor by the clergy and people. The nomination having been ratified by the Emperor St Henry, Lietbertus was ordained priest at Châlon and consecrated bishop by his metropolitan at Rheims. He proved a true father to his people, not only labouring with untiring zeal for their spiritual welfare, but also defending them from the extortions and oppression of the castellan of Cambrai.

In 1054 Lietbertus set forth on a pilgrimage to Jerusalem, accompanied by a number of people. They had reached Laodicea when they learnt to their dismay that the Saracens had closed the Holy Sepulchre to Christians and that it was dangerous for them to travel in Palestine. Many of the pilgrims accordingly returned home, but St Lietbertus and others resolved to persevere. Contrary winds, however, drove their ship to Cyprus, and the sailors, who were afraid of falling into the hands of pirates, brought them back to Laodicea. Other difficulties supervening, the pilgrims were compelled to abandon the enterprise without having set eyes on the Holy Land. After his return to Cambrai, St Lietbertus consoled himself by building a monastery and church to which he gave the name of the Holy Sepulchre. To Rodulphus, a monk of that monastery, we owe an almost contemporary history of the founder. The bishop from thenceforth devoted his days to his pastoral duties, and often at night went barefoot to the churches to pray for his people. His virtues won for him the admiration of every man of goodwill, but his strenuous opposition to evil made him some bitter enemies. On one occasion he was seized and carried off to a prison in the Castle of Oisy by the castellan of Cambrai, Hugh, whom he had excommunicated for his outrageous conduct. He was rescued by Arnulf, count of Flanders, and shortly afterwards Hugh was driven out of Cambrai, to the great relief of the citizens. One last service St Lietbertus is said to have rendered at the very close of his twenty years' episcopate. The town was about to be attacked by raiders when the bishop, who was already very ill, caused himself to be carried in a litter into the enemy's camp, and by his impressive appearance and his eloquence—and his threats— succeeded in inducing the invaders to retire without striking a blow. St Lietbertus died on June 23, 1076.

The monk Rodulphus has elaborated a biography of St Libert from the *Gesta episcoporum Cameracensium*, adding fresh materials of his own. The texts are published in the *Acta Sanctorum*, June, vol. v, and in Pertz, MGH., *Scriptores*, vol. vii, pp. 489–497 and 528–538.

BD PETER OF JULLY (A.D. 1136)

ALTHOUGH he was English by birth and by descent, this Peter is always associated with Jully in Champagne, where his last years were spent. A pious lad of good family, he studied theology in his native land until the death of his parents. He then went to France, probably to continue his studies in Paris, or in one of the great provincial schools. There he became intimate with another young Englishman, St Stephen Harding, who shared his spiritual aspirations. They both wished to dedicate themselves to the service of God, and, in order to discover His will concerning them, they made a pilgrimage to Rome together. On the return journey, as they passed through Burgundy, they stayed at the Cistercian abbey of Molesme, at that time in its primitive simplicity and austerity. Stephen was so impressed by what he saw that he decided to remain at Molesme, but Peter proceeded on his way. After a time, however, he returned, and received the habit and at a later date— presumably—holy orders. He led a most edifying life, acquiring great local fame as a preacher and wonder-worker. Not far from the monastery, at Juilly, or Jully-les-Nonnains, there was a convent which was subject to Molesme, which had as its prioress St Bernard's sister, Bd Humbelina. When their chaplain died the nuns asked if they might have Peter in his place, and the abbot consented. Under his spiritual direction and Humbelina's care the community made rapid progress in the path of perfection. Bd Peter supported Humbelina during her last illness and was beside her when she died. He did not long survive her.

In the *Acta Sanctorum*, June, vol. v, the Bollandists have published the Latin biography of Bd Peter, which seems to have been written about a century after his death.

BD LANFRANC, BISHOP OF PAVIA (A.D. 1194)

LANFRANC was a member of the Beccaria family and a native of Grupello, a village near Pavia, in Lombardy. Although by nature a man of peace, yet during the greater part of his fifteen years' episcopate he was actively engaged in resisting the attempts of the civil authorities to lay hands on the property of the Church.   On one occasion, in the thick of the fray, he disappeared temporarily into the Vallombrosan monastery of San Sepolcro, there to seek strength and guidance ; and his return was followed by a cessation of hostilities.   The peace did not last long, for the city fathers soon put forward the demand that a large proportion of ecclesiastical revenues should be ceded to them for the strengthening of the fortifications of Pavia, and the bishop absolutely refused.   As they proved unable to overcome his resistance, they declared it to be a penal offence for anyone to bake his bread or to supply him with food.   Thus faced with starvation he left the city and made his way to Rome, where he laid his case before Pope Clement III, who threatened the rulers of Pavia with his censure, but advised the bishop to return to his diocese. This Bd Lanfranc was the more ready to do because a man of approved piety, Saracen Salimbene, had recently become chief magistrate, and for a time ruler of the city.   The bishop re-entered Pavia amid general acclamations, and all was peace and amity.   When, however, the old claims were revived Lanfranc felt himself unable to resume the struggle.   He decided to resign and enter the Vallombrosan Order, but before he could carry out his intentions he fell ill and died.. His feast is kept at Pavia, where Lanfranc of Canterbury also was born.

His life was written by Bernard Balbi, his successor in the see of Pavia, who was a famous canonist.   See the *Acta Sanctorum*, June, vol. v, where the life is printed in full.

BD MARY OF OIGNIES, Virgin   (A.D. 1213)

The life of Mary of Oignies was written by Cardinal James de Vitry, who had been her friend, her disciple, and probably at one time her confessor.   It was through her influence that he had been led to take holy orders ; but, when expatiating upon her virtues, he warns his readers that her example is not one to be recommended for general imitation.

She was born of wealthy parents at Nivelles in Brabant, and, though all her aspirations were directed towards the religious life, her parents as soon as she was fourteen gave her in marriage to a worthy young man of good position.   If they anticipated that he would induce her to adopt a more conventional outlook, they were soon disillusioned ; for Mary, young as she was, acquired a great ascendancy over her husband.   At her persuasion he consented not only that they should undertake to live in continency, but also that her house should be turned into a hospital for lepers.   The young couple nursed their patients with their own hands, sometimes sitting up with them all night, and distributed alms so lavishly and indiscriminately as to call forth the remonstrances of relations on both sides.   These activities did not prevent Mary from practising great austerities.   She used the discipline freely, wore a rough rope-girdle next to her skin, and stinted herself of food and sleep.   We are told that throughout an exceptionally rigorous winter, from Martinmas until Easter, she spent every night in a church, lying on the bare ground without extra wraps of any kind, and that she never suffered as much as a headache in consequence.   In her home, when engaged in spinning or other sedentary manual work, she did her best to avoid distractions by keeping before her an open psalter, upon which she could cast her eyes from time to time.   Her biographer lays stress on her abnormal tearfulness, which he and others regarded as a spiritual grace.   Even if in these days we should be more disposed to treat it as the physical reaction from the nervous strain to which she subjected her body, it must not be forgotten that the gift of tears was deemed by many to be a mark of true compunction of heart. To the present time a set of collects, *pro petitione lacrymarum*, stands in the Roman Missal, and St Ignatius Loyola, from a fragment still preserved of his spiritual diary, evidently regarded the days on which he did not shed tears during Mass as a time of desolation when God, so to speak, averted His face. Mary herself maintained that weeping relieved and refreshed her.

The fame of the sanctity of the holy ascetic attracted many visitors, few of whom left her without being edified and helped by her admonitions or counsels ; but a few years before her death she felt the call to retire into solitude. With the consent of her husband she accordingly left Willambroux, and took up her residence in a cell close beside the Austin canons' monastery at Oignies. She had in the past had many visions and ecstasies ; now she seemed to be constantly surrounded by the denizens of Heaven. She died at the age of thirty-eight, on June 23, 1213, after a long and painful illness, which she had long foreseen.

What is perhaps most remarkable about Mary of Oignies is the fact that she and a group of mystics in the Netherlands, notably the Beguines, seem to have anticipated by some few years that change in the spirit of Catholic devotion which is commonly considered to date from the Franciscan movement. Cardinal James de Vitry, in his preface to the Life of Bd Mary, appeals to Bishop Fulk of Toulouse, who had himself been an eye-witness of the extraordinary wave of affective piety of which Belgium was then the nucleus. He undoubtedly had Mary of Oignies most prominently in mind when he addressed Bishop Fulk in these terms :

> I well remember your speaking to me of having left the Egypt of your own diocese, and after passing over a weary desert, of your finding in the country of Liège the promised land. . . . You found, too, as I have heard you say with joy, many holy women amongst us, who mourned more over one venial sin than the people of your own country would have done over a thousand mortal ones. . . . You saw large bands of these holy women, despising earthly delights and the riches of this world through their longing desire after a heavenly kingdom, and clinging to the Eternal Spouse by the bands of poverty and humility. You found them earning a poor subsistence by the work of their hands, and though their parents abounded in wealth, yet preferring to forget their own people and their father's house, and endure the straits of poverty, rather than enjoy ill-gotten affluence.

A tender devotion to the passion of our Lord was specially characteristic of the movement, and it must be remembered that when Mary wept so copiously that, as Vitry says, " her steps might be traced in the church she was walking in by her tears on the pavement ", these tears, so he goes on to tell us, " were poured forth from the wine-press of the Passion ", and that " from this time she could not for a long while either look at a crucifix, or speak of the Passion, or even hear others speak of it, without fainting ".

Equally remarkable was that anticipation of devotion to our Lord's real presence in the Blessed Sacrament of which, up to this date, there is little trace in the devotional literature. But of Mary of Oignies James de Vitry says : " Sometimes she was permitted to take rest in her cell ; but at other times, especially when some great festival was approaching, she could find no rest except in the presence of Christ in the church."

Further, any doubt which might be felt as to the meaning of the words, " in the presence of Christ in the church ", seems to be dispelled by an examination of that other brief account of Mary of Oignies, written by Thomas of Cantimpré, which the Bollandists have printed as an appendix to James de Vitry's biography. In this other narrative reference is made to a very wealthy man who was in some sense a convert of Mary's. She told him, we learn, at a time when he was in great spiritual distress, " to go into the church near by " ; whereupon he obeyed, and " falling on his knees before the holy altar, directed his mental gaze intently upon the pyx containing the Body of Christ, which hung above it ". It then seemed to him in a sort of vision that the pyx three times over moved from its place, came through the air in his direction where he knelt praying, and remained stationary close in front of him. When this happened for the third time, he was rapt out of his senses and held secret communion with God.

The following passage, bearing in mind the date to which it belongs, is in many ways interesting :

> Mary's comfort and great delight, till she arrived at the land of promise, was the manna of life which comes down from Heaven. The sacred Bread strengthened her heart, and the heavenly Wine inebriated and gladdened her soul. She was filled with the holy food of Christ's flesh, and His life-giving blood cleansed and purified her. This was the only comfort she could not endure to be without. To receive Christ's body was the same thing with her as to live, and to die was, in her mind, to be separated from her Lord by not partaking of his blessed Sacrament. . . . The saying, " Unless a man eat the Flesh . . .", so far from being a hard one to her, as it was to the Jews, was most sweet and comforting ; since she experienced not only all interior delight and consolation from receiving Him, but even a sensible sweetness in her mouth, like the taste of honey. . . . And as her thirst for the life-giving Blood of her Lord was so great that she could not bear it, she sometimes entreated that, at least, the bare chalice might be left on the altar after Mass, that she might feast her sight with it.

Mary was also one of the earliest mystics of whom are recorded, in some detail, examples of what we should now be tempted to call psychic gifts. She is said to have known, in certain cases, what was taking place at a distance, she had strange premonitions about the future, and she was believed to be able to discern the past history of relics (hierognosis, psychometry). James de Vitry was undoubtedly speaking of himself when he related her inexplicable knowledge of the details of what passed when " a friend of hers " was ordained in Paris.

It is important to remember that James de Vitry is a most reliable witness. Not only had he spent some five years, from 1208 to her death in 1213, in Mary's company, but his whole career and his writings prove him to have been a man of scrupulous integrity and of sober judgement. He always regarded Mary as his spiritual mother, and considered himself to have been highly honoured by the fact that she looked upon him as her special " preacher " and identified herself with his apostolic work. The biography of Mary seems to have been written shortly after her death and before James became a cardinal, but he retained his devotion to her and to Oignies until the end of his days. She always declared that he had been given to her in answer to her prayers that since she, on account of her sex, could not teach the faithful and draw them to God, she might do it by deputy. There was certainly a great bond between them, and during her last sickness she prayed for him continually, begging first of all that God would so preserve him that when he came to die she might offer up his soul as one which God had entrusted to her and which she restored with usury. She mentioned all the trials and temptations and even the sins of " her preacher ", which he had formerly been guilty of, and then prayed God to keep him from such for the time to come. The prior, who knew his conscience from hearing his confessions, heard her repeat all this ; so he went to him and asked him whether he had told the saint all his sins, for, he added, in the course of her singing she has related all that you have done, just as if she had read it out of a book. " Singing " refers to the extraordinary rapture of Mary's last days when she spoke in Romance rhythmical prose, or possibly verse.

Even the physical conditions under which she lived were extraordinary. Thus we are told that " in the depth of winter she needed no material fire to keep off the cold, but even when the frost was so severe as to turn all the water into ice, she, wonderful to say, burned so in spirit that her body partook of the warmth of her soul, especially in time of prayer ; so that sometimes she even perspired, and her clothes were scented with a sweet aromatic fragrance. Oftentimes also the smell of her clothes was like the smell of incense, while prayers were ascending from the thurible of her heart."

One would suspect such statements, if they depended merely on tradition. But James de Vitry was there himself, and he was undoubtedly a devout and honest man, who told the truth fearlessly.

Practically speaking all that is known of the life of Mary of Oignies will be found in the *Acta Sanctorum*, June, vol. v. To the text of the biography by Cardinal James de Vitry the Bollandists have appended a certain supplementary notice by Thomas de Cantimpré. There is an excellent translation of Vitry printed in the Oratorian series of Lives of the Saints : it is included in the second volume of the *Life of St Jane Frances de Chantal* (1852). See also P. Funk, *Jakob von Vitry* (1909), pp. 113–130 ; and on Oignies, U. Berlière, *Monasticon Belge*, vol. i, pp. 451–452. Further, there is an article in *The Month*, June, 1922, pp. 526–537, by Fr Thurston, from which much of what is written above has been borrowed. An important study of Mary by R. Hanon de Louvet was reviewed in *Analecta Bollandiana*, vol. lxxi (1953), pp. 481–485. Bd Mary had influence on the founding of the Canons Regular of the Holy Cross (Crosiers) by Theodore of Celles, at Clair-Lieu, near Huy, in 1211.

BD THOMAS CORSINI   (A.D. 1345)

THERE is little to record about Bd Thomas Corsini : his life was as uneventful as it was edifying. A native of Orvieto, and a man of education, he was led to join the Servants of Mary by a vision in which he beheld the Mother of God and was invited by her to fight under her banner. At first he hesitated—doubting whether he might not be the victim of a mere hallucination—but when the vision was repeated he concluded that a call had come to him from on high. He promptly obeyed by seeking for admission into the local Servite community. Out of humility he took the habit of a lay-brother, and out of humility he subsequently refused to qualify himself for the priesthood. He chose for himself the office of begging for alms or of attendant upon the brother questor in his daily mendicant rounds. Bd Thomas was endowed with many spiritual graces and gifts, and many miracles were attributed to him. The best-known of these is that when a poor woman was expecting her confinement and expressed to him a longing for some fresh figs, he, though the month was January, went into the garden and found on a tree three ripe figs in perfect condition which he plucked and took to her.   Bd Thomas died in 1345, and was beatified in 1768.

See A. Giani, *Annales Ord. Servorum B.M.V.*, vol. i, pp. 281–282 ; and also Spörr, *Lebensbilder aus dem Serviten Orden* (1892).

BD THOMAS GARNET, Martyr   (A.D. 1608)

THOMAS GARNET was the nephew of the famous Jesuit, Father Henry Garnet, and the son of Mr Richard Garnet, a faithful Catholic who had been a distinguished fellow of Balliol College, Oxford.   His early education Thomas received at Horsham Grammar School, but at the age of sixteen or seventeen he was sent across the Channel to the newly opened College of St Omer.   In January 1595 he and several of the other students set sail for Spain, but not till fourteen months later, after many adventures which included a term of imprisonment in England, did he succeed in reaching his destination—the English Jesuit college at Valladolid.   There, at the close of his theological course, he was ordained priest.   He was then sent on the English Mission with Bd Mark Barkworth.   His manner of life for the next six years he described in a few words in his evidence when on trial : " I wandered from place to place to recover souls which had gone astray and were in error as to the knowledge of the true Catholic Church."

He was arrested near Warwick shortly after the discovery of the Gunpowder Plot, and was imprisoned first in the Gatehouse and then at Newgate.   Because he had been staying in the house of Mr Ambrose Rookwood, who was implicated in the conspiracy, and because he was so closely related to Father Henry Garnet, it was hoped that important information could be extracted from him, but neither threats of the rack nor the strictest cross-examination could elicit any incriminating admission.   After eight or nine months spent in a damp cell with no better bed than the bare ground, he was deported to Flanders with some forty-six other priests. While still in England Bd Thomas had been admitted to the Society of Jesus by his uncle, and he now proceeded to Louvain for his novitiate.   The following year, in September, he returned to England.   Six weeks later he was betrayed by an apostate priest and rearrested.

At the Old Bailey he was charged with high treason on the ground that he had been made a priest by authority derived from Rome and that he had returned to England in defiance of the law.   His priesthood he neither admitted nor denied, but he firmly refused to take the new oath of supremacy.   On the evidence of three witnesses who declared that when he was in the Tower he had signed himself Thomas Garnet, Priest, he was declared guilty and was condemned to death.   On the scaffold he proclaimed himself a priest and a Jesuit, explaining that he had not acknowledged this at his trial lest he should be his own accuser or oblige his judges to condemn him against their consciences.   The Earl of Essex and others tried up to the last to persuade him to save his life by taking the oath, and when the end came and the cart was drawn away they would not allow him to be cut down until it was certain that he was quite dead.

Plenty of information regarding Bd Thomas Garnet is available in Foley, REPSJ., vol. ii, pp. 475–505.   See also Challoner, MMP., pp. 296–299 ; Pollen, *Acts of English Martyrs*, p. 176 ; and Testore, *Il Primato spirituale di Pietro* (1929), pp. 328–332.

ST JOSEPH CAFASSO   (A.D. 1860)

IT is common for St Joseph Cafasso to be referred to as a saint of the Salesian Congregation, and this is understandable, for he was a close friend and spiritual director of St John Bosco. Nevertheless it is a mistake : St Joseph Cafasso was a secular priest, and his full and noble life was in general as deficient in external incident as is the usual lot of the pastoral clergy of the Church.

His birthplace was that of St John Bosco and of several other remarkable ecclesiastics, the small country town of Castelnuovo d'Asti in the Piedmont, where he was born in 1811. His parents, John Cafasso and Ursula Beltramo, were peasants in good circumstances, and he was the third of four children, of whom the last born, Mary Anne, was to be the mother of Canon Joseph Allamano, founder of the missionary priests of the Consolata of Turin. As a boy Joseph Cafasso made his mark at the local school, and he was always willing to help others with their lessons : years afterwards one of his mates said that there was a debt of two black-birds still unpaid from him to Joseph for such services. His father sent him at the age of thirteen to the school at Chieri, from whence he proceeded to the seminary newly opened in the same place by the archbishop of Turin. He was the best student of his time, became prefect of the establishment during his last year, and was ordained priest in 1833, by dispensation on account of his youth.

After his ordination, together with his friend and fellow student John Allamano, Joseph Cafasso took very modest lodgings in Turin in order to pursue further theological studies. He soon became dissatisfied with the metropolitan seminary and with the university, and found his true spiritual home at the institute (*convitto*) attached to the church of St Francis of Assisi, founded for young priests some years before by its rector, the theologian Luigi Guala. After three years of study here Don Cafasso passed the diocesan examination with great distinction, and was straightway engaged as a lecturer at the institute by Don Guala.

When Guala asked his assistant whom to have as lecturer, the reply had been, " Take the little one ", meaning Cafasso. And that he was undersized and some-what deformed by a twist of the spine was what was first noticed about his appear-ance. But his features were fine and regular, his eyes dark and clear, his hair thick and black, and from his mouth, generally lit up by a half smile, came a voice of unusual sonorousness and quality. In spite of his littleness and stoop, Don Cafasso's appearance was striking, almost majestic. His contemporaries frequently refer to St Philip Neri and St Francis de Sales when speaking of him, and they indeed seem to have been his exemplars ; a serene gaiety and kindness distinguished him, and St John Bosco among others remarks on his " undisturbed tranquillity ". And so it soon became talked about that the Institute of St Francis at Turin had a new lecturer who was little in body but very big in soul. His subject was moral theology, and he was not content to instruct without educating : he aimed not only to " teach things ", but by enlightening and directing the understanding to enlighten and direct the heart, to present knowledge not as an abstraction but as a living flame to give life to the spirit.

Don Cafasso was also soon well known as a preacher. He was no rhetorician, for all that words came easily to him : " Jesus Christ, the Infinite Wisdom ", he said to Don Bosco, " used the words and idioms that were in use among those whom He addressed. Do you the same ". And there were not wanting tendencies and teachings to be fought in colloquial words to the multitude as well as in more technical terms to the young clergy. Don Cafasso was outstanding among those

628

who destroyed the remnants of Jansenism in northern Italy, encouraging hope and humble confidence in the love and mercy of God, and fighting a morality that looked on the slightest fault as a grave sin.   " When we hear confessions ", he wrote, " our Lord wants us to be loving and pitiful, to be fatherly towards all who come to us, without reference to who they are or what they have done.   If we repel anybody, if any soul is lost through our fault, we shall be held to account : his blood will be required at our hands."   And Don Cafasso had a big part in bringing up a generation of clergy who should at all points combat and refuse to compromise with civil authorities whose idea of the church-state relationship was one of domination and interference.*

In 1848 Don Guala died, and Don Cafasso was appointed to succeed him as rector of St Francis's church and the annexed institute.   He proved no less a good superior than subordinate ; and the position was not an easy one, for there were some sixty young priests, from several dioceses, of varied education and culture, and, what was important at that time and place, of differing political views.   Don Cafasso made of them a single body, with one heart and mind, and if a strong hand and rigid discipline played its part in this achievement, the holiness of the new rector and his high standards did more.   His love and care for young priests and inexperienced curates, and his insistence that their worst enemy was a spirit of worldliness, had a marked influence on the clergy of Piedmont, nor was his care confined to them : nuns and sisters and lay people, especially the young, all shared in his interest and solicitude.   He had a remarkable intuition in dealing with penitents, and people of all kinds, high and lowly, clerical and lay, flocked to his confessional ; the archdeacon of Ivrea, Mgr Francis Favero, was among those who gave personal testimony to the power of healing the broken spirit that Don Cafasso exercised.

His activities, whether in preaching and ministering to all and sundry, or in guiding and educating the young clergy, were not confined to St Francis's and the institute, and foremost among the places where he was well known was the sanctuary of St Ignatius away in the hills at Lanzo.   At the suppression of the Society of Jesus, this sanctuary came into the hands of the archdiocese of Turin, and in due course Don Luigi Guala was appointed its administrator, to be succeeded at his death by Don Cafasso.   He continued his predecessor's work there of preaching to pilgrims and conducting retreats for both clergy and laity, enlarging the accommodation and finishing the highway to it that Guala had begun.   But of all the activities of Don Cafasso none struck the imagination of the general public more than his work for prisoners and convicts.   The prisons of Turin in those days were horrible institutions, whose inmates were herded together in barbarous conditions likely still more to degrade those who suffered them.   This was a challenge to Don Cafasso, and one which he accepted with both hands.   The best known of his converts in these unpromising circumstances was Peter Mottino, a deserter from the army who had become the leader of a particularly notorious band of brigands.   Executions took place in public, and Don Cafasso accompanied over sixty men to

---

* As an exercise in abuse, Gioberti's views on the Turin institute at this time are worth quoting : " The Institute of St Francis is difficult to define.   It is a college, a seminary, a monastery, a presbytery, a chapter, a penitentiary, a church, a nuisance (*cura*) and a court (*curia*), a tribunal, an academy, a bogus council, a political gang, a seditious conventicle, a business office, a police-station, a laboratory of casuistry, a seed-bed of error, a school of ignorance, a factory of lies, a web of intrigue, a nest of cheats, a warehouse of gossip, a dispensary of trifles, a selling-place of favours. . . ." etc., etc.

the scaffold in various places, no one of whom died impenitent : he called them his " hanged saints ", and asked them to pray for him. Among them was General Jerome Ramorino, who had been an ordnance officer of Napoleon I and then a revolutionary soldier-of-fortune in Spain, Poland and Italy. He was condemned to death for disobedience to orders at the battle of Mortara, and when invited to make his confession on the eve of execution, replied, " My condition is not such that I am in need of that humiliation ". Don Cafasso knew better and persevered —and Ramorino met his death as a good Christian should.

John Bosco and Joseph Cafasso first met on a Sunday in the fall of 1827, when the first was still a lively boy and the second already tonsured. " I've seen him ! I've talked to him ! " announced John, when he got home. " Seen who ? " asked his mother. " Joseph Cafasso. And I tell you, he's a saint." Fourteen years later Don Bosco celebrated his first Mass at the church of St Francis in Turin, and afterwards joined the institute, studying under Cafasso and sharing many of his undertakings, especially the religious instruction of boys. It was Don Cafasso who persuaded him that work for boys was his vocation. And so it came about that a Salesian, John Cagliero, could write, " We love and reverence our dear father and founder Don Bosco, but we love Joseph Cafasso no less, for he was Don Bosco's master, adviser and guide in spiritual things and in his undertakings for over twenty years ; and I venture to say that the goodness, the achievements and the wisdom of Don Bosco are Don Cafasso's glory. It was through him that Don Bosco settled in Turin, through him that boys were brought together in the first Salesian oratory ; the obedience, love and wisdom that he taught have borne fruit in the thousands of youngsters in Europe and Asia and Africa and America who today are being well educated for life in God's Church and in human society." Nor was St John Bosco the only beneficiary in this way. Inspiration and encouragement, help and direction, were found in St Joseph Cafasso by the Marchioness Juliet Falletti di Barolo, who founded a dozen charitable institutions, by Don John Cocchi, who devoted his life to establishing a college for artisans and other good works in Turin, by the priests Dominic Sartoris, who began the Daughters of St Clare, and Peter Merla, who cared for delinquent children, by the founders of the Sisters of the Nativity and the Daughters of St Joseph, Francis Bono and Clement Marchisio respectively, by Laurence Prinotti, who set up an institute for necessitous deaf-mutes, and by Caspar Saccarelli, who organized an establishment for the education of poor girls. All these also may be said to have contributed to the glory of St Joseph Cafasso.

In the spring of 1860 Don Cafasso foretold that death would take him during the year. He drew up a spiritual testament, enlarging on the means of preparation for a good death that he had so often expounded to retreatants at St Ignatius's, namely, a godly and upright life, detachment from the world, and love for Christ crucified. And he made a will disposing of his property, the residuary legatee of which was the rector of the Little House of Divine Providence at Turin, the foundation of St Joseph Cottolengo. Among the other legatees was St John Bosco, who received a sum of money and some land and buildings adjoining the Salesian oratory at Turin. Don Bosco was at this time having difficulties with the civil governor of Piedmont, which was a cause of worry to Don Cafasso and adversely affected his health. After hearing confessions on June 11 he retired to bed, worn out and ill. Pneumonia developed, and he died on Saturday, June 23, 1860, at the hour of the morning angelus.

Enormous crowds attended the funeral, at St Francis's and the parish church of the Holy Martyrs, where, as was fitting, St John Bosco preached. Thirty-five years later the cause of Don Cafasso was introduced in the diocesan court of Turin ; and in 1947 he was canonized.

This is a case where the life of a saint has been written by a saint : *Biografia del sacerdote Giuseppe Cafasso*, by Don Bosco, but the standard biography is *Vita del Ven. G. Cafasso*, in two volumes, by Luigi Nicolis di Robilant. Adequate for all ordinary purposes is Cardinal Salotti's *La Perla del Clero Italiano* (1947) ; but it is rather verbose for English taste. There is also Canon Colombero's *Vita del Servo di Dio Don Giuseppe Cafasso*. See also books on St John Bosco. There still seems to be nothing in English about St Joseph Cafasso except a short reference in Hughes's *Maria Mazzarello* ; but there is a German life by D. W. Mut (Munich, 1925).

24 : THE BIRTHDAY OF ST JOHN THE BAPTIST

ST AUGUSTINE, remarking that the Church celebrates the festivals of saints on the day of their death, which in the true estimate of things is their great birthday, their birthday to eternal life, adds that the birthday of St John the Baptist forms an exception because he was sanctified in his mother's womb, so that he came into the world sinless. Indeed, the majority of divines are disposed to think that he was already invested with sanctifying grace, which would have been imparted by the invisible presence of our divine Redeemer at the time that the Blessed Virgin visited her cousin, St Elizabeth. But in any case the birth of the Forerunner was an event which brought great joy to mankind, announcing that their redemption was at hand.*

John's father, Zachary, was a priest of the Jewish law, and Elizabeth his wife was also descended of the house of Aaron ; and the Holy Scriptures assure us that both of them were just, with a virtue which was sincere and perfect—" and they walked in all commandments and justifications of the Lord without blame." It fell to the lot of Zachary in the turn of his ministration to offer the daily morning and evening sacrifice of incense ; and on a particular day while he did so, and the people were praying outside the sanctuary, he had a vision, the angel Gabriel appearing to him standing on the right side of the altar of incense. Zachary was troubled and stricken with fear, but the angel encouraged him, announcing that his prayer was heard, and that in consequence his wife, although she was called barren, should conceive and bear him a son. The angel told him : " Thou shalt call his name John, and thou shalt have joy and gladness, and many shall rejoice in his birth, for he shall be great before the Lord." The commendations of the Baptist are remarkable in this that they were inspired by God Himself. John was chosen to be the herald and harbinger of the world's Redeemer, the voice to proclaim to men the eternal Word, the morning star to usher in the sun of justice and the light of the world. Other saints are often distinguished by certain privileges belonging to their special character ; but John eminently excelled in graces and was at once a teacher, a virgin and a martyr. He was, moreover, a prophet, and more than a prophet, it being his office to point

---

* To-day is of course the general feast day of the Baptist, and not simply a commemoration of his birth. But for convenience an account of his life is deferred herein until the commemoration of his beheading, on August 29.

out to the world Him whom the ancient prophets had foretold obscurely and at a distance.

Innocence undefiled is a precious grace, and the first-fruits of the heart are particularly due to God. Therefore the angel ordered that the child should be consecrated to the Lord from his very birth, and as an indication of the need to lead a mortified life if virtue is to be protected, no fermented liquor would ever pass his lips. The circumstance of the birth of John proclaimed it an evident miracle, for Elizabeth at that time was advanced in years and according to the course of nature past child-bearing. God had so ordained all things that the event might be seen to be the fruit of long and earnest prayer. Still, Zachary was amazed, and he begged that a sign might be given as an earnest of the realization of these great promises. The angel, to grant his request, and in a measure to rebuke the doubt which it implied, answered that he should continue dumb until such moment as the child was born. Elizabeth conceived ; and in the sixth month of her pregnancy received a visit from the Mother of God, who greeted her kinswoman : " and it came to pass that when Elizabeth heard the salutation of Mary, the infant leaped in her womb."

Elizabeth, when the nine months of her pregnancy were accomplished, brought forth her son, and he was circumcised on the eighth day. Though the family and friends wished him to bear his father's name, Zachary, the mother urged that he should be called John. The father confirmed the desire by writing on a tablet " John is his name " ; and immediately recovering the use of speech, he broke into that great canticle of love and thanksgiving, the *Benedictus*, which the Church sings every day in her office and which she finds it not inappropriate to repeat over the grave of every one of her faithful children when his remains are committed to the earth.

The Birthday of St John the Baptist was one of the earliest feasts to find a definite place in the Church's calendar, no other than where it stands now, June 24. The *Hieronymianum* locates it there, the first edition stressing the point that this commemorates the *earthly* birthday of the Forerunner. The same day is indicated in the Carthaginian Calendar, and before that we have sermons of St Augustine delivered on this particular festival which sufficiently indicate the precise time of year by referring to those words of John reported in the Fourth Gospel : " He must increase, but I must decrease." St Augustine finds this appropriate, for he tells us that after the birthday of St John the days begin to get shorter, whereas after the birthday of our Lord the days begin to grow longer. Duchesne is probably right in urging that the connection of the feast with June 24 must have originated in the West and not in the East. He says : " It is to be noted that the festival is on the 24th and not on the 25th of June, and we may well ask why the latter figure was not adopted, since it would have given the exact interval of six months between the Baptist and Christ. The reason is [he goes on] that the calculation was made according to the Roman calendar ; the 24th of June is the *octavo kalendas Julii*, just as the 25th of December is *octavo kalendas Januarii*." At Antioch, and in the East generally, the days of the month were numbered continuously forward from the first day just as we do, and June 25 would have corresponded with December 25 without attention being paid to the fact that the former month counted thirty days and the latter thirty-one. But just as the Roman date of Christmas was adopted at Antioch (very possibly through St John Chrysostom's acquaintance with St

Jerome) in the last quarter of the fourth century, so it was not very long before the birthday of the Baptist was celebrated at Antioch, Constantinople, and in the other great Eastern churches on the same day as it was in Rome.

St John the Baptist was a very popular saint in the middle ages, and much might be written about the religious orders, institutions, churches and shrines which were placed under his patronage ; but all that we know for certain about his life is to be found in the pages of the four gospels.   The story told in the apocryphal *Protevangelium*, otherwise known as the Gospel of James, which represents Zachary in the capacity of high priest, and as taking a prominent part in the marriage of Mary and Joseph, is altogether unreliable.   Neither can we place unqualified trust in the little additional information which may be gleaned from the historian Josephus ; Dr. Robert Eisler's book, *The Messiah Jesus and John the Baptist* (1931), which purports to be founded on the Slavonic text of Josephus, raises far too many doubts to be taken as a serious contribution to the subject.   There are a number of books on St John the Baptist more or less devotional in character.   One, that of the Abbé Denis Buzy, which has been translated into English, *The Life of St John the Baptist*, discusses the question very fully from the theological and exegetical point of view, and also contains an adequate bibliography.   On liturgical aspects of the subject, see Duchesne's *Christian Worship ;* Schuster, *The Sacramentary*, vol. iv, pp. 265–271 ; DAC., vol. vii, cc. 2167–2184 ; and on the folklore associated especially with Midsummer night, Bächtold-Stäubli, *Handwörterbuch des deutschen Aberglaubens*, vol. iv, pp. 704 *seq.*

THE MARTYRS UNDER NERO   (A.D. 64)

THESE confessors, whose number and names are known only to God, are described in the Roman Martyrology as " the first fruits with which Rome, so fruitful in that seed, had peopled heaven ".   It is interesting to note that the first of the Caesars to persecute Christians was Nero, perhaps the most unprincipled of them all.

In July 64, the tenth year of his reign, a terrible fire devastated Rome.   It began near the Great Circus, in a district of shops and booths full of inflammable goods, and quickly spread in all directions.   After it had raged for six days and seven nights and had been got under by the demolition of numerous buildings, it burst forth again in the garden of Tigellinus, the prefect of the praetorian guard, and continued for three days more.   By the time it had finally died down, two-thirds of Rome was a mass of smouldering ruins.   On the third day of the fire Nero came from Antium to survey the scene.   It is said that, clad in theatrical costume, he went to the top of the Tower of Maecenas, and to the accompaniment of his lyre recited Priam's lament over the burning of Troy.   His savage delight at watching the flames gave rise to the belief that he had ordered the conflagration, or at any rate had prevented it from being extinguished.

The belief rapidly gained ground.   It was said that flaming torches were thrown into houses by mysterious individuals who declared themselves to be acting under orders.   How far Nero was responsible remains a moot point to this day.   In view of the numerous destructive fires which have afflicted Rome throughout the ages, it is more than likely that this, perhaps the worst of them all, was due to accident.   At the time, however, suspicion was so widespread that Nero was alarmed, and sought to divert it from himself by accusing the Christians of setting fire to the city.

Although, as we know from the historian Tacitus, no one believed them to be guilty of the crime, they were seized, exposed to the scorn and derision of the people, and put to death with the utmost cruelty.   Some were sewn up in the skins of wild beasts and delivered to hungry dogs who tore them to pieces ; some were crucified ; others again were smeared over with wax, pitch and other combustible material, and after being impaled with sharp stakes under their chins were ignited to serve as torches. All these barbarities took place at a public nocturnal fête which Nero gave in his own gardens. They served as side-shows whilst the emperor diverted his guests with chariot races, mixing with the crowd in plebeian attire or driving himself in a chariot. Hardened though the Romans were to gladiatorial shows, the savage cruelty of these tortures aroused horror and pity in many of those who witnessed them.

Tacitus, Suetonius, Dio Cassius, Pliny the Elder, and the satirist Juvenal, all make reference to the fire ; but it is only in Tacitus that we have a mention of Nero's attempt to fasten the outrage upon a particular sect. Tacitus definitely specifies the Christians by name, but Gibbon and others maintain that under that designation he included the Jews, because those who had adopted the teaching of our Lord Jesus Christ were not yet sufficiently numerous in Rome to be a source of alarm. This view, however, which seems only prompted by a desire to belittle the influence of Christianity, has not won many adherents. There is an excellent article on the subject in DCB., vol. iv, pp. 24–27.

ST SIMPLICIUS, Bishop of Autun   (Fourth or Fifth Century)

Except that he was bishop of Autun, highly esteemed for his integrity and charity, nothing definite is known about this St Simplicius. He would seem to have succeeded Bishop Egemonius about the year 390. On the other hand, it is possible that he was the Bishop Simplicius mentioned by St Athanasius as one of the signatories to the decrees of the Council of Sardica in 347. According to his legend, as related by Gregory of Tours, he came of a distinguished Gallo-Roman family and married a maiden, young and wealthy like himself, with whom he made a pact that they should live in continence and devote themselves to good works. After Simplicius had been elected bishop, misunderstandings arose and some scandal was caused in the still largely pagan city because the new prelate and his wife continued to dwell under the same roof. To vindicate themselves they voluntarily submitted to an ordeal by fire. They took red-hot coals, laid them in the folds of their clothing, and stood up before the people for an hour without sustaining any injury to themselves or to their garments.

So convincing was this miracle that it led over a thousand pagans to seek baptism. Another wonder, and one equally fruitful in conversions, was wrought by St Simplicius on the day of the goddess Berecynthia, which was always an occasion for disgraceful orgies. The holy bishop met the statue of the deity as it was being conveyed in a chariot to bless the fields, and with a prayer for divine assistance he upraised his hand to make the sign of the cross. Instantly the image fell to the ground, from which no efforts could dislodge it. Moreover, the beasts which drew the chariot refused to proceed any further.

The fantastic story just recounted is to be found in Gregory of Tours, *De Gloria Conf.*, nn. 73–76. There is also a short medieval life of Simplicius (it is printed in the *Catalogus* of Brussels Hagiographical MSS., vol. i, pp. 127–129), and it has been held that this was the source from which Gregory derived his information, but Bruno Krusch (in the *Neues Archiv*, vol. xxxiii, pp. 18–19) denies this. A Simplicius, Bishop of Autun, is commemorated in the *Hieronymianum*, not only today but also on November 19, and there are certain chronological data which suggest that there may have been two bishops of Autun of that name. See also Duchesne, *Fastes Épiscopaux*, vol. ii, pp. 174–178.

ST BARTHOLOMEW OF FARNE   (A.D. 1193)

Of the many pious men who were led by the example of St Cuthbert to become solitaries on the island of Farne, off the Northumbrian coast, not the least remarkable was this Bartholomew, for he spent no less than forty-two years upon that desolate haunt of birds. He was a north-countryman, a native of Whitby. His parents, who may have been of Scandinavian origin, called him Tostig, but because the name 'made him a laughing-stock it was changed to William. He determined to go abroad, and his wanderings led him to Norway, where he remained long enough to receive ordination as a priest. He returned home, and went to Durham, where he took the monastic habit, assuming the name of Bartholomew. A vision he had of St Cuthbert inspired him to dedicate the rest of his life to God in the cell which Cuthbert had once occupied at Farne.

Upon his arrival he found another hermit already installed—a certain Brother Ebwin, who strongly resented his intrusion and who strove by petty persecution to drive him away. Bartholomew attempted no reprisals, but made it quite evident that he had come to stay, and Ebwin eventually retired, leaving him in solitary possession. The mode of life he embraced was one of extreme austerity, modelled upon that of the fathers in the desert. Later he was joined by a former prior of Durham called Thomas ; but they could not agree. Their chief cause of dissension —sad to relate—was the amount of the food ration. Thomas could not manage with as little as Bartholomew, and he went so far as to question the genuineness of what appeared to be his brother's extraordinary abstemiousness. Bartholomew, who seems to have been sensitive to criticism, was so offended at being charged with hypocrisy that he left the island and returned to Durham. There he remained in spite of the apologies of Thomas, until the bishop, a year later, ordered him back to Farne, when a reconciliation then took place. Forewarned of his approaching death, Bartholomew announced it to some monks, who were with him when he died, and buried him in the island. He left a reputation for holiness and miracles, but there is no evidence of liturgical *cultus*.

There is a medieval life which gives Bartholomew's history in some detail, and which was apparently written by a contemporary. It is printed in the *Acta Sanctorum*, June, vol. v. See also Stanton's *Menology*, pp. 287–288 ; T. D. Hardy, *Catalogue of Materials* (Rolls Series), vol. ii, pp. 226–227, where a very different date is suggested for his death ; and a short life in the *Hermit Saints* in the Anglican series edited by J. H. Newman (1844). The Latin text of the saint's miracles is given in *Analecta Bollandiana*, vol. lxx (1952), pp. 5–19.

25 : ST WILLIAM OF VERCELLI, Abbot of Monte Vergine   (A.D. 1142)

THE founder of the religious congregation known as the Hermits of Monte Vergine came of a Piedmontese family and was born at Vercelli in 1085. After the death of his parents, whom he lost in infancy, he was kindly cared for by relations, but at the age of fourteen he abandoned his home and set out as a poor pilgrim for Compostela in Spain. Not satisfied with the hardships such a journey entailed, he had two iron bands fastened round his body. How long William remained in Spain is not recorded. We hear of him next in 1106, when he was at Melfi in the Italian Basilicata, and then at Monte Solicoli, on the slopes of which he remained for two years, leading a penitential life with a hermit. To this period belongs St William's first miracle, the restoration of sight to a blind man. The cure made him famous, and to avoid being acclaimed as a wonder-worker he left the neighbourhood to stay with St John of Matera. They were kindred spirits and became close friends. It was St William's intention to proceed on a pilgrimage to Jerusalem, and he would not allow himself to be deterred by John's assurance that God had other work for him to do. He actually started, but he had not got far when he was attacked by robbers. He took this as a sign that John was right, and relinquished his journey.

He now betook himself to a height between Nola and Benevento, which was then called Monte Virgiliano—possibly after the great Virgil, who is said to have sojourned there. At first William attempted to live there as a hermit, but he was soon joined by would-be disciples, both priests and laymen. He formed them into a community and from the church which he built in 1124, under the name of our Lady, the mountain has derived its present name of Monte Vergine. The rule he instituted was most austere : no wine, meat or dairy produce was allowed, and on three days of the week only vegetables and dry bread. After the first fervour had cooled, murmurs arose and there was a general demand for relaxation. William had no desire to constrain the malcontents, though for himself any relaxation seemed unthinkable. He therefore chose a prior to rule the community, and then departed with five faithful followers. With St John of Matera, who now joined him, he made a second settlement at Monte Laceno, in Apulia. Here, however, the barrenness of the soil, the exposed position and the high altitude made life a misery to all but the most hardy, and even they could with difficulty hold out through the winter. St John had more than once urged removal, when a fire which destroyed their huts compelled them to descend into the valley. There the two holy men parted : John to go east and found one monastery at Pulsano on Monte Gargano, and William to found another on Monte Cognato in the Basilicata.

When that community was well established St William treated it as he had treated the monastery at Monte Vergine—he gave it a prior and left it to govern itself. At Conza, in Apulia, he founded a monastery for men, and at Guglietto, near Nusco, he established two communities, one of men and the other of women. King Roger II of Naples afterwards drew him to Salerno, in order that he might have the benefit of his counsel and help. St William's beneficent influence over the monarch was, however, resented by some of the courtiers who lost no opportunity of discrediting and decrying him as a hypocrite and a humbug. With the knowledge of the king, they set a trap by sending to him, on some specious excuse, a woman of loose life, charged with the task of luring him to sin. William received her in a room at one end of which a great fire was burning ; and as soon as she began to exercise her blandishments he walked away to the fireplace, parted the glowing coals with his bare hands, and then stretched himself down at full length in the space he had cleared, inviting her to lie down with him. Her horror was only exceeded by her amazement, when he presently arose, completely unharmed. The miracle led to her conversion : she gave up her life of sin and took the veil in the convent of Venosa. As for King Roger, he continued to patronize William's foundations, and endowed other houses which he placed under the saint's control.

St William died at Guglietto on June 25, 1142. He left no written constitutions, but a code of regulations bringing the order into conformity with the Benedictine rule was drawn up by the third abbot general, Robert. The only monastery of William's foundation which exists at the present day is that of Monte Vergine. It now belongs to the Benedictine congregation of Subiaco, and has a much venerated picture of our Lady of Constantinople, to which pilgrimages are frequently made.

There is a biography, not devoid of personal touches, which purports to have been written by the saint's disciple, John of Nusco. It is printed from a faulty manuscript in the *Acta*

Sanctorum, June, vol. vii.   A better text, which fills certain lacunae in the earlier copy, was discovered in the present century at Naples and was edited by Dom C. Mercuro in the *Rivista Storica Benedettina*, vol. i (1906), vol. ii (1907), and vol. iii (1908), in several articles, which include an historical commentary, as well as the document itself.   *Cf.* also P. Lugano, *L'Italia Benedettina* (1929), pp. 379–439 ; and E. Capobianco, *Sant' Amato da Nusco* (1936), pp. 145–164.

ST FEBRONIA, Virgin and Martyr   (A.D. 304 ?)

IT must be frankly admitted that the virgin martyr St Febronia is in all probability a purely fictitious personage, but she is venerated by all the churches of the East, including that of Ethiopia, and in the West by such towns as Trani, in Apulia, and Patti, in Sicily. which claim to possess some of her relics.   She is supposed to have suffered at Nisibis in Mesopotamia, somewhere about the year 304, in the persecution under Diocletian.   No genuine records of her life and passion are available, but the legend attributed to her survives in the form of an attractive romance purporting to have been written by Thomaïs, a nun of her convent, who is said to have witnessed the events she describes.   Only a mere outline of the story can be given here.   Febronia, as a child of two, was placed by her parents under the charge of her aunt, Bryene, who ruled a convent of nuns at Nisibis.   There she grew up, lovely in body and in soul, in ignorance of the outside world, and intent only upon adorning herself with virtues to fit her for her heavenly Bridegroom. Bryene took great pains with her education, and, in order to guard her against the temptations likely to assail her, she allowed her niece food only every other day and made her sleep upon a narrow plank of wood.   So well did Febronia profit by the instruction she received that when she was eighteen she was set to read and expound the Holy Scriptures to the nuns every Friday.   Great ladies from the town also attended these readings, but Bryene veiled her from their sight lest their attention should be distracted by Febronia's amazing beauty and also because the girl had never seen anyone but her fellow nuns.

The peaceful life of the convent was brought to a sudden termination by the outbreak of persecution.   At Nisibis the cruel edicts of Diocletian were enforced with great ferocity by the prefect Selenus.   The clergy, together with their bishop, took refuge in flight and their example was followed by all the nuns with the exception of Bryene, of Febronia, who was recovering from a serious illness, and of Thomaïs.   When the prefect's officials came to search the convent, they did not trouble to arrest the two old women, but they carried off Febronia.

The following day she was brought up for trial and Selenus told his nephew, Lysimachus, to cross-examine her.   This the young man proceeded to do courteously and somewhat diffidently, for he was the son of a Christian mother and all his sympathies were with the prisoner.   Selenus interrupted him impatiently and prompted perhaps by a touch of malice, he offered to give Febronia liberty and wealth if she would renounce her religion and consent to marry Lysimachus.   She replied that she had treasure in Heaven—not made with hands : that she was already espoused to an immortal Bridegroom, and possessed a dowry which was the kingdom of Heaven.   Infuriated by her reply, Selenus ordered her to be stripped, to be fastened to four posts over a slow fire, and to be scourged.   Seventeen of her teeth were then pulled out and her breasts were cut off—regardless of the indignant protests of the crowd that filled the court-house.   As the martyr survived all these tortures her limbs were lopped off and she was finally despatched by blows from an axe.   Retribution promptly overtook Selenus : in a sudden fit of madness he struck his head against a marble pillar and fell down, dead.   By order of Lysimachus, Febronia's remains were then reverently gathered up and she was given a magnificent funeral.   Her martyrdom led immense numbers of pagans to seek baptism, amongst them Lysimachus, who became a monk in the days of the Emperor Constantine.

This story, as stated above, had an immense diffusion.   It is to be found not only in Syriac, Greek and Latin, but also in Armenian, Georgian, and other tongues.   In an important article in the *Analecta Bollandiana*, vol. xlii (1924), pp. 69–76, J. Simon has shown that the original was almost certainly Syriac.   He conjectures that the people of Nisibis, in opposition to the monophysites, were anxious to show that they had ancient martyrs who formed part of the old orthodox Byzantine tradition ; and so they, at the end of the sixth or the beginning of the seventh century, invented Febronia.   No trace of such a martyr exists before that period.   The Greek and Latin texts of the story will be found in the *Acta Sanctorum*, June, vol. vii ; the Syriac is printed by Bedjan, *Acta Martyrum et Sanctorum* vol. v, pp. 573–615.

ST GALLICANUS   (A.D. 352 ?)

THERE was a Gallicanus who was an illustrious Roman patrician, and possibly a great benefactor to the Church, in the fourth century.   He was not, however, a martyr, as is asserted in the Roman Martyrology.   In all probability he was the Gallicanus who was consul with Symmachus in 330.   A record has been preserved in the *Liber Pontificalis* of the generosity of Gallicanus to the church of SS. Peter, Paul and John the Baptist, which Constantine had built at Ostia.   Amongst his donations were a silver crown with dolphins, weighing twenty pounds, and a silver cup or chalice with bas-reliefs, weighing fifteen pounds.   He also endowed the church with four landed estates.   This is all that is actually recorded of the patrician of that name.   Despite the abnormally long notice accorded to him in the Roman Martyrology, his reputed " acts " are spurious ; they are a late compilation and abound with anachronisms and inaccuracies.   According to them Gallicanus was a great general who, in the days of Constantine, routed first the Persians and then the Scythians, in two victorious campaigns.   Whilst he was engaged in the second expedition, he was converted to Christianity by the brothers SS. John and Paul.

Retiring from Rome, Gallicanus settled down at Ostia.   He built a church, liberated his slaves, and enlarged his house to make it a hospice for pilgrims.   In all his good works he was assisted by a companion named Hilarinus.   " His fame ", we read, " spread throughout the world, and men came from the east and from the west to see the ex-patrician and ex-consul, the friend of the emperor, washing the feet of pilgrims, laying the table, pouring water on their hands, ministering to the infirm, and generally giving an example of sublime virtue."   These activities are supposed to have been brought to an end by Julian the Apostate, who commanded Gallicanus to sacrifice to the gods or to go into exile.   The saint chose banishment, and withdrew to Egypt, where he joined a group of hermits.   Persecution, however, followed him even into the desert, and he was beheaded, while his friend Hilarinus was scourged to death.

The whole of this story must have been fabricated at a late date, not before the seventh century.   Mgr Duchesne (*Liber Pontificalis*, vol. i, p. 199) has shown that the Acts of Gallicanus were in all probability evolved out of a misinterpretation of what is recorded in the account of St Silvester regarding the donations to the churches made at that time.   In reality, the generous benefactor who here figures as Gallicanus was an entirely different historical personage, *viz.* St Pammachius (August 30), and the hospice for pilgrims mentioned above is an idea borrowed from the *xenodochium* which Pammachius organized, not in Ostia, but at Porto.   What lends point to this interpretation is the fact that the story of Gallicanus is bound up with that of the martyrs SS. John and Paul, whose church in Rome on the Coelian Hill was known as the *titulus Pammachii.*   The gift of the four landed estates is also borrowed from the *Liber Pontificalis,* which mentions such an endowment immediately before the name of Gallicanus occurs, connecting it with the basilica built at Ostia, but the donor was in this case not Gallicanus, but the Emperor Constantine.   The legend of Gallicanus, which really forms part of the Acts of SS. John and Paul, is printed by the Bollandists in the *Acta Sanctorum,* June, vol. vii.   See also J. P. Kirsch, *Die römischen Titelkirchen im Altertum* (1918), pp. 156–158 ; and H. Quentin, *Les Martyrologes historiques,* pp. 431 and 533.

ST PROSPER OF AQUITAINE   (*c.* A.D. 465)

ST PROSPER of Aquitaine, whose feast is kept at Tarbes as The Aquitainian Doctor, is well known in his writings but little known in his life, though there are several ancient references to him as " learned and holy " and the like.   He was neither bishop nor priest (the Roman Martyrology calls him bishop of Reggio by confusion with another Prosper : see below) ;   he seems always to have been a layman, possibly married—a point not settled by the disputed attribution to him of a Poem from a Husband to his Wife, expressive of trust in God whatever befalls.

Prosper went from Aquitaine into Provence, and from Marseilles in 428 wrote, at the instance of his friend Hilary, to St Augustine at Hippo.   The matters raised drew from St Augustine his treatises Concerning Predestination and Concerning the Gift of Perseverance, and Prosper thus became involved in the semi-Pelagian controversy, opposing St John Cassian and perhaps St Vincent of Lerins.   Prosper and Hilary went to Rome, and returned with a letter from Pope St Celestine I to the bishops of Gaul, praising the zeal of the bearers and calling for peace.   But the disputes continued.   Prosper eventually went again to Rome, where he is said to have been secretary to Pope St Leo the Great.   He died there some time after 463.

The writings of Prosper of Aquitaine, whether in verse or prose, are mostly concerned with the controversy about grace and free will in defence of St Augustine's doctrine.   His longest poem is a dogmatic treatise of 1002 hexameters, " A Song about the Graceless " ;   but the most widely known of his works is his *Chronicle,* from the Creation to the capture of Rome by the Vandals in A.D. 455.

L. Valentin, *St Prosper d'Aquitaine* (1900) ;   G. Bardy in DTC.;   H. W. Phillott in DCB. *Cf.* also note to St Prosper of Reggio, below.   An English translation of his treatise on Divine Grace and Free Will, against Cassian, was published in New York in 1950.

ST PROSPER, BISHOP OF REGGIO   (A.D. 466 ?)

THERE is evidence that from the ninth century St Prosper, known as bishop of Reggio (not the Reggio in Calabria), has been much venerated in the Italian province of the Emilia.   He appears to have flourished in the fifth century, but history can tell us little that is definite about him.   An unreliable tradition asserts that he distributed all his goods to the poor in order to fulfil our Lord's precept to the rich young man, and that he died on June 25, 466, in the midst of his priests and deacons after a beneficent episcopate which had lasted twenty-two years.   He was buried in the church of St Apollinaris, which he had built and consecrated, outside the walls of Reggio.   In the year 703 his relics were translated to a great new church erected in his honour by Thomas, Bishop of Reggio, and he is the principal patron of the city. The Roman Martyrology is here gravely at fault, in that it identifies Prosper of Reggio with Prosper of Aquitaine (above). The two were entirely distinct, and there is no trace of any attempt to identify them earlier than the tenth century.

The whole matter has been convincingly dealt with in an article by Dom Germain Morin, in the *Revue Bénédictine*, vol. xii (1895), pp. 241–257, entitled " St Prosper de Reggio ". No serious scholar now defends the identity of these two Prospers, nor did the Bollandists and Tillemont in the eighteenth century. See also J. M. Mercati, in the *Analecta Bollandiana*, vol. xv (1896), pp. 161–256 ; and Lanzoni, *Le Diocesi d'Italia*, vol. i, pp. 615–618.

ST MAXIMUS, BISHOP OF TURIN (*c.* A.D. 467)

MUCH of the literary work of St Maximus of Turin survives, but very little is known about its writer. He appears to have been born about the year 380, and, from inferences drawn from some of his writings, it is conjectured that he was a native either of Vercelli or of some place in the province of Rhaetia. He states that in 397 he witnessed the martyrdom of three missionary bishops at Anaunia, in the Rhaetian Alps. The historian Gennadius in the *Book of Ecclesiastical Writers*, which he compiled towards the end of the fifth century, describes St Maximus, Bishop of Turin, as a profound studen: of the Bible, a preacher well able to instruct the people, and the author of many books, the titles of some of which he specifies. The notice concludes by saying that St Maximus flourished in the reigns of Honorius and of Theodosius the Younger. As a matter of fact he long survived them. In 451 he attended the synod of Milan, presided over by his metropolitan, St Eusebius, and with the other prelates of northern Italy he signed the letter addressed to Pope St Leo the Great, which declared the assembly's adhesion to the orthodox doctrine of the Incarnation as set forth in his so-called " Dogmatic Epistle ". St Maximus was also present at the Council of Rome in 465. His signature on that occasion follows immediately after that of Pope St Hilarus and, as precedence was then regulated by age, it is clear that he must have been a very old man. He is believed to have died shortly afterwards.

A collection made of his reputed writings, as edited by Bruno Bruni in 1784, comprises some 116 sermons, 118 homilies, and six treatises ; but this classification is very arbitrary, and of these probably a considerable number should be assigned to other authorship. They are chiefly interesting for the light they throw on curious old customs and on the condition of the people of Lombardy at the time of the Gothic invasions. He mentions the destruction of Milan by Attila in one of his homilies : in another, which treats of the martyrs Octavius, Solutor and Adventus, whose relics were preserved at Turin, he says : " All the martyrs are to be honoured by us, but especially those whose relics we possess : they preserve us as to our bodies in this life and receive us when we depart hence." In two homilies on thanksgiving he inculcates the duty of daily giving praise to God, and recommends the psalms as being a particularly suitable means to that end. No one, he insists, should ever omit morning and evening prayer, or thanksgiving before and after meals. Maximus exhorts all Christians to make the sign of the cross before every action, " that by the sign of Jesus Christ (devoutly used) a blessing may be insured to us in all things ". Dealing in one of his sermons with abuses in connection with New Year's day, he deprecates the practice of giving presents to the well-off at that season without bestowing alms also on the poor, and denounces the hypocritical

semblance of friendship in which the heart has no share.   Elsewhere he attacks
" heretics who sell the pardon of sins ", whose pretended priests exacted money
for absolving penitents instead of bidding them do penance and weep for their
offences.

In the *Journal of Theological Studies*, vol. xvi, pp. 161–176, and pp. 314–322, as well
as in vol. xvii, pp. 225–232, Professor C. H. Turner was inclined to attribute to St Maximus
certain Latin pieces, the text of which he there edited ; but Dom Capelle, in the *Revue
Bénédictine*, vol. xxxiv, pp. 81–108, has shown pretty conclusively that these are the work
of the Arian bishop Maximinus.   There is a short but good article on St Maximus by E.
Amann, in DTC., vol. x, cc. 464–466.   See also DCB., vol. iii, pp. 881–882 ; and Bardenhewer, *Geschichte der altkirchlichen Literatur*, vol. iv, pp. 610–613.   Cf. E. Dekkens, *Clavis
Patrum Latinorum*.

ST MOLOC, OR LUAN, BISHOP   (A.D. 572 ?)

St Moloc, Molluog, or Murlach was formerly honoured throughout Scotland, and
his widespread *cultus* may be traced in the numerous place-names of which he is
the eponym.   Whether he was a native of Britain or of Ireland is still a moot point.
However, the notice in the Aberdeen Breviary, to the effect that he was of noble
Scottish extraction and a native of Scotland, seems to be borne out by an entry
under the date of June 25 in the *Félire* of Oengus.   It runs : " Sinchell's feast,
Telle's feast : they were heights of Ireland, with Moluoc pure—fair sun of Lismore
of Alba."   The name of the saint's father was Lanneon, and his own was originally
Lugaidh, but it was modified to Moloc, or Moluanus, in Ireland, where he received
his education.   He is said to have been trained at Birr, under St Brendan the Elder.
At what date he returned to Scotland is not known.   Landing in Argyllshire, he
evangelized the inhabitants of Lismore in Loch Linnhe, and, after preaching at
Tyle—wherever that may be—and visiting islands as far north as the Hebrides, he
appears to have devoted the rest of his life to missionary work in Ross and in the
province of Mar.   He died at Rossmarkie, probably about the year 572, but his
relics were translated to Murlach.   King Malcolm II attributed his victory over
the Danes, near Murlach, to the intercessions of our Lady and of St Murlach.   As
an act of thanksgiving, he founded in 1010, at Murlach (Mortlach), under their
joint patronage, an abbey, a cathedral church and an episcopal see.   The bishopric
was subsequently transferred to Aberdeen.   He was apparently a bishop, and the
Duke of Argyll claims to possess the *bacul*, or crozier, of St Moloc, it having been
for generations an heirloom in the family of Livingstone of Lismore.   His feast,
under the form of his name Luan, is still observed in the diocese of Argyll and the
Isles.

It would hardly seem probable that the Moluoc, commemorated in the *Félire* on this
day, June 25, can be identical with the Molua of August 4.   Of the latter, we have three
recensions of a Latin life.   Moreover, in this case the story printed by Whitley Stokes tells
us distinctly that he was " Moluoc of Lismore in Scotland."   Consult, in any case, Forbes,
KSS., pp. 409–411, where the lesson in the Aberdeen Breviary is quoted at length.

ST ADALBERT OF EGMOND   (A.D. 705 OR AFTER 714 ?)

Amongst the band of missionaries who left the monastery of Rathmelsigi in 690,
under the leadership of St Willibrord, to evangelize Friesland, was a deacon named
Adalbert.   He was a Northumbrian, and had followed St Egbert to Ireland in order
to obey our Lord's counsels of perfection.   It was that same aspiration, coupled

with a great love for souls, which prompted him to volunteer for missionary work amongst the heathen. The messengers of the Gospel were assisted by the protection of Pepin of Herstal, and also by the fact that they found little difficulty in making themselves understood by the Frieslanders, but their personality had much to do with their ultimate success. Adalbert's gentleness, his patience and his humility made a deep impression upon those to whom he brought the Christian faith. The nucleus of his activities was Egmond, and he converted the greater part of its inhabitants. It was perhaps out of humility that Adalbert does not seem to have offered himself for the priesthood. St Willibrord is said, indeed, to have appointed him archdeacon of Utrecht, but an archdeacon in those days was simply a chief deacon, and St Willibrord may well have wished to confer upon him some authority.

St Adalbert died in an unknown year. His tomb afterwards became a place of pilgrimage and the scene of many reported miracles. In the tenth century Duke Theodoric built at Egmond a Benedictine abbey dedicated under the name of this Adalbert, and when in recent times the Benedictines of Solesmes restored monastic life at Egmond the same titular was chosen.

The sources upon which we depend for our knowledge of St Adalbert's life are very unsatisfactory. The Latin biography written about 200 years after his death by Rupert, a monk at Mettlach—it is printed in the *Acta Sanctorum*, June, vol. vii—contains little but generalities and the miracles said to have been worked after his death. Another Latin life has been published by C. Pijnacker Hordijk in *Bijdragen voor Vaderlandsche Geschiedenis* (1900), pp. 145–174, but it is little better than an abridgement of the first. Adalbert's claim to the title of archdeacon has been contested by Holder-Egger and others, but, on the other hand, they are disposed to identify him with the Adalbert who succeeded St Willibrord as abbot of Epternach. This last conjecture is rejected by W. Levison. The date of Adalbert's death is quite uncertain. See also DHG., vol. i, c. 441 ; and W. Levison, " Wilhelm Procurator von Egmond . . ." in *Neues Archiv*, vol. xl (1916), pp. 793–804.

ST EUROSIA, Virgin and Martyr   (Eighth Century ?)

In a modern German essay entitled, " An Apocryphal Saint of the Late Middle Ages ", its scholarly writer deals exhaustively and convincingly with St Eurosia, and with the devotion of which she became the centre, first at Jaca in Spain, where it originated in the fifteenth century ; and afterwards in Lombardy also. Father Delehaye, whose own conclusions coincided with those of the author, reviewing the treatise in the *Analecta Bollandiana*, says : " Everything is suspect in the origins of this *cultus* which was propagated in the north of Italy, thanks to the political relations between Spain and Lombardy. . . . A considerable number of places in the dioceses of Como, Cremona, Pavia and Novara possess chapels, altars, images and relics of St Eurosia, who is honoured as the protector of the fruits of the field." Devotion to the new saint would seem to have been spread by Spanish soldiers, and by the religious congregation of the Somaschi, whose headquarters were in the diocese of Cremona. According to the popular tradition, Eurosia was a noble maiden from the province of Bayonne, who, at some time during the eighth century, refused to marry a Moorish chieftain, and was slain by the Saracens in the cavern to which she had fled for safety. Although relics reputed to be hers are preserved in Jaca cathedral, it is not improbable that Eurosia was an entirely fictitious character. She is invoked against bad weather.

Without going quite so far as to say that Eurosia is a pure myth, Fr Papebroch in the *Acta Sanctorum*, June, vol. vii, points out the lack of all early evidence, as well as the contradictions in the legends which were circulated regarding her. The essay above referred to is that of the Swiss E. A. Stückelberg, " Eine apokryphe Heilige des späten Mittelalters ", which appeared in the *Archiv für Religionswissenschaft*, vol. xvii (1914), pp. 159–164. It would seem that already in the sixteenth century there was an office and Mass in honour of Eurosia, though the celebration was then confined to the town of Jaca alone.

SS. GOHARD, Bishop of Nantes, and his Companions, Martyrs (A.D. 843)

The heathen Northmen who raided the coasts of Anglo-Saxon England and of contemporary France seem especially to have singled out for attack religious foundations of all kinds.   In so doing they were animated partly by a hatred to the Christian faith, partly by the expectation of securing, without serious opposition, treasure belonging to the communities or entrusted to their care.   If they met with disappointment or resistance—sometimes if they met with neither—they would destroy the buildings and massacre all connected with them.

In the year 843 a number of Norman ships appeared at the mouth of the Loire, and were piloted up the river by a traitor named Lambert, who had aspired to the countship of Nantes but had been driven out by the citizens.   Great was the alarm felt by the inhabitants when the foreigners reached Nantes.   The monks of a neighbouring monastery carried their ecclesiastical treasure into the church of SS. Peter and Paul, where Gohard, the bishop, was actually engaged in celebrating the feast of the Birthday of St John the Baptist.   Although the sacred edifice was filled with people who had fled there for safety, the Northmen broke down the doors and the windows.   Forcing their way to the altar, they slew St Gohard just as he had reached *Sursum corda* at the beginning of the preface, and the priests who surrounded him were killed by his side.   The monks also were murdered.   After setting fire to the church, the barbarians kidnapped the leading citizens, setting a ransom upon their heads.   Before they finally retired, they had pillaged the whole city.   The body of St Gohard was rescued, and his relics were taken to Angers, his native town.

There is a short Latin life printed in the *Acta Sanctorum*, June, vol. vii (in the Appendix, pp. 682–683), but of no great authority.   See Duchesne, *Fastes Épiscopaux*, vol. iii, p. 369.

BD HENRY ZDIK, Bishop of Olomuc   (A.D. 1150)

Although Bishop Henry Zdik's *cultus* has never been officially approved, yet the great services he rendered to the Church in his own diocese and beyond it have caused him to be honoured as a *beatus* in what is now known as Czechoslovakia. He is said to have been closely connected with the rulers of Bohemia, but what the relationship actually was is a contested point.   All that seems certain about his origin is that he was born in Moravia.   In 1126 he became bishop of Olomuc (Olmütz), and under his auspices Duke Wenceslaus I undertook the rebuilding of the cathedral.   The completion and decoration of the basilica were the bishop's own doing.   In 1137 or 1138 Bd Henry made a pilgrimage to Jerusalem.   While he was there he took the Premonstratensian habit and experienced a spiritual awakening which, in the words of his biographer, led him to return home " a new man ".   His zeal for the Church now expressed itself in various ways.   In 1141 he joined a mission or crusade to convert the Prussians—with what result we are not told.   Two years later we find him associated with others in founding the abbey of Strahov. He entitled it Mount Sion and brought to it Premonstratensians from Steinfeld, near Cologne. At a later date he restored the monastery of Lito-merice, of which he was reckoned the second founder. To this community he gave another name reminiscent of his Palestinian pilgrimage : he called it Mount Olivet. The difficulty he found in bringing his clergy back to regular observance, and especially in enforcing the rule of celibacy, decided him to go to Rome to confer with the pope. Scarcely had he started, however, when he was set upon by would-be assassins, from whose hands he barely escaped with his life. He made no second attempt, for it was rendered unnecessary by the timely arrival in Bohemia of a papal legate, who gave him the support and authority he required to enable him to carry out his reforms. Bd Henry Zdik died in 1150 or 1151, and was buried at Strahov, a monastery that still exists.

An account will be found in the *Acta Sanctorum*, June, vol. vii, but there seems to be no formal biography of this holy bishop dating from the middle ages. See. further, I. van Spilbeeck, *Hagiologium Norbertinum* (1887) ; and A. Zark in *Annales de l'Ordre de Prémontré*, 1908 and 1910.

BD JOHN THE SPANIARD   (A.D. 1160)

THIS John was born in 1123, probably at Almanza, in Leon. He was a studious boy, and at the age of thirteen he went to France with a companion to seek the educational advantages he could not obtain nearer home. The two lads made their way to Arles, where they found excellent teachers, but where they were occasionally reduced to great straits. Later, however, John was befriended by a wealthy man, who took him to live in his own house. His studies completed, John bade farewell to his kind friends, and betook himself to a hermit, under whom he trained for two years and a half. He then obtained admittance to the Carthusian priory of Montrieu, or Mons Rivi, and from the moment he entered the noviciate he set himself to tread faithfully in the footsteps of St Bruno. For six years he filled the office of sacristan, and afterwards he was chosen to be prior. In that capacity he strove to encourage learning, and with his own hand copied and corrected manuscripts—from which last activity it may be judged he was a man of strong nerves.

At the close of his tenure of office—which he appears to have resigned—he was transferred to the Grande Chartreuse. St Anthelm, who was then the superior of that great monastery, held him in very high esteem ; and when Haymo de Fulciano asked that some Carthusians might be sent to make a foundation on one of his estates near the Lake of Geneva, St Anthelm selected Bd John to go as their prior. Not without considerable difficulty was this new charterhouse started, but once it was established it was called Reposoir, from the atmosphere of peace that pervaded it. Another work John performed at the request of St Anthelm was the compilation of a constitution for Carthusian nuns. After ruling the com-munity of Reposoir for nine years, Bd John died in the year 1160. By his express desire he was interred beside two shepherds who had been killed by an avalanche, and whom he had buried. A chapel was built over his tomb, but in 1649 his remains were translated to the sacristy of the monastery church. This was done by Charles Augustus de Sales, Bishop of Geneva, the nephew of St Francis de Sales ; and the formal instrument drawn up by him, with a description of what occurred, is still preserved. Bd John's *cultus* was confirmed in 1864.

There is a very simple straightforward life, containing, however, little detail, which seems to have been compiled at the charterhouse where he died.   It is printed both in the *Acta Sanctorum*, June, vol. vii and in the *Annales Ordinis Cartusiensis* of Dom Le Couteulx, vol. ii, pp. 199–212.

BD GUY MARAMALDI   (A.D. 1391)

AMONG the Dominicans who preached and taught in Italy during the second half of the fourteenth century, Guy Maramaldi deserves a prominent place.   He came of a Neapolitan family, and each of his three brothers—like himself—was a man of mark.   Guy was still a mere stripling when he presented himself at the Neapolitan house of the Order of Preachers, and asked for the habit.   His request was granted, after some hesitation due to the fear that his delicate upbringing would unfit him for the stern discipline of a friary.   The apprehension proved groundless, and in his austerities and obedience, as well as in his studies, he soon outstripped his fellow novices.   In later life he became a great theologian and preacher.   After teaching theology and philosophy at Naples, he went to Ragusa, where the success of his preaching and his fame as a wonder-worker caused him to be acclaimed as an apostle.   Upon his return home he was appointed inquisitor general for the kingdom of Naples—a post which brought him on several occasions into serious danger.   He died in the year 1391, and his *cultus* was approved in 1612.

A short account is to be found in the *Acta Sanctorum*, June, vol. vii.   See also Touron, *Hommes illustres dominicains* (1745), vol. ii, pp. 627–631 ; and *Année dominicaine*, vol. vi (1893), pp. 534–536.

26 : SS. JOHN AND PAUL, MARTYRS   (A.D. 362 ?)

APART from their names, and the fact that they were Christian martyrs of Rome, history can tell us nothing about the two saints, John and Paul, who are commemorated together on this day.   In some quarters, indeed, their very existence is questioned.   This much, however, is generally conceded, *viz.* that at some time in the fourth century, relics, reputed to be theirs, were deposited in the house on the Coelian Hill which Byzantius or his son, St Jerome's friend, St Pammachius, gave to be converted into a Christian church.   The basilica erected over the old foundations in the fifth century may have been originally dedicated to the Apostles John and Paul, but it came to be entirely associated in the popular mind with the two Romans whose tomb it was supposed to contain and whose *cultus* was being propagated by means of their widely-credited, but actually spurious, " acts ".   As a result of that *cultus*, the names of the " brothers ", John and Paul, were inserted in the canon of the Mass, as well as in the litany of the Saints : they were accorded a commemoration with a proper office and Mass in the sacramentaries known as the Gelasianum and the Gregorianum, and they found their way into the Gallican liturgy.   In the Gelasianum we even find their feast preceded by a vigil with fast, but this was abrogated, possibly because of its close proximity to the fasts preceding the great fasts of the Birthday of St John Baptist and of the Apostles Peter and Paul.   The fame of the two brothers reached our own country.   Amongst many medieval itineraries which commend their shrine in the church on the Coelian Hill to the special devotion of pilgrims to Rome is one discovered at Salisbury, in a collection of tenth-century manuscripts.   William of Malmesbury, who wrote during the reign of King Stephen, also mentions it, and the Council of Oxford in 1222 enacted that the feast of SS. John and Paul should be kept as a festival of the third order, with obligation laid on the faithful to assist at Mass that day before going to work.

The so-called " acts " are a pious fiction purporting to be a report taken down from an account given by Terentian, the captain charged with the execution of the two martyrs.   According to this story, John and Paul were brothers, army officers whom the Emperor Constantine assigned to the household of his daughter, Constantia.   She held them in great esteem and appointed the one her steward and the other her major-domo.   They were afterwards recalled by the emperor and commissioned to serve under his general, Gallicanus, in an expeditionary force sent to stem an invasion of Scythians into Thrace.   The barbarians proved to be such formidable opponents that at one time the defeat of the imperial army seemed imminent.   One wing had been cut up and some of the officers had surrendered, when the two brothers approached Gallicanus and assured him of certain victory if he would promise to become a Christian.   He gave the required undertaking and immediately a legion of angels put the enemy to flight.   As long as Constantine and his children were alive, John and Paul continued to serve them and to be honoured by them, but they would have no dealings with the Emperor Julian after his apostasy.   When he summoned them to court they refused to obey and expressed their detestation of his disloyalty to the Christian faith.   A respite of ten days was given them in which to reconsider their refusal.   Then Terentian, captain of the imperial bodyguard, came with some of his men and superintended the execution of the martyrs in their own house on the Coelian Hill.   Their bodies were buried in the garden, but it was given out that they had gone into exile.   The legend adds that the Emperor Jovian built the church dedicated in their honour on the site of their own house.

The present basilica of SS. Giovanni e Paolo, with its twelfth-century Lombard-Romanesque belfry and colonnaded apse, was bestowed by Pope Clement XIV upon St Paul-of-the-Cross, and is still served by the Passionists.   Excavations made in 1887 revealed, beneath the church, rooms of the ancient dwelling-house, with remains of frescoes, some of which belong to the third century.

Fr Delehaye has discussed the question of these saints very thoroughly in his CMH., pp. 336–337.   The spurious *passio* of the martyrs is printed in the *Acta Sanctorum*, June, vol. vii, and elsewhere (*cf*. St Gallicanus, June 25).   See also P. Franchi de' Cavalieri, in *Studi e Testi* ix, pp. 55–65, and xxvii, pp. 41–62 ; J. P. Kirsch, *Die römischen Titelkirchen*, pp. 26–33, 120–124, 156–158 ; Lanzoni, *I Titoli presbiterali di Roma antica*, p. 46 ; *Analecta Bollandiana*, vol. xlviii (1930), pp. 11–16 ; and DAC., vol. ii, cc. 2832–2870, where good pictures are given of the supposed " house of John and Paul " on the Coelian Hill.

ST VIGILIUS, BISHOP OF TRENT, MARTYR   (A.D. 405)

THE principal patron of the Trentino and the Italian Tirol is St Vigilius, who practically completed the conversion of those districts to Christianity.   By race a Roman, he appears to have been born at Trent, where his family through long residence had acquired the rights of citizenship.   He was educated in Athens, but nothing else is known about his movements until after his return to his native city, when in the year 385 he was chosen bishop of Trent at an unusually early age.   One letter addressed to him by his metropolitan, St Ambrose, Archbishop of Milan, is still extant.   In it he is urged vigorously to oppose usury, to discountenance the marriages of Christians with pagans, and to exercise hospitality to strangers, especially to pilgrims.   There were still numerous heathen in the villages of the diocese of Trent : to them St Vigilius went in person to preach the gospel.   He also, through St Ambrose, obtained the help of three other missionaries, SS. Sisinnius, Martyrius and Alexander.   They won the crown of martyrdom on May 29, 395, and St Vigilius wrote an account of their death in a short letter addressed to Ambrose's successor, St Simplician, and in a longer one to St John Chrysostom, whom he had probably known in Athens.   In these epistles he expresses himself as envious of the glory of these apostles, and he laments that his own unworthiness had precluded him from sharing their martyrdom.   The crown he desired, however, was soon to be his.   During a preaching mission in the remote valley of Rendena he was moved, it is said, to overthrow a statue of Saturn ; and the peasants stoned him to death.   Trent still claims to possess his relics, as well as those of St Maxentia, St Claudian and St Majorian, who are reputed to have been his mother and brothers.

See the *Acta Sanctorum*, June, vol. vii, where a *passio* is printed.   This, or some such document, was sent to Rome, and this seems to be the foundation for the statement of Benedict XIV that St Vigilius was the first martyr to be canonized by the Holy See.   See also Perini, *Cenni sulla Vita di S. Vigilio* (1863), and *Scritti di storia e d'arte per il 15 centenario di S. Vigilio* (1905).

ST MAXENTIUS, Abbot   (*c.* A.D. 515)

The French town of Saint-Maixent, in the department of Deux Sèvres, covers the place once occupied by the cell of St Maxentius and the adjacent monastery which he ruled.   The saint was born at Agde, on the Gulf of Lyons, about the year 445, and received in baptism the name of Adjutor.   Under the watchful care of the abbot St Severus, to whom his parents entrusted him as a child, he grew up a model of Christian virtue—extolled by most of his fellow religious, but regarded with jealousy by a few.   Praise was even more distasteful to him than detraction, and to escape the prominence into which he was being thrust, he quietly slipped away from Agde and remained in hiding for two years.   But when at the end of that time he came back to his home he found himself in a position of far greater publicity.   For his return happened to coincide with a break in the weather after a prolonged drought, and he was acclaimed as a saviour and a wonder-worker.   Obviously, he must sever all ties with the past if he was to lead a life of obscurity.   A second time he disappeared and this time he abandoned his native Narbonnaise for good.   He made his way as far as Poitou, where he entered a community in the valley of Vauclair presided over by Abbot Agapitus.   More completely to efface the past, he changed his name to that of Maxentius.

If he could thus conceal his identity, he could not long conceal his sanctity. His austerity was such that he took no food but barley bread and water, he prayed so constantly that his back became bent.   Moreover, he was credited with the gift of miracles.   By the unanimous vote of his brethren he was elected superior about the year 500.   During the war which raged a few years later between Clovis, King of the Franks, and Alaric the Visigoth, the inhabitants of Poitou suffered much from the violence of soldiers and marauders.   One day a band of armed men advanced threateningly upon the monastery of Vauclair and struck terror into the hearts of the monks, who implored St Maxentius to save them.   He reassured them and calmly sallied out to meet the hostile party. One of the soldiers upraised his arm to strike the abbot down with his sword. He found himself unable to lower his arm : it remained as though paralysed until St Maxentius restored it through the application of blessed oil.

Following the example of his predecessor Agapitus, St Maxentius laid down his office at the approach of old age and shut himself up in a cell at a little distance from the monastery; and there he died at the age of seventy, about the year 515.

Two texts or recensions of a medieval life of St Maxentius are preserved. The shorter was printed by Mabillon, in his *Acta Sanctorum O.S.B.* ; the longer by the Bollandists in vol. vii for June. Neither seems very reliable as an historical document. Some time ago, the story of St Maxentius was the subject of animated discussion in the *Revue des Questions Historiques* ; see the years 1883 and 1888. There have been several lives in French.

SS. SALVIUS, or SAUVE, and SUPERIUS   (c. A.D. 768)

ABOUT the year 768, there arrived in Valenciennes a regionary bishop called Salvius accompanied by a disciple. What authority he had and from whence he came remains a mystery, but he was an ardent missionary and through the sermons he preached in the church of St Martin he brought about many conversions. According to the story told of him, he and his companion were murdered by the son of an official for the sake of his handsome cloak and expensive girdle. This story is not well attested—but there is a lesson in it.

The bodies of the victims were taken from the pit into which they had been cast to the church of St Vedast at Valenciennes. The disciple's name was not remembered—if it had ever been known—but because his body was found lying above that of the bishop he was designated St Superus, or Superius. At a later date the bodies of the two martyrs were translated to the village of Brena, which stood on the site now occupied by the town of Saint-Sauve.

The fact that SS. Salvius and Superius are commemorated on this day in the Roman Martyrology unfortunately affords no guarantee for the reliability of this story. There is a *passio*, met with in many manuscripts, which has been printed in the *Acta Sanctorum*, June, vol. vii ; and another version is to be found in the *Analecta Bollandiana*, vol. ii. The writer professes to be a contemporary, but no evidence confirms this. See, on the whole question, Van der Essen, *Étude critique et littéraire sur les Vitae des saints mérovingiens* (1907), pp. 244–249.

ST JOHN, BISHOP OF THE GOTHS   (c. A.D. 800)

THOUGH he has no particular *cultus* in the West, this St John is honoured in the Eastern churches on account of the resistance he opposed to Iconoclasm. He was a native of that district north of the Black Sea which includes the Crimea, and his grandfather was an Armenian legionary. In 761 the then bishop of the Goths in those parts, to gratify the Emperor Constantine Copronymus, who was attempting to abolish the use of sacred images, subscribed to the iconoclastic edicts and was rewarded by being promoted to the more desirable see of Heraclea. His flock, more orthodox than he, asked that John should be appointed in his place. Their request was granted, but they had to await his return from Jerusalem, where he spent three years.

He wrote a defence of the veneration paid to sacred images and relics, and also of the practice of invoking the saints. His arguments were supported by quotations from the Old and New Testaments, as well as by references to the teaching of the fathers. Under the regency of the Empress Irene the ban against sacred images was raised, and John came to Constantinople to attend the synod summoned by St Tarasius ; John was also present in 787 at the second Council of Nicaea, in which the Catholic doctrine with regard to the *cultus* of sacred images was clearly defined. After his return, John's diocese was invaded by the Khazars, and through treachery he became a captive in the hands of their chieftain. He succeeded, however, in escaping and found a refuge at Amastris in Asia Minor, where he was hospitably received by the bishop. He spent there the last four years of his life. Upon being informed that the Khazar chief had died, he turned to his friends and said, " And I, too, shall depart from hence in forty days and will plead my cause with him before God ". The first part of this prophecy was fulfilled to the letter, for on the fortieth day he peacefully expired. His body was conveyed back to his country by Bishop George of Amastris and was deposited in the monastery at Partheniti in the Crimea.

A sufficient account of his activities, together with a Greek biography, is printed in the *Acta Sanctorum*, June, vol. vii. There is also mention of him on the same day in the *Synaxary* of Constantinople. See Delehaye's edition, cc. 772–773.

ST PELAGIUS, MARTYR   (A.D. 925)

THE name of the boy martyr, Pelagius (Pelayo), is still famous throughout Spain, and many churches have been dedicated in his honour. He lived in the days when Abd-ar-Rahman III, the greatest of the Omayyads, was ruling at Cordova, and was left as a hostage in the hands of the Moors by his uncle. He was then a child of ten. Three years went by, the expected exchanges never arrived, and Pelagius remained unredeemed. By this time he had developed into a handsome lad, spirited, and entirely untainted by the corrupt influence of his prison associates. Favourable reports of him having reached Abd-ar-Rahman, he sent for the boy, and told him that he might have his liberty, with horses to ride, fine clothes to wear, money and honours, if he would renounce his faith and acknowledge the prophet Mohammed.

Pelagius, however, stood firm. " All that means nothing to me ", he answered. " A Christian I have been, Christian I am, and Christian I shall continue to be." Promises and threats proving equally unavailing, he was eventually condemned to death. Accounts vary as to the manner of his execution. According to one report he was sentenced to be racked on the iron horse and to be swung up and down till he expired ; according to another, he was suspended from the forked gallows usually reserved for slaves and criminals, and then dismembered, his limbs being thrown into the river Guadalquivir. His remains were rescued by the faithful and preserved in Cordova until 967, when they were translated to Leon ; in 985 the relics were removed for safety to Oviedo.

There is a short Latin *passio*, which has been printed in the *Acta Sanctorum*, June, vol. vii, with a discussion of the historical data and subsequent *cultus*. The story of little St Pelagius was sufficiently famous to rouse the enthusiasm of the poetess, Hroswitha, Abbess of Gandersheim, who about the year 962 narrated the incidents of the martyrdom in Latin verse. The best text of the poem is that edited by P. von Winterfeld in *Deut. Dichter d. Lat. Mittelalters* (1922). There is an English translation of Hroswitha's poems by Christopher St John (1923), and a German version by H. Homeyer (1936).

649

ST ANTHELM, BISHOP OF BELLEY   (A.D. 1178)

ST ANTHELM is justly regarded as one of the greatest ecclesiastics of his age on account of the services he rendered to the Church as bishop of Belley, as minister general of the Carthusian Order at a critical stage of its development, and as an outstanding supporter of the true pope against a pretender backed by all the forces of the emperor.   He was born in 1107 at the castle of Chignin, six miles from Chambéry.   He was a high-principled young priest, hospitable and generous, but interested primarily in the things of this world.   However, he had relatives among the Carthusians, and visits to the monastery of Portes completely changed his outlook.   What he saw of the life of the community and what he learnt from the prior brought home to him a sense of his true vocation, and he accordingly abandoned the world to assume the habit of St Bruno about 1137.   Before he had completed his noviciate he was sent to the Grande Chartreuse which had recently lost the greater part of its buildings through the fall of an avalanche ; and Anthelm did much by his example and business-like qualities to revive the fervour and restore the prosperity of the monastery.   After the resignation of Hugh I in 1139, he was elected seventh prior of the Grande Chartreuse.

He made it his first care to repair the ruined buildings, which he then encircled by a wall.   He brought water through an aqueduct and renewed the farm premises and sheep-folds, and all the time he was enforcing the rule in its primitive simplicity, and had the satisfaction of seeing his efforts crowned with success.   Until his time all the charterhouses had been independent of one another, each one being subject only to the bishop.   He was responsible for summoning the first general chapter. By it the Grande Chartreuse was constituted the mother house, and he became, in fact if not in name, the first minister general of the order.

It is not surprising that his reputation for sanctity and wisdom brought him many recruits ; amongst those who received the habit at his hands were his own father, one of his brothers, and William, Count of Nivernais, who became a lay-brother.   It was St Anthelm, too, who commissioned Bd John the Spaniard to draw up a constitution for a community of women who wished to live under Carthusian rule.

After governing the Grande Chartreuse for twelve years he succeeded in 1152, to his great satisfaction, in resigning an office he had never desired.   He was not allowed to remain long, however, in the seclusion of a solitary cell.   Old age had compelled Bernard, the founder and first prior of Portes, to lay down his charge, and at his request Anthelm was appointed his successor.   The toil of the monks had brought great prosperity to the monastery, whose treasury and barns were full to overflowing.   Such superfluity the new prior regarded as incompatible with evangelical poverty, and in view of the scarcity that prevailed in the surrounding countryside he ordered free distribution to be made to all who were in need.   He even sold some of the ornaments of the church to provide alms.   Two years later he returned to the Grande Chartreuse to live for a while the contemplative life of a simple monk, but it was then that there came to him the first call to deal with ecclesiastical matters outside the order.

In 1159 western Christendom was split into two camps, the one favouring the claims of the true pope, Alexander III, the other supporting the antipope " Victor IV ", who was the nominee of the Emperor Frederick Barbarossa.   Anthelm threw himself into the fray in conjunction with Geoffrey, the learned Cistercian abbot of

Hautecombe. They succeeded in recruiting their own brethren and the religious of other communities, who declared for Alexander and organized his cause in France, in Spain, and even in England. Partly no doubt in recognition of these services, Pope Alexander listened to an appeal made to him regarding the vacant see of Belley, to set aside the selected candidates and to nominate Anthelm. In vain did the Carthusian entreat—even with tears—to be excused : the pope was insistent, and Anthelm was obliged to consent. He was consecrated on September 8, 1163.

There was much in his diocese that called for reform, and he set to work with characteristic thoroughness. In his first synod he made an impassioned appeal to his clergy to live up to their high calling ; the observance of clerical celibacy had largely fallen into abeyance and not a few priests openly lived as married men. At first the bishop used only persuasion and warnings, but after two years, finding that his injunctions were still being disregarded in certain quarters, he made an example of the worst offenders by depriving them of their benefices. He was equally firm in dealing with disorder and oppression among the laity : no previous bishop of Belley had ever been so fearless or so uncompromising. When Humbert III, Count of Maurienne, violating the Church's right of jurisdiction over her clergy, imprisoned a priest accused of misdemeanour, Anthelm sent a prelate to free the prisoner. The priest was killed in the scuffle that followed Humbert's attempt to rearrest him, and the threatened excommunication was pronounced. Not even at the pope's bidding would Anthelm relent ; and when he learnt that Alexander III, with whom the count was somewhat of a favourite, had himself raised the ban, he retired to Portes, indignantly protesting that the pope was acting *ultra vires*, for St Peter himself would not have power to release the impenitent from censure. He was persuaded with difficulty to return to his diocese—but he could not be persuaded to admit Humbert to communion. Nevertheless, his relations with Rome remained so excellent that he was soon chosen for a mission as legate to England, to attempt to bring about a reconciliation between Henry II and St Thomas Becket ; but circumstances prevented him from going.

More remarkable still was the favour shown him by his former opponent, the emperor. But neither honours from the heads of church and state, nor yet the pastoral duties he so adequately fulfilled, could wean his heart from his community or lead him to live otherwise than in Carthusian simplicity. Any leisure time he could secure was spent at the Grande Chartreuse and the houses of his order. Two other institutions were specially dear to him : the one was a community of women solitaries at a place called Bons, the other a leper house where he loved to tend the sufferers with his own hands. Advancing age in no way affected his activities, and he was busily engaged in making a distribution of food during a famine when he was seized with the fever which was to prove fatal. As he lay dying he had the satisfaction of receiving a visit from Count Humbert who had come to beg his forgiveness and to promise amendment. St Anthelm passed away on June 26, 1178, at the age of seventy-two. St Hugh of Lincoln in the last year of his life, returning from a final visit to the Grande Chartreuse, passed through Belley and there venerated the earthly remains of his old friend Anthelm, who was already famous for the miracles wrought at his shrine.

The Bollandists, in the *Acta Sanctorum*, June, vol. vii, have printed a life of St Anthelm, written apparently by a contemporary, a copy of which they obtained from the Grande

Chartreuse. The virtues and activities of Anthelm are discussed also in much detail in the *Annales Ordinis Cartusiensis*, compiled by Dom Le Couteulx, vols. i and ii ; as well as in Le Vasseur, *Ephemerides Ordinis Cartusiensis*, vol. iii, pp. 375–406. A very full and satisfactory life of the saint is available in French : *Vie de St Anthelme*, by the Abbé C. Marchal (1878). Consult further DHG., vol. iii, cc. 523–525.

27 : SS. ZOILUS AND HIS COMPANIONS, MARTYRS (A.D. 304 ?)

IN the Roman Martyrology for this day St Zoilus is commemorated together with nineteen other martyrs, his reputed companions. All are supposed to have perished at Cordova, in Spain, during the persecution of Diocletian. Nothing whatever is known about the rest, but Zoilus is said to have been the son of a local patrician, a Christian from infancy, and to have suffered martyrdom when he was still only a youth. A body identified as his was discovered in the reign of King Reccared, and a church dedicated in his honour was built to enshrine the relics. Shortly before 1083 the remains of St Zoilus and of St Acisclus were translated by Ferdinand, Count of Carrion, to the Benedictine abbey which his mother, Tarasia, had founded at Carrion. Prudentius couples the two saints, Zoilus and Acisclus, in one of his poems. A point that has not escaped the notice of the critics is that the names of the first seven of the companions of St Zoilus appear, and in the same order, in the spurious acts of St Symphorosa, where they are assigned to the Tivoli martyr's seven sons.

The Bollandists in discussing this commemoration, *Acta Sanctorum*, June, vol. vii, do not print any *passio*, but quote various hymns, etc., found in Mozarabic liturgical sources. There are, however, two texts of the *passio*, which, though seemingly of little value, were published by Florez in his *España Sagrada*, vol. x, pp. 502–520. That Zoilus was an authentic martyr may fairly be presumed from the fact that Prudentius in the fifth century already regarded him as one of the glories of Cordova, and also from the insertion of his name in the *Hieronymianum*. See also Dom Férotin, *Le Liber Ordinum*, pp. 468–469, and *Le Liber Sacramentorum*, pp. 373–377, and 824. On the finding of the relics, see *Analecta Bollandiana*, vol. lvi (1938), pp. 361–369.

ST SAMSON OF CONSTANTINOPLE (FIFTH CENTURY)

AT some time during the fifth century, probably about the middle, a rich and philanthropic man named Samson founded at his own expense a great hospital for the sick poor in Constantinople. He is said to have been a physician as well as a priest, and to have ministered himself to those who suffered either in body or in soul. The hospital was called by his name. Honoured during his life as " the hospitable " and " father of the poor ", he was venerated as a saint after his death. In the sixth century his hospital, which had been burnt to the ground some fifty years before, was rebuilt by the Emperor Justinian. At a later period, with sublime indifference to the exigencies of chronology, an attempt was made to connect the two founders. St Samson was represented as having miraculously cured Justinian of an otherwise deadly disease, and as having persuaded him, when he was building the Holy Wisdom church, to erect at the same time a hospital for the poor. It was the only reward which the grateful emperor could induce him to accept. As a matter of fact, St Samson died before 500, and it was not until 527 that Justinian ascended the throne.

A sufficient account, which includes the Greek text of a detailed biography attributed to the Metaphrast, will be found in the *Acta Sanctorum*, June, vol. vii.   See also the *Synaxary* of Constantinople (ed. Delehaye), cc. 773–776 ; Samson is here stated to have been a Roman by birth, and a relative of the Emperor Constantine.   His name was added to the Roman Martyrology by Baronius.

ST JOHN OF CHINON   (Sixth Century)

WHEN Clotaire I was king of Neustria, there was living not far from Chinon a holy hermit of the name of John.   He was a stranger, a native of Brittany, of whose antecedents nothing was known.   Attached to his cell was a little garden, and he would often sit reading or writing under the shelter of some laurels he had planted. Although he led a life of retirement, yet he acquired a great reputation as a healer and a seer.   One day there came to him a messenger from St Radegund, bringing him a present and asking for his hair-shirt and his prayers.   She was then in a state of deep anxiety because she believed that King Clotaire, her brutal husband, was about to drag her from her retreat.   After a whole night spent in prayer, the solitary was able the following morning to send back a reassuring message : he said that she might set her mind at ease, for she had nothing to fear from Clotaire.   St John died a holy death, and was buried in his oratory near the church of St Maximus.

This recluse, who is also known in France as St Jean du Moustier (*Monasterii*), or Jean de Tours, is commemorated on this day in the Roman Martyrology, in which his name was inserted by Baronius.   The Bollandists, however, in the *Acta Sanctorum*, treat of him on May 5.   We know little more than what is to be found in Gregory of Tours, *De gloria confessorum*, ch. xxiii.

ST GEORGE MTASMINDELI, Abbot   (A.D. 1066)

THIS George, whose surname means " of the Black Mountain ", was a doctor of the Georgian (Iberian) Church.   He was born in 1014, and as a young man became a disciple of a monk well known for the holiness of his life, Hilarion Tvaleli ; afterwards he lived as a hermit in Syria.   St George Mtasmindeli's fame rested on his writings and translations into the Iberian language, notably treatises on " The Months " and " The Fasts " and his revision of the biblical translations made by St Euthymius (May 13).   In spite of such work, he spent a rather wandering life, visiting the holy places of Palestine, being for some years abbot of Iviron on Mount Athos, and living on the Black Mountain in Armenia.

A few days before his death on June 27, 1066, he is said to have replied to a question about eucharistic bread, addressed to him by the Emperor Constantine X Dukas, that, " The Greeks use leavened bread out of humility, because they have been several times stained by heresy.   The Latins use unleavened bread, following the example of our Lord and St Peter, as a sign that they have kept the faith pure as Jesus Christ and His apostles taught it."   Whatever may be thought of St George's views on the history of the use of *azyme*, this reply at any rate shows what he thought about events in Constantinople a dozen years earlier, when Rome's " horrible disease " of using unleavened bread at Mass had been one of the excuses for the revolt of the Patriarch Cerularius.

There is nothing easily available about this saint.   References to him may be found in Tamarati, *L'église géorgienne* (1910) ; in Martynov, *Annus ecclesiasticus Graeco-Slavicus ;* in Maltsev, *Menologium ;* and in *Bessarione*, vol. ii, pp. 133 *seq.*

ST LADISLAUS OF HUNGARY (A.D. 1095)

IF Hungary owed the establishment of its monarchy and the organization of its church to St Stephen I, it was almost equally indebted to another sainted king of the same house of Arpad. For Ladislaus extended its borders, kept its enemies at bay, and made it politically a great state. But it is not for such activities that men are canonized (if, indeed, Ladislaus ever was formally canonized, which appears to be doubtful); and it is for his private life and work for Christianity that reverence is due to his memory.

After a childhood and youth whose background was political intrigue and dynastic violence, Ladislaus (Laszlo) came to the Hungarian throne in 1077; but his rights were contested by his kinsman Solomon, whom eventually he defeated in battle. The young prince was said to be the embodiment of the outward graces and inner virtues of the ideal knight of chivalry. Towering head and shoulders above the crowd, he had the strength and courage of a lion, combined with a courteous affability that endeared him to all. His piety, which was as fervent as it was well balanced, expressed itself in his zeal for the faith, in the punctilious fulfilment of his religious obligations, in the strictness of his morals, and in the austerity of his life. Entirely devoid of personal ambition, he accepted the dignity thrust upon him from a sense of duty. In pursuance of a policy dictated alike by his religious and his patriotic instincts, Ladislaus allied himself closely with Pope Gregory VII and the other opponents of the German emperor, Henry IV. He espoused the cause of Henry's rival, Rupert of Swabia, and married Adelaide, the daughter of Rupert's chief supporter, Duke Welf of Bavaria. Within the boundaries of Hungary itself he had to face repeated invasions from the Kumans and others, but he successfully repulsed them all and did his best to win barbarian tribes to Christianity and civilization; at the same time he allowed civil and religious liberty to the Jews and the Ishmaelites, *i.e.* Mohammedans. It was at his solicitation that King Stephen I, his son Emeric, and the martyred bishop Gerard were recognized by the Holy See as worthy of veneration as saints.

Ladislaus governed with a firm hand in both civil and ecclesiastical affairs, as was seen at the diet of Szabolcs and when, in 1091, his sister Helen, the widowed queen of Croatia, appealed to him for help against the murderers of her husband. He marched in, restored some sort of order, and established the see of Zagreb. But when Helen died childless he annexed Croatia and Dalmatia, in the face of remonstrances from the emperor at Constantinople, the republic of Venice and the Holy See. Nevertheless Bd Urban II looked for his help in organizing the First Crusade, and it was Ladislaus who was chosen by the kings of France, Spain and England to be the commander-in-chief of that expedition. However he was not destined to march with the rest, for he died rather suddenly at Nitra in Bohemia in 1095. He was fifty-five years old.

The body of St Ladislaus was taken for burial to Nagy Varad (Oradea Mare in Transylvania)—to the city and the cathedral which he had founded. From the moment of his death he was honoured as a saint and a national hero, and his deeds have formed the theme of many popular Magyar ballads and tales. His relics were solemnly enshrined in 1192.

The Bollandists in the *Acta Sanctorum*, June, vol. vii, print a set of liturgical *legendae*, accompanied with the usual historical dissertation. A more reliable source is probably the life edited by S. L. Endlicher, in his *Rerum Hungaricarum Monumenta Arpadiana* (1849), pp. 235–244, and 324–348. See also *Archiv f. öster. Geschichte* (1902), pp. 46–53, and an article, " St Laszlo ", translated by E. Lindner in the *Ungarische Revue* for 1885. There are several lives published in Magyar, of which that by J. Karacsonyi (1926) is said to be the best. See also *Revue archéologique*, 1925, pp. 315–327, and C. A. Macartney, *The Medieval Hungarian Historians* (1953).

BD BENVENUTO OF GUBBIO (A.D. 1232)

BD BENVENUTO was a native of Gubbio, in Umbria, a soldier by profession and unlettered. Coming under Franciscan influence, he in 1222 took the Minorite habit. From the moment he entered the order, he modelled his life entirely upon that of St Francis. Set in charge of lepers at his own request, he treated them as though they had been our Lord Himself—tending their sores, washing them, and never shrinking from the most repulsive cases or the meanest offices. Always cheerful, always courteous, he waited upon them hand and foot ; his sympathy was perhaps the greater because he suffered much from various infirmities which he bore with unfailing patience. A considerable part of the night he spent in prayer, and often at Mass he had a vision of a beautiful little Child, and would stretch out his arms as though to embrace it. His behaviour was so exemplary that he was never known to merit a reproof of any sort. Yet in the seclusion of a religious life he might well have lived and died unrecognized by the outside world, if he had not been endowed with supernatural gifts of a high order : these spread his fame far and wide. He died at Corneto, in Apulia, in 1232. Within four years of his death, the bishops of Venice and Amalfi approached the Holy See to seek sanction for his *cultus*, and cited many miracles in support ; Pope Gregory IX granted it for their two dioceses.

No independent biography seems to be known, but see the *Acta Sanctorum*, June, vol. vii ; Wadding, *Annales O.M. ;* and Léon, *Auréole Séraphique* (Eng. trans.), vol. ii, pp. 427–429.

BB. MADELEINE FONTAINE AND HER COMPANIONS, VIRGINS AND MARTYRS (A.D. 1794)

THESE four martyrs were Sisters of Charity of St Vincent de Paul of the convent of Arras. They were the superioress, BD MADELEINE FONTAINE, aged 71 ; BD FRANCES LANEL, aged 49 ; BD TERESA FANTOU, a Breton, aged 47 ; and BD JOAN GÉRARD, aged 42. Having, in accordance with the judgement of their ordinary, refused to take the oath tendered by the Convention to clergy and religious in 1793, they were arrested as suspects on February 14 in the following year. On the strength of certain documents " planted " in their convent, they were interrogated about their " counter-revolutionary activity " ; and the notorious apostate priest Joseph Lebon ordered them to be sent to him at Cambrai, where they arrived on June 26. On the same day they were taken before the tribunal, where Sister Madeleine was condemned as " une pieuse contre-révolutionnaire ", and the other three as her accomplices.

Without further delay the sisters went boldly to execution, singing *Ave maris stella ;* and at the scaffold there was a remarkable happening. Sister Madeleine was the last to suffer, and as she approached the guillotine she turned to the crowd and shouted, " Listen, Christians ! We are the last victims. The persecution is going to stop ; the gallows will be destroyed ; the altars of Jesus will rise again gloriously." The prophecy came true. In the face of violent criticism Lebon had to halt the succession of executions ; and within six weeks his own head had fallen into the basket.

These four Sisters of Charity were beatified in 1920, and their feast is kept on June 27.

See L. Misermont, *Les bienheureuses Filles de la Charité d'Arras* (1920), in the series " Les Saints " ; and Baudot and Chaussin, *Vies des saints* . . . t. vi (1948), pp. 448–455.

28 : ST IRENAEUS, BISHOP OF LYONS   (*c.* A.D. 203)

In a Motu Proprio of John XXIII dated July 25, 1960, this feast was transferred to 3 July.

THE writings of St Irenaeus entitle him to a high place amongst the fathers of the Church, for they not only laid the foundations of Christian theology but, by exposing and refuting the errors of the gnostics, they delivered the Catholic faith from the real danger it ran of being leavened by the insidious doctrines of those heretics.   Of his parentage nothing is recorded.   He was born, probably about the year 125, in one of those maritime provinces of Asia Minor where the memory of the Apostles was still cherished and where Christians were numerous.   He received what must have been an exceptionally liberal education, for it gave him a thorough knowledge of the text of Holy Scripture and a good general acquaintance with Greek philosophy and literature.   Moreover, he had the inestimable privilege of sitting at the feet of men who had known the Apostles or their immediate disciples.   Of these the one who influenced him the most was St Polycarp.   So profound indeed was the impression made upon him by the holy bishop of Smyrna that throughout his after life, as he told a friend, he could recall every detail of St Polycarp's appearance, the sound of his voice, and the very words he used when describing his intercourse with the evangelist St John, and others who had seen the Lord, or when he was expounding the doctrine he had learnt from them.   St Gregory of Tours asserts that it was St Polycarp who sent Irenaeus as a missionary to Gaul, but there is no evidence to support this statement.

Commercial relations had existed from early times between the ports of Asia Minor and Marseilles, and in the second century of our era Levantine traders were regularly conveying their wares up the Rhone as far as Lyons, which became in consequence the chief mart of western Europe and the most populous city in Gaul. In the train of the Asiatics, many of whom settled in Lyons, came their priests and missionaries who brought the Gospel to the pagan Gauls and founded a vigorous local church.   To this church of Lyons Irenaeus came to serve as a priest under its first bishop, St Pothinus, an oriental like himself ; to it he was to remain permanently attached.   The high opinion held of him by his brother clergy was evinced in the year 177, when he was dispatched on a somewhat delicate mission to Rome.   It was after the outbreak of the terrible persecution, which is dealt with at some length under June 2 in this volume, and already some of the leaders of the church of Lyons were in prison.   Their captivity, however, did not prevent them from continuing to take a deep interest in their fellow Christians in Asia Minor. Conscious of the sympathetic hearing to which they were entitled as confessors in imminent peril of death, they sent to Pope St Eleutherius, by the hands of Irenaeus, what is described by Eusebius as " a most religious and most orthodox " letter, in which they appealed to him—in the interest of the peace and unity of the Church— to deal leniently with their Montanist brethren in Phrygia.   They commended the bearer of the letter to his notice as a priest " filled with zeal for the testament of Christ ", and as one who was, as his name implied, a lover of peace.

This mission, entailing as it did absence from Lyons, explains how it was that Irenaeus was not called upon to share the martyrdom of St Pothinus and his fellow-sufferers, and does not seem to have witnessed it. How long he remained in Rome we do not know, but when he returned to Lyons it was to occupy its vacant bishopric. By that time the persecution was over and the twenty or more years of his episcopate were years of relative peace. Information about his activities is scanty, but it is clear that in addition to his purely pastoral duties he did much to evangelize the neighbouring lands. He is said to have sent SS. Felix, Fortunatus and Achilleus as missionaries to Valence, and SS. Ferrutius and Ferreolus to Besançon. A small indication of the extent to which he identified himself with his flock is supplied by the fact that he habitually spoke the Celtic language instead of his native Greek. It was the spread of Gnosticism in Gaul, and the ravages it was making amongst the Christians of his diocese, that inspired him to undertake the task of exposing its errors. He began by mastering its tenets—no easy matter, since each gnostic master was inclined to introduce variations of his own. Fortunately for Irenaeus he was, Tertullian tells us, " a curious explorer of all kinds of learning ", and he found the work not uncongenial. He then produced a treatise in five books in which he sets forth fully the inner doctrines of the various sects, and afterwards contrasts them with the teaching of the Apostles and the text of Holy Scripture.

A good example of his method is provided by his treatment of the gnostic doctrine that the visible world has been created, preserved and governed by angelic beings and not by God, who remains unconnected with it, aloof, indifferent, and incapable of activity in the Pleroma (the invisible spiritual world). Irenaeus states the theory, develops it to its logical conclusion, and by an effective *reductio ad absurdum* proceeds to demonstrate its fallacy. The true Christian doctrine of the close relationship between God and the world He has created Irenaeus sets forth in the following terms : " The Father is above all, and He is the head of Christ, but the Word is through all things and He is Himself the head of the Church, whilst the Spirit is in us all ; and His is the living water which the Lord gave to those who believe in Him and love Him and know that there is one Father above all things and through all things and in all things." Concerned as he is to convert rather than to confound, Irenaeus writes with studied moderation and courtesy, but now and then humorous comments escape him. Referring, for instance, to the attitude of the newly " initiated " he says : " As soon as a man has been won over to their way of salvation he becomes so puffed up with conceit and self-importance that he imagines himself to be no longer in Heaven or on earth, but to have already passed into the Pleroma, and with the majestic air of a cock he goes strutting about—as if he had already embraced his angel." Irenaeus was firmly convinced that a great part of the attractiveness of Gnosticism lay in the veil of secrecy with which it surrounded itself, and he was determined to " strip the fox ", as he expressed it. The event proved him to have been right. His work, written in Greek but quickly translated into Latin, was widely circulated and succeeded in dealing to second-century Gnosticism what appears to have been its death-blow. At any rate, from that time onwards, it ceased to offer a serious menace to the Catholic faith.

Thirteen or fourteen years after his mission to Pope Eleutherius, Irenaeus again acted as mediator between a pope and a body of Christians in Asia Minor. Because the Quartodecimans refused to keep Easter in accordance with the Western use they had been excommunicated by Victor III, and there was in consequence a real danger of schism. Irenaeus intervened on their behalf. In a singularly beautiful letter addressed to the pope he pleaded with him to raise the ban, pointing out that they were only following their old tradition, and that a difference of opinion on that very point had not prevented Pope Anicetus and St Polycarp from remaining in communion. The outcome of his representations was the restoration of good relations between the two parties and a peace which proved permanent. After the Council of Nicaea in 325, the Quartodecimans voluntarily conformed to the Roman usage without any pressure from the Holy See.

The date of the death of St Irenaeus is not known : it is usually assigned approximately to the year 202. According to a later tradition he suffered martyrdom, but this is highly improbable. The treatise against the gnostics has come down to us, entire in its Latin version ; and an Armenian translation of an exposition of apostolic preaching has comparatively lately been discovered. Though the rest of his writings have perished, in these two works alone may be found all the elements of a complete system of Christian theology.

The bodily remains of St Irenaeus, as we learn from Gregory of Tours, were buried in a crypt under the altar of what was then called the church of St John, but what was later known by the name of St Irenaeus himself. This tomb or shrine was destroyed by the Calvinists in 1562, and all trace of his relics seems to have perished. It is remarkable that though the feast of St Irenaeus has long been observed in the East (on August 23), it has been general in the Western church only since 1922.

We possess nothing in the nature of an early biography of St Irenaeus, but there is a vast literature dealing with his importance as a witness to early traditions, and as a teacher of orthodox belief. The evidence for and against the supposition that he suffered martyrdom is briefly but clearly summarized by Fr Delehaye in his CMH., pp. 341–342. Much interest was roused in 1904 by the discovery of an Armenian version of a work of which little more than the name was previously known, *viz.*, " Proof of the Apostolic Preaching ". It is mainly an appeal to the prophecies of the Old Testament, and not much fresh information regarding the mind and thought of the author is to be derived from it. A fuller discussion of the theology of Irenaeus would be out of place here ; see the very complete article of F. Vernet (nearly 150 columns) in DTC., vol. vii (1922), cc. 2394–2533, with copious bibliography. There are also good articles in Bardenhewer, and DCB. The originality of St Irenaeus was called in question by T. Loofs in *Texte und Untersuchungen*, vol. xlvi, part II (1932). A convenient little study of St Irenaeus is that of A. Dufourcq in the series " Les Saints " ; and see F. R. M. Hitchcock, *Irenaeus of Lugdunum* (1914).

SS. PLUTARCH, POTAMIAENA AND THEIR COMPANIONS, MARTYRS (*c.* A.D. 202)

THE catechetical school of Origen at Alexandria was a training ground in virtue : for the master, not content with lecturing on the sciences, made a great point of inculcating upon his pupils the loftiest principles of Christian perfection. The school furnished some illustrious martyrs in the persecution of Severus which raged with great fury from 202—the year before Origen was appointed catechist—until the death of the emperor in 211.

The first to suffer was St Plutarch, brother of St Heraclas, afterwards bishop of Alexandria. The two brothers had been converted to the faith together, through listening to the lectures of Origen. Being a prominent personage Plutarch was arrested at an early stage of the persecution. He was visited and encouraged in prison by Origen, who accompanied him to the place of execution and who was nearly lynched by the mob because they held him responsible for Plutarch's death. Serenus, another of the master's disciples, was burnt alive ; Heraclides, a catechumen, and Hero, a neophyte, were beheaded. A second confessor of the name of Serenus was also decapitated after undergoing torture. Women as well as men attended the catechetical school, and three of them suffered martyrdom. Herais, a maiden who was still a catechumen, was baptized by fire—to quote Origen's own words.

The other two, Marcella and Potamiaena, were mother and daughter. Attempts were made to induce Potamiaena to purchase her freedom at the expense of her chastity, for she was young, accomplished and beautiful, but she rejected the proposals with scorn. She was then condemned to be stripped and cast into a cauldron of boiling pitch. Upon hearing her sentence, she said to the judge, " I beg of you, by the life of the emperor whom you honour, not to oblige me to appear unclothed ; rather suffer me to be slowly lowered into the cauldron fully dressed, that you may see the patience which Jesus Christ, whom you know not, bestows upon those who trust Him." The magistrate granted her request and charged Basilides, one of the guards, to lead her to execution. The man treated her with respect, protecting her from the insults and pressure of the crowd. She thanked him for his courtesy and told him that after her death she would obtain his salvation from God. The cruel sentence was then carried out. Her mother suffered at the same time.

Shortly afterwards Basilides surprised his fellow soldiers by refusing to take an oath when called upon to do so : he was a Christian, he said, and could not swear by false gods. At first they thought he was joking, but when he persisted they took him to the prefect, who consigned him to prison. In reply to the inquiries of Christians who came to visit him in gaol, he told them that Potamiaena had appeared to him after her martyrdom and had placed on his head a crown which she said she had won for him by her prayers. He received baptism in prison and, having made a glorious confession of faith before the magistrate, was beheaded. Several other persons in Alexandria are said to have been converted to Christianity as the result of visitations from St Potamiaena who came to them in their dreams.

The authority for this narrative is the *Ecclesiastical History* of Eusebius, bk vi, ch. 5. See also Delehaye, in the *Analecta Bollandiana*, vol. xl (1922), pp. 9, 23, 89 ; and Augar, in *Texte und Untersuchungen*, N.F., vol. xiii, part 4 (1905), pp. 17 *seq.*

ST PAUL I, POPE   (A.D. 767)

THE immediate successor of Pope Stephen III in the chair of St Peter was his younger brother Paul. They had been educated together at the Lateran school, they had been made deacons together by Pope St Zachary, and Paul remained closely associated with his brother, whom he tenderly nursed in his last illness and whose policy he continued to pursue. A contemporary, writing in the *Liber Pontificalis*, pays an eloquent tribute to Paul's personal character, emphasizing his kindness, his clemency and his magnanimity. He was always ready to help those in distress and never did he return evil for evil. Often, under cover of the night, he would visit the sick poor in their homes or in hospitals. Sometimes he would enter the prisons and redeem poor debtors : occasionally he would release prisoners under sentence of death. If he erred, it was always on the side of leniency.

Paul's pontificate of ten years was relatively peaceful abroad, owing to his good relations with King Pepin, and peaceful at home owing to his own firm government :

" firm " is hardly a strong enough word—the severity of Paul's administration is in marked contrast with the kindness of character attributed to him by the *Liber Pontificalis*. At the same time the record of his pontificate is chiefly one long tale of political diplomacy ; in the words of Monsignor Mann : " By unceasing diplomatic effort Paul prevented the Lombards on the one hand and the Greeks on the other from effecting anything of moment against the newly acquired temporal power of the supreme pontiff ; he caused great events never to get beyond the eve of happening." He kept on the best of terms with Pepin, sending him exceedingly polite letters, presents (including an organ) and relics of the martyrs.

In Rome itself the pope's activities took a more concrete form. From catacombs, reduced to ruin by the ravages of time or of the barbarians, he transferred the relics of many saints to churches in the City. Amongst others the remains of St Petronilla, the supposed daughter of St Peter, were brought to a restored mausoleum which became known as the Chapel of the Kings of France. He built or rebuilt a church of SS. Peter and Paul ; he also erected in St Peter's an oratory in honour of our Lady. In his paternal mansion, which he converted into a monastery under the dedication of the popes St Stephen I and St Silvester, he placed Greek monks, refugees from the iconoclast persecution. The adjoining church, entirely rebuilt by him for them, received the name of San Silvestro in Capite, from the head, reputed to be that of St John Baptist, which the monks had brought from the East. Eleven hundred years later that same church (but long since again rebuilt) was given by Pope Leo XIII to the Catholics of England.

Pope Paul was staying at St Paul's outside the Walls, whither he had gone to escape the summer heat in Rome, when he was seized with a fever which proved fatal. He died on June 28, 767.

The *Liber Pontificalis*, in Duchesne's edition (vol. i, pp. 463–467), is the most reliable source for an estimate of the pope's personal character. The letters of Paul I may be studied in MGH., *Epistolae*, vol. iii, in the edition of Gundlach. For English readers, the painstaking account given in Mgr Mann's *Lives of the Popes* (vol. i, part II, pp. 331–360) is the most satisfactory, and easily accessible. See also the *Acta Sanctorum*, June, vol. vii ; Duchesne, *Les premiers temps de l'État Pontifical* (1904), pp. 79–94 ; M. Baumont in *Mélanges d'archéologie et d'histoire*, 1930, pp. 7–24 ; F. H. Seppelt, *Das Papsttum im Früh-mittelalter* (1934), pp. 137–146 ; Fliche and Martin, *Histoire de l'Église*, t. vi (1937), pp. 17–31.

ST HEIMRAD (A.D. 1019)

THE *cultus* of St Heimrad is a purely popular one ; it has never received any official sanction. It arose from reports of miraculous happenings at his tomb, which accordingly became a place of pilgrimage. His career casts a curious light upon social conditions of the age in which he lived. His parents were serfs, attached to a great estate in Swabia ; but Heimrad himself was trained for the priesthood, and appointed chaplain to the great lady on whose property he had been born. The post proving to be one for which he was quite unfitted, he was released at his own request. He then went on pilgrimages, first to Rome and then to Jerusalem, begging his bread as he went, and sharing with other wayfarers whatever he received from charity. After his return, he took to a life of vagrancy, and wandered about, mainly in Thuringia, Hesse and Westphalia. At one time, indeed, he seemed disposed to settle down in the abbey of Hersfeld, where he was allowed to stay on, though he refused to take the habit or to submit to the rule. Before long, however, the old restlessness returned. One day, when the community were at chapter, he flung himself down dramatically in their midst and asked leave to depart.   He was sure, he declared, that he could never find his salvation there.   Far from wishing to detain him, the abbot seems to have been glad to be relieved of his presence, and the malcontent was rather unceremoniously turned out of the monastery.

Heimrad was, or pretended to be, aggrieved, and bewailed aloud the treatment that had been meted out to him.   It was very wrong, he declared, of the abbot and monks to subject him, an emperor's brother, to such indignity.   His biographer insinuates, let us note, that he only meant that he, like the rest of mankind, was a brother of Jesus Christ.   The preposterous claim, however, highly amused the bystanders, but the abbot, when he heard of it, took the matter more seriously, and directed that Heimrad should be whipped.   While a kindly brother was administering a not too severe castigation, the victim, we are told, recited the first half of the *Miserere.*   Afterwards he resumed his nomad existence, and in the course of his peregrinations came to Kirchberg and to Detmold in Westphalia.   Here the parish priest allowed him to take over a disused church, but soon had reason to regret the concession.   For he found himself abandoned by his congregation, who preferred the ministrations of the newcomer, whose abnegation and eccentric ways they, rightly or wrongly, took for sanctity, and transferred to him their customary offerings.   Insult seemed to be added to injury when Heimrad refused a gift from the priest's wife—this was before the strict enforcement of celibacy in the West—on the ground that she was living an immoral life.   This was too much for the incumbent; he set the dogs at his rival, and hounded him out of the place.

Wherever Heimrad went, his gaunt form, emaciated countenance and strange utterances could not fail to attract notice ; but whilst in some quarters he was honoured as a saint, in others he was treated as an impostor or a demoniac.   St Cunegund, when she came to Paderborn with the Emperor St Henry, sentenced him to a flogging, and he fared no better at the hands of St Meinwerk, Bishop of Paderborn, before whom he subsequently appeared.   For the prelate, recognizing him at once, began the proceedings by treating him as an *energumen,* and inquiring where that demoniac had sprung from now.   Then, when Heimrad asserted that he had not a devil, but was a priest and had offered Mass that day, Meinwerk told him to produce the books he had used.   Heimrad obeyed ; but their dirty and dilapidated condition so scandalized the bishop that he consigned them to the flames, and condemned their owner to be beaten.

Heimrad's wanderings came to an end before long—possibly as the result of advancing years and increasing infirmities.   He made a retreat for himself in a wood near the modern town of Wolfhagen in Hesse-Nassau, and there leading an existence of great austerity and destitution, he remained unmolested until his death in the year 1019.   Many miracles are said to have followed, and half a century later, in fulfilment, it is stated, of one of his prophecies, a monastery was erected over his last resting-place, which was dedicated under the names of SS. Peter and Paul and St Heimrad.

The medieval life which relates this strange story was written, seemingly, not much more than fifty years after Heimrad's death, by Egbert, a monk of Hersfeld.   The author claims to have learnt details from his own father, and from others who had known the recluse personally.   The life is printed in the *Acta Sanctorum,* June, vol. vii, and also in MGH., *Scriptores,* vol. x, pp. 598–607.   Egbert seems to suggest that many of the extravagant things recorded of Heimrad were deliberately done by him to draw contempt upon himself.   We must remember that a similar purpose at times animated St Francis of Assisi and his first companions, and may probably be recognized in St Benedict Joseph Labre, who was a sort of professional vagrant nearer our own day, while such a form of ascesis is almost a commonplace in Eastern hagiology.

## SS. SERGIUS AND GERMANUS OF VALAAM, ABBOTS	(DATE UNCERTAIN)

SS. SERGIUS and GERMANUS (Herman) are venerated as Greek monks who founded the great Russian monastery of Valaam (Valamo), on the island of that name in the huge lake called Ladoga in the south-eastern corner of Finland, from whence they evangelized the heathen Karelians on its shores.   This event is commonly put between the years 973 and 992, at the time when the evangelization of the Russians was beginning around Kiev, but there is no solid ground for accepting so early a date.   The monastery was certainly founded before the fifteenth century, and it was re-established by the Tsar Peter the Great in 1718 ; but before then it had been an unoccupied ruin for a century, because of the wars between Sweden and Russia.   Accordingly both written and oral tradition has been broken, and there are only uncertain or obviously mistaken suppositions about the foundation of the house.

A more likely date than 992 is 1329, when Russian monasteries were being planted in the Ladoga region as part of a political consolidation against the Swedes in western Karelia.   There is a story that at this time St Sergius took up his abode in the Vaaga cave, an old site of heathen worship : he was a stranger, from Novgorod or from Byzantium, and according to one version he had been at the head of the powerful trading community in the first-named city.   From his cave he tended the souls and bodies of the people, and for his living and recreation he carved in stone.   As well as becoming head of a monastic community, he was looked on as head-man of the neighbourhood in civil affairs.

There is a legend that St Sergius baptized a Karelian called Munga, who became his successor under the name of Germanus.   It seems that this legend has arisen from confusion with a seventeenth-century Hans Munck, who was a local Swedish governor and a Lutheran, and certainly did not end his days in a monastery.   All that is known about Germanus is that he was a contemporary of St Sergius and his collaborator.   At any rate until the war of 1939, the shrines of the two saints were venerated in the *katholikon* of the Valaam monastery.

SS. Sergius and Germanus are among the Russian saints mentioned under St Sergius of Radonezh on September 25.   Their history is extremely elusive, and for the above notes the writer is principally indebted to Mr Ragnar Rosén, formerly director of the Finnish state archives at Viborg and now director of the municipal archives at Helsinki.   The Valaam monastery of the Russian Orthodox Church is one of those recognized by the Soviet authorities since 1943.   For an account of it before World War II, see an article by Father S. M. Quandalle, in *Russie et Chrétienté*, no. 1 (1938) ; see also C. F. L. St George in *Eastern Churches Quarterly*, vol. iii, no. 3 (1938).

## BD JOHN SOUTHWORTH, MARTYR	(A.D. 1654)

INTEREST in Bd John Southworth was quickened by the discovery of his remains at Douai in 1927, and by their enshrining in the chapel of St George and the English Martyrs in Westminster cathedral.   The Southworths were a Lancashire family which remained staunch to the Catholic faith throughout the penal days, although it suffered much persecution and became greatly impoverished by heavy fines.   John, a member of the younger branch of the house, was sent to Douai

College in 1613 at the age of twenty-one to be trained for the priesthood. After his ordination five years later he tried his vocation for a short time with the Benedictines, but finding that he was not called to the monastic life he decided to remain a secular priest. On December 13, 1619, he was sent on the English mission. All that is known of his whereabouts and activities during the next few years is that he was living in or near London in 1623. The following year he was back in Belgium, first at Douai and then in Brussels, where he was confessor to the Benedictine nuns. Before long, however, he returned to England—this time to his native Lancashire. He laboured there until 1627, when he was arrested and tried on the charge of being a priest and of exercising his sacerdotal functions on English soil. Though condemned to death he was reprieved, and from the window of his cell in Lancaster castle he was able to give absolution to Bd Edmund Arrowsmith as that martyr was being carried to execution.

After three years Mr Southworth was transferred to London and there released, together with some fifteen other priests, at the instance of Queen Henrietta Maria. All of them were ordered to leave the country. Whether Bd John obeyed the injunction is doubtful. He was certainly living in England soon afterwards, and in 1632 he was a prisoner in the Clink. We learn, however, from a complaint made by the Puritan, Prynne, that " he had full liberty to walk abroad at his pleasure as most priests had during their imprisonment ". Of that licence he made full use during a virulent outbreak of plague in 1636. Relief granted to poor sufferers through parish officials was withheld from households known to be Catholic, and their fate would indeed have been tragic had it not been for the devotion of John Southworth and of his fellow martyr, Bd Henry Morse. The two priests visited daily the stricken houses of the Westminster area, distributing the alms provided by the queen and other charitable persons, besides administering the consolations of religion. Some four hundred families were thus assisted. When Morse fell a victim to the prevailing epidemic Southworth carried on alone, until he found himself strictly confined within the prison walls as the result of representations made by the curate of St Margaret's, who had seen him emerge from an infected house and who asserted that he was seducing the people and had recently reconciled two dying men to the Catholic faith. However, an appeal made to the queen led to a restoration of his former privileges ; and not long afterwards, through her influence and that of Windebank, the secretary of state, he was released from captivity.

" Any other particulars relating to Mr Southworth's missionary labours I have not been able to find ", writes Bishop Challoner, " for want of proper memoirs, or any more of him till his final apprehension in 1654 when, upon information of one Jefferies, a pursuivant . . . he was taken out of bed at night by Colonel Worsley, and upon his own confession of having exercised his functions since his reprieve, he was condemned and dragged to Tyburn upon a sledge, between two coiners." Efforts had been made to save him by the foreign ambassadors and even by his judges, who urged him to plead " not guilty " ; but he would not appear to disavow his priesthood, and they had no option but to pass upon him the sentence of death. His martyrdom took place on the eve of the feast of SS. Peter and Paul, 1654, when he was sixty-two years of age. His body was bought by the Spanish ambassador and transported to the chapel of the English College at Douai, where it remained until the confiscation of the establishment by the revolutionary authorities in 1793. To save the martyr's relics from profanation his coffin was secretly removed by four of the students and buried inside the building. In 1927 it was discovered by a workman when he was excavating the foundations of what had once been the college. The contents were identified and Bd John Southworth's partly desiccated remains were brought back to England to rest at St Edmund's College, near Ware, which carries on the work of the old Douai seminary. Four months after the 1929 beatification of English martyrs it was removed to Westminster, and on May 1, 1930, it was solemnly translated to its present place in the cathedral.

Everything that is known concerning Bd John seems to have been brought together in the volume published in 1930 by Fr A. B. Purdie, *The Life of Bd John Southworth*. See also Challoner, MMP., pp. 504–510.

29 : ST PETER, PRINCE OF THE APOSTLES * (A.D. 64 ?)

THE story of St Peter as recounted in the gospels is so familiar that there can be no need to retrace it here in detail. We know that he was a Galilean, that his original home was at Bethsaida, that he was married, a fisherman, and that he was brother to the apostle St Andrew. His name was Simon, but our Lord, on first meeting him, told him that he should be called Kephas, the Aramaic equivalent of the Greek word whose English form is Peter (*i.e.* rock). No one who reads the New Testament can be blind to the predominant rôle which is everywhere accorded to him among the immediate followers of Jesus. It was he who, as spokesman of the rest, made the sublime profession of faith : " Thou art the Christ, the Son of the living God " ; and it was to him personally that our Saviour, with a solemnity of phrase which finds no parallel in the rest of the gospel narrative, addressed the words : " Blessed art thou Simon bar-Jona, because flesh and blood hath not revealed it to thee, but my Father who is in Heaven. And I say to thee, that thou art Peter, and upon this rock I will build my Church, and the gates of Hell shall not prevail against it ; and I will give to thee the keys of the kingdom of Heaven ; and whatsoever thou shalt bind upon earth, it shall be bound also in Heaven ; and whatsoever thou shalt loose on earth, it shall be loosed also in Heaven."

Not less familiar is the story of Peter's triple denial of his Master in spite of the warning he had previously received. The very fact that his fall is recorded by all four evangelists with a fullness of detail which seems out of proportion to its relative insignificance amid the incidents of our Saviour's passion, is itself a tribute to the position which St Peter occupied among his fellows. On the other hand, if our Lord's warning met with no response, we must also remember that it was prefaced by those astounding words, with their strange change from the plural to the singular : " Simon, Simon, behold Satan hath desired to have you that he may sift you as wheat ; but I have prayed for thee, that thy faith fail not, and thou, being once converted, confirm thy brethren." Equally impressive is the triple reparation which our Lord tenderly but almost cruelly extorted from His shamefaced disciple beside the Sea of Galilee. " When therefore they had dined, Jesus saith to Simon

---

* " Prince " is from Latin *princeps*, meaning simply supreme head or leader. The equivalent Greek term is κορυφαῖος, which in Byzantine usage is applied to both St Peter and St Paul ; this term was applied to the leader of the chorus in Attic drama ; hence eventually *coryphée*, the chief dancer in a ballet.

Peter, ' Simon, son of John, lovest thou me more than these ? '   He saith to him :
' Yea, Lord, thou knowest that I love thee.'   He saith to him :   ' Feed my lambs.'
He saith to him again :   ' Simon, son of John, lovest thou me ? '   He saith to Him :
' Yea, Lord, thou knowest that I love thee.'   He saith to him :   ' Feed my lambs.'
He said to him the third time :   ' Simon, son of John, lovest thou me ? '   Peter was
grieved, because He had said to him the third time :   lovest thou me ?   And he
said to Him :   ' Lord, thou knowest all things :   thou knowest that I love thee.'   He
said to him :   ' Feed my sheep '."   But the prophecy which follows is almost more
wonderful ;   for Jesus went on :   " Amen, amen, I say to thee, when thou wast
younger thou didst gird thyself and didst walk where thou wouldst.   But when
thou shalt be old, thou shalt stretch forth thy hands, and another shall gird thee
and lead thee whither thou wouldst not."   " And this," adds the evangelist, " He
said, signifying by what death he should glorify God."

After the Ascension we find St Peter still everywhere taking a leading part.   It
is he who is named first in the group of apostles who, in the upper room, " persevered with one mind in prayer with the women and Mary the mother of Jesus ",
until the coming of the Holy Ghost on the day of the Pentecost.   It was he, also,
who took the initiative in the choosing of a new apostle in the place of Judas, and
he who first addressed the jeering crowd, bearing testimony to " Jesus of Nazareth,
a man approved of God among you, by miracles and wonders and signs which
God did by Him in the midst of you, whom God raised again, whereof all we are
witnesses ".   Further, we are told :   " Now when they had heard these things, they
had compunction in their heart, and said to Peter and to the rest of the apostles :
' What shall we do, men and brethren ? '   Peter said to them :   ' Repent, and be
baptized every one of you in the name of Jesus Christ.' "   Whereupon " they that
received his word were baptized ;   and there were added in that day about three
thousand souls ".   It is Peter, too, who is recorded to have done the first miracle
of healing known in the Christian Church.   A man lame from his birth was lying at
the gate of the Temple when Peter and John went up to pray, and he asked them for
an alms.   " Peter with John fastening his eyes upon him said :   ' Look upon us.'
But he looked earnestly upon them, hoping that he should receive something of
them.   But Peter said :   ' Silver and gold I have none, but what I have, I give thee :
in the name of Jesus Christ of Nazareth, arise and walk.'   And taking him by the
right hand, he lifted him up, and forthwith his feet and soles received strength.
And he leaping up, stood and walked, and went with them into the temple, walking
and leaping and praising God."

When the outbreak of persecution began which culminated in the martyrdom
of St Stephen in the presence of Saul, the future apostle of the Gentiles, the new
converts to Christ's teaching, for the most part, scattered, but the Apostles stood
their ground in Jerusalem until news came of the favourable reception accorded in
Samaria to the preaching of St Philip the Deacon.   Then St Peter and St John
betook themselves to the field of these labours and imposed hands upon (gave
confirmation to ?) those whom St Philip had already baptized.   Among these last
was a man, best known to us as Simon Magus, who claimed to possess occult
powers and had acquired great influence by his sorceries.   Being apparently
impressed by what he witnessed in those who had been newly confirmed, he came
to the Apostles, saying, " Give me also this power, that on whomsoever I shall lay
my hands, he may receive the Holy Ghost."   But, offering them money, he only
met with a stern rebuke ;   for Peter said, " Keep thy money to thyself, to perish

with thee, because thou hast thought that the gift of God may be purchased with money."

In the apocryphal literature known as the " Clementines ", Simon is represented as meeting St Peter at a later date and carrying on a long contest with him and St Clement as they journey from one to another of the maritime cities of Syria on the way to Rome. Earlier still than the Clementines, St Justin Martyr (writing in the year 152) declares that Simon Magus came to Rome and was there honoured as a deity, but it must be admitted that the evidence Justin quotes for this is quite unsatisfactory. Again, in the apocryphal " Acts of St Peter ", there is a dramatic story of the Magus's attempt to gain over the Emperor Nero by a demonstration of his occult power in flying through the air. According to this legend, SS. Peter and Paul were present and by their prayers rendered the sorcerer's magic ineffective. He fell to the ground and died soon afterwards of his injuries. Other, and quite contradictory stories, are repeated by Hippolytus (in the *Philosophumena*) and by other early writers, always turning upon some sort of conflict between Simon and the two great apostles, with Rome as the background of the drama. Unconvincing as the evidence is, there is a general disposition among early Christian writers, such, for instance, as St Irenaeus, to regard Simon Magus as " the father of heresies ", and as in some special way the antagonist of SS. Peter and Paul, the representatives of Christian truth in the capital of the world.

Almost all that we know for certain about the later life of St Peter is derived from the Acts of the Apostles and from slight allusions in his own epistles and those of St Paul. Of special importance is the account of the conversion of the centurion Cornelius ; for this raised the question of the continuance of the rite of circumcision and the maintenance of the prescriptions of the Jewish law in such matters as food and intercourse with the Gentiles. Instructed by a special vision, St Peter, albeit with some hesitancy, came to see that the old dispensation was at an end, and that the Church founded by Christ was to be the Church of the Gentiles as well as of the Jews. He was reproached somewhat later by St Paul, as we learn from the Epistle to the Galatians (ch. ii), with being an opportunist and only half-hearted in acting up to these principles. The incident seems to have been connected with a gathering of certain of the apostles and elders, which has been called the Council of Jerusalem, but whether this preceded or followed St Paul's rebuke to St Peter at Antioch is not quite certain. In any case, it was St Peter's address which guided the decision at which the Jerusalem assembly arrived. The resolution come to was that the Gentile converts to Christianity need not be circumcised or required to observe the law of Moses. On the other hand, to avoid too grievous a shock to Jewish susceptibilities, they were to abstain from blood and from things strangled, as well as from fornication and from idol-offerings. This decision was communicated to Antioch and served to calm the troubled feelings of the fast-growing Christian community in that great city.

It is possible, though we have no really reliable evidence upon the point, that before the Jerusalem council (A.D. 49 ?) St Peter had already, for two years or more, been bishop of Antioch, and that he may even have made his way to Rome, thus taking possession of what was to be his permanent see. A striking incident recorded in the Acts is the violent outbreak of persecution under Herod Agrippa I, probably in the year 43. We are told that Herod " slew James the brother of John with the sword "—this, of course, was the elder James, the apostle whose feast is kept on July 25—and that then he proceeded to arrest Peter also. However, " prayer was earnestly being offered to God by the Church in his behalf ", and Peter, though " he was sleeping between two soldiers bound with two chains, and sentries outside the door were guarding the prison ", was released by an angel and was able to make his way to a safe refuge.   After that we are only told that " he departed and went to another place ", by which might be meant Antioch, or even Rome.   From this point Peter is mentioned no more in the Acts except in connection with the council at Jerusalem as described above.

The passion of St Peter took place in Rome during the reign of Nero (A.D. 54–68), but no written account of it (if there was such a thing) has survived.   According to an old but unverifiable tradition he was confined in the Mamertine prison, where the church of San Pietro in Carcere now stands.   Tertullian (d. *c.* 225) says that the apostle was crucified ; and Eusebius adds, on the authority of Origen (d. 253), that by his own desire he suffered head downwards.   The place has always been believed to be the gardens of Nero, which saw so many scenes of terror and glory at this time.   The, at one time, generally accepted tradition that St Peter's pontificate lasted twenty-five years is probably no more than a deduction based upon inconsistent chronological data.   The beautiful legend that St Peter, departing out of Rome at the earnest request of his flock, met our Lord coming in, and asked Him, " *Domine quo vadis?* " (Lord, whither goest thou ?), is first told by St Ambrose in his sermon against Auxentius.   Our Lord answered, " I am coming to be crucified a second time ", and St Peter at once turned back, realizing that the cross of which the Saviour spoke was that which was destined for himself.   The agreement of this story with the thought expressed in stanzas 4 and 5 of the striking hymn, *Apostolorum passio*, is, as A. S. Walpole pointed out, one among many reasons for attributing the hymn quite definitely to St Ambrose.

This is not the place to discuss objections that have been made from time to time against the tradition of St Peter's episcopate and martyrdom in Rome (*cf.* the feast of his Chair at Rome on January 18).   It is probably true to say that no serious scholar now questions it, for the weight of evidence from both documents and monuments is decisive.   But brief reference may be made to certain early indications of strong popular devotion to Peter and Paul in the City.   According to a view which has been accepted by many Roman archaeologists, the bodies both of St Peter and St Paul were in the year 258 conveyed from their respective tombs beside the Vatican and on the Ostian Way to some hiding-place, *ad catacumbas*, on the Appian Way, close to the site where the basilica of St Sebastian now stands.   Excavations in 1915–1922 were undertaken to find this hiding-place, or at any rate some trace of it, but in this respect the investigation does not seem to have been crowned with success.   There was found, however, the basin or hollow (κύμβη) in the tufa, from which the now familiar name " catacomb " is derived.   The place was called *ad catacumbas* because its most conspicuous original feature was a series of sepulchral chambers constructed in the tufa beside a natural depression in the ground (κατὰ κύμβας).

Close beside these, however, there were found the walls of a large room, open on one side to the air, which must have been constructed about the year 250.   From its decorations and other details it was clearly a place intended for meetings of a more or less convivial and ceremonial character.   There is good reason to suppose that it was the scene of those repasts called *agapae*, the Christian love-feasts of the early centuries.   What is beyond question is that the remains of the plaster coating left here and there on the walls are covered with *graffiti* (scribblings) which can be dated with security as belonging to the second half of the third century. They seem to have been a rather uneducated crowd who scrawled their pious sentiments upon the plaster, but their devotion to Peter and Paul is made everywhere manifest. Here are a specimen or two, selected from a great number, almost all fragmentary :

" PETRO ET PAULO TOMIUS COELIUS REFRIGERIUM FECI."

Refrigerium was the treat or entertainment provided at these reunions by some more affluent person for the benefit of his poorer fellow Christians ; so that we may translate the scribble : " I, Tomius Coelius, made a feast to the honour of Peter and Paul."

" DALMATIUS BOTUM IS PROMISIT REFRIGERIUM." (By way of a vow Dalmatius promised a feast for these.)

Many of the scrawls are simply invocations. Thus :

" PAULE ET PETRE PETITE PRO VICTORE." (Paul and Peter, make intercession for Victor.)

" PETRUS ET PAULUS IN MENTE ABEATIS ANTONIUS BASSUM." (Peter and Paul, do not forget Antonius Bassus.)

These spontaneous and often quite illiterate appeals point clearly to a great popular *cultus* of SS. Peter and Paul at this spot. Most are written in Latin, a few in Greek, but the Latin is often scrawled in Greek letters. As already noticed, the plaster only remains in patches, and many of the scribblings are illegible, but in the case of nearly eighty the names of both apostles can be discerned, sometimes that of Peter standing first, sometimes that of Paul. There can be no possible question that somewhere during the latter half of the third century, and consequently in close accord with an entry in the Philocalian calendar of 354 which commemorates a translation, or at any rate a festival celebration, of the two apostles *ad catacumbas* in 258, there existed precisely in that spot a vigorous popular devotion to the two great Roman patrons conjointly, the evidence of which remains to this day.

Already, at the beginning of the third century, Caius, as quoted by Eusebius, records that the scene of the triumph of St Peter was to be found on the Vatican hill, whereas the martyrdom of St Paul was honoured on the Ostian Way. Father Delehaye and some other distinguished hagiographical experts hold that the bodies of the two apostles were interred there from the beginning and have never since been disturbed ; others suggest that they were temporarily buried at the Appian Way site immediately after their deaths, until permanent tombs near the scene of their respective martyrdoms could be prepared. In either case the inscription set up by Pope St Damasus I (d. 384) at the place near St Sebastian's would then merely commemorate the institution of a festival in 258 which, for convenience or some other reason, was celebrated *ad catacumbas*.

Since the above was written the results of the excavations, begun under St. Peter's basilica in 1938, have been made public. The site and fragmentary remains of the Apostle's tomb there seem to have been established and identified beyond reasonable doubt ; but whether the human remains found in close proximity are those of St Peter can at present, and perhaps for ever, be only a matter of surmise. This discovery on the Vatican hill revives interest in the San Sebastiano site ; but the theory that, after a translation *ad catacumbas* in 258, the bones of St Peter remained there permanently is for several reasons a most unlikely one.

The joint feast of SS. Peter and Paul seems always to have been kept at Rome on June 29, and Duchesne considers that the practice goes back at least to the time of Constantine ; but the celebration in the East was at first commonly assigned to December 28. This was the case at Oxyrhynchus in Egypt, as surviving papyri attest, as late as the year 536, but in Constantinople and elsewhere in the Eastern empire the Roman date for the commemoration gradually won acceptance. The joint feast was kept in Syria in the early fifth century, as we learn from the Syriac *breviarium* of that period, which has an entry in this form : " December 28, in the City of Rome, Paul the Apostle, and Simon Kephas (*i.e.* Peter), the chief of the Apostles of the Lord."

There is, of course, an enormous literature connected with St Peter, which deals with his life and office from every point of view. The commentators on the gospels and on the Acts of the Apostles cover a large part of the ground with which such a work as the present is specially concerned. The little volume *S. Pierre* (in the series " Les Saints "), by L. C. Fillion, forms an excellent introduction to the subject, as it includes the whole range of what is recorded of the apostle ; that of C. Fouard, *St Peter* (Eng. trans.), is more detailed, but it is mainly concerned with the early years of the Christian Church, leaving aside what we are told of St Peter in the gospels. To these may be added R. Aigrain's *St Pierre* (1938) and a popular American work by W. T. Walsh, *St Peter the Apostle* (1950). For St Peter's teaching, G. Thils, *L'enseignement de St Pierre* (1946) may be consulted, and on the early primacy Bishop Besson's *St Pierre et les origines de la primauté Romaine* (1929) is excellent. Among other non-Catholic scholars, see Bishop Lightfoot, *Apostolic Fathers* (1877), W. Ramsay, *The Church and the Roman Empire* (1893), O. Cullmann, *Peter : Disciple, Apostle, Martyr* (1954), and H. Lietzmann, *Petrus und Paulus in Rom* (1927) and *Petrus Römischer Martyrer* (1936) on St Peter in Rome. For a discussion of the catacomb problem, see F. Toletti's article in *Rivista di archeologia cristiana*, 1947–1948 ; Mgr A. S. Barnes, *The Martyrdom of St Peter and St Paul* (1933), on which cf. *Analecta Bollandiana*, vol. lii (1934), pp. 69–72 ; and P. Styger, *Die römischen Katacumben* (1933). Cf. also the *Liber Pontificalis* (ed. Duchesne), vol. i, and Delehaye, *Origines du culte des martyrs* (1933), pp. 263–269. The report of the 1938–1950 excavations has been published in 2 vols., one of text and one of illustrations ; see an article by P. Romanelli in the *Osservatore Romano*, December 19, 1951. Numerous other articles in various languages on the results of the excavations appeared, among them two by J. B. Ward Perkins, in *The Listener*, 25 Sept. 1952, and in the *Journal of Roman Studies*, vol. xlii (1952).

ST PAUL, Apostle of the Gentiles   (A.D. 67 ?)

Of all the saints with whom we are made acquainted through the pages of Holy Writ, St Paul is the most intimately known to us. We possess not merely an exact external record of his doings, furnished by his disciple, St Luke, in the Acts of the Apostles, but we have his own incomparable self-revelation in his letters which, while prompted always by no other purpose than to benefit those to whom he writes, lay bare his very soul.* It would be difficult, without transcribing a great part of the New Testament, to draw a faithful picture of the character of the Apostle of the Gentiles ; and the New Testament, it may be assumed, is in the hands of all. In the first volume of this series, under January 25, St Paul's conversion has been narrated. In the present notice it has seemed best to leave on one side the thirty-two pages which Butler devoted to an account of the apostle's missionary journeys and his writings, and to give a brief summary of what St Luke records in the last fifteen chapters of the Acts.

* There is also some evidence about his physical appearance (*cf.* 2 Corinthians x, 10). A second-century document, the so-called *Acts of Paul and Thecla*, says that he was " a man small in size, bald-headed, bandy-legged, well built, with eyebrows meeting, rather long-nosed, full of grace. For sometimes he seemed like a man, and sometimes he had the countenance of an angel."

When Saul, on his way to Damascus, had been stricken down and converted from a prosecutor into the eager servant of Christ, he withdrew, on recovering from his temporary blindness, to spend three years of seclusion in " Arabia ". Then, returning to Damascus, he began to preach the gospel with fervour. But fury against his teaching was such that he had to make his escape, being let down the city wall in a basket. He directed his steps to Jerusalem, and there, perhaps not unnaturally, he was at first regarded by the Apostles and their converts with considerable suspicion, until the generous support of Barnabas allayed their fears. In Jerusalem, however, he could not stay—the resentment of the Jews against him was too strong—and being warned by a vision which came to him in the temple, Saul went back for a time to his native city of Tarsus. Thither Barnabas went to seek him, and yielding to his persuasion Saul accompanied him to Antioch in Syria, where the two preached with such success that a great community of believers was founded who, in that city for the first time, began to be known as " Christians ".

After a twelve-months' stay Saul, in 44, paid his second visit to Jerusalem, coming with his companion to bring contributions to the brethren who were suffering from famine. By this time all doubts concerning Saul's stability had been laid at rest. By the direction of the Holy Spirit he and Barnabas, after their return to Antioch, were ordained, and forthwith set out on a missionary journey, first to Cyprus and then to Asia Minor. In Cyprus they converted the proconsul, Sergius Paulus, and exposed the false prophet Elymas, by whom he had been duped. Thence crossing to Perga, they made their way through the Taurus mountains to Antioch of Pisidia, and went on to preach in Iconium and then in Lystra, where, healing a cripple, they were at first taken for gods—Barnabas was Jupiter and Paul Mercury, " because he was the chief speaker " ; but enemies among the Jews provoked a revulsion of feeling, Paul, as he now begins to be called by his Gentile name, was stoned and left for dead. They escaped, however, and fled secretly to Derbe, whence in time they pursued their journey to the more peaceful atmosphere of the Syrian Antioch. Two or three years had probably been spent in this first missionary expedition, and it seems to have been in the summer of 49 that Paul came to Jerusalem for the third time, and was present at the meeting in which the question of the attitude of the Christian Church towards Gentile converts was finally decided. The incident in which Paul, as recorded in the second chapter of the Epistle to the Galatians, remonstrated with St Peter at Antioch over his too conservative Judaism, had perhaps occurred in the preceding winter.

Then the years from 49 to 52 were spent by St Paul in his second great missionary journey. Taking Silas with him, he travelled through Derbe to Lystra, regardless of what had previously befallen him in that place, but he was rewarded by the faithful discipleship of Timothy, whose parents dwelt there, Paul, on his part, being seemingly more careful to avoid giving unnecessary offence to the Jews ; for he had Timothy circumcised, as his mother was a Jewess, though his father was a Greek. Accompanied by both Timothy and Silas, St Paul went through Phrygia and Galatia preaching and founding churches. He was, however, prevented from proceeding farther in a northerly direction by a vision which summoned him to Macedonia. Accordingly he crossed over from Troas ; the beloved physician, St Luke, the author of a Gospel and the Acts, being now apparently of the party. At Philippi we have the very interesting episode of the girl with the divining spirit who called after them, " These men are the servants of the most high God ". But though this might have seemed to help the cause, Paul commanded the spirit to go out of her. This put an end to the girl's powers of divining, and her masters, deprived of a source of profit, raised a clamour and brought Paul and Silas before the magistrates. The two missionaries were beaten and thrown into prison, but were miraculously set at liberty. We need not trace the further stages of this journey. The missionaries made their way through Macedonia, Beroea and Athens to Corinth. At Athens we have an account of the address delivered by St Paul on the Areopagus, in which he took occasion to comment upon their altar dedicated " to the unknown god ". In Corinth his preaching made a deeper impression and we are told that he settled there for a year and six months. In the year 52 St Paul seems to have left Corinth to come to Jerusalem—his fourth visit— possibly to be present there for Pentecost, but he remained for only a short time and went on to Antioch.

The third missionary journey is thought ·to have covered the years 52 to 56. St Paul traversed Galatia, the Roman province of " Asia ", Macedonia, Achaia, crossed back to Macedonia, and made a return by sea which allowed him to pay his fifth visit to Jerusalem. During this period he probably spent three winters at Ephesus, and it was at Ephesus that occurred the great disturbance raised by Demetrius the silversmith, when Paul's preaching interfered with the profitable trade which many of the townspeople carried on in making and selling images of Diana. Then at Jerusalem we have the story told in detail of the apostle's reception by the elders and of the intense popular commotion excited by his visit to the Temple. He was arrested, roughly handled, and bound with chains, but before the tribune he defended himself with vigour. The official inquiry ended by his being conveyed to Caesarea, for a plot was discovered in which forty Jews had bound themselves under a curse " that they would neither eat not drink until they should kill Paul ". At Caesarea he was kept in captivity for two years, under the proconsuls Felix and Festus, while the uncertain trial dragged on, for the governors, though all evidence of any real offence was lacking, were unwilling to face the unpopularity and the danger of an outbreak which might occur if they delivered a verdict in his favour. Paul meanwhile " appealed to Caesar " ; in other words, demanded, as a Roman citizen, that the cause should be heard by the emperor himself. In charge of a centurion, Julius, the prisoner was sent to Myra and then conveyed in an Alexandrian wheat-ship to Crete. The vessel, however, was caught in a hurricane and suffered shipwreck at Malta. St Paul, after some delay, was transferred to another ship, brought to Puteoli, and thence by land to Rome. There the book of the Acts of the Apostles leaves him, awaiting his trial before Nero.

The later movements and history of the great apostle are very uncertain. It seems probable that he was tried and acquitted in Rome after a lengthy imprison-ment. We have evidence of yet another, a fourth, missionary journey. It is held by some that he visited Spain, but we can affirm with greater confidence that he found his way to Macedonia once more and probably spent the winter·of 65–66 at Nicopolis. Returning to Rome he was again arrested and imprisoned. Whether he was condemned in company with St Peter is not certain, but as a Roman citizen his punishment was different. There is a strong and seemingly reliable tradition that he was beheaded on the Ostian Way, at a place called Aquae Salviae (now Tre Fontane), near where the basilica of St Paul Outside the Walls stands to-day ; and in that church his burial-place is venerated. It is commonly said that St Paul suffered on the same day of the same year as did St Peter, but there is no certainty about this. Shortly before, he had written to St Timothy those famous words : " I am even now ready to be sacrificed, and the time of my dissolution is at hand. I have fought a good fight ; I have finished my course ; I have kept the faith. As for the rest, there is laid up for me a crown of justice which the Lord, the just judge, will render to me in that day : and not only to me, but to them also that love His coming."

In the case of St Paul again there is a vast literature, which it would be useless to attempt to recapitulate here. As a particularly valuable guide to the many problems involved in the apostle's work and writings, the little volume, *St Paul*, by Fr F. Prat, who has made this study his life-work, may be particularly recommended. It is published in the series " Les Saints ". The *St Paul* of Fouard (Eng. trans.) is also well known, and the apostle's history is therein discussed in great detail. Much help may be obtained from the commentaries on the Epistles by the Anglican Bishop Lightfoot, and from the books of his friend, the archaeological explorer, Sir W. M. Ramsay, notably *St Paul the Traveller* (1908) and *The Church in the Roman Empire* (1893). All the fuller commentaries on the Acts of the Apostles necessarily deal with St Paul's history ; see, for example, E. Jacquier, *Les Actes des Apôtres* (1926), and Camerlynck and Van der Heeren, *Commentarius in Actus Apostolorum* (1923). Other useful books are : K. Pieper, *Paulus, seine missionärische Persönlichkeit* . . . (1926) ; P. Delattre, *Les Épîtres de S. Paul* (1924–1926) ; Tricot, *St Paul* (1928) ; and the indispensable *Theology of St Paul* of Fr Prat (Eng. trans., 2 vols., 1927–1934). Some more recent publications are English translations of Mgr J. Holzner's *Paul of Tarsus* (1944) and I. Giordani's *St Paul, Apostle and Martyr* (1946), a popular work ; a long biography in Italian by D. A. Penna, *San Paulo* (1946) ; E. B. Allo, *Paul, Apôtre de Jésus-Christ* (1946) ; and R. Sencourt's study, *St Paul : Envoy of Grace* (1948). There are many apocryphal writings in which St Paul plays a prominent part, including letters purporting to have been written by him. The *Acts of St Paul* have been edited by W. Schubart and C. Schmidt, from a papyrus manuscript at Hamburg. The *Acts of Paul and Thecla* have been more than once printed : see September 23 herein, under St Thecla, and O. von Gebhardt, in *Texte und Untersuchungen*, vol. vii, part II (1902) ; consult also L. Vouaux, *Les Actes de Paul et ses Lettres apocryphes* (1913). On the burial-place of the apostle in the *confessio* at St Paul's Outside the Walls, see Grisar, *Analecta Romana*, pp. 259 *seq.* No one perhaps has written of St Paul with truer intuition than Cardinal Newman, who was specially fitted to appreciate the secret of the apostle's appeal, his gift of Christian sympathy.

ST CASSIUS, BISHOP OF NARNI   (A.D. 538)

THE little that is known about St Cassius is derived from the pages of St Gregory the Great. In his *Dialogues* he expatiates upon the virtues of this bishop of Narni, upon his exemplary life, his care for his flock and his self-sacrificing generosity to the poor. After it had been revealed to him, through one of his priests, that he would die in Rome on the feast of St Peter and St Paul, he made a point of going annually to the City on the eve of that day. Six times he returned from his pilgrimage, but the seventh year the prophecy was fulfilled. When he had celebrated Mass and given communion to the people, he passed away peacefully to receive his eternal reward. He had composed in advance his own epitaph in verse, and in accordance with its terms he was buried at Narni in the oratory of his predecessor, Juvenalis, beside a certain Fausta, who may have been his wife. In the ninth century Count Adalbert of Tuscany seized Narni and caused the bodies of St Juvenalis, St Cassius and " St " Fausta to be taken to Lucca. There they found a resting-place in the church of St Frediano. Eventually, however, the relics— or part of them—were returned to Narni, where they are still preserved in the cathedral.

Of the life of St Cassius, nothing more is known than what we learn from St Gregory the Great—first of all, in the *Dialogues*, and then in a special sermon of his. All the relevant passages are quoted in the *Acta Sanctorum*, June, vol. vii.

SS. SALOME AND JUDITH (NINTH CENTURY?)

ABOUT the middle of the ninth century, Walter, the abbot of the double monastery of Ober Altaich in Bavaria, caused an anchoress-cell to be built at the west end of the church with an aperture into the choir. In it he enclosed with the customary rites a relation of his own, a stranger from England named Salome. According to a tradition which became current at Altaich, she was an unmarried princess, the niece of a king of England. On her way back from a pilgrimage to Jerusalem she had the misfortune to lose her two attendants, all her possessions, and—temporarily —her sight. After many sufferings and much wandering she arrived at Passau, where she found a temporary home, and from thence she went to Altaich to end her days in seclusion and prayer. Some time later she was joined by a cousin or aunt, a widow called Judith, who—it was popularly believed— had been sent in search of Salome by the king of England. Altaich proved as attractive to her as to her kinswoman, and she also decided to remain there. For her accommodation, a second cell was built, adjoining that of Salome. Thus they lived until Salome's death left Judith in solitude. At times she suffered from diabolical attacks and night terrors, and the shrieks which came from her cell sometimes brought the monks running from the neighbouring abbey to find out if she was being murdered. She was buried beside her niece at Ober Altaich. It is stated that in 907, when the monastery was destroyed by the Hungarians, the relics of both recluses were translated to Nieder Altaich, where they are still venerated.

No contemporary English princess known to history seems to tally with either Salome or Judith, unless, as has been suggested, it be Edburga, the beautiful and wicked daughter of Offa of Mercia. She married Beorhtric, King of the West Saxons, and, after murdering a number of his nobles, she accidentally killed her husband with the poison she had prepared for someone else. She was driven out of England, and she took refuge at the court of Charlemagne. That monarch, in the words of William of Malmesbury, " on account of her wickedness and exceeding beauty, gave her a noble nunnery for women ". Her conduct there, however, was so disgraceful that she was ejected with ignominy, and was reduced to wandering from one city to another with a maidservant as her sole companion. Asser states that he knew people who had seen her begging in the streets of Patavium, *i.e.* Pavia. If Patavium is, indeed, as has been suggested, a copyist's erroneous rendering of Patavia, or Passau, a city within easy reach of Altaich, then Judith the recluse may well have been Edburga ; she would naturally change her name on entering religion, to sever so tangible a link with her discreditable past.

There is a detailed Latin narrative dealing with what purports to be the history of these two recluses, written seemingly by a monk of Nieder Altaich. The Bollandists in 1709 describe him as almost a contemporary of what he records (see the *Acta Sanctorum*, June, vol. vii), but later critics are satisfied that the document which we possess cannot have taken shape earlier than the close of the twelfth century. Moreover, the Walter referred to in the story as abbot of Altaich seems more probably to belong to the eleventh century, in the time of William the Conqueror. See Holder-Egger in MGH., *Scriptores*, vol. xv, pp. 847 *seq.*, who quotes the text in part, and *cf. Forschungen zur deutschen Geschichte*, vol. xviii (1878), pp. 551 *seq.* For Edburga, see R. M. Wilson, *The Lost Literature of Medieval England* (1952), pp. 37 *seq.*

ST EMMA, WIDOW   (*c.* A.D. 1045)

THE little Austrian town of Gurk, in Carinthia, which gives his title to an archbishop, derives its origin from a double monastery and a church founded by St Emma, or Hemma, towards the middle of the eleventh century.   She was related on her mother's side to the Emperor St Henry, at whose court she was trained under the watchful eye of St Cunegund.   She was afterwards given in marriage to William, Landgrave of Friesach, and their union was a happy one.   Emma and her husband had two children, William and Hartwig, to whom when they were old enough the landgrave gave the supervision and charge of the mines from which he drew part of his wealth.   The miners were a wild and lawless band whom the brothers found it difficult to control except by taking measures of extreme severity.   After one of the men had been hanged for gross immorality by order of Count William, a number of his companions rose in rebellion and murdered both their young masters.

When the news was broken to the parents, Emma at first abandoned herself to grief, while the landgrave threatened to destroy all the insurgents, with their wives and children.   Nobler counsels, however, prevailed.   Emma turned to God in fervent prayer, and her husband pardoned all except the actual perpetrators of the murder.   He then undertook a pilgrimage to Rome.   But he fell ill on his way back and died within a short distance of his home.   Thus bereft of her husband and children, St Emma devoted her possessions and the remainder of her life to the service of God and of her fellow creatures.   Besides giving alms liberally to the poor, she founded several religious houses, of which the chief was the monastery mentioned above.   It was located on one of her own estates, and her castle of Gurkhofen formed part of the community buildings.   In the two establishments, which were of course entirely separate, provision was made for twenty monks and seventy nuns.   Between them they kept up the *laus perennis*.*   It is stated that St Emma herself received the veil at Gurk, but this is not certain   She died about the year 1045, and was buried in her own church at Gurk.

Although she certainly founded the abbey of Gurk, the earlier life of St Emma seems to have been in fact different from the medieval tale related above.   It was she who belonged to the Friesach family, and when she was left a widow by the death of Count William of Sanngau *c.* 1015 she had a son living ; he was killed in battle twenty years later, and it was then that her religious benefactions began.   The ancient *cultus* of the Countess Emma was confirmed by the Holy See in 1938; a list supplied by the Congregation of Sacred Rites includes her among the *beatae*, but she is generally called Saint.

The Bollandists print the unsatisfactory medieval Latin biography in the *Acta Sanctorum*, June, vol. vii.   See A. von Jaksch, *Gurker Geschichtsquellen*, vol. i (1896) ; J. Löw, *Hemmabüchlein* (1931) ; and the publication of the Congregation of Rites, *Confirmationis cultus . . . servae Dei Hemmae . . . positio* (1937).

30 : THE COMMEMORATION OF ST PAUL

THE Mass and office of June 29 being principally concerned with St Peter, it is followed the next day by a special commemoration of St Paul.   None the less June 29 is the feast-day of St Paul no less than of St Peter, and the notice of him herein therefore appears under that date.

* The *laus perennis* (continual psalmody) was an arrangement in certain large monasteries whereby relays of monks or nuns sang the Divine Office day and night without intermission. Gurk is a late example of a custom that died out entirely.

ST MARTIAL, Bishop of Limoges (*c.* A.D. 250)

All that is actually known about St Martial is that he was a bishop of Limoges and that he has been venerated from a very early date as the apostle of the Limousin and the founder of the see which he occupied.   In all probability he flourished about A.D. 250.   According to the tradition current in the sixth century, and recorded by St Gregory of Tours, he was one of seven missionaries sent from Rome to Gaul shortly before 250.   St Gatian went to Tours, St Trophimus to Arles, St Paul to Narbonne, St Martial to Limoges, St Dionysius (Denis) to Paris, St Saturninus to Toulouse and St Austremonius to the Auvergne.   Each one evangelized the district he had selected and became its first bishop.   In the early litanies of Limoges, St Martial's name appears as a confessor, but after a time the monks of the local abbey of St Martial (who possessed his relics) began to contend that he must be honoured as an apostle.   His legend had by now developed considerably, and he was being represented not only as the apostle of Aquitaine, but as one of our Lord's immediate followers, the boy with the barley loaves and fishes, and one of the seventy-two disciples.   The question of his title was considered important enough to be brought before several synods.   In the eleventh century St Martial's *cultus* received a great impetus in consequence of the rebuilding of the abbey dedicated under his name, the enshrining of his body, and the dissemination of a fantastic narrative embodying and expanding the various current legends, but purporting to be the saint's original authentic acts as compiled by his immediate successor in the bishopric of Limoges, St Aurelian.

That this extravagant forgery, bristling with anachronisms and improbabilities, should have imposed upon an uncritical age is perhaps not to be wondered at : but it is surprising to find its genuineness still upheld in certain quarters at this present day.   Martial, we are told, was converted at the age of fifteen by our Lord's preaching ; he was baptized by his kinsman, St Peter ; he was present at the raising of Lazarus : he waited on our Lord at the Last Supper, and he received the Holy Ghost with the other disciples at Pentecost.   St Peter, whom he accompanied first to Antioch and then to Rome, sent him to preach the gospel in Gaul.   With St Peter's staff he raised to life his companion, St Austriclinian, who had died on the journey.   After their arrival at Tulle, he delivered his host's daughter from an evil spirit, and resuscitated the son of the Roman governor who had been strangled by a demon.   These miracles led to the conversion and baptism of 3600 persons.   Pagan priests who ventured to attack him were smitten with blindness, until the saint by his prayers restored the use of their eyes.   Others who beat and imprisoned him at Limoges were killed by a thunderbolt, but were brought back to life by him in response to the entreaties of the citizens.   One of the priests thus resuscitated was Aurelian, the reputed author of these so-called " acts ".   Mass conversions followed these miracles also.   Amongst St Martial's penitents was a noble damsel called Valeria.   She determined to consecrate her virginity to our Lord, and was beheaded by order of Duke Stephen to whom she had previously been betrothed.   After the execution she carried her head in her hands to the church where St Martial was.   Duke Stephen himself was subsequently converted, made a pilgrimage to Rome, where he found St Peter engaged in giving instruction to the people at a place called the Vatican.   The duke was able to give him the latest news of St Martial and made a favourable report of the progress of the missions in Gaul.   In the fortieth year after the Resurrection—the seventy-fourth of our era—St Martial was warned in a vision of his impending death, and fifteen days later he breathed his last, surrounded by his brethren.

It is stated that Pope John XIX gave permission for the term " apostle " to be applied to St Martial, but the Congregation of Rites in 1854 refused to ratify this, deciding that he was to be venerated in the Mass, the litanies, and office as an ordinary bishop and confessor. It would seem, however, that the bishop of Limoges, in answer to a remonstrance and appeal addressed to Pius IX in the same year, was gratified with a favourable answer permitting that in that diocese St Martial should enjoy the style and precedence of an apostle.

We have three ancient accounts of the life of St Martial. The first is the very short notice, followed by a few miracles, which we find in the *De gloria confessorum* (cap. xxvii–xxix, and *cf. Hist. Francorum*, i, 28) of St Gregory of Tours. It fixes the coming of St Martial at about A.D. 250. The second is considerably longer, and was written probably in the ninth century. In this, St Martial is said to have been sent to Limoges by St Peter, but his missionary efforts, though crowned with instantaneous success and accompanied with marvels, are limited to the diocese of Limoges. The best text of this was edited by C. F. Bellet, in his book, *L'ancienne vie de St Martial et la prose rythmée* (1897). The third and most extravagant life claims to be written by the saint's successor Aurelian, but borrows much from the *Historia apostolica*, an apocryphal document which was first printed under the name of Abdias. Here, as stated above, St Martial is represented as preaching all over the south of France, with the support of Duke Stephen. There is some reason to think that the story was fabricated by Adhemar de Chabannes, with the object of enhancing the glory of the abbey of Saint-Martial of Limoges, in which he had been brought up. It seems certain that it was Adhemar who forged the supposed bull of Pope John XIX, which authorized the cult of St Martial with all the marks of honour belonging to the twelve authentic Apostles, and he is also gravely suspected of producing other spurious documents of the same kind. All this matter has been very fully investigated by Louis Saltet, in the *Bulletin de littérature ecclés.* (Toulouse, 1925), pp. 161–186, and 279–302 ; 1926, pp. 117–139, and 145–160 ; and 1931, pp. 149–165. See also Duchesne, in the *Annales du Midi*, vol. iv (1892), pp. 289–339 ; as well as his *Fastes Épiscopaux*, vol. ii, pp. 104–117 ; and, finally, a very long article by H. Leclercq in DAC., vol. ix, cc. 1063–1167, which is equipped with a vast and almost bewildering bibliography. The statements made in this article, however, as Saltet has pointed out (*l.c.* 1931, pp. 163–165), are in some respects open to criticism. The saint is referred to as " apostle " in a Winchester litany of the eleventh century (Arundel MS. 60). See *Analecta Bollandiana*, vol. lxiv (1946), pp. 84–86 ; and *cf.* H. M. Colvin, *The White Canons in England* (1951), pp. 51–52.

ST BERTRAND, BISHOP OF LE MANS   (A.D. 623)

ST BERTRAND (Bertichramnus) was born about the middle of the sixth century, but exactly where is uncertain. Eventually he went to Paris, where he received holy orders at the hands of St Germanus and became one of his clergy. Bertrand was conspicuous in the bishop's cathedral school, and had attained the position of archdeacon when, in 587, he was nominated to the bishopric of Le Mans. He was to find his position an uneasy one. At that period, when France was distracted by the rival factions of the kings of Neustria and Austrasia, it was difficult for any prominent person to avoid taking sides, and Bertrand, who was a partisan of the Neustrian princes, shared their changing fortunes. Two or three times he was driven from his diocese, the see on one occasion being occupied by a usurper. In 605, however, he was finally reinstated by King Clotaire II.

He proved a great benefactor to the Church and to the poor. A number of estates were made over to him by landowners, and he used them for the endowment of religious foundations, for the foundation of new ones, and for the enrichment of the church of Le Mans. Agriculture was a subject in which he was greatly

interested.   In the most enlightened and practical way he insisted on the development of land which came under his control.   He was particularly concerned with
the planting of vineyards, and from a few vines which had been given him by his
friend, St Licinius of Angers, he propagated with success a particularly choice kind
of grape.   Amongst his foundations were the abbey of SS. Peter and Paul, a large
hospice for travellers and pilgrims, and a church which he dedicated to St Germanus.   He received the pallium from Rome at the request of King Clotaire,
although he was not an archbishop.   His death took place in the year 623, when he
was about seventy years of age.   Perhaps the most interesting memorial which is
left of this saint is the text of his will, which seems to be accepted as an authentic
document and which disposes of large landed possessions.   It also enables us to
correct in some details the statements too carelessly made by the chronicler who
compiled the account of his episcopate.

A short biography is preserved in the *Actus Pontificum Cenomannensium*, edited by
Mabillon in his *Vetera Analecta*, vol. iii, pp. 109–112.   There is also an account of St
Bertichram in the *Acta Sanctorum*, June, vol. i, under June 6.   But by far the most thorough
study of his life and episcopate is that which has been published by Ambrose Ledru in *La
Province du Maine*, vol. xiv (1906), pp. 369–383, and vol. xv (1907), pp. 20–26, 97–108,
122–134, 142–162, 227–236, 267–271.

ST ERENTRUDE, Virgin   (*c.* A.D. 718)

When St Rupert had been engaged for some years in the task of preaching the
gospel in Bavaria, he paid a visit to his native land, which was in the diocese of
Worms, in order to enlist fresh helpers.   He appealed particularly for the aid of
devoted men and women, prepared to occupy religious houses in the new city of
Salzburg, and amongst those who responded to the call was his kinswoman,
Erentrude, or Erentrudis.   She was probably his niece, the daughter of his
brother, but may possibly have been his sister.   For her and for the women who
accompanied her to Salzburg, or rallied round her after her arrival, he erected a
convent on a hill which is still known by the name of Nonnberg.   She governed
the community as abbess, and by her instruction and example trained them to
great piety.

One day, shortly before St Rupert's death, Erentrude went to visit him at his
special request.   After pledging her to secrecy, he told her that he was about to
die, and asked her to promise that she would continue to intercede for him when
he had departed.   Overcome with emotion, she besought him to pray that she
might be taken first, and not be left orphaned in a strange land.   It was at his
bidding, she reminded him, that she had abandoned her own country.   St Rupert
replied with a gentle reproof.   The disposal of the end of our lives is in the hands
of God, he told her, and it is not right to wish to die before the appointed time.
She accepted the rebuke, and modified her petition.   Would he at least undertake
to ask God, after his death, to allow her soon to follow ?   This he promised to do.
" When they had conversed for a long time on the sweetness of eternal life, amid
tears shed by both, they sadly bade each other a last farewell."   Erentrude's
desire was granted.   One night, shortly after St Rupert's death, she was praying
earnestly for his soul, when he appeared to her and said, " Come, dear sister, come
to the kingdom you have so long been striving to reach."   She fell ill almost
immediately, and the end came within a few days.   She is believed to have died
on June 30, 718.   Three hundred years later, her convent and church, which had

fallen into ruins, were rebuilt by the Emperor St Henry, as a thank-offering for a cure which he attributed to her intervention. St Erentrude's relics, which have been carefully treasured through the centuries, now rest in the crypt of the church on the Nonnberg.

There is a short Latin biography printed by Mabillon, *Acta Sanctorum O.S.B.*, vol. iii, pp. 348–349. In some modern reference books the name is mistakenly given as Ermentrude.

ST THEOBALD, OR THIBAUD, OF PROVINS (A.D. 1066)

THIS Theobald was of the family of the counts of Champagne, son of Count Arnoul, and was born at Provins in Brie in 1017. In his youth he read the lives of the fathers of the desert, and was much struck by the examples of self-denial, contemplation and Christian perfection which were set before him : the lives of St John the Baptist, of St Paul the Hermit, St Antony and St Arsenius in their wildernesses, charmed him, and he greatly desired to imitate them. And when he was ordered to lead a body of troops in the field, he represented so respectfully to Count Arnoul the obligation of a vow by which he had bound himself to quit the world, that he at length obtained his consent.

With another young nobleman, called Walter, he went to the abbey of St Remi at Rheims, and thence they set out in the clothes of beggars. First to Suxy in Ardenne, and then in the forest of Pettingen in Luxemburg they found a convenient solitude for their purpose, and built themselves there two little cells. Manual labour is a necessary duty of an ascetic or penitential life, and not being skilled in the making of mats or baskets or similar work, they went into the neighbouring villages, and there hired themselves by the day to serve the masons, or to work in the fields, to carry stones and mortar, to load and unload wagons, to muck out the stables of the farmers, or to blow the bellows and make charcoal for the forges. With their wages they bought coarse bread, which was their whole subsistence. Whilst they worked with their hands, their hearts were employed in prayer ; and at night they watched long, singing together the divine praises. The reputation of their sanctity became a nuisance to them, so they resolved to leave a place where they were no longer able to live in obscurity. They went on pilgrimage, first to Compostela and then to Rome, and after they had visited all the holy places in Italy, they chose for their retirement a woody place called Salanigo, near Vicenza. Here, after two years, God called Walter to Himself. Theobald looked upon this loss as a warning that he had not long to live, and he redoubled his austerities. A number of disciples gathered round him, and the bishop of Vicenza promoted him to priest's orders, so that they might the more profit by his direction.

His lineage and quality being discovered, his parents were informed that their son was alive, and that the hermit of Salanigo, of whom such stories of sanctity, prophecies and miracles were told, was he whose absence had been the cause of so long a mourning ; and, aged as they were, they journeyed into Italy to see him. Gisela, the saint's mother, obtained her husband's consent to finish her life near her son, who made her a little hut at some distance from his own. St Theobald was shortly after stricken with his last sickness : a painful and repulsive disease which he bore with great patience. A little before his death he sent for an abbot of the Camaldolese hermits from whose hands he had already received the religious habit. To him he made his profession, recommended his mother and his disciples, and, having received viaticum, died in peace on the last day of June, 1066.   He was canonized within less than seven years by Pope Alexander II.

A full contemporary biography by Peter, abbot of Vangadizza, has been printed by Mabillon, and by the Bollandists in the *Acta Sanctorum*, June, vol. vii.   By some curious confusion Theobald has been erroneously honoured as founder of the church and town of Thann in Alsace.   See the *Analecta Bollandiana*, vol. xxiv (1905), p. 159 ; and R. Thompson, *Two Old French Poems on St Thibaut* (1936).   The saint is patron of charcoal-burners, and is sometimes called " le Charbonnier."

BD ARNULF OF VILLERS   (A.D. 1228)

THE story of Bd Arnulf (Arnoul) Cornebout is mainly the history of the heroic mortifications and penitential exercises he practised as a lay-brother in the Cistercian abbey of Villers in Brabant.   Born of middle-class parents at Brussels about the year 1180, he had grown up a careless, pleasure-loving youth, when a sudden conversion completely transformed him.   Every morning he rose betimes to attend Mass, and if by a rare chance he overslept himself, he atoned for his lapse by standing outside the church, however inclement the weather might be.   At the age of twenty-two he received the lay-brother's habit at Villers.   The desire for mortifications greater than those prescribed led him, while still a novice, to gird himself tightly with a horse-hair rope, which cut into his flesh, causing it to become septic ; but he humbly submitted to authority when it was pointed out to him that nothing of the kind must be undertaken without permission.   After his probation was over and his virtue had been tested, Abbot Charles and his successors recognized that Brother Arnulf had a special vocation to penance, and they not only sanctioned his austerities, but also relieved him of some of the manual work incumbent on lay-brothers, in order to allow him ample time for prayer.

Every day he scourged himself severely, now with rods, now with thorny branches, now with a stick covered with a hedgehog's skin.   Brothers whose duties took them near the cell adjoining the fruit-barn which was Arnulf's favourite retreat, asserted that, as each lash descended upon his body he would ejaculate the name of a member of the community, or of some outside person, on behalf of whom he was beseeching God's mercy.   He appeared never to weary of devising fresh forms of discipline, but another side of his character was revealed in his love for the poor.   His greatest joy was to relieve them, and he wished he could be sold as a slave to provide money to be spent in alms.   An anecdote is related by his fellow monk Goswin, who became his biographer.   On a certain occasion he had obtained permission from the abbot to give away forty-two loaves to the poor.   It became known to the community, who cited him to appear before the abbot on a charge of excessive prodigality.   Anxious to screen his superior from adverse criticism, Brother Arnulf refrained from referring the responsibility to him, and took the whole blame on his own shoulders, apologized for his fault, and asked for a punishment.   It took the form of eleven days' exile to an exterior cell situated between the two gates of the abbey.   He received the sentence with satisfaction, and congratulated himself upon becoming a doorkeeper, like St Peter.   (But why did not the abbot " own up " ?)

From the strain imposed upon his nervous system by his austerities, Arnulf developed in his later years symptoms of chorea, or St Vitus's Dance.   He would laugh and dance while scourging himself and sometimes would laugh hysterically in church—scandalizing the young novices who did not know him and were not aware that he had the gifts of miracles and of prophecy. He died on June 30, 1228, and in 1269 his relics were enshrined, at the same time as those of Bd Juliana of Cornillon and others.

All that we know of Bd Arnulf seems to be derived from the life by Goswin de Bossut, who was also a Cistercian at Villers and a contemporary. His biography is printed in the *Acta Sanctorum*, June, vol. vii. A second notice forms part of the *Gesta sanctorum Villariensium*, for which see Pertz, MGH., *Scriptores*, vol. xxv, p. 234.

BD PHILIP POWELL, MARTYR   (A.D. 1646)

BD PHILIP POWELL was born at Trallwng, near Brecon, in 1594 and received his education at the grammar school of Abergavenny. At the age of sixteen he was sent to London to study law under the distinguished lawyer who was afterwards to become still more famous as Father Augustine Baker, the Benedictine writer and director of souls. Between two and three years later Powell had occasion to go to Douai to transact some business, and there he himself became attracted to the Benedictines. In 1619 he received the habit in the monastery of St Gregory at Douai, and on March 7, 1622, he was sent on the English mission. As a precaution against spies it was customary in penal times for English seminarists and missionary priests to bear an *alias*, and Father Powell throughout his later career was usually known by his mother's name of Morgan. After staying for sixteen months with Father Baker he proceeded to Devonshire with an introduction to a Catholic family. For the next twenty years or more he laboured as a priest, administering the sacraments, reconciling the lapsed and converting heretics in the counties of Devon, Somerset and Cornwall. During that time he made his headquarters first with his original host, Mr Risdon, at Bableigh, and then with the family of Mr Risdon's daughter, Mrs Poyntz, at Leighland Barton in Somersetshire.

The outbreak of the Civil War scattered the two households. Father Powell, after some vicissitudes, joined General Goring and served as chaplain to the Catholics in his army until it was disbanded. He was on his way to Wales when the vessel in which he was sailing was boarded and searched by an officer of the Parliamentarian vice-admiral in those seas, Captain Crowther. Two members of the crew recognized Father Powell and denounced him as a Catholic priest who had, as they declared, " seduced the greater part of the parishioners of Yarnscombe and Parkham, in Devonshire, from their allegiance to the Protestant Church ". When Captain Crowther questioned him, off Penarth, he frankly admitted that he was a priest. Thereupon he was consigned to the lower deck, where the sailors stripped him of his upper garments and dressed him in dirty rags. Two months later he was conveyed by sea to London. He was confined for a short time under fairly humane conditions ; but in the common gaol of the King's Bench prison, to which he was afterwards transferred, he suffered much and contracted pleurisy. Two or three times he was brought up before the King's Bench to be examined and tried on a charge based entirely on his own admission that he was a Catholic priest.

In an able and spirited defence he contended that the law against priests did not extend to the high seas, that when his Majesty's flag is flying in civil war all trials of life and death cease, and that the king's person being absent no plot could be executed by anyone against it. But when the verdict was given against him and he was condemned to death he gave thanks to God in the presence of the whole court.   His personality and his conduct in prison had so impressed his fellow-captives that they drew up a kind of testimonial or memorandum of his virtues.   It was signed by twenty-three Protestants and by six Catholics, whom he had reconciled in the gaol.   The officials themselves seem to have regarded him with favour. The man who came to announce the date of his execution was too much overcome to be able to read the notice, but Father Powell, looking over his shoulder, prompted him and then called for a glass of sack in which to drink his health : " Oh what am I ", he cried, " that God thus honours me and will have me to die for His sake ? " In the course of a short address on the scaffold he said that it was the happiest day of his life and that he was suffering for no other reason than that he was a priest and a monk.   After a short prayer he made a sign and received absolution from a priest, Dom Robert Anderton, in the crowd.   He was then strung up.   He was allowed to hang until he was dead and his body was buried in the churchyard at Moorfields.   One of his brethren bought his bloodstained clothes for £4.

There is a full account in Bede Camm, *Nine Martyr Monks* (1931), pp. 318–343 ; and see Challoner, MMP., pp. 474–481 ; and T. P. Ellis, *Catholic Martyrs of Wales* (1933), pp. 100–102, and *Welsh Benedictines of the Terror* (1936), pp. 166–179.

THE example of Christ and His saints ought to encourage us to suffer our trials with patience and even with joy.   We shall soon begin to feel that it is sweet to tread in the steps of the God-man, and we shall find that if we courageously take up our crosses He will make them light by bearing them for us.   The soul will be happy to be abandoned by creatures, learning that they are but vanity and that man himself can be false and treacherous.   Then will she put all her confidence in God alone and cleave to Him with her whole strength.   Then will she find no relish but in Him, who fills her with His grace the more powerfully as she is the more weaned and separated from earthly things, and the more purely clings to Him who never forsakes those who sincerely seek Him.   " O happy exchange ! " exclaims St Francis de Sales, " In the eyes of men the soul is alone and deserted ; but she now has God instead of creatures ."

THE END OF VOLUME II

INDEX

Individual members of groups, e.g. of martyrs, are not entered in this index if they have only a bare mention in the text.